State Rankings 2008

Other titles in the State Fact Finder series

City Crime Rankings

Crime State Rankings

Education State Rankings

Health Care State Rankings

State Trends

State Rankings 2008
A Statistical View of America

Kathleen O'Leary Morgan

and

Scott Morgan

Editors

CQ PRESS

A Division of Congressional Quarterly Inc.
Washington, D.C.

CQ Press
2300 N Street, NW, Suite 800
Washington, DC 20037

Phone: 202-729-1900; toll-free, 1-866-4CQ-PRESS (1-866-427-7737)

Web: www.cqpress.com

Cover design: Silverander Communications

∞ The paper used in this publication exceeds the requirements of the American
National Standard for Information Sciences—Permanence of Paper for Printed
Library Materials, ANSI Z39.48-1992.

Printed and bound in the United States of America

12 11 10 09 08   1 2 3 4 5

ISBN 978-0-87289-926-1 (cloth)
ISBN 978-0-87289-927-8 (paper)
ISSN 1057-3623

Contents

Detailed Table of Contents

XI. HEALTH

XII. HOUSEHOLDS AND HOUSING

XIII. POPULATION

Preface

How much are teachers paid in your state? What percentage of your state's citizens are homeowners? What percentage use their seatbelts? How many have health insurance coverage? What is your state's violent crime rate? How does your state compare with others in generating renewable energy? Find the answers to these and hundreds of other questions in *State Rankings 2008*.

State Rankings is an essential information tool for researchers, librarians, community leaders, and concerned citizens. It provides state-by-state comparisons for taxes, housing, health care, education, crime, government spending, transportation, and more in hundreds of easy-to-understand tables.

Important Notes about *State Rankings 2008*

This book translates complicated and often convoluted statistics to allow meaningful comparisons of state quality of life information. For each new edition, we reexamine every table and update the material as needed. You'll find 569 tables in the 2008 edition.

Although there are changes throughout this new edition of *State Rankings*, the volume's organization and other popular features remain the same. Data are presented in both alphabetical and rank order, so readers can easily locate data for a particular state and quickly learn where that state ranks among the others. National totals, rates, and percentages are prominently displayed at the top of each table. Source information and other important notes are shown clearly at the bottom of each page. Every other line is shaded in gray for easy reading. In addition, we provide numerous information-finding tools: a thorough table of contents, table listings at the beginning of each chapter, and a detailed index. Also included is a directory of data sources we used, showing addresses, phone numbers, and Web sites.

The statistics in *State Rankings* require no additional calculations to convert them from millions, thousands, and so forth. All states are ranked from highest to lowest, with any ties among the states listed alphabetically for a given ranking. Negative numbers are reported in parentheses. In tables with national totals (as opposed to rates, per capita data, or the like) a separate column shows the percentage of the national total represented by each state. This column, "% of USA," is particularly interest-

ing when compared with a state's share of the nation's population for a particular year.

Among the more interesting tables in *State Rankings* are those in which we have combined data from various sources. These tables are sourced as "CQ Press using data from . . ." Many of these editor-generated comparisons are found in the chapters on federal, state, and local government finance.

State Rankings also provides basic information about states in a State Fast Facts table, found on pages xx and xxi. Here you will discover that West Virginia boasts three state songs and that four of the fifty states have adopted the sugar maple as their state tree.

Which State Is Most Livable?

We are often asked which is the best state. While we take great pride in presenting straightforward and unbiased statistics, each year we also conduct an analysis of the numbers in an effort to determine which state is the most livable. The results of this analysis are based on forty-four factors reflecting what we consider to be the keys to a state's quality of life: crime, income, education, employment, energy, environment, health, poverty, social welfare, and transportation. The Most Livable State Award often yields surprising results; this year's rankings can be found on page xviii.

Exciting Changes for Morgan Quitno Press

This edition of *State Rankings* ushers in a new and exciting era for our company and our customers. Effective May 2007, Morgan Quitno's reference books are published by CQ Press in Washington, D.C. A division of Congressional Quarterly Inc., CQ Press is the premier publisher of books, directories, periodicals, and electronic products on American government and politics.

While our publishing structure has changed, our commitment to bringing the highest quality publications to our customers has not. *State Rankings* is one of six titles in our series of easy-to-use, affordable reference publications.

We would like to extend our thanks to the many librarians, government statisticians, and other information keepers who help us compile *State Rankings* year after year. We also must acknowledge the huge contributions of Joe and Joan Williams of Lincoln, Nebraska, the original editors and creators of *State Rankings* who had the vision to create a book that provides meaningful and interesting state information in an easy-to-understand format. We are honored to carry on their mission of creating rankings books that we can all learn from and enjoy.

Finally, thanks to our readers for helping us keep our books relevant and useful. We look forward to providing you with top quality reference titles for many years to come.

Kathleen O'Leary Morgan and Scott Morgan
Editors

The Most Livable State

For the fifth consecutive year, New Hampshire tops the Most Livable State rankings. The Granite State excels in a number of important quality of life measures, boasting low crime, low poverty, and high income levels, as well as a well-educated population. Joining New Hampshire at the top of the rankings are Utah, Wyoming, Minnesota, and Iowa.

At the opposite end of the Most Livable State rankings, Mississippi holds on firmly to last place. It has held this position for nine of the last ten years. Preceding Mississippi are South Carolina, Kentucky, Tennessee, and Arkansas. For the full list of rankings, see page xviii.

Now in its eighteenth year, the Most Livable State Award is issued with the annual publication of *State Rankings*. For each new edition, we reexamine our collection of data and select the factors that reflect a state's basic quality of life. The 2008 award is based on the same forty-four factors used to determine last year's award.

Unlike various other rankings of states, our Most Livable State Award does not focus on any one category of data. Instead, it takes into account a broad range of economic, educational, health-oriented, public safety, and environmental statistics.

To determine a state's "Livability Rating," each state's rankings for forty-four categories are averaged. The scale is one to fifty; the higher the number, the better. Data used are for the most recent year in which comparable numbers are available from most states. All factors are given equal weight. States with no data available for a given category are ranked based only on the remaining factors. In our book, data are listed from highest to lowest. However, for purposes of this award, we inverted rankings for those factors we determined to be "positive." Thus the state with the highest median income in the book (ranking first) would be given a number fifty ranking for this award.

The Most Livable State Award is one of six annual honors announced in conjunction with the publication of our state and city reference books. The Healthiest State Award is based on factors derived from *Health Care State Rankings*. The Most Dangerous and Safest State designations are announced with our *Crime State Rankings* volume. The Safest City/Metro Area Award is based on data from the *City Crime Rankings* volume. The Smartest State Award is determined using data from *Education State Rankings*. The Most Improved State Award is based on statistics from our *State Trends* volume.

While we strive to make our books as objective as possible, these awards give us the opportunity to choose the factors we think tell an interesting story about quality of life in the fifty United States.

Congratulations to the citizens and leaders of New Hampshire on their continued success!

—THE EDITORS

Negative Factors
 1. Percent Change in Number of Crimes: 2005 to 2006 (page 30)
 2. Crime Rate (page 31)
 3. State Prisoner Incarceration Rate (page 61)
 4. Personal Bankruptcy Rate (page 105)
 5. Estimated Pupil-Teacher Ratio in Public Elementary and Secondary Schools (page 126)
 6. Rate of Public Libraries and Branches (page 159)
 7. Unemployment Rate (page 184)
 8. Percent of Nonfarm Employees in Government (page 198)
 9. Average Monthly Electric Bill for Residential Customers (page 218)
10. Hazardous Waste Sites on the National Priority List per 10,000 Square Miles (page 231)
11. State and Local Taxes as a Percent of Personal Income (page 307)
12. Per Capita State and Local Government Debt Outstanding (page 320)
13. Percent of Population Not Covered by Health Insurance (page 385)
14. Births of Low Birthweight as a Percent of All Births (page 395)
15. Teenage Birth Rate (page 396)
16. Infant Mortality Rate (page 402)
17. Age-Adjusted Death Rate by Suicide (page 416)
18. Population per Square Mile (page 458)
19. Poverty Rate (page 519)
20. Percent of Female-Headed Families with Children Living in Poverty (page 523)
21. State and Local Government Spending for Welfare Programs as a Percent of All Spending (page 526)
22. Percent of Households Receiving Food Stamps (page 552)
23. Deficient Bridges as a Percent of Total Bridges (page 570)
24. Highway Fatality Rate (page 573)
25. Fatalities in Alcohol-Related Crashes as a Percent of All Highway Fatalities (page 580)

Positive Factors
26. Per Capita Gross Domestic Product (page 96)
27. Percent Change in Per Capita Gross Domestic Product: 2002 to 2006 (Adjusted to Constant 2000 Dollars) (page 97)
28. Per Capita Personal Income (page 100)
29. Change in Per Capita Personal Income: 2005 to 2006 (page 101)
30. Median Household Income (page 103)
31. Estimated Public High School Graduation Rate (page 134)
32. Percent of Population Graduated from High School (page 135)
33. Expenditures for Education as a Percent of All State and Local Government Expenditures (page 141)
34. Percent of Population With a Bachelor's Degree or More (page 157)
35. Books in Public Libraries Per Capita (page 160)
36. Per Capita State Art Agencies' Legislative Appropriations (page 163)
37. Average Weekly Earnings of Production Workers on Manufacturing Payrolls (page 174)
38. Job Growth: 2006 to 2007 (page 189)
39. Normal Daily Mean Temperature (page 245)
40. Percent of Days That Are Sunny (page 246)
41. Homeownership Rate (page 443)
42. Domestic Migration of Population: 2005 to 2006 (page 496)
43 Marriage Rate (page 502)
44. Percent of Eligible Population Reported Voting (page 516)

The 2008 Most Livable State Award:

New Hampshire Wins Again

RANK	STATE	LIVABILITY RATING	07 RANK	CHANGE
44	Alabama	19.98	42	-2
29	Alaska	23.57	24	-5
36	Arizona	22.64	32	-4
46	Arkansas	19.27	48	2
30	California	23.48	30	0
14	Colorado	29.43	18	4
11	Connecticut	29.91	10	-1
27	Delaware	24.68	21	-6
28	Florida	24.02	27	-1
40	Georgia	21.11	41	1
21	Hawaii	27.25	19	-2
9	Idaho	30.74	14	5
26	Illinois	24.80	26	0
30	Indiana	23.48	35	5
5	Iowa	31.57	6	1
17	Kansas	28.36	17	0
48	Kentucky	17.95	47	-1
45	Louisiana	19.37	49	4
20	Maine	27.32	16	-4
16	Maryland	28.86	15	-1
13	Massachusetts	29.84	8	-5
38	Michigan	22.16	38	0
4	Minnesota	31.82	2	-2
50	Mississippi	15.89	50	0
39	Missouri	22.02	34	-5
19	Montana	27.36	22	3
6	Nebraska	31.32	11	5
35	Nevada	23.02	25	-10
1	New Hampshire	33.61	1	0
7	New Jersey	31.27	5	-2
33	New Mexico	23.14	37	4
24	New York	25.14	29	5
42	North Carolina	20.98	42	0
10	North Dakota	30.57	13	3
40	Ohio	21.11	36	-4
32	Oklahoma	23.27	40	8
22	Oregon	27.05	23	1
34	Pennsylvania	23.11	33	-1
25	Rhode Island	24.89	28	3
49	South Carolina	17.73	46	-3
15	South Dakota	29.11	9	-6
47	Tennessee	18.77	44	-3
37	Texas	22.27	39	2
2	Utah	32.95	4	2
8	Vermont	30.91	7	-1
12	Virginia	29.89	12	0
18	Washington	27.61	31	13
43	West Virginia	20.05	45	2
23	Wisconsin	25.68	20	-3
3	Wyoming	32.16	3	0

RANK	STATE	LIVABILITY RATING	07 RANK	CHANGE
1	New Hampshire	33.61	1	0
2	Utah	32.95	4	2
3	Wyoming	32.16	3	0
4	Minnesota	31.82	2	-2
5	Iowa	31.57	6	1
6	Nebraska	31.32	11	5
7	New Jersey	31.27	5	-2
8	Vermont	30.91	7	-1
9	Idaho	30.74	14	5
10	North Dakota	30.57	13	3
11	Connecticut	29.91	10	-1
12	Virginia	29.89	12	0
13	Massachusetts	29.84	8	-5
14	Colorado	29.43	18	4
15	South Dakota	29.11	9	-6
16	Maryland	28.86	15	-1
17	Kansas	28.36	17	0
18	Washington	27.61	31	13
19	Montana	27.36	22	3
20	Maine	27.32	16	-4
21	Hawaii	27.25	19	-2
22	Oregon	27.05	23	1
23	Wisconsin	25.68	20	-3
24	New York	25.14	29	5
25	Rhode Island	24.89	28	3
26	Illinois	24.80	26	0
27	Delaware	24.68	21	-6
28	Florida	24.02	27	-1
29	Alaska	23.57	24	-5
30	California	23.48	30	0
30	Indiana	23.48	35	5
32	Oklahoma	23.27	40	8
33	New Mexico	23.14	37	4
34	Pennsylvania	23.11	33	-1
35	Nevada	23.02	25	-10
36	Arizona	22.64	32	-4
37	Texas	22.27	39	2
38	Michigan	22.16	38	0
39	Missouri	22.02	34	-5
40	Georgia	21.11	41	1
40	Ohio	21.11	36	-4
42	North Carolina	20.98	42	0
43	West Virginia	20.05	45	2
44	Alabama	19.98	42	-2
45	Louisiana	19.37	49	4
46	Arkansas	19.27	48	2
47	Tennessee	18.77	44	-3
48	Kentucky	17.95	47	-1
49	South Carolina	17.73	46	-3
50	Mississippi	15.89	50	0

Date Each State Admitted to Statehood*

RANK	STATE	DATE OF ADMISSION
22	Alabama	December 14, 1819
49	Alaska	January 3, 1959
48	Arizona	February 14, 1912
25	Arkansas	June 15, 1836
31	California	September 9, 1850
38	Colorado	August 1, 1876
5	Connecticut	January 9, 1788
1	Delaware	December 7, 1787
27	Florida	March 3, 1845
4	Georgia	January 2, 1788
50	Hawaii	August 21, 1959
43	Idaho	July 3, 1890
21	Illinois	December 3, 1818
19	Indiana	December 11, 1816
29	Iowa	December 28, 1846
34	Kansas	January 29, 1861
15	Kentucky	June 1, 1792
18	Louisiana	April 30, 1812
23	Maine	March 15, 1820
7	Maryland	April 28, 1788
6	Massachusetts	February 6, 1788
26	Michigan	January 26, 1837
32	Minnesota	May 11, 1858
20	Mississippi	December 10, 1817
24	Missouri	August 10, 1821
41	Montana	November 8, 1889
37	Nebraska	March 1, 1867
36	Nevada	October 31, 1864
9	New Hampshire	June 21, 1788
3	New Jersey	December 18, 1787
47	New Mexico	January 6, 1912
11	New York	July 26, 1788
12	North Carolina	November 21, 1789
39	North Dakota	November 2, 1889
17	Ohio	March 1, 1803
46	Oklahoma	November 16, 1907
33	Oregon	February 14, 1859
2	Pennsylvania	December 12, 1787
13	Rhode Island	May 29, 1790
8	South Carolina	May 23, 1788
39	South Dakota	November 2, 1889
16	Tennessee	June 1, 1796
28	Texas	December 29, 1845
45	Utah	January 4, 1896
14	Vermont	March 4, 1791
10	Virginia	June 26, 1788
42	Washington	November 11, 1889
35	West Virginia	June 20, 1863
30	Wisconsin	May 29, 1848
44	Wyoming	July 10, 1890

RANK	STATE	DATE OF ADMISSION
1	Delaware	December 7, 1787
2	Pennsylvania	December 12, 1787
3	New Jersey	December 18, 1787
4	Georgia	January 2, 1788
5	Connecticut	January 9, 1788
6	Massachusetts	February 6, 1788
7	Maryland	April 28, 1788
8	South Carolina	May 23, 1788
9	New Hampshire	June 21, 1788
10	Virginia	June 26, 1788
11	New York	July 26, 1788
12	North Carolina	November 21, 1789
13	Rhode Island	May 29, 1790
14	Vermont	March 4, 1791
15	Kentucky	June 1, 1792
16	Tennessee	June 1, 1796
17	Ohio	March 1, 1803
18	Louisiana	April 30, 1812
19	Indiana	December 11, 1816
20	Mississippi	December 10, 1817
21	Illinois	December 3, 1818
22	Alabama	December 14, 1819
23	Maine	March 15, 1820
24	Missouri	August 10, 1821
25	Arkansas	June 15, 1836
26	Michigan	January 26, 1837
27	Florida	March 3, 1845
28	Texas	December 29, 1845
29	Iowa	December 28, 1846
30	Wisconsin	May 29, 1848
31	California	September 9, 1850
32	Minnesota	May 11, 1858
33	Oregon	February 14, 1859
34	Kansas	January 29, 1861
35	West Virginia	June 20, 1863
36	Nevada	October 31, 1864
37	Nebraska	March 1, 1867
38	Colorado	August 1, 1876
39	North Dakota	November 2, 1889
39	South Dakota	November 2, 1889
41	Montana	November 8, 1889
42	Washington	November 11, 1889
43	Idaho	July 3, 1890
44	Wyoming	July 10, 1890
45	Utah	January 4, 1896
46	Oklahoma	November 16, 1907
47	New Mexico	January 6, 1912
48	Arizona	February 14, 1912
49	Alaska	January 3, 1959
50	Hawaii	August 21, 1959

Source: U.S. Bureau of the Census
   "1980 Census of Population" (vol. 1, part A, PC80-1-A)
*First thirteen states show date of ratification of Constitution.

STATE FAST FACTS

STATE	NICKNAME	CAPITAL	POPULATION*	AREA**
Alabama	Heart of Dixie	Montgomery	4,627,851	52,419
Alaska	The Last Frontier	Juneau	683,478	663,267
Arizona	Grand Canyon State	Phoenix	6,338,755	113,998
Arkansas	The Natural State	Little Rock	2,834,797	53,179
California	Golden State	Sacramento	36,553,215	163,696
Colorado	Centennial State	Denver	4,861,515	104,094
Connecticut	Constitution State	Hartford	3,502,309	5,543
Delaware	First State	Dover	864,764	2,489
Florida	Sunshine State	Tallahassee	18,251,243	65,755
Georgia	Peach State	Atlanta	9,544,750	59,425
Hawaii	Aloha State	Honolulu	1,283,388	10,931
Idaho	Gem State	Boise	1,499,402	83,570
Illinois	Land of Lincoln	Springfield	12,852,548	57,914
Indiana	Hoosier State	Indianapolis	6,345,289	36,418
Iowa	Hawkeye State	Des Moines	2,988,046	56,272
Kansas	Sunflower State	Topeka	2,775,997	82,277
Kentucky	Bluegrass State	Frankfort	4,241,474	40,409
Louisiana	Pelican State	Baton Rouge	4,293,204	51,840
Maine	Pine Tree State	Augusta	1,317,207	35,385
Maryland	Free State	Annapolis	5,618,344	12,407
Massachusetts	Bay State	Boston	6,449,755	10,555
Michigan	Great Lake State	Lansing	10,071,822	96,716
Minnesota	North Star State	St. Paul	5,197,621	86,939
Mississippi	Magnolia State	Jackson	2,918,785	48,430
Missouri	Show Me State	Jefferson City	5,878,415	69,704
Montana	Treasure State	Helena	957,861	147,042
Nebraska	Cornhusker State	Lincoln	1,774,571	77,354
Nevada	Silver State	Carson City	2,565,382	110,561
New Hampshire	Granite State	Concord	1,315,828	9,350
New Jersey	Garden State	Trenton	8,685,920	8,721
New Mexico	Land of Enchantment	Santa Fe	1,969,915	121,590
New York	Empire State	Albany	19,297,729	54,556
North Carolina	Tar Heel State	Raleigh	9,061,032	53,819
North Dakota	Peace Garden State	Bismarck	639,715	70,700
Ohio	Buckeye State	Columbus	11,466,917	44,825
Oklahoma	Sooner State	Oklahoma City	3,617,316	69,898
Oregon	Beaver State	Salem	3,747,455	98,381
Pennsylvania	Keystone State	Harrisburg	12,432,792	46,055
Rhode Island	Ocean State	Providence	1,057,832	1,545
South Carolina	Palmetto State	Columbia	4,407,709	32,020
South Dakota	Mount Rushmore State	Pierre	796,214	77,117
Tennessee	Volunteer State	Nashville	6,156,719	42,143
Texas	Lone Star State	Austin	23,904,380	268,581
Utah	Beehive State	Salt Lake City	2,645,330	84,899
Vermont	Green Mountain State	Montpelier	621,254	9,614
Virginia	Old Dominion	Richmond	7,712,091	42,774
Washington	Evergreen State	Olympia	6,468,424	71,300
West Virginia	Mountain State	Charleston	1,812,035	24,230
Wisconsin	Badger State	Madison	5,601,640	65,498
Wyoming	Equality State	Cheyenne	522,830	97,814

*2007 Census resident population estimates.
**Total of land and water area in square miles.

STATE SONG	STATE FLOWER	STATE TREE	STATE BIRD
Alabama	Camellia	Southern Pine	Yellowhammer
Alaska's Flag	Forget-Me-Not	Sitka Spruce	Willow Ptarmigan
Arizona	Saguaro Cactus Blossom	Palo Verde	Cactus Wren
Arkansas	Apple Blossom	Pine	Mockingbird
I Love You, California	Golden Poppy	California Redwood	California Valley Quail
Where the Columbines Grow	Rocky Mountain Columbine	Colorado Blue Spruce	Lark Bunting
Yankee Doodle Dandy	Mountain Laurel	White Oak	American Robin
Our Delaware	Peach Blossom	American Holly	Blue Hen Chicken
Swanee River	Orange Blossom	Sabal Palmetto Palm	Mockingbird
Georgia On My Mind	Cherokee Rose	Live Oak	Brown Thrasher
Hawaii Ponoi	Yellow Hibiscus	Candlenut	Nene
Here We Have Idaho	Syringa	White Pine	Mountain Bluebird
Illinois	Purple Violet	White Oak	Cardinal
On the Banks of the Wabash, Far Away	Peony	Tulip Poplar	Cardinal
The Song of Iowa	Wild Rose	Oak	Eastern Goldfinch
Home on the Range	Sunflower	Cottonwood	Western Meadowlark
My Old Kentucky Home	Goldenrod	Tulip Tree	Cardinal
Give Me Louisiana	Magnolia	Cypress	Eastern Brown Pelican
State of Maine Song	White Pine Cone and Tassel	Eastern White Pine	Chickadee
Maryland, My Maryland	Black-eyed Susan	White Oak	Baltimore Oriole
All Hail to Massachusetts	Mayflower	American Elm	Chickadee
Michigan, My Michigan	Apple Blossom	White Pine	Robin
Hail! Minnesota	Pink and White Lady's Slipper	Red Pine	Common Loon
Go, Mississippi!	Magnolia	Magnolia	Mockingbird
Missouri Waltz	Hawthorn	Dogwood	Bluebird
Montana	Bitterroot	Ponderosa Pine	Western Meadowlark
Beautiful Nebraska	Goldenrod	Cottonwood	Western Meadowlark
Home Means Nevada	Sagebrush	Single-Leaf Pinon	Mountain Bluebird
Old New Hampshire	Purple Lilac	White Birch	Purple Finch
Ode to New Jersey	Purple Violet	Red Oak	Eastern Goldfinch
O Fair New Mexico	Yucca	Pinon	Roadrunner
I Love New York	Rose	Sugar Maple	Bluebird
The Old North State	Dogwood	Pine	Cardinal
North Dakota Hymn	Wild Prairie Rose	American Elm	Western Meadowlark
Beautiful Ohio	Scarlet Carnation	Buckeye	Cardinal
Oklahoma!	Mistletoe	Redbud	Scissortailed Flycatcher
Oregon, My Oregon	Oregon Grape	Douglas Fir	Western Meadowlark
Hail! Pennsylvania	Mountain Laurel	Hemlock	Ruffed Grouse
Rhode Island	Violet	Red Maple	Rhode Island Red
Carolina	Yellow Jessamine	Palmetto	Carolina Wren
Hail, South Dakota	Pasque Flower	Black Hills Spruce	Ringnecked Pheasant
The Tennessee Waltz	Iris	Tulip Poplar	Mockingbird
Texas, Our Texas	Bluebonnet	Pecan	Mockingbird
Utah, We Love Thee	Sego Lily	Blue Spruce	Seagull
Hail, Vermont	Red Clover	Sugar Maple	Hermit Thrush
Carry Me Back to Old Virginia	Dogwood	Dogwood	Cardinal
Washington, My Home	Western Rhododendron	Western Hemlock	Willow Goldfinch
The West Virginia Hills; This Is My West Virginia; and West Virginia, My Home, Sweet Home	Big Rhododendron	Sugar Maple	Cardinal
On Wisconsin!	Wood Violet	Sugar Maple	Robin
Wyoming	Indian Paintbrush	Cottonwood	Meadowlark

I. Agriculture

Number of Farms in 2006

National Total = 2,089,790 Farms*

ALPHA ORDER

RANK ORDER

RANK	STATE	FARMS	% of USA	RANK	STATE	FARMS	% of USA
21	Alabama	43,000	2.1%	1	Texas	230,000	11.0%
50	Alaska	640	0.0%	2	Missouri	105,000	5.0%
38	Arizona	10,000	0.5%	3	Iowa	88,600	4.2%
20	Arkansas	46,500	2.2%	4	Kentucky	84,000	4.0%
9	California	76,000	3.6%	5	Oklahoma	83,000	4.0%
28	Colorado	30,700	1.5%	6	Tennessee	82,000	3.9%
45	Connecticut	4,200	0.2%	7	Minnesota	79,300	3.8%
48	Delaware	2,300	0.1%	8	Ohio	76,200	3.6%
23	Florida	41,000	2.0%	9	California	76,000	3.6%
16	Georgia	49,000	2.3%	9	Wisconsin	76,000	3.6%
44	Hawaii	5,500	0.3%	11	Illinois	72,400	3.5%
32	Idaho	25,000	1.2%	12	Kansas	64,000	3.1%
11	Illinois	72,400	3.5%	13	Indiana	59,000	2.8%
13	Indiana	59,000	2.8%	14	Pennsylvania	58,200	2.8%
3	Iowa	88,600	4.2%	15	Michigan	53,000	2.5%
12	Kansas	64,000	3.1%	16	Georgia	49,000	2.3%
4	Kentucky	84,000	4.0%	17	North Carolina	48,000	2.3%
31	Louisiana	26,800	1.3%	18	Nebraska	47,600	2.3%
41	Maine	7,100	0.3%	19	Virginia	46,800	2.2%
37	Maryland	12,000	0.6%	20	Arkansas	46,500	2.2%
43	Massachusetts	6,100	0.3%	21	Alabama	43,000	2.1%
15	Michigan	53,000	2.5%	22	Mississippi	42,000	2.0%
7	Minnesota	79,300	3.8%	23	Florida	41,000	2.0%
22	Mississippi	42,000	2.0%	24	Oregon	39,300	1.9%
2	Missouri	105,000	5.0%	25	New York	35,000	1.7%
30	Montana	28,100	1.3%	26	Washington	34,000	1.6%
18	Nebraska	47,600	2.3%	27	South Dakota	31,300	1.5%
47	Nevada	3,000	0.1%	28	Colorado	30,700	1.5%
46	New Hampshire	3,400	0.2%	29	North Dakota	30,300	1.4%
39	New Jersey	9,800	0.5%	30	Montana	28,100	1.3%
35	New Mexico	17,500	0.8%	31	Louisiana	26,800	1.3%
25	New York	35,000	1.7%	32	Idaho	25,000	1.2%
17	North Carolina	48,000	2.3%	33	South Carolina	24,600	1.2%
29	North Dakota	30,300	1.4%	34	West Virginia	21,200	1.0%
8	Ohio	76,200	3.6%	35	New Mexico	17,500	0.8%
5	Oklahoma	83,000	4.0%	36	Utah	15,100	0.7%
24	Oregon	39,300	1.9%	37	Maryland	12,000	0.6%
14	Pennsylvania	58,200	2.8%	38	Arizona	10,000	0.5%
49	Rhode Island	850	0.0%	39	New Jersey	9,800	0.5%
33	South Carolina	24,600	1.2%	40	Wyoming	9,100	0.4%
27	South Dakota	31,300	1.5%	41	Maine	7,100	0.3%
6	Tennessee	82,000	3.9%	42	Vermont	6,300	0.3%
1	Texas	230,000	11.0%	43	Massachusetts	6,100	0.3%
36	Utah	15,100	0.7%	44	Hawaii	5,500	0.3%
42	Vermont	6,300	0.3%	45	Connecticut	4,200	0.2%
19	Virginia	46,800	2.2%	46	New Hampshire	3,400	0.2%
26	Washington	34,000	1.6%	47	Nevada	3,000	0.1%
34	West Virginia	21,200	1.0%	48	Delaware	2,300	0.1%
9	Wisconsin	76,000	3.6%	49	Rhode Island	850	0.0%
40	Wyoming	9,100	0.4%	50	Alaska	640	0.0%
					District of Columbia	0	0.0%

Source: U.S. Department of Agriculture, National Agricultural Statistics Service
   "Farms and Land in Farms" (http://usda.mannlib.cornell.edu/usda/current/FarmLandIn/FarmLandIn-02-02-2007.pdf)
*A farm is any establishment from which $1,000 or more of agricultural products were sold or would normally be sold during the year. This includes places with five or more horses, except horses in boarding stables or racetracks.

Land in Farms in 2006

National Total = 932,430,000 Acres*

ALPHA ORDER				RANK ORDER			
RANK	STATE	ACRES	% of USA	RANK	STATE	ACRES	% of USA
32	Alabama	8,600,000	0.9%	1	Texas	129,700,000	13.9%
44	Alaska	900,000	0.1%	2	Montana	60,100,000	6.4%
16	Arizona	26,100,000	2.8%	3	Kansas	47,200,000	5.1%
21	Arkansas	14,300,000	1.5%	4	Nebraska	45,700,000	4.9%
15	California	26,300,000	2.8%	5	New Mexico	44,500,000	4.8%
11	Colorado	30,700,000	3.3%	6	South Dakota	43,700,000	4.7%
49	Connecticut	360,000	0.0%	7	North Dakota	39,400,000	4.2%
47	Delaware	515,000	0.1%	8	Wyoming	34,400,000	3.7%
30	Florida	10,000,000	1.1%	9	Oklahoma	33,700,000	3.6%
28	Georgia	10,800,000	1.2%	10	Iowa	31,500,000	3.4%
42	Hawaii	1,300,000	0.1%	11	Colorado	30,700,000	3.3%
24	Idaho	11,800,000	1.3%	12	Missouri	30,100,000	3.2%
14	Illinois	27,300,000	2.9%	13	Minnesota	27,400,000	2.9%
20	Indiana	15,000,000	1.6%	14	Illinois	27,300,000	2.9%
10	Iowa	31,500,000	3.4%	15	California	26,300,000	2.8%
3	Kansas	47,200,000	5.1%	16	Arizona	26,100,000	2.8%
23	Kentucky	13,700,000	1.5%	17	Oregon	17,100,000	1.8%
34	Louisiana	7,800,000	0.8%	18	Wisconsin	15,300,000	1.6%
41	Maine	1,360,000	0.1%	19	Washington	15,100,000	1.6%
40	Maryland	2,035,000	0.2%	20	Indiana	15,000,000	1.6%
46	Massachusetts	520,000	0.1%	21	Arkansas	14,300,000	1.5%
29	Michigan	10,100,000	1.1%	21	Ohio	14,300,000	1.5%
13	Minnesota	27,400,000	2.9%	23	Kentucky	13,700,000	1.5%
27	Mississippi	11,000,000	1.2%	24	Idaho	11,800,000	1.3%
12	Missouri	30,100,000	3.2%	25	Utah	11,600,000	1.2%
2	Montana	60,100,000	6.4%	26	Tennessee	11,400,000	1.2%
4	Nebraska	45,700,000	4.9%	27	Mississippi	11,000,000	1.2%
37	Nevada	6,300,000	0.7%	28	Georgia	10,800,000	1.2%
48	New Hampshire	450,000	0.0%	29	Michigan	10,100,000	1.1%
45	New Jersey	790,000	0.1%	30	Florida	10,000,000	1.1%
5	New Mexico	44,500,000	4.8%	31	North Carolina	8,800,000	0.9%
36	New York	7,500,000	0.8%	32	Alabama	8,600,000	0.9%
31	North Carolina	8,800,000	0.9%	33	Virginia	8,500,000	0.9%
7	North Dakota	39,400,000	4.2%	34	Louisiana	7,800,000	0.8%
21	Ohio	14,300,000	1.5%	35	Pennsylvania	7,650,000	0.8%
9	Oklahoma	33,700,000	3.6%	36	New York	7,500,000	0.8%
17	Oregon	17,100,000	1.8%	37	Nevada	6,300,000	0.7%
35	Pennsylvania	7,650,000	0.8%	38	South Carolina	4,850,000	0.5%
50	Rhode Island	60,000	0.0%	39	West Virginia	3,600,000	0.4%
38	South Carolina	4,850,000	0.5%	40	Maryland	2,035,000	0.2%
6	South Dakota	43,700,000	4.7%	41	Maine	1,360,000	0.1%
26	Tennessee	11,400,000	1.2%	42	Hawaii	1,300,000	0.1%
1	Texas	129,700,000	13.9%	43	Vermont	1,240,000	0.1%
25	Utah	11,600,000	1.2%	44	Alaska	900,000	0.1%
43	Vermont	1,240,000	0.1%	45	New Jersey	790,000	0.1%
33	Virginia	8,500,000	0.9%	46	Massachusetts	520,000	0.1%
19	Washington	15,100,000	1.6%	47	Delaware	515,000	0.1%
39	West Virginia	3,600,000	0.4%	48	New Hampshire	450,000	0.0%
18	Wisconsin	15,300,000	1.6%	49	Connecticut	360,000	0.0%
8	Wyoming	34,400,000	3.7%	50	Rhode Island	60,000	0.0%
					District of Columbia	0	0.0%

Source: U.S. Department of Agriculture, National Agricultural Statistics Service
"Farms and Land in Farms" (http://usda.mannlib.cornell.edu/usda/current/FarmLandIn/FarmLandIn-02-02-2007.pdf)
*A farm is any establishment from which $1,000 or more of agricultural products were sold or would normally be sold during the year. This includes places with five or more horses, except horses in boarding stables or racetracks.

Average Number of Acres per Farm in 2006

National Average = 446 Acres*

ALPHA ORDER				RANK ORDER		
RANK	STATE	ACRES		RANK	STATE	ACRES
33	Alabama	200		1	Wyoming	3,780
6	Alaska	1,406		2	Arizona	2,610
2	Arizona	2,610		3	New Mexico	2,543
22	Arkansas	308		4	Montana	2,139
20	California	346		5	Nevada	2,100
9	Colorado	1,000		6	Alaska	1,406
47	Connecticut	86		7	South Dakota	1,396
29	Delaware	224		8	North Dakota	1,300
27	Florida	244		9	Colorado	1,000
30	Georgia	220		10	Nebraska	960
28	Hawaii	236		11	Utah	768
14	Idaho	472		12	Kansas	738
18	Illinois	377		13	Texas	564
26	Indiana	254		14	Idaho	472
19	Iowa	356		15	Washington	444
12	Kansas	738		16	Oregon	435
43	Kentucky	163		17	Oklahoma	406
23	Louisiana	291		18	Illinois	377
36	Maine	192		19	Iowa	356
41	Maryland	170		20	California	346
48	Massachusetts	85		20	Minnesota	346
37	Michigan	191		22	Arkansas	308
20	Minnesota	346		23	Louisiana	291
25	Mississippi	262		24	Missouri	287
24	Missouri	287		25	Mississippi	262
4	Montana	2,139		26	Indiana	254
10	Nebraska	960		27	Florida	244
5	Nevada	2,100		28	Hawaii	236
45	New Hampshire	132		29	Delaware	224
49	New Jersey	81		30	Georgia	220
3	New Mexico	2,543		31	New York	214
31	New York	214		32	Wisconsin	201
39	North Carolina	183		33	Alabama	200
8	North Dakota	1,300		34	South Carolina	197
38	Ohio	188		34	Vermont	197
17	Oklahoma	406		36	Maine	192
16	Oregon	435		37	Michigan	191
46	Pennsylvania	131		38	Ohio	188
50	Rhode Island	71		39	North Carolina	183
34	South Carolina	197		40	Virginia	182
7	South Dakota	1,396		41	Maryland	170
44	Tennessee	139		41	West Virginia	170
13	Texas	564		43	Kentucky	163
11	Utah	768		44	Tennessee	139
34	Vermont	197		45	New Hampshire	132
40	Virginia	182		46	Pennsylvania	131
15	Washington	444		47	Connecticut	86
41	West Virginia	170		48	Massachusetts	85
32	Wisconsin	201		49	New Jersey	81
1	Wyoming	3,780		50	Rhode Island	71
				District of Columbia**		NA

Source: U.S. Department of Agriculture, National Agricultural Statistics Service
   "Farms and Land in Farms" (http://usda.mannlib.cornell.edu/usda/current/FarmLandIn/FarmLandIn-02-02-2007.pdf)
*A farm is any establishment from which $1,000 or more of agricultural products were sold or would normally be sold during the year. This includes places with five or more horses, except horses in boarding stables or racetracks.
**Not applicable.

Average per Acre Value of Farmland and Buildings in 2007

National Average = $2,160 per Acre*

ALPHA ORDER				RANK ORDER		
RANK	STATE	PER ACRE VALUE		RANK	STATE	PER ACRE VALUE
22	Alabama	$3,100		1	Rhode Island	$12,500
NA	Alaska**	NA		2	Massachusetts	11,800
19	Arizona	3,400		3	Connecticut	11,700
30	Arkansas	2,300		4	New Jersey	11,300
8	California	6,000		5	Delaware	10,400
39	Colorado	1,250		6	Maryland	9,250
3	Connecticut	11,700		7	Florida	7,570
5	Delaware	10,400		8	California	6,000
7	Florida	7,570		9	Virginia	5,700
12	Georgia	4,500		10	Pennsylvania	5,670
NA	Hawaii**	NA		11	North Carolina	4,600
25	Idaho	2,830		12	Georgia	4,500
13	Illinois	4,330		13	Illinois	4,330
14	Indiana	4,000		14	Indiana	4,000
19	Iowa	3,400		14	New Hampshire	4,000
42	Kansas	1,090		16	Michigan	3,950
24	Kentucky	2,850		17	Ohio	3,800
34	Louisiana	2,120		17	Wisconsin	3,800
33	Maine	2,150		19	Arizona	3,400
6	Maryland	9,250		19	Iowa	3,400
2	Massachusetts	11,800		19	Tennessee	3,400
16	Michigan	3,950		22	Alabama	3,100
26	Minnesota	2,780		23	South Carolina	2,900
35	Mississippi	2,080		24	Kentucky	2,850
31	Missouri	2,280		25	Idaho	2,830
44	Montana	960		26	Minnesota	2,780
40	Nebraska	1,230		27	Vermont	2,700
41	Nevada	1,100		28	Utah	2,550
14	New Hampshire	4,000		29	West Virginia	2,500
4	New Jersey	11,300		30	Arkansas	2,300
47	New Mexico	610		31	Missouri	2,280
32	New York	2,220		32	New York	2,220
11	North Carolina	4,600		33	Maine	2,150
46	North Dakota	650		34	Louisiana	2,120
17	Ohio	3,800		35	Mississippi	2,080
43	Oklahoma	1,080		36	Washington	1,900
37	Oregon	1,650		37	Oregon	1,650
10	Pennsylvania	5,670		38	Texas	1,480
1	Rhode Island	12,500		39	Colorado	1,250
23	South Carolina	2,900		40	Nebraska	1,230
45	South Dakota	820		41	Nevada	1,100
19	Tennessee	3,400		42	Kansas	1,090
38	Texas	1,480		43	Oklahoma	1,080
28	Utah	2,550		44	Montana	960
27	Vermont	2,700		45	South Dakota	820
9	Virginia	5,700		46	North Dakota	650
36	Washington	1,900		47	New Mexico	610
29	West Virginia	2,500		48	Wyoming	560
17	Wisconsin	3,800		NA	Alaska**	NA
48	Wyoming	560		NA	Hawaii**	NA
					District of Columbia**	NA

Source: U.S. Department of Agriculture, National Agricultural Statistics Service
   "Land Values and Cash Rents" (http://usda.mannlib.cornell.edu/MannUsda/viewDocumentInfo.do?documentID=1446)
*As of January 1, 2007. Value of farmland and buildings in nominal dollars.
**Not applicable or available.

Percent Change in Average per Acre Value of Farmland: 2006 to 2007

National Percent Change = 9.9% Increase*

<table>
<tr><td colspan="3">ALPHA ORDER</td><td colspan="3">RANK ORDER</td></tr>
<tr><td>RANK</td><td>STATE</td><td>PERCENT CHANGE</td><td>RANK</td><td>STATE</td><td>PERCENT CHANGE</td></tr>
<tr><td>24</td><td>Alabama</td><td>12.7</td><td>1</td><td>Wyoming</td><td>24.4</td></tr>
<tr><td>NA</td><td>Alaska**</td><td>NA</td><td>2</td><td>Utah</td><td>23.2</td></tr>
<tr><td>28</td><td>Arizona</td><td>11.5</td><td>3</td><td>Nevada</td><td>22.2</td></tr>
<tr><td>26</td><td>Arkansas</td><td>12.2</td><td>4</td><td>Montana</td><td>20.0</td></tr>
<tr><td>30</td><td>California</td><td>11.3</td><td>5</td><td>Wisconsin</td><td>18.8</td></tr>
<tr><td>20</td><td>Colorado</td><td>13.6</td><td>6</td><td>Pennsylvania</td><td>18.4</td></tr>
<tr><td>45</td><td>Connecticut</td><td>2.6</td><td>6</td><td>Texas</td><td>18.4</td></tr>
<tr><td>46</td><td>Delaware</td><td>2.0</td><td>8</td><td>New Mexico</td><td>17.3</td></tr>
<tr><td>41</td><td>Florida</td><td>4.0</td><td>9</td><td>Virginia</td><td>16.3</td></tr>
<tr><td>17</td><td>Georgia</td><td>15.4</td><td>9</td><td>West Virginia</td><td>16.3</td></tr>
<tr><td>NA</td><td>Hawaii**</td><td>NA</td><td>11</td><td>Oregon</td><td>16.2</td></tr>
<tr><td>12</td><td>Idaho</td><td>16.0</td><td>12</td><td>Idaho</td><td>16.0</td></tr>
<tr><td>19</td><td>Illinois</td><td>13.9</td><td>12</td><td>Iowa</td><td>16.0</td></tr>
<tr><td>33</td><td>Indiana</td><td>10.2</td><td>12</td><td>Kansas</td><td>16.0</td></tr>
<tr><td>12</td><td>Iowa</td><td>16.0</td><td>15</td><td>Minnesota</td><td>15.8</td></tr>
<tr><td>12</td><td>Kansas</td><td>16.0</td><td>16</td><td>South Dakota</td><td>15.5</td></tr>
<tr><td>44</td><td>Kentucky</td><td>3.6</td><td>17</td><td>Georgia</td><td>15.4</td></tr>
<tr><td>27</td><td>Louisiana</td><td>11.6</td><td>18</td><td>Missouri</td><td>15.2</td></tr>
<tr><td>40</td><td>Maine</td><td>4.9</td><td>19</td><td>Illinois</td><td>13.9</td></tr>
<tr><td>42</td><td>Maryland</td><td>3.9</td><td>20</td><td>Colorado</td><td>13.6</td></tr>
<tr><td>47</td><td>Massachusetts</td><td>1.7</td><td>21</td><td>North Dakota</td><td>13.0</td></tr>
<tr><td>22</td><td>Michigan</td><td>12.9</td><td>22</td><td>Michigan</td><td>12.9</td></tr>
<tr><td>15</td><td>Minnesota</td><td>15.8</td><td>23</td><td>Nebraska</td><td>12.8</td></tr>
<tr><td>25</td><td>Mississippi</td><td>12.4</td><td>24</td><td>Alabama</td><td>12.7</td></tr>
<tr><td>18</td><td>Missouri</td><td>15.2</td><td>25</td><td>Mississippi</td><td>12.4</td></tr>
<tr><td>4</td><td>Montana</td><td>20.0</td><td>26</td><td>Arkansas</td><td>12.2</td></tr>
<tr><td>23</td><td>Nebraska</td><td>12.8</td><td>27</td><td>Louisiana</td><td>11.6</td></tr>
<tr><td>3</td><td>Nevada</td><td>22.2</td><td>28</td><td>Arizona</td><td>11.5</td></tr>
<tr><td>39</td><td>New Hampshire</td><td>8.1</td><td>28</td><td>South Carolina</td><td>11.5</td></tr>
<tr><td>43</td><td>New Jersey</td><td>3.7</td><td>30</td><td>California</td><td>11.3</td></tr>
<tr><td>8</td><td>New Mexico</td><td>17.3</td><td>30</td><td>Oklahoma</td><td>11.3</td></tr>
<tr><td>37</td><td>New York</td><td>8.3</td><td>32</td><td>Tennessee</td><td>10.7</td></tr>
<tr><td>38</td><td>North Carolina</td><td>8.2</td><td>33</td><td>Indiana</td><td>10.2</td></tr>
<tr><td>21</td><td>North Dakota</td><td>13.0</td><td>33</td><td>Vermont</td><td>10.2</td></tr>
<tr><td>35</td><td>Ohio</td><td>8.9</td><td>35</td><td>Ohio</td><td>8.9</td></tr>
<tr><td>30</td><td>Oklahoma</td><td>11.3</td><td>36</td><td>Washington</td><td>8.6</td></tr>
<tr><td>11</td><td>Oregon</td><td>16.2</td><td>37</td><td>New York</td><td>8.3</td></tr>
<tr><td>6</td><td>Pennsylvania</td><td>18.4</td><td>38</td><td>North Carolina</td><td>8.2</td></tr>
<tr><td>48</td><td>Rhode Island</td><td>0.0</td><td>39</td><td>New Hampshire</td><td>8.1</td></tr>
<tr><td>28</td><td>South Carolina</td><td>11.5</td><td>40</td><td>Maine</td><td>4.9</td></tr>
<tr><td>16</td><td>South Dakota</td><td>15.5</td><td>41</td><td>Florida</td><td>4.0</td></tr>
<tr><td>32</td><td>Tennessee</td><td>10.7</td><td>42</td><td>Maryland</td><td>3.9</td></tr>
<tr><td>6</td><td>Texas</td><td>18.4</td><td>43</td><td>New Jersey</td><td>3.7</td></tr>
<tr><td>2</td><td>Utah</td><td>23.2</td><td>44</td><td>Kentucky</td><td>3.6</td></tr>
<tr><td>33</td><td>Vermont</td><td>10.2</td><td>45</td><td>Connecticut</td><td>2.6</td></tr>
<tr><td>9</td><td>Virginia</td><td>16.3</td><td>46</td><td>Delaware</td><td>2.0</td></tr>
<tr><td>36</td><td>Washington</td><td>8.6</td><td>47</td><td>Massachusetts</td><td>1.7</td></tr>
<tr><td>9</td><td>West Virginia</td><td>16.3</td><td>48</td><td>Rhode Island</td><td>0.0</td></tr>
<tr><td>5</td><td>Wisconsin</td><td>18.8</td><td>NA</td><td>Alaska**</td><td>NA</td></tr>
<tr><td>1</td><td>Wyoming</td><td>24.4</td><td>NA</td><td>Hawaii**</td><td>NA</td></tr>
<tr><td></td><td></td><td></td><td></td><td>District of Columbia**</td><td>NA</td></tr>
</table>

Source: U.S. Department of Agriculture, National Agricultural Statistics Service
"Land Values and Cash Rents" (http://usda.mannlib.cornell.edu/MannUsda/viewDocumentInfo.do?documentID=1446)
*As of January 1, 2007. Value of farmland and buildings in nominal dollars.
**Not applicable or available.

Net Farm Income in 2006

National Total = $59,005,502,000*

ALPHA ORDER

RANK	STATE	FARM INCOME	% of USA
14	Alabama	$1,579,848,173	2.7%
50	Alaska	19,969,268	0.0%
25	Arizona	773,689,374	1.3%
9	Arkansas	1,950,873,049	3.3%
1	California	5,905,654,558	10.0%
29	Colorado	733,993,231	1.2%
41	Connecticut	182,841,059	0.3%
36	Delaware	388,249,217	0.7%
7	Florida	2,340,426,272	4.0%
6	Georgia	2,387,595,956	4.0%
43	Hawaii	105,531,996	0.2%
27	Idaho	758,422,120	1.3%
17	Illinois	1,510,989,333	2.6%
15	Indiana	1,545,389,881	2.6%
4	Iowa	3,274,816,033	5.6%
13	Kansas	1,614,297,915	2.7%
10	Kentucky	1,741,516,250	3.0%
26	Louisiana	765,737,610	1.3%
40	Maine	216,819,637	0.4%
34	Maryland	594,569,213	1.0%
42	Massachusetts	115,414,733	0.2%
18	Michigan	1,321,182,622	2.2%
5	Minnesota	2,493,552,349	4.2%
19	Mississippi	1,230,264,324	2.1%
11	Missouri	1,697,324,608	2.9%
39	Montana	256,840,220	0.4%
8	Nebraska	2,297,014,304	3.9%
45	Nevada	84,619,502	0.1%
48	New Hampshire	42,568,468	0.1%
37	New Jersey	305,394,321	0.5%
35	New Mexico	422,978,783	0.7%
24	New York	868,738,275	1.5%
3	North Carolina	3,702,198,159	6.3%
33	North Dakota	605,882,462	1.0%
12	Ohio	1,614,399,061	2.7%
22	Oklahoma	876,517,333	1.5%
23	Oregon	875,603,412	1.5%
16	Pennsylvania	1,516,419,796	2.6%
49	Rhode Island	26,034,523	0.0%
30	South Carolina	722,213,442	1.2%
28	South Dakota	741,536,708	1.3%
31	Tennessee	721,818,878	1.2%
2	Texas	4,866,321,566	8.2%
38	Utah	263,563,865	0.4%
44	Vermont	103,193,975	0.2%
32	Virginia	678,032,512	1.1%
21	Washington	958,336,709	1.6%
47	West Virginia	49,704,208	0.1%
20	Wisconsin	1,091,383,786	1.8%
46	Wyoming	65,218,901	0.1%

RANK ORDER

RANK	STATE	FARM INCOME	% of USA
1	California	$5,905,654,558	10.0%
2	Texas	4,866,321,566	8.2%
3	North Carolina	3,702,198,159	6.3%
4	Iowa	3,274,816,033	5.6%
5	Minnesota	2,493,552,349	4.2%
6	Georgia	2,387,595,956	4.0%
7	Florida	2,340,426,272	4.0%
8	Nebraska	2,297,014,304	3.9%
9	Arkansas	1,950,873,049	3.3%
10	Kentucky	1,741,516,250	3.0%
11	Missouri	1,697,324,608	2.9%
12	Ohio	1,614,399,061	2.7%
13	Kansas	1,614,297,915	2.7%
14	Alabama	1,579,848,173	2.7%
15	Indiana	1,545,389,881	2.6%
16	Pennsylvania	1,516,419,796	2.6%
17	Illinois	1,510,989,333	2.6%
18	Michigan	1,321,182,622	2.2%
19	Mississippi	1,230,264,324	2.1%
20	Wisconsin	1,091,383,786	1.8%
21	Washington	958,336,709	1.6%
22	Oklahoma	876,517,333	1.5%
23	Oregon	875,603,412	1.5%
24	New York	868,738,275	1.5%
25	Arizona	773,689,374	1.3%
26	Louisiana	765,737,610	1.3%
27	Idaho	758,422,120	1.3%
28	South Dakota	741,536,708	1.3%
29	Colorado	733,993,231	1.2%
30	South Carolina	722,213,442	1.2%
31	Tennessee	721,818,878	1.2%
32	Virginia	678,032,512	1.1%
33	North Dakota	605,882,462	1.0%
34	Maryland	594,569,213	1.0%
35	New Mexico	422,978,783	0.7%
36	Delaware	388,249,217	0.7%
37	New Jersey	305,394,321	0.5%
38	Utah	263,563,865	0.4%
39	Montana	256,840,220	0.4%
40	Maine	216,819,637	0.4%
41	Connecticut	182,841,059	0.3%
42	Massachusetts	115,414,733	0.2%
43	Hawaii	105,531,996	0.2%
44	Vermont	103,193,975	0.2%
45	Nevada	84,619,502	0.1%
46	Wyoming	65,218,901	0.1%
47	West Virginia	49,704,208	0.1%
48	New Hampshire	42,568,468	0.1%
49	Rhode Island	26,034,523	0.0%
50	Alaska	19,969,268	0.0%
	District of Columbia	0	0.0%

Source: U.S. Department of Agriculture, Economic Research Service
"Net Farm Income and Value of Production per Acre for States, 2006
http://www.ers.usda.gov/data/FarmIncome/50State/50stmenu.htm)
*Net farm income is a measure of the net value of production in a given year. It is determined by subtracting total production expenses from gross farm income.

Net Farm Income per Operation in 2006

National Average = $28,235 per Operation

RANK	STATE	PER OPERATION
12	Alabama	$36,741
14	Alaska	31,202
3	Arizona	77,369
10	Arkansas	41,954
2	California	77,706
30	Colorado	23,909
9	Connecticut	43,534
1	Delaware	168,804
5	Florida	57,084
7	Georgia	48,726
38	Hawaii	19,188
18	Idaho	30,337
35	Illinois	20,870
24	Indiana	26,193
11	Iowa	36,962
26	Kansas	25,223
36	Kentucky	20,732
21	Louisiana	28,572
17	Maine	30,538
6	Maryland	49,547
39	Massachusetts	18,920
27	Michigan	24,928
13	Minnesota	31,445
20	Mississippi	29,292
42	Missouri	16,165
47	Montana	9,140
8	Nebraska	48,257
22	Nevada	28,207
45	New Hampshire	12,520
15	New Jersey	31,163
29	New Mexico	24,170
28	New York	24,821
4	North Carolina	77,129
37	North Dakota	19,996
33	Ohio	21,186
46	Oklahoma	10,560
32	Oregon	22,280
25	Pennsylvania	26,055
16	Rhode Island	30,629
19	South Carolina	29,358
31	South Dakota	23,691
48	Tennessee	8,803
34	Texas	21,158
40	Utah	17,455
41	Vermont	16,380
43	Virginia	14,488
23	Washington	28,186
50	West Virginia	2,345
44	Wisconsin	14,360
49	Wyoming	7,167

RANK	STATE	PER OPERATION
1	Delaware	$168,804
2	California	77,706
3	Arizona	77,369
4	North Carolina	77,129
5	Florida	57,084
6	Maryland	49,547
7	Georgia	48,726
8	Nebraska	48,257
9	Connecticut	43,534
10	Arkansas	41,954
11	Iowa	36,962
12	Alabama	36,741
13	Minnesota	31,445
14	Alaska	31,202
15	New Jersey	31,163
16	Rhode Island	30,629
17	Maine	30,538
18	Idaho	30,337
19	South Carolina	29,358
20	Mississippi	29,292
21	Louisiana	28,572
22	Nevada	28,207
23	Washington	28,186
24	Indiana	26,193
25	Pennsylvania	26,055
26	Kansas	25,223
27	Michigan	24,928
28	New York	24,821
29	New Mexico	24,170
30	Colorado	23,909
31	South Dakota	23,691
32	Oregon	22,280
33	Ohio	21,186
34	Texas	21,158
35	Illinois	20,870
36	Kentucky	20,732
37	North Dakota	19,996
38	Hawaii	19,188
39	Massachusetts	18,920
40	Utah	17,455
41	Vermont	16,380
42	Missouri	16,165
43	Virginia	14,488
44	Wisconsin	14,360
45	New Hampshire	12,520
46	Oklahoma	10,560
47	Montana	9,140
48	Tennessee	8,803
49	Wyoming	7,167
50	West Virginia	2,345
	District of Columbia*	NA

Source: U.S. Department of Agriculture, Economic Research Service
"Net Farm Income and Value of Production per Acre for States, 2006"
(http://www.ers.usda.gov/data/FarmIncome/50State/50stmenu.htm)
*Not applicable.

Net Farm Income per Acre in 2006

National Average = $63 per Acre

<table>
<tr><td colspan="3">ALPHA ORDER</td><td colspan="3">RANK ORDER</td></tr>
<tr><td>RANK</td><td>STATE</td><td>PER ACRE</td><td>RANK</td><td>STATE</td><td>PER ACRE</td></tr>
<tr><td>12</td><td>Alabama</td><td>$184</td><td>1</td><td>Delaware</td><td>$754</td></tr>
<tr><td>43</td><td>Alaska</td><td>22</td><td>2</td><td>Connecticut</td><td>508</td></tr>
<tr><td>39</td><td>Arizona</td><td>30</td><td>3</td><td>Rhode Island</td><td>434</td></tr>
<tr><td>15</td><td>Arkansas</td><td>136</td><td>4</td><td>North Carolina</td><td>421</td></tr>
<tr><td>8</td><td>California</td><td>225</td><td>5</td><td>New Jersey</td><td>387</td></tr>
<tr><td>41</td><td>Colorado</td><td>24</td><td>6</td><td>Maryland</td><td>292</td></tr>
<tr><td>2</td><td>Connecticut</td><td>508</td><td>7</td><td>Florida</td><td>234</td></tr>
<tr><td>1</td><td>Delaware</td><td>754</td><td>8</td><td>California</td><td>225</td></tr>
<tr><td>7</td><td>Florida</td><td>234</td><td>9</td><td>Massachusetts</td><td>222</td></tr>
<tr><td>10</td><td>Georgia</td><td>221</td><td>10</td><td>Georgia</td><td>221</td></tr>
<tr><td>27</td><td>Hawaii</td><td>81</td><td>11</td><td>Pennsylvania</td><td>198</td></tr>
<tr><td>30</td><td>Idaho</td><td>64</td><td>12</td><td>Alabama</td><td>184</td></tr>
<tr><td>34</td><td>Illinois</td><td>55</td><td>13</td><td>Maine</td><td>159</td></tr>
<tr><td>22</td><td>Indiana</td><td>103</td><td>14</td><td>South Carolina</td><td>149</td></tr>
<tr><td>21</td><td>Iowa</td><td>104</td><td>15</td><td>Arkansas</td><td>136</td></tr>
<tr><td>38</td><td>Kansas</td><td>34</td><td>16</td><td>Michigan</td><td>131</td></tr>
<tr><td>17</td><td>Kentucky</td><td>127</td><td>17</td><td>Kentucky</td><td>127</td></tr>
<tr><td>23</td><td>Louisiana</td><td>98</td><td>18</td><td>New York</td><td>116</td></tr>
<tr><td>13</td><td>Maine</td><td>159</td><td>19</td><td>Ohio</td><td>113</td></tr>
<tr><td>6</td><td>Maryland</td><td>292</td><td>20</td><td>Mississippi</td><td>112</td></tr>
<tr><td>9</td><td>Massachusetts</td><td>222</td><td>21</td><td>Iowa</td><td>104</td></tr>
<tr><td>16</td><td>Michigan</td><td>131</td><td>22</td><td>Indiana</td><td>103</td></tr>
<tr><td>25</td><td>Minnesota</td><td>91</td><td>23</td><td>Louisiana</td><td>98</td></tr>
<tr><td>20</td><td>Mississippi</td><td>112</td><td>24</td><td>New Hampshire</td><td>95</td></tr>
<tr><td>33</td><td>Missouri</td><td>56</td><td>25</td><td>Minnesota</td><td>91</td></tr>
<tr><td>49</td><td>Montana</td><td>4</td><td>26</td><td>Vermont</td><td>83</td></tr>
<tr><td>36</td><td>Nebraska</td><td>50</td><td>27</td><td>Hawaii</td><td>81</td></tr>
<tr><td>47</td><td>Nevada</td><td>13</td><td>28</td><td>Virginia</td><td>80</td></tr>
<tr><td>24</td><td>New Hampshire</td><td>95</td><td>29</td><td>Wisconsin</td><td>71</td></tr>
<tr><td>5</td><td>New Jersey</td><td>387</td><td>30</td><td>Idaho</td><td>64</td></tr>
<tr><td>48</td><td>New Mexico</td><td>10</td><td>31</td><td>Tennessee</td><td>63</td></tr>
<tr><td>18</td><td>New York</td><td>116</td><td>31</td><td>Washington</td><td>63</td></tr>
<tr><td>4</td><td>North Carolina</td><td>421</td><td>33</td><td>Missouri</td><td>56</td></tr>
<tr><td>45</td><td>North Dakota</td><td>15</td><td>34</td><td>Illinois</td><td>55</td></tr>
<tr><td>19</td><td>Ohio</td><td>113</td><td>35</td><td>Oregon</td><td>51</td></tr>
<tr><td>40</td><td>Oklahoma</td><td>26</td><td>36</td><td>Nebraska</td><td>50</td></tr>
<tr><td>35</td><td>Oregon</td><td>51</td><td>37</td><td>Texas</td><td>38</td></tr>
<tr><td>11</td><td>Pennsylvania</td><td>198</td><td>38</td><td>Kansas</td><td>34</td></tr>
<tr><td>3</td><td>Rhode Island</td><td>434</td><td>39</td><td>Arizona</td><td>30</td></tr>
<tr><td>14</td><td>South Carolina</td><td>149</td><td>40</td><td>Oklahoma</td><td>26</td></tr>
<tr><td>44</td><td>South Dakota</td><td>17</td><td>41</td><td>Colorado</td><td>24</td></tr>
<tr><td>31</td><td>Tennessee</td><td>63</td><td>42</td><td>Utah</td><td>23</td></tr>
<tr><td>37</td><td>Texas</td><td>38</td><td>43</td><td>Alaska</td><td>22</td></tr>
<tr><td>42</td><td>Utah</td><td>23</td><td>44</td><td>South Dakota</td><td>17</td></tr>
<tr><td>26</td><td>Vermont</td><td>83</td><td>45</td><td>North Dakota</td><td>15</td></tr>
<tr><td>28</td><td>Virginia</td><td>80</td><td>46</td><td>West Virginia</td><td>14</td></tr>
<tr><td>31</td><td>Washington</td><td>63</td><td>47</td><td>Nevada</td><td>13</td></tr>
<tr><td>46</td><td>West Virginia</td><td>14</td><td>48</td><td>New Mexico</td><td>10</td></tr>
<tr><td>29</td><td>Wisconsin</td><td>71</td><td>49</td><td>Montana</td><td>4</td></tr>
<tr><td>50</td><td>Wyoming</td><td>2</td><td>50</td><td>Wyoming</td><td>2</td></tr>
<tr><td></td><td></td><td></td><td></td><td>District of Columbia*</td><td>NA</td></tr>
</table>

Source: U.S. Department of Agriculture, Economic Research Service
"Net Farm Income and Value of Production per Acre for States, 2006"
(http://www.ers.usda.gov/data/FarmIncome/50State/50stmenu.htm)
*Not applicable.

Farm Income: Cash Receipts from Commodities in 2006

National Total = $239,271,907,000*

ALPHA ORDER

RANK	STATE	FARM INCOME	% of USA
27	Alabama	$3,739,060,000	1.6%
50	Alaska	64,218,000	0.0%
29	Arizona	2,879,224,000	1.2%
11	Arkansas	6,164,069,000	2.6%
1	California	31,402,706,000	13.1%
16	Colorado	5,614,394,000	2.3%
43	Connecticut	523,611,000	0.2%
39	Delaware	969,124,000	0.4%
9	Florida	6,974,161,000	2.9%
13	Georgia	6,005,101,000	2.5%
42	Hawaii	554,580,000	0.2%
22	Idaho	4,415,602,000	1.8%
7	Illinois	8,635,700,000	3.6%
14	Indiana	5,973,217,000	2.5%
3	Iowa	15,108,261,000	6.3%
5	Kansas	10,335,795,000	4.3%
23	Kentucky	4,007,202,000	1.7%
34	Louisiana	2,186,180,000	0.9%
41	Maine	591,674,000	0.2%
36	Maryland	1,597,699,000	0.7%
47	Massachusetts	433,026,000	0.2%
21	Michigan	4,487,765,000	1.9%
6	Minnesota	9,769,512,000	4.1%
26	Mississippi	3,788,510,000	1.6%
15	Missouri	5,621,258,000	2.3%
33	Montana	2,349,159,000	1.0%
4	Nebraska	12,042,344,000	5.0%
46	Nevada	446,550,000	0.2%
48	New Hampshire	161,804,000	0.1%
40	New Jersey	923,933,000	0.4%
32	New Mexico	2,463,526,000	1.0%
28	New York	3,509,003,000	1.5%
8	North Carolina	8,199,349,000	3.4%
25	North Dakota	3,980,728,000	1.7%
17	Ohio	5,479,712,000	2.3%
18	Oklahoma	5,093,622,000	2.1%
24	Oregon	3,990,617,000	1.7%
20	Pennsylvania	4,691,681,000	2.0%
49	Rhode Island	65,640,000	0.0%
35	South Carolina	1,890,661,000	0.8%
19	South Dakota	4,716,173,000	2.0%
31	Tennessee	2,564,931,000	1.1%
2	Texas	16,026,756,000	6.7%
37	Utah	1,243,673,000	0.5%
44	Vermont	500,792,000	0.2%
30	Virginia	2,688,669,000	1.1%
12	Washington	6,138,973,000	2.6%
45	West Virginia	449,551,000	0.2%
10	Wisconsin	6,791,282,000	2.8%
38	Wyoming	1,021,145,000	0.4%

RANK ORDER

RANK	STATE	FARM INCOME	% of USA
1	California	$31,402,706,000	13.1%
2	Texas	16,026,756,000	6.7%
3	Iowa	15,108,261,000	6.3%
4	Nebraska	12,042,344,000	5.0%
5	Kansas	10,335,795,000	4.3%
6	Minnesota	9,769,512,000	4.1%
7	Illinois	8,635,700,000	3.6%
8	North Carolina	8,199,349,000	3.4%
9	Florida	6,974,161,000	2.9%
10	Wisconsin	6,791,282,000	2.8%
11	Arkansas	6,164,069,000	2.6%
12	Washington	6,138,973,000	2.6%
13	Georgia	6,005,101,000	2.5%
14	Indiana	5,973,217,000	2.5%
15	Missouri	5,621,258,000	2.3%
16	Colorado	5,614,394,000	2.3%
17	Ohio	5,479,712,000	2.3%
18	Oklahoma	5,093,622,000	2.1%
19	South Dakota	4,716,173,000	2.0%
20	Pennsylvania	4,691,681,000	2.0%
21	Michigan	4,487,765,000	1.9%
22	Idaho	4,415,602,000	1.8%
23	Kentucky	4,007,202,000	1.7%
24	Oregon	3,990,617,000	1.7%
25	North Dakota	3,980,728,000	1.7%
26	Mississippi	3,788,510,000	1.6%
27	Alabama	3,739,060,000	1.6%
28	New York	3,509,003,000	1.5%
29	Arizona	2,879,224,000	1.2%
30	Virginia	2,688,669,000	1.1%
31	Tennessee	2,564,931,000	1.1%
32	New Mexico	2,463,526,000	1.0%
33	Montana	2,349,159,000	1.0%
34	Louisiana	2,186,180,000	0.9%
35	South Carolina	1,890,661,000	0.8%
36	Maryland	1,597,699,000	0.7%
37	Utah	1,243,673,000	0.5%
38	Wyoming	1,021,145,000	0.4%
39	Delaware	969,124,000	0.4%
40	New Jersey	923,933,000	0.4%
41	Maine	591,674,000	0.2%
42	Hawaii	554,580,000	0.2%
43	Connecticut	523,611,000	0.2%
44	Vermont	500,792,000	0.2%
45	West Virginia	449,551,000	0.2%
46	Nevada	446,550,000	0.2%
47	Massachusetts	433,026,000	0.2%
48	New Hampshire	161,804,000	0.1%
49	Rhode Island	65,640,000	0.0%
50	Alaska	64,218,000	0.0%
	District of Columbia	0	0.0%

Source: U.S. Department of Agriculture, Economic Research Service
"Farm Marketings" (http://www.ers.usda.gov/data/FarmIncome/firkdmu.htm)
*Commodities include crops and livestock.

Farm Income: Crops in 2006

National Total = $119,951,478,000

RANK	STATE	FARM INCOME	% of USA
36	Alabama	$695,921,000	0.6%
50	Alaska	24,850,000	0.0%
23	Arizona	1,558,497,000	1.3%
17	Arkansas	2,396,712,000	2.0%
1	California	23,787,727,000	19.8%
24	Colorado	1,552,540,000	1.3%
39	Connecticut	372,322,000	0.3%
43	Delaware	182,708,000	0.2%
5	Florida	5,669,269,000	4.7%
18	Georgia	2,240,211,000	1.9%
38	Hawaii	466,875,000	0.4%
21	Idaho	1,999,621,000	1.7%
3	Illinois	6,840,840,000	5.7%
9	Indiana	3,918,946,000	3.3%
2	Iowa	7,229,148,000	6.0%
11	Kansas	3,365,144,000	2.8%
28	Kentucky	1,299,218,000	1.1%
27	Louisiana	1,321,911,000	1.1%
42	Maine	302,766,000	0.3%
35	Maryland	725,556,000	0.6%
40	Massachusetts	343,606,000	0.3%
15	Michigan	2,833,395,000	2.4%
6	Minnesota	5,127,587,000	4.3%
29	Mississippi	1,244,984,000	1.0%
16	Missouri	2,627,578,000	2.2%
30	Montana	1,069,977,000	0.9%
8	Nebraska	4,358,958,000	3.6%
44	Nevada	166,179,000	0.1%
46	New Hampshire	97,765,000	0.1%
34	New Jersey	762,632,000	0.6%
37	New Mexico	602,427,000	0.5%
25	New York	1,527,292,000	1.3%
14	North Carolina	2,925,338,000	2.4%
12	North Dakota	3,088,353,000	2.6%
10	Ohio	3,448,407,000	2.9%
31	Oklahoma	974,121,000	0.8%
13	Oregon	2,960,584,000	2.5%
22	Pennsylvania	1,723,338,000	1.4%
49	Rhode Island	55,550,000	0.0%
33	South Carolina	788,075,000	0.7%
20	South Dakota	2,064,550,000	1.7%
26	Tennessee	1,373,292,000	1.1%
4	Texas	5,703,021,000	4.8%
41	Utah	312,849,000	0.3%
47	Vermont	85,688,000	0.1%
32	Virginia	834,053,000	0.7%
7	Washington	4,524,433,000	3.8%
48	West Virginia	79,749,000	0.1%
19	Wisconsin	2,135,279,000	1.8%
45	Wyoming	161,649,000	0.1%

RANK	STATE	FARM INCOME	% of USA
1	California	$23,787,727,000	19.8%
2	Iowa	7,229,148,000	6.0%
3	Illinois	6,840,840,000	5.7%
4	Texas	5,703,021,000	4.8%
5	Florida	5,669,269,000	4.7%
6	Minnesota	5,127,587,000	4.3%
7	Washington	4,524,433,000	3.8%
8	Nebraska	4,358,958,000	3.6%
9	Indiana	3,918,946,000	3.3%
10	Ohio	3,448,407,000	2.9%
11	Kansas	3,365,144,000	2.8%
12	North Dakota	3,088,353,000	2.6%
13	Oregon	2,960,584,000	2.5%
14	North Carolina	2,925,338,000	2.4%
15	Michigan	2,833,395,000	2.4%
16	Missouri	2,627,578,000	2.2%
17	Arkansas	2,396,712,000	2.0%
18	Georgia	2,240,211,000	1.9%
19	Wisconsin	2,135,279,000	1.8%
20	South Dakota	2,064,550,000	1.7%
21	Idaho	1,999,621,000	1.7%
22	Pennsylvania	1,723,338,000	1.4%
23	Arizona	1,558,497,000	1.3%
24	Colorado	1,552,540,000	1.3%
25	New York	1,527,292,000	1.3%
26	Tennessee	1,373,292,000	1.1%
27	Louisiana	1,321,911,000	1.1%
28	Kentucky	1,299,218,000	1.1%
29	Mississippi	1,244,984,000	1.0%
30	Montana	1,069,977,000	0.9%
31	Oklahoma	974,121,000	0.8%
32	Virginia	834,053,000	0.7%
33	South Carolina	788,075,000	0.7%
34	New Jersey	762,632,000	0.6%
35	Maryland	725,556,000	0.6%
36	Alabama	695,921,000	0.6%
37	New Mexico	602,427,000	0.5%
38	Hawaii	466,875,000	0.4%
39	Connecticut	372,322,000	0.3%
40	Massachusetts	343,606,000	0.3%
41	Utah	312,849,000	0.3%
42	Maine	302,766,000	0.3%
43	Delaware	182,708,000	0.2%
44	Nevada	166,179,000	0.1%
45	Wyoming	161,649,000	0.1%
46	New Hampshire	97,765,000	0.1%
47	Vermont	85,688,000	0.1%
48	West Virginia	79,749,000	0.1%
49	Rhode Island	55,550,000	0.0%
50	Alaska	24,850,000	0.0%
	District of Columbia	0	0.0%

Source: U.S. Department of Agriculture, Economic Research Service
"Farm Marketings" (http://www.ers.usda.gov/data/FarmIncome/firkdmu.htm)

Farm Income: Livestock in 2006

National Total = $119,320,429,000*

ALPHA ORDER

RANK	STATE	FARM INCOME	% of USA
13	Alabama	$3,043,139,000	2.6%
49	Alaska	39,368,000	0.0%
28	Arizona	1,320,727,000	1.1%
11	Arkansas	3,767,357,000	3.2%
4	California	7,614,979,000	6.4%
10	Colorado	4,061,854,000	3.4%
45	Connecticut	151,289,000	0.1%
39	Delaware	786,416,000	0.7%
29	Florida	1,304,892,000	1.1%
12	Georgia	3,764,890,000	3.2%
47	Hawaii	87,705,000	0.1%
19	Idaho	2,415,981,000	2.0%
25	Illinois	1,794,860,000	1.5%
20	Indiana	2,054,271,000	1.7%
2	Iowa	7,879,113,000	6.6%
5	Kansas	6,970,651,000	5.8%
16	Kentucky	2,707,984,000	2.3%
37	Louisiana	864,269,000	0.7%
42	Maine	288,908,000	0.2%
36	Maryland	872,143,000	0.7%
46	Massachusetts	89,420,000	0.1%
26	Michigan	1,654,370,000	1.4%
8	Minnesota	4,641,925,000	3.9%
18	Mississippi	2,543,526,000	2.1%
14	Missouri	2,993,680,000	2.5%
30	Montana	1,279,182,000	1.1%
3	Nebraska	7,683,386,000	6.4%
43	Nevada	280,371,000	0.2%
48	New Hampshire	64,039,000	0.1%
44	New Jersey	161,301,000	0.1%
23	New Mexico	1,861,099,000	1.6%
22	New York	1,981,711,000	1.7%
6	North Carolina	5,274,011,000	4.4%
35	North Dakota	892,375,000	0.7%
21	Ohio	2,031,305,000	1.7%
9	Oklahoma	4,119,501,000	3.5%
33	Oregon	1,030,033,000	0.9%
15	Pennsylvania	2,968,343,000	2.5%
50	Rhode Island	10,090,000	0.0%
32	South Carolina	1,102,586,000	0.9%
17	South Dakota	2,651,623,000	2.2%
31	Tennessee	1,191,639,000	1.0%
1	Texas	10,323,735,000	8.7%
34	Utah	930,824,000	0.8%
40	Vermont	415,104,000	0.3%
24	Virginia	1,854,616,000	1.6%
27	Washington	1,614,540,000	1.4%
41	West Virginia	369,802,000	0.3%
7	Wisconsin	4,656,003,000	3.9%
38	Wyoming	859,496,000	0.7%

RANK ORDER

RANK	STATE	FARM INCOME	% of USA
1	Texas	$10,323,735,000	8.7%
2	Iowa	7,879,113,000	6.6%
3	Nebraska	7,683,386,000	6.4%
4	California	7,614,979,000	6.4%
5	Kansas	6,970,651,000	5.8%
6	North Carolina	5,274,011,000	4.4%
7	Wisconsin	4,656,003,000	3.9%
8	Minnesota	4,641,925,000	3.9%
9	Oklahoma	4,119,501,000	3.5%
10	Colorado	4,061,854,000	3.4%
11	Arkansas	3,767,357,000	3.2%
12	Georgia	3,764,890,000	3.2%
13	Alabama	3,043,139,000	2.6%
14	Missouri	2,993,680,000	2.5%
15	Pennsylvania	2,968,343,000	2.5%
16	Kentucky	2,707,984,000	2.3%
17	South Dakota	2,651,623,000	2.2%
18	Mississippi	2,543,526,000	2.1%
19	Idaho	2,415,981,000	2.0%
20	Indiana	2,054,271,000	1.7%
21	Ohio	2,031,305,000	1.7%
22	New York	1,981,711,000	1.7%
23	New Mexico	1,861,099,000	1.6%
24	Virginia	1,854,616,000	1.6%
25	Illinois	1,794,860,000	1.5%
26	Michigan	1,654,370,000	1.4%
27	Washington	1,614,540,000	1.4%
28	Arizona	1,320,727,000	1.1%
29	Florida	1,304,892,000	1.1%
30	Montana	1,279,182,000	1.1%
31	Tennessee	1,191,639,000	1.0%
32	South Carolina	1,102,586,000	0.9%
33	Oregon	1,030,033,000	0.9%
34	Utah	930,824,000	0.8%
35	North Dakota	892,375,000	0.7%
36	Maryland	872,143,000	0.7%
37	Louisiana	864,269,000	0.7%
38	Wyoming	859,496,000	0.7%
39	Delaware	786,416,000	0.7%
40	Vermont	415,104,000	0.3%
41	West Virginia	369,802,000	0.3%
42	Maine	288,908,000	0.2%
43	Nevada	280,371,000	0.2%
44	New Jersey	161,301,000	0.1%
45	Connecticut	151,289,000	0.1%
46	Massachusetts	89,420,000	0.1%
47	Hawaii	87,705,000	0.1%
48	New Hampshire	64,039,000	0.1%
49	Alaska	39,368,000	0.0%
50	Rhode Island	10,090,000	0.0%
	District of Columbia	0	0.0%

Source: U.S. Department of Agriculture, Economic Research Service
   "Farm Marketings" (http://www.ers.usda.gov/data/FarmIncome/firkdmu.htm)
*Includes livestock products.

Farm Income: Government Payments in 2006

National Total = $15,789,146,000*

ALPHA ORDER

RANK	STATE	PAYMENTS	% of USA
25	Alabama	$219,263,000	1.4%
49	Alaska	3,383,000	0.0%
34	Arizona	109,088,000	0.7%
11	Arkansas	515,613,000	3.3%
10	California	530,193,000	3.4%
23	Colorado	244,612,000	1.5%
45	Connecticut	9,430,000	0.1%
39	Delaware	22,093,000	0.1%
30	Florida	140,767,000	0.9%
14	Georgia	483,093,000	3.1%
48	Hawaii	3,796,000	0.0%
29	Idaho	140,790,000	0.9%
3	Illinois	1,045,199,000	6.6%
9	Indiana	541,283,000	3.4%
2	Iowa	1,252,368,000	7.9%
7	Kansas	648,182,000	4.1%
13	Kentucky	494,867,000	3.1%
19	Louisiana	340,987,000	2.2%
43	Maine	14,948,000	0.1%
36	Maryland	67,445,000	0.4%
44	Massachusetts	12,709,000	0.1%
22	Michigan	247,643,000	1.6%
5	Minnesota	767,576,000	4.9%
8	Mississippi	633,490,000	4.0%
12	Missouri	510,223,000	3.2%
21	Montana	275,301,000	1.7%
4	Nebraska	812,068,000	5.1%
46	Nevada	8,620,000	0.1%
47	New Hampshire	7,558,000	0.0%
41	New Jersey	17,869,000	0.1%
35	New Mexico	82,608,000	0.5%
32	New York	127,873,000	0.8%
6	North Carolina	738,423,000	4.7%
15	North Dakota	453,076,000	2.9%
16	Ohio	441,641,000	2.8%
24	Oklahoma	243,297,000	1.5%
33	Oregon	118,215,000	0.7%
31	Pennsylvania	134,499,000	0.9%
50	Rhode Island	2,576,000	0.0%
27	South Carolina	184,247,000	1.2%
18	South Dakota	411,846,000	2.6%
20	Tennessee	326,258,000	2.1%
1	Texas	1,507,639,000	9.5%
37	Utah	40,184,000	0.3%
40	Vermont	19,844,000	0.1%
28	Virginia	172,422,000	1.1%
26	Washington	196,466,000	1.2%
42	West Virginia	16,188,000	0.1%
17	Wisconsin	414,088,000	2.6%
38	Wyoming	37,299,000	0.2%

RANK ORDER

RANK	STATE	PAYMENTS	% of USA
1	Texas	$1,507,639,000	9.5%
2	Iowa	1,252,368,000	7.9%
3	Illinois	1,045,199,000	6.6%
4	Nebraska	812,068,000	5.1%
5	Minnesota	767,576,000	4.9%
6	North Carolina	738,423,000	4.7%
7	Kansas	648,182,000	4.1%
8	Mississippi	633,490,000	4.0%
9	Indiana	541,283,000	3.4%
10	California	530,193,000	3.4%
11	Arkansas	515,613,000	3.3%
12	Missouri	510,223,000	3.2%
13	Kentucky	494,867,000	3.1%
14	Georgia	483,093,000	3.1%
15	North Dakota	453,076,000	2.9%
16	Ohio	441,641,000	2.8%
17	Wisconsin	414,088,000	2.6%
18	South Dakota	411,846,000	2.6%
19	Louisiana	340,987,000	2.2%
20	Tennessee	326,258,000	2.1%
21	Montana	275,301,000	1.7%
22	Michigan	247,643,000	1.6%
23	Colorado	244,612,000	1.5%
24	Oklahoma	243,297,000	1.5%
25	Alabama	219,263,000	1.4%
26	Washington	196,466,000	1.2%
27	South Carolina	184,247,000	1.2%
28	Virginia	172,422,000	1.1%
29	Idaho	140,790,000	0.9%
30	Florida	140,767,000	0.9%
31	Pennsylvania	134,499,000	0.9%
32	New York	127,873,000	0.8%
33	Oregon	118,215,000	0.7%
34	Arizona	109,088,000	0.7%
35	New Mexico	82,608,000	0.5%
36	Maryland	67,445,000	0.4%
37	Utah	40,184,000	0.3%
38	Wyoming	37,299,000	0.2%
39	Delaware	22,093,000	0.1%
40	Vermont	19,844,000	0.1%
41	New Jersey	17,869,000	0.1%
42	West Virginia	16,188,000	0.1%
43	Maine	14,948,000	0.1%
44	Massachusetts	12,709,000	0.1%
45	Connecticut	9,430,000	0.1%
46	Nevada	8,620,000	0.1%
47	New Hampshire	7,558,000	0.0%
48	Hawaii	3,796,000	0.0%
49	Alaska	3,383,000	0.0%
50	Rhode Island	2,576,000	0.0%
	District of Columbia	0	0.0%

Source: U.S. Department of Agriculture, Economic Research Service
"Farm Income" (http://www.ers.usda.gov/data/FarmIncome/FinfidmuWK4.htm)
*Government payments made directly to farmers in cash.

Acres Planted in 2007

National Total = 319,990,000 Acres*

ALPHA ORDER					RANK ORDER			

RANK	STATE	ACRES	% of USA
31	Alabama	2,068,000	0.6%
NA	Alaska**	NA	NA
38	Arizona	688,000	0.2%
14	Arkansas	8,256,000	2.6%
22	California	4,304,000	1.3%
17	Colorado	6,156,000	1.9%
46	Connecticut	90,000	0.0%
41	Delaware	440,000	0.1%
36	Florida	1,041,000	0.3%
25	Georgia	3,769,000	1.2%
48	Hawaii	23,000	0.0%
23	Idaho	4,294,000	1.3%
2	Illinois	23,201,000	7.3%
10	Indiana	12,305,000	3.8%
1	Iowa	24,410,000	7.6%
3	Kansas	22,941,000	7.2%
18	Kentucky	5,804,000	1.8%
27	Louisiana	3,365,000	1.1%
44	Maine	283,000	0.1%
34	Maryland	1,423,000	0.4%
45	Massachusetts	104,000	0.0%
16	Michigan	6,517,000	2.0%
6	Minnesota	19,543,000	6.1%
20	Mississippi	4,644,000	1.5%
9	Missouri	13,853,000	4.3%
13	Montana	8,864,000	2.8%
7	Nebraska	18,742,000	5.9%
40	Nevada	498,000	0.2%
47	New Hampshire	60,000	0.0%
42	New Jersey	327,000	0.1%
35	New Mexico	1,154,000	0.4%
28	New York	2,864,000	0.9%
19	North Carolina	4,714,000	1.5%
5	North Dakota	22,099,000	6.9%
12	Ohio	10,056,000	3.1%
11	Oklahoma	10,398,000	3.2%
30	Oregon	2,115,000	0.7%
24	Pennsylvania	4,008,000	1.3%
49	Rhode Island	11,000	0.0%
32	South Carolina	1,643,000	0.5%
8	South Dakota	16,688,000	5.2%
21	Tennessee	4,612,000	1.4%
4	Texas	22,621,000	7.1%
37	Utah	1,001,000	0.3%
43	Vermont	312,000	0.1%
29	Virginia	2,792,000	0.9%
26	Washington	3,647,000	1.1%
39	West Virginia	669,000	0.2%
15	Wisconsin	8,100,000	2.5%
33	Wyoming	1,500,000	0.5%

RANK	STATE	ACRES	% of USA
1	Iowa	24,410,000	7.6%
2	Illinois	23,201,000	7.3%
3	Kansas	22,941,000	7.2%
4	Texas	22,621,000	7.1%
5	North Dakota	22,099,000	6.9%
6	Minnesota	19,543,000	6.1%
7	Nebraska	18,742,000	5.9%
8	South Dakota	16,688,000	5.2%
9	Missouri	13,853,000	4.3%
10	Indiana	12,305,000	3.8%
11	Oklahoma	10,398,000	3.2%
12	Ohio	10,056,000	3.1%
13	Montana	8,864,000	2.8%
14	Arkansas	8,256,000	2.6%
15	Wisconsin	8,100,000	2.5%
16	Michigan	6,517,000	2.0%
17	Colorado	6,156,000	1.9%
18	Kentucky	5,804,000	1.8%
19	North Carolina	4,714,000	1.5%
20	Mississippi	4,644,000	1.5%
21	Tennessee	4,612,000	1.4%
22	California	4,304,000	1.3%
23	Idaho	4,294,000	1.3%
24	Pennsylvania	4,008,000	1.3%
25	Georgia	3,769,000	1.2%
26	Washington	3,647,000	1.1%
27	Louisiana	3,365,000	1.1%
28	New York	2,864,000	0.9%
29	Virginia	2,792,000	0.9%
30	Oregon	2,115,000	0.7%
31	Alabama	2,068,000	0.6%
32	South Carolina	1,643,000	0.5%
33	Wyoming	1,500,000	0.5%
34	Maryland	1,423,000	0.4%
35	New Mexico	1,154,000	0.4%
36	Florida	1,041,000	0.3%
37	Utah	1,001,000	0.3%
38	Arizona	688,000	0.2%
39	West Virginia	669,000	0.2%
40	Nevada	498,000	0.2%
41	Delaware	440,000	0.1%
42	New Jersey	327,000	0.1%
43	Vermont	312,000	0.1%
44	Maine	283,000	0.1%
45	Massachusetts	104,000	0.0%
46	Connecticut	90,000	0.0%
47	New Hampshire	60,000	0.0%
48	Hawaii	23,000	0.0%
49	Rhode Island	11,000	0.0%
NA	Alaska**	NA	NA
	District of Columbia**	NA	NA

Source: U.S. Department of Agriculture, National Agricultural Statistics Service
    "Crop Production: 2007 Summary" (Cr Pr 2-1 (07), January 2008)
    (http://usda.mannlib.cornell.edu/MannUsda/viewDocumentInfo.do?documentID=1047)
*Estimated totals.
**No acreage or not available.

Acres Harvested in 2007

National Total = 303,792,000 Acres*

ALPHA ORDER					RANK ORDER			
RANK	STATE	ACRES	% of USA		RANK	STATE	ACRES	% of USA
31	Alabama	1,918,000	0.6%		1	Iowa	24,245,000	8.0%
NA	Alaska**	NA	NA		2	Illinois	22,979,000	7.6%
38	Arizona	679,000	0.2%		3	North Dakota	21,473,000	7.1%
13	Arkansas	8,056,000	2.7%		4	Kansas	20,883,000	6.9%
24	California	3,787,000	1.2%		5	Texas	19,174,000	6.3%
17	Colorado	5,837,000	1.9%		6	Minnesota	19,160,000	6.3%
46	Connecticut	88,000	0.0%		7	Nebraska	18,382,000	6.1%
41	Delaware	428,000	0.1%		8	South Dakota	16,098,000	5.3%
35	Florida	1,014,000	0.3%		9	Missouri	13,501,000	4.4%
26	Georgia	3,331,000	1.1%		10	Indiana	12,198,000	4.0%
48	Hawaii	23,000	0.0%		11	Ohio	9,855,000	3.2%
22	Idaho	4,155,000	1.4%		12	Montana	8,535,000	2.8%
2	Illinois	22,979,000	7.6%		13	Arkansas	8,056,000	2.7%
10	Indiana	12,198,000	4.0%		14	Wisconsin	7,906,000	2.6%
1	Iowa	24,245,000	8.0%		15	Oklahoma	7,644,000	2.5%
4	Kansas	20,883,000	6.9%		16	Michigan	6,444,000	2.1%
18	Kentucky	5,571,000	1.8%		17	Colorado	5,837,000	1.9%
27	Louisiana	3,319,000	1.1%		18	Kentucky	5,571,000	1.8%
44	Maine	278,000	0.1%		19	Mississippi	4,533,000	1.5%
34	Maryland	1,332,000	0.4%		20	North Carolina	4,446,000	1.5%
45	Massachusetts	101,000	0.0%		21	Tennessee	4,359,000	1.4%
16	Michigan	6,444,000	2.1%		22	Idaho	4,155,000	1.4%
6	Minnesota	19,160,000	6.3%		23	Pennsylvania	3,917,000	1.3%
19	Mississippi	4,533,000	1.5%		24	California	3,787,000	1.2%
9	Missouri	13,501,000	4.4%		25	Washington	3,583,000	1.2%
12	Montana	8,535,000	2.8%		26	Georgia	3,331,000	1.1%
7	Nebraska	18,382,000	6.1%		27	Louisiana	3,319,000	1.1%
40	Nevada	486,000	0.2%		28	New York	2,799,000	0.9%
47	New Hampshire	60,000	0.0%		29	Virginia	2,711,000	0.9%
42	New Jersey	319,000	0.1%		30	Oregon	2,045,000	0.7%
36	New Mexico	949,000	0.3%		31	Alabama	1,918,000	0.6%
28	New York	2,799,000	0.9%		32	South Carolina	1,529,000	0.5%
20	North Carolina	4,446,000	1.5%		33	Wyoming	1,436,000	0.5%
3	North Dakota	21,473,000	7.1%		34	Maryland	1,332,000	0.4%
11	Ohio	9,855,000	3.2%		35	Florida	1,014,000	0.3%
15	Oklahoma	7,644,000	2.5%		36	New Mexico	949,000	0.3%
30	Oregon	2,045,000	0.7%		37	Utah	939,000	0.3%
23	Pennsylvania	3,917,000	1.3%		38	Arizona	679,000	0.2%
49	Rhode Island	11,000	0.0%		39	West Virginia	665,000	0.2%
32	South Carolina	1,529,000	0.5%		40	Nevada	486,000	0.2%
8	South Dakota	16,098,000	5.3%		41	Delaware	428,000	0.1%
21	Tennessee	4,359,000	1.4%		42	New Jersey	319,000	0.1%
5	Texas	19,174,000	6.3%		43	Vermont	307,000	0.1%
37	Utah	939,000	0.3%		44	Maine	278,000	0.1%
43	Vermont	307,000	0.1%		45	Massachusetts	101,000	0.0%
29	Virginia	2,711,000	0.9%		46	Connecticut	88,000	0.0%
25	Washington	3,583,000	1.2%		47	New Hampshire	60,000	0.0%
39	West Virginia	665,000	0.2%		48	Hawaii	23,000	0.0%
14	Wisconsin	7,906,000	2.6%		49	Rhode Island	11,000	0.0%
33	Wyoming	1,436,000	0.5%		NA	Alaska**	NA	NA
						District of Columbia**	NA	NA

Source: U.S. Department of Agriculture, National Agricultural Statistics Service
"Crop Production: 2007 Summary" (Cr Pr 2-1 (07), January 2008)
(http://usda.mannlib.cornell.edu/MannUsda/viewDocumentInfo.do?documentID=1047)
*Estimated totals.
**No acreage or not available.

Acres Harvested: Corn in 2007

National Total = 93,600,000 Acres*

ALPHA ORDER

RANK	STATE	ACRES	% of USA
28	Alabama	340,000	0.4%
NA	Alaska**	NA	NA
41	Arizona	55,000	0.1%
23	Arkansas	610,000	0.7%
22	California	650,000	0.7%
16	Colorado	1,200,000	1.3%
44	Connecticut	26,000	0.0%
31	Delaware	195,000	0.2%
38	Florida	75,000	0.1%
26	Georgia	510,000	0.5%
NA	Hawaii**	NA	NA
30	Idaho	310,000	0.3%
2	Illinois	13,200,000	14.1%
5	Indiana	6,500,000	6.9%
1	Iowa	14,200,000	15.2%
8	Kansas	3,900,000	4.2%
14	Kentucky	1,450,000	1.5%
21	Louisiana	740,000	0.8%
43	Maine	28,000	0.0%
25	Maryland	540,000	0.6%
45	Massachusetts	18,000	0.0%
11	Michigan	2,650,000	2.8%
4	Minnesota	8,400,000	9.0%
19	Mississippi	960,000	1.0%
10	Missouri	3,450,000	3.7%
37	Montana	84,000	0.1%
3	Nebraska	9,400,000	10.0%
47	Nevada	5,000	0.0%
46	New Hampshire	14,000	0.0%
34	New Jersey	95,000	0.1%
33	New Mexico	135,000	0.1%
18	New York	1,050,000	1.1%
17	North Carolina	1,100,000	1.2%
12	North Dakota	2,550,000	2.7%
9	Ohio	3,850,000	4.1%
29	Oklahoma	320,000	0.3%
40	Oregon	60,000	0.1%
15	Pennsylvania	1,410,000	1.5%
48	Rhode Island	2,000	0.0%
27	South Carolina	400,000	0.4%
6	South Dakota	5,000,000	5.3%
20	Tennessee	870,000	0.9%
13	Texas	2,150,000	2.3%
39	Utah	70,000	0.1%
36	Vermont	92,000	0.1%
24	Virginia	550,000	0.6%
31	Washington	195,000	0.2%
42	West Virginia	46,000	0.0%
7	Wisconsin	4,050,000	4.3%
34	Wyoming	95,000	0.1%

RANK ORDER

RANK	STATE	ACRES	% of USA
1	Iowa	14,200,000	15.2%
2	Illinois	13,200,000	14.1%
3	Nebraska	9,400,000	10.0%
4	Minnesota	8,400,000	9.0%
5	Indiana	6,500,000	6.9%
6	South Dakota	5,000,000	5.3%
7	Wisconsin	4,050,000	4.3%
8	Kansas	3,900,000	4.2%
9	Ohio	3,850,000	4.1%
10	Missouri	3,450,000	3.7%
11	Michigan	2,650,000	2.8%
12	North Dakota	2,550,000	2.7%
13	Texas	2,150,000	2.3%
14	Kentucky	1,450,000	1.5%
15	Pennsylvania	1,410,000	1.5%
16	Colorado	1,200,000	1.3%
17	North Carolina	1,100,000	1.2%
18	New York	1,050,000	1.1%
19	Mississippi	960,000	1.0%
20	Tennessee	870,000	0.9%
21	Louisiana	740,000	0.8%
22	California	650,000	0.7%
23	Arkansas	610,000	0.7%
24	Virginia	550,000	0.6%
25	Maryland	540,000	0.6%
26	Georgia	510,000	0.5%
27	South Carolina	400,000	0.4%
28	Alabama	340,000	0.4%
29	Oklahoma	320,000	0.3%
30	Idaho	310,000	0.3%
31	Delaware	195,000	0.2%
31	Washington	195,000	0.2%
33	New Mexico	135,000	0.1%
34	New Jersey	95,000	0.1%
34	Wyoming	95,000	0.1%
36	Vermont	92,000	0.1%
37	Montana	84,000	0.1%
38	Florida	75,000	0.1%
39	Utah	70,000	0.1%
40	Oregon	60,000	0.1%
41	Arizona	55,000	0.1%
42	West Virginia	46,000	0.0%
43	Maine	28,000	0.0%
44	Connecticut	26,000	0.0%
45	Massachusetts	18,000	0.0%
46	New Hampshire	14,000	0.0%
47	Nevada	5,000	0.0%
48	Rhode Island	2,000	0.0%
NA	Alaska**	NA	NA
NA	Hawaii**	NA	NA
	District of Columbia**	NA	NA

Source: U.S. Department of Agriculture, National Agricultural Statistics Service
  "Crop Production: 2007 Summary" (Cr Pr 2-1 (07), January 2008)
    (http://usda.mannlib.cornell.edu/MannUsda/viewDocumentInfo.do?documentID=1047)
*Estimated totals. Acres harvested for grain and silage. There were 86,542,000 acres harvested for grain.
**No acreage or not available.

Acres Harvested: Soybeans in 2007

National Total = 62,820,000 Acres*

RANK	STATE	ACRES	% of USA
25	Alabama	180,000	0.3%
NA	Alaska**	NA	NA
NA	Arizona**	NA	NA
10	Arkansas	2,790,000	4.4%
NA	California**	NA	NA
NA	Colorado**	NA	NA
NA	Connecticut**	NA	NA
27	Delaware	145,000	0.2%
31	Florida	12,000	0.0%
23	Georgia	275,000	0.4%
NA	Hawaii**	NA	NA
NA	Idaho**	NA	NA
2	Illinois	8,150,000	13.0%
4	Indiana	4,680,000	7.4%
1	Iowa	8,520,000	13.6%
11	Kansas	2,550,000	4.1%
16	Kentucky	1,080,000	1.7%
18	Louisiana	590,000	0.9%
NA	Maine**	NA	NA
22	Maryland	380,000	0.6%
NA	Massachusetts**	NA	NA
12	Michigan	1,740,000	2.8%
3	Minnesota	6,150,000	9.8%
13	Mississippi	1,420,000	2.3%
5	Missouri	4,550,000	7.2%
NA	Montana**	NA	NA
7	Nebraska	3,770,000	6.0%
NA	Nevada**	NA	NA
NA	New Hampshire**	NA	NA
29	New Jersey	79,000	0.1%
NA	New Mexico**	NA	NA
24	New York	203,000	0.3%
14	North Carolina	1,360,000	2.2%
9	North Dakota	2,990,000	4.8%
6	Ohio	4,130,000	6.6%
26	Oklahoma	175,000	0.3%
NA	Oregon**	NA	NA
21	Pennsylvania	420,000	0.7%
NA	Rhode Island**	NA	NA
20	South Carolina	425,000	0.7%
8	South Dakota	3,180,000	5.1%
17	Tennessee	970,000	1.5%
28	Texas	82,000	0.1%
NA	Utah**	NA	NA
NA	Vermont**	NA	NA
19	Virginia	480,000	0.8%
NA	Washington**	NA	NA
30	West Virginia	14,000	0.0%
15	Wisconsin	1,330,000	2.1%
NA	Wyoming**	NA	NA

RANK	STATE	ACRES	% of USA
1	Iowa	8,520,000	13.6%
2	Illinois	8,150,000	13.0%
3	Minnesota	6,150,000	9.8%
4	Indiana	4,680,000	7.4%
5	Missouri	4,550,000	7.2%
6	Ohio	4,130,000	6.6%
7	Nebraska	3,770,000	6.0%
8	South Dakota	3,180,000	5.1%
9	North Dakota	2,990,000	4.8%
10	Arkansas	2,790,000	4.4%
11	Kansas	2,550,000	4.1%
12	Michigan	1,740,000	2.8%
13	Mississippi	1,420,000	2.3%
14	North Carolina	1,360,000	2.2%
15	Wisconsin	1,330,000	2.1%
16	Kentucky	1,080,000	1.7%
17	Tennessee	970,000	1.5%
18	Louisiana	590,000	0.9%
19	Virginia	480,000	0.8%
20	South Carolina	425,000	0.7%
21	Pennsylvania	420,000	0.7%
22	Maryland	380,000	0.6%
23	Georgia	275,000	0.4%
24	New York	203,000	0.3%
25	Alabama	180,000	0.3%
26	Oklahoma	175,000	0.3%
27	Delaware	145,000	0.2%
28	Texas	82,000	0.1%
29	New Jersey	79,000	0.1%
30	West Virginia	14,000	0.0%
31	Florida	12,000	0.0%
NA	Alaska**	NA	NA
NA	Arizona**	NA	NA
NA	California**	NA	NA
NA	Colorado**	NA	NA
NA	Connecticut**	NA	NA
NA	Hawaii**	NA	NA
NA	Idaho**	NA	NA
NA	Maine**	NA	NA
NA	Massachusetts**	NA	NA
NA	Montana**	NA	NA
NA	Nevada**	NA	NA
NA	New Hampshire**	NA	NA
NA	New Mexico**	NA	NA
NA	Oregon**	NA	NA
NA	Rhode Island**	NA	NA
NA	Utah**	NA	NA
NA	Vermont**	NA	NA
NA	Washington**	NA	NA
NA	Wyoming**	NA	NA
	District of Columbia**	NA	NA

Source: U.S. Department of Agriculture, National Agricultural Statistics Service
   "Crop Production: 2007 Summary" (Cr Pr 2-1 (07), January 2008)
      (http://usda.mannlib.cornell.edu/MannUsda/viewDocumentInfo.do?documentID=1047)
*Estimated totals.
**No acreage or not available.

Acres Harvested: Wheat in 2006

National Total = 51,011,000 Acres*

<table>
<tr><td colspan="4">ALPHA ORDER</td><td colspan="4">RANK ORDER</td></tr>
<tr><th>RANK</th><th>STATE</th><th>ACRES</th><th>% of USA</th><th>RANK</th><th>STATE</th><th>ACRES</th><th>% of USA</th></tr>
<tr><td>36</td><td>Alabama</td><td>80,000</td><td>0.2%</td><td>1</td><td>Kansas</td><td>8,600,000</td><td>16.9%</td></tr>
<tr><td>NA</td><td>Alaska**</td><td>NA</td><td>NA</td><td>2</td><td>North Dakota</td><td>8,405,000</td><td>16.5%</td></tr>
<tr><td>35</td><td>Arizona</td><td>83,000</td><td>0.2%</td><td>3</td><td>Montana</td><td>5,065,000</td><td>9.9%</td></tr>
<tr><td>16</td><td>Arkansas</td><td>700,000</td><td>1.4%</td><td>4</td><td>Texas</td><td>3,800,000</td><td>7.4%</td></tr>
<tr><td>21</td><td>California</td><td>315,000</td><td>0.6%</td><td>5</td><td>Oklahoma</td><td>3,500,000</td><td>6.9%</td></tr>
<tr><td>7</td><td>Colorado</td><td>2,369,000</td><td>4.6%</td><td>6</td><td>South Dakota</td><td>3,328,000</td><td>6.5%</td></tr>
<tr><td>NA</td><td>Connecticut**</td><td>NA</td><td>NA</td><td>7</td><td>Colorado</td><td>2,369,000</td><td>4.6%</td></tr>
<tr><td>37</td><td>Delaware</td><td>55,000</td><td>0.1%</td><td>8</td><td>Washington</td><td>2,137,000</td><td>4.2%</td></tr>
<tr><td>41</td><td>Florida</td><td>9,000</td><td>0.0%</td><td>9</td><td>Nebraska</td><td>1,960,000</td><td>3.8%</td></tr>
<tr><td>26</td><td>Georgia</td><td>230,000</td><td>0.5%</td><td>10</td><td>Minnesota</td><td>1,710,000</td><td>3.4%</td></tr>
<tr><td>NA</td><td>Hawaii**</td><td>NA</td><td>NA</td><td>11</td><td>Idaho</td><td>1,175,000</td><td>2.3%</td></tr>
<tr><td>11</td><td>Idaho</td><td>1,175,000</td><td>2.3%</td><td>12</td><td>Illinois</td><td>890,000</td><td>1.7%</td></tr>
<tr><td>12</td><td>Illinois</td><td>890,000</td><td>1.7%</td><td>13</td><td>Missouri</td><td>880,000</td><td>1.7%</td></tr>
<tr><td>19</td><td>Indiana</td><td>370,000</td><td>0.7%</td><td>14</td><td>Oregon</td><td>855,000</td><td>1.7%</td></tr>
<tr><td>38</td><td>Iowa</td><td>28,000</td><td>0.1%</td><td>15</td><td>Ohio</td><td>730,000</td><td>1.4%</td></tr>
<tr><td>1</td><td>Kansas</td><td>8,600,000</td><td>16.9%</td><td>16</td><td>Arkansas</td><td>700,000</td><td>1.4%</td></tr>
<tr><td>25</td><td>Kentucky</td><td>250,000</td><td>0.5%</td><td>17</td><td>Michigan</td><td>540,000</td><td>1.1%</td></tr>
<tr><td>27</td><td>Louisiana</td><td>220,000</td><td>0.4%</td><td>18</td><td>North Carolina</td><td>500,000</td><td>1.0%</td></tr>
<tr><td>NA</td><td>Maine**</td><td>NA</td><td>NA</td><td>19</td><td>Indiana</td><td>370,000</td><td>0.7%</td></tr>
<tr><td>29</td><td>Maryland</td><td>170,000</td><td>0.3%</td><td>20</td><td>Mississippi</td><td>330,000</td><td>0.6%</td></tr>
<tr><td>NA</td><td>Massachusetts**</td><td>NA</td><td>NA</td><td>21</td><td>California</td><td>315,000</td><td>0.6%</td></tr>
<tr><td>17</td><td>Michigan</td><td>540,000</td><td>1.1%</td><td>22</td><td>New Mexico</td><td>300,000</td><td>0.6%</td></tr>
<tr><td>10</td><td>Minnesota</td><td>1,710,000</td><td>3.4%</td><td>23</td><td>Wisconsin</td><td>278,000</td><td>0.5%</td></tr>
<tr><td>20</td><td>Mississippi</td><td>330,000</td><td>0.6%</td><td>24</td><td>Tennessee</td><td>260,000</td><td>0.5%</td></tr>
<tr><td>13</td><td>Missouri</td><td>880,000</td><td>1.7%</td><td>25</td><td>Kentucky</td><td>250,000</td><td>0.5%</td></tr>
<tr><td>3</td><td>Montana</td><td>5,065,000</td><td>9.9%</td><td>26</td><td>Georgia</td><td>230,000</td><td>0.5%</td></tr>
<tr><td>9</td><td>Nebraska</td><td>1,960,000</td><td>3.8%</td><td>27</td><td>Louisiana</td><td>220,000</td><td>0.4%</td></tr>
<tr><td>40</td><td>Nevada</td><td>13,000</td><td>0.0%</td><td>28</td><td>Virginia</td><td>205,000</td><td>0.4%</td></tr>
<tr><td>NA</td><td>New Hampshire**</td><td>NA</td><td>NA</td><td>29</td><td>Maryland</td><td>170,000</td><td>0.3%</td></tr>
<tr><td>38</td><td>New Jersey</td><td>28,000</td><td>0.1%</td><td>30</td><td>Pennsylvania</td><td>155,000</td><td>0.3%</td></tr>
<tr><td>22</td><td>New Mexico</td><td>300,000</td><td>0.6%</td><td>31</td><td>South Carolina</td><td>135,000</td><td>0.3%</td></tr>
<tr><td>34</td><td>New York</td><td>85,000</td><td>0.2%</td><td>32</td><td>Utah</td><td>132,000</td><td>0.3%</td></tr>
<tr><td>18</td><td>North Carolina</td><td>500,000</td><td>1.0%</td><td>33</td><td>Wyoming</td><td>130,000</td><td>0.3%</td></tr>
<tr><td>2</td><td>North Dakota</td><td>8,405,000</td><td>16.5%</td><td>34</td><td>New York</td><td>85,000</td><td>0.2%</td></tr>
<tr><td>15</td><td>Ohio</td><td>730,000</td><td>1.4%</td><td>35</td><td>Arizona</td><td>83,000</td><td>0.2%</td></tr>
<tr><td>5</td><td>Oklahoma</td><td>3,500,000</td><td>6.9%</td><td>36</td><td>Alabama</td><td>80,000</td><td>0.2%</td></tr>
<tr><td>14</td><td>Oregon</td><td>855,000</td><td>1.7%</td><td>37</td><td>Delaware</td><td>55,000</td><td>0.1%</td></tr>
<tr><td>30</td><td>Pennsylvania</td><td>155,000</td><td>0.3%</td><td>38</td><td>Iowa</td><td>28,000</td><td>0.1%</td></tr>
<tr><td>NA</td><td>Rhode Island**</td><td>NA</td><td>NA</td><td>38</td><td>New Jersey</td><td>28,000</td><td>0.1%</td></tr>
<tr><td>31</td><td>South Carolina</td><td>135,000</td><td>0.3%</td><td>40</td><td>Nevada</td><td>13,000</td><td>0.0%</td></tr>
<tr><td>6</td><td>South Dakota</td><td>3,328,000</td><td>6.5%</td><td>41</td><td>Florida</td><td>9,000</td><td>0.0%</td></tr>
<tr><td>24</td><td>Tennessee</td><td>260,000</td><td>0.5%</td><td>42</td><td>West Virginia</td><td>6,000</td><td>0.0%</td></tr>
<tr><td>4</td><td>Texas</td><td>3,800,000</td><td>7.4%</td><td>NA</td><td>Alaska**</td><td>NA</td><td>NA</td></tr>
<tr><td>32</td><td>Utah</td><td>132,000</td><td>0.3%</td><td>NA</td><td>Connecticut**</td><td>NA</td><td>NA</td></tr>
<tr><td>NA</td><td>Vermont**</td><td>NA</td><td>NA</td><td>NA</td><td>Hawaii**</td><td>NA</td><td>NA</td></tr>
<tr><td>28</td><td>Virginia</td><td>205,000</td><td>0.4%</td><td>NA</td><td>Maine**</td><td>NA</td><td>NA</td></tr>
<tr><td>8</td><td>Washington</td><td>2,137,000</td><td>4.2%</td><td>NA</td><td>Massachusetts**</td><td>NA</td><td>NA</td></tr>
<tr><td>42</td><td>West Virginia</td><td>6,000</td><td>0.0%</td><td>NA</td><td>New Hampshire**</td><td>NA</td><td>NA</td></tr>
<tr><td>23</td><td>Wisconsin</td><td>278,000</td><td>0.5%</td><td>NA</td><td>Rhode Island**</td><td>NA</td><td>NA</td></tr>
<tr><td>33</td><td>Wyoming</td><td>130,000</td><td>0.3%</td><td>NA</td><td>Vermont**</td><td>NA</td><td>NA</td></tr>
<tr><td></td><td></td><td></td><td></td><td></td><td>District of Columbia**</td><td>NA</td><td>NA</td></tr>
</table>

Source: U.S. Department of Agriculture, National Agricultural Statistics Service
   "Crop Production: 2007 Summary" (Cr Pr 2-1 (07), January 2008)
   (http://usda.mannlib.cornell.edu/MannUsda/viewDocumentInfo.do?documentID=1047)
*Estimated totals.
**No acreage or not available.

Cattle on Farms in 2008

National Total = 96,668,600 Cattle*

ALPHA ORDER

RANK	STATE	CATTLE	% of USA
26	Alabama	1,250,000	1.3%
49	Alaska	15,500	0.0%
32	Arizona	970,000	1.0%
16	Arkansas	1,810,000	1.9%
4	California	5,450,000	5.6%
10	Colorado	2,750,000	2.8%
44	Connecticut	50,000	0.1%
48	Delaware	22,000	0.0%
18	Florida	1,710,000	1.8%
28	Georgia	1,130,000	1.2%
42	Hawaii	152,000	0.2%
14	Idaho	2,230,000	2.3%
27	Illinois	1,240,000	1.3%
33	Indiana	890,000	0.9%
7	Iowa	4,000,000	4.1%
2	Kansas	6,700,000	6.9%
12	Kentucky	2,400,000	2.5%
33	Louisiana	890,000	0.9%
43	Maine	89,000	0.1%
41	Maryland	205,000	0.2%
45	Massachusetts	46,000	0.0%
30	Michigan	1,070,000	1.1%
12	Minnesota	2,400,000	2.5%
31	Mississippi	990,000	1.0%
6	Missouri	4,300,000	4.4%
11	Montana	2,600,000	2.7%
3	Nebraska	6,550,000	6.8%
37	Nevada	450,000	0.5%
47	New Hampshire	36,000	0.0%
46	New Jersey	38,000	0.0%
21	New Mexico	1,530,000	1.6%
22	New York	1,450,000	1.5%
36	North Carolina	830,000	0.9%
16	North Dakota	1,810,000	1.9%
25	Ohio	1,270,000	1.3%
5	Oklahoma	5,400,000	5.6%
23	Oregon	1,390,000	1.4%
19	Pennsylvania	1,610,000	1.7%
50	Rhode Island	5,100	0.0%
39	South Carolina	400,000	0.4%
8	South Dakota	3,700,000	3.8%
15	Tennessee	2,130,000	2.2%
1	Texas	13,800,000	14.3%
35	Utah	850,000	0.9%
40	Vermont	265,000	0.3%
20	Virginia	1,570,000	1.6%
29	Washington	1,090,000	1.1%
38	West Virginia	415,000	0.4%
9	Wisconsin	3,400,000	3.5%
24	Wyoming	1,320,000	1.4%

RANK ORDER

RANK	STATE	CATTLE	% of USA
1	Texas	13,800,000	14.3%
2	Kansas	6,700,000	6.9%
3	Nebraska	6,550,000	6.8%
4	California	5,450,000	5.6%
5	Oklahoma	5,400,000	5.6%
6	Missouri	4,300,000	4.4%
7	Iowa	4,000,000	4.1%
8	South Dakota	3,700,000	3.8%
9	Wisconsin	3,400,000	3.5%
10	Colorado	2,750,000	2.8%
11	Montana	2,600,000	2.7%
12	Kentucky	2,400,000	2.5%
12	Minnesota	2,400,000	2.5%
14	Idaho	2,230,000	2.3%
15	Tennessee	2,130,000	2.2%
16	Arkansas	1,810,000	1.9%
16	North Dakota	1,810,000	1.9%
18	Florida	1,710,000	1.8%
19	Pennsylvania	1,610,000	1.7%
20	Virginia	1,570,000	1.6%
21	New Mexico	1,530,000	1.6%
22	New York	1,450,000	1.5%
23	Oregon	1,390,000	1.4%
24	Wyoming	1,320,000	1.4%
25	Ohio	1,270,000	1.3%
26	Alabama	1,250,000	1.3%
27	Illinois	1,240,000	1.3%
28	Georgia	1,130,000	1.2%
29	Washington	1,090,000	1.1%
30	Michigan	1,070,000	1.1%
31	Mississippi	990,000	1.0%
32	Arizona	970,000	1.0%
33	Indiana	890,000	0.9%
33	Louisiana	890,000	0.9%
35	Utah	850,000	0.9%
36	North Carolina	830,000	0.9%
37	Nevada	450,000	0.5%
38	West Virginia	415,000	0.4%
39	South Carolina	400,000	0.4%
40	Vermont	265,000	0.3%
41	Maryland	205,000	0.2%
42	Hawaii	152,000	0.2%
43	Maine	89,000	0.1%
44	Connecticut	50,000	0.1%
45	Massachusetts	46,000	0.0%
46	New Jersey	38,000	0.0%
47	New Hampshire	36,000	0.0%
48	Delaware	22,000	0.0%
49	Alaska	15,500	0.0%
50	Rhode Island	5,100	0.0%
	District of Columbia	0	0.0%

Source: U.S. Department of Agriculture, National Agricultural Statistics Service
   "Cattle" (http://usda.mannlib.cornell.edu/MannUsda/viewDocumentInfo.do?documentID=1017)
*As of January 1, 2008.

Milk Cows on Farms in 2006

National Total = 9,112,000 Milk Cows*

ALPHA ORDER

RANK	STATE	MILK COWS	% of USA
43	Alabama	14,000	0.2%
50	Alaska	800	0.0%
13	Arizona	173,000	1.9%
37	Arkansas	20,000	0.2%
1	California	1,780,000	19.5%
20	Colorado	110,000	1.2%
38	Connecticut	19,000	0.2%
46	Delaware	7,000	0.1%
16	Florida	132,000	1.4%
26	Georgia	77,000	0.8%
48	Hawaii	4,300	0.0%
5	Idaho	488,000	5.4%
21	Illinois	103,000	1.1%
14	Indiana	165,000	1.8%
12	Iowa	205,000	2.2%
19	Kansas	112,000	1.2%
23	Kentucky	98,000	1.1%
32	Louisiana	32,000	0.4%
32	Maine	32,000	0.4%
29	Maryland	64,000	0.7%
41	Massachusetts	16,000	0.2%
9	Michigan	320,000	3.5%
6	Minnesota	450,000	4.9%
36	Mississippi	23,000	0.3%
18	Missouri	115,000	1.3%
38	Montana	19,000	0.2%
30	Nebraska	61,000	0.7%
35	Nevada	27,000	0.3%
42	New Hampshire	15,000	0.2%
45	New Jersey	11,000	0.1%
7	New Mexico	355,000	3.9%
3	New York	638,000	7.0%
31	North Carolina	51,000	0.6%
32	North Dakota	32,000	0.4%
10	Ohio	274,000	3.0%
27	Oklahoma	73,000	0.8%
17	Oregon	118,000	1.3%
4	Pennsylvania	554,000	6.1%
49	Rhode Island	1,100	0.0%
40	South Carolina	17,000	0.2%
25	South Dakota	81,000	0.9%
28	Tennessee	67,000	0.7%
8	Texas	335,000	3.7%
24	Utah	86,000	0.9%
15	Vermont	141,000	1.5%
22	Virginia	102,000	1.1%
11	Washington	237,000	2.6%
44	West Virginia	13,000	0.1%
2	Wisconsin	1,243,000	13.6%
47	Wyoming	6,700	0.1%

RANK ORDER

RANK	STATE	MILK COWS	% of USA
1	California	1,780,000	19.5%
2	Wisconsin	1,243,000	13.6%
3	New York	638,000	7.0%
4	Pennsylvania	554,000	6.1%
5	Idaho	488,000	5.4%
6	Minnesota	450,000	4.9%
7	New Mexico	355,000	3.9%
8	Texas	335,000	3.7%
9	Michigan	320,000	3.5%
10	Ohio	274,000	3.0%
11	Washington	237,000	2.6%
12	Iowa	205,000	2.2%
13	Arizona	173,000	1.9%
14	Indiana	165,000	1.8%
15	Vermont	141,000	1.5%
16	Florida	132,000	1.4%
17	Oregon	118,000	1.3%
18	Missouri	115,000	1.3%
19	Kansas	112,000	1.2%
20	Colorado	110,000	1.2%
21	Illinois	103,000	1.1%
22	Virginia	102,000	1.1%
23	Kentucky	98,000	1.1%
24	Utah	86,000	0.9%
25	South Dakota	81,000	0.9%
26	Georgia	77,000	0.8%
27	Oklahoma	73,000	0.8%
28	Tennessee	67,000	0.7%
29	Maryland	64,000	0.7%
30	Nebraska	61,000	0.7%
31	North Carolina	51,000	0.6%
32	Louisiana	32,000	0.4%
32	Maine	32,000	0.4%
32	North Dakota	32,000	0.4%
35	Nevada	27,000	0.3%
36	Mississippi	23,000	0.3%
37	Arkansas	20,000	0.2%
38	Connecticut	19,000	0.2%
38	Montana	19,000	0.2%
40	South Carolina	17,000	0.2%
41	Massachusetts	16,000	0.2%
42	New Hampshire	15,000	0.2%
43	Alabama	14,000	0.2%
44	West Virginia	13,000	0.1%
45	New Jersey	11,000	0.1%
46	Delaware	7,000	0.1%
47	Wyoming	6,700	0.1%
48	Hawaii	4,300	0.0%
49	Rhode Island	1,100	0.0%
50	Alaska	800	0.0%
	District of Columbia	0	0.0%

Source: U.S. Department of Agriculture, National Agricultural Statistics Service
"Milk Production, Disposition and Income: 2006 Summary" (April 2007)
(http://usda.mannlib.cornell.edu/MannUsda/viewDocumentInfo.do?documentID=1105)
*Average number during year. Excludes heifers not yet fresh.

Milk Production in 2006

National Total = 181,798,000 Pounds of Milk*

ALPHA ORDER

RANK	STATE	POUNDS	% of USA
43	Alabama	203,000,000	0.1%
50	Alaska	9,800,000	0.0%
13	Arizona	3,954,000,000	2.2%
42	Arkansas	265,000,000	0.1%
1	California	38,830,000,000	21.4%
16	Colorado	2,547,000,000	1.4%
36	Connecticut	367,000,000	0.2%
46	Delaware	122,000,000	0.1%
19	Florida	2,167,000,000	1.2%
25	Georgia	1,404,000,000	0.8%
48	Hawaii	57,000,000	0.0%
4	Idaho	10,895,000,000	6.0%
20	Illinois	1,978,000,000	1.1%
14	Indiana	3,299,000,000	1.8%
12	Iowa	4,130,000,000	2.3%
17	Kansas	2,343,000,000	1.3%
26	Kentucky	1,301,000,000	0.7%
35	Louisiana	396,000,000	0.2%
32	Maine	574,000,000	0.3%
29	Maryland	1,093,000,000	0.6%
40	Massachusetts	278,000,000	0.2%
9	Michigan	7,100,000,000	3.9%
6	Minnesota	8,364,000,000	4.6%
38	Mississippi	341,000,000	0.2%
21	Missouri	1,840,000,000	1.0%
37	Montana	354,000,000	0.2%
28	Nebraska	1,118,000,000	0.6%
33	Nevada	558,000,000	0.3%
39	New Hampshire	293,000,000	0.2%
45	New Jersey	178,000,000	0.1%
7	New Mexico	7,638,000,000	4.2%
3	New York	12,045,000,000	6.6%
31	North Carolina	944,000,000	0.5%
34	North Dakota	470,000,000	0.3%
11	Ohio	4,860,000,000	2.7%
27	Oklahoma	1,214,000,000	0.7%
18	Oregon	2,242,000,000	1.2%
5	Pennsylvania	10,742,000,000	5.9%
49	Rhode Island	19,000,000	0.0%
40	South Carolina	278,000,000	0.2%
24	South Dakota	1,505,000,000	0.8%
30	Tennessee	1,049,000,000	0.6%
8	Texas	7,145,000,000	3.9%
23	Utah	1,745,000,000	1.0%
15	Vermont	2,592,000,000	1.4%
22	Virginia	1,771,000,000	1.0%
10	Washington	5,464,000,000	3.0%
44	West Virginia	200,000,000	0.1%
2	Wisconsin	23,398,000,000	12.9%
47	Wyoming	118,000,000	0.1%

RANK ORDER

RANK	STATE	POUNDS	% of USA
1	California	38,830,000,000	21.4%
2	Wisconsin	23,398,000,000	12.9%
3	New York	12,045,000,000	6.6%
4	Idaho	10,895,000,000	6.0%
5	Pennsylvania	10,742,000,000	5.9%
6	Minnesota	8,364,000,000	4.6%
7	New Mexico	7,638,000,000	4.2%
8	Texas	7,145,000,000	3.9%
9	Michigan	7,100,000,000	3.9%
10	Washington	5,464,000,000	3.0%
11	Ohio	4,860,000,000	2.7%
12	Iowa	4,130,000,000	2.3%
13	Arizona	3,954,000,000	2.2%
14	Indiana	3,299,000,000	1.8%
15	Vermont	2,592,000,000	1.4%
16	Colorado	2,547,000,000	1.4%
17	Kansas	2,343,000,000	1.3%
18	Oregon	2,242,000,000	1.2%
19	Florida	2,167,000,000	1.2%
20	Illinois	1,978,000,000	1.1%
21	Missouri	1,840,000,000	1.0%
22	Virginia	1,771,000,000	1.0%
23	Utah	1,745,000,000	1.0%
24	South Dakota	1,505,000,000	0.8%
25	Georgia	1,404,000,000	0.8%
26	Kentucky	1,301,000,000	0.7%
27	Oklahoma	1,214,000,000	0.7%
28	Nebraska	1,118,000,000	0.6%
29	Maryland	1,093,000,000	0.6%
30	Tennessee	1,049,000,000	0.6%
31	North Carolina	944,000,000	0.5%
32	Maine	574,000,000	0.3%
33	Nevada	558,000,000	0.3%
34	North Dakota	470,000,000	0.3%
35	Louisiana	396,000,000	0.2%
36	Connecticut	367,000,000	0.2%
37	Montana	354,000,000	0.2%
38	Mississippi	341,000,000	0.2%
39	New Hampshire	293,000,000	0.2%
40	Massachusetts	278,000,000	0.2%
40	South Carolina	278,000,000	0.2%
42	Arkansas	265,000,000	0.1%
43	Alabama	203,000,000	0.1%
44	West Virginia	200,000,000	0.1%
45	New Jersey	178,000,000	0.1%
46	Delaware	122,000,000	0.1%
47	Wyoming	118,000,000	0.1%
48	Hawaii	57,000,000	0.0%
49	Rhode Island	19,000,000	0.0%
50	Alaska	9,800,000	0.0%
	District of Columbia	0	0.0%

Source: U.S. Department of Agriculture, National Agricultural Statistics Service
"Milk Production, Disposition and Income: 2006 Summary" (April 2007)
(http://usda.mannlib.cornell.edu/MannUsda/viewDocumentInfo.do?documentID=1105)
*Excludes milk sucked by calves.

Milk Production per Milk Cow in 2006

National Average = 19,951 Pounds of Milk per Cow*

ALPHA ORDER

RANK	STATE	POUNDS
45	Alabama	14,500
50	Alaska	12,250
3	Arizona	22,855
48	Arkansas	13,250
6	California	21,815
1	Colorado	23,155
16	Connecticut	19,316
31	Delaware	17,429
37	Florida	16,417
27	Georgia	18,234
47	Hawaii	13,256
4	Idaho	22,326
17	Illinois	19,204
13	Indiana	19,994
12	Iowa	20,146
9	Kansas	20,920
46	Kentucky	13,276
49	Louisiana	12,375
28	Maine	17,938
35	Maryland	17,078
32	Massachusetts	17,375
5	Michigan	22,188
22	Minnesota	18,587
43	Mississippi	14,826
40	Missouri	16,000
21	Montana	18,632
26	Nebraska	18,328
10	Nevada	20,667
14	New Hampshire	19,533
39	New Jersey	16,182
7	New Mexico	21,515
19	New York	18,879
24	North Carolina	18,510
44	North Dakota	14,688
29	Ohio	17,737
36	Oklahoma	16,630
18	Oregon	19,000
15	Pennsylvania	19,390
34	Rhode Island	17,273
38	South Carolina	16,353
23	South Dakota	18,580
41	Tennessee	15,657
8	Texas	21,328
11	Utah	20,291
25	Vermont	18,383
33	Virginia	17,363
2	Washington	23,055
42	West Virginia	15,385
20	Wisconsin	18,824
30	Wyoming	17,612

RANK ORDER

RANK	STATE	POUNDS
1	Colorado	23,155
2	Washington	23,055
3	Arizona	22,855
4	Idaho	22,326
5	Michigan	22,188
6	California	21,815
7	New Mexico	21,515
8	Texas	21,328
9	Kansas	20,920
10	Nevada	20,667
11	Utah	20,291
12	Iowa	20,146
13	Indiana	19,994
14	New Hampshire	19,533
15	Pennsylvania	19,390
16	Connecticut	19,316
17	Illinois	19,204
18	Oregon	19,000
19	New York	18,879
20	Wisconsin	18,824
21	Montana	18,632
22	Minnesota	18,587
23	South Dakota	18,580
24	North Carolina	18,510
25	Vermont	18,383
26	Nebraska	18,328
27	Georgia	18,234
28	Maine	17,938
29	Ohio	17,737
30	Wyoming	17,612
31	Delaware	17,429
32	Massachusetts	17,375
33	Virginia	17,363
34	Rhode Island	17,273
35	Maryland	17,078
36	Oklahoma	16,630
37	Florida	16,417
38	South Carolina	16,353
39	New Jersey	16,182
40	Missouri	16,000
41	Tennessee	15,657
42	West Virginia	15,385
43	Mississippi	14,826
44	North Dakota	14,688
45	Alabama	14,500
46	Kentucky	13,276
47	Hawaii	13,256
48	Arkansas	13,250
49	Louisiana	12,375
50	Alaska	12,250

District of Columbia** NA

Source: U.S. Department of Agriculture, National Agricultural Statistics Service
"Milk Production, Disposition and Income: 2006 Summary" (April 2007)
(http://usda.mannlib.cornell.edu/MannUsda/viewDocumentInfo.do?documentID=1105)
*Excludes milk sucked by calves.
**Not applicable.

Hogs and Pigs on Farms in 2007

National Total = 65,110,000 Hogs and Pigs*

RANK	STATE	HOGS AND PIGS	% of USA
27	Alabama	170,000	0.3%
50	Alaska	900	0.0%
26	Arizona	175,000	0.3%
22	Arkansas	285,000	0.4%
28	California	155,000	0.2%
15	Colorado	850,000	1.3%
44	Connecticut	4,000	0.0%
39	Delaware	11,000	0.0%
36	Florida	20,000	0.0%
23	Georgia	265,000	0.4%
37	Hawaii	15,000	0.0%
34	Idaho	28,000	0.0%
4	Illinois	4,150,000	6.4%
5	Indiana	3,500,000	5.4%
1	Iowa	18,200,000	28.0%
9	Kansas	1,850,000	2.8%
19	Kentucky	350,000	0.5%
39	Louisiana	11,000	0.0%
43	Maine	4,700	0.0%
32	Maryland	31,000	0.0%
38	Massachusetts	12,000	0.0%
14	Michigan	1,020,000	1.6%
3	Minnesota	7,200,000	11.1%
20	Mississippi	345,000	0.5%
7	Missouri	3,050,000	4.7%
25	Montana	180,000	0.3%
6	Nebraska	3,150,000	4.8%
45	Nevada	3,000	0.0%
46	New Hampshire	2,900	0.0%
41	New Jersey	9,000	0.0%
49	New Mexico	2,000	0.0%
31	New York	86,000	0.1%
2	North Carolina	9,900,000	15.2%
24	North Dakota	182,000	0.3%
10	Ohio	1,760,000	2.7%
8	Oklahoma	2,330,000	3.6%
35	Oregon	25,000	0.0%
12	Pennsylvania	1,130,000	1.7%
48	Rhode Island	2,300	0.0%
21	South Carolina	295,000	0.5%
11	South Dakota	1,370,000	2.1%
29	Tennessee	140,000	0.2%
13	Texas	1,120,000	1.7%
16	Utah	790,000	1.2%
47	Vermont	2,700	0.0%
18	Virginia	370,000	0.6%
33	Washington	29,000	0.0%
41	West Virginia	9,000	0.0%
17	Wisconsin	430,000	0.7%
30	Wyoming	89,000	0.1%

RANK	STATE	HOGS AND PIGS	% of USA
1	Iowa	18,200,000	28.0%
2	North Carolina	9,900,000	15.2%
3	Minnesota	7,200,000	11.1%
4	Illinois	4,150,000	6.4%
5	Indiana	3,500,000	5.4%
6	Nebraska	3,150,000	4.8%
7	Missouri	3,050,000	4.7%
8	Oklahoma	2,330,000	3.6%
9	Kansas	1,850,000	2.8%
10	Ohio	1,760,000	2.7%
11	South Dakota	1,370,000	2.1%
12	Pennsylvania	1,130,000	1.7%
13	Texas	1,120,000	1.7%
14	Michigan	1,020,000	1.6%
15	Colorado	850,000	1.3%
16	Utah	790,000	1.2%
17	Wisconsin	430,000	0.7%
18	Virginia	370,000	0.6%
19	Kentucky	350,000	0.5%
20	Mississippi	345,000	0.5%
21	South Carolina	295,000	0.5%
22	Arkansas	285,000	0.4%
23	Georgia	265,000	0.4%
24	North Dakota	182,000	0.3%
25	Montana	180,000	0.3%
26	Arizona	175,000	0.3%
27	Alabama	170,000	0.3%
28	California	155,000	0.2%
29	Tennessee	140,000	0.2%
30	Wyoming	89,000	0.1%
31	New York	86,000	0.1%
32	Maryland	31,000	0.0%
33	Washington	29,000	0.0%
34	Idaho	28,000	0.0%
35	Oregon	25,000	0.0%
36	Florida	20,000	0.0%
37	Hawaii	15,000	0.0%
38	Massachusetts	12,000	0.0%
39	Delaware	11,000	0.0%
39	Louisiana	11,000	0.0%
41	New Jersey	9,000	0.0%
41	West Virginia	9,000	0.0%
43	Maine	4,700	0.0%
44	Connecticut	4,000	0.0%
45	Nevada	3,000	0.0%
46	New Hampshire	2,900	0.0%
47	Vermont	2,700	0.0%
48	Rhode Island	2,300	0.0%
49	New Mexico	2,000	0.0%
50	Alaska	900	0.0%
	District of Columbia	0	0.0%

Source: U.S. Department of Agriculture, National Agricultural Statistics Service
   "Quarterly Hogs and Pigs" (http://usda.mannlib.cornell.edu/MannUsda/viewDocumentInfo.do?documentID=1086)
*As of December 1, 2007.

Chickens in 2006 (Leading States Only)

National Total = 8,882,000,000 Chickens*

<ins>ALPHA ORDER</ins>				<ins>RANK ORDER</ins>			
RANK	STATE	CHICKENS	% of USA	RANK	STATE	CHICKENS	% of USA
3	Alabama	1,053,400,000	11.9%	1	Georgia	1,382,100,000	15.6%
NA	Alaska***	NA	NA	2	Arkansas	1,185,400,000	13.3%
NA	Arizona***	NA	NA	3	Alabama	1,053,400,000	11.9%
2	Arkansas	1,185,400,000	13.3%	4	Mississippi	803,800,000	9.0%
NA	California**	NA	NA	5	North Carolina	749,000,000	8.4%
NA	Colorado***	NA	NA	6	Texas	628,300,000	7.1%
NA	Connecticut***	NA	NA	7	Kentucky	289,000,000	3.3%
9	Delaware	269,100,000	3.0%	8	Maryland	271,800,000	3.1%
16	Florida	75,000,000	0.8%	9	Delaware	269,100,000	3.0%
1	Georgia	1,382,100,000	15.6%	10	Virginia	256,200,000	2.9%
NA	Hawaii***	NA	NA	11	Oklahoma	249,400,000	2.8%
NA	Idaho***	NA	NA	12	South Carolina	227,100,000	2.6%
NA	Illinois***	NA	NA	13	Tennessee	213,500,000	2.4%
NA	Indiana**	NA	NA	14	Pennsylvania	144,900,000	1.6%
NA	Iowa**	NA	NA	15	West Virginia	89,700,000	1.0%
NA	Kansas***	NA	NA	16	Florida	75,000,000	0.8%
7	Kentucky	289,000,000	3.3%	17	Minnesota	45,900,000	0.5%
NA	Louisiana**	NA	NA	18	Ohio	45,600,000	0.5%
NA	Maine***	NA	NA	19	Wisconsin	38,300,000	0.4%
8	Maryland	271,800,000	3.1%	20	Nebraska	5,100,000	0.1%
NA	Massachusetts***	NA	NA	NA	Alaska***	NA	NA
NA	Michigan**	NA	NA	NA	Arizona***	NA	NA
17	Minnesota	45,900,000	0.5%	NA	California**	NA	NA
4	Mississippi	803,800,000	9.0%	NA	Colorado***	NA	NA
NA	Missouri**	NA	NA	NA	Connecticut***	NA	NA
NA	Montana***	NA	NA	NA	Hawaii***	NA	NA
20	Nebraska	5,100,000	0.1%	NA	Idaho***	NA	NA
NA	Nevada***	NA	NA	NA	Illinois***	NA	NA
NA	New Hampshire***	NA	NA	NA	Indiana**	NA	NA
NA	New Jersey***	NA	NA	NA	Iowa**	NA	NA
NA	New Mexico***	NA	NA	NA	Kansas***	NA	NA
NA	New York**	NA	NA	NA	Louisiana**	NA	NA
5	North Carolina	749,000,000	8.4%	NA	Maine***	NA	NA
NA	North Dakota***	NA	NA	NA	Massachusetts***	NA	NA
18	Ohio	45,600,000	0.5%	NA	Michigan**	NA	NA
11	Oklahoma	249,400,000	2.8%	NA	Missouri**	NA	NA
NA	Oregon**	NA	NA	NA	Montana***	NA	NA
14	Pennsylvania	144,900,000	1.6%	NA	Nevada***	NA	NA
NA	Rhode Island***	NA	NA	NA	New Hampshire***	NA	NA
12	South Carolina	227,100,000	2.6%	NA	New Jersey***	NA	NA
NA	South Dakota***	NA	NA	NA	New Mexico***	NA	NA
13	Tennessee	213,500,000	2.4%	NA	New York**	NA	NA
6	Texas	628,300,000	7.1%	NA	North Dakota***	NA	NA
NA	Utah***	NA	NA	NA	Oregon**	NA	NA
NA	Vermont***	NA	NA	NA	Rhode Island***	NA	NA
10	Virginia	256,200,000	2.9%	NA	South Dakota***	NA	NA
NA	Washington**	NA	NA	NA	Utah***	NA	NA
15	West Virginia	89,700,000	1.0%	NA	Vermont***	NA	NA
19	Wisconsin	38,300,000	0.4%	NA	Washington**	NA	NA
NA	Wyoming***	NA	NA	NA	Wyoming***	NA	NA
					District of Columbia	0	0.0%

Source: U.S. Department of Agriculture, National Agricultural Statistics Service
   "Poultry - Production and Value: 2006 Summary"
   (http://usda.mannlib.cornell.edu/MannUsda/viewDocumentInfo.do?documentID=1130)
*Broilers. Total includes numbers for states not shown separately but excludes states producing less than 500,000 birds. **These states produced a combined total of 859,400,000 chickens. They are combined to avoid disclosing individual operations. National total does not include chickens used for egg production. ***Not available.

Eggs Produced in 2006

National Total = 90,877,000,000 Eggs

ALPHA ORDER

RANK	STATE	EGGS	% of USA
14	Alabama	2,002,000,000	2.2%
NA	Alaska*	NA	NA
NA	Arizona*	NA	NA
8	Arkansas	3,267,000,000	3.6%
6	California	4,962,000,000	5.5%
23	Colorado	1,083,000,000	1.2%
28	Connecticut	791,000,000	0.9%
NA	Delaware*	NA	NA
11	Florida	2,938,000,000	3.2%
7	Georgia	4,811,000,000	5.3%
38	Hawaii	98,300,000	0.1%
36	Idaho	182,000,000	0.2%
17	Illinois	1,307,000,000	1.4%
4	Indiana	6,593,000,000	7.3%
1	Iowa	13,811,000,000	15.2%
NA	Kansas*	NA	NA
21	Kentucky	1,150,000,000	1.3%
32	Louisiana	463,000,000	0.5%
24	Maine	1,064,000,000	1.2%
31	Maryland	733,000,000	0.8%
39	Massachusetts	71,000,000	0.1%
13	Michigan	2,391,000,000	2.6%
10	Minnesota	2,940,000,000	3.2%
16	Mississippi	1,546,000,000	1.7%
15	Missouri	1,903,000,000	2.1%
37	Montana	104,000,000	0.1%
9	Nebraska	3,129,000,000	3.4%
NA	Nevada*	NA	NA
41	New Hampshire	36,000,000	0.0%
33	New Jersey	446,000,000	0.5%
NA	New Mexico*	NA	NA
22	New York	1,126,000,000	1.2%
12	North Carolina	2,636,000,000	2.9%
NA	North Dakota*	NA	NA
2	Ohio	7,507,000,000	8.3%
30	Oklahoma	738,000,000	0.8%
29	Oregon	772,000,000	0.8%
3	Pennsylvania	6,687,000,000	7.4%
NA	Rhode Island*	NA	NA
20	South Carolina	1,280,000,000	1.4%
26	South Dakota	865,000,000	1.0%
34	Tennessee	289,000,000	0.3%
5	Texas	5,039,000,000	5.5%
25	Utah	937,000,000	1.0%
40	Vermont	55,000,000	0.1%
27	Virginia	806,000,000	0.9%
18	Washington	1,298,000,000	1.4%
35	West Virginia	274,000,000	0.3%
19	Wisconsin	1,284,000,000	1.4%
42	Wyoming	3,600,000	0.0%

RANK ORDER

RANK	STATE	EGGS	% of USA
1	Iowa	13,811,000,000	15.2%
2	Ohio	7,507,000,000	8.3%
3	Pennsylvania	6,687,000,000	7.4%
4	Indiana	6,593,000,000	7.3%
5	Texas	5,039,000,000	5.5%
6	California	4,962,000,000	5.5%
7	Georgia	4,811,000,000	5.3%
8	Arkansas	3,267,000,000	3.6%
9	Nebraska	3,129,000,000	3.4%
10	Minnesota	2,940,000,000	3.2%
11	Florida	2,938,000,000	3.2%
12	North Carolina	2,636,000,000	2.9%
13	Michigan	2,391,000,000	2.6%
14	Alabama	2,002,000,000	2.2%
15	Missouri	1,903,000,000	2.1%
16	Mississippi	1,546,000,000	1.7%
17	Illinois	1,307,000,000	1.4%
18	Washington	1,298,000,000	1.4%
19	Wisconsin	1,284,000,000	1.4%
20	South Carolina	1,280,000,000	1.4%
21	Kentucky	1,150,000,000	1.3%
22	New York	1,126,000,000	1.2%
23	Colorado	1,083,000,000	1.2%
24	Maine	1,064,000,000	1.2%
25	Utah	937,000,000	1.0%
26	South Dakota	865,000,000	1.0%
27	Virginia	806,000,000	0.9%
28	Connecticut	791,000,000	0.9%
29	Oregon	772,000,000	0.8%
30	Oklahoma	738,000,000	0.8%
31	Maryland	733,000,000	0.8%
32	Louisiana	463,000,000	0.5%
33	New Jersey	446,000,000	0.5%
34	Tennessee	289,000,000	0.3%
35	West Virginia	274,000,000	0.3%
36	Idaho	182,000,000	0.2%
37	Montana	104,000,000	0.1%
38	Hawaii	98,300,000	0.1%
39	Massachusetts	71,000,000	0.1%
40	Vermont	55,000,000	0.1%
41	New Hampshire	36,000,000	0.0%
42	Wyoming	3,600,000	0.0%
NA	Alaska*	NA	NA
NA	Arizona*	NA	NA
NA	Delaware*	NA	NA
NA	Kansas*	NA	NA
NA	Nevada*	NA	NA
NA	New Mexico*	NA	NA
NA	North Dakota*	NA	NA
NA	Rhode Island*	NA	NA
	District of Columbia	0	0.0%

Source: U.S. Department of Agriculture, National Agricultural Statistics Service
"Poultry - Production and Value: 2006 Summary"
(http://usda.mannlib.cornell.edu/MannUsda/viewDocumentInfo.do?documentID=1130)
*These states produced a combined 1,493,000,000 eggs. They are combined to avoid disclosing individual operations.

II. Crime and Law Enforcement

Crimes in 2006

National Total = 11,401,313 Crimes*

ALPHA ORDER

ALPHA ORDER

RANK	STATE	CRIMES	% of USA
21	Alabama	200,578	1.8%
44	Alaska	28,765	0.3%
11	Arizona	316,286	2.8%
28	Arkansas	127,027	1.1%
1	California	1,350,137	11.8%
23	Colorado	182,670	1.6%
33	Connecticut	97,605	0.9%
41	Delaware	34,988	0.3%
3	Florida	849,879	7.5%
7	Georgia	408,289	3.6%
38	Hawaii	57,997	0.5%
40	Idaho	39,096	0.3%
6	Illinois	456,976	4.0%
15	Indiana	241,003	2.1%
35	Iowa	92,034	0.8%
31	Kansas	115,406	1.0%
30	Kentucky	118,086	1.0%
20	Louisiana	201,158	1.8%
42	Maine	34,812	0.3%
16	Maryland	233,586	2.0%
22	Massachusetts	182,688	1.6%
9	Michigan	381,129	3.3%
24	Minnesota	175,242	1.5%
32	Mississippi	102,084	0.9%
14	Missouri	255,450	2.2%
45	Montana	27,784	0.2%
37	Nebraska	64,058	0.6%
29	Nevada	120,544	1.1%
46	New Hampshire	26,466	0.2%
17	New Jersey	230,630	2.0%
36	New Mexico	89,528	0.8%
4	New York	480,270	4.2%
8	North Carolina	407,084	3.6%
50	North Dakota	13,532	0.1%
5	Ohio	462,444	4.1%
26	Oklahoma	146,805	1.3%
27	Oregon	146,268	1.3%
10	Pennsylvania	358,653	3.1%
43	Rhode Island	30,047	0.3%
18	South Carolina	216,400	1.9%
49	South Dakota	14,004	0.1%
13	Tennessee	295,204	2.6%
2	Texas	1,080,838	9.5%
34	Utah	95,393	0.8%
48	Vermont	15,231	0.1%
19	Virginia	210,974	1.9%
12	Washington	308,653	2.7%
39	West Virginia	52,759	0.5%
25	Wisconsin	172,354	1.5%
47	Wyoming	16,584	0.1%

RANK ORDER

RANK	STATE	CRIMES	% of USA
1	California	1,350,137	11.8%
2	Texas	1,080,838	9.5%
3	Florida	849,879	7.5%
4	New York	480,270	4.2%
5	Ohio	462,444	4.1%
6	Illinois	456,976	4.0%
7	Georgia	408,289	3.6%
8	North Carolina	407,084	3.6%
9	Michigan	381,129	3.3%
10	Pennsylvania	358,653	3.1%
11	Arizona	316,286	2.8%
12	Washington	308,653	2.7%
13	Tennessee	295,204	2.6%
14	Missouri	255,450	2.2%
15	Indiana	241,003	2.1%
16	Maryland	233,586	2.0%
17	New Jersey	230,630	2.0%
18	South Carolina	216,400	1.9%
19	Virginia	210,974	1.9%
20	Louisiana	201,158	1.8%
21	Alabama	200,578	1.8%
22	Massachusetts	182,688	1.6%
23	Colorado	182,670	1.6%
24	Minnesota	175,242	1.5%
25	Wisconsin	172,354	1.5%
26	Oklahoma	146,805	1.3%
27	Oregon	146,268	1.3%
28	Arkansas	127,027	1.1%
29	Nevada	120,544	1.1%
30	Kentucky	118,086	1.0%
31	Kansas	115,406	1.0%
32	Mississippi	102,084	0.9%
33	Connecticut	97,605	0.9%
34	Utah	95,393	0.8%
35	Iowa	92,034	0.8%
36	New Mexico	89,528	0.8%
37	Nebraska	64,058	0.6%
38	Hawaii	57,997	0.5%
39	West Virginia	52,759	0.5%
40	Idaho	39,096	0.3%
41	Delaware	34,988	0.3%
42	Maine	34,812	0.3%
43	Rhode Island	30,047	0.3%
44	Alaska	28,765	0.3%
45	Montana	27,784	0.2%
46	New Hampshire	26,466	0.2%
47	Wyoming	16,584	0.1%
48	Vermont	15,231	0.1%
49	South Dakota	14,004	0.1%
50	North Dakota	13,532	0.1%
	District of Columbia	35,835	0.3%

Source: CQ Press using data from Federal Bureau of Investigation
    "Crime in the United States 2006" (Uniform Crime Reports, September 24, 2007)
*Includes murder, rape, robbery, aggravated assault, burglary, larceny-theft, and motor vehicle theft.

Percent Change in Number of Crimes: 2005 to 2006

National Percent Change = 1.4% Decrease*

ALPHA ORDER				RANK ORDER		
RANK	STATE	PERCENT CHANGE		RANK	STATE	PERCENT CHANGE
10	Alabama	1.8		1	Delaware	10.8
9	Alaska	2.1		2	Wisconsin	7.1
22	Arizona	(0.5)		3	Maine	4.3
21	Arkansas	(0.4)		4	Louisiana	4.0
38	California	(2.9)		5	Michigan	3.3
48	Colorado	(11.7)		6	North Carolina	3.2
33	Connecticut	(2.2)		7	Nevada	3.0
1	Delaware	10.8		8	New Hampshire	2.6
13	Florida	1.3		9	Alaska	2.1
35	Georgia	(2.6)		10	Alabama	1.8
47	Hawaii	(9.9)		11	Indiana	1.7
45	Idaho	(7.4)		12	Pennsylvania	1.5
28	Illinois	(1.8)		13	Florida	1.3
11	Indiana	1.7		14	Kentucky	1.2
24	Iowa	(1.1)		15	Minnesota	1.0
18	Kansas	0.1		16	Massachusetts	0.7
14	Kentucky	1.2		17	Ohio	0.3
4	Louisiana	4.0		18	Kansas	0.1
3	Maine	4.3		18	West Virginia	0.1
28	Maryland	(1.8)		20	North Dakota	(0.2)
16	Massachusetts	0.7		21	Arkansas	(0.4)
5	Michigan	3.3		22	Arizona	(0.5)
15	Minnesota	1.0		23	South Carolina	(0.8)
26	Mississippi	(1.2)		24	Iowa	(1.1)
24	Missouri	(1.1)		24	Missouri	(1.1)
49	Montana	(13.3)		26	Mississippi	(1.2)
32	Nebraska	(2.1)		27	New Jersey	(1.6)
7	Nevada	3.0		28	Illinois	(1.8)
8	New Hampshire	2.6		28	Maryland	(1.8)
27	New Jersey	(1.6)		30	Vermont	(1.9)
36	New Mexico	(2.7)		31	Tennessee	(2.0)
34	New York	(2.4)		32	Nebraska	(2.1)
6	North Carolina	3.2		33	Connecticut	(2.2)
20	North Dakota	(0.2)		34	New York	(2.4)
17	Ohio	0.3		35	Georgia	(2.6)
46	Oklahoma	(9.1)		36	New Mexico	(2.7)
50	Oregon	(14.3)		36	Texas	(2.7)
12	Pennsylvania	1.5		38	California	(2.9)
42	Rhode Island	(6.1)		39	Wyoming	(3.8)
23	South Carolina	(0.8)		40	Virginia	(4.9)
44	South Dakota	(7.1)		41	Utah	(5.7)
31	Tennessee	(2.0)		42	Rhode Island	(6.1)
36	Texas	(2.7)		43	Washington	(6.3)
41	Utah	(5.7)		44	South Dakota	(7.1)
30	Vermont	(1.9)		45	Idaho	(7.4)
40	Virginia	(4.9)		46	Oklahoma	(9.1)
43	Washington	(6.3)		47	Hawaii	(9.9)
18	West Virginia	0.1		48	Colorado	(11.7)
2	Wisconsin	7.1		49	Montana	(13.3)
39	Wyoming	(3.8)		50	Oregon	(14.3)

District of Columbia   4.9

Source: CQ Press using data from Federal Bureau of Investigation
  "Crime in the United States 2006" (Uniform Crime Reports, September 24, 2007)
*Includes murder, rape, robbery, aggravated assault, burglary, larceny-theft, and motor vehicle theft.

Crime Rate in 2006

National Rate = 3,808.0 Crimes per 100,000 Population*

ALPHA ORDER				RANK ORDER		
RANK	STATE	RATE		RANK	STATE	RATE
14	Alabama	4,361.3		1	Arizona	5,129.3
16	Alaska	4,292.9		2	South Carolina	5,007.8
1	Arizona	5,129.3		3	Tennessee	4,888.5
11	Arkansas	4,519.1		4	Nevada	4,830.4
27	California	3,703.4		5	Washington	4,825.9
23	Colorado	3,842.9		6	Florida	4,698.1
41	Connecticut	2,784.9		7	Louisiana	4,691.5
20	Delaware	4,099.5		8	Texas	4,597.8
6	Florida	4,698.1		9	North Carolina	4,596.4
15	Georgia	4,360.2		10	New Mexico	4,580.4
12	Hawaii	4,511.6		11	Arkansas	4,519.1
43	Idaho	2,666.0		12	Hawaii	4,511.6
29	Illinois	3,561.2		13	Missouri	4,372.1
24	Indiana	3,817.2		14	Alabama	4,361.3
34	Iowa	3,086.2		15	Georgia	4,360.2
17	Kansas	4,175.2		16	Alaska	4,292.9
40	Kentucky	2,807.5		17	Kansas	4,175.2
7	Louisiana	4,691.5		18	Maryland	4,159.5
45	Maine	2,634.1		19	Oklahoma	4,101.6
18	Maryland	4,159.5		20	Delaware	4,099.5
38	Massachusetts	2,838.0		21	Ohio	4,028.9
25	Michigan	3,775.2		22	Oregon	3,952.4
31	Minnesota	3,391.5		23	Colorado	3,842.9
30	Mississippi	3,507.4		24	Indiana	3,817.2
13	Missouri	4,372.1		25	Michigan	3,775.2
35	Montana	2,941.2		26	Utah	3,740.8
28	Nebraska	3,622.5		27	California	3,703.4
4	Nevada	4,830.4		28	Nebraska	3,622.5
49	New Hampshire	2,012.8		29	Illinois	3,561.2
44	New Jersey	2,643.5		30	Mississippi	3,507.4
10	New Mexico	4,580.4		31	Minnesota	3,391.5
46	New York	2,487.6		32	Wyoming	3,220.2
9	North Carolina	4,596.4		33	Wisconsin	3,101.8
48	North Dakota	2,128.2		34	Iowa	3,086.2
21	Ohio	4,028.9		35	Montana	2,941.2
19	Oklahoma	4,101.6		36	West Virginia	2,901.2
22	Oregon	3,952.4		37	Pennsylvania	2,882.9
37	Pennsylvania	2,882.9		38	Massachusetts	2,838.0
39	Rhode Island	2,814.4		39	Rhode Island	2,814.4
2	South Carolina	5,007.8		40	Kentucky	2,807.5
50	South Dakota	1,791.0		41	Connecticut	2,784.9
3	Tennessee	4,888.5		42	Virginia	2,760.4
8	Texas	4,597.8		43	Idaho	2,666.0
26	Utah	3,740.8		44	New Jersey	2,643.5
47	Vermont	2,441.3		45	Maine	2,634.1
42	Virginia	2,760.4		46	New York	2,487.6
5	Washington	4,825.9		47	Vermont	2,441.3
36	West Virginia	2,901.2		48	North Dakota	2,128.2
33	Wisconsin	3,101.8		49	New Hampshire	2,012.8
32	Wyoming	3,220.2		50	South Dakota	1,791.0
					District of Columbia	6,162.2

Source: CQ Press using data from Federal Bureau of Investigation
  "Crime in the United States 2006" (Uniform Crime Reports, September 24, 2007)
*Includes murder, rape, robbery, aggravated assault, burglary, larceny-theft, and motor vehicle theft.

Percent Change in Crime Rate: 2005 to 2006

National Percent Change = 2.4% Decrease*

ALPHA ORDER

RANK	STATE	PERCENT CHANGE
11	Alabama	0.7
8	Alaska	1.1
35	Arizona	(3.9)
22	Arkansas	(1.7)
34	California	(3.7)
48	Colorado	(13.4)
28	Connecticut	(2.3)
1	Delaware	9.3
18	Florida	(0.5)
37	Georgia	(5.0)
47	Hawaii	(10.8)
45	Idaho	(9.8)
28	Illinois	(2.3)
10	Indiana	0.9
22	Iowa	(1.7)
18	Kansas	(0.5)
13	Kentucky	0.3
1	Louisiana	9.3
4	Maine	4.1
26	Maryland	(2.2)
11	Massachusetts	0.7
5	Michigan	3.4
15	Minnesota	0.2
21	Mississippi	(1.3)
25	Missouri	(1.9)
49	Montana	(14.2)
32	Nebraska	(2.6)
18	Nevada	(0.5)
6	New Hampshire	2.0
24	New Jersey	(1.8)
36	New Mexico	(4.1)
28	New York	(2.3)
9	North Carolina	1.0
17	North Dakota	(0.4)
13	Ohio	0.3
46	Oklahoma	(10.0)
50	Oregon	(15.7)
7	Pennsylvania	1.3
40	Rhode Island	(5.6)
31	South Carolina	(2.5)
44	South Dakota	(8.0)
33	Tennessee	(3.3)
39	Texas	(5.1)
43	Utah	(7.9)
26	Vermont	(2.2)
41	Virginia	(5.9)
42	Washington	(7.8)
16	West Virginia	(0.2)
3	Wisconsin	6.5
37	Wyoming	(5.0)

RANK ORDER

RANK	STATE	PERCENT CHANGE
1	Delaware	9.3
1	Louisiana	9.3
3	Wisconsin	6.5
4	Maine	4.1
5	Michigan	3.4
6	New Hampshire	2.0
7	Pennsylvania	1.3
8	Alaska	1.1
9	North Carolina	1.0
10	Indiana	0.9
11	Alabama	0.7
11	Massachusetts	0.7
13	Kentucky	0.3
13	Ohio	0.3
15	Minnesota	0.2
16	West Virginia	(0.2)
17	North Dakota	(0.4)
18	Florida	(0.5)
18	Kansas	(0.5)
18	Nevada	(0.5)
21	Mississippi	(1.3)
22	Arkansas	(1.7)
22	Iowa	(1.7)
24	New Jersey	(1.8)
25	Missouri	(1.9)
26	Maryland	(2.2)
26	Vermont	(2.2)
28	Connecticut	(2.3)
28	Illinois	(2.3)
28	New York	(2.3)
31	South Carolina	(2.5)
32	Nebraska	(2.6)
33	Tennessee	(3.3)
34	California	(3.7)
35	Arizona	(3.9)
36	New Mexico	(4.1)
37	Georgia	(5.0)
37	Wyoming	(5.0)
39	Texas	(5.1)
40	Rhode Island	(5.6)
41	Virginia	(5.9)
42	Washington	(7.8)
43	Utah	(7.9)
44	South Dakota	(8.0)
45	Idaho	(9.8)
46	Oklahoma	(10.0)
47	Hawaii	(10.8)
48	Colorado	(13.4)
49	Montana	(14.2)
50	Oregon	(15.7)

	District of Columbia	5.0

Source: CQ Press using data from Federal Bureau of Investigation
  "Crime in the United States 2006" (Uniform Crime Reports, September 24, 2007)
*Includes murder, rape, robbery, aggravated assault, burglary, larceny-theft, and motor vehicle theft.

Violent Crimes in 2006

National Total = 1,417,745 Violent Crimes*

ALPHA ORDER

RANK	STATE	VIOLENT CRIMES	% of USA
22	Alabama	19,557	1.4%
40	Alaska	4,610	0.3%
15	Arizona	30,916	2.2%
28	Arkansas	15,506	1.1%
1	California	194,120	13.7%
23	Colorado	18,616	1.3%
33	Connecticut	9,841	0.7%
36	Delaware	5,817	0.4%
2	Florida	128,795	9.1%
9	Georgia	44,106	3.1%
42	Hawaii	3,615	0.3%
41	Idaho	3,625	0.3%
5	Illinois	69,498	4.9%
21	Indiana	19,876	1.4%
35	Iowa	8,455	0.6%
30	Kansas	11,748	0.8%
31	Kentucky	11,063	0.8%
17	Louisiana	29,919	2.1%
46	Maine	1,526	0.1%
12	Maryland	38,110	2.7%
18	Massachusetts	28,775	2.0%
6	Michigan	56,778	4.0%
26	Minnesota	16,123	1.1%
34	Mississippi	8,691	0.6%
14	Missouri	31,880	2.2%
44	Montana	2,397	0.2%
39	Nebraska	4,983	0.4%
24	Nevada	18,508	1.3%
45	New Hampshire	1,824	0.1%
16	New Jersey	30,672	2.2%
29	New Mexico	12,572	0.9%
4	New York	83,966	5.9%
10	North Carolina	42,124	3.0%
50	North Dakota	813	0.1%
11	Ohio	40,209	2.8%
25	Oklahoma	17,803	1.3%
32	Oregon	10,373	0.7%
7	Pennsylvania	54,665	3.9%
43	Rhode Island	2,429	0.2%
13	South Carolina	33,078	2.3%
47	South Dakota	1,340	0.1%
8	Tennessee	45,907	3.2%
3	Texas	121,378	8.6%
37	Utah	5,722	0.4%
49	Vermont	852	0.1%
20	Virginia	21,568	1.5%
19	Washington	22,120	1.6%
38	West Virginia	5,087	0.4%
27	Wisconsin	15,783	1.1%
48	Wyoming	1,234	0.1%

RANK ORDER

RANK	STATE	VIOLENT CRIMES	% of USA
1	California	194,120	13.7%
2	Florida	128,795	9.1%
3	Texas	121,378	8.6%
4	New York	83,966	5.9%
5	Illinois	69,498	4.9%
6	Michigan	56,778	4.0%
7	Pennsylvania	54,665	3.9%
8	Tennessee	45,907	3.2%
9	Georgia	44,106	3.1%
10	North Carolina	42,124	3.0%
11	Ohio	40,209	2.8%
12	Maryland	38,110	2.7%
13	South Carolina	33,078	2.3%
14	Missouri	31,880	2.2%
15	Arizona	30,916	2.2%
16	New Jersey	30,672	2.2%
17	Louisiana	29,919	2.1%
18	Massachusetts	28,775	2.0%
19	Washington	22,120	1.6%
20	Virginia	21,568	1.5%
21	Indiana	19,876	1.4%
22	Alabama	19,557	1.4%
23	Colorado	18,616	1.3%
24	Nevada	18,508	1.3%
25	Oklahoma	17,803	1.3%
26	Minnesota	16,123	1.1%
27	Wisconsin	15,783	1.1%
28	Arkansas	15,506	1.1%
29	New Mexico	12,572	0.9%
30	Kansas	11,748	0.8%
31	Kentucky	11,063	0.8%
32	Oregon	10,373	0.7%
33	Connecticut	9,841	0.7%
34	Mississippi	8,691	0.6%
35	Iowa	8,455	0.6%
36	Delaware	5,817	0.4%
37	Utah	5,722	0.4%
38	West Virginia	5,087	0.4%
39	Nebraska	4,983	0.4%
40	Alaska	4,610	0.3%
41	Idaho	3,625	0.3%
42	Hawaii	3,615	0.3%
43	Rhode Island	2,429	0.2%
44	Montana	2,397	0.2%
45	New Hampshire	1,824	0.1%
46	Maine	1,526	0.1%
47	South Dakota	1,340	0.1%
48	Wyoming	1,234	0.1%
49	Vermont	852	0.1%
50	North Dakota	813	0.1%
	District of Columbia	8,772	0.6%

Source: Federal Bureau of Investigation
   "Crime in the United States 2006" (Uniform Crime Reports, September 24, 2007)
*Violent crimes are offenses of murder, forcible rape, robbery, and aggravated assault.

Percent Change in Number of Violent Crimes: 2005 to 2006

National Percent Change = 1.9% Increase*

<table>
<tr><td colspan="3">ALPHA ORDER</td><td colspan="3">RANK ORDER</td></tr>
<tr><th>RANK</th><th>STATE</th><th>PERCENT CHANGE</th><th>RANK</th><th>STATE</th><th>PERCENT CHANGE</th></tr>
<tr><td>35</td><td>Alabama</td><td>(0.6)</td><td>1</td><td>Nevada</td><td>26.3</td></tr>
<tr><td>6</td><td>Alaska</td><td>9.9</td><td>2</td><td>Wisconsin</td><td>18.1</td></tr>
<tr><td>29</td><td>Arizona</td><td>1.4</td><td>3</td><td>North Dakota</td><td>15.2</td></tr>
<tr><td>13</td><td>Arkansas</td><td>5.7</td><td>4</td><td>Louisiana</td><td>11.3</td></tr>
<tr><td>23</td><td>California</td><td>2.1</td><td>5</td><td>Hawaii</td><td>11.1</td></tr>
<tr><td>31</td><td>Colorado</td><td>0.6</td><td>6</td><td>Alaska</td><td>9.9</td></tr>
<tr><td>19</td><td>Connecticut</td><td>3.1</td><td>7</td><td>Kansas</td><td>9.8</td></tr>
<tr><td>8</td><td>Delaware</td><td>9.1</td><td>8</td><td>Delaware</td><td>9.1</td></tr>
<tr><td>22</td><td>Florida</td><td>2.3</td><td>9</td><td>Vermont</td><td>9.0</td></tr>
<tr><td>10</td><td>Georgia</td><td>8.3</td><td>10</td><td>Georgia</td><td>8.3</td></tr>
<tr><td>5</td><td>Hawaii</td><td>11.1</td><td>11</td><td>Mississippi</td><td>6.9</td></tr>
<tr><td>39</td><td>Idaho</td><td>(1.2)</td><td>12</td><td>Minnesota</td><td>5.8</td></tr>
<tr><td>41</td><td>Illinois</td><td>(1.4)</td><td>13</td><td>Arkansas</td><td>5.7</td></tr>
<tr><td>43</td><td>Indiana</td><td>(2.1)</td><td>14</td><td>Wyoming</td><td>5.3</td></tr>
<tr><td>45</td><td>Iowa</td><td>(2.8)</td><td>15</td><td>Missouri</td><td>4.6</td></tr>
<tr><td>7</td><td>Kansas</td><td>9.8</td><td>16</td><td>New Hampshire</td><td>3.6</td></tr>
<tr><td>35</td><td>Kentucky</td><td>(0.6)</td><td>16</td><td>North Carolina</td><td>3.6</td></tr>
<tr><td>4</td><td>Louisiana</td><td>11.3</td><td>16</td><td>Pennsylvania</td><td>3.6</td></tr>
<tr><td>20</td><td>Maine</td><td>2.9</td><td>19</td><td>Connecticut</td><td>3.1</td></tr>
<tr><td>47</td><td>Maryland</td><td>(3.2)</td><td>20</td><td>Maine</td><td>2.9</td></tr>
<tr><td>46</td><td>Massachusetts</td><td>(2.9)</td><td>21</td><td>West Virginia</td><td>2.4</td></tr>
<tr><td>27</td><td>Michigan</td><td>1.5</td><td>22</td><td>Florida</td><td>2.3</td></tr>
<tr><td>12</td><td>Minnesota</td><td>5.8</td><td>23</td><td>California</td><td>2.1</td></tr>
<tr><td>11</td><td>Mississippi</td><td>6.9</td><td>24</td><td>Utah</td><td>2.0</td></tr>
<tr><td>15</td><td>Missouri</td><td>4.6</td><td>25</td><td>Tennessee</td><td>1.8</td></tr>
<tr><td>49</td><td>Montana</td><td>(9.0)</td><td>26</td><td>Washington</td><td>1.7</td></tr>
<tr><td>41</td><td>Nebraska</td><td>(1.4)</td><td>27</td><td>Michigan</td><td>1.5</td></tr>
<tr><td>1</td><td>Nevada</td><td>26.3</td><td>27</td><td>South Carolina</td><td>1.5</td></tr>
<tr><td>16</td><td>New Hampshire</td><td>3.6</td><td>29</td><td>Arizona</td><td>1.4</td></tr>
<tr><td>38</td><td>New Jersey</td><td>(0.8)</td><td>30</td><td>New Mexico</td><td>1.0</td></tr>
<tr><td>30</td><td>New Mexico</td><td>1.0</td><td>31</td><td>Colorado</td><td>0.6</td></tr>
<tr><td>44</td><td>New York</td><td>(2.2)</td><td>31</td><td>Virginia</td><td>0.6</td></tr>
<tr><td>16</td><td>North Carolina</td><td>3.6</td><td>33</td><td>Texas</td><td>0.2</td></tr>
<tr><td>3</td><td>North Dakota</td><td>15.2</td><td>34</td><td>Ohio</td><td>0.1</td></tr>
<tr><td>34</td><td>Ohio</td><td>0.1</td><td>35</td><td>Alabama</td><td>(0.6)</td></tr>
<tr><td>40</td><td>Oklahoma</td><td>(1.3)</td><td>35</td><td>Kentucky</td><td>(0.6)</td></tr>
<tr><td>37</td><td>Oregon</td><td>(0.7)</td><td>37</td><td>Oregon</td><td>(0.7)</td></tr>
<tr><td>16</td><td>Pennsylvania</td><td>3.6</td><td>38</td><td>New Jersey</td><td>(0.8)</td></tr>
<tr><td>50</td><td>Rhode Island</td><td>(10.4)</td><td>39</td><td>Idaho</td><td>(1.2)</td></tr>
<tr><td>27</td><td>South Carolina</td><td>1.5</td><td>40</td><td>Oklahoma</td><td>(1.3)</td></tr>
<tr><td>48</td><td>South Dakota</td><td>(3.4)</td><td>41</td><td>Illinois</td><td>(1.4)</td></tr>
<tr><td>25</td><td>Tennessee</td><td>1.8</td><td>41</td><td>Nebraska</td><td>(1.4)</td></tr>
<tr><td>33</td><td>Texas</td><td>0.2</td><td>43</td><td>Indiana</td><td>(2.1)</td></tr>
<tr><td>24</td><td>Utah</td><td>2.0</td><td>44</td><td>New York</td><td>(2.2)</td></tr>
<tr><td>9</td><td>Vermont</td><td>9.0</td><td>45</td><td>Iowa</td><td>(2.8)</td></tr>
<tr><td>31</td><td>Virginia</td><td>0.6</td><td>46</td><td>Massachusetts</td><td>(2.9)</td></tr>
<tr><td>26</td><td>Washington</td><td>1.7</td><td>47</td><td>Maryland</td><td>(3.2)</td></tr>
<tr><td>21</td><td>West Virginia</td><td>2.4</td><td>48</td><td>South Dakota</td><td>(3.4)</td></tr>
<tr><td>2</td><td>Wisconsin</td><td>18.1</td><td>49</td><td>Montana</td><td>(9.0)</td></tr>
<tr><td>14</td><td>Wyoming</td><td>5.3</td><td>50</td><td>Rhode Island</td><td>(10.4)</td></tr>
<tr><td></td><td></td><td></td><td></td><td>District of Columbia</td><td>9.2</td></tr>
</table>

Source: Federal Bureau of Investigation
"Crime in the United States 2006" (Uniform Crime Reports, September 24, 2007)
*Violent crimes are offenses of murder, forcible rape, robbery, and aggravated assault.

Violent Crime Rate in 2006

National Rate = 473.5 Violent Crimes per 100,000 Population*

ALPHA ORDER

RANK	STATE	RATE
23	Alabama	425.2
6	Alaska	688.0
16	Arizona	501.4
11	Arkansas	551.6
14	California	532.5
25	Colorado	391.6
37	Connecticut	280.8
7	Delaware	681.6
4	Florida	712.0
19	Georgia	471.0
36	Hawaii	281.2
42	Idaho	247.2
13	Illinois	541.6
29	Indiana	314.8
33	Iowa	283.5
24	Kansas	425.0
40	Kentucky	263.0
5	Louisiana	697.8
50	Maine	115.5
8	Maryland	678.6
20	Massachusetts	447.0
10	Michigan	562.4
30	Minnesota	312.0
31	Mississippi	298.6
12	Missouri	545.6
41	Montana	253.7
35	Nebraska	281.8
3	Nevada	741.6
47	New Hampshire	138.7
26	New Jersey	351.6
9	New Mexico	643.2
22	New York	434.9
18	North Carolina	475.6
49	North Dakota	127.9
27	Ohio	350.3
17	Oklahoma	497.4
38	Oregon	280.3
21	Pennsylvania	439.4
44	Rhode Island	227.5
1	South Carolina	765.5
46	South Dakota	171.4
2	Tennessee	760.2
15	Texas	516.3
45	Utah	224.4
48	Vermont	136.6
34	Virginia	282.2
28	Washington	345.9
39	West Virginia	279.7
32	Wisconsin	284.0
43	Wyoming	239.6

RANK ORDER

RANK	STATE	RATE
1	South Carolina	765.5
2	Tennessee	760.2
3	Nevada	741.6
4	Florida	712.0
5	Louisiana	697.8
6	Alaska	688.0
7	Delaware	681.6
8	Maryland	678.6
9	New Mexico	643.2
10	Michigan	562.4
11	Arkansas	551.6
12	Missouri	545.6
13	Illinois	541.6
14	California	532.5
15	Texas	516.3
16	Arizona	501.4
17	Oklahoma	497.4
18	North Carolina	475.6
19	Georgia	471.0
20	Massachusetts	447.0
21	Pennsylvania	439.4
22	New York	434.9
23	Alabama	425.2
24	Kansas	425.0
25	Colorado	391.6
26	New Jersey	351.6
27	Ohio	350.3
28	Washington	345.9
29	Indiana	314.8
30	Minnesota	312.0
31	Mississippi	298.6
32	Wisconsin	284.0
33	Iowa	283.5
34	Virginia	282.2
35	Nebraska	281.8
36	Hawaii	281.2
37	Connecticut	280.8
38	Oregon	280.3
39	West Virginia	279.7
40	Kentucky	263.0
41	Montana	253.7
42	Idaho	247.2
43	Wyoming	239.6
44	Rhode Island	227.5
45	Utah	224.4
46	South Dakota	171.4
47	New Hampshire	138.7
48	Vermont	136.6
49	North Dakota	127.9
50	Maine	115.5
	District of Columbia	1,508.4

Source: Federal Bureau of Investigation
"Crime in the United States 2006" (Uniform Crime Reports, September 24, 2007)
*Violent crimes are offenses of murder, forcible rape, robbery, and aggravated assault.

Percent Change in Violent Crime Rate: 2005 to 2006

National Percent Change = 1.0% Increase*

ALPHA ORDER				RANK ORDER		
RANK	STATE	PERCENT CHANGE		RANK	STATE	PERCENT CHANGE
35	Alabama	(1.7)		1	Nevada	22.1
7	Alaska	8.8		2	Wisconsin	17.5
38	Arizona	(2.1)		3	Louisiana	17.0
13	Arkansas	4.4		4	North Dakota	14.9
23	California	1.2		5	Hawaii	10.1
33	Colorado	(1.3)		6	Kansas	9.2
17	Connecticut	3.0		7	Alaska	8.8
9	Delaware	7.6		8	Vermont	8.7
24	Florida	0.4		9	Delaware	7.6
11	Georgia	5.6		10	Mississippi	6.8
5	Hawaii	10.1		11	Georgia	5.6
47	Idaho	(3.7)		12	Minnesota	4.9
36	Illinois	(1.9)		13	Arkansas	4.4
43	Indiana	(2.8)		14	Wyoming	4.0
45	Iowa	(3.3)		15	Missouri	3.8
6	Kansas	9.2		16	Pennsylvania	3.3
34	Kentucky	(1.4)		17	Connecticut	3.0
3	Louisiana	17.0		18	New Hampshire	2.9
19	Maine	2.6		19	Maine	2.6
46	Maryland	(3.6)		20	West Virginia	2.1
44	Massachusetts	(3.0)		21	Michigan	1.6
21	Michigan	1.6		22	North Carolina	1.5
12	Minnesota	4.9		23	California	1.2
10	Mississippi	6.8		24	Florida	0.4
15	Missouri	3.8		24	Tennessee	0.4
50	Montana	(10.0)		26	Ohio	0.1
36	Nebraska	(1.9)		26	Washington	0.1
1	Nevada	22.1		28	South Carolina	(0.2)
18	New Hampshire	2.9		29	Utah	(0.4)
32	New Jersey	(1.0)		29	Virginia	(0.4)
31	New Mexico	(0.5)		31	New Mexico	(0.5)
38	New York	(2.1)		32	New Jersey	(1.0)
22	North Carolina	1.5		33	Colorado	(1.3)
4	North Dakota	14.9		34	Kentucky	(1.4)
26	Ohio	0.1		35	Alabama	(1.7)
41	Oklahoma	(2.3)		36	Illinois	(1.9)
41	Oregon	(2.3)		36	Nebraska	(1.9)
16	Pennsylvania	3.3		38	Arizona	(2.1)
49	Rhode Island	(9.9)		38	New York	(2.1)
28	South Carolina	(0.2)		40	Texas	(2.2)
48	South Dakota	(4.3)		41	Oklahoma	(2.3)
24	Tennessee	0.4		41	Oregon	(2.3)
40	Texas	(2.2)		43	Indiana	(2.8)
29	Utah	(0.4)		44	Massachusetts	(3.0)
8	Vermont	8.7		45	Iowa	(3.3)
29	Virginia	(0.4)		46	Maryland	(3.6)
26	Washington	0.1		47	Idaho	(3.7)
20	West Virginia	2.1		48	South Dakota	(4.3)
2	Wisconsin	17.5		49	Rhode Island	(9.9)
14	Wyoming	4.0		50	Montana	(10.0)
					District of Columbia	9.3

Source: Federal Bureau of Investigation
"Crime in the United States 2006" (Uniform Crime Reports, September 24, 2007)
*Violent crimes are offenses of murder, forcible rape, robbery, and aggravated assault.

Murders in 2006

National Total = 17,034 Murders*

ALPHA ORDER

RANK	STATE	MURDERS	% of USA
17	Alabama	382	2.2%
40	Alaska	36	0.2%
13	Arizona	465	2.7%
24	Arkansas	205	1.2%
1	California	2,485	14.6%
29	Colorado	158	0.9%
33	Connecticut	108	0.6%
39	Delaware	42	0.2%
3	Florida	1,129	6.6%
8	Georgia	600	3.5%
44	Hawaii	21	0.1%
40	Idaho	36	0.2%
5	Illinois	780	4.6%
18	Indiana	369	2.2%
36	Iowa	55	0.3%
31	Kansas	127	0.7%
27	Kentucky	168	1.0%
12	Louisiana	530	3.1%
43	Maine	23	0.1%
9	Maryland	546	3.2%
26	Massachusetts	186	1.1%
7	Michigan	713	4.2%
32	Minnesota	125	0.7%
22	Mississippi	223	1.3%
19	Missouri	368	2.2%
45	Montana	17	0.1%
37	Nebraska	50	0.3%
21	Nevada	224	1.3%
46	New Hampshire	13	0.1%
14	New Jersey	428	2.5%
30	New Mexico	132	0.8%
4	New York	921	5.4%
10	North Carolina	540	3.2%
50	North Dakota	8	0.0%
11	Ohio	539	3.2%
23	Oklahoma	207	1.2%
34	Oregon	86	0.5%
6	Pennsylvania	736	4.3%
42	Rhode Island	28	0.2%
20	South Carolina	359	2.1%
48	South Dakota	9	0.1%
15	Tennessee	409	2.4%
2	Texas	1,384	8.1%
38	Utah	46	0.3%
47	Vermont	12	0.1%
16	Virginia	399	2.3%
25	Washington	190	1.1%
35	West Virginia	75	0.4%
28	Wisconsin	164	1.0%
48	Wyoming	9	0.1%

RANK ORDER

RANK	STATE	MURDERS	% of USA
1	California	2,485	14.6%
2	Texas	1,384	8.1%
3	Florida	1,129	6.6%
4	New York	921	5.4%
5	Illinois	780	4.6%
6	Pennsylvania	736	4.3%
7	Michigan	713	4.2%
8	Georgia	600	3.5%
9	Maryland	546	3.2%
10	North Carolina	540	3.2%
11	Ohio	539	3.2%
12	Louisiana	530	3.1%
13	Arizona	465	2.7%
14	New Jersey	428	2.5%
15	Tennessee	409	2.4%
16	Virginia	399	2.3%
17	Alabama	382	2.2%
18	Indiana	369	2.2%
19	Missouri	368	2.2%
20	South Carolina	359	2.1%
21	Nevada	224	1.3%
22	Mississippi	223	1.3%
23	Oklahoma	207	1.2%
24	Arkansas	205	1.2%
25	Washington	190	1.1%
26	Massachusetts	186	1.1%
27	Kentucky	168	1.0%
28	Wisconsin	164	1.0%
29	Colorado	158	0.9%
30	New Mexico	132	0.8%
31	Kansas	127	0.7%
32	Minnesota	125	0.7%
33	Connecticut	108	0.6%
34	Oregon	86	0.5%
35	West Virginia	75	0.4%
36	Iowa	55	0.3%
37	Nebraska	50	0.3%
38	Utah	46	0.3%
39	Delaware	42	0.2%
40	Alaska	36	0.2%
40	Idaho	36	0.2%
42	Rhode Island	28	0.2%
43	Maine	23	0.1%
44	Hawaii	21	0.1%
45	Montana	17	0.1%
46	New Hampshire	13	0.1%
47	Vermont	12	0.1%
48	South Dakota	9	0.1%
48	Wyoming	9	0.1%
50	North Dakota	8	0.0%
	District of Columbia	169	1.0%

Source: Federal Bureau of Investigation
   "Crime in the United States 2006" (Uniform Crime Reports, September 24, 2007)
*Includes nonnegligent manslaughter.

Murder Rate in 2006

National Rate = 5.7 Murders per 100,000 Population*

ALPHA ORDER

RANK	STATE	RATE
4	Alabama	8.3
22	Alaska	5.4
7	Arizona	7.5
8	Arkansas	7.3
10	California	6.8
31	Colorado	3.3
32	Connecticut	3.1
24	Delaware	4.9
15	Florida	6.2
13	Georgia	6.4
47	Hawaii	1.6
38	Idaho	2.5
16	Illinois	6.1
20	Indiana	5.8
42	Iowa	1.8
28	Kansas	4.6
30	Kentucky	4.0
1	Louisiana	12.4
45	Maine	1.7
2	Maryland	9.7
35	Massachusetts	2.9
9	Michigan	7.1
39	Minnesota	2.4
6	Mississippi	7.7
14	Missouri	6.3
42	Montana	1.8
36	Nebraska	2.8
3	Nevada	9.0
50	New Hampshire	1.0
24	New Jersey	4.9
10	New Mexico	6.8
26	New York	4.8
16	North Carolina	6.1
48	North Dakota	1.3
27	Ohio	4.7
20	Oklahoma	5.8
40	Oregon	2.3
18	Pennsylvania	5.9
37	Rhode Island	2.6
4	South Carolina	8.3
49	South Dakota	1.2
10	Tennessee	6.8
18	Texas	5.9
42	Utah	1.8
41	Vermont	1.9
23	Virginia	5.2
33	Washington	3.0
29	West Virginia	4.1
33	Wisconsin	3.0
45	Wyoming	1.7

RANK ORDER

RANK	STATE	RATE
1	Louisiana	12.4
2	Maryland	9.7
3	Nevada	9.0
4	Alabama	8.3
4	South Carolina	8.3
6	Mississippi	7.7
7	Arizona	7.5
8	Arkansas	7.3
9	Michigan	7.1
10	California	6.8
10	New Mexico	6.8
10	Tennessee	6.8
13	Georgia	6.4
14	Missouri	6.3
15	Florida	6.2
16	Illinois	6.1
16	North Carolina	6.1
18	Pennsylvania	5.9
18	Texas	5.9
20	Indiana	5.8
20	Oklahoma	5.8
22	Alaska	5.4
23	Virginia	5.2
24	Delaware	4.9
24	New Jersey	4.9
26	New York	4.8
27	Ohio	4.7
28	Kansas	4.6
29	West Virginia	4.1
30	Kentucky	4.0
31	Colorado	3.3
32	Connecticut	3.1
33	Washington	3.0
33	Wisconsin	3.0
35	Massachusetts	2.9
36	Nebraska	2.8
37	Rhode Island	2.6
38	Idaho	2.5
39	Minnesota	2.4
40	Oregon	2.3
41	Vermont	1.9
42	Iowa	1.8
42	Montana	1.8
42	Utah	1.8
45	Maine	1.7
45	Wyoming	1.7
47	Hawaii	1.6
48	North Dakota	1.3
49	South Dakota	1.2
50	New Hampshire	1.0

District of Columbia		29.1

Source: Federal Bureau of Investigation
   "Crime in the United States 2006" (Uniform Crime Reports, September 24, 2007)
*Includes nonnegligent manslaughter.

Percent of Murders Involving Firearms in 2006

National Percent = 67.9% of Murders*

RANK	STATE	PERCENT
9	Alabama	70.8
26	Alaska	62.9
4	Arizona	74.2
17	Arkansas	66.7
8	California	73.3
37	Colorado	54.5
22	Connecticut	65.0
20	Delaware	65.9
NA	Florida**	NA
7	Georgia	73.5
43	Hawaii	33.3
27	Idaho	61.1
2	Illinois*	80.5
10	Indiana	70.5
42	Iowa	42.6
35	Kansas	55.6
21	Kentucky	65.3
1	Louisiana	81.1
38	Maine	52.2
5	Maryland	73.8
28	Massachusetts	60.0
12	Michigan	70.0
24	Minnesota	64.1
13	Mississippi	69.9
6	Missouri	73.7
48	Montana	23.5
44	Nebraska	31.3
29	Nevada	59.4
45	New Hampshire	25.0
16	New Jersey	67.5
32	New Mexico	57.6
41	New York	43.4
25	North Carolina	63.8
49	North Dakota	12.5
15	Ohio	68.6
23	Oklahoma	64.3
39	Oregon	51.8
3	Pennsylvania	77.1
45	Rhode Island	25.0
10	South Carolina	70.5
45	South Dakota	25.0
18	Tennessee	66.3
14	Texas	68.7
40	Utah	45.7
30	Vermont	58.3
18	Virginia	66.3
33	Washington	57.5
34	West Virginia	56.3
30	Wisconsin	58.3
35	Wyoming	55.6

RANK	STATE	PERCENT
1	Louisiana	81.1
2	Illinois*	80.5
3	Pennsylvania	77.1
4	Arizona	74.2
5	Maryland	73.8
6	Missouri	73.7
7	Georgia	73.5
8	California	73.3
9	Alabama	70.8
10	Indiana	70.5
10	South Carolina	70.5
12	Michigan	70.0
13	Mississippi	69.9
14	Texas	68.7
15	Ohio	68.6
16	New Jersey	67.5
17	Arkansas	66.7
18	Tennessee	66.3
18	Virginia	66.3
20	Delaware	65.9
21	Kentucky	65.3
22	Connecticut	65.0
23	Oklahoma	64.3
24	Minnesota	64.1
25	North Carolina	63.8
26	Alaska	62.9
27	Idaho	61.1
28	Massachusetts	60.0
29	Nevada	59.4
30	Vermont	58.3
30	Wisconsin	58.3
32	New Mexico	57.6
33	Washington	57.5
34	West Virginia	56.3
35	Kansas	55.6
35	Wyoming	55.6
37	Colorado	54.5
38	Maine	52.2
39	Oregon	51.8
40	Utah	45.7
41	New York	43.4
42	Iowa	42.6
43	Hawaii	33.3
44	Nebraska	31.3
45	New Hampshire	25.0
45	Rhode Island	25.0
45	South Dakota	25.0
48	Montana	23.5
49	North Dakota	12.5
NA	Florida**	NA
	District of Columbia**	NA

Source: CQ Press using data from Federal Bureau of Investigation
    "Crime in the United States 2006" (Uniform Crime Reports, September 24, 2007)
*Of the 14,990 murders in 2006 for which supplemental data were received by the F.B.I. There were an additional 2,044 murders
for which the type of murder weapon was not reported to the F.B.I. Includes nonnegligent manslaughter. National and state
rates based on population for reporting jurisdictions only. Illinois' rate is for Chicago only.
**Not available.

Rapes in 2006

National Total = 92,455 Rapes*

ALPHA ORDER

RANK	STATE	RAPES	% of USA
20	Alabama	1,649	1.8%
39	Alaska	509	0.6%
14	Arizona	1,941	2.1%
24	Arkansas	1,308	1.4%
1	California	9,212	10.0%
13	Colorado	2,076	2.2%
36	Connecticut	636	0.7%
40	Delaware	400	0.4%
3	Florida	6,475	7.0%
11	Georgia	2,173	2.4%
42	Hawaii	355	0.4%
37	Idaho	587	0.6%
6	Illinois	4,078	4.4%
15	Indiana	1,835	2.0%
35	Iowa	828	0.9%
26	Kansas	1,238	1.3%
25	Kentucky	1,297	1.4%
22	Louisiana	1,562	1.7%
44	Maine	339	0.4%
29	Maryland	1,178	1.3%
19	Massachusetts	1,742	1.9%
4	Michigan	5,269	5.7%
21	Minnesota	1,645	1.8%
33	Mississippi	1,000	1.1%
17	Missouri	1,764	1.9%
47	Montana	269	0.3%
38	Nebraska	548	0.6%
32	Nevada	1,079	1.2%
43	New Hampshire	344	0.4%
27	New Jersey	1,237	1.3%
31	New Mexico	1,094	1.2%
8	New York	3,169	3.4%
10	North Carolina	2,495	2.7%
48	North Dakota	193	0.2%
5	Ohio	4,548	4.9%
23	Oklahoma	1,488	1.6%
28	Oregon	1,195	1.3%
7	Pennsylvania	3,401	3.7%
46	Rhode Island	285	0.3%
18	South Carolina	1,762	1.9%
45	South Dakota	336	0.4%
12	Tennessee	2,142	2.3%
2	Texas	8,372	9.1%
34	Utah	869	0.9%
49	Vermont	150	0.2%
16	Virginia	1,792	1.9%
9	Washington	2,746	3.0%
41	West Virginia	389	0.4%
30	Wisconsin	1,131	1.2%
50	Wyoming	140	0.2%

RANK ORDER

RANK	STATE	RAPES	% of USA
1	California	9,212	10.0%
2	Texas	8,372	9.1%
3	Florida	6,475	7.0%
4	Michigan	5,269	5.7%
5	Ohio	4,548	4.9%
6	Illinois	4,078	4.4%
7	Pennsylvania	3,401	3.7%
8	New York	3,169	3.4%
9	Washington	2,746	3.0%
10	North Carolina	2,495	2.7%
11	Georgia	2,173	2.4%
12	Tennessee	2,142	2.3%
13	Colorado	2,076	2.2%
14	Arizona	1,941	2.1%
15	Indiana	1,835	2.0%
16	Virginia	1,792	1.9%
17	Missouri	1,764	1.9%
18	South Carolina	1,762	1.9%
19	Massachusetts	1,742	1.9%
20	Alabama	1,649	1.8%
21	Minnesota	1,645	1.8%
22	Louisiana	1,562	1.7%
23	Oklahoma	1,488	1.6%
24	Arkansas	1,308	1.4%
25	Kentucky	1,297	1.4%
26	Kansas	1,238	1.3%
27	New Jersey	1,237	1.3%
28	Oregon	1,195	1.3%
29	Maryland	1,178	1.3%
30	Wisconsin	1,131	1.2%
31	New Mexico	1,094	1.2%
32	Nevada	1,079	1.2%
33	Mississippi	1,000	1.1%
34	Utah	869	0.9%
35	Iowa	828	0.9%
36	Connecticut	636	0.7%
37	Idaho	587	0.6%
38	Nebraska	548	0.6%
39	Alaska	509	0.6%
40	Delaware	400	0.4%
41	West Virginia	389	0.4%
42	Hawaii	355	0.4%
43	New Hampshire	344	0.4%
44	Maine	339	0.4%
45	South Dakota	336	0.4%
46	Rhode Island	285	0.3%
47	Montana	269	0.3%
48	North Dakota	193	0.2%
49	Vermont	150	0.2%
50	Wyoming	140	0.2%
	District of Columbia	185	0.2%

Source: Federal Bureau of Investigation
   "Crime in the United States 2006" (Uniform Crime Reports, September 24, 2007)
*Forcible rape is the carnal knowledge of a female forcibly and against her will. Assaults or attempts to commit rape by force or threat of force are included. However, statutory rape without force and other sex offenses are excluded.

Rape Rate in 2006

National Rate = 30.9 Rapes per 100,000 Population*

ALPHA ORDER

RANK	STATE	RATE
16	Alabama	35.9
1	Alaska	76.0
25	Arizona	31.5
5	Arkansas	46.5
41	California	25.3
7	Colorado	43.7
48	Connecticut	18.1
4	Delaware	46.9
17	Florida	35.8
44	Georgia	23.2
34	Hawaii	27.6
13	Idaho	40.0
23	Illinois	31.8
30	Indiana	29.1
33	Iowa	27.8
6	Kansas	44.8
27	Kentucky	30.8
15	Louisiana	36.4
40	Maine	25.7
46	Maryland	21.0
37	Massachusetts	27.1
3	Michigan	52.2
23	Minnesota	31.8
20	Mississippi	34.4
29	Missouri	30.2
31	Montana	28.5
26	Nebraska	31.0
8	Nevada	43.2
39	New Hampshire	26.2
50	New Jersey	14.2
2	New Mexico	56.0
49	New York	16.4
32	North Carolina	28.2
28	North Dakota	30.4
14	Ohio	39.6
11	Oklahoma	41.6
22	Oregon	32.3
35	Pennsylvania	27.3
38	Rhode Island	26.7
12	South Carolina	40.8
9	South Dakota	43.0
19	Tennessee	35.5
18	Texas	35.6
21	Utah	34.1
42	Vermont	24.0
43	Virginia	23.4
10	Washington	42.9
45	West Virginia	21.4
47	Wisconsin	20.4
36	Wyoming	27.2

RANK ORDER

RANK	STATE	RATE
1	Alaska	76.0
2	New Mexico	56.0
3	Michigan	52.2
4	Delaware	46.9
5	Arkansas	46.5
6	Kansas	44.8
7	Colorado	43.7
8	Nevada	43.2
9	South Dakota	43.0
10	Washington	42.9
11	Oklahoma	41.6
12	South Carolina	40.8
13	Idaho	40.0
14	Ohio	39.6
15	Louisiana	36.4
16	Alabama	35.9
17	Florida	35.8
18	Texas	35.6
19	Tennessee	35.5
20	Mississippi	34.4
21	Utah	34.1
22	Oregon	32.3
23	Illinois	31.8
23	Minnesota	31.8
25	Arizona	31.5
26	Nebraska	31.0
27	Kentucky	30.8
28	North Dakota	30.4
29	Missouri	30.2
30	Indiana	29.1
31	Montana	28.5
32	North Carolina	28.2
33	Iowa	27.8
34	Hawaii	27.6
35	Pennsylvania	27.3
36	Wyoming	27.2
37	Massachusetts	27.1
38	Rhode Island	26.7
39	New Hampshire	26.2
40	Maine	25.7
41	California	25.3
42	Vermont	24.0
43	Virginia	23.4
44	Georgia	23.2
45	West Virginia	21.4
46	Maryland	21.0
47	Wisconsin	20.4
48	Connecticut	18.1
49	New York	16.4
50	New Jersey	14.2
	District of Columbia	31.8

Source: Federal Bureau of Investigation
    "Crime in the United States 2006" (Uniform Crime Reports, September 24, 2007)
*Forcible rape is the carnal knowledge of a female forcibly and against her will. Assaults or attempts to commit rape by force or threat of force are included. However, statutory rape without force and other sex offenses are excluded.

Robberies in 2006

National Total = 447,403 Robberies*

ALPHA ORDER					RANK ORDER			
RANK	STATE	ROBBERIES	% of USA		RANK	STATE	ROBBERIES	% of USA
19	Alabama	7,059	1.6%		1	California	70,968	15.9%
42	Alaska	605	0.1%		2	Texas	37,254	8.3%
14	Arizona	9,226	2.1%		3	New York	34,489	7.7%
31	Arkansas	2,766	0.6%		4	Florida	34,147	7.6%
1	California	70,968	15.9%		5	Illinois	23,782	5.3%
27	Colorado	3,835	0.9%		6	Pennsylvania	20,974	4.7%
26	Connecticut	4,241	0.9%		7	Ohio	19,149	4.3%
35	Delaware	1,735	0.4%		8	Georgia	15,509	3.5%
4	Florida	34,147	7.6%		9	Maryland	14,375	3.2%
8	Georgia	15,509	3.5%		10	Michigan	14,208	3.2%
38	Hawaii	1,143	0.3%		11	North Carolina	13,484	3.0%
45	Idaho	301	0.1%		12	New Jersey	13,357	3.0%
5	Illinois	23,782	5.3%		13	Tennessee	11,129	2.5%
18	Indiana	7,243	1.6%		14	Arizona	9,226	2.1%
36	Iowa	1,298	0.3%		15	Massachusetts	8,047	1.8%
34	Kansas	1,877	0.4%		16	Virginia	7,749	1.7%
28	Kentucky	3,626	0.8%		17	Missouri	7,587	1.7%
23	Louisiana	5,729	1.3%		18	Indiana	7,243	1.6%
44	Maine	384	0.1%		19	Alabama	7,059	1.6%
9	Maryland	14,375	3.2%		20	Nevada	7,027	1.6%
15	Massachusetts	8,047	1.8%		21	Washington	6,405	1.4%
10	Michigan	14,208	3.2%		22	South Carolina	5,899	1.3%
25	Minnesota	5,433	1.2%		23	Louisiana	5,729	1.3%
30	Mississippi	3,118	0.7%		24	Wisconsin	5,567	1.2%
17	Missouri	7,587	1.7%		25	Minnesota	5,433	1.2%
46	Montana	164	0.0%		26	Connecticut	4,241	0.9%
39	Nebraska	1,129	0.3%		27	Colorado	3,835	0.9%
20	Nevada	7,027	1.6%		28	Kentucky	3,626	0.8%
43	New Hampshire	423	0.1%		29	Oklahoma	3,133	0.7%
12	New Jersey	13,357	3.0%		30	Mississippi	3,118	0.7%
33	New Mexico	2,105	0.5%		31	Arkansas	2,766	0.6%
3	New York	34,489	7.7%		32	Oregon	2,689	0.6%
11	North Carolina	13,484	3.0%		33	New Mexico	2,105	0.5%
49	North Dakota	72	0.0%		34	Kansas	1,877	0.4%
7	Ohio	19,149	4.3%		35	Delaware	1,735	0.4%
29	Oklahoma	3,133	0.7%		36	Iowa	1,298	0.3%
32	Oregon	2,689	0.6%		37	Utah	1,245	0.3%
6	Pennsylvania	20,974	4.7%		38	Hawaii	1,143	0.3%
41	Rhode Island	735	0.2%		39	Nebraska	1,129	0.3%
22	South Carolina	5,899	1.3%		40	West Virginia	853	0.2%
47	South Dakota	119	0.0%		41	Rhode Island	735	0.2%
13	Tennessee	11,129	2.5%		42	Alaska	605	0.1%
2	Texas	37,254	8.3%		43	New Hampshire	423	0.1%
37	Utah	1,245	0.3%		44	Maine	384	0.1%
48	Vermont	110	0.0%		45	Idaho	301	0.1%
16	Virginia	7,749	1.7%		46	Montana	164	0.0%
21	Washington	6,405	1.4%		47	South Dakota	119	0.0%
40	West Virginia	853	0.2%		48	Vermont	110	0.0%
24	Wisconsin	5,567	1.2%		49	North Dakota	72	0.0%
49	Wyoming	72	0.0%		49	Wyoming	72	0.0%
					District of Columbia	3,829	0.9%

Source: Federal Bureau of Investigation
"Crime in the United States 2006" (Uniform Crime Reports, September 24, 2007)
*Robbery is the taking or attempting to take anything of value by force or threat of force.

Robbery Rate in 2006

National Rate = 149.4 Robberies per 100,000 Population*

ALPHA ORDER				RANK ORDER		
RANK	**STATE**	**RATE**		**RANK**	**STATE**	**RATE**
13	Alabama	153.5		1	Nevada	281.6
31	Alaska	90.3		2	Maryland	256.0
16	Arizona	149.6		3	Delaware	203.3
30	Arkansas	98.4		4	California	194.7
4	California	194.7		5	Florida	188.8
35	Colorado	80.7		6	Illinois	185.3
22	Connecticut	121.0		7	Tennessee	184.3
3	Delaware	203.3		8	New York	178.6
5	Florida	188.8		9	Pennsylvania	168.6
11	Georgia	165.6		10	Ohio	166.8
32	Hawaii	88.9		11	Georgia	165.6
45	Idaho	20.5		12	Texas	158.5
6	Illinois	185.3		13	Alabama	153.5
23	Indiana	114.7		14	New Jersey	153.1
42	Iowa	43.5		15	North Carolina	152.2
38	Kansas	67.9		16	Arizona	149.6
34	Kentucky	86.2		17	Michigan	140.7
19	Louisiana	133.6		18	South Carolina	136.5
44	Maine	29.1		19	Louisiana	133.6
2	Maryland	256.0		20	Missouri	129.9
21	Massachusetts	125.0		21	Massachusetts	125.0
17	Michigan	140.7		22	Connecticut	121.0
26	Minnesota	105.1		23	Indiana	114.7
25	Mississippi	107.1		24	New Mexico	107.7
20	Missouri	129.9		25	Mississippi	107.1
47	Montana	17.4		26	Minnesota	105.1
39	Nebraska	63.8		27	Virginia	101.4
1	Nevada	281.6		28	Wisconsin	100.2
43	New Hampshire	32.2		29	Washington	100.1
14	New Jersey	153.1		30	Arkansas	98.4
24	New Mexico	107.7		31	Alaska	90.3
8	New York	178.6		32	Hawaii	88.9
15	North Carolina	152.2		33	Oklahoma	87.5
50	North Dakota	11.3		34	Kentucky	86.2
10	Ohio	166.8		35	Colorado	80.7
33	Oklahoma	87.5		36	Oregon	72.7
36	Oregon	72.7		37	Rhode Island	68.8
9	Pennsylvania	168.6		38	Kansas	67.9
37	Rhode Island	68.8		39	Nebraska	63.8
18	South Carolina	136.5		40	Utah	48.8
48	South Dakota	15.2		41	West Virginia	46.9
7	Tennessee	184.3		42	Iowa	43.5
12	Texas	158.5		43	New Hampshire	32.2
40	Utah	48.8		44	Maine	29.1
46	Vermont	17.6		45	Idaho	20.5
27	Virginia	101.4		46	Vermont	17.6
29	Washington	100.1		47	Montana	17.4
41	West Virginia	46.9		48	South Dakota	15.2
28	Wisconsin	100.2		49	Wyoming	14.0
49	Wyoming	14.0		50	North Dakota	11.3
					District of Columbia	658.4

Source: Federal Bureau of Investigation
"Crime in the United States 2006" (Uniform Crime Reports, September 24, 2007)
*Robbery is the taking or attempting to take anything of value by force or threat of force.

Aggravated Assaults in 2006

National Total = 860,853 Aggravated Assaults*

ALPHA ORDER

RANK	STATE	ASSAULTS	% of USA
24	Alabama	10,467	1.2%
39	Alaska	3,460	0.4%
15	Arizona	19,284	2.2%
23	Arkansas	11,227	1.3%
1	California	111,455	12.9%
21	Colorado	12,547	1.5%
34	Connecticut	4,856	0.6%
37	Delaware	3,640	0.4%
2	Florida	87,044	10.1%
9	Georgia	25,824	3.0%
42	Hawaii	2,096	0.2%
41	Idaho	2,701	0.3%
5	Illinois	40,858	4.7%
25	Indiana	10,429	1.2%
32	Iowa	6,274	0.7%
30	Kansas	8,506	1.0%
33	Kentucky	5,972	0.7%
13	Louisiana	22,098	2.6%
48	Maine	780	0.1%
14	Maryland	22,011	2.6%
16	Massachusetts	18,800	2.2%
6	Michigan	36,588	4.3%
29	Minnesota	8,920	1.0%
35	Mississippi	4,350	0.5%
12	Missouri	22,161	2.6%
43	Montana	1,947	0.2%
40	Nebraska	3,256	0.4%
26	Nevada	10,178	1.2%
45	New Hampshire	1,044	0.1%
18	New Jersey	15,650	1.8%
27	New Mexico	9,241	1.1%
4	New York	45,387	5.3%
10	North Carolina	25,605	3.0%
50	North Dakota	540	0.1%
17	Ohio	15,973	1.9%
19	Oklahoma	12,975	1.5%
31	Oregon	6,403	0.7%
8	Pennsylvania	29,554	3.4%
44	Rhode Island	1,381	0.2%
11	South Carolina	25,058	2.9%
47	South Dakota	876	0.1%
7	Tennessee	32,227	3.7%
3	Texas	74,368	8.6%
38	Utah	3,562	0.4%
49	Vermont	580	0.1%
22	Virginia	11,628	1.4%
20	Washington	12,779	1.5%
36	West Virginia	3,770	0.4%
28	Wisconsin	8,921	1.0%
46	Wyoming	1,013	0.1%

RANK ORDER

RANK	STATE	ASSAULTS	% of USA
1	California	111,455	12.9%
2	Florida	87,044	10.1%
3	Texas	74,368	8.6%
4	New York	45,387	5.3%
5	Illinois	40,858	4.7%
6	Michigan	36,588	4.3%
7	Tennessee	32,227	3.7%
8	Pennsylvania	29,554	3.4%
9	Georgia	25,824	3.0%
10	North Carolina	25,605	3.0%
11	South Carolina	25,058	2.9%
12	Missouri	22,161	2.6%
13	Louisiana	22,098	2.6%
14	Maryland	22,011	2.6%
15	Arizona	19,284	2.2%
16	Massachusetts	18,800	2.2%
17	Ohio	15,973	1.9%
18	New Jersey	15,650	1.8%
19	Oklahoma	12,975	1.5%
20	Washington	12,779	1.5%
21	Colorado	12,547	1.5%
22	Virginia	11,628	1.4%
23	Arkansas	11,227	1.3%
24	Alabama	10,467	1.2%
25	Indiana	10,429	1.2%
26	Nevada	10,178	1.2%
27	New Mexico	9,241	1.1%
28	Wisconsin	8,921	1.0%
29	Minnesota	8,920	1.0%
30	Kansas	8,506	1.0%
31	Oregon	6,403	0.7%
32	Iowa	6,274	0.7%
33	Kentucky	5,972	0.7%
34	Connecticut	4,856	0.6%
35	Mississippi	4,350	0.5%
36	West Virginia	3,770	0.4%
37	Delaware	3,640	0.4%
38	Utah	3,562	0.4%
39	Alaska	3,460	0.4%
40	Nebraska	3,256	0.4%
41	Idaho	2,701	0.3%
42	Hawaii	2,096	0.2%
43	Montana	1,947	0.2%
44	Rhode Island	1,381	0.2%
45	New Hampshire	1,044	0.1%
46	Wyoming	1,013	0.1%
47	South Dakota	876	0.1%
48	Maine	780	0.1%
49	Vermont	580	0.1%
50	North Dakota	540	0.1%
	District of Columbia	4,589	0.5%

Source: Federal Bureau of Investigation
"Crime in the United States 2006" (Uniform Crime Reports, September 24, 2007)
*Aggravated assault is an attack for the purpose of inflicting severe bodily injury.

Aggravated Assault Rate in 2006

National Rate = 287.5 Aggravated Assaults per 100,000 Population*

ALPHA ORDER

RANK	STATE	RATE
25	Alabama	227.6
3	Alaska	516.4
16	Arizona	312.7
9	Arkansas	399.4
18	California	305.7
22	Colorado	264.0
44	Connecticut	138.6
7	Delaware	426.5
5	Florida	481.2
21	Georgia	275.8
37	Hawaii	163.0
31	Idaho	184.2
14	Illinois	318.4
36	Indiana	165.2
26	Iowa	210.4
17	Kansas	307.7
41	Kentucky	142.0
4	Louisiana	515.4
50	Maine	59.0
10	Maryland	392.0
19	Massachusetts	292.1
13	Michigan	362.4
35	Minnesota	172.6
40	Mississippi	149.5
11	Missouri	379.3
28	Montana	206.1
32	Nebraska	184.1
8	Nevada	407.8
49	New Hampshire	79.4
33	New Jersey	179.4
6	New Mexico	472.8
24	New York	235.1
20	North Carolina	289.1
48	North Dakota	84.9
43	Ohio	139.2
12	Oklahoma	362.5
34	Oregon	173.0
23	Pennsylvania	237.6
45	Rhode Island	129.4
1	South Carolina	579.9
46	South Dakota	112.0
2	Tennessee	533.7
15	Texas	316.4
42	Utah	139.7
47	Vermont	93.0
39	Virginia	152.1
29	Washington	199.8
27	West Virginia	207.3
38	Wisconsin	160.6
30	Wyoming	196.7

RANK ORDER

RANK	STATE	RATE
1	South Carolina	579.9
2	Tennessee	533.7
3	Alaska	516.4
4	Louisiana	515.4
5	Florida	481.2
6	New Mexico	472.8
7	Delaware	426.5
8	Nevada	407.8
9	Arkansas	399.4
10	Maryland	392.0
11	Missouri	379.3
12	Oklahoma	362.5
13	Michigan	362.4
14	Illinois	318.4
15	Texas	316.4
16	Arizona	312.7
17	Kansas	307.7
18	California	305.7
19	Massachusetts	292.1
20	North Carolina	289.1
21	Georgia	275.8
22	Colorado	264.0
23	Pennsylvania	237.6
24	New York	235.1
25	Alabama	227.6
26	Iowa	210.4
27	West Virginia	207.3
28	Montana	206.1
29	Washington	199.8
30	Wyoming	196.7
31	Idaho	184.2
32	Nebraska	184.1
33	New Jersey	179.4
34	Oregon	173.0
35	Minnesota	172.6
36	Indiana	165.2
37	Hawaii	163.0
38	Wisconsin	160.6
39	Virginia	152.1
40	Mississippi	149.5
41	Kentucky	142.0
42	Utah	139.7
43	Ohio	139.2
44	Connecticut	138.6
45	Rhode Island	129.4
46	South Dakota	112.0
47	Vermont	93.0
48	North Dakota	84.9
49	New Hampshire	79.4
50	Maine	59.0
	District of Columbia	789.1

Source: Federal Bureau of Investigation
   "Crime in the United States 2006" (Uniform Crime Reports, September 24, 2007)
*Aggravated assault is an attack for the purpose of inflicting severe bodily injury.

Property Crimes in 2006

National Total = 9,983,568 Property Crimes*

ALPHA ORDER					RANK ORDER			
RANK	**STATE**		**CRIMES**	**% of USA**	**RANK**	**STATE**	**CRIMES**	**% of USA**
20	Alabama		181,021	1.8%	1	California	1,156,017	11.6%
46	Alaska		24,155	0.2%	2	Texas	959,460	9.6%
12	Arizona		285,370	2.9%	3	Florida	721,084	7.2%
28	Arkansas		111,521	1.1%	4	Ohio	422,235	4.2%
1	California		1,156,017	11.6%	5	New York	396,304	4.0%
22	Colorado		164,054	1.6%	6	Illinois	387,478	3.9%
34	Connecticut		87,764	0.9%	7	North Carolina	364,960	3.7%
42	Delaware		29,171	0.3%	8	Georgia	364,183	3.6%
3	Florida		721,084	7.2%	9	Michigan	324,351	3.2%
8	Georgia		364,183	3.6%	10	Pennsylvania	303,988	3.0%
38	Hawaii		54,382	0.5%	11	Washington	286,533	2.9%
40	Idaho		35,471	0.4%	12	Arizona	285,370	2.9%
6	Illinois		387,478	3.9%	13	Tennessee	249,297	2.5%
15	Indiana		221,127	2.2%	14	Missouri	223,570	2.2%
35	Iowa		83,579	0.8%	15	Indiana	221,127	2.2%
30	Kansas		103,658	1.0%	16	New Jersey	199,958	2.0%
29	Kentucky		107,023	1.1%	17	Maryland	195,476	2.0%
21	Louisiana		171,239	1.7%	18	Virginia	189,406	1.9%
41	Maine		33,286	0.3%	19	South Carolina	183,322	1.8%
17	Maryland		195,476	2.0%	20	Alabama	181,021	1.8%
25	Massachusetts		153,913	1.5%	21	Louisiana	171,239	1.7%
9	Michigan		324,351	3.2%	22	Colorado	164,054	1.6%
23	Minnesota		159,119	1.6%	23	Minnesota	159,119	1.6%
32	Mississippi		93,393	0.9%	24	Wisconsin	156,571	1.6%
14	Missouri		223,570	2.2%	25	Massachusetts	153,913	1.5%
44	Montana		25,387	0.3%	26	Oregon	135,895	1.4%
37	Nebraska		59,075	0.6%	27	Oklahoma	129,002	1.3%
31	Nevada		102,036	1.0%	28	Arkansas	111,521	1.1%
45	New Hampshire		24,642	0.2%	29	Kentucky	107,023	1.1%
16	New Jersey		199,958	2.0%	30	Kansas	103,658	1.0%
36	New Mexico		76,956	0.8%	31	Nevada	102,036	1.0%
5	New York		396,304	4.0%	32	Mississippi	93,393	0.9%
7	North Carolina		364,960	3.7%	33	Utah	89,671	0.9%
49	North Dakota		12,719	0.1%	34	Connecticut	87,764	0.9%
4	Ohio		422,235	4.2%	35	Iowa	83,579	0.8%
27	Oklahoma		129,002	1.3%	36	New Mexico	76,956	0.8%
26	Oregon		135,895	1.4%	37	Nebraska	59,075	0.6%
10	Pennsylvania		303,988	3.0%	38	Hawaii	54,382	0.5%
43	Rhode Island		27,618	0.3%	39	West Virginia	47,672	0.5%
19	South Carolina		183,322	1.8%	40	Idaho	35,471	0.4%
50	South Dakota		12,664	0.1%	41	Maine	33,286	0.3%
13	Tennessee		249,297	2.5%	42	Delaware	29,171	0.3%
2	Texas		959,460	9.6%	43	Rhode Island	27,618	0.3%
33	Utah		89,671	0.9%	44	Montana	25,387	0.3%
48	Vermont		14,379	0.1%	45	New Hampshire	24,642	0.2%
18	Virginia		189,406	1.9%	46	Alaska	24,155	0.2%
11	Washington		286,533	2.9%	47	Wyoming	15,350	0.2%
39	West Virginia		47,672	0.5%	48	Vermont	14,379	0.1%
24	Wisconsin		156,571	1.6%	49	North Dakota	12,719	0.1%
47	Wyoming		15,350	0.2%	50	South Dakota	12,664	0.1%
						District of Columbia	27,063	0.3%

Source: Federal Bureau of Investigation
   "Crime in the United States 2006" (Uniform Crime Reports, September 24, 2007)
*Property crimes are offenses of burglary, larceny-theft, and motor vehicle theft.

Percent Change in Number of Property Crimes: 2005 to 2006

National Percent Change = 1.9% Decrease*

ALPHA ORDER

RANK	STATE	PERCENT CHANGE
8	Alabama	2.0
14	Alaska	0.8
19	Arizona	(0.7)
23	Arkansas	(1.2)
37	California	(3.7)
48	Colorado	(12.9)
34	Connecticut	(2.8)
1	Delaware	11.1
13	Florida	1.1
38	Georgia	(3.8)
47	Hawaii	(11.0)
45	Idaho	(8.0)
27	Illinois	(1.8)
8	Indiana	2.0
20	Iowa	(0.9)
20	Kansas	(0.9)
11	Kentucky	1.3
6	Louisiana	2.8
3	Maine	4.4
25	Maryland	(1.5)
10	Massachusetts	1.4
4	Michigan	3.7
15	Minnesota	0.5
28	Mississippi	(1.9)
28	Missouri	(1.9)
49	Montana	(13.7)
30	Nebraska	(2.1)
18	Nevada	(0.4)
7	New Hampshire	2.5
26	New Jersey	(1.7)
36	New Mexico	(3.3)
31	New York	(2.4)
5	North Carolina	3.1
22	North Dakota	(1.0)
16	Ohio	0.4
46	Oklahoma	(10.0)
50	Oregon	(15.2)
12	Pennsylvania	1.2
41	Rhode Island	(5.7)
23	South Carolina	(1.2)
44	South Dakota	(7.5)
33	Tennessee	(2.7)
35	Texas	(3.1)
42	Utah	(6.1)
32	Vermont	(2.5)
40	Virginia	(5.5)
43	Washington	(6.9)
17	West Virginia	(0.2)
2	Wisconsin	6.1
39	Wyoming	(4.5)

RANK ORDER

RANK	STATE	PERCENT CHANGE
1	Delaware	11.1
2	Wisconsin	6.1
3	Maine	4.4
4	Michigan	3.7
5	North Carolina	3.1
6	Louisiana	2.8
7	New Hampshire	2.5
8	Alabama	2.0
8	Indiana	2.0
10	Massachusetts	1.4
11	Kentucky	1.3
12	Pennsylvania	1.2
13	Florida	1.1
14	Alaska	0.8
15	Minnesota	0.5
16	Ohio	0.4
17	West Virginia	(0.2)
18	Nevada	(0.4)
19	Arizona	(0.7)
20	Iowa	(0.9)
20	Kansas	(0.9)
22	North Dakota	(1.0)
23	Arkansas	(1.2)
23	South Carolina	(1.2)
25	Maryland	(1.5)
26	New Jersey	(1.7)
27	Illinois	(1.8)
28	Mississippi	(1.9)
28	Missouri	(1.9)
30	Nebraska	(2.1)
31	New York	(2.4)
32	Vermont	(2.5)
33	Tennessee	(2.7)
34	Connecticut	(2.8)
35	Texas	(3.1)
36	New Mexico	(3.3)
37	California	(3.7)
38	Georgia	(3.8)
39	Wyoming	(4.5)
40	Virginia	(5.5)
41	Rhode Island	(5.7)
42	Utah	(6.1)
43	Washington	(6.9)
44	South Dakota	(7.5)
45	Idaho	(8.0)
46	Oklahoma	(10.0)
47	Hawaii	(11.0)
48	Colorado	(12.9)
49	Montana	(13.7)
50	Oregon	(15.2)

| | District of Columbia | 3.6 |

Source: Federal Bureau of Investigation
    "Crime in the United States 2006" (Uniform Crime Reports, September 24, 2007)
*Property crimes are offenses of burglary, larceny-theft, and motor vehicle theft.

Property Crime Rate in 2006

National Rate = 3,334.5 Property Crimes per 100,000 Population*

ALPHA ORDER

RANK	STATE	RATE
13	Alabama	3,936.1
19	Alaska	3,604.9
1	Arizona	4,627.9
11	Arkansas	3,967.5
29	California	3,170.9
24	Colorado	3,451.3
40	Connecticut	2,504.1
25	Delaware	3,417.9
10	Florida	3,986.1
14	Georgia	3,889.2
4	Hawaii	4,230.4
43	Idaho	2,418.8
31	Illinois	3,019.6
22	Indiana	3,502.4
34	Iowa	2,802.7
16	Kansas	3,750.2
38	Kentucky	2,544.5
9	Louisiana	3,993.7
39	Maine	2,518.7
23	Maryland	3,480.9
44	Massachusetts	2,391.0
27	Michigan	3,212.8
30	Minnesota	3,079.5
28	Mississippi	3,208.8
15	Missouri	3,826.5
35	Montana	2,687.5
26	Nebraska	3,340.7
7	Nevada	4,088.8
49	New Hampshire	1,874.1
46	New Jersey	2,291.9
12	New Mexico	3,937.2
47	New York	2,052.7
6	North Carolina	4,120.8
48	North Dakota	2,000.3
17	Ohio	3,678.6
20	Oklahoma	3,604.2
18	Oregon	3,672.1
42	Pennsylvania	2,443.5
37	Rhode Island	2,586.9
3	South Carolina	4,242.3
50	South Dakota	1,619.6
5	Tennessee	4,128.3
8	Texas	4,081.5
21	Utah	3,516.4
45	Vermont	2,304.7
41	Virginia	2,478.2
2	Washington	4,480.0
36	West Virginia	2,621.5
33	Wisconsin	2,817.8
32	Wyoming	2,980.6

RANK ORDER

RANK	STATE	RATE
1	Arizona	4,627.9
2	Washington	4,480.0
3	South Carolina	4,242.3
4	Hawaii	4,230.4
5	Tennessee	4,128.3
6	North Carolina	4,120.8
7	Nevada	4,088.8
8	Texas	4,081.5
9	Louisiana	3,993.7
10	Florida	3,986.1
11	Arkansas	3,967.5
12	New Mexico	3,937.2
13	Alabama	3,936.1
14	Georgia	3,889.2
15	Missouri	3,826.5
16	Kansas	3,750.2
17	Ohio	3,678.6
18	Oregon	3,672.1
19	Alaska	3,604.9
20	Oklahoma	3,604.2
21	Utah	3,516.4
22	Indiana	3,502.4
23	Maryland	3,480.9
24	Colorado	3,451.3
25	Delaware	3,417.9
26	Nebraska	3,340.7
27	Michigan	3,212.8
28	Mississippi	3,208.8
29	California	3,170.9
30	Minnesota	3,079.5
31	Illinois	3,019.6
32	Wyoming	2,980.6
33	Wisconsin	2,817.8
34	Iowa	2,802.7
35	Montana	2,687.5
36	West Virginia	2,621.5
37	Rhode Island	2,586.9
38	Kentucky	2,544.5
39	Maine	2,518.7
40	Connecticut	2,504.1
41	Virginia	2,478.2
42	Pennsylvania	2,443.5
43	Idaho	2,418.8
44	Massachusetts	2,391.0
45	Vermont	2,304.7
46	New Jersey	2,291.9
47	New York	2,052.7
48	North Dakota	2,000.3
49	New Hampshire	1,874.1
50	South Dakota	1,619.6
	District of Columbia	4,653.8

Source: Federal Bureau of Investigation
"Crime in the United States 2006" (Uniform Crime Reports, September 24, 2007)
*Property crimes are offenses of burglary, larceny-theft, and motor vehicle theft.

Percent Change in Property Crime Rate: 2005 to 2006

National Percent Change = 2.8% Decrease*

ALPHA ORDER			RANK ORDER		
RANK	STATE	PERCENT CHANGE	RANK	STATE	PERCENT CHANGE
10	Alabama	0.9	1	Delaware	9.6
14	Alaska	(0.3)	2	Louisiana	8.0
34	Arizona	(4.1)	3	Wisconsin	5.6
26	Arkansas	(2.5)	4	Maine	4.1
35	California	(4.5)	5	Michigan	3.7
48	Colorado	(14.6)	6	New Hampshire	1.9
30	Connecticut	(2.9)	7	Massachusetts	1.4
1	Delaware	9.6	8	Indiana	1.2
17	Florida	(0.7)	9	North Carolina	1.0
40	Georgia	(6.2)	10	Alabama	0.9
47	Hawaii	(11.9)	10	Pennsylvania	0.9
45	Idaho	(10.3)	12	Kentucky	0.5
24	Illinois	(2.3)	13	Ohio	0.3
8	Indiana	1.2	14	Alaska	(0.3)
19	Iowa	(1.5)	14	Minnesota	(0.3)
19	Kansas	(1.5)	16	West Virginia	(0.4)
12	Kentucky	0.5	17	Florida	(0.7)
2	Louisiana	8.0	18	North Dakota	(1.2)
4	Maine	4.1	19	Iowa	(1.5)
22	Maryland	(2.0)	19	Kansas	(1.5)
7	Massachusetts	1.4	21	New Jersey	(1.9)
5	Michigan	3.7	22	Maryland	(2.0)
14	Minnesota	(0.3)	22	Mississippi	(2.0)
22	Mississippi	(2.0)	24	Illinois	(2.3)
27	Missouri	(2.6)	24	New York	(2.3)
48	Montana	(14.6)	26	Arkansas	(2.5)
28	Nebraska	(2.7)	27	Missouri	(2.6)
32	Nevada	(3.7)	28	Nebraska	(2.7)
6	New Hampshire	1.9	28	Vermont	(2.7)
21	New Jersey	(1.9)	30	Connecticut	(2.9)
36	New Mexico	(4.7)	30	South Carolina	(2.9)
24	New York	(2.3)	32	Nevada	(3.7)
9	North Carolina	1.0	33	Tennessee	(4.0)
18	North Dakota	(1.2)	34	Arizona	(4.1)
13	Ohio	0.3	35	California	(4.5)
46	Oklahoma	(10.9)	36	New Mexico	(4.7)
50	Oregon	(16.6)	37	Rhode Island	(5.2)
10	Pennsylvania	0.9	38	Texas	(5.5)
37	Rhode Island	(5.2)	39	Wyoming	(5.6)
30	South Carolina	(2.9)	40	Georgia	(6.2)
43	South Dakota	(8.4)	41	Virginia	(6.5)
33	Tennessee	(4.0)	42	Utah	(8.3)
38	Texas	(5.5)	43	South Dakota	(8.4)
42	Utah	(8.3)	43	Washington	(8.4)
28	Vermont	(2.7)	45	Idaho	(10.3)
41	Virginia	(6.5)	46	Oklahoma	(10.9)
43	Washington	(8.4)	47	Hawaii	(11.9)
16	West Virginia	(0.4)	48	Colorado	(14.6)
3	Wisconsin	5.6	48	Montana	(14.6)
39	Wyoming	(5.6)	50	Oregon	(16.6)

District of Columbia   3.7

Source: Federal Bureau of Investigation
    "Crime in the United States 2006" (Uniform Crime Reports, September 24, 2007)
*Property crimes are offenses of burglary, larceny-theft, and motor vehicle theft.

Burglaries in 2006

National Total = 2,183,746 Burglaries*

RANK	STATE	BURGLARIES	% of USA
17	Alabama	44,571	2.0%
45	Alaska	4,136	0.2%
13	Arizona	57,055	2.6%
24	Arkansas	32,042	1.5%
1	California	246,464	11.3%
23	Colorado	32,422	1.5%
36	Connecticut	14,694	0.7%
42	Delaware	6,189	0.3%
3	Florida	170,873	7.8%
6	Georgia	85,117	3.9%
39	Hawaii	8,709	0.4%
40	Idaho	7,526	0.3%
7	Illinois	77,259	3.5%
14	Indiana	46,168	2.1%
34	Iowa	18,017	0.8%
33	Kansas	19,992	0.9%
28	Kentucky	27,122	1.2%
15	Louisiana	44,986	2.1%
41	Maine	6,779	0.3%
20	Maryland	37,457	1.7%
21	Massachusetts	35,181	1.6%
8	Michigan	76,107	3.5%
26	Minnesota	30,173	1.4%
27	Mississippi	27,239	1.2%
16	Missouri	44,647	2.0%
47	Montana	2,935	0.1%
38	Nebraska	9,452	0.4%
30	Nevada	24,820	1.1%
44	New Hampshire	4,358	0.2%
19	New Jersey	39,433	1.8%
32	New Mexico	20,909	1.0%
9	New York	68,565	3.1%
4	North Carolina	107,407	4.9%
49	North Dakota	2,393	0.1%
5	Ohio	104,426	4.8%
22	Oklahoma	34,377	1.6%
31	Oregon	23,879	1.1%
12	Pennsylvania	57,623	2.6%
43	Rhode Island	5,415	0.2%
18	South Carolina	42,772	2.0%
48	South Dakota	2,650	0.1%
10	Tennessee	62,859	2.9%
2	Texas	215,647	9.9%
35	Utah	14,701	0.7%
46	Vermont	3,300	0.2%
25	Virginia	31,913	1.5%
11	Washington	58,307	2.7%
37	West Virginia	11,531	0.5%
29	Wisconsin	26,994	1.2%
50	Wyoming	2,320	0.1%

RANK	STATE	BURGLARIES	% of USA
1	California	246,464	11.3%
2	Texas	215,647	9.9%
3	Florida	170,873	7.8%
4	North Carolina	107,407	4.9%
5	Ohio	104,426	4.8%
6	Georgia	85,117	3.9%
7	Illinois	77,259	3.5%
8	Michigan	76,107	3.5%
9	New York	68,565	3.1%
10	Tennessee	62,859	2.9%
11	Washington	58,307	2.7%
12	Pennsylvania	57,623	2.6%
13	Arizona	57,055	2.6%
14	Indiana	46,168	2.1%
15	Louisiana	44,986	2.1%
16	Missouri	44,647	2.0%
17	Alabama	44,571	2.0%
18	South Carolina	42,772	2.0%
19	New Jersey	39,433	1.8%
20	Maryland	37,457	1.7%
21	Massachusetts	35,181	1.6%
22	Oklahoma	34,377	1.6%
23	Colorado	32,422	1.5%
24	Arkansas	32,042	1.5%
25	Virginia	31,913	1.5%
26	Minnesota	30,173	1.4%
27	Mississippi	27,239	1.2%
28	Kentucky	27,122	1.2%
29	Wisconsin	26,994	1.2%
30	Nevada	24,820	1.1%
31	Oregon	23,879	1.1%
32	New Mexico	20,909	1.0%
33	Kansas	19,992	0.9%
34	Iowa	18,017	0.8%
35	Utah	14,701	0.7%
36	Connecticut	14,694	0.7%
37	West Virginia	11,531	0.5%
38	Nebraska	9,452	0.4%
39	Hawaii	8,709	0.4%
40	Idaho	7,526	0.3%
41	Maine	6,779	0.3%
42	Delaware	6,189	0.3%
43	Rhode Island	5,415	0.2%
44	New Hampshire	4,358	0.2%
45	Alaska	4,136	0.2%
46	Vermont	3,300	0.2%
47	Montana	2,935	0.1%
48	South Dakota	2,650	0.1%
49	North Dakota	2,393	0.1%
50	Wyoming	2,320	0.1%
	District of Columbia	3,835	0.2%

Source: Federal Bureau of Investigation
"Crime in the United States 2006" (Uniform Crime Reports, September 24, 2007)
*Burglary is the unlawful entry of a structure to commit a felony or theft. Attempts are included.

Burglary Rate in 2006

National Rate = 729.4 Burglaries per 100,000 Population*

ALPHA ORDER

RANK	STATE	RATE
8	Alabama	969.1
29	Alaska	617.3
12	Arizona	925.3
2	Arkansas	1,139.9
24	California	676.0
22	Colorado	682.1
44	Connecticut	419.3
20	Delaware	725.2
10	Florida	944.6
16	Georgia	909.0
23	Hawaii	677.5
37	Idaho	513.2
31	Illinois	602.1
19	Indiana	731.3
30	Iowa	604.2
21	Kansas	723.3
27	Kentucky	644.8
4	Louisiana	1,049.2
38	Maine	512.9
25	Maryland	667.0
34	Massachusetts	546.5
18	Michigan	753.9
32	Minnesota	583.9
11	Mississippi	935.9
17	Missouri	764.1
50	Montana	310.7
35	Nebraska	534.5
6	Nevada	994.6
49	New Hampshire	331.4
42	New Jersey	452.0
3	New Mexico	1,069.7
47	New York	355.1
1	North Carolina	1,212.7
46	North Dakota	376.3
15	Ohio	909.8
9	Oklahoma	960.5
26	Oregon	645.2
41	Pennsylvania	463.2
39	Rhode Island	507.2
7	South Carolina	989.8
48	South Dakota	338.9
5	Tennessee	1,040.9
13	Texas	917.3
33	Utah	576.5
36	Vermont	528.9
45	Virginia	417.6
14	Washington	911.6
28	West Virginia	634.1
40	Wisconsin	485.8
43	Wyoming	450.5

RANK ORDER

RANK	STATE	RATE
1	North Carolina	1,212.7
2	Arkansas	1,139.9
3	New Mexico	1,069.7
4	Louisiana	1,049.2
5	Tennessee	1,040.9
6	Nevada	994.6
7	South Carolina	989.8
8	Alabama	969.1
9	Oklahoma	960.5
10	Florida	944.6
11	Mississippi	935.9
12	Arizona	925.3
13	Texas	917.3
14	Washington	911.6
15	Ohio	909.8
16	Georgia	909.0
17	Missouri	764.1
18	Michigan	753.9
19	Indiana	731.3
20	Delaware	725.2
21	Kansas	723.3
22	Colorado	682.1
23	Hawaii	677.5
24	California	676.0
25	Maryland	667.0
26	Oregon	645.2
27	Kentucky	644.8
28	West Virginia	634.1
29	Alaska	617.3
30	Iowa	604.2
31	Illinois	602.1
32	Minnesota	583.9
33	Utah	576.5
34	Massachusetts	546.5
35	Nebraska	534.5
36	Vermont	528.9
37	Idaho	513.2
38	Maine	512.9
39	Rhode Island	507.2
40	Wisconsin	485.8
41	Pennsylvania	463.2
42	New Jersey	452.0
43	Wyoming	450.5
44	Connecticut	419.3
45	Virginia	417.6
46	North Dakota	376.3
47	New York	355.1
48	South Dakota	338.9
49	New Hampshire	331.4
50	Montana	310.7
	District of Columbia	659.5

Source: Federal Bureau of Investigation
"Crime in the United States 2006" (Uniform Crime Reports, September 24, 2007)
*Burglary is the unlawful entry of a structure to commit a felony or theft. Attempts are included.

Larcenies and Thefts in 2006

National Total = 6,607,013 Larcenies and Thefts*

ALPHA ORDER

RANK	STATE	THEFTS	% of USA
20	Alabama	121,610	1.8%
46	Alaska	17,490	0.3%
12	Arizona	173,466	2.6%
29	Arkansas	72,016	1.1%
1	California	666,860	10.1%
23	Colorado	110,837	1.7%
32	Connecticut	62,680	0.9%
43	Delaware	20,166	0.3%
3	Florida	473,774	7.2%
7	Georgia	235,903	3.6%
38	Hawaii	37,910	0.6%
40	Idaho	25,516	0.4%
6	Illinois	272,578	4.1%
15	Indiana	153,093	2.3%
33	Iowa	60,556	0.9%
28	Kansas	74,963	1.1%
30	Kentucky	70,658	1.1%
24	Louisiana	110,613	1.7%
41	Maine	25,167	0.4%
18	Maryland	127,497	1.9%
25	Massachusetts	100,771	1.5%
10	Michigan	198,227	3.0%
21	Minnesota	115,567	1.7%
34	Mississippi	57,807	0.9%
14	Missouri	153,490	2.3%
42	Montana	20,704	0.3%
37	Nebraska	44,585	0.7%
35	Nevada	50,255	0.8%
44	New Hampshire	18,862	0.3%
17	New Jersey	135,801	2.1%
36	New Mexico	46,822	0.7%
4	New York	295,605	4.5%
8	North Carolina	227,427	3.4%
49	North Dakota	9,314	0.1%
5	Ohio	280,384	4.2%
27	Oklahoma	81,267	1.2%
26	Oregon	97,556	1.5%
9	Pennsylvania	216,825	3.3%
45	Rhode Island	18,621	0.3%
19	South Carolina	124,148	1.9%
50	South Dakota	9,296	0.1%
13	Tennessee	163,845	2.5%
2	Texas	648,384	9.8%
31	Utah	66,671	1.0%
48	Vermont	10,493	0.2%
16	Virginia	142,679	2.2%
11	Washington	182,327	2.8%
39	West Virginia	32,220	0.5%
22	Wisconsin	115,546	1.7%
47	Wyoming	12,254	0.2%

RANK ORDER

RANK	STATE	THEFTS	% of USA
1	California	666,860	10.1%
2	Texas	648,384	9.8%
3	Florida	473,774	7.2%
4	New York	295,605	4.5%
5	Ohio	280,384	4.2%
6	Illinois	272,578	4.1%
7	Georgia	235,903	3.6%
8	North Carolina	227,427	3.4%
9	Pennsylvania	216,825	3.3%
10	Michigan	198,227	3.0%
11	Washington	182,327	2.8%
12	Arizona	173,466	2.6%
13	Tennessee	163,845	2.5%
14	Missouri	153,490	2.3%
15	Indiana	153,093	2.3%
16	Virginia	142,679	2.2%
17	New Jersey	135,801	2.1%
18	Maryland	127,497	1.9%
19	South Carolina	124,148	1.9%
20	Alabama	121,610	1.8%
21	Minnesota	115,567	1.7%
22	Wisconsin	115,546	1.7%
23	Colorado	110,837	1.7%
24	Louisiana	110,613	1.7%
25	Massachusetts	100,771	1.5%
26	Oregon	97,556	1.5%
27	Oklahoma	81,267	1.2%
28	Kansas	74,963	1.1%
29	Arkansas	72,016	1.1%
30	Kentucky	70,658	1.1%
31	Utah	66,671	1.0%
32	Connecticut	62,680	0.9%
33	Iowa	60,556	0.9%
34	Mississippi	57,807	0.9%
35	Nevada	50,255	0.8%
36	New Mexico	46,822	0.7%
37	Nebraska	44,585	0.7%
38	Hawaii	37,910	0.6%
39	West Virginia	32,220	0.5%
40	Idaho	25,516	0.4%
41	Maine	25,167	0.4%
42	Montana	20,704	0.3%
43	Delaware	20,166	0.3%
44	New Hampshire	18,862	0.3%
45	Rhode Island	18,621	0.3%
46	Alaska	17,490	0.3%
47	Wyoming	12,254	0.2%
48	Vermont	10,493	0.2%
49	North Dakota	9,314	0.1%
50	South Dakota	9,296	0.1%
	District of Columbia	15,907	0.2%

Source: Federal Bureau of Investigation
"Crime in the United States 2006" (Uniform Crime Reports, September 24, 2007)
*Larceny and theft is the unlawful taking of property without use of force, violence or fraud. Attempts are included. Motor vehicle thefts are excluded.

Larceny and Theft Rate in 2006

National Rate = 2,206.8 Larcenies and Thefts per 100,000 Population*

ALPHA ORDER

RANK	STATE	RATE
8	Alabama	2,644.3
13	Alaska	2,610.2
4	Arizona	2,813.1
16	Arkansas	2,562.1
37	California	1,829.1
24	Colorado	2,331.8
38	Connecticut	1,788.4
23	Delaware	2,362.8
11	Florida	2,619.0
18	Georgia	2,519.3
1	Hawaii	2,949.1
42	Idaho	1,740.0
29	Illinois	2,124.2
20	Indiana	2,424.8
31	Iowa	2,030.7
7	Kansas	2,712.0
44	Kentucky	1,679.9
14	Louisiana	2,579.7
35	Maine	1,904.3
26	Maryland	2,270.4
45	Massachusetts	1,565.4
34	Michigan	1,963.5
27	Minnesota	2,236.6
33	Mississippi	1,986.1
10	Missouri	2,627.0
28	Montana	2,191.8
17	Nebraska	2,521.3
32	Nevada	2,013.8
49	New Hampshire	1,434.5
46	New Jersey	1,556.5
21	New Mexico	2,395.5
47	New York	1,531.1
15	North Carolina	2,567.9
48	North Dakota	1,464.8
19	Ohio	2,442.8
25	Oklahoma	2,270.5
9	Oregon	2,636.1
41	Pennsylvania	1,742.9
40	Rhode Island	1,744.2
2	South Carolina	2,873.0
50	South Dakota	1,188.9
6	Tennessee	2,713.2
5	Texas	2,758.2
12	Utah	2,614.5
43	Vermont	1,681.8
36	Virginia	1,866.8
3	Washington	2,850.7
39	West Virginia	1,771.8
30	Wisconsin	2,079.5
22	Wyoming	2,379.4

RANK ORDER

RANK	STATE	RATE
1	Hawaii	2,949.1
2	South Carolina	2,873.0
3	Washington	2,850.7
4	Arizona	2,813.1
5	Texas	2,758.2
6	Tennessee	2,713.2
7	Kansas	2,712.0
8	Alabama	2,644.3
9	Oregon	2,636.1
10	Missouri	2,627.0
11	Florida	2,619.0
12	Utah	2,614.5
13	Alaska	2,610.2
14	Louisiana	2,579.7
15	North Carolina	2,567.9
16	Arkansas	2,562.1
17	Nebraska	2,521.3
18	Georgia	2,519.3
19	Ohio	2,442.8
20	Indiana	2,424.8
21	New Mexico	2,395.5
22	Wyoming	2,379.4
23	Delaware	2,362.8
24	Colorado	2,331.8
25	Oklahoma	2,270.5
26	Maryland	2,270.4
27	Minnesota	2,236.6
28	Montana	2,191.8
29	Illinois	2,124.2
30	Wisconsin	2,079.5
31	Iowa	2,030.7
32	Nevada	2,013.8
33	Mississippi	1,986.1
34	Michigan	1,963.5
35	Maine	1,904.3
36	Virginia	1,866.8
37	California	1,829.1
38	Connecticut	1,788.4
39	West Virginia	1,771.8
40	Rhode Island	1,744.2
41	Pennsylvania	1,742.9
42	Idaho	1,740.0
43	Vermont	1,681.8
44	Kentucky	1,679.9
45	Massachusetts	1,565.4
46	New Jersey	1,556.5
47	New York	1,531.1
48	North Dakota	1,464.8
49	New Hampshire	1,434.5
50	South Dakota	1,188.9
	District of Columbia	2,735.4

Source: Federal Bureau of Investigation
   "Crime in the United States 2006" (Uniform Crime Reports, September 24, 2007)
*Larceny and theft is the unlawful taking of property without use of force, violence or fraud. Attempts are included. Motor vehicle thefts are excluded.

Motor Vehicle Thefts in 2006

National Total = 1,192,809 Motor Vehicle Thefts*

ALPHA ORDER

RANK	STATE	THEFTS	% of USA
23	Alabama	14,840	1.2%
42	Alaska	2,529	0.2%
4	Arizona	54,849	4.6%
36	Arkansas	7,463	0.6%
1	California	242,693	20.3%
19	Colorado	20,795	1.7%
29	Connecticut	10,390	0.9%
41	Delaware	2,816	0.2%
3	Florida	76,437	6.4%
7	Georgia	43,163	3.6%
35	Hawaii	7,763	0.7%
43	Idaho	2,429	0.2%
8	Illinois	37,641	3.2%
18	Indiana	21,866	1.8%
38	Iowa	5,006	0.4%
32	Kansas	8,703	0.7%
30	Kentucky	9,243	0.8%
22	Louisiana	15,640	1.3%
46	Maine	1,340	0.1%
11	Maryland	30,522	2.6%
20	Massachusetts	17,961	1.5%
5	Michigan	50,017	4.2%
27	Minnesota	13,379	1.1%
33	Mississippi	8,347	0.7%
15	Missouri	25,433	2.1%
44	Montana	1,748	0.1%
37	Nebraska	5,038	0.4%
14	Nevada	26,961	2.3%
45	New Hampshire	1,422	0.1%
16	New Jersey	24,724	2.1%
31	New Mexico	9,225	0.8%
10	New York	32,134	2.7%
12	North Carolina	30,126	2.5%
47	North Dakota	1,012	0.1%
9	Ohio	37,425	3.1%
28	Oklahoma	13,358	1.1%
25	Oregon	14,460	1.2%
13	Pennsylvania	29,540	2.5%
40	Rhode Island	3,582	0.3%
21	South Carolina	16,402	1.4%
49	South Dakota	718	0.1%
17	Tennessee	22,593	1.9%
2	Texas	95,429	8.0%
34	Utah	8,299	0.7%
50	Vermont	586	0.0%
24	Virginia	14,814	1.2%
6	Washington	45,899	3.8%
39	West Virginia	3,921	0.3%
26	Wisconsin	14,031	1.2%
48	Wyoming	776	0.1%

RANK ORDER

RANK	STATE	THEFTS	% of USA
1	California	242,693	20.3%
2	Texas	95,429	8.0%
3	Florida	76,437	6.4%
4	Arizona	54,849	4.6%
5	Michigan	50,017	4.2%
6	Washington	45,899	3.8%
7	Georgia	43,163	3.6%
8	Illinois	37,641	3.2%
9	Ohio	37,425	3.1%
10	New York	32,134	2.7%
11	Maryland	30,522	2.6%
12	North Carolina	30,126	2.5%
13	Pennsylvania	29,540	2.5%
14	Nevada	26,961	2.3%
15	Missouri	25,433	2.1%
16	New Jersey	24,724	2.1%
17	Tennessee	22,593	1.9%
18	Indiana	21,866	1.8%
19	Colorado	20,795	1.7%
20	Massachusetts	17,961	1.5%
21	South Carolina	16,402	1.4%
22	Louisiana	15,640	1.3%
23	Alabama	14,840	1.2%
24	Virginia	14,814	1.2%
25	Oregon	14,460	1.2%
26	Wisconsin	14,031	1.2%
27	Minnesota	13,379	1.1%
28	Oklahoma	13,358	1.1%
29	Connecticut	10,390	0.9%
30	Kentucky	9,243	0.8%
31	New Mexico	9,225	0.8%
32	Kansas	8,703	0.7%
33	Mississippi	8,347	0.7%
34	Utah	8,299	0.7%
35	Hawaii	7,763	0.7%
36	Arkansas	7,463	0.6%
37	Nebraska	5,038	0.4%
38	Iowa	5,006	0.4%
39	West Virginia	3,921	0.3%
40	Rhode Island	3,582	0.3%
41	Delaware	2,816	0.2%
42	Alaska	2,529	0.2%
43	Idaho	2,429	0.2%
44	Montana	1,748	0.1%
45	New Hampshire	1,422	0.1%
46	Maine	1,340	0.1%
47	North Dakota	1,012	0.1%
48	Wyoming	776	0.1%
49	South Dakota	718	0.1%
50	Vermont	586	0.0%
	District of Columbia	7,321	0.6%

Source: Federal Bureau of Investigation
"Crime in the United States 2006" (Uniform Crime Reports, September 24, 2007)
*Includes the theft or attempted theft of a self-propelled vehicle. Excludes motorboats, construction equipment, airplanes, and farming equipment.

Motor Vehicle Theft Rate in 2006

National Rate = 398.4 Motor Vehicle Thefts per 100,000 Population*

ALPHA ORDER

RANK	STATE	RATE
26	Alabama	322.7
16	Alaska	377.4
2	Arizona	889.5
34	Arkansas	265.5
4	California	665.7
10	Colorado	437.5
28	Connecticut	296.4
23	Delaware	329.9
12	Florida	422.5
9	Georgia	460.9
5	Hawaii	603.9
44	Idaho	165.6
29	Illinois	293.3
20	Indiana	346.3
42	Iowa	167.9
27	Kansas	314.9
38	Kentucky	219.8
19	Louisiana	364.8
48	Maine	101.4
6	Maryland	543.5
33	Massachusetts	279.0
7	Michigan	495.4
35	Minnesota	258.9
30	Mississippi	286.8
11	Missouri	435.3
41	Montana	185.0
31	Nebraska	284.9
1	Nevada	1,080.4
47	New Hampshire	108.1
32	New Jersey	283.4
8	New Mexico	472.0
43	New York	166.4
21	North Carolina	340.2
45	North Dakota	159.2
24	Ohio	326.1
18	Oklahoma	373.2
14	Oregon	390.7
37	Pennsylvania	237.4
22	Rhode Island	335.5
15	South Carolina	379.6
50	South Dakota	91.8
17	Tennessee	374.1
13	Texas	405.9
25	Utah	325.4
49	Vermont	93.9
40	Virginia	193.8
3	Washington	717.6
39	West Virginia	215.6
36	Wisconsin	252.5
46	Wyoming	150.7

RANK ORDER

RANK	STATE	RATE
1	Nevada	1,080.4
2	Arizona	889.5
3	Washington	717.6
4	California	665.7
5	Hawaii	603.9
6	Maryland	543.5
7	Michigan	495.4
8	New Mexico	472.0
9	Georgia	460.9
10	Colorado	437.5
11	Missouri	435.3
12	Florida	422.5
13	Texas	405.9
14	Oregon	390.7
15	South Carolina	379.6
16	Alaska	377.4
17	Tennessee	374.1
18	Oklahoma	373.2
19	Louisiana	364.8
20	Indiana	346.3
21	North Carolina	340.2
22	Rhode Island	335.5
23	Delaware	329.9
24	Ohio	326.1
25	Utah	325.4
26	Alabama	322.7
27	Kansas	314.9
28	Connecticut	296.4
29	Illinois	293.3
30	Mississippi	286.8
31	Nebraska	284.9
32	New Jersey	283.4
33	Massachusetts	279.0
34	Arkansas	265.5
35	Minnesota	258.9
36	Wisconsin	252.5
37	Pennsylvania	237.4
38	Kentucky	219.8
39	West Virginia	215.6
40	Virginia	193.8
41	Montana	185.0
42	Iowa	167.9
43	New York	166.4
44	Idaho	165.6
45	North Dakota	159.2
46	Wyoming	150.7
47	New Hampshire	108.1
48	Maine	101.4
49	Vermont	93.9
50	South Dakota	91.8
	District of Columbia	1,258.9

Source: Federal Bureau of Investigation
   "Crime in the United States 2006" (Uniform Crime Reports, September 24, 2007)
*Includes the theft or attempted theft of a self-propelled vehicle. Excludes motorboats, construction equipment, airplanes, and farming equipment.

Rate of Consumer Fraud Complaints in 2006

National Rate = 125.2 Complaints per 100,000 Population*

ALPHA ORDER

RANK	STATE	RATE
44	Alabama	102.4
5	Alaska	161.0
10	Arizona	149.6
47	Arkansas	86.4
16	California	134.6
4	Colorado	161.1
17	Connecticut	134.0
18	Delaware	131.1
12	Florida	143.2
22	Georgia	127.5
7	Hawaii	157.1
13	Idaho	137.2
39	Illinois	108.4
24	Indiana	124.5
46	Iowa	89.4
37	Kansas	111.0
42	Kentucky	106.4
45	Louisiana	92.8
15	Maine	135.5
8	Maryland	154.1
31	Massachusetts	113.9
29	Michigan	115.5
33	Minnesota	113.4
49	Mississippi	79.6
23	Missouri	125.5
14	Montana	136.5
36	Nebraska	111.3
2	Nevada	169.2
11	New Hampshire	149.4
20	New Jersey	129.3
26	New Mexico	123.1
38	New York	109.4
28	North Carolina	116.3
48	North Dakota	85.6
25	Ohio	124.1
43	Oklahoma	103.7
9	Oregon	150.9
19	Pennsylvania	130.6
41	Rhode Island	108.0
35	South Carolina	112.0
50	South Dakota	79.0
32	Tennessee	113.8
40	Texas	108.2
1	Utah	178.9
30	Vermont	115.1
6	Virginia	157.5
3	Washington	163.4
34	West Virginia	113.2
27	Wisconsin	121.0
21	Wyoming	127.6

RANK ORDER

RANK	STATE	RATE
1	Utah	178.9
2	Nevada	169.2
3	Washington	163.4
4	Colorado	161.1
5	Alaska	161.0
6	Virginia	157.5
7	Hawaii	157.1
8	Maryland	154.1
9	Oregon	150.9
10	Arizona	149.6
11	New Hampshire	149.4
12	Florida	143.2
13	Idaho	137.2
14	Montana	136.5
15	Maine	135.5
16	California	134.6
17	Connecticut	134.0
18	Delaware	131.1
19	Pennsylvania	130.6
20	New Jersey	129.3
21	Wyoming	127.6
22	Georgia	127.5
23	Missouri	125.5
24	Indiana	124.5
25	Ohio	124.1
26	New Mexico	123.1
27	Wisconsin	121.0
28	North Carolina	116.3
29	Michigan	115.5
30	Vermont	115.1
31	Massachusetts	113.9
32	Tennessee	113.8
33	Minnesota	113.4
34	West Virginia	113.2
35	South Carolina	112.0
36	Nebraska	111.3
37	Kansas	111.0
38	New York	109.4
39	Illinois	108.4
40	Texas	108.2
41	Rhode Island	108.0
42	Kentucky	106.4
43	Oklahoma	103.7
44	Alabama	102.4
45	Louisiana	92.8
46	Iowa	89.4
47	Arkansas	86.4
48	North Dakota	85.6
49	Mississippi	79.6
50	South Dakota	79.0

District of Columbia	195.9

Source: Federal Trade Commission, Consumer Sentinel
"Consumer Fraud and Identify Theft Complaint Data" (January 2007) (www.consumer.gov/sentinel)
*Figures are for individuals filing complaints. Some complaints result in multiple infractions. Does not include identity theft or "Do Not Call" registry complaints.

Rate of Identity Theft Complaints in 2006

National Rate = 79.9 Complaints per 100,000 Population*

ALPHA ORDER

RANK	STATE	RATE
27	Alabama	60.3
31	Alaska	57.3
1	Arizona	147.8
34	Arkansas	54.7
3	California	113.5
6	Colorado	92.5
18	Connecticut	65.8
17	Delaware	66.7
5	Florida	98.3
7	Georgia	86.3
39	Hawaii	47.8
38	Idaho	49.0
12	Illinois	78.6
24	Indiana	62.2
47	Iowa	34.9
29	Kansas	58.8
44	Kentucky	42.0
35	Louisiana	52.6
45	Maine	39.7
10	Maryland	82.9
22	Massachusetts	63.7
15	Michigan	67.2
33	Minnesota	55.6
36	Mississippi	51.3
21	Missouri	64.2
41	Montana	45.9
37	Nebraska	49.1
2	Nevada	120.0
40	New Hampshire	46.1
14	New Jersey	73.3
10	New Mexico	82.9
8	New York	85.2
19	North Carolina	64.9
49	North Dakota	29.7
28	Ohio	59.9
23	Oklahoma	63.0
13	Oregon	76.1
19	Pennsylvania	64.9
30	Rhode Island	57.6
32	South Carolina	55.7
48	South Dakota	30.2
26	Tennessee	61.3
4	Texas	110.6
25	Utah	61.8
50	Vermont	28.5
15	Virginia	67.2
9	Washington	83.4
46	West Virginia	39.3
42	Wisconsin	45.6
43	Wyoming	42.3

RANK ORDER

RANK	STATE	RATE
1	Arizona	147.8
2	Nevada	120.0
3	California	113.5
4	Texas	110.6
5	Florida	98.3
6	Colorado	92.5
7	Georgia	86.3
8	New York	85.2
9	Washington	83.4
10	Maryland	82.9
10	New Mexico	82.9
12	Illinois	78.6
13	Oregon	76.1
14	New Jersey	73.3
15	Michigan	67.2
15	Virginia	67.2
17	Delaware	66.7
18	Connecticut	65.8
19	North Carolina	64.9
19	Pennsylvania	64.9
21	Missouri	64.2
22	Massachusetts	63.7
23	Oklahoma	63.0
24	Indiana	62.2
25	Utah	61.8
26	Tennessee	61.3
27	Alabama	60.3
28	Ohio	59.9
29	Kansas	58.8
30	Rhode Island	57.6
31	Alaska	57.3
32	South Carolina	55.7
33	Minnesota	55.6
34	Arkansas	54.7
35	Louisiana	52.6
36	Mississippi	51.3
37	Nebraska	49.1
38	Idaho	49.0
39	Hawaii	47.8
40	New Hampshire	46.1
41	Montana	45.9
42	Wisconsin	45.6
43	Wyoming	42.3
44	Kentucky	42.0
45	Maine	39.7
46	West Virginia	39.3
47	Iowa	34.9
48	South Dakota	30.2
49	North Dakota	29.7
50	Vermont	28.5
	District of Columbia	131.5

Source: Federal Trade Commission, Consumer Sentinel
"Consumer Fraud and Identify Theft Complaint Data" (January 2007) (www.consumer.gov/sentinel)
*Figures are for individuals filing complaints. Some complaints result in multiple infractions. Does not include consumer fraud or "Do Not Call" registry complaints.

Reported Arrest Rate in 2006

National Rate = 4,845.0 Reported Arrests per 100,000 Population*

ALPHA ORDER				RANK ORDER		
RANK	STATE	RATE		RANK	STATE	RATE
21	Alabama	5,135.1		1	Louisiana	7,839.1
13	Alaska	5,770.9		2	Wisconsin	7,837.5
20	Arizona	5,220.5		3	Wyoming	7,711.3
11	Arkansas	5,854.7		4	Kentucky	7,468.5
36	California	4,253.9		5	Mississippi	7,391.7
16	Colorado	5,509.0		6	Georgia	7,368.4
30	Connecticut	4,520.2		7	Nevada	6,572.9
27	Delaware	4,667.0		8	Missouri	6,474.1
10	Florida	6,164.5		9	North Carolina	6,470.0
6	Georgia	7,368.4		10	Florida	6,164.5
32	Hawaii	4,440.6		11	Arkansas	5,854.7
19	Idaho	5,332.4		12	Tennessee	5,852.4
NA	Illinois**	NA		13	Alaska	5,770.9
29	Indiana	4,551.3		14	Nebraska	5,739.3
34	Iowa	4,404.7		15	New Mexico	5,685.5
40	Kansas	3,928.4		16	Colorado	5,509.0
4	Kentucky	7,468.5		17	Utah	5,477.7
1	Louisiana	7,839.1		18	Maryland	5,340.5
35	Maine	4,351.5		19	Idaho	5,332.4
18	Maryland	5,340.5		20	Arizona	5,220.5
47	Massachusetts	2,379.8		21	Alabama	5,135.1
44	Michigan	3,444.4		22	North Dakota	4,971.9
NA	Minnesota**	NA		23	South Carolina	4,838.0
5	Mississippi	7,391.7		24	Texas	4,805.4
8	Missouri	6,474.1		25	Washington	4,689.3
NA	Montana**	NA		26	Virginia	4,686.5
14	Nebraska	5,739.3		27	Delaware	4,667.0
7	Nevada	6,572.9		28	New Jersey	4,594.8
33	New Hampshire	4,436.3		29	Indiana	4,551.3
28	New Jersey	4,594.8		30	Connecticut	4,520.2
15	New Mexico	5,685.5		31	Oklahoma	4,460.7
43	New York	3,656.1		32	Hawaii	4,440.6
9	North Carolina	6,470.0		33	New Hampshire	4,436.3
22	North Dakota	4,971.9		34	Iowa	4,404.7
38	Ohio	4,127.9		35	Maine	4,351.5
31	Oklahoma	4,460.7		36	California	4,253.9
39	Oregon	4,021.0		37	Pennsylvania	4,184.7
37	Pennsylvania	4,184.7		38	Ohio	4,127.9
41	Rhode Island	3,773.4		39	Oregon	4,021.0
23	South Carolina	4,838.0		40	Kansas	3,928.4
42	South Dakota	3,742.8		41	Rhode Island	3,773.4
12	Tennessee	5,852.4		42	South Dakota	3,742.8
24	Texas	4,805.4		43	New York	3,656.1
17	Utah	5,477.7		44	Michigan	3,444.4
46	Vermont	2,648.6		45	West Virginia	2,999.1
26	Virginia	4,686.5		46	Vermont	2,648.6
25	Washington	4,689.3		47	Massachusetts	2,379.8
45	West Virginia	2,999.1		NA	Illinois**	NA
2	Wisconsin	7,837.5		NA	Minnesota**	NA
3	Wyoming	7,711.3		NA	Montana**	NA
					District of Columbia**	NA

Source: CQ Press using data from Federal Bureau of Investigation
    "Crime in the United States 2006" (Uniform Crime Reports, September 24, 2007)
*By law enforcement agencies submitting complete reports to the F.B.I. for 12 months in 2006. These rates based on population estimates for areas under the jurisdiction of those agencies reporting. Arrest rate based on the F.B.I. estimate of total arrests is 4,803.1 reported and unreported arrests per 100,000 population. See important note at beginning of this chapter.
**Not available.

Reported Juvenile Arrest Rate in 2006

National Rate = 6,417.1 Reported Arrests per 100,000 Juvenile Population*

<table>
<tr><td colspan="3">ALPHA ORDER</td><td colspan="3">RANK ORDER</td></tr>
<tr><th>RANK</th><th>STATE</th><th>RATE</th><th>RANK</th><th>STATE</th><th>RATE</th></tr>
<tr><td>46</td><td>Alabama</td><td>2,825.4</td><td>1</td><td>Wisconsin</td><td>17,572.3</td></tr>
<tr><td>39</td><td>Alaska</td><td>5,120.6</td><td>2</td><td>Wyoming</td><td>12,189.9</td></tr>
<tr><td>15</td><td>Arizona</td><td>7,552.2</td><td>3</td><td>North Dakota</td><td>11,102.4</td></tr>
<tr><td>38</td><td>Arkansas</td><td>5,279.1</td><td>4</td><td>Idaho</td><td>9,662.3</td></tr>
<tr><td>36</td><td>California</td><td>5,365.9</td><td>5</td><td>Louisiana</td><td>9,446.4</td></tr>
<tr><td>8</td><td>Colorado</td><td>9,103.7</td><td>6</td><td>Utah</td><td>9,241.8</td></tr>
<tr><td>25</td><td>Connecticut</td><td>6,343.2</td><td>7</td><td>Hawaii</td><td>9,172.2</td></tr>
<tr><td>12</td><td>Delaware</td><td>8,006.1</td><td>8</td><td>Colorado</td><td>9,103.7</td></tr>
<tr><td>21</td><td>Florida</td><td>6,594.3</td><td>9</td><td>Pennsylvania</td><td>9,025.7</td></tr>
<tr><td>22</td><td>Georgia</td><td>6,594.2</td><td>10</td><td>Nebraska</td><td>8,579.7</td></tr>
<tr><td>7</td><td>Hawaii</td><td>9,172.2</td><td>11</td><td>Kentucky</td><td>8,228.3</td></tr>
<tr><td>4</td><td>Idaho</td><td>9,662.3</td><td>12</td><td>Delaware</td><td>8,006.1</td></tr>
<tr><td>NA</td><td>Illinois**</td><td>NA</td><td>13</td><td>Maryland</td><td>7,840.4</td></tr>
<tr><td>23</td><td>Indiana</td><td>6,510.4</td><td>14</td><td>Missouri</td><td>7,712.6</td></tr>
<tr><td>19</td><td>Iowa</td><td>7,187.1</td><td>15</td><td>Arizona</td><td>7,552.2</td></tr>
<tr><td>40</td><td>Kansas</td><td>4,936.4</td><td>16</td><td>Oregon</td><td>7,526.1</td></tr>
<tr><td>11</td><td>Kentucky</td><td>8,228.3</td><td>17</td><td>Nevada</td><td>7,456.8</td></tr>
<tr><td>5</td><td>Louisiana</td><td>9,446.4</td><td>18</td><td>New Hampshire</td><td>7,207.9</td></tr>
<tr><td>32</td><td>Maine</td><td>5,611.2</td><td>19</td><td>Iowa</td><td>7,187.1</td></tr>
<tr><td>13</td><td>Maryland</td><td>7,840.4</td><td>20</td><td>Tennessee</td><td>6,625.7</td></tr>
<tr><td>44</td><td>Massachusetts</td><td>3,108.9</td><td>21</td><td>Florida</td><td>6,594.3</td></tr>
<tr><td>43</td><td>Michigan</td><td>4,023.9</td><td>22</td><td>Georgia</td><td>6,594.2</td></tr>
<tr><td>NA</td><td>Minnesota**</td><td>NA</td><td>23</td><td>Indiana</td><td>6,510.4</td></tr>
<tr><td>27</td><td>Mississippi</td><td>6,134.3</td><td>24</td><td>New Jersey</td><td>6,488.9</td></tr>
<tr><td>14</td><td>Missouri</td><td>7,712.6</td><td>25</td><td>Connecticut</td><td>6,343.2</td></tr>
<tr><td>NA</td><td>Montana**</td><td>NA</td><td>26</td><td>Texas</td><td>6,289.4</td></tr>
<tr><td>10</td><td>Nebraska</td><td>8,579.7</td><td>27</td><td>Mississippi</td><td>6,134.3</td></tr>
<tr><td>17</td><td>Nevada</td><td>7,456.8</td><td>28</td><td>North Carolina</td><td>6,131.2</td></tr>
<tr><td>18</td><td>New Hampshire</td><td>7,207.9</td><td>29</td><td>Ohio</td><td>6,039.4</td></tr>
<tr><td>24</td><td>New Jersey</td><td>6,488.9</td><td>30</td><td>Washington</td><td>5,984.3</td></tr>
<tr><td>31</td><td>New Mexico</td><td>5,656.4</td><td>31</td><td>New Mexico</td><td>5,656.4</td></tr>
<tr><td>42</td><td>New York</td><td>4,682.2</td><td>32</td><td>Maine</td><td>5,611.2</td></tr>
<tr><td>28</td><td>North Carolina</td><td>6,131.2</td><td>33</td><td>Oklahoma</td><td>5,589.6</td></tr>
<tr><td>3</td><td>North Dakota</td><td>11,102.4</td><td>34</td><td>Virginia</td><td>5,516.0</td></tr>
<tr><td>29</td><td>Ohio</td><td>6,039.4</td><td>35</td><td>South Carolina</td><td>5,475.6</td></tr>
<tr><td>33</td><td>Oklahoma</td><td>5,589.6</td><td>36</td><td>California</td><td>5,365.9</td></tr>
<tr><td>16</td><td>Oregon</td><td>7,526.1</td><td>37</td><td>South Dakota</td><td>5,314.7</td></tr>
<tr><td>9</td><td>Pennsylvania</td><td>9,025.7</td><td>38</td><td>Arkansas</td><td>5,279.1</td></tr>
<tr><td>41</td><td>Rhode Island</td><td>4,845.4</td><td>39</td><td>Alaska</td><td>5,120.6</td></tr>
<tr><td>35</td><td>South Carolina</td><td>5,475.6</td><td>40</td><td>Kansas</td><td>4,936.4</td></tr>
<tr><td>37</td><td>South Dakota</td><td>5,314.7</td><td>41</td><td>Rhode Island</td><td>4,845.4</td></tr>
<tr><td>20</td><td>Tennessee</td><td>6,625.7</td><td>42</td><td>New York</td><td>4,682.2</td></tr>
<tr><td>26</td><td>Texas</td><td>6,289.4</td><td>43</td><td>Michigan</td><td>4,023.9</td></tr>
<tr><td>6</td><td>Utah</td><td>9,241.8</td><td>44</td><td>Massachusetts</td><td>3,108.9</td></tr>
<tr><td>45</td><td>Vermont</td><td>2,951.1</td><td>45</td><td>Vermont</td><td>2,951.1</td></tr>
<tr><td>34</td><td>Virginia</td><td>5,516.0</td><td>46</td><td>Alabama</td><td>2,825.4</td></tr>
<tr><td>30</td><td>Washington</td><td>5,984.3</td><td>47</td><td>West Virginia</td><td>1,623.4</td></tr>
<tr><td>47</td><td>West Virginia</td><td>1,623.4</td><td>NA</td><td>Illinois**</td><td>NA</td></tr>
<tr><td>1</td><td>Wisconsin</td><td>17,572.3</td><td>NA</td><td>Minnesota**</td><td>NA</td></tr>
<tr><td>2</td><td>Wyoming</td><td>12,189.9</td><td>NA</td><td>Montana**</td><td>NA</td></tr>
<tr><td></td><td></td><td></td><td></td><td>District of Columbia**</td><td>NA</td></tr>
</table>

Source: CQ Press using data from Federal Bureau of Investigation
   "Crime in the United States 2006" (Uniform Crime Reports, September 24, 2007)
*By law enforcement agencies submitting complete reports to the F.B.I. for 12 months in 2006. Arrests of youths 17 years and younger divided into population of 10 to 17 year olds. See important note at beginning of this chapter.
**Not available.

Prisoners in State Correctional Institutions: Year End 2006

National Total = 1,377,815 State Prisoners*

RANK	STATE	PRISONERS	% of USA
15	Alabama	28,241	2.0%
41	Alaska	5,069	0.4%
13	Arizona	35,892	2.6%
28	Arkansas	13,729	1.0%
1	California	175,512	12.7%
23	Colorado	22,481	1.6%
25	Connecticut	20,566	1.5%
35	Delaware	7,206	0.5%
3	Florida	92,969	6.7%
5	Georgia	52,792	3.8%
39	Hawaii	5,967	0.4%
36	Idaho	7,124	0.5%
8	Illinois	45,106	3.3%
18	Indiana	26,091	1.9%
33	Iowa	8,875	0.6%
34	Kansas	8,816	0.6%
26	Kentucky	20,000	1.5%
11	Louisiana	37,012	2.7%
48	Maine	2,120	0.2%
22	Maryland	22,945	1.7%
31	Massachusetts	11,032	0.8%
6	Michigan	51,577	3.7%
32	Minnesota	9,108	0.7%
24	Mississippi	21,068	1.5%
14	Missouri	30,167	2.2%
44	Montana	3,572	0.3%
42	Nebraska	4,407	0.3%
30	Nevada	12,901	0.9%
46	New Hampshire	2,805	0.2%
16	New Jersey	27,371	2.0%
37	New Mexico	6,639	0.5%
4	New York	63,315	4.6%
10	North Carolina	37,460	2.7%
50	North Dakota	1,363	0.1%
7	Ohio	49,166	3.6%
17	Oklahoma	26,243	1.9%
29	Oregon	13,707	1.0%
9	Pennsylvania	44,397	3.2%
43	Rhode Island	3,996	0.3%
20	South Carolina	23,616	1.7%
45	South Dakota	3,359	0.2%
19	Tennessee	25,745	1.9%
2	Texas	172,116	12.5%
38	Utah	6,430	0.5%
47	Vermont	2,215	0.2%
12	Virginia	36,688	2.7%
27	Washington	17,561	1.3%
40	West Virginia	5,733	0.4%
21	Wisconsin	23,431	1.7%
49	Wyoming	2,114	0.2%

RANK	STATE	PRISONERS	% of USA
1	California	175,512	12.7%
2	Texas	172,116	12.5%
3	Florida	92,969	6.7%
4	New York	63,315	4.6%
5	Georgia	52,792	3.8%
6	Michigan	51,577	3.7%
7	Ohio	49,166	3.6%
8	Illinois	45,106	3.3%
9	Pennsylvania	44,397	3.2%
10	North Carolina	37,460	2.7%
11	Louisiana	37,012	2.7%
12	Virginia	36,688	2.7%
13	Arizona	35,892	2.6%
14	Missouri	30,167	2.2%
15	Alabama	28,241	2.0%
16	New Jersey	27,371	2.0%
17	Oklahoma	26,243	1.9%
18	Indiana	26,091	1.9%
19	Tennessee	25,745	1.9%
20	South Carolina	23,616	1.7%
21	Wisconsin	23,431	1.7%
22	Maryland	22,945	1.7%
23	Colorado	22,481	1.6%
24	Mississippi	21,068	1.5%
25	Connecticut	20,566	1.5%
26	Kentucky	20,000	1.5%
27	Washington	17,561	1.3%
28	Arkansas	13,729	1.0%
29	Oregon	13,707	1.0%
30	Nevada	12,901	0.9%
31	Massachusetts	11,032	0.8%
32	Minnesota	9,108	0.7%
33	Iowa	8,875	0.6%
34	Kansas	8,816	0.6%
35	Delaware	7,206	0.5%
36	Idaho	7,124	0.5%
37	New Mexico	6,639	0.5%
38	Utah	6,430	0.5%
39	Hawaii	5,967	0.4%
40	West Virginia	5,733	0.4%
41	Alaska	5,069	0.4%
42	Nebraska	4,407	0.3%
43	Rhode Island	3,996	0.3%
44	Montana	3,572	0.3%
45	South Dakota	3,359	0.2%
46	New Hampshire	2,805	0.2%
47	Vermont	2,215	0.2%
48	Maine	2,120	0.2%
49	Wyoming	2,114	0.2%
50	North Dakota	1,363	0.1%
	District of Columbia**	NA	NA

Source: U.S. Department of Justice, Bureau of Justice Statistics
"Prisoners in 2006" (December 2007, NCJ 219416)

*Advance figures as of December 31, 2006. Totals reflect all prisoners, including those sentenced to a year or less and those unsentenced. National total does not include 193,046 prisoners under federal jurisdiction. State and federal prisoners combined total 1,570,861.

**Responsibility for sentenced felons in D.C. was transferred to the Federal Bureau of Prisons in 2001.

State Prisoner Incarceration Rate in 2006

National Rate = 445 State Prisoners per 100,000 Population*

ALPHA ORDER

RANK	STATE	RATE
5	Alabama	595
19	Alaska	462
10	Arizona	509
14	Arkansas	485
17	California	475
18	Colorado	469
28	Connecticut	392
13	Delaware	488
10	Florida	509
6	Georgia	558
34	Hawaii	338
15	Idaho	480
33	Illinois	350
24	Indiana	411
40	Iowa	296
37	Kansas	318
19	Kentucky	462
1	Louisiana	846
50	Maine	151
26	Maryland	396
44	Massachusetts	243
9	Michigan	511
49	Minnesota	176
4	Mississippi	658
8	Missouri	514
29	Montana	374
45	Nebraska	237
12	Nevada	503
47	New Hampshire	207
39	New Jersey	313
36	New Mexico	323
35	New York	326
31	North Carolina	360
46	North Dakota	214
21	Ohio	428
3	Oklahoma	664
30	Oregon	367
32	Pennsylvania	353
48	Rhode Island	202
7	South Carolina	525
22	South Dakota	426
23	Tennessee	423
2	Texas	683
43	Utah	246
42	Vermont	262
16	Virginia	477
41	Washington	271
38	West Virginia	314
27	Wisconsin	393
25	Wyoming	408

RANK ORDER

RANK	STATE	RATE
1	Louisiana	846
2	Texas	683
3	Oklahoma	664
4	Mississippi	658
5	Alabama	595
6	Georgia	558
7	South Carolina	525
8	Missouri	514
9	Michigan	511
10	Arizona	509
10	Florida	509
12	Nevada	503
13	Delaware	488
14	Arkansas	485
15	Idaho	480
16	Virginia	477
17	California	475
18	Colorado	469
19	Alaska	462
19	Kentucky	462
21	Ohio	428
22	South Dakota	426
23	Tennessee	423
24	Indiana	411
25	Wyoming	408
26	Maryland	396
27	Wisconsin	393
28	Connecticut	392
29	Montana	374
30	Oregon	367
31	North Carolina	360
32	Pennsylvania	353
33	Illinois	350
34	Hawaii	338
35	New York	326
36	New Mexico	323
37	Kansas	318
38	West Virginia	314
39	New Jersey	313
40	Iowa	296
41	Washington	271
42	Vermont	262
43	Utah	246
44	Massachusetts	243
45	Nebraska	237
46	North Dakota	214
47	New Hampshire	207
48	Rhode Island	202
49	Minnesota	176
50	Maine	151
	District of Columbia**	NA

Source: U.S. Department of Justice, Bureau of Justice Statistics
    "Prisoners in 2006" (December 2007, NCJ 219416)
*As of December 31, 2006. Includes only inmates sentenced to more than one year. Does not include federal incarceration rate
of 58 prisoners per 100,000 population. State and federal combined incarceration rate is 501 prisoners per 100,000 population.
**Responsibility for sentenced felons in D.C. was transferred to the Federal Bureau of Prisons in 2001.

Percent Change in Number of State Prisoners: 2005 to 2006

National Percent Change = 2.8% Increase*

ALPHA ORDER				RANK ORDER		
RANK	STATE	PERCENT CHANGE		RANK	STATE	PERCENT CHANGE
33	Alabama	1.3		1	New Hampshire	10.9
11	Alaska	5.3		2	Nevada	9.5
7	Arizona	6.9		3	Rhode Island	9.4
32	Arkansas	1.4		4	Georgia	8.3
24	California	2.8		5	West Virginia	7.9
12	Colorado	4.8		6	Ohio	7.2
10	Connecticut	5.8		7	Arizona	6.9
19	Delaware	3.4		8	Indiana	6.7
18	Florida	3.6		9	Vermont	6.6
4	Georgia	8.3		10	Connecticut	5.8
49	Hawaii	(2.9)		11	Alaska	5.3
15	Idaho	4.5		12	Colorado	4.8
40	Illinois	0.4		12	Maine	4.8
8	Indiana	6.7		12	Pennsylvania	4.8
31	Iowa	1.6		15	Idaho	4.5
48	Kansas	(2.8)		16	Michigan	4.1
30	Kentucky	1.7		17	Virginia	3.8
26	Louisiana	2.6		18	Florida	3.6
12	Maine	4.8		19	Delaware	3.4
37	Maryland	0.9		20	Wyoming	3.3
22	Massachusetts	3.1		21	Wisconsin	3.2
16	Michigan	4.1		22	Massachusetts	3.1
45	Minnesota	(1.9)		23	North Carolina	3.0
25	Mississippi	2.7		24	California	2.8
46	Missouri	(2.1)		25	Mississippi	2.7
34	Montana	1.1		26	Louisiana	2.6
42	Nebraska	(1.1)		27	Oregon	2.2
2	Nevada	9.5		28	South Carolina	2.0
1	New Hampshire	10.9		29	Texas	1.8
41	New Jersey	0.0		30	Kentucky	1.7
35	New Mexico	1.0		31	Iowa	1.6
37	New York	0.9		32	Arkansas	1.4
23	North Carolina	3.0		33	Alabama	1.3
43	North Dakota	(1.6)		34	Montana	1.1
6	Ohio	7.2		35	New Mexico	1.0
43	Oklahoma	(1.6)		35	Washington	1.0
27	Oregon	2.2		37	Maryland	0.9
12	Pennsylvania	4.8		37	New York	0.9
3	Rhode Island	9.4		39	Utah	0.8
28	South Carolina	2.0		40	Illinois	0.4
50	South Dakota	(3.0)		41	New Jersey	0.0
47	Tennessee	(2.4)		42	Nebraska	(1.1)
29	Texas	1.8		43	North Dakota	(1.6)
39	Utah	0.8		43	Oklahoma	(1.6)
9	Vermont	6.6		45	Minnesota	(1.9)
17	Virginia	3.8		46	Missouri	(2.1)
35	Washington	1.0		47	Tennessee	(2.4)
5	West Virginia	7.9		48	Kansas	(2.8)
21	Wisconsin	3.2		49	Hawaii	(2.9)
20	Wyoming	3.3		50	South Dakota	(3.0)
					District of Columbia**	NA

Source: U.S. Department of Justice, Bureau of Justice Statistics
"Prisoners in 2006" (December 2007, NCJ 219416)

*From December 31, 2005 to December 31, 2006. Includes inmates sentenced to more than one year and those sentenced to a year or less or with no sentence. The percent change in number of prisoners under federal jurisdiction during the same period was an 2.9% increase. The combined state and federal increase was 2.8%.

**Responsibility for sentenced felons in D.C. was transferred to the Federal Bureau of Prisons in 2001.

Prisoners Under Sentence of Death in 2006

National Total = 3,186 State Prisoners*

RANK	STATE	PRISONERS	% of USA
5	Alabama	193	6.1%
NA	Alaska**	NA	NA
8	Arizona	110	3.5%
18	Arkansas	36	1.1%
1	California	656	20.6%
32	Colorado	2	0.1%
29	Connecticut	7	0.2%
23	Delaware	16	0.5%
3	Florida	374	11.7%
9	Georgia	105	3.3%
NA	Hawaii**	NA	NA
21	Idaho	18	0.6%
24	Illinois	10	0.3%
22	Indiana	17	0.5%
NA	Iowa**	NA	NA
32	Kansas	2	0.1%
17	Kentucky	40	1.3%
11	Louisiana	86	2.7%
NA	Maine**	NA	NA
30	Maryland	6	0.2%
NA	Massachusetts**	NA	NA
NA	Michigan**	NA	NA
NA	Minnesota**	NA	NA
14	Mississippi	69	2.2%
16	Missouri	47	1.5%
32	Montana	2	0.1%
25	Nebraska	9	0.3%
13	Nevada	82	2.6%
38	New Hampshire	0	0.0%
25	New Jersey	9	0.3%
32	New Mexico	2	0.1%
37	New York	1	0.0%
7	North Carolina	166	5.2%
NA	North Dakota**	NA	NA
6	Ohio	187	5.9%
12	Oklahoma	84	2.6%
19	Oregon	32	1.0%
4	Pennsylvania	219	6.9%
NA	Rhode Island**	NA	NA
15	South Carolina	62	1.9%
31	South Dakota	4	0.1%
10	Tennessee	102	3.2%
2	Texas	391	12.3%
25	Utah	9	0.3%
NA	Vermont**	NA	NA
20	Virginia	20	0.6%
25	Washington	9	0.3%
NA	West Virginia**	NA	NA
NA	Wisconsin**	NA	NA
32	Wyoming	2	0.1%

RANK	STATE	PRISONERS	% of USA
1	California	656	20.6%
2	Texas	391	12.3%
3	Florida	374	11.7%
4	Pennsylvania	219	6.9%
5	Alabama	193	6.1%
6	Ohio	187	5.9%
7	North Carolina	166	5.2%
8	Arizona	110	3.5%
9	Georgia	105	3.3%
10	Tennessee	102	3.2%
11	Louisiana	86	2.7%
12	Oklahoma	84	2.6%
13	Nevada	82	2.6%
14	Mississippi	69	2.2%
15	South Carolina	62	1.9%
16	Missouri	47	1.5%
17	Kentucky	40	1.3%
18	Arkansas	36	1.1%
19	Oregon	32	1.0%
20	Virginia	20	0.6%
21	Idaho	18	0.6%
22	Indiana	17	0.5%
23	Delaware	16	0.5%
24	Illinois	10	0.3%
25	Nebraska	9	0.3%
25	New Jersey	9	0.3%
25	Utah	9	0.3%
25	Washington	9	0.3%
29	Connecticut	7	0.2%
30	Maryland	6	0.2%
31	South Dakota	4	0.1%
32	Colorado	2	0.1%
32	Kansas	2	0.1%
32	Montana	2	0.1%
32	New Mexico	2	0.1%
32	Wyoming	2	0.1%
37	New York	1	0.0%
38	New Hampshire	0	0.0%
NA	Alaska**	NA	NA
NA	Hawaii**	NA	NA
NA	Iowa**	NA	NA
NA	Maine**	NA	NA
NA	Massachusetts**	NA	NA
NA	Michigan**	NA	NA
NA	Minnesota**	NA	NA
NA	North Dakota**	NA	NA
NA	Rhode Island**	NA	NA
NA	Vermont**	NA	NA
NA	West Virginia**	NA	NA
NA	Wisconsin**	NA	NA
	District of Columbia**	NA	NA

Source: U.S. Department of Justice, Bureau of Justice Statistics
    "Capital Punishment 2006" (Bulletin, December 2007, NCJ 220219)
*As of December 31, 2006. Does not include 42 federal prisoners under sentence of death. There were 53 executions in 2006.
**No death penalty as of 12/31/06.

Rate of Full-Time Sworn Officers in Law Enforcement Agencies in 2004

National Rate = 249 Officers per 100,000 Population*

ALPHA ORDER

RANK ORDER

RANK	STATE	RATE		RANK	STATE	RATE
21	Alabama	241		1	Louisiana	399
33	Alaska	215		2	New Jersey	366
30	Arizona	220		3	New York	344
26	Arkansas	230		4	Wyoming	328
36	California	211		5	Illinois	312
21	Colorado	241		6	Virginia	290
27	Connecticut	229		7	Rhode Island	284
23	Delaware	239		8	Massachusetts	283
11	Florida	262		9	Maryland	272
10	Georgia	266		10	Georgia	266
24	Hawaii	238		11	Florida	262
35	Idaho	213		12	Kansas	261
5	Illinois	312		13	Tennessee	258
42	Indiana	194		14	New Mexico	257
46	Iowa	184		15	Nevada	256
12	Kansas	261		15	South Carolina	256
45	Kentucky	185		17	North Carolina	246
1	Louisiana	399		18	Missouri	245
41	Maine	195		19	Texas	244
9	Maryland	272		20	Mississippi	242
8	Massachusetts	283		21	Alabama	241
40	Michigan	205		21	Colorado	241
47	Minnesota	177		23	Delaware	239
20	Mississippi	242		24	Hawaii	238
18	Missouri	245		25	Wisconsin	237
38	Montana	206		26	Arkansas	230
31	Nebraska	217		27	Connecticut	229
15	Nevada	256		28	Oklahoma	227
32	New Hampshire	216		29	Ohio	226
2	New Jersey	366		30	Arizona	220
14	New Mexico	257		31	Nebraska	217
3	New York	344		32	New Hampshire	216
17	North Carolina	246		33	Alaska	215
38	North Dakota	206		33	Pennsylvania	215
29	Ohio	226		35	Idaho	213
28	Oklahoma	227		36	California	211
49	Oregon	176		37	South Dakota	210
33	Pennsylvania	215		38	Montana	206
7	Rhode Island	284		38	North Dakota	206
15	South Carolina	256		40	Michigan	205
37	South Dakota	210		41	Maine	195
13	Tennessee	258		42	Indiana	194
19	Texas	244		43	Utah	191
43	Utah	191		44	Vermont	186
44	Vermont	186		45	Kentucky	185
6	Virginia	290		46	Iowa	184
50	Washington	174		47	Minnesota	177
47	West Virginia	177		47	West Virginia	177
25	Wisconsin	237		49	Oregon	176
4	Wyoming	328		50	Washington	174
					District of Columbia	799

Source: CQ Press using data from U.S. Department of Justice, Bureau of Justice Statistics
"Census of State and Local Law Enforcement Agencies, 2004" (Bulletin, June 2007, NCJ212749)
*Includes state and local police, sheriffs' departments, and special police agencies.

Per Capita State & Local Government Expenditures for Police Protection: 2005

National Per Capita = $252*

ALPHA ORDER

RANK	STATE	PER CAPITA
38	Alabama	$181
6	Alaska	311
12	Arizona	257
43	Arkansas	173
2	California	345
13	Colorado	256
18	Connecticut	240
8	Delaware	282
5	Florida	317
36	Georgia	189
27	Hawaii	210
37	Idaho	182
9	Illinois	281
45	Indiana	168
39	Iowa	180
25	Kansas	212
49	Kentucky	145
19	Louisiana	235
46	Maine	164
11	Maryland	267
17	Massachusetts	244
22	Michigan	225
20	Minnesota	231
40	Mississippi	177
29	Missouri	200
32	Montana	194
44	Nebraska	170
4	Nevada	325
32	New Hampshire	194
3	New Jersey	326
15	New Mexico	247
1	New York	382
32	North Carolina	194
48	North Dakota	157
21	Ohio	229
40	Oklahoma	177
14	Oregon	250
35	Pennsylvania	193
10	Rhode Island	271
42	South Carolina	176
47	South Dakota	161
31	Tennessee	197
29	Texas	200
26	Utah	211
23	Vermont	216
24	Virginia	214
28	Washington	205
50	West Virginia	124
16	Wisconsin	245
7	Wyoming	290

RANK ORDER

RANK	STATE	PER CAPITA
1	New York	$382
2	California	345
3	New Jersey	326
4	Nevada	325
5	Florida	317
6	Alaska	311
7	Wyoming	290
8	Delaware	282
9	Illinois	281
10	Rhode Island	271
11	Maryland	267
12	Arizona	257
13	Colorado	256
14	Oregon	250
15	New Mexico	247
16	Wisconsin	245
17	Massachusetts	244
18	Connecticut	240
19	Louisiana	235
20	Minnesota	231
21	Ohio	229
22	Michigan	225
23	Vermont	216
24	Virginia	214
25	Kansas	212
26	Utah	211
27	Hawaii	210
28	Washington	205
29	Missouri	200
29	Texas	200
31	Tennessee	197
32	Montana	194
32	New Hampshire	194
32	North Carolina	194
35	Pennsylvania	193
36	Georgia	189
37	Idaho	182
38	Alabama	181
39	Iowa	180
40	Mississippi	177
40	Oklahoma	177
42	South Carolina	176
43	Arkansas	173
44	Nebraska	170
45	Indiana	168
46	Maine	164
47	South Dakota	161
48	North Dakota	157
49	Kentucky	145
50	West Virginia	124

| | District of Columbia | 712 |

Source: CQ Press using data from U.S. Bureau of the Census, Governments Division
"State and Local Government Finances 2004-2005" (http://www.census.gov/govs/www/estimate05.html)
*Direct general expenditures.

Per Capita State and Local Government Expenditures for Corrections in 2005

National Per Capita = $200*

ALPHA ORDER

RANK	STATE	PER CAPITA
44	Alabama	$133
2	Alaska	299
13	Arizona	215
28	Arkansas	165
3	California	272
20	Colorado	192
27	Connecticut	166
5	Delaware	259
17	Florida	211
19	Georgia	202
42	Hawaii	134
22	Idaho	175
40	Illinois	135
34	Indiana	152
49	Iowa	110
44	Kansas	133
35	Kentucky	151
18	Louisiana	210
40	Maine	135
4	Maryland	261
32	Massachusetts	161
11	Michigan	224
37	Minnesota	140
46	Mississippi	123
36	Missouri	145
26	Montana	167
29	Nebraska	164
8	Nevada	230
48	New Hampshire	118
15	New Jersey	213
7	New Mexico	239
6	New York	253
22	North Carolina	175
50	North Dakota	106
31	Ohio	162
25	Oklahoma	168
10	Oregon	229
8	Pennsylvania	230
29	Rhode Island	164
39	South Carolina	136
47	South Dakota	119
38	Tennessee	139
21	Texas	187
24	Utah	169
33	Vermont	155
16	Virginia	212
13	Washington	215
42	West Virginia	134
12	Wisconsin	218
1	Wyoming	466

RANK ORDER

RANK	STATE	PER CAPITA
1	Wyoming	$466
2	Alaska	299
3	California	272
4	Maryland	261
5	Delaware	259
6	New York	253
7	New Mexico	239
8	Nevada	230
8	Pennsylvania	230
10	Oregon	229
11	Michigan	224
12	Wisconsin	218
13	Arizona	215
13	Washington	215
15	New Jersey	213
16	Virginia	212
17	Florida	211
18	Louisiana	210
19	Georgia	202
20	Colorado	192
21	Texas	187
22	Idaho	175
22	North Carolina	175
24	Utah	169
25	Oklahoma	168
26	Montana	167
27	Connecticut	166
28	Arkansas	165
29	Nebraska	164
29	Rhode Island	164
31	Ohio	162
32	Massachusetts	161
33	Vermont	155
34	Indiana	152
35	Kentucky	151
36	Missouri	145
37	Minnesota	140
38	Tennessee	139
39	South Carolina	136
40	Illinois	135
40	Maine	135
42	Hawaii	134
42	West Virginia	134
44	Alabama	133
44	Kansas	133
46	Mississippi	123
47	South Dakota	119
48	New Hampshire	118
49	Iowa	110
50	North Dakota	106

District of Columbia 282

Source: CQ Press using data from U.S. Bureau of the Census, Governments Division
"State and Local Government Finances 2004-2005" (http://www.census.gov/govs/www/estimate05.html)
*Direct general expenditures.

Per Capita State and Local Government Expenditures for Judicial and Legal Services in 2005
National Per Capita = $118*

ALPHA ORDER

RANK	STATE	PER CAPITA
44	Alabama	$74
1	Alaska	231
13	Arizona	130
43	Arkansas	75
2	California	202
30	Colorado	93
7	Connecticut	155
6	Delaware	160
18	Florida	113
25	Georgia	99
3	Hawaii	192
27	Idaho	95
27	Illinois	95
48	Indiana	62
32	Iowa	91
26	Kansas	98
35	Kentucky	87
20	Louisiana	111
46	Maine	71
16	Maryland	114
12	Massachusetts	131
15	Michigan	115
19	Minnesota	112
47	Mississippi	64
44	Missouri	74
21	Montana	110
39	Nebraska	81
5	Nevada	163
36	New Hampshire	85
8	New Jersey	153
14	New Mexico	118
4	New York	165
49	North Carolina	59
33	North Dakota	90
11	Ohio	134
42	Oklahoma	76
30	Oregon	93
16	Pennsylvania	114
10	Rhode Island	135
50	South Carolina	58
40	South Dakota	79
38	Tennessee	82
40	Texas	79
21	Utah	110
34	Vermont	88
36	Virginia	85
23	Washington	105
24	West Virginia	100
27	Wisconsin	95
9	Wyoming	150

RANK ORDER

RANK	STATE	PER CAPITA
1	Alaska	$231
2	California	202
3	Hawaii	192
4	New York	165
5	Nevada	163
6	Delaware	160
7	Connecticut	155
8	New Jersey	153
9	Wyoming	150
10	Rhode Island	135
11	Ohio	134
12	Massachusetts	131
13	Arizona	130
14	New Mexico	118
15	Michigan	115
16	Maryland	114
16	Pennsylvania	114
18	Florida	113
19	Minnesota	112
20	Louisiana	111
21	Montana	110
21	Utah	110
23	Washington	105
24	West Virginia	100
25	Georgia	99
26	Kansas	98
27	Idaho	95
27	Illinois	95
27	Wisconsin	95
30	Colorado	93
30	Oregon	93
32	Iowa	91
33	North Dakota	90
34	Vermont	88
35	Kentucky	87
36	New Hampshire	85
36	Virginia	85
38	Tennessee	82
39	Nebraska	81
40	South Dakota	79
40	Texas	79
42	Oklahoma	76
43	Arkansas	75
44	Alabama	74
44	Missouri	74
46	Maine	71
47	Mississippi	64
48	Indiana	62
49	North Carolina	59
50	South Carolina	58

District of Columbia	96

Source: CQ Press using data from U.S. Bureau of the Census, Governments Division
"State and Local Government Finances 2004-2005" (http://www.census.gov/govs/www/estimate05.html)
*Direct general expenditures. Includes Courts, Prosecution and Legal Services, and Public Defense.

III. Defense

Homeland Security Grants in 2007

National Total = $1,666,460,000*

ALPHA ORDER					RANK ORDER			
RANK	STATE	GRANTS	% of USA		RANK	STATE	GRANTS	% of USA
30	Alabama	$11,574,024	0.7%		1	California	$242,244,693	14.5%
36	Alaska	7,194,682	0.4%		2	New York	208,038,833	12.5%
12	Arizona	33,774,130	2.0%		3	Texas	121,628,661	7.3%
34	Arkansas	7,237,952	0.4%		4	Illinois	86,247,804	5.2%
1	California	242,244,693	14.5%		5	Florida	84,742,600	5.1%
22	Colorado	19,898,995	1.2%		6	Pennsylvania	61,306,260	3.7%
32	Connecticut	10,479,178	0.6%		7	New Jersey	61,108,506	3.7%
46	Delaware	6,683,613	0.4%		8	Ohio	46,320,809	2.8%
5	Florida	84,742,600	5.1%		9	Georgia	39,958,802	2.4%
9	Georgia	39,958,802	2.4%		10	Michigan	39,237,379	2.4%
28	Hawaii	12,114,290	0.7%		11	Massachusetts	35,509,322	2.1%
43	Idaho	6,700,613	0.4%		12	Arizona	33,774,130	2.0%
4	Illinois	86,247,804	5.2%		13	Virginia	33,277,688	2.0%
18	Indiana	23,397,497	1.4%		14	Maryland	32,669,855	2.0%
37	Iowa	7,043,386	0.4%		15	Missouri	31,243,804	1.9%
33	Kansas	8,375,096	0.5%		16	Washington	28,926,100	1.7%
29	Kentucky	11,756,573	0.7%		17	North Carolina	25,255,644	1.5%
19	Louisiana	21,873,032	1.3%		18	Indiana	23,397,497	1.4%
44	Maine	6,697,490	0.4%		19	Louisiana	21,873,032	1.3%
14	Maryland	32,669,855	2.0%		20	Minnesota	20,504,426	1.2%
11	Massachusetts	35,509,322	2.1%		21	Tennessee	20,044,817	1.2%
10	Michigan	39,237,379	2.4%		22	Colorado	19,898,995	1.2%
20	Minnesota	20,504,426	1.2%		23	Nevada	19,357,374	1.2%
38	Mississippi	7,002,072	0.4%		24	Wisconsin	17,796,137	1.1%
15	Missouri	31,243,804	1.9%		25	Oregon	16,032,974	1.0%
45	Montana	6,686,289	0.4%		26	Oklahoma	14,198,414	0.9%
35	Nebraska	7,226,474	0.4%		27	Rhode Island	12,118,513	0.7%
23	Nevada	19,357,374	1.2%		28	Hawaii	12,114,290	0.7%
41	New Hampshire	6,955,299	0.4%		29	Kentucky	11,756,573	0.7%
7	New Jersey	61,108,506	3.7%		30	Alabama	11,574,024	0.7%
40	New Mexico	6,973,253	0.4%		31	South Carolina	11,000,800	0.7%
2	New York	208,038,833	12.5%		32	Connecticut	10,479,178	0.6%
17	North Carolina	25,255,644	1.5%		33	Kansas	8,375,096	0.5%
48	North Dakota	6,677,608	0.4%		34	Arkansas	7,237,952	0.4%
8	Ohio	46,320,809	2.8%		35	Nebraska	7,226,474	0.4%
26	Oklahoma	14,198,414	0.9%		36	Alaska	7,194,682	0.4%
25	Oregon	16,032,974	1.0%		37	Iowa	7,043,386	0.4%
6	Pennsylvania	61,306,260	3.7%		38	Mississippi	7,002,072	0.4%
27	Rhode Island	12,118,513	0.7%		39	Utah	6,988,965	0.4%
31	South Carolina	11,000,800	0.7%		40	New Mexico	6,973,253	0.4%
47	South Dakota	6,681,651	0.4%		41	New Hampshire	6,955,299	0.4%
21	Tennessee	20,044,817	1.2%		42	West Virginia	6,711,870	0.4%
3	Texas	121,628,661	7.3%		43	Idaho	6,700,613	0.4%
39	Utah	6,988,965	0.4%		44	Maine	6,697,490	0.4%
49	Vermont	6,677,213	0.4%		45	Montana	6,686,289	0.4%
13	Virginia	33,277,688	2.0%		46	Delaware	6,683,613	0.4%
16	Washington	28,926,100	1.7%		47	South Dakota	6,681,651	0.4%
42	West Virginia	6,711,870	0.4%		48	North Dakota	6,677,608	0.4%
24	Wisconsin	17,796,137	1.1%		49	Vermont	6,677,213	0.4%
50	Wyoming	6,673,910	0.4%		50	Wyoming	6,673,910	0.4%
						District of Columbia	71,985,107	4.3%

Source: CQ Press using data from U.S. Department of Homeland Security
   "State Contacts & Grant Award Information" (http://www.dhs.gov/xgovt/grants/)
*For fiscal year ending September 30. National total includes $15,649,516 in grants to U.S. territories. The Homeland Security Grant Program includes several sub-grant programs such as State Homeland Security, Urban Area Security Initiative, Law Enforcement Terrorism and Prevention Program, and Citizen Corps allocations.

Per Capita Homeland Security Grants in 2007

National Per Capita = $5.47*

ALPHA ORDER

RANK	STATE	PER CAPITA
47	Alabama	$2.50
5	Alaska	10.53
17	Arizona	5.33
46	Arkansas	2.55
14	California	6.63
30	Colorado	4.09
42	Connecticut	2.99
9	Delaware	7.73
24	Florida	4.64
29	Georgia	4.19
7	Hawaii	9.44
25	Idaho	4.47
13	Illinois	6.71
37	Indiana	3.69
50	Iowa	2.36
41	Kansas	3.02
44	Kentucky	2.77
20	Louisiana	5.09
22	Maine	5.08
15	Maryland	5.81
16	Massachusetts	5.51
35	Michigan	3.90
33	Minnesota	3.94
49	Mississippi	2.40
18	Missouri	5.32
12	Montana	6.98
31	Nebraska	4.07
10	Nevada	7.55
19	New Hampshire	5.29
11	New Jersey	7.04
38	New Mexico	3.54
3	New York	10.78
43	North Carolina	2.79
6	North Dakota	10.44
32	Ohio	4.04
34	Oklahoma	3.93
28	Oregon	4.28
23	Pennsylvania	4.93
2	Rhode Island	11.46
47	South Carolina	2.50
8	South Dakota	8.39
39	Tennessee	3.26
20	Texas	5.09
45	Utah	2.64
4	Vermont	10.75
27	Virginia	4.32
25	Washington	4.47
36	West Virginia	3.70
40	Wisconsin	3.18
1	Wyoming	12.76

RANK ORDER

RANK	STATE	PER CAPITA
1	Wyoming	$12.76
2	Rhode Island	11.46
3	New York	10.78
4	Vermont	10.75
5	Alaska	10.53
6	North Dakota	10.44
7	Hawaii	9.44
8	South Dakota	8.39
9	Delaware	7.73
10	Nevada	7.55
11	New Jersey	7.04
12	Montana	6.98
13	Illinois	6.71
14	California	6.63
15	Maryland	5.81
16	Massachusetts	5.51
17	Arizona	5.33
18	Missouri	5.32
19	New Hampshire	5.29
20	Louisiana	5.09
20	Texas	5.09
22	Maine	5.08
23	Pennsylvania	4.93
24	Florida	4.64
25	Idaho	4.47
25	Washington	4.47
27	Virginia	4.32
28	Oregon	4.28
29	Georgia	4.19
30	Colorado	4.09
31	Nebraska	4.07
32	Ohio	4.04
33	Minnesota	3.94
34	Oklahoma	3.93
35	Michigan	3.90
36	West Virginia	3.70
37	Indiana	3.69
38	New Mexico	3.54
39	Tennessee	3.26
40	Wisconsin	3.18
41	Kansas	3.02
42	Connecticut	2.99
43	North Carolina	2.79
44	Kentucky	2.77
45	Utah	2.64
46	Arkansas	2.55
47	Alabama	2.50
47	South Carolina	2.50
49	Mississippi	2.40
50	Iowa	2.36

District of Columbia   122.36

Source: CQ Press using data from U.S. Department of Homeland Security
    "State Contacts & Grant Award Information" (http://www.dhs.gov/xgovt/grants/)
*For fiscal year ending September 30. National per capita does not include grants to U.S. territories. The Homeland Security Grant Program includes several sub-grant programs such as State Homeland Security, Urban Area Security Initiative, Law Enforcement Terrorism and Prevention Program, and Citizen Corps allocations.

U.S. Department of Defense Domestic Expenditures in 2006

National Total = $408,248,512,000*

ALPHA ORDER

ALPHA ORDER

RANK	STATE	CONTRACTS	% of USA
11	Alabama	$10,520,824,000	2.6%
31	Alaska	3,338,712,000	0.8%
7	Arizona	12,430,407,000	3.0%
35	Arkansas	2,025,375,000	0.5%
1	California	47,745,405,000	11.7%
19	Colorado	7,383,018,000	1.8%
16	Connecticut	8,602,489,000	2.1%
49	Delaware	566,121,000	0.1%
4	Florida	19,701,629,000	4.8%
6	Georgia	12,978,124,000	3.2%
23	Hawaii	6,104,108,000	1.5%
47	Idaho	746,151,000	0.2%
22	Illinois	6,219,503,000	1.5%
24	Indiana	6,052,234,000	1.5%
40	Iowa	1,431,564,000	0.4%
30	Kansas	3,578,408,000	0.9%
17	Kentucky	8,371,759,000	2.1%
21	Louisiana	7,199,143,000	1.8%
37	Maine	1,866,110,000	0.5%
5	Maryland	15,792,267,000	3.9%
13	Massachusetts	10,329,906,000	2.5%
27	Michigan	5,302,955,000	1.3%
34	Minnesota	2,357,207,000	0.6%
20	Mississippi	7,305,762,000	1.8%
8	Missouri	11,871,166,000	2.9%
48	Montana	686,787,000	0.2%
38	Nebraska	1,690,211,000	0.4%
36	Nevada	1,915,957,000	0.5%
39	New Hampshire	1,461,423,000	0.4%
18	New Jersey	8,231,918,000	2.0%
33	New Mexico	2,569,718,000	0.6%
10	New York	10,838,944,000	2.7%
14	North Carolina	9,922,182,000	2.4%
45	North Dakota	778,091,000	0.2%
15	Ohio	9,106,810,000	2.2%
26	Oklahoma	5,362,128,000	1.3%
41	Oregon	1,370,119,000	0.3%
9	Pennsylvania	10,891,896,000	2.7%
42	Rhode Island	1,125,562,000	0.3%
25	South Carolina	5,672,629,000	1.4%
46	South Dakota	750,136,000	0.2%
28	Tennessee	4,441,121,000	1.1%
3	Texas	39,177,926,000	9.6%
29	Utah	4,064,930,000	1.0%
43	Vermont	1,018,904,000	0.2%
2	Virginia	46,024,057,000	11.3%
12	Washington	10,478,189,000	2.6%
44	West Virginia	800,575,000	0.2%
32	Wisconsin	2,901,851,000	0.7%
50	Wyoming	479,657,000	0.1%

RANK ORDER

RANK	STATE	CONTRACTS	% of USA
1	California	$47,745,405,000	11.7%
2	Virginia	46,024,057,000	11.3%
3	Texas	39,177,926,000	9.6%
4	Florida	19,701,629,000	4.8%
5	Maryland	15,792,267,000	3.9%
6	Georgia	12,978,124,000	3.2%
7	Arizona	12,430,407,000	3.0%
8	Missouri	11,871,166,000	2.9%
9	Pennsylvania	10,891,896,000	2.7%
10	New York	10,838,944,000	2.7%
11	Alabama	10,520,824,000	2.6%
12	Washington	10,478,189,000	2.6%
13	Massachusetts	10,329,906,000	2.5%
14	North Carolina	9,922,182,000	2.4%
15	Ohio	9,106,810,000	2.2%
16	Connecticut	8,602,489,000	2.1%
17	Kentucky	8,371,759,000	2.1%
18	New Jersey	8,231,918,000	2.0%
19	Colorado	7,383,018,000	1.8%
20	Mississippi	7,305,762,000	1.8%
21	Louisiana	7,199,143,000	1.8%
22	Illinois	6,219,503,000	1.5%
23	Hawaii	6,104,108,000	1.5%
24	Indiana	6,052,234,000	1.5%
25	South Carolina	5,672,629,000	1.4%
26	Oklahoma	5,362,128,000	1.3%
27	Michigan	5,302,955,000	1.3%
28	Tennessee	4,441,121,000	1.1%
29	Utah	4,064,930,000	1.0%
30	Kansas	3,578,408,000	0.9%
31	Alaska	3,338,712,000	0.8%
32	Wisconsin	2,901,851,000	0.7%
33	New Mexico	2,569,718,000	0.6%
34	Minnesota	2,357,207,000	0.6%
35	Arkansas	2,025,375,000	0.5%
36	Nevada	1,915,957,000	0.5%
37	Maine	1,866,110,000	0.5%
38	Nebraska	1,690,211,000	0.4%
39	New Hampshire	1,461,423,000	0.4%
40	Iowa	1,431,564,000	0.4%
41	Oregon	1,370,119,000	0.3%
42	Rhode Island	1,125,562,000	0.3%
43	Vermont	1,018,904,000	0.2%
44	West Virginia	800,575,000	0.2%
45	North Dakota	778,091,000	0.2%
46	South Dakota	750,136,000	0.2%
47	Idaho	746,151,000	0.2%
48	Montana	686,787,000	0.2%
49	Delaware	566,121,000	0.1%
50	Wyoming	479,657,000	0.1%
	District of Columbia	6,666,444,000	1.6%

Source: U.S. Department of Defense
"Atlas/Data Abstract for the United States" (http://siadapp.dior.whs.mil/personnel/L03/fy06/atlas_2006.pdf)
*Expenditures for payroll, grants, and prime contracts ($25,000 or more) for civil and military functions. Does not include payroll, contracts, or grants to U.S. territories and other countries.

Per Capita U.S. Department of Defense Domestic Expenditures in 2006

National Per Capita = $1,367*

ALPHA ORDER

RANK	STATE	PER CAPITA
7	Alabama	$2,292
2	Alaska	4,928
9	Arizona	2,016
40	Arkansas	721
22	California	1,317
17	Colorado	1,549
6	Connecticut	2,461
41	Delaware	664
28	Florida	1,091
20	Georgia	1,389
3	Hawaii	4,774
45	Idaho	510
46	Illinois	487
30	Indiana	960
47	Iowa	482
24	Kansas	1,298
10	Kentucky	1,991
11	Louisiana	1,697
19	Maine	1,419
4	Maryland	2,819
15	Massachusetts	1,605
43	Michigan	525
48	Minnesota	457
5	Mississippi	2,520
8	Missouri	2,034
39	Montana	725
31	Nebraska	958
37	Nevada	769
27	New Hampshire	1,114
33	New Jersey	950
21	New Mexico	1,323
42	New York	562
26	North Carolina	1,119
25	North Dakota	1,221
36	Ohio	794
18	Oklahoma	1,499
50	Oregon	371
35	Pennsylvania	878
29	Rhode Island	1,060
23	South Carolina	1,310
32	South Dakota	951
38	Tennessee	731
12	Texas	1,674
16	Utah	1,576
14	Vermont	1,641
1	Virginia	6,024
13	Washington	1,644
49	West Virginia	443
44	Wisconsin	521
34	Wyoming	935

RANK ORDER

RANK	STATE	PER CAPITA
1	Virginia	$6,024
2	Alaska	4,928
3	Hawaii	4,774
4	Maryland	2,819
5	Mississippi	2,520
6	Connecticut	2,461
7	Alabama	2,292
8	Missouri	2,034
9	Arizona	2,016
10	Kentucky	1,991
11	Louisiana	1,697
12	Texas	1,674
13	Washington	1,644
14	Vermont	1,641
15	Massachusetts	1,605
16	Utah	1,576
17	Colorado	1,549
18	Oklahoma	1,499
19	Maine	1,419
20	Georgia	1,389
21	New Mexico	1,323
22	California	1,317
23	South Carolina	1,310
24	Kansas	1,298
25	North Dakota	1,221
26	North Carolina	1,119
27	New Hampshire	1,114
28	Florida	1,091
29	Rhode Island	1,060
30	Indiana	960
31	Nebraska	958
32	South Dakota	951
33	New Jersey	950
34	Wyoming	935
35	Pennsylvania	878
36	Ohio	794
37	Nevada	769
38	Tennessee	731
39	Montana	725
40	Arkansas	721
41	Delaware	664
42	New York	562
43	Michigan	525
44	Wisconsin	521
45	Idaho	510
46	Illinois	487
47	Iowa	482
48	Minnesota	457
49	West Virginia	443
50	Oregon	371
	District of Columbia	11,387

Source: CQ Press using data from U.S. Department of Defense
   "Atlas/Data Abstract for the United States" (http://siadapp.dior.whs.mil/personnel/L03/fy06/atlas_2006.pdf)
*Expenditures for payroll, grants, and prime contracts ($25,000 or more) for civil and military functions. Does not include payroll, contracts, or grants to U.S. territories and other countries.

U.S. Department of Defense Total Contracts in 2006

National Total = $257,456,798,000*

<table>
<tr><td colspan="4">ALPHA ORDER</td><td colspan="4">RANK ORDER</td></tr>
<tr><td>RANK</td><td>STATE</td><td>CONTRACTS</td><td>% of USA</td><td>RANK</td><td>STATE</td><td>CONTRACTS</td><td>% of USA</td></tr>
<tr><td>12</td><td>Alabama</td><td>$6,953,772,000</td><td>2.7%</td><td>1</td><td>California</td><td>$32,126,109,000</td><td>12.5%</td></tr>
<tr><td>32</td><td>Alaska</td><td>1,655,627,000</td><td>0.6%</td><td>2</td><td>Virginia</td><td>29,246,034,000</td><td>11.4%</td></tr>
<tr><td>6</td><td>Arizona</td><td>9,695,948,000</td><td>3.8%</td><td>3</td><td>Texas</td><td>27,101,956,000</td><td>10.5%</td></tr>
<tr><td>38</td><td>Arkansas</td><td>881,346,000</td><td>0.3%</td><td>4</td><td>Florida</td><td>10,706,644,000</td><td>4.2%</td></tr>
<tr><td>1</td><td>California</td><td>32,126,109,000</td><td>12.5%</td><td>5</td><td>Maryland</td><td>10,244,137,000</td><td>4.0%</td></tr>
<tr><td>21</td><td>Colorado</td><td>4,127,154,000</td><td>1.6%</td><td>6</td><td>Arizona</td><td>9,695,948,000</td><td>3.8%</td></tr>
<tr><td>10</td><td>Connecticut</td><td>7,780,823,000</td><td>3.0%</td><td>7</td><td>Missouri</td><td>9,392,852,000</td><td>3.6%</td></tr>
<tr><td>50</td><td>Delaware</td><td>124,776,000</td><td>0.0%</td><td>8</td><td>Massachusetts</td><td>9,077,395,000</td><td>3.5%</td></tr>
<tr><td>4</td><td>Florida</td><td>10,706,644,000</td><td>4.2%</td><td>9</td><td>New York</td><td>8,020,492,000</td><td>3.1%</td></tr>
<tr><td>15</td><td>Georgia</td><td>5,515,093,000</td><td>2.1%</td><td>10</td><td>Connecticut</td><td>7,780,823,000</td><td>3.0%</td></tr>
<tr><td>30</td><td>Hawaii</td><td>1,963,468,000</td><td>0.8%</td><td>11</td><td>Pennsylvania</td><td>7,514,783,000</td><td>2.9%</td></tr>
<tr><td>48</td><td>Idaho</td><td>168,321,000</td><td>0.1%</td><td>12</td><td>Alabama</td><td>6,953,772,000</td><td>2.7%</td></tr>
<tr><td>23</td><td>Illinois</td><td>3,273,844,000</td><td>1.3%</td><td>13</td><td>New Jersey</td><td>6,151,133,000</td><td>2.4%</td></tr>
<tr><td>20</td><td>Indiana</td><td>4,627,372,000</td><td>1.8%</td><td>14</td><td>Ohio</td><td>5,980,221,000</td><td>2.3%</td></tr>
<tr><td>37</td><td>Iowa</td><td>944,483,000</td><td>0.4%</td><td>15</td><td>Georgia</td><td>5,515,093,000</td><td>2.1%</td></tr>
<tr><td>31</td><td>Kansas</td><td>1,705,691,000</td><td>0.7%</td><td>16</td><td>Mississippi</td><td>5,477,261,000</td><td>2.1%</td></tr>
<tr><td>17</td><td>Kentucky</td><td>5,394,692,000</td><td>2.1%</td><td>17</td><td>Kentucky</td><td>5,394,692,000</td><td>2.1%</td></tr>
<tr><td>18</td><td>Louisiana</td><td>5,154,128,000</td><td>2.0%</td><td>18</td><td>Louisiana</td><td>5,154,128,000</td><td>2.0%</td></tr>
<tr><td>36</td><td>Maine</td><td>1,019,801,000</td><td>0.4%</td><td>19</td><td>Washington</td><td>4,765,782,000</td><td>1.9%</td></tr>
<tr><td>5</td><td>Maryland</td><td>10,244,137,000</td><td>4.0%</td><td>20</td><td>Indiana</td><td>4,627,372,000</td><td>1.8%</td></tr>
<tr><td>8</td><td>Massachusetts</td><td>9,077,395,000</td><td>3.5%</td><td>21</td><td>Colorado</td><td>4,127,154,000</td><td>1.6%</td></tr>
<tr><td>22</td><td>Michigan</td><td>3,897,649,000</td><td>1.5%</td><td>22</td><td>Michigan</td><td>3,897,649,000</td><td>1.5%</td></tr>
<tr><td>33</td><td>Minnesota</td><td>1,525,731,000</td><td>0.6%</td><td>23</td><td>Illinois</td><td>3,273,844,000</td><td>1.3%</td></tr>
<tr><td>16</td><td>Mississippi</td><td>5,477,261,000</td><td>2.1%</td><td>24</td><td>Tennessee</td><td>2,865,761,000</td><td>1.1%</td></tr>
<tr><td>7</td><td>Missouri</td><td>9,392,852,000</td><td>3.6%</td><td>25</td><td>North Carolina</td><td>2,690,120,000</td><td>1.0%</td></tr>
<tr><td>46</td><td>Montana</td><td>247,146,000</td><td>0.1%</td><td>26</td><td>Utah</td><td>2,303,676,000</td><td>0.9%</td></tr>
<tr><td>41</td><td>Nebraska</td><td>718,281,000</td><td>0.3%</td><td>27</td><td>South Carolina</td><td>2,197,034,000</td><td>0.9%</td></tr>
<tr><td>40</td><td>Nevada</td><td>750,415,000</td><td>0.3%</td><td>28</td><td>Wisconsin</td><td>2,165,275,000</td><td>0.8%</td></tr>
<tr><td>34</td><td>New Hampshire</td><td>1,105,518,000</td><td>0.4%</td><td>29</td><td>Oklahoma</td><td>2,069,823,000</td><td>0.8%</td></tr>
<tr><td>13</td><td>New Jersey</td><td>6,151,133,000</td><td>2.4%</td><td>30</td><td>Hawaii</td><td>1,963,468,000</td><td>0.8%</td></tr>
<tr><td>35</td><td>New Mexico</td><td>1,074,568,000</td><td>0.4%</td><td>31</td><td>Kansas</td><td>1,705,691,000</td><td>0.7%</td></tr>
<tr><td>9</td><td>New York</td><td>8,020,492,000</td><td>3.1%</td><td>32</td><td>Alaska</td><td>1,655,627,000</td><td>0.6%</td></tr>
<tr><td>25</td><td>North Carolina</td><td>2,690,120,000</td><td>1.0%</td><td>33</td><td>Minnesota</td><td>1,525,731,000</td><td>0.6%</td></tr>
<tr><td>47</td><td>North Dakota</td><td>240,478,000</td><td>0.1%</td><td>34</td><td>New Hampshire</td><td>1,105,518,000</td><td>0.4%</td></tr>
<tr><td>14</td><td>Ohio</td><td>5,980,221,000</td><td>2.3%</td><td>35</td><td>New Mexico</td><td>1,074,568,000</td><td>0.4%</td></tr>
<tr><td>29</td><td>Oklahoma</td><td>2,069,823,000</td><td>0.8%</td><td>36</td><td>Maine</td><td>1,019,801,000</td><td>0.4%</td></tr>
<tr><td>42</td><td>Oregon</td><td>562,475,000</td><td>0.2%</td><td>37</td><td>Iowa</td><td>944,483,000</td><td>0.4%</td></tr>
<tr><td>11</td><td>Pennsylvania</td><td>7,514,783,000</td><td>2.9%</td><td>38</td><td>Arkansas</td><td>881,346,000</td><td>0.3%</td></tr>
<tr><td>43</td><td>Rhode Island</td><td>430,736,000</td><td>0.2%</td><td>39</td><td>Vermont</td><td>829,033,000</td><td>0.3%</td></tr>
<tr><td>27</td><td>South Carolina</td><td>2,197,034,000</td><td>0.9%</td><td>40</td><td>Nevada</td><td>750,415,000</td><td>0.3%</td></tr>
<tr><td>45</td><td>South Dakota</td><td>371,727,000</td><td>0.1%</td><td>41</td><td>Nebraska</td><td>718,281,000</td><td>0.3%</td></tr>
<tr><td>24</td><td>Tennessee</td><td>2,865,761,000</td><td>1.1%</td><td>42</td><td>Oregon</td><td>562,475,000</td><td>0.2%</td></tr>
<tr><td>3</td><td>Texas</td><td>27,101,956,000</td><td>10.5%</td><td>43</td><td>Rhode Island</td><td>430,736,000</td><td>0.2%</td></tr>
<tr><td>26</td><td>Utah</td><td>2,303,676,000</td><td>0.9%</td><td>44</td><td>West Virginia</td><td>392,274,000</td><td>0.2%</td></tr>
<tr><td>39</td><td>Vermont</td><td>829,033,000</td><td>0.3%</td><td>45</td><td>South Dakota</td><td>371,727,000</td><td>0.1%</td></tr>
<tr><td>2</td><td>Virginia</td><td>29,246,034,000</td><td>11.4%</td><td>46</td><td>Montana</td><td>247,146,000</td><td>0.1%</td></tr>
<tr><td>19</td><td>Washington</td><td>4,765,782,000</td><td>1.9%</td><td>47</td><td>North Dakota</td><td>240,478,000</td><td>0.1%</td></tr>
<tr><td>44</td><td>West Virginia</td><td>392,274,000</td><td>0.2%</td><td>48</td><td>Idaho</td><td>168,321,000</td><td>0.1%</td></tr>
<tr><td>28</td><td>Wisconsin</td><td>2,165,275,000</td><td>0.8%</td><td>49</td><td>Wyoming</td><td>161,156,000</td><td>0.1%</td></tr>
<tr><td>49</td><td>Wyoming</td><td>161,156,000</td><td>0.1%</td><td>50</td><td>Delaware</td><td>124,776,000</td><td>0.0%</td></tr>
<tr><td></td><td></td><td></td><td></td><td></td><td>District of Columbia</td><td>4,066,784,000</td><td>1.6%</td></tr>
</table>

Source: U.S. Department of Defense
"Atlas/Data Abstract for the United States" (http://siadapp.dior.whs.mil/personnel/L03/fy06/atlas_2006.pdf)
*Includes prime contracts ($25,000 or more) for civil and military functions. Does not include contracts to U.S. territories and other countries.

Per Capita U.S. Department of Defense Total Contracts in 2006

National Per Capita = $862*

ALPHA ORDER

RANK	STATE	PER CAPITA
9	Alabama	$1,515
2	Alaska	2,444
7	Arizona	1,573
40	Arkansas	314
16	California	886
17	Colorado	866
3	Connecticut	2,226
49	Delaware	146
25	Florida	593
26	Georgia	590
8	Hawaii	1,536
50	Idaho	115
46	Illinois	256
21	Indiana	734
39	Iowa	318
23	Kansas	619
12	Kentucky	1,283
13	Louisiana	1,215
19	Maine	776
5	Maryland	1,829
10	Massachusetts	1,411
37	Michigan	386
44	Minnesota	296
4	Mississippi	1,889
6	Missouri	1,609
45	Montana	261
34	Nebraska	407
43	Nevada	301
18	New Hampshire	843
22	New Jersey	710
28	New Mexico	553
33	New York	416
42	North Carolina	303
38	North Dakota	377
29	Ohio	522
27	Oklahoma	579
48	Oregon	152
24	Pennsylvania	606
35	Rhode Island	406
30	South Carolina	507
32	South Dakota	471
31	Tennessee	472
14	Texas	1,158
15	Utah	893
11	Vermont	1,335
1	Virginia	3,828
20	Washington	748
47	West Virginia	217
36	Wisconsin	389
40	Wyoming	314

RANK ORDER

RANK	STATE	PER CAPITA
1	Virginia	$3,828
2	Alaska	2,444
3	Connecticut	2,226
4	Mississippi	1,889
5	Maryland	1,829
6	Missouri	1,609
7	Arizona	1,573
8	Hawaii	1,536
9	Alabama	1,515
10	Massachusetts	1,411
11	Vermont	1,335
12	Kentucky	1,283
13	Louisiana	1,215
14	Texas	1,158
15	Utah	893
16	California	886
17	Colorado	866
18	New Hampshire	843
19	Maine	776
20	Washington	748
21	Indiana	734
22	New Jersey	710
23	Kansas	619
24	Pennsylvania	606
25	Florida	593
26	Georgia	590
27	Oklahoma	579
28	New Mexico	553
29	Ohio	522
30	South Carolina	507
31	Tennessee	472
32	South Dakota	471
33	New York	416
34	Nebraska	407
35	Rhode Island	406
36	Wisconsin	389
37	Michigan	386
38	North Dakota	377
39	Iowa	318
40	Arkansas	314
40	Wyoming	314
42	North Carolina	303
43	Nevada	301
44	Minnesota	296
45	Montana	261
46	Illinois	256
47	West Virginia	217
48	Oregon	152
49	Delaware	146
50	Idaho	115

District of Columbia   6,946

Source: CQ Press using data from U.S. Department of Defense
"Atlas/Data Abstract for the United States" (http://siadapp.dior.whs.mil/personnel/L03/fy06/atlas_2006.pdf)
*Includes prime contracts ($25,000 or more) for civil and military functions. Does not include contracts to U.S. territories and other countries.

U.S. Department of Defense Contracts for Military Functions in 2006

National Total = $251,711,336,000*

ALPHA ORDER

RANK	STATE	CONTRACTS	% of USA
12	Alabama	$6,888,153,000	2.7%
32	Alaska	1,634,533,000	0.6%
6	Arizona	9,669,500,000	3.8%
39	Arkansas	826,193,000	0.3%
1	California	32,057,308,000	12.7%
20	Colorado	4,104,257,000	1.6%
10	Connecticut	7,777,852,000	3.1%
50	Delaware	113,557,000	0.0%
4	Florida	10,381,646,000	4.1%
15	Georgia	5,403,192,000	2.1%
30	Hawaii	1,960,916,000	0.8%
48	Idaho	162,973,000	0.1%
22	Illinois	3,138,284,000	1.2%
19	Indiana	4,604,445,000	1.8%
37	Iowa	913,017,000	0.4%
31	Kansas	1,680,207,000	0.7%
16	Kentucky	5,284,745,000	2.1%
24	Louisiana	2,670,063,000	1.1%
36	Maine	1,010,420,000	0.4%
5	Maryland	10,202,357,000	4.1%
8	Massachusetts	9,051,608,000	3.6%
21	Michigan	3,883,043,000	1.5%
33	Minnesota	1,490,045,000	0.6%
17	Mississippi	4,791,680,000	1.9%
7	Missouri	9,272,302,000	3.7%
46	Montana	232,801,000	0.1%
41	Nebraska	704,032,000	0.3%
40	Nevada	748,857,000	0.3%
34	New Hampshire	1,100,844,000	0.4%
13	New Jersey	6,024,591,000	2.4%
35	New Mexico	1,060,874,000	0.4%
9	New York	7,904,239,000	3.1%
25	North Carolina	2,621,873,000	1.0%
47	North Dakota	216,403,000	0.1%
14	Ohio	5,965,423,000	2.4%
29	Oklahoma	2,062,770,000	0.8%
42	Oregon	501,378,000	0.2%
11	Pennsylvania	7,444,329,000	3.0%
43	Rhode Island	427,301,000	0.2%
27	South Carolina	2,152,909,000	0.9%
44	South Dakota	353,420,000	0.1%
23	Tennessee	2,811,931,000	1.1%
3	Texas	26,755,028,000	10.6%
26	Utah	2,291,170,000	0.9%
38	Vermont	827,758,000	0.3%
2	Virginia	29,190,030,000	11.6%
18	Washington	4,665,563,000	1.9%
45	West Virginia	322,681,000	0.1%
28	Wisconsin	2,145,446,000	0.9%
49	Wyoming	159,391,000	0.1%

RANK ORDER

RANK	STATE	CONTRACTS	% of USA
1	California	$32,057,308,000	12.7%
2	Virginia	29,190,030,000	11.6%
3	Texas	26,755,028,000	10.6%
4	Florida	10,381,646,000	4.1%
5	Maryland	10,202,357,000	4.1%
6	Arizona	9,669,500,000	3.8%
7	Missouri	9,272,302,000	3.7%
8	Massachusetts	9,051,608,000	3.6%
9	New York	7,904,239,000	3.1%
10	Connecticut	7,777,852,000	3.1%
11	Pennsylvania	7,444,329,000	3.0%
12	Alabama	6,888,153,000	2.7%
13	New Jersey	6,024,591,000	2.4%
14	Ohio	5,965,423,000	2.4%
15	Georgia	5,403,192,000	2.1%
16	Kentucky	5,284,745,000	2.1%
17	Mississippi	4,791,680,000	1.9%
18	Washington	4,665,563,000	1.9%
19	Indiana	4,604,445,000	1.8%
20	Colorado	4,104,257,000	1.6%
21	Michigan	3,883,043,000	1.5%
22	Illinois	3,138,284,000	1.2%
23	Tennessee	2,811,931,000	1.1%
24	Louisiana	2,670,063,000	1.1%
25	North Carolina	2,621,873,000	1.0%
26	Utah	2,291,170,000	0.9%
27	South Carolina	2,152,909,000	0.9%
28	Wisconsin	2,145,446,000	0.9%
29	Oklahoma	2,062,770,000	0.8%
30	Hawaii	1,960,916,000	0.8%
31	Kansas	1,680,207,000	0.7%
32	Alaska	1,634,533,000	0.6%
33	Minnesota	1,490,045,000	0.6%
34	New Hampshire	1,100,844,000	0.4%
35	New Mexico	1,060,874,000	0.4%
36	Maine	1,010,420,000	0.4%
37	Iowa	913,017,000	0.4%
38	Vermont	827,758,000	0.3%
39	Arkansas	826,193,000	0.3%
40	Nevada	748,857,000	0.3%
41	Nebraska	704,032,000	0.3%
42	Oregon	501,378,000	0.2%
43	Rhode Island	427,301,000	0.2%
44	South Dakota	353,420,000	0.1%
45	West Virginia	322,681,000	0.1%
46	Montana	232,801,000	0.1%
47	North Dakota	216,403,000	0.1%
48	Idaho	162,973,000	0.1%
49	Wyoming	159,391,000	0.1%
50	Delaware	113,557,000	0.0%
	District of Columbia	4,047,998,000	1.6%

Source: U.S. Department of Defense
"Atlas/Data Abstract for the United States" (http://siadapp.dior.whs.mil/personnel/L03/fy06/atlas_2006.pdf)
*Includes prime contracts ($25,000 or more). Does not include contracts to U.S. territories and other countries.

U.S. Department of Defense Contracts for Civil Functions in 2006

National Total = $5,745,462,000*

ALPHA ORDER

RANK ORDER

RANK	STATE	CONTRACTS	% of USA	RANK	STATE	CONTRACTS	% of USA
16	Alabama	$65,619,000	1.1%	1	Louisiana	$2,484,065,000	43.2%
31	Alaska	21,094,000	0.4%	2	Mississippi	685,581,000	11.9%
25	Arizona	26,448,000	0.5%	3	Texas	346,928,000	6.0%
19	Arkansas	55,153,000	1.0%	4	Florida	324,998,000	5.7%
14	California	68,801,000	1.2%	5	Illinois	135,560,000	2.4%
30	Colorado	22,897,000	0.4%	6	New Jersey	126,542,000	2.2%
46	Connecticut	2,971,000	0.1%	7	Missouri	120,550,000	2.1%
40	Delaware	11,219,000	0.2%	8	New York	116,253,000	2.0%
4	Florida	324,998,000	5.7%	9	Georgia	111,901,000	1.9%
9	Georgia	111,901,000	1.9%	10	Kentucky	109,947,000	1.9%
47	Hawaii	2,552,000	0.0%	11	Washington	100,219,000	1.7%
43	Idaho	5,348,000	0.1%	12	Pennsylvania	70,454,000	1.2%
5	Illinois	135,560,000	2.4%	13	West Virginia	69,593,000	1.2%
29	Indiana	22,927,000	0.4%	14	California	68,801,000	1.2%
24	Iowa	31,466,000	0.5%	15	North Carolina	68,247,000	1.2%
27	Kansas	25,484,000	0.4%	16	Alabama	65,619,000	1.1%
10	Kentucky	109,947,000	1.9%	17	Oregon	61,097,000	1.1%
1	Louisiana	2,484,065,000	43.2%	18	Virginia	56,004,000	1.0%
41	Maine	9,381,000	0.2%	19	Arkansas	55,153,000	1.0%
22	Maryland	41,780,000	0.7%	20	Tennessee	53,830,000	0.9%
26	Massachusetts	25,787,000	0.4%	21	South Carolina	44,125,000	0.8%
35	Michigan	14,606,000	0.3%	22	Maryland	41,780,000	0.7%
23	Minnesota	35,686,000	0.6%	23	Minnesota	35,686,000	0.6%
2	Mississippi	685,581,000	11.9%	24	Iowa	31,466,000	0.5%
7	Missouri	120,550,000	2.1%	25	Arizona	26,448,000	0.5%
36	Montana	14,345,000	0.2%	26	Massachusetts	25,787,000	0.4%
37	Nebraska	14,249,000	0.2%	27	Kansas	25,484,000	0.4%
49	Nevada	1,558,000	0.0%	28	North Dakota	24,075,000	0.4%
44	New Hampshire	4,674,000	0.1%	29	Indiana	22,927,000	0.4%
6	New Jersey	126,542,000	2.2%	30	Colorado	22,897,000	0.4%
38	New Mexico	13,694,000	0.2%	31	Alaska	21,094,000	0.4%
8	New York	116,253,000	2.0%	32	Wisconsin	19,829,000	0.3%
15	North Carolina	68,247,000	1.2%	33	South Dakota	18,307,000	0.3%
28	North Dakota	24,075,000	0.4%	34	Ohio	14,798,000	0.3%
34	Ohio	14,798,000	0.3%	35	Michigan	14,606,000	0.3%
42	Oklahoma	7,053,000	0.1%	36	Montana	14,345,000	0.2%
17	Oregon	61,097,000	1.1%	37	Nebraska	14,249,000	0.2%
12	Pennsylvania	70,454,000	1.2%	38	New Mexico	13,694,000	0.2%
45	Rhode Island	3,435,000	0.1%	39	Utah	12,506,000	0.2%
21	South Carolina	44,125,000	0.8%	40	Delaware	11,219,000	0.2%
33	South Dakota	18,307,000	0.3%	41	Maine	9,381,000	0.2%
20	Tennessee	53,830,000	0.9%	42	Oklahoma	7,053,000	0.1%
3	Texas	346,928,000	6.0%	43	Idaho	5,348,000	0.1%
39	Utah	12,506,000	0.2%	44	New Hampshire	4,674,000	0.1%
50	Vermont	1,275,000	0.0%	45	Rhode Island	3,435,000	0.1%
18	Virginia	56,004,000	1.0%	46	Connecticut	2,971,000	0.1%
11	Washington	100,219,000	1.7%	47	Hawaii	2,552,000	0.0%
13	West Virginia	69,593,000	1.2%	48	Wyoming	1,765,000	0.0%
32	Wisconsin	19,829,000	0.3%	49	Nevada	1,558,000	0.0%
48	Wyoming	1,765,000	0.0%	50	Vermont	1,275,000	0.0%
					District of Columbia	18,786,000	0.3%

Source: U.S. Department of Defense
   "Atlas/Data Abstract for the United States" (http://siadapp.dior.whs.mil/personnel/L03/fy06/atlas_2006.pdf)
*Includes prime contracts ($25,000 or more). Does not include contracts to U.S. territories and other countries.

U.S. Department of Defense Domestic Personnel in 2006

National Total = 2,840,064 Personnel*

ALPHA ORDER					RANK ORDER			

RANK	STATE	PERSONNEL	% of USA		RANK	STATE	PERSONNEL	% of USA
17	Alabama	62,066	2.2%		1	California	289,542	10.2%
29	Alaska	31,102	1.1%		2	Virginia	245,525	8.6%
20	Arizona	49,540	1.7%		3	Texas	233,593	8.2%
32	Arkansas	26,680	0.9%		4	North Carolina	150,323	5.3%
1	California	289,542	10.2%		5	Georgia	137,940	4.9%
18	Colorado	56,951	2.0%		6	Florida	133,898	4.7%
38	Connecticut	17,157	0.6%		7	Washington	100,313	3.5%
46	Delaware	10,251	0.4%		8	Maryland	81,962	2.9%
6	Florida	133,898	4.7%		9	New York	76,738	2.7%
5	Georgia	137,940	4.9%		10	Hawaii	73,782	2.6%
10	Hawaii	73,782	2.6%		11	Pennsylvania	71,723	2.5%
42	Idaho	12,659	0.4%		12	Illinois	70,932	2.5%
12	Illinois	70,932	2.5%		13	South Carolina	69,407	2.4%
26	Indiana	32,714	1.2%		14	Oklahoma	65,002	2.3%
39	Iowa	16,314	0.6%		15	Ohio	63,708	2.2%
23	Kansas	39,668	1.4%		16	Kentucky	63,524	2.2%
16	Kentucky	63,524	2.2%		17	Alabama	62,066	2.2%
21	Louisiana	43,362	1.5%		18	Colorado	56,951	2.0%
41	Maine	14,133	0.5%		19	Missouri	51,450	1.8%
8	Maryland	81,962	2.9%		20	Arizona	49,540	1.7%
31	Massachusetts	27,582	1.0%		21	Louisiana	43,362	1.5%
27	Michigan	32,094	1.1%		22	New Jersey	40,312	1.4%
30	Minnesota	27,888	1.0%		23	Kansas	39,668	1.4%
24	Mississippi	37,924	1.3%		24	Mississippi	37,924	1.3%
19	Missouri	51,450	1.8%		25	Utah	34,039	1.2%
45	Montana	10,708	0.4%		26	Indiana	32,714	1.2%
35	Nebraska	19,111	0.7%		27	Michigan	32,094	1.1%
36	Nevada	18,699	0.7%		28	Tennessee	31,470	1.1%
49	New Hampshire	6,531	0.2%		29	Alaska	31,102	1.1%
22	New Jersey	40,312	1.4%		30	Minnesota	27,888	1.0%
33	New Mexico	25,039	0.9%		31	Massachusetts	27,582	1.0%
9	New York	76,738	2.7%		32	Arkansas	26,680	0.9%
4	North Carolina	150,323	5.3%		33	New Mexico	25,039	0.9%
40	North Dakota	14,506	0.5%		34	Wisconsin	23,414	0.8%
15	Ohio	63,708	2.2%		35	Nebraska	19,111	0.7%
14	Oklahoma	65,002	2.3%		36	Nevada	18,699	0.7%
37	Oregon	17,220	0.6%		37	Oregon	17,220	0.6%
11	Pennsylvania	71,723	2.5%		38	Connecticut	17,157	0.6%
44	Rhode Island	11,728	0.4%		39	Iowa	16,314	0.6%
13	South Carolina	69,407	2.4%		40	North Dakota	14,506	0.5%
47	South Dakota	10,055	0.4%		41	Maine	14,133	0.5%
28	Tennessee	31,470	1.1%		42	Idaho	12,659	0.4%
3	Texas	233,593	8.2%		43	West Virginia	12,186	0.4%
25	Utah	34,039	1.2%		44	Rhode Island	11,728	0.4%
50	Vermont	4,808	0.2%		45	Montana	10,708	0.4%
2	Virginia	245,525	8.6%		46	Delaware	10,251	0.4%
7	Washington	100,313	3.5%		47	South Dakota	10,055	0.4%
43	West Virginia	12,186	0.4%		48	Wyoming	7,784	0.3%
34	Wisconsin	23,414	0.8%		49	New Hampshire	6,531	0.2%
48	Wyoming	7,784	0.3%		50	Vermont	4,808	0.2%
						District of Columbia	35,007	1.2%

Source: U.S. Department of Defense

"Atlas/Data Abstract for the United States" (http://siadapp.dior.whs.mil/personnel/L03/fy06/atlas_2006.pdf)

*Includes Active Duty Military, Civilian, Reserve, and National Guard personnel. Does not include personnel in U.S. territories or in other countries.

U.S. Department of Defense Active Duty Military Personnel in 2006

National Total = 1,156,308 Personnel*

ALPHA ORDER

RANK	STATE	PERSONNEL	% of USA
23	Alabama	9,742	0.8%
17	Alaska	20,363	1.8%
16	Arizona	21,997	1.9%
31	Arkansas	4,905	0.4%
1	California	149,481	12.9%
11	Colorado	29,932	2.6%
28	Connecticut	6,594	0.6%
34	Delaware	3,297	0.3%
6	Florida	58,100	5.0%
5	Georgia	68,928	6.0%
8	Hawaii	45,366	3.9%
32	Idaho	4,042	0.3%
15	Illinois	24,536	2.1%
44	Indiana	805	0.1%
48	Iowa	390	0.0%
18	Kansas	17,645	1.5%
9	Kentucky	38,799	3.4%
20	Louisiana	15,069	1.3%
41	Maine	2,096	0.2%
12	Maryland	29,626	2.6%
40	Massachusetts	2,175	0.2%
42	Michigan	1,073	0.1%
45	Minnesota	729	0.1%
22	Mississippi	10,158	0.9%
19	Missouri	16,241	1.4%
33	Montana	3,589	0.3%
27	Nebraska	6,784	0.6%
24	Nevada	9,127	0.8%
43	New Hampshire	912	0.1%
29	New Jersey	6,293	0.5%
21	New Mexico	10,834	0.9%
13	New York	26,240	2.3%
4	North Carolina	102,845	8.9%
25	North Dakota	7,013	0.6%
26	Ohio	6,845	0.6%
14	Oklahoma	25,064	2.2%
46	Oregon	558	0.0%
37	Pennsylvania	2,979	0.3%
39	Rhode Island	2,403	0.2%
10	South Carolina	38,090	3.3%
35	South Dakota	3,150	0.3%
38	Tennessee	2,441	0.2%
3	Texas	119,176	10.3%
30	Utah	5,188	0.4%
50	Vermont	70	0.0%
2	Virginia	128,515	11.1%
7	Washington	49,887	4.3%
49	West Virginia	373	0.0%
47	Wisconsin	449	0.0%
36	Wyoming	3,043	0.3%

RANK ORDER

RANK	STATE	PERSONNEL	% of USA
1	California	149,481	12.9%
2	Virginia	128,515	11.1%
3	Texas	119,176	10.3%
4	North Carolina	102,845	8.9%
5	Georgia	68,928	6.0%
6	Florida	58,100	5.0%
7	Washington	49,887	4.3%
8	Hawaii	45,366	3.9%
9	Kentucky	38,799	3.4%
10	South Carolina	38,090	3.3%
11	Colorado	29,932	2.6%
12	Maryland	29,626	2.6%
13	New York	26,240	2.3%
14	Oklahoma	25,064	2.2%
15	Illinois	24,536	2.1%
16	Arizona	21,997	1.9%
17	Alaska	20,363	1.8%
18	Kansas	17,645	1.5%
19	Missouri	16,241	1.4%
20	Louisiana	15,069	1.3%
21	New Mexico	10,834	0.9%
22	Mississippi	10,158	0.9%
23	Alabama	9,742	0.8%
24	Nevada	9,127	0.8%
25	North Dakota	7,013	0.6%
26	Ohio	6,845	0.6%
27	Nebraska	6,784	0.6%
28	Connecticut	6,594	0.6%
29	New Jersey	6,293	0.5%
30	Utah	5,188	0.4%
31	Arkansas	4,905	0.4%
32	Idaho	4,042	0.3%
33	Montana	3,589	0.3%
34	Delaware	3,297	0.3%
35	South Dakota	3,150	0.3%
36	Wyoming	3,043	0.3%
37	Pennsylvania	2,979	0.3%
38	Tennessee	2,441	0.2%
39	Rhode Island	2,403	0.2%
40	Massachusetts	2,175	0.2%
41	Maine	2,096	0.2%
42	Michigan	1,073	0.1%
43	New Hampshire	912	0.1%
44	Indiana	805	0.1%
45	Minnesota	729	0.1%
46	Oregon	558	0.0%
47	Wisconsin	449	0.0%
48	Iowa	390	0.0%
49	West Virginia	373	0.0%
50	Vermont	70	0.0%
	District of Columbia	12,351	1.1%

Source: U.S. Department of Defense
"Atlas/Data Abstract for the United States" (http://siadapp.dior.whs.mil/personnel/L03/fy06/atlas_2006.pdf)
*Does not include active duty personnel in U.S. territories, in other countries or others undistributed.

U.S. Department of Defense Domestic Civilian Personnel in 2006

National Total = 642,214 Personnel*

ALPHA ORDER

RANK	STATE	PERSONNEL	% of USA
9	Alabama	22,312	3.5%
32	Alaska	4,894	0.8%
23	Arizona	9,047	1.4%
34	Arkansas	3,977	0.6%
2	California	55,709	8.7%
18	Colorado	10,907	1.7%
39	Connecticut	2,388	0.4%
44	Delaware	1,564	0.2%
6	Florida	26,072	4.1%
4	Georgia	32,862	5.1%
13	Hawaii	17,079	2.7%
45	Idaho	1,522	0.2%
16	Illinois	13,617	2.1%
21	Indiana	9,281	1.4%
43	Iowa	1,582	0.2%
27	Kansas	6,577	1.0%
22	Kentucky	9,170	1.4%
30	Louisiana	6,212	1.0%
29	Maine	6,445	1.0%
5	Maryland	30,749	4.8%
28	Massachusetts	6,491	1.0%
25	Michigan	8,147	1.3%
38	Minnesota	2,522	0.4%
24	Mississippi	8,630	1.3%
20	Missouri	9,483	1.5%
46	Montana	1,358	0.2%
35	Nebraska	3,774	0.6%
40	Nevada	2,178	0.3%
48	New Hampshire	1,069	0.2%
15	New Jersey	13,959	2.2%
26	New Mexico	6,863	1.1%
17	New York	11,145	1.7%
12	North Carolina	17,447	2.7%
41	North Dakota	1,853	0.3%
10	Ohio	21,789	3.4%
11	Oklahoma	21,539	3.4%
36	Oregon	3,241	0.5%
7	Pennsylvania	25,266	3.9%
33	Rhode Island	4,213	0.7%
19	South Carolina	9,640	1.5%
47	South Dakota	1,237	0.2%
31	Tennessee	5,334	0.8%
3	Texas	41,462	6.5%
14	Utah	15,081	2.3%
50	Vermont	608	0.1%
1	Virginia	81,342	12.7%
8	Washington	24,501	3.8%
42	West Virginia	1,745	0.3%
37	Wisconsin	2,695	0.4%
49	Wyoming	1,002	0.2%

RANK ORDER

RANK	STATE	PERSONNEL	% of USA
1	Virginia	81,342	12.7%
2	California	55,709	8.7%
3	Texas	41,462	6.5%
4	Georgia	32,862	5.1%
5	Maryland	30,749	4.8%
6	Florida	26,072	4.1%
7	Pennsylvania	25,266	3.9%
8	Washington	24,501	3.8%
9	Alabama	22,312	3.5%
10	Ohio	21,789	3.4%
11	Oklahoma	21,539	3.4%
12	North Carolina	17,447	2.7%
13	Hawaii	17,079	2.7%
14	Utah	15,081	2.3%
15	New Jersey	13,959	2.2%
16	Illinois	13,617	2.1%
17	New York	11,145	1.7%
18	Colorado	10,907	1.7%
19	South Carolina	9,640	1.5%
20	Missouri	9,483	1.5%
21	Indiana	9,281	1.4%
22	Kentucky	9,170	1.4%
23	Arizona	9,047	1.4%
24	Mississippi	8,630	1.3%
25	Michigan	8,147	1.3%
26	New Mexico	6,863	1.1%
27	Kansas	6,577	1.0%
28	Massachusetts	6,491	1.0%
29	Maine	6,445	1.0%
30	Louisiana	6,212	1.0%
31	Tennessee	5,334	0.8%
32	Alaska	4,894	0.8%
33	Rhode Island	4,213	0.7%
34	Arkansas	3,977	0.6%
35	Nebraska	3,774	0.6%
36	Oregon	3,241	0.5%
37	Wisconsin	2,695	0.4%
38	Minnesota	2,522	0.4%
39	Connecticut	2,388	0.4%
40	Nevada	2,178	0.3%
41	North Dakota	1,853	0.3%
42	West Virginia	1,745	0.3%
43	Iowa	1,582	0.2%
44	Delaware	1,564	0.2%
45	Idaho	1,522	0.2%
46	Montana	1,358	0.2%
47	South Dakota	1,237	0.2%
48	New Hampshire	1,069	0.2%
49	Wyoming	1,002	0.2%
50	Vermont	608	0.1%
	District of Columbia	14,634	2.3%

Source: U.S. Department of Defense
 "Atlas/Data Abstract for the United States" (http://siadapp.dior.whs.mil/personnel/L03/fy06/atlas_2006.pdf)
*Does not include civilian personnel in U.S. territories or civilian personnel in other countries. Includes military and civil functions.

U.S. Department of Defense Reserve and National Guard Personnel in 2006

National Total = 1,041,542 Personnel*

ALPHA ORDER

RANK	STATE	PERSONNEL	% of USA
11	Alabama	30,012	2.9%
41	Alaska	5,845	0.6%
25	Arizona	18,496	1.8%
27	Arkansas	17,798	1.7%
1	California	84,352	8.1%
28	Colorado	16,112	1.5%
37	Connecticut	8,175	0.8%
46	Delaware	5,390	0.5%
3	Florida	49,726	4.8%
6	Georgia	36,150	3.5%
34	Hawaii	11,337	1.1%
40	Idaho	7,095	0.7%
9	Illinois	32,779	3.1%
17	Indiana	22,628	2.2%
31	Iowa	14,342	1.4%
30	Kansas	15,446	1.5%
29	Kentucky	15,555	1.5%
18	Louisiana	22,081	2.1%
45	Maine	5,592	0.5%
20	Maryland	21,587	2.1%
24	Massachusetts	18,916	1.8%
16	Michigan	22,874	2.2%
14	Minnesota	24,637	2.4%
23	Mississippi	19,136	1.8%
13	Missouri	25,726	2.5%
42	Montana	5,761	0.6%
36	Nebraska	8,553	0.8%
38	Nevada	7,394	0.7%
48	New Hampshire	4,550	0.4%
22	New Jersey	20,060	1.9%
39	New Mexico	7,342	0.7%
5	New York	39,353	3.8%
10	North Carolina	30,031	2.9%
44	North Dakota	5,640	0.5%
8	Ohio	35,074	3.4%
26	Oklahoma	18,399	1.8%
33	Oregon	13,421	1.3%
4	Pennsylvania	43,478	4.2%
47	Rhode Island	5,112	0.5%
19	South Carolina	21,677	2.1%
43	South Dakota	5,668	0.5%
15	Tennessee	23,695	2.3%
2	Texas	72,955	7.0%
32	Utah	13,770	1.3%
49	Vermont	4,130	0.4%
7	Virginia	35,668	3.4%
12	Washington	25,925	2.5%
35	West Virginia	10,068	1.0%
21	Wisconsin	20,270	1.9%
50	Wyoming	3,739	0.4%

RANK ORDER

RANK	STATE	PERSONNEL	% of USA
1	California	84,352	8.1%
2	Texas	72,955	7.0%
3	Florida	49,726	4.8%
4	Pennsylvania	43,478	4.2%
5	New York	39,353	3.8%
6	Georgia	36,150	3.5%
7	Virginia	35,668	3.4%
8	Ohio	35,074	3.4%
9	Illinois	32,779	3.1%
10	North Carolina	30,031	2.9%
11	Alabama	30,012	2.9%
12	Washington	25,925	2.5%
13	Missouri	25,726	2.5%
14	Minnesota	24,637	2.4%
15	Tennessee	23,695	2.3%
16	Michigan	22,874	2.2%
17	Indiana	22,628	2.2%
18	Louisiana	22,081	2.1%
19	South Carolina	21,677	2.1%
20	Maryland	21,587	2.1%
21	Wisconsin	20,270	1.9%
22	New Jersey	20,060	1.9%
23	Mississippi	19,136	1.8%
24	Massachusetts	18,916	1.8%
25	Arizona	18,496	1.8%
26	Oklahoma	18,399	1.8%
27	Arkansas	17,798	1.7%
28	Colorado	16,112	1.5%
29	Kentucky	15,555	1.5%
30	Kansas	15,446	1.5%
31	Iowa	14,342	1.4%
32	Utah	13,770	1.3%
33	Oregon	13,421	1.3%
34	Hawaii	11,337	1.1%
35	West Virginia	10,068	1.0%
36	Nebraska	8,553	0.8%
37	Connecticut	8,175	0.8%
38	Nevada	7,394	0.7%
39	New Mexico	7,342	0.7%
40	Idaho	7,095	0.7%
41	Alaska	5,845	0.6%
42	Montana	5,761	0.6%
43	South Dakota	5,668	0.5%
44	North Dakota	5,640	0.5%
45	Maine	5,592	0.5%
46	Delaware	5,390	0.5%
47	Rhode Island	5,112	0.5%
48	New Hampshire	4,550	0.4%
49	Vermont	4,130	0.4%
50	Wyoming	3,739	0.4%
	District of Columbia	8,022	0.8%

Source: U.S. Department of Defense
"Atlas/Data Abstract for the United States" (http://siadapp.dior.whs.mil/personnel/L03/fy06/atlas_2006.pdf)
*Does not include reserve and national guard personnel in U.S. territories.

U.S. Department of Defense Total Compensation in 2006

National Total = $146,857,505,000*

ALPHA ORDER

RANK	STATE	TOTAL PAY	% of USA
10	Alabama	$3,503,330,000	2.4%
26	Alaska	1,639,960,000	1.1%
19	Arizona	2,655,501,000	1.8%
33	Arkansas	1,080,151,000	0.7%
2	California	15,269,710,000	10.4%
13	Colorado	3,210,364,000	2.2%
38	Connecticut	757,759,000	0.5%
44	Delaware	419,848,000	0.3%
4	Florida	8,863,769,000	6.0%
5	Georgia	7,409,373,000	5.0%
9	Hawaii	4,064,063,000	2.8%
41	Idaho	541,290,000	0.4%
17	Illinois	2,838,406,000	1.9%
29	Indiana	1,360,874,000	0.9%
43	Iowa	444,967,000	0.3%
22	Kansas	1,827,165,000	1.2%
16	Kentucky	2,959,047,000	2.0%
24	Louisiana	1,734,325,000	1.2%
35	Maine	827,224,000	0.6%
8	Maryland	5,333,575,000	3.6%
32	Massachusetts	1,097,587,000	0.7%
30	Michigan	1,307,212,000	0.9%
36	Minnesota	761,594,000	0.5%
25	Mississippi	1,702,149,000	1.2%
20	Missouri	2,432,471,000	1.7%
45	Montana	407,142,000	0.3%
34	Nebraska	960,998,000	0.7%
31	Nevada	1,145,774,000	0.8%
48	New Hampshire	324,356,000	0.2%
21	New Jersey	2,004,030,000	1.4%
28	New Mexico	1,465,574,000	1.0%
18	New York	2,668,950,000	1.8%
6	North Carolina	7,131,669,000	4.9%
42	North Dakota	500,849,000	0.3%
15	Ohio	3,030,082,000	2.1%
12	Oklahoma	3,259,656,000	2.2%
37	Oregon	760,465,000	0.5%
14	Pennsylvania	3,077,484,000	2.1%
40	Rhode Island	677,943,000	0.5%
11	South Carolina	3,430,778,000	2.3%
47	South Dakota	357,662,000	0.2%
27	Tennessee	1,519,720,000	1.0%
3	Texas	11,908,183,000	8.1%
23	Utah	1,739,346,000	1.2%
50	Vermont	168,378,000	0.1%
1	Virginia	16,692,841,000	11.4%
7	Washington	5,652,251,000	3.8%
46	West Virginia	383,624,000	0.3%
39	Wisconsin	680,804,000	0.5%
49	Wyoming	306,051,000	0.2%

RANK ORDER

RANK	STATE	TOTAL PAY	% of USA
1	Virginia	$16,692,841,000	11.4%
2	California	15,269,710,000	10.4%
3	Texas	11,908,183,000	8.1%
4	Florida	8,863,769,000	6.0%
5	Georgia	7,409,373,000	5.0%
6	North Carolina	7,131,669,000	4.9%
7	Washington	5,652,251,000	3.8%
8	Maryland	5,333,575,000	3.6%
9	Hawaii	4,064,063,000	2.8%
10	Alabama	3,503,330,000	2.4%
11	South Carolina	3,430,778,000	2.3%
12	Oklahoma	3,259,656,000	2.2%
13	Colorado	3,210,364,000	2.2%
14	Pennsylvania	3,077,484,000	2.1%
15	Ohio	3,030,082,000	2.1%
16	Kentucky	2,959,047,000	2.0%
17	Illinois	2,838,406,000	1.9%
18	New York	2,668,950,000	1.8%
19	Arizona	2,655,501,000	1.8%
20	Missouri	2,432,471,000	1.7%
21	New Jersey	2,004,030,000	1.4%
22	Kansas	1,827,165,000	1.2%
23	Utah	1,739,346,000	1.2%
24	Louisiana	1,734,325,000	1.2%
25	Mississippi	1,702,149,000	1.2%
26	Alaska	1,639,960,000	1.1%
27	Tennessee	1,519,720,000	1.0%
28	New Mexico	1,465,574,000	1.0%
29	Indiana	1,360,874,000	0.9%
30	Michigan	1,307,212,000	0.9%
31	Nevada	1,145,774,000	0.8%
32	Massachusetts	1,097,587,000	0.7%
33	Arkansas	1,080,151,000	0.7%
34	Nebraska	960,998,000	0.7%
35	Maine	827,224,000	0.6%
36	Minnesota	761,594,000	0.5%
37	Oregon	760,465,000	0.5%
38	Connecticut	757,759,000	0.5%
39	Wisconsin	680,804,000	0.5%
40	Rhode Island	677,943,000	0.5%
41	Idaho	541,290,000	0.4%
42	North Dakota	500,849,000	0.3%
43	Iowa	444,967,000	0.3%
44	Delaware	419,848,000	0.3%
45	Montana	407,142,000	0.3%
46	West Virginia	383,624,000	0.3%
47	South Dakota	357,662,000	0.2%
48	New Hampshire	324,356,000	0.2%
49	Wyoming	306,051,000	0.2%
50	Vermont	168,378,000	0.1%
	District of Columbia	2,561,181,000	1.7%

Source: U.S. Department of Defense
  "Atlas/Data Abstract for the United States" (http://siadapp.dior.whs.mil/personnel/L03/fy06/atlas_2006.pdf)
*Includes Civilian Pay, Military Active Duty Pay, Reserve, National Guard Pay, and Retired Military Pay. Based on location
of recipient. Does not include recipients in U.S. territories and other countries.

U.S. Department of Defense Military Active Duty Pay in 2006

National Total = $55,829,079,000*

ALPHA ORDER

RANK	STATE	PAYROLL	% of USA
21	Alabama	$569,010,000	1.0%
15	Alaska	1,110,957,000	2.0%
17	Arizona	988,064,000	1.8%
31	Arkansas	239,529,000	0.4%
1	California	6,867,014,000	12.3%
12	Colorado	1,385,576,000	2.5%
27	Connecticut	332,517,000	0.6%
33	Delaware	164,925,000	0.3%
6	Florida	2,981,817,000	5.3%
5	Georgia	3,389,947,000	6.1%
8	Hawaii	2,302,847,000	4.1%
32	Idaho	183,991,000	0.3%
16	Illinois	1,051,183,000	1.9%
44	Indiana	50,898,000	0.1%
49	Iowa	27,964,000	0.1%
18	Kansas	889,660,000	1.6%
9	Kentucky	1,837,451,000	3.3%
20	Louisiana	694,143,000	1.2%
41	Maine	120,494,000	0.2%
11	Maryland	1,543,652,000	2.8%
35	Massachusetts	156,754,000	0.3%
42	Michigan	72,771,000	0.1%
46	Minnesota	48,548,000	0.1%
23	Mississippi	486,587,000	0.9%
19	Missouri	723,735,000	1.3%
36	Montana	146,235,000	0.3%
26	Nebraska	370,865,000	0.7%
24	Nevada	454,457,000	0.8%
43	New Hampshire	53,193,000	0.1%
28	New Jersey	327,314,000	0.6%
22	New Mexico	505,378,000	0.9%
14	New York	1,154,161,000	2.1%
4	North Carolina	4,372,597,000	7.8%
29	North Dakota	281,641,000	0.5%
25	Ohio	446,008,000	0.8%
13	Oklahoma	1,160,016,000	2.1%
45	Oregon	49,199,000	0.1%
34	Pennsylvania	161,921,000	0.3%
39	Rhode Island	136,077,000	0.2%
10	South Carolina	1,696,223,000	3.0%
40	South Dakota	128,497,000	0.2%
37	Tennessee	145,512,000	0.3%
3	Texas	5,254,027,000	9.4%
30	Utah	245,002,000	0.4%
50	Vermont	11,934,000	0.0%
2	Virginia	6,770,183,000	12.1%
7	Washington	2,416,778,000	4.3%
48	West Virginia	28,073,000	0.1%
47	Wisconsin	40,501,000	0.1%
38	Wyoming	140,149,000	0.3%

RANK ORDER

RANK	STATE	PAYROLL	% of USA
1	California	$6,867,014,000	12.3%
2	Virginia	6,770,183,000	12.1%
3	Texas	5,254,027,000	9.4%
4	North Carolina	4,372,597,000	7.8%
5	Georgia	3,389,947,000	6.1%
6	Florida	2,981,817,000	5.3%
7	Washington	2,416,778,000	4.3%
8	Hawaii	2,302,847,000	4.1%
9	Kentucky	1,837,451,000	3.3%
10	South Carolina	1,696,223,000	3.0%
11	Maryland	1,543,652,000	2.8%
12	Colorado	1,385,576,000	2.5%
13	Oklahoma	1,160,016,000	2.1%
14	New York	1,154,161,000	2.1%
15	Alaska	1,110,957,000	2.0%
16	Illinois	1,051,183,000	1.9%
17	Arizona	988,064,000	1.8%
18	Kansas	889,660,000	1.6%
19	Missouri	723,735,000	1.3%
20	Louisiana	694,143,000	1.2%
21	Alabama	569,010,000	1.0%
22	New Mexico	505,378,000	0.9%
23	Mississippi	486,587,000	0.9%
24	Nevada	454,457,000	0.8%
25	Ohio	446,008,000	0.8%
26	Nebraska	370,865,000	0.7%
27	Connecticut	332,517,000	0.6%
28	New Jersey	327,314,000	0.6%
29	North Dakota	281,641,000	0.5%
30	Utah	245,002,000	0.4%
31	Arkansas	239,529,000	0.4%
32	Idaho	183,991,000	0.3%
33	Delaware	164,925,000	0.3%
34	Pennsylvania	161,921,000	0.3%
35	Massachusetts	156,754,000	0.3%
36	Montana	146,235,000	0.3%
37	Tennessee	145,512,000	0.3%
38	Wyoming	140,149,000	0.3%
39	Rhode Island	136,077,000	0.2%
40	South Dakota	128,497,000	0.2%
41	Maine	120,494,000	0.2%
42	Michigan	72,771,000	0.1%
43	New Hampshire	53,193,000	0.1%
44	Indiana	50,898,000	0.1%
45	Oregon	49,199,000	0.1%
46	Minnesota	48,548,000	0.1%
47	Wisconsin	40,501,000	0.1%
48	West Virginia	28,073,000	0.1%
49	Iowa	27,964,000	0.1%
50	Vermont	11,934,000	0.0%
	District of Columbia	1,113,104,000	2.0%

Source: U.S. Department of Defense
   "Atlas/Data Abstract for the United States" (http://siadapp.dior.whs.mil/personnel/L03/fy06/atlas_2006.pdf)
*Based on location of recipient. Does not include recipients in U.S. territories and other countries.

U.S. Department of Defense Civilian Pay in 2006

National Total = $45,104,515,000*

ALPHA ORDER

ALPHA ORDER

RANK	STATE	PAYROLL	% of USA
9	Alabama	$1,670,119,000	3.7%
32	Alaska	329,885,000	0.7%
21	Arizona	584,603,000	1.3%
35	Arkansas	229,025,000	0.5%
2	California	4,206,698,000	9.3%
18	Colorado	703,932,000	1.6%
37	Connecticut	165,681,000	0.4%
44	Delaware	84,651,000	0.2%
6	Florida	1,818,427,000	4.0%
5	Georgia	2,076,349,000	4.6%
12	Hawaii	1,300,936,000	2.9%
45	Idaho	76,985,000	0.2%
16	Illinois	955,047,000	2.1%
20	Indiana	641,770,000	1.4%
43	Iowa	84,877,000	0.2%
31	Kansas	373,136,000	0.8%
25	Kentucky	520,752,000	1.2%
29	Louisiana	396,019,000	0.9%
28	Maine	466,352,000	1.0%
3	Maryland	2,603,595,000	5.8%
27	Massachusetts	475,160,000	1.1%
19	Michigan	645,074,000	1.4%
38	Minnesota	144,383,000	0.3%
23	Mississippi	556,078,000	1.2%
24	Missouri	551,544,000	1.2%
46	Montana	70,226,000	0.2%
34	Nebraska	238,572,000	0.5%
40	Nevada	129,995,000	0.3%
48	New Hampshire	64,214,000	0.1%
13	New Jersey	1,196,165,000	2.7%
26	New Mexico	482,932,000	1.1%
17	New York	710,978,000	1.6%
15	North Carolina	1,027,413,000	2.3%
42	North Dakota	96,606,000	0.2%
10	Ohio	1,645,451,000	3.6%
11	Oklahoma	1,402,273,000	3.1%
36	Oregon	220,103,000	0.5%
7	Pennsylvania	1,738,680,000	3.9%
30	Rhode Island	373,754,000	0.8%
22	South Carolina	581,680,000	1.3%
47	South Dakota	65,809,000	0.1%
33	Tennessee	323,292,000	0.7%
4	Texas	2,516,962,000	5.6%
14	Utah	1,034,204,000	2.3%
50	Vermont	28,895,000	0.1%
1	Virginia	6,157,809,000	13.7%
8	Washington	1,723,931,000	3.8%
41	West Virginia	103,560,000	0.2%
39	Wisconsin	143,907,000	0.3%
49	Wyoming	55,905,000	0.1%

RANK ORDER

RANK	STATE	PAYROLL	% of USA
1	Virginia	$6,157,809,000	13.7%
2	California	4,206,698,000	9.3%
3	Maryland	2,603,595,000	5.8%
4	Texas	2,516,962,000	5.6%
5	Georgia	2,076,349,000	4.6%
6	Florida	1,818,427,000	4.0%
7	Pennsylvania	1,738,680,000	3.9%
8	Washington	1,723,931,000	3.8%
9	Alabama	1,670,119,000	3.7%
10	Ohio	1,645,451,000	3.6%
11	Oklahoma	1,402,273,000	3.1%
12	Hawaii	1,300,936,000	2.9%
13	New Jersey	1,196,165,000	2.7%
14	Utah	1,034,204,000	2.3%
15	North Carolina	1,027,413,000	2.3%
16	Illinois	955,047,000	2.1%
17	New York	710,978,000	1.6%
18	Colorado	703,932,000	1.6%
19	Michigan	645,074,000	1.4%
20	Indiana	641,770,000	1.4%
21	Arizona	584,603,000	1.3%
22	South Carolina	581,680,000	1.3%
23	Mississippi	556,078,000	1.2%
24	Missouri	551,544,000	1.2%
25	Kentucky	520,752,000	1.2%
26	New Mexico	482,932,000	1.1%
27	Massachusetts	475,160,000	1.1%
28	Maine	466,352,000	1.0%
29	Louisiana	396,019,000	0.9%
30	Rhode Island	373,754,000	0.8%
31	Kansas	373,136,000	0.8%
32	Alaska	329,885,000	0.7%
33	Tennessee	323,292,000	0.7%
34	Nebraska	238,572,000	0.5%
35	Arkansas	229,025,000	0.5%
36	Oregon	220,103,000	0.5%
37	Connecticut	165,681,000	0.4%
38	Minnesota	144,383,000	0.3%
39	Wisconsin	143,907,000	0.3%
40	Nevada	129,995,000	0.3%
41	West Virginia	103,560,000	0.2%
42	North Dakota	96,606,000	0.2%
43	Iowa	84,877,000	0.2%
44	Delaware	84,651,000	0.2%
45	Idaho	76,985,000	0.2%
46	Montana	70,226,000	0.2%
47	South Dakota	65,809,000	0.1%
48	New Hampshire	64,214,000	0.1%
49	Wyoming	55,905,000	0.1%
50	Vermont	28,895,000	0.1%
	District of Columbia	1,310,121,000	2.9%

Source: U.S. Department of Defense
 "Atlas/Data Abstract for the United States" (http://siadapp.dior.whs.mil/personnel/L03/fy06/atlas_2006.pdf)
*Based on location of recipient. Does not include recipients in U.S. territories and other countries.

U.S. Department of Defense Reserve and National Guard Pay in 2006

National Total = $10,123,084,000*

ALPHA ORDER

RANK	STATE	PAYROLL	% of USA
9	Alabama	$323,668,000	3.2%
46	Alaska	49,961,000	0.5%
40	Arizona	68,707,000	0.7%
22	Arkansas	201,668,000	2.0%
2	California	660,546,000	6.5%
33	Colorado	120,474,000	1.2%
36	Connecticut	81,827,000	0.8%
48	Delaware	37,929,000	0.4%
6	Florida	341,721,000	3.4%
4	Georgia	417,753,000	4.1%
31	Hawaii	151,745,000	1.5%
37	Idaho	72,606,000	0.7%
13	Illinois	253,758,000	2.5%
8	Indiana	325,316,000	3.2%
26	Iowa	171,199,000	1.7%
23	Kansas	201,183,000	2.0%
25	Kentucky	195,495,000	1.9%
19	Louisiana	213,759,000	2.1%
47	Maine	46,442,000	0.5%
27	Maryland	170,867,000	1.7%
28	Massachusetts	162,097,000	1.6%
24	Michigan	200,523,000	2.0%
7	Minnesota	326,760,000	3.2%
15	Mississippi	240,066,000	2.4%
3	Missouri	583,169,000	5.8%
43	Montana	57,373,000	0.6%
34	Nebraska	107,682,000	1.1%
45	Nevada	55,720,000	0.6%
49	New Hampshire	31,523,000	0.3%
29	New Jersey	159,175,000	1.6%
38	New Mexico	72,537,000	0.7%
10	New York	300,831,000	3.0%
11	North Carolina	277,907,000	2.7%
44	North Dakota	56,702,000	0.6%
14	Ohio	240,236,000	2.4%
30	Oklahoma	152,985,000	1.5%
32	Oregon	128,472,000	1.3%
5	Pennsylvania	410,026,000	4.1%
41	Rhode Island	60,929,000	0.6%
21	South Carolina	207,426,000	2.0%
42	South Dakota	57,821,000	0.6%
16	Tennessee	235,262,000	2.3%
1	Texas	675,960,000	6.7%
20	Utah	212,721,000	2.1%
39	Vermont	72,465,000	0.7%
12	Virginia	270,631,000	2.7%
18	Washington	216,610,000	2.1%
35	West Virginia	97,464,000	1.0%
17	Wisconsin	234,117,000	2.3%
50	Wyoming	30,701,000	0.3%

RANK ORDER

RANK	STATE	PAYROLL	% of USA
1	Texas	$675,960,000	6.7%
2	California	660,546,000	6.5%
3	Missouri	583,169,000	5.8%
4	Georgia	417,753,000	4.1%
5	Pennsylvania	410,026,000	4.1%
6	Florida	341,721,000	3.4%
7	Minnesota	326,760,000	3.2%
8	Indiana	325,316,000	3.2%
9	Alabama	323,668,000	3.2%
10	New York	300,831,000	3.0%
11	North Carolina	277,907,000	2.7%
12	Virginia	270,631,000	2.7%
13	Illinois	253,758,000	2.5%
14	Ohio	240,236,000	2.4%
15	Mississippi	240,066,000	2.4%
16	Tennessee	235,262,000	2.3%
17	Wisconsin	234,117,000	2.3%
18	Washington	216,610,000	2.1%
19	Louisiana	213,759,000	2.1%
20	Utah	212,721,000	2.1%
21	South Carolina	207,426,000	2.0%
22	Arkansas	201,668,000	2.0%
23	Kansas	201,183,000	2.0%
24	Michigan	200,523,000	2.0%
25	Kentucky	195,495,000	1.9%
26	Iowa	171,199,000	1.7%
27	Maryland	170,867,000	1.7%
28	Massachusetts	162,097,000	1.6%
29	New Jersey	159,175,000	1.6%
30	Oklahoma	152,985,000	1.5%
31	Hawaii	151,745,000	1.5%
32	Oregon	128,472,000	1.3%
33	Colorado	120,474,000	1.2%
34	Nebraska	107,682,000	1.1%
35	West Virginia	97,464,000	1.0%
36	Connecticut	81,827,000	0.8%
37	Idaho	72,606,000	0.7%
38	New Mexico	72,537,000	0.7%
39	Vermont	72,465,000	0.7%
40	Arizona	68,707,000	0.7%
41	Rhode Island	60,929,000	0.6%
42	South Dakota	57,821,000	0.6%
43	Montana	57,373,000	0.6%
44	North Dakota	56,702,000	0.6%
45	Nevada	55,720,000	0.6%
46	Alaska	49,961,000	0.5%
47	Maine	46,442,000	0.5%
48	Delaware	37,929,000	0.4%
49	New Hampshire	31,523,000	0.3%
50	Wyoming	30,701,000	0.3%
	District of Columbia	80,569,000	0.8%

Source: U.S. Department of Defense
"Atlas/Data Abstract for the United States" (http://siadapp.dior.whs.mil/personnel/L03/fy06/atlas_2006.pdf)
*Based on location of recipient. Does not include recipients in U.S. territories and other countries.

U.S. Department of Defense Retired Military Pay in 2006

National Total = $35,800,827,000*

RANK	STATE	PAYROLL	% of USA
12	Alabama	$940,533,000	2.6%
43	Alaska	149,157,000	0.4%
9	Arizona	1,014,127,000	2.8%
23	Arkansas	409,929,000	1.1%
2	California	3,535,452,000	9.9%
10	Colorado	1,000,382,000	2.8%
39	Connecticut	177,734,000	0.5%
45	Delaware	132,343,000	0.4%
1	Florida	3,721,804,000	10.4%
5	Georgia	1,525,324,000	4.3%
31	Hawaii	308,535,000	0.9%
37	Idaho	207,708,000	0.6%
16	Illinois	578,418,000	1.6%
29	Indiana	342,890,000	1.0%
41	Iowa	160,927,000	0.4%
27	Kansas	363,186,000	1.0%
24	Kentucky	405,349,000	1.1%
21	Louisiana	430,404,000	1.2%
38	Maine	193,936,000	0.5%
8	Maryland	1,015,461,000	2.8%
32	Massachusetts	303,576,000	0.8%
26	Michigan	388,844,000	1.1%
36	Minnesota	241,903,000	0.7%
22	Mississippi	419,418,000	1.2%
17	Missouri	574,023,000	1.6%
44	Montana	133,308,000	0.4%
35	Nebraska	243,879,000	0.7%
19	Nevada	505,602,000	1.4%
40	New Hampshire	175,426,000	0.5%
30	New Jersey	321,376,000	0.9%
25	New Mexico	404,727,000	1.1%
20	New York	502,980,000	1.4%
6	North Carolina	1,453,752,000	4.1%
49	North Dakota	65,900,000	0.2%
15	Ohio	698,387,000	2.0%
18	Oklahoma	544,382,000	1.5%
28	Oregon	362,691,000	1.0%
14	Pennsylvania	766,857,000	2.1%
46	Rhode Island	107,183,000	0.3%
11	South Carolina	945,449,000	2.6%
47	South Dakota	105,535,000	0.3%
13	Tennessee	815,654,000	2.3%
4	Texas	3,461,234,000	9.7%
34	Utah	247,419,000	0.7%
50	Vermont	55,084,000	0.2%
3	Virginia	3,494,218,000	9.8%
7	Washington	1,294,932,000	3.6%
42	West Virginia	154,527,000	0.4%
33	Wisconsin	262,279,000	0.7%
48	Wyoming	79,296,000	0.2%

RANK	STATE	PAYROLL	% of USA
1	Florida	$3,721,804,000	10.4%
2	California	3,535,452,000	9.9%
3	Virginia	3,494,218,000	9.8%
4	Texas	3,461,234,000	9.7%
5	Georgia	1,525,324,000	4.3%
6	North Carolina	1,453,752,000	4.1%
7	Washington	1,294,932,000	3.6%
8	Maryland	1,015,461,000	2.8%
9	Arizona	1,014,127,000	2.8%
10	Colorado	1,000,382,000	2.8%
11	South Carolina	945,449,000	2.6%
12	Alabama	940,533,000	2.6%
13	Tennessee	815,654,000	2.3%
14	Pennsylvania	766,857,000	2.1%
15	Ohio	698,387,000	2.0%
16	Illinois	578,418,000	1.6%
17	Missouri	574,023,000	1.6%
18	Oklahoma	544,382,000	1.5%
19	Nevada	505,602,000	1.4%
20	New York	502,980,000	1.4%
21	Louisiana	430,404,000	1.2%
22	Mississippi	419,418,000	1.2%
23	Arkansas	409,929,000	1.1%
24	Kentucky	405,349,000	1.1%
25	New Mexico	404,727,000	1.1%
26	Michigan	388,844,000	1.1%
27	Kansas	363,186,000	1.0%
28	Oregon	362,691,000	1.0%
29	Indiana	342,890,000	1.0%
30	New Jersey	321,376,000	0.9%
31	Hawaii	308,535,000	0.9%
32	Massachusetts	303,576,000	0.8%
33	Wisconsin	262,279,000	0.7%
34	Utah	247,419,000	0.7%
35	Nebraska	243,879,000	0.7%
36	Minnesota	241,903,000	0.7%
37	Idaho	207,708,000	0.6%
38	Maine	193,936,000	0.5%
39	Connecticut	177,734,000	0.5%
40	New Hampshire	175,426,000	0.5%
41	Iowa	160,927,000	0.4%
42	West Virginia	154,527,000	0.4%
43	Alaska	149,157,000	0.4%
44	Montana	133,308,000	0.4%
45	Delaware	132,343,000	0.4%
46	Rhode Island	107,183,000	0.3%
47	South Dakota	105,535,000	0.3%
48	Wyoming	79,296,000	0.2%
49	North Dakota	65,900,000	0.2%
50	Vermont	55,084,000	0.2%
	District of Columbia	57,387,000	0.2%

Source: U.S. Department of Defense
"Atlas/Data Abstract for the United States" (http://siadapp.dior.whs.mil/personnel/L03/fy06/atlas_2006.pdf)
*Based on location of recipient. Does not include recipients in U.S. territories and other countries.

Veterans in 2007

National Total = 23,531,672 Veterans*

ALPHA ORDER

RANK	STATE	VETERANS	% of USA
22	Alabama	412,232	1.8%
47	Alaska	64,821	0.3%
13	Arizona	545,960	2.3%
29	Arkansas	259,246	1.1%
1	California	2,147,769	9.1%
21	Colorado	415,020	1.8%
32	Connecticut	243,469	1.0%
45	Delaware	77,986	0.3%
2	Florida	1,722,691	7.3%
9	Georgia	753,321	3.2%
42	Hawaii	99,768	0.4%
40	Idaho	130,777	0.6%
7	Illinois	829,660	3.5%
17	Indiana	524,835	2.2%
30	Iowa	249,043	1.1%
34	Kansas	232,837	1.0%
27	Kentucky	346,179	1.5%
26	Louisiana	350,504	1.5%
39	Maine	136,513	0.6%
18	Maryland	462,106	2.0%
20	Massachusetts	447,649	1.9%
8	Michigan	786,700	3.3%
24	Minnesota	401,548	1.7%
33	Mississippi	233,888	1.0%
14	Missouri	529,192	2.2%
43	Montana	98,852	0.4%
37	Nebraska	150,766	0.6%
31	Nevada	243,710	1.0%
41	New Hampshire	125,406	0.5%
16	New Jersey	526,651	2.2%
36	New Mexico	173,477	0.7%
5	New York	1,055,882	4.5%
10	North Carolina	748,758	3.2%
50	North Dakota	51,806	0.2%
6	Ohio	991,671	4.2%
28	Oklahoma	341,691	1.5%
25	Oregon	352,037	1.5%
4	Pennsylvania	1,058,615	4.5%
44	Rhode Island	83,861	0.4%
23	South Carolina	407,200	1.7%
46	South Dakota	69,648	0.3%
15	Tennessee	526,671	2.2%
3	Texas	1,633,507	6.9%
38	Utah	144,252	0.6%
48	Vermont	54,531	0.2%
11	Virginia	728,755	3.1%
12	Washington	608,908	2.6%
35	West Virginia	179,092	0.8%
19	Wisconsin	448,324	1.9%
49	Wyoming	52,961	0.2%

RANK ORDER

RANK	STATE	VETERANS	% of USA
1	California	2,147,769	9.1%
2	Florida	1,722,691	7.3%
3	Texas	1,633,507	6.9%
4	Pennsylvania	1,058,615	4.5%
5	New York	1,055,882	4.5%
6	Ohio	991,671	4.2%
7	Illinois	829,660	3.5%
8	Michigan	786,700	3.3%
9	Georgia	753,321	3.2%
10	North Carolina	748,758	3.2%
11	Virginia	728,755	3.1%
12	Washington	608,908	2.6%
13	Arizona	545,960	2.3%
14	Missouri	529,192	2.2%
15	Tennessee	526,671	2.2%
16	New Jersey	526,651	2.2%
17	Indiana	524,835	2.2%
18	Maryland	462,106	2.0%
19	Wisconsin	448,324	1.9%
20	Massachusetts	447,649	1.9%
21	Colorado	415,020	1.8%
22	Alabama	412,232	1.8%
23	South Carolina	407,200	1.7%
24	Minnesota	401,548	1.7%
25	Oregon	352,037	1.5%
26	Louisiana	350,504	1.5%
27	Kentucky	346,179	1.5%
28	Oklahoma	341,691	1.5%
29	Arkansas	259,246	1.1%
30	Iowa	249,043	1.1%
31	Nevada	243,710	1.0%
32	Connecticut	243,469	1.0%
33	Mississippi	233,888	1.0%
34	Kansas	232,837	1.0%
35	West Virginia	179,092	0.8%
36	New Mexico	173,477	0.7%
37	Nebraska	150,766	0.6%
38	Utah	144,252	0.6%
39	Maine	136,513	0.6%
40	Idaho	130,777	0.6%
41	New Hampshire	125,406	0.5%
42	Hawaii	99,768	0.4%
43	Montana	98,852	0.4%
44	Rhode Island	83,861	0.4%
45	Delaware	77,986	0.3%
46	South Dakota	69,648	0.3%
47	Alaska	64,821	0.3%
48	Vermont	54,531	0.2%
49	Wyoming	52,961	0.2%
50	North Dakota	51,806	0.2%
	District of Columbia	33,567	0.1%

Source: U.S. Department of Veteran Affairs
   "Veteran Data and Information" (http://www1.va.gov/vetdata/page.cfm?pg=2)
*Estimates based on 2004 data. Includes 237,357 veterans in U.S. territories or other countries.

Percent of Adult Population Who are Veterans: 2007

National Percent = 10.3%*

ALPHA ORDER

RANK	STATE	PERCENT
21	Alabama	11.8
3	Alaska	13.3
16	Arizona	12.0
13	Arkansas	12.2
48	California	8.0
22	Colorado	11.6
44	Connecticut	9.1
16	Delaware	12.0
13	Florida	12.2
33	Georgia	10.9
41	Hawaii	10.1
13	Idaho	12.2
46	Illinois	8.6
28	Indiana	11.1
30	Iowa	11.0
26	Kansas	11.3
36	Kentucky	10.8
30	Louisiana	11.0
4	Maine	13.1
33	Maryland	10.9
45	Massachusetts	9.0
39	Michigan	10.3
39	Minnesota	10.3
33	Mississippi	10.9
16	Missouri	12.0
1	Montana	13.6
24	Nebraska	11.4
4	Nevada	13.1
12	New Hampshire	12.3
49	New Jersey	7.9
16	New Mexico	12.0
50	New York	7.1
27	North Carolina	11.2
37	North Dakota	10.6
24	Ohio	11.4
6	Oklahoma	12.7
10	Oregon	12.4
30	Pennsylvania	11.0
41	Rhode Island	10.1
10	South Carolina	12.4
20	South Dakota	11.9
23	Tennessee	11.5
43	Texas	9.6
47	Utah	8.2
28	Vermont	11.1
7	Virginia	12.5
7	Washington	12.5
7	West Virginia	12.5
37	Wisconsin	10.6
2	Wyoming	13.5

RANK ORDER

RANK	STATE	PERCENT
1	Montana	13.6
2	Wyoming	13.5
3	Alaska	13.3
4	Maine	13.1
4	Nevada	13.1
6	Oklahoma	12.7
7	Virginia	12.5
7	Washington	12.5
7	West Virginia	12.5
10	Oregon	12.4
10	South Carolina	12.4
12	New Hampshire	12.3
13	Arkansas	12.2
13	Florida	12.2
13	Idaho	12.2
16	Arizona	12.0
16	Delaware	12.0
16	Missouri	12.0
16	New Mexico	12.0
20	South Dakota	11.9
21	Alabama	11.8
22	Colorado	11.6
23	Tennessee	11.5
24	Nebraska	11.4
24	Ohio	11.4
26	Kansas	11.3
27	North Carolina	11.2
28	Indiana	11.1
28	Vermont	11.1
30	Iowa	11.0
30	Louisiana	11.0
30	Pennsylvania	11.0
33	Georgia	10.9
33	Maryland	10.9
33	Mississippi	10.9
36	Kentucky	10.8
37	North Dakota	10.6
37	Wisconsin	10.6
39	Michigan	10.3
39	Minnesota	10.3
41	Hawaii	10.1
41	Rhode Island	10.1
43	Texas	9.6
44	Connecticut	9.1
45	Massachusetts	9.0
46	Illinois	8.6
47	Utah	8.2
48	California	8.0
49	New Jersey	7.9
50	New York	7.1

	District of Columbia	7.2

Source: CQ Press using data from U.S. Department of Veteran Affairs
   "Veteran Data and Information" (http://www1.va.gov/vetdata/page.cfm?pg=2)
*Estimates based on 2004 data. National figures does not include veterans in U.S. territories or other countries. Percent calculated with population 18 years old and older in 2006.

U.S. Military Fatalities in Iraq as of January 28, 2008

National Total = 3,923 Fatalities*

ALPHA ORDER

RANK	STATE	FATALITIES	% of USA
22	Alabama	66	1.7%
46	Alaska	17	0.4%
12	Arizona	88	2.2%
26	Arkansas	59	1.5%
1	California	422	10.8%
28	Colorado	54	1.4%
36	Connecticut	29	0.7%
48	Delaware	13	0.3%
5	Florida	167	4.3%
9	Georgia	120	3.1%
38	Hawaii	22	0.6%
36	Idaho	29	0.7%
8	Illinois	141	3.6%
13	Indiana	85	2.2%
31	Iowa	45	1.1%
32	Kansas	44	1.1%
24	Kentucky	63	1.6%
17	Louisiana	77	2.0%
38	Maine	22	0.6%
18	Maryland	71	1.8%
23	Massachusetts	64	1.6%
7	Michigan	148	3.8%
27	Minnesota	58	1.5%
30	Mississippi	46	1.2%
18	Missouri	71	1.8%
38	Montana	22	0.6%
33	Nebraska	43	1.1%
35	Nevada	34	0.9%
43	New Hampshire	20	0.5%
20	New Jersey	69	1.8%
34	New Mexico	35	0.9%
4	New York	173	4.4%
11	North Carolina	90	2.3%
47	North Dakota	14	0.4%
6	Ohio	165	4.2%
24	Oklahoma	63	1.6%
21	Oregon	67	1.7%
3	Pennsylvania	178	4.5%
49	Rhode Island	12	0.3%
29	South Carolina	49	1.2%
45	South Dakota	18	0.5%
14	Tennessee	84	2.1%
2	Texas	362	9.2%
42	Utah	21	0.5%
44	Vermont	19	0.5%
10	Virginia	111	2.8%
16	Washington	81	2.1%
38	West Virginia	22	0.6%
15	Wisconsin	83	2.1%
50	Wyoming	11	0.3%

RANK ORDER

RANK	STATE	FATALITIES	% of USA
1	California	422	10.8%
2	Texas	362	9.2%
3	Pennsylvania	178	4.5%
4	New York	173	4.4%
5	Florida	167	4.3%
6	Ohio	165	4.2%
7	Michigan	148	3.8%
8	Illinois	141	3.6%
9	Georgia	120	3.1%
10	Virginia	111	2.8%
11	North Carolina	90	2.3%
12	Arizona	88	2.2%
13	Indiana	85	2.2%
14	Tennessee	84	2.1%
15	Wisconsin	83	2.1%
16	Washington	81	2.1%
17	Louisiana	77	2.0%
18	Maryland	71	1.8%
18	Missouri	71	1.8%
20	New Jersey	69	1.8%
21	Oregon	67	1.7%
22	Alabama	66	1.7%
23	Massachusetts	64	1.6%
24	Kentucky	63	1.6%
24	Oklahoma	63	1.6%
26	Arkansas	59	1.5%
27	Minnesota	58	1.5%
28	Colorado	54	1.4%
29	South Carolina	49	1.2%
30	Mississippi	46	1.2%
31	Iowa	45	1.1%
32	Kansas	44	1.1%
33	Nebraska	43	1.1%
34	New Mexico	35	0.9%
35	Nevada	34	0.9%
36	Connecticut	29	0.7%
36	Idaho	29	0.7%
38	Hawaii	22	0.6%
38	Maine	22	0.6%
38	Montana	22	0.6%
38	West Virginia	22	0.6%
42	Utah	21	0.5%
43	New Hampshire	20	0.5%
44	Vermont	19	0.5%
45	South Dakota	18	0.5%
46	Alaska	17	0.4%
47	North Dakota	14	0.4%
48	Delaware	13	0.3%
49	Rhode Island	12	0.3%
50	Wyoming	11	0.3%
	District of Columbia	4	0.1%

Source: Iraq Coalition Casualty Count
    "U.S. Fatalities by State" (http://icasualties.org/oif/Statecity.aspx)
*As of January 28, 2008. Total includes 52 deaths of soldiers from U.S. territories. Total does not include deaths of United Kingdom soldiers or other coalition nations. Includes combat and noncombat deaths. Does not include 482 U.S. military deaths from efforts in Afghanistan.

Rate of U.S. Military Fatalities in Iraq as of January 28, 2008

National Rate = 1.28 Fatalities per 100,000 Population*

ALPHA ORDER

RANK	STATE	RATE
27	Alabama	1.43
2	Alaska	2.49
29	Arizona	1.39
8	Arkansas	2.08
38	California	1.15
41	Colorado	1.11
48	Connecticut	0.83
21	Delaware	1.50
46	Florida	0.92
33	Georgia	1.26
14	Hawaii	1.71
9	Idaho	1.93
43	Illinois	1.10
31	Indiana	1.34
19	Iowa	1.51
16	Kansas	1.59
22	Kentucky	1.49
10	Louisiana	1.79
15	Maine	1.67
33	Maryland	1.26
44	Massachusetts	0.99
24	Michigan	1.47
40	Minnesota	1.12
17	Mississippi	1.58
36	Missouri	1.21
4	Montana	2.30
3	Nebraska	2.42
32	Nevada	1.33
18	New Hampshire	1.52
49	New Jersey	0.79
12	New Mexico	1.78
47	New York	0.90
44	North Carolina	0.99
6	North Dakota	2.19
25	Ohio	1.44
13	Oklahoma	1.74
10	Oregon	1.79
27	Pennsylvania	1.43
39	Rhode Island	1.13
41	South Carolina	1.11
5	South Dakota	2.26
30	Tennessee	1.36
19	Texas	1.51
49	Utah	0.79
1	Vermont	3.06
25	Virginia	1.44
35	Washington	1.25
36	West Virginia	1.21
23	Wisconsin	1.48
7	Wyoming	2.10

RANK ORDER

RANK	STATE	RATE
1	Vermont	3.06
2	Alaska	2.49
3	Nebraska	2.42
4	Montana	2.30
5	South Dakota	2.26
6	North Dakota	2.19
7	Wyoming	2.10
8	Arkansas	2.08
9	Idaho	1.93
10	Louisiana	1.79
10	Oregon	1.79
12	New Mexico	1.78
13	Oklahoma	1.74
14	Hawaii	1.71
15	Maine	1.67
16	Kansas	1.59
17	Mississippi	1.58
18	New Hampshire	1.52
19	Iowa	1.51
19	Texas	1.51
21	Delaware	1.50
22	Kentucky	1.49
23	Wisconsin	1.48
24	Michigan	1.47
25	Ohio	1.44
25	Virginia	1.44
27	Alabama	1.43
27	Pennsylvania	1.43
29	Arizona	1.39
30	Tennessee	1.36
31	Indiana	1.34
32	Nevada	1.33
33	Georgia	1.26
33	Maryland	1.26
35	Washington	1.25
36	Missouri	1.21
36	West Virginia	1.21
38	California	1.15
39	Rhode Island	1.13
40	Minnesota	1.12
41	Colorado	1.11
41	South Carolina	1.11
43	Illinois	1.10
44	Massachusetts	0.99
44	North Carolina	0.99
46	Florida	0.92
47	New York	0.90
48	Connecticut	0.83
49	New Jersey	0.79
49	Utah	0.79
	District of Columbia	0.68

Source: CQ Press using data from Iraq Coalition Casualty Count
"U.S. Fatalities by State" (http://icasualties.org/oif/Statecity.aspx)

*As of January 28, 2008. National rate does not include deaths of soldiers from U.S. territories. Includes combat and noncombat deaths. Does not include U.S. military deaths from efforts in Afghanistan. Calculated with 2007 population estimates.

IV. Economy

Gross Domestic Product in 2006

National Total = $13,149,033,000,000*

ALPHA ORDER

RANK	STATE	G.D.P.	% of USA
25	Alabama	$160,569,000,000	1.2%
45	Alaska	41,105,000,000	0.3%
19	Arizona	232,463,000,000	1.8%
34	Arkansas	91,837,000,000	0.7%
1	California	1,727,355,000,000	13.1%
20	Colorado	230,478,000,000	1.8%
23	Connecticut	204,134,000,000	1.6%
38	Delaware	60,361,000,000	0.5%
4	Florida	713,505,000,000	5.4%
10	Georgia	379,550,000,000	2.9%
39	Hawaii	58,307,000,000	0.4%
42	Idaho	49,907,000,000	0.4%
5	Illinois	589,598,000,000	4.5%
16	Indiana	248,915,000,000	1.9%
30	Iowa	123,970,000,000	0.9%
32	Kansas	111,699,000,000	0.8%
28	Kentucky	145,959,000,000	1.1%
24	Louisiana	193,138,000,000	1.5%
43	Maine	46,973,000,000	0.4%
15	Maryland	257,815,000,000	2.0%
13	Massachusetts	337,570,000,000	2.6%
9	Michigan	381,003,000,000	2.9%
17	Minnesota	244,546,000,000	1.9%
35	Mississippi	84,225,000,000	0.6%
22	Missouri	225,876,000,000	1.7%
47	Montana	32,322,000,000	0.2%
37	Nebraska	75,700,000,000	0.6%
31	Nevada	118,399,000,000	0.9%
40	New Hampshire	56,276,000,000	0.4%
8	New Jersey	453,177,000,000	3.4%
36	New Mexico	75,910,000,000	0.6%
3	New York	1,021,944,000,000	7.8%
11	North Carolina	374,525,000,000	2.8%
49	North Dakota	26,385,000,000	0.2%
7	Ohio	461,302,000,000	3.5%
29	Oklahoma	134,651,000,000	1.0%
26	Oregon	151,301,000,000	1.2%
6	Pennsylvania	510,293,000,000	3.9%
44	Rhode Island	45,660,000,000	0.3%
27	South Carolina	149,214,000,000	1.1%
46	South Dakota	32,330,000,000	0.2%
18	Tennessee	238,029,000,000	1.8%
2	Texas	1,065,891,000,000	8.1%
33	Utah	97,749,000,000	0.7%
50	Vermont	24,213,000,000	0.2%
12	Virginia	369,260,000,000	2.8%
14	Washington	293,531,000,000	2.2%
41	West Virginia	55,658,000,000	0.4%
21	Wisconsin	227,230,000,000	1.7%
48	Wyoming	29,561,000,000	0.2%

RANK ORDER

RANK	STATE	G.D.P.	% of USA
1	California	$1,727,355,000,000	13.1%
2	Texas	1,065,891,000,000	8.1%
3	New York	1,021,944,000,000	7.8%
4	Florida	713,505,000,000	5.4%
5	Illinois	589,598,000,000	4.5%
6	Pennsylvania	510,293,000,000	3.9%
7	Ohio	461,302,000,000	3.5%
8	New Jersey	453,177,000,000	3.4%
9	Michigan	381,003,000,000	2.9%
10	Georgia	379,550,000,000	2.9%
11	North Carolina	374,525,000,000	2.8%
12	Virginia	369,260,000,000	2.8%
13	Massachusetts	337,570,000,000	2.6%
14	Washington	293,531,000,000	2.2%
15	Maryland	257,815,000,000	2.0%
16	Indiana	248,915,000,000	1.9%
17	Minnesota	244,546,000,000	1.9%
18	Tennessee	238,029,000,000	1.8%
19	Arizona	232,463,000,000	1.8%
20	Colorado	230,478,000,000	1.8%
21	Wisconsin	227,230,000,000	1.7%
22	Missouri	225,876,000,000	1.7%
23	Connecticut	204,134,000,000	1.6%
24	Louisiana	193,138,000,000	1.5%
25	Alabama	160,569,000,000	1.2%
26	Oregon	151,301,000,000	1.2%
27	South Carolina	149,214,000,000	1.1%
28	Kentucky	145,959,000,000	1.1%
29	Oklahoma	134,651,000,000	1.0%
30	Iowa	123,970,000,000	0.9%
31	Nevada	118,399,000,000	0.9%
32	Kansas	111,699,000,000	0.8%
33	Utah	97,749,000,000	0.7%
34	Arkansas	91,837,000,000	0.7%
35	Mississippi	84,225,000,000	0.6%
36	New Mexico	75,910,000,000	0.6%
37	Nebraska	75,700,000,000	0.6%
38	Delaware	60,361,000,000	0.5%
39	Hawaii	58,307,000,000	0.4%
40	New Hampshire	56,276,000,000	0.4%
41	West Virginia	55,658,000,000	0.4%
42	Idaho	49,907,000,000	0.4%
43	Maine	46,973,000,000	0.4%
44	Rhode Island	45,660,000,000	0.3%
45	Alaska	41,105,000,000	0.3%
46	South Dakota	32,330,000,000	0.2%
47	Montana	32,322,000,000	0.2%
48	Wyoming	29,561,000,000	0.2%
49	North Dakota	26,385,000,000	0.2%
50	Vermont	24,213,000,000	0.2%
	District of Columbia	87,664,000,000	0.7%

Source: U.S. Department of Commerce, Bureau of Economic Analysis
   "Gross Domestic Product Data" (http://www.bea.gov/regional/gsp/)
*G.D.P. is the market value of goods and services produced by the labor and property located in a state. It is the state counterpart to the nation's Gross Domestic Product. This was formerly known as Gross State Product (G.S.P.).

Percent Change in Gross Domestic Product: 2002 to 2006
(Adjusted to Constant 2000 Dollars)
National Percent Change = 13.1% Increase*

ALPHA ORDER

RANK	STATE	PERCENT CHANGE
14	Alabama	15.6
49	Alaska	4.6
3	Arizona	23.6
20	Arkansas	13.7
12	California	17.0
24	Colorado	13.2
29	Connecticut	11.2
10	Delaware	17.8
4	Florida	22.6
27	Georgia	12.6
8	Hawaii	19.1
2	Idaho	26.9
41	Illinois	8.8
38	Indiana	9.2
15	Iowa	14.6
31	Kansas	11.0
43	Kentucky	8.7
41	Louisiana	8.8
39	Maine	9.1
20	Maryland	13.7
36	Massachusetts	9.4
50	Michigan	0.3
28	Minnesota	11.6
44	Mississippi	8.5
45	Missouri	8.1
9	Montana	18.6
24	Nebraska	13.2
1	Nevada	28.9
30	New Hampshire	11.1
36	New Jersey	9.4
5	New Mexico	21.1
20	New York	13.7
17	North Carolina	14.4
13	North Dakota	16.4
47	Ohio	6.4
19	Oklahoma	13.8
5	Oregon	21.1
46	Pennsylvania	7.5
31	Rhode Island	11.0
33	South Carolina	10.7
33	South Dakota	10.7
24	Tennessee	13.2
18	Texas	14.1
7	Utah	19.4
20	Vermont	13.7
11	Virginia	17.5
15	Washington	14.6
48	West Virginia	6.0
40	Wisconsin	9.0
35	Wyoming	9.6

RANK ORDER

RANK	STATE	PERCENT CHANGE
1	Nevada	28.9
2	Idaho	26.9
3	Arizona	23.6
4	Florida	22.6
5	New Mexico	21.1
5	Oregon	21.1
7	Utah	19.4
8	Hawaii	19.1
9	Montana	18.6
10	Delaware	17.8
11	Virginia	17.5
12	California	17.0
13	North Dakota	16.4
14	Alabama	15.6
15	Iowa	14.6
15	Washington	14.6
17	North Carolina	14.4
18	Texas	14.1
19	Oklahoma	13.8
20	Arkansas	13.7
20	Maryland	13.7
20	New York	13.7
20	Vermont	13.7
24	Colorado	13.2
24	Nebraska	13.2
24	Tennessee	13.2
27	Georgia	12.6
28	Minnesota	11.6
29	Connecticut	11.2
30	New Hampshire	11.1
31	Kansas	11.0
31	Rhode Island	11.0
33	South Carolina	10.7
33	South Dakota	10.7
35	Wyoming	9.6
36	Massachusetts	9.4
36	New Jersey	9.4
38	Indiana	9.2
39	Maine	9.1
40	Wisconsin	9.0
41	Illinois	8.8
41	Louisiana	8.8
43	Kentucky	8.7
44	Mississippi	8.5
45	Missouri	8.1
46	Pennsylvania	7.5
47	Ohio	6.4
48	West Virginia	6.0
49	Alaska	4.6
50	Michigan	0.3

District of Columbia	15.1

Source: CQ Press using data from U.S. Department of Commerce, Bureau of Economic Analysis
  "Gross Domestic Product Data" (http://www.bea.gov/regional/gsp/)
*G.D.P. is the market value of goods and services produced by the labor and property located in a state. It is the state counterpart to the nation's Gross Domestic Product. This was formerly known as Gross State Product (G.S.P.). Adjusted for inflation using chained 2000 dollars.

Average Annual Change in Gross Domestic Product: 2002 to 2006
(Adjusted to Constant 2000 Dollars)
National Annual Percent Change = 2.5% Increase*

ALPHA ORDER

RANK	STATE	PERCENT CHANGE
14	Alabama	2.9
49	Alaska	0.9
3	Arizona	4.3
19	Arkansas	2.6
12	California	3.2
24	Colorado	2.5
29	Connecticut	2.1
10	Delaware	3.3
4	Florida	4.2
27	Georgia	2.4
7	Hawaii	3.6
2	Idaho	4.9
40	Illinois	1.7
35	Indiana	1.8
15	Iowa	2.8
29	Kansas	2.1
40	Kentucky	1.7
40	Louisiana	1.7
35	Maine	1.8
19	Maryland	2.6
35	Massachusetts	1.8
50	Michigan	0.1
28	Minnesota	2.2
44	Mississippi	1.6
44	Missouri	1.6
9	Montana	3.5
24	Nebraska	2.5
1	Nevada	5.2
29	New Hampshire	2.1
35	New Jersey	1.8
5	New Mexico	3.9
19	New York	2.6
17	North Carolina	2.7
13	North Dakota	3.1
47	Ohio	1.2
19	Oklahoma	2.6
5	Oregon	3.9
46	Pennsylvania	1.5
29	Rhode Island	2.1
29	South Carolina	2.1
29	South Dakota	2.1
24	Tennessee	2.5
17	Texas	2.7
7	Utah	3.6
19	Vermont	2.6
10	Virginia	3.3
15	Washington	2.8
47	West Virginia	1.2
40	Wisconsin	1.7
35	Wyoming	1.8

RANK ORDER

RANK	STATE	PERCENT CHANGE
1	Nevada	5.2
2	Idaho	4.9
3	Arizona	4.3
4	Florida	4.2
5	New Mexico	3.9
5	Oregon	3.9
7	Hawaii	3.6
7	Utah	3.6
9	Montana	3.5
10	Delaware	3.3
10	Virginia	3.3
12	California	3.2
13	North Dakota	3.1
14	Alabama	2.9
15	Iowa	2.8
15	Washington	2.8
17	North Carolina	2.7
17	Texas	2.7
19	Arkansas	2.6
19	Maryland	2.6
19	New York	2.6
19	Oklahoma	2.6
19	Vermont	2.6
24	Colorado	2.5
24	Nebraska	2.5
24	Tennessee	2.5
27	Georgia	2.4
28	Minnesota	2.2
29	Connecticut	2.1
29	Kansas	2.1
29	New Hampshire	2.1
29	Rhode Island	2.1
29	South Carolina	2.1
29	South Dakota	2.1
35	Indiana	1.8
35	Maine	1.8
35	Massachusetts	1.8
35	New Jersey	1.8
35	Wyoming	1.8
40	Illinois	1.7
40	Kentucky	1.7
40	Louisiana	1.7
40	Wisconsin	1.7
44	Mississippi	1.6
44	Missouri	1.6
46	Pennsylvania	1.5
47	Ohio	1.2
47	West Virginia	1.2
49	Alaska	0.9
50	Michigan	0.1
	District of Columbia	2.9

Source: CQ Press using data from U.S. Department of Commerce, Bureau of Economic Analysis
   "Gross Domestic Product Data" (http://www.bea.gov/regional/gsp/)
*G.D.P. is the market value of goods and services produced by the labor and property located in a state. It is the state counterpart to the nation's Gross Domestic Product. This was formerly known as Gross State Product (G.S.P.). Adjusted for inflation using chained 2000 dollars.

Per Capita Gross Domestic Product in 2006

National Per Capita = $44,013*

ALPHA ORDER

RANK	STATE	PER CAPITA
43	Alabama	$34,981
2	Alaska	60,676
40	Arizona	37,703
48	Arkansas	32,693
10	California	47,651
8	Colorado	48,356
3	Connecticut	58,395
1	Delaware	70,784
32	Florida	39,513
29	Georgia	40,628
16	Hawaii	45,601
47	Idaho	34,092
13	Illinois	46,145
33	Indiana	39,494
23	Iowa	41,705
30	Kansas	40,532
44	Kentucky	34,715
18	Louisiana	45,516
42	Maine	35,723
15	Maryland	46,022
6	Massachusetts	52,463
39	Michigan	37,714
12	Minnesota	47,442
50	Mississippi	29,052
37	Missouri	38,693
46	Montana	34,138
20	Nebraska	42,920
11	Nevada	47,503
21	New Hampshire	42,899
7	New Jersey	52,293
35	New Mexico	39,082
5	New York	53,000
22	North Carolina	42,226
24	North Dakota	41,391
31	Ohio	40,241
41	Oklahoma	37,638
27	Oregon	40,991
25	Pennsylvania	41,143
19	Rhode Island	43,009
45	South Carolina	34,460
26	South Dakota	41,004
34	Tennessee	39,182
17	Texas	45,536
38	Utah	37,894
36	Vermont	39,004
9	Virginia	48,331
14	Washington	46,045
49	West Virginia	30,772
28	Wisconsin	40,776
4	Wyoming	57,651

RANK ORDER

RANK	STATE	PER CAPITA
1	Delaware	$70,784
2	Alaska	60,676
3	Connecticut	58,395
4	Wyoming	57,651
5	New York	53,000
6	Massachusetts	52,463
7	New Jersey	52,293
8	Colorado	48,356
9	Virginia	48,331
10	California	47,651
11	Nevada	47,503
12	Minnesota	47,442
13	Illinois	46,145
14	Washington	46,045
15	Maryland	46,022
16	Hawaii	45,601
17	Texas	45,536
18	Louisiana	45,516
19	Rhode Island	43,009
20	Nebraska	42,920
21	New Hampshire	42,899
22	North Carolina	42,226
23	Iowa	41,705
24	North Dakota	41,391
25	Pennsylvania	41,143
26	South Dakota	41,004
27	Oregon	40,991
28	Wisconsin	40,776
29	Georgia	40,628
30	Kansas	40,532
31	Ohio	40,241
32	Florida	39,513
33	Indiana	39,494
34	Tennessee	39,182
35	New Mexico	39,082
36	Vermont	39,004
37	Missouri	38,693
38	Utah	37,894
39	Michigan	37,714
40	Arizona	37,703
41	Oklahoma	37,638
42	Maine	35,723
43	Alabama	34,981
44	Kentucky	34,715
45	South Carolina	34,460
46	Montana	34,138
47	Idaho	34,092
48	Arkansas	32,693
49	West Virginia	30,772
50	Mississippi	29,052

	District of Columbia	149,736

Source: CQ Press using data from U.S. Department of Commerce, Bureau of Economic Analysis
  "Gross Domestic Product Data" (http://www.bea.gov/regional/gsp/)
*G.D.P. is the market value of goods and services produced by the labor and property located in a state. It is the state counterpart to the nation's Gross Domestic Product. This was formerly known as Gross State Product (G.S.P.).

Percent Change in Per Capita Gross Domestic Product: 2002 to 2006
(Adjusted to Constant 2000 Dollars)
National Percent Change = 8.9% Increase*

ALPHA ORDER

RANK	STATE	PERCENT CHANGE
11	Alabama	12.5
49	Alaska	0.0
24	Arizona	9.1
22	Arkansas	9.5
12	California	12.4
34	Colorado	7.2
21	Connecticut	9.7
16	Delaware	11.2
8	Florida	13.1
48	Georgia	3.4
5	Hawaii	14.3
1	Idaho	16.4
36	Illinois	6.8
39	Indiana	6.5
10	Iowa	12.8
25	Kansas	9.0
43	Kentucky	5.7
7	Louisiana	13.4
35	Maine	7.0
20	Maryland	10.1
23	Massachusetts	9.3
50	Michigan	(0.3)
28	Minnesota	8.6
37	Mississippi	6.7
46	Missouri	5.1
5	Montana	14.3
19	Nebraska	10.5
14	Nevada	12.0
30	New Hampshire	7.7
32	New Jersey	7.6
4	New Mexico	14.9
9	New York	12.9
33	North Carolina	7.4
2	North Dakota	16.0
42	Ohio	5.8
18	Oklahoma	10.9
3	Oregon	15.3
39	Pennsylvania	6.5
17	Rhode Island	11.1
46	South Carolina	5.1
30	South Dakota	7.7
29	Tennessee	8.5
44	Texas	5.6
26	Utah	8.9
13	Vermont	12.3
14	Virginia	12.0
27	Washington	8.8
45	West Virginia	5.2
37	Wisconsin	6.7
41	Wyoming	6.1

RANK ORDER

RANK	STATE	PERCENT CHANGE
1	Idaho	16.4
2	North Dakota	16.0
3	Oregon	15.3
4	New Mexico	14.9
5	Hawaii	14.3
5	Montana	14.3
7	Louisiana	13.4
8	Florida	13.1
9	New York	12.9
10	Iowa	12.8
11	Alabama	12.5
12	California	12.4
13	Vermont	12.3
14	Nevada	12.0
14	Virginia	12.0
16	Delaware	11.2
17	Rhode Island	11.1
18	Oklahoma	10.9
19	Nebraska	10.5
20	Maryland	10.1
21	Connecticut	9.7
22	Arkansas	9.5
23	Massachusetts	9.3
24	Arizona	9.1
25	Kansas	9.0
26	Utah	8.9
27	Washington	8.8
28	Minnesota	8.6
29	Tennessee	8.5
30	New Hampshire	7.7
30	South Dakota	7.7
32	New Jersey	7.6
33	North Carolina	7.4
34	Colorado	7.2
35	Maine	7.0
36	Illinois	6.8
37	Mississippi	6.7
37	Wisconsin	6.7
39	Indiana	6.5
39	Pennsylvania	6.5
41	Wyoming	6.1
42	Ohio	5.8
43	Kentucky	5.7
44	Texas	5.6
45	West Virginia	5.2
46	Missouri	5.1
46	South Carolina	5.1
48	Georgia	3.4
49	Alaska	0.0
50	Michigan	(0.3)

	District of Columbia	14.6

Source: CQ Press using data from U.S. Department of Commerce, Bureau of Economic Analysis
  "Gross Domestic Product Data" (http://www.bea.gov/regional/gsp/)
*G.D.P. is the market value of goods and services produced by the labor and property located in a state. It is the state
counterpart to the nation's Gross Domestic Product. This was formerly known as Gross State Product (G.S.P.). Adjusted for
inflation using chained 2000 dollars.

Personal Income in 2006

National Total = $10,966,808,000,000*

RANK	STATE	INCOME	% of USA
24	Alabama	$141,838,062,000	1.3%
46	Alaska	25,878,837,000	0.2%
18	Arizona	197,008,991,000	1.8%
33	Arkansas	79,951,163,000	0.7%
1	California	1,434,909,558,000	13.1%
22	Colorado	188,173,243,000	1.7%
23	Connecticut	177,997,159,000	1.6%
44	Delaware	33,271,963,000	0.3%
4	Florida	663,260,710,000	6.0%
11	Georgia	299,884,835,000	2.7%
40	Hawaii	47,339,410,000	0.4%
41	Idaho	43,917,216,000	0.4%
5	Illinois	491,421,726,000	4.5%
16	Indiana	203,457,453,000	1.9%
30	Iowa	98,458,684,000	0.9%
32	Kansas	96,034,329,000	0.9%
27	Kentucky	125,000,728,000	1.1%
25	Louisiana	134,504,614,000	1.2%
42	Maine	42,199,321,000	0.4%
14	Maryland	245,821,150,000	2.2%
12	Massachusetts	297,754,674,000	2.7%
9	Michigan	341,075,070,000	3.1%
17	Minnesota	200,232,153,000	1.8%
34	Mississippi	78,317,451,000	0.7%
20	Missouri	191,601,916,000	1.7%
45	Montana	29,175,827,000	0.3%
36	Nebraska	60,801,061,000	0.6%
31	Nevada	97,362,540,000	0.9%
38	New Hampshire	52,141,774,000	0.5%
7	New Jersey	404,192,118,000	3.7%
37	New Mexico	58,101,012,000	0.5%
2	New York	848,744,137,000	7.7%
13	North Carolina	286,404,526,000	2.6%
49	North Dakota	21,005,256,000	0.2%
8	Ohio	381,260,142,000	3.5%
29	Oklahoma	115,959,812,000	1.1%
28	Oregon	123,059,010,000	1.1%
6	Pennsylvania	456,429,169,000	4.2%
43	Rhode Island	39,780,445,000	0.4%
26	South Carolina	128,290,812,000	1.2%
47	South Dakota	25,338,251,000	0.2%
19	Tennessee	195,085,114,000	1.8%
3	Texas	824,144,412,000	7.5%
35	Utah	75,913,503,000	0.7%
48	Vermont	21,601,346,000	0.2%
10	Virginia	302,381,894,000	2.8%
15	Washington	243,471,226,000	2.2%
39	West Virginia	51,038,834,000	0.5%
21	Wisconsin	191,566,836,000	1.7%
50	Wyoming	20,892,944,000	0.2%

RANK	STATE	INCOME	% of USA
1	California	$1,434,909,558,000	13.1%
2	New York	848,744,137,000	7.7%
3	Texas	824,144,412,000	7.5%
4	Florida	663,260,710,000	6.0%
5	Illinois	491,421,726,000	4.5%
6	Pennsylvania	456,429,169,000	4.2%
7	New Jersey	404,192,118,000	3.7%
8	Ohio	381,260,142,000	3.5%
9	Michigan	341,075,070,000	3.1%
10	Virginia	302,381,894,000	2.8%
11	Georgia	299,884,835,000	2.7%
12	Massachusetts	297,754,674,000	2.7%
13	North Carolina	286,404,526,000	2.6%
14	Maryland	245,821,150,000	2.2%
15	Washington	243,471,226,000	2.2%
16	Indiana	203,457,453,000	1.9%
17	Minnesota	200,232,153,000	1.8%
18	Arizona	197,008,991,000	1.8%
19	Tennessee	195,085,114,000	1.8%
20	Missouri	191,601,916,000	1.7%
21	Wisconsin	191,566,836,000	1.7%
22	Colorado	188,173,243,000	1.7%
23	Connecticut	177,997,159,000	1.6%
24	Alabama	141,838,062,000	1.3%
25	Louisiana	134,504,614,000	1.2%
26	South Carolina	128,290,812,000	1.2%
27	Kentucky	125,000,728,000	1.1%
28	Oregon	123,059,010,000	1.1%
29	Oklahoma	115,959,812,000	1.1%
30	Iowa	98,458,684,000	0.9%
31	Nevada	97,362,540,000	0.9%
32	Kansas	96,034,329,000	0.9%
33	Arkansas	79,951,163,000	0.7%
34	Mississippi	78,317,451,000	0.7%
35	Utah	75,913,503,000	0.7%
36	Nebraska	60,801,061,000	0.6%
37	New Mexico	58,101,012,000	0.5%
38	New Hampshire	52,141,774,000	0.5%
39	West Virginia	51,038,834,000	0.5%
40	Hawaii	47,339,410,000	0.4%
41	Idaho	43,917,216,000	0.4%
42	Maine	42,199,321,000	0.4%
43	Rhode Island	39,780,445,000	0.4%
44	Delaware	33,271,963,000	0.3%
45	Montana	29,175,827,000	0.3%
46	Alaska	25,878,837,000	0.2%
47	South Dakota	25,338,251,000	0.2%
48	Vermont	21,601,346,000	0.2%
49	North Dakota	21,005,256,000	0.2%
50	Wyoming	20,892,944,000	0.2%
	District of Columbia	33,355,583,000	0.3%

Source: U.S. Department of Commerce, Bureau of Economic Analysis
"Annual State Personal Income" (http://www.bea.gov/regional/spi/)
*The national total shown here is the sum of the state estimates. It differs from the national income and product accounts (NIPA) estimate of personal income because it omits the earnings of federal civilian and military personnel stationed abroad and of U.S. residents employed abroad temporarily by private U.S. firms.

Change in Personal Income: 2005 to 2006

National Percent Change = 6.6% Increase*

ALPHA ORDER

RANK	STATE	PERCENT CHANGE
21	Alabama	6.6
24	Alaska	6.5
3	Arizona	8.9
18	Arkansas	6.8
24	California	6.5
16	Colorado	7.0
21	Connecticut	6.6
21	Delaware	6.6
11	Florida	7.5
37	Georgia	5.6
18	Hawaii	6.8
5	Idaho	8.7
31	Illinois	5.9
43	Indiana	5.1
38	Iowa	5.5
16	Kansas	7.0
33	Kentucky	5.7
1	Louisiana	20.4
46	Maine	3.9
33	Maryland	5.7
30	Massachusetts	6.2
49	Michigan	3.2
43	Minnesota	5.1
32	Mississippi	5.8
39	Missouri	5.3
18	Montana	6.8
39	Nebraska	5.3
9	Nevada	7.9
24	New Hampshire	6.5
15	New Jersey	7.2
10	New Mexico	7.6
12	New York	7.4
13	North Carolina	7.3
48	North Dakota	3.3
45	Ohio	4.4
3	Oklahoma	8.9
13	Oregon	7.3
33	Pennsylvania	5.7
47	Rhode Island	3.6
28	South Carolina	6.3
50	South Dakota	2.8
33	Tennessee	5.7
6	Texas	8.4
8	Utah	8.2
28	Vermont	6.3
39	Virginia	5.3
7	Washington	8.3
27	West Virginia	6.4
39	Wisconsin	5.3
2	Wyoming	10.5

RANK ORDER

RANK	STATE	PERCENT CHANGE
1	Louisiana	20.4
2	Wyoming	10.5
3	Arizona	8.9
3	Oklahoma	8.9
5	Idaho	8.7
6	Texas	8.4
7	Washington	8.3
8	Utah	8.2
9	Nevada	7.9
10	New Mexico	7.6
11	Florida	7.5
12	New York	7.4
13	North Carolina	7.3
13	Oregon	7.3
15	New Jersey	7.2
16	Colorado	7.0
16	Kansas	7.0
18	Arkansas	6.8
18	Hawaii	6.8
18	Montana	6.8
21	Alabama	6.6
21	Connecticut	6.6
21	Delaware	6.6
24	Alaska	6.5
24	California	6.5
24	New Hampshire	6.5
27	West Virginia	6.4
28	South Carolina	6.3
28	Vermont	6.3
30	Massachusetts	6.2
31	Illinois	5.9
32	Mississippi	5.8
33	Kentucky	5.7
33	Maryland	5.7
33	Pennsylvania	5.7
33	Tennessee	5.7
37	Georgia	5.6
38	Iowa	5.5
39	Missouri	5.3
39	Nebraska	5.3
39	Virginia	5.3
39	Wisconsin	5.3
43	Indiana	5.1
43	Minnesota	5.1
45	Ohio	4.4
46	Maine	3.9
47	Rhode Island	3.6
48	North Dakota	3.3
49	Michigan	3.2
50	South Dakota	2.8

| | District of Columbia | 6.9 |

Source: CQ Press using data from U.S. Department of Commerce, Bureau of Economic Analysis
    "Annual State Personal Income" (http://www.bea.gov/regional/spi/)
*Based on revised 2005 figures.

Per Capita Personal Income in 2006

National Per Capita = $36,629*

ALPHA ORDER

RANK	STATE	PER CAPITA
42	Alabama	$30,841
14	Alaska	38,622
38	Arizona	31,949
48	Arkansas	28,444
10	California	39,358
8	Colorado	39,587
1	Connecticut	50,787
12	Delaware	38,984
20	Florida	36,665
37	Georgia	32,025
18	Hawaii	36,826
43	Idaho	29,948
15	Illinois	38,297
36	Indiana	32,226
30	Iowa	33,017
22	Kansas	34,744
46	Kentucky	29,719
40	Louisiana	31,369
39	Maine	31,931
5	Maryland	43,774
3	Massachusetts	46,255
26	Michigan	33,784
13	Minnesota	38,751
50	Mississippi	26,908
31	Missouri	32,793
41	Montana	30,886
25	Nebraska	34,383
11	Nevada	39,015
7	New Hampshire	39,655
2	New Jersey	46,328
45	New Mexico	29,725
4	New York	43,962
34	North Carolina	32,338
29	North Dakota	33,034
28	Ohio	33,217
33	Oklahoma	32,398
27	Oregon	33,252
19	Pennsylvania	36,689
17	Rhode Island	37,261
47	South Carolina	29,688
32	South Dakota	32,405
35	Tennessee	32,305
21	Texas	35,058
44	Utah	29,769
23	Vermont	34,623
9	Virginia	39,564
16	Washington	38,067
49	West Virginia	28,067
24	Wisconsin	34,476
6	Wyoming	40,569

RANK ORDER

RANK	STATE	PER CAPITA
1	Connecticut	$50,787
2	New Jersey	46,328
3	Massachusetts	46,255
4	New York	43,962
5	Maryland	43,774
6	Wyoming	40,569
7	New Hampshire	39,655
8	Colorado	39,587
9	Virginia	39,564
10	California	39,358
11	Nevada	39,015
12	Delaware	38,984
13	Minnesota	38,751
14	Alaska	38,622
15	Illinois	38,297
16	Washington	38,067
17	Rhode Island	37,261
18	Hawaii	36,826
19	Pennsylvania	36,689
20	Florida	36,665
21	Texas	35,058
22	Kansas	34,744
23	Vermont	34,623
24	Wisconsin	34,476
25	Nebraska	34,383
26	Michigan	33,784
27	Oregon	33,252
28	Ohio	33,217
29	North Dakota	33,034
30	Iowa	33,017
31	Missouri	32,793
32	South Dakota	32,405
33	Oklahoma	32,398
34	North Carolina	32,338
35	Tennessee	32,305
36	Indiana	32,226
37	Georgia	32,025
38	Arizona	31,949
39	Maine	31,931
40	Louisiana	31,369
41	Montana	30,886
42	Alabama	30,841
43	Idaho	29,948
44	Utah	29,769
45	New Mexico	29,725
46	Kentucky	29,719
47	South Carolina	29,688
48	Arkansas	28,444
49	West Virginia	28,067
50	Mississippi	26,908

District of Columbia 57,358

Source: U.S. Department of Commerce, Bureau of Economic Analysis
"Annual State Personal Income" (http://www.bea.gov/regional/spi/)
*The national total shown here is the sum of the state estimates. It differs from the national income and product accounts (NIPA) estimate of personal income because it omits the earnings of federal civilian and military personnel stationed abroad and of U.S. residents employed abroad temporarily by private U.S. firms.

Change in Per Capita Personal Income: 2005 to 2006

National Percent Change = 5.6% Increase*

ALPHA ORDER				RANK ORDER		
RANK	STATE	PERCENT CHANGE		RANK	STATE	PERCENT CHANGE
24	Alabama	5.4		1	Louisiana	26.6
24	Alaska	5.4		2	Wyoming	9.2
29	Arizona	5.2		3	Oklahoma	7.8
22	Arkansas	5.5		4	New York	7.4
20	California	5.6		5	New Jersey	6.9
31	Colorado	5.0		6	Connecticut	6.5
6	Connecticut	6.5		6	Washington	6.5
30	Delaware	5.1		8	Kansas	6.4
20	Florida	5.6		9	West Virginia	6.2
49	Georgia	3.0		10	Massachusetts	6.1
14	Hawaii	5.8		11	New Mexico	6.0
13	Idaho	5.9		11	Vermont	6.0
27	Illinois	5.3		13	Idaho	5.9
39	Indiana	4.3		14	Hawaii	5.8
33	Iowa	4.9		14	New Hampshire	5.8
8	Kansas	6.4		16	Mississippi	5.7
34	Kentucky	4.8		16	Montana	5.7
1	Louisiana	26.6		16	Texas	5.7
46	Maine	3.6		16	Utah	5.7
27	Maryland	5.3		20	California	5.6
10	Massachusetts	6.1		20	Florida	5.6
47	Michigan	3.3		22	Arkansas	5.5
39	Minnesota	4.3		22	Oregon	5.5
16	Mississippi	5.7		24	Alabama	5.4
37	Missouri	4.5		24	Alaska	5.4
16	Montana	5.7		24	Pennsylvania	5.4
35	Nebraska	4.7		27	Illinois	5.3
39	Nevada	4.3		27	Maryland	5.3
14	New Hampshire	5.8		29	Arizona	5.2
5	New Jersey	6.9		30	Delaware	5.1
11	New Mexico	6.0		31	Colorado	5.0
4	New York	7.4		31	North Carolina	5.0
31	North Carolina	5.0		33	Iowa	4.9
48	North Dakota	3.1		34	Kentucky	4.8
39	Ohio	4.3		35	Nebraska	4.7
3	Oklahoma	7.8		35	Wisconsin	4.7
22	Oregon	5.5		37	Missouri	4.5
24	Pennsylvania	5.4		38	South Carolina	4.4
43	Rhode Island	4.2		39	Indiana	4.3
38	South Carolina	4.4		39	Minnesota	4.3
50	South Dakota	1.9		39	Nevada	4.3
43	Tennessee	4.2		39	Ohio	4.3
16	Texas	5.7		43	Rhode Island	4.2
16	Utah	5.7		43	Tennessee	4.2
11	Vermont	6.0		43	Virginia	4.2
43	Virginia	4.2		46	Maine	3.6
6	Washington	6.5		47	Michigan	3.3
9	West Virginia	6.2		48	North Dakota	3.1
35	Wisconsin	4.7		49	Georgia	3.0
2	Wyoming	9.2		50	South Dakota	1.9
					District of Columbia	7.0

Source: CQ Press using data from U.S. Department of Commerce, Bureau of Economic Analysis
    "Annual State Personal Income" (http://www.bea.gov/regional/spi/)
*Based on revised 2005 figures.

Per Capita Disposable Personal Income in 2006

National Per Capita = $32,111*

ALPHA ORDER

RANK	STATE	PER CAPITA
41	Alabama	$27,764
8	Alaska	35,021
40	Arizona	28,204
48	Arkansas	25,643
13	California	33,801
9	Colorado	34,711
1	Connecticut	42,014
14	Delaware	33,770
19	Florida	32,343
39	Georgia	28,244
18	Hawaii	32,377
45	Idaho	26,558
16	Illinois	33,597
35	Indiana	28,759
28	Iowa	29,647
22	Kansas	30,856
44	Kentucky	26,571
36	Louisiana	28,643
38	Maine	28,353
4	Maryland	37,494
3	Massachusetts	39,317
26	Michigan	30,233
15	Minnesota	33,672
50	Mississippi	24,829
32	Missouri	29,181
42	Montana	27,615
24	Nebraska	30,703
10	Nevada	34,178
7	New Hampshire	35,377
2	New Jersey	39,857
43	New Mexico	26,845
5	New York	37,039
37	North Carolina	28,494
27	North Dakota	30,014
31	Ohio	29,244
33	Oklahoma	29,003
34	Oregon	28,940
20	Pennsylvania	32,254
17	Rhode Island	32,777
46	South Carolina	26,517
29	South Dakota	29,605
30	Tennessee	29,519
21	Texas	31,671
47	Utah	26,285
23	Vermont	30,765
11	Virginia	34,124
12	Washington	34,096
49	West Virginia	25,387
25	Wisconsin	30,320
6	Wyoming	35,904

RANK ORDER

RANK	STATE	PER CAPITA
1	Connecticut	$42,014
2	New Jersey	39,857
3	Massachusetts	39,317
4	Maryland	37,494
5	New York	37,039
6	Wyoming	35,904
7	New Hampshire	35,377
8	Alaska	35,021
9	Colorado	34,711
10	Nevada	34,178
11	Virginia	34,124
12	Washington	34,096
13	California	33,801
14	Delaware	33,770
15	Minnesota	33,672
16	Illinois	33,597
17	Rhode Island	32,777
18	Hawaii	32,377
19	Florida	32,343
20	Pennsylvania	32,254
21	Texas	31,671
22	Kansas	30,856
23	Vermont	30,765
24	Nebraska	30,703
25	Wisconsin	30,320
26	Michigan	30,233
27	North Dakota	30,014
28	Iowa	29,647
29	South Dakota	29,605
30	Tennessee	29,519
31	Ohio	29,244
32	Missouri	29,181
33	Oklahoma	29,003
34	Oregon	28,940
35	Indiana	28,759
36	Louisiana	28,643
37	North Carolina	28,494
38	Maine	28,353
39	Georgia	28,244
40	Arizona	28,204
41	Alabama	27,764
42	Montana	27,615
43	New Mexico	26,845
44	Kentucky	26,571
45	Idaho	26,558
46	South Carolina	26,517
47	Utah	26,285
48	Arkansas	25,643
49	West Virginia	25,387
50	Mississippi	24,829
	District of Columbia	49,297

Source: U.S. Department of Commerce, Bureau of Economic Analysis
   "Annual State Personal Income" (http://www.bea.gov/regional/spi/)
*Disposable personal income is personal income less personal tax and nontax payments. It is the income available to persons for spending or saving.

Median Household Income in 2006

National Median = $48,200*

RANK	STATE	INCOME
45	Alabama	$38,473
6	Alaska	57,639
27	Arizona	46,729
48	Arkansas	37,420
12	California	53,770
11	Colorado	54,039
5	Connecticut	59,972
14	Delaware	52,214
35	Florida	44,448
26	Georgia	46,841
3	Hawaii	60,681
28	Idaho	46,395
18	Illinois	49,280
32	Indiana	44,806
23	Iowa	47,489
36	Kansas	44,264
46	Kentucky	38,466
47	Louisiana	37,943
31	Maine	45,040
2	Maryland	62,372
8	Massachusetts	56,236
25	Michigan	47,064
7	Minnesota	57,363
50	Mississippi	35,261
33	Missouri	44,651
44	Montana	38,629
21	Nebraska	48,126
17	Nevada	50,819
4	New Hampshire	60,489
1	New Jersey	64,169
40	New Mexico	40,827
20	New York	48,201
39	North Carolina	42,061
38	North Dakota	42,162
29	Ohio	45,837
43	Oklahoma	40,001
30	Oregon	45,485
22	Pennsylvania	47,791
15	Rhode Island	52,003
41	South Carolina	40,822
34	South Dakota	44,624
42	Tennessee	40,676
37	Texas	43,425
9	Utah	55,179
16	Vermont	51,622
10	Virginia	55,108
13	Washington	53,439
49	West Virginia	37,227
19	Wisconsin	48,874
24	Wyoming	47,227

RANK	STATE	INCOME
1	New Jersey	$64,169
2	Maryland	62,372
3	Hawaii	60,681
4	New Hampshire	60,489
5	Connecticut	59,972
6	Alaska	57,639
7	Minnesota	57,363
8	Massachusetts	56,236
9	Utah	55,179
10	Virginia	55,108
11	Colorado	54,039
12	California	53,770
13	Washington	53,439
14	Delaware	52,214
15	Rhode Island	52,003
16	Vermont	51,622
17	Nevada	50,819
18	Illinois	49,280
19	Wisconsin	48,874
20	New York	48,201
21	Nebraska	48,126
22	Pennsylvania	47,791
23	Iowa	47,489
24	Wyoming	47,227
25	Michigan	47,064
26	Georgia	46,841
27	Arizona	46,729
28	Idaho	46,395
29	Ohio	45,837
30	Oregon	45,485
31	Maine	45,040
32	Indiana	44,806
33	Missouri	44,651
34	South Dakota	44,624
35	Florida	44,448
36	Kansas	44,264
37	Texas	43,425
38	North Dakota	42,162
39	North Carolina	42,061
40	New Mexico	40,827
41	South Carolina	40,822
42	Tennessee	40,676
43	Oklahoma	40,001
44	Montana	38,629
45	Alabama	38,473
46	Kentucky	38,466
47	Louisiana	37,943
48	Arkansas	37,420
49	West Virginia	37,227
50	Mississippi	35,261
	District of Columbia**	NA

Source: U.S. Bureau of the Census
   "Income 2005" (http://www.census.gov/hhes/www/income/income06/statemhi.html)
*Three-year average: 2004-2006.
**Not available.

Bankruptcy Filings in 2007

National Total = 801,269 Bankruptcies*

ALPHA ORDER

RANK	STATE	BANKRUPTCIES	% of USA
12	Alabama	23,176	2.9%
50	Alaska	696	0.1%
27	Arizona	9,749	1.2%
24	Arkansas	11,494	1.4%
1	California	62,951	7.9%
20	Colorado	14,238	1.8%
35	Connecticut	5,572	0.7%
44	Delaware	1,897	0.2%
9	Florida	36,572	4.6%
3	Georgia	48,104	6.0%
46	Hawaii	1,281	0.2%
38	Idaho	3,716	0.5%
6	Illinois	39,147	4.9%
10	Indiana	29,656	3.7%
33	Iowa	6,660	0.8%
31	Kansas	7,730	1.0%
17	Kentucky	16,216	2.0%
21	Louisiana	13,534	1.7%
42	Maine	2,143	0.3%
23	Maryland	12,509	1.6%
22	Massachusetts	13,011	1.6%
4	Michigan	43,806	5.5%
25	Minnesota	11,139	1.4%
26	Mississippi	10,789	1.3%
13	Missouri	20,141	2.5%
43	Montana	1,934	0.2%
36	Nebraska	5,204	0.6%
28	Nevada	9,445	1.2%
40	New Hampshire	2,804	0.3%
15	New Jersey	18,702	2.3%
39	New Mexico	3,232	0.4%
7	New York	38,823	4.8%
14	North Carolina	19,420	2.4%
47	North Dakota	1,090	0.1%
2	Ohio	48,527	6.1%
30	Oklahoma	8,966	1.1%
29	Oregon	8,993	1.1%
11	Pennsylvania	29,111	3.6%
41	Rhode Island	2,521	0.3%
32	South Carolina	7,139	0.9%
45	South Dakota	1,302	0.2%
8	Tennessee	37,779	4.7%
5	Texas	42,487	5.3%
34	Utah	6,182	0.8%
48	Vermont	849	0.1%
16	Virginia	17,893	2.2%
19	Washington	14,632	1.8%
37	West Virginia	4,230	0.5%
18	Wisconsin	14,952	1.9%
49	Wyoming	784	0.1%

RANK ORDER

RANK	STATE	BANKRUPTCIES	% of USA
1	California	62,951	7.9%
2	Ohio	48,527	6.1%
3	Georgia	48,104	6.0%
4	Michigan	43,806	5.5%
5	Texas	42,487	5.3%
6	Illinois	39,147	4.9%
7	New York	38,823	4.8%
8	Tennessee	37,779	4.7%
9	Florida	36,572	4.6%
10	Indiana	29,656	3.7%
11	Pennsylvania	29,111	3.6%
12	Alabama	23,176	2.9%
13	Missouri	20,141	2.5%
14	North Carolina	19,420	2.4%
15	New Jersey	18,702	2.3%
16	Virginia	17,893	2.2%
17	Kentucky	16,216	2.0%
18	Wisconsin	14,952	1.9%
19	Washington	14,632	1.8%
20	Colorado	14,238	1.8%
21	Louisiana	13,534	1.7%
22	Massachusetts	13,011	1.6%
23	Maryland	12,509	1.6%
24	Arkansas	11,494	1.4%
25	Minnesota	11,139	1.4%
26	Mississippi	10,789	1.3%
27	Arizona	9,749	1.2%
28	Nevada	9,445	1.2%
29	Oregon	8,993	1.1%
30	Oklahoma	8,966	1.1%
31	Kansas	7,730	1.0%
32	South Carolina	7,139	0.9%
33	Iowa	6,660	0.8%
34	Utah	6,182	0.8%
35	Connecticut	5,572	0.7%
36	Nebraska	5,204	0.6%
37	West Virginia	4,230	0.5%
38	Idaho	3,716	0.5%
39	New Mexico	3,232	0.4%
40	New Hampshire	2,804	0.3%
41	Rhode Island	2,521	0.3%
42	Maine	2,143	0.3%
43	Montana	1,934	0.2%
44	Delaware	1,897	0.2%
45	South Dakota	1,302	0.2%
46	Hawaii	1,281	0.2%
47	North Dakota	1,090	0.1%
48	Vermont	849	0.1%
49	Wyoming	784	0.1%
50	Alaska	696	0.1%
	District of Columbia	670	0.1%

Source: CQ Press using data from Administrative Office of the U.S. Courts
   "Table F-2, U.S. Bankruptcy Courts" (press release, November 19, 2007)
*For 12 months through September 2007. Includes business (25,925) and non-business (775,344) filings. Includes all chapters of bankruptcy. National total includes 7,671 bankruptcies in U.S. territories.

Personal Bankruptcy Rate in 2007

National Rate = 255 Personal Bankruptcies per 100,000 Population*

ALPHA ORDER

RANK	STATE	RATE
2	Alabama	495
50	Alaska	92
46	Arizona	148
7	Arkansas	393
39	California	164
15	Colorado	281
43	Connecticut	153
37	Delaware	186
35	Florida	191
3	Georgia	489
49	Hawaii	96
18	Idaho	241
13	Illinois	297
4	Indiana	459
28	Iowa	215
16	Kansas	271
8	Kentucky	376
12	Louisiana	304
43	Maine	153
27	Maryland	216
32	Massachusetts	196
5	Michigan	424
31	Minnesota	205
9	Mississippi	361
11	Missouri	337
32	Montana	196
14	Nebraska	282
10	Nevada	358
36	New Hampshire	188
30	New Jersey	206
42	New Mexico	158
34	New York	194
29	North Carolina	208
40	North Dakota	161
6	Ohio	412
19	Oklahoma	238
20	Oregon	232
23	Pennsylvania	227
21	Rhode Island	231
41	South Carolina	159
43	South Dakota	153
1	Tennessee	605
38	Texas	168
22	Utah	228
48	Vermont	126
25	Virginia	225
26	Washington	219
24	West Virginia	226
17	Wisconsin	260
47	Wyoming	143

RANK ORDER

RANK	STATE	RATE
1	Tennessee	605
2	Alabama	495
3	Georgia	489
4	Indiana	459
5	Michigan	424
6	Ohio	412
7	Arkansas	393
8	Kentucky	376
9	Mississippi	361
10	Nevada	358
11	Missouri	337
12	Louisiana	304
13	Illinois	297
14	Nebraska	282
15	Colorado	281
16	Kansas	271
17	Wisconsin	260
18	Idaho	241
19	Oklahoma	238
20	Oregon	232
21	Rhode Island	231
22	Utah	228
23	Pennsylvania	227
24	West Virginia	226
25	Virginia	225
26	Washington	219
27	Maryland	216
28	Iowa	215
29	North Carolina	208
30	New Jersey	206
31	Minnesota	205
32	Massachusetts	196
32	Montana	196
34	New York	194
35	Florida	191
36	New Hampshire	188
37	Delaware	186
38	Texas	168
39	California	164
40	North Dakota	161
41	South Carolina	159
42	New Mexico	158
43	Connecticut	153
43	Maine	153
43	South Dakota	153
46	Arizona	148
47	Wyoming	143
48	Vermont	126
49	Hawaii	96
50	Alaska	92

District of Columbia   108

Source: CQ Press using data from Administrative Office of the U.S. Courts
"Table F-2, U.S. Bankruptcy Courts" (press release, November 19, 2007)
*For 12 months through September 2007. National rate does not include bankruptcies or population in U.S. territories. Includes all nonbusiness bankruptcies.

Percent Change in Personal Bankruptcy Rate: 2006 to 2007

National Percent Change = 29.2% Decrease*

ALPHA ORDER

RANK	STATE	PERCENT CHANGE
6	Alabama	(17.1)
48	Alaska	(50.3)
46	Arizona	(46.8)
17	Arkansas	(28.4)
16	California	(27.4)
35	Colorado	(37.7)
36	Connecticut	(38.1)
26	Delaware	(32.4)
22	Florida	(32.0)
1	Georgia	(6.9)
43	Hawaii	(43.5)
37	Idaho	(38.8)
25	Illinois	(32.2)
32	Indiana	(34.5)
15	Iowa	(27.1)
34	Kansas	(37.3)
18	Kentucky	(28.7)
24	Louisiana	(32.1)
22	Maine	(32.0)
27	Maryland	(32.9)
4	Massachusetts	(15.2)
8	Michigan	(18.3)
7	Minnesota	(17.7)
10	Mississippi	(18.7)
21	Missouri	(30.9)
42	Montana	(41.8)
11	Nebraska	(22.7)
19	Nevada	(28.8)
3	New Hampshire	(14.2)
20	New Jersey	(29.2)
41	New Mexico	(41.3)
28	New York	(33.1)
12	North Carolina	(23.5)
37	North Dakota	(38.8)
30	Ohio	(33.5)
50	Oklahoma	(55.3)
44	Oregon	(45.0)
29	Pennsylvania	(33.2)
5	Rhode Island	(16.3)
9	South Carolina	(18.5)
31	South Dakota	(34.3)
2	Tennessee	(9.4)
33	Texas	(37.1)
40	Utah	(40.3)
45	Vermont	(45.5)
13	Virginia	(24.0)
39	Washington	(39.7)
47	West Virginia	(48.5)
14	Wisconsin	(25.7)
49	Wyoming	(52.3)

RANK ORDER

RANK	STATE	PERCENT CHANGE
1	Georgia	(6.9)
2	Tennessee	(9.4)
3	New Hampshire	(14.2)
4	Massachusetts	(15.2)
5	Rhode Island	(16.3)
6	Alabama	(17.1)
7	Minnesota	(17.7)
8	Michigan	(18.3)
9	South Carolina	(18.5)
10	Mississippi	(18.7)
11	Nebraska	(22.7)
12	North Carolina	(23.5)
13	Virginia	(24.0)
14	Wisconsin	(25.7)
15	Iowa	(27.1)
16	California	(27.4)
17	Arkansas	(28.4)
18	Kentucky	(28.7)
19	Nevada	(28.8)
20	New Jersey	(29.2)
21	Missouri	(30.9)
22	Florida	(32.0)
22	Maine	(32.0)
24	Louisiana	(32.1)
25	Illinois	(32.2)
26	Delaware	(32.4)
27	Maryland	(32.9)
28	New York	(33.1)
29	Pennsylvania	(33.2)
30	Ohio	(33.5)
31	South Dakota	(34.3)
32	Indiana	(34.5)
33	Texas	(37.1)
34	Kansas	(37.3)
35	Colorado	(37.7)
36	Connecticut	(38.1)
37	Idaho	(38.8)
37	North Dakota	(38.8)
39	Washington	(39.7)
40	Utah	(40.3)
41	New Mexico	(41.3)
42	Montana	(41.8)
43	Hawaii	(43.5)
44	Oregon	(45.0)
45	Vermont	(45.5)
46	Arizona	(46.8)
47	West Virginia	(48.5)
48	Alaska	(50.3)
49	Wyoming	(52.3)
50	Oklahoma	(55.3)

District of Columbia (50.9)

Source: CQ Press using data from Administrative Office of the U.S. Courts
  "Table F-2, U.S. Bankruptcy Courts" (press release, November 19, 2007)
*Twelve months ending in September 2006 to 12 months ending in September 2007. National rate does not include bankruptcies
or population in U.S. territories. Includes all nonbusiness bankruptcies.

Total Tax Burden as a Percentage of Income in 2007

National Percent = 32.7% of Income*

RANK	STATE	PERCENT
49	Alabama	28.0
47	Alaska	28.1
24	Arizona	31.3
31	Arkansas	30.7
8	California	34.3
22	Colorado	31.8
1	Connecticut	38.3
26	Delaware	31.2
12	Florida	33.6
28	Georgia	30.9
16	Hawaii	33.0
42	Idaho	29.6
14	Illinois	33.2
29	Indiana	30.8
33	Iowa	30.6
27	Kansas	31.0
34	Kentucky	30.4
44	Louisiana	29.1
10	Maine	33.9
15	Maryland	33.1
7	Massachusetts	34.4
20	Michigan	31.9
10	Minnesota	33.9
47	Mississippi	28.1
37	Missouri	30.2
39	Montana	29.8
22	Nebraska	31.8
4	Nevada	35.2
29	New Hampshire	30.8
3	New Jersey	35.6
45	New Mexico	28.8
2	New York	37.1
24	North Carolina	31.3
37	North Dakota	30.2
18	Ohio	32.4
50	Oklahoma	27.8
31	Oregon	30.7
20	Pennsylvania	31.9
5	Rhode Island	35.1
35	South Carolina	30.3
43	South Dakota	29.3
45	Tennessee	28.8
39	Texas	29.8
35	Utah	30.3
5	Vermont	35.1
17	Virginia	32.9
9	Washington	34.0
39	West Virginia	29.8
13	Wisconsin	33.3
19	Wyoming	32.1

RANK	STATE	PERCENT
1	Connecticut	38.3
2	New York	37.1
3	New Jersey	35.6
4	Nevada	35.2
5	Rhode Island	35.1
5	Vermont	35.1
7	Massachusetts	34.4
8	California	34.3
9	Washington	34.0
10	Maine	33.9
10	Minnesota	33.9
12	Florida	33.6
13	Wisconsin	33.3
14	Illinois	33.2
15	Maryland	33.1
16	Hawaii	33.0
17	Virginia	32.9
18	Ohio	32.4
19	Wyoming	32.1
20	Michigan	31.9
20	Pennsylvania	31.9
22	Colorado	31.8
22	Nebraska	31.8
24	Arizona	31.3
24	North Carolina	31.3
26	Delaware	31.2
27	Kansas	31.0
28	Georgia	30.9
29	Indiana	30.8
29	New Hampshire	30.8
31	Arkansas	30.7
31	Oregon	30.7
33	Iowa	30.6
34	Kentucky	30.4
35	South Carolina	30.3
35	Utah	30.3
37	Missouri	30.2
37	North Dakota	30.2
39	Montana	29.8
39	Texas	29.8
39	West Virginia	29.8
42	Idaho	29.6
43	South Dakota	29.3
44	Louisiana	29.1
45	New Mexico	28.8
45	Tennessee	28.8
47	Alaska	28.1
47	Mississippi	28.1
49	Alabama	28.0
50	Oklahoma	27.8

District of Columbia   36.4

Source: The Tax Foundation
"State and Local Tax Burdens Compared to Other U.S. States, 1970-2007" (http://www.taxfoundation.org/research/)
*This table attempts to allocate federal tax revenue among the states based on who ultimately bears the burden of taxes as opposed to simply the states where taxes are collected. State and local taxes are then added to determine the "total tax burden."

State Business Tax Climate Index 2008

National Average Score = 5.00*

<u>ALPHA ORDER</u>

RANK	STATE	SCORE
21	Alabama	5.37
4	Alaska	7.19
25	Arizona	5.19
35	Arkansas	4.94
47	California	4.12
13	Colorado	5.89
38	Connecticut	4.89
9	Delaware	6.03
5	Florida	7.03
20	Georgia	5.38
22	Hawaii	5.33
31	Idaho	5.06
28	Illinois	5.14
12	Indiana	5.93
44	Iowa	4.54
33	Kansas	4.97
35	Kentucky	4.94
32	Louisiana	5.02
41	Maine	4.69
24	Maryland	5.25
34	Massachusetts	4.96
29	Michigan	5.13
42	Minnesota	4.60
17	Mississippi	5.44
15	Missouri	5.58
6	Montana	6.34
43	Nebraska	4.56
3	Nevada	7.35
7	New Hampshire	6.24
49	New Jersey	3.88
23	New Mexico	5.28
48	New York	4.11
40	North Carolina	4.73
30	North Dakota	5.08
46	Ohio	4.14
19	Oklahoma	5.42
10	Oregon	5.98
27	Pennsylvania	5.15
50	Rhode Island	3.78
26	South Carolina	5.18
2	South Dakota	7.46
16	Tennessee	5.53
8	Texas	6.23
17	Utah	5.44
44	Vermont	4.54
14	Virginia	5.69
11	Washington	5.95
37	West Virginia	4.90
39	Wisconsin	4.77
1	Wyoming	7.71

<u>RANK ORDER</u>

RANK	STATE	SCORE
1	Wyoming	7.71
2	South Dakota	7.46
3	Nevada	7.35
4	Alaska	7.19
5	Florida	7.03
6	Montana	6.34
7	New Hampshire	6.24
8	Texas	6.23
9	Delaware	6.03
10	Oregon	5.98
11	Washington	5.95
12	Indiana	5.93
13	Colorado	5.89
14	Virginia	5.69
15	Missouri	5.58
16	Tennessee	5.53
17	Mississippi	5.44
17	Utah	5.44
19	Oklahoma	5.42
20	Georgia	5.38
21	Alabama	5.37
22	Hawaii	5.33
23	New Mexico	5.28
24	Maryland	5.25
25	Arizona	5.19
26	South Carolina	5.18
27	Pennsylvania	5.15
28	Illinois	5.14
29	Michigan	5.13
30	North Dakota	5.08
31	Idaho	5.06
32	Louisiana	5.02
33	Kansas	4.97
34	Massachusetts	4.96
35	Arkansas	4.94
35	Kentucky	4.94
37	West Virginia	4.90
38	Connecticut	4.89
39	Wisconsin	4.77
40	North Carolina	4.73
41	Maine	4.69
42	Minnesota	4.60
43	Nebraska	4.56
44	Iowa	4.54
44	Vermont	4.54
46	Ohio	4.14
47	California	4.12
48	New York	4.11
49	New Jersey	3.88
50	Rhode Island	3.78
	District of Columbia	4.49

Source: The Tax Foundation
   "State Business Tax Climate Index" (October 2007, http://www.taxfoundation.org/publications/show/22658.html)
*This index looks at levels of taxation and complexity of compliance to compare the states on how "business friendly" each state is compared to the others. The scale for each factor considered is one to ten, with ten being the "best."

Fortune 500 Companies in 2006

National Total = 500 Companies*

ALPHA ORDER

RANK	STATE	COMPANIES	% of USA
32	Alabama	1	0.2%
41	Alaska	0	0.0%
26	Arizona	4	0.8%
23	Arkansas	5	1.0%
3	California	52	10.4%
13	Colorado	12	2.4%
15	Connecticut	11	2.2%
32	Delaware	1	0.2%
13	Florida	12	2.4%
11	Georgia	15	3.0%
41	Hawaii	0	0.0%
29	Idaho	2	0.4%
4	Illinois	33	6.6%
23	Indiana	5	1.0%
32	Iowa	1	0.2%
32	Kansas	1	0.2%
21	Kentucky	6	1.2%
28	Louisiana	3	0.6%
32	Maine	1	0.2%
21	Maryland	6	1.2%
16	Massachusetts	10	2.0%
8	Michigan	22	4.4%
9	Minnesota	20	4.0%
41	Mississippi	0	0.0%
16	Missouri	10	2.0%
41	Montana	0	0.0%
23	Nebraska	5	1.0%
29	Nevada	2	0.4%
32	New Hampshire	1	0.2%
7	New Jersey	24	4.8%
41	New Mexico	0	0.0%
1	New York	56	11.2%
12	North Carolina	14	2.8%
41	North Dakota	0	0.0%
5	Ohio	28	5.6%
26	Oklahoma	4	0.8%
32	Oregon	1	0.2%
6	Pennsylvania	25	5.0%
29	Rhode Island	2	0.4%
32	South Carolina	1	0.2%
41	South Dakota	0	0.0%
19	Tennessee	9	1.8%
1	Texas	56	11.2%
32	Utah	1	0.2%
41	Vermont	0	0.0%
10	Virginia	17	3.4%
16	Washington	10	2.0%
41	West Virginia	0	0.0%
19	Wisconsin	9	1.8%
41	Wyoming	0	0.0%

RANK ORDER

RANK	STATE	COMPANIES	% of USA
1	New York	56	11.2%
1	Texas	56	11.2%
3	California	52	10.4%
4	Illinois	33	6.6%
5	Ohio	28	5.6%
6	Pennsylvania	25	5.0%
7	New Jersey	24	4.8%
8	Michigan	22	4.4%
9	Minnesota	20	4.0%
10	Virginia	17	3.4%
11	Georgia	15	3.0%
12	North Carolina	14	2.8%
13	Colorado	12	2.4%
13	Florida	12	2.4%
15	Connecticut	11	2.2%
16	Massachusetts	10	2.0%
16	Missouri	10	2.0%
16	Washington	10	2.0%
19	Tennessee	9	1.8%
19	Wisconsin	9	1.8%
21	Kentucky	6	1.2%
21	Maryland	6	1.2%
23	Arkansas	5	1.0%
23	Indiana	5	1.0%
23	Nebraska	5	1.0%
26	Arizona	4	0.8%
26	Oklahoma	4	0.8%
28	Louisiana	3	0.6%
29	Idaho	2	0.4%
29	Nevada	2	0.4%
29	Rhode Island	2	0.4%
32	Alabama	1	0.2%
32	Delaware	1	0.2%
32	Iowa	1	0.2%
32	Kansas	1	0.2%
32	Maine	1	0.2%
32	New Hampshire	1	0.2%
32	Oregon	1	0.2%
32	South Carolina	1	0.2%
32	Utah	1	0.2%
41	Alaska	0	0.0%
41	Hawaii	0	0.0%
41	Mississippi	0	0.0%
41	Montana	0	0.0%
41	New Mexico	0	0.0%
41	North Dakota	0	0.0%
41	South Dakota	0	0.0%
41	Vermont	0	0.0%
41	West Virginia	0	0.0%
41	Wyoming	0	0.0%
	District of Columbia	2	0.4%

Source: Fortune Magazine
   "Fortune 500 Ranked Within States" (April 30, 2007)
*By state where each company's headquarters is located.

Employer Firms in 2006

National Total = 6,080,000 Firms*

ALPHA ORDER

RANK	STATE	FIRMS	% of USA
27	Alabama	86,813	1.4%
50	Alaska	17,125	0.3%
20	Arizona	128,786	2.1%
33	Arkansas	66,021	1.1%
1	California	1,146,269	18.9%
15	Colorado	156,866	2.6%
25	Connecticut	99,042	1.6%
45	Delaware	26,068	0.4%
3	Florida	489,452	8.1%
10	Georgia	212,713	3.5%
44	Hawaii	31,152	0.5%
36	Idaho	49,463	0.8%
5	Illinois	295,322	4.9%
21	Indiana	128,096	2.1%
30	Iowa	71,394	1.2%
31	Kansas	70,707	1.2%
28	Kentucky	85,134	1.4%
24	Louisiana	99,981	1.6%
39	Maine	42,008	0.7%
16	Maryland	141,726	2.3%
13	Massachusetts	184,093	3.0%
9	Michigan	219,140	3.6%
18	Minnesota	134,083	2.2%
35	Mississippi	55,178	0.9%
17	Missouri	138,583	2.3%
42	Montana	36,632	0.6%
37	Nebraska	47,600	0.8%
34	Nevada	57,512	0.9%
40	New Hampshire	41,019	0.7%
7	New Jersey	261,759	4.3%
38	New Mexico	45,220	0.7%
2	New York	491,433	8.1%
12	North Carolina	192,761	3.2%
49	North Dakota	19,962	0.3%
8	Ohio	227,244	3.7%
29	Oklahoma	79,895	1.3%
23	Oregon	110,907	1.8%
6	Pennsylvania	284,770	4.7%
43	Rhode Island	33,855	0.6%
26	South Carolina	98,732	1.6%
46	South Dakota	24,797	0.4%
22	Tennessee	113,862	1.9%
4	Texas	424,308	7.0%
32	Utah	67,169	1.1%
47	Vermont	21,618	0.4%
14	Virginia	181,039	3.0%
11	Washington	198,195	3.3%
41	West Virginia	36,797	0.6%
19	Wisconsin	129,967	2.1%
48	Wyoming	21,116	0.3%

RANK ORDER

RANK	STATE	FIRMS	% of USA
1	California	1,146,269	18.9%
2	New York	491,433	8.1%
3	Florida	489,452	8.1%
4	Texas	424,308	7.0%
5	Illinois	295,322	4.9%
6	Pennsylvania	284,770	4.7%
7	New Jersey	261,759	4.3%
8	Ohio	227,244	3.7%
9	Michigan	219,140	3.6%
10	Georgia	212,713	3.5%
11	Washington	198,195	3.3%
12	North Carolina	192,761	3.2%
13	Massachusetts	184,093	3.0%
14	Virginia	181,039	3.0%
15	Colorado	156,866	2.6%
16	Maryland	141,726	2.3%
17	Missouri	138,583	2.3%
18	Minnesota	134,083	2.2%
19	Wisconsin	129,967	2.1%
20	Arizona	128,786	2.1%
21	Indiana	128,096	2.1%
22	Tennessee	113,862	1.9%
23	Oregon	110,907	1.8%
24	Louisiana	99,981	1.6%
25	Connecticut	99,042	1.6%
26	South Carolina	98,732	1.6%
27	Alabama	86,813	1.4%
28	Kentucky	85,134	1.4%
29	Oklahoma	79,895	1.3%
30	Iowa	71,394	1.2%
31	Kansas	70,707	1.2%
32	Utah	67,169	1.1%
33	Arkansas	66,021	1.1%
34	Nevada	57,512	0.9%
35	Mississippi	55,178	0.9%
36	Idaho	49,463	0.8%
37	Nebraska	47,600	0.8%
38	New Mexico	45,220	0.7%
39	Maine	42,008	0.7%
40	New Hampshire	41,019	0.7%
41	West Virginia	36,797	0.6%
42	Montana	36,632	0.6%
43	Rhode Island	33,855	0.6%
44	Hawaii	31,152	0.5%
45	Delaware	26,068	0.4%
46	South Dakota	24,797	0.4%
47	Vermont	21,618	0.4%
48	Wyoming	21,116	0.3%
49	North Dakota	19,962	0.3%
50	Alaska	17,125	0.3%
	District of Columbia	28,485	0.5%

Source: U.S. Small Business Administration
"The Small Business Economy" (2006, http://www.sba.gov/advo/research/sb_econ2007.pdf)
*State totals do not add to the U.S. figure as firms can be in more than one state.

New Employer Firms in 2006

National Total = 649,700 New Firms*

ALPHA ORDER

RANK	STATE	FIRMS	% of USA
28	Alabama	10,096	1.6%
49	Alaska	1,904	0.3%
15	Arizona	21,555	3.3%
30	Arkansas	9,551	1.5%
1	California	115,684	17.8%
13	Colorado	22,708	3.5%
31	Connecticut	9,516	1.5%
45	Delaware	3,153	0.5%
2	Florida	79,870	12.3%
8	Georgia	31,677	4.9%
43	Hawaii	3,813	0.6%
32	Idaho	9,159	1.4%
9	Illinois	30,230	4.7%
21	Indiana	14,653	2.3%
36	Iowa	5,877	0.9%
34	Kansas	6,973	1.1%
33	Kentucky	8,973	1.4%
26	Louisiana	11,034	1.7%
41	Maine	4,497	0.7%
16	Maryland	21,535	3.3%
17	Massachusetts	17,800	2.7%
12	Michigan	23,508	3.6%
22	Minnesota	13,739	2.1%
35	Mississippi	6,862	1.1%
19	Missouri	15,805	2.4%
39	Montana	4,727	0.7%
38	Nebraska	4,820	0.7%
27	Nevada	10,743	1.7%
40	New Hampshire	4,703	0.7%
5	New Jersey	36,258	5.6%
37	New Mexico	5,536	0.9%
3	New York	61,718	9.5%
10	North Carolina	26,729	4.1%
50	North Dakota	1,821	0.3%
14	Ohio	22,213	3.4%
29	Oklahoma	9,962	1.5%
20	Oregon	15,085	2.3%
6	Pennsylvania	34,928	5.4%
44	Rhode Island	3,739	0.6%
25	South Carolina	12,373	1.9%
47	South Dakota	2,003	0.3%
18	Tennessee	17,207	2.6%
4	Texas	58,943	9.1%
23	Utah	13,379	2.1%
48	Vermont	1,957	0.3%
11	Virginia	23,686	3.6%
7	Washington	32,726	5.0%
42	West Virginia	3,823	0.6%
24	Wisconsin	13,371	2.1%
46	Wyoming	2,570	0.4%

RANK ORDER

RANK	STATE	FIRMS	% of USA
1	California	115,684	17.8%
2	Florida	79,870	12.3%
3	New York	61,718	9.5%
4	Texas	58,943	9.1%
5	New Jersey	36,258	5.6%
6	Pennsylvania	34,928	5.4%
7	Washington	32,726	5.0%
8	Georgia	31,677	4.9%
9	Illinois	30,230	4.7%
10	North Carolina	26,729	4.1%
11	Virginia	23,686	3.6%
12	Michigan	23,508	3.6%
13	Colorado	22,708	3.5%
14	Ohio	22,213	3.4%
15	Arizona	21,555	3.3%
16	Maryland	21,535	3.3%
17	Massachusetts	17,800	2.7%
18	Tennessee	17,207	2.6%
19	Missouri	15,805	2.4%
20	Oregon	15,085	2.3%
21	Indiana	14,653	2.3%
22	Minnesota	13,739	2.1%
23	Utah	13,379	2.1%
24	Wisconsin	13,371	2.1%
25	South Carolina	12,373	1.9%
26	Louisiana	11,034	1.7%
27	Nevada	10,743	1.7%
28	Alabama	10,096	1.6%
29	Oklahoma	9,962	1.5%
30	Arkansas	9,551	1.5%
31	Connecticut	9,516	1.5%
32	Idaho	9,159	1.4%
33	Kentucky	8,973	1.4%
34	Kansas	6,973	1.1%
35	Mississippi	6,862	1.1%
36	Iowa	5,877	0.9%
37	New Mexico	5,536	0.9%
38	Nebraska	4,820	0.7%
39	Montana	4,727	0.7%
40	New Hampshire	4,703	0.7%
41	Maine	4,497	0.7%
42	West Virginia	3,823	0.6%
43	Hawaii	3,813	0.6%
44	Rhode Island	3,739	0.6%
45	Delaware	3,153	0.5%
46	Wyoming	2,570	0.4%
47	South Dakota	2,003	0.3%
48	Vermont	1,957	0.3%
49	Alaska	1,904	0.3%
50	North Dakota	1,821	0.3%
	District of Columbia	4,232	0.7%

Source: U.S. Small Business Administration
   "The Small Business Economy" (2006, http://www.sba.gov/advo/research/sb_econ2007.pdf)
*State totals do not add to the U.S. figure as firms can be in more than one state.

Rate of New Employer Firms in 2006

National Rate = 10.8% of Existing Firms*

ALPHA ORDER				RANK ORDER		
RANK	**STATE**	**RATE**		**RANK**	**STATE**	**RATE**
30	Alabama	11.4		1	Utah	21.3
31	Alaska	11.3		2	Idaho	19.8
4	Arizona	18.2		3	Nevada	19.7
10	Arkansas	15.2		4	Arizona	18.2
36	California	10.8		5	Florida	16.9
11	Colorado	14.9		6	Washington	16.8
44	Connecticut	9.7		7	Maryland	15.4
26	Delaware	12.2		7	Tennessee	15.4
5	Florida	16.9		9	Georgia	15.3
9	Georgia	15.3		10	Arkansas	15.2
23	Hawaii	12.5		11	Colorado	14.9
2	Idaho	19.8		12	North Carolina	14.3
39	Illinois	10.4		12	Texas	14.3
27	Indiana	11.7		14	Oregon	14.1
49	Iowa	8.3		15	New Jersey	14.0
43	Kansas	10.0		16	Montana	13.3
37	Kentucky	10.6		16	Virginia	13.3
31	Louisiana	11.3		18	South Carolina	12.9
34	Maine	11.0		19	New Mexico	12.8
7	Maryland	15.4		19	Oklahoma	12.8
44	Massachusetts	9.7		21	New York	12.7
34	Michigan	11.0		22	Mississippi	12.6
41	Minnesota	10.3		23	Hawaii	12.5
22	Mississippi	12.6		23	Pennsylvania	12.5
28	Missouri	11.6		25	Wyoming	12.4
16	Montana	13.3		26	Delaware	12.2
42	Nebraska	10.2		27	Indiana	11.7
3	Nevada	19.7		28	Missouri	11.6
28	New Hampshire	11.6		28	New Hampshire	11.6
15	New Jersey	14.0		30	Alabama	11.4
19	New Mexico	12.8		31	Alaska	11.3
21	New York	12.7		31	Louisiana	11.3
12	North Carolina	14.3		33	Rhode Island	11.1
47	North Dakota	9.3		34	Maine	11.0
46	Ohio	9.6		34	Michigan	11.0
19	Oklahoma	12.8		36	California	10.8
14	Oregon	14.1		37	Kentucky	10.6
23	Pennsylvania	12.5		38	Wisconsin	10.5
33	Rhode Island	11.1		39	Illinois	10.4
18	South Carolina	12.9		39	West Virginia	10.4
50	South Dakota	8.2		41	Minnesota	10.3
7	Tennessee	15.4		42	Nebraska	10.2
12	Texas	14.3		43	Kansas	10.0
1	Utah	21.3		44	Connecticut	9.7
48	Vermont	9.1		44	Massachusetts	9.7
16	Virginia	13.3		46	Ohio	9.6
6	Washington	16.8		47	North Dakota	9.3
39	West Virginia	10.4		48	Vermont	9.1
38	Wisconsin	10.5		49	Iowa	8.3
25	Wyoming	12.4		50	South Dakota	8.2
					District of Columbia	15.3

Source: CQ Press using data from U.S. Small Business Administration
"The Small Business Economy" (2006, http://www.sba.gov/advo/research/sb_econ2007.pdf)
*Firms can be in more than one state. Rate figure represents the number of employer firms started in 2006 as a percent of existing firms at the beginning of 2006.

Employer Firm Terminations in 2006

National Total = 564,900 Terminations*

ALPHA ORDER

RANK	STATE	FIRMS	% of USA
27	Alabama	11,128	2.0%
49	Alaska	2,239	0.4%
5	Arizona	52,375	9.3%
33	Arkansas	7,289	1.3%
1	California	149,212	26.4%
12	Colorado	24,158	4.3%
25	Connecticut	11,214	2.0%
45	Delaware	3,295	0.6%
2	Florida	64,423	11.4%
10	Georgia	29,787	5.3%
44	Hawaii	3,789	0.7%
36	Idaho	6,713	1.2%
8	Illinois	33,426	5.9%
22	Indiana	13,851	2.5%
34	Iowa	7,248	1.3%
35	Kansas	7,000	1.2%
28	Kentucky	10,230	1.8%
29	Louisiana	8,972	1.6%
41	Maine	4,769	0.8%
17	Maryland	20,745	3.7%
14	Massachusetts	22,376	4.0%
15	Michigan	21,268	3.8%
20	Minnesota	14,403	2.5%
31	Mississippi	7,898	1.4%
18	Missouri	18,124	3.2%
43	Montana	4,469	0.8%
39	Nebraska	5,117	0.9%
30	Nevada	8,423	1.5%
37	New Hampshire	5,481	1.0%
9	New Jersey	32,959	5.8%
38	New Mexico	5,274	0.9%
3	New York	61,190	10.8%
13	North Carolina	23,165	4.1%
50	North Dakota	2,181	0.4%
11	Ohio	25,412	4.5%
32	Oklahoma	7,829	1.4%
21	Oregon	14,039	2.5%
7	Pennsylvania	35,805	6.3%
42	Rhode Island	4,572	0.8%
24	South Carolina	11,661	2.1%
47	South Dakota	2,449	0.4%
19	Tennessee	16,395	2.9%
4	Texas	54,479	9.6%
26	Utah	11,190	2.0%
48	Vermont	2,365	0.4%
16	Virginia	20,972	3.7%
6	Washington	36,331	6.4%
40	West Virginia	4,854	0.9%
23	Wisconsin	13,060	2.3%
46	Wyoming	2,773	0.5%

RANK ORDER

RANK	STATE	FIRMS	% of USA
1	California	149,212	26.4%
2	Florida	64,423	11.4%
3	New York	61,190	10.8%
4	Texas	54,479	9.6%
5	Arizona	52,375	9.3%
6	Washington	36,331	6.4%
7	Pennsylvania	35,805	6.3%
8	Illinois	33,426	5.9%
9	New Jersey	32,959	5.8%
10	Georgia	29,787	5.3%
11	Ohio	25,412	4.5%
12	Colorado	24,158	4.3%
13	North Carolina	23,165	4.1%
14	Massachusetts	22,376	4.0%
15	Michigan	21,268	3.8%
16	Virginia	20,972	3.7%
17	Maryland	20,745	3.7%
18	Missouri	18,124	3.2%
19	Tennessee	16,395	2.9%
20	Minnesota	14,403	2.5%
21	Oregon	14,039	2.5%
22	Indiana	13,851	2.5%
23	Wisconsin	13,060	2.3%
24	South Carolina	11,661	2.1%
25	Connecticut	11,214	2.0%
26	Utah	11,190	2.0%
27	Alabama	11,128	2.0%
28	Kentucky	10,230	1.8%
29	Louisiana	8,972	1.6%
30	Nevada	8,423	1.5%
31	Mississippi	7,898	1.4%
32	Oklahoma	7,829	1.4%
33	Arkansas	7,289	1.3%
34	Iowa	7,248	1.3%
35	Kansas	7,000	1.2%
36	Idaho	6,713	1.2%
37	New Hampshire	5,481	1.0%
38	New Mexico	5,274	0.9%
39	Nebraska	5,117	0.9%
40	West Virginia	4,854	0.9%
41	Maine	4,769	0.8%
42	Rhode Island	4,572	0.8%
43	Montana	4,469	0.8%
44	Hawaii	3,789	0.7%
45	Delaware	3,295	0.6%
46	Wyoming	2,773	0.5%
47	South Dakota	2,449	0.4%
48	Vermont	2,365	0.4%
49	Alaska	2,239	0.4%
50	North Dakota	2,181	0.4%
	District of Columbia	3,111	0.6%

Source: U.S. Small Business Administration
   "The Small Business Economy" (2006, http://www.sba.gov/advo/research/sb_econ2007.pdf)
*State totals do not add to the U.S. figure as firms can be in more than one state.

Rate of Employer Firm Terminations in 2006

National Rate = 9.4% of Existing Firms*

ALPHA ORDER

RANK	STATE	RATE
24	Alabama	12.6
17	Alaska	13.2
1	Arizona	44.3
34	Arkansas	11.6
11	California	13.9
4	Colorado	15.8
37	Connecticut	11.4
21	Delaware	12.8
12	Florida	13.6
9	Georgia	14.4
27	Hawaii	12.4
8	Idaho	14.5
36	Illinois	11.5
39	Indiana	11.0
44	Iowa	10.3
48	Kansas	10.0
32	Kentucky	12.0
50	Louisiana	9.2
34	Maine	11.6
6	Maryland	14.9
29	Massachusetts	12.2
49	Michigan	9.9
43	Minnesota	10.8
9	Mississippi	14.4
16	Missouri	13.3
24	Montana	12.6
42	Nebraska	10.9
5	Nevada	15.4
14	New Hampshire	13.5
23	New Jersey	12.7
29	New Mexico	12.2
24	New York	12.6
27	North Carolina	12.4
38	North Dakota	11.1
39	Ohio	11.0
46	Oklahoma	10.1
20	Oregon	13.1
21	Pennsylvania	12.8
12	Rhode Island	13.6
29	South Carolina	12.2
46	South Dakota	10.1
7	Tennessee	14.7
17	Texas	13.2
3	Utah	17.8
39	Vermont	11.0
33	Virginia	11.8
2	Washington	18.6
17	West Virginia	13.2
45	Wisconsin	10.2
15	Wyoming	13.4

RANK ORDER

RANK	STATE	RATE
1	Arizona	44.3
2	Washington	18.6
3	Utah	17.8
4	Colorado	15.8
5	Nevada	15.4
6	Maryland	14.9
7	Tennessee	14.7
8	Idaho	14.5
9	Georgia	14.4
9	Mississippi	14.4
11	California	13.9
12	Florida	13.6
12	Rhode Island	13.6
14	New Hampshire	13.5
15	Wyoming	13.4
16	Missouri	13.3
17	Alaska	13.2
17	Texas	13.2
17	West Virginia	13.2
20	Oregon	13.1
21	Delaware	12.8
21	Pennsylvania	12.8
23	New Jersey	12.7
24	Alabama	12.6
24	Montana	12.6
24	New York	12.6
27	Hawaii	12.4
27	North Carolina	12.4
29	Massachusetts	12.2
29	New Mexico	12.2
29	South Carolina	12.2
32	Kentucky	12.0
33	Virginia	11.8
34	Arkansas	11.6
34	Maine	11.6
36	Illinois	11.5
37	Connecticut	11.4
38	North Dakota	11.1
39	Indiana	11.0
39	Ohio	11.0
39	Vermont	11.0
42	Nebraska	10.9
43	Minnesota	10.8
44	Iowa	10.3
45	Wisconsin	10.2
46	Oklahoma	10.1
46	South Dakota	10.1
48	Kansas	10.0
49	Michigan	9.9
50	Louisiana	9.2

	District of Columbia	11.2

Source: CQ Press using data from U.S. Small Business Administration
"The Small Business Economy" (2006, http://www.sba.gov/advo/research/sb_econ2007.pdf)
*Firms can be in more than one state. Firms with paid employees ceasing operations in 2006 as a percent of employer firms existing in 2006. Some state terminations result in successor firms which are not listed as new firms, thus making terminations higher than formations for most states.

Percent of Businesses Owned by Women in 2002

National Percent = 28.3% of Businesses*

ALPHA ORDER

RANK ORDER

RANK	STATE	PERCENT	RANK	STATE	PERCENT
28	Alabama	26.5	1	Maryland	31.0
33	Alaska	26.2	2	New Mexico	30.9
13	Arizona	28.8	3	Hawaii	30.1
47	Arkansas	23.8	4	California	30.0
4	California	30.0	5	Illinois	29.8
11	Colorado	29.1	6	Virginia	29.7
22	Connecticut	27.2	7	Michigan	29.6
45	Delaware	24.2	7	New York	29.6
15	Florida	28.4	9	Oregon	29.5
11	Georgia	29.1	10	Washington	29.4
3	Hawaii	30.1	11	Colorado	29.1
48	Idaho	23.7	11	Georgia	29.1
5	Illinois	29.8	13	Arizona	28.8
20	Indiana	27.4	14	Massachusetts	28.7
25	Iowa	27.0	15	Florida	28.4
22	Kansas	27.2	16	Nevada	28.1
38	Kentucky	25.7	16	Ohio	28.1
31	Louisiana	26.4	18	Minnesota	27.9
46	Maine	24.0	19	West Virginia	27.7
1	Maryland	31.0	20	Indiana	27.4
14	Massachusetts	28.7	20	Missouri	27.4
7	Michigan	29.6	22	Connecticut	27.2
18	Minnesota	27.9	22	Kansas	27.2
40	Mississippi	25.1	24	North Carolina	27.1
20	Missouri	27.4	25	Iowa	27.0
43	Montana	24.4	25	Texas	27.0
27	Nebraska	26.6	27	Nebraska	26.6
16	Nevada	28.1	28	Alabama	26.5
42	New Hampshire	24.7	28	Rhode Island	26.5
33	New Jersey	26.2	28	Wisconsin	26.5
2	New Mexico	30.9	31	Louisiana	26.4
7	New York	29.6	32	Vermont	26.3
24	North Carolina	27.1	33	Alaska	26.2
49	North Dakota	23.2	33	New Jersey	26.2
16	Ohio	28.1	33	South Carolina	26.2
38	Oklahoma	25.7	36	Pennsylvania	26.0
9	Oregon	29.5	36	Tennessee	26.0
36	Pennsylvania	26.0	38	Kentucky	25.7
28	Rhode Island	26.5	38	Oklahoma	25.7
33	South Carolina	26.2	40	Mississippi	25.1
50	South Dakota	22.4	40	Utah	25.1
36	Tennessee	26.0	42	New Hampshire	24.7
25	Texas	27.0	43	Montana	24.4
40	Utah	25.1	43	Wyoming	24.4
32	Vermont	26.3	45	Delaware	24.2
6	Virginia	29.7	46	Maine	24.0
10	Washington	29.4	47	Arkansas	23.8
19	West Virginia	27.7	48	Idaho	23.7
28	Wisconsin	26.5	49	North Dakota	23.2
43	Wyoming	24.4	50	South Dakota	22.4

District of Columbia 33.2

Source: CQ Press using data from U.S. Bureau of the Census
"2002 Survey of Business Owners" (http://www.census.gov/csd/sbo/index.html)
*Based on survey of firms with at least $1,000 in receipts. Ownership is defined as having 51 percent or more of the stock or equity in a business.

Percent of Businesses Owned by Minorities in 2002

National Percent = 17.9% of Businesses*

<table>
<tr><td colspan="3">ALPHA ORDER</td><td colspan="3">RANK ORDER</td></tr>
<tr><td>RANK</td><td>STATE</td><td>PERCENT</td><td>RANK</td><td>STATE</td><td>PERCENT</td></tr>
<tr><td>19</td><td>Alabama</td><td>12.4</td><td>1</td><td>Hawaii</td><td>58.8</td></tr>
<tr><td>15</td><td>Alaska</td><td>14.9</td><td>2</td><td>California</td><td>33.0</td></tr>
<tr><td>14</td><td>Arizona</td><td>15.4</td><td>3</td><td>New Mexico</td><td>29.6</td></tr>
<tr><td>29</td><td>Arkansas</td><td>7.4</td><td>4</td><td>Texas</td><td>29.1</td></tr>
<tr><td>2</td><td>California</td><td>33.0</td><td>5</td><td>Florida</td><td>27.4</td></tr>
<tr><td>24</td><td>Colorado</td><td>10.0</td><td>6</td><td>New York</td><td>26.7</td></tr>
<tr><td>25</td><td>Connecticut</td><td>9.4</td><td>7</td><td>Maryland</td><td>25.9</td></tr>
<tr><td>21</td><td>Delaware</td><td>11.6</td><td>8</td><td>Georgia</td><td>20.8</td></tr>
<tr><td>5</td><td>Florida</td><td>27.4</td><td>9</td><td>New Jersey</td><td>19.9</td></tr>
<tr><td>8</td><td>Georgia</td><td>20.8</td><td>10</td><td>Louisiana</td><td>17.9</td></tr>
<tr><td>1</td><td>Hawaii</td><td>58.8</td><td>11</td><td>Virginia</td><td>17.7</td></tr>
<tr><td>41</td><td>Idaho</td><td>4.5</td><td>12</td><td>Illinois</td><td>16.4</td></tr>
<tr><td>12</td><td>Illinois</td><td>16.4</td><td>13</td><td>Mississippi</td><td>16.0</td></tr>
<tr><td>34</td><td>Indiana</td><td>6.4</td><td>14</td><td>Arizona</td><td>15.4</td></tr>
<tr><td>48</td><td>Iowa</td><td>2.4</td><td>15</td><td>Alaska</td><td>14.9</td></tr>
<tr><td>34</td><td>Kansas</td><td>6.4</td><td>15</td><td>Nevada</td><td>14.9</td></tr>
<tr><td>38</td><td>Kentucky</td><td>4.7</td><td>17</td><td>South Carolina</td><td>12.8</td></tr>
<tr><td>10</td><td>Louisiana</td><td>17.9</td><td>18</td><td>North Carolina</td><td>12.6</td></tr>
<tr><td>49</td><td>Maine</td><td>1.9</td><td>19</td><td>Alabama</td><td>12.4</td></tr>
<tr><td>7</td><td>Maryland</td><td>25.9</td><td>20</td><td>Oklahoma</td><td>12.0</td></tr>
<tr><td>27</td><td>Massachusetts</td><td>8.8</td><td>21</td><td>Delaware</td><td>11.6</td></tr>
<tr><td>23</td><td>Michigan</td><td>10.2</td><td>22</td><td>Washington</td><td>10.8</td></tr>
<tr><td>37</td><td>Minnesota</td><td>5.0</td><td>23</td><td>Michigan</td><td>10.2</td></tr>
<tr><td>13</td><td>Mississippi</td><td>16.0</td><td>24</td><td>Colorado</td><td>10.0</td></tr>
<tr><td>33</td><td>Missouri</td><td>6.9</td><td>25</td><td>Connecticut</td><td>9.4</td></tr>
<tr><td>43</td><td>Montana</td><td>3.7</td><td>26</td><td>Tennessee</td><td>9.2</td></tr>
<tr><td>42</td><td>Nebraska</td><td>4.1</td><td>27</td><td>Massachusetts</td><td>8.8</td></tr>
<tr><td>15</td><td>Nevada</td><td>14.9</td><td>28</td><td>Rhode Island</td><td>8.2</td></tr>
<tr><td>46</td><td>New Hampshire</td><td>2.8</td><td>29</td><td>Arkansas</td><td>7.4</td></tr>
<tr><td>9</td><td>New Jersey</td><td>19.9</td><td>30</td><td>Ohio</td><td>7.3</td></tr>
<tr><td>3</td><td>New Mexico</td><td>29.6</td><td>31</td><td>Oregon</td><td>7.0</td></tr>
<tr><td>6</td><td>New York</td><td>26.7</td><td>31</td><td>Pennsylvania</td><td>7.0</td></tr>
<tr><td>18</td><td>North Carolina</td><td>12.6</td><td>33</td><td>Missouri</td><td>6.9</td></tr>
<tr><td>47</td><td>North Dakota</td><td>2.5</td><td>34</td><td>Indiana</td><td>6.4</td></tr>
<tr><td>30</td><td>Ohio</td><td>7.3</td><td>34</td><td>Kansas</td><td>6.4</td></tr>
<tr><td>20</td><td>Oklahoma</td><td>12.0</td><td>36</td><td>Utah</td><td>5.3</td></tr>
<tr><td>31</td><td>Oregon</td><td>7.0</td><td>37</td><td>Minnesota</td><td>5.0</td></tr>
<tr><td>31</td><td>Pennsylvania</td><td>7.0</td><td>38</td><td>Kentucky</td><td>4.7</td></tr>
<tr><td>28</td><td>Rhode Island</td><td>8.2</td><td>39</td><td>Wisconsin</td><td>4.6</td></tr>
<tr><td>17</td><td>South Carolina</td><td>12.8</td><td>39</td><td>Wyoming</td><td>4.6</td></tr>
<tr><td>45</td><td>South Dakota</td><td>3.0</td><td>41</td><td>Idaho</td><td>4.5</td></tr>
<tr><td>26</td><td>Tennessee</td><td>9.2</td><td>42</td><td>Nebraska</td><td>4.1</td></tr>
<tr><td>4</td><td>Texas</td><td>29.1</td><td>43</td><td>Montana</td><td>3.7</td></tr>
<tr><td>36</td><td>Utah</td><td>5.3</td><td>44</td><td>West Virginia</td><td>3.4</td></tr>
<tr><td>49</td><td>Vermont</td><td>1.9</td><td>45</td><td>South Dakota</td><td>3.0</td></tr>
<tr><td>11</td><td>Virginia</td><td>17.7</td><td>46</td><td>New Hampshire</td><td>2.8</td></tr>
<tr><td>22</td><td>Washington</td><td>10.8</td><td>47</td><td>North Dakota</td><td>2.5</td></tr>
<tr><td>44</td><td>West Virginia</td><td>3.4</td><td>48</td><td>Iowa</td><td>2.4</td></tr>
<tr><td>39</td><td>Wisconsin</td><td>4.6</td><td>49</td><td>Maine</td><td>1.9</td></tr>
<tr><td>39</td><td>Wyoming</td><td>4.6</td><td>49</td><td>Vermont</td><td>1.9</td></tr>
<tr><td></td><td></td><td></td><td></td><td>District of Columbia</td><td>36.0</td></tr>
</table>

Source: CQ Press using data from U.S. Bureau of the Census
   "2002 Survey of Business Owners" (http://www.census.gov/csd/sbo/index.html)
*Based on survey of firms with at least $1,000 in receipts. Ownership is defined as having 51 percent or more of the stock or equity in a business.

V. Education

Estimated Percent of School-Age Population in Public Schools in 2006

National Percent = 92.1%*

ALPHA ORDER

RANK	STATE	PERCENT
32	Alabama	91.0
1	Alaska	101.2
7	Arizona	95.4
8	Arkansas	95.2
11	California	93.9
10	Colorado	94.2
15	Connecticut	93.4
50	Delaware	82.5
22	Florida	92.3
30	Georgia	91.2
46	Hawaii	86.7
18	Idaho	93.1
35	Illinois	90.7
37	Indiana	90.3
16	Iowa	93.3
18	Kansas	93.1
11	Kentucky	93.9
49	Louisiana	83.0
20	Maine	92.8
46	Maryland	86.7
27	Massachusetts	91.6
9	Michigan	94.7
24	Minnesota	92.0
39	Mississippi	90.0
40	Missouri	89.1
33	Montana	90.9
37	Nebraska	90.3
28	Nevada	91.5
25	New Hampshire	91.8
30	New Jersey	91.2
41	New Mexico	89.0
48	New York	85.5
26	North Carolina	91.7
16	North Dakota	93.3
36	Ohio	90.4
2	Oklahoma	99.3
42	Oregon	88.3
43	Pennsylvania	88.0
44	Rhode Island	87.4
20	South Carolina	92.8
45	South Dakota	87.2
29	Tennessee	91.3
3	Texas	99.1
13	Utah	93.6
5	Vermont	96.1
13	Virginia	93.6
22	Washington	92.3
4	West Virginia	98.9
34	Wisconsin	90.8
6	Wyoming	95.7

RANK ORDER

RANK	STATE	PERCENT
1	Alaska	101.2
2	Oklahoma	99.3
3	Texas	99.1
4	West Virginia	98.9
5	Vermont	96.1
6	Wyoming	95.7
7	Arizona	95.4
8	Arkansas	95.2
9	Michigan	94.7
10	Colorado	94.2
11	California	93.9
11	Kentucky	93.9
13	Utah	93.6
13	Virginia	93.6
15	Connecticut	93.4
16	Iowa	93.3
16	North Dakota	93.3
18	Idaho	93.1
18	Kansas	93.1
20	Maine	92.8
20	South Carolina	92.8
22	Florida	92.3
22	Washington	92.3
24	Minnesota	92.0
25	New Hampshire	91.8
26	North Carolina	91.7
27	Massachusetts	91.6
28	Nevada	91.5
29	Tennessee	91.3
30	Georgia	91.2
30	New Jersey	91.2
32	Alabama	91.0
33	Montana	90.9
34	Wisconsin	90.8
35	Illinois	90.7
36	Ohio	90.4
37	Indiana	90.3
37	Nebraska	90.3
39	Mississippi	90.0
40	Missouri	89.1
41	New Mexico	89.0
42	Oregon	88.3
43	Pennsylvania	88.0
44	Rhode Island	87.4
45	South Dakota	87.2
46	Hawaii	86.7
46	Maryland	86.7
48	New York	85.5
49	Louisiana	83.0
50	Delaware	82.5

District of Columbia — 96.2

Source: CQ Press using data from U.S. Department of Education, National Center for Education Statistics
"Common Core of Data (CCD) Database" (http://nces.ed.gov/ccd/)

*Estimate based on 2006 Census population estimates for five to 17 year olds compared to estimated 2005-2006 school year public school student membership. Student membership figures include counts for pre-kindergarten programs. Figures higher than 100 percent reflect using different sources for population and for student membership.

Regular Public Elementary and Secondary School Districts in 2006

National Total = 14,199 Districts*

ALPHA ORDER					RANK ORDER			
RANK	STATE	DISTRICTS	% of USA		RANK	STATE	DISTRICTS	% of USA
32	Alabama	165	1.2%		1	Texas	1,035	7.3%
43	Alaska	54	0.4%		2	California	987	7.0%
23	Arizona	218	1.5%		3	Illinois	875	6.2%
22	Arkansas	253	1.8%		4	New York	730	5.1%
2	California	987	7.0%		5	New Jersey	615	4.3%
27	Colorado	179	1.3%		6	Ohio	614	4.3%
31	Connecticut	166	1.2%		7	Michigan	552	3.9%
48	Delaware	19	0.1%		8	Oklahoma	540	3.8%
41	Florida	67	0.5%		9	Missouri	524	3.7%
26	Georgia	180	1.3%		10	Pennsylvania	501	3.5%
50	Hawaii	1	0.0%		11	Nebraska	474	3.3%
36	Idaho	122	0.9%		12	Wisconsin	440	3.1%
3	Illinois	875	6.2%		13	Montana	430	3.0%
20	Indiana	294	2.1%		14	Iowa	365	2.6%
14	Iowa	365	2.6%		15	Massachusetts	350	2.5%
18	Kansas	300	2.1%		16	Minnesota	343	2.4%
29	Kentucky	176	1.2%		17	Vermont	302	2.1%
40	Louisiana	68	0.5%		18	Kansas	300	2.1%
21	Maine	285	2.0%		19	Washington	296	2.1%
47	Maryland	24	0.2%		20	Indiana	294	2.1%
15	Massachusetts	350	2.5%		21	Maine	285	2.0%
7	Michigan	552	3.9%		22	Arkansas	253	1.8%
16	Minnesota	343	2.4%		23	Arizona	218	1.5%
33	Mississippi	152	1.1%		24	North Dakota	204	1.4%
9	Missouri	524	3.7%		25	Oregon	200	1.4%
13	Montana	430	3.0%		26	Georgia	180	1.3%
11	Nebraska	474	3.3%		27	Colorado	179	1.3%
49	Nevada	17	0.1%		27	New Hampshire	179	1.3%
27	New Hampshire	179	1.3%		29	Kentucky	176	1.2%
5	New Jersey	615	4.3%		30	South Dakota	168	1.2%
38	New Mexico	89	0.6%		31	Connecticut	166	1.2%
4	New York	730	5.1%		32	Alabama	165	1.2%
37	North Carolina	115	0.8%		33	Mississippi	152	1.1%
24	North Dakota	204	1.4%		34	Tennessee	136	1.0%
6	Ohio	614	4.3%		35	Virginia	134	0.9%
8	Oklahoma	540	3.8%		36	Idaho	122	0.9%
25	Oregon	200	1.4%		37	North Carolina	115	0.8%
10	Pennsylvania	501	3.5%		38	New Mexico	89	0.6%
46	Rhode Island	32	0.2%		39	South Carolina	85	0.6%
39	South Carolina	85	0.6%		40	Louisiana	68	0.5%
30	South Dakota	168	1.2%		41	Florida	67	0.5%
34	Tennessee	136	1.0%		42	West Virginia	55	0.4%
1	Texas	1,035	7.3%		43	Alaska	54	0.4%
45	Utah	40	0.3%		44	Wyoming	48	0.3%
17	Vermont	302	2.1%		45	Utah	40	0.3%
35	Virginia	134	0.9%		46	Rhode Island	32	0.2%
19	Washington	296	2.1%		47	Maryland	24	0.2%
42	West Virginia	55	0.4%		48	Delaware	19	0.1%
12	Wisconsin	440	3.1%		49	Nevada	17	0.1%
44	Wyoming	48	0.3%		50	Hawaii	1	0.0%
						District of Columbia	1	0.0%

Source: U.S. Department of Education, National Center for Education Statistics
   "Common Core of Data (CCD) Database" (http://nces.ed.gov/ccd/)
*For school year 2005-2006. Regular school districts are agencies responsible for providing free public education for school-age children residing within their jurisdiction. Included in these figures are 367 districts that reported having no students. This can occur when a small district has no pupils or contracts with another district to educate the students under its jurisdiction.

Public Elementary and Secondary Schools in 2006

National Total = 97,382 Schools*

ALPHA ORDER

RANK ORDER

RANK	STATE	SCHOOLS	% of USA	RANK	STATE	SCHOOLS	% of USA
23	Alabama	1,585	1.6%	1	California	9,650	9.9%
44	Alaska	502	0.5%	2	Texas	8,517	8.7%
17	Arizona	2,078	2.1%	3	New York	4,669	4.8%
32	Arkansas	1,138	1.2%	4	Illinois	4,401	4.5%
1	California	9,650	9.9%	5	Michigan	4,090	4.2%
21	Colorado	1,707	1.8%	6	Ohio	4,007	4.1%
33	Connecticut	1,111	1.1%	7	Florida	3,723	3.8%
50	Delaware	222	0.2%	8	Pennsylvania	3,250	3.3%
7	Florida	3,723	3.8%	9	Minnesota	2,644	2.7%
11	Georgia	2,389	2.5%	10	New Jersey	2,474	2.5%
49	Hawaii	285	0.3%	11	Georgia	2,389	2.5%
40	Idaho	706	0.7%	12	Missouri	2,361	2.4%
4	Illinois	4,401	4.5%	13	North Carolina	2,347	2.4%
18	Indiana	1,977	2.0%	14	Washington	2,269	2.3%
24	Iowa	1,512	1.6%	15	Wisconsin	2,246	2.3%
27	Kansas	1,407	1.4%	16	Virginia	2,079	2.1%
26	Kentucky	1,409	1.4%	17	Arizona	2,078	2.1%
28	Louisiana	1,390	1.4%	18	Indiana	1,977	2.0%
41	Maine	679	0.7%	19	Massachusetts	1,879	1.9%
25	Maryland	1,430	1.5%	20	Oklahoma	1,788	1.8%
19	Massachusetts	1,879	1.9%	21	Colorado	1,707	1.8%
5	Michigan	4,090	4.2%	22	Tennessee	1,700	1.7%
9	Minnesota	2,644	2.7%	23	Alabama	1,585	1.6%
34	Mississippi	1,051	1.1%	24	Iowa	1,512	1.6%
12	Missouri	2,361	2.4%	25	Maryland	1,430	1.5%
37	Montana	840	0.9%	26	Kentucky	1,409	1.4%
30	Nebraska	1,225	1.3%	27	Kansas	1,407	1.4%
42	Nevada	557	0.6%	28	Louisiana	1,390	1.4%
45	New Hampshire	480	0.5%	29	Oregon	1,260	1.3%
10	New Jersey	2,474	2.5%	30	Nebraska	1,225	1.3%
36	New Mexico	854	0.9%	31	South Carolina	1,152	1.2%
3	New York	4,669	4.8%	32	Arkansas	1,138	1.2%
13	North Carolina	2,347	2.4%	33	Connecticut	1,111	1.1%
43	North Dakota	539	0.6%	34	Mississippi	1,051	1.1%
6	Ohio	4,007	4.1%	35	Utah	956	1.0%
20	Oklahoma	1,788	1.8%	36	New Mexico	854	0.9%
29	Oregon	1,260	1.3%	37	Montana	840	0.9%
8	Pennsylvania	3,250	3.3%	38	West Virginia	784	0.8%
48	Rhode Island	338	0.3%	39	South Dakota	725	0.7%
31	South Carolina	1,152	1.2%	40	Idaho	706	0.7%
39	South Dakota	725	0.7%	41	Maine	679	0.7%
22	Tennessee	1,700	1.7%	42	Nevada	557	0.6%
2	Texas	8,517	8.7%	43	North Dakota	539	0.6%
35	Utah	956	1.0%	44	Alaska	502	0.5%
46	Vermont	392	0.4%	45	New Hampshire	480	0.5%
16	Virginia	2,079	2.1%	46	Vermont	392	0.4%
14	Washington	2,269	2.3%	47	Wyoming	379	0.4%
38	West Virginia	784	0.8%	48	Rhode Island	338	0.3%
15	Wisconsin	2,246	2.3%	49	Hawaii	285	0.3%
47	Wyoming	379	0.4%	50	Delaware	222	0.2%
					District of Columbia	229	0.2%

Source: U.S. Department of Education, National Center for Education Statistics
    "Common Core of Data (CCD) Database" (http://nces.ed.gov/ccd/)
*For school year 2005-2006. Includes 2,579 schools without membership and 958 schools whose membership is reported for some other school.

Private Elementary and Secondary Schools in 2004

National Total = 28,384 Schools*

ALPHA ORDER

RANK	STATE	SCHOOLS	% of USA
22	Alabama	408	1.4%
48	Alaska	75	0.3%
28	Arizona	292	1.0%
33	Arkansas	189	0.7%
1	California	3,377	11.9%
26	Colorado	345	1.2%
25	Connecticut	361	1.3%
42	Delaware	121	0.4%
4	Florida	1,803	6.4%
14	Georgia	665	2.3%
40	Hawaii	133	0.5%
45	Idaho	107	0.4%
5	Illinois	1,346	4.7%
11	Indiana	784	2.8%
29	Iowa	266	0.9%
32	Kansas	229	0.8%
23	Kentucky	368	1.3%
21	Louisiana	440	1.6%
38	Maine	151	0.5%
12	Maryland	727	2.6%
13	Massachusetts	688	2.4%
9	Michigan	983	3.5%
18	Minnesota	568	2.0%
31	Mississippi	240	0.8%
16	Missouri	633	2.2%
46	Montana	104	0.4%
30	Nebraska	242	0.9%
43	Nevada	111	0.4%
37	New Hampshire	165	0.6%
10	New Jersey	964	3.4%
34	New Mexico	176	0.6%
3	New York	1,959	6.9%
15	North Carolina	661	2.3%
49	North Dakota	52	0.2%
8	Ohio	987	3.5%
35	Oklahoma	168	0.6%
24	Oregon	362	1.3%
2	Pennsylvania	2,009	7.1%
39	Rhode Island	139	0.5%
26	South Carolina	345	1.2%
47	South Dakota	95	0.3%
20	Tennessee	551	1.9%
6	Texas	1,282	4.5%
44	Utah	108	0.4%
41	Vermont	123	0.4%
17	Virginia	604	2.1%
19	Washington	556	2.0%
36	West Virginia	166	0.6%
7	Wisconsin	1,041	3.7%
50	Wyoming	35	0.1%

RANK ORDER

RANK	STATE	SCHOOLS	% of USA
1	California	3,377	11.9%
2	Pennsylvania	2,009	7.1%
3	New York	1,959	6.9%
4	Florida	1,803	6.4%
5	Illinois	1,346	4.7%
6	Texas	1,282	4.5%
7	Wisconsin	1,041	3.7%
8	Ohio	987	3.5%
9	Michigan	983	3.5%
10	New Jersey	964	3.4%
11	Indiana	784	2.8%
12	Maryland	727	2.6%
13	Massachusetts	688	2.4%
14	Georgia	665	2.3%
15	North Carolina	661	2.3%
16	Missouri	633	2.2%
17	Virginia	604	2.1%
18	Minnesota	568	2.0%
19	Washington	556	2.0%
20	Tennessee	551	1.9%
21	Louisiana	440	1.6%
22	Alabama	408	1.4%
23	Kentucky	368	1.3%
24	Oregon	362	1.3%
25	Connecticut	361	1.3%
26	Colorado	345	1.2%
26	South Carolina	345	1.2%
28	Arizona	292	1.0%
29	Iowa	266	0.9%
30	Nebraska	242	0.9%
31	Mississippi	240	0.8%
32	Kansas	229	0.8%
33	Arkansas	189	0.7%
34	New Mexico	176	0.6%
35	Oklahoma	168	0.6%
36	West Virginia	166	0.6%
37	New Hampshire	165	0.6%
38	Maine	151	0.5%
39	Rhode Island	139	0.5%
40	Hawaii	133	0.5%
41	Vermont	123	0.4%
42	Delaware	121	0.4%
43	Nevada	111	0.4%
44	Utah	108	0.4%
45	Idaho	107	0.4%
46	Montana	104	0.4%
47	South Dakota	95	0.3%
48	Alaska	75	0.3%
49	North Dakota	52	0.2%
50	Wyoming	35	0.1%
	District of Columbia	82	0.3%

Source: U.S. Department of Education, Institute of Education Sciences
"Characteristics of Private Schools in the United States" (NCES 2006-319, http://nces.ed.gov/pubs2006/2006319.pdf)
*For school year 2003-2004.

Percent of Elementary/Secondary School Students in Private Schools in 2004

National Percent = 9.6% of Students*

RANK	STATE	PERCENT		RANK	STATE	PERCENT
	ALPHA ORDER				RANK ORDER	
23	Alabama	9.2		1	Delaware	18.3
44	Alaska	4.5		2	Hawaii	17.7
46	Arizona	4.2		3	Louisiana	16.7
41	Arkansas	5.6		4	Rhode Island	15.4
26	California	8.9		5	Pennsylvania	14.9
38	Colorado	6.0		6	Maryland	14.6
12	Connecticut	11.9		7	Wisconsin	13.9
1	Delaware	18.3		8	New York	13.8
17	Florida	11.1		9	New Jersey	13.0
34	Georgia	7.3		10	Massachusetts	12.6
2	Hawaii	17.7		10	Nebraska	12.6
48	Idaho	4.1		12	Connecticut	11.9
16	Illinois	11.5		13	Missouri	11.8
22	Indiana	9.3		13	Vermont	11.8
25	Iowa	9.1		15	Ohio	11.7
29	Kansas	8.4		16	Illinois	11.5
20	Kentucky	10.0		17	Florida	11.1
3	Louisiana	16.7		18	Minnesota	10.3
21	Maine	9.6		19	New Hampshire	10.2
6	Maryland	14.6		20	Kentucky	10.0
10	Massachusetts	12.6		21	Maine	9.6
28	Michigan	8.5		22	Indiana	9.3
18	Minnesota	10.3		23	Alabama	9.2
23	Mississippi	9.2		23	Mississippi	9.2
13	Missouri	11.8		25	Iowa	9.1
40	Montana	5.7		26	California	8.9
10	Nebraska	12.6		27	Tennessee	8.6
46	Nevada	4.2		28	Michigan	8.5
19	New Hampshire	10.2		29	Kansas	8.4
9	New Jersey	13.0		30	Virginia	8.0
37	New Mexico	6.2		31	South Carolina	7.8
8	New York	13.8		31	South Dakota	7.8
36	North Carolina	6.8		33	Oregon	7.5
38	North Dakota	6.0		34	Georgia	7.3
15	Ohio	11.7		35	Washington	7.2
44	Oklahoma	4.5		36	North Carolina	6.8
33	Oregon	7.5		37	New Mexico	6.2
5	Pennsylvania	14.9		38	Colorado	6.0
4	Rhode Island	15.4		38	North Dakota	6.0
31	South Carolina	7.8		40	Montana	5.7
31	South Dakota	7.8		41	Arkansas	5.6
27	Tennessee	8.6		42	West Virginia	5.1
43	Texas	5.0		43	Texas	5.0
49	Utah	3.1		44	Alaska	4.5
13	Vermont	11.8		44	Oklahoma	4.5
30	Virginia	8.0		46	Arizona	4.2
35	Washington	7.2		46	Nevada	4.2
42	West Virginia	5.1		48	Idaho	4.1
7	Wisconsin	13.9		49	Utah	3.1
50	Wyoming	2.4		50	Wyoming	2.4
					District of Columbia	22.0

Source: CQ Press using data from U.S. Department of Education, Institute of Education Sciences
"Characteristics of Private Schools in the United States"
*Estimate for 2003-2004. Calculated using 5-17 year old population estimates for 2004.

Estimated Enrollment in Public Elementary and Secondary Schools in 2007

National Total = 48,892,573 Students*

ALPHA ORDER

RANK	STATE	STUDENTS	% of USA
23	Alabama	739,554	1.5%
45	Alaska	132,841	0.3%
14	Arizona	1,033,680	2.1%
34	Arkansas	454,788	0.9%
1	California	6,283,835	12.9%
22	Colorado	794,026	1.6%
28	Connecticut	573,768	1.2%
46	Delaware	122,263	0.3%
4	Florida	2,663,697	5.4%
9	Georgia	1,629,157	3.3%
42	Hawaii	180,720	0.4%
39	Idaho	267,533	0.5%
5	Illinois	2,118,276	4.3%
13	Indiana	1,035,296	2.1%
32	Iowa	483,122	1.0%
33	Kansas	470,996	1.0%
26	Kentucky	646,544	1.3%
25	Louisiana	675,851	1.4%
41	Maine	195,802	0.4%
20	Maryland	851,138	1.7%
16	Massachusetts	968,097	2.0%
8	Michigan	1,734,237	3.5%
21	Minnesota	828,601	1.7%
30	Mississippi	494,135	1.0%
18	Missouri	898,373	1.8%
44	Montana	144,418	0.3%
37	Nebraska	287,141	0.6%
35	Nevada	426,436	0.9%
40	New Hampshire	205,861	0.4%
11	New Jersey	1,388,535	2.8%
36	New Mexico	328,568	0.7%
3	New York	2,809,590	5.7%
10	North Carolina	1,403,196	2.9%
48	North Dakota	95,600	0.2%
6	Ohio	1,865,524	3.8%
27	Oklahoma	639,023	1.3%
29	Oregon	562,828	1.2%
7	Pennsylvania	1,821,383	3.7%
43	Rhode Island	162,259	0.3%
24	South Carolina	689,668	1.4%
47	South Dakota	120,278	0.2%
17	Tennessee	950,570	1.9%
2	Texas	4,576,933	9.4%
31	Utah	485,839	1.0%
49	Vermont	92,571	0.2%
12	Virginia	1,229,808	2.5%
15	Washington	1,028,377	2.1%
38	West Virginia	281,297	0.6%
19	Wisconsin	876,700	1.8%
50	Wyoming	84,611	0.2%

RANK ORDER

RANK	STATE	STUDENTS	% of USA
1	California	6,283,835	12.9%
2	Texas	4,576,933	9.4%
3	New York	2,809,590	5.7%
4	Florida	2,663,697	5.4%
5	Illinois	2,118,276	4.3%
6	Ohio	1,865,524	3.8%
7	Pennsylvania	1,821,383	3.7%
8	Michigan	1,734,237	3.5%
9	Georgia	1,629,157	3.3%
10	North Carolina	1,403,196	2.9%
11	New Jersey	1,388,535	2.8%
12	Virginia	1,229,808	2.5%
13	Indiana	1,035,296	2.1%
14	Arizona	1,033,680	2.1%
15	Washington	1,028,377	2.1%
16	Massachusetts	968,097	2.0%
17	Tennessee	950,570	1.9%
18	Missouri	898,373	1.8%
19	Wisconsin	876,700	1.8%
20	Maryland	851,138	1.7%
21	Minnesota	828,601	1.7%
22	Colorado	794,026	1.6%
23	Alabama	739,554	1.5%
24	South Carolina	689,668	1.4%
25	Louisiana	675,851	1.4%
26	Kentucky	646,544	1.3%
27	Oklahoma	639,023	1.3%
28	Connecticut	573,768	1.2%
29	Oregon	562,828	1.2%
30	Mississippi	494,135	1.0%
31	Utah	485,839	1.0%
32	Iowa	483,122	1.0%
33	Kansas	470,996	1.0%
34	Arkansas	454,788	0.9%
35	Nevada	426,436	0.9%
36	New Mexico	328,568	0.7%
37	Nebraska	287,141	0.6%
38	West Virginia	281,297	0.6%
39	Idaho	267,533	0.5%
40	New Hampshire	205,861	0.4%
41	Maine	195,802	0.4%
42	Hawaii	180,720	0.4%
43	Rhode Island	162,259	0.3%
44	Montana	144,418	0.3%
45	Alaska	132,841	0.3%
46	Delaware	122,263	0.3%
47	South Dakota	120,278	0.2%
48	North Dakota	95,600	0.2%
49	Vermont	92,571	0.2%
50	Wyoming	84,611	0.2%
	District of Columbia	59,228	0.1%

Source: National Education Association, Washington, D.C.
   "Rankings & Estimates, December 2007" (Copyright © 2007, NEA, used with permission)
*Estimates for school year 2006-2007.

Estimated Public Elementary and Secondary School Teachers in 2007

National Total = 3,174,354 Teachers*

ALPHA ORDER				RANK ORDER			
RANK	STATE	TEACHERS	% of USA	RANK	STATE	TEACHERS	% of USA
21	Alabama	49,985	1.6%	1	Texas	311,654	9.8%
48	Alaska	8,017	0.3%	2	California	304,152	9.6%
22	Arizona	47,087	1.5%	3	New York	229,257	7.2%
31	Arkansas	34,139	1.1%	4	Florida	167,775	5.3%
2	California	304,152	9.6%	5	Illinois	131,926	4.2%
23	Colorado	46,959	1.5%	6	Pennsylvania	123,150	3.9%
26	Connecticut	42,533	1.3%	7	Ohio	119,250	3.8%
47	Delaware	8,041	0.3%	8	New Jersey	114,994	3.6%
4	Florida	167,775	5.3%	9	Georgia	112,861	3.6%
9	Georgia	112,861	3.6%	10	Michigan	109,946	3.5%
43	Hawaii	11,477	0.4%	11	North Carolina	95,542	3.0%
42	Idaho	14,770	0.5%	12	Virginia	93,553	2.9%
5	Illinois	131,926	4.2%	13	Massachusetts	73,176	2.3%
16	Indiana	61,183	1.9%	14	Missouri	66,840	2.1%
29	Iowa	35,405	1.1%	15	Tennessee	61,824	1.9%
30	Kansas	34,351	1.1%	16	Indiana	61,183	1.9%
28	Kentucky	41,331	1.3%	17	Maryland	59,322	1.9%
25	Louisiana	46,406	1.5%	18	Wisconsin	59,291	1.9%
39	Maine	16,395	0.5%	19	Washington	53,951	1.7%
17	Maryland	59,322	1.9%	20	Minnesota	50,237	1.6%
13	Massachusetts	73,176	2.3%	21	Alabama	49,985	1.6%
10	Michigan	109,946	3.5%	22	Arizona	47,087	1.5%
20	Minnesota	50,237	1.6%	23	Colorado	46,959	1.5%
32	Mississippi	33,494	1.1%	24	South Carolina	46,951	1.5%
14	Missouri	66,840	2.1%	25	Louisiana	46,406	1.5%
44	Montana	10,518	0.3%	26	Connecticut	42,533	1.3%
37	Nebraska	21,293	0.7%	27	Oklahoma	42,183	1.3%
34	Nevada	22,133	0.7%	28	Kentucky	41,331	1.3%
40	New Hampshire	15,800	0.5%	29	Iowa	35,405	1.1%
8	New Jersey	114,994	3.6%	30	Kansas	34,351	1.1%
36	New Mexico	21,667	0.7%	31	Arkansas	34,139	1.1%
3	New York	229,257	7.2%	32	Mississippi	33,494	1.1%
11	North Carolina	95,542	3.0%	33	Oregon	29,336	0.9%
49	North Dakota	7,569	0.2%	34	Nevada	22,133	0.7%
7	Ohio	119,250	3.8%	35	Utah	21,786	0.7%
27	Oklahoma	42,183	1.3%	36	New Mexico	21,667	0.7%
33	Oregon	29,336	0.9%	37	Nebraska	21,293	0.7%
6	Pennsylvania	123,150	3.9%	38	West Virginia	19,881	0.6%
41	Rhode Island	14,945	0.5%	39	Maine	16,395	0.5%
24	South Carolina	46,951	1.5%	40	New Hampshire	15,800	0.5%
46	South Dakota	9,024	0.3%	41	Rhode Island	14,945	0.5%
15	Tennessee	61,824	1.9%	42	Idaho	14,770	0.5%
1	Texas	311,654	9.8%	43	Hawaii	11,477	0.4%
35	Utah	21,786	0.7%	44	Montana	10,518	0.3%
45	Vermont	9,035	0.3%	45	Vermont	9,035	0.3%
12	Virginia	93,553	2.9%	46	South Dakota	9,024	0.3%
19	Washington	53,951	1.7%	47	Delaware	8,041	0.3%
38	West Virginia	19,881	0.6%	48	Alaska	8,017	0.3%
18	Wisconsin	59,291	1.9%	49	North Dakota	7,569	0.2%
50	Wyoming	6,457	0.2%	50	Wyoming	6,457	0.2%
					District of Columbia	5,503	0.2%

Source: National Education Association, Washington, D.C.
"Rankings & Estimates, December 2007" (Copyright © 2007, NEA, used with permission)
*Estimates for school year 2006-2007.

Estimated Pupil-Teacher Ratio in
Public Elementary and Secondary Schools in 2007
National Ratio = 15.4 Pupils per Teacher*

ALPHA ORDER

RANK	STATE	RATIO
22	Alabama	14.8
10	Alaska	16.6
2	Arizona	22.0
39	Arkansas	13.3
3	California	20.7
8	Colorado	16.9
36	Connecticut	13.5
19	Delaware	15.2
13	Florida	15.9
30	Georgia	14.4
15	Hawaii	15.7
7	Idaho	18.1
12	Illinois	16.1
8	Indiana	16.9
35	Iowa	13.6
33	Kansas	13.7
16	Kentucky	15.6
29	Louisiana	14.6
48	Maine	11.9
31	Maryland	14.3
41	Massachusetts	13.2
14	Michigan	15.8
11	Minnesota	16.5
22	Mississippi	14.8
38	Missouri	13.4
33	Montana	13.7
36	Nebraska	13.5
4	Nevada	19.3
44	New Hampshire	13.0
47	New Jersey	12.1
19	New Mexico	15.2
46	New York	12.3
26	North Carolina	14.7
45	North Dakota	12.6
16	Ohio	15.6
21	Oklahoma	15.1
5	Oregon	19.2
22	Pennsylvania	14.8
49	Rhode Island	10.9
26	South Carolina	14.7
39	South Dakota	13.3
18	Tennessee	15.4
26	Texas	14.7
1	Utah	22.3
50	Vermont	10.2
42	Virginia	13.1
6	Washington	19.1
32	West Virginia	14.1
22	Wisconsin	14.8
42	Wyoming	13.1

RANK ORDER

RANK	STATE	RATIO
1	Utah	22.3
2	Arizona	22.0
3	California	20.7
4	Nevada	19.3
5	Oregon	19.2
6	Washington	19.1
7	Idaho	18.1
8	Colorado	16.9
8	Indiana	16.9
10	Alaska	16.6
11	Minnesota	16.5
12	Illinois	16.1
13	Florida	15.9
14	Michigan	15.8
15	Hawaii	15.7
16	Kentucky	15.6
16	Ohio	15.6
18	Tennessee	15.4
19	Delaware	15.2
19	New Mexico	15.2
21	Oklahoma	15.1
22	Alabama	14.8
22	Mississippi	14.8
22	Pennsylvania	14.8
22	Wisconsin	14.8
26	North Carolina	14.7
26	South Carolina	14.7
26	Texas	14.7
29	Louisiana	14.6
30	Georgia	14.4
31	Maryland	14.3
32	West Virginia	14.1
33	Kansas	13.7
33	Montana	13.7
35	Iowa	13.6
36	Connecticut	13.5
36	Nebraska	13.5
38	Missouri	13.4
39	Arkansas	13.3
39	South Dakota	13.3
41	Massachusetts	13.2
42	Virginia	13.1
42	Wyoming	13.1
44	New Hampshire	13.0
45	North Dakota	12.6
46	New York	12.3
47	New Jersey	12.1
48	Maine	11.9
49	Rhode Island	10.9
50	Vermont	10.2

District of Columbia   10.8

Source: CQ Press using data from National Education Association, Washington, D.C.
"Rankings & Estimates, December 2007" (Copyright © 2007, NEA, used with permission)
*Estimates for school year 2006-2007.

Estimated Average Salary of Public School Classroom Teachers in 2007
(National Education Association)
National Average = $50,816*

ALPHA ORDER

RANK	STATE	SALARY
35	Alabama	$43,389
12	Alaska	54,658
25	Arizona	45,941
31	Arkansas	44,245
1	California	63,640
26	Colorado	45,833
2	Connecticut	60,822
11	Delaware	54,680
28	Florida	45,308
17	Georgia	49,905
14	Hawaii	51,922
39	Idaho	42,798
6	Illinois	58,246
22	Indiana	47,831
37	Iowa	43,130
36	Kansas	43,334
34	Kentucky	43,646
38	Louisiana	42,816
44	Maine	41,596
7	Maryland	56,927
4	Massachusetts	58,624
10	Michigan	54,895
18	Minnesota	49,634
48	Mississippi	40,182
43	Missouri	41,839
45	Montana	41,225
42	Nebraska	42,044
27	Nevada	45,342
23	New Hampshire	46,527
3	New Jersey	59,920
40	New Mexico	42,780
5	New York	58,537
24	North Carolina	46,410
49	North Dakota	38,822
13	Ohio	51,937
41	Oklahoma	42,379
15	Oregon	50,911
9	Pennsylvania	54,970
8	Rhode Island	55,956
32	South Carolina	44,133
50	South Dakota	35,378
33	Tennessee	43,816
29	Texas	44,897
46	Utah	40,566
19	Vermont	48,370
30	Virginia	44,727
21	Washington	47,882
47	West Virginia	40,531
20	Wisconsin	47,901
16	Wyoming	50,692

RANK ORDER

RANK	STATE	SALARY
1	California	$63,640
2	Connecticut	60,822
3	New Jersey	59,920
4	Massachusetts	58,624
5	New York	58,537
6	Illinois	58,246
7	Maryland	56,927
8	Rhode Island	55,956
9	Pennsylvania	54,970
10	Michigan	54,895
11	Delaware	54,680
12	Alaska	54,658
13	Ohio	51,937
14	Hawaii	51,922
15	Oregon	50,911
16	Wyoming	50,692
17	Georgia	49,905
18	Minnesota	49,634
19	Vermont	48,370
20	Wisconsin	47,901
21	Washington	47,882
22	Indiana	47,831
23	New Hampshire	46,527
24	North Carolina	46,410
25	Arizona	45,941
26	Colorado	45,833
27	Nevada	45,342
28	Florida	45,308
29	Texas	44,897
30	Virginia	44,727
31	Arkansas	44,245
32	South Carolina	44,133
33	Tennessee	43,816
34	Kentucky	43,646
35	Alabama	43,389
36	Kansas	43,334
37	Iowa	43,130
38	Louisiana	42,816
39	Idaho	42,798
40	New Mexico	42,780
41	Oklahoma	42,379
42	Nebraska	42,044
43	Missouri	41,839
44	Maine	41,596
45	Montana	41,225
46	Utah	40,566
47	West Virginia	40,531
48	Mississippi	40,182
49	North Dakota	38,822
50	South Dakota	35,378
	District of Columbia	59,000

Source: National Education Association, Washington, D.C.
  "Rankings & Estimates, December 2007" (Copyright © 2007, NEA, used with permission)
*Estimates for school year 2006-2007.

Average Teacher's Salary as a Percent of Average Annual Pay in 2006

National Average = 117.4% of Average Annual Pay*

ALPHA ORDER

RANK	STATE	PERCENT
34	Alabama	115.6
11	Alaska	129.6
39	Arizona	113.2
2	Arkansas	134.3
17	California	127.7
48	Colorado	103.7
45	Connecticut	109.6
31	Delaware	117.7
35	Florida	115.1
25	Georgia	121.6
3	Hawaii	133.9
13	Idaho	128.8
14	Illinois	128.1
9	Indiana	130.1
19	Iowa	122.7
30	Kansas	118.8
20	Kentucky	122.5
39	Louisiana	113.2
24	Maine	121.8
27	Maryland	120.5
44	Massachusetts	109.7
10	Michigan	130.0
32	Minnesota	116.3
12	Mississippi	129.4
42	Missouri	110.8
7	Montana	132.5
23	Nebraska	121.9
41	Nevada	112.0
46	New Hampshire	108.1
38	New Jersey	114.3
22	New Mexico	122.1
47	New York	104.4
26	North Carolina	120.6
21	North Dakota	122.3
5	Ohio	132.6
29	Oklahoma	119.3
5	Oregon	132.6
8	Pennsylvania	131.8
1	Rhode Island	136.8
18	South Carolina	127.1
33	South Dakota	115.7
36	Tennessee	114.9
49	Texas	102.0
37	Utah	114.7
4	Vermont	133.6
50	Virginia	100.5
43	Washington	109.8
28	West Virginia	120.4
16	Wisconsin	128.0
14	Wyoming	128.1

RANK ORDER

RANK	STATE	PERCENT
1	Rhode Island	136.8
2	Arkansas	134.3
3	Hawaii	133.9
4	Vermont	133.6
5	Ohio	132.6
5	Oregon	132.6
7	Montana	132.5
8	Pennsylvania	131.8
9	Indiana	130.1
10	Michigan	130.0
11	Alaska	129.6
12	Mississippi	129.4
13	Idaho	128.8
14	Illinois	128.1
14	Wyoming	128.1
16	Wisconsin	128.0
17	California	127.7
18	South Carolina	127.1
19	Iowa	122.7
20	Kentucky	122.5
21	North Dakota	122.3
22	New Mexico	122.1
23	Nebraska	121.9
24	Maine	121.8
25	Georgia	121.6
26	North Carolina	120.6
27	Maryland	120.5
28	West Virginia	120.4
29	Oklahoma	119.3
30	Kansas	118.8
31	Delaware	117.7
32	Minnesota	116.3
33	South Dakota	115.7
34	Alabama	115.6
35	Florida	115.1
36	Tennessee	114.9
37	Utah	114.7
38	New Jersey	114.3
39	Arizona	113.2
39	Louisiana	113.2
41	Nevada	112.0
42	Missouri	110.8
43	Washington	109.8
44	Massachusetts	109.7
45	Connecticut	109.6
46	New Hampshire	108.1
47	New York	104.4
48	Colorado	103.7
49	Texas	102.0
50	Virginia	100.5

District of Columbia — 84.1

Source: CQ Press using data from National Education Association, Washington, D.C.
"Rankings & Estimates" (Copyright © 2007, NEA, used with permission) and
"Quarterly Census of Employment and Wages" (http://www.bls.gov/cew/home.htm)
*Average of public elementary and secondary teacher salary for school years 2005-2006 and 2006-2007 compared to each state's 2006 average annual pay for all workers covered by federal unemployment.

Percent of Public School Fourth Graders
Proficient or Better in Reading in 2007
National Percent = 32%*

ALPHA ORDER

RANK	STATE	PERCENT
34	Alabama	29
34	Alaska	29
45	Arizona	24
34	Arkansas	29
48	California	23
10	Colorado	36
3	Connecticut	41
23	Delaware	34
23	Florida	34
38	Georgia	28
43	Hawaii	26
20	Idaho	35
29	Illinois	32
27	Indiana	33
10	Iowa	36
10	Kansas	36
27	Kentucky	33
49	Louisiana	20
10	Maine	36
10	Maryland	36
1	Massachusetts	49
29	Michigan	32
9	Minnesota	37
50	Mississippi	19
29	Missouri	32
7	Montana	39
20	Nebraska	35
45	Nevada	24
3	New Hampshire	41
2	New Jersey	43
45	New Mexico	24
10	New York	36
34	North Carolina	29
20	North Dakota	35
10	Ohio	36
41	Oklahoma	27
38	Oregon	28
6	Pennsylvania	40
32	Rhode Island	31
43	South Carolina	26
23	South Dakota	34
41	Tennessee	27
33	Texas	30
23	Utah	34
3	Vermont	41
8	Virginia	38
10	Washington	36
38	West Virginia	28
10	Wisconsin	36
10	Wyoming	36

RANK ORDER

RANK	STATE	PERCENT
1	Massachusetts	49
2	New Jersey	43
3	Connecticut	41
3	New Hampshire	41
3	Vermont	41
6	Pennsylvania	40
7	Montana	39
8	Virginia	38
9	Minnesota	37
10	Colorado	36
10	Iowa	36
10	Kansas	36
10	Maine	36
10	Maryland	36
10	New York	36
10	Ohio	36
10	Washington	36
10	Wisconsin	36
10	Wyoming	36
20	Idaho	35
20	Nebraska	35
20	North Dakota	35
23	Delaware	34
23	Florida	34
23	South Dakota	34
23	Utah	34
27	Indiana	33
27	Kentucky	33
29	Illinois	32
29	Michigan	32
29	Missouri	32
32	Rhode Island	31
33	Texas	30
34	Alabama	29
34	Alaska	29
34	Arkansas	29
34	North Carolina	29
38	Georgia	28
38	Oregon	28
38	West Virginia	28
41	Oklahoma	27
41	Tennessee	27
43	Hawaii	26
43	South Carolina	26
45	Arizona	24
45	Nevada	24
45	New Mexico	24
48	California	23
49	Louisiana	20
50	Mississippi	19
	District of Columbia	14

Source: U.S. Department of Education, National Center for Education Statistics
    "NAEP 2007: Reading Report Card for the Nation and the States" (NCES 2007-496)
*There are four achievement levels: Below Basic, Basic, Proficient, and Advanced. Proficient represents solid academic
mastery for 4th graders. Students reaching this level have demonstrated competency over challenging subject matter, including
subject matter knowledge, application of such knowledge to real-world situations, and analytical skills appropriate to the subject
matter.

Percent of Public School Eighth Graders
Proficient or Better in Reading in 2007
National Percent = 29%*

ALPHA ORDER

ALPHA ORDER

RANK	STATE	PERCENT
45	Alabama	21
35	Alaska	27
42	Arizona	24
40	Arkansas	25
45	California	21
13	Colorado	35
5	Connecticut	37
25	Delaware	31
30	Florida	28
37	Georgia	26
47	Hawaii	20
22	Idaho	32
28	Illinois	30
25	Indiana	31
10	Iowa	36
13	Kansas	35
30	Kentucky	28
48	Louisiana	19
5	Maine	37
19	Maryland	33
1	Massachusetts	43
30	Michigan	28
5	Minnesota	37
49	Mississippi	17
25	Missouri	31
3	Montana	39
13	Nebraska	35
44	Nevada	22
5	New Hampshire	37
3	New Jersey	39
49	New Mexico	17
22	New York	32
30	North Carolina	28
22	North Dakota	32
10	Ohio	36
37	Oklahoma	26
16	Oregon	34
10	Pennsylvania	36
35	Rhode Island	27
40	South Carolina	25
5	South Dakota	37
37	Tennessee	26
30	Texas	28
28	Utah	30
2	Vermont	42
16	Virginia	34
16	Washington	34
43	West Virginia	23
19	Wisconsin	33
19	Wyoming	33

RANK ORDER

RANK	STATE	PERCENT
1	Massachusetts	43
2	Vermont	42
3	Montana	39
3	New Jersey	39
5	Connecticut	37
5	Maine	37
5	Minnesota	37
5	New Hampshire	37
5	South Dakota	37
10	Iowa	36
10	Ohio	36
10	Pennsylvania	36
13	Colorado	35
13	Kansas	35
13	Nebraska	35
16	Oregon	34
16	Virginia	34
16	Washington	34
19	Maryland	33
19	Wisconsin	33
19	Wyoming	33
22	Idaho	32
22	New York	32
22	North Dakota	32
25	Delaware	31
25	Indiana	31
25	Missouri	31
28	Illinois	30
28	Utah	30
30	Florida	28
30	Kentucky	28
30	Michigan	28
30	North Carolina	28
30	Texas	28
35	Alaska	27
35	Rhode Island	27
37	Georgia	26
37	Oklahoma	26
37	Tennessee	26
40	Arkansas	25
40	South Carolina	25
42	Arizona	24
43	West Virginia	23
44	Nevada	22
45	Alabama	21
45	California	21
47	Hawaii	20
48	Louisiana	19
49	Mississippi	17
49	New Mexico	17

| | District of Columbia | 12 |

Source: U.S. Department of Education, National Center for Education Statistics
   "NAEP 2007: Reading Report Card for the Nation and the States" (NCES 2007-496)
*There are four achievement levels: Below Basic, Basic, Proficient, and Advanced. Proficient represents solid academic mastery for 8th graders. Students reaching this level have demonstrated competency over challenging subject matter, including subject matter knowledge, application of such knowledge to real-world situations, and analytical skills appropriate to the subject matter.

Percent of Public School Fourth Graders Proficient or Better in Mathematics in 2007
National Percent = 39%*

ALPHA ORDER

RANK	STATE	PERCENT
47	Alabama	26
29	Alaska	38
42	Arizona	31
32	Arkansas	37
44	California	30
20	Colorado	41
12	Connecticut	45
23	Delaware	40
23	Florida	40
41	Georgia	32
38	Hawaii	33
23	Idaho	40
34	Illinois	36
9	Indiana	46
16	Iowa	43
4	Kansas	51
42	Kentucky	31
48	Louisiana	24
18	Maine	42
23	Maryland	40
1	Massachusetts	58
32	Michigan	37
4	Minnesota	51
50	Mississippi	21
29	Missouri	38
13	Montana	44
29	Nebraska	38
44	Nevada	30
2	New Hampshire	52
2	New Jersey	52
48	New Mexico	24
16	New York	43
20	North Carolina	41
9	North Dakota	46
9	Ohio	46
38	Oklahoma	33
36	Oregon	35
7	Pennsylvania	47
37	Rhode Island	34
34	South Carolina	36
20	South Dakota	41
46	Tennessee	29
23	Texas	40
28	Utah	39
6	Vermont	49
18	Virginia	42
13	Washington	44
38	West Virginia	33
7	Wisconsin	47
13	Wyoming	44

RANK ORDER

RANK	STATE	PERCENT
1	Massachusetts	58
2	New Hampshire	52
2	New Jersey	52
4	Kansas	51
4	Minnesota	51
6	Vermont	49
7	Pennsylvania	47
7	Wisconsin	47
9	Indiana	46
9	North Dakota	46
9	Ohio	46
12	Connecticut	45
13	Montana	44
13	Washington	44
13	Wyoming	44
16	Iowa	43
16	New York	43
18	Maine	42
18	Virginia	42
20	Colorado	41
20	North Carolina	41
20	South Dakota	41
23	Delaware	40
23	Florida	40
23	Idaho	40
23	Maryland	40
23	Texas	40
28	Utah	39
29	Alaska	38
29	Missouri	38
29	Nebraska	38
32	Arkansas	37
32	Michigan	37
34	Illinois	36
34	South Carolina	36
36	Oregon	35
37	Rhode Island	34
38	Hawaii	33
38	Oklahoma	33
38	West Virginia	33
41	Georgia	32
42	Arizona	31
42	Kentucky	31
44	California	30
44	Nevada	30
46	Tennessee	29
47	Alabama	26
48	Louisiana	24
48	New Mexico	24
50	Mississippi	21
	District of Columbia	14

Source: U.S. Department of Education, National Center for Education Statistics
    "NAEP 2007: The Nation's Report Card, Mathematics 2007" (NCES 2007-494)

*There are four achievement levels: Below Basic, Basic, Proficient, and Advanced. Proficient represents solid academic mastery for 4th graders. Students reaching this level have demonstrated competency over challenging subject matter, including subject matter knowledge, application of such knowledge to real-world situations, and analytical skills appropriate to the subject matter.

Percent of Public School Eighth Graders Proficient or Better in Mathematics in 2007
National Percent = 31%*

ALPHA ORDER

RANK	STATE	PERCENT
48	Alabama	18
27	Alaska	32
38	Arizona	26
40	Arkansas	24
40	California	24
11	Colorado	37
17	Connecticut	35
30	Delaware	31
36	Florida	27
39	Georgia	25
44	Hawaii	21
24	Idaho	34
30	Illinois	31
17	Indiana	35
17	Iowa	35
5	Kansas	40
36	Kentucky	27
46	Louisiana	19
24	Maine	34
11	Maryland	37
1	Massachusetts	51
34	Michigan	29
2	Minnesota	43
50	Mississippi	14
32	Missouri	30
8	Montana	38
17	Nebraska	35
42	Nevada	23
8	New Hampshire	38
5	New Jersey	40
49	New Mexico	17
32	New York	30
24	North Carolina	34
3	North Dakota	41
17	Ohio	35
44	Oklahoma	21
17	Oregon	35
8	Pennsylvania	38
35	Rhode Island	28
27	South Carolina	32
7	South Dakota	39
42	Tennessee	23
17	Texas	35
27	Utah	32
3	Vermont	41
11	Virginia	37
15	Washington	36
46	West Virginia	19
11	Wisconsin	37
15	Wyoming	36

RANK ORDER

RANK	STATE	PERCENT
1	Massachusetts	51
2	Minnesota	43
3	North Dakota	41
3	Vermont	41
5	Kansas	40
5	New Jersey	40
7	South Dakota	39
8	Montana	38
8	New Hampshire	38
8	Pennsylvania	38
11	Colorado	37
11	Maryland	37
11	Virginia	37
11	Wisconsin	37
15	Washington	36
15	Wyoming	36
17	Connecticut	35
17	Indiana	35
17	Iowa	35
17	Nebraska	35
17	Ohio	35
17	Oregon	35
17	Texas	35
24	Idaho	34
24	Maine	34
24	North Carolina	34
27	Alaska	32
27	South Carolina	32
27	Utah	32
30	Delaware	31
30	Illinois	31
32	Missouri	30
32	New York	30
34	Michigan	29
35	Rhode Island	28
36	Florida	27
36	Kentucky	27
38	Arizona	26
39	Georgia	25
40	Arkansas	24
40	California	24
42	Nevada	23
42	Tennessee	23
44	Hawaii	21
44	Oklahoma	21
46	Louisiana	19
46	West Virginia	19
48	Alabama	18
49	New Mexico	17
50	Mississippi	14
	District of Columbia	8

Source: U.S. Department of Education, National Center for Education Statistics
   "NAEP 2007: The Nation's Report Card, Mathematics 2007" (NCES 2007-494)
*There are four achievement levels: Below Basic, Basic, Proficient, and Advanced. Proficient represents solid academic mastery for 8th graders. Students reaching this level have demonstrated competency over challenging subject matter, including subject matter knowledge, application of such knowledge to real-world situations, and analytical skills appropriate to the subject matter.

Estimated Public High School Graduates in 2007

National Total = 2,904,641 Graduates*

ALPHA ORDER

RANK	STATE	GRADUATES	% of USA
25	Alabama	37,789	1.3%
46	Alaska	7,886	0.3%
13	Arizona	68,141	2.3%
32	Arkansas	28,965	1.0%
1	California	361,206	12.4%
22	Colorado	47,361	1.6%
27	Connecticut	36,222	1.2%
48	Delaware	7,392	0.3%
4	Florida	134,307	4.6%
10	Georgia	85,939	3.0%
42	Hawaii	10,700	0.4%
39	Idaho	15,901	0.5%
6	Illinois	127,349	4.4%
21	Indiana	55,829	1.9%
29	Iowa	33,912	1.2%
31	Kansas	29,800	1.0%
24	Kentucky	38,769	1.3%
30	Louisiana	33,123	1.1%
41	Maine	14,216	0.5%
18	Maryland	58,166	2.0%
15	Massachusetts	63,900	2.2%
8	Michigan	103,708	3.6%
16	Minnesota	63,304	2.2%
34	Mississippi	23,813	0.8%
17	Missouri	60,351	2.1%
43	Montana	10,283	0.4%
36	Nebraska	19,870	0.7%
35	Nevada	20,290	0.7%
40	New Hampshire	14,724	0.5%
9	New Jersey	89,858	3.1%
37	New Mexico	17,472	0.6%
3	New York	163,673	5.6%
11	North Carolina	79,248	2.7%
49	North Dakota	7,013	0.2%
7	Ohio	117,541	4.0%
26	Oklahoma	36,536	1.3%
28	Oregon	34,287	1.2%
5	Pennsylvania	129,800	4.5%
44	Rhode Island	9,190	0.3%
23	South Carolina	39,107	1.3%
45	South Dakota	8,292	0.3%
20	Tennessee	56,630	1.9%
2	Texas	241,256	8.3%
33	Utah	27,951	1.0%
47	Vermont	7,636	0.3%
12	Virginia	78,548	2.7%
19	Washington	58,120	2.0%
38	West Virginia	17,378	0.6%
14	Wisconsin	64,345	2.2%
50	Wyoming	5,525	0.2%

RANK ORDER

RANK	STATE	GRADUATES	% of USA
1	California	361,206	12.4%
2	Texas	241,256	8.3%
3	New York	163,673	5.6%
4	Florida	134,307	4.6%
5	Pennsylvania	129,800	4.5%
6	Illinois	127,349	4.4%
7	Ohio	117,541	4.0%
8	Michigan	103,708	3.6%
9	New Jersey	89,858	3.1%
10	Georgia	85,939	3.0%
11	North Carolina	79,248	2.7%
12	Virginia	78,548	2.7%
13	Arizona	68,141	2.3%
14	Wisconsin	64,345	2.2%
15	Massachusetts	63,900	2.2%
16	Minnesota	63,304	2.2%
17	Missouri	60,351	2.1%
18	Maryland	58,166	2.0%
19	Washington	58,120	2.0%
20	Tennessee	56,630	1.9%
21	Indiana	55,829	1.9%
22	Colorado	47,361	1.6%
23	South Carolina	39,107	1.3%
24	Kentucky	38,769	1.3%
25	Alabama	37,789	1.3%
26	Oklahoma	36,536	1.3%
27	Connecticut	36,222	1.2%
28	Oregon	34,287	1.2%
29	Iowa	33,912	1.2%
30	Louisiana	33,123	1.1%
31	Kansas	29,800	1.0%
32	Arkansas	28,965	1.0%
33	Utah	27,951	1.0%
34	Mississippi	23,813	0.8%
35	Nevada	20,290	0.7%
36	Nebraska	19,870	0.7%
37	New Mexico	17,472	0.6%
38	West Virginia	17,378	0.6%
39	Idaho	15,901	0.5%
40	New Hampshire	14,724	0.5%
41	Maine	14,216	0.5%
42	Hawaii	10,700	0.4%
43	Montana	10,283	0.4%
44	Rhode Island	9,190	0.3%
45	South Dakota	8,292	0.3%
46	Alaska	7,886	0.3%
47	Vermont	7,636	0.3%
48	Delaware	7,392	0.3%
49	North Dakota	7,013	0.2%
50	Wyoming	5,525	0.2%
	District of Columbia	2,018	0.1%

Source: National Education Association, Washington, D.C.
 "Rankings & Estimates, December 2007" (Copyright © 2007, NEA, used with permission)
*Estimates for school year 2006-2007.

Estimated Public High School Graduation Rate in 2007

National Rate = 69.3% Graduated*

ALPHA ORDER

RANK	STATE	PERCENT
44	Alabama	60.3
35	Alaska	66.8
14	Arizona	77.8
15	Arkansas	77.7
32	California	68.3
21	Colorado	74.8
22	Connecticut	74.5
34	Delaware	67.1
50	Florida	53.0
42	Georgia	63.6
38	Hawaii	65.0
18	Idaho	76.6
29	Illinois	73.0
36	Indiana	65.7
4	Iowa	83.8
17	Kansas	77.0
31	Kentucky	70.8
48	Louisiana	56.6
3	Maine	84.2
24	Maryland	73.9
19	Massachusetts	76.3
33	Michigan	67.5
1	Minnesota	90.8
45	Mississippi	60.2
13	Missouri	78.2
11	Montana	79.6
7	Nebraska	81.5
47	Nevada	58.3
8	New Hampshire	80.5
5	New Jersey	82.8
46	New Mexico	58.6
42	New York	63.6
40	North Carolina	64.7
12	North Dakota	78.3
28	Ohio	73.1
25	Oklahoma	73.8
23	Oregon	74.2
9	Pennsylvania	80.1
39	Rhode Island	64.8
49	South Carolina	56.3
10	South Dakota	79.9
30	Tennessee	71.5
41	Texas	63.8
16	Utah	77.6
2	Vermont	90.7
26	Virginia	73.4
37	Washington	65.4
27	West Virginia	73.3
6	Wisconsin	82.7
20	Wyoming	75.2

RANK ORDER

RANK	STATE	PERCENT
1	Minnesota	90.8
2	Vermont	90.7
3	Maine	84.2
4	Iowa	83.8
5	New Jersey	82.8
6	Wisconsin	82.7
7	Nebraska	81.5
8	New Hampshire	80.5
9	Pennsylvania	80.1
10	South Dakota	79.9
11	Montana	79.6
12	North Dakota	78.3
13	Missouri	78.2
14	Arizona	77.8
15	Arkansas	77.7
16	Utah	77.6
17	Kansas	77.0
18	Idaho	76.6
19	Massachusetts	76.3
20	Wyoming	75.2
21	Colorado	74.8
22	Connecticut	74.5
23	Oregon	74.2
24	Maryland	73.9
25	Oklahoma	73.8
26	Virginia	73.4
27	West Virginia	73.3
28	Ohio	73.1
29	Illinois	73.0
30	Tennessee	71.5
31	Kentucky	70.8
32	California	68.3
33	Michigan	67.5
34	Delaware	67.1
35	Alaska	66.8
36	Indiana	65.7
37	Washington	65.4
38	Hawaii	65.0
39	Rhode Island	64.8
40	North Carolina	64.7
41	Texas	63.8
42	Georgia	63.6
42	New York	63.6
44	Alabama	60.3
45	Mississippi	60.2
46	New Mexico	58.6
47	Nevada	58.3
48	Louisiana	56.6
49	South Carolina	56.3
50	Florida	53.0

| | District of Columbia | 35.7 |

Source: CQ Press using data from National Education Association, Washington, D.C.
"Rankings & Estimates" (Copyright © 2007, NEA, used with permission) and
National Center for Education Statistics, "Common Core of Data (CCD) Database" (http://nces.ed.gov/ccd/)
*Calculated by comparing estimated number of public high school graduates in 2006-2007 with 9th grade enrollment in 2003-2004.
Data exclude ungraded pupils and have not been adjusted for interstate migration or switching to or from private schools.

Percent of Population Graduated from High School in 2006

National Percent = 85.5%*

RANK	STATE	PERCENT
42	Alabama	82.1
2	Alaska	92.0
39	Arizona	83.1
41	Arkansas	82.5
46	California	80.8
13	Colorado	90.0
22	Connecticut	88.4
33	Delaware	86.0
30	Florida	86.7
36	Georgia	84.2
20	Hawaii	88.7
19	Idaho	88.9
25	Illinois	87.6
23	Indiana	88.2
11	Iowa	90.4
12	Kansas	90.2
48	Kentucky	79.9
49	Louisiana	79.7
18	Maine	89.3
28	Maryland	87.2
14	Massachusetts	89.9
16	Michigan	89.7
1	Minnesota	93.0
45	Mississippi	81.1
29	Missouri	87.1
4	Montana	91.4
9	Nebraska	91.0
34	Nevada	85.6
3	New Hampshire	91.6
30	New Jersey	86.7
43	New Mexico	81.8
35	New York	85.1
36	North Carolina	84.2
20	North Dakota	88.7
24	Ohio	88.1
26	Oklahoma	87.5
16	Oregon	89.7
26	Pennsylvania	87.5
38	Rhode Island	84.0
39	South Carolina	83.1
14	South Dakota	89.9
47	Tennessee	80.7
50	Texas	78.7
5	Utah	91.2
9	Vermont	91.0
32	Virginia	86.5
6	Washington	91.1
44	West Virginia	81.5
6	Wisconsin	91.1
6	Wyoming	91.1

RANK	STATE	PERCENT
1	Minnesota	93.0
2	Alaska	92.0
3	New Hampshire	91.6
4	Montana	91.4
5	Utah	91.2
6	Washington	91.1
6	Wisconsin	91.1
6	Wyoming	91.1
9	Nebraska	91.0
9	Vermont	91.0
11	Iowa	90.4
12	Kansas	90.2
13	Colorado	90.0
14	Massachusetts	89.9
14	South Dakota	89.9
16	Michigan	89.7
16	Oregon	89.7
18	Maine	89.3
19	Idaho	88.9
20	Hawaii	88.7
20	North Dakota	88.7
22	Connecticut	88.4
23	Indiana	88.2
24	Ohio	88.1
25	Illinois	87.6
26	Oklahoma	87.5
26	Pennsylvania	87.5
28	Maryland	87.2
29	Missouri	87.1
30	Florida	86.7
30	New Jersey	86.7
32	Virginia	86.5
33	Delaware	86.0
34	Nevada	85.6
35	New York	85.1
36	Georgia	84.2
36	North Carolina	84.2
38	Rhode Island	84.0
39	Arizona	83.1
39	South Carolina	83.1
41	Arkansas	82.5
42	Alabama	82.1
43	New Mexico	81.8
44	West Virginia	81.5
45	Mississippi	81.1
46	California	80.8
47	Tennessee	80.7
48	Kentucky	79.9
49	Louisiana	79.7
50	Texas	78.7

District of Columbia		83.3

Source: U.S. Bureau of the Census, American Community Survey
"Educational Attainment in the United States: 2006"
(http://www.census.gov/population/www/socdemo/education/cps2006.html)
*Persons age 25 and older. Includes equivalency status.

Averaged Freshman Graduation Rate for Public High Schools in 2005

National Average = 74.7%*

ALPHA ORDER

RANK	STATE	PERCENT
41	Alabama	65.9
45	Alaska	64.1
8	Arizona	84.7
30	Arkansas	75.7
33	California	74.6
27	Colorado	76.7
14	Connecticut	80.9
37	Delaware	73.1
44	Florida	64.6
48	Georgia	61.7
31	Hawaii	75.1
13	Idaho	81.0
19	Illinois	79.4
36	Indiana	73.2
3	Iowa	86.6
21	Kansas	79.2
29	Kentucky	75.9
46	Louisiana	63.9
23	Maine	78.6
20	Maryland	79.3
22	Massachusetts	78.7
38	Michigan	73.0
6	Minnesota	85.9
47	Mississippi	63.3
15	Missouri	80.6
12	Montana	81.5
1	Nebraska	87.8
50	Nevada	55.8
17	New Hampshire	80.1
7	New Jersey	85.1
42	New Mexico	65.4
43	New York	65.3
39	North Carolina	72.6
5	North Dakota	86.3
16	Ohio	80.2
26	Oklahoma	76.9
34	Oregon	74.2
10	Pennsylvania	82.5
24	Rhode Island	78.4
49	South Carolina	60.1
11	South Dakota	82.3
40	Tennessee	68.5
35	Texas	74.0
9	Utah	84.4
4	Vermont	86.5
18	Virginia	79.6
32	Washington	75.0
25	West Virginia	77.3
2	Wisconsin	86.7
27	Wyoming	76.7

RANK ORDER

RANK	STATE	PERCENT
1	Nebraska	87.8
2	Wisconsin	86.7
3	Iowa	86.6
4	Vermont	86.5
5	North Dakota	86.3
6	Minnesota	85.9
7	New Jersey	85.1
8	Arizona	84.7
9	Utah	84.4
10	Pennsylvania	82.5
11	South Dakota	82.3
12	Montana	81.5
13	Idaho	81.0
14	Connecticut	80.9
15	Missouri	80.6
16	Ohio	80.2
17	New Hampshire	80.1
18	Virginia	79.6
19	Illinois	79.4
20	Maryland	79.3
21	Kansas	79.2
22	Massachusetts	78.7
23	Maine	78.6
24	Rhode Island	78.4
25	West Virginia	77.3
26	Oklahoma	76.9
27	Colorado	76.7
27	Wyoming	76.7
29	Kentucky	75.9
30	Arkansas	75.7
31	Hawaii	75.1
32	Washington	75.0
33	California	74.6
34	Oregon	74.2
35	Texas	74.0
36	Indiana	73.2
37	Delaware	73.1
38	Michigan	73.0
39	North Carolina	72.6
40	Tennessee	68.5
41	Alabama	65.9
42	New Mexico	65.4
43	New York	65.3
44	Florida	64.6
45	Alaska	64.1
46	Louisiana	63.9
47	Mississippi	63.3
48	Georgia	61.7
49	South Carolina	60.1
50	Nevada	55.8

District of Columbia   68.8

Source: U.S. Department of Education, National Center for Education Statistics
"Public Elementary and Secondary School Student Enrollment, High School Completions" (NCES 2007352)
*This rate is calculated by comparing the incoming freshman class enrollment of school year 2001-2002 with the number of graduates with regular diplomas four years later (2004-2005). The incoming class enrollment figure is an average of the eighth grade from five years earlier, the ninth grade four years earlier, and the tenth grade from three years earlier.

Public High School Drop Out Rate in 2005

National Rate = 3.9%*

ALPHA ORDER

RANK	STATE	PERCENT
35	Alabama	2.8
1	Alaska	8.2
4	Arizona	6.2
15	Arkansas	4.3
32	California	3.1
2	Colorado	7.8
NA	Connecticut**	NA
8	Delaware	5.3
25	Florida	3.5
7	Georgia	5.6
11	Hawaii	4.7
33	Idaho	3.0
12	Illinois	4.5
41	Indiana	2.5
44	Iowa	2.2
45	Kansas	2.1
25	Kentucky	3.5
3	Louisiana	7.5
35	Maine	2.8
19	Maryland	3.9
21	Massachusetts	3.8
19	Michigan	3.9
NA	Minnesota**	NA
35	Mississippi	2.8
22	Missouri	3.7
30	Montana	3.4
38	Nebraska	2.7
5	Nevada	5.8
25	New Hampshire	3.5
NA	New Jersey**	NA
16	New Mexico	4.2
6	New York	5.7
9	North Carolina	5.2
46	North Dakota	1.9
25	Ohio	3.5
25	Oklahoma	3.5
NA	Oregon**	NA
34	Pennsylvania	2.9
17	Rhode Island	4.1
31	South Carolina	3.3
14	South Dakota	4.4
38	Tennessee	2.7
24	Texas	3.6
22	Utah	3.7
40	Vermont	2.6
41	Virginia	2.5
12	Washington	4.5
17	West Virginia	4.1
43	Wisconsin	2.4
10	Wyoming	4.8

RANK ORDER

RANK	STATE	PERCENT
1	Alaska	8.2
2	Colorado	7.8
3	Louisiana	7.5
4	Arizona	6.2
5	Nevada	5.8
6	New York	5.7
7	Georgia	5.6
8	Delaware	5.3
9	North Carolina	5.2
10	Wyoming	4.8
11	Hawaii	4.7
12	Illinois	4.5
12	Washington	4.5
14	South Dakota	4.4
15	Arkansas	4.3
16	New Mexico	4.2
17	Rhode Island	4.1
17	West Virginia	4.1
19	Maryland	3.9
19	Michigan	3.9
21	Massachusetts	3.8
22	Missouri	3.7
22	Utah	3.7
24	Texas	3.6
25	Florida	3.5
25	Kentucky	3.5
25	New Hampshire	3.5
25	Ohio	3.5
25	Oklahoma	3.5
30	Montana	3.4
31	South Carolina	3.3
32	California	3.1
33	Idaho	3.0
34	Pennsylvania	2.9
35	Alabama	2.8
35	Maine	2.8
35	Mississippi	2.8
38	Nebraska	2.7
38	Tennessee	2.7
40	Vermont	2.6
41	Indiana	2.5
41	Virginia	2.5
43	Wisconsin	2.4
44	Iowa	2.2
45	Kansas	2.1
46	North Dakota	1.9
NA	Connecticut**	NA
NA	Minnesota**	NA
NA	New Jersey**	NA
NA	Oregon**	NA
	District of Columbia**	NA

Source: U.S. Department of Education, National Center for Education Statistics
    "Numbers and Rates of Public High School Dropouts" (NCES 2008-305, December 2007)
*School year 2004-2005. "Event" dropout rates showing the number of 9-12th grade dropouts divided by the number of students enrolled at the beginning of the school year in those grades. National rate is the median of reporting states.
**Not available.

ACT Average Composite Score in 2007

National Average = 21.2*

ALPHA ORDER

RANK	STATE	AVERAGE SCORE
44	Alabama	20.3
34	Alaska	21.2
21	Arizona	21.8
40	Arkansas	20.5
13	California	22.1
43	Colorado	20.4
2	Connecticut	23.2
23	Delaware	21.7
48	Florida	19.9
44	Georgia	20.3
9	Hawaii	22.3
32	Idaho	21.4
40	Illinois	20.5
15	Indiana	22.0
9	Iowa	22.3
18	Kansas	21.9
36	Kentucky	20.7
47	Louisiana	20.1
7	Maine	22.5
25	Maryland	21.6
1	Massachusetts	23.5
29	Michigan	21.5
7	Minnesota	22.5
50	Mississippi	18.9
25	Missouri	21.6
18	Montana	21.9
13	Nebraska	22.1
29	Nevada	21.5
4	New Hampshire	22.9
12	New Jersey	22.2
46	New Mexico	20.2
4	New York	22.9
35	North Carolina	21.0
25	North Dakota	21.6
25	Ohio	21.6
36	Oklahoma	20.7
15	Oregon	22.0
15	Pennsylvania	22.0
21	Rhode Island	21.8
49	South Carolina	19.6
18	South Dakota	21.9
36	Tennessee	20.7
40	Texas	20.5
23	Utah	21.7
6	Vermont	22.8
32	Virginia	21.4
3	Washington	23.1
39	West Virginia	20.6
9	Wisconsin	22.3
29	Wyoming	21.5

RANK ORDER

RANK	STATE	AVERAGE SCORE
1	Massachusetts	23.5
2	Connecticut	23.2
3	Washington	23.1
4	New Hampshire	22.9
4	New York	22.9
6	Vermont	22.8
7	Maine	22.5
7	Minnesota	22.5
9	Hawaii	22.3
9	Iowa	22.3
9	Wisconsin	22.3
12	New Jersey	22.2
13	California	22.1
13	Nebraska	22.1
15	Indiana	22.0
15	Oregon	22.0
15	Pennsylvania	22.0
18	Kansas	21.9
18	Montana	21.9
18	South Dakota	21.9
21	Arizona	21.8
21	Rhode Island	21.8
23	Delaware	21.7
23	Utah	21.7
25	Maryland	21.6
25	Missouri	21.6
25	North Dakota	21.6
25	Ohio	21.6
29	Michigan	21.5
29	Nevada	21.5
29	Wyoming	21.5
32	Idaho	21.4
32	Virginia	21.4
34	Alaska	21.2
35	North Carolina	21.0
36	Kentucky	20.7
36	Oklahoma	20.7
36	Tennessee	20.7
39	West Virginia	20.6
40	Arkansas	20.5
40	Illinois	20.5
40	Texas	20.5
43	Colorado	20.4
44	Alabama	20.3
44	Georgia	20.3
46	New Mexico	20.2
47	Louisiana	20.1
48	Florida	19.9
49	South Carolina	19.6
50	Mississippi	18.9
	District of Columbia	18.7

Source: The American College Testing Program (copyright 2007)
   "Average ACT Scores by State" (http://www.act.org/news/data/07/states-text.html)
*The ACT score range is 1 to 36. Approximately 1.3 million 2007 U.S. high school students took the test. Caution should be used in using ACT scores to compare states. The percentage of high school students taking the test varies greatly from one state to another. For example, all 11th grade students in Colorado and Illinois are required to take the test.

Education Expenditures by State and Local Governments in 2005

National Total = $689,375,633,000*

ALPHA ORDER			
RANK	STATE	EXPENDITURES	% of USA
23	Alabama	$9,877,109,000	1.4%
45	Alaska	2,361,342,000	0.3%
20	Arizona	10,878,202,000	1.6%
32	Arkansas	5,914,853,000	0.9%
1	California	88,631,217,000	12.9%
22	Colorado	10,131,048,000	1.5%
25	Connecticut	9,097,107,000	1.3%
44	Delaware	2,395,567,000	0.3%
4	Florida	32,042,662,000	4.6%
10	Georgia	19,915,890,000	2.9%
43	Hawaii	2,648,452,000	0.4%
41	Idaho	2,772,249,000	0.4%
6	Illinois	28,667,152,000	4.2%
15	Indiana	14,615,774,000	2.1%
30	Iowa	7,259,124,000	1.1%
31	Kansas	6,280,339,000	0.9%
27	Kentucky	8,249,235,000	1.2%
26	Louisiana	8,981,368,000	1.3%
40	Maine	2,865,681,000	0.4%
17	Maryland	13,549,330,000	2.0%
13	Massachusetts	16,095,935,000	2.3%
8	Michigan	27,160,939,000	3.9%
18	Minnesota	12,196,896,000	1.8%
33	Mississippi	5,860,381,000	0.9%
19	Missouri	11,279,161,000	1.6%
46	Montana	1,979,076,000	0.3%
37	Nebraska	4,135,829,000	0.6%
36	Nevada	4,485,331,000	0.7%
39	New Hampshire	2,894,134,000	0.4%
9	New Jersey	26,576,943,000	3.9%
35	New Mexico	4,879,448,000	0.7%
2	New York	53,848,722,000	7.8%
11	North Carolina	18,633,889,000	2.7%
48	North Dakota	1,599,781,000	0.2%
7	Ohio	27,508,583,000	4.0%
29	Oklahoma	7,556,741,000	1.1%
28	Oregon	7,880,059,000	1.1%
5	Pennsylvania	30,193,395,000	4.4%
42	Rhode Island	2,669,636,000	0.4%
24	South Carolina	9,762,718,000	1.4%
50	South Dakota	1,519,604,000	0.2%
21	Tennessee	10,286,078,000	1.5%
3	Texas	52,817,668,000	7.7%
34	Utah	5,522,305,000	0.8%
47	Vermont	1,904,780,000	0.3%
12	Virginia	17,584,863,000	2.6%
14	Washington	14,711,065,000	2.1%
38	West Virginia	3,964,566,000	0.6%
16	Wisconsin	13,800,986,000	2.0%
49	Wyoming	1,596,125,000	0.2%

RANK ORDER			
RANK	STATE	EXPENDITURES	% of USA
1	California	$88,631,217,000	12.9%
2	New York	53,848,722,000	7.8%
3	Texas	52,817,668,000	7.7%
4	Florida	32,042,662,000	4.6%
5	Pennsylvania	30,193,395,000	4.4%
6	Illinois	28,667,152,000	4.2%
7	Ohio	27,508,583,000	4.0%
8	Michigan	27,160,939,000	3.9%
9	New Jersey	26,576,943,000	3.9%
10	Georgia	19,915,890,000	2.9%
11	North Carolina	18,633,889,000	2.7%
12	Virginia	17,584,863,000	2.6%
13	Massachusetts	16,095,935,000	2.3%
14	Washington	14,711,065,000	2.1%
15	Indiana	14,615,774,000	2.1%
16	Wisconsin	13,800,986,000	2.0%
17	Maryland	13,549,330,000	2.0%
18	Minnesota	12,196,896,000	1.8%
19	Missouri	11,279,161,000	1.6%
20	Arizona	10,878,202,000	1.6%
21	Tennessee	10,286,078,000	1.5%
22	Colorado	10,131,048,000	1.5%
23	Alabama	9,877,109,000	1.4%
24	South Carolina	9,762,718,000	1.4%
25	Connecticut	9,097,107,000	1.3%
26	Louisiana	8,981,368,000	1.3%
27	Kentucky	8,249,235,000	1.2%
28	Oregon	7,880,059,000	1.1%
29	Oklahoma	7,556,741,000	1.1%
30	Iowa	7,259,124,000	1.1%
31	Kansas	6,280,339,000	0.9%
32	Arkansas	5,914,853,000	0.9%
33	Mississippi	5,860,381,000	0.9%
34	Utah	5,522,305,000	0.8%
35	New Mexico	4,879,448,000	0.7%
36	Nevada	4,485,331,000	0.7%
37	Nebraska	4,135,829,000	0.6%
38	West Virginia	3,964,566,000	0.6%
39	New Hampshire	2,894,134,000	0.4%
40	Maine	2,865,681,000	0.4%
41	Idaho	2,772,249,000	0.4%
42	Rhode Island	2,669,636,000	0.4%
43	Hawaii	2,648,452,000	0.4%
44	Delaware	2,395,567,000	0.3%
45	Alaska	2,361,342,000	0.3%
46	Montana	1,979,076,000	0.3%
47	Vermont	1,904,780,000	0.3%
48	North Dakota	1,599,781,000	0.2%
49	Wyoming	1,596,125,000	0.2%
50	South Dakota	1,519,604,000	0.2%
	District of Columbia	1,336,295,000	0.2%

Source: U.S. Bureau of the Census, Governments Division
"State and Local Government Finances: 2004-2005" (http://www.census.gov/govs/www/estimate05.html)
*Direct general expenditures for higher, secondary, elementary, and, "other" education. Includes capital outlays.

Per Capita State and Local Government Expenditures for Education in 2005

National Per Capita = $2,330*

RANK	STATE	PER CAPITA
33	Alabama	$2,176
1	Alaska	3,527
48	Arizona	1,828
38	Arkansas	2,134
14	California	2,463
35	Colorado	2,168
8	Connecticut	2,609
5	Delaware	2,850
49	Florida	1,807
31	Georgia	2,187
40	Hawaii	2,089
46	Idaho	1,944
27	Illinois	2,254
22	Indiana	2,336
15	Iowa	2,456
26	Kansas	2,291
43	Kentucky	1,978
42	Louisiana	1,998
32	Maine	2,184
17	Maryland	2,431
11	Massachusetts	2,504
7	Michigan	2,687
19	Minnesota	2,385
41	Mississippi	2,021
44	Missouri	1,949
39	Montana	2,115
20	Nebraska	2,358
47	Nevada	1,862
28	New Hampshire	2,221
4	New Jersey	3,070
9	New Mexico	2,546
6	New York	2,796
36	North Carolina	2,147
10	North Dakota	2,516
18	Ohio	2,400
37	Oklahoma	2,137
34	Oregon	2,171
16	Pennsylvania	2,441
12	Rhode Island	2,503
25	South Carolina	2,294
45	South Dakota	1,948
50	Tennessee	1,717
24	Texas	2,312
29	Utah	2,205
3	Vermont	3,074
23	Virginia	2,327
21	Washington	2,346
30	West Virginia	2,196
13	Wisconsin	2,491
2	Wyoming	3,151

RANK	STATE	PER CAPITA
1	Alaska	$3,527
2	Wyoming	3,151
3	Vermont	3,074
4	New Jersey	3,070
5	Delaware	2,850
6	New York	2,796
7	Michigan	2,687
8	Connecticut	2,609
9	New Mexico	2,546
10	North Dakota	2,516
11	Massachusetts	2,504
12	Rhode Island	2,503
13	Wisconsin	2,491
14	California	2,463
15	Iowa	2,456
16	Pennsylvania	2,441
17	Maryland	2,431
18	Ohio	2,400
19	Minnesota	2,385
20	Nebraska	2,358
21	Washington	2,346
22	Indiana	2,336
23	Virginia	2,327
24	Texas	2,312
25	South Carolina	2,294
26	Kansas	2,291
27	Illinois	2,254
28	New Hampshire	2,221
29	Utah	2,205
30	West Virginia	2,196
31	Georgia	2,187
32	Maine	2,184
33	Alabama	2,176
34	Oregon	2,171
35	Colorado	2,168
36	North Carolina	2,147
37	Oklahoma	2,137
38	Arkansas	2,134
39	Montana	2,115
40	Hawaii	2,089
41	Mississippi	2,021
42	Louisiana	1,998
43	Kentucky	1,978
44	Missouri	1,949
45	South Dakota	1,948
46	Idaho	1,944
47	Nevada	1,862
48	Arizona	1,828
49	Florida	1,807
50	Tennessee	1,717

District of Columbia   2,296

Source: CQ Press using data from U.S. Bureau of the Census, Governments Division
"State and Local Government Finances: 2004-2005" (http://www.census.gov/govs/www/estimate05.html)
*Direct general expenditures for higher, secondary, elementary, and "other" education. Includes capital outlays.

Expenditures for Education as a Percent of All State and Local Government Expenditures in 2005
National Percent = 34.3%*

ALPHA ORDER

RANK	STATE	PERCENT
33	Alabama	34.0
50	Alaska	26.8
37	Arizona	33.0
8	Arkansas	38.1
40	California	32.1
24	Colorado	34.9
27	Connecticut	34.7
22	Delaware	35.1
48	Florida	28.4
6	Georgia	39.3
48	Hawaii	28.4
30	Idaho	34.4
24	Illinois	34.9
7	Indiana	38.3
13	Iowa	37.3
12	Kansas	37.4
21	Kentucky	35.2
42	Louisiana	31.5
45	Maine	30.1
14	Maryland	37.0
39	Massachusetts	32.4
1	Michigan	40.5
40	Minnesota	32.1
38	Mississippi	32.8
28	Missouri	34.6
30	Montana	34.4
10	Nebraska	37.7
46	Nevada	30.0
15	New Hampshire	36.9
2	New Jersey	40.3
28	New Mexico	34.6
47	New York	29.2
19	North Carolina	35.4
16	North Dakota	36.8
20	Ohio	35.3
5	Oklahoma	39.6
34	Oregon	33.2
23	Pennsylvania	35.0
34	Rhode Island	33.2
24	South Carolina	34.9
32	South Dakota	34.2
44	Tennessee	30.3
4	Texas	40.2
9	Utah	38.0
2	Vermont	40.3
10	Virginia	37.7
34	Washington	33.2
18	West Virginia	35.7
17	Wisconsin	36.6
43	Wyoming	31.4

RANK ORDER

RANK	STATE	PERCENT
1	Michigan	40.5
2	New Jersey	40.3
2	Vermont	40.3
4	Texas	40.2
5	Oklahoma	39.6
6	Georgia	39.3
7	Indiana	38.3
8	Arkansas	38.1
9	Utah	38.0
10	Nebraska	37.7
10	Virginia	37.7
12	Kansas	37.4
13	Iowa	37.3
14	Maryland	37.0
15	New Hampshire	36.9
16	North Dakota	36.8
17	Wisconsin	36.6
18	West Virginia	35.7
19	North Carolina	35.4
20	Ohio	35.3
21	Kentucky	35.2
22	Delaware	35.1
23	Pennsylvania	35.0
24	Colorado	34.9
24	Illinois	34.9
24	South Carolina	34.9
27	Connecticut	34.7
28	Missouri	34.6
28	New Mexico	34.6
30	Idaho	34.4
30	Montana	34.4
32	South Dakota	34.2
33	Alabama	34.0
34	Oregon	33.2
34	Rhode Island	33.2
34	Washington	33.2
37	Arizona	33.0
38	Mississippi	32.8
39	Massachusetts	32.4
40	California	32.1
40	Minnesota	32.1
42	Louisiana	31.5
43	Wyoming	31.4
44	Tennessee	30.3
45	Maine	30.1
46	Nevada	30.0
47	New York	29.2
48	Florida	28.4
48	Hawaii	28.4
50	Alaska	26.8

District of Columbia	18.4

Source: CQ Press using data from U.S. Bureau of the Census, Governments Division
"State and Local Government Finances: 2004-2005" (http://www.census.gov/govs/www/estimate05.html)
*Direct general expenditures for higher, secondary, elementary, and "other" education as a percent of all direct general expenditures. Includes capital outlays.

State and Local Government Expenditures for Elementary and Secondary Education in 2005
National Total = $473,520,388,000*

ALPHA ORDER

RANK	STATE	EXPENDITURES	% of USA
26	Alabama	$5,805,289,000	1.2%
43	Alaska	1,729,461,000	0.4%
21	Arizona	6,941,626,000	1.5%
31	Arkansas	3,845,468,000	0.8%
1	California	61,759,507,000	13.1%
22	Colorado	6,916,656,000	1.5%
23	Connecticut	6,780,845,000	1.4%
45	Delaware	1,452,134,000	0.3%
4	Florida	23,314,184,000	4.9%
10	Georgia	14,179,193,000	3.0%
44	Hawaii	1,728,202,000	0.4%
42	Idaho	1,779,385,000	0.4%
7	Illinois	19,848,664,000	4.2%
14	Indiana	9,639,395,000	2.0%
30	Iowa	4,377,757,000	0.9%
32	Kansas	3,803,986,000	0.8%
27	Kentucky	4,954,520,000	1.0%
25	Louisiana	5,872,082,000	1.2%
40	Maine	2,054,411,000	0.4%
17	Maryland	8,960,278,000	1.9%
12	Massachusetts	11,006,603,000	2.3%
9	Michigan	18,547,108,000	3.9%
18	Minnesota	8,381,483,000	1.8%
33	Mississippi	3,545,210,000	0.8%
19	Missouri	7,843,642,000	1.7%
46	Montana	1,249,065,000	0.3%
37	Nebraska	2,603,104,000	0.6%
34	Nevada	3,291,621,000	0.7%
39	New Hampshire	2,133,346,000	0.5%
5	New Jersey	20,963,993,000	4.4%
36	New Mexico	2,967,115,000	0.6%
2	New York	42,402,279,000	9.0%
13	North Carolina	10,734,175,000	2.3%
50	North Dakota	915,225,000	0.2%
8	Ohio	19,104,649,000	4.0%
29	Oklahoma	4,710,354,000	1.0%
28	Oregon	4,897,083,000	1.0%
6	Pennsylvania	20,771,409,000	4.4%
41	Rhode Island	1,839,307,000	0.4%
24	South Carolina	6,382,790,000	1.4%
49	South Dakota	1,018,709,000	0.2%
20	Tennessee	6,994,633,000	1.5%
3	Texas	36,201,432,000	7.7%
35	Utah	3,113,563,000	0.7%
47	Vermont	1,203,707,000	0.3%
11	Virginia	12,054,757,000	2.6%
15	Washington	9,232,094,000	2.0%
38	West Virginia	2,443,481,000	0.5%
16	Wisconsin	8,961,006,000	1.9%
48	Wyoming	1,029,638,000	0.2%

RANK ORDER

RANK	STATE	EXPENDITURES	% of USA
1	California	$61,759,507,000	13.1%
2	New York	42,402,279,000	9.0%
3	Texas	36,201,432,000	7.7%
4	Florida	23,314,184,000	4.9%
5	New Jersey	20,963,993,000	4.4%
6	Pennsylvania	20,771,409,000	4.4%
7	Illinois	19,848,664,000	4.2%
8	Ohio	19,104,649,000	4.0%
9	Michigan	18,547,108,000	3.9%
10	Georgia	14,179,193,000	3.0%
11	Virginia	12,054,757,000	2.6%
12	Massachusetts	11,006,603,000	2.3%
13	North Carolina	10,734,175,000	2.3%
14	Indiana	9,639,395,000	2.0%
15	Washington	9,232,094,000	2.0%
16	Wisconsin	8,961,006,000	1.9%
17	Maryland	8,960,278,000	1.9%
18	Minnesota	8,381,483,000	1.8%
19	Missouri	7,843,642,000	1.7%
20	Tennessee	6,994,633,000	1.5%
21	Arizona	6,941,626,000	1.5%
22	Colorado	6,916,656,000	1.5%
23	Connecticut	6,780,845,000	1.4%
24	South Carolina	6,382,790,000	1.4%
25	Louisiana	5,872,082,000	1.2%
26	Alabama	5,805,289,000	1.2%
27	Kentucky	4,954,520,000	1.0%
28	Oregon	4,897,083,000	1.0%
29	Oklahoma	4,710,354,000	1.0%
30	Iowa	4,377,757,000	0.9%
31	Arkansas	3,845,468,000	0.8%
32	Kansas	3,803,986,000	0.8%
33	Mississippi	3,545,210,000	0.8%
34	Nevada	3,291,621,000	0.7%
35	Utah	3,113,563,000	0.7%
36	New Mexico	2,967,115,000	0.6%
37	Nebraska	2,603,104,000	0.6%
38	West Virginia	2,443,481,000	0.5%
39	New Hampshire	2,133,346,000	0.5%
40	Maine	2,054,411,000	0.4%
41	Rhode Island	1,839,307,000	0.4%
42	Idaho	1,779,385,000	0.4%
43	Alaska	1,729,461,000	0.4%
44	Hawaii	1,728,202,000	0.4%
45	Delaware	1,452,134,000	0.3%
46	Montana	1,249,065,000	0.3%
47	Vermont	1,203,707,000	0.3%
48	Wyoming	1,029,638,000	0.2%
49	South Dakota	1,018,709,000	0.2%
50	North Dakota	915,225,000	0.2%
	District of Columbia	1,234,764,000	0.3%

Source: U.S. Bureau of the Census, Governments Division
   "State and Local Government Finances 2004-2005" (http://www.census.gov/govs/www/estimate05.html)
*Direct general expenditures. Includes capital outlays.

Per Capita State and Local Government Expenditures for Elementary and Secondary Education in 2005
National Per Capita = $1,597*

ALPHA ORDER

RANK	STATE	PER CAPITA
43	Alabama	$1,276
1	Alaska	2,608
50	Arizona	1,166
31	Arkansas	1,385
11	California	1,708
26	Colorado	1,483
5	Connecticut	1,937
8	Delaware	1,725
41	Florida	1,312
22	Georgia	1,553
34	Hawaii	1,357
45	Idaho	1,245
21	Illinois	1,555
24	Indiana	1,538
28	Iowa	1,476
32	Kansas	1,384
48	Kentucky	1,187
42	Louisiana	1,303
20	Maine	1,558
17	Maryland	1,603
10	Massachusetts	1,711
7	Michigan	1,836
14	Minnesota	1,635
47	Mississippi	1,219
35	Missouri	1,353
38	Montana	1,336
27	Nebraska	1,481
33	Nevada	1,365
15	New Hampshire	1,632
2	New Jersey	2,409
23	New Mexico	1,541
3	New York	2,195
46	North Carolina	1,238
30	North Dakota	1,442
13	Ohio	1,666
39	Oklahoma	1,329
37	Oregon	1,346
12	Pennsylvania	1,674
9	Rhode Island	1,713
25	South Carolina	1,503
40	South Dakota	1,315
49	Tennessee	1,174
19	Texas	1,579
44	Utah	1,250
6	Vermont	1,934
18	Virginia	1,594
29	Washington	1,467
36	West Virginia	1,347
16	Wisconsin	1,621
4	Wyoming	2,024

RANK ORDER

RANK	STATE	PER CAPITA
1	Alaska	$2,608
2	New Jersey	2,409
3	New York	2,195
4	Wyoming	2,024
5	Connecticut	1,937
6	Vermont	1,934
7	Michigan	1,836
8	Delaware	1,725
9	Rhode Island	1,713
10	Massachusetts	1,711
11	California	1,708
12	Pennsylvania	1,674
13	Ohio	1,666
14	Minnesota	1,635
15	New Hampshire	1,632
16	Wisconsin	1,621
17	Maryland	1,603
18	Virginia	1,594
19	Texas	1,579
20	Maine	1,558
21	Illinois	1,555
22	Georgia	1,553
23	New Mexico	1,541
24	Indiana	1,538
25	South Carolina	1,503
26	Colorado	1,483
27	Nebraska	1,481
28	Iowa	1,476
29	Washington	1,467
30	North Dakota	1,442
31	Arkansas	1,385
32	Kansas	1,384
33	Nevada	1,365
34	Hawaii	1,357
35	Missouri	1,353
36	West Virginia	1,347
37	Oregon	1,346
38	Montana	1,336
39	Oklahoma	1,329
40	South Dakota	1,315
41	Florida	1,312
42	Louisiana	1,303
43	Alabama	1,276
44	Utah	1,250
45	Idaho	1,245
46	North Carolina	1,238
47	Mississippi	1,219
48	Kentucky	1,187
49	Tennessee	1,174
50	Arizona	1,166

District of Columbia   2,121

Source: CQ Press using data from U.S. Bureau of the Census, Governments Division
"State and Local Government Finances 2004-2005" (http://www.census.gov/govs/www/estimate05.html)
*Direct general expenditures. Includes capital outlays.

State and Local Government Expenditures for Elementary and Secondary Education as a Percent of All Education Expenditures in 2005
National Percent = 68.7%*

RANK	STATE	PERCENT
47	Alabama	58.8
6	Alaska	73.2
33	Arizona	63.8
29	Arkansas	65.0
10	California	69.7
20	Colorado	68.3
3	Connecticut	74.5
42	Delaware	60.6
7	Florida	72.8
9	Georgia	71.2
28	Hawaii	65.3
32	Idaho	64.2
13	Illinois	69.2
25	Indiana	66.0
45	Iowa	60.3
42	Kansas	60.6
46	Kentucky	60.1
26	Louisiana	65.4
8	Maine	71.7
24	Maryland	66.1
19	Massachusetts	68.4
20	Michigan	68.3
16	Minnesota	68.7
44	Mississippi	60.5
11	Missouri	69.5
35	Montana	63.1
36	Nebraska	62.9
5	Nevada	73.4
4	New Hampshire	73.7
1	New Jersey	78.9
41	New Mexico	60.8
2	New York	78.7
48	North Carolina	57.6
49	North Dakota	57.2
12	Ohio	69.4
38	Oklahoma	62.3
39	Oregon	62.1
15	Pennsylvania	68.8
14	Rhode Island	68.9
26	South Carolina	65.4
23	South Dakota	67.0
22	Tennessee	68.0
18	Texas	68.5
50	Utah	56.4
34	Vermont	63.2
17	Virginia	68.6
37	Washington	62.8
40	West Virginia	61.6
30	Wisconsin	64.9
31	Wyoming	64.5

RANK	STATE	PERCENT
1	New Jersey	78.9
2	New York	78.7
3	Connecticut	74.5
4	New Hampshire	73.7
5	Nevada	73.4
6	Alaska	73.2
7	Florida	72.8
8	Maine	71.7
9	Georgia	71.2
10	California	69.7
11	Missouri	69.5
12	Ohio	69.4
13	Illinois	69.2
14	Rhode Island	68.9
15	Pennsylvania	68.8
16	Minnesota	68.7
17	Virginia	68.6
18	Texas	68.5
19	Massachusetts	68.4
20	Colorado	68.3
20	Michigan	68.3
22	Tennessee	68.0
23	South Dakota	67.0
24	Maryland	66.1
25	Indiana	66.0
26	Louisiana	65.4
26	South Carolina	65.4
28	Hawaii	65.3
29	Arkansas	65.0
30	Wisconsin	64.9
31	Wyoming	64.5
32	Idaho	64.2
33	Arizona	63.8
34	Vermont	63.2
35	Montana	63.1
36	Nebraska	62.9
37	Washington	62.8
38	Oklahoma	62.3
39	Oregon	62.1
40	West Virginia	61.6
41	New Mexico	60.8
42	Delaware	60.6
42	Kansas	60.6
44	Mississippi	60.5
45	Iowa	60.3
46	Kentucky	60.1
47	Alabama	58.8
48	North Carolina	57.6
49	North Dakota	57.2
50	Utah	56.4
	District of Columbia	92.4

Source: CQ Press using data from U.S. Bureau of the Census, Governments Division
"State and Local Government Finances 2004-2005" (http://www.census.gov/govs/www/estimate05.html)
*Direct general expenditures. Includes capital outlays.

Estimated Per Pupil Public Elementary and
Secondary School Current Expenditures in 2007
National Per Pupil = $9,557*

ALPHA ORDER

RANK	STATE	PER PUPIL
43	Alabama	$7,672
16	Alaska	10,392
49	Arizona	5,696
26	Arkansas	8,905
28	California	8,834
27	Colorado	8,895
6	Connecticut	13,005
7	Delaware	12,565
34	Florida	8,493
30	Georgia	8,799
14	Hawaii	10,431
45	Idaho	7,176
15	Illinois	10,404
22	Indiana	9,330
40	Iowa	8,141
29	Kansas	8,804
35	Kentucky	8,459
33	Louisiana	8,657
8	Maine	12,063
17	Maryland	10,298
5	Massachusetts	13,294
18	Michigan	10,209
19	Minnesota	10,143
48	Mississippi	6,866
39	Missouri	8,170
32	Montana	8,682
36	Nebraska	8,309
47	Nevada	6,963
11	New Hampshire	10,792
1	New Jersey	14,675
24	New Mexico	9,036
2	New York	14,206
42	North Carolina	8,000
38	North Dakota	8,228
12	Ohio	10,563
46	Oklahoma	7,084
25	Oregon	8,989
10	Pennsylvania	11,304
9	Rhode Island	11,503
23	South Carolina	9,274
37	South Dakota	8,237
44	Tennessee	7,255
41	Texas	8,048
50	Utah	5,551
3	Vermont	13,385
21	Virginia	9,785
31	Washington	8,730
20	West Virginia	10,071
13	Wisconsin	10,432
4	Wyoming	13,328

RANK ORDER

RANK	STATE	PER PUPIL
1	New Jersey	$14,675
2	New York	14,206
3	Vermont	13,385
4	Wyoming	13,328
5	Massachusetts	13,294
6	Connecticut	13,005
7	Delaware	12,565
8	Maine	12,063
9	Rhode Island	11,503
10	Pennsylvania	11,304
11	New Hampshire	10,792
12	Ohio	10,563
13	Wisconsin	10,432
14	Hawaii	10,431
15	Illinois	10,404
16	Alaska	10,392
17	Maryland	10,298
18	Michigan	10,209
19	Minnesota	10,143
20	West Virginia	10,071
21	Virginia	9,785
22	Indiana	9,330
23	South Carolina	9,274
24	New Mexico	9,036
25	Oregon	8,989
26	Arkansas	8,905
27	Colorado	8,895
28	California	8,834
29	Kansas	8,804
30	Georgia	8,799
31	Washington	8,730
32	Montana	8,682
33	Louisiana	8,657
34	Florida	8,493
35	Kentucky	8,459
36	Nebraska	8,309
37	South Dakota	8,237
38	North Dakota	8,228
39	Missouri	8,170
40	Iowa	8,141
41	Texas	8,048
42	North Carolina	8,000
43	Alabama	7,672
44	Tennessee	7,255
45	Idaho	7,176
46	Oklahoma	7,084
47	Nevada	6,963
48	Mississippi	6,866
49	Arizona	5,696
50	Utah	5,551
	District of Columbia	16,540

Source: National Education Association, Washington, D.C.
   "Rankings & Estimates, December 2007" (Copyright © 2007, NEA, used with permission)
*Estimates for school year 2006-2007. Based on student membership.

Higher Education Expenditures by State and Local Governments in 2005

National Total = $182,267,983,000*

ALPHA ORDER

RANK	STATE	EXPENDITURES	% of USA
17	Alabama	$3,491,000,000	1.9%
47	Alaska	546,488,000	0.3%
18	Arizona	3,448,303,000	1.9%
34	Arkansas	1,706,055,000	0.9%
1	California	23,272,008,000	12.8%
21	Colorado	2,917,296,000	1.6%
33	Connecticut	1,955,136,000	1.1%
41	Delaware	780,613,000	0.4%
7	Florida	7,165,777,000	3.9%
13	Georgia	4,435,577,000	2.4%
39	Hawaii	880,427,000	0.5%
40	Idaho	858,137,000	0.5%
5	Illinois	7,505,948,000	4.1%
15	Indiana	4,240,922,000	2.3%
27	Iowa	2,533,630,000	1.4%
30	Kansas	2,282,995,000	1.3%
26	Kentucky	2,565,655,000	1.4%
29	Louisiana	2,377,166,000	1.3%
43	Maine	669,102,000	0.4%
16	Maryland	3,867,454,000	2.1%
19	Massachusetts	3,175,645,000	1.7%
4	Michigan	7,891,207,000	4.3%
20	Minnesota	3,117,798,000	1.7%
32	Mississippi	2,023,152,000	1.1%
22	Missouri	2,897,349,000	1.6%
45	Montana	613,932,000	0.3%
36	Nebraska	1,378,850,000	0.8%
38	Nevada	1,060,658,000	0.6%
42	New Hampshire	673,391,000	0.4%
11	New Jersey	4,783,216,000	2.6%
35	New Mexico	1,704,960,000	0.9%
3	New York	9,429,429,000	5.2%
6	North Carolina	7,402,294,000	4.1%
44	North Dakota	633,918,000	0.3%
8	Ohio	6,744,666,000	3.7%
28	Oklahoma	2,505,256,000	1.4%
24	Oregon	2,730,234,000	1.5%
9	Pennsylvania	6,546,458,000	3.6%
48	Rhode Island	516,054,000	0.3%
25	South Carolina	2,602,177,000	1.4%
50	South Dakota	423,875,000	0.2%
23	Tennessee	2,735,434,000	1.5%
2	Texas	14,955,151,000	8.2%
31	Utah	2,183,331,000	1.2%
46	Vermont	585,892,000	0.3%
10	Virginia	4,876,841,000	2.7%
12	Washington	4,526,685,000	2.5%
37	West Virginia	1,098,475,000	0.6%
14	Wisconsin	4,375,836,000	2.4%
49	Wyoming	474,599,000	0.3%

RANK ORDER

RANK	STATE	EXPENDITURES	% of USA
1	California	$23,272,008,000	12.8%
2	Texas	14,955,151,000	8.2%
3	New York	9,429,429,000	5.2%
4	Michigan	7,891,207,000	4.3%
5	Illinois	7,505,948,000	4.1%
6	North Carolina	7,402,294,000	4.1%
7	Florida	7,165,777,000	3.9%
8	Ohio	6,744,666,000	3.7%
9	Pennsylvania	6,546,458,000	3.6%
10	Virginia	4,876,841,000	2.7%
11	New Jersey	4,783,216,000	2.6%
12	Washington	4,526,685,000	2.5%
13	Georgia	4,435,577,000	2.4%
14	Wisconsin	4,375,836,000	2.4%
15	Indiana	4,240,922,000	2.3%
16	Maryland	3,867,454,000	2.1%
17	Alabama	3,491,000,000	1.9%
18	Arizona	3,448,303,000	1.9%
19	Massachusetts	3,175,645,000	1.7%
20	Minnesota	3,117,798,000	1.7%
21	Colorado	2,917,296,000	1.6%
22	Missouri	2,897,349,000	1.6%
23	Tennessee	2,735,434,000	1.5%
24	Oregon	2,730,234,000	1.5%
25	South Carolina	2,602,177,000	1.4%
26	Kentucky	2,565,655,000	1.4%
27	Iowa	2,533,630,000	1.4%
28	Oklahoma	2,505,256,000	1.4%
29	Louisiana	2,377,166,000	1.3%
30	Kansas	2,282,995,000	1.3%
31	Utah	2,183,331,000	1.2%
32	Mississippi	2,023,152,000	1.1%
33	Connecticut	1,955,136,000	1.1%
34	Arkansas	1,706,055,000	0.9%
35	New Mexico	1,704,960,000	0.9%
36	Nebraska	1,378,850,000	0.8%
37	West Virginia	1,098,475,000	0.6%
38	Nevada	1,060,658,000	0.6%
39	Hawaii	880,427,000	0.5%
40	Idaho	858,137,000	0.5%
41	Delaware	780,613,000	0.4%
42	New Hampshire	673,391,000	0.4%
43	Maine	669,102,000	0.4%
44	North Dakota	633,918,000	0.3%
45	Montana	613,932,000	0.3%
46	Vermont	585,892,000	0.3%
47	Alaska	546,488,000	0.3%
48	Rhode Island	516,054,000	0.3%
49	Wyoming	474,599,000	0.3%
50	South Dakota	423,875,000	0.2%
	District of Columbia	101,531,000	0.1%

Source: U.S. Bureau of the Census, Governments Division
   "State and Local Government Finances: 2004-2005" (http://www.census.gov/govs/www/estimate05.html)
*Direct general expenditures. Includes capital outlays.

Per Capita State and Local Government Expenditures for Higher Education in 2005
National Per Capita = $616*

ALPHA ORDER

RANK	STATE	PER CAPITA
14	Alabama	$769
10	Alaska	816
35	Arizona	579
27	Arkansas	615
24	California	647
26	Colorado	624
36	Connecticut	561
4	Delaware	929
50	Florida	404
46	Georgia	487
19	Hawaii	695
32	Idaho	602
33	Illinois	590
21	Indiana	678
7	Iowa	857
9	Kansas	833
27	Kentucky	615
39	Louisiana	529
42	Maine	510
20	Maryland	694
44	Massachusetts	494
13	Michigan	781
30	Minnesota	610
18	Mississippi	698
43	Missouri	501
22	Montana	656
12	Nebraska	786
49	Nevada	440
41	New Hampshire	517
37	New Jersey	552
5	New Mexico	890
45	New York	490
8	North Carolina	853
1	North Dakota	997
34	Ohio	589
17	Oklahoma	709
15	Oregon	752
39	Pennsylvania	529
47	Rhode Island	484
29	South Carolina	612
38	South Dakota	543
48	Tennessee	457
23	Texas	655
6	Utah	872
2	Vermont	945
25	Virginia	645
16	Washington	722
31	West Virginia	608
11	Wisconsin	790
3	Wyoming	937

RANK ORDER

RANK	STATE	PER CAPITA
1	North Dakota	$997
2	Vermont	945
3	Wyoming	937
4	Delaware	929
5	New Mexico	890
6	Utah	872
7	Iowa	857
8	North Carolina	853
9	Kansas	833
10	Alaska	816
11	Wisconsin	790
12	Nebraska	786
13	Michigan	781
14	Alabama	769
15	Oregon	752
16	Washington	722
17	Oklahoma	709
18	Mississippi	698
19	Hawaii	695
20	Maryland	694
21	Indiana	678
22	Montana	656
23	Texas	655
24	California	647
25	Virginia	645
26	Colorado	624
27	Arkansas	615
27	Kentucky	615
29	South Carolina	612
30	Minnesota	610
31	West Virginia	608
32	Idaho	602
33	Illinois	590
34	Ohio	589
35	Arizona	579
36	Connecticut	561
37	New Jersey	552
38	South Dakota	543
39	Louisiana	529
39	Pennsylvania	529
41	New Hampshire	517
42	Maine	510
43	Missouri	501
44	Massachusetts	494
45	New York	490
46	Georgia	487
47	Rhode Island	484
48	Tennessee	457
49	Nevada	440
50	Florida	404

District of Columbia — 174

Source: CQ Press using data from U.S. Bureau of the Census, Governments Division
"State and Local Government Finances: 2004-2005" (http://www.census.gov/govs/www/estimate05.html)
*Direct general expenditures. Includes capital outlays.

Expenditures for Higher Education as a Percent of All State and Local Government Expenditures in 2005
National Percent = 9.1%*

<table>
<tr><th colspan="3">ALPHA ORDER</th><th colspan="3">RANK ORDER</th></tr>
<tr><th>RANK</th><th>STATE</th><th>PERCENT</th><th>RANK</th><th>STATE</th><th>PERCENT</th></tr>
<tr><td>10</td><td>Alabama</td><td>12.0</td><td>1</td><td>Utah</td><td>15.0</td></tr>
<tr><td>49</td><td>Alaska</td><td>6.2</td><td>2</td><td>North Dakota</td><td>14.6</td></tr>
<tr><td>23</td><td>Arizona</td><td>10.5</td><td>3</td><td>North Carolina</td><td>14.1</td></tr>
<tr><td>18</td><td>Arkansas</td><td>11.0</td><td>4</td><td>Kansas</td><td>13.6</td></tr>
<tr><td>37</td><td>California</td><td>8.4</td><td>5</td><td>Oklahoma</td><td>13.1</td></tr>
<tr><td>26</td><td>Colorado</td><td>10.1</td><td>6</td><td>Iowa</td><td>13.0</td></tr>
<tr><td>42</td><td>Connecticut</td><td>7.5</td><td>7</td><td>Nebraska</td><td>12.6</td></tr>
<tr><td>14</td><td>Delaware</td><td>11.4</td><td>8</td><td>Vermont</td><td>12.4</td></tr>
<tr><td>46</td><td>Florida</td><td>6.4</td><td>9</td><td>New Mexico</td><td>12.1</td></tr>
<tr><td>34</td><td>Georgia</td><td>8.7</td><td>10</td><td>Alabama</td><td>12.0</td></tr>
<tr><td>29</td><td>Hawaii</td><td>9.4</td><td>11</td><td>Michigan</td><td>11.8</td></tr>
<tr><td>21</td><td>Idaho</td><td>10.6</td><td>12</td><td>Wisconsin</td><td>11.6</td></tr>
<tr><td>32</td><td>Illinois</td><td>9.1</td><td>13</td><td>Oregon</td><td>11.5</td></tr>
<tr><td>17</td><td>Indiana</td><td>11.1</td><td>14</td><td>Delaware</td><td>11.4</td></tr>
<tr><td>6</td><td>Iowa</td><td>13.0</td><td>14</td><td>Texas</td><td>11.4</td></tr>
<tr><td>4</td><td>Kansas</td><td>13.6</td><td>16</td><td>Mississippi</td><td>11.3</td></tr>
<tr><td>19</td><td>Kentucky</td><td>10.9</td><td>17</td><td>Indiana</td><td>11.1</td></tr>
<tr><td>38</td><td>Louisiana</td><td>8.3</td><td>18</td><td>Arkansas</td><td>11.0</td></tr>
<tr><td>45</td><td>Maine</td><td>7.0</td><td>19</td><td>Kentucky</td><td>10.9</td></tr>
<tr><td>21</td><td>Maryland</td><td>10.6</td><td>20</td><td>Montana</td><td>10.7</td></tr>
<tr><td>46</td><td>Massachusetts</td><td>6.4</td><td>21</td><td>Idaho</td><td>10.6</td></tr>
<tr><td>11</td><td>Michigan</td><td>11.8</td><td>21</td><td>Maryland</td><td>10.6</td></tr>
<tr><td>39</td><td>Minnesota</td><td>8.2</td><td>23</td><td>Arizona</td><td>10.5</td></tr>
<tr><td>16</td><td>Mississippi</td><td>11.3</td><td>23</td><td>Virginia</td><td>10.5</td></tr>
<tr><td>33</td><td>Missouri</td><td>8.9</td><td>25</td><td>Washington</td><td>10.2</td></tr>
<tr><td>20</td><td>Montana</td><td>10.7</td><td>26</td><td>Colorado</td><td>10.1</td></tr>
<tr><td>7</td><td>Nebraska</td><td>12.6</td><td>27</td><td>West Virginia</td><td>9.9</td></tr>
<tr><td>44</td><td>Nevada</td><td>7.1</td><td>28</td><td>South Dakota</td><td>9.5</td></tr>
<tr><td>36</td><td>New Hampshire</td><td>8.6</td><td>29</td><td>Hawaii</td><td>9.4</td></tr>
<tr><td>43</td><td>New Jersey</td><td>7.2</td><td>30</td><td>South Carolina</td><td>9.3</td></tr>
<tr><td>9</td><td>New Mexico</td><td>12.1</td><td>30</td><td>Wyoming</td><td>9.3</td></tr>
<tr><td>50</td><td>New York</td><td>5.1</td><td>32</td><td>Illinois</td><td>9.1</td></tr>
<tr><td>3</td><td>North Carolina</td><td>14.1</td><td>33</td><td>Missouri</td><td>8.9</td></tr>
<tr><td>2</td><td>North Dakota</td><td>14.6</td><td>34</td><td>Georgia</td><td>8.7</td></tr>
<tr><td>34</td><td>Ohio</td><td>8.7</td><td>34</td><td>Ohio</td><td>8.7</td></tr>
<tr><td>5</td><td>Oklahoma</td><td>13.1</td><td>36</td><td>New Hampshire</td><td>8.6</td></tr>
<tr><td>13</td><td>Oregon</td><td>11.5</td><td>37</td><td>California</td><td>8.4</td></tr>
<tr><td>41</td><td>Pennsylvania</td><td>7.6</td><td>38</td><td>Louisiana</td><td>8.3</td></tr>
<tr><td>46</td><td>Rhode Island</td><td>6.4</td><td>39</td><td>Minnesota</td><td>8.2</td></tr>
<tr><td>30</td><td>South Carolina</td><td>9.3</td><td>40</td><td>Tennessee</td><td>8.1</td></tr>
<tr><td>28</td><td>South Dakota</td><td>9.5</td><td>41</td><td>Pennsylvania</td><td>7.6</td></tr>
<tr><td>40</td><td>Tennessee</td><td>8.1</td><td>42</td><td>Connecticut</td><td>7.5</td></tr>
<tr><td>14</td><td>Texas</td><td>11.4</td><td>43</td><td>New Jersey</td><td>7.2</td></tr>
<tr><td>1</td><td>Utah</td><td>15.0</td><td>44</td><td>Nevada</td><td>7.1</td></tr>
<tr><td>8</td><td>Vermont</td><td>12.4</td><td>45</td><td>Maine</td><td>7.0</td></tr>
<tr><td>23</td><td>Virginia</td><td>10.5</td><td>46</td><td>Florida</td><td>6.4</td></tr>
<tr><td>25</td><td>Washington</td><td>10.2</td><td>46</td><td>Massachusetts</td><td>6.4</td></tr>
<tr><td>27</td><td>West Virginia</td><td>9.9</td><td>46</td><td>Rhode Island</td><td>6.4</td></tr>
<tr><td>12</td><td>Wisconsin</td><td>11.6</td><td>49</td><td>Alaska</td><td>6.2</td></tr>
<tr><td>30</td><td>Wyoming</td><td>9.3</td><td>50</td><td>New York</td><td>5.1</td></tr>
</table>

District of Columbia   1.4

Source: CQ Press using data from U.S. Bureau of the Census, Governments Division
"State and Local Government Finances: 2004-2005" (http://www.census.gov/govs/www/estimate05.html)
*Direct general expenditures for higher education as a percent of all direct general expenditures. Includes capital outlays.

Average Faculty Salary at Institutions of Higher Education in 2006

National Average = $66,172*

ALPHA ORDER

RANK ORDER

RANK	STATE	AVERAGE SALARY		RANK	STATE	AVERAGE SALARY
36	Alabama	$56,542		1	Massachusetts	$81,355
29	Alaska	59,309		2	Connecticut	80,368
11	Arizona	69,344		3	New Jersey	78,502
48	Arkansas	50,398		4	California	78,292
4	California	78,292		5	Delaware	76,668
25	Colorado	61,734		6	Rhode Island	75,146
2	Connecticut	80,368		7	New York	73,760
5	Delaware	76,668		8	Pennsylvania	70,936
23	Florida	62,485		9	Michigan	70,308
27	Georgia	61,093		10	Nevada	69,790
17	Hawaii	64,403		11	Arizona	69,344
46	Idaho	51,057		12	New Hampshire	68,522
13	Illinois	68,314		13	Illinois	68,314
21	Indiana	63,341		14	Maryland	66,871
31	Iowa	58,504		15	Utah	64,644
37	Kansas	56,527		16	Washington	64,563
41	Kentucky	55,386		17	Hawaii	64,403
42	Louisiana	55,146		18	Virginia	64,272
28	Maine	60,601		19	Minnesota	64,140
14	Maryland	66,871		20	Ohio	63,592
1	Massachusetts	81,355		21	Indiana	63,341
9	Michigan	70,308		22	Wisconsin	62,866
19	Minnesota	64,140		23	Florida	62,485
49	Mississippi	49,182		24	Texas	62,273
30	Missouri	58,962		25	Colorado	61,734
45	Montana	51,192		26	Vermont	61,644
32	Nebraska	58,204		27	Georgia	61,093
10	Nevada	69,790		28	Maine	60,601
12	New Hampshire	68,522		29	Alaska	59,309
3	New Jersey	78,502		30	Missouri	58,962
39	New Mexico	56,415		31	Iowa	58,504
7	New York	73,760		32	Nebraska	58,204
34	North Carolina	57,638		33	Tennessee	57,891
50	North Dakota	47,422		34	North Carolina	57,638
20	Ohio	63,592		35	Oregon	57,589
43	Oklahoma	54,515		36	Alabama	56,542
35	Oregon	57,589		37	Kansas	56,527
8	Pennsylvania	70,936		38	South Carolina	56,472
6	Rhode Island	75,146		39	New Mexico	56,415
38	South Carolina	56,472		40	Wyoming	56,149
47	South Dakota	50,822		41	Kentucky	55,386
33	Tennessee	57,891		42	Louisiana	55,146
24	Texas	62,273		43	Oklahoma	54,515
15	Utah	64,644		44	West Virginia	51,456
26	Vermont	61,644		45	Montana	51,192
18	Virginia	64,272		46	Idaho	51,057
16	Washington	64,563		47	South Dakota	50,822
44	West Virginia	51,456		48	Arkansas	50,398
22	Wisconsin	62,866		49	Mississippi	49,182
40	Wyoming	56,149		50	North Dakota	47,422
					District of Columbia	79,713

Source: U.S. Department of Education, National Center for Education Statistics
   "Digest of Education Statistics 2006" (NCES 2007-017, July 2007)
*For 2005-2006 school year. For full-time instructional faculty on 9-month contracts at four-year and two-year public and private degree-granting institutions.

Average Student Costs at Public Institutions of Higher Education in 2006

National Average = $12,108*

RANK	STATE	AVERAGE COSTS
40	Alabama	$9,625
30	Alaska	10,620
25	Arizona	11,480
45	Arkansas	9,192
13	California	13,685
24	Colorado	11,569
7	Connecticut	14,658
9	Delaware	14,326
33	Florida	10,141
34	Georgia	10,062
46	Hawaii	9,042
47	Idaho	8,982
11	Illinois	13,976
19	Indiana	12,388
21	Iowa	12,329
36	Kansas	9,980
29	Kentucky	10,663
50	Louisiana	8,506
18	Maine	12,568
6	Maryland	14,793
8	Massachusetts	14,651
12	Michigan	13,693
16	Minnesota	12,777
43	Mississippi	9,461
23	Missouri	11,861
31	Montana	10,613
26	Nebraska	11,286
28	Nevada	10,865
4	New Hampshire	15,479
1	New Jersey	17,708
41	New Mexico	9,579
14	New York	13,275
39	North Carolina	9,675
38	North Dakota	9,829
3	Ohio	16,032
44	Oklahoma	9,404
17	Oregon	12,720
5	Pennsylvania	15,464
10	Rhode Island	14,315
15	South Carolina	13,145
42	South Dakota	9,493
37	Tennessee	9,956
27	Texas	10,973
49	Utah	8,745
2	Vermont	16,571
22	Virginia	12,279
20	Washington	12,384
35	West Virginia	9,992
32	Wisconsin	10,560
48	Wyoming	8,946

RANK	STATE	AVERAGE COSTS
1	New Jersey	$17,708
2	Vermont	16,571
3	Ohio	16,032
4	New Hampshire	15,479
5	Pennsylvania	15,464
6	Maryland	14,793
7	Connecticut	14,658
8	Massachusetts	14,651
9	Delaware	14,326
10	Rhode Island	14,315
11	Illinois	13,976
12	Michigan	13,693
13	California	13,685
14	New York	13,275
15	South Carolina	13,145
16	Minnesota	12,777
17	Oregon	12,720
18	Maine	12,568
19	Indiana	12,388
20	Washington	12,384
21	Iowa	12,329
22	Virginia	12,279
23	Missouri	11,861
24	Colorado	11,569
25	Arizona	11,480
26	Nebraska	11,286
27	Texas	10,973
28	Nevada	10,865
29	Kentucky	10,663
30	Alaska	10,620
31	Montana	10,613
32	Wisconsin	10,560
33	Florida	10,141
34	Georgia	10,062
35	West Virginia	9,992
36	Kansas	9,980
37	Tennessee	9,956
38	North Dakota	9,829
39	North Carolina	9,675
40	Alabama	9,625
41	New Mexico	9,579
42	South Dakota	9,493
43	Mississippi	9,461
44	Oklahoma	9,404
45	Arkansas	9,192
46	Hawaii	9,042
47	Idaho	8,982
48	Wyoming	8,946
49	Utah	8,745
50	Louisiana	8,506

District of Columbia**	NA

Source: U.S. Department of Education, National Center for Education Statistics
   "Digest of Education Statistics 2006" (NCES 2007-017, July 2007)
*Data for 2005-2006 school year. Based on average in-state tuition, room and board, and fees for full-time students in public four-year institutions for an entire academic year.
**Not available.

Average Student Costs at Private Institutions of Higher Education in 2006

National Average = $27,317*

ALPHA ORDER

ALPHA ORDER

RANK	STATE	AVERAGE COSTS
41	Alabama	$18,520
29	Alaska	21,651
40	Arizona	18,734
43	Arkansas	18,122
8	California	31,266
14	Colorado	27,779
2	Connecticut	36,026
42	Delaware	18,176
22	Florida	24,985
20	Georgia	26,081
38	Hawaii	19,437
48	Idaho	11,614
13	Illinois	27,875
15	Indiana	27,582
24	Iowa	23,444
31	Kansas	20,741
33	Kentucky	20,674
45	Louisiana	17,207
10	Maine	29,550
4	Maryland	32,617
1	Massachusetts	37,282
37	Michigan	19,732
16	Minnesota	27,314
46	Mississippi	17,112
27	Missouri	22,441
44	Montana	18,093
30	Nebraska	21,017
32	Nevada	20,691
9	New Hampshire	31,154
7	New Jersey	31,335
35	New Mexico	20,006
5	New York	32,478
19	North Carolina	26,411
47	North Dakota	13,553
18	Ohio	26,906
34	Oklahoma	20,113
12	Oregon	27,945
6	Pennsylvania	31,963
3	Rhode Island	33,101
28	South Carolina	22,170
39	South Dakota	18,930
26	Tennessee	23,039
25	Texas	23,440
49	Utah	11,275
11	Vermont	29,072
23	Virginia	23,823
17	Washington	27,280
36	West Virginia	20,002
21	Wisconsin	25,656
NA	Wyoming**	NA

RANK ORDER

RANK	STATE	AVERAGE COSTS
1	Massachusetts	$37,282
2	Connecticut	36,026
3	Rhode Island	33,101
4	Maryland	32,617
5	New York	32,478
6	Pennsylvania	31,963
7	New Jersey	31,335
8	California	31,266
9	New Hampshire	31,154
10	Maine	29,550
11	Vermont	29,072
12	Oregon	27,945
13	Illinois	27,875
14	Colorado	27,779
15	Indiana	27,582
16	Minnesota	27,314
17	Washington	27,280
18	Ohio	26,906
19	North Carolina	26,411
20	Georgia	26,081
21	Wisconsin	25,656
22	Florida	24,985
23	Virginia	23,823
24	Iowa	23,444
25	Texas	23,440
26	Tennessee	23,039
27	Missouri	22,441
28	South Carolina	22,170
29	Alaska	21,651
30	Nebraska	21,017
31	Kansas	20,741
32	Nevada	20,691
33	Kentucky	20,674
34	Oklahoma	20,113
35	New Mexico	20,006
36	West Virginia	20,002
37	Michigan	19,732
38	Hawaii	19,437
39	South Dakota	18,930
40	Arizona	18,734
41	Alabama	18,520
42	Delaware	18,176
43	Arkansas	18,122
44	Montana	18,093
45	Louisiana	17,207
46	Mississippi	17,112
47	North Dakota	13,553
48	Idaho	11,614
49	Utah	11,275
NA	Wyoming**	NA
	District of Columbia	32,556

Source: U.S. Department of Education, National Center for Education Statistics
   "Digest of Education Statistics 2006" (NCES 2007-017, July 2007)
*Data for 2005-2006 school year. Based on average in-state tuition, room and board, and fees for full-time students in private four-year institutions for an entire academic year.
**Not available or not applicable.

Institutions of Higher Education in 2006

National Total = 4,276 Institutions*

ALPHA ORDER				RANK ORDER			
RANK	STATE	INSTITUTIONS	% of USA	RANK	STATE	INSTITUTIONS	% of USA
23	Alabama	66	1.5%	1	California	408	9.5%
50	Alaska	8	0.2%	2	New York	308	7.2%
20	Arizona	76	1.8%	3	Pennsylvania	259	6.1%
31	Arkansas	48	1.1%	4	Texas	213	5.0%
1	California	408	9.5%	5	Ohio	200	4.7%
19	Colorado	78	1.8%	6	Illinois	172	4.0%
32	Connecticut	44	1.0%	7	Florida	169	4.0%
48	Delaware	10	0.2%	8	Georgia	132	3.1%
7	Florida	169	4.0%	9	Missouri	128	3.0%
8	Georgia	132	3.1%	9	North Carolina	128	3.0%
42	Hawaii	23	0.5%	11	Massachusetts	121	2.8%
46	Idaho	14	0.3%	12	Minnesota	109	2.5%
6	Illinois	172	4.0%	13	Virginia	107	2.5%
15	Indiana	100	2.3%	14	Michigan	104	2.4%
24	Iowa	65	1.5%	15	Indiana	100	2.3%
26	Kansas	62	1.4%	16	Tennessee	98	2.3%
20	Kentucky	76	1.8%	17	Louisiana	90	2.1%
17	Louisiana	90	2.1%	18	Washington	80	1.9%
38	Maine	30	0.7%	19	Colorado	78	1.8%
29	Maryland	58	1.4%	20	Arizona	76	1.8%
11	Massachusetts	121	2.8%	20	Kentucky	76	1.8%
14	Michigan	104	2.4%	22	Wisconsin	68	1.6%
12	Minnesota	109	2.5%	23	Alabama	66	1.5%
35	Mississippi	41	1.0%	24	Iowa	65	1.5%
9	Missouri	128	3.0%	25	South Carolina	64	1.5%
42	Montana	23	0.5%	26	Kansas	62	1.4%
36	Nebraska	39	0.9%	27	Oregon	60	1.4%
42	Nevada	23	0.5%	28	New Jersey	59	1.4%
39	New Hampshire	26	0.6%	29	Maryland	58	1.4%
28	New Jersey	59	1.4%	30	Oklahoma	57	1.3%
34	New Mexico	42	1.0%	31	Arkansas	48	1.1%
2	New York	308	7.2%	32	Connecticut	44	1.0%
9	North Carolina	128	3.0%	32	West Virginia	44	1.0%
45	North Dakota	22	0.5%	34	New Mexico	42	1.0%
5	Ohio	200	4.7%	35	Mississippi	41	1.0%
30	Oklahoma	57	1.3%	36	Nebraska	39	0.9%
27	Oregon	60	1.4%	37	Utah	31	0.7%
3	Pennsylvania	259	6.1%	38	Maine	30	0.7%
46	Rhode Island	14	0.3%	39	New Hampshire	26	0.6%
25	South Carolina	64	1.5%	40	Vermont	25	0.6%
41	South Dakota	24	0.6%	41	South Dakota	24	0.6%
16	Tennessee	98	2.3%	42	Hawaii	23	0.5%
4	Texas	213	5.0%	42	Montana	23	0.5%
37	Utah	31	0.7%	42	Nevada	23	0.5%
40	Vermont	25	0.6%	45	North Dakota	22	0.5%
13	Virginia	107	2.5%	46	Idaho	14	0.3%
18	Washington	80	1.9%	46	Rhode Island	14	0.3%
32	West Virginia	44	1.0%	48	Delaware	10	0.2%
22	Wisconsin	68	1.6%	48	Wyoming	10	0.2%
48	Wyoming	10	0.2%	50	Alaska	8	0.2%
					District of Columbia	15	0.4%

Source: U.S. Department of Education, National Center for Education Statistics
    "Digest of Education Statistics 2006" (NCES 2007-017, July 2007)
*For 2005-2006 school year. Consists of 2,582 four-year and 1,694 two-year public and private degree-granting institutions.
Includes five U.S. Service Schools not shown by state.

Enrollment in Institutions of Higher Education in 2005

National Total = 17,487,475 Students*

ALPHA ORDER

RANK	STATE	STUDENTS	% of USA
23	Alabama	256,389	1.5%
50	Alaska	30,231	0.2%
9	Arizona	545,597	3.1%
34	Arkansas	143,272	0.8%
1	California	2,399,833	13.7%
21	Colorado	302,672	1.7%
32	Connecticut	174,675	1.0%
44	Delaware	51,612	0.3%
4	Florida	872,662	5.0%
13	Georgia	426,650	2.4%
42	Hawaii	67,083	0.4%
40	Idaho	77,708	0.4%
5	Illinois	832,967	4.8%
17	Indiana	361,253	2.1%
25	Iowa	227,722	1.3%
31	Kansas	191,752	1.1%
24	Kentucky	244,969	1.4%
30	Louisiana	197,713	1.1%
43	Maine	65,551	0.4%
20	Maryland	314,151	1.8%
11	Massachusetts	443,316	2.5%
7	Michigan	626,751	3.6%
16	Minnesota	361,701	2.1%
33	Mississippi	150,457	0.9%
15	Missouri	374,445	2.1%
47	Montana	47,850	0.3%
36	Nebraska	121,236	0.7%
37	Nevada	110,705	0.6%
41	New Hampshire	69,893	0.4%
14	New Jersey	379,758	2.2%
35	New Mexico	131,337	0.8%
3	New York	1,152,081	6.6%
10	North Carolina	484,392	2.8%
45	North Dakota	49,389	0.3%
8	Ohio	616,350	3.5%
27	Oklahoma	208,053	1.2%
29	Oregon	200,033	1.1%
6	Pennsylvania	692,340	4.0%
39	Rhode Island	81,382	0.5%
26	South Carolina	210,444	1.2%
46	South Dakota	48,768	0.3%
22	Tennessee	283,070	1.6%
2	Texas	1,240,707	7.1%
28	Utah	200,691	1.1%
48	Vermont	39,915	0.2%
12	Virginia	439,166	2.5%
18	Washington	348,482	2.0%
38	West Virginia	99,547	0.6%
19	Wisconsin	335,258	1.9%
49	Wyoming	35,334	0.2%

RANK ORDER

RANK	STATE	STUDENTS	% of USA
1	California	2,399,833	13.7%
2	Texas	1,240,707	7.1%
3	New York	1,152,081	6.6%
4	Florida	872,662	5.0%
5	Illinois	832,967	4.8%
6	Pennsylvania	692,340	4.0%
7	Michigan	626,751	3.6%
8	Ohio	616,350	3.5%
9	Arizona	545,597	3.1%
10	North Carolina	484,392	2.8%
11	Massachusetts	443,316	2.5%
12	Virginia	439,166	2.5%
13	Georgia	426,650	2.4%
14	New Jersey	379,758	2.2%
15	Missouri	374,445	2.1%
16	Minnesota	361,701	2.1%
17	Indiana	361,253	2.1%
18	Washington	348,482	2.0%
19	Wisconsin	335,258	1.9%
20	Maryland	314,151	1.8%
21	Colorado	302,672	1.7%
22	Tennessee	283,070	1.6%
23	Alabama	256,389	1.5%
24	Kentucky	244,969	1.4%
25	Iowa	227,722	1.3%
26	South Carolina	210,444	1.2%
27	Oklahoma	208,053	1.2%
28	Utah	200,691	1.1%
29	Oregon	200,033	1.1%
30	Louisiana	197,713	1.1%
31	Kansas	191,752	1.1%
32	Connecticut	174,675	1.0%
33	Mississippi	150,457	0.9%
34	Arkansas	143,272	0.8%
35	New Mexico	131,337	0.8%
36	Nebraska	121,236	0.7%
37	Nevada	110,705	0.6%
38	West Virginia	99,547	0.6%
39	Rhode Island	81,382	0.5%
40	Idaho	77,708	0.4%
41	New Hampshire	69,893	0.4%
42	Hawaii	67,083	0.4%
43	Maine	65,551	0.4%
44	Delaware	51,612	0.3%
45	North Dakota	49,389	0.3%
46	South Dakota	48,768	0.3%
47	Montana	47,850	0.3%
48	Vermont	39,915	0.2%
49	Wyoming	35,334	0.2%
50	Alaska	30,231	0.2%
	District of Columbia	104,897	0.6%

Source: U.S. Department of Education, National Center for Education Statistics
    "Digest of Education Statistics 2006" (NCES 2007-017, July 2007)
*Fall 2005 enrollment. Includes full-time and part-time students at Title IV eligible, degree-granting four-year and two-year institutions. National total includes 15,265 students at U.S. Service Schools not shown by state.

Enrollment Rate in Institutions of Higher Education in 2005

National Rate = 597 Students per 1,000 Population 18 to 24 Years Old*

ALPHA ORDER

RANK	STATE	RATE
28	Alabama	567
50	Alaska	392
1	Arizona	931
39	Arkansas	513
6	California	669
9	Colorado	653
32	Connecticut	553
18	Delaware	621
34	Florida	549
48	Georgia	464
37	Hawaii	524
45	Idaho	487
7	Illinois	665
26	Indiana	581
4	Iowa	734
10	Kansas	645
20	Kentucky	601
49	Louisiana	397
38	Maine	521
22	Maryland	590
3	Massachusetts	750
13	Michigan	633
5	Minnesota	678
47	Mississippi	477
12	Missouri	635
46	Montana	479
11	Nebraska	636
41	Nevada	505
28	New Hampshire	567
42	New Jersey	502
15	New Mexico	628
13	New York	633
25	North Carolina	584
8	North Dakota	660
33	Ohio	551
35	Oklahoma	544
28	Oregon	567
23	Pennsylvania	587
2	Rhode Island	756
43	South Carolina	494
31	South Dakota	566
44	Tennessee	491
39	Texas	513
15	Utah	628
17	Vermont	627
26	Virginia	581
36	Washington	540
21	West Virginia	592
24	Wisconsin	586
19	Wyoming	620

RANK ORDER

RANK	STATE	RATE
1	Arizona	931
2	Rhode Island	756
3	Massachusetts	750
4	Iowa	734
5	Minnesota	678
6	California	669
7	Illinois	665
8	North Dakota	660
9	Colorado	653
10	Kansas	645
11	Nebraska	636
12	Missouri	635
13	Michigan	633
13	New York	633
15	New Mexico	628
15	Utah	628
17	Vermont	627
18	Delaware	621
19	Wyoming	620
20	Kentucky	601
21	West Virginia	592
22	Maryland	590
23	Pennsylvania	587
24	Wisconsin	586
25	North Carolina	584
26	Indiana	581
26	Virginia	581
28	Alabama	567
28	New Hampshire	567
28	Oregon	567
31	South Dakota	566
32	Connecticut	553
33	Ohio	551
34	Florida	549
35	Oklahoma	544
36	Washington	540
37	Hawaii	524
38	Maine	521
39	Arkansas	513
39	Texas	513
41	Nevada	505
42	New Jersey	502
43	South Carolina	494
44	Tennessee	491
45	Idaho	487
46	Montana	479
47	Mississippi	477
48	Georgia	464
49	Louisiana	397
50	Alaska	392

District of Columbia 2,016

Source: CQ Press using data from U.S. Department of Education, National Center for Education Statistics
"Digest of Education Statistics 2006" (NCES 2007-017, July 2007)

*Based on fall 2005 enrollment. National rate includes U.S. Service Schools. Includes students at four-year and two-year public and private degree-granting institutions. Enrollment based on location of institution. Population based on residence.

Enrollment in Public Institutions of Higher Education in 2005

National Total = 13,021,834 Students*

ALPHA ORDER

RANK	STATE	STUDENTS	% of USA
20	Alabama	228,153	1.8%
49	Alaska	28,866	0.2%
12	Arizona	320,865	2.5%
33	Arkansas	128,117	1.0%
1	California	2,008,155	15.4%
19	Colorado	234,509	1.8%
35	Connecticut	111,705	0.9%
46	Delaware	38,682	0.3%
3	Florida	648,999	5.0%
11	Georgia	342,012	2.6%
40	Hawaii	50,157	0.4%
39	Idaho	60,303	0.5%
5	Illinois	555,149	4.3%
16	Indiana	267,298	2.1%
31	Iowa	148,907	1.1%
28	Kansas	170,319	1.3%
22	Kentucky	201,579	1.5%
25	Louisiana	181,043	1.4%
41	Maine	47,519	0.4%
17	Maryland	256,073	2.0%
24	Massachusetts	188,295	1.4%
6	Michigan	505,586	3.9%
18	Minnesota	240,853	1.8%
32	Mississippi	135,896	1.0%
21	Missouri	217,722	1.7%
42	Montana	42,997	0.3%
37	Nebraska	93,181	0.7%
36	Nevada	100,043	0.8%
44	New Hampshire	41,007	0.3%
13	New Jersey	304,315	2.3%
34	New Mexico	120,976	0.9%
4	New York	626,222	4.8%
8	North Carolina	396,755	3.0%
43	North Dakota	42,808	0.3%
7	Ohio	453,001	3.5%
26	Oklahoma	179,225	1.4%
29	Oregon	163,752	1.3%
9	Pennsylvania	380,271	2.9%
45	Rhode Island	40,008	0.3%
27	South Carolina	174,686	1.3%
47	South Dakota	37,548	0.3%
23	Tennessee	200,394	1.5%
2	Texas	1,081,335	8.3%
30	Utah	148,960	1.1%
50	Vermont	24,090	0.2%
10	Virginia	349,195	2.7%
14	Washington	296,756	2.3%
38	West Virginia	85,148	0.7%
15	Wisconsin	268,928	2.1%
48	Wyoming	32,611	0.3%

RANK ORDER

RANK	STATE	STUDENTS	% of USA
1	California	2,008,155	15.4%
2	Texas	1,081,335	8.3%
3	Florida	648,999	5.0%
4	New York	626,222	4.8%
5	Illinois	555,149	4.3%
6	Michigan	505,586	3.9%
7	Ohio	453,001	3.5%
8	North Carolina	396,755	3.0%
9	Pennsylvania	380,271	2.9%
10	Virginia	349,195	2.7%
11	Georgia	342,012	2.6%
12	Arizona	320,865	2.5%
13	New Jersey	304,315	2.3%
14	Washington	296,756	2.3%
15	Wisconsin	268,928	2.1%
16	Indiana	267,298	2.1%
17	Maryland	256,073	2.0%
18	Minnesota	240,853	1.8%
19	Colorado	234,509	1.8%
20	Alabama	228,153	1.8%
21	Missouri	217,722	1.7%
22	Kentucky	201,579	1.5%
23	Tennessee	200,394	1.5%
24	Massachusetts	188,295	1.4%
25	Louisiana	181,043	1.4%
26	Oklahoma	179,225	1.4%
27	South Carolina	174,686	1.3%
28	Kansas	170,319	1.3%
29	Oregon	163,752	1.3%
30	Utah	148,960	1.1%
31	Iowa	148,907	1.1%
32	Mississippi	135,896	1.0%
33	Arkansas	128,117	1.0%
34	New Mexico	120,976	0.9%
35	Connecticut	111,705	0.9%
36	Nevada	100,043	0.8%
37	Nebraska	93,181	0.7%
38	West Virginia	85,148	0.7%
39	Idaho	60,303	0.5%
40	Hawaii	50,157	0.4%
41	Maine	47,519	0.4%
42	Montana	42,997	0.3%
43	North Dakota	42,808	0.3%
44	New Hampshire	41,007	0.3%
45	Rhode Island	40,008	0.3%
46	Delaware	38,682	0.3%
47	South Dakota	37,548	0.3%
48	Wyoming	32,611	0.3%
49	Alaska	28,866	0.2%
50	Vermont	24,090	0.2%
	District of Columbia	5,595	0.0%

Source: U.S. Department of Education, National Center for Education Statistics
    "Digest of Education Statistics 2006" (NCES 2007-017, July 2007)
*Fall 2005 enrollment. Includes full-time and part-time students at Title IV eligible, degree-granting four-year and two-year institutions. National total includes 15,265 students at U.S. Service Schools not shown by state.

Enrollment in Private Institutions of Higher Education in 2005

National Total = 4,465,641 Students*

ALPHA ORDER

RANK	STATE	STUDENTS	% of USA
32	Alabama	28,236	0.6%
50	Alaska	1,365	0.0%
6	Arizona	224,732	5.0%
40	Arkansas	15,155	0.3%
2	California	391,678	8.8%
20	Colorado	68,163	1.5%
22	Connecticut	62,970	1.4%
43	Delaware	12,930	0.3%
7	Florida	223,663	5.0%
16	Georgia	84,638	1.9%
37	Hawaii	16,926	0.4%
36	Idaho	17,405	0.4%
4	Illinois	277,818	6.2%
13	Indiana	93,955	2.1%
18	Iowa	78,815	1.8%
34	Kansas	21,433	0.5%
26	Kentucky	43,390	1.0%
38	Louisiana	16,670	0.4%
35	Maine	18,032	0.4%
23	Maryland	58,078	1.3%
5	Massachusetts	255,021	5.7%
11	Michigan	121,165	2.7%
12	Minnesota	120,848	2.7%
41	Mississippi	14,561	0.3%
10	Missouri	156,723	3.5%
48	Montana	4,853	0.1%
33	Nebraska	28,055	0.6%
45	Nevada	10,662	0.2%
30	New Hampshire	28,886	0.6%
19	New Jersey	75,443	1.7%
46	New Mexico	10,361	0.2%
1	New York	525,859	11.8%
15	North Carolina	87,637	2.0%
47	North Dakota	6,581	0.1%
8	Ohio	163,349	3.7%
31	Oklahoma	28,828	0.6%
28	Oregon	36,281	0.8%
3	Pennsylvania	312,069	7.0%
27	Rhode Island	41,374	0.9%
29	South Carolina	35,758	0.8%
44	South Dakota	11,220	0.3%
17	Tennessee	82,676	1.9%
9	Texas	159,372	3.6%
24	Utah	51,731	1.2%
39	Vermont	15,825	0.4%
14	Virginia	89,971	2.0%
25	Washington	51,726	1.2%
42	West Virginia	14,399	0.3%
21	Wisconsin	66,330	1.5%
49	Wyoming	2,723	0.1%

RANK ORDER

RANK	STATE	STUDENTS	% of USA
1	New York	525,859	11.8%
2	California	391,678	8.8%
3	Pennsylvania	312,069	7.0%
4	Illinois	277,818	6.2%
5	Massachusetts	255,021	5.7%
6	Arizona	224,732	5.0%
7	Florida	223,663	5.0%
8	Ohio	163,349	3.7%
9	Texas	159,372	3.6%
10	Missouri	156,723	3.5%
11	Michigan	121,165	2.7%
12	Minnesota	120,848	2.7%
13	Indiana	93,955	2.1%
14	Virginia	89,971	2.0%
15	North Carolina	87,637	2.0%
16	Georgia	84,638	1.9%
17	Tennessee	82,676	1.9%
18	Iowa	78,815	1.8%
19	New Jersey	75,443	1.7%
20	Colorado	68,163	1.5%
21	Wisconsin	66,330	1.5%
22	Connecticut	62,970	1.4%
23	Maryland	58,078	1.3%
24	Utah	51,731	1.2%
25	Washington	51,726	1.2%
26	Kentucky	43,390	1.0%
27	Rhode Island	41,374	0.9%
28	Oregon	36,281	0.8%
29	South Carolina	35,758	0.8%
30	New Hampshire	28,886	0.6%
31	Oklahoma	28,828	0.6%
32	Alabama	28,236	0.6%
33	Nebraska	28,055	0.6%
34	Kansas	21,433	0.5%
35	Maine	18,032	0.4%
36	Idaho	17,405	0.4%
37	Hawaii	16,926	0.4%
38	Louisiana	16,670	0.4%
39	Vermont	15,825	0.4%
40	Arkansas	15,155	0.3%
41	Mississippi	14,561	0.3%
42	West Virginia	14,399	0.3%
43	Delaware	12,930	0.3%
44	South Dakota	11,220	0.3%
45	Nevada	10,662	0.2%
46	New Mexico	10,361	0.2%
47	North Dakota	6,581	0.1%
48	Montana	4,853	0.1%
49	Wyoming	2,723	0.1%
50	Alaska	1,365	0.0%
	District of Columbia	99,302	2.2%

Source: U.S. Department of Education, National Center for Education Statistics
    "Digest of Education Statistics 2006" (NCES 2007-017, July 2007)
*Fall 2005 enrollment. Includes full-time and part-time students at Title IV eligible, degree-granting four-year and two-year institutions.

Percent of Population With a Bachelor's Degree or More in 2006

National Percent = 28.0%*

RANK ORDER

ALPHA ORDER

RANK	STATE	PERCENT
45	Alabama	20.8
20	Alaska	27.7
36	Arizona	24.5
49	Arkansas	19.0
16	California	29.8
2	Colorado	36.4
3	Connecticut	36.0
27	Delaware	26.2
21	Florida	27.2
19	Georgia	28.1
8	Hawaii	32.3
32	Idaho	25.1
14	Illinois	31.2
42	Indiana	21.9
34	Iowa	24.7
12	Kansas	31.6
48	Kentucky	20.2
43	Louisiana	21.2
24	Maine	26.9
4	Maryland	35.7
1	Massachusetts	40.4
28	Michigan	26.1
7	Minnesota	33.5
44	Mississippi	21.1
37	Missouri	24.3
32	Montana	25.1
21	Nebraska	27.2
45	Nevada	20.8
10	New Hampshire	32.1
5	New Jersey	35.6
25	New Mexico	26.7
9	New York	32.2
29	North Carolina	25.6
17	North Dakota	28.7
38	Ohio	23.3
39	Oklahoma	22.9
18	Oregon	28.3
26	Pennsylvania	26.6
15	Rhode Island	30.9
40	South Carolina	22.6
31	South Dakota	25.3
41	Tennessee	22.0
30	Texas	25.5
23	Utah	27.0
6	Vermont	34.0
10	Virginia	32.1
13	Washington	31.4
50	West Virginia	15.9
35	Wisconsin	24.6
45	Wyoming	20.8

RANK ORDER

RANK	STATE	PERCENT
1	Massachusetts	40.4
2	Colorado	36.4
3	Connecticut	36.0
4	Maryland	35.7
5	New Jersey	35.6
6	Vermont	34.0
7	Minnesota	33.5
8	Hawaii	32.3
9	New York	32.2
10	New Hampshire	32.1
10	Virginia	32.1
12	Kansas	31.6
13	Washington	31.4
14	Illinois	31.2
15	Rhode Island	30.9
16	California	29.8
17	North Dakota	28.7
18	Oregon	28.3
19	Georgia	28.1
20	Alaska	27.7
21	Florida	27.2
21	Nebraska	27.2
23	Utah	27.0
24	Maine	26.9
25	New Mexico	26.7
26	Pennsylvania	26.6
27	Delaware	26.2
28	Michigan	26.1
29	North Carolina	25.6
30	Texas	25.5
31	South Dakota	25.3
32	Idaho	25.1
32	Montana	25.1
34	Iowa	24.7
35	Wisconsin	24.6
36	Arizona	24.5
37	Missouri	24.3
38	Ohio	23.3
39	Oklahoma	22.9
40	South Carolina	22.6
41	Tennessee	22.0
42	Indiana	21.9
43	Louisiana	21.2
44	Mississippi	21.1
45	Alabama	20.8
45	Nevada	20.8
45	Wyoming	20.8
48	Kentucky	20.2
49	Arkansas	19.0
50	West Virginia	15.9
	District of Columbia	49.1

Source: U.S. Bureau of the Census
"Educational Attainment of the Population 25 Years and Over, By State"
(http://www.census.gov/population/www/socdemo/education/cps2006.html)
*Persons age 25 and older.

Public Libraries and Branches in 2005

National Total = 16,543 Libraries and Branches*

RANK	STATE	LIBRARIES	% of USA
	ALPHA ORDER		
24	Alabama	285	1.7%
44	Alaska	106	0.6%
34	Arizona	191	1.2%
30	Arkansas	213	1.3%
1	California	1,093	6.6%
27	Colorado	242	1.5%
26	Connecticut	244	1.5%
50	Delaware	33	0.2%
9	Florida	502	3.0%
16	Georgia	370	2.2%
49	Hawaii	51	0.3%
40	Idaho	139	0.8%
4	Illinois	783	4.7%
13	Indiana	438	2.6%
8	Iowa	563	3.4%
15	Kansas	374	2.3%
33	Kentucky	193	1.2%
20	Louisiana	335	2.0%
25	Maine	278	1.7%
37	Maryland	178	1.1%
10	Massachusetts	483	2.9%
6	Michigan	656	4.0%
17	Minnesota	359	2.2%
28	Mississippi	241	1.5%
18	Missouri	358	2.2%
43	Montana	109	0.7%
23	Nebraska	286	1.7%
46	Nevada	85	0.5%
29	New Hampshire	237	1.4%
12	New Jersey	453	2.7%
41	New Mexico	114	0.7%
2	New York	1,068	6.5%
14	North Carolina	383	2.3%
45	North Dakota	91	0.6%
5	Ohio	718	4.3%
32	Oklahoma	204	1.2%
31	Oregon	212	1.3%
7	Pennsylvania	635	3.8%
48	Rhode Island	73	0.4%
35	South Carolina	185	1.1%
39	South Dakota	144	0.9%
22	Tennessee	289	1.7%
3	Texas	851	5.1%
41	Utah	114	0.7%
35	Vermont	185	1.1%
19	Virginia	343	2.1%
21	Washington	329	2.0%
38	West Virginia	173	1.0%
11	Wisconsin	457	2.8%
47	Wyoming	74	0.4%

RANK	STATE	LIBRARIES	% of USA
	RANK ORDER		
1	California	1,093	6.6%
2	New York	1,068	6.5%
3	Texas	851	5.1%
4	Illinois	783	4.7%
5	Ohio	718	4.3%
6	Michigan	656	4.0%
7	Pennsylvania	635	3.8%
8	Iowa	563	3.4%
9	Florida	502	3.0%
10	Massachusetts	483	2.9%
11	Wisconsin	457	2.8%
12	New Jersey	453	2.7%
13	Indiana	438	2.6%
14	North Carolina	383	2.3%
15	Kansas	374	2.3%
16	Georgia	370	2.2%
17	Minnesota	359	2.2%
18	Missouri	358	2.2%
19	Virginia	343	2.1%
20	Louisiana	335	2.0%
21	Washington	329	2.0%
22	Tennessee	289	1.7%
23	Nebraska	286	1.7%
24	Alabama	285	1.7%
25	Maine	278	1.7%
26	Connecticut	244	1.5%
27	Colorado	242	1.5%
28	Mississippi	241	1.5%
29	New Hampshire	237	1.4%
30	Arkansas	213	1.3%
31	Oregon	212	1.3%
32	Oklahoma	204	1.2%
33	Kentucky	193	1.2%
34	Arizona	191	1.2%
35	South Carolina	185	1.1%
35	Vermont	185	1.1%
37	Maryland	178	1.1%
38	West Virginia	173	1.0%
39	South Dakota	144	0.9%
40	Idaho	139	0.8%
41	New Mexico	114	0.7%
41	Utah	114	0.7%
43	Montana	109	0.7%
44	Alaska	106	0.6%
45	North Dakota	91	0.6%
46	Nevada	85	0.5%
47	Wyoming	74	0.4%
48	Rhode Island	73	0.4%
49	Hawaii	51	0.3%
50	Delaware	33	0.2%
	District of Columbia	23	0.1%

Source: U.S. Dept. of Education, Office of Educational Research and Improvement
"Public Libraries in the United States: FY 2005" (NCES 2008-301, November 2007)
*For fiscal year 2005. Total of central and branch outlets. Does not include 825 bookmobiles. There are 9,198 public libraries.

Rate of Public Libraries and Branches in 2005

National Average = 17,886 Population per Library*

ALPHA ORDER				RANK ORDER		
RANK	STATE	RATE		RANK	STATE	RATE
27	Alabama	15,928		1	Florida	35,331
44	Alaska	6,315		2	California	32,928
4	Arizona	31,163		3	Maryland	31,310
35	Arkansas	13,015		4	Arizona	31,163
2	California	32,928		5	Nevada	28,341
17	Colorado	19,313		6	Texas	26,844
30	Connecticut	14,289		7	Delaware	25,471
7	Delaware	25,471		8	Hawaii	24,855
1	Florida	35,331		9	Georgia	24,615
9	Georgia	24,615		10	South Carolina	23,000
8	Hawaii	24,855		11	North Carolina	22,661
39	Idaho	10,258		12	Virginia	22,034
24	Illinois	16,245		13	Utah	21,974
31	Indiana	14,286		14	Kentucky	21,611
48	Iowa	5,250		15	Tennessee	20,724
41	Kansas	7,331		16	Pennsylvania	19,476
14	Kentucky	21,611		17	Colorado	19,313
33	Louisiana	13,420		18	New Jersey	19,111
49	Maine	4,720		19	Washington	19,060
3	Maryland	31,310		20	New York	18,036
34	Massachusetts	13,311		21	Oklahoma	17,333
28	Michigan	15,408		22	Oregon	17,122
32	Minnesota	14,245		23	New Mexico	16,810
37	Mississippi	12,035		24	Illinois	16,245
25	Missouri	16,167		25	Missouri	16,167
40	Montana	8,585		26	Ohio	15,961
45	Nebraska	6,133		27	Alabama	15,928
5	Nevada	28,341		28	Michigan	15,408
46	New Hampshire	5,498		29	Rhode Island	14,613
18	New Jersey	19,111		30	Connecticut	14,289
23	New Mexico	16,810		31	Indiana	14,286
20	New York	18,036		32	Minnesota	14,245
11	North Carolina	22,661		33	Louisiana	13,420
42	North Dakota	6,988		34	Massachusetts	13,311
26	Ohio	15,961		35	Arkansas	13,015
21	Oklahoma	17,333		36	Wisconsin	12,124
22	Oregon	17,122		37	Mississippi	12,035
16	Pennsylvania	19,476		38	West Virginia	10,437
29	Rhode Island	14,613		39	Idaho	10,258
10	South Carolina	23,000		40	Montana	8,585
47	South Dakota	5,417		41	Kansas	7,331
15	Tennessee	20,724		42	North Dakota	6,988
6	Texas	26,844		43	Wyoming	6,845
13	Utah	21,974		44	Alaska	6,315
50	Vermont	3,350		45	Nebraska	6,133
12	Virginia	22,034		46	New Hampshire	5,498
19	Washington	19,060		47	South Dakota	5,417
38	West Virginia	10,437		48	Iowa	5,250
36	Wisconsin	12,124		49	Maine	4,720
43	Wyoming	6,845		50	Vermont	3,350
					District of Columbia	25,306

Source: CQ Press using data from U.S. Dept. of Education, Office of Educational Research and Improvement
  "Public Libraries in the United States: FY 2005" (NCES 2008-301, November 2007)
*For fiscal year 2005. Total of central and branch outlets. Does not include 825 bookmobiles. There are 9,198 public libraries.

Books in Public Libraries Per Capita in 2005

National Per Capita = 2.8 Books*

RANK	STATE	BOOKS PER CAPITA
40	Alabama	2.1
19	Alaska	3.5
48	Arizona	1.8
37	Arkansas	2.3
38	California	2.2
30	Colorado	2.6
9	Connecticut	4.3
38	Delaware	2.2
44	Florida	1.9
49	Georgia	1.7
33	Hawaii	2.5
22	Idaho	3.2
17	Illinois	3.7
9	Indiana	4.3
13	Iowa	4.1
4	Kansas	4.8
40	Kentucky	2.1
33	Louisiana	2.5
1	Maine	5.4
30	Maryland	2.6
3	Massachusetts	5.0
21	Michigan	3.4
23	Minnesota	3.1
44	Mississippi	1.9
18	Missouri	3.6
23	Montana	3.1
6	Nebraska	4.7
50	Nevada	1.6
8	New Hampshire	4.6
16	New Jersey	3.8
25	New Mexico	3.0
15	New York	3.9
44	North Carolina	1.9
11	North Dakota	4.2
11	Ohio	4.2
36	Oklahoma	2.4
27	Oregon	2.8
33	Pennsylvania	2.5
14	Rhode Island	4.0
40	South Carolina	2.1
2	South Dakota	5.3
44	Tennessee	1.9
40	Texas	2.1
28	Utah	2.7
6	Vermont	4.7
30	Virginia	2.6
26	Washington	2.9
28	West Virginia	2.7
19	Wisconsin	3.5
4	Wyoming	4.8

RANK	STATE	BOOKS PER CAPITA
1	Maine	5.4
2	South Dakota	5.3
3	Massachusetts	5.0
4	Kansas	4.8
4	Wyoming	4.8
6	Nebraska	4.7
6	Vermont	4.7
8	New Hampshire	4.6
9	Connecticut	4.3
9	Indiana	4.3
11	North Dakota	4.2
11	Ohio	4.2
13	Iowa	4.1
14	Rhode Island	4.0
15	New York	3.9
16	New Jersey	3.8
17	Illinois	3.7
18	Missouri	3.6
19	Alaska	3.5
19	Wisconsin	3.5
21	Michigan	3.4
22	Idaho	3.2
23	Minnesota	3.1
23	Montana	3.1
25	New Mexico	3.0
26	Washington	2.9
27	Oregon	2.8
28	Utah	2.7
28	West Virginia	2.7
30	Colorado	2.6
30	Maryland	2.6
30	Virginia	2.6
33	Hawaii	2.5
33	Louisiana	2.5
33	Pennsylvania	2.5
36	Oklahoma	2.4
37	Arkansas	2.3
38	California	2.2
38	Delaware	2.2
40	Alabama	2.1
40	Kentucky	2.1
40	South Carolina	2.1
40	Texas	2.1
44	Florida	1.9
44	Mississippi	1.9
44	North Carolina	1.9
44	Tennessee	1.9
48	Arizona	1.8
49	Georgia	1.7
50	Nevada	1.6
	District of Columbia	4.1

Source: U.S. Dept. of Education, Office of Educational Research and Improvement
   "Public Libraries in the United States: FY 2005" (NCES 2008-301, November 2007)
*For fiscal year 2005. Includes serial volumes but not serial subscriptions.

Internet Terminals in Public Libraries: 2005

National Total = 185,179 Terminals*

ALPHA ORDER					RANK ORDER			
RANK	STATE	TERMINALS	% of USA		RANK	STATE	TERMINALS	% of USA
19	Alabama	3,614	2.0%		1	California	14,209	7.7%
46	Alaska	562	0.3%		2	Texas	12,848	6.9%
24	Arizona	2,906	1.6%		3	New York	12,045	6.5%
35	Arkansas	1,311	0.7%		4	Illinois	11,110	6.0%
1	California	14,209	7.7%		5	Ohio	10,404	5.6%
25	Colorado	2,812	1.5%		6	Florida	9,555	5.2%
27	Connecticut	2,622	1.4%		7	Michigan	7,822	4.2%
50	Delaware	351	0.2%		8	Pennsylvania	7,012	3.8%
6	Florida	9,555	5.2%		9	Indiana	5,979	3.2%
10	Georgia	5,598	3.0%		10	Georgia	5,598	3.0%
47	Hawaii	518	0.3%		11	New Jersey	5,275	2.8%
42	Idaho	843	0.5%		12	North Carolina	5,062	2.7%
4	Illinois	11,110	6.0%		13	Massachusetts	4,381	2.4%
9	Indiana	5,979	3.2%		14	Wisconsin	4,310	2.3%
23	Iowa	2,926	1.6%		15	Virginia	4,238	2.3%
28	Kansas	2,565	1.4%		16	Washington	4,037	2.2%
29	Kentucky	2,373	1.3%		17	Missouri	3,923	2.1%
22	Louisiana	2,935	1.6%		18	Minnesota	3,685	2.0%
36	Maine	1,249	0.7%		19	Alabama	3,614	2.0%
21	Maryland	3,177	1.7%		20	Tennessee	3,228	1.7%
13	Massachusetts	4,381	2.4%		21	Maryland	3,177	1.7%
7	Michigan	7,822	4.2%		22	Louisiana	2,935	1.6%
18	Minnesota	3,685	2.0%		23	Iowa	2,926	1.6%
33	Mississippi	1,630	0.9%		24	Arizona	2,906	1.6%
17	Missouri	3,923	2.1%		25	Colorado	2,812	1.5%
45	Montana	744	0.4%		26	South Carolina	2,670	1.4%
32	Nebraska	1,685	0.9%		27	Connecticut	2,622	1.4%
39	Nevada	949	0.5%		28	Kansas	2,565	1.4%
40	New Hampshire	925	0.5%		29	Kentucky	2,373	1.3%
11	New Jersey	5,275	2.8%		30	Oregon	2,014	1.1%
37	New Mexico	1,126	0.6%		31	Oklahoma	1,940	1.0%
3	New York	12,045	6.5%		32	Nebraska	1,685	0.9%
12	North Carolina	5,062	2.7%		33	Mississippi	1,630	0.9%
49	North Dakota	443	0.2%		34	Utah	1,379	0.7%
5	Ohio	10,404	5.6%		35	Arkansas	1,311	0.7%
31	Oklahoma	1,940	1.0%		36	Maine	1,249	0.7%
30	Oregon	2,014	1.1%		37	New Mexico	1,126	0.6%
8	Pennsylvania	7,012	3.8%		38	West Virginia	1,010	0.5%
41	Rhode Island	886	0.5%		39	Nevada	949	0.5%
26	South Carolina	2,670	1.4%		40	New Hampshire	925	0.5%
43	South Dakota	798	0.4%		41	Rhode Island	886	0.5%
20	Tennessee	3,228	1.7%		42	Idaho	843	0.5%
2	Texas	12,848	6.9%		43	South Dakota	798	0.4%
34	Utah	1,379	0.7%		44	Vermont	786	0.4%
44	Vermont	786	0.4%		45	Montana	744	0.4%
15	Virginia	4,238	2.3%		46	Alaska	562	0.3%
16	Washington	4,037	2.2%		47	Hawaii	518	0.3%
38	West Virginia	1,010	0.5%		48	Wyoming	495	0.3%
14	Wisconsin	4,310	2.3%		49	North Dakota	443	0.2%
48	Wyoming	495	0.3%		50	Delaware	351	0.2%
						District of Columbia	214	0.1%

Source: U.S. Dept. of Education, Office of Educational Research and Improvement
   "Public Libraries in the United States: FY 2005" (NCES 2008-301, November 2007)
*For fiscal year 2005. Total of public-use internet terminals in central and branch outlets.

Rate of Internet Terminals in Public Libraries: 2005

National Rate = 11.2 Terminals per Library*

ALPHA ORDER

RANK	STATE	RATE
12	Alabama	12.7
45	Alaska	5.3
3	Arizona	15.2
40	Arkansas	6.2
11	California	13.0
19	Colorado	11.6
26	Connecticut	10.7
27	Delaware	10.6
1	Florida	19.0
4	Georgia	15.1
29	Hawaii	10.2
41	Idaho	6.1
8	Illinois	14.2
9	Indiana	13.7
46	Iowa	5.2
36	Kansas	6.9
14	Kentucky	12.3
35	Louisiana	8.8
48	Maine	4.5
2	Maryland	17.8
34	Massachusetts	9.1
18	Michigan	11.9
28	Minnesota	10.3
37	Mississippi	6.8
24	Missouri	11.0
37	Montana	6.8
42	Nebraska	5.9
22	Nevada	11.2
50	New Hampshire	3.9
19	New Jersey	11.6
30	New Mexico	9.9
21	New York	11.3
10	North Carolina	13.2
47	North Dakota	4.9
6	Ohio	14.5
31	Oklahoma	9.5
31	Oregon	9.5
24	Pennsylvania	11.0
16	Rhode Island	12.1
7	South Carolina	14.4
44	South Dakota	5.5
22	Tennessee	11.2
4	Texas	15.1
16	Utah	12.1
49	Vermont	4.2
13	Virginia	12.4
14	Washington	12.3
43	West Virginia	5.8
33	Wisconsin	9.4
39	Wyoming	6.7

RANK ORDER

RANK	STATE	RATE
1	Florida	19.0
2	Maryland	17.8
3	Arizona	15.2
4	Georgia	15.1
4	Texas	15.1
6	Ohio	14.5
7	South Carolina	14.4
8	Illinois	14.2
9	Indiana	13.7
10	North Carolina	13.2
11	California	13.0
12	Alabama	12.7
13	Virginia	12.4
14	Kentucky	12.3
14	Washington	12.3
16	Rhode Island	12.1
16	Utah	12.1
18	Michigan	11.9
19	Colorado	11.6
19	New Jersey	11.6
21	New York	11.3
22	Nevada	11.2
22	Tennessee	11.2
24	Missouri	11.0
24	Pennsylvania	11.0
26	Connecticut	10.7
27	Delaware	10.6
28	Minnesota	10.3
29	Hawaii	10.2
30	New Mexico	9.9
31	Oklahoma	9.5
31	Oregon	9.5
33	Wisconsin	9.4
34	Massachusetts	9.1
35	Louisiana	8.8
36	Kansas	6.9
37	Mississippi	6.8
37	Montana	6.8
39	Wyoming	6.7
40	Arkansas	6.2
41	Idaho	6.1
42	Nebraska	5.9
43	West Virginia	5.8
44	South Dakota	5.5
45	Alaska	5.3
46	Iowa	5.2
47	North Dakota	4.9
48	Maine	4.5
49	Vermont	4.2
50	New Hampshire	3.9
	District of Columbia	9.3

Source: U.S. Dept. of Education, Office of Educational Research and Improvement
"Public Libraries in the United States: FY 2005" (NCES 2008-301, November 2007)
*For fiscal year 2005. Total of public-use internet terminals in central and branch outlets divided by the number of outlets.

Per Capita State Art Agencies' Legislative Appropriations in 2007

National Per Capita = $1.01*

ALPHA ORDER			RANK ORDER		
RANK	STATE	PER CAPITA	RANK	STATE	PER CAPITA
24	Alabama	$0.85	1	Hawaii	$5.32
26	Alaska	0.81	2	New Jersey	3.42
32	Arizona	0.59	3	Rhode Island	3.04
36	Arkansas	0.54	4	New York	2.35
50	California	0.06	5	Delaware	2.09
49	Colorado	0.15	6	Connecticut	2.02
6	Connecticut	2.02	7	Maryland	2.01
5	Delaware	2.09	8	Minnesota	1.66
9	Florida	1.63	9	Florida	1.63
43	Georgia	0.42	10	Illinois	1.54
1	Hawaii	5.32	11	Massachusetts	1.51
33	Idaho	0.58	12	West Virginia	1.33
10	Illinois	1.54	13	Wyoming	1.27
36	Indiana	0.54	14	Oklahoma	1.19
44	Iowa	0.40	15	Louisiana	1.17
36	Kansas	0.54	15	Pennsylvania	1.17
21	Kentucky	0.98	17	Tennessee	1.10
15	Louisiana	1.17	18	Utah	1.06
33	Maine	0.58	19	Michigan	1.04
7	Maryland	2.01	20	New Mexico	1.00
11	Massachusetts	1.51	21	Kentucky	0.98
19	Michigan	1.04	21	Ohio	0.98
8	Minnesota	1.66	23	North Carolina	0.90
36	Mississippi	0.54	24	Alabama	0.85
46	Missouri	0.20	25	South Carolina	0.83
42	Montana	0.43	26	Alaska	0.81
29	Nebraska	0.77	27	North Dakota	0.79
31	Nevada	0.68	27	Vermont	0.79
35	New Hampshire	0.55	29	Nebraska	0.77
2	New Jersey	3.42	29	South Dakota	0.77
20	New Mexico	1.00	31	Nevada	0.68
4	New York	2.35	32	Arizona	0.59
23	North Carolina	0.90	33	Idaho	0.58
27	North Dakota	0.79	33	Maine	0.58
21	Ohio	0.98	35	New Hampshire	0.55
14	Oklahoma	1.19	36	Arkansas	0.54
47	Oregon	0.17	36	Indiana	0.54
15	Pennsylvania	1.17	36	Kansas	0.54
3	Rhode Island	3.04	36	Mississippi	0.54
25	South Carolina	0.83	40	Virginia	0.46
29	South Dakota	0.77	41	Wisconsin	0.44
17	Tennessee	1.10	42	Montana	0.43
47	Texas	0.17	43	Georgia	0.42
18	Utah	1.06	44	Iowa	0.40
27	Vermont	0.79	45	Washington	0.36
40	Virginia	0.46	46	Missouri	0.20
45	Washington	0.36	47	Oregon	0.17
12	West Virginia	1.33	47	Texas	0.17
41	Wisconsin	0.44	49	Colorado	0.15
13	Wyoming	1.27	50	California	0.06
				District of Columbia	14.71

Source: CQ Press using data from National Assembly of State Arts Agencies
"State Arts Funding Grows in Fiscal Year 2007" (Press Release, February 7, 2007)
*Preliminary figures for fiscal year 2007. Includes line item appropriations. Line items are legislative appropriations that are not controlled by the state art agencies but are passed through their budgets directly to another entity. Calculated using 2006 census population estimates. National per capita does not include appropriations or population in U.S. territories.

Federal Allocations for Head Start Program in 2006

National Total = $6,554,737,000*

<table>
<tr><td colspan="4">ALPHA ORDER</td><td colspan="4">RANK ORDER</td></tr>
<tr><td>RANK</td><td>STATE</td><td>ALLOCATIONS</td><td>% of USA</td><td>RANK</td><td>STATE</td><td>ALLOCATIONS</td><td>% of USA</td></tr>
<tr><td>18</td><td>Alabama</td><td>$105,467,527</td><td>1.6%</td><td>1</td><td>California</td><td>$822,593,768</td><td>12.5%</td></tr>
<tr><td>49</td><td>Alaska</td><td>12,336,713</td><td>0.2%</td><td>2</td><td>Texas</td><td>473,492,116</td><td>7.2%</td></tr>
<tr><td>19</td><td>Arizona</td><td>102,373,122</td><td>1.6%</td><td>3</td><td>New York</td><td>428,470,291</td><td>6.5%</td></tr>
<tr><td>29</td><td>Arkansas</td><td>63,823,662</td><td>1.0%</td><td>4</td><td>Illinois</td><td>267,812,098</td><td>4.1%</td></tr>
<tr><td>1</td><td>California</td><td>822,593,768</td><td>12.5%</td><td>5</td><td>Florida</td><td>260,267,233</td><td>4.0%</td></tr>
<tr><td>28</td><td>Colorado</td><td>67,594,321</td><td>1.0%</td><td>6</td><td>Ohio</td><td>244,204,960</td><td>3.7%</td></tr>
<tr><td>32</td><td>Connecticut</td><td>51,332,832</td><td>0.8%</td><td>7</td><td>Michigan</td><td>231,993,266</td><td>3.5%</td></tr>
<tr><td>48</td><td>Delaware</td><td>13,091,612</td><td>0.2%</td><td>8</td><td>Pennsylvania</td><td>225,684,989</td><td>3.4%</td></tr>
<tr><td>5</td><td>Florida</td><td>260,267,233</td><td>4.0%</td><td>9</td><td>Georgia</td><td>166,671,579</td><td>2.5%</td></tr>
<tr><td>9</td><td>Georgia</td><td>166,671,579</td><td>2.5%</td><td>10</td><td>Mississippi</td><td>159,927,300</td><td>2.4%</td></tr>
<tr><td>40</td><td>Hawaii</td><td>22,636,682</td><td>0.3%</td><td>11</td><td>Louisiana</td><td>144,311,959</td><td>2.2%</td></tr>
<tr><td>41</td><td>Idaho</td><td>22,565,199</td><td>0.3%</td><td>12</td><td>North Carolina</td><td>139,734,909</td><td>2.1%</td></tr>
<tr><td>4</td><td>Illinois</td><td>267,812,098</td><td>4.1%</td><td>13</td><td>New Jersey</td><td>127,606,975</td><td>1.9%</td></tr>
<tr><td>22</td><td>Indiana</td><td>95,151,487</td><td>1.5%</td><td>14</td><td>Tennessee</td><td>118,039,184</td><td>1.8%</td></tr>
<tr><td>33</td><td>Iowa</td><td>50,987,675</td><td>0.8%</td><td>15</td><td>Missouri</td><td>117,694,689</td><td>1.8%</td></tr>
<tr><td>34</td><td>Kansas</td><td>50,371,658</td><td>0.8%</td><td>16</td><td>Massachusetts</td><td>107,169,026</td><td>1.6%</td></tr>
<tr><td>17</td><td>Kentucky</td><td>106,670,143</td><td>1.6%</td><td>17</td><td>Kentucky</td><td>106,670,143</td><td>1.6%</td></tr>
<tr><td>11</td><td>Louisiana</td><td>144,311,959</td><td>2.2%</td><td>18</td><td>Alabama</td><td>105,467,527</td><td>1.6%</td></tr>
<tr><td>38</td><td>Maine</td><td>27,309,854</td><td>0.4%</td><td>19</td><td>Arizona</td><td>102,373,122</td><td>1.6%</td></tr>
<tr><td>26</td><td>Maryland</td><td>77,183,646</td><td>1.2%</td><td>20</td><td>Washington</td><td>99,268,177</td><td>1.5%</td></tr>
<tr><td>16</td><td>Massachusetts</td><td>107,169,026</td><td>1.6%</td><td>21</td><td>Virginia</td><td>98,071,628</td><td>1.5%</td></tr>
<tr><td>7</td><td>Michigan</td><td>231,993,266</td><td>3.5%</td><td>22</td><td>Indiana</td><td>95,151,487</td><td>1.5%</td></tr>
<tr><td>27</td><td>Minnesota</td><td>71,218,555</td><td>1.1%</td><td>23</td><td>Wisconsin</td><td>89,887,220</td><td>1.4%</td></tr>
<tr><td>10</td><td>Mississippi</td><td>159,927,300</td><td>2.4%</td><td>24</td><td>South Carolina</td><td>81,602,767</td><td>1.2%</td></tr>
<tr><td>15</td><td>Missouri</td><td>117,694,689</td><td>1.8%</td><td>25</td><td>Oklahoma</td><td>80,166,186</td><td>1.2%</td></tr>
<tr><td>43</td><td>Montana</td><td>20,720,770</td><td>0.3%</td><td>26</td><td>Maryland</td><td>77,183,646</td><td>1.2%</td></tr>
<tr><td>37</td><td>Nebraska</td><td>35,665,489</td><td>0.5%</td><td>27</td><td>Minnesota</td><td>71,218,555</td><td>1.1%</td></tr>
<tr><td>39</td><td>Nevada</td><td>24,015,210</td><td>0.4%</td><td>28</td><td>Colorado</td><td>67,594,321</td><td>1.0%</td></tr>
<tr><td>47</td><td>New Hampshire</td><td>13,240,062</td><td>0.2%</td><td>29</td><td>Arkansas</td><td>63,823,662</td><td>1.0%</td></tr>
<tr><td>13</td><td>New Jersey</td><td>127,606,975</td><td>1.9%</td><td>30</td><td>Oregon</td><td>58,820,971</td><td>0.9%</td></tr>
<tr><td>31</td><td>New Mexico</td><td>51,729,545</td><td>0.8%</td><td>31</td><td>New Mexico</td><td>51,729,545</td><td>0.8%</td></tr>
<tr><td>3</td><td>New York</td><td>428,470,291</td><td>6.5%</td><td>32</td><td>Connecticut</td><td>51,332,832</td><td>0.8%</td></tr>
<tr><td>12</td><td>North Carolina</td><td>139,734,909</td><td>2.1%</td><td>33</td><td>Iowa</td><td>50,987,675</td><td>0.8%</td></tr>
<tr><td>45</td><td>North Dakota</td><td>16,987,597</td><td>0.3%</td><td>34</td><td>Kansas</td><td>50,371,658</td><td>0.8%</td></tr>
<tr><td>6</td><td>Ohio</td><td>244,204,960</td><td>3.7%</td><td>35</td><td>West Virginia</td><td>50,091,048</td><td>0.8%</td></tr>
<tr><td>25</td><td>Oklahoma</td><td>80,166,186</td><td>1.2%</td><td>36</td><td>Utah</td><td>37,352,635</td><td>0.6%</td></tr>
<tr><td>30</td><td>Oregon</td><td>58,820,971</td><td>0.9%</td><td>37</td><td>Nebraska</td><td>35,665,489</td><td>0.5%</td></tr>
<tr><td>8</td><td>Pennsylvania</td><td>225,684,989</td><td>3.4%</td><td>38</td><td>Maine</td><td>27,309,854</td><td>0.4%</td></tr>
<tr><td>42</td><td>Rhode Island</td><td>21,775,158</td><td>0.3%</td><td>39</td><td>Nevada</td><td>24,015,210</td><td>0.4%</td></tr>
<tr><td>24</td><td>South Carolina</td><td>81,602,767</td><td>1.2%</td><td>40</td><td>Hawaii</td><td>22,636,682</td><td>0.3%</td></tr>
<tr><td>44</td><td>South Dakota</td><td>18,620,111</td><td>0.3%</td><td>41</td><td>Idaho</td><td>22,565,199</td><td>0.3%</td></tr>
<tr><td>14</td><td>Tennessee</td><td>118,039,184</td><td>1.8%</td><td>42</td><td>Rhode Island</td><td>21,775,158</td><td>0.3%</td></tr>
<tr><td>2</td><td>Texas</td><td>473,492,116</td><td>7.2%</td><td>43</td><td>Montana</td><td>20,720,770</td><td>0.3%</td></tr>
<tr><td>36</td><td>Utah</td><td>37,352,635</td><td>0.6%</td><td>44</td><td>South Dakota</td><td>18,620,111</td><td>0.3%</td></tr>
<tr><td>46</td><td>Vermont</td><td>13,411,517</td><td>0.2%</td><td>45</td><td>North Dakota</td><td>16,987,597</td><td>0.3%</td></tr>
<tr><td>21</td><td>Virginia</td><td>98,071,628</td><td>1.5%</td><td>46</td><td>Vermont</td><td>13,411,517</td><td>0.2%</td></tr>
<tr><td>20</td><td>Washington</td><td>99,268,177</td><td>1.5%</td><td>47</td><td>New Hampshire</td><td>13,240,062</td><td>0.2%</td></tr>
<tr><td>35</td><td>West Virginia</td><td>50,091,048</td><td>0.8%</td><td>48</td><td>Delaware</td><td>13,091,612</td><td>0.2%</td></tr>
<tr><td>23</td><td>Wisconsin</td><td>89,887,220</td><td>1.4%</td><td>49</td><td>Alaska</td><td>12,336,713</td><td>0.2%</td></tr>
<tr><td>50</td><td>Wyoming</td><td>12,236,450</td><td>0.2%</td><td>50</td><td>Wyoming</td><td>12,236,450</td><td>0.2%</td></tr>
<tr><td></td><td></td><td></td><td></td><td></td><td>District of Columbia</td><td>24,834,071</td><td>0.4%</td></tr>
</table>

Source: U.S. Department of Health and Human Services, Administration for Children and Families
   "Head Start Fact Sheet" (http://www.acf.hhs.gov/programs/hsb/about/fy2007.html)
*For fiscal year 2006. National total includes $468,764,522 to Migrant and Native American programs and $261,740,886 to U.S. territories. Does not include $222,047,000 in "support activities" expenditures.

Head Start Program Enrollment in 2006

National Total = 909,201 Children*

RANK	STATE	CHILDREN	% of USA
15	Alabama	16,374	1.8%
49	Alaska	1,580	0.2%
22	Arizona	13,175	1.4%
26	Arkansas	10,778	1.2%
1	California	98,395	10.8%
29	Colorado	9,820	1.1%
35	Connecticut	7,126	0.8%
46	Delaware	2,071	0.2%
6	Florida	35,514	3.9%
10	Georgia	23,508	2.6%
40	Hawaii	3,049	0.3%
41	Idaho	2,951	0.3%
4	Illinois	39,640	4.4%
18	Indiana	14,231	1.6%
32	Iowa	7,710	0.8%
31	Kansas	8,335	0.9%
16	Kentucky	16,071	1.8%
11	Louisiana	21,910	2.4%
38	Maine	3,913	0.4%
27	Maryland	10,347	1.1%
23	Massachusetts	12,819	1.4%
8	Michigan	35,069	3.9%
28	Minnesota	10,332	1.1%
9	Mississippi	26,657	2.9%
13	Missouri	17,451	1.9%
42	Montana	2,929	0.3%
37	Nebraska	5,080	0.6%
44	Nevada	2,754	0.3%
48	New Hampshire	1,632	0.2%
17	New Jersey	14,582	1.6%
34	New Mexico	7,451	0.8%
3	New York	48,818	5.4%
12	North Carolina	18,963	2.1%
45	North Dakota	2,353	0.3%
5	Ohio	38,021	4.2%
21	Oklahoma	13,474	1.5%
30	Oregon	8,804	1.0%
7	Pennsylvania	35,372	3.9%
39	Rhode Island	3,135	0.3%
24	South Carolina	12,248	1.3%
43	South Dakota	2,827	0.3%
14	Tennessee	16,397	1.8%
2	Texas	67,875	7.5%
36	Utah	5,518	0.6%
50	Vermont	1,552	0.2%
19	Virginia	13,679	1.5%
25	Washington	11,190	1.2%
33	West Virginia	7,610	0.8%
20	Wisconsin	13,538	1.5%
47	Wyoming	1,792	0.2%

RANK	STATE	CHILDREN	% of USA
1	California	98,395	10.8%
2	Texas	67,875	7.5%
3	New York	48,818	5.4%
4	Illinois	39,640	4.4%
5	Ohio	38,021	4.2%
6	Florida	35,514	3.9%
7	Pennsylvania	35,372	3.9%
8	Michigan	35,069	3.9%
9	Mississippi	26,657	2.9%
10	Georgia	23,508	2.6%
11	Louisiana	21,910	2.4%
12	North Carolina	18,963	2.1%
13	Missouri	17,451	1.9%
14	Tennessee	16,397	1.8%
15	Alabama	16,374	1.8%
16	Kentucky	16,071	1.8%
17	New Jersey	14,582	1.6%
18	Indiana	14,231	1.6%
19	Virginia	13,679	1.5%
20	Wisconsin	13,538	1.5%
21	Oklahoma	13,474	1.5%
22	Arizona	13,175	1.4%
23	Massachusetts	12,819	1.4%
24	South Carolina	12,248	1.3%
25	Washington	11,190	1.2%
26	Arkansas	10,778	1.2%
27	Maryland	10,347	1.1%
28	Minnesota	10,332	1.1%
29	Colorado	9,820	1.1%
30	Oregon	8,804	1.0%
31	Kansas	8,335	0.9%
32	Iowa	7,710	0.8%
33	West Virginia	7,610	0.8%
34	New Mexico	7,451	0.8%
35	Connecticut	7,126	0.8%
36	Utah	5,518	0.6%
37	Nebraska	5,080	0.6%
38	Maine	3,913	0.4%
39	Rhode Island	3,135	0.3%
40	Hawaii	3,049	0.3%
41	Idaho	2,951	0.3%
42	Montana	2,929	0.3%
43	South Dakota	2,827	0.3%
44	Nevada	2,754	0.3%
45	North Dakota	2,353	0.3%
46	Delaware	2,071	0.2%
47	Wyoming	1,792	0.2%
48	New Hampshire	1,632	0.2%
49	Alaska	1,580	0.2%
50	Vermont	1,552	0.2%
	District of Columbia	3,403	0.4%

Source: U.S. Department of Health and Human Services, Administration for Children and Families
    "Head Start Fact Sheet" (http://www.acf.hhs.gov/programs/hsb/about/fy2007.html)
*For fiscal year 2006. National total includes 58,534 enrollees in Migrant and Native American programs and 40,844 enrollees in
U.S. territories.

VI. Employment and Labor

Average Annual Pay in 2006

National Average = $42,535*

RANK	STATE	ANNUAL PAY
33	Alabama	$36,204
16	Alaska	41,750
21	Arizona	40,019
46	Arkansas	32,389
5	California	48,345
10	Colorado	43,506
2	Connecticut	54,814
6	Delaware	46,285
23	Florida	38,485
19	Georgia	40,370
25	Hawaii	37,799
45	Idaho	32,580
8	Illinois	45,650
32	Indiana	36,553
39	Iowa	34,320
34	Kansas	35,696
36	Kentucky	35,201
31	Louisiana	36,604
43	Maine	33,794
7	Maryland	46,162
3	Massachusetts	52,435
15	Michigan	42,157
14	Minnesota	42,185
48	Mississippi	31,194
28	Missouri	37,143
49	Montana	30,596
42	Nebraska	33,814
20	Nevada	40,070
13	New Hampshire	42,447
4	New Jersey	51,645
38	New Mexico	34,567
1	New York	55,479
27	North Carolina	37,439
47	North Dakota	31,316
22	Ohio	38,568
41	Oklahoma	34,022
24	Oregon	38,077
17	Pennsylvania	41,349
18	Rhode Island	40,454
40	South Carolina	34,281
50	South Dakota	30,291
26	Tennessee	37,564
12	Texas	42,458
37	Utah	35,130
35	Vermont	35,542
9	Virginia	44,051
11	Washington	42,897
44	West Virginia	32,728
29	Wisconsin	36,821
30	Wyoming	36,662

RANK	STATE	ANNUAL PAY
1	New York	$55,479
2	Connecticut	54,814
3	Massachusetts	52,435
4	New Jersey	51,645
5	California	48,345
6	Delaware	46,285
7	Maryland	46,162
8	Illinois	45,650
9	Virginia	44,051
10	Colorado	43,506
11	Washington	42,897
12	Texas	42,458
13	New Hampshire	42,447
14	Minnesota	42,185
15	Michigan	42,157
16	Alaska	41,750
17	Pennsylvania	41,349
18	Rhode Island	40,454
19	Georgia	40,370
20	Nevada	40,070
21	Arizona	40,019
22	Ohio	38,568
23	Florida	38,485
24	Oregon	38,077
25	Hawaii	37,799
26	Tennessee	37,564
27	North Carolina	37,439
28	Missouri	37,143
29	Wisconsin	36,821
30	Wyoming	36,662
31	Louisiana	36,604
32	Indiana	36,553
33	Alabama	36,204
34	Kansas	35,696
35	Vermont	35,542
36	Kentucky	35,201
37	Utah	35,130
38	New Mexico	34,567
39	Iowa	34,320
40	South Carolina	34,281
41	Oklahoma	34,022
42	Nebraska	33,814
43	Maine	33,794
44	West Virginia	32,728
45	Idaho	32,580
46	Arkansas	32,389
47	North Dakota	31,316
48	Mississippi	31,194
49	Montana	30,596
50	South Dakota	30,291
	District of Columbia	70,151

Source: U.S. Department of Labor, Bureau of Labor Statistics
   "Quarterly Census of Employment and Wages" (http://www.bls.gov/cew/home.htm)
*Computed by dividing total annual wages of employees covered by unemployment insurance programs by the average monthly number of these employees. Includes bonuses, cash value of meals and lodging, tips and, in many states, employer contributions to certain deferred compensation plans such as 401(k) plans.

Percent Change in Average Annual Pay: 2005 to 2006

National Percent Change = 4.6% Increase*

ALPHA ORDER				RANK ORDER		
RANK	STATE	PERCENT CHANGE		RANK	STATE	PERCENT CHANGE
17	Alabama	4.6		1	Wyoming	10.3
36	Alaska	3.8		2	Louisiana	9.1
12	Arizona	4.9		3	Oklahoma	7.3
40	Arkansas	3.6		4	New York	6.8
17	California	4.6		5	New Mexico	6.0
17	Colorado	4.6		6	Idaho	5.9
42	Connecticut	3.5		7	Texas	5.7
39	Delaware	3.7		8	Kansas	5.4
17	Florida	4.6		8	Utah	5.4
45	Georgia	3.3		10	Washington	5.3
32	Hawaii	4.0		11	Montana	5.0
6	Idaho	5.9		12	Arizona	4.9
22	Illinois	4.4		13	Mississippi	4.8
49	Indiana	3.2		14	Massachusetts	4.7
36	Iowa	3.8		14	New Hampshire	4.7
8	Kansas	5.4		14	Tennessee	4.7
40	Kentucky	3.6		17	Alabama	4.6
2	Louisiana	9.1		17	California	4.6
45	Maine	3.3		17	Colorado	4.6
32	Maryland	4.0		17	Florida	4.6
14	Massachusetts	4.7		21	North Dakota	4.5
50	Michigan	2.3		22	Illinois	4.4
43	Minnesota	3.4		22	New Jersey	4.4
13	Mississippi	4.8		22	Rhode Island	4.4
45	Missouri	3.3		22	West Virginia	4.4
11	Montana	5.0		26	Nebraska	4.3
26	Nebraska	4.3		26	North Carolina	4.3
43	Nevada	3.4		26	Pennsylvania	4.3
14	New Hampshire	4.7		29	Virginia	4.2
22	New Jersey	4.4		30	Oregon	4.1
5	New Mexico	6.0		30	South Carolina	4.1
4	New York	6.8		32	Hawaii	4.0
26	North Carolina	4.3		32	Maryland	4.0
21	North Dakota	4.5		34	South Dakota	3.9
45	Ohio	3.3		34	Vermont	3.9
3	Oklahoma	7.3		36	Alaska	3.8
30	Oregon	4.1		36	Iowa	3.8
26	Pennsylvania	4.3		36	Wisconsin	3.8
22	Rhode Island	4.4		39	Delaware	3.7
30	South Carolina	4.1		40	Arkansas	3.6
34	South Dakota	3.9		40	Kentucky	3.6
14	Tennessee	4.7		42	Connecticut	3.5
7	Texas	5.7		43	Minnesota	3.4
8	Utah	5.4		43	Nevada	3.4
34	Vermont	3.9		45	Georgia	3.3
29	Virginia	4.2		45	Maine	3.3
10	Washington	5.3		45	Missouri	3.3
22	West Virginia	4.4		45	Ohio	3.3
36	Wisconsin	3.8		49	Indiana	3.2
1	Wyoming	10.3		50	Michigan	2.3
					District of Columbia	5.2

Source: CQ Press using data from U.S. Department of Labor, Bureau of Labor Statistics
"Quarterly Census of Employment and Wages" (http://www.bls.gov/cew/home.htm)
*Includes bonuses, cash value of meals and lodging, tips and, in many states, employer contributions to certain deferred compensation plans such as 401(k) plans.

Median Earnings of Male Full-Time Workers in 2006

National Median = $42,210

RANK	STATE	EARNINGS
35	Alabama	$39,528
5	Alaska	48,703
32	Arizona	40,056
49	Arkansas	35,144
16	California	44,905
15	Colorado	45,017
2	Connecticut	52,372
12	Delaware	46,043
39	Florida	38,005
27	Georgia	40,646
22	Hawaii	41,821
37	Idaho	38,278
10	Illinois	46,526
20	Indiana	41,991
33	Iowa	39,753
28	Kansas	40,595
34	Kentucky	39,595
26	Louisiana	40,765
31	Maine	40,116
4	Maryland	51,316
3	Massachusetts	51,960
8	Michigan	47,329
11	Minnesota	46,349
48	Mississippi	35,617
29	Missouri	40,443
47	Montana	36,378
40	Nebraska	37,828
23	Nevada	41,717
7	New Hampshire	48,254
1	New Jersey	52,487
45	New Mexico	37,064
13	New York	45,833
43	North Carolina	37,545
38	North Dakota	38,179
19	Ohio	42,346
46	Oklahoma	36,655
24	Oregon	41,536
17	Pennsylvania	43,402
14	Rhode Island	45,544
44	South Carolina	37,194
50	South Dakota	34,937
42	Tennessee	37,589
36	Texas	38,797
25	Utah	41,475
30	Vermont	40,119
9	Virginia	47,063
6	Washington	48,331
41	West Virginia	37,622
18	Wisconsin	42,380
21	Wyoming	41,913

RANK	STATE	EARNINGS
1	New Jersey	$52,487
2	Connecticut	52,372
3	Massachusetts	51,960
4	Maryland	51,316
5	Alaska	48,703
6	Washington	48,331
7	New Hampshire	48,254
8	Michigan	47,329
9	Virginia	47,063
10	Illinois	46,526
11	Minnesota	46,349
12	Delaware	46,043
13	New York	45,833
14	Rhode Island	45,544
15	Colorado	45,017
16	California	44,905
17	Pennsylvania	43,402
18	Wisconsin	42,380
19	Ohio	42,346
20	Indiana	41,991
21	Wyoming	41,913
22	Hawaii	41,821
23	Nevada	41,717
24	Oregon	41,536
25	Utah	41,475
26	Louisiana	40,765
27	Georgia	40,646
28	Kansas	40,595
29	Missouri	40,443
30	Vermont	40,119
31	Maine	40,116
32	Arizona	40,056
33	Iowa	39,753
34	Kentucky	39,595
35	Alabama	39,528
36	Texas	38,797
37	Idaho	38,278
38	North Dakota	38,179
39	Florida	38,005
40	Nebraska	37,828
41	West Virginia	37,622
42	Tennessee	37,589
43	North Carolina	37,545
44	South Carolina	37,194
45	New Mexico	37,064
46	Oklahoma	36,655
47	Montana	36,378
48	Mississippi	35,617
49	Arkansas	35,144
50	South Dakota	34,937
	District of Columbia	49,544

Source: U.S. Bureau of the Census
"2006 American Community Survey" (http://www.census.gov/acs/www/index.html)

Median Earnings of Female Full-Time Workers in 2006

National Median = $32,649

<table>
<tr><td colspan="3">ALPHA ORDER</td><td colspan="3">RANK ORDER</td></tr>
<tr><td>RANK</td><td>STATE</td><td>EARNINGS</td><td>RANK</td><td>STATE</td><td>EARNINGS</td></tr>
<tr><td>43</td><td>Alabama</td><td>$27,893</td><td>1</td><td>Connecticut</td><td>$41,831</td></tr>
<tr><td>7</td><td>Alaska</td><td>36,655</td><td>2</td><td>Maryland</td><td>41,761</td></tr>
<tr><td>18</td><td>Arizona</td><td>32,468</td><td>3</td><td>New Jersey</td><td>41,100</td></tr>
<tr><td>47</td><td>Arkansas</td><td>26,277</td><td>4</td><td>Massachusetts</td><td>40,174</td></tr>
<tr><td>5</td><td>California</td><td>37,019</td><td>5</td><td>California</td><td>37,019</td></tr>
<tr><td>10</td><td>Colorado</td><td>35,847</td><td>6</td><td>New York</td><td>36,769</td></tr>
<tr><td>1</td><td>Connecticut</td><td>41,831</td><td>7</td><td>Alaska</td><td>36,655</td></tr>
<tr><td>13</td><td>Delaware</td><td>35,506</td><td>8</td><td>Washington</td><td>36,158</td></tr>
<tr><td>27</td><td>Florida</td><td>30,896</td><td>9</td><td>Virginia</td><td>36,062</td></tr>
<tr><td>24</td><td>Georgia</td><td>31,637</td><td>10</td><td>Colorado</td><td>35,847</td></tr>
<tr><td>16</td><td>Hawaii</td><td>33,780</td><td>11</td><td>Minnesota</td><td>35,611</td></tr>
<tr><td>41</td><td>Idaho</td><td>28,019</td><td>12</td><td>Rhode Island</td><td>35,510</td></tr>
<tr><td>14</td><td>Illinois</td><td>35,092</td><td>13</td><td>Delaware</td><td>35,506</td></tr>
<tr><td>30</td><td>Indiana</td><td>30,537</td><td>14</td><td>Illinois</td><td>35,092</td></tr>
<tr><td>33</td><td>Iowa</td><td>29,824</td><td>15</td><td>New Hampshire</td><td>34,719</td></tr>
<tr><td>29</td><td>Kansas</td><td>30,552</td><td>16</td><td>Hawaii</td><td>33,780</td></tr>
<tr><td>36</td><td>Kentucky</td><td>29,362</td><td>17</td><td>Michigan</td><td>33,748</td></tr>
<tr><td>45</td><td>Louisiana</td><td>27,000</td><td>18</td><td>Arizona</td><td>32,468</td></tr>
<tr><td>31</td><td>Maine</td><td>30,338</td><td>19</td><td>Oregon</td><td>32,390</td></tr>
<tr><td>2</td><td>Maryland</td><td>41,761</td><td>20</td><td>Pennsylvania</td><td>32,190</td></tr>
<tr><td>4</td><td>Massachusetts</td><td>40,174</td><td>21</td><td>Nevada</td><td>31,915</td></tr>
<tr><td>17</td><td>Michigan</td><td>33,748</td><td>22</td><td>Vermont</td><td>31,763</td></tr>
<tr><td>11</td><td>Minnesota</td><td>35,611</td><td>23</td><td>Ohio</td><td>31,748</td></tr>
<tr><td>49</td><td>Mississippi</td><td>25,849</td><td>24</td><td>Georgia</td><td>31,637</td></tr>
<tr><td>32</td><td>Missouri</td><td>30,127</td><td>25</td><td>Wisconsin</td><td>31,539</td></tr>
<tr><td>48</td><td>Montana</td><td>26,007</td><td>26</td><td>Texas</td><td>30,954</td></tr>
<tr><td>35</td><td>Nebraska</td><td>29,467</td><td>27</td><td>Florida</td><td>30,896</td></tr>
<tr><td>21</td><td>Nevada</td><td>31,915</td><td>28</td><td>North Carolina</td><td>30,600</td></tr>
<tr><td>15</td><td>New Hampshire</td><td>34,719</td><td>29</td><td>Kansas</td><td>30,552</td></tr>
<tr><td>3</td><td>New Jersey</td><td>41,100</td><td>30</td><td>Indiana</td><td>30,537</td></tr>
<tr><td>38</td><td>New Mexico</td><td>28,884</td><td>31</td><td>Maine</td><td>30,338</td></tr>
<tr><td>6</td><td>New York</td><td>36,769</td><td>32</td><td>Missouri</td><td>30,127</td></tr>
<tr><td>28</td><td>North Carolina</td><td>30,600</td><td>33</td><td>Iowa</td><td>29,824</td></tr>
<tr><td>46</td><td>North Dakota</td><td>26,583</td><td>34</td><td>Utah</td><td>29,623</td></tr>
<tr><td>23</td><td>Ohio</td><td>31,748</td><td>35</td><td>Nebraska</td><td>29,467</td></tr>
<tr><td>44</td><td>Oklahoma</td><td>27,626</td><td>36</td><td>Kentucky</td><td>29,362</td></tr>
<tr><td>19</td><td>Oregon</td><td>32,390</td><td>37</td><td>Tennessee</td><td>29,300</td></tr>
<tr><td>20</td><td>Pennsylvania</td><td>32,190</td><td>38</td><td>New Mexico</td><td>28,884</td></tr>
<tr><td>12</td><td>Rhode Island</td><td>35,510</td><td>39</td><td>South Carolina</td><td>28,696</td></tr>
<tr><td>39</td><td>South Carolina</td><td>28,696</td><td>40</td><td>South Dakota</td><td>28,158</td></tr>
<tr><td>40</td><td>South Dakota</td><td>28,158</td><td>41</td><td>Idaho</td><td>28,019</td></tr>
<tr><td>37</td><td>Tennessee</td><td>29,300</td><td>42</td><td>Wyoming</td><td>27,926</td></tr>
<tr><td>26</td><td>Texas</td><td>30,954</td><td>43</td><td>Alabama</td><td>27,893</td></tr>
<tr><td>34</td><td>Utah</td><td>29,623</td><td>44</td><td>Oklahoma</td><td>27,626</td></tr>
<tr><td>22</td><td>Vermont</td><td>31,763</td><td>45</td><td>Louisiana</td><td>27,000</td></tr>
<tr><td>9</td><td>Virginia</td><td>36,062</td><td>46</td><td>North Dakota</td><td>26,583</td></tr>
<tr><td>8</td><td>Washington</td><td>36,158</td><td>47</td><td>Arkansas</td><td>26,277</td></tr>
<tr><td>50</td><td>West Virginia</td><td>25,758</td><td>48</td><td>Montana</td><td>26,007</td></tr>
<tr><td>25</td><td>Wisconsin</td><td>31,539</td><td>49</td><td>Mississippi</td><td>25,849</td></tr>
<tr><td>42</td><td>Wyoming</td><td>27,926</td><td>50</td><td>West Virginia</td><td>25,758</td></tr>
<tr><td></td><td></td><td></td><td></td><td>District of Columbia</td><td>48,586</td></tr>
</table>

Source: U.S. Bureau of the Census
  "2006 American Community Survey" (http://www.census.gov/acs/www/index.html)

State Minimum Wage Rates in 2008

National Rate = $5.85 per Hour*

ALPHA ORDER				RANK ORDER		
RANK	STATE	MINIMUM WAGE		RANK	STATE	MINIMUM WAGE
NA	Alabama**	NA		1	Washington	$8.07
11	Alaska	7.15		2	California	8.00
20	Arizona	6.90		2	Massachusetts	8.00
28	Arkansas	6.25		4	Oregon	7.95
2	California	8.00		5	Vermont	7.68
17	Colorado	7.02		6	Connecticut	7.65
6	Connecticut	7.65		7	Illinois	7.50
11	Delaware	7.15		8	Rhode Island	7.40
21	Florida	6.79		9	Hawaii	7.25
43	Georgia	5.15		9	Iowa	7.25
9	Hawaii	7.25		11	Alaska	7.15
33	Idaho	5.85		11	Delaware	7.15
7	Illinois	7.50		11	Michigan	7.15
33	Indiana	5.85		11	New Jersey	7.15
9	Iowa	7.25		11	New York	7.15
45	Kansas	2.65		11	Pennsylvania	7.15
33	Kentucky	5.85		17	Colorado	7.02
NA	Louisiana**	NA		18	Maine	7.00
18	Maine	7.00		18	Ohio	7.00
30	Maryland	6.15		20	Arizona	6.90
2	Massachusetts	8.00		21	Florida	6.79
11	Michigan	7.15		22	Missouri	6.65
30	Minnesota	6.15		23	West Virginia	6.55
NA	Mississippi**	NA		24	New Hampshire	6.50
22	Missouri	6.65		24	New Mexico	6.50
28	Montana	6.25		24	Wisconsin	6.50
33	Nebraska	5.85		27	Nevada	6.33
27	Nevada	6.33		28	Arkansas	6.25
24	New Hampshire	6.50		28	Montana	6.25
11	New Jersey	7.15		30	Maryland	6.15
24	New Mexico	6.50		30	Minnesota	6.15
11	New York	7.15		30	North Carolina	6.15
30	North Carolina	6.15		33	Idaho	5.85
33	North Dakota	5.85		33	Indiana	5.85
18	Ohio	7.00		33	Kentucky	5.85
33	Oklahoma	5.85		33	Nebraska	5.85
4	Oregon	7.95		33	North Dakota	5.85
11	Pennsylvania	7.15		33	Oklahoma	5.85
8	Rhode Island	7.40		33	South Dakota	5.85
NA	South Carolina**	NA		33	Texas	5.85
33	South Dakota	5.85		33	Utah	5.85
NA	Tennessee**	NA		33	Virginia	5.85
33	Texas	5.85		43	Georgia	5.15
33	Utah	5.85		43	Wyoming	5.15
5	Vermont	7.68		45	Kansas	2.65
33	Virginia	5.85		NA	Alabama**	NA
1	Washington	8.07		NA	Louisiana**	NA
23	West Virginia	6.55		NA	Mississippi**	NA
24	Wisconsin	6.50		NA	South Carolina**	NA
43	Wyoming	5.15		NA	Tennessee**	NA
					District of Columbia	7.00

Source: U.S. Department of Labor, Employment Standards Administration
"Minimum Wage Laws in the States" (http://www.dol.gov/esa/minwage/america.htm)
*As of January 1, 2008. The federal and many states rates are scheduled to rise to $6.55 on July 24, 2008. State minimum wage rates are for those employers and jobs not covered by the federal program.
**No separate state program.

Average Hourly Earnings of Production Workers
on Manufacturing Payrolls in 2007
National Average = $17.45*

ALPHA ORDER

RANK	STATE	HOURLY EARNINGS
31	Alabama	$15.56
43	Alaska	14.30
38	Arizona	14.88
50	Arkansas	13.35
26	California	15.95
20	Colorado	16.58
3	Connecticut	19.78
9	Delaware	18.13
40	Florida	14.75
41	Georgia	14.74
28	Hawaii	15.89
18	Idaho	16.89
25	Illinois	16.03
5	Indiana	18.57
24	Iowa	16.40
13	Kansas	17.68
17	Kentucky	16.92
10	Louisiana	17.94
5	Maine	18.57
12	Maryland	17.87
8	Massachusetts	18.26
1	Michigan	21.83
15	Minnesota	17.23
47	Mississippi	13.78
16	Missouri	17.16
27	Montana	15.90
35	Nebraska	15.04
32	Nevada	15.47
21	New Hampshire	16.56
22	New Jersey	16.55
44	New Mexico	14.06
7	New York	18.29
42	North Carolina	14.57
37	North Dakota	14.97
4	Ohio	19.16
39	Oklahoma	14.77
30	Oregon	15.57
33	Pennsylvania	15.37
49	Rhode Island	13.42
36	South Carolina	15.03
48	South Dakota	13.75
45	Tennessee	14.04
46	Texas	14.01
34	Utah	15.25
29	Vermont	15.79
19	Virginia	16.75
2	Washington	19.90
11	West Virginia	17.89
23	Wisconsin	16.54
14	Wyoming	17.44

RANK ORDER

RANK	STATE	HOURLY EARNINGS
1	Michigan	$21.83
2	Washington	19.90
3	Connecticut	19.78
4	Ohio	19.16
5	Indiana	18.57
5	Maine	18.57
7	New York	18.29
8	Massachusetts	18.26
9	Delaware	18.13
10	Louisiana	17.94
11	West Virginia	17.89
12	Maryland	17.87
13	Kansas	17.68
14	Wyoming	17.44
15	Minnesota	17.23
16	Missouri	17.16
17	Kentucky	16.92
18	Idaho	16.89
19	Virginia	16.75
20	Colorado	16.58
21	New Hampshire	16.56
22	New Jersey	16.55
23	Wisconsin	16.54
24	Iowa	16.40
25	Illinois	16.03
26	California	15.95
27	Montana	15.90
28	Hawaii	15.89
29	Vermont	15.79
30	Oregon	15.57
31	Alabama	15.56
32	Nevada	15.47
33	Pennsylvania	15.37
34	Utah	15.25
35	Nebraska	15.04
36	South Carolina	15.03
37	North Dakota	14.97
38	Arizona	14.88
39	Oklahoma	14.77
40	Florida	14.75
41	Georgia	14.74
42	North Carolina	14.57
43	Alaska	14.30
44	New Mexico	14.06
45	Tennessee	14.04
46	Texas	14.01
47	Mississippi	13.78
48	South Dakota	13.75
49	Rhode Island	13.42
50	Arkansas	13.35
	District of Columbia**	NA

Source: U.S. Department of Labor, Bureau of Labor Statistics
    "Current Employment Statistics Survey" (http://www.bls.gov/sae/home.htm)
*Preliminary data for December 2007. Not seasonally adjusted.
**Not available.

Average Weekly Earnings of Production Workers on Manufacturing Payrolls in 2007
National Average = $729.41*

<table>
<tr><td colspan="3"><u>ALPHA ORDER</u></td><td colspan="3"><u>RANK ORDER</u></td></tr>
<tr><td>RANK</td><td>STATE</td><td>WEEKLY EARNINGS</td><td>RANK</td><td>STATE</td><td>WEEKLY EARNINGS</td></tr>
<tr><td>27</td><td>Alabama</td><td>$636.40</td><td>1</td><td>Michigan</td><td>$921.23</td></tr>
<tr><td>43</td><td>Alaska</td><td>579.15</td><td>2</td><td>Connecticut</td><td>834.72</td></tr>
<tr><td>38</td><td>Arizona</td><td>604.13</td><td>3</td><td>Washington</td><td>807.94</td></tr>
<tr><td>48</td><td>Arkansas</td><td>547.35</td><td>4</td><td>Ohio</td><td>793.22</td></tr>
<tr><td>26</td><td>California</td><td>644.38</td><td>5</td><td>Indiana</td><td>774.37</td></tr>
<tr><td>25</td><td>Colorado</td><td>649.94</td><td>6</td><td>Louisiana</td><td>771.42</td></tr>
<tr><td>2</td><td>Connecticut</td><td>834.72</td><td>7</td><td>Maine</td><td>768.80</td></tr>
<tr><td>13</td><td>Delaware</td><td>723.39</td><td>8</td><td>Kansas</td><td>760.24</td></tr>
<tr><td>36</td><td>Florida</td><td>612.13</td><td>9</td><td>New York</td><td>751.72</td></tr>
<tr><td>42</td><td>Georgia</td><td>582.23</td><td>10</td><td>Massachusetts</td><td>743.18</td></tr>
<tr><td>35</td><td>Hawaii</td><td>613.35</td><td>11</td><td>West Virginia</td><td>738.86</td></tr>
<tr><td>16</td><td>Idaho</td><td>704.31</td><td>12</td><td>Maryland</td><td>725.52</td></tr>
<tr><td>24</td><td>Illinois</td><td>658.83</td><td>13</td><td>Delaware</td><td>723.39</td></tr>
<tr><td>5</td><td>Indiana</td><td>774.37</td><td>14</td><td>Wyoming</td><td>718.53</td></tr>
<tr><td>20</td><td>Iowa</td><td>687.16</td><td>15</td><td>Minnesota</td><td>706.43</td></tr>
<tr><td>8</td><td>Kansas</td><td>760.24</td><td>16</td><td>Idaho</td><td>704.31</td></tr>
<tr><td>18</td><td>Kentucky</td><td>695.41</td><td>17</td><td>New Jersey</td><td>696.76</td></tr>
<tr><td>6</td><td>Louisiana</td><td>771.42</td><td>18</td><td>Kentucky</td><td>695.41</td></tr>
<tr><td>7</td><td>Maine</td><td>768.80</td><td>19</td><td>Virginia</td><td>691.78</td></tr>
<tr><td>12</td><td>Maryland</td><td>725.52</td><td>20</td><td>Iowa</td><td>687.16</td></tr>
<tr><td>10</td><td>Massachusetts</td><td>743.18</td><td>21</td><td>New Hampshire</td><td>682.27</td></tr>
<tr><td>1</td><td>Michigan</td><td>921.23</td><td>22</td><td>Missouri</td><td>674.39</td></tr>
<tr><td>15</td><td>Minnesota</td><td>706.43</td><td>23</td><td>Wisconsin</td><td>673.18</td></tr>
<tr><td>49</td><td>Mississippi</td><td>542.93</td><td>24</td><td>Illinois</td><td>658.83</td></tr>
<tr><td>22</td><td>Missouri</td><td>674.39</td><td>25</td><td>Colorado</td><td>649.94</td></tr>
<tr><td>28</td><td>Montana</td><td>636.00</td><td>26</td><td>California</td><td>644.38</td></tr>
<tr><td>34</td><td>Nebraska</td><td>615.14</td><td>27</td><td>Alabama</td><td>636.40</td></tr>
<tr><td>37</td><td>Nevada</td><td>609.52</td><td>28</td><td>Montana</td><td>636.00</td></tr>
<tr><td>21</td><td>New Hampshire</td><td>682.27</td><td>29</td><td>Oregon</td><td>630.59</td></tr>
<tr><td>17</td><td>New Jersey</td><td>696.76</td><td>30</td><td>Pennsylvania</td><td>627.10</td></tr>
<tr><td>47</td><td>New Mexico</td><td>551.15</td><td>31</td><td>Utah</td><td>626.78</td></tr>
<tr><td>9</td><td>New York</td><td>751.72</td><td>32</td><td>Vermont</td><td>625.28</td></tr>
<tr><td>41</td><td>North Carolina</td><td>582.80</td><td>33</td><td>South Carolina</td><td>616.23</td></tr>
<tr><td>40</td><td>North Dakota</td><td>583.83</td><td>34</td><td>Nebraska</td><td>615.14</td></tr>
<tr><td>4</td><td>Ohio</td><td>793.22</td><td>35</td><td>Hawaii</td><td>613.35</td></tr>
<tr><td>39</td><td>Oklahoma</td><td>589.32</td><td>36</td><td>Florida</td><td>612.13</td></tr>
<tr><td>29</td><td>Oregon</td><td>630.59</td><td>37</td><td>Nevada</td><td>609.52</td></tr>
<tr><td>30</td><td>Pennsylvania</td><td>627.10</td><td>38</td><td>Arizona</td><td>604.13</td></tr>
<tr><td>50</td><td>Rhode Island</td><td>522.04</td><td>39</td><td>Oklahoma</td><td>589.32</td></tr>
<tr><td>33</td><td>South Carolina</td><td>616.23</td><td>40</td><td>North Dakota</td><td>583.83</td></tr>
<tr><td>44</td><td>South Dakota</td><td>578.88</td><td>41</td><td>North Carolina</td><td>582.80</td></tr>
<tr><td>46</td><td>Tennessee</td><td>553.18</td><td>42</td><td>Georgia</td><td>582.23</td></tr>
<tr><td>45</td><td>Texas</td><td>573.01</td><td>43</td><td>Alaska</td><td>579.15</td></tr>
<tr><td>31</td><td>Utah</td><td>626.78</td><td>44</td><td>South Dakota</td><td>578.88</td></tr>
<tr><td>32</td><td>Vermont</td><td>625.28</td><td>45</td><td>Texas</td><td>573.01</td></tr>
<tr><td>19</td><td>Virginia</td><td>691.78</td><td>46</td><td>Tennessee</td><td>553.18</td></tr>
<tr><td>3</td><td>Washington</td><td>807.94</td><td>47</td><td>New Mexico</td><td>551.15</td></tr>
<tr><td>11</td><td>West Virginia</td><td>738.86</td><td>48</td><td>Arkansas</td><td>547.35</td></tr>
<tr><td>23</td><td>Wisconsin</td><td>673.18</td><td>49</td><td>Mississippi</td><td>542.93</td></tr>
<tr><td>14</td><td>Wyoming</td><td>718.53</td><td>50</td><td>Rhode Island</td><td>522.04</td></tr>
<tr><td></td><td></td><td></td><td colspan="2">District of Columbia**</td><td>NA</td></tr>
</table>

Source: U.S. Department of Labor, Bureau of Labor Statistics
　　"Current Employment Statistics Survey" (http://www.bls.gov/sae/home.htm)
*Preliminary data for December 2007. Not seasonally adjusted.
**Not available.

Average Work Week of Production Workers
on Manufacturing Payrolls in 2007
National Average = 41.8 Hours per Week*

RANK	STATE	WEEKLY HOURS
24	Alabama	40.9
33	Alaska	40.5
30	Arizona	40.6
21	Arkansas	41.0
35	California	40.4
46	Colorado	39.2
3	Connecticut	42.2
38	Delaware	39.9
10	Florida	41.5
41	Georgia	39.5
50	Hawaii	38.6
8	Idaho	41.7
17	Illinois	41.1
8	Indiana	41.7
7	Iowa	41.9
1	Kansas	43.0
17	Kentucky	41.1
1	Louisiana	43.0
11	Maine	41.4
30	Maryland	40.6
28	Massachusetts	40.7
3	Michigan	42.2
21	Minnesota	41.0
42	Mississippi	39.4
45	Missouri	39.3
36	Montana	40.0
24	Nebraska	40.9
42	Nevada	39.4
15	New Hampshire	41.2
5	New Jersey	42.1
46	New Mexico	39.2
17	New York	41.1
36	North Carolina	40.0
48	North Dakota	39.0
11	Ohio	41.4
38	Oklahoma	39.9
33	Oregon	40.5
27	Pennsylvania	40.8
49	Rhode Island	38.9
21	South Carolina	41.0
5	South Dakota	42.1
42	Tennessee	39.4
24	Texas	40.9
17	Utah	41.1
40	Vermont	39.6
13	Virginia	41.3
30	Washington	40.6
13	West Virginia	41.3
28	Wisconsin	40.7
15	Wyoming	41.2

RANK	STATE	WEEKLY HOURS
1	Kansas	43.0
1	Louisiana	43.0
3	Connecticut	42.2
3	Michigan	42.2
5	New Jersey	42.1
5	South Dakota	42.1
7	Iowa	41.9
8	Idaho	41.7
8	Indiana	41.7
10	Florida	41.5
11	Maine	41.4
11	Ohio	41.4
13	Virginia	41.3
13	West Virginia	41.3
15	New Hampshire	41.2
15	Wyoming	41.2
17	Illinois	41.1
17	Kentucky	41.1
17	New York	41.1
17	Utah	41.1
21	Arkansas	41.0
21	Minnesota	41.0
21	South Carolina	41.0
24	Alabama	40.9
24	Nebraska	40.9
24	Texas	40.9
27	Pennsylvania	40.8
28	Massachusetts	40.7
28	Wisconsin	40.7
30	Arizona	40.6
30	Maryland	40.6
30	Washington	40.6
33	Alaska	40.5
33	Oregon	40.5
35	California	40.4
36	Montana	40.0
36	North Carolina	40.0
38	Delaware	39.9
38	Oklahoma	39.9
40	Vermont	39.6
41	Georgia	39.5
42	Mississippi	39.4
42	Nevada	39.4
42	Tennessee	39.4
45	Missouri	39.3
46	Colorado	39.2
46	New Mexico	39.2
48	North Dakota	39.0
49	Rhode Island	38.9
50	Hawaii	38.6

District of Columbia** NA

Source: U.S. Department of Labor, Bureau of Labor Statistics
    "Current Employment Statistics Survey" (http://www.bls.gov/sae/home.htm)
*Preliminary data for December 2007. Not seasonally adjusted.
**Not available

Average Weekly Unemployment Benefit in 2007

National Average = $287.54 a Week

ALPHA ORDER

RANK	STATE	BENEFIT
49	Alabama	$185.01
47	Alaska	198.20
46	Arizona	199.72
34	Arkansas	245.91
12	California	292.14
7	Colorado	316.10
9	Connecticut	305.36
32	Delaware	251.31
38	Florida	232.74
30	Georgia	256.47
1	Hawaii	370.12
35	Idaho	244.50
11	Illinois	292.70
15	Indiana	285.50
17	Iowa	283.07
13	Kansas	290.30
24	Kentucky	271.77
48	Louisiana	194.90
33	Maine	247.95
20	Maryland	276.55
2	Massachusetts	369.63
10	Michigan	293.61
5	Minnesota	332.80
50	Mississippi	183.70
44	Missouri	215.36
45	Montana	213.13
40	Nebraska	230.01
19	Nevada	276.80
27	New Hampshire	259.75
3	New Jersey	347.81
36	New Mexico	242.90
16	New York	283.87
25	North Carolina	268.22
31	North Dakota	252.30
14	Ohio	287.94
37	Oklahoma	235.99
23	Oregon	274.00
8	Pennsylvania	306.35
4	Rhode Island	347.34
41	South Carolina	225.01
42	South Dakota	218.71
43	Tennessee	216.78
22	Texas	275.56
18	Utah	280.56
21	Vermont	275.95
29	Virginia	258.51
6	Washington	326.72
39	West Virginia	231.98
28	Wisconsin	259.03
26	Wyoming	260.63

RANK ORDER

RANK	STATE	BENEFIT
1	Hawaii	$370.12
2	Massachusetts	369.63
3	New Jersey	347.81
4	Rhode Island	347.34
5	Minnesota	332.80
6	Washington	326.72
7	Colorado	316.10
8	Pennsylvania	306.35
9	Connecticut	305.36
10	Michigan	293.61
11	Illinois	292.70
12	California	292.14
13	Kansas	290.30
14	Ohio	287.94
15	Indiana	285.50
16	New York	283.87
17	Iowa	283.07
18	Utah	280.56
19	Nevada	276.80
20	Maryland	276.55
21	Vermont	275.95
22	Texas	275.56
23	Oregon	274.00
24	Kentucky	271.77
25	North Carolina	268.22
26	Wyoming	260.63
27	New Hampshire	259.75
28	Wisconsin	259.03
29	Virginia	258.51
30	Georgia	256.47
31	North Dakota	252.30
32	Delaware	251.31
33	Maine	247.95
34	Arkansas	245.91
35	Idaho	244.50
36	New Mexico	242.90
37	Oklahoma	235.99
38	Florida	232.74
39	West Virginia	231.98
40	Nebraska	230.01
41	South Carolina	225.01
42	South Dakota	218.71
43	Tennessee	216.78
44	Missouri	215.36
45	Montana	213.13
46	Arizona	199.72
47	Alaska	198.20
48	Louisiana	194.90
49	Alabama	185.01
50	Mississippi	183.70
	District of Columbia	283.93

Source: CQ Press using data from U.S. Department of Labor, Bureau of Labor Statistics
"Unemployment Insurance Data Summary" (http://workforcesecurity.doleta.gov/unemploy/content/data.asp)

Workers' Compensation Benefit Payments in 2005

National Total = $55,307,176,000*

ALPHA ORDER

ALPHA ORDER

RANK	STATE	PAYMENTS	% of USA
27	Alabama	$608,522	1.1%
44	Alaska	189,212	0.3%
30	Arizona	535,539	1.0%
43	Arkansas	208,021	0.4%
1	California	10,938,475	19.8%
17	Colorado	896,430	1.6%
22	Connecticut	713,275	1.3%
45	Delaware	168,146	0.3%
2	Florida	2,899,301	5.2%
12	Georgia	1,197,521	2.2%
37	Hawaii	250,779	0.5%
38	Idaho	243,168	0.4%
6	Illinois	2,404,456	4.3%
26	Indiana	609,596	1.1%
31	Iowa	473,724	0.9%
33	Kansas	383,283	0.7%
23	Kentucky	705,802	1.3%
25	Louisiana	667,097	1.2%
36	Maine	268,936	0.5%
20	Maryland	769,563	1.4%
16	Massachusetts	903,555	1.6%
10	Michigan	1,473,598	2.7%
15	Minnesota	945,888	1.7%
34	Mississippi	311,796	0.6%
14	Missouri	1,050,889	1.9%
40	Montana	239,498	0.4%
35	Nebraska	298,366	0.5%
32	Nevada	394,373	0.7%
42	New Hampshire	216,968	0.4%
8	New Jersey	1,608,345	2.9%
41	New Mexico	230,591	0.4%
3	New York	2,895,331	5.2%
11	North Carolina	1,398,001	2.5%
50	North Dakota	82,282	0.1%
5	Ohio	2,447,038	4.4%
28	Oklahoma	587,523	1.1%
29	Oregon	550,878	1.0%
4	Pennsylvania	2,677,899	4.8%
46	Rhode Island	142,170	0.3%
21	South Carolina	769,553	1.4%
49	South Dakota	85,889	0.2%
18	Tennessee	880,100	1.6%
9	Texas	1,554,796	2.8%
39	Utah	240,767	0.4%
47	Vermont	122,160	0.2%
19	Virginia	853,877	1.5%
7	Washington	1,864,015	3.4%
24	West Virginia	695,771	1.3%
13	Wisconsin	1,188,459	2.1%
48	Wyoming	116,528	0.2%

RANK ORDER

RANK	STATE	PAYMENTS	% of USA
1	California	$10,938,475	19.8%
2	Florida	2,899,301	5.2%
3	New York	2,895,331	5.2%
4	Pennsylvania	2,677,899	4.8%
5	Ohio	2,447,038	4.4%
6	Illinois	2,404,456	4.3%
7	Washington	1,864,015	3.4%
8	New Jersey	1,608,345	2.9%
9	Texas	1,554,796	2.8%
10	Michigan	1,473,598	2.7%
11	North Carolina	1,398,001	2.5%
12	Georgia	1,197,521	2.2%
13	Wisconsin	1,188,459	2.1%
14	Missouri	1,050,889	1.9%
15	Minnesota	945,888	1.7%
16	Massachusetts	903,555	1.6%
17	Colorado	896,430	1.6%
18	Tennessee	880,100	1.6%
19	Virginia	853,877	1.5%
20	Maryland	769,563	1.4%
21	South Carolina	769,553	1.4%
22	Connecticut	713,275	1.3%
23	Kentucky	705,802	1.3%
24	West Virginia	695,771	1.3%
25	Louisiana	667,097	1.2%
26	Indiana	609,596	1.1%
27	Alabama	608,522	1.1%
28	Oklahoma	587,523	1.1%
29	Oregon	550,878	1.0%
30	Arizona	535,539	1.0%
31	Iowa	473,724	0.9%
32	Nevada	394,373	0.7%
33	Kansas	383,283	0.7%
34	Mississippi	311,796	0.6%
35	Nebraska	298,366	0.5%
36	Maine	268,936	0.5%
37	Hawaii	250,779	0.5%
38	Idaho	243,168	0.4%
39	Utah	240,767	0.4%
40	Montana	239,498	0.4%
41	New Mexico	230,591	0.4%
42	New Hampshire	216,968	0.4%
43	Arkansas	208,021	0.4%
44	Alaska	189,212	0.3%
45	Delaware	168,146	0.3%
46	Rhode Island	142,170	0.3%
47	Vermont	122,160	0.2%
48	Wyoming	116,528	0.2%
49	South Dakota	85,889	0.2%
50	North Dakota	82,282	0.1%
	District of Columbia	91,270	0.2%

Source: National Academy of Social Insurance (Washington, DC)
    "Workers' Compensation: Benefits, Coverage, and Costs, 2005" (http://www.nasi.org)
*Estimated payments from private insurance, state and federal funds, and self insurance. National total includes payments for federal civilian employee program, Black Lung Program, and other federal programs.

Workers' Compensation Benefit Payment per Covered Worker in 2005

National Average = $432*

ALPHA ORDER

RANK	STATE	AVERAGE
31	Alabama	$345
4	Alaska	664
47	Arizona	220
50	Arkansas	190
2	California	730
15	Colorado	423
12	Connecticut	439
21	Delaware	408
23	Florida	397
38	Georgia	319
13	Hawaii	438
22	Idaho	405
14	Illinois	425
48	Indiana	216
34	Iowa	332
41	Kansas	301
20	Kentucky	411
25	Louisiana	369
9	Maine	463
36	Maryland	324
42	Massachusetts	291
27	Michigan	355
26	Minnesota	363
40	Mississippi	302
16	Missouri	421
5	Montana	599
32	Nebraska	341
35	Nevada	329
28	New Hampshire	354
17	New Jersey	417
37	New Mexico	320
29	New York	352
24	North Carolina	377
43	North Dakota	260
8	Ohio	468
18	Oklahoma	414
33	Oregon	339
6	Pennsylvania	492
39	Rhode Island	304
11	South Carolina	446
45	South Dakota	235
30	Tennessee	347
48	Texas	216
46	Utah	223
18	Vermont	414
44	Virginia	255
3	Washington	691
1	West Virginia	1,034
10	Wisconsin	447
7	Wyoming	472

RANK ORDER

RANK	STATE	AVERAGE
1	West Virginia	$1,034
2	California	730
3	Washington	691
4	Alaska	664
5	Montana	599
6	Pennsylvania	492
7	Wyoming	472
8	Ohio	468
9	Maine	463
10	Wisconsin	447
11	South Carolina	446
12	Connecticut	439
13	Hawaii	438
14	Illinois	425
15	Colorado	423
16	Missouri	421
17	New Jersey	417
18	Oklahoma	414
18	Vermont	414
20	Kentucky	411
21	Delaware	408
22	Idaho	405
23	Florida	397
24	North Carolina	377
25	Louisiana	369
26	Minnesota	363
27	Michigan	355
28	New Hampshire	354
29	New York	352
30	Tennessee	347
31	Alabama	345
32	Nebraska	341
33	Oregon	339
34	Iowa	332
35	Nevada	329
36	Maryland	324
37	New Mexico	320
38	Georgia	319
39	Rhode Island	304
40	Mississippi	302
41	Kansas	301
42	Massachusetts	291
43	North Dakota	260
44	Virginia	255
45	South Dakota	235
46	Utah	223
47	Arizona	220
48	Indiana	216
48	Texas	216
50	Arkansas	190

| | District of Columbia | 193 |

Source: CQ Press using data from National Academy of Social Insurance (Washington, DC)
"Workers' Compensation: Benefits, Coverage, and Costs, 2005" (http://www.nasi.org)
*Estimated payments from private insurance, state and federal funds, and self insurance. National rate includes payments for federal civilian employee program, Black Lung Program, and other federal programs. Total divided by number of workers covered by workers' compensation.

Percent Change in Workers' Compensation Benefit Payments: 2004 to 2005

National Percent Change = 1.4% Decrease*

ALPHA ORDER

RANK	STATE	PERCENT CHANGE
18	Alabama	5.7
29	Alaska	1.1
38	Arizona	(2.3)
47	Arkansas	(8.5)
49	California	(12.2)
16	Colorado	6.3
32	Connecticut	0.3
15	Delaware	6.8
13	Florida	7.0
10	Georgia	7.5
45	Hawaii	(7.6)
23	Idaho	3.0
13	Illinois	7.0
24	Indiana	2.4
17	Iowa	5.9
20	Kansas	3.3
36	Kentucky	(1.9)
46	Louisiana	(8.1)
32	Maine	0.3
37	Maryland	(2.2)
44	Massachusetts	(6.7)
39	Michigan	(2.9)
26	Minnesota	1.6
30	Mississippi	0.6
43	Missouri	(6.2)
12	Montana	7.4
19	Nebraska	5.6
8	Nevada	9.9
25	New Hampshire	2.3
9	New Jersey	8.8
2	New Mexico	17.6
48	New York	(11.7)
1	North Carolina	20.6
34	North Dakota	(1.1)
31	Ohio	0.5
28	Oklahoma	1.3
21	Oregon	3.2
21	Pennsylvania	3.2
41	Rhode Island	(3.7)
5	South Carolina	11.8
7	South Dakota	11.0
10	Tennessee	7.5
42	Texas	(5.2)
6	Utah	11.2
35	Vermont	(1.3)
4	Virginia	13.3
27	Washington	1.5
50	West Virginia	(12.7)
3	Wisconsin	14.4
39	Wyoming	(2.9)

RANK ORDER

RANK	STATE	PERCENT CHANGE
1	North Carolina	20.6
2	New Mexico	17.6
3	Wisconsin	14.4
4	Virginia	13.3
5	South Carolina	11.8
6	Utah	11.2
7	South Dakota	11.0
8	Nevada	9.9
9	New Jersey	8.8
10	Georgia	7.5
10	Tennessee	7.5
12	Montana	7.4
13	Florida	7.0
13	Illinois	7.0
15	Delaware	6.8
16	Colorado	6.3
17	Iowa	5.9
18	Alabama	5.7
19	Nebraska	5.6
20	Kansas	3.3
21	Oregon	3.2
21	Pennsylvania	3.2
23	Idaho	3.0
24	Indiana	2.4
25	New Hampshire	2.3
26	Minnesota	1.6
27	Washington	1.5
28	Oklahoma	1.3
29	Alaska	1.1
30	Mississippi	0.6
31	Ohio	0.5
32	Connecticut	0.3
32	Maine	0.3
34	North Dakota	(1.1)
35	Vermont	(1.3)
36	Kentucky	(1.9)
37	Maryland	(2.2)
38	Arizona	(2.3)
39	Michigan	(2.9)
39	Wyoming	(2.9)
41	Rhode Island	(3.7)
42	Texas	(5.2)
43	Missouri	(6.2)
44	Massachusetts	(6.7)
45	Hawaii	(7.6)
46	Louisiana	(8.1)
47	Arkansas	(8.5)
48	New York	(11.7)
49	California	(12.2)
50	West Virginia	(12.7)
	District of Columbia	(5.1)

Source: National Academy of Social Insurance (Washington, DC)
  "Workers' Compensation: Benefits, Coverage, and Costs, 2005" (http://www.nasi.org)
*Estimated payments from private insurance, state and federal funds, and self insurance. National rate includes payments for federal civilian employee program, Black Lung Program, and other federal programs.

Civilian Labor Force in 2007

National Total = 153,866,000 Workers*

RANK	STATE	EMPLOYEES	% of USA
23	Alabama	2,219,300	1.4%
49	Alaska	350,800	0.2%
19	Arizona	3,052,400	2.0%
32	Arkansas	1,384,100	0.9%
1	California	18,433,300	12.0%
22	Colorado	2,724,200	1.8%
28	Connecticut	1,899,300	1.2%
45	Delaware	446,800	0.3%
4	Florida	9,311,700	6.1%
9	Georgia	4,899,300	3.2%
42	Hawaii	647,600	0.4%
39	Idaho	761,000	0.5%
5	Illinois	6,794,900	4.4%
15	Indiana	3,231,700	2.1%
30	Iowa	1,678,700	1.1%
31	Kansas	1,490,300	1.0%
25	Kentucky	2,051,700	1.3%
26	Louisiana	2,028,300	1.3%
41	Maine	712,500	0.5%
20	Maryland	3,015,700	2.0%
14	Massachusetts	3,398,500	2.2%
8	Michigan	5,012,100	3.3%
21	Minnesota	2,951,600	1.9%
35	Mississippi	1,348,200	0.9%
17	Missouri	3,059,500	2.0%
44	Montana	502,600	0.3%
36	Nebraska	993,300	0.6%
33	Nevada	1,370,000	0.9%
40	New Hampshire	747,900	0.5%
10	New Jersey	4,529,900	2.9%
37	New Mexico	945,200	0.6%
3	New York	9,529,900	6.2%
11	North Carolina	4,526,000	2.9%
47	North Dakota	366,400	0.2%
7	Ohio	6,018,600	3.9%
29	Oklahoma	1,735,400	1.1%
27	Oregon	1,957,200	1.3%
6	Pennsylvania	6,345,500	4.1%
43	Rhode Island	579,500	0.4%
24	South Carolina	2,159,000	1.4%
46	South Dakota	440,100	0.3%
18	Tennessee	3,058,400	2.0%
2	Texas	11,643,200	7.6%
34	Utah	1,356,500	0.9%
48	Vermont	355,900	0.2%
12	Virginia	4,093,600	2.7%
13	Washington	3,469,500	2.3%
38	West Virginia	818,800	0.5%
16	Wisconsin	3,100,500	2.0%
50	Wyoming	290,000	0.2%

RANK	STATE	EMPLOYEES	% of USA
1	California	18,433,300	12.0%
2	Texas	11,643,200	7.6%
3	New York	9,529,900	6.2%
4	Florida	9,311,700	6.1%
5	Illinois	6,794,900	4.4%
6	Pennsylvania	6,345,500	4.1%
7	Ohio	6,018,600	3.9%
8	Michigan	5,012,100	3.3%
9	Georgia	4,899,300	3.2%
10	New Jersey	4,529,900	2.9%
11	North Carolina	4,526,000	2.9%
12	Virginia	4,093,600	2.7%
13	Washington	3,469,500	2.3%
14	Massachusetts	3,398,500	2.2%
15	Indiana	3,231,700	2.1%
16	Wisconsin	3,100,500	2.0%
17	Missouri	3,059,500	2.0%
18	Tennessee	3,058,400	2.0%
19	Arizona	3,052,400	2.0%
20	Maryland	3,015,700	2.0%
21	Minnesota	2,951,600	1.9%
22	Colorado	2,724,200	1.8%
23	Alabama	2,219,300	1.4%
24	South Carolina	2,159,000	1.4%
25	Kentucky	2,051,700	1.3%
26	Louisiana	2,028,300	1.3%
27	Oregon	1,957,200	1.3%
28	Connecticut	1,899,300	1.2%
29	Oklahoma	1,735,400	1.1%
30	Iowa	1,678,700	1.1%
31	Kansas	1,490,300	1.0%
32	Arkansas	1,384,100	0.9%
33	Nevada	1,370,000	0.9%
34	Utah	1,356,500	0.9%
35	Mississippi	1,348,200	0.9%
36	Nebraska	993,300	0.6%
37	New Mexico	945,200	0.6%
38	West Virginia	818,800	0.5%
39	Idaho	761,000	0.5%
40	New Hampshire	747,900	0.5%
41	Maine	712,500	0.5%
42	Hawaii	647,600	0.4%
43	Rhode Island	579,500	0.4%
44	Montana	502,600	0.3%
45	Delaware	446,800	0.3%
46	South Dakota	440,100	0.3%
47	North Dakota	366,400	0.2%
48	Vermont	355,900	0.2%
49	Alaska	350,800	0.2%
50	Wyoming	290,000	0.2%
	District of Columbia	321,000	0.2%

Source: U.S. Department of Labor, Bureau of Labor Statistics
"Regional and State Employment and Unemployment" (press release, January 18, 2008)
*Seasonally adjusted preliminary data as of December 2007. National total calculated through a different formula.

Employed Civilian Labor Force in 2007

National Total = 146,211,000 Employed Workers*

ALPHA ORDER					RANK ORDER			
RANK	STATE	EMPLOYED	% of USA		RANK	STATE	EMPLOYED	% of USA
23	Alabama	2,129,500	1.5%		1	California	17,307,000	11.8%
49	Alaska	327,800	0.2%		2	Texas	11,119,000	7.6%
17	Arizona	2,908,600	2.0%		3	New York	9,061,600	6.2%
33	Arkansas	1,303,100	0.9%		4	Florida	8,870,900	6.1%
1	California	17,307,000	11.8%		5	Illinois	6,422,900	4.4%
22	Colorado	2,602,700	1.8%		6	Pennsylvania	6,048,200	4.1%
28	Connecticut	1,804,400	1.2%		7	Ohio	5,657,900	3.9%
45	Delaware	429,800	0.3%		8	Georgia	4,662,800	3.2%
4	Florida	8,870,900	6.1%		9	Michigan	4,629,100	3.2%
8	Georgia	4,662,800	3.2%		10	New Jersey	4,327,100	3.0%
42	Hawaii	626,800	0.4%		11	North Carolina	4,301,000	2.9%
39	Idaho	738,000	0.5%		12	Virginia	3,951,400	2.7%
5	Illinois	6,422,900	4.4%		13	Washington	3,303,500	2.3%
15	Indiana	3,083,300	2.1%		14	Massachusetts	3,247,100	2.2%
30	Iowa	1,611,100	1.1%		15	Indiana	3,083,300	2.1%
31	Kansas	1,425,300	1.0%		16	Wisconsin	2,946,300	2.0%
26	Kentucky	1,935,000	1.3%		17	Arizona	2,908,600	2.0%
25	Louisiana	1,943,200	1.3%		18	Maryland	2,900,900	2.0%
41	Maine	675,900	0.5%		19	Tennessee	2,895,000	2.0%
18	Maryland	2,900,900	2.0%		20	Missouri	2,890,300	2.0%
14	Massachusetts	3,247,100	2.2%		21	Minnesota	2,806,000	1.9%
9	Michigan	4,629,100	3.2%		22	Colorado	2,602,700	1.8%
21	Minnesota	2,806,000	1.9%		23	Alabama	2,129,500	1.5%
35	Mississippi	1,256,000	0.9%		24	South Carolina	2,016,200	1.4%
20	Missouri	2,890,300	2.0%		25	Louisiana	1,943,200	1.3%
44	Montana	484,400	0.3%		26	Kentucky	1,935,000	1.3%
36	Nebraska	961,800	0.7%		27	Oregon	1,846,900	1.3%
34	Nevada	1,290,300	0.9%		28	Connecticut	1,804,400	1.2%
40	New Hampshire	721,300	0.5%		29	Oklahoma	1,658,200	1.1%
10	New Jersey	4,327,100	3.0%		30	Iowa	1,611,100	1.1%
37	New Mexico	910,600	0.6%		31	Kansas	1,425,300	1.0%
3	New York	9,061,600	6.2%		32	Utah	1,312,800	0.9%
11	North Carolina	4,301,000	2.9%		33	Arkansas	1,303,100	0.9%
47	North Dakota	354,300	0.2%		34	Nevada	1,290,300	0.9%
7	Ohio	5,657,900	3.9%		35	Mississippi	1,256,000	0.9%
29	Oklahoma	1,658,200	1.1%		36	Nebraska	961,800	0.7%
27	Oregon	1,846,900	1.3%		37	New Mexico	910,600	0.6%
6	Pennsylvania	6,048,200	4.1%		38	West Virginia	778,800	0.5%
43	Rhode Island	547,700	0.4%		39	Idaho	738,000	0.5%
24	South Carolina	2,016,200	1.4%		40	New Hampshire	721,300	0.5%
46	South Dakota	426,800	0.3%		41	Maine	675,900	0.5%
19	Tennessee	2,895,000	2.0%		42	Hawaii	626,800	0.4%
2	Texas	11,119,000	7.6%		43	Rhode Island	547,700	0.4%
32	Utah	1,312,800	0.9%		44	Montana	484,400	0.3%
48	Vermont	341,600	0.2%		45	Delaware	429,800	0.3%
12	Virginia	3,951,400	2.7%		46	South Dakota	426,800	0.3%
13	Washington	3,303,500	2.3%		47	North Dakota	354,300	0.2%
38	West Virginia	778,800	0.5%		48	Vermont	341,600	0.2%
16	Wisconsin	2,946,300	2.0%		49	Alaska	327,800	0.2%
50	Wyoming	281,000	0.2%		50	Wyoming	281,000	0.2%
						District of Columbia	301,300	0.2%

Source: CQ Press using data from U.S. Department of Labor, Bureau of Labor Statistics
   "Regional and State Employment and Unemployment" (press release, January 18, 2008)
*Seasonally adjusted preliminary data as of December 2007. National total calculated through a different formula.

Employment to Population Ratio in 2007

National Percent = 62.4% of Population 16 Years and Older Employed*

ALPHA ORDER

RANK	STATE	PERCENT
45	Alabama	58.9
22	Alaska	64.1
35	Arizona	61.7
42	Arkansas	59.2
34	California	61.8
2	Colorado	70.1
19	Connecticut	64.7
23	Delaware	63.8
37	Florida	61.0
18	Georgia	64.9
36	Hawaii	61.4
14	Idaho	66.0
20	Illinois	64.3
28	Indiana	62.7
8	Iowa	68.3
13	Kansas	66.3
48	Kentucky	58.2
46	Louisiana	58.4
28	Maine	62.7
15	Maryland	65.6
25	Massachusetts	62.9
46	Michigan	58.4
6	Minnesota	69.1
49	Mississippi	56.1
25	Missouri	62.9
21	Montana	64.2
3	Nebraska	69.9
12	Nevada	66.8
8	New Hampshire	68.3
25	New Jersey	62.9
39	New Mexico	60.5
44	New York	59.1
33	North Carolina	61.9
5	North Dakota	69.6
31	Ohio	62.6
41	Oklahoma	59.5
31	Oregon	62.6
39	Pennsylvania	60.5
24	Rhode Island	63.7
42	South Carolina	59.2
3	South Dakota	69.9
38	Tennessee	60.8
28	Texas	62.7
1	Utah	71.3
10	Vermont	67.1
17	Virginia	65.3
16	Washington	65.4
50	West Virginia	52.7
11	Wisconsin	66.9
7	Wyoming	68.8

RANK ORDER

RANK	STATE	PERCENT
1	Utah	71.3
2	Colorado	70.1
3	Nebraska	69.9
3	South Dakota	69.9
5	North Dakota	69.6
6	Minnesota	69.1
7	Wyoming	68.8
8	Iowa	68.3
8	New Hampshire	68.3
10	Vermont	67.1
11	Wisconsin	66.9
12	Nevada	66.8
13	Kansas	66.3
14	Idaho	66.0
15	Maryland	65.6
16	Washington	65.4
17	Virginia	65.3
18	Georgia	64.9
19	Connecticut	64.7
20	Illinois	64.3
21	Montana	64.2
22	Alaska	64.1
23	Delaware	63.8
24	Rhode Island	63.7
25	Massachusetts	62.9
25	Missouri	62.9
25	New Jersey	62.9
28	Indiana	62.7
28	Maine	62.7
28	Texas	62.7
31	Ohio	62.6
31	Oregon	62.6
33	North Carolina	61.9
34	California	61.8
35	Arizona	61.7
36	Hawaii	61.4
37	Florida	61.0
38	Tennessee	60.8
39	New Mexico	60.5
39	Pennsylvania	60.5
41	Oklahoma	59.5
42	Arkansas	59.2
42	South Carolina	59.2
44	New York	59.1
45	Alabama	58.9
46	Louisiana	58.4
46	Michigan	58.4
48	Kentucky	58.2
49	Mississippi	56.1
50	West Virginia	52.7

District of Columbia	62.8

Source: CQ Press using data from U.S. Department of Labor, Bureau of Labor Statistics
"Regional and State Employment and Unemployment" (press release, January 18, 2008)
*Seasonally adjusted preliminary data as of December 2007. Calculated with 2006 population data.

Unemployed Civilian Labor Force in 2007

National Total = 7,655,000 Unemployed Workers*

ALPHA ORDER

RANK	STATE	UNEMPLOYED	% of USA
28	Alabama	89,800	1.2%
42	Alaska	23,000	0.3%
19	Arizona	143,800	1.9%
30	Arkansas	81,000	1.1%
1	California	1,126,300	14.7%
22	Colorado	121,500	1.6%
26	Connecticut	94,900	1.2%
46	Delaware	17,000	0.2%
4	Florida	440,800	5.8%
9	Georgia	236,500	3.1%
44	Hawaii	20,800	0.3%
42	Idaho	23,000	0.3%
6	Illinois	372,000	4.9%
17	Indiana	148,400	1.9%
33	Iowa	67,600	0.9%
34	Kansas	65,000	0.8%
23	Kentucky	116,700	1.5%
29	Louisiana	85,100	1.1%
37	Maine	36,600	0.5%
24	Maryland	114,800	1.5%
16	Massachusetts	151,400	2.0%
5	Michigan	383,000	5.0%
18	Minnesota	145,600	1.9%
27	Mississippi	92,200	1.2%
12	Missouri	169,200	2.2%
45	Montana	18,200	0.2%
40	Nebraska	31,500	0.4%
31	Nevada	79,700	1.0%
41	New Hampshire	26,600	0.3%
11	New Jersey	202,800	2.6%
38	New Mexico	34,600	0.5%
3	New York	468,300	6.1%
10	North Carolina	225,000	2.9%
49	North Dakota	12,100	0.2%
7	Ohio	360,700	4.7%
32	Oklahoma	77,200	1.0%
25	Oregon	110,300	1.4%
8	Pennsylvania	297,300	3.9%
39	Rhode Island	31,800	0.4%
20	South Carolina	142,800	1.9%
48	South Dakota	13,300	0.2%
14	Tennessee	163,400	2.1%
2	Texas	524,200	6.8%
35	Utah	43,700	0.6%
47	Vermont	14,300	0.2%
21	Virginia	142,200	1.9%
13	Washington	166,000	2.2%
36	West Virginia	40,000	0.5%
15	Wisconsin	154,200	2.0%
50	Wyoming	9,000	0.1%

RANK ORDER

RANK	STATE	UNEMPLOYED	% of USA
1	California	1,126,300	14.7%
2	Texas	524,200	6.8%
3	New York	468,300	6.1%
4	Florida	440,800	5.8%
5	Michigan	383,000	5.0%
6	Illinois	372,000	4.9%
7	Ohio	360,700	4.7%
8	Pennsylvania	297,300	3.9%
9	Georgia	236,500	3.1%
10	North Carolina	225,000	2.9%
11	New Jersey	202,800	2.6%
12	Missouri	169,200	2.2%
13	Washington	166,000	2.2%
14	Tennessee	163,400	2.1%
15	Wisconsin	154,200	2.0%
16	Massachusetts	151,400	2.0%
17	Indiana	148,400	1.9%
18	Minnesota	145,600	1.9%
19	Arizona	143,800	1.9%
20	South Carolina	142,800	1.9%
21	Virginia	142,200	1.9%
22	Colorado	121,500	1.6%
23	Kentucky	116,700	1.5%
24	Maryland	114,800	1.5%
25	Oregon	110,300	1.4%
26	Connecticut	94,900	1.2%
27	Mississippi	92,200	1.2%
28	Alabama	89,800	1.2%
29	Louisiana	85,100	1.1%
30	Arkansas	81,000	1.1%
31	Nevada	79,700	1.0%
32	Oklahoma	77,200	1.0%
33	Iowa	67,600	0.9%
34	Kansas	65,000	0.8%
35	Utah	43,700	0.6%
36	West Virginia	40,000	0.5%
37	Maine	36,600	0.5%
38	New Mexico	34,600	0.5%
39	Rhode Island	31,800	0.4%
40	Nebraska	31,500	0.4%
41	New Hampshire	26,600	0.3%
42	Alaska	23,000	0.3%
42	Idaho	23,000	0.3%
44	Hawaii	20,800	0.3%
45	Montana	18,200	0.2%
46	Delaware	17,000	0.2%
47	Vermont	14,300	0.2%
48	South Dakota	13,300	0.2%
49	North Dakota	12,100	0.2%
50	Wyoming	9,000	0.1%
	District of Columbia	19,700	0.3%

Source: U.S. Department of Labor, Bureau of Labor Statistics
    "Regional and State Employment and Unemployment" (press release, January 18, 2008)
*Seasonally adjusted preliminary data as of December 2007. National total calculated through a different formula.

Unemployment Rate in 2007

National Rate = 5.0% of Labor Force Unemployed*

ALPHA ORDER

RANK	STATE	PERCENT
35	Alabama	4.0
4	Alaska	6.5
24	Arizona	4.7
7	Arkansas	5.9
5	California	6.1
28	Colorado	4.5
16	Connecticut	5.0
38	Delaware	3.8
24	Florida	4.7
22	Georgia	4.8
45	Hawaii	3.2
49	Idaho	3.0
11	Illinois	5.5
27	Indiana	4.6
35	Iowa	4.0
33	Kansas	4.4
9	Kentucky	5.7
34	Louisiana	4.2
15	Maine	5.1
38	Maryland	3.8
28	Massachusetts	4.5
1	Michigan	7.6
19	Minnesota	4.9
2	Mississippi	6.8
11	Missouri	5.5
41	Montana	3.6
45	Nebraska	3.2
8	Nevada	5.8
41	New Hampshire	3.6
28	New Jersey	4.5
40	New Mexico	3.7
19	New York	4.9
16	North Carolina	5.0
44	North Dakota	3.3
6	Ohio	6.0
28	Oklahoma	4.5
10	Oregon	5.6
24	Pennsylvania	4.7
11	Rhode Island	5.5
3	South Carolina	6.6
49	South Dakota	3.0
14	Tennessee	5.3
28	Texas	4.5
45	Utah	3.2
35	Vermont	4.0
43	Virginia	3.5
22	Washington	4.8
19	West Virginia	4.9
16	Wisconsin	5.0
48	Wyoming	3.1

RANK ORDER

RANK	STATE	PERCENT
1	Michigan	7.6
2	Mississippi	6.8
3	South Carolina	6.6
4	Alaska	6.5
5	California	6.1
6	Ohio	6.0
7	Arkansas	5.9
8	Nevada	5.8
9	Kentucky	5.7
10	Oregon	5.6
11	Illinois	5.5
11	Missouri	5.5
11	Rhode Island	5.5
14	Tennessee	5.3
15	Maine	5.1
16	Connecticut	5.0
16	North Carolina	5.0
16	Wisconsin	5.0
19	Minnesota	4.9
19	New York	4.9
19	West Virginia	4.9
22	Georgia	4.8
22	Washington	4.8
24	Arizona	4.7
24	Florida	4.7
24	Pennsylvania	4.7
27	Indiana	4.6
28	Colorado	4.5
28	Massachusetts	4.5
28	New Jersey	4.5
28	Oklahoma	4.5
28	Texas	4.5
33	Kansas	4.4
34	Louisiana	4.2
35	Alabama	4.0
35	Iowa	4.0
35	Vermont	4.0
38	Delaware	3.8
38	Maryland	3.8
40	New Mexico	3.7
41	Montana	3.6
41	New Hampshire	3.6
43	Virginia	3.5
44	North Dakota	3.3
45	Hawaii	3.2
45	Nebraska	3.2
45	Utah	3.2
48	Wyoming	3.1
49	Idaho	3.0
49	South Dakota	3.0
	District of Columbia	6.1

Source: U.S. Department of Labor, Bureau of Labor Statistics
   "Regional and State Employment and Unemployment" (press release, January 18, 2008)
*Seasonally adjusted preliminary data as of December 2007. National rate calculated through a different formula.

Women in Civilian Labor Force in 2006

National Total = 70,173,000 Women*

ALPHA ORDER				RANK ORDER			
RANK	STATE	WOMEN	% of USA	RANK	STATE	WOMEN	% of USA
23	Alabama	1,031,000	1.5%	1	California	7,875,000	11.2%
49	Alaska	162,000	0.2%	2	Texas	5,075,000	7.2%
21	Arizona	1,310,000	1.9%	3	New York	4,497,000	6.4%
32	Arkansas	650,000	0.9%	4	Florida	4,254,000	6.1%
1	California	7,875,000	11.2%	5	Illinois	3,015,000	4.3%
22	Colorado	1,186,000	1.7%	6	Pennsylvania	2,948,000	4.2%
27	Connecticut	876,000	1.2%	7	Ohio	2,854,000	4.1%
45	Delaware	215,000	0.3%	8	Michigan	2,387,000	3.4%
4	Florida	4,254,000	6.1%	9	Georgia	2,183,000	3.1%
9	Georgia	2,183,000	3.1%	10	North Carolina	2,073,000	3.0%
42	Hawaii	315,000	0.4%	11	New Jersey	2,063,000	2.9%
40	Idaho	343,000	0.5%	12	Virginia	1,895,000	2.7%
5	Illinois	3,015,000	4.3%	13	Massachusetts	1,598,000	2.3%
15	Indiana	1,502,000	2.1%	14	Washington	1,543,000	2.2%
29	Iowa	806,000	1.1%	15	Indiana	1,502,000	2.1%
31	Kansas	693,000	1.0%	16	Missouri	1,465,000	2.1%
25	Kentucky	965,000	1.4%	17	Wisconsin	1,464,000	2.1%
26	Louisiana	919,000	1.3%	18	Maryland	1,453,000	2.1%
41	Maine	342,000	0.5%	19	Minnesota	1,399,000	2.0%
18	Maryland	1,453,000	2.1%	20	Tennessee	1,388,000	2.0%
13	Massachusetts	1,598,000	2.3%	21	Arizona	1,310,000	1.9%
8	Michigan	2,387,000	3.4%	22	Colorado	1,186,000	1.7%
19	Minnesota	1,399,000	2.0%	23	Alabama	1,031,000	1.5%
33	Mississippi	615,000	0.9%	24	South Carolina	1,009,000	1.4%
16	Missouri	1,465,000	2.1%	25	Kentucky	965,000	1.4%
44	Montana	240,000	0.3%	26	Louisiana	919,000	1.3%
36	Nebraska	458,000	0.7%	27	Connecticut	876,000	1.2%
34	Nevada	580,000	0.8%	28	Oregon	865,000	1.2%
39	New Hampshire	349,000	0.5%	29	Iowa	806,000	1.1%
11	New Jersey	2,063,000	2.9%	30	Oklahoma	797,000	1.1%
37	New Mexico	445,000	0.6%	31	Kansas	693,000	1.0%
3	New York	4,497,000	6.4%	32	Arkansas	650,000	0.9%
10	North Carolina	2,073,000	3.0%	33	Mississippi	615,000	0.9%
47	North Dakota	176,000	0.3%	34	Nevada	580,000	0.8%
7	Ohio	2,854,000	4.1%	35	Utah	574,000	0.8%
30	Oklahoma	797,000	1.1%	36	Nebraska	458,000	0.7%
28	Oregon	865,000	1.2%	37	New Mexico	445,000	0.6%
6	Pennsylvania	2,948,000	4.2%	38	West Virginia	382,000	0.5%
43	Rhode Island	278,000	0.4%	39	New Hampshire	349,000	0.5%
24	South Carolina	1,009,000	1.4%	40	Idaho	343,000	0.5%
46	South Dakota	206,000	0.3%	41	Maine	342,000	0.5%
20	Tennessee	1,388,000	2.0%	42	Hawaii	315,000	0.4%
2	Texas	5,075,000	7.2%	43	Rhode Island	278,000	0.4%
35	Utah	574,000	0.8%	44	Montana	240,000	0.3%
47	Vermont	176,000	0.3%	45	Delaware	215,000	0.3%
12	Virginia	1,895,000	2.7%	46	South Dakota	206,000	0.3%
14	Washington	1,543,000	2.2%	47	North Dakota	176,000	0.3%
38	West Virginia	382,000	0.5%	47	Vermont	176,000	0.3%
17	Wisconsin	1,464,000	2.1%	49	Alaska	162,000	0.2%
50	Wyoming	130,000	0.2%	50	Wyoming	130,000	0.2%
					District of Columbia	151,000	0.2%

Source: U.S. Department of Labor, Bureau of Labor Statistics
   "Geographic Profiles of Employment and Unemployment, 2006" (http://www.bls.gov/gps/)
*Annual averages.

Percent of Women in the Civilian Labor Force in 2006

National Percent = 59.4% of Women*

RANK	STATE	PERCENT
47	Alabama	55.2
6	Alaska	66.8
46	Arizona	56.3
35	Arkansas	58.0
44	California	56.7
9	Colorado	65.6
24	Connecticut	61.4
21	Delaware	61.5
39	Florida	57.5
28	Georgia	60.9
26	Hawaii	61.0
21	Idaho	61.5
30	Illinois	59.8
29	Indiana	60.8
4	Iowa	67.2
11	Kansas	64.5
42	Kentucky	57.2
48	Louisiana	55.0
20	Maine	61.6
13	Maryland	63.7
26	Massachusetts	61.0
32	Michigan	59.2
2	Minnesota	68.3
49	Mississippi	53.6
17	Missouri	62.3
14	Montana	63.1
7	Nebraska	66.1
21	Nevada	61.5
10	New Hampshire	65.3
33	New Jersey	58.7
39	New Mexico	57.5
41	New York	57.3
31	North Carolina	59.5
1	North Dakota	69.0
19	Ohio	61.7
45	Oklahoma	56.4
33	Oregon	58.7
38	Pennsylvania	57.6
15	Rhode Island	63.0
36	South Carolina	57.9
5	South Dakota	67.1
43	Tennessee	56.9
37	Texas	57.7
16	Utah	62.8
3	Vermont	68.0
17	Virginia	62.3
25	Washington	61.1
50	West Virginia	50.8
8	Wisconsin	65.8
12	Wyoming	63.8

RANK	STATE	PERCENT
1	North Dakota	69.0
2	Minnesota	68.3
3	Vermont	68.0
4	Iowa	67.2
5	South Dakota	67.1
6	Alaska	66.8
7	Nebraska	66.1
8	Wisconsin	65.8
9	Colorado	65.6
10	New Hampshire	65.3
11	Kansas	64.5
12	Wyoming	63.8
13	Maryland	63.7
14	Montana	63.1
15	Rhode Island	63.0
16	Utah	62.8
17	Missouri	62.3
17	Virginia	62.3
19	Ohio	61.7
20	Maine	61.6
21	Delaware	61.5
21	Idaho	61.5
21	Nevada	61.5
24	Connecticut	61.4
25	Washington	61.1
26	Hawaii	61.0
26	Massachusetts	61.0
28	Georgia	60.9
29	Indiana	60.8
30	Illinois	59.8
31	North Carolina	59.5
32	Michigan	59.2
33	New Jersey	58.7
33	Oregon	58.7
35	Arkansas	58.0
36	South Carolina	57.9
37	Texas	57.7
38	Pennsylvania	57.6
39	Florida	57.5
39	New Mexico	57.5
41	New York	57.3
42	Kentucky	57.2
43	Tennessee	56.9
44	California	56.7
45	Oklahoma	56.4
46	Arizona	56.3
47	Alabama	55.2
48	Louisiana	55.0
49	Mississippi	53.6
50	West Virginia	50.8
	District of Columbia	64.3

Source: U.S. Department of Labor, Bureau of Labor Statistics
   "Geographic Profiles of Employment and Unemployment, 2006" (http://www.bls.gov/gps/)
*Annual averages.

Percent of Civilian Labor Force Comprised of Women in 2006

National Percent = 46.3% of Civilian Labor Force*

ALPHA ORDER

RANK	STATE	PERCENT
31	Alabama	46.7
35	Alaska	46.4
49	Arizona	44.1
20	Arkansas	47.3
47	California	44.4
43	Colorado	45.4
22	Connecticut	47.1
4	Delaware	48.0
25	Florida	47.0
34	Georgia	46.5
5	Hawaii	47.9
45	Idaho	45.2
40	Illinois	45.8
37	Indiana	46.2
18	Iowa	47.4
29	Kansas	46.8
20	Kentucky	47.3
26	Louisiana	46.9
6	Maine	47.8
1	Maryland	48.4
18	Massachusetts	47.4
26	Michigan	46.9
9	Minnesota	47.7
12	Mississippi	47.5
9	Missouri	47.7
12	Montana	47.5
33	Nebraska	46.6
46	Nevada	44.8
22	New Hampshire	47.1
39	New Jersey	45.9
22	New Mexico	47.1
12	New York	47.5
29	North Carolina	46.8
6	North Dakota	47.8
6	Ohio	47.8
38	Oklahoma	46.0
42	Oregon	45.6
31	Pennsylvania	46.7
2	Rhode Island	48.2
12	South Carolina	47.5
12	South Dakota	47.5
40	Tennessee	45.8
48	Texas	44.3
50	Utah	43.9
2	Vermont	48.2
9	Virginia	47.7
36	Washington	46.3
26	West Virginia	46.9
12	Wisconsin	47.5
44	Wyoming	45.3

RANK ORDER

RANK	STATE	PERCENT
1	Maryland	48.4
2	Rhode Island	48.2
2	Vermont	48.2
4	Delaware	48.0
5	Hawaii	47.9
6	Maine	47.8
6	North Dakota	47.8
6	Ohio	47.8
9	Minnesota	47.7
9	Missouri	47.7
9	Virginia	47.7
12	Mississippi	47.5
12	Montana	47.5
12	New York	47.5
12	South Carolina	47.5
12	South Dakota	47.5
12	Wisconsin	47.5
18	Iowa	47.4
18	Massachusetts	47.4
20	Arkansas	47.3
20	Kentucky	47.3
22	Connecticut	47.1
22	New Hampshire	47.1
22	New Mexico	47.1
25	Florida	47.0
26	Louisiana	46.9
26	Michigan	46.9
26	West Virginia	46.9
29	Kansas	46.8
29	North Carolina	46.8
31	Alabama	46.7
31	Pennsylvania	46.7
33	Nebraska	46.6
34	Georgia	46.5
35	Alaska	46.4
36	Washington	46.3
37	Indiana	46.2
38	Oklahoma	46.0
39	New Jersey	45.9
40	Illinois	45.8
40	Tennessee	45.8
42	Oregon	45.6
43	Colorado	45.4
44	Wyoming	45.3
45	Idaho	45.2
46	Nevada	44.8
47	California	44.4
48	Texas	44.3
49	Arizona	44.1
50	Utah	43.9

| | District of Columbia | 51.9 |

Source: CQ Press using data from U.S. Department of Labor, Bureau of Labor Statistics
"Geographic Profiles of Employment and Unemployment, 2006" (http://www.bls.gov/gps/)
*Annual averages.

Percent of Children Under 6 Years Old With All Parents Working: 2006

National Percent = 61.6%

ALPHA ORDER

RANK	STATE	PERCENT
18	Alabama	65.0
44	Alaska	58.2
46	Arizona	57.2
17	Arkansas	65.6
47	California	56.1
39	Colorado	60.0
30	Connecticut	62.0
14	Delaware	65.9
23	Florida	63.7
32	Georgia	61.8
12	Hawaii	66.2
48	Idaho	56.0
34	Illinois	61.7
15	Indiana	65.8
3	Iowa	72.0
15	Kansas	65.8
35	Kentucky	61.6
18	Louisiana	65.0
26	Maine	63.5
8	Maryland	67.3
22	Massachusetts	63.8
24	Michigan	63.6
6	Minnesota	69.7
20	Mississippi	64.3
13	Missouri	66.1
30	Montana	62.0
4	Nebraska	71.1
40	Nevada	59.8
32	New Hampshire	61.8
37	New Jersey	60.9
28	New Mexico	62.6
42	New York	58.8
20	North Carolina	64.3
2	North Dakota	72.8
11	Ohio	66.3
36	Oklahoma	61.2
43	Oregon	58.6
28	Pennsylvania	62.6
27	Rhode Island	63.0
9	South Carolina	66.7
1	South Dakota	74.0
37	Tennessee	60.9
45	Texas	57.6
50	Utah	49.3
7	Vermont	68.0
24	Virginia	63.6
41	Washington	59.6
49	West Virginia	55.1
5	Wisconsin	70.7
10	Wyoming	66.6

RANK ORDER

RANK	STATE	PERCENT
1	South Dakota	74.0
2	North Dakota	72.8
3	Iowa	72.0
4	Nebraska	71.1
5	Wisconsin	70.7
6	Minnesota	69.7
7	Vermont	68.0
8	Maryland	67.3
9	South Carolina	66.7
10	Wyoming	66.6
11	Ohio	66.3
12	Hawaii	66.2
13	Missouri	66.1
14	Delaware	65.9
15	Indiana	65.8
15	Kansas	65.8
17	Arkansas	65.6
18	Alabama	65.0
18	Louisiana	65.0
20	Mississippi	64.3
20	North Carolina	64.3
22	Massachusetts	63.8
23	Florida	63.7
24	Michigan	63.6
24	Virginia	63.6
26	Maine	63.5
27	Rhode Island	63.0
28	New Mexico	62.6
28	Pennsylvania	62.6
30	Connecticut	62.0
30	Montana	62.0
32	Georgia	61.8
32	New Hampshire	61.8
34	Illinois	61.7
35	Kentucky	61.6
36	Oklahoma	61.2
37	New Jersey	60.9
37	Tennessee	60.9
39	Colorado	60.0
40	Nevada	59.8
41	Washington	59.6
42	New York	58.8
43	Oregon	58.6
44	Alaska	58.2
45	Texas	57.6
46	Arizona	57.2
47	California	56.1
48	Idaho	56.0
49	West Virginia	55.1
50	Utah	49.3

	District of Columbia	63.5

Source: U.S. Bureau of the Census
"2006 American Community Survey" (http://www.census.gov/acs/www/index.html)

Job Growth: 2006 to 2007

National Percent Change = 1.0% Increase*

ALPHA ORDER

RANK	STATE	PERCENT CHANGE
17	Alabama	1.3
39	Alaska	0.5
17	Arizona	1.3
42	Arkansas	0.4
39	California	0.5
6	Colorado	2.0
23	Connecticut	1.0
39	Delaware	0.5
21	Florida	1.1
10	Georgia	1.6
10	Hawaii	1.6
17	Idaho	1.3
32	Illinois	0.7
47	Indiana	0.2
17	Iowa	1.3
21	Kansas	1.1
44	Kentucky	0.3
4	Louisiana	2.2
32	Maine	0.7
15	Maryland	1.4
32	Massachusetts	0.7
50	Michigan	(1.8)
48	Minnesota	0.0
15	Mississippi	1.4
44	Missouri	0.3
2	Montana	3.4
13	Nebraska	1.5
38	Nevada	0.6
27	New Hampshire	0.9
32	New Jersey	0.7
27	New Mexico	0.9
29	New York	0.8
8	North Carolina	1.7
23	North Dakota	1.0
49	Ohio	(0.3)
13	Oklahoma	1.5
10	Oregon	1.6
32	Pennsylvania	0.7
32	Rhode Island	0.7
23	South Carolina	1.0
23	South Dakota	1.0
29	Tennessee	0.8
5	Texas	2.1
1	Utah	4.0
44	Vermont	0.3
8	Virginia	1.7
6	Washington	2.0
42	West Virginia	0.4
29	Wisconsin	0.8
2	Wyoming	3.4

RANK ORDER

RANK	STATE	PERCENT CHANGE
1	Utah	4.0
2	Montana	3.4
2	Wyoming	3.4
4	Louisiana	2.2
5	Texas	2.1
6	Colorado	2.0
6	Washington	2.0
8	North Carolina	1.7
8	Virginia	1.7
10	Georgia	1.6
10	Hawaii	1.6
10	Oregon	1.6
13	Nebraska	1.5
13	Oklahoma	1.5
15	Maryland	1.4
15	Mississippi	1.4
17	Alabama	1.3
17	Arizona	1.3
17	Idaho	1.3
17	Iowa	1.3
21	Florida	1.1
21	Kansas	1.1
23	Connecticut	1.0
23	North Dakota	1.0
23	South Carolina	1.0
23	South Dakota	1.0
27	New Hampshire	0.9
27	New Mexico	0.9
29	New York	0.8
29	Tennessee	0.8
29	Wisconsin	0.8
32	Illinois	0.7
32	Maine	0.7
32	Massachusetts	0.7
32	New Jersey	0.7
32	Pennsylvania	0.7
32	Rhode Island	0.7
38	Nevada	0.6
39	Alaska	0.5
39	California	0.5
39	Delaware	0.5
42	Arkansas	0.4
42	West Virginia	0.4
44	Kentucky	0.3
44	Missouri	0.3
44	Vermont	0.3
47	Indiana	0.2
48	Minnesota	0.0
49	Ohio	(0.3)
50	Michigan	(1.8)

District of Columbia   1.5

Source: CQ Press using data from U.S. Department of Labor, Bureau of Labor Statistics
"Regional and State Employment and Unemployment" (press release, January 18, 2008)
*Nonfarm jobs. December 2006 to December 2007, seasonally adjusted. National figure based on nonfarm employment from a different survey.

Employees on Nonfarm Payrolls in 2007

National Total = 138,495,000 Employees*

ALPHA ORDER

ALPHA ORDER

RANK	STATE	EMPLOYEES	% of USA
23	Alabama	2,021,700	1.5%
48	Alaska	317,100	0.2%
20	Arizona	2,720,100	2.0%
34	Arkansas	1,208,100	0.9%
1	California	15,291,400	11.0%
22	Colorado	2,345,600	1.7%
28	Connecticut	1,702,600	1.2%
45	Delaware	441,100	0.3%
4	Florida	8,155,400	5.9%
9	Georgia	4,171,000	3.0%
41	Hawaii	632,200	0.5%
39	Idaho	659,300	0.5%
5	Illinois	5,991,400	4.3%
14	Indiana	2,986,400	2.2%
30	Iowa	1,527,800	1.1%
31	Kansas	1,383,700	1.0%
26	Kentucky	1,857,300	1.3%
25	Louisiana	1,929,100	1.4%
42	Maine	619,500	0.4%
21	Maryland	2,636,100	1.9%
13	Massachusetts	3,282,100	2.4%
8	Michigan	4,247,900	3.1%
19	Minnesota	2,768,100	2.0%
35	Mississippi	1,171,200	0.8%
18	Missouri	2,797,000	2.0%
44	Montana	449,600	0.3%
36	Nebraska	969,100	0.7%
32	Nevada	1,308,200	0.9%
40	New Hampshire	648,100	0.5%
11	New Jersey	4,114,900	3.0%
37	New Mexico	848,100	0.6%
3	New York	8,723,200	6.3%
10	North Carolina	4,133,100	3.0%
47	North Dakota	361,000	0.3%
7	Ohio	5,427,500	3.9%
29	Oklahoma	1,585,800	1.1%
27	Oregon	1,738,800	1.3%
6	Pennsylvania	5,817,800	4.2%
43	Rhode Island	499,200	0.4%
24	South Carolina	1,938,500	1.4%
46	South Dakota	408,500	0.3%
17	Tennessee	2,816,800	2.0%
2	Texas	10,389,900	7.5%
33	Utah	1,271,600	0.9%
49	Vermont	309,200	0.2%
12	Virginia	3,809,600	2.8%
15	Washington	2,949,300	2.1%
38	West Virginia	762,800	0.6%
16	Wisconsin	2,892,700	2.1%
50	Wyoming	290,700	0.2%

RANK ORDER

RANK	STATE	EMPLOYEES	% of USA
1	California	15,291,400	11.0%
2	Texas	10,389,900	7.5%
3	New York	8,723,200	6.3%
4	Florida	8,155,400	5.9%
5	Illinois	5,991,400	4.3%
6	Pennsylvania	5,817,800	4.2%
7	Ohio	5,427,500	3.9%
8	Michigan	4,247,900	3.1%
9	Georgia	4,171,000	3.0%
10	North Carolina	4,133,100	3.0%
11	New Jersey	4,114,900	3.0%
12	Virginia	3,809,600	2.8%
13	Massachusetts	3,282,100	2.4%
14	Indiana	2,986,400	2.2%
15	Washington	2,949,300	2.1%
16	Wisconsin	2,892,700	2.1%
17	Tennessee	2,816,800	2.0%
18	Missouri	2,797,000	2.0%
19	Minnesota	2,768,100	2.0%
20	Arizona	2,720,100	2.0%
21	Maryland	2,636,100	1.9%
22	Colorado	2,345,600	1.7%
23	Alabama	2,021,700	1.5%
24	South Carolina	1,938,500	1.4%
25	Louisiana	1,929,100	1.4%
26	Kentucky	1,857,300	1.3%
27	Oregon	1,738,800	1.3%
28	Connecticut	1,702,600	1.2%
29	Oklahoma	1,585,800	1.1%
30	Iowa	1,527,800	1.1%
31	Kansas	1,383,700	1.0%
32	Nevada	1,308,200	0.9%
33	Utah	1,271,600	0.9%
34	Arkansas	1,208,100	0.9%
35	Mississippi	1,171,200	0.8%
36	Nebraska	969,100	0.7%
37	New Mexico	848,100	0.6%
38	West Virginia	762,800	0.6%
39	Idaho	659,300	0.5%
40	New Hampshire	648,100	0.5%
41	Hawaii	632,200	0.5%
42	Maine	619,500	0.4%
43	Rhode Island	499,200	0.4%
44	Montana	449,600	0.3%
45	Delaware	441,100	0.3%
46	South Dakota	408,500	0.3%
47	North Dakota	361,000	0.3%
48	Alaska	317,100	0.2%
49	Vermont	309,200	0.2%
50	Wyoming	290,700	0.2%
	District of Columbia	704,100	0.5%

Source: U.S. Department of Labor, Bureau of Labor Statistics
"Regional and State Employment and Unemployment" (press release, January 18, 2008)
*Seasonally adjusted preliminary data as of December 2007. National total calculated through a different formula.

Employees in Construction in 2007

National Total = 7,489,000 Employees*

ALPHA ORDER

RANK	STATE	EMPLOYEES	% of USA
26	Alabama	114,300	1.5%
49	Alaska	17,300	0.2%
10	Arizona	227,600	3.0%
36	Arkansas	56,200	0.8%
1	California	899,500	12.0%
15	Colorado	164,200	2.2%
32	Connecticut	68,100	0.9%
44	Delaware**	29,500	0.4%
3	Florida	618,000	8.3%
11	Georgia	225,300	3.0%
40	Hawaii**	38,600	0.5%
37	Idaho	51,900	0.7%
5	Illinois	272,600	3.6%
17	Indiana	152,600	2.0%
30	Iowa	77,500	1.0%
33	Kansas	64,900	0.9%
29	Kentucky	84,200	1.1%
20	Louisiana	138,200	1.8%
42	Maine	30,500	0.4%
13	Maryland**	194,600	2.6%
21	Massachusetts	137,100	1.8%
16	Michigan	159,900	2.1%
24	Minnesota	123,900	1.7%
34	Mississippi	63,100	0.8%
18	Missouri	150,300	2.0%
41	Montana	33,200	0.4%
38	Nebraska**	51,000	0.7%
22	Nevada	134,400	1.8%
43	New Hampshire	29,600	0.4%
14	New Jersey	171,500	2.3%
35	New Mexico	58,800	0.8%
4	New York	347,400	4.6%
7	North Carolina	255,500	3.4%
48	North Dakota	19,000	0.3%
9	Ohio	227,700	3.0%
31	Oklahoma	72,800	1.0%
28	Oregon	98,100	1.3%
6	Pennsylvania	261,100	3.5%
46	Rhode Island	24,500	0.3%
25	South Carolina	123,300	1.6%
47	South Dakota	22,200	0.3%
19	Tennessee	140,300	1.9%
2	Texas	628,800	8.4%
27	Utah	108,200	1.4%
50	Vermont	17,100	0.2%
8	Virginia	252,300	3.4%
12	Washington	207,300	2.8%
39	West Virginia	39,600	0.5%
23	Wisconsin	125,400	1.7%
45	Wyoming	27,000	0.4%

RANK ORDER

RANK	STATE	EMPLOYEES	% of USA
1	California	899,500	12.0%
2	Texas	628,800	8.4%
3	Florida	618,000	8.3%
4	New York	347,400	4.6%
5	Illinois	272,600	3.6%
6	Pennsylvania	261,100	3.5%
7	North Carolina	255,500	3.4%
8	Virginia	252,300	3.4%
9	Ohio	227,700	3.0%
10	Arizona	227,600	3.0%
11	Georgia	225,300	3.0%
12	Washington	207,300	2.8%
13	Maryland**	194,600	2.6%
14	New Jersey	171,500	2.3%
15	Colorado	164,200	2.2%
16	Michigan	159,900	2.1%
17	Indiana	152,600	2.0%
18	Missouri	150,300	2.0%
19	Tennessee	140,300	1.9%
20	Louisiana	138,200	1.8%
21	Massachusetts	137,100	1.8%
22	Nevada	134,400	1.8%
23	Wisconsin	125,400	1.7%
24	Minnesota	123,900	1.7%
25	South Carolina	123,300	1.6%
26	Alabama	114,300	1.5%
27	Utah	108,200	1.4%
28	Oregon	98,100	1.3%
29	Kentucky	84,200	1.1%
30	Iowa	77,500	1.0%
31	Oklahoma	72,800	1.0%
32	Connecticut	68,100	0.9%
33	Kansas	64,900	0.9%
34	Mississippi	63,100	0.8%
35	New Mexico	58,800	0.8%
36	Arkansas	56,200	0.8%
37	Idaho	51,900	0.7%
38	Nebraska**	51,000	0.7%
39	West Virginia	39,600	0.5%
40	Hawaii**	38,600	0.5%
41	Montana	33,200	0.4%
42	Maine	30,500	0.4%
43	New Hampshire	29,600	0.4%
44	Delaware**	29,500	0.4%
45	Wyoming	27,000	0.4%
46	Rhode Island	24,500	0.3%
47	South Dakota	22,200	0.3%
48	North Dakota	19,000	0.3%
49	Alaska	17,300	0.2%
50	Vermont	17,100	0.2%
	District of Columbia**	13,000	0.2%

Source: U.S. Department of Labor, Bureau of Labor Statistics
   "Regional and State Employment and Unemployment" (press release, January 18, 2008)
*Seasonally adjusted preliminary data as of December 2007. National total calculated through a different formula.
**Figures for Delaware, DC, Hawaii, Maryland, and Nebraska include employees in natural resources and mining.

Percent of Nonfarm Employees in Construction in 2007

National Percent = 5.4% of Employees*

ALPHA ORDER

RANK	STATE	PERCENT
20	Alabama	5.7
22	Alaska	5.5
4	Arizona	8.4
36	Arkansas	4.7
19	California	5.9
10	Colorado	7.0
48	Connecticut	4.0
13	Delaware**	6.7
6	Florida	7.6
24	Georgia	5.4
17	Hawaii**	6.1
5	Idaho	7.9
40	Illinois	4.5
31	Indiana	5.1
31	Iowa	5.1
36	Kansas	4.7
40	Kentucky	4.5
9	Louisiana	7.2
34	Maine	4.9
7	Maryland**	7.4
45	Massachusetts	4.2
50	Michigan	3.8
40	Minnesota	4.5
24	Mississippi	5.4
24	Missouri	5.4
7	Montana	7.4
28	Nebraska**	5.3
1	Nevada	10.3
38	New Hampshire	4.6
45	New Jersey	4.2
12	New Mexico	6.9
48	New York	4.0
16	North Carolina	6.2
28	North Dakota	5.3
45	Ohio	4.2
38	Oklahoma	4.6
21	Oregon	5.6
40	Pennsylvania	4.5
34	Rhode Island	4.9
15	South Carolina	6.4
24	South Dakota	5.4
33	Tennessee	5.0
17	Texas	6.1
3	Utah	8.5
22	Vermont	5.5
14	Virginia	6.6
10	Washington	7.0
30	West Virginia	5.2
44	Wisconsin	4.3
2	Wyoming	9.3

RANK ORDER

RANK	STATE	PERCENT
1	Nevada	10.3
2	Wyoming	9.3
3	Utah	8.5
4	Arizona	8.4
5	Idaho	7.9
6	Florida	7.6
7	Maryland**	7.4
7	Montana	7.4
9	Louisiana	7.2
10	Colorado	7.0
10	Washington	7.0
12	New Mexico	6.9
13	Delaware**	6.7
14	Virginia	6.6
15	South Carolina	6.4
16	North Carolina	6.2
17	Hawaii**	6.1
17	Texas	6.1
19	California	5.9
20	Alabama	5.7
21	Oregon	5.6
22	Alaska	5.5
22	Vermont	5.5
24	Georgia	5.4
24	Mississippi	5.4
24	Missouri	5.4
24	South Dakota	5.4
28	Nebraska**	5.3
28	North Dakota	5.3
30	West Virginia	5.2
31	Indiana	5.1
31	Iowa	5.1
33	Tennessee	5.0
34	Maine	4.9
34	Rhode Island	4.9
36	Arkansas	4.7
36	Kansas	4.7
38	New Hampshire	4.6
38	Oklahoma	4.6
40	Illinois	4.5
40	Kentucky	4.5
40	Minnesota	4.5
40	Pennsylvania	4.5
44	Wisconsin	4.3
45	Massachusetts	4.2
45	New Jersey	4.2
45	Ohio	4.2
48	Connecticut	4.0
48	New York	4.0
50	Michigan	3.8
	District of Columbia**	1.8

Source: CQ Press using data from U.S. Department of Labor, Bureau of Labor Statistics
    "Regional and State Employment and Unemployment" (press release, January 18, 2008)
*Seasonally adjusted preliminary data as of December 2007. National figure calculated through a different formula.
**Figures for Delaware, DC, Hawaii, Maryland, and Nebraska include employees in natural resources and mining.

Employees in Education and Health Services in 2007

National Total = 18,627,000 Employees*

ALPHA ORDER

RANK	STATE	EMPLOYEES	% of USA
27	Alabama	209,500	1.1%
48	Alaska	37,600	0.2%
21	Arizona	307,400	1.7%
32	Arkansas	155,600	0.8%
1	California	1,696,900	9.1%
24	Colorado	244,200	1.3%
22	Connecticut	289,100	1.6%
45	Delaware	59,000	0.3%
5	Florida	1,014,800	5.4%
12	Georgia	455,700	2.4%
42	Hawaii	72,800	0.4%
NA	Idaho**	NA	NA
7	Illinois	781,800	4.2%
16	Indiana	391,500	2.1%
29	Iowa	204,500	1.1%
31	Kansas	169,900	0.9%
25	Kentucky	241,500	1.3%
23	Louisiana	246,600	1.3%
36	Maine	117,600	0.6%
18	Maryland	373,900	2.0%
8	Massachusetts	624,000	3.3%
9	Michigan	599,700	3.2%
13	Minnesota	425,400	2.3%
35	Mississippi	124,800	0.7%
17	Missouri	386,700	2.1%
44	Montana	59,600	0.3%
34	Nebraska	135,900	0.7%
41	Nevada	93,900	0.5%
39	New Hampshire	104,900	0.6%
10	New Jersey	586,900	3.2%
38	New Mexico	112,900	0.6%
2	New York	1,615,800	8.7%
11	North Carolina	516,100	2.8%
47	North Dakota	51,800	0.3%
6	Ohio	792,700	4.3%
30	Oklahoma	192,000	1.0%
26	Oregon	213,400	1.1%
4	Pennsylvania	1,096,200	5.9%
40	Rhode Island	98,800	0.5%
28	South Carolina	205,200	1.1%
43	South Dakota	60,800	0.3%
20	Tennessee	349,200	1.9%
3	Texas	1,262,800	6.8%
33	Utah	141,700	0.8%
46	Vermont	56,300	0.3%
14	Virginia	415,400	2.2%
19	Washington	351,000	1.9%
37	West Virginia	114,800	0.6%
15	Wisconsin	400,000	2.1%
NA	Wyoming**	NA	NA

RANK ORDER

RANK	STATE	EMPLOYEES	% of USA
1	California	1,696,900	9.1%
2	New York	1,615,800	8.7%
3	Texas	1,262,800	6.8%
4	Pennsylvania	1,096,200	5.9%
5	Florida	1,014,800	5.4%
6	Ohio	792,700	4.3%
7	Illinois	781,800	4.2%
8	Massachusetts	624,000	3.3%
9	Michigan	599,700	3.2%
10	New Jersey	586,900	3.2%
11	North Carolina	516,100	2.8%
12	Georgia	455,700	2.4%
13	Minnesota	425,400	2.3%
14	Virginia	415,400	2.2%
15	Wisconsin	400,000	2.1%
16	Indiana	391,500	2.1%
17	Missouri	386,700	2.1%
18	Maryland	373,900	2.0%
19	Washington	351,000	1.9%
20	Tennessee	349,200	1.9%
21	Arizona	307,400	1.7%
22	Connecticut	289,100	1.6%
23	Louisiana	246,600	1.3%
24	Colorado	244,200	1.3%
25	Kentucky	241,500	1.3%
26	Oregon	213,400	1.1%
27	Alabama	209,500	1.1%
28	South Carolina	205,200	1.1%
29	Iowa	204,500	1.1%
30	Oklahoma	192,000	1.0%
31	Kansas	169,900	0.9%
32	Arkansas	155,600	0.8%
33	Utah	141,700	0.8%
34	Nebraska	135,900	0.7%
35	Mississippi	124,800	0.7%
36	Maine	117,600	0.6%
37	West Virginia	114,800	0.6%
38	New Mexico	112,900	0.6%
39	New Hampshire	104,900	0.6%
40	Rhode Island	98,800	0.5%
41	Nevada	93,900	0.5%
42	Hawaii	72,800	0.4%
43	South Dakota	60,800	0.3%
44	Montana	59,600	0.3%
45	Delaware	59,000	0.3%
46	Vermont	56,300	0.3%
47	North Dakota	51,800	0.3%
48	Alaska	37,600	0.2%
NA	Idaho**	NA	NA
NA	Wyoming**	NA	NA
	District of Columbia**	NA	NA

Source: U.S. Department of Labor, Bureau of Labor Statistics
"Regional and State Employment and Unemployment" (press release, January 18, 2008)
*Seasonally adjusted preliminary data as of December 2007. National total calculated through a different formula.
**The Bureau of Labor Statistics does not publish seasonally adjusted figures in this category for these states.

Percent of Nonfarm Employees in Education and Health Services in 2007

National Percent = 13.4% of Employees*

ALPHA ORDER				RANK ORDER		
RANK	STATE	PERCENT		RANK	STATE	PERCENT
46	Alabama	10.4		1	Rhode Island	19.8
36	Alaska	11.9		2	Maine	19.0
39	Arizona	11.3		2	Massachusetts	19.0
27	Arkansas	12.9		4	Pennsylvania	18.8
40	California	11.1		5	New York	18.5
46	Colorado	10.4		6	Vermont	18.2
7	Connecticut	17.0		7	Connecticut	17.0
20	Delaware	13.4		8	New Hampshire	16.2
30	Florida	12.4		9	Minnesota	15.4
42	Georgia	10.9		10	West Virginia	15.0
38	Hawaii	11.5		11	South Dakota	14.9
NA	Idaho**	NA		12	Ohio	14.6
25	Illinois	13.0		13	New Jersey	14.3
24	Indiana	13.1		13	North Dakota	14.3
20	Iowa	13.4		15	Maryland	14.2
32	Kansas	12.3		16	Michigan	14.1
25	Kentucky	13.0		17	Nebraska	14.0
28	Louisiana	12.8		18	Missouri	13.8
2	Maine	19.0		18	Wisconsin	13.8
15	Maryland	14.2		20	Delaware	13.4
2	Massachusetts	19.0		20	Iowa	13.4
16	Michigan	14.1		22	Montana	13.3
9	Minnesota	15.4		22	New Mexico	13.3
44	Mississippi	10.7		24	Indiana	13.1
18	Missouri	13.8		25	Illinois	13.0
22	Montana	13.3		25	Kentucky	13.0
17	Nebraska	14.0		27	Arkansas	12.9
48	Nevada	7.2		28	Louisiana	12.8
8	New Hampshire	16.2		29	North Carolina	12.5
13	New Jersey	14.3		30	Florida	12.4
22	New Mexico	13.3		30	Tennessee	12.4
5	New York	18.5		32	Kansas	12.3
29	North Carolina	12.5		32	Oregon	12.3
13	North Dakota	14.3		34	Texas	12.2
12	Ohio	14.6		35	Oklahoma	12.1
35	Oklahoma	12.1		36	Alaska	11.9
32	Oregon	12.3		36	Washington	11.9
4	Pennsylvania	18.8		38	Hawaii	11.5
1	Rhode Island	19.8		39	Arizona	11.3
45	South Carolina	10.6		40	California	11.1
11	South Dakota	14.9		40	Utah	11.1
30	Tennessee	12.4		42	Georgia	10.9
34	Texas	12.2		42	Virginia	10.9
40	Utah	11.1		44	Mississippi	10.7
6	Vermont	18.2		45	South Carolina	10.6
42	Virginia	10.9		46	Alabama	10.4
36	Washington	11.9		46	Colorado	10.4
10	West Virginia	15.0		48	Nevada	7.2
18	Wisconsin	13.8		NA	Idaho**	NA
NA	Wyoming**	NA		NA	Wyoming**	NA
					District of Columbia**	NA

Source: CQ Press using data from U.S. Department of Labor, Bureau of Labor Statistics
    "Regional and State Employment and Unemployment" (press release, January 18, 2008)
*Seasonally adjusted preliminary data as of December 2007. National figure calculated through a different formula.
**The Bureau of Labor Statistics does not publish seasonally adjusted figures in this category for these states.

Employees in Financial Activities in 2007

National Total = 8,417,000 Employees*

ALPHA ORDER

RANK	STATE	EMPLOYEES	% of USA
27	Alabama	98,500	1.2%
45	Alaska	14,700	0.2%
14	Arizona	184,300	2.2%
35	Arkansas	54,000	0.6%
1	California	917,400	10.9%
18	Colorado	161,300	1.9%
22	Connecticut	144,300	1.7%
36	Delaware	43,800	0.5%
4	Florida	555,000	6.6%
9	Georgia	231,400	2.7%
NA	Hawaii**	NA	NA
NA	Idaho**	NA	NA
5	Illinois	410,800	4.9%
23	Indiana	140,000	1.7%
26	Iowa	103,600	1.2%
32	Kansas	73,400	0.9%
29	Kentucky	92,200	1.1%
28	Louisiana	97,400	1.2%
40	Maine	33,300	0.4%
19	Maryland	161,100	1.9%
10	Massachusetts	224,400	2.7%
12	Michigan	210,100	2.5%
15	Minnesota	183,000	2.2%
NA	Mississippi**	NA	NA
16	Missouri	165,700	2.0%
43	Montana	23,200	0.3%
33	Nebraska	66,800	0.8%
34	Nevada	65,300	0.8%
37	New Hampshire	40,400	0.5%
8	New Jersey	280,600	3.3%
39	New Mexico	35,500	0.4%
2	New York	740,600	8.8%
11	North Carolina	217,400	2.6%
44	North Dakota	19,800	0.2%
7	Ohio	303,600	3.6%
30	Oklahoma	84,800	1.0%
25	Oregon	105,500	1.3%
6	Pennsylvania	334,300	4.0%
38	Rhode Island	35,800	0.4%
24	South Carolina	106,400	1.3%
41	South Dakota	31,000	0.4%
21	Tennessee	144,900	1.7%
3	Texas	652,100	7.7%
31	Utah	75,600	0.9%
46	Vermont	13,300	0.2%
13	Virginia	199,000	2.4%
20	Washington	157,600	1.9%
42	West Virginia	30,000	0.4%
17	Wisconsin	162,000	1.9%
NA	Wyoming**	NA	NA

RANK ORDER

RANK	STATE	EMPLOYEES	% of USA
1	California	917,400	10.9%
2	New York	740,600	8.8%
3	Texas	652,100	7.7%
4	Florida	555,000	6.6%
5	Illinois	410,800	4.9%
6	Pennsylvania	334,300	4.0%
7	Ohio	303,600	3.6%
8	New Jersey	280,600	3.3%
9	Georgia	231,400	2.7%
10	Massachusetts	224,400	2.7%
11	North Carolina	217,400	2.6%
12	Michigan	210,100	2.5%
13	Virginia	199,000	2.4%
14	Arizona	184,300	2.2%
15	Minnesota	183,000	2.2%
16	Missouri	165,700	2.0%
17	Wisconsin	162,000	1.9%
18	Colorado	161,300	1.9%
19	Maryland	161,100	1.9%
20	Washington	157,600	1.9%
21	Tennessee	144,900	1.7%
22	Connecticut	144,300	1.7%
23	Indiana	140,000	1.7%
24	South Carolina	106,400	1.3%
25	Oregon	105,500	1.3%
26	Iowa	103,600	1.2%
27	Alabama	98,500	1.2%
28	Louisiana	97,400	1.2%
29	Kentucky	92,200	1.1%
30	Oklahoma	84,800	1.0%
31	Utah	75,600	0.9%
32	Kansas	73,400	0.9%
33	Nebraska	66,800	0.8%
34	Nevada	65,300	0.8%
35	Arkansas	54,000	0.6%
36	Delaware	43,800	0.5%
37	New Hampshire	40,400	0.5%
38	Rhode Island	35,800	0.4%
39	New Mexico	35,500	0.4%
40	Maine	33,300	0.4%
41	South Dakota	31,000	0.4%
42	West Virginia	30,000	0.4%
43	Montana	23,200	0.3%
44	North Dakota	19,800	0.2%
45	Alaska	14,700	0.2%
46	Vermont	13,300	0.2%
NA	Hawaii**	NA	NA
NA	Idaho**	NA	NA
NA	Mississippi**	NA	NA
NA	Wyoming**	NA	NA
	District of Columbia	30,800	0.4%

Source: U.S. Department of Labor, Bureau of Labor Statistics
  "Regional and State Employment and Unemployment" (press release, January 18, 2008)
*Seasonally adjusted preliminary data as of December 2007. National total calculated through a different formula. Financial activities include insurance and real estate.
**The Bureau of Labor Statistics does not publish seasonally adjusted figures in this category for these states.

Percent of Nonfarm Employees in Financial Activities in 2007

National Percent = 6.1% of Employees*

ALPHA ORDER

ALPHA ORDER

RANK ORDER

RANK	STATE	PERCENT
39	Alabama	4.9
42	Alaska	4.6
9	Arizona	6.8
43	Arkansas	4.5
19	California	6.0
6	Colorado	6.9
2	Connecticut	8.5
1	Delaware	9.9
9	Florida	6.8
25	Georgia	5.5
NA	Hawaii**	NA
NA	Idaho**	NA
6	Illinois	6.9
41	Indiana	4.7
9	Iowa	6.8
29	Kansas	5.3
36	Kentucky	5.0
36	Louisiana	5.0
28	Maine	5.4
17	Maryland	6.1
9	Massachusetts	6.8
39	Michigan	4.9
14	Minnesota	6.6
NA	Mississippi**	NA
20	Missouri	5.9
33	Montana	5.2
6	Nebraska	6.9
36	Nevada	5.0
16	New Hampshire	6.2
9	New Jersey	6.8
45	New Mexico	4.2
2	New York	8.5
29	North Carolina	5.3
25	North Dakota	5.5
23	Ohio	5.6
29	Oklahoma	5.3
17	Oregon	6.1
22	Pennsylvania	5.7
5	Rhode Island	7.2
25	South Carolina	5.5
4	South Dakota	7.6
35	Tennessee	5.1
15	Texas	6.3
20	Utah	5.9
44	Vermont	4.3
33	Virginia	5.2
29	Washington	5.3
46	West Virginia	3.9
23	Wisconsin	5.6
NA	Wyoming**	NA

RANK	STATE	PERCENT
1	Delaware	9.9
2	Connecticut	8.5
2	New York	8.5
4	South Dakota	7.6
5	Rhode Island	7.2
6	Colorado	6.9
6	Illinois	6.9
6	Nebraska	6.9
9	Arizona	6.8
9	Florida	6.8
9	Iowa	6.8
9	Massachusetts	6.8
9	New Jersey	6.8
14	Minnesota	6.6
15	Texas	6.3
16	New Hampshire	6.2
17	Maryland	6.1
17	Oregon	6.1
19	California	6.0
20	Missouri	5.9
20	Utah	5.9
22	Pennsylvania	5.7
23	Ohio	5.6
23	Wisconsin	5.6
25	Georgia	5.5
25	North Dakota	5.5
25	South Carolina	5.5
28	Maine	5.4
29	Kansas	5.3
29	North Carolina	5.3
29	Oklahoma	5.3
29	Washington	5.3
33	Montana	5.2
33	Virginia	5.2
35	Tennessee	5.1
36	Kentucky	5.0
36	Louisiana	5.0
36	Nevada	5.0
39	Alabama	4.9
39	Michigan	4.9
41	Indiana	4.7
42	Alaska	4.6
43	Arkansas	4.5
44	Vermont	4.3
45	New Mexico	4.2
46	West Virginia	3.9
NA	Hawaii**	NA
NA	Idaho**	NA
NA	Mississippi**	NA
NA	Wyoming**	NA

District of Columbia	4.4

Source: CQ Press using data from U.S. Department of Labor, Bureau of Labor Statistics
    "Regional and State Employment and Unemployment" (press release, January 18, 2008)
*Seasonally adjusted preliminary data as of December 2007. National figure calculated through a different formula. Financial activities include insurance and real estate.
**The Bureau of Labor Statistics does not publish seasonally adjusted figures in this category for these states.

Employees in Government in 2007

National Total = 22,388,000 Employees*

ALPHA ORDER

RANK	STATE	EMPLOYEES	% of USA
22	Alabama	378,200	1.7%
43	Alaska	82,200	0.4%
18	Arizona	419,900	1.9%
33	Arkansas	211,900	0.9%
1	California	2,516,600	11.2%
23	Colorado	376,100	1.7%
31	Connecticut	248,800	1.1%
48	Delaware	60,800	0.3%
4	Florida	1,125,400	5.0%
8	Georgia	690,300	3.1%
39	Hawaii	123,600	0.6%
NA	Idaho**	NA	NA
5	Illinois	843,700	3.8%
17	Indiana	430,000	1.9%
30	Iowa	250,300	1.1%
29	Kansas	260,100	1.2%
26	Kentucky	325,600	1.5%
24	Louisiana	361,500	1.6%
40	Maine	105,200	0.5%
14	Maryland	478,600	2.1%
16	Massachusetts	435,500	1.9%
12	Michigan	647,700	2.9%
21	Minnesota	413,900	1.8%
32	Mississippi	248,300	1.1%
15	Missouri	436,100	1.9%
42	Montana	86,800	0.4%
36	Nebraska	162,100	0.7%
37	Nevada	158,700	0.7%
41	New Hampshire	91,600	0.4%
11	New Jersey	657,600	2.9%
35	New Mexico	197,000	0.9%
3	New York	1,497,000	6.7%
10	North Carolina	676,800	3.0%
44	North Dakota	75,700	0.3%
6	Ohio	800,800	3.6%
27	Oklahoma	324,900	1.5%
28	Oregon	294,900	1.3%
7	Pennsylvania	745,400	3.3%
47	Rhode Island	64,300	0.3%
25	South Carolina	339,900	1.5%
45	South Dakota	75,600	0.3%
20	Tennessee	417,300	1.9%
2	Texas	1,748,400	7.8%
34	Utah	208,400	0.9%
49	Vermont	53,700	0.2%
9	Virginia	686,000	3.1%
13	Washington	531,300	2.4%
38	West Virginia	144,200	0.6%
19	Wisconsin	417,900	1.9%
46	Wyoming	67,000	0.3%

RANK ORDER

RANK	STATE	EMPLOYEES	% of USA
1	California	2,516,600	11.2%
2	Texas	1,748,400	7.8%
3	New York	1,497,000	6.7%
4	Florida	1,125,400	5.0%
5	Illinois	843,700	3.8%
6	Ohio	800,800	3.6%
7	Pennsylvania	745,400	3.3%
8	Georgia	690,300	3.1%
9	Virginia	686,000	3.1%
10	North Carolina	676,800	3.0%
11	New Jersey	657,600	2.9%
12	Michigan	647,700	2.9%
13	Washington	531,300	2.4%
14	Maryland	478,600	2.1%
15	Missouri	436,100	1.9%
16	Massachusetts	435,500	1.9%
17	Indiana	430,000	1.9%
18	Arizona	419,900	1.9%
19	Wisconsin	417,900	1.9%
20	Tennessee	417,300	1.9%
21	Minnesota	413,900	1.8%
22	Alabama	378,200	1.7%
23	Colorado	376,100	1.7%
24	Louisiana	361,500	1.6%
25	South Carolina	339,900	1.5%
26	Kentucky	325,600	1.5%
27	Oklahoma	324,900	1.5%
28	Oregon	294,900	1.3%
29	Kansas	260,100	1.2%
30	Iowa	250,300	1.1%
31	Connecticut	248,800	1.1%
32	Mississippi	248,300	1.1%
33	Arkansas	211,900	0.9%
34	Utah	208,400	0.9%
35	New Mexico	197,000	0.9%
36	Nebraska	162,100	0.7%
37	Nevada	158,700	0.7%
38	West Virginia	144,200	0.6%
39	Hawaii	123,600	0.6%
40	Maine	105,200	0.5%
41	New Hampshire	91,600	0.4%
42	Montana	86,800	0.4%
43	Alaska	82,200	0.4%
44	North Dakota	75,700	0.3%
45	South Dakota	75,600	0.3%
46	Wyoming	67,000	0.3%
47	Rhode Island	64,300	0.3%
48	Delaware	60,800	0.3%
49	Vermont	53,700	0.2%
NA	Idaho**	NA	NA
	District of Columbia	234,200	1.0%

Source: U.S. Department of Labor, Bureau of Labor Statistics
    "Regional and State Employment and Unemployment" (press release, January 18, 2008)
*Seasonally adjusted preliminary data as of December 2007. National total calculated through a different formula.
**The Bureau of Labor Statistics does not publish seasonally adjusted figures in this category for this state.

Percent of Nonfarm Employees in Government in 2007

National Percent = 16.2% of Employees*

ALPHA ORDER				RANK ORDER		
RANK	STATE	PERCENT		RANK	STATE	PERCENT
11	Alabama	18.7		1	Alaska	25.9
1	Alaska	25.9		2	New Mexico	23.2
34	Arizona	15.4		3	Wyoming	23.0
17	Arkansas	17.5		4	Mississippi	21.2
26	California	16.5		5	North Dakota	21.0
31	Colorado	16.0		6	Oklahoma	20.5
39	Connecticut	14.6		7	Hawaii	19.6
44	Delaware	13.8		8	Montana	19.3
44	Florida	13.8		9	West Virginia	18.9
26	Georgia	16.5		10	Kansas	18.8
7	Hawaii	19.6		11	Alabama	18.7
NA	Idaho**	NA		11	Louisiana	18.7
42	Illinois	14.1		13	South Dakota	18.5
40	Indiana	14.4		14	Maryland	18.2
28	Iowa	16.4		15	Virginia	18.0
10	Kansas	18.8		15	Washington	18.0
17	Kentucky	17.5		17	Arkansas	17.5
11	Louisiana	18.7		17	Kentucky	17.5
22	Maine	17.0		17	South Carolina	17.5
14	Maryland	18.2		20	Vermont	17.4
46	Massachusetts	13.3		21	New York	17.2
35	Michigan	15.2		22	Maine	17.0
36	Minnesota	15.0		22	Oregon	17.0
4	Mississippi	21.2		24	Texas	16.8
33	Missouri	15.6		25	Nebraska	16.7
8	Montana	19.3		26	California	16.5
25	Nebraska	16.7		26	Georgia	16.5
49	Nevada	12.1		28	Iowa	16.4
42	New Hampshire	14.1		28	North Carolina	16.4
31	New Jersey	16.0		28	Utah	16.4
2	New Mexico	23.2		31	Colorado	16.0
21	New York	17.2		31	New Jersey	16.0
28	North Carolina	16.4		33	Missouri	15.6
5	North Dakota	21.0		34	Arizona	15.4
37	Ohio	14.8		35	Michigan	15.2
6	Oklahoma	20.5		36	Minnesota	15.0
22	Oregon	17.0		37	Ohio	14.8
48	Pennsylvania	12.8		37	Tennessee	14.8
47	Rhode Island	12.9		39	Connecticut	14.6
17	South Carolina	17.5		40	Indiana	14.4
13	South Dakota	18.5		40	Wisconsin	14.4
37	Tennessee	14.8		42	Illinois	14.1
24	Texas	16.8		42	New Hampshire	14.1
28	Utah	16.4		44	Delaware	13.8
20	Vermont	17.4		44	Florida	13.8
15	Virginia	18.0		46	Massachusetts	13.3
15	Washington	18.0		47	Rhode Island	12.9
9	West Virginia	18.9		48	Pennsylvania	12.8
40	Wisconsin	14.4		49	Nevada	12.1
3	Wyoming	23.0		NA	Idaho**	NA
					District of Columbia	33.3

Source: CQ Press using data from U.S. Department of Labor, Bureau of Labor Statistics
"Regional and State Employment and Unemployment" (press release, January 18, 2008)
*Seasonally adjusted preliminary data as of December 2007. National figure calculated through a different formula.
**The Bureau of Labor Statistics does not publish seasonally adjusted figures in this category for this state.

Employees in Leisure and Hospitality in 2007

National Total = 13,734,000 Employees*

ALPHA ORDER

RANK	STATE	EMPLOYEES	% of USA
26	Alabama	176,100	1.3%
49	Alaska	31,100	0.2%
17	Arizona	282,600	2.1%
36	Arkansas	101,500	0.7%
1	California	1,574,400	11.5%
20	Colorado	274,400	2.0%
31	Connecticut	135,100	1.0%
45	Delaware	41,600	0.3%
3	Florida	943,500	6.9%
9	Georgia	396,700	2.9%
35	Hawaii	109,900	0.8%
NA	Idaho**	NA	NA
5	Illinois	538,700	3.9%
16	Indiana	284,200	2.1%
30	Iowa	136,400	1.0%
33	Kansas	117,600	0.9%
28	Kentucky	169,400	1.2%
25	Louisiana	199,500	1.5%
41	Maine	60,900	0.4%
23	Maryland	239,900	1.7%
14	Massachusetts	300,700	2.2%
8	Michigan	407,500	3.0%
22	Minnesota	249,500	1.8%
32	Mississippi	125,900	0.9%
15	Missouri	288,900	2.1%
42	Montana	57,700	0.4%
38	Nebraska	83,800	0.6%
12	Nevada	346,100	2.5%
40	New Hampshire	63,800	0.5%
13	New Jersey	342,200	2.5%
37	New Mexico	88,200	0.6%
4	New York	691,800	5.0%
10	North Carolina	392,700	2.9%
48	North Dakota	32,200	0.2%
7	Ohio	496,100	3.6%
29	Oklahoma	138,900	1.0%
27	Oregon	175,500	1.3%
6	Pennsylvania	500,400	3.6%
43	Rhode Island	51,600	0.4%
24	South Carolina	216,200	1.6%
44	South Dakota	42,800	0.3%
19	Tennessee	281,500	2.0%
2	Texas	1,001,700	7.3%
34	Utah	113,800	0.8%
47	Vermont	33,700	0.2%
11	Virginia	348,000	2.5%
18	Washington	281,800	2.1%
39	West Virginia	71,900	0.5%
21	Wisconsin	267,600	1.9%
46	Wyoming	34,000	0.2%

RANK ORDER

RANK	STATE	EMPLOYEES	% of USA
1	California	1,574,400	11.5%
2	Texas	1,001,700	7.3%
3	Florida	943,500	6.9%
4	New York	691,800	5.0%
5	Illinois	538,700	3.9%
6	Pennsylvania	500,400	3.6%
7	Ohio	496,100	3.6%
8	Michigan	407,500	3.0%
9	Georgia	396,700	2.9%
10	North Carolina	392,700	2.9%
11	Virginia	348,000	2.5%
12	Nevada	346,100	2.5%
13	New Jersey	342,200	2.5%
14	Massachusetts	300,700	2.2%
15	Missouri	288,900	2.1%
16	Indiana	284,200	2.1%
17	Arizona	282,600	2.1%
18	Washington	281,800	2.1%
19	Tennessee	281,500	2.0%
20	Colorado	274,400	2.0%
21	Wisconsin	267,600	1.9%
22	Minnesota	249,500	1.8%
23	Maryland	239,900	1.7%
24	South Carolina	216,200	1.6%
25	Louisiana	199,500	1.5%
26	Alabama	176,100	1.3%
27	Oregon	175,500	1.3%
28	Kentucky	169,400	1.2%
29	Oklahoma	138,900	1.0%
30	Iowa	136,400	1.0%
31	Connecticut	135,100	1.0%
32	Mississippi	125,900	0.9%
33	Kansas	117,600	0.9%
34	Utah	113,800	0.8%
35	Hawaii	109,900	0.8%
36	Arkansas	101,500	0.7%
37	New Mexico	88,200	0.6%
38	Nebraska	83,800	0.6%
39	West Virginia	71,900	0.5%
40	New Hampshire	63,800	0.5%
41	Maine	60,900	0.4%
42	Montana	57,700	0.4%
43	Rhode Island	51,600	0.4%
44	South Dakota	42,800	0.3%
45	Delaware	41,600	0.3%
46	Wyoming	34,000	0.2%
47	Vermont	33,700	0.2%
48	North Dakota	32,200	0.2%
49	Alaska	31,100	0.2%
NA	Idaho**	NA	NA
	District of Columbia	55,000	0.4%

Source: U.S. Department of Labor, Bureau of Labor Statistics
   "Regional and State Employment and Unemployment" (press release, January 18, 2008)
*Seasonally adjusted preliminary data as of December 2007. National total calculated through a different formula.
**The Bureau of Labor Statistics does not publish seasonally adjusted figures in this category for this state.

Percent of Nonfarm Employees in Leisure and Hospitality in 2007

National Percent = 9.9% of Employees*

ALPHA ORDER

RANK	STATE	PERCENT
42	Alabama	8.7
19	Alaska	9.8
11	Arizona	10.4
46	Arkansas	8.4
13	California	10.3
4	Colorado	11.7
48	Connecticut	7.9
28	Delaware	9.4
6	Florida	11.6
25	Georgia	9.5
2	Hawaii	17.4
NA	Idaho**	NA
36	Illinois	9.0
25	Indiana	9.5
38	Iowa	8.9
45	Kansas	8.5
32	Kentucky	9.1
13	Louisiana	10.3
19	Maine	9.8
32	Maryland	9.1
31	Massachusetts	9.2
22	Michigan	9.6
36	Minnesota	9.0
9	Mississippi	10.7
13	Missouri	10.3
3	Montana	12.8
43	Nebraska	8.6
1	Nevada	26.5
19	New Hampshire	9.8
47	New Jersey	8.3
11	New Mexico	10.4
48	New York	7.9
25	North Carolina	9.5
38	North Dakota	8.9
32	Ohio	9.1
41	Oklahoma	8.8
17	Oregon	10.1
43	Pennsylvania	8.6
13	Rhode Island	10.3
7	South Carolina	11.2
10	South Dakota	10.5
18	Tennessee	10.0
22	Texas	9.6
38	Utah	8.9
8	Vermont	10.9
32	Virginia	9.1
22	Washington	9.6
28	West Virginia	9.4
30	Wisconsin	9.3
4	Wyoming	11.7

RANK ORDER

RANK	STATE	PERCENT
1	Nevada	26.5
2	Hawaii	17.4
3	Montana	12.8
4	Colorado	11.7
4	Wyoming	11.7
6	Florida	11.6
7	South Carolina	11.2
8	Vermont	10.9
9	Mississippi	10.7
10	South Dakota	10.5
11	Arizona	10.4
11	New Mexico	10.4
13	California	10.3
13	Louisiana	10.3
13	Missouri	10.3
13	Rhode Island	10.3
17	Oregon	10.1
18	Tennessee	10.0
19	Alaska	9.8
19	Maine	9.8
19	New Hampshire	9.8
22	Michigan	9.6
22	Texas	9.6
22	Washington	9.6
25	Georgia	9.5
25	Indiana	9.5
25	North Carolina	9.5
28	Delaware	9.4
28	West Virginia	9.4
30	Wisconsin	9.3
31	Massachusetts	9.2
32	Kentucky	9.1
32	Maryland	9.1
32	Ohio	9.1
32	Virginia	9.1
36	Illinois	9.0
36	Minnesota	9.0
38	Iowa	8.9
38	North Dakota	8.9
38	Utah	8.9
41	Oklahoma	8.8
42	Alabama	8.7
43	Nebraska	8.6
43	Pennsylvania	8.6
45	Kansas	8.5
46	Arkansas	8.4
47	New Jersey	8.3
48	Connecticut	7.9
48	New York	7.9
NA	Idaho**	NA

District of Columbia 7.8

Source: CQ Press using data from U.S. Department of Labor, Bureau of Labor Statistics
   "Regional and State Employment and Unemployment" (press release, January 18, 2008)
*Seasonally adjusted preliminary data as of December 2007. National figure calculated through a different formula.
**The Bureau of Labor Statistics does not publish seasonally adjusted figures in this category for this state.

Employees in Manufacturing in 2007

National Total = 13,919,000 Employees*

ALPHA ORDER

RANK	STATE	EMPLOYEES	% of USA
NA	Alabama**	NA	NA
45	Alaska	12,800	0.1%
27	Arizona	186,500	1.3%
25	Arkansas	187,400	1.3%
1	California	1,492,600	10.7%
30	Colorado	142,800	1.0%
24	Connecticut	190,600	1.4%
NA	Delaware**	NA	NA
12	Florida	390,200	2.8%
11	Georgia	431,800	3.1%
NA	Hawaii**	NA	NA
35	Idaho	63,600	0.5%
4	Illinois	673,100	4.8%
7	Indiana	553,900	4.0%
22	Iowa	230,500	1.7%
26	Kansas	186,900	1.3%
20	Kentucky	252,700	1.8%
29	Louisiana	154,000	1.1%
37	Maine	57,800	0.4%
31	Maryland	133,800	1.0%
18	Massachusetts	294,000	2.1%
6	Michigan	605,900	4.4%
14	Minnesota	336,400	2.4%
28	Mississippi	172,000	1.2%
17	Missouri	294,400	2.1%
44	Montana	20,900	0.2%
33	Nebraska	101,400	0.7%
38	Nevada	51,800	0.4%
34	New Hampshire	74,800	0.5%
15	New Jersey	315,900	2.3%
41	New Mexico	36,400	0.3%
8	New York	541,000	3.9%
9	North Carolina	540,000	3.9%
43	North Dakota	26,000	0.2%
3	Ohio	774,300	5.6%
NA	Oklahoma**	NA	NA
23	Oregon	204,400	1.5%
5	Pennsylvania	655,300	4.7%
39	Rhode Island	50,200	0.4%
21	South Carolina	240,100	1.7%
40	South Dakota	42,800	0.3%
13	Tennessee	387,100	2.8%
2	Texas	927,400	6.7%
32	Utah	129,400	0.9%
42	Vermont	35,500	0.3%
19	Virginia	285,500	2.1%
16	Washington	295,500	2.1%
36	West Virginia	58,600	0.4%
10	Wisconsin	496,400	3.6%
NA	Wyoming**	NA	NA

RANK ORDER

RANK	STATE	EMPLOYEES	% of USA
1	California	1,492,600	10.7%
2	Texas	927,400	6.7%
3	Ohio	774,300	5.6%
4	Illinois	673,100	4.8%
5	Pennsylvania	655,300	4.7%
6	Michigan	605,900	4.4%
7	Indiana	553,900	4.0%
8	New York	541,000	3.9%
9	North Carolina	540,000	3.9%
10	Wisconsin	496,400	3.6%
11	Georgia	431,800	3.1%
12	Florida	390,200	2.8%
13	Tennessee	387,100	2.8%
14	Minnesota	336,400	2.4%
15	New Jersey	315,900	2.3%
16	Washington	295,500	2.1%
17	Missouri	294,400	2.1%
18	Massachusetts	294,000	2.1%
19	Virginia	285,500	2.1%
20	Kentucky	252,700	1.8%
21	South Carolina	240,100	1.7%
22	Iowa	230,500	1.7%
23	Oregon	204,400	1.5%
24	Connecticut	190,600	1.4%
25	Arkansas	187,400	1.3%
26	Kansas	186,900	1.3%
27	Arizona	186,500	1.3%
28	Mississippi	172,000	1.2%
29	Louisiana	154,000	1.1%
30	Colorado	142,800	1.0%
31	Maryland	133,800	1.0%
32	Utah	129,400	0.9%
33	Nebraska	101,400	0.7%
34	New Hampshire	74,800	0.5%
35	Idaho	63,600	0.5%
36	West Virginia	58,600	0.4%
37	Maine	57,800	0.4%
38	Nevada	51,800	0.4%
39	Rhode Island	50,200	0.4%
40	South Dakota	42,800	0.3%
41	New Mexico	36,400	0.3%
42	Vermont	35,500	0.3%
43	North Dakota	26,000	0.2%
44	Montana	20,900	0.2%
45	Alaska	12,800	0.1%
NA	Alabama**	NA	NA
NA	Delaware**	NA	NA
NA	Hawaii**	NA	NA
NA	Oklahoma**	NA	NA
NA	Wyoming**	NA	NA
	District of Columbia**	NA	NA

Source: U.S. Department of Labor, Bureau of Labor Statistics
"Regional and State Employment and Unemployment" (press release, January 18, 2008)
*Seasonally adjusted preliminary data as of December 2007. National total calculated through a different formula.
**The Bureau of Labor Statistics does not publish seasonally adjusted figures in this category for these states.

Percent of Nonfarm Employees in Manufacturing in 2007

National Percent = 10.1% of Employees*

ALPHA ORDER				RANK ORDER		
RANK	STATE	PERCENT		RANK	STATE	PERCENT
NA	Alabama**	NA		1	Indiana	18.5
44	Alaska	4.0		2	Wisconsin	17.2
37	Arizona	6.9		3	Arkansas	15.5
3	Arkansas	15.5		4	Iowa	15.1
27	California	9.8		5	Mississippi	14.7
39	Colorado	6.1		6	Michigan	14.3
18	Connecticut	11.2		6	Ohio	14.3
NA	Delaware**	NA		8	Tennessee	13.7
41	Florida	4.8		9	Kentucky	13.6
23	Georgia	10.4		10	Kansas	13.5
NA	Hawaii**	NA		11	North Carolina	13.1
28	Idaho	9.6		12	South Carolina	12.4
18	Illinois	11.2		13	Minnesota	12.2
1	Indiana	18.5		14	Oregon	11.8
4	Iowa	15.1		15	New Hampshire	11.5
10	Kansas	13.5		15	Vermont	11.5
9	Kentucky	13.6		17	Pennsylvania	11.3
32	Louisiana	8.0		18	Connecticut	11.2
29	Maine	9.3		18	Illinois	11.2
40	Maryland	5.1		20	Missouri	10.5
30	Massachusetts	9.0		20	Nebraska	10.5
6	Michigan	14.3		20	South Dakota	10.5
13	Minnesota	12.2		23	Georgia	10.4
5	Mississippi	14.7		24	Utah	10.2
20	Missouri	10.5		25	Rhode Island	10.1
42	Montana	4.6		26	Washington	10.0
20	Nebraska	10.5		27	California	9.8
44	Nevada	4.0		28	Idaho	9.6
15	New Hampshire	11.5		29	Maine	9.3
33	New Jersey	7.7		30	Massachusetts	9.0
43	New Mexico	4.3		31	Texas	8.9
38	New York	6.2		32	Louisiana	8.0
11	North Carolina	13.1		33	New Jersey	7.7
36	North Dakota	7.2		33	West Virginia	7.7
6	Ohio	14.3		35	Virginia	7.5
NA	Oklahoma**	NA		36	North Dakota	7.2
14	Oregon	11.8		37	Arizona	6.9
17	Pennsylvania	11.3		38	New York	6.2
25	Rhode Island	10.1		39	Colorado	6.1
12	South Carolina	12.4		40	Maryland	5.1
20	South Dakota	10.5		41	Florida	4.8
8	Tennessee	13.7		42	Montana	4.6
31	Texas	8.9		43	New Mexico	4.3
24	Utah	10.2		44	Alaska	4.0
15	Vermont	11.5		44	Nevada	4.0
35	Virginia	7.5		NA	Alabama**	NA
26	Washington	10.0		NA	Delaware**	NA
33	West Virginia	7.7		NA	Hawaii**	NA
2	Wisconsin	17.2		NA	Oklahoma**	NA
NA	Wyoming**	NA		NA	Wyoming**	NA
					District of Columbia**	NA

Source: CQ Press using data from U.S. Department of Labor, Bureau of Labor Statistics
    "Regional and State Employment and Unemployment" (press release, January 18, 2008)
*Seasonally adjusted preliminary data as of December 2007. National figure calculated through a different formula.
**The Bureau of Labor Statistics does not publish seasonally adjusted figures in this category for these states.

Employees in Natural Resources and Mining in 2007

National Total = 734,000 Employees*

ALPHA ORDER

RANK	STATE	EMPLOYEES	% of USA
12	Alabama	13,000	1.8%
11	Alaska	14,200	1.9%
13	Arizona	12,400	1.7%
20	Arkansas	9,700	1.3%
7	California	25,900	3.5%
6	Colorado	26,900	3.7%
45	Connecticut	700	0.1%
NA	Delaware**	NA	NA
29	Florida	6,400	0.9%
15	Georgia	11,900	1.6%
NA	Hawaii**	NA	NA
34	Idaho	4,900	0.7%
19	Illinois	10,300	1.4%
27	Indiana	6,900	0.9%
39	Iowa	2,000	0.3%
22	Kansas	8,800	1.2%
8	Kentucky	24,200	3.3%
2	Louisiana	50,600	6.9%
38	Maine	2,900	0.4%
NA	Maryland**	NA	NA
40	Massachusetts	1,800	0.2%
26	Michigan	7,500	1.0%
31	Minnesota	5,500	0.7%
20	Mississippi	9,700	1.3%
33	Missouri	5,200	0.7%
23	Montana	8,600	1.2%
NA	Nebraska**	NA	NA
14	Nevada	12,000	1.6%
43	New Hampshire	900	0.1%
40	New Jersey	1,800	0.2%
10	New Mexico	20,000	2.7%
30	New York	5,800	0.8%
28	North Carolina	6,800	0.9%
32	North Dakota	5,300	0.7%
18	Ohio	11,200	1.5%
3	Oklahoma	47,500	6.5%
24	Oregon	8,400	1.1%
9	Pennsylvania	21,800	3.0%
46	Rhode Island	300	0.0%
35	South Carolina	4,800	0.7%
43	South Dakota	900	0.1%
36	Tennessee	4,200	0.6%
1	Texas	209,600	28.6%
16	Utah	11,500	1.6%
42	Vermont	1,000	0.1%
17	Virginia	11,400	1.6%
25	Washington	7,900	1.1%
4	West Virginia	29,600	4.0%
37	Wisconsin	3,700	0.5%
5	Wyoming	27,400	3.7%

RANK ORDER

RANK	STATE	EMPLOYEES	% of USA
1	Texas	209,600	28.6%
2	Louisiana	50,600	6.9%
3	Oklahoma	47,500	6.5%
4	West Virginia	29,600	4.0%
5	Wyoming	27,400	3.7%
6	Colorado	26,900	3.7%
7	California	25,900	3.5%
8	Kentucky	24,200	3.3%
9	Pennsylvania	21,800	3.0%
10	New Mexico	20,000	2.7%
11	Alaska	14,200	1.9%
12	Alabama	13,000	1.8%
13	Arizona	12,400	1.7%
14	Nevada	12,000	1.6%
15	Georgia	11,900	1.6%
16	Utah	11,500	1.6%
17	Virginia	11,400	1.6%
18	Ohio	11,200	1.5%
19	Illinois	10,300	1.4%
20	Arkansas	9,700	1.3%
20	Mississippi	9,700	1.3%
22	Kansas	8,800	1.2%
23	Montana	8,600	1.2%
24	Oregon	8,400	1.1%
25	Washington	7,900	1.1%
26	Michigan	7,500	1.0%
27	Indiana	6,900	0.9%
28	North Carolina	6,800	0.9%
29	Florida	6,400	0.9%
30	New York	5,800	0.8%
31	Minnesota	5,500	0.7%
32	North Dakota	5,300	0.7%
33	Missouri	5,200	0.7%
34	Idaho	4,900	0.7%
35	South Carolina	4,800	0.7%
36	Tennessee	4,200	0.6%
37	Wisconsin	3,700	0.5%
38	Maine	2,900	0.4%
39	Iowa	2,000	0.3%
40	Massachusetts	1,800	0.2%
40	New Jersey	1,800	0.2%
42	Vermont	1,000	0.1%
43	New Hampshire	900	0.1%
43	South Dakota	900	0.1%
45	Connecticut	700	0.1%
46	Rhode Island	300	0.0%
NA	Delaware**	NA	NA
NA	Hawaii**	NA	NA
NA	Maryland**	NA	NA
NA	Nebraska**	NA	NA
	District of Columbia**	NA	NA

Source: U.S. Department of Labor, Bureau of Labor Statistics
  "Regional and State Employment and Unemployment" (press release, January 18, 2008)
*Not seasonally adjusted preliminary data as of December 2007. National total calculated through a different formula.
**Natural resources and mining is combined with construction for these states.

Percent of Nonfarm Employees in Natural Resources and Mining in 2007

National Percent = 0.5% of Employees*

RANK	STATE	PERCENT
17	Alabama	0.6
2	Alaska	4.5
19	Arizona	0.5
14	Arkansas	0.8
27	California	0.2
11	Colorado	1.1
45	Connecticut	0.0
NA	Delaware**	NA
37	Florida	0.1
23	Georgia	0.3
NA	Hawaii**	NA
16	Idaho	0.7
27	Illinois	0.2
27	Indiana	0.2
37	Iowa	0.1
17	Kansas	0.6
10	Kentucky	1.3
5	Louisiana	2.6
19	Maine	0.5
NA	Maryland**	NA
37	Massachusetts	0.1
27	Michigan	0.2
27	Minnesota	0.2
14	Mississippi	0.8
27	Missouri	0.2
8	Montana	1.9
NA	Nebraska**	NA
12	Nevada	0.9
37	New Hampshire	0.1
45	New Jersey	0.0
6	New Mexico	2.4
37	New York	0.1
27	North Carolina	0.2
9	North Dakota	1.5
27	Ohio	0.2
4	Oklahoma	3.0
19	Oregon	0.5
22	Pennsylvania	0.4
37	Rhode Island	0.1
27	South Carolina	0.2
27	South Dakota	0.2
37	Tennessee	0.1
7	Texas	2.0
12	Utah	0.9
23	Vermont	0.3
23	Virginia	0.3
23	Washington	0.3
3	West Virginia	3.9
37	Wisconsin	0.1
1	Wyoming	9.4

RANK	STATE	PERCENT
1	Wyoming	9.4
2	Alaska	4.5
3	West Virginia	3.9
4	Oklahoma	3.0
5	Louisiana	2.6
6	New Mexico	2.4
7	Texas	2.0
8	Montana	1.9
9	North Dakota	1.5
10	Kentucky	1.3
11	Colorado	1.1
12	Nevada	0.9
12	Utah	0.9
14	Arkansas	0.8
14	Mississippi	0.8
16	Idaho	0.7
17	Alabama	0.6
17	Kansas	0.6
19	Arizona	0.5
19	Maine	0.5
19	Oregon	0.5
22	Pennsylvania	0.4
23	Georgia	0.3
23	Vermont	0.3
23	Virginia	0.3
23	Washington	0.3
27	California	0.2
27	Illinois	0.2
27	Indiana	0.2
27	Michigan	0.2
27	Minnesota	0.2
27	Missouri	0.2
27	North Carolina	0.2
27	Ohio	0.2
27	South Carolina	0.2
27	South Dakota	0.2
37	Florida	0.1
37	Iowa	0.1
37	Massachusetts	0.1
37	New Hampshire	0.1
37	New York	0.1
37	Rhode Island	0.1
37	Tennessee	0.1
37	Wisconsin	0.1
45	Connecticut	0.0
45	New Jersey	0.0
NA	Delaware**	NA
NA	Hawaii**	NA
NA	Maryland**	NA
NA	Nebraska**	NA
	District of Columbia**	NA

Source: CQ Press using data from U.S. Department of Labor, Bureau of Labor Statistics
  "Regional and State Employment and Unemployment" (press release, January 18, 2008)
*Not seasonally adjusted preliminary data as of December 2007. National figure calculated through a different formula.
**Natural resources and mining is combined with construction for these states.

Employees in Professional and Business Services in 2007

National Total = 18,106,000 Employees*

ALPHA ORDER					RANK ORDER			
RANK	STATE	EMPLOYEES	% of USA		RANK	STATE	EMPLOYEES	% of USA
23	Alabama	224,300	1.2%		1	California	2,280,200	12.6%
46	Alaska	24,800	0.1%		2	Florida	1,374,900	7.6%
14	Arizona	417,800	2.3%		3	Texas	1,308,800	7.2%
34	Arkansas	118,500	0.7%		4	New York	1,139,400	6.3%
1	California	2,280,200	12.6%		5	Illinois	881,800	4.9%
16	Colorado	351,600	1.9%		6	Pennsylvania	699,100	3.9%
25	Connecticut	210,500	1.2%		7	Ohio	667,600	3.7%
38	Delaware	64,100	0.4%		8	Virginia	652,100	3.6%
2	Florida	1,374,900	7.6%		9	New Jersey	620,500	3.4%
11	Georgia	564,600	3.1%		10	Michigan	586,100	3.2%
NA	Hawaii**	NA	NA		11	Georgia	564,600	3.1%
NA	Idaho**	NA	NA		12	North Carolina	497,500	2.7%
5	Illinois	881,800	4.9%		13	Massachusetts	484,900	2.7%
21	Indiana	283,500	1.6%		14	Arizona	417,800	2.3%
33	Iowa	121,100	0.7%		15	Maryland	406,800	2.2%
32	Kansas	144,100	0.8%		16	Colorado	351,600	1.9%
28	Kentucky	182,000	1.0%		17	Washington	346,300	1.9%
26	Louisiana	200,900	1.1%		18	Missouri	334,000	1.8%
42	Maine	53,100	0.3%		19	Minnesota	324,000	1.8%
15	Maryland	406,800	2.2%		20	Tennessee	323,900	1.8%
13	Massachusetts	484,900	2.7%		21	Indiana	283,500	1.6%
10	Michigan	586,100	3.2%		22	Wisconsin	283,000	1.6%
19	Minnesota	324,000	1.8%		23	Alabama	224,300	1.2%
37	Mississippi	98,000	0.5%		24	South Carolina	220,300	1.2%
18	Missouri	334,000	1.8%		25	Connecticut	210,500	1.2%
43	Montana	42,500	0.2%		26	Louisiana	200,900	1.1%
36	Nebraska	108,300	0.6%		27	Oregon	195,500	1.1%
31	Nevada	159,800	0.9%		28	Kentucky	182,000	1.0%
39	New Hampshire	63,000	0.3%		29	Oklahoma	180,200	1.0%
9	New Jersey	620,500	3.4%		30	Utah	164,400	0.9%
35	New Mexico	108,400	0.6%		31	Nevada	159,800	0.9%
4	New York	1,139,400	6.3%		32	Kansas	144,100	0.8%
12	North Carolina	497,500	2.7%		33	Iowa	121,100	0.7%
44	North Dakota	30,800	0.2%		34	Arkansas	118,500	0.7%
7	Ohio	667,600	3.7%		35	New Mexico	108,400	0.6%
29	Oklahoma	180,200	1.0%		36	Nebraska	108,300	0.6%
27	Oregon	195,500	1.1%		37	Mississippi	98,000	0.5%
6	Pennsylvania	699,100	3.9%		38	Delaware	64,100	0.4%
41	Rhode Island	58,900	0.3%		39	New Hampshire	63,000	0.3%
24	South Carolina	220,300	1.2%		40	West Virginia	61,400	0.3%
45	South Dakota	27,900	0.2%		41	Rhode Island	58,900	0.3%
20	Tennessee	323,900	1.8%		42	Maine	53,100	0.3%
3	Texas	1,308,800	7.2%		43	Montana	42,500	0.2%
30	Utah	164,400	0.9%		44	North Dakota	30,800	0.2%
47	Vermont	22,600	0.1%		45	South Dakota	27,900	0.2%
8	Virginia	652,100	3.6%		46	Alaska	24,800	0.1%
17	Washington	346,300	1.9%		47	Vermont	22,600	0.1%
40	West Virginia	61,400	0.3%		48	Wyoming	18,600	0.1%
22	Wisconsin	283,000	1.6%		NA	Hawaii**	NA	NA
48	Wyoming	18,600	0.1%		NA	Idaho**	NA	NA
						District of Columbia	161,100	0.9%

Source: U.S. Department of Labor, Bureau of Labor Statistics
   "Regional and State Employment and Unemployment" (press release, January 18, 2008)
*Seasonally adjusted preliminary data as of December 2007. National total calculated through a different formula.
**The Bureau of Labor Statistics does not publish seasonally adjusted figures in this category for these states.

Percent of Nonfarm Employees in Professional and Business Services in 2007

National Percent = 13.1% of Employees*

ALPHA ORDER			RANK ORDER		
RANK	**STATE**	**PERCENT**	**RANK**	**STATE**	**PERCENT**
31	Alabama	11.1	1	Virginia	17.1
45	Alaska	7.8	2	Florida	16.9
3	Arizona	15.4	3	Arizona	15.4
34	Arkansas	9.8	3	Maryland	15.4
7	California	14.9	5	New Jersey	15.1
6	Colorado	15.0	6	Colorado	15.0
17	Connecticut	12.4	7	California	14.9
10	Delaware	14.5	8	Massachusetts	14.8
2	Florida	16.9	9	Illinois	14.7
12	Georgia	13.5	10	Delaware	14.5
NA	Hawaii**	NA	11	Michigan	13.8
NA	Idaho**	NA	12	Georgia	13.5
9	Illinois	14.7	13	New York	13.1
38	Indiana	9.5	14	Utah	12.9
44	Iowa	7.9	15	New Mexico	12.8
32	Kansas	10.4	16	Texas	12.6
34	Kentucky	9.8	17	Connecticut	12.4
32	Louisiana	10.4	18	Ohio	12.3
40	Maine	8.6	19	Nevada	12.2
3	Maryland	15.4	20	North Carolina	12.0
8	Massachusetts	14.8	20	Pennsylvania	12.0
11	Michigan	13.8	22	Missouri	11.9
24	Minnesota	11.7	23	Rhode Island	11.8
42	Mississippi	8.4	24	Minnesota	11.7
22	Missouri	11.9	24	Washington	11.7
38	Montana	9.5	26	Tennessee	11.5
29	Nebraska	11.2	27	Oklahoma	11.4
19	Nevada	12.2	27	South Carolina	11.4
37	New Hampshire	9.7	29	Nebraska	11.2
5	New Jersey	15.1	29	Oregon	11.2
15	New Mexico	12.8	31	Alabama	11.1
13	New York	13.1	32	Kansas	10.4
20	North Carolina	12.0	32	Louisiana	10.4
41	North Dakota	8.5	34	Arkansas	9.8
18	Ohio	12.3	34	Kentucky	9.8
27	Oklahoma	11.4	34	Wisconsin	9.8
29	Oregon	11.2	37	New Hampshire	9.7
20	Pennsylvania	12.0	38	Indiana	9.5
23	Rhode Island	11.8	38	Montana	9.5
27	South Carolina	11.4	40	Maine	8.6
47	South Dakota	6.8	41	North Dakota	8.5
26	Tennessee	11.5	42	Mississippi	8.4
16	Texas	12.6	43	West Virginia	8.0
14	Utah	12.9	44	Iowa	7.9
46	Vermont	7.3	45	Alaska	7.8
1	Virginia	17.1	46	Vermont	7.3
24	Washington	11.7	47	South Dakota	6.8
43	West Virginia	8.0	48	Wyoming	6.4
34	Wisconsin	9.8	NA	Hawaii**	NA
48	Wyoming	6.4	NA	Idaho**	NA

District of Columbia   22.9

Source: CQ Press using data from U.S. Department of Labor, Bureau of Labor Statistics
     "Regional and State Employment and Unemployment" (press release, January 18, 2008)
*Seasonally adjusted preliminary data as of December 2007. National figure calculated through a different formula.
**The Bureau of Labor Statistics does not publish seasonally adjusted figures in this category for these states.

Employees in Trade, Transportation and Public Utilities in 2007

National Total = 26,526,000 Employees*

ALPHA ORDER

RANK	STATE	EMPLOYEES	% of USA
23	Alabama	397,000	1.5%
48	Alaska	63,900	0.2%
20	Arizona	531,000	2.0%
33	Arkansas	248,500	0.9%
1	California	2,894,600	10.9%
22	Colorado	434,000	1.6%
28	Connecticut	312,700	1.2%
44	Delaware	82,700	0.3%
3	Florida	1,610,900	6.1%
8	Georgia	886,800	3.3%
42	Hawaii	120,600	0.5%
40	Idaho	133,000	0.5%
5	Illinois	1,202,000	4.5%
14	Indiana	591,400	2.2%
29	Iowa	312,200	1.2%
31	Kansas	264,900	1.0%
25	Kentucky	379,300	1.4%
24	Louisiana	384,700	1.5%
41	Maine	127,100	0.5%
21	Maryland	478,000	1.8%
15	Massachusetts	572,700	2.2%
10	Michigan	781,200	2.9%
19	Minnesota	534,200	2.0%
35	Mississippi	231,500	0.9%
17	Missouri	552,600	2.1%
43	Montana	92,000	0.3%
36	Nebraska	204,200	0.8%
34	Nevada	232,200	0.9%
38	New Hampshire	144,600	0.5%
9	New Jersey	876,300	3.3%
37	New Mexico	144,700	0.5%
4	New York	1,512,900	5.7%
11	North Carolina	770,500	2.9%
47	North Dakota	77,400	0.3%
7	Ohio	1,044,800	3.9%
30	Oklahoma	287,900	1.1%
27	Oregon	343,200	1.3%
6	Pennsylvania	1,135,900	4.3%
46	Rhode Island	80,100	0.3%
26	South Carolina	375,100	1.4%
45	South Dakota	81,400	0.3%
13	Tennessee	615,000	2.3%
2	Texas	2,078,300	7.8%
32	Utah	250,800	0.9%
49	Vermont	60,000	0.2%
12	Virginia	681,900	2.6%
16	Washington	559,000	2.1%
39	West Virginia	144,000	0.5%
18	Wisconsin	549,200	2.1%
50	Wyoming	55,700	0.2%

RANK ORDER

RANK	STATE	EMPLOYEES	% of USA
1	California	2,894,600	10.9%
2	Texas	2,078,300	7.8%
3	Florida	1,610,900	6.1%
4	New York	1,512,900	5.7%
5	Illinois	1,202,000	4.5%
6	Pennsylvania	1,135,900	4.3%
7	Ohio	1,044,800	3.9%
8	Georgia	886,800	3.3%
9	New Jersey	876,300	3.3%
10	Michigan	781,200	2.9%
11	North Carolina	770,500	2.9%
12	Virginia	681,900	2.6%
13	Tennessee	615,000	2.3%
14	Indiana	591,400	2.2%
15	Massachusetts	572,700	2.2%
16	Washington	559,000	2.1%
17	Missouri	552,600	2.1%
18	Wisconsin	549,200	2.1%
19	Minnesota	534,200	2.0%
20	Arizona	531,000	2.0%
21	Maryland	478,000	1.8%
22	Colorado	434,000	1.6%
23	Alabama	397,000	1.5%
24	Louisiana	384,700	1.5%
25	Kentucky	379,300	1.4%
26	South Carolina	375,100	1.4%
27	Oregon	343,200	1.3%
28	Connecticut	312,700	1.2%
29	Iowa	312,200	1.2%
30	Oklahoma	287,900	1.1%
31	Kansas	264,900	1.0%
32	Utah	250,800	0.9%
33	Arkansas	248,500	0.9%
34	Nevada	232,200	0.9%
35	Mississippi	231,500	0.9%
36	Nebraska	204,200	0.8%
37	New Mexico	144,700	0.5%
38	New Hampshire	144,600	0.5%
39	West Virginia	144,000	0.5%
40	Idaho	133,000	0.5%
41	Maine	127,100	0.5%
42	Hawaii	120,600	0.5%
43	Montana	92,000	0.3%
44	Delaware	82,700	0.3%
45	South Dakota	81,400	0.3%
46	Rhode Island	80,100	0.3%
47	North Dakota	77,400	0.3%
48	Alaska	63,900	0.2%
49	Vermont	60,000	0.2%
50	Wyoming	55,700	0.2%
	District of Columbia**	NA	NA

Source: U.S. Department of Labor, Bureau of Labor Statistics
   "Regional and State Employment and Unemployment" (press release, January 18, 2008)
*Seasonally adjusted preliminary data as of December 2007. National total calculated through a different formula.
**The Bureau of Labor Statistics does not publish seasonally adjusted figures in this category for the District.

Percent of Nonfarm Employees in
Trade, Transportation and Public Utilities in 2007
National Percent = 19.2% of Employees*

ALPHA ORDER

RANK ORDER

RANK	STATE	PERCENT		RANK	STATE	PERCENT
24	Alabama	19.6		1	New Hampshire	22.3
12	Alaska	20.2		2	Tennessee	21.8
25	Arizona	19.5		3	North Dakota	21.4
7	Arkansas	20.6		4	Georgia	21.3
36	California	18.9		4	New Jersey	21.3
40	Colorado	18.5		6	Nebraska	21.1
41	Connecticut	18.4		7	Arkansas	20.6
38	Delaware	18.7		8	Maine	20.5
18	Florida	19.8		8	Montana	20.5
4	Georgia	21.3		10	Iowa	20.4
32	Hawaii	19.1		10	Kentucky	20.4
12	Idaho	20.2		12	Alaska	20.2
14	Illinois	20.1		12	Idaho	20.2
18	Indiana	19.8		14	Illinois	20.1
10	Iowa	20.4		15	Texas	20.0
32	Kansas	19.1		16	Louisiana	19.9
10	Kentucky	20.4		16	South Dakota	19.9
16	Louisiana	19.9		18	Florida	19.8
8	Maine	20.5		18	Indiana	19.8
44	Maryland	18.1		18	Mississippi	19.8
47	Massachusetts	17.4		18	Missouri	19.8
41	Michigan	18.4		22	Oregon	19.7
29	Minnesota	19.3		22	Utah	19.7
18	Mississippi	19.8		24	Alabama	19.6
18	Missouri	19.8		25	Arizona	19.5
8	Montana	20.5		25	Pennsylvania	19.5
6	Nebraska	21.1		27	South Carolina	19.4
46	Nevada	17.7		27	Vermont	19.4
1	New Hampshire	22.3		29	Minnesota	19.3
4	New Jersey	21.3		29	Ohio	19.3
49	New Mexico	17.1		31	Wyoming	19.2
48	New York	17.3		32	Hawaii	19.1
39	North Carolina	18.6		32	Kansas	19.1
3	North Dakota	21.4		34	Washington	19.0
29	Ohio	19.3		34	Wisconsin	19.0
43	Oklahoma	18.2		36	California	18.9
22	Oregon	19.7		36	West Virginia	18.9
25	Pennsylvania	19.5		38	Delaware	18.7
50	Rhode Island	16.0		39	North Carolina	18.6
27	South Carolina	19.4		40	Colorado	18.5
16	South Dakota	19.9		41	Connecticut	18.4
2	Tennessee	21.8		41	Michigan	18.4
15	Texas	20.0		43	Oklahoma	18.2
22	Utah	19.7		44	Maryland	18.1
27	Vermont	19.4		45	Virginia	17.9
45	Virginia	17.9		46	Nevada	17.7
34	Washington	19.0		47	Massachusetts	17.4
36	West Virginia	18.9		48	New York	17.3
34	Wisconsin	19.0		49	New Mexico	17.1
31	Wyoming	19.2		50	Rhode Island	16.0

District of Columbia** NA

Source: CQ Press using data from U.S. Department of Labor, Bureau of Labor Statistics
    "Regional and State Employment and Unemployment" (press release, January 18, 2008)
*Seasonally adjusted preliminary data as of December 2007. National figure calculated through a different formula.
**The Bureau of Labor Statistics does not publish seasonally adjusted figures in this category for the District.

VII. Energy and Environment

Energy Consumption in 2004

National Total = 100,278,600,000,000,000 BTUs*

ALPHA ORDER

RANK	STATE	BTUs	% of USA
16	Alabama	2,159,700,000,000,000	2.2%
35	Alaska	779,100,000,000,000	0.8%
26	Arizona	1,436,600,000,000,000	1.4%
30	Arkansas	1,135,900,000,000,000	1.1%
2	California	8,364,600,000,000,000	8.3%
27	Colorado	1,383,900,000,000,000	1.4%
33	Connecticut	923,800,000,000,000	0.9%
47	Delaware	304,800,000,000,000	0.3%
3	Florida	4,452,500,000,000,000	4.4%
9	Georgia	3,141,100,000,000,000	3.1%
46	Hawaii	323,500,000,000,000	0.3%
40	Idaho	499,800,000,000,000	0.5%
7	Illinois	3,960,500,000,000,000	3.9%
11	Indiana	2,945,700,000,000,000	2.9%
29	Iowa	1,205,800,000,000,000	1.2%
31	Kansas	1,103,500,000,000,000	1.1%
18	Kentucky	1,956,400,000,000,000	2.0%
8	Louisiana	3,816,300,000,000,000	3.8%
41	Maine	480,300,000,000,000	0.5%
24	Maryland	1,526,600,000,000,000	1.5%
23	Massachusetts	1,542,900,000,000,000	1.5%
10	Michigan	3,119,400,000,000,000	3.1%
21	Minnesota	1,826,300,000,000,000	1.8%
28	Mississippi	1,214,300,000,000,000	1.2%
19	Missouri	1,849,300,000,000,000	1.8%
43	Montana	402,900,000,000,000	0.4%
39	Nebraska	651,900,000,000,000	0.7%
37	Nevada	693,700,000,000,000	0.7%
45	New Hampshire	340,700,000,000,000	0.3%
13	New Jersey	2,630,200,000,000,000	2.6%
38	New Mexico	682,300,000,000,000	0.7%
4	New York	4,254,000,000,000,000	4.2%
12	North Carolina	2,715,600,000,000,000	2.7%
44	North Dakota	402,300,000,000,000	0.4%
6	Ohio	4,022,800,000,000,000	4.0%
25	Oklahoma	1,485,900,000,000,000	1.5%
32	Oregon	1,093,600,000,000,000	1.1%
5	Pennsylvania	4,049,400,000,000,000	4.0%
49	Rhode Island	226,400,000,000,000	0.2%
22	South Carolina	1,717,500,000,000,000	1.7%
48	South Dakota	263,600,000,000,000	0.3%
15	Tennessee	2,297,700,000,000,000	2.3%
1	Texas	11,971,400,000,000,000	11.9%
36	Utah	740,200,000,000,000	0.7%
50	Vermont	169,300,000,000,000	0.2%
14	Virginia	2,558,200,000,000,000	2.6%
17	Washington	2,004,800,000,000,000	2.0%
34	West Virginia	821,300,000,000,000	0.8%
20	Wisconsin	1,847,700,000,000,000	1.8%
42	Wyoming	454,400,000,000,000	0.5%

RANK ORDER

RANK	STATE	BTUs	% of USA
1	Texas	11,971,400,000,000,000	11.9%
2	California	8,364,600,000,000,000	8.3%
3	Florida	4,452,500,000,000,000	4.4%
4	New York	4,254,000,000,000,000	4.2%
5	Pennsylvania	4,049,400,000,000,000	4.0%
6	Ohio	4,022,800,000,000,000	4.0%
7	Illinois	3,960,500,000,000,000	3.9%
8	Louisiana	3,816,300,000,000,000	3.8%
9	Georgia	3,141,100,000,000,000	3.1%
10	Michigan	3,119,400,000,000,000	3.1%
11	Indiana	2,945,700,000,000,000	2.9%
12	North Carolina	2,715,600,000,000,000	2.7%
13	New Jersey	2,630,200,000,000,000	2.6%
14	Virginia	2,558,200,000,000,000	2.6%
15	Tennessee	2,297,700,000,000,000	2.3%
16	Alabama	2,159,700,000,000,000	2.2%
17	Washington	2,004,800,000,000,000	2.0%
18	Kentucky	1,956,400,000,000,000	2.0%
19	Missouri	1,849,300,000,000,000	1.8%
20	Wisconsin	1,847,700,000,000,000	1.8%
21	Minnesota	1,826,300,000,000,000	1.8%
22	South Carolina	1,717,500,000,000,000	1.7%
23	Massachusetts	1,542,900,000,000,000	1.5%
24	Maryland	1,526,600,000,000,000	1.5%
25	Oklahoma	1,485,900,000,000,000	1.5%
26	Arizona	1,436,600,000,000,000	1.4%
27	Colorado	1,383,900,000,000,000	1.4%
28	Mississippi	1,214,300,000,000,000	1.2%
29	Iowa	1,205,800,000,000,000	1.2%
30	Arkansas	1,135,900,000,000,000	1.1%
31	Kansas	1,103,500,000,000,000	1.1%
32	Oregon	1,093,600,000,000,000	1.1%
33	Connecticut	923,800,000,000,000	0.9%
34	West Virginia	821,300,000,000,000	0.8%
35	Alaska	779,100,000,000,000	0.8%
36	Utah	740,200,000,000,000	0.7%
37	Nevada	693,700,000,000,000	0.7%
38	New Mexico	682,300,000,000,000	0.7%
39	Nebraska	651,900,000,000,000	0.7%
40	Idaho	499,800,000,000,000	0.5%
41	Maine	480,300,000,000,000	0.5%
42	Wyoming	454,400,000,000,000	0.5%
43	Montana	402,900,000,000,000	0.4%
44	North Dakota	402,300,000,000,000	0.4%
45	New Hampshire	340,700,000,000,000	0.3%
46	Hawaii	323,500,000,000,000	0.3%
47	Delaware	304,800,000,000,000	0.3%
48	South Dakota	263,600,000,000,000	0.3%
49	Rhode Island	226,400,000,000,000	0.2%
50	Vermont	169,300,000,000,000	0.2%
	District of Columbia	190,300,000,000,000	0.2%

Source: U.S. Department of Energy, Energy Information Administration
"State Energy Data 2004: Consumption" (http://www.eia.doe.gov/emeu/states/_seds.html)
*British Thermal Units: The amount of heat required to raise the temperature of one pound of water one degree. National total includes 137.8 trillion Btu of net imports of coal coke that is not allocated to the states.

Per Capita Energy Consumption in 2004

National Per Capita = 342,024,227 BTUs*

RANK	STATE	BTUs
6	Alabama	479,024,252
1	Alaska	1,177,491,193
46	Arizona	250,088,478
13	Arkansas	414,124,040
48	California	234,158,281
38	Colorado	300,243,162
42	Connecticut	265,315,676
19	Delaware	368,262,268
45	Florida	256,737,404
24	Georgia	352,087,140
44	Hawaii	257,939,102
22	Idaho	359,115,963
33	Illinois	312,340,966
7	Indiana	473,671,795
14	Iowa	409,299,496
16	Kansas	404,089,895
8	Kentucky	472,576,481
3	Louisiana	850,340,667
20	Maine	366,951,590
40	Maryland	275,675,908
47	Massachusetts	239,816,242
34	Michigan	308,768,332
23	Minnesota	359,110,167
12	Mississippi	420,630,027
31	Missouri	321,911,142
10	Montana	434,758,681
18	Nebraska	373,805,731
39	Nevada	297,730,433
43	New Hampshire	263,234,141
37	New Jersey	304,377,789
21	New Mexico	360,588,992
49	New York	220,889,718
32	North Carolina	318,046,355
4	North Dakota	631,738,624
25	Ohio	351,250,104
11	Oklahoma	422,544,583
35	Oregon	305,216,790
29	Pennsylvania	327,923,335
50	Rhode Island	211,024,934
15	South Carolina	408,788,707
27	South Dakota	340,511,723
17	Tennessee	388,646,061
5	Texas	533,132,966
36	Utah	304,503,668
41	Vermont	273,596,706
26	Virginia	342,736,963
30	Washington	323,884,076
9	West Virginia	455,110,167
28	Wisconsin	335,323,643
2	Wyoming	902,916,595

RANK	STATE	BTUs
1	Alaska	1,177,491,193
2	Wyoming	902,916,595
3	Louisiana	850,340,667
4	North Dakota	631,738,624
5	Texas	533,132,966
6	Alabama	479,024,252
7	Indiana	473,671,795
8	Kentucky	472,576,481
9	West Virginia	455,110,167
10	Montana	434,758,681
11	Oklahoma	422,544,583
12	Mississippi	420,630,027
13	Arkansas	414,124,040
14	Iowa	409,299,496
15	South Carolina	408,788,707
16	Kansas	404,089,895
17	Tennessee	388,646,061
18	Nebraska	373,805,731
19	Delaware	368,262,268
20	Maine	366,951,590
21	New Mexico	360,588,992
22	Idaho	359,115,963
23	Minnesota	359,110,167
24	Georgia	352,087,140
25	Ohio	351,250,104
26	Virginia	342,736,963
27	South Dakota	340,511,723
28	Wisconsin	335,323,643
29	Pennsylvania	327,923,335
30	Washington	323,884,076
31	Missouri	321,911,142
32	North Carolina	318,046,355
33	Illinois	312,340,966
34	Michigan	308,768,332
35	Oregon	305,216,790
36	Utah	304,503,668
37	New Jersey	304,377,789
38	Colorado	300,243,162
39	Nevada	297,730,433
40	Maryland	275,675,908
41	Vermont	273,596,706
42	Connecticut	265,315,676
43	New Hampshire	263,234,141
44	Hawaii	257,939,102
45	Florida	256,737,404
46	Arizona	250,088,478
47	Massachusetts	239,816,242
48	California	234,158,281
49	New York	220,889,718
50	Rhode Island	211,024,934
	District of Columbia	328,317,987

Source: CQ Press using data from U.S. Department of Energy, Energy Information Administration
"State Energy Data 2004: Consumption" (http://www.eia.doe.gov/emeu/states/_seds.html)
*British Thermal Units: The amount of heat required to raise the temperature of one pound of water one degree. National total includes 137.8 trillion Btu of net imports of coal coke that is not allocated to the states.

Energy Prices in 2004

National Rate = $12.91 per Million BTUs*

ALPHA ORDER				RANK ORDER		
RANK	STATE	RATE		RANK	STATE	RATE
44	Alabama	$11.29		1	Hawaii	$18.05
45	Alaska	11.09		2	Massachusetts	16.18
9	Arizona	15.24		3	Rhode Island	15.95
38	Arkansas	11.89		4	Connecticut	15.86
11	California	15.12		5	Vermont	15.83
24	Colorado	12.54		6	New York	15.65
4	Connecticut	15.86		7	New Hampshire	15.52
14	Delaware	13.64		8	Nevada	15.43
10	Florida	15.21		9	Arizona	15.24
30	Georgia	12.42		10	Florida	15.21
1	Hawaii	18.05		11	California	15.12
39	Idaho	11.82		12	Maryland	14.11
28	Illinois	12.46		13	New Jersey	14.07
48	Indiana	10.19		14	Delaware	13.64
40	Iowa	11.80		15	North Carolina	13.60
29	Kansas	12.44		16	New Mexico	13.48
43	Kentucky	11.30		17	Pennsylvania	13.05
49	Louisiana	10.09		18	Missouri	12.89
21	Maine	12.80		19	Ohio	12.85
12	Maryland	14.11		19	Oregon	12.85
2	Massachusetts	16.18		21	Maine	12.80
32	Michigan	12.24		22	Wisconsin	12.69
35	Minnesota	12.17		23	Virginia	12.64
27	Mississippi	12.51		24	Colorado	12.54
18	Missouri	12.89		24	South Dakota	12.54
37	Montana	12.12		26	South Carolina	12.53
34	Nebraska	12.18		27	Mississippi	12.51
8	Nevada	15.43		28	Illinois	12.46
7	New Hampshire	15.52		29	Kansas	12.44
13	New Jersey	14.07		30	Georgia	12.42
16	New Mexico	13.48		31	Washington	12.32
6	New York	15.65		32	Michigan	12.24
15	North Carolina	13.60		32	Oklahoma	12.24
50	North Dakota	9.18		34	Nebraska	12.18
19	Ohio	12.85		35	Minnesota	12.17
32	Oklahoma	12.24		36	Tennessee	12.16
19	Oregon	12.85		37	Montana	12.12
17	Pennsylvania	13.05		38	Arkansas	11.89
3	Rhode Island	15.95		39	Idaho	11.82
26	South Carolina	12.53		40	Iowa	11.80
24	South Dakota	12.54		41	Texas	11.50
36	Tennessee	12.16		42	Utah	11.39
41	Texas	11.50		43	Kentucky	11.30
42	Utah	11.39		44	Alabama	11.29
5	Vermont	15.83		45	Alaska	11.09
23	Virginia	12.64		46	West Virginia	10.66
31	Washington	12.32		47	Wyoming	10.29
46	West Virginia	10.66		48	Indiana	10.19
22	Wisconsin	12.69		49	Louisiana	10.09
47	Wyoming	10.29		50	North Dakota	9.18
					District of Columbia	16.87

Source: U.S. Department of Energy, Energy Information Administration
   "State Energy Data 2004: Prices and Expenditures" (http://www.eia.doe.gov/emeu/states/_seds.html)
*British Thermal Units: The amount of heat required to raise the temperature of one pound of water one degree.

Energy Expenditures in 2004

National Total = $869,318,600,000*

ALPHA ORDER				RANK ORDER			
RANK	STATE	EXPENDITURES	% of USA	RANK	STATE	EXPENDITURES	% of USA
21	Alabama	$15,180,200,000	1.7%	1	Texas	$95,122,100,000	10.9%
40	Alaska	4,163,600,000	0.5%	2	California	90,260,400,000	10.4%
24	Arizona	13,778,700,000	1.6%	3	New York	48,504,100,000	5.6%
33	Arkansas	8,718,100,000	1.0%	4	Florida	41,112,300,000	4.7%
2	California	90,260,400,000	10.4%	5	Pennsylvania	36,069,100,000	4.1%
26	Colorado	11,804,500,000	1.4%	6	Ohio	34,943,900,000	4.0%
28	Connecticut	10,595,000,000	1.2%	7	Illinois	34,067,400,000	3.9%
48	Delaware	2,540,900,000	0.3%	8	Michigan	27,062,900,000	3.1%
4	Florida	41,112,300,000	4.7%	9	New Jersey	27,060,000,000	3.1%
10	Georgia	25,658,700,000	3.0%	10	Georgia	25,658,700,000	3.0%
41	Hawaii	4,038,200,000	0.5%	11	Louisiana	24,401,700,000	2.8%
43	Idaho	3,736,300,000	0.4%	12	North Carolina	23,225,000,000	2.7%
7	Illinois	34,067,400,000	3.9%	13	Virginia	21,298,100,000	2.4%
14	Indiana	20,932,200,000	2.4%	14	Indiana	20,932,200,000	2.4%
29	Iowa	10,111,000,000	1.2%	15	Massachusetts	17,854,800,000	2.1%
32	Kansas	8,953,800,000	1.0%	16	Tennessee	17,665,500,000	2.0%
23	Kentucky	13,882,100,000	1.6%	17	Missouri	16,370,100,000	1.9%
11	Louisiana	24,401,700,000	2.8%	18	Wisconsin	16,068,900,000	1.8%
39	Maine	4,471,000,000	0.5%	19	Washington	15,561,100,000	1.8%
22	Maryland	14,167,400,000	1.6%	20	Minnesota	15,228,700,000	1.8%
15	Massachusetts	17,854,800,000	2.1%	21	Alabama	15,180,200,000	1.7%
8	Michigan	27,062,900,000	3.1%	22	Maryland	14,167,400,000	1.6%
20	Minnesota	15,228,700,000	1.8%	23	Kentucky	13,882,100,000	1.6%
30	Mississippi	9,453,300,000	1.1%	24	Arizona	13,778,700,000	1.6%
17	Missouri	16,370,100,000	1.9%	25	South Carolina	13,396,600,000	1.5%
44	Montana	3,182,300,000	0.4%	26	Colorado	11,804,500,000	1.4%
37	Nebraska	5,404,100,000	0.6%	27	Oklahoma	11,274,400,000	1.3%
34	Nevada	6,878,400,000	0.8%	28	Connecticut	10,595,000,000	1.2%
42	New Hampshire	3,928,100,000	0.5%	29	Iowa	10,111,000,000	1.2%
9	New Jersey	27,060,000,000	3.1%	30	Mississippi	9,453,300,000	1.1%
38	New Mexico	5,216,900,000	0.6%	31	Oregon	9,129,400,000	1.1%
3	New York	48,504,100,000	5.6%	32	Kansas	8,953,800,000	1.0%
12	North Carolina	23,225,000,000	2.7%	33	Arkansas	8,718,100,000	1.0%
46	North Dakota	2,649,900,000	0.3%	34	Nevada	6,878,400,000	0.8%
6	Ohio	34,943,900,000	4.0%	35	West Virginia	5,844,900,000	0.7%
27	Oklahoma	11,274,400,000	1.3%	36	Utah	5,672,600,000	0.7%
31	Oregon	9,129,400,000	1.1%	37	Nebraska	5,404,100,000	0.6%
5	Pennsylvania	36,069,100,000	4.1%	38	New Mexico	. 5,216,900,000	0.6%
47	Rhode Island	2,634,300,000	0.3%	39	Maine	4,471,000,000	0.5%
25	South Carolina	13,396,600,000	1.5%	40	Alaska	4,163,600,000	0.5%
49	South Dakota	2,317,100,000	0.3%	41	Hawaii	4,038,200,000	0.5%
16	Tennessee	17,665,500,000	2.0%	42	New Hampshire	3,928,100,000	0.5%
1	Texas	95,122,100,000	10.9%	43	Idaho	3,736,300,000	0.4%
36	Utah	5,672,600,000	0.7%	44	Montana	3,182,300,000	0.4%
50	Vermont	1,968,000,000	0.2%	45	Wyoming	2,906,300,000	0.3%
13	Virginia	21,298,100,000	2.4%	46	North Dakota	2,649,900,000	0.3%
19	Washington	15,561,100,000	1.8%	47	Rhode Island	2,634,300,000	0.3%
35	West Virginia	5,844,900,000	0.7%	48	Delaware	2,540,900,000	0.3%
18	Wisconsin	16,068,900,000	1.8%	49	South Dakota	2,317,100,000	0.3%
45	Wyoming	2,906,300,000	0.3%	50	Vermont	1,968,000,000	0.2%
					District of Columbia	1,729,400,000	0.2%

Source: U.S. Department of Energy, Energy Information Administration
   "State Energy Data 2004: Prices and Expenditures" (http://www.eia.doe.gov/emeu/states/_seds.html)
*The national total includes $1,124.6 million for coal coke net imports, which are not allocated to the states.

Per Capita Energy Expenditures in 2004

National Per Capita = $2,965

ALPHA ORDER

ALPHA ORDER

RANK	STATE	PER CAPITA
9	Alabama	$3,367
1	Alaska	6,293
48	Arizona	2,399
19	Arkansas	3,178
44	California	2,527
41	Colorado	2,561
24	Connecticut	3,043
22	Delaware	3,070
49	Florida	2,371
32	Georgia	2,876
15	Hawaii	3,220
39	Idaho	2,685
38	Illinois	2,687
10	Indiana	3,366
7	Iowa	3,432
12	Kansas	3,279
11	Kentucky	3,353
3	Louisiana	5,437
8	Maine	3,416
42	Maryland	2,558
35	Massachusetts	2,775
40	Michigan	2,679
26	Minnesota	2,994
13	Mississippi	3,275
34	Missouri	2,850
6	Montana	3,434
21	Nebraska	3,099
29	Nevada	2,952
25	New Hampshire	3,035
20	New Jersey	3,131
36	New Mexico	2,757
45	New York	2,519
37	North Carolina	2,720
5	North Dakota	4,161
23	Ohio	3,051
16	Oklahoma	3,206
43	Oregon	2,548
30	Pennsylvania	2,921
47	Rhode Island	2,455
17	South Carolina	3,189
27	South Dakota	2,993
28	Tennessee	2,988
4	Texas	4,236
50	Utah	2,334
18	Vermont	3,180
33	Virginia	2,853
46	Washington	2,514
14	West Virginia	3,239
31	Wisconsin	2,916
2	Wyoming	5,775

RANK ORDER

RANK	STATE	PER CAPITA
1	Alaska	$6,293
2	Wyoming	5,775
3	Louisiana	5,437
4	Texas	4,236
5	North Dakota	4,161
6	Montana	3,434
7	Iowa	3,432
8	Maine	3,416
9	Alabama	3,367
10	Indiana	3,366
11	Kentucky	3,353
12	Kansas	3,279
13	Mississippi	3,275
14	West Virginia	3,239
15	Hawaii	3,220
16	Oklahoma	3,206
17	South Carolina	3,189
18	Vermont	3,180
19	Arkansas	3,178
20	New Jersey	3,131
21	Nebraska	3,099
22	Delaware	3,070
23	Ohio	3,051
24	Connecticut	3,043
25	New Hampshire	3,035
26	Minnesota	2,994
27	South Dakota	2,993
28	Tennessee	2,988
29	Nevada	2,952
30	Pennsylvania	2,921
31	Wisconsin	2,916
32	Georgia	2,876
33	Virginia	2,853
34	Missouri	2,850
35	Massachusetts	2,775
36	New Mexico	2,757
37	North Carolina	2,720
38	Illinois	2,687
39	Idaho	2,685
40	Michigan	2,679
41	Colorado	2,561
42	Maryland	2,558
43	Oregon	2,548
44	California	2,527
45	New York	2,519
46	Washington	2,514
47	Rhode Island	2,455
48	Arizona	2,399
49	Florida	2,371
50	Utah	2,334
	District of Columbia	2,984

Source: CQ Press using data from U.S. Department of Energy, Energy Information Administration
"State Energy Data 2004: Prices and Expenditures" (http://www.eia.doe.gov/emeu/states/_seds.html)

Average Monthly Electric Bill for Industrial Customers in 2006

National Average = $6,836 a Month

<table>
<tr><td colspan="3"><u>ALPHA ORDER</u></td><td colspan="3"><u>RANK ORDER</u></td></tr>
<tr><td>RANK</td><td>STATE</td><td>MONTHLY BILL</td><td>RANK</td><td>STATE</td><td>MONTHLY BILL</td></tr>
<tr><td>10</td><td>Alabama</td><td>$16,690</td><td>1</td><td>Hawaii</td><td>$84,610</td></tr>
<tr><td>24</td><td>Alaska</td><td>8,643</td><td>2</td><td>Tennessee</td><td>71,813</td></tr>
<tr><td>25</td><td>Arizona</td><td>7,858</td><td>3</td><td>Delaware</td><td>32,462</td></tr>
<tr><td>47</td><td>Arkansas</td><td>2,501</td><td>4</td><td>Vermont</td><td>28,142</td></tr>
<tr><td>33</td><td>California</td><td>5,425</td><td>5</td><td>South Carolina</td><td>27,655</td></tr>
<tr><td>37</td><td>Colorado</td><td>4,607</td><td>6</td><td>Illinois</td><td>26,945</td></tr>
<tr><td>23</td><td>Connecticut</td><td>8,965</td><td>7</td><td>Nevada</td><td>26,771</td></tr>
<tr><td>3</td><td>Delaware</td><td>32,462</td><td>8</td><td>Kentucky</td><td>23,688</td></tr>
<tr><td>39</td><td>Florida</td><td>4,110</td><td>9</td><td>Wisconsin</td><td>17,824</td></tr>
<tr><td>19</td><td>Georgia</td><td>10,227</td><td>10</td><td>Alabama</td><td>16,690</td></tr>
<tr><td>1</td><td>Hawaii</td><td>84,610</td><td>11</td><td>Virginia</td><td>14,342</td></tr>
<tr><td>49</td><td>Idaho</td><td>1,040</td><td>12</td><td>Iowa</td><td>12,985</td></tr>
<tr><td>6</td><td>Illinois</td><td>26,945</td><td>13</td><td>Michigan</td><td>12,899</td></tr>
<tr><td>18</td><td>Indiana</td><td>10,669</td><td>14</td><td>New York</td><td>12,860</td></tr>
<tr><td>12</td><td>Iowa</td><td>12,985</td><td>15</td><td>Ohio</td><td>12,122</td></tr>
<tr><td>46</td><td>Kansas</td><td>2,810</td><td>16</td><td>Minnesota</td><td>11,744</td></tr>
<tr><td>8</td><td>Kentucky</td><td>23,688</td><td>17</td><td>North Carolina</td><td>11,738</td></tr>
<tr><td>26</td><td>Louisiana</td><td>7,692</td><td>18</td><td>Indiana</td><td>10,669</td></tr>
<tr><td>21</td><td>Maine</td><td>9,899</td><td>19</td><td>Georgia</td><td>10,227</td></tr>
<tr><td>35</td><td>Maryland</td><td>4,912</td><td>20</td><td>Mississippi</td><td>10,044</td></tr>
<tr><td>27</td><td>Massachusetts</td><td>7,415</td><td>21</td><td>Maine</td><td>9,899</td></tr>
<tr><td>13</td><td>Michigan</td><td>12,899</td><td>22</td><td>Pennsylvania</td><td>9,370</td></tr>
<tr><td>16</td><td>Minnesota</td><td>11,744</td><td>23</td><td>Connecticut</td><td>8,965</td></tr>
<tr><td>20</td><td>Mississippi</td><td>10,044</td><td>24</td><td>Alaska</td><td>8,643</td></tr>
<tr><td>29</td><td>Missouri</td><td>6,635</td><td>25</td><td>Arizona</td><td>7,858</td></tr>
<tr><td>38</td><td>Montana</td><td>4,264</td><td>26</td><td>Louisiana</td><td>7,692</td></tr>
<tr><td>50</td><td>Nebraska</td><td>884</td><td>27</td><td>Massachusetts</td><td>7,415</td></tr>
<tr><td>7</td><td>Nevada</td><td>26,771</td><td>28</td><td>New Jersey</td><td>7,060</td></tr>
<tr><td>30</td><td>New Hampshire</td><td>6,482</td><td>29</td><td>Missouri</td><td>6,635</td></tr>
<tr><td>28</td><td>New Jersey</td><td>7,060</td><td>30</td><td>New Hampshire</td><td>6,482</td></tr>
<tr><td>32</td><td>New Mexico</td><td>5,759</td><td>31</td><td>North Dakota</td><td>5,833</td></tr>
<tr><td>14</td><td>New York</td><td>12,860</td><td>32</td><td>New Mexico</td><td>5,759</td></tr>
<tr><td>17</td><td>North Carolina</td><td>11,738</td><td>33</td><td>California</td><td>5,425</td></tr>
<tr><td>31</td><td>North Dakota</td><td>5,833</td><td>34</td><td>Rhode Island</td><td>5,424</td></tr>
<tr><td>15</td><td>Ohio</td><td>12,122</td><td>35</td><td>Maryland</td><td>4,912</td></tr>
<tr><td>40</td><td>Oklahoma</td><td>3,833</td><td>36</td><td>Texas</td><td>4,904</td></tr>
<tr><td>48</td><td>Oregon</td><td>2,412</td><td>37</td><td>Colorado</td><td>4,607</td></tr>
<tr><td>22</td><td>Pennsylvania</td><td>9,370</td><td>38</td><td>Montana</td><td>4,264</td></tr>
<tr><td>34</td><td>Rhode Island</td><td>5,424</td><td>39</td><td>Florida</td><td>4,110</td></tr>
<tr><td>5</td><td>South Carolina</td><td>27,655</td><td>40</td><td>Oklahoma</td><td>3,833</td></tr>
<tr><td>43</td><td>South Dakota</td><td>3,336</td><td>41</td><td>West Virginia</td><td>3,655</td></tr>
<tr><td>2</td><td>Tennessee</td><td>71,813</td><td>42</td><td>Wyoming</td><td>3,494</td></tr>
<tr><td>36</td><td>Texas</td><td>4,904</td><td>43</td><td>South Dakota</td><td>3,336</td></tr>
<tr><td>44</td><td>Utah</td><td>3,200</td><td>44</td><td>Utah</td><td>3,200</td></tr>
<tr><td>4</td><td>Vermont</td><td>28,142</td><td>45</td><td>Washington</td><td>3,150</td></tr>
<tr><td>11</td><td>Virginia</td><td>14,342</td><td>46</td><td>Kansas</td><td>2,810</td></tr>
<tr><td>45</td><td>Washington</td><td>3,150</td><td>47</td><td>Arkansas</td><td>2,501</td></tr>
<tr><td>41</td><td>West Virginia</td><td>3,655</td><td>48</td><td>Oregon</td><td>2,412</td></tr>
<tr><td>9</td><td>Wisconsin</td><td>17,824</td><td>49</td><td>Idaho</td><td>1,040</td></tr>
<tr><td>42</td><td>Wyoming</td><td>3,494</td><td>50</td><td>Nebraska</td><td>884</td></tr>
</table>

District of Columbia   3,483,833

Source: U.S. Department of Energy, Energy Information Administration
"Electric Sales and Revenue" (http://www.eia.doe.gov/cneaf/electricity/esr/esr_sum.html)

Average Monthly Electric Bill for Commercial Customers in 2006

National Average = $596 a Month

ALPHA ORDER

ALPHA ORDER

RANK	STATE	MONTHLY BILL
34	Alabama	$419
13	Alaska	613
11	Arizona	683
41	Arkansas	393
8	California	744
43	Colorado	365
2	Connecticut	1,040
7	Delaware	758
10	Florida	692
17	Georgia	560
3	Hawaii	1,016
49	Idaho	270
15	Illinois	590
31	Indiana	431
45	Iowa	343
40	Kansas	394
44	Kentucky	351
12	Louisiana	639
24	Maine	495
1	Maryland	1,106
5	Massachusetts	908
18	Michigan	542
23	Minnesota	498
27	Mississippi	463
33	Missouri	420
48	Montana	301
47	Nebraska	312
21	Nevada	529
20	New Hampshire	531
6	New Jersey	828
34	New Mexico	419
4	New York	978
32	North Carolina	428
37	North Dakota	403
19	Ohio	536
29	Oklahoma	445
39	Oregon	397
22	Pennsylvania	511
9	Rhode Island	738
38	South Carolina	402
46	South Dakota	341
30	Tennessee	432
14	Texas	612
28	Utah	462
36	Vermont	407
15	Virginia	590
26	Washington	467
50	West Virginia	260
25	Wisconsin	490
42	Wyoming	388

RANK ORDER

RANK	STATE	MONTHLY BILL
1	Maryland	$1,106
2	Connecticut	1,040
3	Hawaii	1,016
4	New York	978
5	Massachusetts	908
6	New Jersey	828
7	Delaware	758
8	California	744
9	Rhode Island	738
10	Florida	692
11	Arizona	683
12	Louisiana	639
13	Alaska	613
14	Texas	612
15	Illinois	590
15	Virginia	590
17	Georgia	560
18	Michigan	542
19	Ohio	536
20	New Hampshire	531
21	Nevada	529
22	Pennsylvania	511
23	Minnesota	498
24	Maine	495
25	Wisconsin	490
26	Washington	467
27	Mississippi	463
28	Utah	462
29	Oklahoma	445
30	Tennessee	432
31	Indiana	431
32	North Carolina	428
33	Missouri	420
34	Alabama	419
34	New Mexico	419
36	Vermont	407
37	North Dakota	403
38	South Carolina	402
39	Oregon	397
40	Kansas	394
41	Arkansas	393
42	Wyoming	388
43	Colorado	365
44	Kentucky	351
45	Iowa	343
46	South Dakota	341
47	Nebraska	312
48	Montana	301
49	Idaho	270
50	West Virginia	260
	District of Columbia	3,140

Source: U.S. Department of Energy, Energy Information Administration
"Electric Sales and Revenue" (http://www.eia.doe.gov/cneaf/electricity/esr/esr_sum.html)

Average Monthly Electric Bill for Residential Customers in 2006

National Average = $95.66 a Month

ALPHA ORDER

RANK	STATE	MONTHLY BILL
7	Alabama	$113.99
16	Alaska	100.18
12	Arizona	103.76
19	Arkansas	98.08
26	California	84.56
48	Colorado	62.74
4	Connecticut	126.64
8	Delaware	110.18
3	Florida	133.30
13	Georgia	103.16
1	Hawaii	154.18
44	Idaho	66.36
47	Illinois	64.85
28	Indiana	81.65
29	Iowa	81.52
33	Kansas	77.14
30	Kentucky	79.91
6	Louisiana	115.23
39	Maine	73.01
14	Maryland	101.68
11	Massachusetts	103.97
45	Michigan	65.55
41	Minnesota	70.85
5	Mississippi	121.27
31	Missouri	79.48
43	Montana	67.50
38	Nebraska	73.32
9	Nevada	108.19
22	New Hampshire	91.59
23	New Jersey	90.84
50	New Mexico	55.60
18	New York	99.83
17	North Carolina	100.10
37	North Dakota	73.91
27	Ohio	81.78
21	Oklahoma	95.56
34	Oregon	74.97
25	Pennsylvania	86.04
24	Rhode Island	88.62
10	South Carolina	107.89
35	South Dakota	74.90
15	Tennessee	100.88
2	Texas	149.29
49	Utah	58.79
32	Vermont	77.95
20	Virginia	98.03
40	Washington	72.42
42	West Virginia	68.27
36	Wisconsin	74.79
46	Wyoming	65.50

RANK ORDER

RANK	STATE	MONTHLY BILL
1	Hawaii	$154.18
2	Texas	149.29
3	Florida	133.30
4	Connecticut	126.64
5	Mississippi	121.27
6	Louisiana	115.23
7	Alabama	113.99
8	Delaware	110.18
9	Nevada	108.19
10	South Carolina	107.89
11	Massachusetts	103.97
12	Arizona	103.76
13	Georgia	103.16
14	Maryland	101.68
15	Tennessee	100.88
16	Alaska	100.18
17	North Carolina	100.10
18	New York	99.83
19	Arkansas	98.08
20	Virginia	98.03
21	Oklahoma	95.56
22	New Hampshire	91.59
23	New Jersey	90.84
24	Rhode Island	88.62
25	Pennsylvania	86.04
26	California	84.56
27	Ohio	81.78
28	Indiana	81.65
29	Iowa	81.52
30	Kentucky	79.91
31	Missouri	79.48
32	Vermont	77.95
33	Kansas	77.14
34	Oregon	74.97
35	South Dakota	74.90
36	Wisconsin	74.79
37	North Dakota	73.91
38	Nebraska	73.32
39	Maine	73.01
40	Washington	72.42
41	Minnesota	70.85
42	West Virginia	68.27
43	Montana	67.50
44	Idaho	66.36
45	Michigan	65.55
46	Wyoming	65.50
47	Illinois	64.85
48	Colorado	62.74
49	Utah	58.79
50	New Mexico	55.60
	District of Columbia	71.66

Source: U.S. Department of Energy, Energy Information Administration
"Electric Sales and Revenue" (http://www.eia.doe.gov/cneaf/electricity/esr/esr_sum.html)

Electricity Generated Through Renewable Sources in 2005

National Total = 365,253,632,000 Kilowatthours*

ALPHA ORDER

RANK	STATE	KWH	% of USA
5	Alabama	13,916,046,000	3.8%
38	Alaska	1,469,785,000	0.4%
13	Arizona	6,484,059,000	1.8%
16	Arkansas	4,832,497,000	1.3%
2	California	63,492,788,000	17.4%
31	Colorado	2,225,857,000	0.6%
32	Connecticut	1,961,130,000	0.5%
50	Delaware	0	0.0%
14	Florida	5,901,757,000	1.6%
10	Georgia	7,310,952,000	2.0%
46	Hawaii	784,146,000	0.2%
8	Idaho	9,119,161,000	2.5%
44	Illinois	951,751,000	0.3%
47	Indiana	523,540,000	0.1%
29	Iowa	2,735,076,000	0.7%
48	Kansas	437,160,000	0.1%
23	Kentucky	3,400,551,000	0.9%
22	Louisiana	3,604,813,000	1.0%
9	Maine	8,511,414,000	2.3%
30	Maryland	2,610,047,000	0.7%
26	Massachusetts	3,072,548,000	0.8%
19	Michigan	4,281,637,000	1.2%
21	Minnesota	3,700,133,000	1.0%
36	Mississippi	1,530,338,000	0.4%
40	Missouri	1,238,311,000	0.3%
7	Montana	9,652,594,000	2.6%
41	Nebraska	1,010,727,000	0.3%
27	Nevada	2,965,087,000	0.8%
28	New Hampshire	2,799,264,000	0.8%
39	New Jersey	1,385,623,000	0.4%
43	New Mexico	964,267,000	0.3%
4	New York	28,752,053,000	7.9%
11	North Carolina	7,308,125,000	2.0%
35	North Dakota	1,572,158,000	0.4%
45	Ohio	916,769,000	0.3%
20	Oklahoma	3,767,351,000	1.0%
3	Oregon	32,630,445,000	8.9%
15	Pennsylvania	5,270,706,000	1.4%
49	Rhode Island	6,734,000	0.0%
17	South Carolina	4,813,635,000	1.3%
24	South Dakota	3,232,691,000	0.9%
6	Tennessee	9,868,426,000	2.7%
12	Texas	6,666,970,000	1.8%
42	Utah	976,316,000	0.3%
33	Vermont	1,632,788,000	0.4%
18	Virginia	4,462,959,000	1.2%
1	Washington	74,255,371,000	20.3%
34	West Virginia	1,613,386,000	0.4%
25	Wisconsin	3,108,051,000	0.9%
37	Wyoming	1,525,639,000	0.4%

RANK ORDER

RANK	STATE	KWH	% of USA
1	Washington	74,255,371,000	20.3%
2	California	63,492,788,000	17.4%
3	Oregon	32,630,445,000	8.9%
4	New York	28,752,053,000	7.9%
5	Alabama	13,916,046,000	3.8%
6	Tennessee	9,868,426,000	2.7%
7	Montana	9,652,594,000	2.6%
8	Idaho	9,119,161,000	2.5%
9	Maine	8,511,414,000	2.3%
10	Georgia	7,310,952,000	2.0%
11	North Carolina	7,308,125,000	2.0%
12	Texas	6,666,970,000	1.8%
13	Arizona	6,484,059,000	1.8%
14	Florida	5,901,757,000	1.6%
15	Pennsylvania	5,270,706,000	1.4%
16	Arkansas	4,832,497,000	1.3%
17	South Carolina	4,813,635,000	1.3%
18	Virginia	4,462,959,000	1.2%
19	Michigan	4,281,637,000	1.2%
20	Oklahoma	3,767,351,000	1.0%
21	Minnesota	3,700,133,000	1.0%
22	Louisiana	3,604,813,000	1.0%
23	Kentucky	3,400,551,000	0.9%
24	South Dakota	3,232,691,000	0.9%
25	Wisconsin	3,108,051,000	0.9%
26	Massachusetts	3,072,548,000	0.8%
27	Nevada	2,965,087,000	0.8%
28	New Hampshire	2,799,264,000	0.8%
29	Iowa	2,735,076,000	0.7%
30	Maryland	2,610,047,000	0.7%
31	Colorado	2,225,857,000	0.6%
32	Connecticut	1,961,130,000	0.5%
33	Vermont	1,632,788,000	0.4%
34	West Virginia	1,613,386,000	0.4%
35	North Dakota	1,572,158,000	0.4%
36	Mississippi	1,530,338,000	0.4%
37	Wyoming	1,525,639,000	0.4%
38	Alaska	1,469,785,000	0.4%
39	New Jersey	1,385,623,000	0.4%
40	Missouri	1,238,311,000	0.3%
41	Nebraska	1,010,727,000	0.3%
42	Utah	976,316,000	0.3%
43	New Mexico	964,267,000	0.3%
44	Illinois	951,751,000	0.3%
45	Ohio	916,769,000	0.3%
46	Hawaii	784,146,000	0.2%
47	Indiana	523,540,000	0.1%
48	Kansas	437,160,000	0.1%
49	Rhode Island	6,734,000	0.0%
50	Delaware	0	0.0%
	District of Columbia	0	0.0%

Source: U.S. Department of Energy, Energy Information Administration
 "Renewable Energy Trends, 2005" (http://www.eia.doe.gov/cneaf/solar.renewables/page/trends/rentrends.html)
*Includes hydroelectric, geothermal, solar, wind, MSW/landfill gas, wood/wood waste and other biomass.

Percent of Electricity Generated Through Renewable Sources in 2005

National Percent = 9.0%*

ALPHA ORDER			RANK ORDER		
RANK	STATE	PERCENT	RANK	STATE	PERCENT
13	Alabama	10.1	1	Idaho	84.2
9	Alaska	22.3	2	Washington	72.8
19	Arizona	6.4	3	Oregon	66.2
13	Arkansas	10.1	4	South Dakota	49.6
7	California	31.7	5	Maine	45.2
30	Colorado	4.5	6	Montana	34.5
21	Connecticut	5.8	7	California	31.7
50	Delaware	0.0	8	Vermont	28.6
37	Florida	2.7	9	Alaska	22.3
25	Georgia	5.3	10	New York	19.6
17	Hawaii	6.8	11	New Hampshire	11.4
1	Idaho	84.2	12	Tennessee	10.2
47	Illinois	0.5	13	Alabama	10.1
48	Indiana	0.4	13	Arkansas	10.1
20	Iowa	6.2	15	Nevada	7.4
45	Kansas	1.0	16	Minnesota	7.0
32	Kentucky	3.5	17	Hawaii	6.8
31	Louisiana	3.9	18	Massachusetts	6.5
5	Maine	45.2	19	Arizona	6.4
26	Maryland	5.0	20	Iowa	6.2
18	Massachusetts	6.5	21	Connecticut	5.8
32	Michigan	3.5	22	Virginia	5.7
16	Minnesota	7.0	23	North Carolina	5.6
34	Mississippi	3.4	24	Oklahoma	5.5
44	Missouri	1.4	25	Georgia	5.3
6	Montana	34.5	26	Maryland	5.0
36	Nebraska	3.2	26	Wisconsin	5.0
15	Nevada	7.4	28	North Dakota	4.9
11	New Hampshire	11.4	29	South Carolina	4.7
41	New Jersey	2.3	30	Colorado	4.5
37	New Mexico	2.7	31	Louisiana	3.9
10	New York	19.6	32	Kentucky	3.5
23	North Carolina	5.6	32	Michigan	3.5
28	North Dakota	4.9	34	Mississippi	3.4
46	Ohio	0.6	35	Wyoming	3.3
24	Oklahoma	5.5	36	Nebraska	3.2
3	Oregon	66.2	37	Florida	2.7
40	Pennsylvania	2.4	37	New Mexico	2.7
49	Rhode Island	0.1	39	Utah	2.6
29	South Carolina	4.7	40	Pennsylvania	2.4
4	South Dakota	49.6	41	New Jersey	2.3
12	Tennessee	10.2	42	Texas	1.7
42	Texas	1.7	42	West Virginia	1.7
39	Utah	2.6	44	Missouri	1.4
8	Vermont	28.6	45	Kansas	1.0
22	Virginia	5.7	46	Ohio	0.6
2	Washington	72.8	47	Illinois	0.5
42	West Virginia	1.7	48	Indiana	0.4
26	Wisconsin	5.0	49	Rhode Island	0.1
35	Wyoming	3.3	50	Delaware	0.0
				District of Columbia	0.0

Source: U.S. Department of Energy, Energy Information Administration
"Renewable Energy Trends, 2005" (http://www.eia.doe.gov/cneaf/solar.renewables/page/trends/rentrends.html)
*Includes hydroelectric, geothermal, solar, wind, MSW/landfill gas, wood/wood waste and other biomass.

Average Price of Natural Gas Delivered to Industrial Customers in 2006

National Average = $7.86 per Thousand Cubic Feet

ALPHA ORDER			RANK ORDER		
RANK	STATE	RATE	RANK	STATE	RATE
29	Alabama	$9.46	1	Hawaii	$18.49
50	Alaska	3.70	2	Massachusetts	14.88
22	Arizona	9.90	3	Maine	14.39
27	Arkansas	9.51	4	Rhode Island	13.32
34	California	9.30	5	Maryland	12.86
14	Colorado	11.53	6	New Hampshire	12.55
16	Connecticut	10.86	7	Missouri	12.40
10	Delaware	11.94	8	Pennsylvania	12.30
11	Florida	11.66	9	Nevada	12.00
27	Georgia	9.51	10	Delaware	11.94
1	Hawaii	18.49	11	Florida	11.66
19	Idaho	10.05	12	Montana	11.63
31	Illinois	9.44	13	Ohio	11.60
32	Indiana	9.38	14	Colorado	11.53
42	Iowa	8.47	15	North Carolina	10.99
47	Kansas	6.83	16	Connecticut	10.86
26	Kentucky	9.64	17	New York	10.56
46	Louisiana	7.43	18	New Jersey	10.28
3	Maine	14.39	19	Idaho	10.05
5	Maryland	12.86	20	Tennessee	10.00
2	Massachusetts	14.88	21	Virginia	9.98
22	Michigan	9.90	22	Arizona	9.90
44	Minnesota	8.09	22	Michigan	9.90
35	Mississippi	9.27	24	Washington	9.87
7	Missouri	12.40	25	Oklahoma	9.66
12	Montana	11.63	26	Kentucky	9.64
43	Nebraska	8.37	27	Arkansas	9.51
9	Nevada	12.00	27	Georgia	9.51
6	New Hampshire	12.55	29	Alabama	9.46
18	New Jersey	10.28	29	Wisconsin	9.46
40	New Mexico	8.92	31	Illinois	9.44
17	New York	10.56	32	Indiana	9.38
15	North Carolina	10.99	33	South Dakota	9.32
49	North Dakota	6.54	34	California	9.30
13	Ohio	11.60	35	Mississippi	9.27
25	Oklahoma	9.66	36	Vermont	9.25
38	Oregon	9.16	37	South Carolina	9.21
8	Pennsylvania	12.30	38	Oregon	9.16
4	Rhode Island	13.32	39	West Virginia	8.98
37	South Carolina	9.21	40	New Mexico	8.92
33	South Dakota	9.32	41	Wyoming	8.90
20	Tennessee	10.00	42	Iowa	8.47
48	Texas	6.69	43	Nebraska	8.37
45	Utah	8.02	44	Minnesota	8.09
36	Vermont	9.25	45	Utah	8.02
21	Virginia	9.98	46	Louisiana	7.43
24	Washington	9.87	47	Kansas	6.83
39	West Virginia	8.98	48	Texas	6.69
29	Wisconsin	9.46	49	North Dakota	6.54
41	Wyoming	8.90	50	Alaska	3.70
				District of Columbia*	NA

Source: U.S. Department of Energy, Energy Information Administration
"Natural Gas Annual 2006" (http://www.eia.doe.gov/oil_gas/natural_gas/info_glance/natural_gas.html)
*Not applicable.

Average Price of Natural Gas Delivered to Commercial Customers in 2006

National Average = $11.99 per Thousand Cubic Feet

ALPHA ORDER				RANK ORDER		
RANK	STATE	RATE		RANK	STATE	RATE
3	Alabama	$15.82		1	Hawaii	$29.29
50	Alaska	4.75		2	Rhode Island	15.94
27	Arizona	12.11		3	Alabama	15.82
37	Arkansas	10.72		4	Massachusetts	15.74
39	California	10.43		5	Maine	15.66
47	Colorado	9.61		6	Delaware	15.33
14	Connecticut	13.60		7	New Hampshire	15.03
6	Delaware	15.33		8	West Virginia	14.38
13	Florida	13.91		9	Pennsylvania	14.30
12	Georgia	13.99		10	South Carolina	14.09
1	Hawaii	29.29		11	North Carolina	14.06
32	Idaho	11.49		12	Georgia	13.99
35	Illinois	10.91		13	Florida	13.91
31	Indiana	11.55		14	Connecticut	13.60
40	Iowa	10.38		15	Maryland	13.28
23	Kansas	12.44		16	Kentucky	13.22
16	Kentucky	13.22		17	Tennessee	13.06
30	Louisiana	11.84		18	New Jersey	12.98
5	Maine	15.66		19	Missouri	12.94
15	Maryland	13.28		19	Oregon	12.94
4	Massachusetts	15.74		21	Ohio	12.83
36	Michigan	10.75		22	Virginia	12.46
41	Minnesota	10.31		23	Kansas	12.44
24	Mississippi	12.25		24	Mississippi	12.25
19	Missouri	12.94		25	Oklahoma	12.17
34	Montana	11.12		26	Nevada	12.12
46	Nebraska	9.62		27	Arizona	12.11
26	Nevada	12.12		28	Washington	11.97
7	New Hampshire	15.03		29	New York	11.91
18	New Jersey	12.98		30	Louisiana	11.84
38	New Mexico	10.65		31	Indiana	11.55
29	New York	11.91		32	Idaho	11.49
11	North Carolina	14.06		33	Vermont	11.13
45	North Dakota	9.68		34	Montana	11.12
21	Ohio	12.83		35	Illinois	10.91
25	Oklahoma	12.17		36	Michigan	10.75
19	Oregon	12.94		37	Arkansas	10.72
9	Pennsylvania	14.30		38	New Mexico	10.65
2	Rhode Island	15.94		39	California	10.43
10	South Carolina	14.09		40	Iowa	10.38
49	South Dakota	9.46		41	Minnesota	10.31
17	Tennessee	13.06		42	Wyoming	10.30
44	Texas	10.25		43	Wisconsin	10.27
47	Utah	9.61		44	Texas	10.25
33	Vermont	11.13		45	North Dakota	9.68
22	Virginia	12.46		46	Nebraska	9.62
28	Washington	11.97		47	Colorado	9.61
8	West Virginia	14.38		47	Utah	9.61
43	Wisconsin	10.27		49	South Dakota	9.46
42	Wyoming	10.30		50	Alaska	4.75
					District of Columbia	14.67

Source: U.S. Department of Energy, Energy Information Administration
"Natural Gas Annual 2006" (http://www.eia.doe.gov/oil_gas/natural_gas/info_glance/natural_gas.html)

Average Price of Natural Gas Delivered to Residential Customers in 2006

National Average = $13.75 per Thousand Cubic Feet

ALPHA ORDER

RANK	STATE	RATE
3	Alabama	$18.80
50	Alaska	6.84
15	Arizona	16.32
28	Arkansas	14.15
40	California	11.79
49	Colorado	10.45
6	Connecticut	17.71
10	Delaware	16.93
2	Florida	21.54
4	Georgia	18.20
1	Hawaii	35.28
37	Idaho	12.25
45	Illinois	11.18
34	Indiana	13.07
36	Iowa	12.42
32	Kansas	13.19
29	Kentucky	14.14
21	Louisiana	14.67
5	Maine	17.90
14	Maryland	16.36
7	Massachusetts	17.66
39	Michigan	11.97
41	Minnesota	11.67
22	Mississippi	14.65
26	Missouri	14.25
44	Montana	11.26
43	Nebraska	11.30
25	Nevada	14.31
13	New Hampshire	16.38
19	New Jersey	15.33
35	New Mexico	12.64
18	New York	15.35
10	North Carolina	16.93
48	North Dakota	10.80
24	Ohio	14.39
30	Oklahoma	13.40
23	Oregon	14.53
12	Pennsylvania	16.45
8	Rhode Island	17.58
9	South Carolina	17.36
46	South Dakota	11.11
20	Tennessee	14.74
33	Texas	13.11
47	Utah	11.02
27	Vermont	14.18
16	Virginia	16.20
31	Washington	13.36
17	West Virginia	15.74
38	Wisconsin	12.17
42	Wyoming	11.60

RANK ORDER

RANK	STATE	RATE
1	Hawaii	$35.28
2	Florida	21.54
3	Alabama	18.80
4	Georgia	18.20
5	Maine	17.90
6	Connecticut	17.71
7	Massachusetts	17.66
8	Rhode Island	17.58
9	South Carolina	17.36
10	Delaware	16.93
10	North Carolina	16.93
12	Pennsylvania	16.45
13	New Hampshire	16.38
14	Maryland	16.36
15	Arizona	16.32
16	Virginia	16.20
17	West Virginia	15.74
18	New York	15.35
19	New Jersey	15.33
20	Tennessee	14.74
21	Louisiana	14.67
22	Mississippi	14.65
23	Oregon	14.53
24	Ohio	14.39
25	Nevada	14.31
26	Missouri	14.25
27	Vermont	14.18
28	Arkansas	14.15
29	Kentucky	14.14
30	Oklahoma	13.40
31	Washington	13.36
32	Kansas	13.19
33	Texas	13.11
34	Indiana	13.07
35	New Mexico	12.64
36	Iowa	12.42
37	Idaho	12.25
38	Wisconsin	12.17
39	Michigan	11.97
40	California	11.79
41	Minnesota	11.67
42	Wyoming	11.60
43	Nebraska	11.30
44	Montana	11.26
45	Illinois	11.18
46	South Dakota	11.11
47	Utah	11.02
48	North Dakota	10.80
49	Colorado	10.45
50	Alaska	6.84
	District of Columbia	16.96

Source: U.S. Department of Energy, Energy Information Administration
"Natural Gas Annual 2006" (http://www.eia.doe.gov/oil_gas/natural_gas/info_glance/natural_gas.html)

Natural Gas Consumption in 2006

National Total = 21,653,086,000,000 Cubic Feet*

ALPHA ORDER

RANK	STATE	CUBIC FEET	% of USA
15	Alabama	391,098,000,000	1.8%
16	Alaska	379,791,000,000	1.8%
19	Arizona	358,136,000,000	1.7%
28	Arkansas	233,640,000,000	1.1%
2	California	2,292,056,000,000	10.6%
13	Colorado	449,830,000,000	2.1%
37	Connecticut	172,707,000,000	0.8%
47	Delaware	43,194,000,000	0.2%
6	Florida	891,607,000,000	4.1%
14	Georgia	419,908,000,000	1.9%
50	Hawaii	2,784,000,000	0.0%
42	Idaho	75,728,000,000	0.3%
5	Illinois	892,129,000,000	4.1%
12	Indiana	496,332,000,000	2.3%
27	Iowa	238,495,000,000	1.1%
24	Kansas	258,363,000,000	1.2%
33	Kentucky	211,067,000,000	1.0%
3	Louisiana	1,222,720,000,000	5.6%
46	Maine	49,605,000,000	0.2%
35	Maryland	182,057,000,000	0.8%
18	Massachusetts	370,789,000,000	1.7%
7	Michigan	809,099,000,000	3.7%
20	Minnesota	352,576,000,000	1.6%
21	Mississippi	307,293,000,000	1.4%
25	Missouri	250,797,000,000	1.2%
43	Montana	73,882,000,000	0.3%
38	Nebraska	121,756,000,000	0.6%
26	Nevada	249,683,000,000	1.2%
44	New Hampshire	62,549,000,000	0.3%
11	New Jersey	547,908,000,000	2.5%
29	New Mexico	224,103,000,000	1.0%
4	New York	1,097,040,000,000	5.1%
30	North Carolina	223,038,000,000	1.0%
45	North Dakota	53,338,000,000	0.2%
8	Ohio	742,440,000,000	3.4%
10	Oklahoma	618,714,000,000	2.9%
31	Oregon	222,643,000,000	1.0%
9	Pennsylvania	659,848,000,000	3.0%
41	Rhode Island	77,197,000,000	0.4%
36	South Carolina	174,805,000,000	0.8%
48	South Dakota	40,739,000,000	0.2%
32	Tennessee	220,426,000,000	1.0%
1	Texas	3,433,863,000,000	15.9%
34	Utah	187,537,000,000	0.9%
49	Vermont	8,056,000,000	0.0%
22	Virginia	274,055,000,000	1.3%
23	Washington	263,467,000,000	1.2%
39	West Virginia	113,085,000,000	0.5%
17	Wisconsin	372,457,000,000	1.7%
40	Wyoming	107,363,000,000	0.5%

RANK ORDER

RANK	STATE	CUBIC FEET	% of USA
1	Texas	3,433,863,000,000	15.9%
2	California	2,292,056,000,000	10.6%
3	Louisiana	1,222,720,000,000	5.6%
4	New York	1,097,040,000,000	5.1%
5	Illinois	892,129,000,000	4.1%
6	Florida	891,607,000,000	4.1%
7	Michigan	809,099,000,000	3.7%
8	Ohio	742,440,000,000	3.4%
9	Pennsylvania	659,848,000,000	3.0%
10	Oklahoma	618,714,000,000	2.9%
11	New Jersey	547,908,000,000	2.5%
12	Indiana	496,332,000,000	2.3%
13	Colorado	449,830,000,000	2.1%
14	Georgia	419,908,000,000	1.9%
15	Alabama	391,098,000,000	1.8%
16	Alaska	379,791,000,000	1.8%
17	Wisconsin	372,457,000,000	1.7%
18	Massachusetts	370,789,000,000	1.7%
19	Arizona	358,136,000,000	1.7%
20	Minnesota	352,576,000,000	1.6%
21	Mississippi	307,293,000,000	1.4%
22	Virginia	274,055,000,000	1.3%
23	Washington	263,467,000,000	1.2%
24	Kansas	258,363,000,000	1.2%
25	Missouri	250,797,000,000	1.2%
26	Nevada	249,683,000,000	1.2%
27	Iowa	238,495,000,000	1.1%
28	Arkansas	233,640,000,000	1.1%
29	New Mexico	224,103,000,000	1.0%
30	North Carolina	223,038,000,000	1.0%
31	Oregon	222,643,000,000	1.0%
32	Tennessee	220,426,000,000	1.0%
33	Kentucky	211,067,000,000	1.0%
34	Utah	187,537,000,000	0.9%
35	Maryland	182,057,000,000	0.8%
36	South Carolina	174,805,000,000	0.8%
37	Connecticut	172,707,000,000	0.8%
38	Nebraska	121,756,000,000	0.6%
39	West Virginia	113,085,000,000	0.5%
40	Wyoming	107,363,000,000	0.5%
41	Rhode Island	77,197,000,000	0.4%
42	Idaho	75,728,000,000	0.3%
43	Montana	73,882,000,000	0.3%
44	New Hampshire	62,549,000,000	0.3%
45	North Dakota	53,338,000,000	0.2%
46	Maine	49,605,000,000	0.2%
47	Delaware	43,194,000,000	0.2%
48	South Dakota	40,739,000,000	0.2%
49	Vermont	8,056,000,000	0.0%
50	Hawaii	2,784,000,000	0.0%
	District of Columbia	29,052,000,000	0.1%

Source: U.S. Department of Energy, Energy Information Administration
"Natural Gas Annual 2006" (http://www.eia.doe.gov/oil_gas/natural_gas/info_glance/natural_gas.html)
*National total includes 102,242,000,000 cubic feet of consumption in the Gulf of Mexico not shown by state.

Coal Mines in 2006

National Total = 1,438

ALPHA ORDER

RANK	STATE	MINES	% of USA
5	Alabama	57	4.0%
23	Alaska	1	0.1%
23	Arizona	1	0.1%
19	Arkansas	2	0.1%
NA	California**	NA	NA
13	Colorado	12	0.8%
NA	Connecticut**	NA	NA
NA	Delaware**	NA	NA
NA	Florida**	NA	NA
NA	Georgia**	NA	NA
NA	Hawaii**	NA	NA
NA	Idaho**	NA	NA
9	Illinois	22	1.5%
7	Indiana	28	1.9%
NA	Iowa**	NA	NA
19	Kansas	2	0.1%
1	Kentucky	442	30.7%
19	Louisiana	2	0.1%
NA	Maine**	NA	NA
11	Maryland	19	1.3%
NA	Massachusetts**	NA	NA
NA	Michigan**	NA	NA
NA	Minnesota**	NA	NA
23	Mississippi	1	0.1%
19	Missouri	2	0.1%
16	Montana	6	0.4%
NA	Nebraska**	NA	NA
NA	Nevada**	NA	NA
NA	New Hampshire**	NA	NA
NA	New Jersey**	NA	NA
17	New Mexico	4	0.3%
NA	New York**	NA	NA
NA	North Carolina**	NA	NA
17	North Dakota	4	0.3%
6	Ohio	52	3.6%
15	Oklahoma	10	0.7%
NA	Oregon**	NA	NA
3	Pennsylvania	270	18.8%
NA	Rhode Island**	NA	NA
NA	South Carolina**	NA	NA
NA	South Dakota**	NA	NA
8	Tennessee	23	1.6%
13	Texas	12	0.8%
12	Utah	13	0.9%
NA	Vermont**	NA	NA
4	Virginia	127	8.8%
23	Washington	1	0.1%
2	West Virginia	290	20.2%
NA	Wisconsin**	NA	NA
10	Wyoming	21	1.5%

RANK ORDER

RANK	STATE	MINES	% of USA
1	Kentucky	442	30.7%
2	West Virginia	290	20.2%
3	Pennsylvania	270	18.8%
4	Virginia	127	8.8%
5	Alabama	57	4.0%
6	Ohio	52	3.6%
7	Indiana	28	1.9%
8	Tennessee	23	1.6%
9	Illinois	22	1.5%
10	Wyoming	21	1.5%
11	Maryland	19	1.3%
12	Utah	13	0.9%
13	Colorado	12	0.8%
13	Texas	12	0.8%
15	Oklahoma	10	0.7%
16	Montana	6	0.4%
17	New Mexico	4	0.3%
17	North Dakota	4	0.3%
19	Arkansas	2	0.1%
19	Kansas	2	0.1%
19	Louisiana	2	0.1%
19	Missouri	2	0.1%
23	Alaska	1	0.1%
23	Arizona	1	0.1%
23	Mississippi	1	0.1%
23	Washington	1	0.1%
NA	California**	NA	NA
NA	Connecticut**	NA	NA
NA	Delaware**	NA	NA
NA	Florida**	NA	NA
NA	Georgia**	NA	NA
NA	Hawaii**	NA	NA
NA	Idaho**	NA	NA
NA	Iowa**	NA	NA
NA	Maine**	NA	NA
NA	Massachusetts**	NA	NA
NA	Michigan**	NA	NA
NA	Minnesota**	NA	NA
NA	Nebraska**	NA	NA
NA	Nevada**	NA	NA
NA	New Hampshire**	NA	NA
NA	New Jersey**	NA	NA
NA	New York**	NA	NA
NA	North Carolina**	NA	NA
NA	Oregon**	NA	NA
NA	Rhode Island**	NA	NA
NA	South Carolina**	NA	NA
NA	South Dakota**	NA	NA
NA	Vermont**	NA	NA
NA	Wisconsin**	NA	NA

District of Columbia** — NA — NA

Source: U.S. Department of Energy, Energy Information Administration
   "Annual Coal Report" (http://www.eia.doe.gov/cneaf/coal/page/acr/acr_sum.html)
*National total includes 14 coal mines in refuse recovery not shown by state.
**Not available or no mines.

Coal Production in 2006

National Total = 1,162,750,000 Short Tons*

RANK	STATE	SHORT TONS	% of USA
15	Alabama	18,830,000	1.6%
23	Alaska	1,425,000	0.1%
16	Arizona	8,216,000	0.7%
26	Arkansas	23,000	0.0%
NA	California**	NA	NA
7	Colorado	36,322,000	3.1%
NA	Connecticut**	NA	NA
NA	Delaware**	NA	NA
NA	Florida**	NA	NA
NA	Georgia**	NA	NA
NA	Hawaii**	NA	NA
NA	Idaho**	NA	NA
9	Illinois	32,729,000	2.8%
8	Indiana	35,119,000	3.0%
NA	Iowa**	NA	NA
24	Kansas	426,000	0.0%
3	Kentucky	120,848,000	10.4%
18	Louisiana	4,114,000	0.4%
NA	Maine**	NA	NA
17	Maryland	5,054,000	0.4%
NA	Massachusetts**	NA	NA
NA	Michigan**	NA	NA
NA	Minnesota**	NA	NA
19	Mississippi	3,797,000	0.3%
25	Missouri	394,000	0.0%
6	Montana	41,823,000	3.6%
NA	Nebraska**	NA	NA
NA	Nevada**	NA	NA
NA	New Hampshire**	NA	NA
NA	New Jersey**	NA	NA
13	New Mexico	25,913,000	2.2%
NA	New York**	NA	NA
NA	North Carolina**	NA	NA
10	North Dakota	30,411,000	2.6%
14	Ohio	22,722,000	2.0%
22	Oklahoma	1,998,000	0.2%
NA	Oregon**	NA	NA
4	Pennsylvania	66,029,000	5.7%
NA	Rhode Island**	NA	NA
NA	South Carolina**	NA	NA
NA	South Dakota**	NA	NA
20	Tennessee	2,804,000	0.2%
5	Texas	45,548,000	3.9%
12	Utah	26,018,000	2.2%
NA	Vermont**	NA	NA
11	Virginia	29,740,000	2.6%
21	Washington	2,580,000	0.2%
2	West Virginia	152,374,000	13.1%
NA	Wisconsin**	NA	NA
1	Wyoming	446,742,000	38.4%

RANK	STATE	SHORT TONS	% of USA
1	Wyoming	446,742,000	38.4%
2	West Virginia	152,374,000	13.1%
3	Kentucky	120,848,000	10.4%
4	Pennsylvania	66,029,000	5.7%
5	Texas	45,548,000	3.9%
6	Montana	41,823,000	3.6%
7	Colorado	36,322,000	3.1%
8	Indiana	35,119,000	3.0%
9	Illinois	32,729,000	2.8%
10	North Dakota	30,411,000	2.6%
11	Virginia	29,740,000	2.6%
12	Utah	26,018,000	2.2%
13	New Mexico	25,913,000	2.2%
14	Ohio	22,722,000	2.0%
15	Alabama	18,830,000	1.6%
16	Arizona	8,216,000	0.7%
17	Maryland	5,054,000	0.4%
18	Louisiana	4,114,000	0.4%
19	Mississippi	3,797,000	0.3%
20	Tennessee	2,804,000	0.2%
21	Washington	2,580,000	0.2%
22	Oklahoma	1,998,000	0.2%
23	Alaska	1,425,000	0.1%
24	Kansas	426,000	0.0%
25	Missouri	394,000	0.0%
26	Arkansas	23,000	0.0%
NA	California**	NA	NA
NA	Connecticut**	NA	NA
NA	Delaware**	NA	NA
NA	Florida**	NA	NA
NA	Georgia**	NA	NA
NA	Hawaii**	NA	NA
NA	Idaho**	NA	NA
NA	Iowa**	NA	NA
NA	Maine**	NA	NA
NA	Massachusetts**	NA	NA
NA	Michigan**	NA	NA
NA	Minnesota**	NA	NA
NA	Nebraska**	NA	NA
NA	Nevada**	NA	NA
NA	New Hampshire**	NA	NA
NA	New Jersey**	NA	NA
NA	New York**	NA	NA
NA	North Carolina**	NA	NA
NA	Oregon**	NA	NA
NA	Rhode Island**	NA	NA
NA	South Carolina**	NA	NA
NA	South Dakota**	NA	NA
NA	Vermont**	NA	NA
NA	Wisconsin**	NA	NA
	District of Columbia**	NA	NA

Source: U.S. Department of Energy, Energy Information Administration
"Annual Coal Report" (http://www.eia.doe.gov/cneaf/coal/page/acr/acr_sum.html)
*National total includes 752,000 short tons from refuse recovery not shown by state.
**Not available or no production.

Gasoline Used in 2005

National Total = 139,988,554,000 Gallons*

ALPHA ORDER

ALPHA ORDER

RANK	STATE	GALLONS	% of USA
21	Alabama	2,629,805,000	1.9%
50	Alaska	299,484,000	0.2%
17	Arizona	2,827,962,000	2.0%
32	Arkansas	1,444,285,000	1.0%
1	California	15,953,544,000	11.4%
26	Colorado	2,149,600,000	1.5%
30	Connecticut	1,621,416,000	1.2%
44	Delaware	446,400,000	0.3%
3	Florida	8,688,392,000	6.2%
8	Georgia	5,119,288,000	3.7%
43	Hawaii	460,712,000	0.3%
41	Idaho	622,214,000	0.4%
6	Illinois	5,211,550,000	3.7%
14	Indiana	3,224,630,000	2.3%
29	Iowa	1,644,758,000	1.2%
33	Kansas	1,186,646,000	0.8%
25	Kentucky	2,254,889,000	1.6%
24	Louisiana	2,377,518,000	1.7%
39	Maine	725,420,000	0.5%
20	Maryland	2,702,478,000	1.9%
16	Massachusetts	2,848,206,000	2.0%
9	Michigan	4,999,437,000	3.6%
19	Minnesota	2,707,472,000	1.9%
28	Mississippi	1,663,258,000	1.2%
13	Missouri	3,225,434,000	2.3%
42	Montana	493,946,000	0.4%
38	Nebraska	845,607,000	0.6%
34	Nevada	1,140,200,000	0.8%
40	New Hampshire	709,588,000	0.5%
11	New Jersey	4,314,114,000	3.1%
36	New Mexico	964,204,000	0.7%
4	New York	5,750,908,000	4.1%
10	North Carolina	4,425,595,000	3.2%
47	North Dakota	367,259,000	0.3%
5	Ohio	5,214,309,000	3.7%
27	Oklahoma	1,889,136,000	1.3%
31	Oregon	1,572,881,000	1.1%
7	Pennsylvania	5,176,664,000	3.7%
46	Rhode Island	385,591,000	0.3%
23	South Carolina	2,481,868,000	1.8%
45	South Dakota	430,597,000	0.3%
15	Tennessee	3,111,613,000	2.2%
2	Texas	11,652,049,000	8.3%
35	Utah	1,035,953,000	0.7%
49	Vermont	352,451,000	0.3%
12	Virginia	3,992,108,000	2.9%
18	Washington	2,736,786,000	2.0%
37	West Virginia	848,234,000	0.6%
22	Wisconsin	2,567,465,000	1.8%
48	Wyoming	353,831,000	0.3%

RANK ORDER

RANK	STATE	GALLONS	% of USA
1	California	15,953,544,000	11.4%
2	Texas	11,652,049,000	8.3%
3	Florida	8,688,392,000	6.2%
4	New York	5,750,908,000	4.1%
5	Ohio	5,214,309,000	3.7%
6	Illinois	5,211,550,000	3.7%
7	Pennsylvania	5,176,664,000	3.7%
8	Georgia	5,119,288,000	3.7%
9	Michigan	4,999,437,000	3.6%
10	North Carolina	4,425,595,000	3.2%
11	New Jersey	4,314,114,000	3.1%
12	Virginia	3,992,108,000	2.9%
13	Missouri	3,225,434,000	2.3%
14	Indiana	3,224,630,000	2.3%
15	Tennessee	3,111,613,000	2.2%
16	Massachusetts	2,848,206,000	2.0%
17	Arizona	2,827,962,000	2.0%
18	Washington	2,736,786,000	2.0%
19	Minnesota	2,707,472,000	1.9%
20	Maryland	2,702,478,000	1.9%
21	Alabama	2,629,805,000	1.9%
22	Wisconsin	2,567,465,000	1.8%
23	South Carolina	2,481,868,000	1.8%
24	Louisiana	2,377,518,000	1.7%
25	Kentucky	2,254,889,000	1.6%
26	Colorado	2,149,600,000	1.5%
27	Oklahoma	1,889,136,000	1.3%
28	Mississippi	1,663,258,000	1.2%
29	Iowa	1,644,758,000	1.2%
30	Connecticut	1,621,416,000	1.2%
31	Oregon	1,572,881,000	1.1%
32	Arkansas	1,444,285,000	1.0%
33	Kansas	1,186,646,000	0.8%
34	Nevada	1,140,200,000	0.8%
35	Utah	1,035,953,000	0.7%
36	New Mexico	964,204,000	0.7%
37	West Virginia	848,234,000	0.6%
38	Nebraska	845,607,000	0.6%
39	Maine	725,420,000	0.5%
40	New Hampshire	709,588,000	0.5%
41	Idaho	622,214,000	0.4%
42	Montana	493,946,000	0.4%
43	Hawaii	460,712,000	0.3%
44	Delaware	446,400,000	0.3%
45	South Dakota	430,597,000	0.3%
46	Rhode Island	385,591,000	0.3%
47	North Dakota	367,259,000	0.3%
48	Wyoming	353,831,000	0.3%
49	Vermont	352,451,000	0.3%
50	Alaska	299,484,000	0.2%
	District of Columbia	140,799,000	0.1%

Source: U.S. Department of Transportation, Federal Highway Administration
"Highway Statistics 2005" (Table MF-21) (http://www.fhwa.dot.gov/policy/ohpi/hss/index.htm)
*Includes gasoline for highway and nonhighway uses. "Gasoline" includes gasohol but excludes "special fuels" such as diesel.

Per Capita Gasoline Used in 2005

National Per Capita = 472 Gallons*

ALPHA ORDER

RANK	STATE	GALLONS
4	Alabama	578
38	Alaska	452
31	Arizona	475
21	Arkansas	520
40	California	441
36	Colorado	461
35	Connecticut	463
15	Delaware	530
28	Florida	489
7	Georgia	561
48	Hawaii	362
41	Idaho	435
47	Illinois	408
22	Indiana	515
10	Iowa	555
43	Kansas	432
13	Kentucky	540
19	Louisiana	527
11	Maine	550
29	Maryland	483
39	Massachusetts	443
27	Michigan	495
16	Minnesota	528
5	Mississippi	572
8	Missouri	556
16	Montana	528
30	Nebraska	481
32	Nevada	473
12	New Hampshire	543
26	New Jersey	496
25	New Mexico	501
50	New York	298
23	North Carolina	510
3	North Dakota	579
37	Ohio	455
14	Oklahoma	533
43	Oregon	432
45	Pennsylvania	417
49	Rhode Island	359
2	South Carolina	584
8	South Dakota	556
20	Tennessee	522
24	Texas	508
46	Utah	416
6	Vermont	566
16	Virginia	528
41	Washington	435
33	West Virginia	468
34	Wisconsin	464
1	Wyoming	695

RANK ORDER

RANK	STATE	GALLONS
1	Wyoming	695
2	South Carolina	584
3	North Dakota	579
4	Alabama	578
5	Mississippi	572
6	Vermont	566
7	Georgia	561
8	Missouri	556
8	South Dakota	556
10	Iowa	555
11	Maine	550
12	New Hampshire	543
13	Kentucky	540
14	Oklahoma	533
15	Delaware	530
16	Minnesota	528
16	Montana	528
16	Virginia	528
19	Louisiana	527
20	Tennessee	522
21	Arkansas	520
22	Indiana	515
23	North Carolina	510
24	Texas	508
25	New Mexico	501
26	New Jersey	496
27	Michigan	495
28	Florida	489
29	Maryland	483
30	Nebraska	481
31	Arizona	475
32	Nevada	473
33	West Virginia	468
34	Wisconsin	464
35	Connecticut	463
36	Colorado	461
37	Ohio	455
38	Alaska	452
39	Massachusetts	443
40	California	441
41	Idaho	435
41	Washington	435
43	Kansas	432
43	Oregon	432
45	Pennsylvania	417
46	Utah	416
47	Illinois	408
48	Hawaii	362
49	Rhode Island	359
50	New York	298
	District of Columbia	242

Source: CQ Press using data from U.S. Department of Transportation, Federal Highway Administration
"Highway Statistics 2005" (Table MF-21) (http://www.fhwa.dot.gov/policy/ohpi/hss/index.htm)
*Includes gasoline for highway and nonhighway uses. "Gasoline" includes gasohol but excludes "special fuels" such as diesel.

Daily Production of Crude Oil in 2006

National Total = 5,102,079 Barrels a Day*

RANK	STATE	BARRELS	% of USA		RANK	STATE	BARRELS	% of USA
15	Alabama	20,633	0.4%		1	Texas	1,088,274	21.3%
2	Alaska	741,058	14.5%		2	Alaska	741,058	14.5%
30	Arizona	151	0.0%		3	California	612,189	12.0%
16	Arkansas	16,723	0.3%		4	Louisiana	202,400	4.0%
3	California	612,189	12.0%		5	Oklahoma	172,167	3.4%
11	Colorado	64,082	1.3%		6	New Mexico	163,885	3.2%
NA	Connecticut**	NA	NA		7	Wyoming	144,942	2.8%
NA	Delaware**	NA	NA		8	North Dakota	109,345	2.1%
20	Florida	6,466	0.1%		9	Montana	99,348	1.9%
NA	Georgia**	NA	NA		10	Kansas	97,674	1.9%
NA	Hawaii**	NA	NA		11	Colorado	64,082	1.3%
NA	Idaho**	NA	NA		12	Utah	49,068	1.0%
14	Illinois	28,282	0.6%		13	Mississippi	47,551	0.9%
24	Indiana	4,742	0.1%		14	Illinois	28,282	0.6%
NA	Iowa**	NA	NA		15	Alabama	20,633	0.4%
10	Kansas	97,674	1.9%		16	Arkansas	16,723	0.3%
21	Kentucky	6,411	0.1%		17	Ohio	14,855	0.3%
4	Louisiana	202,400	4.0%		18	Michigan	13,953	0.3%
NA	Maine**	NA	NA		19	Pennsylvania	9,934	0.2%
NA	Maryland**	NA	NA		20	Florida	6,466	0.1%
NA	Massachusetts**	NA	NA		21	Kentucky	6,411	0.1%
18	Michigan	13,953	0.3%		22	Nebraska	6,337	0.1%
NA	Minnesota**	NA	NA		23	West Virginia	4,792	0.1%
13	Mississippi	47,551	0.9%		24	Indiana	4,742	0.1%
29	Missouri	238	0.0%		25	South Dakota	3,819	0.1%
9	Montana	99,348	1.9%		26	Nevada	1,167	0.0%
22	Nebraska	6,337	0.1%		27	New York	874	0.0%
26	Nevada	1,167	0.0%		28	Tennessee	526	0.0%
NA	New Hampshire**	NA	NA		29	Missouri	238	0.0%
NA	New Jersey**	NA	NA		30	Arizona	151	0.0%
6	New Mexico	163,885	3.2%		31	Virginia	19	0.0%
27	New York	874	0.0%		NA	Connecticut**	NA	NA
NA	North Carolina**	NA	NA		NA	Delaware**	NA	NA
8	North Dakota	109,345	2.1%		NA	Georgia**	NA	NA
17	Ohio	14,855	0.3%		NA	Hawaii**	NA	NA
5	Oklahoma	172,167	3.4%		NA	Idaho**	NA	NA
NA	Oregon**	NA	NA		NA	Iowa**	NA	NA
19	Pennsylvania	9,934	0.2%		NA	Maine**	NA	NA
NA	Rhode Island**	NA	NA		NA	Maryland**	NA	NA
NA	South Carolina**	NA	NA		NA	Massachusetts**	NA	NA
25	South Dakota	3,819	0.1%		NA	Minnesota**	NA	NA
28	Tennessee	526	0.0%		NA	New Hampshire**	NA	NA
1	Texas	1,088,274	21.3%		NA	New Jersey**	NA	NA
12	Utah	49,068	1.0%		NA	North Carolina**	NA	NA
NA	Vermont**	NA	NA		NA	Oregon**	NA	NA
31	Virginia	19	0.0%		NA	Rhode Island**	NA	NA
NA	Washington**	NA	NA		NA	South Carolina**	NA	NA
23	West Virginia	4,792	0.1%		NA	Vermont**	NA	NA
NA	Wisconsin**	NA	NA		NA	Washington**	NA	NA
7	Wyoming	144,942	2.8%		NA	Wisconsin**	NA	NA
						District of Columbia**	NA	NA

ALPHA ORDER — RANK ORDER

Source: CQ Press using data from U.S. Department of Energy, Energy Information Administration
   "Petroleum Supply Annual, Volume 1: Production of Crude Oil by PAD District and State, 2006"
*National total includes 1,370,173 barrels a day in federal offshore production. Figures for Alaska, California, Louisiana, and Texas include state offshore production.
**No reported production.

Hazardous Waste Sites on the National Priority List in 2007

National Total = 1,311 Sites*

ALPHA ORDER

RANK	STATE	SITES	% of USA
24	Alabama	15	1.1%
45	Alaska	5	0.4%
43	Arizona	8	0.6%
40	Arkansas	10	0.8%
2	California	96	7.3%
20	Colorado	19	1.4%
24	Connecticut	15	1.1%
27	Delaware	14	1.1%
6	Florida	49	3.7%
23	Georgia	16	1.2%
46	Hawaii	3	0.2%
41	Idaho	9	0.7%
6	Illinois	49	3.7%
12	Indiana	32	2.4%
33	Iowa	12	0.9%
33	Kansas	12	0.9%
27	Kentucky	14	1.1%
27	Louisiana	14	1.1%
33	Maine	12	0.9%
22	Maryland	18	1.4%
12	Massachusetts	32	2.4%
5	Michigan	67	5.1%
17	Minnesota	25	1.9%
44	Mississippi	6	0.5%
16	Missouri	29	2.2%
24	Montana	15	1.1%
32	Nebraska	13	1.0%
49	Nevada	1	0.1%
19	New Hampshire	21	1.6%
1	New Jersey	116	8.8%
27	New Mexico	14	1.1%
4	New York	87	6.6%
14	North Carolina	31	2.4%
50	North Dakota	0	0.0%
10	Ohio	38	2.9%
38	Oklahoma	11	0.8%
33	Oregon	12	0.9%
2	Pennsylvania	96	7.3%
33	Rhode Island	12	0.9%
17	South Carolina	25	1.9%
47	South Dakota	2	0.2%
27	Tennessee	14	1.1%
9	Texas	47	3.6%
20	Utah	19	1.4%
38	Vermont	11	0.8%
15	Virginia	30	2.3%
8	Washington	48	3.7%
41	West Virginia	9	0.7%
10	Wisconsin	38	2.9%
47	Wyoming	2	0.2%

RANK ORDER

RANK	STATE	SITES	% of USA
1	New Jersey	116	8.8%
2	California	96	7.3%
2	Pennsylvania	96	7.3%
4	New York	87	6.6%
5	Michigan	67	5.1%
6	Florida	49	3.7%
6	Illinois	49	3.7%
8	Washington	48	3.7%
9	Texas	47	3.6%
10	Ohio	38	2.9%
10	Wisconsin	38	2.9%
12	Indiana	32	2.4%
12	Massachusetts	32	2.4%
14	North Carolina	31	2.4%
15	Virginia	30	2.3%
16	Missouri	29	2.2%
17	Minnesota	25	1.9%
17	South Carolina	25	1.9%
19	New Hampshire	21	1.6%
20	Colorado	19	1.4%
20	Utah	19	1.4%
22	Maryland	18	1.4%
23	Georgia	16	1.2%
24	Alabama	15	1.1%
24	Connecticut	15	1.1%
24	Montana	15	1.1%
27	Delaware	14	1.1%
27	Kentucky	14	1.1%
27	Louisiana	14	1.1%
27	New Mexico	14	1.1%
27	Tennessee	14	1.1%
32	Nebraska	13	1.0%
33	Iowa	12	0.9%
33	Kansas	12	0.9%
33	Maine	12	0.9%
33	Oregon	12	0.9%
33	Rhode Island	12	0.9%
38	Oklahoma	11	0.8%
38	Vermont	11	0.8%
40	Arkansas	10	0.8%
41	Idaho	9	0.7%
41	West Virginia	9	0.7%
43	Arizona	8	0.6%
44	Mississippi	6	0.5%
45	Alaska	5	0.4%
46	Hawaii	3	0.2%
47	South Dakota	2	0.2%
47	Wyoming	2	0.2%
49	Nevada	1	0.1%
50	North Dakota	0	0.0%
	District of Columbia	1	0.1%

Source: U.S. Environmental Protection Agency
"National Priorities List (NPL) Sites in the United States" (www.epa.gov/superfund/sites/npl/npl.htm)
*As of October 2007. Includes final and proposed General Superfund and Federal Facilities Sites. National total includes 15 sites in Puerto Rico, two in Guam, and five in the other U.S. territories.

Hazardous Waste Sites on the National Priority List
per 10,000 Square Miles in 2007
National Rate = 3.4 Sites per 10,000 Square Miles*

ALPHA ORDER

RANK	STATE	RATE
27	Alabama	2.9
48	Alaska	0.1
45	Arizona	0.7
34	Arkansas	1.9
19	California	5.9
35	Colorado	1.8
5	Connecticut	27.1
3	Delaware	56.2
15	Florida	7.5
29	Georgia	2.7
29	Hawaii	2.7
43	Idaho	1.1
12	Illinois	8.5
11	Indiana	8.8
33	Iowa	2.1
39	Kansas	1.5
24	Kentucky	3.5
29	Louisiana	2.7
25	Maine	3.4
9	Maryland	14.5
4	Massachusetts	30.3
17	Michigan	6.9
27	Minnesota	2.9
40	Mississippi	1.2
22	Missouri	4.2
44	Montana	1.0
36	Nebraska	1.7
48	Nevada	0.1
6	New Hampshire	22.5
1	New Jersey	133.0
40	New Mexico	1.2
8	New York	15.9
20	North Carolina	5.8
50	North Dakota	0.0
12	Ohio	8.5
38	Oklahoma	1.6
40	Oregon	1.2
7	Pennsylvania	20.8
2	Rhode Island	77.7
14	South Carolina	7.8
46	South Dakota	0.3
26	Tennessee	3.3
36	Texas	1.7
32	Utah	2.2
10	Vermont	11.4
16	Virginia	7.0
18	Washington	6.7
23	West Virginia	3.7
20	Wisconsin	5.8
47	Wyoming	0.2

RANK ORDER

RANK	STATE	RATE
1	New Jersey	133.0
2	Rhode Island	77.7
3	Delaware	56.2
4	Massachusetts	30.3
5	Connecticut	27.1
6	New Hampshire	22.5
7	Pennsylvania	20.8
8	New York	15.9
9	Maryland	14.5
10	Vermont	11.4
11	Indiana	8.8
12	Illinois	8.5
12	Ohio	8.5
14	South Carolina	7.8
15	Florida	7.5
16	Virginia	7.0
17	Michigan	6.9
18	Washington	6.7
19	California	5.9
20	North Carolina	5.8
20	Wisconsin	5.8
22	Missouri	4.2
23	West Virginia	3.7
24	Kentucky	3.5
25	Maine	3.4
26	Tennessee	3.3
27	Alabama	2.9
27	Minnesota	2.9
29	Georgia	2.7
29	Hawaii	2.7
29	Louisiana	2.7
32	Utah	2.2
33	Iowa	2.1
34	Arkansas	1.9
35	Colorado	1.8
36	Nebraska	1.7
36	Texas	1.7
38	Oklahoma	1.6
39	Kansas	1.5
40	Mississippi	1.2
40	New Mexico	1.2
40	Oregon	1.2
43	Idaho	1.1
44	Montana	1.0
45	Arizona	0.7
46	South Dakota	0.3
47	Wyoming	0.2
48	Alaska	0.1
48	Nevada	0.1
50	North Dakota	0.0

District of Columbia**   NA

Source: CQ Press using data from U.S. Environmental Protection Agency
"National Priorities List (NPL) Sites in the United States"

*As of October 2007. Includes final and proposed General Superfund and Federal Facilities Sites. National rate excludes sites and square miles in Puerto Rico, Guam and the Virgin Islands. Based on land and water area of states.
**The District of Columbia has one site in its 68 square miles.

Hazardous Waste Sites Deleted from the National Priorities List as of 2007

National Total = 324 Sites*

ALPHA ORDER

RANK	STATE	SITES	% of USA
42	Alabama	1	0.3%
29	Alaska	3	0.9%
29	Arizona	3	0.9%
18	Arkansas	5	1.5%
8	California	11	3.4%
29	Colorado	3	0.9%
29	Connecticut	3	0.9%
14	Delaware	6	1.9%
4	Florida	22	6.8%
21	Georgia	4	1.2%
42	Hawaii	1	0.3%
29	Idaho	3	0.9%
36	Illinois	2	0.6%
12	Indiana	8	2.5%
9	Iowa	10	3.1%
18	Kansas	5	1.5%
14	Kentucky	6	1.9%
11	Louisiana	9	2.8%
36	Maine	2	0.6%
21	Maryland	4	1.2%
21	Massachusetts	4	1.2%
6	Michigan	17	5.2%
5	Minnesota	21	6.5%
29	Mississippi	3	0.9%
18	Missouri	5	1.5%
48	Montana	0	0.0%
42	Nebraska	1	0.3%
48	Nevada	0	0.0%
48	New Hampshire	0	0.0%
2	New Jersey	24	7.4%
21	New Mexico	4	1.2%
3	New York	23	7.1%
42	North Carolina	1	0.3%
36	North Dakota	2	0.6%
13	Ohio	7	2.2%
29	Oklahoma	3	0.9%
21	Oregon	4	1.2%
1	Pennsylvania	27	8.3%
42	Rhode Island	1	0.3%
21	South Carolina	4	1.2%
36	South Dakota	2	0.6%
14	Tennessee	6	1.9%
9	Texas	10	3.1%
21	Utah	4	1.2%
36	Vermont	2	0.6%
21	Virginia	4	1.2%
6	Washington	17	5.2%
36	West Virginia	2	0.6%
14	Wisconsin	6	1.9%
42	Wyoming	1	0.3%

RANK ORDER

RANK	STATE	SITES	% of USA
1	Pennsylvania	27	8.3%
2	New Jersey	24	7.4%
3	New York	23	7.1%
4	Florida	22	6.8%
5	Minnesota	21	6.5%
6	Michigan	17	5.2%
6	Washington	17	5.2%
8	California	11	3.4%
9	Iowa	10	3.1%
9	Texas	10	3.1%
11	Louisiana	9	2.8%
12	Indiana	8	2.5%
13	Ohio	7	2.2%
14	Delaware	6	1.9%
14	Kentucky	6	1.9%
14	Tennessee	6	1.9%
14	Wisconsin	6	1.9%
18	Arkansas	5	1.5%
18	Kansas	5	1.5%
18	Missouri	5	1.5%
21	Georgia	4	1.2%
21	Maryland	4	1.2%
21	Massachusetts	4	1.2%
21	New Mexico	4	1.2%
21	Oregon	4	1.2%
21	South Carolina	4	1.2%
21	Utah	4	1.2%
21	Virginia	4	1.2%
29	Alaska	3	0.9%
29	Arizona	3	0.9%
29	Colorado	3	0.9%
29	Connecticut	3	0.9%
29	Idaho	3	0.9%
29	Mississippi	3	0.9%
29	Oklahoma	3	0.9%
36	Illinois	2	0.6%
36	Maine	2	0.6%
36	North Dakota	2	0.6%
36	South Dakota	2	0.6%
36	Vermont	2	0.6%
36	West Virginia	2	0.6%
42	Alabama	1	0.3%
42	Hawaii	1	0.3%
42	Nebraska	1	0.3%
42	North Carolina	1	0.3%
42	Rhode Island	1	0.3%
42	Wyoming	1	0.3%
48	Montana	0	0.0%
48	Nevada	0	0.0%
48	New Hampshire	0	0.0%
	District of Columbia	0	0.0%

Source: U.S. Environmental Protection Agency
"National Priorities List (NPL) Sites in the United States" (www.epa.gov/superfund/sites/npl/npl.htm)
*Cumulative total as of October 2007. National total includes five sites in Puerto Rico and three in other U.S. territories.

Toxic Releases: Total Pollution Released in 2005

National Total = 4,330,751,852 Pounds of Toxins*

ALPHA ORDER

RANK	STATE	POUNDS	% of USA
13	Alabama	122,888,800	2.8%
1	Alaska	548,692,097	12.7%
22	Arizona	65,121,394	1.5%
25	Arkansas	49,461,442	1.1%
27	California	43,653,705	1.0%
36	Colorado	25,665,802	0.6%
47	Connecticut	4,793,559	0.1%
42	Delaware	12,778,539	0.3%
11	Florida	129,866,857	3.0%
10	Georgia	130,424,788	3.0%
48	Hawaii	3,106,186	0.1%
21	Idaho	66,009,099	1.5%
14	Illinois	122,338,475	2.8%
5	Indiana	249,202,754	5.8%
30	Iowa	40,133,662	0.9%
33	Kansas	29,646,258	0.7%
16	Kentucky	102,888,597	2.4%
12	Louisiana	125,244,675	2.9%
43	Maine	11,513,052	0.3%
28	Maryland	42,762,778	1.0%
45	Massachusetts	7,656,873	0.2%
17	Michigan	101,887,835	2.4%
35	Minnesota	27,271,909	0.6%
24	Mississippi	58,618,046	1.4%
15	Missouri	121,271,906	2.8%
23	Montana	59,012,894	1.4%
31	Nebraska	37,457,819	0.9%
2	Nevada	326,116,592	7.5%
46	New Hampshire	5,254,593	0.1%
38	New Jersey	23,912,385	0.6%
41	New Mexico	15,105,066	0.3%
29	New York	42,447,044	1.0%
9	North Carolina	139,459,424	3.2%
39	North Dakota	23,035,677	0.5%
3	Ohio	276,920,721	6.4%
34	Oklahoma	27,299,988	0.6%
37	Oregon	23,914,899	0.6%
7	Pennsylvania	156,651,991	3.6%
49	Rhode Island	582,689	0.0%
19	South Carolina	75,927,679	1.8%
44	South Dakota	7,926,408	0.2%
8	Tennessee	143,793,237	3.3%
4	Texas	261,872,877	6.0%
6	Utah	172,622,269	4.0%
50	Vermont	425,115	0.0%
20	Virginia	73,947,822	1.7%
32	Washington	35,852,716	0.8%
18	West Virginia	97,061,444	2.2%
26	Wisconsin	45,588,444	1.1%
40	Wyoming	15,623,107	0.4%

RANK ORDER

RANK	STATE	POUNDS	% of USA
1	Alaska	548,692,097	12.7%
2	Nevada	326,116,592	7.5%
3	Ohio	276,920,721	6.4%
4	Texas	261,872,877	6.0%
5	Indiana	249,202,754	5.8%
6	Utah	172,622,269	4.0%
7	Pennsylvania	156,651,991	3.6%
8	Tennessee	143,793,237	3.3%
9	North Carolina	139,459,424	3.2%
10	Georgia	130,424,788	3.0%
11	Florida	129,866,857	3.0%
12	Louisiana	125,244,675	2.9%
13	Alabama	122,888,800	2.8%
14	Illinois	122,338,475	2.8%
15	Missouri	121,271,906	2.8%
16	Kentucky	102,888,597	2.4%
17	Michigan	101,887,835	2.4%
18	West Virginia	97,061,444	2.2%
19	South Carolina	75,927,679	1.8%
20	Virginia	73,947,822	1.7%
21	Idaho	66,009,099	1.5%
22	Arizona	65,121,394	1.5%
23	Montana	59,012,894	1.4%
24	Mississippi	58,618,046	1.4%
25	Arkansas	49,461,442	1.1%
26	Wisconsin	45,588,444	1.1%
27	California	43,653,705	1.0%
28	Maryland	42,762,778	1.0%
29	New York	42,447,044	1.0%
30	Iowa	40,133,662	0.9%
31	Nebraska	37,457,819	0.9%
32	Washington	35,852,716	0.8%
33	Kansas	29,646,258	0.7%
34	Oklahoma	27,299,988	0.6%
35	Minnesota	27,271,909	0.6%
36	Colorado	25,665,802	0.6%
37	Oregon	23,914,899	0.6%
38	New Jersey	23,912,385	0.6%
39	North Dakota	23,035,677	0.5%
40	Wyoming	15,623,107	0.4%
41	New Mexico	15,105,066	0.3%
42	Delaware	12,778,539	0.3%
43	Maine	11,513,052	0.3%
44	South Dakota	7,926,408	0.2%
45	Massachusetts	7,656,873	0.2%
46	New Hampshire	5,254,593	0.1%
47	Connecticut	4,793,559	0.1%
48	Hawaii	3,106,186	0.1%
49	Rhode Island	582,689	0.0%
50	Vermont	425,115	0.0%
	District of Columbia	39,864	0.0%

Source: U.S. Environmental Protection Agency, Office of Pollution Prevention and Toxics Information Management
    "2005 Toxics Release Inventory" (http://www.epa.gov/tri/tridata/tri05/)
*National total does not include 8,711,898 pounds of toxins in U.S. territories. Includes discharges to air, surface water, underground injection, and surface land. Includes both original (or manufacturing) industries and those added by EPA since it began tracking releases.

Toxic Releases: Total Air Emissions in 2005

National Total = 1,503,898,559 Pounds*

RANK	STATE	POUNDS	% of USA
13	Alabama	51,642,618	3.4%
43	Alaska	2,583,755	0.2%
38	Arizona	4,175,605	0.3%
20	Arkansas	21,939,710	1.5%
24	California	17,334,498	1.2%
41	Colorado	2,973,328	0.2%
42	Connecticut	2,763,616	0.2%
33	Delaware	6,399,004	0.4%
9	Florida	68,900,432	4.6%
3	Georgia	96,824,944	6.4%
44	Hawaii	2,311,630	0.2%
39	Idaho	4,024,870	0.3%
14	Illinois	51,331,483	3.4%
7	Indiana	73,665,394	4.9%
19	Iowa	24,629,050	1.6%
28	Kansas	12,561,234	0.8%
10	Kentucky	65,826,604	4.4%
15	Louisiana	50,560,703	3.4%
34	Maine	5,498,050	0.4%
17	Maryland	35,344,370	2.4%
35	Massachusetts	5,213,299	0.3%
12	Michigan	52,565,194	3.5%
29	Minnesota	12,393,314	0.8%
18	Mississippi	24,765,858	1.6%
21	Missouri	21,609,987	1.4%
37	Montana	4,190,586	0.3%
32	Nebraska	8,417,455	0.6%
46	Nevada	1,979,411	0.1%
36	New Hampshire	4,811,898	0.3%
26	New Jersey	13,487,632	0.9%
48	New Mexico	924,583	0.1%
23	New York	19,757,161	1.3%
2	North Carolina	104,581,619	7.0%
40	North Dakota	3,703,311	0.2%
1	Ohio	126,254,637	8.4%
25	Oklahoma	15,507,429	1.0%
27	Oregon	12,958,932	0.9%
4	Pennsylvania	85,556,674	5.7%
49	Rhode Island	387,781	0.0%
11	South Carolina	54,540,367	3.6%
47	South Dakota	1,707,173	0.1%
6	Tennessee	81,508,511	5.4%
5	Texas	81,998,187	5.5%
31	Utah	10,012,328	0.7%
50	Vermont	49,078	0.0%
16	Virginia	50,157,341	3.3%
30	Washington	10,145,020	0.7%
8	West Virginia	70,574,581	4.7%
22	Wisconsin	20,723,917	1.4%
45	Wyoming	2,123,078	0.1%

RANK	STATE	POUNDS	% of USA
1	Ohio	126,254,637	8.4%
2	North Carolina	104,581,619	7.0%
3	Georgia	96,824,944	6.4%
4	Pennsylvania	85,556,674	5.7%
5	Texas	81,998,187	5.5%
6	Tennessee	81,508,511	5.4%
7	Indiana	73,665,394	4.9%
8	West Virginia	70,574,581	4.7%
9	Florida	68,900,432	4.6%
10	Kentucky	65,826,604	4.4%
11	South Carolina	54,540,367	3.6%
12	Michigan	52,565,194	3.5%
13	Alabama	51,642,618	3.4%
14	Illinois	51,331,483	3.4%
15	Louisiana	50,560,703	3.4%
16	Virginia	50,157,341	3.3%
17	Maryland	35,344,370	2.4%
18	Mississippi	24,765,858	1.6%
19	Iowa	24,629,050	1.6%
20	Arkansas	21,939,710	1.5%
21	Missouri	21,609,987	1.4%
22	Wisconsin	20,723,917	1.4%
23	New York	19,757,161	1.3%
24	California	17,334,498	1.2%
25	Oklahoma	15,507,429	1.0%
26	New Jersey	13,487,632	0.9%
27	Oregon	12,958,932	0.9%
28	Kansas	12,561,234	0.8%
29	Minnesota	12,393,314	0.8%
30	Washington	10,145,020	0.7%
31	Utah	10,012,328	0.7%
32	Nebraska	8,417,455	0.6%
33	Delaware	6,399,004	0.4%
34	Maine	5,498,050	0.4%
35	Massachusetts	5,213,299	0.3%
36	New Hampshire	4,811,898	0.3%
37	Montana	4,190,586	0.3%
38	Arizona	4,175,605	0.3%
39	Idaho	4,024,870	0.3%
40	North Dakota	3,703,311	0.2%
41	Colorado	2,973,328	0.2%
42	Connecticut	2,763,616	0.2%
43	Alaska	2,583,755	0.2%
44	Hawaii	2,311,630	0.2%
45	Wyoming	2,123,078	0.1%
46	Nevada	1,979,411	0.1%
47	South Dakota	1,707,173	0.1%
48	New Mexico	924,583	0.1%
49	Rhode Island	387,781	0.0%
50	Vermont	49,078	0.0%
	District of Columbia	1,319	0.0%

Source: U.S. Environmental Protection Agency, Office of Pollution Prevention and Toxics Information Management
    "2005 Toxics Release Inventory" (http://www.epa.gov/tri/tridata/tri05/)
*National total does not include 7,791,872 pounds of emissions in U.S. territories. Includes both original (or manufacturing) industries and those added by EPA since it began tracking releases.

Toxic Releases: Total Surface Water Discharges in 2005

National Total = 239,909,018 Pounds*

ALPHA ORDER

RANK	STATE	POUNDS	% of USA
5	Alabama	10,605,294	4.4%
43	Alaska	92,060	0.0%
49	Arizona	6,337	0.0%
6	Arkansas	10,600,872	4.4%
22	California	3,563,106	1.5%
19	Colorado	3,754,546	1.6%
38	Connecticut	466,971	0.2%
34	Delaware	1,211,798	0.5%
28	Florida	2,380,520	1.0%
8	Georgia	9,858,919	4.1%
37	Hawaii	522,217	0.2%
26	Idaho	2,592,830	1.1%
12	Illinois	8,600,252	3.6%
1	Indiana	27,554,609	11.5%
27	Iowa	2,490,029	1.0%
36	Kansas	570,092	0.2%
17	Kentucky	4,906,826	2.0%
4	Louisiana	11,541,781	4.8%
21	Maine	3,672,441	1.5%
33	Maryland	1,920,165	0.8%
47	Massachusetts	18,078	0.0%
35	Michigan	665,327	0.3%
32	Minnesota	2,106,204	0.9%
10	Mississippi	9,241,139	3.9%
31	Missouri	2,114,037	0.9%
41	Montana	141,625	0.1%
2	Nebraska	21,082,285	8.8%
42	Nevada	110,556	0.0%
46	New Hampshire	50,943	0.0%
15	New Jersey	6,551,620	2.7%
44	New Mexico	56,069	0.0%
9	New York	9,812,179	4.1%
13	North Carolina	8,252,513	3.4%
39	North Dakota	208,853	0.1%
14	Ohio	6,943,424	2.9%
25	Oklahoma	3,174,323	1.3%
30	Oregon	2,225,592	0.9%
11	Pennsylvania	8,995,388	3.7%
50	Rhode Island	6,029	0.0%
20	South Carolina	3,740,885	1.6%
24	South Dakota	3,274,427	1.4%
23	Tennessee	3,340,595	1.4%
3	Texas	17,763,109	7.4%
45	Utah	54,524	0.0%
40	Vermont	149,172	0.1%
7	Virginia	10,169,542	4.2%
29	Washington	2,331,142	1.0%
18	West Virginia	4,382,837	1.8%
16	Wisconsin	5,994,722	2.5%
48	Wyoming	12,012	0.0%

RANK ORDER

RANK	STATE	POUNDS	% of USA
1	Indiana	27,554,609	11.5%
2	Nebraska	21,082,285	8.8%
3	Texas	17,763,109	7.4%
4	Louisiana	11,541,781	4.8%
5	Alabama	10,605,294	4.4%
6	Arkansas	10,600,872	4.4%
7	Virginia	10,169,542	4.2%
8	Georgia	9,858,919	4.1%
9	New York	9,812,179	4.1%
10	Mississippi	9,241,139	3.9%
11	Pennsylvania	8,995,388	3.7%
12	Illinois	8,600,252	3.6%
13	North Carolina	8,252,513	3.4%
14	Ohio	6,943,424	2.9%
15	New Jersey	6,551,620	2.7%
16	Wisconsin	5,994,722	2.5%
17	Kentucky	4,906,826	2.0%
18	West Virginia	4,382,837	1.8%
19	Colorado	3,754,546	1.6%
20	South Carolina	3,740,885	1.6%
21	Maine	3,672,441	1.5%
22	California	3,563,106	1.5%
23	Tennessee	3,340,595	1.4%
24	South Dakota	3,274,427	1.4%
25	Oklahoma	3,174,323	1.3%
26	Idaho	2,592,830	1.1%
27	Iowa	2,490,029	1.0%
28	Florida	2,380,520	1.0%
29	Washington	2,331,142	1.0%
30	Oregon	2,225,592	0.9%
31	Missouri	2,114,037	0.9%
32	Minnesota	2,106,204	0.9%
33	Maryland	1,920,165	0.8%
34	Delaware	1,211,798	0.5%
35	Michigan	665,327	0.3%
36	Kansas	570,092	0.2%
37	Hawaii	522,217	0.2%
38	Connecticut	466,971	0.2%
39	North Dakota	208,853	0.1%
40	Vermont	149,172	0.1%
41	Montana	141,625	0.1%
42	Nevada	110,556	0.0%
43	Alaska	92,060	0.0%
44	New Mexico	56,069	0.0%
45	Utah	54,524	0.0%
46	New Hampshire	50,943	0.0%
47	Massachusetts	18,078	0.0%
48	Wyoming	12,012	0.0%
49	Arizona	6,337	0.0%
50	Rhode Island	6,029	0.0%
	District of Columbia	28,202	0.0%

Source: U.S. Environmental Protection Agency, Office of Pollution Prevention and Toxics Information Management
   "2005 Toxics Release Inventory" (http://www.epa.gov/tri/tridata/tri05/)
*National total does not include 337,083 pounds of discharges in U.S. territories. Includes both original (or manufacturing) industries and those added by EPA since it began tracking releases.

Pollution Released by Manufacturing Plants in 2005

National Total = 1,921,627,152 Pounds of Toxins*

ALPHA ORDER

RANK	STATE	POUNDS	% of USA
6	Alabama	78,661,232	4.1%
45	Alaska	2,474,844	0.1%
31	Arizona	16,718,064	0.9%
17	Arkansas	43,028,781	2.2%
23	California	31,695,916	1.6%
37	Colorado	6,258,278	0.3%
40	Connecticut	4,026,685	0.2%
36	Delaware	7,054,584	0.4%
9	Florida	67,892,289	3.5%
10	Georgia	63,059,949	3.3%
48	Hawaii	1,081,270	0.1%
32	Idaho	14,571,556	0.8%
5	Illinois	79,781,831	4.2%
2	Indiana	168,494,164	8.8%
21	Iowa	37,870,888	2.0%
27	Kansas	20,222,101	1.1%
22	Kentucky	37,175,135	1.9%
4	Louisiana	118,766,002	6.2%
34	Maine	11,462,898	0.6%
35	Maryland	11,332,337	0.6%
42	Massachusetts	3,618,590	0.2%
13	Michigan	53,466,228	2.8%
29	Minnesota	19,323,873	1.0%
15	Mississippi	52,714,998	2.7%
19	Missouri	39,978,900	2.1%
41	Montana	4,001,901	0.2%
18	Nebraska	40,915,671	2.1%
43	Nevada	2,527,132	0.1%
46	New Hampshire	1,292,445	0.1%
33	New Jersey	14,021,319	0.7%
47	New Mexico	1,237,020	0.1%
24	New York	27,779,815	1.4%
11	North Carolina	56,550,161	2.9%
44	North Dakota	2,517,428	0.1%
3	Ohio	138,832,118	7.2%
28	Oklahoma	20,106,406	1.0%
25	Oregon	23,150,437	1.2%
7	Pennsylvania	76,020,946	4.0%
49	Rhode Island	510,637	0.0%
12	South Carolina	54,590,037	2.8%
38	South Dakota	4,951,280	0.3%
8	Tennessee	72,519,114	3.8%
1	Texas	205,024,760	10.7%
16	Utah	49,150,083	2.6%
50	Vermont	426,198	0.0%
14	Virginia	52,782,781	2.7%
30	Washington	16,723,701	0.9%
26	West Virginia	20,548,801	1.1%
20	Wisconsin	39,854,894	2.1%
39	Wyoming	4,820,813	0.3%

RANK ORDER

RANK	STATE	POUNDS	% of USA
1	Texas	205,024,760	10.7%
2	Indiana	168,494,164	8.8%
3	Ohio	138,832,118	7.2%
4	Louisiana	118,766,002	6.2%
5	Illinois	79,781,831	4.2%
6	Alabama	78,661,232	4.1%
7	Pennsylvania	76,020,946	4.0%
8	Tennessee	72,519,114	3.8%
9	Florida	67,892,289	3.5%
10	Georgia	63,059,949	3.3%
11	North Carolina	56,550,161	2.9%
12	South Carolina	54,590,037	2.8%
13	Michigan	53,466,228	2.8%
14	Virginia	52,782,781	2.7%
15	Mississippi	52,714,998	2.7%
16	Utah	49,150,083	2.6%
17	Arkansas	43,028,781	2.2%
18	Nebraska	40,915,671	2.1%
19	Missouri	39,978,900	2.1%
20	Wisconsin	39,854,894	2.1%
21	Iowa	37,870,888	2.0%
22	Kentucky	37,175,135	1.9%
23	California	31,695,916	1.6%
24	New York	27,779,815	1.4%
25	Oregon	23,150,437	1.2%
26	West Virginia	20,548,801	1.1%
27	Kansas	20,222,101	1.1%
28	Oklahoma	20,106,406	1.0%
29	Minnesota	19,323,873	1.0%
30	Washington	16,723,701	0.9%
31	Arizona	16,718,064	0.9%
32	Idaho	14,571,556	0.8%
33	New Jersey	14,021,319	0.7%
34	Maine	11,462,898	0.6%
35	Maryland	11,332,337	0.6%
36	Delaware	7,054,584	0.4%
37	Colorado	6,258,278	0.3%
38	South Dakota	4,951,280	0.3%
39	Wyoming	4,820,813	0.3%
40	Connecticut	4,026,685	0.2%
41	Montana	4,001,901	0.2%
42	Massachusetts	3,618,590	0.2%
43	Nevada	2,527,132	0.1%
44	North Dakota	2,517,428	0.1%
45	Alaska	2,474,844	0.1%
46	New Hampshire	1,292,445	0.1%
47	New Mexico	1,237,020	0.1%
48	Hawaii	1,081,270	0.1%
49	Rhode Island	510,637	0.0%
50	Vermont	426,198	0.0%
	District of Columbia	39,861	0.0%

Source: U.S. Environmental Protection Agency, Office of Pollution Prevention and Toxics Information Management
"Toxics Release Inventory (TRI)" (http://www.epa.gov/tri/)
*National total does not include 2,948,232 pounds of toxins in U.S. territories. Includes discharges to air, surface water, underground injection and surface land by what are labeled by the EPA as "original industries" for which data have been collected since 1988. An additional 2,409,124,700 pounds (excluding territories) of toxins were released by industries that have been added by EPA (see page 233).

VIII. Geography

Total Area of States in Square Miles in 2007

National Total = 3,794,083 Square Miles*

ALPHA ORDER

RANK	STATE	MILES	% of USA
30	Alabama	52,419	1.4%
1	Alaska	663,267	17.5%
6	Arizona	113,998	3.0%
29	Arkansas	53,179	1.4%
3	California	163,696	4.3%
8	Colorado	104,094	2.7%
48	Connecticut	5,543	0.1%
49	Delaware	2,489	0.1%
22	Florida	65,755	1.7%
24	Georgia	59,425	1.6%
43	Hawaii	10,931	0.3%
14	Idaho	83,570	2.2%
25	Illinois	57,914	1.5%
38	Indiana	36,418	1.0%
26	Iowa	56,272	1.5%
15	Kansas	82,277	2.2%
37	Kentucky	40,409	1.1%
31	Louisiana	51,840	1.4%
39	Maine	35,385	0.9%
42	Maryland	12,407	0.3%
44	Massachusetts	10,555	0.3%
11	Michigan	96,716	2.5%
12	Minnesota	86,939	2.3%
32	Mississippi	48,430	1.3%
21	Missouri	69,704	1.8%
4	Montana	147,042	3.9%
16	Nebraska	77,354	2.0%
7	Nevada	110,561	2.9%
46	New Hampshire	9,350	0.2%
47	New Jersey	8,721	0.2%
5	New Mexico	121,590	3.2%
27	New York	54,556	1.4%
28	North Carolina	53,819	1.4%
19	North Dakota	70,700	1.9%
34	Ohio	44,825	1.2%
20	Oklahoma	69,898	1.8%
9	Oregon	98,381	2.6%
33	Pennsylvania	46,055	1.2%
50	Rhode Island	1,545	0.0%
40	South Carolina	32,020	0.8%
17	South Dakota	77,117	2.0%
36	Tennessee	42,143	1.1%
2	Texas	268,581	7.1%
13	Utah	84,899	2.2%
45	Vermont	9,614	0.3%
35	Virginia	42,774	1.1%
18	Washington	71,300	1.9%
41	West Virginia	24,230	0.6%
23	Wisconsin	65,498	1.7%
10	Wyoming	97,814	2.6%

RANK ORDER

RANK	STATE	MILES	% of USA
1	Alaska	663,267	17.5%
2	Texas	268,581	7.1%
3	California	163,696	4.3%
4	Montana	147,042	3.9%
5	New Mexico	121,590	3.2%
6	Arizona	113,998	3.0%
7	Nevada	110,561	2.9%
8	Colorado	104,094	2.7%
9	Oregon	98,381	2.6%
10	Wyoming	97,814	2.6%
11	Michigan	96,716	2.5%
12	Minnesota	86,939	2.3%
13	Utah	84,899	2.2%
14	Idaho	83,570	2.2%
15	Kansas	82,277	2.2%
16	Nebraska	77,354	2.0%
17	South Dakota	77,117	2.0%
18	Washington	71,300	1.9%
19	North Dakota	70,700	1.9%
20	Oklahoma	69,898	1.8%
21	Missouri	69,704	1.8%
22	Florida	65,755	1.7%
23	Wisconsin	65,498	1.7%
24	Georgia	59,425	1.6%
25	Illinois	57,914	1.5%
26	Iowa	56,272	1.5%
27	New York	54,556	1.4%
28	North Carolina	53,819	1.4%
29	Arkansas	53,179	1.4%
30	Alabama	52,419	1.4%
31	Louisiana	51,840	1.4%
32	Mississippi	48,430	1.3%
33	Pennsylvania	46,055	1.2%
34	Ohio	44,825	1.2%
35	Virginia	42,774	1.1%
36	Tennessee	42,143	1.1%
37	Kentucky	40,409	1.1%
38	Indiana	36,418	1.0%
39	Maine	35,385	0.9%
40	South Carolina	32,020	0.8%
41	West Virginia	24,230	0.6%
42	Maryland	12,407	0.3%
43	Hawaii	10,931	0.3%
44	Massachusetts	10,555	0.3%
45	Vermont	9,614	0.3%
46	New Hampshire	9,350	0.2%
47	New Jersey	8,721	0.2%
48	Connecticut	5,543	0.1%
49	Delaware	2,489	0.1%
50	Rhode Island	1,545	0.0%
	District of Columbia	68	0.0%

Source: U.S. Bureau of the Census
    "2000 Census of Population and Housing" (Series PHC-1)
*Total of land and water area.

Land Area of States in Square Miles in 2007

National Total = 3,537,438 Square Miles of Land Area*

ALPHA ORDER

RANK	STATE	MILES	% of USA
28	Alabama	50,744	1.4%
1	Alaska	571,951	16.2%
6	Arizona	113,635	3.2%
27	Arkansas	52,068	1.5%
3	California	155,959	4.4%
8	Colorado	103,718	2.9%
48	Connecticut	4,845	0.1%
49	Delaware	1,954	0.1%
26	Florida	53,927	1.5%
21	Georgia	57,906	1.6%
47	Hawaii	6,423	0.2%
11	Idaho	82,747	2.3%
24	Illinois	55,584	1.6%
38	Indiana	35,867	1.0%
23	Iowa	55,869	1.6%
13	Kansas	81,815	2.3%
36	Kentucky	39,728	1.1%
33	Louisiana	43,562	1.2%
39	Maine	30,862	0.9%
42	Maryland	9,774	0.3%
45	Massachusetts	7,840	0.2%
22	Michigan	56,804	1.6%
14	Minnesota	79,610	2.3%
31	Mississippi	46,907	1.3%
18	Missouri	68,886	1.9%
4	Montana	145,552	4.1%
15	Nebraska	76,872	2.2%
7	Nevada	109,826	3.1%
44	New Hampshire	8,968	0.3%
46	New Jersey	7,417	0.2%
5	New Mexico	121,356	3.4%
30	New York	47,214	1.3%
29	North Carolina	48,711	1.4%
17	North Dakota	68,976	1.9%
35	Ohio	40,948	1.2%
19	Oklahoma	68,667	1.9%
10	Oregon	95,997	2.7%
32	Pennsylvania	44,817	1.3%
50	Rhode Island	1,045	0.0%
40	South Carolina	30,110	0.9%
16	South Dakota	75,885	2.1%
34	Tennessee	41,217	1.2%
2	Texas	261,797	7.4%
12	Utah	82,144	2.3%
43	Vermont	9,250	0.3%
37	Virginia	39,594	1.1%
20	Washington	66,544	1.9%
41	West Virginia	24,078	0.7%
25	Wisconsin	54,310	1.5%
9	Wyoming	97,100	2.7%

RANK ORDER

RANK	STATE	MILES	% of USA
1	Alaska	571,951	16.2%
2	Texas	261,797	7.4%
3	California	155,959	4.4%
4	Montana	145,552	4.1%
5	New Mexico	121,356	3.4%
6	Arizona	113,635	3.2%
7	Nevada	109,826	3.1%
8	Colorado	103,718	2.9%
9	Wyoming	97,100	2.7%
10	Oregon	95,997	2.7%
11	Idaho	82,747	2.3%
12	Utah	82,144	2.3%
13	Kansas	81,815	2.3%
14	Minnesota	79,610	2.3%
15	Nebraska	76,872	2.2%
16	South Dakota	75,885	2.1%
17	North Dakota	68,976	1.9%
18	Missouri	68,886	1.9%
19	Oklahoma	68,667	1.9%
20	Washington	66,544	1.9%
21	Georgia	57,906	1.6%
22	Michigan	56,804	1.6%
23	Iowa	55,869	1.6%
24	Illinois	55,584	1.6%
25	Wisconsin	54,310	1.5%
26	Florida	53,927	1.5%
27	Arkansas	52,068	1.5%
28	Alabama	50,744	1.4%
29	North Carolina	48,711	1.4%
30	New York	47,214	1.3%
31	Mississippi	46,907	1.3%
32	Pennsylvania	44,817	1.3%
33	Louisiana	43,562	1.2%
34	Tennessee	41,217	1.2%
35	Ohio	40,948	1.2%
36	Kentucky	39,728	1.1%
37	Virginia	39,594	1.1%
38	Indiana	35,867	1.0%
39	Maine	30,862	0.9%
40	South Carolina	30,110	0.9%
41	West Virginia	24,078	0.7%
42	Maryland	9,774	0.3%
43	Vermont	9,250	0.3%
44	New Hampshire	8,968	0.3%
45	Massachusetts	7,840	0.2%
46	New Jersey	7,417	0.2%
47	Hawaii	6,423	0.2%
48	Connecticut	4,845	0.1%
49	Delaware	1,954	0.1%
50	Rhode Island	1,045	0.0%
	District of Columbia	61	0.0%

Source: U.S. Bureau of the Census
   "2000 Census of Population and Housing" (Series PHC-1)
*Includes dry land temporarily or partially covered by water, such as marshland, swamps, etc.; streams and canals under one-eighth mile wide; and lakes, reservoirs, and ponds under 40 acres.

Water Area of States in Square Miles in 2007

National Total = 256,645 Square Miles of Water*

ALPHA ORDER

RANK	STATE	MILES	% of USA
23	Alabama	1,675	0.7%
1	Alaska	91,316	35.6%
48	Arizona	364	0.1%
31	Arkansas	1,110	0.4%
6	California	7,736	3.0%
46	Colorado	376	0.1%
37	Connecticut	699	0.3%
40	Delaware	536	0.2%
3	Florida	11,828	4.6%
25	Georgia	1,519	0.6%
13	Hawaii	4,508	1.8%
33	Idaho	823	0.3%
20	Illinois	2,331	0.9%
39	Indiana	551	0.2%
44	Iowa	402	0.2%
43	Kansas	462	0.2%
38	Kentucky	681	0.3%
5	Louisiana	8,278	3.2%
12	Maine	4,523	1.8%
18	Maryland	2,633	1.0%
17	Massachusetts	2,715	1.1%
2	Michigan	39,912	15.6%
8	Minnesota	7,329	2.9%
24	Mississippi	1,523	0.6%
34	Missouri	818	0.3%
26	Montana	1,490	0.6%
42	Nebraska	481	0.2%
35	Nevada	735	0.3%
45	New Hampshire	382	0.1%
27	New Jersey	1,304	0.5%
49	New Mexico	234	0.1%
7	New York	7,342	2.9%
10	North Carolina	5,108	2.0%
22	North Dakota	1,724	0.7%
14	Ohio	3,877	1.5%
30	Oklahoma	1,231	0.5%
19	Oregon	2,384	0.9%
28	Pennsylvania	1,239	0.5%
41	Rhode Island	500	0.2%
21	South Carolina	1,911	0.7%
29	South Dakota	1,232	0.5%
32	Tennessee	926	0.4%
9	Texas	6,784	2.6%
16	Utah	2,755	1.1%
47	Vermont	365	0.1%
15	Virginia	3,180	1.2%
11	Washington	4,756	1.9%
50	West Virginia	152	0.1%
4	Wisconsin	11,188	4.4%
36	Wyoming	713	0.3%

RANK ORDER

RANK	STATE	MILES	% of USA
1	Alaska	91,316	35.6%
2	Michigan	39,912	15.6%
3	Florida	11,828	4.6%
4	Wisconsin	11,188	4.4%
5	Louisiana	8,278	3.2%
6	California	7,736	3.0%
7	New York	7,342	2.9%
8	Minnesota	7,329	2.9%
9	Texas	6,784	2.6%
10	North Carolina	5,108	2.0%
11	Washington	4,756	1.9%
12	Maine	4,523	1.8%
13	Hawaii	4,508	1.8%
14	Ohio	3,877	1.5%
15	Virginia	3,180	1.2%
16	Utah	2,755	1.1%
17	Massachusetts	2,715	1.1%
18	Maryland	2,633	1.0%
19	Oregon	2,384	0.9%
20	Illinois	2,331	0.9%
21	South Carolina	1,911	0.7%
22	North Dakota	1,724	0.7%
23	Alabama	1,675	0.7%
24	Mississippi	1,523	0.6%
25	Georgia	1,519	0.6%
26	Montana	1,490	0.6%
27	New Jersey	1,304	0.5%
28	Pennsylvania	1,239	0.5%
29	South Dakota	1,232	0.5%
30	Oklahoma	1,231	0.5%
31	Arkansas	1,110	0.4%
32	Tennessee	926	0.4%
33	Idaho	823	0.3%
34	Missouri	818	0.3%
35	Nevada	735	0.3%
36	Wyoming	713	0.3%
37	Connecticut	699	0.3%
38	Kentucky	681	0.3%
39	Indiana	551	0.2%
40	Delaware	536	0.2%
41	Rhode Island	500	0.2%
42	Nebraska	481	0.2%
43	Kansas	462	0.2%
44	Iowa	402	0.2%
45	New Hampshire	382	0.1%
46	Colorado	376	0.1%
47	Vermont	365	0.1%
48	Arizona	364	0.1%
49	New Mexico	234	0.1%
50	West Virginia	152	0.1%
	District of Columbia	7	0.0%

Source: U.S. Bureau of the Census
    "2000 Census of Population and Housing" (Series PHC-1)
*Includes permanent inland water surface, such as lakes, reservoirs, and ponds having an area of 40 acres or more, canals one-eighth mile or more in width; coastal waters behind or sheltered by headlands or islands separated by less than 1 nautical mile of water, and islands under 40 acres in area. Excludes areas of oceans, bays, etc., lying within U.S. jurisdiction but not defined as inland water.

Highest Point of Elevation in Feet

National High Point = 20,320 Feet Above Sea Level (Mt. McKinley, Alaska)

ALPHA ORDER

RANK	STATE	HIGHEST POINT
35	Alabama	2,407
1	Alaska	20,320
12	Arizona	12,633
34	Arkansas	2,753
2	California	14,494
3	Colorado	14,433
36	Connecticut	2,380
49	Delaware	448
50	Florida	345
25	Georgia	4,784
6	Hawaii	13,796
11	Idaho	12,662
45	Illinois	1,235
44	Indiana	1,257
42	Iowa	1,670
28	Kansas	4,039
27	Kentucky	4,145
48	Louisiana	535
22	Maine	5,268
32	Maryland	3,360
31	Massachusetts	3,491
38	Michigan	1,979
37	Minnesota	2,301
47	Mississippi	806
41	Missouri	1,772
10	Montana	12,799
20	Nebraska	5,424
9	Nevada	13,140
18	New Hampshire	6,288
40	New Jersey	1,803
8	New Mexico	13,161
21	New York	5,344
16	North Carolina	6,684
30	North Dakota	3,506
43	Ohio	1,550
23	Oklahoma	4,973
13	Oregon	11,239
33	Pennsylvania	3,213
46	Rhode Island	812
29	South Carolina	3,560
15	South Dakota	7,242
17	Tennessee	6,643
14	Texas	8,749
7	Utah	13,528
26	Vermont	4,393
19	Virginia	5,729
4	Washington	14,411
24	West Virginia	4,863
39	Wisconsin	1,951
5	Wyoming	13,804

RANK ORDER

RANK	STATE	HIGHEST POINT
1	Alaska	20,320
2	California	14,494
3	Colorado	14,433
4	Washington	14,411
5	Wyoming	13,804
6	Hawaii	13,796
7	Utah	13,528
8	New Mexico	13,161
9	Nevada	13,140
10	Montana	12,799
11	Idaho	12,662
12	Arizona	12,633
13	Oregon	11,239
14	Texas	8,749
15	South Dakota	7,242
16	North Carolina	6,684
17	Tennessee	6,643
18	New Hampshire	6,288
19	Virginia	5,729
20	Nebraska	5,424
21	New York	5,344
22	Maine	5,268
23	Oklahoma	4,973
24	West Virginia	4,863
25	Georgia	4,784
26	Vermont	4,393
27	Kentucky	4,145
28	Kansas	4,039
29	South Carolina	3,560
30	North Dakota	3,506
31	Massachusetts	3,491
32	Maryland	3,360
33	Pennsylvania	3,213
34	Arkansas	2,753
35	Alabama	2,407
36	Connecticut	2,380
37	Minnesota	2,301
38	Michigan	1,979
39	Wisconsin	1,951
40	New Jersey	1,803
41	Missouri	1,772
42	Iowa	1,670
43	Ohio	1,550
44	Indiana	1,257
45	Illinois	1,235
46	Rhode Island	812
47	Mississippi	806
48	Louisiana	535
49	Delaware	448
50	Florida	345

District of Columbia — 410

Source: U.S. Department of Interior, U.S. Geological Survey
"Elevations and Distances in the United States" (http://erg.usgs.gov/isb/pubs/booklets/elvadist/elvadist.html)

Lowest Point of Elevation in Feet

National Low Point = 282 Feet Below Sea Level (Death Valley, California)*

ALPHA ORDER

RANK	STATE	LOWEST POINT
3	Alabama	0
3	Alaska	0
26	Arizona	70
25	Arkansas	55
1	California	(282)
50	Colorado	3,315
3	Connecticut	0
3	Delaware	0
3	Florida	0
3	Georgia	0
3	Hawaii	0
42	Idaho	710
32	Illinois	279
34	Indiana	320
37	Iowa	480
41	Kansas	679
31	Kentucky	257
2	Louisiana	(8)
3	Maine	0
3	Maryland	0
3	Massachusetts	0
38	Michigan	571
40	Minnesota	601
3	Mississippi	0
29	Missouri	230
46	Montana	1,800
44	Nebraska	840
36	Nevada	479
3	New Hampshire	0
3	New Jersey	0
48	New Mexico	2,842
3	New York	0
3	North Carolina	0
43	North Dakota	750
35	Ohio	455
33	Oklahoma	289
3	Oregon	0
3	Pennsylvania	0
3	Rhode Island	0
3	South Carolina	0
45	South Dakota	966
28	Tennessee	178
3	Texas	0
47	Utah	2,000
27	Vermont	95
3	Virginia	0
3	Washington	0
30	West Virginia	240
39	Wisconsin	579
49	Wyoming	3,099

RANK ORDER

RANK	STATE	LOWEST POINT
1	California	(282)
2	Louisiana	(8)
3	Alabama*	0
3	Alaska	0
3	Connecticut	0
3	Delaware	0
3	Florida	0
3	Georgia	0
3	Hawaii	0
3	Maine	0
3	Maryland	0
3	Massachusetts	0
3	Mississippi	0
3	New Hampshire	0
3	New Jersey	0
3	New York	0
3	North Carolina	0
3	Oregon	0
3	Pennsylvania	0
3	Rhode Island	0
3	South Carolina	0
3	Texas	0
3	Virginia	0
3	Washington	0
25	Arkansas	55
26	Arizona	70
27	Vermont	95
28	Tennessee	178
29	Missouri	230
30	West Virginia	240
31	Kentucky	257
32	Illinois	279
33	Oklahoma	289
34	Indiana	320
35	Ohio	455
36	Nevada	479
37	Iowa	480
38	Michigan	571
39	Wisconsin	579
40	Minnesota	601
41	Kansas	679
42	Idaho	710
43	North Dakota	750
44	Nebraska	840
45	South Dakota	966
46	Montana	1,800
47	Utah	2,000
48	New Mexico	2,842
49	Wyoming	3,099
50	Colorado	3,315

District of Columbia   1

Source: U.S. Department of Interior, U.S. Geological Survey
    "Elevations and Distances in the United States" (http://erg.usgs.gov/isb/pubs/booklets/elvadist/elvadist.html)
*States with "0" have sea level as lowest point.

Approximate Mean Elevation in Feet

Approximate National Mean Elevation = 2,500 Feet Above Sea Level

ALPHA ORDER

RANK	STATE	MEAN ELEVATION
40	Alabama	500
15	Alaska	1,900
7	Arizona	4,100
36	Arkansas	650
11	California	2,900
1	Colorado	6,800
40	Connecticut	500
50	Delaware	60
48	Florida	100
37	Georgia	600
10	Hawaii	3,030
6	Idaho	5,000
37	Illinois	600
34	Indiana	700
22	Iowa	1,100
14	Kansas	2,000
33	Kentucky	750
48	Louisiana	100
37	Maine	600
43	Maryland	350
40	Massachusetts	500
29	Michigan	900
21	Minnesota	1,200
45	Mississippi	300
32	Missouri	800
8	Montana	3,400
12	Nebraska	2,600
5	Nevada	5,500
25	New Hampshire	1,000
46	New Jersey	250
4	New Mexico	5,700
25	New York	1,000
34	North Carolina	700
15	North Dakota	1,900
31	Ohio	850
20	Oklahoma	1,300
9	Oregon	3,300
22	Pennsylvania	1,100
47	Rhode Island	200
43	South Carolina	350
13	South Dakota	2,200
29	Tennessee	900
17	Texas	1,700
3	Utah	6,100
25	Vermont	1,000
28	Virginia	950
17	Washington	1,700
19	West Virginia	1,500
24	Wisconsin	1,050
2	Wyoming	6,700

RANK ORDER

RANK	STATE	MEAN ELEVATION
1	Colorado	6,800
2	Wyoming	6,700
3	Utah	6,100
4	New Mexico	5,700
5	Nevada	5,500
6	Idaho	5,000
7	Arizona	4,100
8	Montana	3,400
9	Oregon	3,300
10	Hawaii	3,030
11	California	2,900
12	Nebraska	2,600
13	South Dakota	2,200
14	Kansas	2,000
15	Alaska	1,900
15	North Dakota	1,900
17	Texas	1,700
17	Washington	1,700
19	West Virginia	1,500
20	Oklahoma	1,300
21	Minnesota	1,200
22	Iowa	1,100
22	Pennsylvania	1,100
24	Wisconsin	1,050
25	New Hampshire	1,000
25	New York	1,000
25	Vermont	1,000
28	Virginia	950
29	Michigan	900
29	Tennessee	900
31	Ohio	850
32	Missouri	800
33	Kentucky	750
34	Indiana	700
34	North Carolina	700
36	Arkansas	650
37	Georgia	600
37	Illinois	600
37	Maine	600
40	Alabama	500
40	Connecticut	500
40	Massachusetts	500
43	Maryland	350
43	South Carolina	350
45	Mississippi	300
46	New Jersey	250
47	Rhode Island	200
48	Florida	100
48	Louisiana	100
50	Delaware	60

District of Columbia	150

Source: U.S. Department of Interior, U.S. Geological Survey
"Elevations and Distances in the United States" (http://erg.usgs.gov/isb/pubs/booklets/elvadist/elvadist.html)

Normal Daily Mean Temperature*

<table>
<tr><td colspan="3">ALPHA ORDER</td></tr>
<tr><td>RANK</td><td>STATE</td><td>MEAN TEMPERATURE</td></tr>
<tr><td>5</td><td>Alabama</td><td>66.8</td></tr>
<tr><td>50</td><td>Alaska</td><td>41.5</td></tr>
<tr><td>2</td><td>Arizona</td><td>72.9</td></tr>
<tr><td>10</td><td>Arkansas</td><td>62.1</td></tr>
<tr><td>11</td><td>California**</td><td>61.5</td></tr>
<tr><td>35</td><td>Colorado</td><td>50.1</td></tr>
<tr><td>34</td><td>Connecticut</td><td>50.2</td></tr>
<tr><td>22</td><td>Delaware</td><td>54.4</td></tr>
<tr><td>3</td><td>Florida**</td><td>72.4</td></tr>
<tr><td>9</td><td>Georgia</td><td>62.2</td></tr>
<tr><td>1</td><td>Hawaii</td><td>77.5</td></tr>
<tr><td>28</td><td>Idaho</td><td>52.0</td></tr>
<tr><td>37</td><td>Illinois**</td><td>50.0</td></tr>
<tr><td>26</td><td>Indiana</td><td>52.5</td></tr>
<tr><td>37</td><td>Iowa</td><td>50.0</td></tr>
<tr><td>18</td><td>Kansas</td><td>56.4</td></tr>
<tr><td>16</td><td>Kentucky</td><td>57.0</td></tr>
<tr><td>4</td><td>Louisiana</td><td>68.8</td></tr>
<tr><td>42</td><td>Maine</td><td>45.8</td></tr>
<tr><td>20</td><td>Maryland</td><td>54.6</td></tr>
<tr><td>30</td><td>Massachusetts</td><td>51.6</td></tr>
<tr><td>45</td><td>Michigan**</td><td>45.0</td></tr>
<tr><td>48</td><td>Minnesota**</td><td>42.3</td></tr>
<tr><td>7</td><td>Mississippi</td><td>64.1</td></tr>
<tr><td>19</td><td>Missouri**</td><td>55.3</td></tr>
<tr><td>47</td><td>Montana</td><td>43.8</td></tr>
<tr><td>33</td><td>Nebraska</td><td>50.7</td></tr>
<tr><td>31</td><td>Nevada</td><td>51.3</td></tr>
<tr><td>41</td><td>New Hampshire</td><td>45.9</td></tr>
<tr><td>23</td><td>New Jersey</td><td>53.5</td></tr>
<tr><td>17</td><td>New Mexico</td><td>56.8</td></tr>
<tr><td>35</td><td>New York**</td><td>50.1</td></tr>
<tr><td>13</td><td>North Carolina**</td><td>60.5</td></tr>
<tr><td>48</td><td>North Dakota</td><td>42.3</td></tr>
<tr><td>27</td><td>Ohio**</td><td>52.3</td></tr>
<tr><td>14</td><td>Oklahoma</td><td>60.1</td></tr>
<tr><td>23</td><td>Oregon</td><td>53.5</td></tr>
<tr><td>25</td><td>Pennsylvania**</td><td>53.2</td></tr>
<tr><td>32</td><td>Rhode Island</td><td>51.1</td></tr>
<tr><td>8</td><td>South Carolina</td><td>63.6</td></tr>
<tr><td>44</td><td>South Dakota</td><td>45.1</td></tr>
<tr><td>12</td><td>Tennessee**</td><td>60.7</td></tr>
<tr><td>6</td><td>Texas**</td><td>66.3</td></tr>
<tr><td>28</td><td>Utah</td><td>52.0</td></tr>
<tr><td>43</td><td>Vermont</td><td>45.2</td></tr>
<tr><td>15</td><td>Virginia**</td><td>58.6</td></tr>
<tr><td>39</td><td>Washington**</td><td>49.8</td></tr>
<tr><td>21</td><td>West Virginia</td><td>54.5</td></tr>
<tr><td>40</td><td>Wisconsin</td><td>47.5</td></tr>
<tr><td>45</td><td>Wyoming</td><td>45.0</td></tr>
</table>

<table>
<tr><td colspan="3">RANK ORDER</td></tr>
<tr><td>RANK</td><td>STATE</td><td>MEAN TEMPERATURE</td></tr>
<tr><td>1</td><td>Hawaii</td><td>77.5</td></tr>
<tr><td>2</td><td>Arizona</td><td>72.9</td></tr>
<tr><td>3</td><td>Florida**</td><td>72.4</td></tr>
<tr><td>4</td><td>Louisiana</td><td>68.8</td></tr>
<tr><td>5</td><td>Alabama</td><td>66.8</td></tr>
<tr><td>6</td><td>Texas**</td><td>66.3</td></tr>
<tr><td>7</td><td>Mississippi</td><td>64.1</td></tr>
<tr><td>8</td><td>South Carolina</td><td>63.6</td></tr>
<tr><td>9</td><td>Georgia</td><td>62.2</td></tr>
<tr><td>10</td><td>Arkansas</td><td>62.1</td></tr>
<tr><td>11</td><td>California**</td><td>61.5</td></tr>
<tr><td>12</td><td>Tennessee**</td><td>60.7</td></tr>
<tr><td>13</td><td>North Carolina**</td><td>60.5</td></tr>
<tr><td>14</td><td>Oklahoma</td><td>60.1</td></tr>
<tr><td>15</td><td>Virginia**</td><td>58.6</td></tr>
<tr><td>16</td><td>Kentucky</td><td>57.0</td></tr>
<tr><td>17</td><td>New Mexico</td><td>56.8</td></tr>
<tr><td>18</td><td>Kansas</td><td>56.4</td></tr>
<tr><td>19</td><td>Missouri**</td><td>55.3</td></tr>
<tr><td>20</td><td>Maryland</td><td>54.6</td></tr>
<tr><td>21</td><td>West Virginia</td><td>54.5</td></tr>
<tr><td>22</td><td>Delaware</td><td>54.4</td></tr>
<tr><td>23</td><td>New Jersey</td><td>53.5</td></tr>
<tr><td>23</td><td>Oregon</td><td>53.5</td></tr>
<tr><td>25</td><td>Pennsylvania**</td><td>53.2</td></tr>
<tr><td>26</td><td>Indiana</td><td>52.5</td></tr>
<tr><td>27</td><td>Ohio**</td><td>52.3</td></tr>
<tr><td>28</td><td>Idaho</td><td>52.0</td></tr>
<tr><td>28</td><td>Utah</td><td>52.0</td></tr>
<tr><td>30</td><td>Massachusetts</td><td>51.6</td></tr>
<tr><td>31</td><td>Nevada</td><td>51.3</td></tr>
<tr><td>32</td><td>Rhode Island</td><td>51.1</td></tr>
<tr><td>33</td><td>Nebraska</td><td>50.7</td></tr>
<tr><td>34</td><td>Connecticut</td><td>50.2</td></tr>
<tr><td>35</td><td>Colorado</td><td>50.1</td></tr>
<tr><td>35</td><td>New York**</td><td>50.1</td></tr>
<tr><td>37</td><td>Illinois**</td><td>50.0</td></tr>
<tr><td>37</td><td>Iowa</td><td>50.0</td></tr>
<tr><td>39</td><td>Washington**</td><td>49.8</td></tr>
<tr><td>40</td><td>Wisconsin</td><td>47.5</td></tr>
<tr><td>41</td><td>New Hampshire</td><td>45.9</td></tr>
<tr><td>42</td><td>Maine</td><td>45.8</td></tr>
<tr><td>43</td><td>Vermont</td><td>45.2</td></tr>
<tr><td>44</td><td>South Dakota</td><td>45.1</td></tr>
<tr><td>45</td><td>Michigan**</td><td>45.0</td></tr>
<tr><td>45</td><td>Wyoming</td><td>45.0</td></tr>
<tr><td>47</td><td>Montana</td><td>43.8</td></tr>
<tr><td>48</td><td>Minnesota**</td><td>42.3</td></tr>
<tr><td>48</td><td>North Dakota</td><td>42.3</td></tr>
<tr><td>50</td><td>Alaska</td><td>41.5</td></tr>
<tr><td></td><td>District of Columbia</td><td>57.5</td></tr>
</table>

Source: U.S. Department of Commerce, National Oceanic and Atmospheric Administration
"Climatography of the United States" (No. 81) (www.ncdc.noaa.gov/oa/climate/online/ccd/nrmmax.txt)
*Based on standard 30 year period, 1971-2000.
**Temperatures from multiple reporting cities within one state were averaged to determine a state's mean temperature.

Percent of Days That Are Sunny*

ALPHA ORDER

RANK	STATE	PERCENT OF DAYS SUNNY
28	Alabama	58.0
50	Alaska	37.7
1	Arizona	84.5
10	Arkansas	65.3
5	California	71.9
4	Colorado	72.0
34	Connecticut**	56.0
36	Delaware**	55.1
7	Florida	67.0
17	Georgia	62.7
23	Hawaii	59.3
13	Idaho	64.0
31	Illinois	57.0
30	Indiana	57.7
22	Iowa	60.0
8	Kansas	65.8
39	Kentucky	54.7
13	Louisiana	64.0
31	Maine**	57.0
31	Maryland**	57.0
37	Massachusetts	55.0
44	Michigan	49.3
37	Minnesota	55.0
18	Mississippi	62.5
26	Missouri	58.3
25	Montana	58.8
15	Nebraska	63.3
2	Nevada	76.3
48	New Hampshire	43.5
34	New Jersey**	56.0
3	New Mexico	75.0
43	New York	50.8
21	North Carolina	60.3
24	North Dakota	59.0
42	Ohio	51.0
12	Oklahoma	65.0
46	Oregon**	48.0
41	Pennsylvania	53.3
28	Rhode Island**	58.0
19	South Carolina	62.3
16	South Dakota	63.0
26	Tennessee	58.3
10	Texas	65.3
6	Utah	68.0
45	Vermont**	49.0
20	Virginia	60.7
47	Washington	44.5
49	West Virginia**	40.0
40	Wisconsin	54.0
9	Wyoming	65.7

RANK ORDER

RANK	STATE	PERCENT OF DAYS SUNNY
1	Arizona	84.5
2	Nevada	76.3
3	New Mexico	75.0
4	Colorado	72.0
5	California	71.9
6	Utah	68.0
7	Florida	67.0
8	Kansas	65.8
9	Wyoming	65.7
10	Arkansas	65.3
10	Texas	65.3
12	Oklahoma	65.0
13	Idaho	64.0
13	Louisiana	64.0
15	Nebraska	63.3
16	South Dakota	63.0
17	Georgia	62.7
18	Mississippi	62.5
19	South Carolina	62.3
20	Virginia	60.7
21	North Carolina	60.3
22	Iowa	60.0
23	Hawaii	59.3
24	North Dakota	59.0
25	Montana	58.8
26	Missouri	58.3
26	Tennessee	58.3
28	Alabama	58.0
28	Rhode Island**	58.0
30	Indiana	57.7
31	Illinois	57.0
31	Maine**	57.0
31	Maryland**	57.0
34	Connecticut**	56.0
34	New Jersey**	56.0
36	Delaware**	55.1
37	Massachusetts	55.0
37	Minnesota	55.0
39	Kentucky	54.7
40	Wisconsin	54.0
41	Pennsylvania	53.3
42	Ohio	51.0
43	New York	50.8
44	Michigan	49.3
45	Vermont**	49.0
46	Oregon**	48.0
47	Washington	44.5
48	New Hampshire	43.5
49	West Virginia**	40.0
50	Alaska	37.7
	District of Columbia**	56.0

Source: CQ Press using data from U.S. Department of Commerce, National Oceanic and Atmospheric Administration
   "Comparative Climatic Data" (annual)
*Averages over various years.
**Percentages from these states are from a single location. All other states are from two or more reporting cities within each
state, which were averaged to determine each state's average percentage of sunny days.

Average Wind Speed (M.P.H.)*

ALPHA ORDER

RANK	STATE	MILES PER HOUR
29	Alabama	8.8
39	Alaska	8.2
49	Arizona	6.2
43	Arkansas	7.8
39	California**	8.2
34	Colorado	8.6
36	Connecticut	8.4
24	Delaware	9.0
35	Florida**	8.5
22	Georgia	9.1
7	Hawaii	11.3
32	Idaho	8.7
14	Illinois**	10.1
19	Indiana	9.6
10	Iowa	10.7
4	Kansas	12.2
38	Kentucky	8.3
39	Louisiana	8.2
32	Maine	8.7
29	Maryland	8.8
3	Massachusetts	12.4
18	Michigan**	9.7
9	Minnesota**	10.8
45	Mississippi	6.9
14	Missouri**	10.1
2	Montana	12.5
11	Nebraska	10.5
48	Nevada	6.6
47	New Hampshire	6.7
17	New Jersey	9.8
27	New Mexico	8.9
16	New York**	10.0
44	North Carolina**	7.5
13	North Dakota	10.2
20	Ohio**	9.3
4	Oklahoma	12.2
42	Oregon	7.9
20	Pennsylvania**	9.3
12	Rhode Island	10.4
46	South Carolina	6.8
8	South Dakota	11.0
36	Tennessee**	8.4
24	Texas**	9.0
29	Utah	8.8
24	Vermont	9.0
22	Virginia**	9.1
27	Washington**	8.9
50	West Virginia	5.8
6	Wisconsin	11.5
1	Wyoming	12.9

RANK ORDER

RANK	STATE	MILES PER HOUR
1	Wyoming	12.9
2	Montana	12.5
3	Massachusetts	12.4
4	Kansas	12.2
4	Oklahoma	12.2
6	Wisconsin	11.5
7	Hawaii	11.3
8	South Dakota	11.0
9	Minnesota**	10.8
10	Iowa	10.7
11	Nebraska	10.5
12	Rhode Island	10.4
13	North Dakota	10.2
14	Illinois**	10.1
14	Missouri**	10.1
16	New York**	10.0
17	New Jersey	9.8
18	Michigan**	9.7
19	Indiana	9.6
20	Ohio**	9.3
20	Pennsylvania**	9.3
22	Georgia	9.1
22	Virginia**	9.1
24	Delaware	9.0
24	Texas**	9.0
24	Vermont	9.0
27	New Mexico	8.9
27	Washington**	8.9
29	Alabama	8.8
29	Maryland	8.8
29	Utah	8.8
32	Idaho	8.7
32	Maine	8.7
34	Colorado	8.6
35	Florida**	8.5
36	Connecticut	8.4
36	Tennessee**	8.4
38	Kentucky	8.3
39	Alaska	8.2
39	California**	8.2
39	Louisiana	8.2
42	Oregon	7.9
43	Arkansas	7.8
44	North Carolina**	7.5
45	Mississippi	6.9
46	South Carolina	6.8
47	New Hampshire	6.7
48	Nevada	6.6
49	Arizona	6.2
50	West Virginia	5.8
	District of Columbia	9.4

Source: U.S. Department of Commerce, National Oceanic and Atmospheric Administration
   "Comparative Climatic Data" (annual)
*Averages over various years.
**Wind speeds from multiple reporting cities within one state were averaged to determine a state's average wind speed.

Tornadoes in 2006

National Total = 1,120 Tornadoes*

RANK	STATE	TORNADOES	% of USA
5	Alabama	69	6.2%
46	Alaska	0	0.0%
31	Arizona	6	0.5%
15	Arkansas	25	2.2%
27	California	9	0.8%
22	Colorado	20	1.8%
39	Connecticut	1	0.1%
46	Delaware	0	0.0%
6	Florida	42	3.8%
20	Georgia	21	1.9%
35	Hawaii	2	0.2%
27	Idaho	9	0.8%
1	Illinois	123	11.0%
15	Indiana	25	2.2%
8	Iowa	38	3.4%
4	Kansas	93	8.3%
23	Kentucky	19	1.7%
7	Louisiana	40	3.6%
39	Maine	1	0.1%
34	Maryland	3	0.3%
39	Massachusetts	1	0.1%
26	Michigan	10	0.9%
15	Minnesota	25	2.2%
11	Mississippi	32	2.9%
3	Missouri	103	9.2%
39	Montana	1	0.1%
19	Nebraska	22	2.0%
39	Nevada	1	0.1%
35	New Hampshire	2	0.2%
39	New Jersey	1	0.1%
32	New Mexico	5	0.4%
29	New York	8	0.7%
12	North Carolina	31	2.8%
20	North Dakota	21	1.9%
9	Ohio	36	3.2%
13	Oklahoma	27	2.4%
33	Oregon	4	0.4%
29	Pennsylvania	8	0.7%
46	Rhode Island	0	0.0%
9	South Carolina	36	3.2%
13	South Dakota	27	2.4%
15	Tennessee	25	2.2%
2	Texas	114	10.2%
35	Utah	2	0.2%
46	Vermont	0	0.0%
24	Virginia	16	1.4%
35	Washington	2	0.2%
46	West Virginia	0	0.0%
25	Wisconsin	13	1.2%
39	Wyoming	1	0.1%

RANK	STATE	TORNADOES	% of USA
1	Illinois	123	11.0%
2	Texas	114	10.2%
3	Missouri	103	9.2%
4	Kansas	93	8.3%
5	Alabama	69	6.2%
6	Florida	42	3.8%
7	Louisiana	40	3.6%
8	Iowa	38	3.4%
9	Ohio	36	3.2%
9	South Carolina	36	3.2%
11	Mississippi	32	2.9%
12	North Carolina	31	2.8%
13	Oklahoma	27	2.4%
13	South Dakota	27	2.4%
15	Arkansas	25	2.2%
15	Indiana	25	2.2%
15	Minnesota	25	2.2%
15	Tennessee	25	2.2%
19	Nebraska	22	2.0%
20	Georgia	21	1.9%
20	North Dakota	21	1.9%
22	Colorado	20	1.8%
23	Kentucky	19	1.7%
24	Virginia	16	1.4%
25	Wisconsin	13	1.2%
26	Michigan	10	0.9%
27	California	9	0.8%
27	Idaho	9	0.8%
29	New York	8	0.7%
29	Pennsylvania	8	0.7%
31	Arizona	6	0.5%
32	New Mexico	5	0.4%
33	Oregon	4	0.4%
34	Maryland	3	0.3%
35	Hawaii	2	0.2%
35	New Hampshire	2	0.2%
35	Utah	2	0.2%
35	Washington	2	0.2%
39	Connecticut	1	0.1%
39	Maine	1	0.1%
39	Massachusetts	1	0.1%
39	Montana	1	0.1%
39	Nevada	1	0.1%
39	New Jersey	1	0.1%
39	Wyoming	1	0.1%
46	Alaska	0	0.0%
46	Delaware	0	0.0%
46	Rhode Island	0	0.0%
46	Vermont	0	0.0%
46	West Virginia	0	0.0%
	District of Columbia	0	0.0%

Source: National Weather Service, Storm Prediction Center
   unpublished data (www.spc.noaa.gov)
*National total includes 15 tornadoes tracking in more than one state.

Hazardous Weather Fatalities in 2006

National Total = 558 Fatalities*

ALPHA ORDER

RANK	STATE	FATALITIES	% of USA
33	Alabama	2	0.4%
33	Alaska	2	0.4%
9	Arizona	21	3.8%
18	Arkansas	6	1.1%
1	California	79	14.2%
13	Colorado	10	1.8%
43	Connecticut	1	0.2%
33	Delaware	2	0.4%
10	Florida	20	3.6%
33	Georgia	2	0.4%
17	Hawaii	7	1.3%
43	Idaho	1	0.2%
4	Illinois	45	8.1%
18	Indiana	6	1.1%
33	Iowa	2	0.4%
21	Kansas	5	0.9%
16	Kentucky	8	1.4%
15	Louisiana	9	1.6%
33	Maine	2	0.4%
11	Maryland	15	2.7%
25	Massachusetts	4	0.7%
21	Michigan	5	0.9%
33	Minnesota	2	0.4%
25	Mississippi	4	0.7%
6	Missouri	33	5.9%
33	Montana	2	0.4%
43	Nebraska	1	0.2%
30	Nevada	3	0.5%
43	New Hampshire	1	0.2%
13	New Jersey	10	1.8%
30	New Mexico	3	0.5%
2	New York	48	8.6%
11	North Carolina	15	2.7%
33	North Dakota	2	0.4%
18	Ohio	6	1.1%
8	Oklahoma	26	4.7%
25	Oregon	4	0.7%
3	Pennsylvania	46	8.2%
48	Rhode Island	0	0.0%
25	South Carolina	4	0.7%
33	South Dakota	2	0.4%
5	Tennessee	40	7.2%
7	Texas	32	5.7%
25	Utah	4	0.7%
48	Vermont	0	0.0%
30	Virginia	3	0.5%
21	Washington	5	0.9%
48	West Virginia	0	0.0%
21	Wisconsin	5	0.9%
43	Wyoming	1	0.2%

RANK ORDER

RANK	STATE	FATALITIES	% of USA
1	California	79	14.2%
2	New York	48	8.6%
3	Pennsylvania	46	8.2%
4	Illinois	45	8.1%
5	Tennessee	40	7.2%
6	Missouri	33	5.9%
7	Texas	32	5.7%
8	Oklahoma	26	4.7%
9	Arizona	21	3.8%
10	Florida	20	3.6%
11	Maryland	15	2.7%
11	North Carolina	15	2.7%
13	Colorado	10	1.8%
13	New Jersey	10	1.8%
15	Louisiana	9	1.6%
16	Kentucky	8	1.4%
17	Hawaii	7	1.3%
18	Arkansas	6	1.1%
18	Indiana	6	1.1%
18	Ohio	6	1.1%
21	Kansas	5	0.9%
21	Michigan	5	0.9%
21	Washington	5	0.9%
21	Wisconsin	5	0.9%
25	Massachusetts	4	0.7%
25	Mississippi	4	0.7%
25	Oregon	4	0.7%
25	South Carolina	4	0.7%
25	Utah	4	0.7%
30	Nevada	3	0.5%
30	New Mexico	3	0.5%
30	Virginia	3	0.5%
33	Alabama	2	0.4%
33	Alaska	2	0.4%
33	Delaware	2	0.4%
33	Georgia	2	0.4%
33	Iowa	2	0.4%
33	Maine	2	0.4%
33	Minnesota	2	0.4%
33	Montana	2	0.4%
33	North Dakota	2	0.4%
33	South Dakota	2	0.4%
43	Connecticut	1	0.2%
43	Idaho	1	0.2%
43	Nebraska	1	0.2%
43	New Hampshire	1	0.2%
43	Wyoming	1	0.2%
48	Rhode Island	0	0.0%
48	Vermont	0	0.0%
48	West Virginia	0	0.0%
	District of Columbia	2	0.4%

Source: National Weather Service, Water and Weather Services
    "2006 Summary of Hazardous Weather Fatalities" (http://www.nws.noaa.gov/om/hazstats/state06.pdf)
*Includes lightning, tornado, thunderstorm, extreme temperature, flood, coastal storm, rip current, hurricane, winter storm, fog, avalanche, and other weather events. National total does not include six fatalities in U.S. territories.

Cost of Damage from Hazardous Weather in 2006

National Total = $126,322,800,000*

ALPHA ORDER

RANK	STATE	DAMAGE	% of USA
37	Alabama	$16,600,000	0.0%
22	Alaska	63,600,000	0.1%
14	Arizona	159,500,000	0.1%
21	Arkansas	65,600,000	0.1%
1	California	116,168,900,000	92.0%
34	Colorado	22,100,000	0.0%
47	Connecticut	2,800,000	0.0%
48	Delaware	2,300,000	0.0%
18	Florida	82,500,000	0.1%
26	Georgia	44,100,000	0.0%
50	Hawaii	100,000	0.0%
43	Idaho	4,400,000	0.0%
20	Illinois	67,200,000	0.1%
28	Indiana	41,500,000	0.0%
27	Iowa	41,600,000	0.0%
17	Kansas	108,900,000	0.1%
24	Kentucky	51,400,000	0.0%
6	Louisiana	675,900,000	0.5%
40	Maine	12,000,000	0.0%
29	Maryland	39,400,000	0.0%
33	Massachusetts	22,600,000	0.0%
38	Michigan	15,100,000	0.0%
11	Minnesota	217,200,000	0.2%
15	Mississippi	157,400,000	0.1%
7	Missouri	619,300,000	0.5%
41	Montana	7,100,000	0.0%
16	Nebraska	114,900,000	0.1%
44	Nevada	3,200,000	0.0%
35	New Hampshire	18,200,000	0.0%
25	New Jersey	47,500,000	0.0%
31	New Mexico	24,500,000	0.0%
3	New York	1,164,100,000	0.9%
23	North Carolina	56,400,000	0.0%
32	North Dakota	24,100,000	0.0%
4	Ohio	861,200,000	0.7%
10	Oklahoma	229,900,000	0.2%
19	Oregon	80,800,000	0.1%
8	Pennsylvania	544,500,000	0.4%
49	Rhode Island	800,000	0.0%
42	South Carolina	6,900,000	0.0%
30	South Dakota	27,200,000	0.0%
13	Tennessee	165,800,000	0.1%
2	Texas	3,007,500,000	2.4%
36	Utah	18,000,000	0.0%
44	Vermont	3,200,000	0.0%
12	Virginia	212,200,000	0.2%
9	Washington	241,400,000	0.2%
39	West Virginia	13,900,000	0.0%
5	Wisconsin	733,800,000	0.6%
46	Wyoming	3,100,000	0.0%

RANK ORDER

RANK	STATE	DAMAGE	% of USA
1	California	$116,168,900,000	92.0%
2	Texas	3,007,500,000	2.4%
3	New York	1,164,100,000	0.9%
4	Ohio	861,200,000	0.7%
5	Wisconsin	733,800,000	0.6%
6	Louisiana	675,900,000	0.5%
7	Missouri	619,300,000	0.5%
8	Pennsylvania	544,500,000	0.4%
9	Washington	241,400,000	0.2%
10	Oklahoma	229,900,000	0.2%
11	Minnesota	217,200,000	0.2%
12	Virginia	212,200,000	0.2%
13	Tennessee	165,800,000	0.1%
14	Arizona	159,500,000	0.1%
15	Mississippi	157,400,000	0.1%
16	Nebraska	114,900,000	0.1%
17	Kansas	108,900,000	0.1%
18	Florida	82,500,000	0.1%
19	Oregon	80,800,000	0.1%
20	Illinois	67,200,000	0.1%
21	Arkansas	65,600,000	0.1%
22	Alaska	63,600,000	0.1%
23	North Carolina	56,400,000	0.0%
24	Kentucky	51,400,000	0.0%
25	New Jersey	47,500,000	0.0%
26	Georgia	44,100,000	0.0%
27	Iowa	41,600,000	0.0%
28	Indiana	41,500,000	0.0%
29	Maryland	39,400,000	0.0%
30	South Dakota	27,200,000	0.0%
31	New Mexico	24,500,000	0.0%
32	North Dakota	24,100,000	0.0%
33	Massachusetts	22,600,000	0.0%
34	Colorado	22,100,000	0.0%
35	New Hampshire	18,200,000	0.0%
36	Utah	18,000,000	0.0%
37	Alabama	16,600,000	0.0%
38	Michigan	15,100,000	0.0%
39	West Virginia	13,900,000	0.0%
40	Maine	12,000,000	0.0%
41	Montana	7,100,000	0.0%
42	South Carolina	6,900,000	0.0%
43	Idaho	4,400,000	0.0%
44	Nevada	3,200,000	0.0%
44	Vermont	3,200,000	0.0%
46	Wyoming	3,100,000	0.0%
47	Connecticut	2,800,000	0.0%
48	Delaware	2,300,000	0.0%
49	Rhode Island	800,000	0.0%
50	Hawaii	100,000	0.0%
	District of Columbia	10,600,000	0.0%

Source: National Weather Service, Water and Weather Services
"2006 Summary of Hazardous Weather Fatalities" (http://www.nws.noaa.gov/om/hazstats/state06.pdf)
*Includes lightning, tornado, thunderstorm, extreme temperature, flood, coastal storm, rip current, hurricane, winter storm, fog, avalanche, and other weather events. National total does not include damage costs in U.S. territories.

Acres Owned by the Federal Government in 2004

National Total = 653,299,090 Acres*

ALPHA ORDER

RANK	STATE	ACRES	% of USA
38	Alabama	513,913	0.1%
1	Alaska	252,495,811	38.6%
4	Arizona	34,933,236	5.3%
20	Arkansas	2,407,948	0.4%
3	California	45,393,238	6.9%
11	Colorado	24,354,713	3.7%
49	Connecticut	13,938	0.0%
48	Delaware	25,874	0.0%
18	Florida	2,858,782	0.4%
26	Georgia	1,409,406	0.2%
31	Hawaii	796,726	0.1%
9	Idaho	26,565,412	4.1%
35	Illinois	641,959	0.1%
39	Indiana	463,245	0.1%
42	Iowa	273,954	0.0%
36	Kansas	631,351	0.1%
27	Kentucky	1,378,677	0.2%
25	Louisiana	1,474,788	0.2%
44	Maine	208,422	0.0%
45	Maryland	178,527	0.0%
47	Massachusetts	93,950	0.0%
14	Michigan	3,637,873	0.6%
17	Minnesota	2,873,517	0.4%
22	Mississippi	2,196,940	0.3%
21	Missouri	2,224,788	0.3%
8	Montana	27,910,152	4.3%
34	Nebraska	665,481	0.1%
2	Nevada	59,362,643	9.1%
32	New Hampshire	775,665	0.1%
46	New Jersey	148,441	0.0%
6	New Mexico	32,483,877	5.0%
43	New York	233,533	0.0%
13	North Carolina	3,710,338	0.6%
28	North Dakota	1,185,777	0.2%
40	Ohio	448,381	0.1%
24	Oklahoma	1,586,148	0.2%
5	Oregon	32,715,514	5.0%
33	Pennsylvania	719,864	0.1%
50	Rhode Island	2,923	0.0%
37	South Carolina	560,956	0.1%
16	South Dakota	3,028,003	0.5%
30	Tennessee	865,837	0.1%
15	Texas	3,130,345	0.5%
7	Utah	30,271,905	4.6%
41	Vermont	443,249	0.1%
19	Virginia	2,534,178	0.4%
12	Washington	12,949,662	2.0%
29	West Virginia	1,146,211	0.2%
23	Wisconsin	1,971,902	0.3%
10	Wyoming	26,391,487	4.0%

RANK ORDER

RANK	STATE	ACRES	% of USA
1	Alaska	252,495,811	38.6%
2	Nevada	59,362,643	9.1%
3	California	45,393,238	6.9%
4	Arizona	34,933,236	5.3%
5	Oregon	32,715,514	5.0%
6	New Mexico	32,483,877	5.0%
7	Utah	30,271,905	4.6%
8	Montana	27,910,152	4.3%
9	Idaho	26,565,412	4.1%
10	Wyoming	26,391,487	4.0%
11	Colorado	24,354,713	3.7%
12	Washington	12,949,662	2.0%
13	North Carolina	3,710,338	0.6%
14	Michigan	3,637,873	0.6%
15	Texas	3,130,345	0.5%
16	South Dakota	3,028,003	0.5%
17	Minnesota	2,873,517	0.4%
18	Florida	2,858,782	0.4%
19	Virginia	2,534,178	0.4%
20	Arkansas	2,407,948	0.4%
21	Missouri	2,224,788	0.3%
22	Mississippi	2,196,940	0.3%
23	Wisconsin	1,971,902	0.3%
24	Oklahoma	1,586,148	0.2%
25	Louisiana	1,474,788	0.2%
26	Georgia	1,409,406	0.2%
27	Kentucky	1,378,677	0.2%
28	North Dakota	1,185,777	0.2%
29	West Virginia	1,146,211	0.2%
30	Tennessee	865,837	0.1%
31	Hawaii	796,726	0.1%
32	New Hampshire	775,665	0.1%
33	Pennsylvania	719,864	0.1%
34	Nebraska	665,481	0.1%
35	Illinois	641,959	0.1%
36	Kansas	631,351	0.1%
37	South Carolina	560,956	0.1%
38	Alabama	513,913	0.1%
39	Indiana	463,245	0.1%
40	Ohio	448,381	0.1%
41	Vermont	443,249	0.1%
42	Iowa	273,954	0.0%
43	New York	233,533	0.0%
44	Maine	208,422	0.0%
45	Maryland	178,527	0.0%
46	New Jersey	148,441	0.0%
47	Massachusetts	93,950	0.0%
48	Delaware	25,874	0.0%
49	Connecticut	13,938	0.0%
50	Rhode Island	2,923	0.0%
	District of Columbia	9,631	0.0%

Source: Government Services Administration, Office of Governmentwide Real Property Policy
"Federal Real Property Profile" (http://www.gsa.gov/realpropertyprofile)
*As of September 30, 2004. Does not include land owned by the federal government in U.S. territories or in foreign countries.

Percent of Land Owned by the Federal Government in 2004

National Percent = 28.8%*

ALPHA ORDER

RANK	STATE	PERCENT
43	Alabama	1.6
2	Alaska	69.1
6	Arizona	48.1
22	Arkansas	7.2
7	California	45.3
10	Colorado	36.6
49	Connecticut	0.4
37	Delaware	2.0
18	Florida	8.2
29	Georgia	3.8
13	Hawaii	19.4
5	Idaho	50.2
41	Illinois	1.8
37	Indiana	2.0
47	Iowa	0.8
45	Kansas	1.2
26	Kentucky	5.4
27	Louisiana	5.1
46	Maine	1.1
34	Maryland	2.8
39	Massachusetts	1.9
16	Michigan	10.0
24	Minnesota	5.6
21	Mississippi	7.3
28	Missouri	5.0
12	Montana	29.9
44	Nebraska	1.4
1	Nevada	84.5
14	New Hampshire	13.5
32	New Jersey	3.1
9	New Mexico	41.8
47	New York	0.8
15	North Carolina	11.8
35	North Dakota	2.7
42	Ohio	1.7
30	Oklahoma	3.6
4	Oregon	53.1
36	Pennsylvania	2.5
49	Rhode Island	0.4
33	South Carolina	2.9
23	South Dakota	6.2
31	Tennessee	3.2
39	Texas	1.9
3	Utah	57.5
19	Vermont	7.5
17	Virginia	9.9
11	Washington	30.3
20	West Virginia	7.4
24	Wisconsin	5.6
8	Wyoming	42.3

RANK ORDER

RANK	STATE	PERCENT
1	Nevada	84.5
2	Alaska	69.1
3	Utah	57.5
4	Oregon	53.1
5	Idaho	50.2
6	Arizona	48.1
7	California	45.3
8	Wyoming	42.3
9	New Mexico	41.8
10	Colorado	36.6
11	Washington	30.3
12	Montana	29.9
13	Hawaii	19.4
14	New Hampshire	13.5
15	North Carolina	11.8
16	Michigan	10.0
17	Virginia	9.9
18	Florida	8.2
19	Vermont	7.5
20	West Virginia	7.4
21	Mississippi	7.3
22	Arkansas	7.2
23	South Dakota	6.2
24	Minnesota	5.6
24	Wisconsin	5.6
26	Kentucky	5.4
27	Louisiana	5.1
28	Missouri	5.0
29	Georgia	3.8
30	Oklahoma	3.6
31	Tennessee	3.2
32	New Jersey	3.1
33	South Carolina	2.9
34	Maryland	2.8
35	North Dakota	2.7
36	Pennsylvania	2.5
37	Delaware	2.0
37	Indiana	2.0
39	Massachusetts	1.9
39	Texas	1.9
41	Illinois	1.8
42	Ohio	1.7
43	Alabama	1.6
44	Nebraska	1.4
45	Kansas	1.2
46	Maine	1.1
47	Iowa	0.8
47	New York	0.8
49	Connecticut	0.4
49	Rhode Island	0.4

District of Columbia	24.7

Source: Government Services Administration, Office of Governmentwide Real Property Policy
    "Federal Real Property Profile" (http://www.gsa.gov/realpropertyprofile)
*As of September 30, 2004. Does not include land owned by the federal government in U.S. territories or in foreign countries.

National Park Service Land in 2007

National Total = 84,323,151 Acres*

ALPHA ORDER

RANK	STATE	ACRES	% of USA
41	Alabama	21,081	0.0%
1	Alaska	54,638,803	64.8%
3	Arizona	2,962,853	3.5%
25	Arkansas	104,976	0.1%
2	California	8,107,244	9.6%
12	Colorado	673,296	0.8%
46	Connecticut	7,782	0.0%
50	Delaware	0	0.0%
4	Florida	2,637,755	3.1%
34	Georgia	62,923	0.1%
17	Hawaii	364,999	0.4%
13	Idaho	517,904	0.6%
48	Illinois	13	0.0%
43	Indiana	15,317	0.0%
47	Iowa	2,713	0.0%
44	Kansas	11,792	0.0%
27	Kentucky	95,415	0.1%
40	Louisiana	21,126	0.0%
29	Maine	90,257	0.1%
33	Maryland	71,857	0.1%
35	Massachusetts	57,897	0.1%
11	Michigan	718,187	0.9%
20	Minnesota	301,333	0.4%
24	Mississippi	117,629	0.1%
30	Missouri	83,471	0.1%
8	Montana	1,274,374	1.5%
38	Nebraska	29,748	0.0%
10	Nevada	778,512	0.9%
42	New Hampshire	15,897	0.0%
26	New Jersey	99,096	0.1%
15	New Mexico	391,029	0.5%
32	New York	72,426	0.1%
14	North Carolina	405,793	0.5%
31	North Dakota	72,581	0.1%
36	Ohio	34,157	0.0%
45	Oklahoma	10,241	0.0%
21	Oregon	199,087	0.2%
22	Pennsylvania	136,745	0.2%
49	Rhode Island	5	0.0%
37	South Carolina	32,618	0.0%
19	South Dakota	307,377	0.4%
16	Tennessee	383,545	0.5%
9	Texas	1,236,625	1.5%
6	Utah	2,117,038	2.5%
39	Vermont	22,178	0.0%
18	Virginia	362,554	0.4%
7	Washington	1,965,395	2.3%
28	West Virginia	92,604	0.1%
23	Wisconsin	133,754	0.2%
5	Wyoming	2,396,340	2.8%

RANK ORDER

RANK	STATE	ACRES	% of USA
1	Alaska	54,638,803	64.8%
2	California	8,107,244	9.6%
3	Arizona	2,962,853	3.5%
4	Florida	2,637,755	3.1%
5	Wyoming	2,396,340	2.8%
6	Utah	2,117,038	2.5%
7	Washington	1,965,395	2.3%
8	Montana	1,274,374	1.5%
9	Texas	1,236,625	1.5%
10	Nevada	778,512	0.9%
11	Michigan	718,187	0.9%
12	Colorado	673,296	0.8%
13	Idaho	517,904	0.6%
14	North Carolina	405,793	0.5%
15	New Mexico	391,029	0.5%
16	Tennessee	383,545	0.5%
17	Hawaii	364,999	0.4%
18	Virginia	362,554	0.4%
19	South Dakota	307,377	0.4%
20	Minnesota	301,333	0.4%
21	Oregon	199,087	0.2%
22	Pennsylvania	136,745	0.2%
23	Wisconsin	133,754	0.2%
24	Mississippi	117,629	0.1%
25	Arkansas	104,976	0.1%
26	New Jersey	99,096	0.1%
27	Kentucky	95,415	0.1%
28	West Virginia	92,604	0.1%
29	Maine	90,257	0.1%
30	Missouri	83,471	0.1%
31	North Dakota	72,581	0.1%
32	New York	72,426	0.1%
33	Maryland	71,857	0.1%
34	Georgia	62,923	0.1%
35	Massachusetts	57,897	0.1%
36	Ohio	34,157	0.0%
37	South Carolina	32,618	0.0%
38	Nebraska	29,748	0.0%
39	Vermont	22,178	0.0%
40	Louisiana	21,126	0.0%
41	Alabama	21,081	0.0%
42	New Hampshire	15,897	0.0%
43	Indiana	15,317	0.0%
44	Kansas	11,792	0.0%
45	Oklahoma	10,241	0.0%
46	Connecticut	7,782	0.0%
47	Iowa	2,713	0.0%
48	Illinois	13	0.0%
49	Rhode Island	5	0.0%
50	Delaware	0	0.0%
	District of Columbia	7,088	0.0%

Source: National Park Service
    "Listing of Acreage by State" (unpublished data)
*As of December 31, 2007. Includes federal and nonfederal land in national parks, monuments, historic sites, recreation areas, preserves, battlefields, grasslands, seashores, parkways, trails, and rivers. Does not include land in national forest or wildlife areas. Includes 59,716 acres in U.S. territories.

Recreation Visits to National Park Service Areas in 2006

National Total = 272,623,980 Visits*

RANK	STATE	VISITS	% of USA
36	Alabama	790,039	0.3%
26	Alaska	2,471,970	0.9%
5	Arizona	10,543,205	3.9%
25	Arkansas	2,556,666	0.9%
1	California	32,906,849	12.1%
19	Colorado	5,289,308	1.9%
49	Connecticut	11,795	0.0%
50	Delaware	0	0.0%
8	Florida	7,983,175	2.9%
12	Georgia	6,462,784	2.4%
17	Hawaii	5,323,425	2.0%
40	Idaho	435,806	0.2%
41	Illinois	388,887	0.1%
27	Indiana	2,190,492	0.8%
44	Iowa	225,179	0.1%
45	Kansas	125,408	0.0%
29	Kentucky	1,924,683	0.7%
42	Louisiana	333,508	0.1%
28	Maine	2,083,588	0.8%
23	Maryland	3,249,642	1.2%
6	Massachusetts	9,813,899	3.6%
31	Michigan	1,649,394	0.6%
37	Minnesota	605,606	0.2%
13	Mississippi	6,016,266	2.2%
20	Missouri	4,302,533	1.6%
21	Montana	3,897,415	1.4%
43	Nebraska	225,937	0.1%
14	Nevada	5,911,839	2.2%
47	New Hampshire	25,858	0.0%
15	New Jersey	5,708,286	2.1%
32	New Mexico	1,620,457	0.6%
4	New York	15,154,997	5.6%
3	North Carolina	20,091,486	7.4%
38	North Dakota	472,986	0.2%
24	Ohio	2,704,686	1.0%
34	Oklahoma	1,358,201	0.5%
35	Oregon	806,344	0.3%
7	Pennsylvania	8,842,235	3.2%
46	Rhode Island	52,671	0.0%
33	South Carolina	1,383,500	0.5%
22	South Dakota	3,703,047	1.4%
10	Tennessee	7,758,199	2.8%
16	Texas	5,488,711	2.0%
9	Utah	7,840,356	2.9%
48	Vermont	22,484	0.0%
2	Virginia	22,944,011	8.4%
11	Washington	6,518,791	2.4%
30	West Virginia	1,737,487	0.6%
39	Wisconsin	442,472	0.2%
18	Wyoming	5,322,531	2.0%

RANK	STATE	VISITS	% of USA
1	California	32,906,849	12.1%
2	Virginia	22,944,011	8.4%
3	North Carolina	20,091,486	7.4%
4	New York	15,154,997	5.6%
5	Arizona	10,543,205	3.9%
6	Massachusetts	9,813,899	3.6%
7	Pennsylvania	8,842,235	3.2%
8	Florida	7,983,175	2.9%
9	Utah	7,840,356	2.9%
10	Tennessee	7,758,199	2.8%
11	Washington	6,518,791	2.4%
12	Georgia	6,462,784	2.4%
13	Mississippi	6,016,266	2.2%
14	Nevada	5,911,839	2.2%
15	New Jersey	5,708,286	2.1%
16	Texas	5,488,711	2.0%
17	Hawaii	5,323,425	2.0%
18	Wyoming	5,322,531	2.0%
19	Colorado	5,289,308	1.9%
20	Missouri	4,302,533	1.6%
21	Montana	3,897,415	1.4%
22	South Dakota	3,703,047	1.4%
23	Maryland	3,249,642	1.2%
24	Ohio	2,704,686	1.0%
25	Arkansas	2,556,666	0.9%
26	Alaska	2,471,970	0.9%
27	Indiana	2,190,492	0.8%
28	Maine	2,083,588	0.8%
29	Kentucky	1,924,683	0.7%
30	West Virginia	1,737,487	0.6%
31	Michigan	1,649,394	0.6%
32	New Mexico	1,620,457	0.6%
33	South Carolina	1,383,500	0.5%
34	Oklahoma	1,358,201	0.5%
35	Oregon	806,344	0.3%
36	Alabama	790,039	0.3%
37	Minnesota	605,606	0.2%
38	North Dakota	472,986	0.2%
39	Wisconsin	442,472	0.2%
40	Idaho	435,806	0.2%
41	Illinois	388,887	0.1%
42	Louisiana	333,508	0.1%
43	Nebraska	225,937	0.1%
44	Iowa	225,179	0.1%
45	Kansas	125,408	0.0%
46	Rhode Island	52,671	0.0%
47	New Hampshire	25,858	0.0%
48	Vermont	22,484	0.0%
49	Connecticut	11,795	0.0%
50	Delaware	0	0.0%
	District of Columbia	32,867,947	12.1%

Source: National Park Service, Public Use Statistics Office
"National Park Service Statistical Abstract 2006" (http://www2.nature.nps.gov/stats/abst2006.pdf)
*National total includes 2,036,941 visits in U.S. territories.

Percent Change in National Park Service Recreation Visits: 2005-2006

National Percent Change = 0.3% Decrease*

ALPHA ORDER

RANK	STATE	PERCENT CHANGE
5	Alabama	5.4
6	Alaska	4.6
30	Arizona	(2.4)
20	Arkansas	0.4
26	California	(1.5)
25	Colorado	(1.2)
3	Connecticut	5.6
NA	Delaware**	NA
13	Florida	2.4
1	Georgia	12.5
27	Hawaii	(1.7)
31	Idaho	(2.5)
41	Illinois	(7.9)
43	Indiana	(9.7)
40	Iowa	(6.9)
12	Kansas	3.2
49	Kentucky	(71.0)
48	Louisiana	(49.5)
15	Maine	1.5
21	Maryland	0.2
2	Massachusetts	7.4
37	Michigan	(4.1)
36	Minnesota	(3.7)
7	Mississippi	4.5
45	Missouri	(11.9)
19	Montana	0.5
23	Nebraska	(0.4)
17	Nevada	1.1
38	New Hampshire	(4.2)
8	New Jersey	3.9
29	New Mexico	(1.9)
39	New York	(5.8)
10	North Carolina	3.5
46	North Dakota	(14.4)
35	Ohio	(3.5)
10	Oklahoma	3.5
44	Oregon	(11.8)
34	Pennsylvania	(3.1)
9	Rhode Island	3.8
27	South Carolina	(1.7)
24	South Dakota	(0.8)
18	Tennessee	1.0
14	Texas	2.1
33	Utah	(2.6)
47	Vermont	(27.5)
22	Virginia	(0.2)
42	Washington	(8.8)
4	West Virginia	5.5
16	Wisconsin	1.4
31	Wyoming	(2.5)

RANK ORDER

RANK	STATE	PERCENT CHANGE
1	Georgia	12.5
2	Massachusetts	7.4
3	Connecticut	5.6
4	West Virginia	5.5
5	Alabama	5.4
6	Alaska	4.6
7	Mississippi	4.5
8	New Jersey	3.9
9	Rhode Island	3.8
10	North Carolina	3.5
10	Oklahoma	3.5
12	Kansas	3.2
13	Florida	2.4
14	Texas	2.1
15	Maine	1.5
16	Wisconsin	1.4
17	Nevada	1.1
18	Tennessee	1.0
19	Montana	0.5
20	Arkansas	0.4
21	Maryland	0.2
22	Virginia	(0.2)
23	Nebraska	(0.4)
24	South Dakota	(0.8)
25	Colorado	(1.2)
26	California	(1.5)
27	Hawaii	(1.7)
27	South Carolina	(1.7)
29	New Mexico	(1.9)
30	Arizona	(2.4)
31	Idaho	(2.5)
31	Wyoming	(2.5)
33	Utah	(2.6)
34	Pennsylvania	(3.1)
35	Ohio	(3.5)
36	Minnesota	(3.7)
37	Michigan	(4.1)
38	New Hampshire	(4.2)
39	New York	(5.8)
40	Iowa	(6.9)
41	Illinois	(7.9)
42	Washington	(8.8)
43	Indiana	(9.7)
44	Oregon	(11.8)
45	Missouri	(11.9)
46	North Dakota	(14.4)
47	Vermont	(27.5)
48	Louisiana	(49.5)
49	Kentucky	(71.0)
NA	Delaware**	NA
	District of Columbia	4.1

Source: National Park Service, Public Use Statistics Office
"National Park Service Statistical Abstract 2006" (http://www2.nature.nps.gov/stats/abst2006.pdf)
*National percent change includes visits in U.S. territories.
**Not applicable.

State Parks, Recreation Areas and Natural Areas in 2005

National Total = 5,842 Areas*

ALPHA ORDER

RANK	STATE	AREAS	% of USA
50	Alabama	22	0.4%
12	Alaska	139	2.4%
45	Arizona	31	0.5%
34	Arkansas	51	0.9%
4	California	278	4.8%
11	Colorado	146	2.5%
13	Connecticut	137	2.3%
41	Delaware	34	0.6%
10	Florida	159	2.7%
26	Georgia	72	1.2%
27	Hawaii	69	1.2%
43	Idaho	32	0.5%
3	Illinois	300	5.1%
41	Indiana	34	0.6%
9	Iowa	181	3.1%
49	Kansas	25	0.4%
37	Kentucky	50	0.9%
30	Louisiana	57	1.0%
14	Maine	134	2.3%
34	Maryland	51	0.9%
5	Massachusetts	245	4.2%
20	Michigan	97	1.7%
8	Minnesota	198	3.4%
47	Mississippi	28	0.5%
23	Missouri	84	1.4%
2	Montana	379	6.5%
22	Nebraska	85	1.5%
48	Nevada	26	0.4%
21	New Hampshire	89	1.5%
18	New Jersey	116	2.0%
43	New Mexico	32	0.5%
1	New York	879	15.0%
29	North Carolina	64	1.1%
46	North Dakota	30	0.5%
24	Ohio	74	1.3%
34	Oklahoma	51	0.9%
7	Oregon	233	4.0%
16	Pennsylvania	120	2.1%
24	Rhode Island	74	1.3%
31	South Carolina	55	0.9%
15	South Dakota	130	2.2%
32	Tennessee	53	0.9%
16	Texas	120	2.1%
33	Utah	52	0.9%
19	Vermont	103	1.8%
39	Virginia	37	0.6%
6	Washington	235	4.0%
38	West Virginia	47	0.8%
28	Wisconsin	68	1.2%
40	Wyoming	36	0.6%

RANK ORDER

RANK	STATE	AREAS	% of USA
1	New York	879	15.0%
2	Montana	379	6.5%
3	Illinois	300	5.1%
4	California	278	4.8%
5	Massachusetts	245	4.2%
6	Washington	235	4.0%
7	Oregon	233	4.0%
8	Minnesota	198	3.4%
9	Iowa	181	3.1%
10	Florida	159	2.7%
11	Colorado	146	2.5%
12	Alaska	139	2.4%
13	Connecticut	137	2.3%
14	Maine	134	2.3%
15	South Dakota	130	2.2%
16	Pennsylvania	120	2.1%
16	Texas	120	2.1%
18	New Jersey	116	2.0%
19	Vermont	103	1.8%
20	Michigan	97	1.7%
21	New Hampshire	89	1.5%
22	Nebraska	85	1.5%
23	Missouri	84	1.4%
24	Ohio	74	1.3%
24	Rhode Island	74	1.3%
26	Georgia	72	1.2%
27	Hawaii	69	1.2%
28	Wisconsin	68	1.2%
29	North Carolina	64	1.1%
30	Louisiana	57	1.0%
31	South Carolina	55	0.9%
32	Tennessee	53	0.9%
33	Utah	52	0.9%
34	Arkansas	51	0.9%
34	Maryland	51	0.9%
34	Oklahoma	51	0.9%
37	Kentucky	50	0.9%
38	West Virginia	47	0.8%
39	Virginia	37	0.6%
40	Wyoming	36	0.6%
41	Delaware	34	0.6%
41	Indiana	34	0.6%
43	Idaho	32	0.5%
43	New Mexico	32	0.5%
45	Arizona	31	0.5%
46	North Dakota	30	0.5%
47	Mississippi	28	0.5%
48	Nevada	26	0.4%
49	Kansas	25	0.4%
50	Alabama	22	0.4%
	District of Columbia**	NA	NA

Source: The National Association of State Parks Directors
   "The 2006 Annual Information Exchange" (http://www.naspd.org/)
*For the period July 1, 2004 through June 30, 2005. Includes operating and nonoperating state parks, recreation areas, natural areas, and other areas.
**Not applicable.

Visitors to State Parks and Recreation Areas in 2005

National Total = 708,602,410 Visitors*

ALPHA ORDER

RANK	STATE	VISITORS	% of USA
44	Alabama	2,699,454	0.4%
36	Alaska	4,334,192	0.6%
45	Arizona	2,286,324	0.3%
21	Arkansas	10,455,102	1.5%
1	California	77,049,170	10.9%
20	Colorado	11,203,691	1.6%
31	Connecticut	6,814,390	1.0%
40	Delaware	3,470,731	0.5%
10	Florida	17,380,803	2.5%
19	Georgia	11,487,932	1.6%
25	Hawaii	9,221,298	1.3%
43	Idaho	2,782,272	0.4%
4	Illinois	44,357,795	6.3%
12	Indiana	17,049,527	2.4%
15	Iowa	14,128,797	2.0%
28	Kansas	7,623,191	1.1%
30	Kentucky	7,134,087	1.0%
46	Louisiana	2,183,421	0.3%
47	Maine	2,093,843	0.3%
18	Maryland	11,537,907	1.6%
23	Massachusetts	9,785,378	1.4%
9	Michigan	20,446,568	2.9%
26	Minnesota	8,039,468	1.1%
42	Mississippi	2,941,988	0.4%
11	Missouri	17,317,876	2.4%
35	Montana	5,255,684	0.7%
22	Nebraska	10,085,789	1.4%
38	Nevada	4,148,777	0.6%
NA	New Hampshire**	NA	NA
13	New Jersey	15,945,324	2.3%
39	New Mexico	3,840,234	0.5%
2	New York	53,605,395	7.6%
17	North Carolina	11,770,923	1.7%
48	North Dakota	965,989	0.1%
3	Ohio	51,440,085	7.3%
16	Oklahoma	12,742,046	1.8%
5	Oregon	44,253,075	6.2%
7	Pennsylvania	35,095,476	5.0%
34	Rhode Island	5,470,736	0.8%
33	South Carolina	6,507,624	0.9%
29	South Dakota	7,148,091	1.0%
8	Tennessee	29,228,449	4.1%
24	Texas	9,654,221	1.4%
37	Utah	4,273,707	0.6%
49	Vermont	694,458	0.1%
32	Virginia	6,543,387	0.9%
6	Washington	40,330,551	5.7%
27	West Virginia	7,969,348	1.1%
14	Wisconsin	14,492,246	2.0%
41	Wyoming	3,315,590	0.5%

RANK ORDER

RANK	STATE	VISITORS	% of USA
1	California	77,049,170	10.9%
2	New York	53,605,395	7.6%
3	Ohio	51,440,085	7.3%
4	Illinois	44,357,795	6.3%
5	Oregon	44,253,075	6.2%
6	Washington	40,330,551	5.7%
7	Pennsylvania	35,095,476	5.0%
8	Tennessee	29,228,449	4.1%
9	Michigan	20,446,568	2.9%
10	Florida	17,380,803	2.5%
11	Missouri	17,317,876	2.4%
12	Indiana	17,049,527	2.4%
13	New Jersey	15,945,324	2.3%
14	Wisconsin	14,492,246	2.0%
15	Iowa	14,128,797	2.0%
16	Oklahoma	12,742,046	1.8%
17	North Carolina	11,770,923	1.7%
18	Maryland	11,537,907	1.6%
19	Georgia	11,487,932	1.6%
20	Colorado	11,203,691	1.6%
21	Arkansas	10,455,102	1.5%
22	Nebraska	10,085,789	1.4%
23	Massachusetts	9,785,378	1.4%
24	Texas	9,654,221	1.4%
25	Hawaii	9,221,298	1.3%
26	Minnesota	8,039,468	1.1%
27	West Virginia	7,969,348	1.1%
28	Kansas	7,623,191	1.1%
29	South Dakota	7,148,091	1.0%
30	Kentucky	7,134,087	1.0%
31	Connecticut	6,814,390	1.0%
32	Virginia	6,543,387	0.9%
33	South Carolina	6,507,624	0.9%
34	Rhode Island	5,470,736	0.8%
35	Montana	5,255,684	0.7%
36	Alaska	4,334,192	0.6%
37	Utah	4,273,707	0.6%
38	Nevada	4,148,777	0.6%
39	New Mexico	3,840,234	0.5%
40	Delaware	3,470,731	0.5%
41	Wyoming	3,315,590	0.5%
42	Mississippi	2,941,988	0.4%
43	Idaho	2,782,272	0.4%
44	Alabama	2,699,454	0.4%
45	Arizona	2,286,324	0.3%
46	Louisiana	2,183,421	0.3%
47	Maine	2,093,843	0.3%
48	North Dakota	965,989	0.1%
49	Vermont	694,458	0.1%
NA	New Hampshire**	NA	NA
	District of Columbia**	NA	NA

Source: The National Association of State Parks Directors
   "The 2005 Annual Information Exchange" (http://www.naspd.org/)
*For the period July 1, 2004 through June 30, 2005. Includes operating and nonoperating state parks, recreation areas, natural areas, and other areas. Includes day and overnight visitors.
**Not available.

Percent of Land That is Developed: 2003

National Percent = 5.6%*

ALPHA ORDER

RANK	STATE	PERCENT
20	Alabama	8.1
NA	Alaska**	NA
38	Arizona	2.6
33	Arkansas	4.7
25	California	5.8
37	Colorado	2.8
2	Connecticut	29.5
5	Delaware	17.3
7	Florida	15.6
12	Georgia	12.1
NA	Hawaii**	NA
44	Idaho	1.5
19	Illinois	9.3
16	Indiana	10.5
31	Iowa	4.9
36	Kansas	3.8
21	Kentucky	7.7
26	Louisiana	5.7
35	Maine	3.9
6	Maryland	17.1
2	Massachusetts	29.5
16	Michigan	10.5
34	Minnesota	4.3
29	Mississippi	5.5
24	Missouri	6.1
46	Montana	1.1
39	Nebraska	2.5
48	Nevada	0.7
15	New Hampshire	10.7
1	New Jersey	36.9
43	New Mexico	1.8
13	New York	11.1
10	North Carolina	13.8
40	North Dakota	2.2
9	Ohio	14.6
32	Oklahoma	4.8
41	Oregon	2.1
8	Pennsylvania	14.7
4	Rhode Island	27.0
11	South Carolina	12.4
42	South Dakota	2.0
18	Tennessee	9.7
27	Texas	5.6
45	Utah	1.4
27	Vermont	5.6
14	Virginia	10.8
30	Washington	5.2
23	West Virginia	6.5
22	Wisconsin	7.2
47	Wyoming	1.0

RANK ORDER

RANK	STATE	PERCENT
1	New Jersey	36.9
2	Connecticut	29.5
2	Massachusetts	29.5
4	Rhode Island	27.0
5	Delaware	17.3
6	Maryland	17.1
7	Florida	15.6
8	Pennsylvania	14.7
9	Ohio	14.6
10	North Carolina	13.8
11	South Carolina	12.4
12	Georgia	12.1
13	New York	11.1
14	Virginia	10.8
15	New Hampshire	10.7
16	Indiana	10.5
16	Michigan	10.5
18	Tennessee	9.7
19	Illinois	9.3
20	Alabama	8.1
21	Kentucky	7.7
22	Wisconsin	7.2
23	West Virginia	6.5
24	Missouri	6.1
25	California	5.8
26	Louisiana	5.7
27	Texas	5.6
27	Vermont	5.6
29	Mississippi	5.5
30	Washington	5.2
31	Iowa	4.9
32	Oklahoma	4.8
33	Arkansas	4.7
34	Minnesota	4.3
35	Maine	3.9
36	Kansas	3.8
37	Colorado	2.8
38	Arizona	2.6
39	Nebraska	2.5
40	North Dakota	2.2
41	Oregon	2.1
42	South Dakota	2.0
43	New Mexico	1.8
44	Idaho	1.5
45	Utah	1.4
46	Montana	1.1
47	Wyoming	1.0
48	Nevada	0.7
NA	Alaska**	NA
NA	Hawaii**	NA
	District of Columbia**	NA

Source: CQ Press using data from U.S. Department of Agriculture, Natural Resources Conservation Service
"2003 Annual NRI (http://www.nrcs.usda.gov/Technical/nri/2003/nri03landuse-mrb.html)
*National percent does not include land in Alaska, Hawaii or the District of Columbia. "Developed" does not include cropland, water areas, or federal land.

IX. Government Finances: Federal

Internal Revenue Service Gross Collections in 2006

National Total = $2,518,680,230,000*

ALPHA ORDER

RANK	STATE	COLLECTIONS	% of USA
29	Alabama	$22,179,707,000	0.9%
47	Alaska	4,057,755,000	0.2%
23	Arizona	32,638,677,000	1.3%
26	Arkansas	27,697,303,000	1.1%
1	California	299,521,281,000	11.9%
20	Colorado	42,308,861,000	1.7%
17	Connecticut	50,450,286,000	2.0%
35	Delaware	17,222,467,000	0.7%
4	Florida	131,261,303,000	5.2%
9	Georgia	74,824,364,000	3.0%
42	Hawaii	7,122,326,000	0.3%
40	Idaho	8,279,632,000	0.3%
5	Illinois	129,891,703,000	5.2%
22	Indiana	39,851,966,000	1.6%
33	Iowa	17,400,565,000	0.7%
31	Kansas	20,126,901,000	0.8%
30	Kentucky	21,709,969,000	0.9%
27	Louisiana	27,323,703,000	1.1%
43	Maine	6,300,230,000	0.3%
16	Maryland	51,243,026,000	2.0%
12	Massachusetts	69,628,887,000	2.8%
11	Michigan	70,036,186,000	2.8%
10	Minnesota	72,065,501,000	2.9%
38	Mississippi	9,803,730,000	0.4%
19	Missouri	44,460,802,000	1.8%
46	Montana	4,081,168,000	0.2%
34	Nebraska	17,381,221,000	0.7%
32	Nevada	19,123,140,000	0.8%
39	New Hampshire	9,112,460,000	0.4%
6	New Jersey	108,541,003,000	4.3%
41	New Mexico	7,513,621,000	0.3%
2	New York	214,937,242,000	8.5%
13	North Carolina	69,364,463,000	2.8%
50	North Dakota	3,333,405,000	0.1%
8	Ohio	90,623,355,000	3.6%
24	Oklahoma	31,148,116,000	1.2%
28	Oregon	23,119,047,000	0.9%
7	Pennsylvania	102,512,063,000	4.1%
37	Rhode Island	10,392,995,000	0.4%
25	South Carolina	31,111,506,000	1.2%
45	South Dakota	4,377,098,000	0.2%
18	Tennessee	47,392,686,000	1.9%
3	Texas	204,736,871,000	8.1%
36	Utah	13,240,911,000	0.5%
49	Vermont	3,605,629,000	0.1%
14	Virginia	61,307,121,000	2.4%
15	Washington	56,732,059,000	2.3%
44	West Virginia	6,179,043,000	0.2%
21	Wisconsin	41,685,918,000	1.7%
48	Wyoming	3,956,255,000	0.2%

RANK ORDER

RANK	STATE	COLLECTIONS	% of USA
1	California	$299,521,281,000	11.9%
2	New York	214,937,242,000	8.5%
3	Texas	204,736,871,000	8.1%
4	Florida	131,261,303,000	5.2%
5	Illinois	129,891,703,000	5.2%
6	New Jersey	108,541,003,000	4.3%
7	Pennsylvania	102,512,063,000	4.1%
8	Ohio	90,623,355,000	3.6%
9	Georgia	74,824,364,000	3.0%
10	Minnesota	72,065,501,000	2.9%
11	Michigan	70,036,186,000	2.8%
12	Massachusetts	69,628,887,000	2.8%
13	North Carolina	69,364,463,000	2.8%
14	Virginia	61,307,121,000	2.4%
15	Washington	56,732,059,000	2.3%
16	Maryland	51,243,026,000	2.0%
17	Connecticut	50,450,286,000	2.0%
18	Tennessee	47,392,686,000	1.9%
19	Missouri	44,460,802,000	1.8%
20	Colorado	42,308,861,000	1.7%
21	Wisconsin	41,685,918,000	1.7%
22	Indiana	39,851,966,000	1.6%
23	Arizona	32,638,677,000	1.3%
24	Oklahoma	31,148,116,000	1.2%
25	South Carolina	31,111,506,000	1.2%
26	Arkansas	27,697,303,000	1.1%
27	Louisiana	27,323,703,000	1.1%
28	Oregon	23,119,047,000	0.9%
29	Alabama	22,179,707,000	0.9%
30	Kentucky	21,709,969,000	0.9%
31	Kansas	20,126,901,000	0.8%
32	Nevada	19,123,140,000	0.8%
33	Iowa	17,400,565,000	0.7%
34	Nebraska	17,381,221,000	0.7%
35	Delaware	17,222,467,000	0.7%
36	Utah	13,240,911,000	0.5%
37	Rhode Island	10,392,995,000	0.4%
38	Mississippi	9,803,730,000	0.4%
39	New Hampshire	9,112,460,000	0.4%
40	Idaho	8,279,632,000	0.3%
41	New Mexico	7,513,621,000	0.3%
42	Hawaii	7,122,326,000	0.3%
43	Maine	6,300,230,000	0.3%
44	West Virginia	6,179,043,000	0.2%
45	South Dakota	4,377,098,000	0.2%
46	Montana	4,081,168,000	0.2%
47	Alaska	4,057,755,000	0.2%
48	Wyoming	3,956,255,000	0.2%
49	Vermont	3,605,629,000	0.1%
50	North Dakota	3,333,405,000	0.1%
	District of Columbia	17,458,924,000	0.7%

Source: U.S. Department of the Treasury, Internal Revenue Service
"FY2006 IRS Data Book" (http://www.irs.gov/taxstats/index.html)
*Total includes $18,305,774,000 from U.S. citizens abroad and other miscellaneous returns not shown separately.

Per Capita Internal Revenue Service Gross Collections in 2006

National Per Capita = $8,369*

RANK	STATE	PER CAPITA
45	Alabama	$4,832
35	Alaska	5,990
41	Arizona	5,294
8	Arkansas	9,860
17	California	8,263
13	Colorado	8,877
2	Connecticut	14,432
1	Delaware	20,196
28	Florida	7,269
19	Georgia	8,009
39	Hawaii	5,570
38	Idaho	5,656
7	Illinois	10,166
33	Indiana	6,323
36	Iowa	5,854
27	Kansas	7,303
43	Kentucky	5,164
32	Louisiana	6,439
46	Maine	4,791
11	Maryland	9,147
6	Massachusetts	10,821
31	Michigan	6,933
3	Minnesota	13,981
50	Mississippi	3,382
25	Missouri	7,616
47	Montana	4,311
9	Nebraska	9,855
24	Nevada	7,672
30	New Hampshire	6,946
4	New Jersey	12,525
48	New Mexico	3,868
5	New York	11,147
21	North Carolina	7,821
42	North Dakota	5,229
20	Ohio	7,905
15	Oklahoma	8,707
34	Oregon	6,263
16	Pennsylvania	8,265
10	Rhode Island	9,790
29	South Carolina	7,185
40	South Dakota	5,551
22	Tennessee	7,801
14	Texas	8,747
44	Utah	5,133
37	Vermont	5,808
18	Virginia	8,024
12	Washington	8,899
49	West Virginia	3,416
26	Wisconsin	7,480
23	Wyoming	7,716

RANK	STATE	PER CAPITA
1	Delaware	$20,196
2	Connecticut	14,432
3	Minnesota	13,981
4	New Jersey	12,525
5	New York	11,147
6	Massachusetts	10,821
7	Illinois	10,166
8	Arkansas	9,860
9	Nebraska	9,855
10	Rhode Island	9,790
11	Maryland	9,147
12	Washington	8,899
13	Colorado	8,877
14	Texas	8,747
15	Oklahoma	8,707
16	Pennsylvania	8,265
17	California	8,263
18	Virginia	8,024
19	Georgia	8,009
20	Ohio	7,905
21	North Carolina	7,821
22	Tennessee	7,801
23	Wyoming	7,716
24	Nevada	7,672
25	Missouri	7,616
26	Wisconsin	7,480
27	Kansas	7,303
28	Florida	7,269
29	South Carolina	7,185
30	New Hampshire	6,946
31	Michigan	6,933
32	Louisiana	6,439
33	Indiana	6,323
34	Oregon	6,263
35	Alaska	5,990
36	Iowa	5,854
37	Vermont	5,808
38	Idaho	5,656
39	Hawaii	5,570
40	South Dakota	5,551
41	Arizona	5,294
42	North Dakota	5,229
43	Kentucky	5,164
44	Utah	5,133
45	Alabama	4,832
46	Maine	4,791
47	Montana	4,311
48	New Mexico	3,868
49	West Virginia	3,416
50	Mississippi	3,382
	District of Columbia	29,821

Source: CQ Press using data from U.S. Department of the Treasury, Internal Revenue Service
   "FY2006 IRS Data Book" (http://www.irs.gov/taxstats/index.html)
*National per capita does not include collections from U.S. citizens abroad and other miscellaneous returns not shown separately.

Federal Individual Income Tax Collections in 2006

National Total = $2,051,078,590,000*

ALPHA ORDER					RANK ORDER			

RANK	STATE	COLLECTIONS	% of USA		RANK	STATE	COLLECTIONS	% of USA
28	Alabama	$19,271,581,000	0.9%		1	California	$246,839,791,000	12.0%
47	Alaska	3,682,979,000	0.2%		2	New York	171,788,322,000	8.4%
24	Arizona	28,922,345,000	1.4%		3	Texas	145,758,275,000	7.1%
29	Arkansas	18,511,007,000	0.9%		4	Florida	118,062,123,000	5.8%
1	California	246,839,791,000	12.0%		5	Illinois	102,622,203,000	5.0%
19	Colorado	37,328,243,000	1.8%		6	New Jersey	88,833,131,000	4.3%
18	Connecticut	39,058,058,000	1.9%		7	Pennsylvania	86,218,915,000	4.2%
34	Delaware	12,182,555,000	0.6%		8	Ohio	72,968,398,000	3.6%
4	Florida	118,062,123,000	5.8%		9	Michigan	61,290,112,000	3.0%
11	Georgia	56,641,155,000	2.8%		10	Massachusetts	61,248,266,000	3.0%
42	Hawaii	6,184,056,000	0.3%		11	Georgia	56,641,155,000	2.8%
40	Idaho	7,592,855,000	0.4%		12	Minnesota	56,057,690,000	2.7%
5	Illinois	102,622,203,000	5.0%		13	Virginia	50,433,386,000	2.5%
22	Indiana	34,002,874,000	1.7%		14	North Carolina	48,217,766,000	2.4%
33	Iowa	15,058,800,000	0.7%		15	Washington	46,430,144,000	2.3%
31	Kansas	15,846,823,000	0.8%		16	Maryland	46,283,133,000	2.3%
27	Kentucky	19,756,820,000	1.0%		17	Tennessee	39,590,480,000	1.9%
25	Louisiana	25,666,190,000	1.3%		18	Connecticut	39,058,058,000	1.9%
43	Maine	5,556,418,000	0.3%		19	Colorado	37,328,243,000	1.8%
16	Maryland	46,283,133,000	2.3%		20	Missouri	37,113,741,000	1.8%
10	Massachusetts	61,248,266,000	3.0%		21	Wisconsin	34,934,539,000	1.7%
9	Michigan	61,290,112,000	3.0%		22	Indiana	34,002,874,000	1.7%
12	Minnesota	56,057,690,000	2.7%		23	South Carolina	29,271,051,000	1.4%
37	Mississippi	8,641,413,000	0.4%		24	Arizona	28,922,345,000	1.4%
20	Missouri	37,113,741,000	1.8%		25	Louisiana	25,666,190,000	1.3%
46	Montana	3,784,622,000	0.2%		26	Oregon	20,482,070,000	1.0%
35	Nebraska	11,936,550,000	0.6%		27	Kentucky	19,756,820,000	1.0%
32	Nevada	15,597,007,000	0.8%		28	Alabama	19,271,581,000	0.9%
38	New Hampshire	8,331,695,000	0.4%		29	Arkansas	18,511,007,000	0.9%
6	New Jersey	88,833,131,000	4.3%		30	Oklahoma	16,377,931,000	0.8%
41	New Mexico	7,066,973,000	0.3%		31	Kansas	15,846,823,000	0.8%
2	New York	171,788,322,000	8.4%		32	Nevada	15,597,007,000	0.8%
14	North Carolina	48,217,766,000	2.4%		33	Iowa	15,058,800,000	0.7%
50	North Dakota	2,995,155,000	0.1%		34	Delaware	12,182,555,000	0.6%
8	Ohio	72,968,398,000	3.6%		35	Nebraska	11,936,550,000	0.6%
30	Oklahoma	16,377,931,000	0.8%		36	Utah	11,358,072,000	0.6%
26	Oregon	20,482,070,000	1.0%		37	Mississippi	8,641,413,000	0.4%
7	Pennsylvania	86,218,915,000	4.2%		38	New Hampshire	8,331,695,000	0.4%
39	Rhode Island	7,899,398,000	0.4%		39	Rhode Island	7,899,398,000	0.4%
23	South Carolina	29,271,051,000	1.4%		40	Idaho	7,592,855,000	0.4%
45	South Dakota	4,017,121,000	0.2%		41	New Mexico	7,066,973,000	0.3%
17	Tennessee	39,590,480,000	1.9%		42	Hawaii	6,184,056,000	0.3%
3	Texas	145,758,275,000	7.1%		43	Maine	5,556,418,000	0.3%
36	Utah	11,358,072,000	0.6%		44	West Virginia	5,432,759,000	0.3%
48	Vermont	3,334,454,000	0.2%		45	South Dakota	4,017,121,000	0.2%
13	Virginia	50,433,386,000	2.5%		46	Montana	3,784,622,000	0.2%
15	Washington	46,430,144,000	2.3%		47	Alaska	3,682,979,000	0.2%
44	West Virginia	5,432,759,000	0.3%		48	Vermont	3,334,454,000	0.2%
21	Wisconsin	34,934,539,000	1.7%		49	Wyoming	3,127,814,000	0.2%
49	Wyoming	3,127,814,000	0.2%		50	North Dakota	2,995,155,000	0.1%
						District of Columbia	16,213,546,000	0.8%

Source: U.S. Department of the Treasury, Internal Revenue Service
"FY2006 IRS Data Book" (http://www.irs.gov/taxstats/index.html)
*Total includes $17,741,245,000 from U.S. citizens abroad and other miscellaneous returns not shown separately.

Average Revenue Collection per Federal Individual Income Tax Return in 2006

National Average = $15,316 per Return*

<table>
<tr><td colspan="3">ALPHA ORDER</td><td colspan="3">RANK ORDER</td></tr>
<tr><td>RANK</td><td>STATE</td><td>AVERAGE</td><td>RANK</td><td>STATE</td><td>AVERAGE</td></tr>
<tr><td>44</td><td>Alabama</td><td>$9,974</td><td>1</td><td>Delaware</td><td>$30,422</td></tr>
<tr><td>42</td><td>Alaska</td><td>10,716</td><td>2</td><td>Connecticut</td><td>23,422</td></tr>
<tr><td>35</td><td>Arizona</td><td>11,825</td><td>3</td><td>Minnesota</td><td>23,052</td></tr>
<tr><td>10</td><td>Arkansas</td><td>16,179</td><td>4</td><td>New Jersey</td><td>21,562</td></tr>
<tr><td>11</td><td>California</td><td>16,027</td><td>5</td><td>Massachusetts</td><td>20,000</td></tr>
<tr><td>8</td><td>Colorado</td><td>17,506</td><td>6</td><td>New York</td><td>19,860</td></tr>
<tr><td>2</td><td>Connecticut</td><td>23,422</td><td>7</td><td>Illinois</td><td>17,703</td></tr>
<tr><td>1</td><td>Delaware</td><td>30,422</td><td>8</td><td>Colorado</td><td>17,506</td></tr>
<tr><td>23</td><td>Florida</td><td>14,255</td><td>9</td><td>Maryland</td><td>17,452</td></tr>
<tr><td>20</td><td>Georgia</td><td>14,634</td><td>10</td><td>Arkansas</td><td>16,179</td></tr>
<tr><td>43</td><td>Hawaii</td><td>10,021</td><td>11</td><td>California</td><td>16,027</td></tr>
<tr><td>33</td><td>Idaho</td><td>12,471</td><td>12</td><td>Washington</td><td>16,022</td></tr>
<tr><td>7</td><td>Illinois</td><td>17,703</td><td>13</td><td>Rhode Island</td><td>15,830</td></tr>
<tr><td>34</td><td>Indiana</td><td>11,837</td><td>14</td><td>South Carolina</td><td>15,669</td></tr>
<tr><td>36</td><td>Iowa</td><td>11,221</td><td>15</td><td>Louisiana</td><td>15,260</td></tr>
<tr><td>29</td><td>Kansas</td><td>12,855</td><td>16</td><td>Texas</td><td>15,209</td></tr>
<tr><td>37</td><td>Kentucky</td><td>11,182</td><td>17</td><td>Tennessee</td><td>15,059</td></tr>
<tr><td>15</td><td>Louisiana</td><td>15,260</td><td>18</td><td>Pennsylvania</td><td>14,771</td></tr>
<tr><td>46</td><td>Maine</td><td>9,011</td><td>19</td><td>Nebraska</td><td>14,711</td></tr>
<tr><td>9</td><td>Maryland</td><td>17,452</td><td>20</td><td>Georgia</td><td>14,634</td></tr>
<tr><td>5</td><td>Massachusetts</td><td>20,000</td><td>21</td><td>Virginia</td><td>14,370</td></tr>
<tr><td>25</td><td>Michigan</td><td>13,488</td><td>22</td><td>Missouri</td><td>14,301</td></tr>
<tr><td>3</td><td>Minnesota</td><td>23,052</td><td>23</td><td>Florida</td><td>14,255</td></tr>
<tr><td>49</td><td>Mississippi</td><td>7,567</td><td>24</td><td>Nevada</td><td>13,710</td></tr>
<tr><td>22</td><td>Missouri</td><td>14,301</td><td>25</td><td>Michigan</td><td>13,488</td></tr>
<tr><td>47</td><td>Montana</td><td>8,524</td><td>26</td><td>Ohio</td><td>13,442</td></tr>
<tr><td>19</td><td>Nebraska</td><td>14,711</td><td>27</td><td>Wisconsin</td><td>13,227</td></tr>
<tr><td>24</td><td>Nevada</td><td>13,710</td><td>28</td><td>New Hampshire</td><td>12,919</td></tr>
<tr><td>28</td><td>New Hampshire</td><td>12,919</td><td>29</td><td>Kansas</td><td>12,855</td></tr>
<tr><td>4</td><td>New Jersey</td><td>21,562</td><td>30</td><td>Wyoming</td><td>12,729</td></tr>
<tr><td>48</td><td>New Mexico</td><td>8,452</td><td>31</td><td>Oregon</td><td>12,571</td></tr>
<tr><td>6</td><td>New York</td><td>19,860</td><td>32</td><td>North Carolina</td><td>12,567</td></tr>
<tr><td>32</td><td>North Carolina</td><td>12,567</td><td>33</td><td>Idaho</td><td>12,471</td></tr>
<tr><td>45</td><td>North Dakota</td><td>9,801</td><td>34</td><td>Indiana</td><td>11,837</td></tr>
<tr><td>26</td><td>Ohio</td><td>13,442</td><td>35</td><td>Arizona</td><td>11,825</td></tr>
<tr><td>39</td><td>Oklahoma</td><td>11,050</td><td>36</td><td>Iowa</td><td>11,221</td></tr>
<tr><td>31</td><td>Oregon</td><td>12,571</td><td>37</td><td>Kentucky</td><td>11,182</td></tr>
<tr><td>18</td><td>Pennsylvania</td><td>14,771</td><td>38</td><td>Utah</td><td>11,118</td></tr>
<tr><td>13</td><td>Rhode Island</td><td>15,830</td><td>39</td><td>Oklahoma</td><td>11,050</td></tr>
<tr><td>14</td><td>South Carolina</td><td>15,669</td><td>40</td><td>South Dakota</td><td>11,015</td></tr>
<tr><td>40</td><td>South Dakota</td><td>11,015</td><td>41</td><td>Vermont</td><td>10,840</td></tr>
<tr><td>17</td><td>Tennessee</td><td>15,059</td><td>42</td><td>Alaska</td><td>10,716</td></tr>
<tr><td>16</td><td>Texas</td><td>15,209</td><td>43</td><td>Hawaii</td><td>10,021</td></tr>
<tr><td>38</td><td>Utah</td><td>11,118</td><td>44</td><td>Alabama</td><td>9,974</td></tr>
<tr><td>41</td><td>Vermont</td><td>10,840</td><td>45</td><td>North Dakota</td><td>9,801</td></tr>
<tr><td>21</td><td>Virginia</td><td>14,370</td><td>46</td><td>Maine</td><td>9,011</td></tr>
<tr><td>12</td><td>Washington</td><td>16,022</td><td>47</td><td>Montana</td><td>8,524</td></tr>
<tr><td>50</td><td>West Virginia</td><td>7,251</td><td>48</td><td>New Mexico</td><td>8,452</td></tr>
<tr><td>27</td><td>Wisconsin</td><td>13,227</td><td>49</td><td>Mississippi</td><td>7,567</td></tr>
<tr><td>30</td><td>Wyoming</td><td>12,729</td><td>50</td><td>West Virginia</td><td>7,251</td></tr>
<tr><td></td><td></td><td></td><td></td><td>District of Columbia</td><td>57,931</td></tr>
</table>

Source: CQ Press using data from U.S. Department of the Treasury, Internal Revenue Service
"FY2006 IRS Data Book" (http://www.irs.gov/taxstats/index.html)
*Total includes collections and returns from U.S. citizens abroad and other miscellaneous returns not shown separately.

Adjusted Gross Income in 2005

National Total = $7,364,640,131,000*

ALPHA ORDER

RANK	STATE	A.G.I.	% of USA
24	Alabama	$88,628,735,000	1.2%
46	Alaska	16,725,880,000	0.2%
17	Arizona	135,510,440,000	1.8%
34	Arkansas	47,857,444,000	0.6%
1	California	970,448,917,000	13.2%
21	Colorado	125,994,344,000	1.7%
19	Connecticut	132,285,344,000	1.8%
44	Delaware	23,183,670,000	0.3%
4	Florida	481,888,152,000	6.5%
12	Georgia	199,214,881,000	2.7%
39	Hawaii	31,284,219,000	0.4%
41	Idaho	28,226,440,000	0.4%
5	Illinois	335,321,455,000	4.6%
18	Indiana	134,324,776,000	1.8%
31	Iowa	61,643,860,000	0.8%
32	Kansas	60,483,659,000	0.8%
27	Kentucky	77,639,797,000	1.1%
28	Louisiana	77,629,149,000	1.1%
42	Maine	27,763,882,000	0.4%
14	Maryland	170,124,868,000	2.3%
11	Massachusetts	206,948,515,000	2.8%
9	Michigan	226,438,921,000	3.1%
16	Minnesota	137,232,136,000	1.9%
35	Mississippi	45,340,179,000	0.6%
23	Missouri	122,774,783,000	1.7%
45	Montana	18,315,335,000	0.2%
36	Nebraska	37,830,701,000	0.5%
29	Nevada	72,209,472,000	1.0%
37	New Hampshire	37,533,740,000	0.5%
7	New Jersey	282,306,218,000	3.8%
38	New Mexico	35,785,778,000	0.5%
2	New York	552,244,486,000	7.5%
13	North Carolina	186,047,795,000	2.5%
50	North Dakota	12,970,269,000	0.2%
8	Ohio	252,434,762,000	3.4%
30	Oklahoma	66,783,183,000	0.9%
26	Oregon	81,023,741,000	1.1%
6	Pennsylvania	299,493,501,000	4.1%
43	Rhode Island	26,529,043,000	0.4%
25	South Carolina	84,321,938,000	1.1%
47	South Dakota	16,165,957,000	0.2%
22	Tennessee	123,251,823,000	1.7%
3	Texas	507,165,219,000	6.9%
33	Utah	51,060,650,000	0.7%
48	Vermont	14,703,594,000	0.2%
10	Virginia	214,671,763,000	2.9%
15	Washington	168,672,520,000	2.3%
40	West Virginia	30,318,090,000	0.4%
20	Wisconsin	132,137,153,000	1.8%
49	Wyoming	14,299,375,000	0.2%

RANK ORDER

RANK	STATE	A.G.I.	% of USA
1	California	$970,448,917,000	13.2%
2	New York	552,244,486,000	7.5%
3	Texas	507,165,219,000	6.9%
4	Florida	481,888,152,000	6.5%
5	Illinois	335,321,455,000	4.6%
6	Pennsylvania	299,493,501,000	4.1%
7	New Jersey	282,306,218,000	3.8%
8	Ohio	252,434,762,000	3.4%
9	Michigan	226,438,921,000	3.1%
10	Virginia	214,671,763,000	2.9%
11	Massachusetts	206,948,515,000	2.8%
12	Georgia	199,214,881,000	2.7%
13	North Carolina	186,047,795,000	2.5%
14	Maryland	170,124,868,000	2.3%
15	Washington	168,672,520,000	2.3%
16	Minnesota	137,232,136,000	1.9%
17	Arizona	135,510,440,000	1.8%
18	Indiana	134,324,776,000	1.8%
19	Connecticut	132,285,344,000	1.8%
20	Wisconsin	132,137,153,000	1.8%
21	Colorado	125,994,344,000	1.7%
22	Tennessee	123,251,823,000	1.7%
23	Missouri	122,774,783,000	1.7%
24	Alabama	88,628,735,000	1.2%
25	South Carolina	84,321,938,000	1.1%
26	Oregon	81,023,741,000	1.1%
27	Kentucky	77,639,797,000	1.1%
28	Louisiana	77,629,149,000	1.1%
29	Nevada	72,209,472,000	1.0%
30	Oklahoma	66,783,183,000	0.9%
31	Iowa	61,643,860,000	0.8%
32	Kansas	60,483,659,000	0.8%
33	Utah	51,060,650,000	0.7%
34	Arkansas	47,857,444,000	0.6%
35	Mississippi	45,340,179,000	0.6%
36	Nebraska	37,830,701,000	0.5%
37	New Hampshire	37,533,740,000	0.5%
38	New Mexico	35,785,778,000	0.5%
39	Hawaii	31,284,219,000	0.4%
40	West Virginia	30,318,090,000	0.4%
41	Idaho	28,226,440,000	0.4%
42	Maine	27,763,882,000	0.4%
43	Rhode Island	26,529,043,000	0.4%
44	Delaware	23,183,670,000	0.3%
45	Montana	18,315,335,000	0.2%
46	Alaska	16,725,880,000	0.2%
47	South Dakota	16,165,957,000	0.2%
48	Vermont	14,703,594,000	0.2%
49	Wyoming	14,299,375,000	0.2%
50	North Dakota	12,970,269,000	0.2%
	District of Columbia	19,712,600,000	0.3%

Source: U.S. Department of the Treasury, Internal Revenue Service
"Individual Tax Statistics, State Income" (http://www.irs.gov/)
*Total includes $61,736,977,000 from U.S. citizens abroad and other miscellaneous returns not shown separately.

Per Capita Adjusted Gross Income in 2005

National Per Capita = $24,681*

ALPHA ORDER

RANK	STATE	PER CAPITA
43	Alabama	$19,523
17	Alaska	24,986
23	Arizona	22,767
48	Arkansas	17,264
12	California	26,964
13	Colorado	26,958
1	Connecticut	37,942
10	Delaware	27,581
11	Florida	27,170
29	Georgia	21,873
19	Hawaii	24,680
41	Idaho	19,796
16	Illinois	26,363
31	Indiana	21,468
35	Iowa	20,857
27	Kansas	22,061
46	Kentucky	18,614
47	Louisiana	17,268
34	Maine	21,158
4	Maryland	30,526
3	Massachusetts	32,189
24	Michigan	22,402
15	Minnesota	26,836
50	Mississippi	15,632
33	Missouri	21,212
42	Montana	19,572
30	Nebraska	21,568
5	Nevada	29,976
6	New Hampshire	28,803
2	New Jersey	32,608
45	New Mexico	18,674
7	New York	28,669
32	North Carolina	21,436
38	North Dakota	20,395
28	Ohio	22,028
44	Oklahoma	18,887
25	Oregon	22,321
20	Pennsylvania	24,217
18	Rhode Island	24,870
40	South Carolina	19,817
36	South Dakota	20,724
37	Tennessee	20,579
26	Texas	22,201
39	Utah	20,383
22	Vermont	23,726
8	Virginia	28,405
14	Washington	26,898
49	West Virginia	16,791
21	Wisconsin	23,849
9	Wyoming	28,229

RANK ORDER

RANK	STATE	PER CAPITA
1	Connecticut	$37,942
2	New Jersey	32,608
3	Massachusetts	32,189
4	Maryland	30,526
5	Nevada	29,976
6	New Hampshire	28,803
7	New York	28,669
8	Virginia	28,405
9	Wyoming	28,229
10	Delaware	27,581
11	Florida	27,170
12	California	26,964
13	Colorado	26,958
14	Washington	26,898
15	Minnesota	26,836
16	Illinois	26,363
17	Alaska	24,986
18	Rhode Island	24,870
19	Hawaii	24,680
20	Pennsylvania	24,217
21	Wisconsin	23,849
22	Vermont	23,726
23	Arizona	22,767
24	Michigan	22,402
25	Oregon	22,321
26	Texas	22,201
27	Kansas	22,061
28	Ohio	22,028
29	Georgia	21,873
30	Nebraska	21,568
31	Indiana	21,468
32	North Carolina	21,436
33	Missouri	21,212
34	Maine	21,158
35	Iowa	20,857
36	South Dakota	20,724
37	Tennessee	20,579
38	North Dakota	20,395
39	Utah	20,383
40	South Carolina	19,817
41	Idaho	19,796
42	Montana	19,572
43	Alabama	19,523
44	Oklahoma	18,887
45	New Mexico	18,674
46	Kentucky	18,614
47	Louisiana	17,268
48	Arkansas	17,264
49	West Virginia	16,791
50	Mississippi	15,632
	District of Columbia	33,868

Source: CQ Press using data from U.S. Department of the Treasury, Internal Revenue Service
"Individual Tax Statistics, State Income" (http://www.irs.gov/)
*National per capita does not include income from U.S. citizens abroad and other miscellaneous returns not shown separately.

Federal Corporate Income Tax Collections in 2006

National Total = $380,924,573,000*

ALPHA ORDER

RANK	STATE	COLLECTIONS	% of USA
30	Alabama	$2,433,131,000	0.6%
46	Alaska	310,985,000	0.1%
28	Arizona	2,795,459,000	0.7%
18	Arkansas	6,823,206,000	1.8%
1	California	44,419,490,000	11.7%
27	Colorado	3,180,315,000	0.8%
11	Connecticut	10,350,897,000	2.7%
24	Delaware	4,838,043,000	1.3%
12	Florida	9,900,660,000	2.6%
8	Georgia	14,582,950,000	3.8%
39	Hawaii	655,818,000	0.2%
40	Idaho	603,353,000	0.2%
4	Illinois	24,143,928,000	6.3%
23	Indiana	5,179,590,000	1.4%
33	Iowa	1,981,102,000	0.5%
29	Kansas	2,671,506,000	0.7%
34	Kentucky	1,606,303,000	0.4%
36	Louisiana	1,165,111,000	0.3%
44	Maine	490,185,000	0.1%
25	Maryland	4,242,760,000	1.1%
17	Massachusetts	7,006,102,000	1.8%
16	Michigan	7,636,529,000	2.0%
9	Minnesota	14,252,702,000	3.7%
38	Mississippi	765,810,000	0.2%
21	Missouri	5,820,070,000	1.5%
50	Montana	193,276,000	0.1%
22	Nebraska	5,211,131,000	1.4%
26	Nevada	3,270,070,000	0.9%
41	New Hampshire	580,687,000	0.2%
6	New Jersey	17,386,979,000	4.6%
45	New Mexico	346,719,000	0.1%
2	New York	39,114,058,000	10.3%
5	North Carolina	20,343,866,000	5.3%
47	North Dakota	305,275,000	0.1%
7	Ohio	16,380,204,000	4.3%
13	Oklahoma	8,961,139,000	2.4%
32	Oregon	2,138,547,000	0.6%
10	Pennsylvania	12,561,651,000	3.3%
31	Rhode Island	2,383,388,000	0.6%
35	South Carolina	1,177,975,000	0.3%
48	South Dakota	261,933,000	0.1%
19	Tennessee	6,663,979,000	1.7%
3	Texas	37,004,514,000	9.7%
37	Utah	1,143,559,000	0.3%
49	Vermont	193,703,000	0.1%
14	Virginia	8,867,884,000	2.3%
15	Washington	8,737,224,000	2.3%
42	West Virginia	531,996,000	0.1%
20	Wisconsin	6,102,472,000	1.6%
43	Wyoming	525,501,000	0.1%

RANK ORDER

RANK	STATE	COLLECTIONS	% of USA
1	California	$44,419,490,000	11.7%
2	New York	39,114,058,000	10.3%
3	Texas	37,004,514,000	9.7%
4	Illinois	24,143,928,000	6.3%
5	North Carolina	20,343,866,000	5.3%
6	New Jersey	17,386,979,000	4.6%
7	Ohio	16,380,204,000	4.3%
8	Georgia	14,582,950,000	3.8%
9	Minnesota	14,252,702,000	3.7%
10	Pennsylvania	12,561,651,000	3.3%
11	Connecticut	10,350,897,000	2.7%
12	Florida	9,900,660,000	2.6%
13	Oklahoma	8,961,139,000	2.4%
14	Virginia	8,867,884,000	2.3%
15	Washington	8,737,224,000	2.3%
16	Michigan	7,636,529,000	2.0%
17	Massachusetts	7,006,102,000	1.8%
18	Arkansas	6,823,206,000	1.8%
19	Tennessee	6,663,979,000	1.7%
20	Wisconsin	6,102,472,000	1.6%
21	Missouri	5,820,070,000	1.5%
22	Nebraska	5,211,131,000	1.4%
23	Indiana	5,179,590,000	1.4%
24	Delaware	4,838,043,000	1.3%
25	Maryland	4,242,760,000	1.1%
26	Nevada	3,270,070,000	0.9%
27	Colorado	3,180,315,000	0.8%
28	Arizona	2,795,459,000	0.7%
29	Kansas	2,671,506,000	0.7%
30	Alabama	2,433,131,000	0.6%
31	Rhode Island	2,383,388,000	0.6%
32	Oregon	2,138,547,000	0.6%
33	Iowa	1,981,102,000	0.5%
34	Kentucky	1,606,303,000	0.4%
35	South Carolina	1,177,975,000	0.3%
36	Louisiana	1,165,111,000	0.3%
37	Utah	1,143,559,000	0.3%
38	Mississippi	765,810,000	0.2%
39	Hawaii	655,818,000	0.2%
40	Idaho	603,353,000	0.2%
41	New Hampshire	580,687,000	0.2%
42	West Virginia	531,996,000	0.1%
43	Wyoming	525,501,000	0.1%
44	Maine	490,185,000	0.1%
45	New Mexico	346,719,000	0.1%
46	Alaska	310,985,000	0.1%
47	North Dakota	305,275,000	0.1%
48	South Dakota	261,933,000	0.1%
49	Vermont	193,703,000	0.1%
50	Montana	193,276,000	0.1%
	District of Columbia	1,124,379,000	0.3%

Source: U.S. Department of the Treasury, Internal Revenue Service
   "FY2006 IRS Data Book" (http://www.irs.gov/taxstats/index.html)
*Total includes collections and returns from international sources and others not distributed by state.

Average Revenue Collection per Federal Corporate Income Tax Return in 2006

National Average = $60,672 per Return*

ALPHA ORDER			RANK ORDER		
RANK	STATE	AVERAGE	RANK	STATE	AVERAGE
27	Alabama	$37,703	1	Delaware	$201,896
32	Alaska	28,141	2	Connecticut	185,483
33	Arizona	26,306	3	Oklahoma	134,849
4	Arkansas	130,893	4	Arkansas	130,893
16	California	71,166	5	Nebraska	129,798
39	Colorado	23,248	6	North Carolina	117,420
2	Connecticut	185,483	7	Minnesota	116,520
1	Delaware	201,896	8	Tennessee	100,081
47	Florida	13,944	9	Texas	99,142
15	Georgia	71,420	10	Rhode Island	92,001
35	Hawaii	24,510	11	Ohio	87,127
42	Idaho	19,424	12	Illinois	78,679
12	Illinois	78,679	13	New Jersey	77,507
25	Indiana	45,599	14	Washington	71,512
30	Iowa	33,947	15	Georgia	71,420
22	Kansas	52,764	16	California	71,166
37	Kentucky	23,735	17	New York	68,154
43	Louisiana	16,215	18	Wisconsin	65,170
44	Maine	16,059	19	Pennsylvania	59,747
29	Maryland	35,366	20	Virginia	58,586
23	Massachusetts	47,502	21	Missouri	57,498
26	Michigan	37,877	22	Kansas	52,764
7	Minnesota	116,520	23	Massachusetts	47,502
40	Mississippi	20,586	24	Nevada	46,753
21	Missouri	57,498	25	Indiana	45,599
50	Montana	6,603	26	Michigan	37,877
5	Nebraska	129,798	27	Alabama	37,703
24	Nevada	46,753	28	Wyoming	36,415
38	New Hampshire	23,606	29	Maryland	35,366
13	New Jersey	77,507	30	Iowa	33,947
48	New Mexico	12,236	31	Oregon	29,248
17	New York	68,154	32	Alaska	28,141
6	North Carolina	117,420	33	Arizona	26,306
36	North Dakota	23,977	34	West Virginia	25,585
11	Ohio	87,127	35	Hawaii	24,510
3	Oklahoma	134,849	36	North Dakota	23,977
31	Oregon	29,248	37	Kentucky	23,735
19	Pennsylvania	59,747	38	New Hampshire	23,606
10	Rhode Island	92,001	39	Colorado	23,248
46	South Carolina	14,886	40	Mississippi	20,586
45	South Dakota	15,893	41	Utah	19,502
8	Tennessee	100,081	42	Idaho	19,424
9	Texas	99,142	43	Louisiana	16,215
41	Utah	19,502	44	Maine	16,059
49	Vermont	11,566	45	South Dakota	15,893
20	Virginia	58,586	46	South Carolina	14,886
14	Washington	71,512	47	Florida	13,944
34	West Virginia	25,585	48	New Mexico	12,236
18	Wisconsin	65,170	49	Vermont	11,566
28	Wyoming	36,415	50	Montana	6,603
				District of Columbia	72,452

Source: CQ Press using data from U.S. Department of the Treasury, Internal Revenue Service
"FY2006 IRS Data Book" (http://www.irs.gov/taxstats/index.html)
*National rate includes collections and returns from U.S. citizens abroad and other miscellaneous returns not shown separately.

Federal Tax Returns Filed in 2006

National Total = 228,145,029 Returns*

ALPHA ORDER

RANK	STATE	RETURNS	% of USA
23	Alabama	3,015,495	1.3%
48	Alaska	566,359	0.2%
20	Arizona	4,162,522	1.8%
33	Arkansas	1,896,354	0.8%
1	California	26,955,122	11.8%
22	Colorado	3,954,233	1.7%
25	Connecticut	2,970,651	1.3%
45	Delaware	721,652	0.3%
3	Florida	15,131,316	6.6%
10	Georgia	6,347,242	2.8%
42	Hawaii	1,069,903	0.5%
41	Idaho	1,091,086	0.5%
5	Illinois	9,785,843	4.3%
15	Indiana	4,580,183	2.0%
30	Iowa	2,326,440	1.0%
31	Kansas	2,140,125	0.9%
27	Kentucky	2,824,578	1.2%
28	Louisiana	2,716,848	1.2%
40	Maine	1,101,215	0.5%
16	Maryland	4,472,902	2.0%
13	Massachusetts	5,456,071	2.4%
8	Michigan	7,342,098	3.2%
19	Minnesota	4,204,084	1.8%
35	Mississippi	1,750,778	0.8%
18	Missouri	4,390,250	1.9%
44	Montana	866,914	0.4%
36	Nebraska	1,412,524	0.6%
32	Nevada	1,907,366	0.8%
39	New Hampshire	1,116,112	0.5%
9	New Jersey	7,319,893	3.2%
37	New Mexico	1,366,441	0.6%
4	New York	15,089,612	6.6%
11	North Carolina	6,326,367	2.8%
49	North Dakota	558,342	0.2%
7	Ohio	8,699,892	3.8%
29	Oklahoma	2,612,692	1.1%
26	Oregon	2,958,526	1.3%
6	Pennsylvania	9,568,227	4.2%
43	Rhode Island	872,759	0.4%
24	South Carolina	3,004,403	1.3%
46	South Dakota	669,919	0.3%
21	Tennessee	4,098,749	1.8%
2	Texas	15,757,892	6.9%
34	Utah	1,764,449	0.8%
47	Vermont	579,609	0.3%
12	Virginia	5,898,239	2.6%
14	Washington	5,123,051	2.2%
38	West Virginia	1,169,188	0.5%
17	Wisconsin	4,424,146	1.9%
50	Wyoming	476,756	0.2%

RANK ORDER

RANK	STATE	RETURNS	% of USA
1	California	26,955,122	11.8%
2	Texas	15,757,892	6.9%
3	Florida	15,131,316	6.6%
4	New York	15,089,612	6.6%
5	Illinois	9,785,843	4.3%
6	Pennsylvania	9,568,227	4.2%
7	Ohio	8,699,892	3.8%
8	Michigan	7,342,098	3.2%
9	New Jersey	7,319,893	3.2%
10	Georgia	6,347,242	2.8%
11	North Carolina	6,326,367	2.8%
12	Virginia	5,898,239	2.6%
13	Massachusetts	5,456,071	2.4%
14	Washington	5,123,051	2.2%
15	Indiana	4,580,183	2.0%
16	Maryland	4,472,902	2.0%
17	Wisconsin	4,424,146	1.9%
18	Missouri	4,390,250	1.9%
19	Minnesota	4,204,084	1.8%
20	Arizona	4,162,522	1.8%
21	Tennessee	4,098,749	1.8%
22	Colorado	3,954,233	1.7%
23	Alabama	3,015,495	1.3%
24	South Carolina	3,004,403	1.3%
25	Connecticut	2,970,651	1.3%
26	Oregon	2,958,526	1.3%
27	Kentucky	2,824,578	1.2%
28	Louisiana	2,716,848	1.2%
29	Oklahoma	2,612,692	1.1%
30	Iowa	2,326,440	1.0%
31	Kansas	2,140,125	0.9%
32	Nevada	1,907,366	0.8%
33	Arkansas	1,896,354	0.8%
34	Utah	1,764,449	0.8%
35	Mississippi	1,750,778	0.8%
36	Nebraska	1,412,524	0.6%
37	New Mexico	1,366,441	0.6%
38	West Virginia	1,169,188	0.5%
39	New Hampshire	1,116,112	0.5%
40	Maine	1,101,215	0.5%
41	Idaho	1,091,086	0.5%
42	Hawaii	1,069,903	0.5%
43	Rhode Island	872,759	0.4%
44	Montana	866,914	0.4%
45	Delaware	721,652	0.3%
46	South Dakota	669,919	0.3%
47	Vermont	579,609	0.3%
48	Alaska	566,359	0.2%
49	North Dakota	558,342	0.2%
50	Wyoming	476,756	0.2%
	District of Columbia	957,154	0.4%

Source: U.S. Department of the Treasury, Internal Revenue Service
"FY2006 IRS Data Book" (http://www.irs.gov/taxstats/index.html)
*Total includes returns from international sources and other miscellaneous returns not shown separately.

Federal Individual Income Tax Returns Filed in 2006

National Total = 133,917,068 Returns*

ALPHA ORDER					RANK ORDER			
RANK	STATE	RETURNS	% of USA		RANK	STATE	RETURNS	% of USA
23	Alabama	1,932,097	1.4%		1	California	15,401,847	11.5%
47	Alaska	343,687	0.3%		2	Texas	9,583,785	7.2%
20	Arizona	2,445,889	1.8%		3	New York	8,649,945	6.5%
32	Arkansas	1,144,171	0.9%		4	Florida	8,282,359	6.2%
1	California	15,401,847	11.5%		5	Pennsylvania	5,837,127	4.4%
22	Colorado	2,132,363	1.6%		6	Illinois	5,796,754	4.3%
27	Connecticut	1,667,612	1.2%		7	Ohio	5,428,221	4.1%
45	Delaware	400,453	0.3%		8	Michigan	4,544,045	3.4%
4	Florida	8,282,359	6.2%		9	New Jersey	4,119,915	3.1%
10	Georgia	3,870,442	2.9%		10	Georgia	3,870,442	2.9%
40	Hawaii	617,089	0.5%		11	North Carolina	3,836,959	2.9%
42	Idaho	608,842	0.5%		12	Virginia	3,509,616	2.6%
6	Illinois	5,796,754	4.3%		13	Massachusetts	3,062,454	2.3%
15	Indiana	2,872,625	2.1%		14	Washington	2,897,838	2.2%
30	Iowa	1,342,065	1.0%		15	Indiana	2,872,625	2.1%
31	Kansas	1,232,747	0.9%		16	Maryland	2,652,044	2.0%
25	Kentucky	1,766,852	1.3%		17	Wisconsin	2,641,248	2.0%
26	Louisiana	1,681,881	1.3%		18	Tennessee	2,629,091	2.0%
41	Maine	616,618	0.5%		19	Missouri	2,595,210	1.9%
16	Maryland	2,652,044	2.0%		20	Arizona	2,445,889	1.8%
13	Massachusetts	3,062,454	2.3%		21	Minnesota	2,431,768	1.8%
8	Michigan	4,544,045	3.4%		22	Colorado	2,132,363	1.6%
21	Minnesota	2,431,768	1.8%		23	Alabama	1,932,097	1.4%
33	Mississippi	1,142,042	0.9%		24	South Carolina	1,868,046	1.4%
19	Missouri	2,595,210	1.9%		25	Kentucky	1,766,852	1.3%
44	Montana	444,015	0.3%		26	Louisiana	1,681,881	1.3%
37	Nebraska	811,397	0.6%		27	Connecticut	1,667,612	1.2%
34	Nevada	1,137,633	0.8%		28	Oregon	1,629,305	1.2%
39	New Hampshire	644,931	0.5%		29	Oklahoma	1,482,139	1.1%
9	New Jersey	4,119,915	3.1%		30	Iowa	1,342,065	1.0%
36	New Mexico	836,083	0.6%		31	Kansas	1,232,747	0.9%
3	New York	8,649,945	6.5%		32	Arkansas	1,144,171	0.9%
11	North Carolina	3,836,959	2.9%		33	Mississippi	1,142,042	0.9%
49	North Dakota	305,584	0.2%		34	Nevada	1,137,633	0.8%
7	Ohio	5,428,221	4.1%		35	Utah	1,021,593	0.8%
29	Oklahoma	1,482,139	1.1%		36	New Mexico	836,083	0.6%
28	Oregon	1,629,305	1.2%		37	Nebraska	811,397	0.6%
5	Pennsylvania	5,837,127	4.4%		38	West Virginia	749,210	0.6%
43	Rhode Island	499,005	0.4%		39	New Hampshire	644,931	0.5%
24	South Carolina	1,868,046	1.4%		40	Hawaii	617,089	0.5%
46	South Dakota	364,697	0.3%		41	Maine	616,618	0.5%
18	Tennessee	2,629,091	2.0%		42	Idaho	608,842	0.5%
2	Texas	9,583,785	7.2%		43	Rhode Island	499,005	0.4%
35	Utah	1,021,593	0.8%		44	Montana	444,015	0.3%
48	Vermont	307,608	0.2%		45	Delaware	400,453	0.3%
12	Virginia	3,509,616	2.6%		46	South Dakota	364,697	0.3%
14	Washington	2,897,838	2.2%		47	Alaska	343,687	0.3%
38	West Virginia	749,210	0.6%		48	Vermont	307,608	0.2%
17	Wisconsin	2,641,248	2.0%		49	North Dakota	305,584	0.2%
50	Wyoming	245,733	0.2%		50	Wyoming	245,733	0.2%
						District of Columbia	279,878	0.2%

Source: U.S. Department of the Treasury, Internal Revenue Service
  "FY2006 IRS Data Book" (http://www.irs.gov/taxstats/index.html)
*Total includes returns from international sources and other miscellaneous returns not shown separately.

Federal Corporate Income Tax Returns Filed in 2006

National Total = 6,278,399 Returns*

ALPHA ORDER					RANK ORDER			
RANK	STATE	RETURNS	% of USA		RANK	STATE	RETURNS	% of USA
29	Alabama	64,534	1.0%		1	Florida	710,040	11.3%
50	Alaska	11,051	0.2%		2	California	624,165	9.9%
19	Arizona	106,266	1.7%		3	New York	573,907	9.1%
33	Arkansas	52,128	0.8%		4	Texas	373,248	5.9%
2	California	624,165	9.9%		5	Illinois	306,865	4.9%
14	Colorado	136,800	2.2%		6	New Jersey	224,329	3.6%
32	Connecticut	55,805	0.9%		7	Pennsylvania	210,249	3.3%
44	Delaware	23,963	0.4%		8	Georgia	204,185	3.3%
1	Florida	710,040	11.3%		9	Michigan	201,613	3.2%
8	Georgia	204,185	3.3%		10	Ohio	188,003	3.0%
41	Hawaii	26,757	0.4%		11	North Carolina	173,257	2.8%
37	Idaho	31,063	0.5%		12	Virginia	151,366	2.4%
5	Illinois	306,865	4.9%		13	Massachusetts	147,492	2.3%
18	Indiana	113,589	1.8%		14	Colorado	136,800	2.2%
31	Iowa	58,359	0.9%		15	Minnesota	122,320	1.9%
34	Kansas	50,631	0.8%		16	Washington	122,179	1.9%
26	Kentucky	67,676	1.1%		17	Maryland	119,966	1.9%
24	Louisiana	71,853	1.1%		18	Indiana	113,589	1.8%
38	Maine	30,524	0.5%		19	Arizona	106,266	1.7%
17	Maryland	119,966	1.9%		20	Missouri	101,222	1.6%
13	Massachusetts	147,492	2.3%		21	Wisconsin	93,640	1.5%
9	Michigan	201,613	3.2%		22	South Carolina	79,134	1.3%
15	Minnesota	122,320	1.9%		23	Oregon	73,118	1.2%
36	Mississippi	37,200	0.6%		24	Louisiana	71,853	1.1%
20	Missouri	101,222	1.6%		25	Nevada	69,944	1.1%
39	Montana	29,271	0.5%		26	Kentucky	67,676	1.1%
35	Nebraska	40,148	0.6%		27	Tennessee	66,586	1.1%
25	Nevada	69,944	1.1%		28	Oklahoma	66,453	1.1%
43	New Hampshire	24,599	0.4%		29	Alabama	64,534	1.0%
6	New Jersey	224,329	3.6%		30	Utah	58,638	0.9%
40	New Mexico	28,337	0.5%		31	Iowa	58,359	0.9%
3	New York	573,907	9.1%		32	Connecticut	55,805	0.9%
11	North Carolina	173,257	2.8%		33	Arkansas	52,128	0.8%
49	North Dakota	12,732	0.2%		34	Kansas	50,631	0.8%
10	Ohio	188,003	3.0%		35	Nebraska	40,148	0.6%
28	Oklahoma	66,453	1.1%		36	Mississippi	37,200	0.6%
23	Oregon	73,118	1.2%		37	Idaho	31,063	0.5%
7	Pennsylvania	210,249	3.3%		38	Maine	30,524	0.5%
42	Rhode Island	25,906	0.4%		39	Montana	29,271	0.5%
22	South Carolina	79,134	1.3%		40	New Mexico	28,337	0.5%
47	South Dakota	16,481	0.3%		41	Hawaii	26,757	0.4%
27	Tennessee	66,586	1.1%		42	Rhode Island	25,906	0.4%
4	Texas	373,248	5.9%		43	New Hampshire	24,599	0.4%
30	Utah	58,638	0.9%		44	Delaware	23,963	0.4%
46	Vermont	16,747	0.3%		45	West Virginia	20,793	0.3%
12	Virginia	151,366	2.4%		46	Vermont	16,747	0.3%
16	Washington	122,179	1.9%		47	South Dakota	16,481	0.3%
45	West Virginia	20,793	0.3%		48	Wyoming	14,431	0.2%
21	Wisconsin	93,640	1.5%		49	North Dakota	12,732	0.2%
48	Wyoming	14,431	0.2%		50	Alaska	11,051	0.2%
						District of Columbia	15,519	0.2%

Source: U.S. Department of the Treasury, Internal Revenue Service
   "FY2006 IRS Data Book" (http://www.irs.gov/taxstats/index.html)
*Total includes returns from international sources and other miscellaneous returns not shown separately.

Federal Tax Refunds in 2006

National Total = 110,810,589 Refunds*

<u>ALPHA ORDER</u>

RANK	STATE	REFUNDS	% of USA
23	Alabama	1,656,941	1.5%
47	Alaska	265,482	0.2%
20	Arizona	1,978,455	1.8%
34	Arkansas	955,126	0.9%
1	California	12,392,511	11.2%
22	Colorado	1,699,853	1.5%
27	Connecticut	1,336,231	1.2%
45	Delaware	334,993	0.3%
4	Florida	6,944,596	6.3%
10	Georgia	3,314,315	3.0%
41	Hawaii	500,775	0.5%
42	Idaho	491,764	0.4%
6	Illinois	4,837,057	4.4%
14	Indiana	2,457,422	2.2%
30	Iowa	1,064,276	1.0%
32	Kansas	989,376	0.9%
26	Kentucky	1,495,484	1.3%
25	Louisiana	1,500,608	1.4%
40	Maine	505,406	0.5%
17	Maryland	2,183,810	2.0%
13	Massachusetts	2,474,654	2.2%
8	Michigan	3,787,822	3.4%
21	Minnesota	1,932,659	1.7%
31	Mississippi	999,402	0.9%
18	Missouri	2,140,738	1.9%
44	Montana	345,907	0.3%
38	Nebraska	651,887	0.6%
33	Nevada	961,170	0.9%
39	New Hampshire	533,776	0.5%
9	New Jersey	3,349,874	3.0%
36	New Mexico	697,278	0.6%
3	New York	7,129,206	6.4%
11	North Carolina	3,180,786	2.9%
49	North Dakota	236,637	0.2%
7	Ohio	4,561,748	4.1%
29	Oklahoma	1,212,564	1.1%
28	Oregon	1,268,717	1.1%
5	Pennsylvania	4,871,899	4.4%
43	Rhode Island	421,031	0.4%
24	South Carolina	1,564,609	1.4%
46	South Dakota	290,175	0.3%
16	Tennessee	2,253,351	2.0%
2	Texas	8,255,845	7.5%
35	Utah	857,172	0.8%
48	Vermont	247,927	0.2%
12	Virginia	2,892,800	2.6%
15	Washington	2,407,643	2.2%
37	West Virginia	653,507	0.6%
19	Wisconsin	2,140,034	1.9%
50	Wyoming	203,917	0.2%

<u>RANK ORDER</u>

RANK	STATE	REFUNDS	% of USA
1	California	12,392,511	11.2%
2	Texas	8,255,845	7.5%
3	New York	7,129,206	6.4%
4	Florida	6,944,596	6.3%
5	Pennsylvania	4,871,899	4.4%
6	Illinois	4,837,057	4.4%
7	Ohio	4,561,748	4.1%
8	Michigan	3,787,822	3.4%
9	New Jersey	3,349,874	3.0%
10	Georgia	3,314,315	3.0%
11	North Carolina	3,180,786	2.9%
12	Virginia	2,892,800	2.6%
13	Massachusetts	2,474,654	2.2%
14	Indiana	2,457,422	2.2%
15	Washington	2,407,643	2.2%
16	Tennessee	2,253,351	2.0%
17	Maryland	2,183,810	2.0%
18	Missouri	2,140,738	1.9%
19	Wisconsin	2,140,034	1.9%
20	Arizona	1,978,455	1.8%
21	Minnesota	1,932,659	1.7%
22	Colorado	1,699,853	1.5%
23	Alabama	1,656,941	1.5%
24	South Carolina	1,564,609	1.4%
25	Louisiana	1,500,608	1.4%
26	Kentucky	1,495,484	1.3%
27	Connecticut	1,336,231	1.2%
28	Oregon	1,268,717	1.1%
29	Oklahoma	1,212,564	1.1%
30	Iowa	1,064,276	1.0%
31	Mississippi	999,402	0.9%
32	Kansas	989,376	0.9%
33	Nevada	961,170	0.9%
34	Arkansas	955,126	0.9%
35	Utah	857,172	0.8%
36	New Mexico	697,278	0.6%
37	West Virginia	653,507	0.6%
38	Nebraska	651,887	0.6%
39	New Hampshire	533,776	0.5%
40	Maine	505,406	0.5%
41	Hawaii	500,775	0.5%
42	Idaho	491,764	0.4%
43	Rhode Island	421,031	0.4%
44	Montana	345,907	0.3%
45	Delaware	334,993	0.3%
46	South Dakota	290,175	0.3%
47	Alaska	265,482	0.2%
48	Vermont	247,927	0.2%
49	North Dakota	236,637	0.2%
50	Wyoming	203,917	0.2%
	District of Columbia	232,695	0.2%

Source: U.S. Department of the Treasury, Internal Revenue Service
  "FY2006 IRS Data Book" (http://www.irs.gov/taxstats/index.html)
*Total includes refunds to international sources and other miscellaneous refunds not shown separately.

Value of Federal Tax Refunds in 2006

National Total = $280,393,087,000*

ALPHA ORDER

RANK	STATE	REFUNDS	% of USA
24	Alabama	$3,927,882,000	1.4%
46	Alaska	554,652,000	0.2%
21	Arizona	4,177,180,000	1.5%
33	Arkansas	2,060,770,000	0.7%
1	California	31,843,097,000	11.4%
25	Colorado	3,696,625,000	1.3%
23	Connecticut	4,056,894,000	1.4%
35	Delaware	1,940,311,000	0.7%
4	Florida	16,316,127,000	5.8%
10	Georgia	8,282,980,000	3.0%
41	Hawaii	983,897,000	0.4%
42	Idaho	950,165,000	0.3%
5	Illinois	14,199,344,000	5.1%
17	Indiana	5,292,070,000	1.9%
31	Iowa	2,355,412,000	0.8%
34	Kansas	1,977,435,000	0.7%
27	Kentucky	3,117,375,000	1.1%
22	Louisiana	4,096,658,000	1.5%
44	Maine	930,379,000	0.3%
18	Maryland	5,208,585,000	1.9%
13	Massachusetts	6,213,026,000	2.2%
9	Michigan	9,311,068,000	3.3%
16	Minnesota	5,321,687,000	1.9%
29	Mississippi	2,411,766,000	0.9%
19	Missouri	4,635,569,000	1.7%
45	Montana	583,160,000	0.2%
37	Nebraska	1,404,951,000	0.5%
32	Nevada	2,287,665,000	0.8%
40	New Hampshire	1,167,303,000	0.4%
8	New Jersey	9,839,029,000	3.5%
38	New Mexico	1,359,378,000	0.5%
2	New York	21,797,693,000	7.8%
11	North Carolina	6,991,927,000	2.5%
49	North Dakota	408,404,000	0.1%
7	Ohio	10,587,898,000	3.8%
28	Oklahoma	2,511,556,000	0.9%
30	Oregon	2,394,740,000	0.9%
6	Pennsylvania	11,001,987,000	3.9%
43	Rhode Island	944,128,000	0.3%
26	South Carolina	3,245,435,000	1.2%
47	South Dakota	546,040,000	0.2%
15	Tennessee	5,584,924,000	2.0%
3	Texas	20,879,927,000	7.4%
36	Utah	1,744,072,000	0.6%
48	Vermont	480,078,000	0.2%
12	Virginia	6,539,180,000	2.3%
14	Washington	5,873,121,000	2.1%
39	West Virginia	1,254,825,000	0.4%
20	Wisconsin	4,464,618,000	1.6%
50	Wyoming	407,004,000	0.1%

RANK ORDER

RANK	STATE	REFUNDS	% of USA
1	California	$31,843,097,000	11.4%
2	New York	21,797,693,000	7.8%
3	Texas	20,879,927,000	7.4%
4	Florida	16,316,127,000	5.8%
5	Illinois	14,199,344,000	5.1%
6	Pennsylvania	11,001,987,000	3.9%
7	Ohio	10,587,898,000	3.8%
8	New Jersey	9,839,029,000	3.5%
9	Michigan	9,311,068,000	3.3%
10	Georgia	8,282,980,000	3.0%
11	North Carolina	6,991,927,000	2.5%
12	Virginia	6,539,180,000	2.3%
13	Massachusetts	6,213,026,000	2.2%
14	Washington	5,873,121,000	2.1%
15	Tennessee	5,584,924,000	2.0%
16	Minnesota	5,321,687,000	1.9%
17	Indiana	5,292,070,000	1.9%
18	Maryland	5,208,585,000	1.9%
19	Missouri	4,635,569,000	1.7%
20	Wisconsin	4,464,618,000	1.6%
21	Arizona	4,177,180,000	1.5%
22	Louisiana	4,096,658,000	1.5%
23	Connecticut	4,056,894,000	1.4%
24	Alabama	3,927,882,000	1.4%
25	Colorado	3,696,625,000	1.3%
26	South Carolina	3,245,435,000	1.2%
27	Kentucky	3,117,375,000	1.1%
28	Oklahoma	2,511,556,000	0.9%
29	Mississippi	2,411,766,000	0.9%
30	Oregon	2,394,740,000	0.9%
31	Iowa	2,355,412,000	0.8%
32	Nevada	2,287,665,000	0.8%
33	Arkansas	2,060,770,000	0.7%
34	Kansas	1,977,435,000	0.7%
35	Delaware	1,940,311,000	0.7%
36	Utah	1,744,072,000	0.6%
37	Nebraska	1,404,951,000	0.5%
38	New Mexico	1,359,378,000	0.5%
39	West Virginia	1,254,825,000	0.4%
40	New Hampshire	1,167,303,000	0.4%
41	Hawaii	983,897,000	0.4%
42	Idaho	950,165,000	0.3%
43	Rhode Island	944,128,000	0.3%
44	Maine	930,379,000	0.3%
45	Montana	583,160,000	0.2%
46	Alaska	554,652,000	0.2%
47	South Dakota	546,040,000	0.2%
48	Vermont	480,078,000	0.2%
49	North Dakota	408,404,000	0.1%
50	Wyoming	407,004,000	0.1%
	District of Columbia	626,891,000	0.2%

Source: U.S. Department of the Treasury, Internal Revenue Service
   "FY2006 IRS Data Book" (http://www.irs.gov/taxstats/index.html)
*Total includes refunds to international sources and other miscellaneous refunds not shown separately.

Average Value of Federal Tax Refunds in 2006

National Average = $2,530*

ALPHA ORDER

RANK	STATE	REFUNDS
18	Alabama	$2,371
33	Alaska	2,089
32	Arizona	2,111
29	Arkansas	2,158
8	California	2,570
27	Colorado	2,175
3	Connecticut	3,036
1	Delaware	5,792
19	Florida	2,349
11	Georgia	2,499
41	Hawaii	1,965
44	Idaho	1,932
5	Illinois	2,936
31	Indiana	2,154
24	Iowa	2,213
39	Kansas	1,999
35	Kentucky	2,085
7	Louisiana	2,730
48	Maine	1,841
16	Maryland	2,385
10	Massachusetts	2,511
13	Michigan	2,458
6	Minnesota	2,754
15	Mississippi	2,413
28	Missouri	2,165
50	Montana	1,686
30	Nebraska	2,155
17	Nevada	2,380
26	New Hampshire	2,187
4	New Jersey	2,937
42	New Mexico	1,950
2	New York	3,058
25	North Carolina	2,198
49	North Dakota	1,726
20	Ohio	2,321
37	Oklahoma	2,071
46	Oregon	1,888
22	Pennsylvania	2,258
23	Rhode Island	2,242
36	South Carolina	2,074
47	South Dakota	1,882
12	Tennessee	2,478
9	Texas	2,529
38	Utah	2,035
43	Vermont	1,936
21	Virginia	2,261
14	Washington	2,439
45	West Virginia	1,920
34	Wisconsin	2,086
40	Wyoming	1,996

RANK ORDER

RANK	STATE	REFUNDS
1	Delaware	$5,792
2	New York	3,058
3	Connecticut	3,036
4	New Jersey	2,937
5	Illinois	2,936
6	Minnesota	2,754
7	Louisiana	2,730
8	California	2,570
9	Texas	2,529
10	Massachusetts	2,511
11	Georgia	2,499
12	Tennessee	2,478
13	Michigan	2,458
14	Washington	2,439
15	Mississippi	2,413
16	Maryland	2,385
17	Nevada	2,380
18	Alabama	2,371
19	Florida	2,349
20	Ohio	2,321
21	Virginia	2,261
22	Pennsylvania	2,258
23	Rhode Island	2,242
24	Iowa	2,213
25	North Carolina	2,198
26	New Hampshire	2,187
27	Colorado	2,175
28	Missouri	2,165
29	Arkansas	2,158
30	Nebraska	2,155
31	Indiana	2,154
32	Arizona	2,111
33	Alaska	2,089
34	Wisconsin	2,086
35	Kentucky	2,085
36	South Carolina	2,074
37	Oklahoma	2,071
38	Utah	2,035
39	Kansas	1,999
40	Wyoming	1,996
41	Hawaii	1,965
42	New Mexico	1,950
43	Vermont	1,936
44	Idaho	1,932
45	West Virginia	1,920
46	Oregon	1,888
47	South Dakota	1,882
48	Maine	1,841
49	North Dakota	1,726
50	Montana	1,686

District of Columbia   2,694

Source: CQ Press using data from U.S. Department of the Treasury, Internal Revenue Service
"FY2006 IRS Data Book" (http://www.irs.gov/taxstats/index.html)
*National average includes refunds to international sources and other miscellaneous refunds not shown separately.

Value of Federal Individual Income Tax Refunds in 2006

National Total = $242,630,468,000*

ALPHA ORDER

RANK	STATE	REFUNDS	% of USA
21	Alabama	$3,653,233,000	1.5%
46	Alaska	529,703,000	0.2%
19	Arizona	4,008,793,000	1.7%
32	Arkansas	1,953,238,000	0.8%
1	California	28,085,609,000	11.6%
24	Colorado	3,380,529,000	1.4%
25	Connecticut	3,186,167,000	1.3%
44	Delaware	713,971,000	0.3%
4	Florida	15,253,441,000	6.3%
10	Georgia	7,346,600,000	3.0%
40	Hawaii	924,085,000	0.4%
42	Idaho	881,519,000	0.4%
5	Illinois	11,070,441,000	4.6%
14	Indiana	5,004,844,000	2.1%
33	Iowa	1,936,105,000	0.8%
34	Kansas	1,854,443,000	0.8%
27	Kentucky	2,969,099,000	1.2%
23	Louisiana	3,586,107,000	1.5%
41	Maine	883,080,000	0.4%
16	Maryland	4,865,259,000	2.0%
13	Massachusetts	5,498,621,000	2.3%
9	Michigan	7,929,859,000	3.3%
22	Minnesota	3,599,995,000	1.5%
29	Mississippi	2,329,901,000	1.0%
18	Missouri	4,188,516,000	1.7%
45	Montana	562,537,000	0.2%
38	Nebraska	1,198,974,000	0.5%
31	Nevada	2,177,067,000	0.9%
39	New Hampshire	1,089,399,000	0.4%
8	New Jersey	8,112,243,000	3.3%
36	New Mexico	1,302,824,000	0.5%
3	New York	16,674,090,000	6.9%
11	North Carolina	6,374,602,000	2.6%
50	North Dakota	383,280,000	0.2%
7	Ohio	8,895,016,000	3.7%
28	Oklahoma	2,335,142,000	1.0%
30	Oregon	2,229,181,000	0.9%
6	Pennsylvania	9,741,173,000	4.0%
43	Rhode Island	853,592,000	0.4%
26	South Carolina	3,099,512,000	1.3%
47	South Dakota	511,735,000	0.2%
17	Tennessee	4,718,450,000	1.9%
2	Texas	18,789,329,000	7.7%
35	Utah	1,610,412,000	0.7%
48	Vermont	430,884,000	0.2%
12	Virginia	6,076,076,000	2.5%
15	Washington	4,875,358,000	2.0%
37	West Virginia	1,217,261,000	0.5%
20	Wisconsin	3,888,603,000	1.6%
49	Wyoming	389,476,000	0.2%

RANK ORDER

RANK	STATE	REFUNDS	% of USA
1	California	$28,085,609,000	11.6%
2	Texas	18,789,329,000	7.7%
3	New York	16,674,090,000	6.9%
4	Florida	15,253,441,000	6.3%
5	Illinois	11,070,441,000	4.6%
6	Pennsylvania	9,741,173,000	4.0%
7	Ohio	8,895,016,000	3.7%
8	New Jersey	8,112,243,000	3.3%
9	Michigan	7,929,859,000	3.3%
10	Georgia	7,346,600,000	3.0%
11	North Carolina	6,374,602,000	2.6%
12	Virginia	6,076,076,000	2.5%
13	Massachusetts	5,498,621,000	2.3%
14	Indiana	5,004,844,000	2.1%
15	Washington	4,875,358,000	2.0%
16	Maryland	4,865,259,000	2.0%
17	Tennessee	4,718,450,000	1.9%
18	Missouri	4,188,516,000	1.7%
19	Arizona	4,008,793,000	1.7%
20	Wisconsin	3,888,603,000	1.6%
21	Alabama	3,653,233,000	1.5%
22	Minnesota	3,599,995,000	1.5%
23	Louisiana	3,586,107,000	1.5%
24	Colorado	3,380,529,000	1.4%
25	Connecticut	3,186,167,000	1.3%
26	South Carolina	3,099,512,000	1.3%
27	Kentucky	2,969,099,000	1.2%
28	Oklahoma	2,335,142,000	1.0%
29	Mississippi	2,329,901,000	1.0%
30	Oregon	2,229,181,000	0.9%
31	Nevada	2,177,067,000	0.9%
32	Arkansas	1,953,238,000	0.8%
33	Iowa	1,936,105,000	0.8%
34	Kansas	1,854,443,000	0.8%
35	Utah	1,610,412,000	0.7%
36	New Mexico	1,302,824,000	0.5%
37	West Virginia	1,217,261,000	0.5%
38	Nebraska	1,198,974,000	0.5%
39	New Hampshire	1,089,399,000	0.4%
40	Hawaii	924,085,000	0.4%
41	Maine	883,080,000	0.4%
42	Idaho	881,519,000	0.4%
43	Rhode Island	853,592,000	0.4%
44	Delaware	713,971,000	0.3%
45	Montana	562,537,000	0.2%
46	Alaska	529,703,000	0.2%
47	South Dakota	511,735,000	0.2%
48	Vermont	430,884,000	0.2%
49	Wyoming	389,476,000	0.2%
50	North Dakota	383,280,000	0.2%
	District of Columbia	557,842,000	0.2%

Source: U.S. Department of the Treasury, Internal Revenue Service
"FY2006 IRS Data Book" (http://www.irs.gov/taxstats/index.html)
*Total includes refunds to international sources and other miscellaneous refunds not shown separately.

Average Value of Federal Individual Income Tax Refunds in 2006

National Average = $2,246*

ALPHA ORDER

RANK	STATE	REFUNDS
14	Alabama	$2,258
24	Alaska	2,070
23	Arizona	2,076
19	Arkansas	2,103
9	California	2,326
27	Colorado	2,048
3	Connecticut	2,444
15	Delaware	2,188
13	Florida	2,267
11	Georgia	2,273
41	Hawaii	1,895
44	Idaho	1,856
6	Illinois	2,343
22	Indiana	2,077
42	Iowa	1,870
36	Kansas	1,928
30	Kentucky	2,027
2	Louisiana	2,462
48	Maine	1,790
10	Maryland	2,280
12	Massachusetts	2,270
18	Michigan	2,140
38	Minnesota	1,911
5	Mississippi	2,392
31	Missouri	2,006
49	Montana	1,697
40	Nebraska	1,898
8	Nevada	2,328
20	New Hampshire	2,099
1	New Jersey	2,489
37	New Mexico	1,917
4	New York	2,402
26	North Carolina	2,051
50	North Dakota	1,680
33	Ohio	1,986
34	Oklahoma	1,979
46	Oregon	1,808
28	Pennsylvania	2,038
25	Rhode Island	2,062
29	South Carolina	2,028
45	South Dakota	1,828
17	Tennessee	2,147
7	Texas	2,341
35	Utah	1,932
47	Vermont	1,797
16	Virginia	2,153
21	Washington	2,088
39	West Virginia	1,906
43	Wisconsin	1,860
32	Wyoming	1,999

RANK ORDER

RANK	STATE	REFUNDS
1	New Jersey	$2,489
2	Louisiana	2,462
3	Connecticut	2,444
4	New York	2,402
5	Mississippi	2,392
6	Illinois	2,343
7	Texas	2,341
8	Nevada	2,328
9	California	2,326
10	Maryland	2,280
11	Georgia	2,273
12	Massachusetts	2,270
13	Florida	2,267
14	Alabama	2,258
15	Delaware	2,188
16	Virginia	2,153
17	Tennessee	2,147
18	Michigan	2,140
19	Arkansas	2,103
20	New Hampshire	2,099
21	Washington	2,088
22	Indiana	2,077
23	Arizona	2,076
24	Alaska	2,070
25	Rhode Island	2,062
26	North Carolina	2,051
27	Colorado	2,048
28	Pennsylvania	2,038
29	South Carolina	2,028
30	Kentucky	2,027
31	Missouri	2,006
32	Wyoming	1,999
33	Ohio	1,986
34	Oklahoma	1,979
35	Utah	1,932
36	Kansas	1,928
37	New Mexico	1,917
38	Minnesota	1,911
39	West Virginia	1,906
40	Nebraska	1,898
41	Hawaii	1,895
42	Iowa	1,870
43	Wisconsin	1,860
44	Idaho	1,856
45	South Dakota	1,828
46	Oregon	1,808
47	Vermont	1,797
48	Maine	1,790
49	Montana	1,697
50	North Dakota	1,680
	District of Columbia	2,471

Source: U.S. Department of the Treasury, Internal Revenue Service
"FY2006 IRS Data Book" (http://www.irs.gov/taxstats/index.html)
*National average includes refunds to international sources and other miscellaneous refunds not shown separately.

Value of Federal Corporate Income Tax Refunds in 2006

National Total = $29,831,391,000*

ALPHA ORDER

RANK	STATE	REFUNDS	% of USA
25	Alabama	$221,279,000	0.7%
48	Alaska	16,002,000	0.1%
32	Arizona	112,252,000	0.4%
35	Arkansas	85,819,000	0.3%
2	California	3,212,830,000	10.8%
26	Colorado	216,720,000	0.7%
14	Connecticut	796,764,000	2.7%
9	Delaware	1,202,552,000	4.0%
12	Florida	816,980,000	2.7%
13	Georgia	814,423,000	2.7%
42	Hawaii	43,092,000	0.1%
40	Idaho	55,626,000	0.2%
3	Illinois	2,950,624,000	9.9%
24	Indiana	247,276,000	0.8%
21	Iowa	381,211,000	1.3%
33	Kansas	98,640,000	0.3%
31	Kentucky	114,348,000	0.4%
19	Louisiana	476,032,000	1.6%
44	Maine	38,748,000	0.1%
23	Maryland	262,950,000	0.9%
16	Massachusetts	627,217,000	2.1%
8	Michigan	1,288,527,000	4.3%
5	Minnesota	1,597,875,000	5.4%
39	Mississippi	64,722,000	0.2%
20	Missouri	390,755,000	1.3%
49	Montana	13,335,000	0.0%
27	Nebraska	187,239,000	0.6%
37	Nevada	75,350,000	0.3%
38	New Hampshire	65,208,000	0.2%
7	New Jersey	1,431,290,000	4.8%
43	New Mexico	42,806,000	0.1%
1	New York	4,644,700,000	15.6%
17	North Carolina	534,004,000	1.8%
47	North Dakota	20,204,000	0.1%
6	Ohio	1,596,177,000	5.4%
29	Oklahoma	125,948,000	0.4%
28	Oregon	127,921,000	0.4%
10	Pennsylvania	1,143,060,000	3.8%
36	Rhode Island	84,378,000	0.3%
30	South Carolina	118,005,000	0.4%
45	South Dakota	25,658,000	0.1%
15	Tennessee	795,698,000	2.7%
4	Texas	1,766,988,000	5.9%
34	Utah	98,232,000	0.3%
41	Vermont	43,204,000	0.1%
22	Virginia	345,073,000	1.2%
11	Washington	901,737,000	3.0%
46	West Virginia	21,650,000	0.1%
18	Wisconsin	527,407,000	1.8%
50	Wyoming	9,859,000	0.0%

RANK ORDER

RANK	STATE	REFUNDS	% of USA
1	New York	$4,644,700,000	15.6%
2	California	3,212,830,000	10.8%
3	Illinois	2,950,624,000	9.9%
4	Texas	1,766,988,000	5.9%
5	Minnesota	1,597,875,000	5.4%
6	Ohio	1,596,177,000	5.4%
7	New Jersey	1,431,290,000	4.8%
8	Michigan	1,288,527,000	4.3%
9	Delaware	1,202,552,000	4.0%
10	Pennsylvania	1,143,060,000	3.8%
11	Washington	901,737,000	3.0%
12	Florida	816,980,000	2.7%
13	Georgia	814,423,000	2.7%
14	Connecticut	796,764,000	2.7%
15	Tennessee	795,698,000	2.7%
16	Massachusetts	627,217,000	2.1%
17	North Carolina	534,004,000	1.8%
18	Wisconsin	527,407,000	1.8%
19	Louisiana	476,032,000	1.6%
20	Missouri	390,755,000	1.3%
21	Iowa	381,211,000	1.3%
22	Virginia	345,073,000	1.2%
23	Maryland	262,950,000	0.9%
24	Indiana	247,276,000	0.8%
25	Alabama	221,279,000	0.7%
26	Colorado	216,720,000	0.7%
27	Nebraska	187,239,000	0.6%
28	Oregon	127,921,000	0.4%
29	Oklahoma	125,948,000	0.4%
30	South Carolina	118,005,000	0.4%
31	Kentucky	114,348,000	0.4%
32	Arizona	112,252,000	0.4%
33	Kansas	98,640,000	0.3%
34	Utah	98,232,000	0.3%
35	Arkansas	85,819,000	0.3%
36	Rhode Island	84,378,000	0.3%
37	Nevada	75,350,000	0.3%
38	New Hampshire	65,208,000	0.2%
39	Mississippi	64,722,000	0.2%
40	Idaho	55,626,000	0.2%
41	Vermont	43,204,000	0.1%
42	Hawaii	43,092,000	0.1%
43	New Mexico	42,806,000	0.1%
44	Maine	38,748,000	0.1%
45	South Dakota	25,658,000	0.1%
46	West Virginia	21,650,000	0.1%
47	North Dakota	20,204,000	0.1%
48	Alaska	16,002,000	0.1%
49	Montana	13,335,000	0.0%
50	Wyoming	9,859,000	0.0%
	District of Columbia	49,198,000	0.2%

Source: U.S. Department of the Treasury, Internal Revenue Service
   "FY2006 IRS Data Book" (http://www.irs.gov/taxstats/index.html)
*Total includes refunds to international sources and other miscellaneous refunds not shown separately.

Average Value of Federal Corporate Income Tax Refunds in 2006

National Average = $67,033*

ALPHA ORDER

RANK	STATE	REFUNDS
21	Alabama	$47,566
41	Alaska	17,318
39	Arizona	17,900
36	Arkansas	22,867
16	California	58,215
30	Colorado	29,466
5	Connecticut	158,592
1	Delaware	693,114
29	Florida	31,657
13	Georgia	69,013
44	Hawaii	15,004
35	Idaho	23,782
4	Illinois	160,867
24	Indiana	37,252
20	Iowa	48,267
42	Kansas	16,556
31	Kentucky	27,232
10	Louisiana	84,794
43	Maine	16,012
28	Maryland	31,927
15	Massachusetts	64,257
12	Michigan	74,036
2	Minnesota	174,708
40	Mississippi	17,502
22	Missouri	42,162
50	Montana	3,821
23	Nebraska	40,249
45	Nevada	14,965
33	New Hampshire	25,866
11	New Jersey	80,032
38	New Mexico	17,918
3	New York	168,366
19	North Carolina	49,601
48	North Dakota	10,132
7	Ohio	104,210
34	Oklahoma	24,995
37	Oregon	20,666
8	Pennsylvania	90,561
14	Rhode Island	65,308
32	South Carolina	26,518
46	South Dakota	11,626
6	Tennessee	106,891
17	Texas	53,032
25	Utah	34,287
26	Vermont	32,656
27	Virginia	32,481
9	Washington	89,334
47	West Virginia	11,341
18	Wisconsin	51,130
49	Wyoming	5,921

RANK ORDER

RANK	STATE	REFUNDS
1	Delaware	$693,114
2	Minnesota	174,708
3	New York	168,366
4	Illinois	160,867
5	Connecticut	158,592
6	Tennessee	106,891
7	Ohio	104,210
8	Pennsylvania	90,561
9	Washington	89,334
10	Louisiana	84,794
11	New Jersey	80,032
12	Michigan	74,036
13	Georgia	69,013
14	Rhode Island	65,308
15	Massachusetts	64,257
16	California	58,215
17	Texas	53,032
18	Wisconsin	51,130
19	North Carolina	49,601
20	Iowa	48,267
21	Alabama	47,566
22	Missouri	42,162
23	Nebraska	40,249
24	Indiana	37,252
25	Utah	34,287
26	Vermont	32,656
27	Virginia	32,481
28	Maryland	31,927
29	Florida	31,657
30	Colorado	29,466
31	Kentucky	27,232
32	South Carolina	26,518
33	New Hampshire	25,866
34	Oklahoma	24,995
35	Idaho	23,782
36	Arkansas	22,867
37	Oregon	20,666
38	New Mexico	17,918
39	Arizona	17,900
40	Mississippi	17,502
41	Alaska	17,318
42	Kansas	16,556
43	Maine	16,012
44	Hawaii	15,004
45	Nevada	14,965
46	South Dakota	11,626
47	West Virginia	11,341
48	North Dakota	10,132
49	Wyoming	5,921
50	Montana	3,821

District of Columbia	43,043

Source: CQ Press using data from U.S. Department of the Treasury, Internal Revenue Service
"FY2006 IRS Data Book" (http://www.irs.gov/taxstats/index.html)
*National average includes refunds to international sources and other miscellaneous refunds not shown separately.

Federal Expenditures per Dollar of Federal Taxes in 2005

National Median = $1.09 Received for Each Dollar Sent*

ALPHA ORDER

RANK	STATE	PER DOLLAR
7	Alabama	$1.66
3	Alaska	1.84
21	Arizona	1.19
14	Arkansas	1.41
43	California	0.78
41	Colorado	0.81
48	Connecticut	0.69
44	Delaware	0.77
34	Florida	0.97
32	Georgia	1.01
12	Hawaii	1.44
20	Idaho	1.21
45	Illinois	0.75
30	Indiana	1.05
24	Iowa	1.10
22	Kansas	1.12
9	Kentucky	1.51
4	Louisiana	1.78
13	Maine	1.41
18	Maryland	1.30
40	Massachusetts	0.82
37	Michigan	0.92
46	Minnesota	0.72
2	Mississippi	2.02
17	Missouri	1.32
11	Montana	1.47
25	Nebraska	1.10
49	Nevada	0.65
47	New Hampshire	0.71
50	New Jersey	0.61
1	New Mexico	2.03
42	New York	0.79
27	North Carolina	1.08
6	North Dakota	1.68
31	Ohio	1.05
15	Oklahoma	1.36
36	Oregon	0.93
28	Pennsylvania	1.07
33	Rhode Island	1.00
16	South Carolina	1.35
8	South Dakota	1.53
19	Tennessee	1.27
35	Texas	0.94
29	Utah	1.07
26	Vermont	1.08
10	Virginia	1.51
38	Washington	0.88
5	West Virginia	1.76
39	Wisconsin	0.86
23	Wyoming	1.11

RANK ORDER

RANK	STATE	PER DOLLAR
1	New Mexico	$2.03
2	Mississippi	2.02
3	Alaska	1.84
4	Louisiana	1.78
5	West Virginia	1.76
6	North Dakota	1.68
7	Alabama	1.66
8	South Dakota	1.53
9	Kentucky	1.51
10	Virginia	1.51
11	Montana	1.47
12	Hawaii	1.44
13	Maine	1.41
14	Arkansas	1.41
15	Oklahoma	1.36
16	South Carolina	1.35
17	Missouri	1.32
18	Maryland	1.30
19	Tennessee	1.27
20	Idaho	1.21
21	Arizona	1.19
22	Kansas	1.12
23	Wyoming	1.11
24	Iowa	1.10
25	Nebraska	1.10
26	Vermont	1.08
27	North Carolina	1.08
28	Pennsylvania	1.07
29	Utah	1.07
30	Indiana	1.05
31	Ohio	1.05
32	Georgia	1.01
33	Rhode Island	1.00
34	Florida	0.97
35	Texas	0.94
36	Oregon	0.93
37	Michigan	0.92
38	Washington	0.88
39	Wisconsin	0.86
40	Massachusetts	0.82
41	Colorado	0.81
42	New York	0.79
43	California	0.78
44	Delaware	0.77
45	Illinois	0.75
46	Minnesota	0.72
47	New Hampshire	0.71
48	Connecticut	0.69
49	Nevada	0.65
50	New Jersey	0.61

District of Columbia 5.55

Source: The Tax Foundation
"Federal Spending in Each State Per Dollar of Federal Taxes" (http://www.taxfoundation.org/taxdata/)
*Fiscal year 2005. This table shows how much the federal government spent in each state compared to how much the federal government receives from each state.

Federal Government Expenditures in 2005

National Total = $2,284,760,000,000*

ALPHA ORDER

RANK	STATE	EXPENDITURES	% of USA
20	Alabama	$42,061,000,000	1.8%
42	Alaska	9,230,000,000	0.4%
18	Arizona	44,639,000,000	2.0%
33	Arkansas	20,387,000,000	0.9%
1	California	242,023,000,000	10.6%
25	Colorado	31,173,000,000	1.4%
27	Connecticut	30,774,000,000	1.3%
48	Delaware	5,495,000,000	0.2%
4	Florida	134,544,000,000	5.9%
11	Georgia	59,846,000,000	2.6%
39	Hawaii	12,699,000,000	0.6%
41	Idaho	9,598,000,000	0.4%
7	Illinois	80,778,000,000	3.5%
19	Indiana	42,347,000,000	1.9%
34	Iowa	20,345,000,000	0.9%
32	Kansas	20,492,000,000	0.9%
22	Kentucky	34,653,000,000	1.5%
21	Louisiana	39,628,000,000	1.7%
40	Maine	11,356,000,000	0.5%
9	Maryland	66,720,000,000	2.9%
14	Massachusetts	55,830,000,000	2.4%
10	Michigan	64,787,000,000	2.8%
26	Minnesota	31,067,000,000	1.4%
29	Mississippi	26,181,000,000	1.1%
16	Missouri	48,273,000,000	2.1%
45	Montana	7,814,000,000	0.3%
38	Nebraska	12,785,000,000	0.6%
37	Nevada	14,089,000,000	0.6%
44	New Hampshire	8,331,000,000	0.4%
13	New Jersey	58,617,000,000	2.6%
31	New Mexico	20,604,000,000	0.9%
3	New York	144,876,000,000	6.3%
12	North Carolina	59,162,000,000	2.6%
47	North Dakota	6,608,000,000	0.3%
8	Ohio	77,881,000,000	3.4%
28	Oklahoma	27,637,000,000	1.2%
30	Oregon	22,792,000,000	1.0%
5	Pennsylvania	99,503,000,000	4.4%
43	Rhode Island	8,423,000,000	0.4%
24	South Carolina	32,044,000,000	1.4%
46	South Dakota	7,481,000,000	0.3%
15	Tennessee	48,288,000,000	2.1%
2	Texas	148,683,000,000	6.5%
36	Utah	14,823,000,000	0.6%
50	Vermont	4,645,000,000	0.2%
6	Virginia	95,097,000,000	4.2%
17	Washington	46,338,000,000	2.0%
35	West Virginia	16,087,000,000	0.7%
23	Wisconsin	33,749,000,000	1.5%
49	Wyoming	4,782,000,000	0.2%

RANK ORDER

RANK	STATE	EXPENDITURES	% of USA
1	California	$242,023,000,000	10.6%
2	Texas	148,683,000,000	6.5%
3	New York	144,876,000,000	6.3%
4	Florida	134,544,000,000	5.9%
5	Pennsylvania	99,503,000,000	4.4%
6	Virginia	95,097,000,000	4.2%
7	Illinois	80,778,000,000	3.5%
8	Ohio	77,881,000,000	3.4%
9	Maryland	66,720,000,000	2.9%
10	Michigan	64,787,000,000	2.8%
11	Georgia	59,846,000,000	2.6%
12	North Carolina	59,162,000,000	2.6%
13	New Jersey	58,617,000,000	2.6%
14	Massachusetts	55,830,000,000	2.4%
15	Tennessee	48,288,000,000	2.1%
16	Missouri	48,273,000,000	2.1%
17	Washington	46,338,000,000	2.0%
18	Arizona	44,639,000,000	2.0%
19	Indiana	42,347,000,000	1.9%
20	Alabama	42,061,000,000	1.8%
21	Louisiana	39,628,000,000	1.7%
22	Kentucky	34,653,000,000	1.5%
23	Wisconsin	33,749,000,000	1.5%
24	South Carolina	32,044,000,000	1.4%
25	Colorado	31,173,000,000	1.4%
26	Minnesota	31,067,000,000	1.4%
27	Connecticut	30,774,000,000	1.3%
28	Oklahoma	27,637,000,000	1.2%
29	Mississippi	26,181,000,000	1.1%
30	Oregon	22,792,000,000	1.0%
31	New Mexico	20,604,000,000	0.9%
32	Kansas	20,492,000,000	0.9%
33	Arkansas	20,387,000,000	0.9%
34	Iowa	20,345,000,000	0.9%
35	West Virginia	16,087,000,000	0.7%
36	Utah	14,823,000,000	0.6%
37	Nevada	14,089,000,000	0.6%
38	Nebraska	12,785,000,000	0.6%
39	Hawaii	12,699,000,000	0.6%
40	Maine	11,356,000,000	0.5%
41	Idaho	9,598,000,000	0.4%
42	Alaska	9,230,000,000	0.4%
43	Rhode Island	8,423,000,000	0.4%
44	New Hampshire	8,331,000,000	0.4%
45	Montana	7,814,000,000	0.3%
46	South Dakota	7,481,000,000	0.3%
47	North Dakota	6,608,000,000	0.3%
48	Delaware	5,495,000,000	0.2%
49	Wyoming	4,782,000,000	0.2%
50	Vermont	4,645,000,000	0.2%
	District of Columbia	37,859,000,000	1.7%

Source: U.S. Bureau of the Census
   "Consolidated Federal Funds Report: 2005" (CFFR/05, Sept 2007, http://www.census.gov/govs/www/cffr05.html)
*Total includes $18,998,000,000 in U.S. territories ($16,174,000,000 in Puerto Rico) and $21,839,000,000 in expenditures not distributed by state.

Per Capita Federal Government Expenditures in 2005

National Per Capita = $7,583*

<table>
<tr><th colspan="3">ALPHA ORDER</th><th colspan="3">RANK ORDER</th></tr>
<tr><th>RANK</th><th>STATE</th><th>PER CAPITA</th><th>RANK</th><th>STATE</th><th>PER CAPITA</th></tr>
<tr><td>9</td><td>Alabama</td><td>$9,265</td><td>1</td><td>Alaska</td><td>$13,788</td></tr>
<tr><td>1</td><td>Alaska</td><td>13,788</td><td>2</td><td>Virginia</td><td>12,583</td></tr>
<tr><td>26</td><td>Arizona</td><td>7,500</td><td>3</td><td>Maryland</td><td>11,972</td></tr>
<tr><td>30</td><td>Arkansas</td><td>7,354</td><td>4</td><td>New Mexico</td><td>10,752</td></tr>
<tr><td>38</td><td>California</td><td>6,725</td><td>5</td><td>North Dakota</td><td>10,391</td></tr>
<tr><td>39</td><td>Colorado</td><td>6,670</td><td>6</td><td>Hawaii</td><td>10,018</td></tr>
<tr><td>12</td><td>Connecticut</td><td>8,827</td><td>7</td><td>South Dakota</td><td>9,590</td></tr>
<tr><td>41</td><td>Delaware</td><td>6,537</td><td>8</td><td>Wyoming</td><td>9,440</td></tr>
<tr><td>23</td><td>Florida</td><td>7,586</td><td>9</td><td>Alabama</td><td>9,265</td></tr>
<tr><td>40</td><td>Georgia</td><td>6,571</td><td>10</td><td>Mississippi</td><td>9,027</td></tr>
<tr><td>6</td><td>Hawaii</td><td>10,018</td><td>11</td><td>West Virginia</td><td>8,909</td></tr>
<tr><td>37</td><td>Idaho</td><td>6,731</td><td>12</td><td>Connecticut</td><td>8,827</td></tr>
<tr><td>45</td><td>Illinois</td><td>6,351</td><td>13</td><td>Louisiana</td><td>8,815</td></tr>
<tr><td>36</td><td>Indiana</td><td>6,768</td><td>14</td><td>Massachusetts</td><td>8,684</td></tr>
<tr><td>32</td><td>Iowa</td><td>6,884</td><td>15</td><td>Maine</td><td>8,654</td></tr>
<tr><td>28</td><td>Kansas</td><td>7,474</td><td>16</td><td>Montana</td><td>8,350</td></tr>
<tr><td>18</td><td>Kentucky</td><td>8,308</td><td>17</td><td>Missouri</td><td>8,340</td></tr>
<tr><td>13</td><td>Louisiana</td><td>8,815</td><td>18</td><td>Kentucky</td><td>8,308</td></tr>
<tr><td>15</td><td>Maine</td><td>8,654</td><td>19</td><td>Tennessee</td><td>8,062</td></tr>
<tr><td>3</td><td>Maryland</td><td>11,972</td><td>20</td><td>Pennsylvania</td><td>8,046</td></tr>
<tr><td>14</td><td>Massachusetts</td><td>8,684</td><td>21</td><td>Rhode Island</td><td>7,896</td></tr>
<tr><td>43</td><td>Michigan</td><td>6,410</td><td>22</td><td>Oklahoma</td><td>7,816</td></tr>
<tr><td>48</td><td>Minnesota</td><td>6,075</td><td>23</td><td>Florida</td><td>7,586</td></tr>
<tr><td>10</td><td>Mississippi</td><td>9,027</td><td>24</td><td>South Carolina</td><td>7,531</td></tr>
<tr><td>17</td><td>Missouri</td><td>8,340</td><td>25</td><td>New York</td><td>7,521</td></tr>
<tr><td>16</td><td>Montana</td><td>8,350</td><td>26</td><td>Arizona</td><td>7,500</td></tr>
<tr><td>31</td><td>Nebraska</td><td>7,289</td><td>27</td><td>Vermont</td><td>7,495</td></tr>
<tr><td>50</td><td>Nevada</td><td>5,849</td><td>28</td><td>Kansas</td><td>7,474</td></tr>
<tr><td>44</td><td>New Hampshire</td><td>6,393</td><td>29</td><td>Washington</td><td>7,389</td></tr>
<tr><td>35</td><td>New Jersey</td><td>6,771</td><td>30</td><td>Arkansas</td><td>7,354</td></tr>
<tr><td>4</td><td>New Mexico</td><td>10,752</td><td>31</td><td>Nebraska</td><td>7,289</td></tr>
<tr><td>25</td><td>New York</td><td>7,521</td><td>32</td><td>Iowa</td><td>6,884</td></tr>
<tr><td>33</td><td>North Carolina</td><td>6,817</td><td>33</td><td>North Carolina</td><td>6,817</td></tr>
<tr><td>5</td><td>North Dakota</td><td>10,391</td><td>34</td><td>Ohio</td><td>6,796</td></tr>
<tr><td>34</td><td>Ohio</td><td>6,796</td><td>35</td><td>New Jersey</td><td>6,771</td></tr>
<tr><td>22</td><td>Oklahoma</td><td>7,816</td><td>36</td><td>Indiana</td><td>6,768</td></tr>
<tr><td>46</td><td>Oregon</td><td>6,279</td><td>37</td><td>Idaho</td><td>6,731</td></tr>
<tr><td>20</td><td>Pennsylvania</td><td>8,046</td><td>38</td><td>California</td><td>6,725</td></tr>
<tr><td>21</td><td>Rhode Island</td><td>7,896</td><td>39</td><td>Colorado</td><td>6,670</td></tr>
<tr><td>24</td><td>South Carolina</td><td>7,531</td><td>40</td><td>Georgia</td><td>6,571</td></tr>
<tr><td>7</td><td>South Dakota</td><td>9,590</td><td>41</td><td>Delaware</td><td>6,537</td></tr>
<tr><td>19</td><td>Tennessee</td><td>8,062</td><td>42</td><td>Texas</td><td>6,509</td></tr>
<tr><td>42</td><td>Texas</td><td>6,509</td><td>43</td><td>Michigan</td><td>6,410</td></tr>
<tr><td>49</td><td>Utah</td><td>5,917</td><td>44</td><td>New Hampshire</td><td>6,393</td></tr>
<tr><td>27</td><td>Vermont</td><td>7,495</td><td>45</td><td>Illinois</td><td>6,351</td></tr>
<tr><td>2</td><td>Virginia</td><td>12,583</td><td>46</td><td>Oregon</td><td>6,279</td></tr>
<tr><td>29</td><td>Washington</td><td>7,389</td><td>47</td><td>Wisconsin</td><td>6,091</td></tr>
<tr><td>11</td><td>West Virginia</td><td>8,909</td><td>48</td><td>Minnesota</td><td>6,075</td></tr>
<tr><td>47</td><td>Wisconsin</td><td>6,091</td><td>49</td><td>Utah</td><td>5,917</td></tr>
<tr><td>8</td><td>Wyoming</td><td>9,440</td><td>50</td><td>Nevada</td><td>5,849</td></tr>
<tr><td></td><td></td><td></td><td></td><td>District of Columbia</td><td>65,044</td></tr>
</table>

Source: CQ Press using data from U.S. Bureau of the Census
"Consolidated Federal Funds Report: 2005" (CFFR/05, Sept 2007, http://www.census.gov/govs/www/cffr05.html)
*National per capita excludes expenditures and population for territories and undistributed amounts.

Federal Government Grants in 2005

National Total = $469,579,000,000*

<table>
<tr><td colspan="4">ALPHA ORDER</td><td colspan="4">RANK ORDER</td></tr>
<tr><td>RANK</td><td>STATE</td><td>EXPENDITURES</td><td>% of USA</td><td>RANK</td><td>STATE</td><td>EXPENDITURES</td><td>% of USA</td></tr>
<tr><td>23</td><td>Alabama</td><td>$7,346,000,000</td><td>1.6%</td><td>1</td><td>California</td><td>$55,334,000,000</td><td>11.8%</td></tr>
<tr><td>36</td><td>Alaska</td><td>3,131,000,000</td><td>0.7%</td><td>2</td><td>New York</td><td>45,631,000,000</td><td>9.7%</td></tr>
<tr><td>18</td><td>Arizona</td><td>8,603,000,000</td><td>1.8%</td><td>3</td><td>Texas</td><td>28,912,000,000</td><td>6.2%</td></tr>
<tr><td>31</td><td>Arkansas</td><td>4,682,000,000</td><td>1.0%</td><td>4</td><td>Florida</td><td>22,552,000,000</td><td>4.8%</td></tr>
<tr><td>1</td><td>California</td><td>55,334,000,000</td><td>11.8%</td><td>5</td><td>Pennsylvania</td><td>19,869,000,000</td><td>4.2%</td></tr>
<tr><td>30</td><td>Colorado</td><td>5,433,000,000</td><td>1.2%</td><td>6</td><td>Ohio</td><td>17,152,000,000</td><td>3.7%</td></tr>
<tr><td>29</td><td>Connecticut</td><td>5,439,000,000</td><td>1.2%</td><td>7</td><td>Illinois</td><td>16,635,000,000</td><td>3.5%</td></tr>
<tr><td>50</td><td>Delaware</td><td>1,265,000,000</td><td>0.3%</td><td>8</td><td>Massachusetts</td><td>13,749,000,000</td><td>2.9%</td></tr>
<tr><td>4</td><td>Florida</td><td>22,552,000,000</td><td>4.8%</td><td>9</td><td>Michigan</td><td>13,313,000,000</td><td>2.8%</td></tr>
<tr><td>12</td><td>Georgia</td><td>11,166,000,000</td><td>2.4%</td><td>10</td><td>North Carolina</td><td>12,959,000,000</td><td>2.8%</td></tr>
<tr><td>42</td><td>Hawaii</td><td>2,168,000,000</td><td>0.5%</td><td>11</td><td>Louisiana</td><td>11,389,000,000</td><td>2.4%</td></tr>
<tr><td>44</td><td>Idaho</td><td>2,093,000,000</td><td>0.4%</td><td>12</td><td>Georgia</td><td>11,166,000,000</td><td>2.4%</td></tr>
<tr><td>7</td><td>Illinois</td><td>16,635,000,000</td><td>3.5%</td><td>13</td><td>New Jersey</td><td>11,124,000,000</td><td>2.4%</td></tr>
<tr><td>19</td><td>Indiana</td><td>8,065,000,000</td><td>1.7%</td><td>14</td><td>Tennessee</td><td>9,985,000,000</td><td>2.1%</td></tr>
<tr><td>33</td><td>Iowa</td><td>4,035,000,000</td><td>0.9%</td><td>15</td><td>Washington</td><td>9,047,000,000</td><td>1.9%</td></tr>
<tr><td>35</td><td>Kansas</td><td>3,618,000,000</td><td>0.8%</td><td>16</td><td>Missouri</td><td>8,930,000,000</td><td>1.9%</td></tr>
<tr><td>24</td><td>Kentucky</td><td>6,634,000,000</td><td>1.4%</td><td>17</td><td>Maryland</td><td>8,643,000,000</td><td>1.8%</td></tr>
<tr><td>11</td><td>Louisiana</td><td>11,389,000,000</td><td>2.4%</td><td>18</td><td>Arizona</td><td>8,603,000,000</td><td>1.8%</td></tr>
<tr><td>39</td><td>Maine</td><td>2,773,000,000</td><td>0.6%</td><td>19</td><td>Indiana</td><td>8,065,000,000</td><td>1.7%</td></tr>
<tr><td>17</td><td>Maryland</td><td>8,643,000,000</td><td>1.8%</td><td>20</td><td>Virginia</td><td>7,745,000,000</td><td>1.6%</td></tr>
<tr><td>8</td><td>Massachusetts</td><td>13,749,000,000</td><td>2.9%</td><td>21</td><td>Wisconsin</td><td>7,538,000,000</td><td>1.6%</td></tr>
<tr><td>9</td><td>Michigan</td><td>13,313,000,000</td><td>2.8%</td><td>22</td><td>Minnesota</td><td>7,484,000,000</td><td>1.6%</td></tr>
<tr><td>22</td><td>Minnesota</td><td>7,484,000,000</td><td>1.6%</td><td>23</td><td>Alabama</td><td>7,346,000,000</td><td>1.6%</td></tr>
<tr><td>25</td><td>Mississippi</td><td>6,567,000,000</td><td>1.4%</td><td>24</td><td>Kentucky</td><td>6,634,000,000</td><td>1.4%</td></tr>
<tr><td>16</td><td>Missouri</td><td>8,930,000,000</td><td>1.9%</td><td>25</td><td>Mississippi</td><td>6,567,000,000</td><td>1.4%</td></tr>
<tr><td>43</td><td>Montana</td><td>2,140,000,000</td><td>0.5%</td><td>26</td><td>South Carolina</td><td>6,324,000,000</td><td>1.3%</td></tr>
<tr><td>40</td><td>Nebraska</td><td>2,596,000,000</td><td>0.6%</td><td>27</td><td>Oklahoma</td><td>5,502,000,000</td><td>1.2%</td></tr>
<tr><td>38</td><td>Nevada</td><td>2,926,000,000</td><td>0.6%</td><td>28</td><td>Oregon</td><td>5,466,000,000</td><td>1.2%</td></tr>
<tr><td>46</td><td>New Hampshire</td><td>1,795,000,000</td><td>0.4%</td><td>29</td><td>Connecticut</td><td>5,439,000,000</td><td>1.2%</td></tr>
<tr><td>13</td><td>New Jersey</td><td>11,124,000,000</td><td>2.4%</td><td>30</td><td>Colorado</td><td>5,433,000,000</td><td>1.2%</td></tr>
<tr><td>32</td><td>New Mexico</td><td>4,564,000,000</td><td>1.0%</td><td>31</td><td>Arkansas</td><td>4,682,000,000</td><td>1.0%</td></tr>
<tr><td>2</td><td>New York</td><td>45,631,000,000</td><td>9.7%</td><td>32</td><td>New Mexico</td><td>4,564,000,000</td><td>1.0%</td></tr>
<tr><td>10</td><td>North Carolina</td><td>12,959,000,000</td><td>2.8%</td><td>33</td><td>Iowa</td><td>4,035,000,000</td><td>0.9%</td></tr>
<tr><td>48</td><td>North Dakota</td><td>1,666,000,000</td><td>0.4%</td><td>34</td><td>West Virginia</td><td>3,809,000,000</td><td>0.8%</td></tr>
<tr><td>6</td><td>Ohio</td><td>17,152,000,000</td><td>3.7%</td><td>35</td><td>Kansas</td><td>3,618,000,000</td><td>0.8%</td></tr>
<tr><td>27</td><td>Oklahoma</td><td>5,502,000,000</td><td>1.2%</td><td>36</td><td>Alaska</td><td>3,131,000,000</td><td>0.7%</td></tr>
<tr><td>28</td><td>Oregon</td><td>5,466,000,000</td><td>1.2%</td><td>37</td><td>Utah</td><td>3,038,000,000</td><td>0.6%</td></tr>
<tr><td>5</td><td>Pennsylvania</td><td>19,869,000,000</td><td>4.2%</td><td>38</td><td>Nevada</td><td>2,926,000,000</td><td>0.6%</td></tr>
<tr><td>41</td><td>Rhode Island</td><td>2,325,000,000</td><td>0.5%</td><td>39</td><td>Maine</td><td>2,773,000,000</td><td>0.6%</td></tr>
<tr><td>26</td><td>South Carolina</td><td>6,324,000,000</td><td>1.3%</td><td>40</td><td>Nebraska</td><td>2,596,000,000</td><td>0.6%</td></tr>
<tr><td>47</td><td>South Dakota</td><td>1,742,000,000</td><td>0.4%</td><td>41</td><td>Rhode Island</td><td>2,325,000,000</td><td>0.5%</td></tr>
<tr><td>14</td><td>Tennessee</td><td>9,985,000,000</td><td>2.1%</td><td>42</td><td>Hawaii</td><td>2,168,000,000</td><td>0.5%</td></tr>
<tr><td>3</td><td>Texas</td><td>28,912,000,000</td><td>6.2%</td><td>43</td><td>Montana</td><td>2,140,000,000</td><td>0.5%</td></tr>
<tr><td>37</td><td>Utah</td><td>3,038,000,000</td><td>0.6%</td><td>44</td><td>Idaho</td><td>2,093,000,000</td><td>0.4%</td></tr>
<tr><td>49</td><td>Vermont</td><td>1,324,000,000</td><td>0.3%</td><td>45</td><td>Wyoming</td><td>1,899,000,000</td><td>0.4%</td></tr>
<tr><td>20</td><td>Virginia</td><td>7,745,000,000</td><td>1.6%</td><td>46</td><td>New Hampshire</td><td>1,795,000,000</td><td>0.4%</td></tr>
<tr><td>15</td><td>Washington</td><td>9,047,000,000</td><td>1.9%</td><td>47</td><td>South Dakota</td><td>1,742,000,000</td><td>0.4%</td></tr>
<tr><td>34</td><td>West Virginia</td><td>3,809,000,000</td><td>0.8%</td><td>48</td><td>North Dakota</td><td>1,666,000,000</td><td>0.4%</td></tr>
<tr><td>21</td><td>Wisconsin</td><td>7,538,000,000</td><td>1.6%</td><td>49</td><td>Vermont</td><td>1,324,000,000</td><td>0.3%</td></tr>
<tr><td>45</td><td>Wyoming</td><td>1,899,000,000</td><td>0.4%</td><td>50</td><td>Delaware</td><td>1,265,000,000</td><td>0.3%</td></tr>
<tr><td></td><td></td><td></td><td></td><td></td><td>District of Columbia</td><td>4,325,000,000</td><td>0.9%</td></tr>
</table>

Source: U.S. Bureau of the Census
   "Consolidated Federal Funds Report: 2005" (CFFR/05, Sept 2007, http://www.census.gov/govs/www/cffr05.html)
*Total includes $7,111,000,000 in U.S. territories ($5,973,000,000 in Puerto Rico) and $18,000,000 in expenditures not distributed by state.

Per Capita Expenditures for Federal Government Grants in 2005

National Per Capita = $1,563*

ALPHA ORDER

RANK	STATE	PER CAPITA
18	Alabama	$1,618
1	Alaska	4,677
34	Arizona	1,445
16	Arkansas	1,689
25	California	1,537
49	Colorado	1,162
21	Connecticut	1,560
27	Delaware	1,505
44	Florida	1,272
46	Georgia	1,226
15	Hawaii	1,710
32	Idaho	1,468
41	Illinois	1,308
42	Indiana	1,289
37	Iowa	1,365
39	Kansas	1,320
20	Kentucky	1,590
4	Louisiana	2,533
13	Maine	2,113
23	Maryland	1,551
11	Massachusetts	2,139
40	Michigan	1,317
33	Minnesota	1,463
8	Mississippi	2,264
24	Missouri	1,543
7	Montana	2,287
31	Nebraska	1,480
47	Nevada	1,215
36	New Hampshire	1,377
43	New Jersey	1,285
5	New Mexico	2,382
6	New York	2,369
29	North Carolina	1,493
3	North Dakota	2,620
28	Ohio	1,497
22	Oklahoma	1,556
26	Oregon	1,506
19	Pennsylvania	1,607
10	Rhode Island	2,180
30	South Carolina	1,486
9	South Dakota	2,233
17	Tennessee	1,667
45	Texas	1,266
48	Utah	1,213
12	Vermont	2,136
50	Virginia	1,025
35	Washington	1,443
14	West Virginia	2,110
38	Wisconsin	1,361
2	Wyoming	3,749

RANK ORDER

RANK	STATE	PER CAPITA
1	Alaska	$4,677
2	Wyoming	3,749
3	North Dakota	2,620
4	Louisiana	2,533
5	New Mexico	2,382
6	New York	2,369
7	Montana	2,287
8	Mississippi	2,264
9	South Dakota	2,233
10	Rhode Island	2,180
11	Massachusetts	2,139
12	Vermont	2,136
13	Maine	2,113
14	West Virginia	2,110
15	Hawaii	1,710
16	Arkansas	1,689
17	Tennessee	1,667
18	Alabama	1,618
19	Pennsylvania	1,607
20	Kentucky	1,590
21	Connecticut	1,560
22	Oklahoma	1,556
23	Maryland	1,551
24	Missouri	1,543
25	California	1,537
26	Oregon	1,506
27	Delaware	1,505
28	Ohio	1,497
29	North Carolina	1,493
30	South Carolina	1,486
31	Nebraska	1,480
32	Idaho	1,468
33	Minnesota	1,463
34	Arizona	1,445
35	Washington	1,443
36	New Hampshire	1,377
37	Iowa	1,365
38	Wisconsin	1,361
39	Kansas	1,320
40	Michigan	1,317
41	Illinois	1,308
42	Indiana	1,289
43	New Jersey	1,285
44	Florida	1,272
45	Texas	1,266
46	Georgia	1,226
47	Nevada	1,215
48	Utah	1,213
49	Colorado	1,162
50	Virginia	1,025
	District of Columbia	7,431

Source: CQ Press using data from U.S. Bureau of the Census
"Consolidated Federal Funds Report: 2005" (CFFR/05, Sept 2007, http://www.census.gov/govs/www/cffr05.html)
*National per capita excludes expenditures and population for territories and undistributed amounts.

Federal Government Procurement Contract Awards in 2005

National Total = $380,984,000,000*

ALPHA ORDER

RANK	STATE	EXPENDITURES	% of USA
14	Alabama	$8,557,000,000	2.2%
33	Alaska	2,412,000,000	0.6%
6	Arizona	10,756,000,000	2.8%
42	Arkansas	1,154,000,000	0.3%
1	California	43,267,000,000	11.4%
20	Colorado	6,253,000,000	1.6%
10	Connecticut	9,364,000,000	2.5%
50	Delaware	292,000,000	0.1%
5	Florida	14,296,000,000	3.8%
12	Georgia	8,964,000,000	2.4%
34	Hawaii	2,322,000,000	0.6%
38	Idaho	1,619,000,000	0.4%
18	Illinois	7,321,000,000	1.9%
23	Indiana	5,771,000,000	1.5%
37	Iowa	1,636,000,000	0.4%
30	Kansas	2,964,000,000	0.8%
21	Kentucky	6,130,000,000	1.6%
24	Louisiana	5,074,000,000	1.3%
35	Maine	1,917,000,000	0.5%
4	Maryland	21,843,000,000	5.7%
7	Massachusetts	10,430,000,000	2.7%
22	Michigan	5,849,000,000	1.5%
31	Minnesota	2,863,000,000	0.8%
27	Mississippi	4,145,000,000	1.1%
13	Missouri	8,762,000,000	2.3%
45	Montana	561,000,000	0.1%
43	Nebraska	793,000,000	0.2%
36	Nevada	1,912,000,000	0.5%
41	New Hampshire	1,185,000,000	0.3%
16	New Jersey	7,965,000,000	2.1%
19	New Mexico	6,402,000,000	1.7%
9	New York	9,604,000,000	2.5%
25	North Carolina	4,912,000,000	1.3%
48	North Dakota	504,000,000	0.1%
15	Ohio	8,195,000,000	2.2%
32	Oklahoma	2,767,000,000	0.7%
39	Oregon	1,427,000,000	0.4%
8	Pennsylvania	10,398,000,000	2.7%
46	Rhode Island	554,000,000	0.1%
26	South Carolina	4,844,000,000	1.3%
44	South Dakota	590,000,000	0.2%
11	Tennessee	9,080,000,000	2.4%
3	Texas	28,117,000,000	7.4%
29	Utah	2,978,000,000	0.8%
47	Vermont	523,000,000	0.1%
2	Virginia	38,610,000,000	10.1%
17	Washington	7,795,000,000	2.0%
40	West Virginia	1,188,000,000	0.3%
28	Wisconsin	3,607,000,000	0.9%
49	Wyoming	452,000,000	0.1%

RANK ORDER

RANK	STATE	EXPENDITURES	% of USA
1	California	$43,267,000,000	11.4%
2	Virginia	38,610,000,000	10.1%
3	Texas	28,117,000,000	7.4%
4	Maryland	21,843,000,000	5.7%
5	Florida	14,296,000,000	3.8%
6	Arizona	10,756,000,000	2.8%
7	Massachusetts	10,430,000,000	2.7%
8	Pennsylvania	10,398,000,000	2.7%
9	New York	9,604,000,000	2.5%
10	Connecticut	9,364,000,000	2.5%
11	Tennessee	9,080,000,000	2.4%
12	Georgia	8,964,000,000	2.4%
13	Missouri	8,762,000,000	2.3%
14	Alabama	8,557,000,000	2.2%
15	Ohio	8,195,000,000	2.2%
16	New Jersey	7,965,000,000	2.1%
17	Washington	7,795,000,000	2.0%
18	Illinois	7,321,000,000	1.9%
19	New Mexico	6,402,000,000	1.7%
20	Colorado	6,253,000,000	1.6%
21	Kentucky	6,130,000,000	1.6%
22	Michigan	5,849,000,000	1.5%
23	Indiana	5,771,000,000	1.5%
24	Louisiana	5,074,000,000	1.3%
25	North Carolina	4,912,000,000	1.3%
26	South Carolina	4,844,000,000	1.3%
27	Mississippi	4,145,000,000	1.1%
28	Wisconsin	3,607,000,000	0.9%
29	Utah	2,978,000,000	0.8%
30	Kansas	2,964,000,000	0.8%
31	Minnesota	2,863,000,000	0.8%
32	Oklahoma	2,767,000,000	0.7%
33	Alaska	2,412,000,000	0.6%
34	Hawaii	2,322,000,000	0.6%
35	Maine	1,917,000,000	0.5%
36	Nevada	1,912,000,000	0.5%
37	Iowa	1,636,000,000	0.4%
38	Idaho	1,619,000,000	0.4%
39	Oregon	1,427,000,000	0.4%
40	West Virginia	1,188,000,000	0.3%
41	New Hampshire	1,185,000,000	0.3%
42	Arkansas	1,154,000,000	0.3%
43	Nebraska	793,000,000	0.2%
44	South Dakota	590,000,000	0.2%
45	Montana	561,000,000	0.1%
46	Rhode Island	554,000,000	0.1%
47	Vermont	523,000,000	0.1%
48	North Dakota	504,000,000	0.1%
49	Wyoming	452,000,000	0.1%
50	Delaware	292,000,000	0.1%
	District of Columbia	13,324,000,000	3.5%

Source: U.S. Bureau of the Census
"Consolidated Federal Funds Report: 2005" (CFFR/05, Sept 2007, http://www.census.gov/govs/www/cffr05.html)
*Total includes $1,122,000,000 in U.S. territories ($506,000,000 in Puerto Rico) and $17,617,000,000 in expenditures not distributed by state.

Per Capita Expenditures for Federal Government Procurement Contract Awards in 2005
National Per Capita = $1,224*

ALPHA ORDER

RANK	STATE	PER CAPITA
6	Alabama	$1,885
3	Alaska	3,603
8	Arizona	1,807
48	Arkansas	416
18	California	1,202
15	Colorado	1,338
5	Connecticut	2,686
50	Delaware	347
31	Florida	806
24	Georgia	984
7	Hawaii	1,832
21	Idaho	1,135
41	Illinois	576
25	Indiana	922
44	Iowa	554
23	Kansas	1,081
12	Kentucky	1,470
22	Louisiana	1,129
13	Maine	1,461
2	Maryland	3,919
9	Massachusetts	1,622
40	Michigan	579
43	Minnesota	560
14	Mississippi	1,429
11	Missouri	1,514
39	Montana	599
47	Nebraska	452
32	Nevada	794
27	New Hampshire	909
26	New Jersey	920
4	New Mexico	3,341
46	New York	499
42	North Carolina	566
33	North Dakota	793
36	Ohio	715
34	Oklahoma	783
49	Oregon	393
30	Pennsylvania	841
45	Rhode Island	519
20	South Carolina	1,138
35	South Dakota	756
10	Tennessee	1,516
17	Texas	1,231
19	Utah	1,189
29	Vermont	844
1	Virginia	5,109
16	Washington	1,243
37	West Virginia	658
38	Wisconsin	651
28	Wyoming	892

RANK ORDER

RANK	STATE	PER CAPITA
1	Virginia	$5,109
2	Maryland	3,919
3	Alaska	3,603
4	New Mexico	3,341
5	Connecticut	2,686
6	Alabama	1,885
7	Hawaii	1,832
8	Arizona	1,807
9	Massachusetts	1,622
10	Tennessee	1,516
11	Missouri	1,514
12	Kentucky	1,470
13	Maine	1,461
14	Mississippi	1,429
15	Colorado	1,338
16	Washington	1,243
17	Texas	1,231
18	California	1,202
19	Utah	1,189
20	South Carolina	1,138
21	Idaho	1,135
22	Louisiana	1,129
23	Kansas	1,081
24	Georgia	984
25	Indiana	922
26	New Jersey	920
27	New Hampshire	909
28	Wyoming	892
29	Vermont	844
30	Pennsylvania	841
31	Florida	806
32	Nevada	794
33	North Dakota	793
34	Oklahoma	783
35	South Dakota	756
36	Ohio	715
37	West Virginia	658
38	Wisconsin	651
39	Montana	599
40	Michigan	579
41	Illinois	576
42	North Carolina	566
43	Minnesota	560
44	Iowa	554
45	Rhode Island	519
46	New York	499
47	Nebraska	452
48	Arkansas	416
49	Oregon	393
50	Delaware	347
	District of Columbia	22,892

Source: CQ Press using data from U.S. Bureau of the Census
"Consolidated Federal Funds Report: 2005" (CFFR/05, Sept 2007, http://www.census.gov/govs/www/cffr05.html)
*National per capita excludes expenditures and population for territories and undistributed amounts.

Federal Government Direct Payments for Retirement and Disability in 2005
National Total = $702,758,000,000*

ALPHA ORDER

RANK	STATE	PAYMENTS	% of USA
20	Alabama	$13,657,000,000	1.9%
50	Alaska	1,154,000,000	0.2%
19	Arizona	13,760,000,000	2.0%
30	Arkansas	7,835,000,000	1.1%
1	California	67,208,000,000	9.6%
27	Colorado	9,291,000,000	1.3%
29	Connecticut	8,122,000,000	1.2%
45	Delaware	2,226,000,000	0.3%
2	Florida	50,477,000,000	7.2%
12	Georgia	18,804,000,000	2.7%
40	Hawaii	3,319,000,000	0.5%
41	Idaho	3,260,000,000	0.5%
7	Illinois	27,356,000,000	3.9%
18	Indiana	14,818,000,000	2.1%
32	Iowa	7,294,000,000	1.0%
33	Kansas	6,678,000,000	1.0%
23	Kentucky	11,277,000,000	1.6%
25	Louisiana	10,520,000,000	1.5%
39	Maine	3,766,000,000	0.5%
16	Maryland	14,829,000,000	2.1%
15	Massachusetts	14,903,000,000	2.1%
8	Michigan	24,369,000,000	3.5%
24	Minnesota	10,640,000,000	1.5%
31	Mississippi	7,718,000,000	1.1%
17	Missouri	14,824,000,000	2.1%
44	Montana	2,515,000,000	0.4%
38	Nebraska	4,224,000,000	0.6%
35	Nevada	5,394,000,000	0.8%
42	New Hampshire	3,184,000,000	0.5%
11	New Jersey	19,846,000,000	2.8%
36	New Mexico	4,947,000,000	0.7%
4	New York	43,459,000,000	6.2%
10	North Carolina	21,478,000,000	3.1%
47	North Dakota	1,531,000,000	0.2%
6	Ohio	27,558,000,000	3.9%
26	Oklahoma	9,629,000,000	1.4%
28	Oregon	8,954,000,000	1.3%
5	Pennsylvania	34,732,000,000	4.9%
43	Rhode Island	2,727,000,000	0.4%
22	South Carolina	11,446,000,000	1.6%
46	South Dakota	1,929,000,000	0.3%
13	Tennessee	15,499,000,000	2.2%
3	Texas	44,113,000,000	6.3%
37	Utah	4,384,000,000	0.6%
48	Vermont	1,496,000,000	0.2%
9	Virginia	21,705,000,000	3.1%
14	Washington	15,199,000,000	2.2%
34	West Virginia	6,198,000,000	0.9%
21	Wisconsin	12,753,000,000	1.8%
49	Wyoming	1,248,000,000	0.2%

RANK ORDER

RANK	STATE	PAYMENTS	% of USA
1	California	$67,208,000,000	9.6%
2	Florida	50,477,000,000	7.2%
3	Texas	44,113,000,000	6.3%
4	New York	43,459,000,000	6.2%
5	Pennsylvania	34,732,000,000	4.9%
6	Ohio	27,558,000,000	3.9%
7	Illinois	27,356,000,000	3.9%
8	Michigan	24,369,000,000	3.5%
9	Virginia	21,705,000,000	3.1%
10	North Carolina	21,478,000,000	3.1%
11	New Jersey	19,846,000,000	2.8%
12	Georgia	18,804,000,000	2.7%
13	Tennessee	15,499,000,000	2.2%
14	Washington	15,199,000,000	2.2%
15	Massachusetts	14,903,000,000	2.1%
16	Maryland	14,829,000,000	2.1%
17	Missouri	14,824,000,000	2.1%
18	Indiana	14,818,000,000	2.1%
19	Arizona	13,760,000,000	2.0%
20	Alabama	13,657,000,000	1.9%
21	Wisconsin	12,753,000,000	1.8%
22	South Carolina	11,446,000,000	1.6%
23	Kentucky	11,277,000,000	1.6%
24	Minnesota	10,640,000,000	1.5%
25	Louisiana	10,520,000,000	1.5%
26	Oklahoma	9,629,000,000	1.4%
27	Colorado	9,291,000,000	1.3%
28	Oregon	8,954,000,000	1.3%
29	Connecticut	8,122,000,000	1.2%
30	Arkansas	7,835,000,000	1.1%
31	Mississippi	7,718,000,000	1.1%
32	Iowa	7,294,000,000	1.0%
33	Kansas	6,678,000,000	1.0%
34	West Virginia	6,198,000,000	0.9%
35	Nevada	5,394,000,000	0.8%
36	New Mexico	4,947,000,000	0.7%
37	Utah	4,384,000,000	0.6%
38	Nebraska	4,224,000,000	0.6%
39	Maine	3,766,000,000	0.5%
40	Hawaii	3,319,000,000	0.5%
41	Idaho	3,260,000,000	0.5%
42	New Hampshire	3,184,000,000	0.5%
43	Rhode Island	2,727,000,000	0.4%
44	Montana	2,515,000,000	0.4%
45	Delaware	2,226,000,000	0.3%
46	South Dakota	1,929,000,000	0.3%
47	North Dakota	1,531,000,000	0.2%
48	Vermont	1,496,000,000	0.2%
49	Wyoming	1,248,000,000	0.2%
50	Alaska	1,154,000,000	0.2%
	District of Columbia	2,046,000,000	0.3%

Source: U.S. Bureau of the Census
"Consolidated Federal Funds Report: 2005" (CFFR/05, Sept 2007, http://www.census.gov/govs/www/cffr05.html)
*Total includes $6,440,000,000 in U.S. territories ($5,973,000,000 in Puerto Rico) and $17,000,000 in expenditures not distributed by state. "Direct Payments for Retirement and Disability" include Social Security, federal retirement and disability payments, and veterans benefits.

Per Capita Federal Government Direct Payments for Retirement and Disability in 2005
National Per Capita = $2,353*

ALPHA ORDER

RANK	STATE	PER CAPITA
2	Alabama	$3,008
50	Alaska	1,724
37	Arizona	2,312
6	Arkansas	2,826
48	California	1,867
46	Colorado	1,988
35	Connecticut	2,330
14	Delaware	2,648
5	Florida	2,846
45	Georgia	2,065
15	Hawaii	2,618
40	Idaho	2,286
43	Illinois	2,151
33	Indiana	2,368
22	Iowa	2,468
26	Kansas	2,436
9	Kentucky	2,704
34	Louisiana	2,340
4	Maine	2,870
12	Maryland	2,661
36	Massachusetts	2,318
29	Michigan	2,411
44	Minnesota	2,081
12	Mississippi	2,661
18	Missouri	2,561
11	Montana	2,688
30	Nebraska	2,408
42	Nevada	2,239
25	New Hampshire	2,443
39	New Jersey	2,292
17	New Mexico	2,581
41	New York	2,256
20	North Carolina	2,475
31	North Dakota	2,407
32	Ohio	2,405
8	Oklahoma	2,723
23	Oregon	2,467
7	Pennsylvania	2,808
19	Rhode Island	2,556
10	South Carolina	2,690
21	South Dakota	2,473
16	Tennessee	2,588
47	Texas	1,931
49	Utah	1,750
28	Vermont	2,414
3	Virginia	2,872
27	Washington	2,424
1	West Virginia	3,433
38	Wisconsin	2,302
24	Wyoming	2,464

RANK ORDER

RANK	STATE	PER CAPITA
1	West Virginia	$3,433
2	Alabama	3,008
3	Virginia	2,872
4	Maine	2,870
5	Florida	2,846
6	Arkansas	2,826
7	Pennsylvania	2,808
8	Oklahoma	2,723
9	Kentucky	2,704
10	South Carolina	2,690
11	Montana	2,688
12	Maryland	2,661
12	Mississippi	2,661
14	Delaware	2,648
15	Hawaii	2,618
16	Tennessee	2,588
17	New Mexico	2,581
18	Missouri	2,561
19	Rhode Island	2,556
20	North Carolina	2,475
21	South Dakota	2,473
22	Iowa	2,468
23	Oregon	2,467
24	Wyoming	2,464
25	New Hampshire	2,443
26	Kansas	2,436
27	Washington	2,424
28	Vermont	2,414
29	Michigan	2,411
30	Nebraska	2,408
31	North Dakota	2,407
32	Ohio	2,405
33	Indiana	2,368
34	Louisiana	2,340
35	Connecticut	2,330
36	Massachusetts	2,318
37	Arizona	2,312
38	Wisconsin	2,302
39	New Jersey	2,292
40	Idaho	2,286
41	New York	2,256
42	Nevada	2,239
43	Illinois	2,151
44	Minnesota	2,081
45	Georgia	2,065
46	Colorado	1,988
47	Texas	1,931
48	California	1,867
49	Utah	1,750
50	Alaska	1,724

District of Columbia 3,515

Source: CQ Press using data from U.S. Bureau of the Census

"Consolidated Federal Funds Report: 2005" (CFFR/05, Sept 2007, http://www.census.gov/govs/www/cffr05.html)

*National per capita excludes expenditures and population for territories and undistributed amounts. "Direct Payments for Retirement and Disability" include Social Security, federal retirement and disability payments, and veterans benefits.

Federal Government "Other" Direct Payments in 2005

National Total = $499,928,000,000*

ALPHA ORDER

RANK	STATE	PAYMENTS	% of USA
19	Alabama	$8,919,000,000	1.8%
49	Alaska	684,000,000	0.1%
22	Arizona	7,752,000,000	1.6%
31	Arkansas	5,128,000,000	1.0%
1	California	53,841,000,000	10.8%
30	Colorado	5,498,000,000	1.1%
26	Connecticut	6,136,000,000	1.2%
47	Delaware	1,201,000,000	0.2%
3	Florida	36,557,000,000	7.3%
11	Georgia	12,322,000,000	2.5%
45	Hawaii	1,652,000,000	0.3%
43	Idaho	1,706,000,000	0.3%
6	Illinois	22,279,000,000	4.5%
14	Indiana	11,135,000,000	2.2%
28	Iowa	6,067,000,000	1.2%
33	Kansas	4,954,000,000	1.0%
24	Kentucky	7,127,000,000	1.4%
18	Louisiana	9,846,000,000	2.0%
42	Maine	1,955,000,000	0.4%
16	Maryland	10,611,000,000	2.1%
10	Massachusetts	13,057,000,000	2.6%
8	Michigan	17,533,000,000	3.5%
23	Minnesota	7,708,000,000	1.5%
29	Mississippi	5,738,000,000	1.1%
13	Missouri	11,515,000,000	2.3%
44	Montana	1,678,000,000	0.3%
34	Nebraska	3,839,000,000	0.8%
37	Nevada	2,440,000,000	0.5%
46	New Hampshire	1,479,000,000	0.3%
9	New Jersey	15,239,000,000	3.0%
36	New Mexico	2,585,000,000	0.5%
2	New York	36,590,000,000	7.3%
12	North Carolina	12,103,000,000	2.4%
40	North Dakota	2,102,000,000	0.4%
7	Ohio	19,252,000,000	3.9%
25	Oklahoma	6,212,000,000	1.2%
32	Oregon	5,008,000,000	1.0%
5	Pennsylvania	27,764,000,000	5.6%
41	Rhode Island	1,990,000,000	0.4%
27	South Carolina	6,129,000,000	1.2%
38	South Dakota	2,423,000,000	0.5%
17	Tennessee	10,200,000,000	2.0%
4	Texas	32,394,000,000	6.5%
39	Utah	2,178,000,000	0.4%
48	Vermont	873,000,000	0.2%
15	Virginia	11,037,000,000	2.2%
20	Washington	8,166,000,000	1.6%
35	West Virginia	3,469,000,000	0.7%
21	Wisconsin	7,898,000,000	1.6%
50	Wyoming	642,000,000	0.1%

RANK ORDER

RANK	STATE	PAYMENTS	% of USA
1	California	$53,841,000,000	10.8%
2	New York	36,590,000,000	7.3%
3	Florida	36,557,000,000	7.3%
4	Texas	32,394,000,000	6.5%
5	Pennsylvania	27,764,000,000	5.6%
6	Illinois	22,279,000,000	4.5%
7	Ohio	19,252,000,000	3.9%
8	Michigan	17,533,000,000	3.5%
9	New Jersey	15,239,000,000	3.0%
10	Massachusetts	13,057,000,000	2.6%
11	Georgia	12,322,000,000	2.5%
12	North Carolina	12,103,000,000	2.4%
13	Missouri	11,515,000,000	2.3%
14	Indiana	11,135,000,000	2.2%
15	Virginia	11,037,000,000	2.2%
16	Maryland	10,611,000,000	2.1%
17	Tennessee	10,200,000,000	2.0%
18	Louisiana	9,846,000,000	2.0%
19	Alabama	8,919,000,000	1.8%
20	Washington	8,166,000,000	1.6%
21	Wisconsin	7,898,000,000	1.6%
22	Arizona	7,752,000,000	1.6%
23	Minnesota	7,708,000,000	1.5%
24	Kentucky	7,127,000,000	1.4%
25	Oklahoma	6,212,000,000	1.2%
26	Connecticut	6,136,000,000	1.2%
27	South Carolina	6,129,000,000	1.2%
28	Iowa	6,067,000,000	1.2%
29	Mississippi	5,738,000,000	1.1%
30	Colorado	5,498,000,000	1.1%
31	Arkansas	5,128,000,000	1.0%
32	Oregon	5,008,000,000	1.0%
33	Kansas	4,954,000,000	1.0%
34	Nebraska	3,839,000,000	0.8%
35	West Virginia	3,469,000,000	0.7%
36	New Mexico	2,585,000,000	0.5%
37	Nevada	2,440,000,000	0.5%
38	South Dakota	2,423,000,000	0.5%
39	Utah	2,178,000,000	0.4%
40	North Dakota	2,102,000,000	0.4%
41	Rhode Island	1,990,000,000	0.4%
42	Maine	1,955,000,000	0.4%
43	Idaho	1,706,000,000	0.3%
44	Montana	1,678,000,000	0.3%
45	Hawaii	1,652,000,000	0.3%
46	New Hampshire	1,479,000,000	0.3%
47	Delaware	1,201,000,000	0.2%
48	Vermont	873,000,000	0.2%
49	Alaska	684,000,000	0.1%
50	Wyoming	642,000,000	0.1%
	District of Columbia	2,353,000,000	0.5%

Source: U.S. Bureau of the Census
"Consolidated Federal Funds Report: 2005" (CFFR/05, Sept 2007, http://www.census.gov/govs/www/cffr05.html)
*Total includes $2,856,000,000 in U.S. territories ($2,662,000,000 in Puerto Rico) and $107,000,000 in expenditures not distributed by state. "Other Direct Payments" include direct payments for programs other than retirement and disability. These include Medicare, excess earned income tax credits, unemployment compensation, food stamps, housing assistance, and agricultural assistance.

Per Capita Expenditures for Federal Government "Other" Direct Payments in 2005
National Per Capita = $1,680*

ALPHA ORDER

RANK	STATE	PER CAPITA
11	Alabama	$1,965
48	Alaska	1,022
42	Arizona	1,302
16	Arkansas	1,850
29	California	1,496
46	Colorado	1,176
20	Connecticut	1,760
33	Delaware	1,429
6	Florida	2,061
39	Georgia	1,353
41	Hawaii	1,303
45	Idaho	1,196
23	Illinois	1,752
19	Indiana	1,780
7	Iowa	2,053
17	Kansas	1,807
25	Kentucky	1,709
4	Louisiana	2,190
30	Maine	1,490
13	Maryland	1,904
8	Massachusetts	2,031
24	Michigan	1,735
28	Minnesota	1,507
10	Mississippi	1,978
9	Missouri	1,990
18	Montana	1,793
5	Nebraska	2,189
49	Nevada	1,013
47	New Hampshire	1,135
20	New Jersey	1,760
40	New Mexico	1,349
14	New York	1,900
37	North Carolina	1,395
1	North Dakota	3,305
27	Ohio	1,680
22	Oklahoma	1,757
38	Oregon	1,380
3	Pennsylvania	2,245
15	Rhode Island	1,866
32	South Carolina	1,440
2	South Dakota	3,106
26	Tennessee	1,703
35	Texas	1,418
50	Utah	869
36	Vermont	1,409
31	Virginia	1,460
42	Washington	1,302
12	West Virginia	1,921
34	Wisconsin	1,426
44	Wyoming	1,267

RANK ORDER

RANK	STATE	PER CAPITA
1	North Dakota	$3,305
2	South Dakota	3,106
3	Pennsylvania	2,245
4	Louisiana	2,190
5	Nebraska	2,189
6	Florida	2,061
7	Iowa	2,053
8	Massachusetts	2,031
9	Missouri	1,990
10	Mississippi	1,978
11	Alabama	1,965
12	West Virginia	1,921
13	Maryland	1,904
14	New York	1,900
15	Rhode Island	1,866
16	Arkansas	1,850
17	Kansas	1,807
18	Montana	1,793
19	Indiana	1,780
20	Connecticut	1,760
20	New Jersey	1,760
22	Oklahoma	1,757
23	Illinois	1,752
24	Michigan	1,735
25	Kentucky	1,709
26	Tennessee	1,703
27	Ohio	1,680
28	Minnesota	1,507
29	California	1,496
30	Maine	1,490
31	Virginia	1,460
32	South Carolina	1,440
33	Delaware	1,429
34	Wisconsin	1,426
35	Texas	1,418
36	Vermont	1,409
37	North Carolina	1,395
38	Oregon	1,380
39	Georgia	1,353
40	New Mexico	1,349
41	Hawaii	1,303
42	Arizona	1,302
42	Washington	1,302
44	Wyoming	1,267
45	Idaho	1,196
46	Colorado	1,176
47	New Hampshire	1,135
48	Alaska	1,022
49	Nevada	1,013
50	Utah	869

District of Columbia 4,043

Source: CQ Press using data from U.S. Bureau of the Census
"Consolidated Federal Funds Report: 2005" (CFFR/05, Sept 2007, http://www.census.gov/govs/www/cffr05.html)
*National per capita excludes expenditures and population for territories and undistributed amounts. "Other Direct Payments" include direct payments for programs other than retirement and disability. These include Medicare, excess earned income tax credits, unemployment compensation, food stamps, housing assistance, and agricultural assistance.

Federal Government Expenditures for Salaries and Wages in 2005

National Total = $231,511,000,000*

ALPHA ORDER

RANK	STATE	SALARIES	% of USA
19	Alabama	$3,581,000,000	1.5%
34	Alaska	1,848,000,000	0.8%
16	Arizona	3,768,000,000	1.6%
36	Arkansas	1,589,000,000	0.7%
1	California	22,373,000,000	9.7%
13	Colorado	4,697,000,000	2.0%
35	Connecticut	1,712,000,000	0.7%
49	Delaware	511,000,000	0.2%
5	Florida	10,662,000,000	4.6%
7	Georgia	8,589,000,000	3.7%
24	Hawaii	3,238,000,000	1.4%
42	Idaho	920,000,000	0.4%
9	Illinois	7,188,000,000	3.1%
26	Indiana	2,559,000,000	1.1%
40	Iowa	1,312,000,000	0.6%
28	Kansas	2,278,000,000	1.0%
22	Kentucky	3,485,000,000	1.5%
25	Louisiana	2,800,000,000	1.2%
41	Maine	945,000,000	0.4%
4	Maryland	10,794,000,000	4.7%
18	Massachusetts	3,692,000,000	1.6%
17	Michigan	3,722,000,000	1.6%
27	Minnesota	2,372,000,000	1.0%
31	Mississippi	2,012,000,000	0.9%
15	Missouri	4,242,000,000	1.8%
42	Montana	920,000,000	0.4%
39	Nebraska	1,334,000,000	0.6%
38	Nevada	1,417,000,000	0.6%
47	New Hampshire	688,000,000	0.3%
14	New Jersey	4,442,000,000	1.9%
30	New Mexico	2,105,000,000	0.9%
6	New York	9,592,000,000	4.1%
8	North Carolina	7,711,000,000	3.3%
45	North Dakota	806,000,000	0.3%
12	Ohio	5,724,000,000	2.5%
20	Oklahoma	3,527,000,000	1.5%
33	Oregon	1,936,000,000	0.8%
10	Pennsylvania	6,739,000,000	2.9%
44	Rhode Island	827,000,000	0.4%
23	South Carolina	3,301,000,000	1.4%
46	South Dakota	798,000,000	0.3%
21	Tennessee	3,524,000,000	1.5%
3	Texas	15,146,000,000	6.5%
29	Utah	2,244,000,000	1.0%
50	Vermont	429,000,000	0.2%
2	Virginia	16,001,000,000	6.9%
11	Washington	6,132,000,000	2.6%
37	West Virginia	1,423,000,000	0.6%
32	Wisconsin	1,953,000,000	0.8%
48	Wyoming	541,000,000	0.2%

RANK ORDER

RANK	STATE	SALARIES	% of USA
1	California	$22,373,000,000	9.7%
2	Virginia	16,001,000,000	6.9%
3	Texas	15,146,000,000	6.5%
4	Maryland	10,794,000,000	4.7%
5	Florida	10,662,000,000	4.6%
6	New York	9,592,000,000	4.1%
7	Georgia	8,589,000,000	3.7%
8	North Carolina	7,711,000,000	3.3%
9	Illinois	7,188,000,000	3.1%
10	Pennsylvania	6,739,000,000	2.9%
11	Washington	6,132,000,000	2.6%
12	Ohio	5,724,000,000	2.5%
13	Colorado	4,697,000,000	2.0%
14	New Jersey	4,442,000,000	1.9%
15	Missouri	4,242,000,000	1.8%
16	Arizona	3,768,000,000	1.6%
17	Michigan	3,722,000,000	1.6%
18	Massachusetts	3,692,000,000	1.6%
19	Alabama	3,581,000,000	1.5%
20	Oklahoma	3,527,000,000	1.5%
21	Tennessee	3,524,000,000	1.5%
22	Kentucky	3,485,000,000	1.5%
23	South Carolina	3,301,000,000	1.4%
24	Hawaii	3,238,000,000	1.4%
25	Louisiana	2,800,000,000	1.2%
26	Indiana	2,559,000,000	1.1%
27	Minnesota	2,372,000,000	1.0%
28	Kansas	2,278,000,000	1.0%
29	Utah	2,244,000,000	1.0%
30	New Mexico	2,105,000,000	0.9%
31	Mississippi	2,012,000,000	0.9%
32	Wisconsin	1,953,000,000	0.8%
33	Oregon	1,936,000,000	0.8%
34	Alaska	1,848,000,000	0.8%
35	Connecticut	1,712,000,000	0.7%
36	Arkansas	1,589,000,000	0.7%
37	West Virginia	1,423,000,000	0.6%
38	Nevada	1,417,000,000	0.6%
39	Nebraska	1,334,000,000	0.6%
40	Iowa	1,312,000,000	0.6%
41	Maine	945,000,000	0.4%
42	Idaho	920,000,000	0.4%
42	Montana	920,000,000	0.4%
44	Rhode Island	827,000,000	0.4%
45	North Dakota	806,000,000	0.3%
46	South Dakota	798,000,000	0.3%
47	New Hampshire	688,000,000	0.3%
48	Wyoming	541,000,000	0.2%
49	Delaware	511,000,000	0.2%
50	Vermont	429,000,000	0.2%
	District of Columbia	15,811,000,000	6.8%

Source: U.S. Bureau of the Census

"Consolidated Federal Funds Report: 2005" (CFFR/05, Sept 2007, http://www.census.gov/govs/www/cffr05.html)

*Total includes $1,472,000,000 in U.S. territories ($1,061,000,000 in Puerto Rico) and $4,080,000,000 in expenditures not distributed by state.

Per Capita Expenditures for Federal Government Salaries and Wages in 2005

National Per Capita = $764*

RANK	STATE	PER CAPITA		RANK	STATE	PER CAPITA
ALPHA ORDER				RANK ORDER		
18	Alabama	$789		1	Alaska	$2,761
1	Alaska	2,761		2	Hawaii	2,554
29	Arizona	633		3	Virginia	2,117
37	Arkansas	573		4	Maryland	1,937
31	California	622		5	North Dakota	1,267
9	Colorado	1,005		6	New Mexico	1,098
45	Connecticut	491		7	Wyoming	1,068
32	Delaware	608		8	South Dakota	1,023
33	Florida	601		9	Colorado	1,005
13	Georgia	943		10	Oklahoma	997
2	Hawaii	2,554		11	Montana	983
28	Idaho	645		12	Washington	978
38	Illinois	565		13	Georgia	943
48	Indiana	409		14	Utah	896
47	Iowa	444		15	North Carolina	888
17	Kansas	831		16	Kentucky	836
16	Kentucky	836		17	Kansas	831
30	Louisiana	623		18	Alabama	789
24	Maine	720		19	West Virginia	788
4	Maryland	1,937		20	South Carolina	776
36	Massachusetts	574		21	Rhode Island	775
49	Michigan	368		22	Nebraska	761
46	Minnesota	464		23	Missouri	733
25	Mississippi	694		24	Maine	720
23	Missouri	733		25	Mississippi	694
11	Montana	983		26	Vermont	692
22	Nebraska	761		27	Texas	663
34	Nevada	588		28	Idaho	645
41	New Hampshire	528		29	Arizona	633
42	New Jersey	513		30	Louisiana	623
6	New Mexico	1,098		31	California	622
44	New York	498		32	Delaware	608
15	North Carolina	888		33	Florida	601
5	North Dakota	1,267		34	Nevada	588
43	Ohio	499		34	Tennessee	588
10	Oklahoma	997		36	Massachusetts	574
40	Oregon	533		37	Arkansas	573
39	Pennsylvania	545		38	Illinois	565
21	Rhode Island	775		39	Pennsylvania	545
20	South Carolina	776		40	Oregon	533
8	South Dakota	1,023		41	New Hampshire	528
34	Tennessee	588		42	New Jersey	513
27	Texas	663		43	Ohio	499
14	Utah	896		44	New York	498
26	Vermont	692		45	Connecticut	491
3	Virginia	2,117		46	Minnesota	464
12	Washington	978		47	Iowa	444
19	West Virginia	788		48	Indiana	409
50	Wisconsin	352		49	Michigan	368
7	Wyoming	1,068		50	Wisconsin	352
				District of Columbia		27,164

Source: CQ Press using data from U.S. Bureau of the Census

"Consolidated Federal Funds Report: 2005" (CFFR/05, Sept 2007, http://www.census.gov/govs/www/cffr05.html)

*National per capita excludes expenditures and population for territories and undistributed amounts.

Average Salary of Federal Civilian Employees in 2004

National Average = $60,772*

ALPHA ORDER

RANK	STATE	SALARY		RANK	STATE	SALARY
13	Alabama	$60,364		1	Maryland	$72,636
31	Alaska	53,499		2	New Hampshire	70,174
44	Arizona	51,372		3	Virginia	67,482
46	Arkansas	50,972		4	Rhode Island	66,594
11	California	60,904		5	New Jersey	66,118
8	Colorado	62,289		6	Ohio	62,683
10	Connecticut	61,242		7	Illinois	62,388
37	Delaware	53,017		8	Colorado	62,289
20	Florida	56,151		9	Massachusetts	61,351
17	Georgia	57,216		10	Connecticut	61,242
42	Hawaii	52,057		11	California	60,904
27	Idaho	54,292		12	Michigan	60,536
7	Illinois	62,388		13	Alabama	60,364
18	Indiana	56,381		14	New York	59,700
40	Iowa	52,354		15	Minnesota	58,304
28	Kansas	54,104		16	Washington	58,124
50	Kentucky	49,526		17	Georgia	57,216
33	Louisiana	53,285		18	Indiana	56,381
35	Maine	53,208		19	Oregon	56,305
1	Maryland	72,636		20	Florida	56,151
9	Massachusetts	61,351		21	Nevada	55,901
12	Michigan	60,536		22	Texas	55,726
15	Minnesota	58,304		23	Tennessee	55,661
34	Mississippi	53,242		24	West Virginia	55,544
36	Missouri	53,083		25	Pennsylvania	54,754
41	Montana	52,261		26	New Mexico	54,650
30	Nebraska	53,537		27	Idaho	54,292
21	Nevada	55,901		28	Kansas	54,104
2	New Hampshire	70,174		29	South Carolina	53,680
5	New Jersey	66,118		30	Nebraska	53,537
26	New Mexico	54,650		31	Alaska	53,499
14	New York	59,700		32	Wisconsin	53,348
39	North Carolina	52,523		33	Louisiana	53,285
48	North Dakota	50,482		34	Mississippi	53,242
6	Ohio	62,683		35	Maine	53,208
38	Oklahoma	52,855		36	Missouri	53,083
19	Oregon	56,305		37	Delaware	53,017
25	Pennsylvania	54,754		38	Oklahoma	52,855
4	Rhode Island	66,594		39	North Carolina	52,523
29	South Carolina	53,680		40	Iowa	52,354
49	South Dakota	49,605		41	Montana	52,261
23	Tennessee	55,661		42	Hawaii	52,057
22	Texas	55,726		43	Vermont	51,723
47	Utah	50,538		44	Arizona	51,372
43	Vermont	51,723		45	Wyoming	51,079
3	Virginia	67,482		46	Arkansas	50,972
16	Washington	58,124		47	Utah	50,538
24	West Virginia	55,544		48	North Dakota	50,482
32	Wisconsin	53,348		49	South Dakota	49,605
45	Wyoming	51,079		50	Kentucky	49,526
					District of Columbia	79,680

Source: Office of Personnel Management
"The Fact Book: 2005 Edition" (http://www.opm.gov/feddata/factbook/)
*Full-time employees. National average includes employees not shown by state.

Federal Civilian Employees in 2004

National Total = 1,690,528 Full-Time Employees*

RANK	STATE	EMPLOYEES	% of USA
12	Alabama	35,695	2.1%
34	Alaska	12,053	0.7%
16	Arizona	32,822	1.9%
35	Arkansas	11,791	0.7%
1	California	143,772	8.5%
13	Colorado	33,627	2.0%
44	Connecticut	6,970	0.4%
50	Delaware	2,583	0.2%
5	Florida	70,684	4.2%
6	Georgia	64,282	3.8%
25	Hawaii	20,758	1.2%
41	Idaho	8,056	0.5%
10	Illinois	42,809	2.5%
27	Indiana	18,595	1.1%
42	Iowa	7,268	0.4%
31	Kansas	15,410	0.9%
24	Kentucky	20,783	1.2%
26	Louisiana	19,931	1.2%
37	Maine	9,083	0.5%
4	Maryland	104,087	6.2%
21	Massachusetts	25,118	1.5%
22	Michigan	23,582	1.4%
32	Minnesota	14,313	0.8%
29	Mississippi	16,734	1.0%
17	Missouri	32,792	1.9%
39	Montana	8,971	0.5%
40	Nebraska	8,624	0.5%
38	Nevada	9,048	0.5%
49	New Hampshire	3,224	0.2%
19	New Jersey	27,223	1.6%
23	New Mexico	21,700	1.3%
8	New York	58,958	3.5%
18	North Carolina	32,406	1.9%
46	North Dakota	5,517	0.3%
11	Ohio	41,791	2.5%
14	Oklahoma	33,421	2.0%
28	Oregon	18,440	1.1%
7	Pennsylvania	62,821	3.7%
45	Rhode Island	6,120	0.4%
30	South Carolina	16,249	1.0%
43	South Dakota	7,059	0.4%
15	Tennessee	33,143	2.0%
3	Texas	108,071	6.4%
20	Utah	27,018	1.6%
48	Vermont	3,696	0.2%
2	Virginia	119,184	7.1%
9	Washington	45,538	2.7%
33	West Virginia	12,605	0.7%
36	Wisconsin	11,637	0.7%
47	Wyoming	4,870	0.3%

RANK	STATE	EMPLOYEES	% of USA
1	California	143,772	8.5%
2	Virginia	119,184	7.1%
3	Texas	108,071	6.4%
4	Maryland	104,087	6.2%
5	Florida	70,684	4.2%
6	Georgia	64,282	3.8%
7	Pennsylvania	62,821	3.7%
8	New York	58,958	3.5%
9	Washington	45,538	2.7%
10	Illinois	42,809	2.5%
11	Ohio	41,791	2.5%
12	Alabama	35,695	2.1%
13	Colorado	33,627	2.0%
14	Oklahoma	33,421	2.0%
15	Tennessee	33,143	2.0%
16	Arizona	32,822	1.9%
17	Missouri	32,792	1.9%
18	North Carolina	32,406	1.9%
19	New Jersey	27,223	1.6%
20	Utah	27,018	1.6%
21	Massachusetts	25,118	1.5%
22	Michigan	23,582	1.4%
23	New Mexico	21,700	1.3%
24	Kentucky	20,783	1.2%
25	Hawaii	20,758	1.2%
26	Louisiana	19,931	1.2%
27	Indiana	18,595	1.1%
28	Oregon	18,440	1.1%
29	Mississippi	16,734	1.0%
30	South Carolina	16,249	1.0%
31	Kansas	15,410	0.9%
32	Minnesota	14,313	0.8%
33	West Virginia	12,605	0.7%
34	Alaska	12,053	0.7%
35	Arkansas	11,791	0.7%
36	Wisconsin	11,637	0.7%
37	Maine	9,083	0.5%
38	Nevada	9,048	0.5%
39	Montana	8,971	0.5%
40	Nebraska	8,624	0.5%
41	Idaho	8,056	0.5%
42	Iowa	7,268	0.4%
43	South Dakota	7,059	0.4%
44	Connecticut	6,970	0.4%
45	Rhode Island	6,120	0.4%
46	North Dakota	5,517	0.3%
47	Wyoming	4,870	0.3%
48	Vermont	3,696	0.2%
49	New Hampshire	3,224	0.2%
50	Delaware	2,583	0.2%
	District of Columbia	150,631	8.9%

Source: Office of Personnel Management
"The Fact Book: 2005 Edition" (http://www.opm.gov/feddata/factbook/)
*Full-time employees. National total includes 18,965 employees not shown by state.

Rate of Federal Civilian Employees in 2004

National Rate = 58 Full-Time Employees per 10,000 Population*

ALPHA ORDER				RANK ORDER		
RANK	STATE	RATE		RANK	STATE	RATE
12	Alabama	79		1	Maryland	187
2	Alaska	184		2	Alaska	184
21	Arizona	57		3	Hawaii	165
32	Arkansas	43		4	Virginia	159
34	California	40		5	New Mexico	114
13	Colorado	73		6	Utah	112
50	Connecticut	20		7	Montana	97
41	Delaware	31		8	Wyoming	96
33	Florida	41		9	Oklahoma	95
15	Georgia	72		10	South Dakota	92
3	Hawaii	165		11	North Dakota	87
19	Idaho	58		12	Alabama	79
40	Illinois	34		13	Colorado	73
44	Indiana	30		13	Washington	73
46	Iowa	25		15	Georgia	72
24	Kansas	56		16	West Virginia	70
28	Kentucky	50		17	Maine	69
31	Louisiana	44		18	Vermont	60
17	Maine	69		19	Idaho	58
1	Maryland	187		19	Mississippi	58
35	Massachusetts	39		21	Arizona	57
48	Michigan	23		21	Missouri	57
45	Minnesota	28		21	Rhode Island	57
19	Mississippi	58		24	Kansas	56
21	Missouri	57		24	Tennessee	56
7	Montana	97		26	Oregon	51
29	Nebraska	49		26	Pennsylvania	51
35	Nevada	39		28	Kentucky	50
46	New Hampshire	25		29	Nebraska	49
41	New Jersey	31		30	Texas	48
5	New Mexico	114		31	Louisiana	44
41	New York	31		32	Arkansas	43
38	North Carolina	38		33	Florida	41
11	North Dakota	87		34	California	40
39	Ohio	36		35	Massachusetts	39
9	Oklahoma	95		35	Nevada	39
26	Oregon	51		35	South Carolina	39
26	Pennsylvania	51		38	North Carolina	38
21	Rhode Island	57		39	Ohio	36
35	South Carolina	39		40	Illinois	34
10	South Dakota	92		41	Delaware	31
24	Tennessee	56		41	New Jersey	31
30	Texas	48		41	New York	31
6	Utah	112		44	Indiana	30
18	Vermont	60		45	Minnesota	28
4	Virginia	159		46	Iowa	25
13	Washington	73		46	New Hampshire	25
16	West Virginia	70		48	Michigan	23
49	Wisconsin	21		49	Wisconsin	21
8	Wyoming	96		50	Connecticut	20
					District of Columbia	2,598

Source: CQ Press using data from Office of Personnel Management
   "The Fact Book: 2005 Edition" (http://www.opm.gov/feddata/factbook/)
*Full-time employees. National rate includes employees not shown by state.

X. Government Finances: State and Local

A Note About Fiscal Years

State and Local
Data in these tables relate to the state and local governments' 12-month fiscal years. The data reflect individual government fiscal years that ended between July 1 and the following June 30.

State
The statistics show state government data for fiscal years that end on June 30, except for four states with other ending dates: Alabama and Michigan (September 30), New York (March 31) and Texas (August 31).

State and Local Government Total Revenue in 2005

National Total = $2,523,005,780,000*

ALPHA ORDER					RANK ORDER			

RANK	STATE	REVENUE	% of USA
24	Alabama	$33,606,093,000	1.3%
40	Alaska	11,334,457,000	0.4%
21	Arizona	41,134,826,000	1.6%
35	Arkansas	18,876,794,000	0.7%
1	California	380,476,699,000	15.1%
22	Colorado	38,930,181,000	1.5%
27	Connecticut	30,584,258,000	1.2%
46	Delaware	7,638,188,000	0.3%
4	Florida	135,338,670,000	5.4%
12	Georgia	60,292,959,000	2.4%
41	Hawaii	11,000,269,000	0.4%
42	Idaho	10,003,867,000	0.4%
7	Illinois	100,447,028,000	4.0%
18	Indiana	43,792,014,000	1.7%
30	Iowa	23,249,871,000	0.9%
32	Kansas	19,921,338,000	0.8%
28	Kentucky	28,043,814,000	1.1%
23	Louisiana	35,847,751,000	1.4%
39	Maine	11,346,337,000	0.4%
17	Maryland	45,327,471,000	1.8%
11	Massachusetts	61,507,149,000	2.4%
8	Michigan	81,370,429,000	3.2%
16	Minnesota	45,464,495,000	1.8%
31	Mississippi	21,092,104,000	0.8%
20	Missouri	41,339,990,000	1.6%
47	Montana	7,438,139,000	0.3%
37	Nebraska	15,883,267,000	0.6%
34	Nevada	18,953,181,000	0.8%
44	New Hampshire	8,924,491,000	0.4%
9	New Jersey	77,812,162,000	3.1%
36	New Mexico	16,649,605,000	0.7%
2	New York	231,011,453,000	9.2%
10	North Carolina	64,823,562,000	2.6%
50	North Dakota	5,240,123,000	0.2%
6	Ohio	102,601,496,000	4.1%
29	Oklahoma	24,552,073,000	1.0%
26	Oregon	32,392,874,000	1.3%
5	Pennsylvania	103,730,295,000	4.1%
43	Rhode Island	9,729,274,000	0.4%
25	South Carolina	33,276,639,000	1.3%
48	South Dakota	5,824,750,000	0.2%
19	Tennessee	43,686,248,000	1.7%
3	Texas	163,057,453,000	6.5%
33	Utah	19,186,196,000	0.8%
49	Vermont	5,392,814,000	0.2%
14	Virginia	56,858,890,000	2.3%
13	Washington	57,586,458,000	2.3%
38	West Virginia	14,739,417,000	0.6%
15	Wisconsin	48,429,818,000	1.9%
45	Wyoming	7,931,306,000	0.3%

RANK	STATE	REVENUE	% of USA
1	California	$380,476,699,000	15.1%
2	New York	231,011,453,000	9.2%
3	Texas	163,057,453,000	6.5%
4	Florida	135,338,670,000	5.4%
5	Pennsylvania	103,730,295,000	4.1%
6	Ohio	102,601,496,000	4.1%
7	Illinois	100,447,028,000	4.0%
8	Michigan	81,370,429,000	3.2%
9	New Jersey	77,812,162,000	3.1%
10	North Carolina	64,823,562,000	2.6%
11	Massachusetts	61,507,149,000	2.4%
12	Georgia	60,292,959,000	2.4%
13	Washington	57,586,458,000	2.3%
14	Virginia	56,858,890,000	2.3%
15	Wisconsin	48,429,818,000	1.9%
16	Minnesota	45,464,495,000	1.8%
17	Maryland	45,327,471,000	1.8%
18	Indiana	43,792,014,000	1.7%
19	Tennessee	43,686,248,000	1.7%
20	Missouri	41,339,990,000	1.6%
21	Arizona	41,134,826,000	1.6%
22	Colorado	38,930,181,000	1.5%
23	Louisiana	35,847,751,000	1.4%
24	Alabama	33,606,093,000	1.3%
25	South Carolina	33,276,639,000	1.3%
26	Oregon	32,392,874,000	1.3%
27	Connecticut	30,584,258,000	1.2%
28	Kentucky	28,043,814,000	1.1%
29	Oklahoma	24,552,073,000	1.0%
30	Iowa	23,249,871,000	0.9%
31	Mississippi	21,092,104,000	0.8%
32	Kansas	19,921,338,000	0.8%
33	Utah	19,186,196,000	0.8%
34	Nevada	18,953,181,000	0.8%
35	Arkansas	18,876,794,000	0.7%
36	New Mexico	16,649,605,000	0.7%
37	Nebraska	15,883,267,000	0.6%
38	West Virginia	14,739,417,000	0.6%
39	Maine	11,346,337,000	0.4%
40	Alaska	11,334,457,000	0.4%
41	Hawaii	11,000,269,000	0.4%
42	Idaho	10,003,867,000	0.4%
43	Rhode Island	9,729,274,000	0.4%
44	New Hampshire	8,924,491,000	0.4%
45	Wyoming	7,931,306,000	0.3%
46	Delaware	7,638,188,000	0.3%
47	Montana	7,438,139,000	0.3%
48	South Dakota	5,824,750,000	0.2%
49	Vermont	5,392,814,000	0.2%
50	North Dakota	5,240,123,000	0.2%
	District of Columbia	9,326,744,000	0.4%

Source: U.S. Bureau of the Census, Governments Division
  "State and Local Government Finances: 2004-2005" (http://www.census.gov/govs/www/estimate05.html)
*Total revenue includes all money received from external sources. This includes taxes, intergovernmental transfers and insurance trust revenue, and revenue from government owned utilities and other commercial or auxiliary enterprise.

Per Capita State and Local Government Revenue in 2005

National Per Capita = $8,527*

<table>
<tr><td colspan="3">ALPHA ORDER</td><td colspan="3">RANK ORDER</td></tr>
<tr><td>RANK</td><td>STATE</td><td>PER CAPITA</td><td>RANK</td><td>STATE</td><td>PER CAPITA</td></tr>
<tr><td>37</td><td>Alabama</td><td>$7,403</td><td>1</td><td>Alaska</td><td>$16,932</td></tr>
<tr><td>1</td><td>Alaska</td><td>16,932</td><td>2</td><td>Wyoming</td><td>15,658</td></tr>
<tr><td>46</td><td>Arizona</td><td>6,911</td><td>3</td><td>New York</td><td>11,993</td></tr>
<tr><td>48</td><td>Arkansas</td><td>6,809</td><td>4</td><td>California</td><td>10,572</td></tr>
<tr><td>4</td><td>California</td><td>10,572</td><td>5</td><td>Massachusetts</td><td>9,567</td></tr>
<tr><td>21</td><td>Colorado</td><td>8,330</td><td>6</td><td>Washington</td><td>9,183</td></tr>
<tr><td>14</td><td>Connecticut</td><td>8,772</td><td>7</td><td>Rhode Island</td><td>9,121</td></tr>
<tr><td>8</td><td>Delaware</td><td>9,087</td><td>8</td><td>Delaware</td><td>9,087</td></tr>
<tr><td>33</td><td>Florida</td><td>7,631</td><td>9</td><td>Nebraska</td><td>9,055</td></tr>
<tr><td>50</td><td>Georgia</td><td>6,620</td><td>10</td><td>New Jersey</td><td>8,988</td></tr>
<tr><td>18</td><td>Hawaii</td><td>8,678</td><td>11</td><td>Ohio</td><td>8,953</td></tr>
<tr><td>43</td><td>Idaho</td><td>7,016</td><td>12</td><td>Oregon</td><td>8,924</td></tr>
<tr><td>28</td><td>Illinois</td><td>7,897</td><td>13</td><td>Minnesota</td><td>8,891</td></tr>
<tr><td>44</td><td>Indiana</td><td>6,999</td><td>14</td><td>Connecticut</td><td>8,772</td></tr>
<tr><td>30</td><td>Iowa</td><td>7,866</td><td>15</td><td>Wisconsin</td><td>8,741</td></tr>
<tr><td>40</td><td>Kansas</td><td>7,266</td><td>16</td><td>Vermont</td><td>8,702</td></tr>
<tr><td>49</td><td>Kentucky</td><td>6,723</td><td>17</td><td>New Mexico</td><td>8,688</td></tr>
<tr><td>26</td><td>Louisiana</td><td>7,974</td><td>18</td><td>Hawaii</td><td>8,678</td></tr>
<tr><td>19</td><td>Maine</td><td>8,647</td><td>19</td><td>Maine</td><td>8,647</td></tr>
<tr><td>24</td><td>Maryland</td><td>8,133</td><td>20</td><td>Pennsylvania</td><td>8,387</td></tr>
<tr><td>5</td><td>Massachusetts</td><td>9,567</td><td>21</td><td>Colorado</td><td>8,330</td></tr>
<tr><td>25</td><td>Michigan</td><td>8,050</td><td>22</td><td>North Dakota</td><td>8,240</td></tr>
<tr><td>13</td><td>Minnesota</td><td>8,891</td><td>23</td><td>West Virginia</td><td>8,163</td></tr>
<tr><td>39</td><td>Mississippi</td><td>7,272</td><td>24</td><td>Maryland</td><td>8,133</td></tr>
<tr><td>41</td><td>Missouri</td><td>7,143</td><td>25</td><td>Michigan</td><td>8,050</td></tr>
<tr><td>27</td><td>Montana</td><td>7,949</td><td>26</td><td>Louisiana</td><td>7,974</td></tr>
<tr><td>9</td><td>Nebraska</td><td>9,055</td><td>27</td><td>Montana</td><td>7,949</td></tr>
<tr><td>29</td><td>Nevada</td><td>7,868</td><td>28</td><td>Illinois</td><td>7,897</td></tr>
<tr><td>47</td><td>New Hampshire</td><td>6,849</td><td>29</td><td>Nevada</td><td>7,868</td></tr>
<tr><td>10</td><td>New Jersey</td><td>8,988</td><td>30</td><td>Iowa</td><td>7,866</td></tr>
<tr><td>17</td><td>New Mexico</td><td>8,688</td><td>31</td><td>South Carolina</td><td>7,821</td></tr>
<tr><td>3</td><td>New York</td><td>11,993</td><td>32</td><td>Utah</td><td>7,659</td></tr>
<tr><td>35</td><td>North Carolina</td><td>7,469</td><td>33</td><td>Florida</td><td>7,631</td></tr>
<tr><td>22</td><td>North Dakota</td><td>8,240</td><td>34</td><td>Virginia</td><td>7,523</td></tr>
<tr><td>11</td><td>Ohio</td><td>8,953</td><td>35</td><td>North Carolina</td><td>7,469</td></tr>
<tr><td>45</td><td>Oklahoma</td><td>6,944</td><td>36</td><td>South Dakota</td><td>7,467</td></tr>
<tr><td>12</td><td>Oregon</td><td>8,924</td><td>37</td><td>Alabama</td><td>7,403</td></tr>
<tr><td>20</td><td>Pennsylvania</td><td>8,387</td><td>38</td><td>Tennessee</td><td>7,294</td></tr>
<tr><td>7</td><td>Rhode Island</td><td>9,121</td><td>39</td><td>Mississippi</td><td>7,272</td></tr>
<tr><td>31</td><td>South Carolina</td><td>7,821</td><td>40</td><td>Kansas</td><td>7,266</td></tr>
<tr><td>36</td><td>South Dakota</td><td>7,467</td><td>41</td><td>Missouri</td><td>7,143</td></tr>
<tr><td>38</td><td>Tennessee</td><td>7,294</td><td>42</td><td>Texas</td><td>7,138</td></tr>
<tr><td>42</td><td>Texas</td><td>7,138</td><td>43</td><td>Idaho</td><td>7,016</td></tr>
<tr><td>32</td><td>Utah</td><td>7,659</td><td>44</td><td>Indiana</td><td>6,999</td></tr>
<tr><td>16</td><td>Vermont</td><td>8,702</td><td>45</td><td>Oklahoma</td><td>6,944</td></tr>
<tr><td>34</td><td>Virginia</td><td>7,523</td><td>46</td><td>Arizona</td><td>6,911</td></tr>
<tr><td>6</td><td>Washington</td><td>9,183</td><td>47</td><td>New Hampshire</td><td>6,849</td></tr>
<tr><td>23</td><td>West Virginia</td><td>8,163</td><td>48</td><td>Arkansas</td><td>6,809</td></tr>
<tr><td>15</td><td>Wisconsin</td><td>8,741</td><td>49</td><td>Kentucky</td><td>6,723</td></tr>
<tr><td>2</td><td>Wyoming</td><td>15,658</td><td>50</td><td>Georgia</td><td>6,620</td></tr>
<tr><td></td><td></td><td></td><td></td><td>District of Columbia</td><td>16,024</td></tr>
</table>

Source: CQ Press using data from U.S. Bureau of the Census, Governments Division
"State and Local Government Finances: 2004-2005" (http://www.census.gov/govs/www/estimate05.html)
*Total revenue includes all money received from external sources. This includes taxes, intergovernmental transfers and insurance trust revenue, and revenue from government owned utilities and other commercial or auxiliary enterprise.

State and Local Government Revenue from the Federal Government in 2005

National Total = $438,155,977,000

ALPHA ORDER

RANK	STATE	REVENUE	% of USA
19	Alabama	$7,437,692,000	1.7%
40	Alaska	2,553,249,000	0.6%
16	Arizona	8,238,501,000	1.9%
32	Arkansas	4,338,891,000	1.0%
1	California	54,578,422,000	12.5%
29	Colorado	5,102,276,000	1.2%
30	Connecticut	4,448,985,000	1.0%
50	Delaware	1,184,432,000	0.3%
4	Florida	21,097,833,000	4.8%
11	Georgia	10,573,988,000	2.4%
44	Hawaii	1,964,554,000	0.4%
45	Idaho	1,876,814,000	0.4%
7	Illinois	15,387,326,000	3.5%
21	Indiana	7,192,834,000	1.6%
31	Iowa	4,380,491,000	1.0%
35	Kansas	3,402,605,000	0.8%
25	Kentucky	6,115,805,000	1.4%
17	Louisiana	7,848,173,000	1.8%
39	Maine	2,647,192,000	0.6%
18	Maryland	7,540,629,000	1.7%
12	Massachusetts	9,198,142,000	2.1%
8	Michigan	14,195,442,000	3.2%
20	Minnesota	7,307,853,000	1.7%
26	Mississippi	5,987,016,000	1.4%
14	Missouri	8,573,060,000	2.0%
43	Montana	2,002,965,000	0.5%
38	Nebraska	2,668,570,000	0.6%
41	Nevada	2,240,559,000	0.5%
46	New Hampshire	1,625,172,000	0.4%
10	New Jersey	10,626,825,000	2.4%
33	New Mexico	4,258,072,000	1.0%
2	New York	45,701,539,000	10.4%
9	North Carolina	13,066,924,000	3.0%
49	North Dakota	1,311,019,000	0.3%
6	Ohio	17,182,975,000	3.9%
28	Oklahoma	5,179,250,000	1.2%
27	Oregon	5,257,787,000	1.2%
5	Pennsylvania	19,258,927,000	4.4%
42	Rhode Island	2,106,180,000	0.5%
22	South Carolina	7,100,845,000	1.6%
47	South Dakota	1,369,870,000	0.3%
13	Tennessee	9,071,470,000	2.1%
3	Texas	28,960,854,000	6.6%
36	Utah	3,219,817,000	0.7%
48	Vermont	1,313,181,000	0.3%
24	Virginia	6,934,683,000	1.6%
15	Washington	8,336,629,000	1.9%
34	West Virginia	3,540,319,000	0.8%
23	Wisconsin	7,100,591,000	1.6%
37	Wyoming	2,734,175,000	0.6%

RANK ORDER

RANK	STATE	REVENUE	% of USA
1	California	$54,578,422,000	12.5%
2	New York	45,701,539,000	10.4%
3	Texas	28,960,854,000	6.6%
4	Florida	21,097,833,000	4.8%
5	Pennsylvania	19,258,927,000	4.4%
6	Ohio	17,182,975,000	3.9%
7	Illinois	15,387,326,000	3.5%
8	Michigan	14,195,442,000	3.2%
9	North Carolina	13,066,924,000	3.0%
10	New Jersey	10,626,825,000	2.4%
11	Georgia	10,573,988,000	2.4%
12	Massachusetts	9,198,142,000	2.1%
13	Tennessee	9,071,470,000	2.1%
14	Missouri	8,573,060,000	2.0%
15	Washington	8,336,629,000	1.9%
16	Arizona	8,238,501,000	1.9%
17	Louisiana	7,848,173,000	1.8%
18	Maryland	7,540,629,000	1.7%
19	Alabama	7,437,692,000	1.7%
20	Minnesota	7,307,853,000	1.7%
21	Indiana	7,192,834,000	1.6%
22	South Carolina	7,100,845,000	1.6%
23	Wisconsin	7,100,591,000	1.6%
24	Virginia	6,934,683,000	1.6%
25	Kentucky	6,115,805,000	1.4%
26	Mississippi	5,987,016,000	1.4%
27	Oregon	5,257,787,000	1.2%
28	Oklahoma	5,179,250,000	1.2%
29	Colorado	5,102,276,000	1.2%
30	Connecticut	4,448,985,000	1.0%
31	Iowa	4,380,491,000	1.0%
32	Arkansas	4,338,891,000	1.0%
33	New Mexico	4,258,072,000	1.0%
34	West Virginia	3,540,319,000	0.8%
35	Kansas	3,402,605,000	0.8%
36	Utah	3,219,817,000	0.7%
37	Wyoming	2,734,175,000	0.6%
38	Nebraska	2,668,570,000	0.6%
39	Maine	2,647,192,000	0.6%
40	Alaska	2,553,249,000	0.6%
41	Nevada	2,240,559,000	0.5%
42	Rhode Island	2,106,180,000	0.5%
43	Montana	2,002,965,000	0.5%
44	Hawaii	1,964,554,000	0.4%
45	Idaho	1,876,814,000	0.4%
46	New Hampshire	1,625,172,000	0.4%
47	South Dakota	1,369,870,000	0.3%
48	Vermont	1,313,181,000	0.3%
49	North Dakota	1,311,019,000	0.3%
50	Delaware	1,184,432,000	0.3%
	District of Columbia	2,814,574,000	0.6%

Source: U.S. Bureau of the Census, Governments Division
"State and Local Government Finances: 2004-2005" (http://www.census.gov/govs/www/estimate05.html)

Per Capita State and Local Government Revenue from the Federal Government in 2005
National Per Capita = $1,481

ALPHA ORDER

RANK	STATE	PER CAPITA
15	Alabama	$1,638
2	Alaska	3,814
33	Arizona	1,384
16	Arkansas	1,565
20	California	1,516
48	Colorado	1,092
39	Connecticut	1,276
31	Delaware	1,409
45	Florida	1,190
46	Georgia	1,161
18	Hawaii	1,550
36	Idaho	1,316
44	Illinois	1,210
47	Indiana	1,150
24	Iowa	1,482
42	Kansas	1,241
26	Kentucky	1,466
13	Louisiana	1,746
9	Maine	2,017
34	Maryland	1,353
29	Massachusetts	1,431
32	Michigan	1,404
30	Minnesota	1,429
7	Mississippi	2,064
25	Missouri	1,481
5	Montana	2,140
19	Nebraska	1,521
49	Nevada	930
41	New Hampshire	1,247
43	New Jersey	1,227
4	New Mexico	2,222
3	New York	2,373
22	North Carolina	1,506
8	North Dakota	2,062
23	Ohio	1,499
27	Oklahoma	1,465
28	Oregon	1,448
17	Pennsylvania	1,557
10	Rhode Island	1,974
14	South Carolina	1,669
12	South Dakota	1,756
21	Tennessee	1,515
40	Texas	1,268
37	Utah	1,285
6	Vermont	2,119
50	Virginia	918
35	Washington	1,329
11	West Virginia	1,961
38	Wisconsin	1,282
1	Wyoming	5,398

RANK ORDER

RANK	STATE	PER CAPITA
1	Wyoming	$5,398
2	Alaska	3,814
3	New York	2,373
4	New Mexico	2,222
5	Montana	2,140
6	Vermont	2,119
7	Mississippi	2,064
8	North Dakota	2,062
9	Maine	2,017
10	Rhode Island	1,974
11	West Virginia	1,961
12	South Dakota	1,756
13	Louisiana	1,746
14	South Carolina	1,669
15	Alabama	1,638
16	Arkansas	1,565
17	Pennsylvania	1,557
18	Hawaii	1,550
19	Nebraska	1,521
20	California	1,516
21	Tennessee	1,515
22	North Carolina	1,506
23	Ohio	1,499
24	Iowa	1,482
25	Missouri	1,481
26	Kentucky	1,466
27	Oklahoma	1,465
28	Oregon	1,448
29	Massachusetts	1,431
30	Minnesota	1,429
31	Delaware	1,409
32	Michigan	1,404
33	Arizona	1,384
34	Maryland	1,353
35	Washington	1,329
36	Idaho	1,316
37	Utah	1,285
38	Wisconsin	1,282
39	Connecticut	1,276
40	Texas	1,268
41	New Hampshire	1,247
42	Kansas	1,241
43	New Jersey	1,227
44	Illinois	1,210
45	Florida	1,190
46	Georgia	1,161
47	Indiana	1,150
48	Colorado	1,092
49	Nevada	930
50	Virginia	918

District of Columbia 4,836

Source: CQ Press using data from U.S. Bureau of the Census, Governments Division
"State and Local Government Finances: 2004-2005" (http://www.census.gov/govs/www/estimate05.html)

Percent of State and Local Government Revenue from the Federal Government in 2005
National Percent = 17.4%*

ALPHA ORDER

RANK	STATE	PERCENT
12	Alabama	22.1
11	Alaska	22.5
21	Arizona	20.0
10	Arkansas	23.0
46	California	14.3
48	Colorado	13.1
44	Connecticut	14.5
40	Delaware	15.5
39	Florida	15.6
29	Georgia	17.5
27	Hawaii	17.9
23	Idaho	18.8
41	Illinois	15.3
36	Indiana	16.4
23	Iowa	18.8
31	Kansas	17.1
14	Kentucky	21.8
13	Louisiana	21.9
9	Maine	23.3
35	Maryland	16.6
42	Massachusetts	15.0
30	Michigan	17.4
38	Minnesota	16.1
2	Mississippi	28.4
19	Missouri	20.7
3	Montana	26.9
32	Nebraska	16.8
50	Nevada	11.8
26	New Hampshire	18.2
47	New Jersey	13.7
4	New Mexico	25.6
22	New York	19.8
20	North Carolina	20.2
5	North Dakota	25.0
34	Ohio	16.7
17	Oklahoma	21.1
37	Oregon	16.2
25	Pennsylvania	18.6
15	Rhode Island	21.6
16	South Carolina	21.3
8	South Dakota	23.5
18	Tennessee	20.8
28	Texas	17.8
32	Utah	16.8
6	Vermont	24.4
49	Virginia	12.2
44	Washington	14.5
7	West Virginia	24.0
43	Wisconsin	14.7
1	Wyoming	34.5

RANK ORDER

RANK	STATE	PERCENT
1	Wyoming	34.5
2	Mississippi	28.4
3	Montana	26.9
4	New Mexico	25.6
5	North Dakota	25.0
6	Vermont	24.4
7	West Virginia	24.0
8	South Dakota	23.5
9	Maine	23.3
10	Arkansas	23.0
11	Alaska	22.5
12	Alabama	22.1
13	Louisiana	21.9
14	Kentucky	21.8
15	Rhode Island	21.6
16	South Carolina	21.3
17	Oklahoma	21.1
18	Tennessee	20.8
19	Missouri	20.7
20	North Carolina	20.2
21	Arizona	20.0
22	New York	19.8
23	Idaho	18.8
23	Iowa	18.8
25	Pennsylvania	18.6
26	New Hampshire	18.2
27	Hawaii	17.9
28	Texas	17.8
29	Georgia	17.5
30	Michigan	17.4
31	Kansas	17.1
32	Nebraska	16.8
32	Utah	16.8
34	Ohio	16.7
35	Maryland	16.6
36	Indiana	16.4
37	Oregon	16.2
38	Minnesota	16.1
39	Florida	15.6
40	Delaware	15.5
41	Illinois	15.3
42	Massachusetts	15.0
43	Wisconsin	14.7
44	Connecticut	14.5
44	Washington	14.5
46	California	14.3
47	New Jersey	13.7
48	Colorado	13.1
49	Virginia	12.2
50	Nevada	11.8
	District of Columbia	30.2

Source: CQ Press using data from U.S. Bureau of the Census, Governments Division
"State and Local Government Finances: 2004-2005" (http://www.census.gov/govs/www/estimate05.html)
*As a percent of total revenue.

State and Local Government Own Source Revenue in 2005

National Total = $1,582,770,336,000*

ALPHA ORDER

RANK	STATE	REVENUE	% of USA
26	Alabama	$20,161,798,000	1.3%
40	Alaska	7,271,531,000	0.5%
19	Arizona	25,537,702,000	1.6%
35	Arkansas	11,695,272,000	0.7%
1	California	215,525,860,000	13.6%
21	Colorado	24,686,249,000	1.6%
23	Connecticut	23,170,157,000	1.5%
45	Delaware	5,458,638,000	0.3%
4	Florida	90,961,726,000	5.7%
13	Georgia	39,606,449,000	2.5%
39	Hawaii	7,589,945,000	0.5%
42	Idaho	6,422,573,000	0.4%
5	Illinois	65,361,025,000	4.1%
15	Indiana	31,917,234,000	2.0%
30	Iowa	15,041,662,000	1.0%
31	Kansas	13,517,874,000	0.9%
28	Kentucky	17,715,421,000	1.1%
24	Louisiana	22,029,418,000	1.4%
41	Maine	7,207,005,000	0.5%
16	Maryland	31,733,051,000	2.0%
11	Massachusetts	39,929,655,000	2.5%
9	Michigan	52,789,980,000	3.3%
17	Minnesota	30,084,307,000	1.9%
34	Mississippi	11,792,838,000	0.7%
20	Missouri	25,367,538,000	1.6%
46	Montana	4,285,177,000	0.3%
37	Nebraska	9,594,272,000	0.6%
32	Nevada	13,134,124,000	0.8%
43	New Hampshire	6,088,713,000	0.4%
8	New Jersey	55,811,593,000	3.5%
36	New Mexico	9,749,736,000	0.6%
2	New York	144,874,167,000	9.2%
12	North Carolina	39,827,610,000	2.5%
49	North Dakota	3,275,586,000	0.2%
7	Ohio	59,980,947,000	3.8%
29	Oklahoma	15,242,407,000	1.0%
27	Oregon	18,070,350,000	1.1%
6	Pennsylvania	64,776,955,000	4.1%
44	Rhode Island	6,041,168,000	0.4%
25	South Carolina	20,520,703,000	1.3%
50	South Dakota	3,153,314,000	0.2%
22	Tennessee	24,595,799,000	1.6%
3	Texas	103,334,700,000	6.5%
33	Utah	11,793,916,000	0.7%
48	Vermont	3,511,496,000	0.2%
10	Virginia	40,613,930,000	2.6%
14	Washington	33,934,887,000	2.1%
38	West Virginia	8,804,542,000	0.6%
18	Wisconsin	29,620,064,000	1.9%
47	Wyoming	4,268,875,000	0.3%

RANK ORDER

RANK	STATE	REVENUE	% of USA
1	California	$215,525,860,000	13.6%
2	New York	144,874,167,000	9.2%
3	Texas	103,334,700,000	6.5%
4	Florida	90,961,726,000	5.7%
5	Illinois	65,361,025,000	4.1%
6	Pennsylvania	64,776,955,000	4.1%
7	Ohio	59,980,947,000	3.8%
8	New Jersey	55,811,593,000	3.5%
9	Michigan	52,789,980,000	3.3%
10	Virginia	40,613,930,000	2.6%
11	Massachusetts	39,929,655,000	2.5%
12	North Carolina	39,827,610,000	2.5%
13	Georgia	39,606,449,000	2.5%
14	Washington	33,934,887,000	2.1%
15	Indiana	31,917,234,000	2.0%
16	Maryland	31,733,051,000	2.0%
17	Minnesota	30,084,307,000	1.9%
18	Wisconsin	29,620,064,000	1.9%
19	Arizona	25,537,702,000	1.6%
20	Missouri	25,367,538,000	1.6%
21	Colorado	24,686,249,000	1.6%
22	Tennessee	24,595,799,000	1.6%
23	Connecticut	23,170,157,000	1.5%
24	Louisiana	22,029,418,000	1.4%
25	South Carolina	20,520,703,000	1.3%
26	Alabama	20,161,798,000	1.3%
27	Oregon	18,070,350,000	1.1%
28	Kentucky	17,715,421,000	1.1%
29	Oklahoma	15,242,407,000	1.0%
30	Iowa	15,041,662,000	1.0%
31	Kansas	13,517,874,000	0.9%
32	Nevada	13,134,124,000	0.8%
33	Utah	11,793,916,000	0.7%
34	Mississippi	11,792,838,000	0.7%
35	Arkansas	11,695,272,000	0.7%
36	New Mexico	9,749,736,000	0.6%
37	Nebraska	9,594,272,000	0.6%
38	West Virginia	8,804,542,000	0.6%
39	Hawaii	7,589,945,000	0.5%
40	Alaska	7,271,531,000	0.5%
41	Maine	7,207,005,000	0.5%
42	Idaho	6,422,573,000	0.4%
43	New Hampshire	6,088,713,000	0.4%
44	Rhode Island	6,041,168,000	0.4%
45	Delaware	5,458,638,000	0.3%
46	Montana	4,285,177,000	0.3%
47	Wyoming	4,268,875,000	0.3%
48	Vermont	3,511,496,000	0.2%
49	North Dakota	3,275,586,000	0.2%
50	South Dakota	3,153,314,000	0.2%
	District of Columbia	5,290,397,000	0.3%

Source: U.S. Bureau of the Census, Governments Division
"State and Local Government Finances: 2004-2005" (http://www.census.gov/govs/www/estimate05.html)
*Own source revenue includes taxes, current charges, and miscellaneous general revenue. Excluded are intergovernmental transfers, insurance trust revenue, and revenue from government owned utilities and other commercial or auxiliary enterprise.

Per Capita State and Local Government Own Source Revenue in 2005

National Per Capita = $5,349*

ALPHA ORDER

RANK	STATE	PER CAPITA
41	Alabama	$4,441
1	Alaska	10,863
45	Arizona	4,291
47	Arkansas	4,219
8	California	5,988
20	Colorado	5,282
4	Connecticut	6,646
5	Delaware	6,494
26	Florida	5,129
43	Georgia	4,349
8	Hawaii	5,988
40	Idaho	4,504
25	Illinois	5,139
27	Indiana	5,101
28	Iowa	5,089
31	Kansas	4,931
46	Kentucky	4,247
32	Louisiana	4,900
14	Maine	5,492
11	Maryland	5,694
7	Massachusetts	6,211
23	Michigan	5,223
10	Minnesota	5,883
49	Mississippi	4,066
42	Missouri	4,383
38	Montana	4,579
15	Nebraska	5,470
16	Nevada	5,452
36	New Hampshire	4,672
6	New Jersey	6,447
29	New Mexico	5,088
3	New York	7,521
37	North Carolina	4,589
24	North Dakota	5,151
22	Ohio	5,234
44	Oklahoma	4,311
30	Oregon	4,978
21	Pennsylvania	5,238
13	Rhode Island	5,663
34	South Carolina	4,823
50	South Dakota	4,042
48	Tennessee	4,107
39	Texas	4,523
35	Utah	4,708
12	Vermont	5,666
18	Virginia	5,374
17	Washington	5,412
33	West Virginia	4,876
19	Wisconsin	5,346
2	Wyoming	8,428

RANK ORDER

RANK	STATE	PER CAPITA
1	Alaska	$10,863
2	Wyoming	8,428
3	New York	7,521
4	Connecticut	6,646
5	Delaware	6,494
6	New Jersey	6,447
7	Massachusetts	6,211
8	California	5,988
8	Hawaii	5,988
10	Minnesota	5,883
11	Maryland	5,694
12	Vermont	5,666
13	Rhode Island	5,663
14	Maine	5,492
15	Nebraska	5,470
16	Nevada	5,452
17	Washington	5,412
18	Virginia	5,374
19	Wisconsin	5,346
20	Colorado	5,282
21	Pennsylvania	5,238
22	Ohio	5,234
23	Michigan	5,223
24	North Dakota	5,151
25	Illinois	5,139
26	Florida	5,129
27	Indiana	5,101
28	Iowa	5,089
29	New Mexico	5,088
30	Oregon	4,978
31	Kansas	4,931
32	Louisiana	4,900
33	West Virginia	4,876
34	South Carolina	4,823
35	Utah	4,708
36	New Hampshire	4,672
37	North Carolina	4,589
38	Montana	4,579
39	Texas	4,523
40	Idaho	4,504
41	Alabama	4,441
42	Missouri	4,383
43	Georgia	4,349
44	Oklahoma	4,311
45	Arizona	4,291
46	Kentucky	4,247
47	Arkansas	4,219
48	Tennessee	4,107
49	Mississippi	4,066
50	South Dakota	4,042
	District of Columbia	9,089

Source: CQ Press using data from U.S. Bureau of the Census, Governments Division
"State and Local Government Finances: 2004-2005" (http://www.census.gov/govs/www/estimate05.html)
*Own source revenue includes taxes, current charges, and miscellaneous general revenue. Excluded are intergovernmental transfers, insurance trust revenue, and revenue from government owned utilities and other commercial or auxiliary enterprise.

State and Local Government Tax Revenue in 2005

National Total = $1,096,384,739,000

RANK	STATE	TAX REVENUE	% of USA
27	Alabama	$11,686,675,000	1.1%
45	Alaska	2,947,034,000	0.3%
20	Arizona	18,331,117,000	1.7%
33	Arkansas	8,053,926,000	0.7%
1	California	146,616,887,000	13.4%
23	Colorado	15,680,821,000	1.4%
19	Connecticut	18,896,812,000	1.7%
44	Delaware	3,277,387,000	0.3%
4	Florida	59,863,884,000	5.5%
12	Georgia	27,486,109,000	2.5%
39	Hawaii	5,523,747,000	0.5%
43	Idaho	4,182,546,000	0.4%
5	Illinois	49,138,495,000	4.5%
17	Indiana	21,337,077,000	1.9%
30	Iowa	9,704,861,000	0.9%
31	Kansas	9,385,496,000	0.9%
25	Kentucky	12,261,812,000	1.1%
24	Louisiana	14,301,995,000	1.3%
40	Maine	5,219,708,000	0.5%
14	Maryland	23,899,055,000	2.2%
10	Massachusetts	28,756,962,000	2.6%
9	Michigan	35,295,158,000	3.2%
18	Minnesota	20,956,639,000	1.9%
34	Mississippi	7,490,681,000	0.7%
21	Missouri	17,374,264,000	1.6%
46	Montana	2,722,702,000	0.2%
36	Nebraska	6,586,238,000	0.6%
32	Nevada	9,043,570,000	0.8%
42	New Hampshire	4,319,777,000	0.4%
7	New Jersey	42,557,354,000	3.9%
37	New Mexico	6,069,328,000	0.6%
2	New York	111,107,619,000	10.1%
13	North Carolina	27,307,108,000	2.5%
49	North Dakota	2,121,388,000	0.2%
8	Ohio	41,714,754,000	3.8%
29	Oklahoma	10,073,102,000	0.9%
28	Oregon	11,106,991,000	1.0%
6	Pennsylvania	46,019,258,000	4.2%
41	Rhode Island	4,499,624,000	0.4%
26	South Carolina	11,800,640,000	1.1%
50	South Dakota	2,103,820,000	0.2%
22	Tennessee	15,993,136,000	1.5%
3	Texas	69,133,862,000	6.3%
35	Utah	7,303,964,000	0.7%
48	Vermont	2,574,761,000	0.2%
11	Virginia	27,659,186,000	2.5%
15	Washington	22,974,042,000	2.1%
38	West Virginia	5,550,746,000	0.5%
16	Wisconsin	21,403,526,000	2.0%
47	Wyoming	2,671,853,000	0.2%

RANK	STATE	TAX REVENUE	% of USA
1	California	$146,616,887,000	13.4%
2	New York	111,107,619,000	10.1%
3	Texas	69,133,862,000	6.3%
4	Florida	59,863,884,000	5.5%
5	Illinois	49,138,495,000	4.5%
6	Pennsylvania	46,019,258,000	4.2%
7	New Jersey	42,557,354,000	3.9%
8	Ohio	41,714,754,000	3.8%
9	Michigan	35,295,158,000	3.2%
10	Massachusetts	28,756,962,000	2.6%
11	Virginia	27,659,186,000	2.5%
12	Georgia	27,486,109,000	2.5%
13	North Carolina	27,307,108,000	2.5%
14	Maryland	23,899,055,000	2.2%
15	Washington	22,974,042,000	2.1%
16	Wisconsin	21,403,526,000	2.0%
17	Indiana	21,337,077,000	1.9%
18	Minnesota	20,956,639,000	1.9%
19	Connecticut	18,896,812,000	1.7%
20	Arizona	18,331,117,000	1.7%
21	Missouri	17,374,264,000	1.6%
22	Tennessee	15,993,136,000	1.5%
23	Colorado	15,680,821,000	1.4%
24	Louisiana	14,301,995,000	1.3%
25	Kentucky	12,261,812,000	1.1%
26	South Carolina	11,800,640,000	1.1%
27	Alabama	11,686,675,000	1.1%
28	Oregon	11,106,991,000	1.0%
29	Oklahoma	10,073,102,000	0.9%
30	Iowa	9,704,861,000	0.9%
31	Kansas	9,385,496,000	0.9%
32	Nevada	9,043,570,000	0.8%
33	Arkansas	8,053,926,000	0.7%
34	Mississippi	7,490,681,000	0.7%
35	Utah	7,303,964,000	0.7%
36	Nebraska	6,586,238,000	0.6%
37	New Mexico	6,069,328,000	0.6%
38	West Virginia	5,550,746,000	0.5%
39	Hawaii	5,523,747,000	0.5%
40	Maine	5,219,708,000	0.5%
41	Rhode Island	4,499,624,000	0.4%
42	New Hampshire	4,319,777,000	0.4%
43	Idaho	4,182,546,000	0.4%
44	Delaware	3,277,387,000	0.3%
45	Alaska	2,947,034,000	0.3%
46	Montana	2,722,702,000	0.2%
47	Wyoming	2,671,853,000	0.2%
48	Vermont	2,574,761,000	0.2%
49	North Dakota	2,121,388,000	0.2%
50	South Dakota	2,103,820,000	0.2%
	District of Columbia	4,297,242,000	0.4%

Source: U.S. Bureau of the Census, Governments Division
"State and Local Government Finances: 2004-2005" (http://www.census.gov/govs/www/estimate05.html)

Per Capita State and Local Government Tax Revenue in 2005

National Per Capita = $3,705

ALPHA ORDER			RANK ORDER		
RANK	STATE	PER CAPITA	RANK	STATE	PER CAPITA
50	Alabama	$2,574	1	New York	$5,768
6	Alaska	4,402	2	Connecticut	5,420
34	Arizona	3,080	3	Wyoming	5,275
44	Arkansas	2,905	4	New Jersey	4,916
12	California	4,074	5	Massachusetts	4,473
27	Colorado	3,355	6	Alaska	4,402
2	Connecticut	5,420	7	Hawaii	4,358
14	Delaware	3,899	8	Maryland	4,288
26	Florida	3,375	9	Rhode Island	4,218
38	Georgia	3,018	10	Vermont	4,155
7	Hawaii	4,358	11	Minnesota	4,098
41	Idaho	2,933	12	California	4,074
15	Illinois	3,863	13	Maine	3,978
25	Indiana	3,410	14	Delaware	3,899
30	Iowa	3,284	15	Illinois	3,863
24	Kansas	3,423	15	Wisconsin	3,863
40	Kentucky	2,940	17	Nebraska	3,755
31	Louisiana	3,181	18	Nevada	3,754
13	Maine	3,978	19	Pennsylvania	3,721
8	Maryland	4,288	20	Washington	3,664
5	Massachusetts	4,473	21	Virginia	3,660
23	Michigan	3,492	22	Ohio	3,640
11	Minnesota	4,098	23	Michigan	3,492
49	Mississippi	2,583	24	Kansas	3,423
39	Missouri	3,002	25	Indiana	3,410
43	Montana	2,910	26	Florida	3,375
17	Nebraska	3,755	27	Colorado	3,355
18	Nevada	3,754	28	North Dakota	3,336
29	New Hampshire	3,315	29	New Hampshire	3,315
4	New Jersey	4,916	30	Iowa	3,284
32	New Mexico	3,167	31	Louisiana	3,181
1	New York	5,768	32	New Mexico	3,167
33	North Carolina	3,146	33	North Carolina	3,146
28	North Dakota	3,336	34	Arizona	3,080
22	Ohio	3,640	35	West Virginia	3,074
45	Oklahoma	2,849	36	Oregon	3,060
36	Oregon	3,060	37	Texas	3,026
19	Pennsylvania	3,721	38	Georgia	3,018
9	Rhode Island	4,218	39	Missouri	3,002
46	South Carolina	2,773	40	Kentucky	2,940
47	South Dakota	2,697	41	Idaho	2,933
48	Tennessee	2,670	42	Utah	2,916
37	Texas	3,026	43	Montana	2,910
42	Utah	2,916	44	Arkansas	2,905
10	Vermont	4,155	45	Oklahoma	2,849
21	Virginia	3,660	46	South Carolina	2,773
20	Washington	3,664	47	South Dakota	2,697
35	West Virginia	3,074	48	Tennessee	2,670
15	Wisconsin	3,863	49	Mississippi	2,583
3	Wyoming	5,275	50	Alabama	2,574
				District of Columbia	7,383

Source: CQ Press using data from U.S. Bureau of the Census, Governments Division
"State and Local Government Finances: 2004-2005" (http://www.census.gov/govs/www/estimate05.html)

Percent of State and Local Government Revenue from Taxes in 2005

National Percent = 43.5%

RANK	STATE	PERCENT
47	Alabama	34.8
50	Alaska	26.0
18	Arizona	44.6
25	Arkansas	42.7
38	California	38.5
35	Colorado	40.3
1	Connecticut	61.8
24	Delaware	42.9
20	Florida	44.2
17	Georgia	45.6
4	Hawaii	50.2
29	Idaho	41.8
5	Illinois	48.9
6	Indiana	48.7
30	Iowa	41.7
12	Kansas	47.1
22	Kentucky	43.7
36	Louisiana	39.9
16	Maine	46.0
3	Maryland	52.7
13	Massachusetts	46.8
23	Michigan	43.4
15	Minnesota	46.1
45	Mississippi	35.5
28	Missouri	42.0
41	Montana	36.6
31	Nebraska	41.5
10	Nevada	47.7
8	New Hampshire	48.4
2	New Jersey	54.7
43	New Mexico	36.5
9	New York	48.1
27	North Carolina	42.1
34	North Dakota	40.5
33	Ohio	40.7
32	Oklahoma	41.0
48	Oregon	34.3
19	Pennsylvania	44.4
14	Rhode Island	46.2
45	South Carolina	35.5
44	South Dakota	36.1
41	Tennessee	36.6
26	Texas	42.4
39	Utah	38.1
10	Vermont	47.7
7	Virginia	48.6
36	Washington	39.9
40	West Virginia	37.7
20	Wisconsin	44.2
49	Wyoming	33.7

RANK	STATE	PERCENT
1	Connecticut	61.8
2	New Jersey	54.7
3	Maryland	52.7
4	Hawaii	50.2
5	Illinois	48.9
6	Indiana	48.7
7	Virginia	48.6
8	New Hampshire	48.4
9	New York	48.1
10	Nevada	47.7
10	Vermont	47.7
12	Kansas	47.1
13	Massachusetts	46.8
14	Rhode Island	46.2
15	Minnesota	46.1
16	Maine	46.0
17	Georgia	45.6
18	Arizona	44.6
19	Pennsylvania	44.4
20	Florida	44.2
20	Wisconsin	44.2
22	Kentucky	43.7
23	Michigan	43.4
24	Delaware	42.9
25	Arkansas	42.7
26	Texas	42.4
27	North Carolina	42.1
28	Missouri	42.0
29	Idaho	41.8
30	Iowa	41.7
31	Nebraska	41.5
32	Oklahoma	41.0
33	Ohio	40.7
34	North Dakota	40.5
35	Colorado	40.3
36	Louisiana	39.9
36	Washington	39.9
38	California	38.5
39	Utah	38.1
40	West Virginia	37.7
41	Montana	36.6
41	Tennessee	36.6
43	New Mexico	36.5
44	South Dakota	36.1
45	Mississippi	35.5
45	South Carolina	35.5
47	Alabama	34.8
48	Oregon	34.3
49	Wyoming	33.7
50	Alaska	26.0

District of Columbia	46.1

Source: CQ Press using data from U.S. Bureau of the Census, Governments Division
"State and Local Government Finances: 2004-2005" (http://www.census.gov/govs/www/estimate05.html)

State and Local Government Tax Revenue
as a Percent of Personal Income in 2005
National Percent = 10.7% of Personal Income*

RANK	STATE	PERCENT
47	Alabama	8.8
7	Alaska	12.1
34	Arizona	10.1
19	Arkansas	10.8
18	California	10.9
46	Colorado	8.9
13	Connecticut	11.3
23	Delaware	10.5
39	Florida	9.7
39	Georgia	9.7
6	Hawaii	12.5
29	Idaho	10.3
22	Illinois	10.6
16	Indiana	11.0
25	Iowa	10.4
23	Kansas	10.5
25	Kentucky	10.4
3	Louisiana	12.8
3	Maine	12.8
29	Maryland	10.3
29	Massachusetts	10.3
20	Michigan	10.7
16	Minnesota	11.0
34	Mississippi	10.1
43	Missouri	9.5
36	Montana	10.0
11	Nebraska	11.4
36	Nevada	10.0
47	New Hampshire	8.8
13	New Jersey	11.3
15	New Mexico	11.2
1	New York	14.1
32	North Carolina	10.2
25	North Dakota	10.4
11	Ohio	11.4
43	Oklahoma	9.5
39	Oregon	9.7
20	Pennsylvania	10.7
9	Rhode Island	11.7
38	South Carolina	9.8
50	South Dakota	8.5
49	Tennessee	8.7
45	Texas	9.1
25	Utah	10.4
5	Vermont	12.7
42	Virginia	9.6
32	Washington	10.2
10	West Virginia	11.6
8	Wisconsin	11.8
1	Wyoming	14.1

RANK	STATE	PERCENT
1	New York	14.1
1	Wyoming	14.1
3	Louisiana	12.8
3	Maine	12.8
5	Vermont	12.7
6	Hawaii	12.5
7	Alaska	12.1
8	Wisconsin	11.8
9	Rhode Island	11.7
10	West Virginia	11.6
11	Nebraska	11.4
11	Ohio	11.4
13	Connecticut	11.3
13	New Jersey	11.3
15	New Mexico	11.2
16	Indiana	11.0
16	Minnesota	11.0
18	California	10.9
19	Arkansas	10.8
20	Michigan	10.7
20	Pennsylvania	10.7
22	Illinois	10.6
23	Delaware	10.5
23	Kansas	10.5
25	Iowa	10.4
25	Kentucky	10.4
25	North Dakota	10.4
25	Utah	10.4
29	Idaho	10.3
29	Maryland	10.3
29	Massachusetts	10.3
32	North Carolina	10.2
32	Washington	10.2
34	Arizona	10.1
34	Mississippi	10.1
36	Montana	10.0
36	Nevada	10.0
38	South Carolina	9.8
39	Florida	9.7
39	Georgia	9.7
39	Oregon	9.7
42	Virginia	9.6
43	Missouri	9.5
43	Oklahoma	9.5
45	Texas	9.1
46	Colorado	8.9
47	Alabama	8.8
47	New Hampshire	8.8
49	Tennessee	8.7
50	South Dakota	8.5

	District of Columbia	13.8

Source:CQ Press using data from Bureau of Economic Analysis and U.S. Census Bureau
"State Personal Income" and "State and Local Government Finances: 2004-2005"

*The personal income total used for this table is the sum of state estimates. This total differs from the national income and product accounts (NIPA) estimate of personal income because it omits the earnings of federal civilian and military personnel stationed abroad and of U.S. residents employed abroad temporarily by private U.S. firms.

State and Local Government General Sales Tax Revenue in 2005

National Total = $262,954,969,000*

ALPHA ORDER					RANK ORDER			
RANK	STATE	REVENUE	% of USA		RANK	STATE	REVENUE	% of USA
23	Alabama	$3,533,309,000	1.3%		1	California	$37,574,729,000	14.3%
46	Alaska	157,364,000	0.1%		2	New York	21,100,839,000	8.0%
12	Arizona	7,026,285,000	2.7%		3	Texas	20,248,178,000	7.7%
24	Arkansas	3,327,742,000	1.3%		4	Florida	20,078,780,000	7.6%
1	California	37,574,729,000	14.3%		5	Washington	10,645,361,000	4.0%
18	Colorado	4,390,974,000	1.7%		6	Ohio	9,649,733,000	3.7%
25	Connecticut	3,267,726,000	1.2%		7	Illinois	8,361,402,000	3.2%
47	Delaware	0	0.0%		8	Pennsylvania	8,257,856,000	3.1%
4	Florida	20,078,780,000	7.6%		9	Michigan	8,074,095,000	3.1%
10	Georgia	7,663,648,000	2.9%		10	Georgia	7,663,648,000	2.9%
36	Hawaii	2,136,604,000	0.8%		11	Tennessee	7,569,457,000	2.9%
38	Idaho	1,128,485,000	0.4%		12	Arizona	7,026,285,000	2.7%
7	Illinois	8,361,402,000	3.2%		13	New Jersey	6,552,200,000	2.5%
16	Indiana	5,001,049,000	1.9%		14	North Carolina	6,242,129,000	2.4%
34	Iowa	2,159,655,000	0.8%		15	Louisiana	5,677,694,000	2.2%
32	Kansas	2,519,819,000	1.0%		16	Indiana	5,001,049,000	1.9%
30	Kentucky	2,605,165,000	1.0%		17	Missouri	4,859,476,000	1.8%
15	Louisiana	5,677,694,000	2.2%		18	Colorado	4,390,974,000	1.7%
40	Maine	934,848,000	0.4%		19	Wisconsin	4,299,914,000	1.6%
29	Maryland	2,889,997,000	1.1%		20	Minnesota	4,269,450,000	1.6%
22	Massachusetts	3,890,945,000	1.5%		21	Virginia	4,046,895,000	1.5%
9	Michigan	8,074,095,000	3.1%		22	Massachusetts	3,890,945,000	1.5%
20	Minnesota	4,269,450,000	1.6%		23	Alabama	3,533,309,000	1.3%
31	Mississippi	2,588,972,000	1.0%		24	Arkansas	3,327,742,000	1.3%
17	Missouri	4,859,476,000	1.8%		25	Connecticut	3,267,726,000	1.2%
47	Montana	0	0.0%		26	Nevada	3,061,987,000	1.2%
37	Nebraska	1,768,202,000	0.7%		27	South Carolina	3,030,925,000	1.2%
26	Nevada	3,061,987,000	1.2%		28	Oklahoma	2,929,587,000	1.1%
47	New Hampshire	0	0.0%		29	Maryland	2,889,997,000	1.1%
13	New Jersey	6,552,200,000	2.5%		30	Kentucky	2,605,165,000	1.0%
35	New Mexico	2,155,330,000	0.8%		31	Mississippi	2,588,972,000	1.0%
2	New York	21,100,839,000	8.0%		32	Kansas	2,519,819,000	1.0%
14	North Carolina	6,242,129,000	2.4%		33	Utah	2,181,820,000	0.8%
44	North Dakota	478,934,000	0.2%		34	Iowa	2,159,655,000	0.8%
6	Ohio	9,649,733,000	3.7%		35	New Mexico	2,155,330,000	0.8%
28	Oklahoma	2,929,587,000	1.1%		36	Hawaii	2,136,604,000	0.8%
47	Oregon	0	0.0%		37	Nebraska	1,768,202,000	0.7%
8	Pennsylvania	8,257,856,000	3.1%		38	Idaho	1,128,485,000	0.4%
41	Rhode Island	844,087,000	0.3%		39	West Virginia	1,095,341,000	0.4%
27	South Carolina	3,030,925,000	1.2%		40	Maine	934,848,000	0.4%
42	South Dakota	833,586,000	0.3%		41	Rhode Island	844,087,000	0.3%
11	Tennessee	7,569,457,000	2.9%		42	South Dakota	833,586,000	0.3%
3	Texas	20,248,178,000	7.7%		43	Wyoming	682,253,000	0.3%
33	Utah	2,181,820,000	0.8%		44	North Dakota	478,934,000	0.2%
45	Vermont	315,233,000	0.1%		45	Vermont	315,233,000	0.1%
21	Virginia	4,046,895,000	1.5%		46	Alaska	157,364,000	0.1%
5	Washington	10,645,361,000	4.0%		47	Delaware	0	0.0%
39	West Virginia	1,095,341,000	0.4%		47	Montana	0	0.0%
19	Wisconsin	4,299,914,000	1.6%		47	New Hampshire	0	0.0%
43	Wyoming	682,253,000	0.3%		47	Oregon	0	0.0%
						District of Columbia	846,909,000	0.3%

Source: U.S. Bureau of the Census, Governments Division
"State and Local Government Finances: 2004-2005" (http://www.census.gov/govs/www/estimate05.html)
*Does not include special sales taxes such as those on sale of alcohol, gasoline, or tobacco.

Per Capita State and Local Government General Sales Tax Revenue in 2005

National Per Capita = $889*

ALPHA ORDER

RANK	STATE	PER CAPITA
30	Alabama	$778
46	Alaska	235
8	Arizona	1,180
7	Arkansas	1,200
13	California	1,044
15	Colorado	940
16	Connecticut	937
47	Delaware	0
9	Florida	1,132
22	Georgia	841
2	Hawaii	1,686
28	Idaho	791
39	Illinois	657
26	Indiana	799
34	Iowa	731
17	Kansas	919
40	Kentucky	625
6	Louisiana	1,263
36	Maine	712
44	Maryland	519
42	Massachusetts	605
26	Michigan	799
24	Minnesota	835
18	Mississippi	893
23	Missouri	840
47	Montana	0
14	Nebraska	1,008
4	Nevada	1,271
47	New Hampshire	0
32	New Jersey	757
10	New Mexico	1,125
11	New York	1,095
35	North Carolina	719
33	North Dakota	753
21	Ohio	842
25	Oklahoma	829
47	Oregon	0
38	Pennsylvania	668
28	Rhode Island	791
36	South Carolina	712
12	South Dakota	1,069
5	Tennessee	1,264
19	Texas	886
20	Utah	871
45	Vermont	509
43	Virginia	535
1	Washington	1,698
41	West Virginia	607
31	Wisconsin	776
3	Wyoming	1,347

RANK ORDER

RANK	STATE	PER CAPITA
1	Washington	$1,698
2	Hawaii	1,686
3	Wyoming	1,347
4	Nevada	1,271
5	Tennessee	1,264
6	Louisiana	1,263
7	Arkansas	1,200
8	Arizona	1,180
9	Florida	1,132
10	New Mexico	1,125
11	New York	1,095
12	South Dakota	1,069
13	California	1,044
14	Nebraska	1,008
15	Colorado	940
16	Connecticut	937
17	Kansas	919
18	Mississippi	893
19	Texas	886
20	Utah	871
21	Ohio	842
22	Georgia	841
23	Missouri	840
24	Minnesota	835
25	Oklahoma	829
26	Indiana	799
26	Michigan	799
28	Idaho	791
28	Rhode Island	791
30	Alabama	778
31	Wisconsin	776
32	New Jersey	757
33	North Dakota	753
34	Iowa	731
35	North Carolina	719
36	Maine	712
36	South Carolina	712
38	Pennsylvania	668
39	Illinois	657
40	Kentucky	625
41	West Virginia	607
42	Massachusetts	605
43	Virginia	535
44	Maryland	519
45	Vermont	509
46	Alaska	235
47	Delaware	0
47	Montana	0
47	New Hampshire	0
47	Oregon	0

District of Columbia 1,455

Source: CQ Press using data from U.S. Bureau of the Census, Governments Division
    "State and Local Government Finances: 2004-2005" (http://www.census.gov/govs/www/estimate05.html)
*Does not include special sales taxes such as those on sale of alcohol, gasoline, or tobacco.

State and Local Government Property Tax Revenue in 2005

National Total = $335,678,019,000

ALPHA ORDER

RANK	STATE	REVENUE	% of USA
37	Alabama	$1,792,320,000	0.5%
44	Alaska	892,307,000	0.3%
20	Arizona	5,126,076,000	1.5%
39	Arkansas	1,172,261,000	0.3%
2	California	34,058,299,000	10.1%
21	Colorado	4,940,398,000	1.5%
15	Connecticut	7,155,644,000	2.1%
50	Delaware	485,848,000	0.1%
4	Florida	20,389,149,000	6.1%
12	Georgia	8,214,542,000	2.4%
47	Hawaii	818,239,000	0.2%
40	Idaho	1,153,841,000	0.3%
6	Illinois	18,690,132,000	5.6%
14	Indiana	7,638,992,000	2.3%
26	Iowa	3,302,265,000	1.0%
27	Kansas	3,090,403,000	0.9%
31	Kentucky	2,246,867,000	0.7%
29	Louisiana	2,429,386,000	0.7%
32	Maine	2,151,968,000	0.6%
18	Maryland	5,594,371,000	1.7%
10	Massachusetts	10,341,126,000	3.1%
8	Michigan	12,918,887,000	3.8%
19	Minnesota	5,250,869,000	1.6%
34	Mississippi	1,967,447,000	0.6%
22	Missouri	4,695,477,000	1.4%
43	Montana	997,447,000	0.3%
33	Nebraska	2,101,827,000	0.6%
30	Nevada	2,320,774,000	0.7%
28	New Hampshire	2,650,326,000	0.8%
5	New Jersey	19,196,599,000	5.7%
46	New Mexico	863,071,000	0.3%
1	New York	34,149,967,000	10.2%
17	North Carolina	6,449,622,000	1.9%
49	North Dakota	619,912,000	0.2%
9	Ohio	11,973,971,000	3.6%
38	Oklahoma	1,718,634,000	0.5%
25	Oregon	3,562,960,000	1.1%
7	Pennsylvania	13,390,534,000	4.0%
35	Rhode Island	1,819,413,000	0.5%
24	South Carolina	3,738,818,000	1.1%
48	South Dakota	730,122,000	0.2%
23	Tennessee	3,894,418,000	1.2%
3	Texas	30,275,679,000	9.0%
36	Utah	1,792,451,000	0.5%
41	Vermont	1,056,355,000	0.3%
11	Virginia	8,390,045,000	2.5%
16	Washington	6,637,299,000	2.0%
42	West Virginia	1,008,409,000	0.3%
13	Wisconsin	7,796,015,000	2.3%
45	Wyoming	890,710,000	0.3%

RANK ORDER

RANK	STATE	REVENUE	% of USA
1	New York	$34,149,967,000	10.2%
2	California	34,058,299,000	10.1%
3	Texas	30,275,679,000	9.0%
4	Florida	20,389,149,000	6.1%
5	New Jersey	19,196,599,000	5.7%
6	Illinois	18,690,132,000	5.6%
7	Pennsylvania	13,390,534,000	4.0%
8	Michigan	12,918,887,000	3.8%
9	Ohio	11,973,971,000	3.6%
10	Massachusetts	10,341,126,000	3.1%
11	Virginia	8,390,045,000	2.5%
12	Georgia	8,214,542,000	2.4%
13	Wisconsin	7,796,015,000	2.3%
14	Indiana	7,638,992,000	2.3%
15	Connecticut	7,155,644,000	2.1%
16	Washington	6,637,299,000	2.0%
17	North Carolina	6,449,622,000	1.9%
18	Maryland	5,594,371,000	1.7%
19	Minnesota	5,250,869,000	1.6%
20	Arizona	5,126,076,000	1.5%
21	Colorado	4,940,398,000	1.5%
22	Missouri	4,695,477,000	1.4%
23	Tennessee	3,894,418,000	1.2%
24	South Carolina	3,738,818,000	1.1%
25	Oregon	3,562,960,000	1.1%
26	Iowa	3,302,265,000	1.0%
27	Kansas	3,090,403,000	0.9%
28	New Hampshire	2,650,326,000	0.8%
29	Louisiana	2,429,386,000	0.7%
30	Nevada	2,320,774,000	0.7%
31	Kentucky	2,246,867,000	0.7%
32	Maine	2,151,968,000	0.6%
33	Nebraska	2,101,827,000	0.6%
34	Mississippi	1,967,447,000	0.6%
35	Rhode Island	1,819,413,000	0.5%
36	Utah	1,792,451,000	0.5%
37	Alabama	1,792,320,000	0.5%
38	Oklahoma	1,718,634,000	0.5%
39	Arkansas	1,172,261,000	0.3%
40	Idaho	1,153,841,000	0.3%
41	Vermont	1,056,355,000	0.3%
42	West Virginia	1,008,409,000	0.3%
43	Montana	997,447,000	0.3%
44	Alaska	892,307,000	0.3%
45	Wyoming	890,710,000	0.3%
46	New Mexico	863,071,000	0.3%
47	Hawaii	818,239,000	0.2%
48	South Dakota	730,122,000	0.2%
49	North Dakota	619,912,000	0.2%
50	Delaware	485,848,000	0.1%
	District of Columbia	1,135,527,000	0.3%

Source: U.S. Bureau of the Census, Governments Division
"State and Local Government Finances: 2004-2005" (http://www.census.gov/govs/www/estimate05.html)

Per Capita State and Local Government Property Tax Revenue in 2005

National Per Capita = $1,134

ALPHA ORDER

RANK	STATE	PER CAPITA
50	Alabama	$395
12	Alaska	1,333
35	Arizona	861
49	Arkansas	423
31	California	946
24	Colorado	1,057
2	Connecticut	2,052
43	Delaware	578
17	Florida	1,150
33	Georgia	902
42	Hawaii	646
37	Idaho	809
10	Illinois	1,469
15	Indiana	1,221
19	Iowa	1,117
18	Kansas	1,127
46	Kentucky	539
45	Louisiana	540
8	Maine	1,640
27	Maryland	1,004
9	Massachusetts	1,608
14	Michigan	1,278
26	Minnesota	1,027
40	Mississippi	678
36	Missouri	811
22	Montana	1,066
16	Nebraska	1,198
30	Nevada	963
3	New Hampshire	2,034
1	New Jersey	2,217
48	New Mexico	450
4	New York	1,773
38	North Carolina	743
29	North Dakota	975
25	Ohio	1,045
47	Oklahoma	486
28	Oregon	982
21	Pennsylvania	1,083
6	Rhode Island	1,706
34	South Carolina	879
32	South Dakota	936
41	Tennessee	650
13	Texas	1,325
39	Utah	716
7	Vermont	1,705
20	Virginia	1,110
23	Washington	1,058
44	West Virginia	558
11	Wisconsin	1,407
5	Wyoming	1,758

RANK ORDER

RANK	STATE	PER CAPITA
1	New Jersey	$2,217
2	Connecticut	2,052
3	New Hampshire	2,034
4	New York	1,773
5	Wyoming	1,758
6	Rhode Island	1,706
7	Vermont	1,705
8	Maine	1,640
9	Massachusetts	1,608
10	Illinois	1,469
11	Wisconsin	1,407
12	Alaska	1,333
13	Texas	1,325
14	Michigan	1,278
15	Indiana	1,221
16	Nebraska	1,198
17	Florida	1,150
18	Kansas	1,127
19	Iowa	1,117
20	Virginia	1,110
21	Pennsylvania	1,083
22	Montana	1,066
23	Washington	1,058
24	Colorado	1,057
25	Ohio	1,045
26	Minnesota	1,027
27	Maryland	1,004
28	Oregon	982
29	North Dakota	975
30	Nevada	963
31	California	946
32	South Dakota	936
33	Georgia	902
34	South Carolina	879
35	Arizona	861
36	Missouri	811
37	Idaho	809
38	North Carolina	743
39	Utah	716
40	Mississippi	678
41	Tennessee	650
42	Hawaii	646
43	Delaware	578
44	West Virginia	558
45	Louisiana	540
46	Kentucky	539
47	Oklahoma	486
48	New Mexico	450
49	Arkansas	423
50	Alabama	395

| | District of Columbia | 1,951 |

Source: CQ Press using data from U.S. Bureau of the Census, Governments Division
"State and Local Government Finances: 2004-2005" (http://www.census.gov/govs/www/estimate05.html)

State and Local Government Property Tax as a Percent of State and Local Government Total Revenue in 2005
National Percent = 13.3%

RANK	STATE	PERCENT
49	Alabama	5.3
42	Alaska	7.9
23	Arizona	12.5
48	Arkansas	6.2
39	California	9.0
22	Colorado	12.7
3	Connecticut	23.4
47	Delaware	6.4
14	Florida	15.1
18	Georgia	13.6
43	Hawaii	7.4
29	Idaho	11.5
7	Illinois	18.6
9	Indiana	17.4
17	Iowa	14.2
13	Kansas	15.5
41	Kentucky	8.0
45	Louisiana	6.8
5	Maine	19.0
25	Maryland	12.3
10	Massachusetts	16.8
12	Michigan	15.9
29	Minnesota	11.5
37	Mississippi	9.3
32	Missouri	11.4
19	Montana	13.4
20	Nebraska	13.2
26	Nevada	12.2
1	New Hampshire	29.7
2	New Jersey	24.7
50	New Mexico	5.2
15	New York	14.8
36	North Carolina	9.9
27	North Dakota	11.8
28	Ohio	11.7
44	Oklahoma	7.0
35	Oregon	11.0
21	Pennsylvania	12.9
6	Rhode Island	18.7
33	South Carolina	11.2
23	South Dakota	12.5
40	Tennessee	8.9
7	Texas	18.6
37	Utah	9.3
4	Vermont	19.6
15	Virginia	14.8
29	Washington	11.5
45	West Virginia	6.8
11	Wisconsin	16.1
33	Wyoming	11.2

RANK	STATE	PERCENT
1	New Hampshire	29.7
2	New Jersey	24.7
3	Connecticut	23.4
4	Vermont	19.6
5	Maine	19.0
6	Rhode Island	18.7
7	Illinois	18.6
7	Texas	18.6
9	Indiana	17.4
10	Massachusetts	16.8
11	Wisconsin	16.1
12	Michigan	15.9
13	Kansas	15.5
14	Florida	15.1
15	New York	14.8
15	Virginia	14.8
17	Iowa	14.2
18	Georgia	13.6
19	Montana	13.4
20	Nebraska	13.2
21	Pennsylvania	12.9
22	Colorado	12.7
23	Arizona	12.5
23	South Dakota	12.5
25	Maryland	12.3
26	Nevada	12.2
27	North Dakota	11.8
28	Ohio	11.7
29	Idaho	11.5
29	Minnesota	11.5
29	Washington	11.5
32	Missouri	11.4
33	South Carolina	11.2
33	Wyoming	11.2
35	Oregon	11.0
36	North Carolina	9.9
37	Mississippi	9.3
37	Utah	9.3
39	California	9.0
40	Tennessee	8.9
41	Kentucky	8.0
42	Alaska	7.9
43	Hawaii	7.4
44	Oklahoma	7.0
45	Louisiana	6.8
45	West Virginia	6.8
47	Delaware	6.4
48	Arkansas	6.2
49	Alabama	5.3
50	New Mexico	5.2

District of Columbia	12.2

Source: CQ Press using data from U.S. Bureau of the Census, Governments Division
"State and Local Government Finances: 2004-2005" (http://www.census.gov/govs/www/estimate05.html)

State and Local Government Property Tax Revenue as a Percent of State and Local Government Own Source Revenue in 2005
National Percent = 21.2%*

ALPHA ORDER

RANK	STATE	PERCENT
48	Alabama	8.9
42	Alaska	12.3
24	Arizona	20.1
47	Arkansas	10.0
38	California	15.8
25	Colorado	20.0
3	Connecticut	30.9
48	Delaware	8.9
17	Florida	22.4
21	Georgia	20.7
46	Hawaii	10.8
32	Idaho	18.0
8	Illinois	28.6
12	Indiana	23.9
18	Iowa	22.0
16	Kansas	22.9
41	Kentucky	12.7
45	Louisiana	11.0
6	Maine	29.9
34	Maryland	17.6
10	Massachusetts	25.9
11	Michigan	24.5
35	Minnesota	17.5
36	Mississippi	16.7
30	Missouri	18.5
14	Montana	23.3
19	Nebraska	21.9
33	Nevada	17.7
1	New Hampshire	43.5
2	New Jersey	34.4
48	New Mexico	8.9
13	New York	23.6
37	North Carolina	16.2
29	North Dakota	18.9
25	Ohio	20.0
44	Oklahoma	11.3
27	Oregon	19.7
21	Pennsylvania	20.7
4	Rhode Island	30.1
31	South Carolina	18.2
15	South Dakota	23.2
38	Tennessee	15.8
7	Texas	29.3
40	Utah	15.2
4	Vermont	30.1
21	Virginia	20.7
28	Washington	19.6
43	West Virginia	11.5
9	Wisconsin	26.3
20	Wyoming	20.9

RANK ORDER

RANK	STATE	PERCENT
1	New Hampshire	43.5
2	New Jersey	34.4
3	Connecticut	30.9
4	Rhode Island	30.1
4	Vermont	30.1
6	Maine	29.9
7	Texas	29.3
8	Illinois	28.6
9	Wisconsin	26.3
10	Massachusetts	25.9
11	Michigan	24.5
12	Indiana	23.9
13	New York	23.6
14	Montana	23.3
15	South Dakota	23.2
16	Kansas	22.9
17	Florida	22.4
18	Iowa	22.0
19	Nebraska	21.9
20	Wyoming	20.9
21	Georgia	20.7
21	Pennsylvania	20.7
21	Virginia	20.7
24	Arizona	20.1
25	Colorado	20.0
25	Ohio	20.0
27	Oregon	19.7
28	Washington	19.6
29	North Dakota	18.9
30	Missouri	18.5
31	South Carolina	18.2
32	Idaho	18.0
33	Nevada	17.7
34	Maryland	17.6
35	Minnesota	17.5
36	Mississippi	16.7
37	North Carolina	16.2
38	California	15.8
38	Tennessee	15.8
40	Utah	15.2
41	Kentucky	12.7
42	Alaska	12.3
43	West Virginia	11.5
44	Oklahoma	11.3
45	Louisiana	11.0
46	Hawaii	10.8
47	Arkansas	10.0
48	Alabama	8.9
48	Delaware	8.9
48	New Mexico	8.9
	District of Columbia	21.5

Source: CQ Press using data from U.S. Bureau of the Census, Governments Division
   "State and Local Government Finances: 2004-2005" (http://www.census.gov/govs/www/estimate05.html)
*Own source revenue includes taxes, current charges, and miscellaneous general revenue. Excluded are intergovernmental transfers, insurance trust revenue, and revenue from government owned utilities and other commercial or auxiliary enterprise.

State and Local Tax Burden as a Percentage of Income in 2007

National Percent = 11.0% of Income*

ALPHA ORDER				RANK ORDER		
RANK	STATE	PERCENT		RANK	STATE	PERCENT
46	Alabama	8.8		1	Vermont	14.1
50	Alaska	6.6		2	Maine	14.0
31	Arizona	10.3		3	New York	13.8
13	Arkansas	11.3		4	Rhode Island	12.7
11	California	11.5		5	Hawaii	12.4
30	Colorado	10.4		5	Ohio	12.4
8	Connecticut	12.2		7	Wisconsin	12.3
46	Delaware	8.8		8	Connecticut	12.2
37	Florida	10.0		9	Nebraska	11.9
31	Georgia	10.3		10	New Jersey	11.6
5	Hawaii	12.4		11	California	11.5
34	Idaho	10.1		11	Minnesota	11.5
22	Illinois	10.8		13	Arkansas	11.3
25	Indiana	10.7		14	Kansas	11.2
17	Iowa	11.0		14	Michigan	11.2
14	Kansas	11.2		16	Washington	11.1
20	Kentucky	10.9		17	Iowa	11.0
17	Louisiana	11.0		17	Louisiana	11.0
2	Maine	14.0		17	North Carolina	11.0
22	Maryland	10.8		20	Kentucky	10.9
28	Massachusetts	10.6		20	West Virginia	10.9
14	Michigan	11.2		22	Illinois	10.8
11	Minnesota	11.5		22	Maryland	10.8
29	Mississippi	10.5		22	Pennsylvania	10.8
34	Missouri	10.1		25	Indiana	10.7
41	Montana	9.7		25	South Carolina	10.7
9	Nebraska	11.9		25	Utah	10.7
34	Nevada	10.1		28	Massachusetts	10.6
49	New Hampshire	8.0		29	Mississippi	10.5
10	New Jersey	11.6		30	Colorado	10.4
40	New Mexico	9.8		31	Arizona	10.3
3	New York	13.8		31	Georgia	10.3
17	North Carolina	11.0		33	Virginia	10.2
39	North Dakota	9.9		34	Idaho	10.1
5	Ohio	12.4		34	Missouri	10.1
44	Oklahoma	9.0		34	Nevada	10.1
37	Oregon	10.0		37	Florida	10.0
22	Pennsylvania	10.8		37	Oregon	10.0
4	Rhode Island	12.7		39	North Dakota	9.9
25	South Carolina	10.7		40	New Mexico	9.8
44	South Dakota	9.0		41	Montana	9.7
48	Tennessee	8.5		42	Wyoming	9.5
43	Texas	9.3		43	Texas	9.3
25	Utah	10.7		44	Oklahoma	9.0
1	Vermont	14.1		44	South Dakota	9.0
33	Virginia	10.2		46	Alabama	8.8
16	Washington	11.1		46	Delaware	8.8
20	West Virginia	10.9		48	Tennessee	8.5
7	Wisconsin	12.3		49	New Hampshire	8.0
42	Wyoming	9.5		50	Alaska	6.6

	District of Columbia	12.5

Source: The Tax Foundation
   "State and Local Tax Burdens Compared to Other U.S. States, 1970-2007" (www.taxfoundation.org/research/show/335.html)
*All state and local taxes. Rankings based on rounded percentages.

State and Local Government Total Expenditures in 2005

National Total = $2,372,079,901,000*

ALPHA ORDER

RANK	STATE	EXPENDITURES	% of USA
23	Alabama	$33,223,624,000	1.4%
41	Alaska	10,026,866,000	0.4%
20	Arizona	39,259,444,000	1.7%
35	Arkansas	17,253,392,000	0.7%
1	California	343,493,753,000	14.5%
22	Colorado	35,096,165,000	1.5%
26	Connecticut	29,929,966,000	1.3%
45	Delaware	7,573,343,000	0.3%
4	Florida	130,363,162,000	5.5%
12	Georgia	58,901,679,000	2.5%
39	Hawaii	10,533,933,000	0.4%
43	Idaho	8,908,551,000	0.4%
6	Illinois	98,011,030,000	4.1%
18	Indiana	42,099,353,000	1.8%
30	Iowa	21,731,111,000	0.9%
32	Kansas	18,897,393,000	0.8%
28	Kentucky	26,964,382,000	1.1%
25	Louisiana	32,568,396,000	1.4%
40	Maine	10,221,371,000	0.4%
19	Maryland	41,273,875,000	1.7%
11	Massachusetts	59,040,717,000	2.5%
9	Michigan	76,538,413,000	3.2%
15	Minnesota	43,545,029,000	1.8%
31	Mississippi	20,041,617,000	0.8%
21	Missouri	37,186,146,000	1.6%
46	Montana	6,407,010,000	0.3%
37	Nebraska	14,266,846,000	0.6%
33	Nevada	17,404,534,000	0.7%
44	New Hampshire	8,661,571,000	0.4%
8	New Jersey	77,457,590,000	3.3%
36	New Mexico	15,572,278,000	0.7%
2	New York	227,985,299,000	9.6%
10	North Carolina	60,758,249,000	2.6%
50	North Dakota	4,796,172,000	0.2%
7	Ohio	91,932,549,000	3.9%
29	Oklahoma	22,005,087,000	0.9%
27	Oregon	29,084,143,000	1.2%
5	Pennsylvania	100,436,544,000	4.2%
42	Rhode Island	9,380,377,000	0.4%
24	South Carolina	33,010,572,000	1.4%
49	South Dakota	4,953,093,000	0.2%
17	Tennessee	42,911,391,000	1.8%
3	Texas	151,960,889,000	6.4%
34	Utah	17,269,401,000	0.7%
48	Vermont	5,179,203,000	0.2%
14	Virginia	51,595,278,000	2.2%
13	Washington	56,213,842,000	2.4%
38	West Virginia	12,267,018,000	0.5%
16	Wisconsin	43,146,506,000	1.8%
47	Wyoming	5,642,152,000	0.2%

RANK ORDER

RANK	STATE	EXPENDITURES	% of USA
1	California	$343,493,753,000	14.5%
2	New York	227,985,299,000	9.6%
3	Texas	151,960,889,000	6.4%
4	Florida	130,363,162,000	5.5%
5	Pennsylvania	100,436,544,000	4.2%
6	Illinois	98,011,030,000	4.1%
7	Ohio	91,932,549,000	3.9%
8	New Jersey	77,457,590,000	3.3%
9	Michigan	76,538,413,000	3.2%
10	North Carolina	60,758,249,000	2.6%
11	Massachusetts	59,040,717,000	2.5%
12	Georgia	58,901,679,000	2.5%
13	Washington	56,213,842,000	2.4%
14	Virginia	51,595,278,000	2.2%
15	Minnesota	43,545,029,000	1.8%
16	Wisconsin	43,146,506,000	1.8%
17	Tennessee	42,911,391,000	1.8%
18	Indiana	42,099,353,000	1.8%
19	Maryland	41,273,875,000	1.7%
20	Arizona	39,259,444,000	1.7%
21	Missouri	37,186,146,000	1.6%
22	Colorado	35,096,165,000	1.5%
23	Alabama	33,223,624,000	1.4%
24	South Carolina	33,010,572,000	1.4%
25	Louisiana	32,568,396,000	1.4%
26	Connecticut	29,929,966,000	1.3%
27	Oregon	29,084,143,000	1.2%
28	Kentucky	26,964,382,000	1.1%
29	Oklahoma	22,005,087,000	0.9%
30	Iowa	21,731,111,000	0.9%
31	Mississippi	20,041,617,000	0.8%
32	Kansas	18,897,393,000	0.8%
33	Nevada	17,404,534,000	0.7%
34	Utah	17,269,401,000	0.7%
35	Arkansas	17,253,392,000	0.7%
36	New Mexico	15,572,278,000	0.7%
37	Nebraska	14,266,846,000	0.6%
38	West Virginia	12,267,018,000	0.5%
39	Hawaii	10,533,933,000	0.4%
40	Maine	10,221,371,000	0.4%
41	Alaska	10,026,866,000	0.4%
42	Rhode Island	9,380,377,000	0.4%
43	Idaho	8,908,551,000	0.4%
44	New Hampshire	8,661,571,000	0.4%
45	Delaware	7,573,343,000	0.3%
46	Montana	6,407,010,000	0.3%
47	Wyoming	5,642,152,000	0.2%
48	Vermont	5,179,203,000	0.2%
49	South Dakota	4,953,093,000	0.2%
50	North Dakota	4,796,172,000	0.2%
	District of Columbia	9,099,596,000	0.4%

Source: U.S. Bureau of the Census, Governments Division
"State and Local Government Finances: 2004-2005" (http://www.census.gov/govs/www/estimate05.html)
*Total expenditures includes all money paid other than for retirement of debt and extension of loans. Includes payments from all sources of funds including current revenues and proceeds from borrowing and prior year fund balances. Includes intergovernmental transfers and expenditures for government owned utilities and other commercial or auxiliary enterprise, and insurance trust expenditures.

Per Capita State and Local Government Total Expenditures in 2005

National Per Capita = $8,017*

ALPHA ORDER

RANK	STATE	PER CAPITA
29	Alabama	$7,319
1	Alaska	14,979
43	Arizona	6,596
49	Arkansas	6,224
4	California	9,544
25	Colorado	7,509
10	Connecticut	8,585
6	Delaware	9,010
28	Florida	7,350
44	Georgia	6,467
13	Hawaii	8,310
48	Idaho	6,248
22	Illinois	7,706
40	Indiana	6,728
27	Iowa	7,353
36	Kansas	6,893
45	Kentucky	6,465
30	Louisiana	7,244
19	Maine	7,789
26	Maryland	7,406
5	Massachusetts	9,183
23	Michigan	7,572
11	Minnesota	8,515
34	Mississippi	6,910
46	Missouri	6,425
37	Montana	6,847
14	Nebraska	8,134
31	Nevada	7,225
42	New Hampshire	6,647
8	New Jersey	8,947
15	New Mexico	8,126
2	New York	11,836
33	North Carolina	7,001
24	North Dakota	7,542
17	Ohio	8,022
50	Oklahoma	6,223
18	Oregon	8,012
16	Pennsylvania	8,121
9	Rhode Island	8,794
21	South Carolina	7,758
47	South Dakota	6,350
32	Tennessee	7,165
41	Texas	6,652
35	Utah	6,894
12	Vermont	8,357
38	Virginia	6,827
7	Washington	8,964
39	West Virginia	6,794
20	Wisconsin	7,788
3	Wyoming	11,139

RANK ORDER

RANK	STATE	PER CAPITA
1	Alaska	$14,979
2	New York	11,836
3	Wyoming	11,139
4	California	9,544
5	Massachusetts	9,183
6	Delaware	9,010
7	Washington	8,964
8	New Jersey	8,947
9	Rhode Island	8,794
10	Connecticut	8,585
11	Minnesota	8,515
12	Vermont	8,357
13	Hawaii	8,310
14	Nebraska	8,134
15	New Mexico	8,126
16	Pennsylvania	8,121
17	Ohio	8,022
18	Oregon	8,012
19	Maine	7,789
20	Wisconsin	7,788
21	South Carolina	7,758
22	Illinois	7,706
23	Michigan	7,572
24	North Dakota	7,542
25	Colorado	7,509
26	Maryland	7,406
27	Iowa	7,353
28	Florida	7,350
29	Alabama	7,319
30	Louisiana	7,244
31	Nevada	7,225
32	Tennessee	7,165
33	North Carolina	7,001
34	Mississippi	6,910
35	Utah	6,894
36	Kansas	6,893
37	Montana	6,847
38	Virginia	6,827
39	West Virginia	6,794
40	Indiana	6,728
41	Texas	6,652
42	New Hampshire	6,647
43	Arizona	6,596
44	Georgia	6,467
45	Kentucky	6,465
46	Missouri	6,425
47	South Dakota	6,350
48	Idaho	6,248
49	Arkansas	6,224
50	Oklahoma	6,223

District of Columbia	15,634

Source: CQ Press using data from U.S. Bureau of the Census, Governments Division
"State and Local Government Finances: 2004-2005" (http://www.census.gov/govs/www/estimate05.html)
*Total expenditures includes all money paid other than for retirement of debt and extension of loans. Includes payments from all sources of funds including current revenues and proceeds from borrowing and prior year fund balances. Includes intergovernmental transfers and expenditures for government owned utilities and other commercial or auxiliary enterprise, and insurance trust expenditures.

State and Local Government Direct General Expenditures in 2005

National Total = $2,009,643,948,000*

ALPHA ORDER

RANK	STATE	EXPENDITURES	% of USA
22	Alabama	$29,029,453,000	1.4%
41	Alaska	8,795,450,000	0.4%
20	Arizona	32,928,754,000	1.6%
33	Arkansas	15,504,364,000	0.8%
1	California	275,715,075,000	13.7%
23	Colorado	28,991,387,000	1.4%
26	Connecticut	26,211,818,000	1.3%
45	Delaware	6,822,379,000	0.3%
4	Florida	112,637,220,000	5.6%
11	Georgia	50,700,848,000	2.5%
40	Hawaii	9,329,110,000	0.5%
42	Idaho	8,062,213,000	0.4%
6	Illinois	82,258,357,000	4.1%
15	Indiana	38,197,018,000	1.9%
29	Iowa	19,456,400,000	1.0%
32	Kansas	16,796,017,000	0.8%
28	Kentucky	23,442,445,000	1.2%
24	Louisiana	28,527,886,000	1.4%
39	Maine	9,512,051,000	0.5%
18	Maryland	36,654,548,000	1.8%
12	Massachusetts	49,735,294,000	2.5%
8	Michigan	67,107,847,000	3.3%
16	Minnesota	38,008,771,000	1.9%
31	Mississippi	17,846,506,000	0.9%
21	Missouri	32,614,003,000	1.6%
46	Montana	5,746,548,000	0.3%
38	Nebraska	10,964,144,000	0.5%
34	Nevada	14,933,368,000	0.7%
44	New Hampshire	7,833,884,000	0.4%
9	New Jersey	65,991,631,000	3.3%
36	New Mexico	14,092,748,000	0.7%
2	New York	184,121,449,000	9.2%
10	North Carolina	52,596,377,000	2.6%
50	North Dakota	4,349,445,000	0.2%
7	Ohio	77,930,439,000	3.9%
30	Oklahoma	19,081,155,000	0.9%
27	Oregon	23,726,302,000	1.2%
5	Pennsylvania	86,302,826,000	4.3%
43	Rhode Island	8,043,284,000	0.4%
25	South Carolina	28,001,544,000	1.4%
49	South Dakota	4,445,966,000	0.2%
19	Tennessee	33,892,752,000	1.7%
3	Texas	131,336,182,000	6.5%
35	Utah	14,521,599,000	0.7%
48	Vermont	4,728,618,000	0.2%
13	Virginia	46,603,950,000	2.3%
14	Washington	44,360,102,000	2.2%
37	West Virginia	11,109,069,000	0.6%
17	Wisconsin	37,723,732,000	1.9%
47	Wyoming	5,077,315,000	0.3%

RANK ORDER

RANK	STATE	EXPENDITURES	% of USA
1	California	$275,715,075,000	13.7%
2	New York	184,121,449,000	9.2%
3	Texas	131,336,182,000	6.5%
4	Florida	112,637,220,000	5.6%
5	Pennsylvania	86,302,826,000	4.3%
6	Illinois	82,258,357,000	4.1%
7	Ohio	77,930,439,000	3.9%
8	Michigan	67,107,847,000	3.3%
9	New Jersey	65,991,631,000	3.3%
10	North Carolina	52,596,377,000	2.6%
11	Georgia	50,700,848,000	2.5%
12	Massachusetts	49,735,294,000	2.5%
13	Virginia	46,603,950,000	2.3%
14	Washington	44,360,102,000	2.2%
15	Indiana	38,197,018,000	1.9%
16	Minnesota	38,008,771,000	1.9%
17	Wisconsin	37,723,732,000	1.9%
18	Maryland	36,654,548,000	1.8%
19	Tennessee	33,892,752,000	1.7%
20	Arizona	32,928,754,000	1.6%
21	Missouri	32,614,003,000	1.6%
22	Alabama	29,029,453,000	1.4%
23	Colorado	28,991,387,000	1.4%
24	Louisiana	28,527,886,000	1.4%
25	South Carolina	28,001,544,000	1.4%
26	Connecticut	26,211,818,000	1.3%
27	Oregon	23,726,302,000	1.2%
28	Kentucky	23,442,445,000	1.2%
29	Iowa	19,456,400,000	1.0%
30	Oklahoma	19,081,155,000	0.9%
31	Mississippi	17,846,506,000	0.9%
32	Kansas	16,796,017,000	0.8%
33	Arkansas	15,504,364,000	0.8%
34	Nevada	14,933,368,000	0.7%
35	Utah	14,521,599,000	0.7%
36	New Mexico	14,092,748,000	0.7%
37	West Virginia	11,109,069,000	0.6%
38	Nebraska	10,964,144,000	0.5%
39	Maine	9,512,051,000	0.5%
40	Hawaii	9,329,110,000	0.5%
41	Alaska	8,795,450,000	0.4%
42	Idaho	8,062,213,000	0.4%
43	Rhode Island	8,043,284,000	0.4%
44	New Hampshire	7,833,884,000	0.4%
45	Delaware	6,822,379,000	0.3%
46	Montana	5,746,548,000	0.3%
47	Wyoming	5,077,315,000	0.3%
48	Vermont	4,728,618,000	0.2%
49	South Dakota	4,445,966,000	0.2%
50	North Dakota	4,349,445,000	0.2%
	District of Columbia	7,244,305,000	0.4%

Source: U.S. Bureau of the Census, Governments Division
  "State and Local Government Finances: 2004-2005" (http://www.census.gov/govs/www/estimate05.html)
*Direct general expenditures include expenditures for current operations, assistance and subsidies, interest on debt, and capital outlay. Excludes intergovernmental transfers, expenditures for government owned utilities and other commercial or auxiliary enterprise, and insurance trust expenditures.

Per Capita State and Local Government Direct General Expenditures in 2005

National Per Capita = $6,792*

ALPHA ORDER

RANK	STATE	PER CAPITA
26	Alabama	$6,395
1	Alaska	13,139
49	Arizona	5,532
47	Arkansas	5,593
6	California	7,661
30	Colorado	6,203
10	Connecticut	7,518
4	Delaware	8,116
27	Florida	6,351
48	Georgia	5,567
12	Hawaii	7,360
44	Idaho	5,654
25	Illinois	6,467
37	Indiana	6,105
21	Iowa	6,583
36	Kansas	6,126
46	Kentucky	5,620
28	Louisiana	6,346
14	Maine	7,249
23	Maryland	6,577
5	Massachusetts	7,736
20	Michigan	6,639
11	Minnesota	7,433
33	Mississippi	6,153
45	Missouri	5,635
35	Montana	6,141
29	Nebraska	6,251
31	Nevada	6,199
39	New Hampshire	6,012
8	New Jersey	7,623
13	New Mexico	7,354
3	New York	9,559
38	North Carolina	6,060
17	North Dakota	6,839
19	Ohio	6,800
50	Oklahoma	5,396
24	Oregon	6,536
16	Pennsylvania	6,978
9	Rhode Island	7,540
22	South Carolina	6,581
42	South Dakota	5,700
43	Tennessee	5,659
41	Texas	5,749
40	Utah	5,797
7	Vermont	7,630
32	Virginia	6,167
15	Washington	7,074
34	West Virginia	6,152
18	Wisconsin	6,809
2	Wyoming	10,024

RANK ORDER

RANK	STATE	PER CAPITA
1	Alaska	$13,139
2	Wyoming	10,024
3	New York	9,559
4	Delaware	8,116
5	Massachusetts	7,736
6	California	7,661
7	Vermont	7,630
8	New Jersey	7,623
9	Rhode Island	7,540
10	Connecticut	7,518
11	Minnesota	7,433
12	Hawaii	7,360
13	New Mexico	7,354
14	Maine	7,249
15	Washington	7,074
16	Pennsylvania	6,978
17	North Dakota	6,839
18	Wisconsin	6,809
19	Ohio	6,800
20	Michigan	6,639
21	Iowa	6,583
22	South Carolina	6,581
23	Maryland	6,577
24	Oregon	6,536
25	Illinois	6,467
26	Alabama	6,395
27	Florida	6,351
28	Louisiana	6,346
29	Nebraska	6,251
30	Colorado	6,203
31	Nevada	6,199
32	Virginia	6,167
33	Mississippi	6,153
34	West Virginia	6,152
35	Montana	6,141
36	Kansas	6,126
37	Indiana	6,105
38	North Carolina	6,060
39	New Hampshire	6,012
40	Utah	5,797
41	Texas	5,749
42	South Dakota	5,700
43	Tennessee	5,659
44	Idaho	5,654
45	Missouri	5,635
46	Kentucky	5,620
47	Arkansas	5,593
48	Georgia	5,567
49	Arizona	5,532
50	Oklahoma	5,396

District of Columbia	12,446

Source: CQ Press using data from U.S. Bureau of the Census, Governments Division
   "State and Local Government Finances: 2004-2005" (http://www.census.gov/govs/www/estimate05.html)
*Direct general expenditures include expenditures for current operations, assistance and subsidies, interest on debt, and capital outlay. Excludes intergovernmental transfers, expenditures for government owned utilities and other commercial or auxiliary enterprise, and insurance trust expenditures.

State and Local Government Debt Outstanding in 2005

National Total = $2,066,755,086,000*

ALPHA ORDER

RANK	STATE	DEBT	% of USA
28	Alabama	$22,531,730,000	1.1%
39	Alaska	8,758,496,000	0.4%
18	Arizona	32,829,830,000	1.6%
34	Arkansas	11,202,611,000	0.5%
1	California	283,699,007,000	13.7%
14	Colorado	39,107,926,000	1.9%
20	Connecticut	31,049,942,000	1.5%
44	Delaware	6,227,033,000	0.3%
4	Florida	110,713,236,000	5.4%
15	Georgia	37,917,360,000	1.8%
37	Hawaii	9,292,140,000	0.4%
46	Idaho	3,978,636,000	0.2%
5	Illinois	103,685,805,000	5.0%
21	Indiana	30,525,519,000	1.5%
33	Iowa	11,649,016,000	0.6%
30	Kansas	17,552,547,000	0.8%
22	Kentucky	30,197,179,000	1.5%
27	Louisiana	24,754,276,000	1.2%
43	Maine	6,961,914,000	0.3%
24	Maryland	27,956,720,000	1.4%
7	Massachusetts	77,989,984,000	3.8%
9	Michigan	68,817,529,000	3.3%
17	Minnesota	36,262,165,000	1.8%
36	Mississippi	10,189,289,000	0.5%
19	Missouri	31,333,437,000	1.5%
45	Montana	5,097,210,000	0.2%
41	Nebraska	8,555,830,000	0.4%
29	Nevada	18,494,186,000	0.9%
38	New Hampshire	9,292,099,000	0.4%
8	New Jersey	72,894,132,000	3.5%
35	New Mexico	10,443,324,000	0.5%
2	New York	233,107,491,000	11.3%
13	North Carolina	40,906,463,000	2.0%
49	North Dakota	3,314,088,000	0.2%
10	Ohio	60,648,565,000	2.9%
32	Oklahoma	14,412,990,000	0.7%
25	Oregon	25,856,952,000	1.3%
6	Pennsylvania	100,591,286,000	4.9%
40	Rhode Island	8,698,729,000	0.4%
23	South Carolina	29,917,129,000	1.4%
47	South Dakota	3,839,762,000	0.2%
26	Tennessee	25,572,989,000	1.2%
3	Texas	150,605,604,000	7.3%
31	Utah	14,830,829,000	0.7%
48	Vermont	3,640,270,000	0.2%
12	Virginia	44,535,283,000	2.2%
11	Washington	53,049,067,000	2.6%
42	West Virginia	8,433,275,000	0.4%
16	Wisconsin	36,925,377,000	1.8%
50	Wyoming	1,899,320,000	0.1%

RANK ORDER

RANK	STATE	DEBT	% of USA
1	California	$283,699,007,000	13.7%
2	New York	233,107,491,000	11.3%
3	Texas	150,605,604,000	7.3%
4	Florida	110,713,236,000	5.4%
5	Illinois	103,685,805,000	5.0%
6	Pennsylvania	100,591,286,000	4.9%
7	Massachusetts	77,989,984,000	3.8%
8	New Jersey	72,894,132,000	3.5%
9	Michigan	68,817,529,000	3.3%
10	Ohio	60,648,565,000	2.9%
11	Washington	53,049,067,000	2.6%
12	Virginia	44,535,283,000	2.2%
13	North Carolina	40,906,463,000	2.0%
14	Colorado	39,107,926,000	1.9%
15	Georgia	37,917,360,000	1.8%
16	Wisconsin	36,925,377,000	1.8%
17	Minnesota	36,262,165,000	1.8%
18	Arizona	32,829,830,000	1.6%
19	Missouri	31,333,437,000	1.5%
20	Connecticut	31,049,942,000	1.5%
21	Indiana	30,525,519,000	1.5%
22	Kentucky	30,197,179,000	1.5%
23	South Carolina	29,917,129,000	1.4%
24	Maryland	27,956,720,000	1.4%
25	Oregon	25,856,952,000	1.3%
26	Tennessee	25,572,989,000	1.2%
27	Louisiana	24,754,276,000	1.2%
28	Alabama	22,531,730,000	1.1%
29	Nevada	18,494,186,000	0.9%
30	Kansas	17,552,547,000	0.8%
31	Utah	14,830,829,000	0.7%
32	Oklahoma	14,412,990,000	0.7%
33	Iowa	11,649,016,000	0.6%
34	Arkansas	11,202,611,000	0.5%
35	New Mexico	10,443,324,000	0.5%
36	Mississippi	10,189,289,000	0.5%
37	Hawaii	9,292,140,000	0.4%
38	New Hampshire	9,292,099,000	0.4%
39	Alaska	8,758,496,000	0.4%
40	Rhode Island	8,698,729,000	0.4%
41	Nebraska	8,555,830,000	0.4%
42	West Virginia	8,433,275,000	0.4%
43	Maine	6,961,914,000	0.3%
44	Delaware	6,227,033,000	0.3%
45	Montana	5,097,210,000	0.2%
46	Idaho	3,978,636,000	0.2%
47	South Dakota	3,839,762,000	0.2%
48	Vermont	3,640,270,000	0.2%
49	North Dakota	3,314,088,000	0.2%
50	Wyoming	1,899,320,000	0.1%
	District of Columbia	6,009,509,000	0.3%

Source: U.S. Bureau of the Census, Governments Division
"State and Local Government Finances: 2004-2005" (http://www.census.gov/govs/www/estimate05.html)
*Includes short-term, long-term, full faith and credit, nonguaranteed, and public debt for private purposes.

Per Capita State and Local Government Debt Outstanding in 2005

National Per Capita = $6,985*

<table>
<tr><td colspan="3">ALPHA ORDER</td><td colspan="3">RANK ORDER</td></tr>
<tr><th>RANK</th><th>STATE</th><th>PER CAPITA</th><th>RANK</th><th>STATE</th><th>PER CAPITA</th></tr>
<tr><td>37</td><td>Alabama</td><td>$4,963</td><td>1</td><td>Alaska</td><td>$13,084</td></tr>
<tr><td>1</td><td>Alaska</td><td>13,084</td><td>2</td><td>Massachusetts</td><td>12,131</td></tr>
<tr><td>28</td><td>Arizona</td><td>5,516</td><td>3</td><td>New York</td><td>12,102</td></tr>
<tr><td>46</td><td>Arkansas</td><td>4,041</td><td>4</td><td>Connecticut</td><td>8,906</td></tr>
<tr><td>11</td><td>California</td><td>7,883</td><td>5</td><td>Washington</td><td>8,460</td></tr>
<tr><td>7</td><td>Colorado</td><td>8,368</td><td>6</td><td>New Jersey</td><td>8,420</td></tr>
<tr><td>4</td><td>Connecticut</td><td>8,906</td><td>7</td><td>Colorado</td><td>8,368</td></tr>
<tr><td>13</td><td>Delaware</td><td>7,408</td><td>8</td><td>Rhode Island</td><td>8,155</td></tr>
<tr><td>24</td><td>Florida</td><td>6,242</td><td>9</td><td>Illinois</td><td>8,152</td></tr>
<tr><td>44</td><td>Georgia</td><td>4,163</td><td>10</td><td>Pennsylvania</td><td>8,134</td></tr>
<tr><td>14</td><td>Hawaii</td><td>7,331</td><td>11</td><td>California</td><td>7,883</td></tr>
<tr><td>50</td><td>Idaho</td><td>2,790</td><td>12</td><td>Nevada</td><td>7,677</td></tr>
<tr><td>9</td><td>Illinois</td><td>8,152</td><td>13</td><td>Delaware</td><td>7,408</td></tr>
<tr><td>39</td><td>Indiana</td><td>4,879</td><td>14</td><td>Hawaii</td><td>7,331</td></tr>
<tr><td>47</td><td>Iowa</td><td>3,941</td><td>15</td><td>Kentucky</td><td>7,240</td></tr>
<tr><td>23</td><td>Kansas</td><td>6,402</td><td>16</td><td>New Hampshire</td><td>7,131</td></tr>
<tr><td>15</td><td>Kentucky</td><td>7,240</td><td>17</td><td>Oregon</td><td>7,123</td></tr>
<tr><td>29</td><td>Louisiana</td><td>5,506</td><td>18</td><td>Minnesota</td><td>7,091</td></tr>
<tr><td>33</td><td>Maine</td><td>5,305</td><td>19</td><td>South Carolina</td><td>7,031</td></tr>
<tr><td>36</td><td>Maryland</td><td>5,016</td><td>20</td><td>Michigan</td><td>6,808</td></tr>
<tr><td>2</td><td>Massachusetts</td><td>12,131</td><td>21</td><td>Wisconsin</td><td>6,665</td></tr>
<tr><td>20</td><td>Michigan</td><td>6,808</td><td>22</td><td>Texas</td><td>6,593</td></tr>
<tr><td>18</td><td>Minnesota</td><td>7,091</td><td>23</td><td>Kansas</td><td>6,402</td></tr>
<tr><td>49</td><td>Mississippi</td><td>3,513</td><td>24</td><td>Florida</td><td>6,242</td></tr>
<tr><td>32</td><td>Missouri</td><td>5,414</td><td>25</td><td>Utah</td><td>5,920</td></tr>
<tr><td>31</td><td>Montana</td><td>5,447</td><td>26</td><td>Virginia</td><td>5,893</td></tr>
<tr><td>40</td><td>Nebraska</td><td>4,878</td><td>27</td><td>Vermont</td><td>5,874</td></tr>
<tr><td>12</td><td>Nevada</td><td>7,677</td><td>28</td><td>Arizona</td><td>5,516</td></tr>
<tr><td>16</td><td>New Hampshire</td><td>7,131</td><td>29</td><td>Louisiana</td><td>5,506</td></tr>
<tr><td>6</td><td>New Jersey</td><td>8,420</td><td>30</td><td>New Mexico</td><td>5,450</td></tr>
<tr><td>30</td><td>New Mexico</td><td>5,450</td><td>31</td><td>Montana</td><td>5,447</td></tr>
<tr><td>3</td><td>New York</td><td>12,102</td><td>32</td><td>Missouri</td><td>5,414</td></tr>
<tr><td>41</td><td>North Carolina</td><td>4,713</td><td>33</td><td>Maine</td><td>5,305</td></tr>
<tr><td>35</td><td>North Dakota</td><td>5,211</td><td>34</td><td>Ohio</td><td>5,292</td></tr>
<tr><td>34</td><td>Ohio</td><td>5,292</td><td>35</td><td>North Dakota</td><td>5,211</td></tr>
<tr><td>45</td><td>Oklahoma</td><td>4,076</td><td>36</td><td>Maryland</td><td>5,016</td></tr>
<tr><td>17</td><td>Oregon</td><td>7,123</td><td>37</td><td>Alabama</td><td>4,963</td></tr>
<tr><td>10</td><td>Pennsylvania</td><td>8,134</td><td>38</td><td>South Dakota</td><td>4,922</td></tr>
<tr><td>8</td><td>Rhode Island</td><td>8,155</td><td>39</td><td>Indiana</td><td>4,879</td></tr>
<tr><td>19</td><td>South Carolina</td><td>7,031</td><td>40</td><td>Nebraska</td><td>4,878</td></tr>
<tr><td>38</td><td>South Dakota</td><td>4,922</td><td>41</td><td>North Carolina</td><td>4,713</td></tr>
<tr><td>43</td><td>Tennessee</td><td>4,270</td><td>42</td><td>West Virginia</td><td>4,671</td></tr>
<tr><td>22</td><td>Texas</td><td>6,593</td><td>43</td><td>Tennessee</td><td>4,270</td></tr>
<tr><td>25</td><td>Utah</td><td>5,920</td><td>44</td><td>Georgia</td><td>4,163</td></tr>
<tr><td>27</td><td>Vermont</td><td>5,874</td><td>45</td><td>Oklahoma</td><td>4,076</td></tr>
<tr><td>26</td><td>Virginia</td><td>5,893</td><td>46</td><td>Arkansas</td><td>4,041</td></tr>
<tr><td>5</td><td>Washington</td><td>8,460</td><td>47</td><td>Iowa</td><td>3,941</td></tr>
<tr><td>42</td><td>West Virginia</td><td>4,671</td><td>48</td><td>Wyoming</td><td>3,750</td></tr>
<tr><td>21</td><td>Wisconsin</td><td>6,665</td><td>49</td><td>Mississippi</td><td>3,513</td></tr>
<tr><td>48</td><td>Wyoming</td><td>3,750</td><td>50</td><td>Idaho</td><td>2,790</td></tr>
<tr><td></td><td></td><td></td><td></td><td>District of Columbia</td><td>10,325</td></tr>
</table>

Source: CQ Press using data from U.S. Bureau of the Census, Governments Division

"State and Local Government Finances: 2004-2005" (http://www.census.gov/govs/www/estimate05.html)

*Includes short-term, long-term, full faith and credit, nonguaranteed, and public debt for private purposes.

State and Local Government Full-Time Equivalent Employees in 2006

National Total = 16,135,699 FTE Employees*

ALPHA ORDER					RANK ORDER			
RANK	STATE	EMPLOYEES	% of USA		RANK	STATE	EMPLOYEES	% of USA
22	Alabama	272,535	1.7%		1	California	1,818,732	11.3%
44	Alaska	52,631	0.3%		2	Texas	1,315,006	8.1%
20	Arizona	285,084	1.8%		3	New York	1,190,287	7.4%
33	Arkansas	161,923	1.0%		4	Florida	867,259	5.4%
1	California	1,818,732	11.3%		5	Illinois	634,990	3.9%
24	Colorado	255,002	1.6%		6	Ohio	616,739	3.8%
29	Connecticut	188,222	1.2%		7	Pennsylvania	568,350	3.5%
46	Delaware	49,488	0.3%		8	New Jersey	511,755	3.2%
4	Florida	867,259	5.4%		9	North Carolina	511,263	3.2%
10	Georgia	505,644	3.1%		10	Georgia	505,644	3.1%
42	Hawaii	69,594	0.4%		11	Michigan	486,697	3.0%
39	Idaho	79,413	0.5%		12	Virginia	430,621	2.7%
5	Illinois	634,990	3.9%		13	Washington	333,196	2.1%
14	Indiana	332,849	2.1%		14	Indiana	332,849	2.1%
30	Iowa	185,921	1.2%		15	Massachusetts	332,072	2.1%
31	Kansas	184,943	1.1%		16	Tennessee	323,673	2.0%
26	Kentucky	243,798	1.5%		17	Missouri	320,083	2.0%
21	Louisiana	275,776	1.7%		18	Maryland	291,140	1.8%
40	Maine	77,605	0.5%		19	Wisconsin	288,073	1.8%
18	Maryland	291,140	1.8%		20	Arizona	285,084	1.8%
15	Massachusetts	332,072	2.1%		21	Louisiana	275,776	1.7%
11	Michigan	486,697	3.0%		22	Alabama	272,535	1.7%
23	Minnesota	272,394	1.7%		23	Minnesota	272,394	1.7%
28	Mississippi	188,905	1.2%		24	Colorado	255,002	1.6%
17	Missouri	320,083	2.0%		25	South Carolina	248,966	1.5%
43	Montana	54,188	0.3%		26	Kentucky	243,798	1.5%
36	Nebraska	117,496	0.7%		27	Oklahoma	214,343	1.3%
37	Nevada	103,304	0.6%		28	Mississippi	188,905	1.2%
41	New Hampshire	69,777	0.4%		29	Connecticut	188,222	1.2%
8	New Jersey	511,755	3.2%		30	Iowa	185,921	1.2%
35	New Mexico	127,929	0.8%		31	Kansas	184,943	1.1%
3	New York	1,190,287	7.4%		32	Oregon	181,711	1.1%
9	North Carolina	511,263	3.2%		33	Arkansas	161,923	1.0%
49	North Dakota	41,173	0.3%		34	Utah	128,785	0.8%
6	Ohio	616,739	3.8%		35	New Mexico	127,929	0.8%
27	Oklahoma	214,343	1.3%		36	Nebraska	117,496	0.7%
32	Oregon	181,711	1.1%		37	Nevada	103,304	0.6%
7	Pennsylvania	568,350	3.5%		38	West Virginia	97,391	0.6%
45	Rhode Island	51,232	0.3%		39	Idaho	79,413	0.5%
25	South Carolina	248,966	1.5%		40	Maine	77,605	0.5%
48	South Dakota	45,186	0.3%		41	New Hampshire	69,777	0.4%
16	Tennessee	323,673	2.0%		42	Hawaii	69,594	0.4%
2	Texas	1,315,006	8.1%		43	Montana	54,188	0.3%
34	Utah	128,785	0.8%		44	Alaska	52,631	0.3%
50	Vermont	40,142	0.2%		45	Rhode Island	51,232	0.3%
12	Virginia	430,621	2.7%		46	Delaware	49,488	0.3%
13	Washington	333,196	2.1%		47	Wyoming	45,802	0.3%
38	West Virginia	97,391	0.6%		48	South Dakota	45,186	0.3%
19	Wisconsin	288,073	1.8%		49	North Dakota	41,173	0.3%
47	Wyoming	45,802	0.3%		50	Vermont	40,142	0.2%
						District of Columbia	46,611	0.3%

Source: U.S. Bureau of the Census, Governments Division
"State and Local Employment and Payroll - March 2006" (http://www.census.gov/govs/www/apesstl06.html)
*As of March 2006.

Rate of State and Local Government Full-Time Equivalent Employees in 2006

National Rate = 540 State/Local Government Employees per 10,000 Population*

ALPHA ORDER

RANK	STATE	RATE
13	Alabama	594
2	Alaska	777
48	Arizona	462
18	Arkansas	576
41	California	502
32	Colorado	535
29	Connecticut	538
16	Delaware	580
47	Florida	480
28	Georgia	541
26	Hawaii	544
27	Idaho	542
43	Illinois	497
35	Indiana	528
10	Iowa	625
3	Kansas	671
16	Kentucky	580
7	Louisiana	650
15	Maine	590
38	Maryland	520
40	Massachusetts	516
46	Michigan	482
35	Minnesota	528
6	Mississippi	652
25	Missouri	548
22	Montana	572
4	Nebraska	666
50	Nevada	414
34	New Hampshire	532
14	New Jersey	591
5	New Mexico	659
11	New York	617
18	North Carolina	576
9	North Dakota	646
29	Ohio	538
12	Oklahoma	599
44	Oregon	492
49	Pennsylvania	458
45	Rhode Island	483
20	South Carolina	575
21	South Dakota	573
33	Tennessee	533
24	Texas	562
42	Utah	499
8	Vermont	647
23	Virginia	564
37	Washington	523
29	West Virginia	538
39	Wisconsin	517
1	Wyoming	893

RANK ORDER

RANK	STATE	RATE
1	Wyoming	893
2	Alaska	777
3	Kansas	671
4	Nebraska	666
5	New Mexico	659
6	Mississippi	652
7	Louisiana	650
8	Vermont	647
9	North Dakota	646
10	Iowa	625
11	New York	617
12	Oklahoma	599
13	Alabama	594
14	New Jersey	591
15	Maine	590
16	Delaware	580
16	Kentucky	580
18	Arkansas	576
18	North Carolina	576
20	South Carolina	575
21	South Dakota	573
22	Montana	572
23	Virginia	564
24	Texas	562
25	Missouri	548
26	Hawaii	544
27	Idaho	542
28	Georgia	541
29	Connecticut	538
29	Ohio	538
29	West Virginia	538
32	Colorado	535
33	Tennessee	533
34	New Hampshire	532
35	Indiana	528
35	Minnesota	528
37	Washington	523
38	Maryland	520
39	Wisconsin	517
40	Massachusetts	516
41	California	502
42	Utah	499
43	Illinois	497
44	Oregon	492
45	Rhode Island	483
46	Michigan	482
47	Florida	480
48	Arizona	462
49	Pennsylvania	458
50	Nevada	414

District of Columbia 796

Source: CQ Press using data from U.S. Bureau of the Census, Governments Division
"State and Local Employment and Payroll - March 2006" (http://www.census.gov/govs/www/apesstl06.html)
*As of March 2006.

Average Annual Earnings of Full-Time State and Local Government Employees in 2006
National Average = $46,588*

ALPHA ORDER

RANK	STATE	EARNINGS
37	Alabama	$37,654
9	Alaska	51,508
20	Arizona	45,894
50	Arkansas	34,455
1	California	61,871
15	Colorado	48,170
3	Connecticut	56,545
14	Delaware	48,513
23	Florida	43,059
32	Georgia	39,373
17	Hawaii	47,243
41	Idaho	37,219
13	Illinois	48,947
29	Indiana	40,840
24	Iowa	42,766
39	Kansas	37,647
45	Kentucky	36,275
46	Louisiana	35,931
34	Maine	38,972
8	Maryland	52,395
10	Massachusetts	51,426
12	Michigan	49,600
11	Minnesota	50,490
49	Mississippi	34,470
42	Missouri	36,974
40	Montana	37,406
30	Nebraska	40,476
7	Nevada	53,139
25	New Hampshire	41,674
2	New Jersey	57,725
43	New Mexico	36,894
4	New York	56,255
33	North Carolina	39,288
28	North Dakota	40,978
21	Ohio	44,656
47	Oklahoma	34,964
19	Oregon	46,671
18	Pennsylvania	47,028
5	Rhode Island	54,940
38	South Carolina	37,652
44	South Dakota	36,361
36	Tennessee	37,951
35	Texas	38,782
26	Utah	41,368
27	Vermont	41,346
22	Virginia	43,418
6	Washington	53,657
48	West Virginia	34,869
16	Wisconsin	47,780
31	Wyoming	40,072

RANK ORDER

RANK	STATE	EARNINGS
1	California	$61,871
2	New Jersey	57,725
3	Connecticut	56,545
4	New York	56,255
5	Rhode Island	54,940
6	Washington	53,657
7	Nevada	53,139
8	Maryland	52,395
9	Alaska	51,508
10	Massachusetts	51,426
11	Minnesota	50,490
12	Michigan	49,600
13	Illinois	48,947
14	Delaware	48,513
15	Colorado	48,170
16	Wisconsin	47,780
17	Hawaii	47,243
18	Pennsylvania	47,028
19	Oregon	46,671
20	Arizona	45,894
21	Ohio	44,656
22	Virginia	43,418
23	Florida	43,059
24	Iowa	42,766
25	New Hampshire	41,674
26	Utah	41,368
27	Vermont	41,346
28	North Dakota	40,978
29	Indiana	40,840
30	Nebraska	40,476
31	Wyoming	40,072
32	Georgia	39,373
33	North Carolina	39,288
34	Maine	38,972
35	Texas	38,782
36	Tennessee	37,951
37	Alabama	37,654
38	South Carolina	37,652
39	Kansas	37,647
40	Montana	37,406
41	Idaho	37,219
42	Missouri	36,974
43	New Mexico	36,894
44	South Dakota	36,361
45	Kentucky	36,275
46	Louisiana	35,931
47	Oklahoma	34,964
48	West Virginia	34,869
49	Mississippi	34,470
50	Arkansas	34,455
	District of Columbia	59,901

Source: CQ Press using data from U.S. Bureau of the Census, Governments Division
"State and Local Employment and Payroll - March 2006" (http://www.census.gov/govs/www/apesstl06.html)
*March 2006 full-time payroll (multiplied by 12) divided by full-time employees.

State Government Total Revenue in 2005

National Total = $1,637,791,549,000*

ALPHA ORDER

RANK	STATE	REVENUE	% of USA
25	Alabama	$22,538,186,000	1.4%
38	Alaska	9,115,808,000	0.6%
20	Arizona	25,310,938,000	1.5%
32	Arkansas	14,931,481,000	0.9%
1	California	249,057,158,000	15.2%
26	Colorado	22,473,929,000	1.4%
28	Connecticut	20,550,806,000	1.3%
44	Delaware	6,166,083,000	0.4%
4	Florida	77,077,664,000	4.7%
14	Georgia	36,111,681,000	2.2%
39	Hawaii	9,091,681,000	0.6%
43	Idaho	7,204,275,000	0.4%
7	Illinois	60,061,672,000	3.7%
18	Indiana	27,324,685,000	1.7%
30	Iowa	15,677,109,000	1.0%
35	Kansas	12,514,724,000	0.8%
27	Kentucky	21,248,450,000	1.3%
21	Louisiana	24,841,345,000	1.5%
41	Maine	8,419,502,000	0.5%
17	Maryland	28,889,827,000	1.8%
11	Massachusetts	41,747,484,000	2.5%
8	Michigan	55,726,406,000	3.4%
16	Minnesota	31,723,566,000	1.9%
31	Mississippi	15,518,347,000	0.9%
19	Missouri	26,820,654,000	1.6%
47	Montana	5,688,525,000	0.3%
40	Nebraska	8,711,002,000	0.5%
37	Nevada	11,535,175,000	0.7%
45	New Hampshire	6,150,551,000	0.4%
9	New Jersey	51,348,019,000	3.1%
33	New Mexico	13,337,333,000	0.8%
2	New York	140,222,453,000	8.6%
10	North Carolina	44,892,190,000	2.7%
50	North Dakota	3,877,194,000	0.2%
5	Ohio	72,202,876,000	4.4%
29	Oklahoma	17,873,970,000	1.1%
24	Oregon	22,589,057,000	1.4%
6	Pennsylvania	69,760,398,000	4.3%
42	Rhode Island	7,252,620,000	0.4%
23	South Carolina	22,990,747,000	1.4%
49	South Dakota	4,059,264,000	0.2%
22	Tennessee	24,660,867,000	1.5%
3	Texas	96,134,134,000	5.9%
34	Utah	13,122,463,000	0.8%
48	Vermont	4,599,312,000	0.3%
12	Virginia	37,267,917,000	2.3%
13	Washington	36,831,190,000	2.2%
36	West Virginia	12,170,191,000	0.7%
15	Wisconsin	34,437,923,000	2.1%
46	Wyoming	5,932,717,000	0.4%

RANK ORDER

RANK	STATE	REVENUE	% of USA
1	California	$249,057,158,000	15.2%
2	New York	140,222,453,000	8.6%
3	Texas	96,134,134,000	5.9%
4	Florida	77,077,664,000	4.7%
5	Ohio	72,202,876,000	4.4%
6	Pennsylvania	69,760,398,000	4.3%
7	Illinois	60,061,672,000	3.7%
8	Michigan	55,726,406,000	3.4%
9	New Jersey	51,348,019,000	3.1%
10	North Carolina	44,892,190,000	2.7%
11	Massachusetts	41,747,484,000	2.5%
12	Virginia	37,267,917,000	2.3%
13	Washington	36,831,190,000	2.2%
14	Georgia	36,111,681,000	2.2%
15	Wisconsin	34,437,923,000	2.1%
16	Minnesota	31,723,566,000	1.9%
17	Maryland	28,889,827,000	1.8%
18	Indiana	27,324,685,000	1.7%
19	Missouri	26,820,654,000	1.6%
20	Arizona	25,310,938,000	1.5%
21	Louisiana	24,841,345,000	1.5%
22	Tennessee	24,660,867,000	1.5%
23	South Carolina	22,990,747,000	1.4%
24	Oregon	22,589,057,000	1.4%
25	Alabama	22,538,186,000	1.4%
26	Colorado	22,473,929,000	1.4%
27	Kentucky	21,248,450,000	1.3%
28	Connecticut	20,550,806,000	1.3%
29	Oklahoma	17,873,970,000	1.1%
30	Iowa	15,677,109,000	1.0%
31	Mississippi	15,518,347,000	0.9%
32	Arkansas	14,931,481,000	0.9%
33	New Mexico	13,337,333,000	0.8%
34	Utah	13,122,463,000	0.8%
35	Kansas	12,514,724,000	0.8%
36	West Virginia	12,170,191,000	0.7%
37	Nevada	11,535,175,000	0.7%
38	Alaska	9,115,808,000	0.6%
39	Hawaii	9,091,681,000	0.6%
40	Nebraska	8,711,002,000	0.5%
41	Maine	8,419,502,000	0.5%
42	Rhode Island	7,252,620,000	0.4%
43	Idaho	7,204,275,000	0.4%
44	Delaware	6,166,083,000	0.4%
45	New Hampshire	6,150,551,000	0.4%
46	Wyoming	5,932,717,000	0.4%
47	Montana	5,688,525,000	0.3%
48	Vermont	4,599,312,000	0.3%
49	South Dakota	4,059,264,000	0.2%
50	North Dakota	3,877,194,000	0.2%
	District of Columbia**	NA	NA

Source: U.S. Bureau of the Census, Governments Division
   "State and Local Government Finances: 2004-2005" (http://www.census.gov/govs/www/estimate05.html)
*Total revenue includes all money received from external sources. This includes taxes, intergovernmental transfers and insurance trust revenue, and revenue from government owned utilities and other commercial or auxiliary enterprise.
**Not applicable.

Per Capita State Government Total Revenue in 2005

National Per Capita = $5,546*

ALPHA ORDER

RANK	STATE	PER CAPITA
37	Alabama	$4,965
1	Alaska	13,618
47	Arizona	4,252
26	Arkansas	5,386
8	California	6,920
39	Colorado	4,809
20	Connecticut	5,894
4	Delaware	7,336
46	Florida	4,346
50	Georgia	3,965
6	Hawaii	7,172
35	Idaho	5,052
41	Illinois	4,722
45	Indiana	4,367
28	Iowa	5,304
44	Kansas	4,565
33	Kentucky	5,094
23	Louisiana	5,526
12	Maine	6,416
31	Maryland	5,184
11	Massachusetts	6,493
24	Michigan	5,513
16	Minnesota	6,203
27	Mississippi	5,350
43	Missouri	4,634
18	Montana	6,079
36	Nebraska	4,966
40	Nevada	4,788
42	New Hampshire	4,720
19	New Jersey	5,931
7	New Mexico	6,960
5	New York	7,280
32	North Carolina	5,172
17	North Dakota	6,097
13	Ohio	6,301
34	Oklahoma	5,055
14	Oregon	6,223
22	Pennsylvania	5,641
9	Rhode Island	6,799
25	South Carolina	5,403
30	South Dakota	5,204
49	Tennessee	4,117
48	Texas	4,208
29	Utah	5,238
3	Vermont	7,421
38	Virginia	4,931
21	Washington	5,873
10	West Virginia	6,740
15	Wisconsin	6,216
2	Wyoming	11,712

RANK ORDER

RANK	STATE	PER CAPITA
1	Alaska	$13,618
2	Wyoming	11,712
3	Vermont	7,421
4	Delaware	7,336
5	New York	7,280
6	Hawaii	7,172
7	New Mexico	6,960
8	California	6,920
9	Rhode Island	6,799
10	West Virginia	6,740
11	Massachusetts	6,493
12	Maine	6,416
13	Ohio	6,301
14	Oregon	6,223
15	Wisconsin	6,216
16	Minnesota	6,203
17	North Dakota	6,097
18	Montana	6,079
19	New Jersey	5,931
20	Connecticut	5,894
21	Washington	5,873
22	Pennsylvania	5,641
23	Louisiana	5,526
24	Michigan	5,513
25	South Carolina	5,403
26	Arkansas	5,386
27	Mississippi	5,350
28	Iowa	5,304
29	Utah	5,238
30	South Dakota	5,204
31	Maryland	5,184
32	North Carolina	5,172
33	Kentucky	5,094
34	Oklahoma	5,055
35	Idaho	5,052
36	Nebraska	4,966
37	Alabama	4,965
38	Virginia	4,931
39	Colorado	4,809
40	Nevada	4,788
41	Illinois	4,722
42	New Hampshire	4,720
43	Missouri	4,634
44	Kansas	4,565
45	Indiana	4,367
46	Florida	4,346
47	Arizona	4,252
48	Texas	4,208
49	Tennessee	4,117
50	Georgia	3,965

District of Columbia**   NA

Source: CQ Press using data from U.S. Bureau of the Census, Governments Division
"State and Local Government Finances: 2004-2005" (http://www.census.gov/govs/www/estimate05.html)
*Total revenue includes all money received from external sources. This includes taxes, intergovernmental transfers and insurance trust revenue, and revenue from government owned utilities and other commercial or auxiliary enterprise.
**Not applicable.

State Government Intergovernmental Revenue in 2005

National Total = $408,449,375,000*

ALPHA ORDER

RANK	STATE	REVENUE	% of USA
16	Alabama	$7,460,913,000	1.8%
40	Alaska	2,317,180,000	0.6%
15	Arizona	7,566,075,000	1.9%
30	Arkansas	4,110,258,000	1.0%
1	California	51,163,273,000	12.5%
28	Colorado	4,536,117,000	1.1%
32	Connecticut	4,012,708,000	1.0%
50	Delaware	1,157,400,000	0.3%
4	Florida	18,287,697,000	4.5%
11	Georgia	9,861,216,000	2.4%
44	Hawaii	1,785,979,000	0.4%
45	Idaho	1,749,617,000	0.4%
7	Illinois	13,894,704,000	3.4%
20	Indiana	6,949,410,000	1.7%
31	Iowa	4,104,190,000	1.0%
35	Kansas	3,219,968,000	0.8%
25	Kentucky	5,840,378,000	1.4%
19	Louisiana	7,087,581,000	1.7%
38	Maine	2,528,819,000	0.6%
21	Maryland	6,705,276,000	1.6%
13	Massachusetts	8,423,035,000	2.1%
8	Michigan	12,992,812,000	3.2%
23	Minnesota	6,575,048,000	1.6%
26	Mississippi	5,769,398,000	1.4%
14	Missouri	7,904,419,000	1.9%
43	Montana	1,813,841,000	0.4%
39	Nebraska	2,502,664,000	0.6%
42	Nevada	1,900,554,000	0.5%
46	New Hampshire	1,738,974,000	0.4%
10	New Jersey	10,258,349,000	2.5%
33	New Mexico	3,978,116,000	1.0%
2	New York	47,756,868,000	11.7%
9	North Carolina	12,841,936,000	3.1%
49	North Dakota	1,204,744,000	0.3%
6	Ohio	15,745,517,000	3.9%
27	Oklahoma	4,909,074,000	1.2%
29	Oregon	4,474,091,000	1.1%
5	Pennsylvania	16,656,455,000	4.1%
41	Rhode Island	2,078,598,000	0.5%
18	South Carolina	7,180,316,000	1.8%
48	South Dakota	1,235,882,000	0.3%
12	Tennessee	8,645,708,000	2.1%
3	Texas	26,701,366,000	6.5%
36	Utah	2,961,509,000	0.7%
47	Vermont	1,260,499,000	0.3%
24	Virginia	6,414,447,000	1.6%
17	Washington	7,397,857,000	1.8%
34	West Virginia	3,338,846,000	0.8%
22	Wisconsin	6,693,670,000	1.6%
37	Wyoming	2,756,023,000	0.7%

RANK ORDER

RANK	STATE	REVENUE	% of USA
1	California	$51,163,273,000	12.5%
2	New York	47,756,868,000	11.7%
3	Texas	26,701,366,000	6.5%
4	Florida	18,287,697,000	4.5%
5	Pennsylvania	16,656,455,000	4.1%
6	Ohio	15,745,517,000	3.9%
7	Illinois	13,894,704,000	3.4%
8	Michigan	12,992,812,000	3.2%
9	North Carolina	12,841,936,000	3.1%
10	New Jersey	10,258,349,000	2.5%
11	Georgia	9,861,216,000	2.4%
12	Tennessee	8,645,708,000	2.1%
13	Massachusetts	8,423,035,000	2.1%
14	Missouri	7,904,419,000	1.9%
15	Arizona	7,566,075,000	1.9%
16	Alabama	7,460,913,000	1.8%
17	Washington	7,397,857,000	1.8%
18	South Carolina	7,180,316,000	1.8%
19	Louisiana	7,087,581,000	1.7%
20	Indiana	6,949,410,000	1.7%
21	Maryland	6,705,276,000	1.6%
22	Wisconsin	6,693,670,000	1.6%
23	Minnesota	6,575,048,000	1.6%
24	Virginia	6,414,447,000	1.6%
25	Kentucky	5,840,378,000	1.4%
26	Mississippi	5,769,398,000	1.4%
27	Oklahoma	4,909,074,000	1.2%
28	Colorado	4,536,117,000	1.1%
29	Oregon	4,474,091,000	1.1%
30	Arkansas	4,110,258,000	1.0%
31	Iowa	4,104,190,000	1.0%
32	Connecticut	4,012,708,000	1.0%
33	New Mexico	3,978,116,000	1.0%
34	West Virginia	3,338,846,000	0.8%
35	Kansas	3,219,968,000	0.8%
36	Utah	2,961,509,000	0.7%
37	Wyoming	2,756,023,000	0.7%
38	Maine	2,528,819,000	0.6%
39	Nebraska	2,502,664,000	0.6%
40	Alaska	2,317,180,000	0.6%
41	Rhode Island	2,078,598,000	0.5%
42	Nevada	1,900,554,000	0.5%
43	Montana	1,813,841,000	0.4%
44	Hawaii	1,785,979,000	0.4%
45	Idaho	1,749,617,000	0.4%
46	New Hampshire	1,738,974,000	0.4%
47	Vermont	1,260,499,000	0.3%
48	South Dakota	1,235,882,000	0.3%
49	North Dakota	1,204,744,000	0.3%
50	Delaware	1,157,400,000	0.3%
	District of Columbia**	NA	NA

Source: U.S. Bureau of the Census, Governments Division
     "State and Local Government Finances: 2004-2005" (http://www.census.gov/govs/www/estimate05.html)
*Includes revenue from federal and local government sources.
**Not applicable.

Per Capita State Government Intergovernmental Revenue in 2005

National Per Capita = $1,383*

ALPHA ORDER

RANK	STATE	PER CAPITA
13	Alabama	$1,644
2	Alaska	3,462
33	Arizona	1,271
16	Arkansas	1,483
20	California	1,422
48	Colorado	971
43	Connecticut	1,151
25	Delaware	1,377
47	Florida	1,031
46	Georgia	1,083
21	Hawaii	1,409
35	Idaho	1,227
45	Illinois	1,092
44	Indiana	1,111
23	Iowa	1,389
41	Kansas	1,174
22	Kentucky	1,400
15	Louisiana	1,577
9	Maine	1,927
37	Maryland	1,203
30	Massachusetts	1,310
32	Michigan	1,285
31	Minnesota	1,286
6	Mississippi	1,989
27	Missouri	1,366
8	Montana	1,938
19	Nebraska	1,427
50	Nevada	789
29	New Hampshire	1,334
38	New Jersey	1,185
4	New Mexico	2,076
3	New York	2,479
17	North Carolina	1,480
10	North Dakota	1,894
26	Ohio	1,374
24	Oklahoma	1,388
34	Oregon	1,233
28	Pennsylvania	1,347
7	Rhode Island	1,949
12	South Carolina	1,688
14	South Dakota	1,584
18	Tennessee	1,444
42	Texas	1,169
39	Utah	1,182
5	Vermont	2,034
49	Virginia	849
40	Washington	1,180
11	West Virginia	1,849
36	Wisconsin	1,208
1	Wyoming	5,441

RANK ORDER

RANK	STATE	PER CAPITA
1	Wyoming	$5,441
2	Alaska	3,462
3	New York	2,479
4	New Mexico	2,076
5	Vermont	2,034
6	Mississippi	1,989
7	Rhode Island	1,949
8	Montana	1,938
9	Maine	1,927
10	North Dakota	1,894
11	West Virginia	1,849
12	South Carolina	1,688
13	Alabama	1,644
14	South Dakota	1,584
15	Louisiana	1,577
16	Arkansas	1,483
17	North Carolina	1,480
18	Tennessee	1,444
19	Nebraska	1,427
20	California	1,422
21	Hawaii	1,409
22	Kentucky	1,400
23	Iowa	1,389
24	Oklahoma	1,388
25	Delaware	1,377
26	Ohio	1,374
27	Missouri	1,366
28	Pennsylvania	1,347
29	New Hampshire	1,334
30	Massachusetts	1,310
31	Minnesota	1,286
32	Michigan	1,285
33	Arizona	1,271
34	Oregon	1,233
35	Idaho	1,227
36	Wisconsin	1,208
37	Maryland	1,203
38	New Jersey	1,185
39	Utah	1,182
40	Washington	1,180
41	Kansas	1,174
42	Texas	1,169
43	Connecticut	1,151
44	Indiana	1,111
45	Illinois	1,092
46	Georgia	1,083
47	Florida	1,031
48	Colorado	971
49	Virginia	849
50	Nevada	789

District of Columbia**   NA

Source: CQ Press using data from U.S. Bureau of the Census, Governments Division
"State and Local Government Finances: 2004-2005" (http://www.census.gov/govs/www/estimate05.html)
*Includes revenue from federal and local government sources.
**Not applicable.

State Government Own Source Revenue in 2004

National Total = $873,869,115,000*

RANK	STATE	REVENUE	% of USA
25	Alabama	$11,690,547,000	1.3%
39	Alaska	5,563,360,000	0.6%
20	Arizona	13,925,466,000	1.6%
30	Arkansas	8,737,492,000	1.0%
1	California	119,402,242,000	13.7%
27	Colorado	11,327,702,000	1.3%
19	Connecticut	14,609,972,000	1.7%
42	Delaware	4,312,307,000	0.5%
4	Florida	43,797,521,000	5.0%
13	Georgia	20,192,050,000	2.3%
38	Hawaii	6,078,397,000	0.7%
43	Idaho	3,929,660,000	0.4%
6	Illinois	33,812,464,000	3.9%
18	Indiana	17,515,802,000	2.0%
31	Iowa	8,468,430,000	1.0%
33	Kansas	7,321,975,000	0.8%
24	Kentucky	12,316,671,000	1.4%
23	Louisiana	13,079,655,000	1.5%
41	Maine	4,488,621,000	0.5%
16	Maryland	17,967,919,000	2.1%
10	Massachusetts	26,086,778,000	3.0%
8	Michigan	32,967,044,000	3.8%
15	Minnesota	19,214,969,000	2.2%
35	Mississippi	7,047,838,000	0.8%
21	Missouri	13,520,624,000	1.5%
47	Montana	2,807,301,000	0.3%
40	Nebraska	5,284,428,000	0.6%
36	Nevada	6,872,941,000	0.8%
45	New Hampshire	3,302,364,000	0.4%
9	New Jersey	30,612,084,000	3.5%
34	New Mexico	7,148,181,000	0.8%
2	New York	63,228,136,000	7.2%
12	North Carolina	23,460,672,000	2.7%
49	North Dakota	2,138,296,000	0.2%
7	Ohio	33,291,147,000	3.8%
29	Oklahoma	9,699,664,000	1.1%
28	Oregon	10,294,532,000	1.2%
5	Pennsylvania	37,438,318,000	4.3%
44	Rhode Island	3,818,290,000	0.4%
26	South Carolina	11,562,222,000	1.3%
50	South Dakota	1,759,145,000	0.2%
22	Tennessee	13,445,510,000	1.5%
3	Texas	49,402,954,000	5.7%
32	Utah	7,452,805,000	0.9%
46	Vermont	2,961,492,000	0.3%
11	Virginia	24,018,211,000	2.7%
14	Washington	19,581,029,000	2.2%
37	West Virginia	6,627,158,000	0.8%
17	Wisconsin	17,917,533,000	2.1%
48	Wyoming	2,369,196,000	0.3%

RANK	STATE	REVENUE	% of USA
1	California	$119,402,242,000	13.7%
2	New York	63,228,136,000	7.2%
3	Texas	49,402,954,000	5.7%
4	Florida	43,797,521,000	5.0%
5	Pennsylvania	37,438,318,000	4.3%
6	Illinois	33,812,464,000	3.9%
7	Ohio	33,291,147,000	3.8%
8	Michigan	32,967,044,000	3.8%
9	New Jersey	30,612,084,000	3.5%
10	Massachusetts	26,086,778,000	3.0%
11	Virginia	24,018,211,000	2.7%
12	North Carolina	23,460,672,000	2.7%
13	Georgia	20,192,050,000	2.3%
14	Washington	19,581,029,000	2.2%
15	Minnesota	19,214,969,000	2.2%
16	Maryland	17,967,919,000	2.1%
17	Wisconsin	17,917,533,000	2.1%
18	Indiana	17,515,802,000	2.0%
19	Connecticut	14,609,972,000	1.7%
20	Arizona	13,925,466,000	1.6%
21	Missouri	13,520,624,000	1.5%
22	Tennessee	13,445,510,000	1.5%
23	Louisiana	13,079,655,000	1.5%
24	Kentucky	12,316,671,000	1.4%
25	Alabama	11,690,547,000	1.3%
26	South Carolina	11,562,222,000	1.3%
27	Colorado	11,327,702,000	1.3%
28	Oregon	10,294,532,000	1.2%
29	Oklahoma	9,699,664,000	1.1%
30	Arkansas	8,737,492,000	1.0%
31	Iowa	8,468,430,000	1.0%
32	Utah	7,452,805,000	0.9%
33	Kansas	7,321,975,000	0.8%
34	New Mexico	7,148,181,000	0.8%
35	Mississippi	7,047,838,000	0.8%
36	Nevada	6,872,941,000	0.8%
37	West Virginia	6,627,158,000	0.8%
38	Hawaii	6,078,397,000	0.7%
39	Alaska	5,563,360,000	0.6%
40	Nebraska	5,284,428,000	0.6%
41	Maine	4,488,621,000	0.5%
42	Delaware	4,312,307,000	0.5%
43	Idaho	3,929,660,000	0.4%
44	Rhode Island	3,818,290,000	0.4%
45	New Hampshire	3,302,364,000	0.4%
46	Vermont	2,961,492,000	0.3%
47	Montana	2,807,301,000	0.3%
48	Wyoming	2,369,196,000	0.3%
49	North Dakota	2,138,296,000	0.2%
50	South Dakota	1,759,145,000	0.2%
	District of Columbia**	NA	NA

Source: U.S. Bureau of the Census, Governments Division
"State and Local Government Finances: 2004-2005" (http://www.census.gov/govs/www/estimate05.html)
*Own source revenue includes taxes, current charges, and miscellaneous general revenue. Excluded are intergovernmental transfers, insurance trust revenue, and revenue from government owned utilities and other commercial or auxiliary enterprise.
**Not applicable.

Per Capita State Government Own Source Revenue in 2005

National Per Capita = $2,959*

ALPHA ORDER		
RANK	STATE	PER CAPITA
40	Alabama	$2,575
1	Alaska	8,311
45	Arizona	2,340
21	Arkansas	3,152
15	California	3,318
44	Colorado	2,424
6	Connecticut	4,190
2	Delaware	5,130
42	Florida	2,469
49	Georgia	2,217
3	Hawaii	4,795
34	Idaho	2,756
39	Illinois	2,658
33	Indiana	2,799
30	Iowa	2,865
38	Kansas	2,671
27	Kentucky	2,953
28	Louisiana	2,909
13	Maine	3,421
19	Maryland	3,224
7	Massachusetts	4,058
17	Michigan	3,261
8	Minnesota	3,757
43	Mississippi	2,430
46	Missouri	2,336
25	Montana	3,000
24	Nebraska	3,013
31	Nevada	2,853
41	New Hampshire	2,534
12	New Jersey	3,536
9	New Mexico	3,730
16	New York	3,282
37	North Carolina	2,703
14	North Dakota	3,362
29	Ohio	2,905
35	Oklahoma	2,743
32	Oregon	2,836
23	Pennsylvania	3,027
11	Rhode Island	3,579
36	South Carolina	2,717
47	South Dakota	2,255
48	Tennessee	2,245
50	Texas	2,163
26	Utah	2,975
4	Vermont	4,779
20	Virginia	3,178
22	Washington	3,123
10	West Virginia	3,670
18	Wisconsin	3,234
5	Wyoming	4,677

RANK ORDER		
RANK	STATE	PER CAPITA
1	Alaska	$8,311
2	Delaware	5,130
3	Hawaii	4,795
4	Vermont	4,779
5	Wyoming	4,677
6	Connecticut	4,190
7	Massachusetts	4,058
8	Minnesota	3,757
9	New Mexico	3,730
10	West Virginia	3,670
11	Rhode Island	3,579
12	New Jersey	3,536
13	Maine	3,421
14	North Dakota	3,362
15	California	3,318
16	New York	3,282
17	Michigan	3,261
18	Wisconsin	3,234
19	Maryland	3,224
20	Virginia	3,178
21	Arkansas	3,152
22	Washington	3,123
23	Pennsylvania	3,027
24	Nebraska	3,013
25	Montana	3,000
26	Utah	2,975
27	Kentucky	2,953
28	Louisiana	2,909
29	Ohio	2,905
30	Iowa	2,865
31	Nevada	2,853
32	Oregon	2,836
33	Indiana	2,799
34	Idaho	2,756
35	Oklahoma	2,743
36	South Carolina	2,717
37	North Carolina	2,703
38	Kansas	2,671
39	Illinois	2,658
40	Alabama	2,575
41	New Hampshire	2,534
42	Florida	2,469
43	Mississippi	2,430
44	Colorado	2,424
45	Arizona	2,340
46	Missouri	2,336
47	South Dakota	2,255
48	Tennessee	2,245
49	Georgia	2,217
50	Texas	2,163

District of Columbia**   NA

Source: CQ Press using data from U.S. Bureau of the Census, Governments Division

"State and Local Government Finances: 2004-2005" (http://www.census.gov/govs/www/estimate05.html)

*Own source revenue includes taxes, current charges, and miscellaneous general revenue. Excluded are intergovernmental transfers, insurance trust revenue, and revenue from government owned utilities and other commercial or auxiliary enterprise.

**Not applicable.

Profits of State Lotteries in 2006

National Total = $16,986,220,000*

ALPHA ORDER

RANK ORDER

RANK	STATE	PROFITS	% of USA	RANK	STATE	PROFITS	% of USA
NA	Alabama**	NA	NA	1	New York	$2,203,000,000	13.0%
NA	Alaska**	NA	NA	2	California	1,240,570,000	7.3%
25	Arizona	141,120,000	0.8%	3	Florida	1,230,000,000	7.2%
NA	Arkansas**	NA	NA	4	Texas	1,036,110,000	6.1%
2	California	1,240,570,000	7.3%	5	Pennsylvania	975,850,000	5.7%
26	Colorado	125,600,000	0.7%	6	Massachusetts	951,240,000	5.6%
18	Connecticut	284,870,000	1.7%	7	New Jersey	849,250,000	5.0%
21	Delaware	248,800,000	1.5%	8	Georgia	822,400,000	4.8%
3	Florida	1,230,000,000	7.2%	9	Michigan	688,020,000	4.1%
8	Georgia	822,400,000	4.8%	10	Ohio	646,300,000	3.8%
NA	Hawaii**	NA	NA	11	Illinois	637,670,000	3.8%
38	Idaho	33,000,000	0.2%	12	West Virginia	610,000,000	3.6%
11	Illinois	637,670,000	3.8%	13	Maryland	500,970,000	2.9%
22	Indiana	218,000,000	1.3%	14	Oregon	483,000,000	2.8%
31	Iowa	80,880,000	0.5%	15	Virginia	454,900,000	2.7%
34	Kansas	67,090,000	0.4%	16	Rhode Island	323,900,000	1.9%
23	Kentucky	204,300,000	1.2%	17	South Carolina	319,400,000	1.9%
29	Louisiana	118,760,000	0.7%	18	Connecticut	284,870,000	1.7%
36	Maine	51,700,000	0.3%	19	Tennessee	277,660,000	1.6%
13	Maryland	500,970,000	2.9%	20	Missouri	260,670,000	1.5%
6	Massachusetts	951,240,000	5.6%	21	Delaware	248,800,000	1.5%
9	Michigan	688,020,000	4.1%	22	Indiana	218,000,000	1.3%
27	Minnesota	121,300,000	0.7%	23	Kentucky	204,300,000	1.2%
NA	Mississippi**	NA	NA	24	Wisconsin	150,600,000	0.9%
20	Missouri	260,670,000	1.5%	25	Arizona	141,120,000	0.8%
41	Montana	9,110,000	0.1%	26	Colorado	125,600,000	0.7%
39	Nebraska	30,320,000	0.2%	27	Minnesota	121,300,000	0.7%
NA	Nevada**	NA	NA	28	South Dakota	118,990,000	0.7%
32	New Hampshire	80,320,000	0.5%	29	Louisiana	118,760,000	0.7%
7	New Jersey	849,250,000	5.0%	30	Washington	116,950,000	0.7%
37	New Mexico	36,860,000	0.2%	31	Iowa	80,880,000	0.5%
1	New York	2,203,000,000	13.0%	32	New Hampshire	80,320,000	0.5%
35	North Carolina	64,590,000	0.4%	33	Oklahoma	68,950,000	0.4%
42	North Dakota	6,920,000	0.0%	34	Kansas	67,090,000	0.4%
10	Ohio	646,300,000	3.8%	35	North Carolina	64,590,000	0.4%
33	Oklahoma	68,950,000	0.4%	36	Maine	51,700,000	0.3%
14	Oregon	483,000,000	2.8%	37	New Mexico	36,860,000	0.2%
5	Pennsylvania	975,850,000	5.7%	38	Idaho	33,000,000	0.2%
16	Rhode Island	323,900,000	1.9%	39	Nebraska	30,320,000	0.2%
17	South Carolina	319,400,000	1.9%	40	Vermont	22,880,000	0.1%
28	South Dakota	118,990,000	0.7%	41	Montana	9,110,000	0.1%
19	Tennessee	277,660,000	1.6%	42	North Dakota	6,920,000	0.0%
4	Texas	1,036,110,000	6.1%	NA	Alabama**	NA	NA
NA	Utah**	NA	NA	NA	Alaska**	NA	NA
40	Vermont	22,880,000	0.1%	NA	Arkansas**	NA	NA
15	Virginia	454,900,000	2.7%	NA	Hawaii**	NA	NA
30	Washington	116,950,000	0.7%	NA	Mississippi**	NA	NA
12	West Virginia	610,000,000	3.6%	NA	Nevada**	NA	NA
24	Wisconsin	150,600,000	0.9%	NA	Utah**	NA	NA
NA	Wyoming**	NA	NA	NA	Wyoming**	NA	NA
					District of Columbia	73,400,000	0.4%

Source: North American Association of State and Provincial Lotteries, Willoughby Hills, OH
    "Sales and Profits" (http://www.naspl.org/index.cfm?fuseaction=content&PageID=3&PageCategory=3)
*Reported profits for fiscal year 2006 on sales of $57,101,180,000. National total does not include $115,200,000 in profits for Puerto Rico.
**No lottery as of fiscal year 2006.

Per Capita Profits of State Lotteries in 2006

National Per Capita = $60.47*

ALPHA ORDER				RANK ORDER		
RANK	STATE	PER CAPITA		RANK	STATE	PER CAPITA
NA	Alabama**	NA		1	West Virginia	$337.26
NA	Alaska**	NA		2	Rhode Island	305.09
34	Arizona	22.89		3	Delaware	291.76
NA	Arkansas**	NA		4	South Dakota	150.91
27	California	34.22		5	Massachusetts	147.84
31	Colorado	26.35		6	Oregon	130.86
11	Connecticut	81.49		7	New York	114.25
3	Delaware	291.76		8	New Jersey	98.00
14	Florida	68.12		9	Maryland	89.43
10	Georgia	88.03		10	Georgia	88.03
NA	Hawaii**	NA		11	Connecticut	81.49
35	Idaho	22.54		12	Pennsylvania	78.68
19	Illinois	49.91		13	South Carolina	73.76
26	Indiana	34.59		14	Florida	68.12
29	Iowa	27.21		15	Michigan	68.11
32	Kansas	24.34		16	New Hampshire	61.23
20	Kentucky	48.59		17	Virginia	59.54
28	Louisiana	27.99		18	Ohio	56.38
24	Maine	39.32		19	Illinois	49.91
9	Maryland	89.43		20	Kentucky	48.59
5	Massachusetts	147.84		21	Tennessee	45.71
15	Michigan	68.11		22	Missouri	44.65
33	Minnesota	23.53		23	Texas	44.26
NA	Mississippi**	NA		24	Maine	39.32
22	Missouri	44.65		25	Vermont	36.86
41	Montana	9.62		26	Indiana	34.59
39	Nebraska	17.19		27	California	34.22
NA	Nevada**	NA		28	Louisiana	27.99
16	New Hampshire	61.23		29	Iowa	27.21
8	New Jersey	98.00		30	Wisconsin	27.02
37	New Mexico	18.98		31	Colorado	26.35
7	New York	114.25		32	Kansas	24.34
42	North Carolina	7.28		33	Minnesota	23.53
40	North Dakota	10.86		34	Arizona	22.89
18	Ohio	56.38		35	Idaho	22.54
36	Oklahoma	19.27		36	Oklahoma	19.27
6	Oregon	130.86		37	New Mexico	18.98
12	Pennsylvania	78.68		38	Washington	18.35
2	Rhode Island	305.09		39	Nebraska	17.19
13	South Carolina	73.76		40	North Dakota	10.86
4	South Dakota	150.91		41	Montana	9.62
21	Tennessee	45.71		42	North Carolina	7.28
23	Texas	44.26		NA	Alabama**	NA
NA	Utah**	NA		NA	Alaska**	NA
25	Vermont	36.86		NA	Arkansas**	NA
17	Virginia	59.54		NA	Hawaii**	NA
38	Washington	18.35		NA	Mississippi**	NA
1	West Virginia	337.26		NA	Nevada**	NA
30	Wisconsin	27.02		NA	Utah**	NA
NA	Wyoming**	NA		NA	Wyoming**	NA
					District of Columbia	125.37

Source: CQ Press using data from North American Association of State and Provincial Lotteries, Willoughby Hills, OH
"Sales and Profits" (http://www.naspl.org/index.cfm?fuseaction=content&PageID=3&PageCategory=3)
*For fiscal year 2006. National rate is based on population of states with a lottery.
**No lottery as of fiscal year 2006.

Projected vs. Actual State Tax Collections in 2007

National Percent = 103.3% of Projected Taxes*

ALPHA ORDER

RANK	STATE	PERCENT
16	Alabama	106.3
6	Alaska	111.8
47	Arizona	97.3
31	Arkansas	102.1
26	California	103.3
10	Colorado	108.8
22	Connecticut	104.4
50	Delaware	93.3
48	Florida	97.0
19	Georgia	105.1
46	Hawaii	98.7
41	Idaho	100.0
30	Illinois	102.3
38	Indiana	100.9
19	Iowa	105.1
33	Kansas	101.6
31	Kentucky	102.1
2	Louisiana	125.4
40	Maine	100.6
44	Maryland	99.3
23	Massachusetts	104.1
49	Michigan	96.6
36	Minnesota	101.1
13	Mississippi	107.6
24	Missouri	103.9
3	Montana	123.9
18	Nebraska	105.5
44	Nevada	99.3
9	New Hampshire	108.9
37	New Jersey	101.0
8	New Mexico	109.6
28	New York	102.7
12	North Carolina	107.8
1	North Dakota	127.1
35	Ohio	101.4
21	Oklahoma	104.6
7	Oregon	110.7
34	Pennsylvania	101.5
43	Rhode Island	99.5
11	South Carolina	108.6
42	South Dakota	99.7
27	Tennessee	103.1
5	Texas	112.3
15	Utah	106.7
13	Vermont	107.6
28	Virginia	102.7
17	Washington	106.1
25	West Virginia	103.6
38	Wisconsin	100.9
4	Wyoming	114.0

RANK ORDER

RANK	STATE	PERCENT
1	North Dakota	127.1
2	Louisiana	125.4
3	Montana	123.9
4	Wyoming	114.0
5	Texas	112.3
6	Alaska	111.8
7	Oregon	110.7
8	New Mexico	109.6
9	New Hampshire	108.9
10	Colorado	108.8
11	South Carolina	108.6
12	North Carolina	107.8
13	Mississippi	107.6
13	Vermont	107.6
15	Utah	106.7
16	Alabama	106.3
17	Washington	106.1
18	Nebraska	105.5
19	Georgia	105.1
19	Iowa	105.1
21	Oklahoma	104.6
22	Connecticut	104.4
23	Massachusetts	104.1
24	Missouri	103.9
25	West Virginia	103.6
26	California	103.3
27	Tennessee	103.1
28	New York	102.7
28	Virginia	102.7
30	Illinois	102.3
31	Arkansas	102.1
31	Kentucky	102.1
33	Kansas	101.6
34	Pennsylvania	101.5
35	Ohio	101.4
36	Minnesota	101.1
37	New Jersey	101.0
38	Indiana	100.9
38	Wisconsin	100.9
40	Maine	100.6
41	Idaho	100.0
42	South Dakota	99.7
43	Rhode Island	99.5
44	Maryland	99.3
44	Nevada	99.3
46	Hawaii	98.7
47	Arizona	97.3
48	Florida	97.0
49	Michigan	96.6
50	Delaware	93.3

District of Columbia**   NA

Source: CQ Press using data from National Association of State Budget Officers
   "The Fiscal Survey of States" (December 2007, http://www.nasbo.org/publications.php#fss2007)
*For fiscal year 2007. This table compares sales, personal, and corporate income tax collections projected in adopting budgets with the amount collected.
**Not available.

State Government Tax Revenue in 2006

National Total = $706,334,858,000

ALPHA ORDER

RANK	STATE	STATE TAXES	% of USA
25	Alabama	$8,529,676,000	1.2%
44	Alaska	2,484,422,000	0.4%
20	Arizona	11,713,167,000	1.7%
30	Arkansas	6,959,438,000	1.0%
1	California	111,346,857,000	15.8%
26	Colorado	8,522,307,000	1.2%
19	Connecticut	12,131,894,000	1.7%
42	Delaware	2,860,749,000	0.4%
3	Florida	37,201,518,000	5.3%
14	Georgia	17,033,651,000	2.4%
37	Hawaii	4,918,655,000	0.7%
41	Idaho	3,142,663,000	0.4%
6	Illinois	28,128,749,000	4.0%
18	Indiana	13,625,667,000	1.9%
33	Iowa	6,118,897,000	0.9%
31	Kansas	6,275,075,000	0.9%
23	Kentucky	9,953,098,000	1.4%
24	Louisiana	9,651,457,000	1.4%
40	Maine	3,590,334,000	0.5%
16	Maryland	14,549,632,000	2.1%
11	Massachusetts	19,395,270,000	2.7%
9	Michigan	23,714,514,000	3.4%
12	Minnesota	17,331,413,000	2.5%
34	Mississippi	5,989,603,000	0.8%
22	Missouri	10,180,045,000	1.4%
46	Montana	2,126,324,000	0.3%
39	Nebraska	3,961,093,000	0.6%
32	Nevada	6,152,980,000	0.9%
48	New Hampshire	2,080,573,000	0.3%
7	New Jersey	24,848,825,000	3.5%
36	New Mexico	5,110,683,000	0.7%
2	New York	54,549,027,000	7.7%
10	North Carolina	20,602,549,000	2.9%
49	North Dakota	1,621,912,000	0.2%
8	Ohio	24,636,910,000	3.5%
27	Oklahoma	7,784,453,000	1.1%
29	Oregon	7,590,306,000	1.1%
5	Pennsylvania	29,050,577,000	4.1%
43	Rhode Island	2,741,734,000	0.4%
28	South Carolina	7,759,797,000	1.1%
50	South Dakota	1,182,027,000	0.2%
21	Tennessee	10,650,350,000	1.5%
4	Texas	36,591,749,000	5.2%
35	Utah	5,459,091,000	0.8%
45	Vermont	2,406,661,000	0.3%
13	Virginia	17,192,007,000	2.4%
15	Washington	16,410,977,000	2.3%
38	West Virginia	4,558,219,000	0.6%
17	Wisconsin	13,795,044,000	2.0%
47	Wyoming	2,122,239,000	0.3%

RANK ORDER

RANK	STATE	STATE TAXES	% of USA
1	California	$111,346,857,000	15.8%
2	New York	54,549,027,000	7.7%
3	Florida	37,201,518,000	5.3%
4	Texas	36,591,749,000	5.2%
5	Pennsylvania	29,050,577,000	4.1%
6	Illinois	28,128,749,000	4.0%
7	New Jersey	24,848,825,000	3.5%
8	Ohio	24,636,910,000	3.5%
9	Michigan	23,714,514,000	3.4%
10	North Carolina	20,602,549,000	2.9%
11	Massachusetts	19,395,270,000	2.7%
12	Minnesota	17,331,413,000	2.5%
13	Virginia	17,192,007,000	2.4%
14	Georgia	17,033,651,000	2.4%
15	Washington	16,410,977,000	2.3%
16	Maryland	14,549,632,000	2.1%
17	Wisconsin	13,795,044,000	2.0%
18	Indiana	13,625,667,000	1.9%
19	Connecticut	12,131,894,000	1.7%
20	Arizona	11,713,167,000	1.7%
21	Tennessee	10,650,350,000	1.5%
22	Missouri	10,180,045,000	1.4%
23	Kentucky	9,953,098,000	1.4%
24	Louisiana	9,651,457,000	1.4%
25	Alabama	8,529,676,000	1.2%
26	Colorado	8,522,307,000	1.2%
27	Oklahoma	7,784,453,000	1.1%
28	South Carolina	7,759,797,000	1.1%
29	Oregon	7,590,306,000	1.1%
30	Arkansas	6,959,438,000	1.0%
31	Kansas	6,275,075,000	0.9%
32	Nevada	6,152,980,000	0.9%
33	Iowa	6,118,897,000	0.9%
34	Mississippi	5,989,603,000	0.8%
35	Utah	5,459,091,000	0.8%
36	New Mexico	5,110,683,000	0.7%
37	Hawaii	4,918,655,000	0.7%
38	West Virginia	4,558,219,000	0.6%
39	Nebraska	3,961,093,000	0.6%
40	Maine	3,590,334,000	0.5%
41	Idaho	3,142,663,000	0.4%
42	Delaware	2,860,749,000	0.4%
43	Rhode Island	2,741,734,000	0.4%
44	Alaska	2,484,422,000	0.4%
45	Vermont	2,406,661,000	0.3%
46	Montana	2,126,324,000	0.3%
47	Wyoming	2,122,239,000	0.3%
48	New Hampshire	2,080,573,000	0.3%
49	North Dakota	1,621,912,000	0.2%
50	South Dakota	1,182,027,000	0.2%
	District of Columbia*	NA	NA

Source: U.S. Bureau of the Census, Governments Division
"2006 State Government Tax Collections" (http://www.census.gov/govs/www/statetax06.html)
*Not applicable.

Per Capita State Government Tax Revenue in 2006

National Per Capita = $2,364

<table>
<tr><td colspan="3">ALPHA ORDER</td><td colspan="3">RANK ORDER</td></tr>
<tr><td>RANK</td><td>STATE</td><td>PER CAPITA</td><td>RANK</td><td>STATE</td><td>PER CAPITA</td></tr>
<tr><td>42</td><td>Alabama</td><td>$1,858</td><td>1</td><td>Wyoming</td><td>$4,139</td></tr>
<tr><td>4</td><td>Alaska</td><td>3,667</td><td>2</td><td>Vermont</td><td>3,877</td></tr>
<tr><td>41</td><td>Arizona</td><td>1,900</td><td>3</td><td>Hawaii</td><td>3,847</td></tr>
<tr><td>19</td><td>Arkansas</td><td>2,477</td><td>4</td><td>Alaska</td><td>3,667</td></tr>
<tr><td>8</td><td>California</td><td>3,072</td><td>5</td><td>Connecticut</td><td>3,470</td></tr>
<tr><td>45</td><td>Colorado</td><td>1,788</td><td>6</td><td>Minnesota</td><td>3,362</td></tr>
<tr><td>5</td><td>Connecticut</td><td>3,470</td><td>7</td><td>Delaware</td><td>3,355</td></tr>
<tr><td>7</td><td>Delaware</td><td>3,355</td><td>8</td><td>California</td><td>3,072</td></tr>
<tr><td>38</td><td>Florida</td><td>2,060</td><td>9</td><td>Massachusetts</td><td>3,014</td></tr>
<tr><td>43</td><td>Georgia</td><td>1,823</td><td>10</td><td>New Jersey</td><td>2,867</td></tr>
<tr><td>3</td><td>Hawaii</td><td>3,847</td><td>11</td><td>New York</td><td>2,829</td></tr>
<tr><td>35</td><td>Idaho</td><td>2,147</td><td>12</td><td>Maine</td><td>2,730</td></tr>
<tr><td>31</td><td>Illinois</td><td>2,202</td><td>13</td><td>New Mexico</td><td>2,631</td></tr>
<tr><td>33</td><td>Indiana</td><td>2,162</td><td>14</td><td>Maryland</td><td>2,597</td></tr>
<tr><td>39</td><td>Iowa</td><td>2,058</td><td>15</td><td>Rhode Island</td><td>2,583</td></tr>
<tr><td>26</td><td>Kansas</td><td>2,277</td><td>16</td><td>Washington</td><td>2,574</td></tr>
<tr><td>22</td><td>Kentucky</td><td>2,367</td><td>17</td><td>North Dakota</td><td>2,544</td></tr>
<tr><td>27</td><td>Louisiana</td><td>2,275</td><td>18</td><td>West Virginia</td><td>2,520</td></tr>
<tr><td>12</td><td>Maine</td><td>2,730</td><td>19</td><td>Arkansas</td><td>2,477</td></tr>
<tr><td>14</td><td>Maryland</td><td>2,597</td><td>20</td><td>Wisconsin</td><td>2,475</td></tr>
<tr><td>9</td><td>Massachusetts</td><td>3,014</td><td>21</td><td>Nevada</td><td>2,469</td></tr>
<tr><td>23</td><td>Michigan</td><td>2,347</td><td>22</td><td>Kentucky</td><td>2,367</td></tr>
<tr><td>6</td><td>Minnesota</td><td>3,362</td><td>23</td><td>Michigan</td><td>2,347</td></tr>
<tr><td>37</td><td>Mississippi</td><td>2,066</td><td>24</td><td>Pennsylvania</td><td>2,342</td></tr>
<tr><td>47</td><td>Missouri</td><td>1,744</td><td>25</td><td>North Carolina</td><td>2,323</td></tr>
<tr><td>29</td><td>Montana</td><td>2,246</td><td>26</td><td>Kansas</td><td>2,277</td></tr>
<tr><td>29</td><td>Nebraska</td><td>2,246</td><td>27</td><td>Louisiana</td><td>2,275</td></tr>
<tr><td>21</td><td>Nevada</td><td>2,469</td><td>28</td><td>Virginia</td><td>2,250</td></tr>
<tr><td>48</td><td>New Hampshire</td><td>1,586</td><td>29</td><td>Montana</td><td>2,246</td></tr>
<tr><td>10</td><td>New Jersey</td><td>2,867</td><td>29</td><td>Nebraska</td><td>2,246</td></tr>
<tr><td>13</td><td>New Mexico</td><td>2,631</td><td>31</td><td>Illinois</td><td>2,202</td></tr>
<tr><td>11</td><td>New York</td><td>2,829</td><td>32</td><td>Oklahoma</td><td>2,176</td></tr>
<tr><td>25</td><td>North Carolina</td><td>2,323</td><td>33</td><td>Indiana</td><td>2,162</td></tr>
<tr><td>17</td><td>North Dakota</td><td>2,544</td><td>34</td><td>Ohio</td><td>2,149</td></tr>
<tr><td>34</td><td>Ohio</td><td>2,149</td><td>35</td><td>Idaho</td><td>2,147</td></tr>
<tr><td>32</td><td>Oklahoma</td><td>2,176</td><td>36</td><td>Utah</td><td>2,116</td></tr>
<tr><td>40</td><td>Oregon</td><td>2,056</td><td>37</td><td>Mississippi</td><td>2,066</td></tr>
<tr><td>24</td><td>Pennsylvania</td><td>2,342</td><td>38</td><td>Florida</td><td>2,060</td></tr>
<tr><td>15</td><td>Rhode Island</td><td>2,583</td><td>39</td><td>Iowa</td><td>2,058</td></tr>
<tr><td>44</td><td>South Carolina</td><td>1,792</td><td>40</td><td>Oregon</td><td>2,056</td></tr>
<tr><td>50</td><td>South Dakota</td><td>1,499</td><td>41</td><td>Arizona</td><td>1,900</td></tr>
<tr><td>46</td><td>Tennessee</td><td>1,753</td><td>42</td><td>Alabama</td><td>1,858</td></tr>
<tr><td>49</td><td>Texas</td><td>1,563</td><td>43</td><td>Georgia</td><td>1,823</td></tr>
<tr><td>36</td><td>Utah</td><td>2,116</td><td>44</td><td>South Carolina</td><td>1,792</td></tr>
<tr><td>2</td><td>Vermont</td><td>3,877</td><td>45</td><td>Colorado</td><td>1,788</td></tr>
<tr><td>28</td><td>Virginia</td><td>2,250</td><td>46</td><td>Tennessee</td><td>1,753</td></tr>
<tr><td>16</td><td>Washington</td><td>2,574</td><td>47</td><td>Missouri</td><td>1,744</td></tr>
<tr><td>18</td><td>West Virginia</td><td>2,520</td><td>48</td><td>New Hampshire</td><td>1,586</td></tr>
<tr><td>20</td><td>Wisconsin</td><td>2,475</td><td>49</td><td>Texas</td><td>1,563</td></tr>
<tr><td>1</td><td>Wyoming</td><td>4,139</td><td>50</td><td>South Dakota</td><td>1,499</td></tr>
</table>

District of Columbia*   NA

Source: CQ Press using data from U.S. Bureau of the Census, Governments Division
"2006 State Government Tax Collections" (http://www.census.gov/govs/www/statetax06.html)
*Not applicable.

State Government Tax Revenue as a Percent of Personal Income in 2006

National Percent = 6.5% of Personal Income*

ALPHA ORDER

RANK	STATE	PERCENT
37	Alabama	6.0
4	Alaska	9.6
39	Arizona	5.9
7	Arkansas	8.7
12	California	7.8
48	Colorado	4.5
23	Connecticut	6.8
9	Delaware	8.6
44	Florida	5.6
41	Georgia	5.7
2	Hawaii	10.4
16	Idaho	7.2
41	Illinois	5.7
24	Indiana	6.7
34	Iowa	6.2
27	Kansas	6.5
11	Kentucky	8.0
16	Louisiana	7.2
10	Maine	8.5
39	Maryland	5.9
27	Massachusetts	6.5
21	Michigan	7.0
7	Minnesota	8.7
14	Mississippi	7.6
46	Missouri	5.3
15	Montana	7.3
27	Nebraska	6.5
33	Nevada	6.3
50	New Hampshire	4.0
36	New Jersey	6.1
6	New Mexico	8.8
31	New York	6.4
16	North Carolina	7.2
13	North Dakota	7.7
27	Ohio	6.5
24	Oklahoma	6.7
34	Oregon	6.2
31	Pennsylvania	6.4
22	Rhode Island	6.9
37	South Carolina	6.0
47	South Dakota	4.7
45	Tennessee	5.5
49	Texas	4.4
16	Utah	7.2
1	Vermont	11.1
41	Virginia	5.7
24	Washington	6.7
5	West Virginia	8.9
16	Wisconsin	7.2
3	Wyoming	10.2

RANK ORDER

RANK	STATE	PERCENT
1	Vermont	11.1
2	Hawaii	10.4
3	Wyoming	10.2
4	Alaska	9.6
5	West Virginia	8.9
6	New Mexico	8.8
7	Arkansas	8.7
7	Minnesota	8.7
9	Delaware	8.6
10	Maine	8.5
11	Kentucky	8.0
12	California	7.8
13	North Dakota	7.7
14	Mississippi	7.6
15	Montana	7.3
16	Idaho	7.2
16	Louisiana	7.2
16	North Carolina	7.2
16	Utah	7.2
16	Wisconsin	7.2
21	Michigan	7.0
22	Rhode Island	6.9
23	Connecticut	6.8
24	Indiana	6.7
24	Oklahoma	6.7
24	Washington	6.7
27	Kansas	6.5
27	Massachusetts	6.5
27	Nebraska	6.5
27	Ohio	6.5
31	New York	6.4
31	Pennsylvania	6.4
33	Nevada	6.3
34	Iowa	6.2
34	Oregon	6.2
36	New Jersey	6.1
37	Alabama	6.0
37	South Carolina	6.0
39	Arizona	5.9
39	Maryland	5.9
41	Georgia	5.7
41	Illinois	5.7
41	Virginia	5.7
44	Florida	5.6
45	Tennessee	5.5
46	Missouri	5.3
47	South Dakota	4.7
48	Colorado	4.5
49	Texas	4.4
50	New Hampshire	4.0

District of Columbia**   NA

Source: CQ Press using data from U.S. Bureau of the Census, Governments Division
"2006 State Government Tax Collections" (http://www.census.gov/govs/www/statetax06.html)
U.S. Department of Commerce, Bureau of Economic Analysis
"Annual State Personal Income" (http://www.bea.doc.gov/bea/regional/spi/)
*National figure does not include personal income or taxes from the District of Columbia.
**Not applicable.

State Government Individual Income Tax Revenue in 2006

National Total = $244,370,415,000

ALPHA ORDER

ALPHA ORDER

RANK	STATE	INCOME TAX	% of USA
22	Alabama	$2,766,239,000	1.1%
44	Alaska	0	0.0%
20	Arizona	3,253,279,000	1.3%
29	Arkansas	2,012,835,000	0.8%
1	California	51,219,823,000	21.0%
19	Colorado	4,258,944,000	1.7%
15	Connecticut	5,777,636,000	2.4%
38	Delaware	1,018,633,000	0.4%
44	Florida	0	0.0%
10	Georgia	8,040,366,000	3.3%
30	Hawaii	1,550,757,000	0.6%
35	Idaho	1,222,569,000	0.5%
9	Illinois	8,635,104,000	3.5%
18	Indiana	4,381,548,000	1.8%
26	Iowa	2,413,775,000	1.0%
27	Kansas	2,401,128,000	1.0%
21	Kentucky	2,918,536,000	1.2%
25	Louisiana	2,501,120,000	1.0%
32	Maine	1,368,927,000	0.6%
13	Maryland	6,151,365,000	2.5%
3	Massachusetts	10,483,437,000	4.3%
12	Michigan	6,226,304,000	2.5%
11	Minnesota	6,862,953,000	2.8%
34	Mississippi	1,254,733,000	0.5%
17	Missouri	4,491,428,000	1.8%
39	Montana	768,911,000	0.3%
31	Nebraska	1,545,024,000	0.6%
44	Nevada	0	0.0%
43	New Hampshire	80,931,000	0.0%
6	New Jersey	9,091,658,000	3.7%
36	New Mexico	1,123,954,000	0.5%
2	New York	30,812,924,000	12.6%
5	North Carolina	9,467,278,000	3.9%
41	North Dakota	275,630,000	0.1%
4	Ohio	9,859,712,000	4.0%
24	Oklahoma	2,658,272,000	1.1%
16	Oregon	5,416,466,000	2.2%
8	Pennsylvania	9,021,917,000	3.7%
37	Rhode Island	1,019,482,000	0.4%
23	South Carolina	2,727,251,000	1.1%
44	South Dakota	0	0.0%
42	Tennessee	192,764,000	0.1%
44	Texas	0	0.0%
28	Utah	2,277,478,000	0.9%
40	Vermont	542,012,000	0.2%
7	Virginia	9,073,077,000	3.7%
44	Washington	0	0.0%
33	West Virginia	1,297,720,000	0.5%
14	Wisconsin	5,906,515,000	2.4%
44	Wyoming	0	0.0%

RANK ORDER

RANK	STATE	INCOME TAX	% of USA
1	California	$51,219,823,000	21.0%
2	New York	30,812,924,000	12.6%
3	Massachusetts	10,483,437,000	4.3%
4	Ohio	9,859,712,000	4.0%
5	North Carolina	9,467,278,000	3.9%
6	New Jersey	9,091,658,000	3.7%
7	Virginia	9,073,077,000	3.7%
8	Pennsylvania	9,021,917,000	3.7%
9	Illinois	8,635,104,000	3.5%
10	Georgia	8,040,366,000	3.3%
11	Minnesota	6,862,953,000	2.8%
12	Michigan	6,226,304,000	2.5%
13	Maryland	6,151,365,000	2.5%
14	Wisconsin	5,906,515,000	2.4%
15	Connecticut	5,777,636,000	2.4%
16	Oregon	5,416,466,000	2.2%
17	Missouri	4,491,428,000	1.8%
18	Indiana	4,381,548,000	1.8%
19	Colorado	4,258,944,000	1.7%
20	Arizona	3,253,279,000	1.3%
21	Kentucky	2,918,536,000	1.2%
22	Alabama	2,766,239,000	1.1%
23	South Carolina	2,727,251,000	1.1%
24	Oklahoma	2,658,272,000	1.1%
25	Louisiana	2,501,120,000	1.0%
26	Iowa	2,413,775,000	1.0%
27	Kansas	2,401,128,000	1.0%
28	Utah	2,277,478,000	0.9%
29	Arkansas	2,012,835,000	0.8%
30	Hawaii	1,550,757,000	0.6%
31	Nebraska	1,545,024,000	0.6%
32	Maine	1,368,927,000	0.6%
33	West Virginia	1,297,720,000	0.5%
34	Mississippi	1,254,733,000	0.5%
35	Idaho	1,222,569,000	0.5%
36	New Mexico	1,123,954,000	0.5%
37	Rhode Island	1,019,482,000	0.4%
38	Delaware	1,018,633,000	0.4%
39	Montana	768,911,000	0.3%
40	Vermont	542,012,000	0.2%
41	North Dakota	275,630,000	0.1%
42	Tennessee	192,764,000	0.1%
43	New Hampshire	80,931,000	0.0%
44	Alaska	0	0.0%
44	Florida	0	0.0%
44	Nevada	0	0.0%
44	South Dakota	0	0.0%
44	Texas	0	0.0%
44	Washington	0	0.0%
44	Wyoming	0	0.0%
	District of Columbia*	NA	NA

Source: U.S. Bureau of the Census, Governments Division
   "2006 State Government Tax Collections" (http://www.census.gov/govs/www/statetax06.html)
*Not applicable.

Per Capita State Government Individual Income Tax Revenue in 2006

National Per Capita = $818

ALPHA ORDER

RANK	STATE	PER CAPITA
36	Alabama	$603
44	Alaska	0
39	Arizona	528
29	Arkansas	717
5	California	1,413
16	Colorado	894
1	Connecticut	1,653
8	Delaware	1,195
44	Florida	0
21	Georgia	861
7	Hawaii	1,213
23	Idaho	835
33	Illinois	676
31	Indiana	695
24	Iowa	812
20	Kansas	871
32	Kentucky	694
37	Louisiana	589
14	Maine	1,041
10	Maryland	1,098
2	Massachusetts	1,629
35	Michigan	616
6	Minnesota	1,331
40	Mississippi	433
26	Missouri	769
24	Montana	812
18	Nebraska	876
44	Nevada	0
42	New Hampshire	62
13	New Jersey	1,049
38	New Mexico	579
3	New York	1,598
11	North Carolina	1,067
41	North Dakota	432
22	Ohio	860
27	Oklahoma	743
4	Oregon	1,467
28	Pennsylvania	727
15	Rhode Island	960
34	South Carolina	630
44	South Dakota	0
43	Tennessee	32
44	Texas	0
17	Utah	883
19	Vermont	873
9	Virginia	1,188
44	Washington	0
29	West Virginia	717
12	Wisconsin	1,060
44	Wyoming	0

RANK ORDER

RANK	STATE	PER CAPITA
1	Connecticut	$1,653
2	Massachusetts	1,629
3	New York	1,598
4	Oregon	1,467
5	California	1,413
6	Minnesota	1,331
7	Hawaii	1,213
8	Delaware	1,195
9	Virginia	1,188
10	Maryland	1,098
11	North Carolina	1,067
12	Wisconsin	1,060
13	New Jersey	1,049
14	Maine	1,041
15	Rhode Island	960
16	Colorado	894
17	Utah	883
18	Nebraska	876
19	Vermont	873
20	Kansas	871
21	Georgia	861
22	Ohio	860
23	Idaho	835
24	Iowa	812
24	Montana	812
26	Missouri	769
27	Oklahoma	743
28	Pennsylvania	727
29	Arkansas	717
29	West Virginia	717
31	Indiana	695
32	Kentucky	694
33	Illinois	676
34	South Carolina	630
35	Michigan	616
36	Alabama	603
37	Louisiana	589
38	New Mexico	579
39	Arizona	528
40	Mississippi	433
41	North Dakota	432
42	New Hampshire	62
43	Tennessee	32
44	Alaska	0
44	Florida	0
44	Nevada	0
44	South Dakota	0
44	Texas	0
44	Washington	0
44	Wyoming	0
	District of Columbia*	NA

Source: CQ Press using data from U.S. Bureau of the Census, Governments Division
   "2006 State Government Tax Collections" (http://www.census.gov/govs/www/statetax06.html)
*Not applicable.

State Government Corporation Net Income Tax Revenue in 2006

National Total = $47,392,347,000

ALPHA ORDER

RANK	STATE	REVENUE	% of USA
22	Alabama	$558,768,000	1.2%
19	Alaska	821,664,000	1.7%
16	Arizona	890,004,000	1.9%
30	Arkansas	368,523,000	0.8%
1	California	10,316,467,000	21.8%
26	Colorado	457,673,000	1.0%
21	Connecticut	634,990,000	1.3%
35	Delaware	295,577,000	0.6%
4	Florida	2,405,863,000	5.1%
15	Georgia	890,732,000	1.9%
43	Hawaii	148,084,000	0.3%
39	Idaho	198,302,000	0.4%
5	Illinois	2,400,270,000	5.1%
12	Indiana	1,043,873,000	2.2%
36	Iowa	284,976,000	0.6%
28	Kansas	381,259,000	0.8%
13	Kentucky	1,001,619,000	2.1%
25	Louisiana	506,174,000	1.1%
40	Maine	188,016,000	0.4%
18	Maryland	846,863,000	1.8%
8	Massachusetts	1,859,009,000	3.9%
7	Michigan	1,886,168,000	4.0%
11	Minnesota	1,071,884,000	2.3%
33	Mississippi	316,981,000	0.7%
32	Missouri	343,689,000	0.7%
42	Montana	153,675,000	0.3%
37	Nebraska	262,296,000	0.6%
47	Nevada	0	0.0%
23	New Hampshire	542,644,000	1.1%
3	New Jersey	2,508,428,000	5.3%
29	New Mexico	377,185,000	0.8%
2	New York	4,018,199,000	8.5%
9	North Carolina	1,308,022,000	2.8%
44	North Dakota	120,113,000	0.3%
10	Ohio	1,102,351,000	2.3%
38	Oklahoma	231,206,000	0.5%
27	Oregon	438,255,000	0.9%
6	Pennsylvania	2,116,954,000	4.5%
41	Rhode Island	169,865,000	0.4%
34	South Carolina	296,753,000	0.6%
46	South Dakota	61,865,000	0.1%
14	Tennessee	928,349,000	2.0%
47	Texas	0	0.0%
31	Utah	348,129,000	0.7%
45	Vermont	86,083,000	0.2%
17	Virginia	863,320,000	1.8%
47	Washington	0	0.0%
24	West Virginia	533,027,000	1.1%
20	Wisconsin	808,200,000	1.7%
47	Wyoming	0	0.0%

RANK ORDER

RANK	STATE	REVENUE	% of USA
1	California	$10,316,467,000	21.8%
2	New York	4,018,199,000	8.5%
3	New Jersey	2,508,428,000	5.3%
4	Florida	2,405,863,000	5.1%
5	Illinois	2,400,270,000	5.1%
6	Pennsylvania	2,116,954,000	4.5%
7	Michigan	1,886,168,000	4.0%
8	Massachusetts	1,859,009,000	3.9%
9	North Carolina	1,308,022,000	2.8%
10	Ohio	1,102,351,000	2.3%
11	Minnesota	1,071,884,000	2.3%
12	Indiana	1,043,873,000	2.2%
13	Kentucky	1,001,619,000	2.1%
14	Tennessee	928,349,000	2.0%
15	Georgia	890,732,000	1.9%
16	Arizona	890,004,000	1.9%
17	Virginia	863,320,000	1.8%
18	Maryland	846,863,000	1.8%
19	Alaska	821,664,000	1.7%
20	Wisconsin	808,200,000	1.7%
21	Connecticut	634,990,000	1.3%
22	Alabama	558,768,000	1.2%
23	New Hampshire	542,644,000	1.1%
24	West Virginia	533,027,000	1.1%
25	Louisiana	506,174,000	1.1%
26	Colorado	457,673,000	1.0%
27	Oregon	438,255,000	0.9%
28	Kansas	381,259,000	0.8%
29	New Mexico	377,185,000	0.8%
30	Arkansas	368,523,000	0.8%
31	Utah	348,129,000	0.7%
32	Missouri	343,689,000	0.7%
33	Mississippi	316,981,000	0.7%
34	South Carolina	296,753,000	0.6%
35	Delaware	295,577,000	0.6%
36	Iowa	284,976,000	0.6%
37	Nebraska	262,296,000	0.6%
38	Oklahoma	231,206,000	0.5%
39	Idaho	198,302,000	0.4%
40	Maine	188,016,000	0.4%
41	Rhode Island	169,865,000	0.4%
42	Montana	153,675,000	0.3%
43	Hawaii	148,084,000	0.3%
44	North Dakota	120,113,000	0.3%
45	Vermont	86,083,000	0.2%
46	South Dakota	61,865,000	0.1%
47	Nevada	0	0.0%
47	Texas	0	0.0%
47	Washington	0	0.0%
47	Wyoming	0	0.0%
	District of Columbia*	NA	NA

Source: U.S. Bureau of the Census, Governments Division
"2006 State Government Tax Collections" (http://www.census.gov/govs/www/statetax06.html)
*Not applicable.

Per Capita State Government Corporation Net Income Tax Revenue in 2006

National Per Capita = $159

<table>
<tr><td colspan="3">ALPHA ORDER</td><td colspan="3">RANK ORDER</td></tr>
<tr><td>RANK</td><td>STATE</td><td>PER CAPITA</td><td>RANK</td><td>STATE</td><td>PER CAPITA</td></tr>
<tr><td>33</td><td>Alabama</td><td>$122</td><td>1</td><td>Alaska</td><td>$1,213</td></tr>
<tr><td>1</td><td>Alaska</td><td>1,213</td><td>2</td><td>New Hampshire</td><td>414</td></tr>
<tr><td>25</td><td>Arizona</td><td>144</td><td>3</td><td>Delaware</td><td>347</td></tr>
<tr><td>32</td><td>Arkansas</td><td>131</td><td>4</td><td>West Virginia</td><td>295</td></tr>
<tr><td>7</td><td>California</td><td>285</td><td>5</td><td>Massachusetts</td><td>289</td></tr>
<tr><td>39</td><td>Colorado</td><td>96</td><td>5</td><td>New Jersey</td><td>289</td></tr>
<tr><td>15</td><td>Connecticut</td><td>182</td><td>7</td><td>California</td><td>285</td></tr>
<tr><td>3</td><td>Delaware</td><td>347</td><td>8</td><td>Kentucky</td><td>238</td></tr>
<tr><td>31</td><td>Florida</td><td>133</td><td>9</td><td>Minnesota</td><td>208</td></tr>
<tr><td>42</td><td>Georgia</td><td>95</td><td>9</td><td>New York</td><td>208</td></tr>
<tr><td>36</td><td>Hawaii</td><td>116</td><td>11</td><td>New Mexico</td><td>194</td></tr>
<tr><td>29</td><td>Idaho</td><td>135</td><td>12</td><td>Illinois</td><td>188</td></tr>
<tr><td>12</td><td>Illinois</td><td>188</td><td>12</td><td>North Dakota</td><td>188</td></tr>
<tr><td>17</td><td>Indiana</td><td>166</td><td>14</td><td>Michigan</td><td>187</td></tr>
<tr><td>39</td><td>Iowa</td><td>96</td><td>15</td><td>Connecticut</td><td>182</td></tr>
<tr><td>28</td><td>Kansas</td><td>138</td><td>16</td><td>Pennsylvania</td><td>171</td></tr>
<tr><td>8</td><td>Kentucky</td><td>238</td><td>17</td><td>Indiana</td><td>166</td></tr>
<tr><td>34</td><td>Louisiana</td><td>119</td><td>18</td><td>Montana</td><td>162</td></tr>
<tr><td>26</td><td>Maine</td><td>143</td><td>19</td><td>Rhode Island</td><td>160</td></tr>
<tr><td>21</td><td>Maryland</td><td>151</td><td>20</td><td>Tennessee</td><td>153</td></tr>
<tr><td>5</td><td>Massachusetts</td><td>289</td><td>21</td><td>Maryland</td><td>151</td></tr>
<tr><td>14</td><td>Michigan</td><td>187</td><td>22</td><td>Nebraska</td><td>149</td></tr>
<tr><td>9</td><td>Minnesota</td><td>208</td><td>23</td><td>North Carolina</td><td>147</td></tr>
<tr><td>38</td><td>Mississippi</td><td>109</td><td>24</td><td>Wisconsin</td><td>145</td></tr>
<tr><td>46</td><td>Missouri</td><td>59</td><td>25</td><td>Arizona</td><td>144</td></tr>
<tr><td>18</td><td>Montana</td><td>162</td><td>26</td><td>Maine</td><td>143</td></tr>
<tr><td>22</td><td>Nebraska</td><td>149</td><td>27</td><td>Vermont</td><td>139</td></tr>
<tr><td>47</td><td>Nevada</td><td>0</td><td>28</td><td>Kansas</td><td>138</td></tr>
<tr><td>2</td><td>New Hampshire</td><td>414</td><td>29</td><td>Idaho</td><td>135</td></tr>
<tr><td>5</td><td>New Jersey</td><td>289</td><td>29</td><td>Utah</td><td>135</td></tr>
<tr><td>11</td><td>New Mexico</td><td>194</td><td>31</td><td>Florida</td><td>133</td></tr>
<tr><td>9</td><td>New York</td><td>208</td><td>32</td><td>Arkansas</td><td>131</td></tr>
<tr><td>23</td><td>North Carolina</td><td>147</td><td>33</td><td>Alabama</td><td>122</td></tr>
<tr><td>12</td><td>North Dakota</td><td>188</td><td>34</td><td>Louisiana</td><td>119</td></tr>
<tr><td>39</td><td>Ohio</td><td>96</td><td>34</td><td>Oregon</td><td>119</td></tr>
<tr><td>45</td><td>Oklahoma</td><td>65</td><td>36</td><td>Hawaii</td><td>116</td></tr>
<tr><td>34</td><td>Oregon</td><td>119</td><td>37</td><td>Virginia</td><td>113</td></tr>
<tr><td>16</td><td>Pennsylvania</td><td>171</td><td>38</td><td>Mississippi</td><td>109</td></tr>
<tr><td>19</td><td>Rhode Island</td><td>160</td><td>39</td><td>Colorado</td><td>96</td></tr>
<tr><td>44</td><td>South Carolina</td><td>69</td><td>39</td><td>Iowa</td><td>96</td></tr>
<tr><td>43</td><td>South Dakota</td><td>78</td><td>39</td><td>Ohio</td><td>96</td></tr>
<tr><td>20</td><td>Tennessee</td><td>153</td><td>42</td><td>Georgia</td><td>95</td></tr>
<tr><td>47</td><td>Texas</td><td>0</td><td>43</td><td>South Dakota</td><td>78</td></tr>
<tr><td>29</td><td>Utah</td><td>135</td><td>44</td><td>South Carolina</td><td>69</td></tr>
<tr><td>27</td><td>Vermont</td><td>139</td><td>45</td><td>Oklahoma</td><td>65</td></tr>
<tr><td>37</td><td>Virginia</td><td>113</td><td>46</td><td>Missouri</td><td>59</td></tr>
<tr><td>47</td><td>Washington</td><td>0</td><td>47</td><td>Nevada</td><td>0</td></tr>
<tr><td>4</td><td>West Virginia</td><td>295</td><td>47</td><td>Texas</td><td>0</td></tr>
<tr><td>24</td><td>Wisconsin</td><td>145</td><td>47</td><td>Washington</td><td>0</td></tr>
<tr><td>47</td><td>Wyoming</td><td>0</td><td>47</td><td>Wyoming</td><td>0</td></tr>
<tr><td colspan="3"></td><td colspan="2">District of Columbia*</td><td>NA</td></tr>
</table>

Source: CQ Press using data from U.S. Bureau of the Census, Governments Division
"2006 State Government Tax Collections" (http://www.census.gov/govs/www/statetax06.html)
*Not applicable.

State Government General Sales Tax Revenue in 2006

National Total = $226,523,438,000*

ALPHA ORDER

RANK	STATE	SALES TAX	% of USA
30	Alabama	$2,221,506,000	1.0%
46	Alaska	0	0.0%
14	Arizona	5,189,786,000	2.3%
27	Arkansas	2,772,131,000	1.2%
1	California	32,199,800,000	14.2%
32	Colorado	2,105,049,000	0.9%
26	Connecticut	3,040,683,000	1.3%
46	Delaware	0	0.0%
2	Florida	20,788,525,000	9.2%
12	Georgia	5,802,913,000	2.6%
29	Hawaii	2,355,316,000	1.0%
39	Idaho	1,078,543,000	0.5%
8	Illinois	7,760,590,000	3.4%
13	Indiana	5,334,275,000	2.4%
34	Iowa	1,800,829,000	0.8%
31	Kansas	2,127,597,000	0.9%
28	Kentucky	2,748,643,000	1.2%
19	Louisiana	3,427,486,000	1.5%
40	Maine	1,041,216,000	0.5%
20	Maryland	3,381,694,000	1.5%
18	Massachusetts	4,009,371,000	1.8%
7	Michigan	8,080,905,000	3.6%
16	Minnesota	4,437,407,000	2.0%
25	Mississippi	3,047,837,000	1.3%
24	Missouri	3,100,045,000	1.4%
46	Montana	0	0.0%
37	Nebraska	1,409,015,000	0.6%
23	Nevada	3,163,832,000	1.4%
46	New Hampshire	0	0.0%
10	New Jersey	6,853,418,000	3.0%
36	New Mexico	1,741,673,000	0.8%
4	New York	11,263,576,000	5.0%
15	North Carolina	5,021,648,000	2.2%
44	North Dakota	427,487,000	0.2%
9	Ohio	7,733,133,000	3.4%
35	Oklahoma	1,799,947,000	0.8%
46	Oregon	0	0.0%
6	Pennsylvania	8,403,283,000	3.7%
41	Rhode Island	854,257,000	0.4%
22	South Carolina	3,186,306,000	1.4%
42	South Dakota	679,162,000	0.3%
11	Tennessee	6,451,838,000	2.8%
3	Texas	18,275,210,000	8.1%
33	Utah	1,890,793,000	0.8%
45	Vermont	326,055,000	0.1%
21	Virginia	3,263,647,000	1.4%
5	Washington	10,048,349,000	4.4%
38	West Virginia	1,125,766,000	0.5%
17	Wisconsin	4,127,972,000	1.8%
43	Wyoming	624,924,000	0.3%

RANK ORDER

RANK	STATE	SALES TAX	% of USA
1	California	$32,199,800,000	14.2%
2	Florida	20,788,525,000	9.2%
3	Texas	18,275,210,000	8.1%
4	New York	11,263,576,000	5.0%
5	Washington	10,048,349,000	4.4%
6	Pennsylvania	8,403,283,000	3.7%
7	Michigan	8,080,905,000	3.6%
8	Illinois	7,760,590,000	3.4%
9	Ohio	7,733,133,000	3.4%
10	New Jersey	6,853,418,000	3.0%
11	Tennessee	6,451,838,000	2.8%
12	Georgia	5,802,913,000	2.6%
13	Indiana	5,334,275,000	2.4%
14	Arizona	5,189,786,000	2.3%
15	North Carolina	5,021,648,000	2.2%
16	Minnesota	4,437,407,000	2.0%
17	Wisconsin	4,127,972,000	1.8%
18	Massachusetts	4,009,371,000	1.8%
19	Louisiana	3,427,486,000	1.5%
20	Maryland	3,381,694,000	1.5%
21	Virginia	3,263,647,000	1.4%
22	South Carolina	3,186,306,000	1.4%
23	Nevada	3,163,832,000	1.4%
24	Missouri	3,100,045,000	1.4%
25	Mississippi	3,047,837,000	1.3%
26	Connecticut	3,040,683,000	1.3%
27	Arkansas	2,772,131,000	1.2%
28	Kentucky	2,748,643,000	1.2%
29	Hawaii	2,355,316,000	1.0%
30	Alabama	2,221,506,000	1.0%
31	Kansas	2,127,597,000	0.9%
32	Colorado	2,105,049,000	0.9%
33	Utah	1,890,793,000	0.8%
34	Iowa	1,800,829,000	0.8%
35	Oklahoma	1,799,947,000	0.8%
36	New Mexico	1,741,673,000	0.8%
37	Nebraska	1,409,015,000	0.6%
38	West Virginia	1,125,766,000	0.5%
39	Idaho	1,078,543,000	0.5%
40	Maine	1,041,216,000	0.5%
41	Rhode Island	854,257,000	0.4%
42	South Dakota	679,162,000	0.3%
43	Wyoming	624,924,000	0.3%
44	North Dakota	427,487,000	0.2%
45	Vermont	326,055,000	0.1%
46	Alaska	0	0.0%
46	Delaware	0	0.0%
46	Montana	0	0.0%
46	New Hampshire	0	0.0%
46	Oregon	0	0.0%
	District of Columbia**	NA	NA

Source: U.S. Bureau of the Census, Governments Division
     "2006 State Government Tax Collections" (http://www.census.gov/govs/www/statetax06.html)
*Does not include special sales taxes such as those on sale of alcohol, gasoline, or tobacco.
**Not applicable.

Per Capita State Government General Sales Tax Revenue in 2006

National Per Capita = $758*

ALPHA ORDER

RANK	STATE	PER CAPITA
43	Alabama	$484
46	Alaska	0
15	Arizona	842
8	Arkansas	987
10	California	888
44	Colorado	442
11	Connecticut	870
46	Delaware	0
5	Florida	1,151
34	Georgia	621
1	Hawaii	1,842
25	Idaho	737
35	Illinois	607
14	Indiana	846
36	Iowa	606
23	Kansas	772
31	Kentucky	654
16	Louisiana	808
20	Maine	792
37	Maryland	604
32	Massachusetts	623
18	Michigan	800
12	Minnesota	861
7	Mississippi	1,051
40	Missouri	531
46	Montana	0
19	Nebraska	799
3	Nevada	1,269
46	New Hampshire	0
21	New Jersey	791
9	New Mexico	897
38	New York	584
39	North Carolina	566
30	North Dakota	671
29	Ohio	675
42	Oklahoma	503
46	Oregon	0
28	Pennsylvania	678
17	Rhode Island	805
26	South Carolina	736
12	South Dakota	861
6	Tennessee	1,062
22	Texas	781
27	Utah	733
41	Vermont	525
45	Virginia	427
2	Washington	1,576
33	West Virginia	622
24	Wisconsin	741
4	Wyoming	1,219

RANK ORDER

RANK	STATE	PER CAPITA
1	Hawaii	$1,842
2	Washington	1,576
3	Nevada	1,269
4	Wyoming	1,219
5	Florida	1,151
6	Tennessee	1,062
7	Mississippi	1,051
8	Arkansas	987
9	New Mexico	897
10	California	888
11	Connecticut	870
12	Minnesota	861
12	South Dakota	861
14	Indiana	846
15	Arizona	842
16	Louisiana	808
17	Rhode Island	805
18	Michigan	800
19	Nebraska	799
20	Maine	792
21	New Jersey	791
22	Texas	781
23	Kansas	772
24	Wisconsin	741
25	Idaho	737
26	South Carolina	736
27	Utah	733
28	Pennsylvania	678
29	Ohio	675
30	North Dakota	671
31	Kentucky	654
32	Massachusetts	623
33	West Virginia	622
34	Georgia	621
35	Illinois	607
36	Iowa	606
37	Maryland	604
38	New York	584
39	North Carolina	566
40	Missouri	531
41	Vermont	525
42	Oklahoma	503
43	Alabama	484
44	Colorado	442
45	Virginia	427
46	Alaska	0
46	Delaware	0
46	Montana	0
46	New Hampshire	0
46	Oregon	0
	District of Columbia**	NA

Source: CQ Press using data from U.S. Bureau of the Census, Governments Division
"2006 State Government Tax Collections" (http://www.census.gov/govs/www/statetax06.html)
*Does not include special sales taxes such as those on sale of alcohol, gasoline, or tobacco.
**Not applicable.

State Government Motor Fuels Sales Tax Revenue in 2006

National Total = $35,754,616,000

ALPHA ORDER

RANK	STATE	FUEL TAX	% of USA
22	Alabama	$566,700,000	1.6%
50	Alaska	42,087,000	0.1%
15	Arizona	772,849,000	2.2%
27	Arkansas	456,377,000	1.3%
1	California	3,393,381,000	9.5%
21	Colorado	589,533,000	1.6%
31	Connecticut	432,948,000	1.2%
46	Delaware	120,090,000	0.3%
3	Florida	2,264,350,000	6.3%
12	Georgia	899,222,000	2.5%
47	Hawaii	87,476,000	0.2%
40	Idaho	228,140,000	0.6%
7	Illinois	1,445,821,000	4.0%
14	Indiana	838,295,000	2.3%
29	Iowa	441,867,000	1.2%
32	Kansas	432,530,000	1.2%
24	Kentucky	533,534,000	1.5%
19	Louisiana	648,621,000	1.8%
39	Maine	229,066,000	0.6%
16	Maryland	768,742,000	2.2%
18	Massachusetts	671,844,000	1.9%
8	Michigan	1,061,656,000	3.0%
20	Minnesota	646,453,000	1.8%
28	Mississippi	442,881,000	1.2%
17	Missouri	738,690,000	2.1%
41	Montana	207,256,000	0.6%
37	Nebraska	304,217,000	0.9%
36	Nevada	311,888,000	0.9%
44	New Hampshire	128,357,000	0.4%
25	New Jersey	519,491,000	1.5%
38	New Mexico	240,599,000	0.7%
23	New York	533,618,000	1.5%
6	North Carolina	1,494,367,000	4.2%
42	North Dakota	133,607,000	0.4%
5	Ohio	1,792,544,000	5.0%
30	Oklahoma	441,456,000	1.2%
33	Oregon	415,249,000	1.2%
4	Pennsylvania	2,092,822,000	5.9%
43	Rhode Island	133,200,000	0.4%
26	South Carolina	511,834,000	1.4%
45	South Dakota	125,367,000	0.4%
13	Tennessee	848,348,000	2.4%
2	Texas	2,993,570,000	8.4%
34	Utah	359,218,000	1.0%
48	Vermont	86,018,000	0.2%
11	Virginia	933,207,000	2.6%
9	Washington	1,030,005,000	2.9%
35	West Virginia	320,734,000	0.9%
10	Wisconsin	975,646,000	2.7%
49	Wyoming	68,845,000	0.2%

RANK ORDER

RANK	STATE	FUEL TAX	% of USA
1	California	$3,393,381,000	9.5%
2	Texas	2,993,570,000	8.4%
3	Florida	2,264,350,000	6.3%
4	Pennsylvania	2,092,822,000	5.9%
5	Ohio	1,792,544,000	5.0%
6	North Carolina	1,494,367,000	4.2%
7	Illinois	1,445,821,000	4.0%
8	Michigan	1,061,656,000	3.0%
9	Washington	1,030,005,000	2.9%
10	Wisconsin	975,646,000	2.7%
11	Virginia	933,207,000	2.6%
12	Georgia	899,222,000	2.5%
13	Tennessee	848,348,000	2.4%
14	Indiana	838,295,000	2.3%
15	Arizona	772,849,000	2.2%
16	Maryland	768,742,000	2.2%
17	Missouri	738,690,000	2.1%
18	Massachusetts	671,844,000	1.9%
19	Louisiana	648,621,000	1.8%
20	Minnesota	646,453,000	1.8%
21	Colorado	589,533,000	1.6%
22	Alabama	566,700,000	1.6%
23	New York	533,618,000	1.5%
24	Kentucky	533,534,000	1.5%
25	New Jersey	519,491,000	1.5%
26	South Carolina	511,834,000	1.4%
27	Arkansas	456,377,000	1.3%
28	Mississippi	442,881,000	1.2%
29	Iowa	441,867,000	1.2%
30	Oklahoma	441,456,000	1.2%
31	Connecticut	432,948,000	1.2%
32	Kansas	432,530,000	1.2%
33	Oregon	415,249,000	1.2%
34	Utah	359,218,000	1.0%
35	West Virginia	320,734,000	0.9%
36	Nevada	311,888,000	0.9%
37	Nebraska	304,217,000	0.9%
38	New Mexico	240,599,000	0.7%
39	Maine	229,066,000	0.6%
40	Idaho	228,140,000	0.6%
41	Montana	207,256,000	0.6%
42	North Dakota	133,607,000	0.4%
43	Rhode Island	133,200,000	0.4%
44	New Hampshire	128,357,000	0.4%
45	South Dakota	125,367,000	0.4%
46	Delaware	120,090,000	0.3%
47	Hawaii	87,476,000	0.2%
48	Vermont	86,018,000	0.2%
49	Wyoming	68,845,000	0.2%
50	Alaska	42,087,000	0.1%
	District of Columbia*	NA	NA

Source: U.S. Bureau of the Census, Governments Division
    "2006 State Government Tax Collections" (http://www.census.gov/govs/www/statetax06.html)
*Not applicable.

Per Capita State Government Motor Fuel Sales Tax Revenue in 2006

National Per Capita = $120

ALPHA ORDER			RANK ORDER		
RANK	STATE	PER CAPITA	RANK	STATE	PER CAPITA
36	Alabama	$123	1	Montana	$219
48	Alaska	62	2	North Dakota	210
28	Arizona	125	3	West Virginia	177
9	Arkansas	162	4	Wisconsin	175
46	California	94	5	Maine	174
33	Colorado	124	6	Nebraska	172
33	Connecticut	124	7	Pennsylvania	169
18	Delaware	141	8	North Carolina	168
28	Florida	125	9	Arkansas	162
45	Georgia	96	9	Washington	162
47	Hawaii	68	11	South Dakota	159
13	Idaho	156	12	Kansas	157
40	Illinois	113	13	Idaho	156
24	Indiana	133	13	Ohio	156
17	Iowa	149	15	Louisiana	153
12	Kansas	157	15	Mississippi	153
26	Kentucky	127	17	Iowa	149
15	Louisiana	153	18	Delaware	141
5	Maine	174	19	Tennessee	140
22	Maryland	137	20	Utah	139
43	Massachusetts	104	20	Vermont	139
42	Michigan	105	22	Maryland	137
28	Minnesota	125	23	Wyoming	134
15	Mississippi	153	24	Indiana	133
26	Missouri	127	25	Texas	128
1	Montana	219	26	Kentucky	127
6	Nebraska	172	26	Missouri	127
28	Nevada	125	28	Arizona	125
44	New Hampshire	98	28	Florida	125
49	New Jersey	60	28	Minnesota	125
33	New Mexico	124	28	Nevada	125
50	New York	28	28	Rhode Island	125
8	North Carolina	168	33	Colorado	124
2	North Dakota	210	33	Connecticut	124
13	Ohio	156	33	New Mexico	124
36	Oklahoma	123	36	Alabama	123
40	Oregon	113	36	Oklahoma	123
7	Pennsylvania	169	38	Virginia	122
28	Rhode Island	125	39	South Carolina	118
39	South Carolina	118	40	Illinois	113
11	South Dakota	159	40	Oregon	113
19	Tennessee	140	42	Michigan	105
25	Texas	128	43	Massachusetts	104
20	Utah	139	44	New Hampshire	98
20	Vermont	139	45	Georgia	96
38	Virginia	122	46	California	94
9	Washington	162	47	Hawaii	68
3	West Virginia	177	48	Alaska	62
4	Wisconsin	175	49	New Jersey	60
23	Wyoming	134	50	New York	28

District of Columbia*   NA

Source: CQ Press using data from U.S. Bureau of the Census, Governments Division
"2006 State Government Tax Collections" (http://www.census.gov/govs/www/statetax06.html)
*Not applicable.

State Tax Rates on Gasoline in 2007

National Median = 21.00 Cents per Gallon*

ALPHA ORDER

RANK	STATE	CENTS PER GALLON
37	Alabama	18.00
50	Alaska	8.00
37	Arizona	18.00
23	Arkansas	21.50
37	California	18.00
21	Colorado	22.00
11	Connecticut	25.00
19	Delaware	23.00
46	Florida	15.30
47	Georgia	15.20
44	Hawaii	16.00
11	Idaho	25.00
27	Illinois	20.10
37	Indiana	18.00
25	Iowa	21.00
16	Kansas	24.00
32	Kentucky	19.70
28	Louisiana	20.00
10	Maine	26.80
18	Maryland	23.50
25	Massachusetts	21.00
34	Michigan	19.00
28	Minnesota	20.00
36	Mississippi	18.40
41	Missouri	17.55
9	Montana	27.00
7	Nebraska	28.00
13	Nevada	24.81
33	New Hampshire	19.63
48	New Jersey	14.50
35	New Mexico	18.88
14	New York	24.60
6	North Carolina	30.15
19	North Dakota	23.00
7	Ohio	28.00
43	Oklahoma	17.00
16	Oregon	24.00
4	Pennsylvania	31.20
5	Rhode Island	31.00
44	South Carolina	16.00
21	South Dakota	22.00
24	Tennessee	21.40
28	Texas	20.00
15	Utah	24.50
28	Vermont	20.00
42	Virginia	17.50
1	Washington	34.00
3	West Virginia	31.50
2	Wisconsin	32.90
49	Wyoming	14.00

RANK ORDER

RANK	STATE	CENTS PER GALLON
1	Washington	34.00
2	Wisconsin	32.90
3	West Virginia	31.50
4	Pennsylvania	31.20
5	Rhode Island	31.00
6	North Carolina	30.15
7	Nebraska	28.00
7	Ohio	28.00
9	Montana	27.00
10	Maine	26.80
11	Connecticut	25.00
11	Idaho	25.00
13	Nevada	24.81
14	New York	24.60
15	Utah	24.50
16	Kansas	24.00
16	Oregon	24.00
18	Maryland	23.50
19	Delaware	23.00
19	North Dakota	23.00
21	Colorado	22.00
21	South Dakota	22.00
23	Arkansas	21.50
24	Tennessee	21.40
25	Iowa	21.00
25	Massachusetts	21.00
27	Illinois	20.10
28	Louisiana	20.00
28	Minnesota	20.00
28	Texas	20.00
28	Vermont	20.00
32	Kentucky	19.70
33	New Hampshire	19.63
34	Michigan	19.00
35	New Mexico	18.88
36	Mississippi	18.40
37	Alabama	18.00
37	Arizona	18.00
37	California	18.00
37	Indiana	18.00
41	Missouri	17.55
42	Virginia	17.50
43	Oklahoma	17.00
44	Hawaii	16.00
44	South Carolina	16.00
46	Florida	15.30
47	Georgia	15.20
48	New Jersey	14.50
49	Wyoming	14.00
50	Alaska	8.00
	District of Columbia	20.00

Source: Federation of Tax Administrators
    "Motor Fuel Excise Tax Rates" (http://www.taxadmin.org/fta/rate/motor_fl.html)
*As of January 1, 2007. Federal gasoline tax rate is an additional 18.4 cents per gallon. Many states also allow additional local option taxes on gasoline.

State Government Motor Vehicle and Operators' License Tax Revenue in 2006

National Total = $21,153,510,000

ALPHA ORDER

RANK	STATE	REVENUE	% of USA
25	Alabama	$237,543,000	1.1%
48	Alaska	52,494,000	0.2%
28	Arizona	214,448,000	1.0%
35	Arkansas	144,621,000	0.7%
1	California	2,811,928,000	13.3%
27	Colorado	214,486,000	1.0%
24	Connecticut	265,792,000	1.3%
50	Delaware	36,393,000	0.2%
4	Florida	1,366,866,000	6.5%
21	Georgia	321,277,000	1.5%
39	Hawaii	108,495,000	0.5%
37	Idaho	123,818,000	0.6%
2	Illinois	1,537,095,000	7.3%
18	Indiana	384,418,000	1.8%
16	Iowa	405,533,000	1.9%
30	Kansas	187,632,000	0.9%
26	Kentucky	222,894,000	1.1%
36	Louisiana	144,041,000	0.7%
41	Maine	93,700,000	0.4%
14	Maryland	472,463,000	2.2%
19	Massachusetts	368,775,000	1.7%
6	Michigan	955,824,000	4.5%
11	Minnesota	566,782,000	2.7%
34	Mississippi	148,599,000	0.7%
23	Missouri	298,423,000	1.4%
33	Montana	150,235,000	0.7%
40	Nebraska	99,725,000	0.5%
32	Nevada	177,527,000	0.8%
42	New Hampshire	93,658,000	0.4%
13	New Jersey	478,884,000	2.3%
31	New Mexico	184,635,000	0.9%
5	New York	1,001,109,000	4.7%
9	North Carolina	690,172,000	3.3%
44	North Dakota	73,627,000	0.3%
8	Ohio	873,799,000	4.1%
10	Oklahoma	576,603,000	2.7%
12	Oregon	511,770,000	2.4%
7	Pennsylvania	888,279,000	4.2%
47	Rhode Island	57,342,000	0.3%
29	South Carolina	202,307,000	1.0%
49	South Dakota	47,160,000	0.2%
22	Tennessee	308,838,000	1.5%
3	Texas	1,483,753,000	7.0%
38	Utah	123,663,000	0.6%
45	Vermont	64,254,000	0.3%
17	Virginia	400,968,000	1.9%
15	Washington	467,182,000	2.2%
43	West Virginia	87,955,000	0.4%
20	Wisconsin	367,105,000	1.7%
46	Wyoming	58,620,000	0.3%

RANK ORDER

RANK	STATE	REVENUE	% of USA
1	California	$2,811,928,000	13.3%
2	Illinois	1,537,095,000	7.3%
3	Texas	1,483,753,000	7.0%
4	Florida	1,366,866,000	6.5%
5	New York	1,001,109,000	4.7%
6	Michigan	955,824,000	4.5%
7	Pennsylvania	888,279,000	4.2%
8	Ohio	873,799,000	4.1%
9	North Carolina	690,172,000	3.3%
10	Oklahoma	576,603,000	2.7%
11	Minnesota	566,782,000	2.7%
12	Oregon	511,770,000	2.4%
13	New Jersey	478,884,000	2.3%
14	Maryland	472,463,000	2.2%
15	Washington	467,182,000	2.2%
16	Iowa	405,533,000	1.9%
17	Virginia	400,968,000	1.9%
18	Indiana	384,418,000	1.8%
19	Massachusetts	368,775,000	1.7%
20	Wisconsin	367,105,000	1.7%
21	Georgia	321,277,000	1.5%
22	Tennessee	308,838,000	1.5%
23	Missouri	298,423,000	1.4%
24	Connecticut	265,792,000	1.3%
25	Alabama	237,543,000	1.1%
26	Kentucky	222,894,000	1.1%
27	Colorado	214,486,000	1.0%
28	Arizona	214,448,000	1.0%
29	South Carolina	202,307,000	1.0%
30	Kansas	187,632,000	0.9%
31	New Mexico	184,635,000	0.9%
32	Nevada	177,527,000	0.8%
33	Montana	150,235,000	0.7%
34	Mississippi	148,599,000	0.7%
35	Arkansas	144,621,000	0.7%
36	Louisiana	144,041,000	0.7%
37	Idaho	123,818,000	0.6%
38	Utah	123,663,000	0.6%
39	Hawaii	108,495,000	0.5%
40	Nebraska	99,725,000	0.5%
41	Maine	93,700,000	0.4%
42	New Hampshire	93,658,000	0.4%
43	West Virginia	87,955,000	0.4%
44	North Dakota	73,627,000	0.3%
45	Vermont	64,254,000	0.3%
46	Wyoming	58,620,000	0.3%
47	Rhode Island	57,342,000	0.3%
48	Alaska	52,494,000	0.2%
49	South Dakota	47,160,000	0.2%
50	Delaware	36,393,000	0.2%
	District of Columbia*	NA	NA

Source: U.S. Bureau of the Census, Governments Division
   "2006 State Government Tax Collections" (http://www.census.gov/govs/www/statetax06.html)
*Not applicable.

Per Capita State Government Motor Vehicle and Operators' License Tax Revenue in 2006
National Per Capita = $70.81

ALPHA ORDER

RANK	STATE	PER CAPITA
38	Alabama	$51.75
17	Alaska	77.49
48	Arizona	34.78
39	Arkansas	51.48
16	California	77.57
46	Colorado	45.00
19	Connecticut	76.03
47	Delaware	42.68
20	Florida	75.70
49	Georgia	34.39
12	Hawaii	84.85
13	Idaho	84.58
5	Illinois	120.30
29	Indiana	60.99
4	Iowa	136.43
26	Kansas	68.09
35	Kentucky	53.01
50	Louisiana	33.95
24	Maine	71.26
14	Maryland	84.34
31	Massachusetts	57.31
11	Michigan	94.61
8	Minnesota	109.96
40	Mississippi	51.26
41	Missouri	51.12
2	Montana	158.68
32	Nebraska	56.54
25	Nevada	71.23
23	New Hampshire	71.40
33	New Jersey	55.26
10	New Mexico	95.06
37	New York	51.92
15	North Carolina	77.81
6	North Dakota	115.50
18	Ohio	76.22
1	Oklahoma	161.17
3	Oregon	138.65
22	Pennsylvania	71.62
34	Rhode Island	54.01
45	South Carolina	46.72
30	South Dakota	59.81
42	Tennessee	50.84
28	Texas	63.39
44	Utah	47.94
9	Vermont	103.51
36	Virginia	52.48
21	Washington	73.28
43	West Virginia	48.63
27	Wisconsin	65.88
7	Wyoming	114.32

RANK ORDER

RANK	STATE	PER CAPITA
1	Oklahoma	$161.17
2	Montana	158.68
3	Oregon	138.65
4	Iowa	136.43
5	Illinois	120.30
6	North Dakota	115.50
7	Wyoming	114.32
8	Minnesota	109.96
9	Vermont	103.51
10	New Mexico	95.06
11	Michigan	94.61
12	Hawaii	84.85
13	Idaho	84.58
14	Maryland	84.34
15	North Carolina	77.81
16	California	77.57
17	Alaska	77.49
18	Ohio	76.22
19	Connecticut	76.03
20	Florida	75.70
21	Washington	73.28
22	Pennsylvania	71.62
23	New Hampshire	71.40
24	Maine	71.26
25	Nevada	71.23
26	Kansas	68.09
27	Wisconsin	65.88
28	Texas	63.39
29	Indiana	60.99
30	South Dakota	59.81
31	Massachusetts	57.31
32	Nebraska	56.54
33	New Jersey	55.26
34	Rhode Island	54.01
35	Kentucky	53.01
36	Virginia	52.48
37	New York	51.92
38	Alabama	51.75
39	Arkansas	51.48
40	Mississippi	51.26
41	Missouri	51.12
42	Tennessee	50.84
43	West Virginia	48.63
44	Utah	47.94
45	South Carolina	46.72
46	Colorado	45.00
47	Delaware	42.68
48	Arizona	34.78
49	Georgia	34.39
50	Louisiana	33.95

District of Columbia*　　　　　　　　NA

Source: CQ Press using data from U.S. Bureau of the Census, Governments Division
"2006 State Government Tax Collections" (http://www.census.gov/govs/www/statetax06.html)
*Not applicable.

State Government Tobacco Product Sales Tax Revenue in 2006

National Total = $14,479,660,000

ALPHA ORDER

RANK	STATE	REVENUE	% of USA
26	Alabama	$154,321,000	1.1%
41	Alaska	64,106,000	0.4%
15	Arizona	298,001,000	2.1%
28	Arkansas	148,879,000	1.0%
2	California	1,088,703,000	7.5%
20	Colorado	229,207,000	1.6%
18	Connecticut	256,397,000	1.8%
38	Delaware	88,526,000	0.6%
10	Florida	456,794,000	3.2%
19	Georgia	243,540,000	1.7%
39	Hawaii	88,261,000	0.6%
44	Idaho	53,525,000	0.4%
7	Illinois	640,333,000	4.4%
13	Indiana	355,525,000	2.5%
35	Iowa	98,936,000	0.7%
32	Kansas	122,991,000	0.8%
22	Kentucky	193,242,000	1.3%
36	Louisiana	96,762,000	0.7%
25	Maine	154,825,000	1.1%
16	Maryland	280,307,000	1.9%
12	Massachusetts	435,336,000	3.0%
1	Michigan	1,171,889,000	8.1%
11	Minnesota	446,117,000	3.1%
43	Mississippi	58,098,000	0.4%
34	Missouri	111,322,000	0.8%
37	Montana	89,299,000	0.6%
40	Nebraska	67,026,000	0.5%
29	Nevada	138,813,000	1.0%
27	New Hampshire	149,985,000	1.0%
6	New Jersey	801,439,000	5.5%
46	New Mexico	48,405,000	0.3%
5	New York	971,330,000	6.7%
24	North Carolina	171,672,000	1.2%
50	North Dakota	23,490,000	0.2%
3	Ohio	1,086,712,000	7.5%
21	Oklahoma	222,898,000	1.5%
17	Oregon	269,922,000	1.9%
4	Pennsylvania	1,033,480,000	7.1%
30	Rhode Island	125,911,000	0.9%
47	South Carolina	32,056,000	0.2%
48	South Dakota	28,185,000	0.2%
31	Tennessee	124,923,000	0.9%
8	Texas	545,904,000	3.8%
42	Utah	60,300,000	0.4%
45	Vermont	48,931,000	0.3%
23	Virginia	172,192,000	1.2%
9	Washington	474,907,000	3.3%
33	West Virginia	112,027,000	0.8%
14	Wisconsin	317,911,000	2.2%
49	Wyoming	25,999,000	0.2%

RANK ORDER

RANK	STATE	REVENUE	% of USA
1	Michigan	$1,171,889,000	8.1%
2	California	1,088,703,000	7.5%
3	Ohio	1,086,712,000	7.5%
4	Pennsylvania	1,033,480,000	7.1%
5	New York	971,330,000	6.7%
6	New Jersey	801,439,000	5.5%
7	Illinois	640,333,000	4.4%
8	Texas	545,904,000	3.8%
9	Washington	474,907,000	3.3%
10	Florida	456,794,000	3.2%
11	Minnesota	446,117,000	3.1%
12	Massachusetts	435,336,000	3.0%
13	Indiana	355,525,000	2.5%
14	Wisconsin	317,911,000	2.2%
15	Arizona	298,001,000	2.1%
16	Maryland	280,307,000	1.9%
17	Oregon	269,922,000	1.9%
18	Connecticut	256,397,000	1.8%
19	Georgia	243,540,000	1.7%
20	Colorado	229,207,000	1.6%
21	Oklahoma	222,898,000	1.5%
22	Kentucky	193,242,000	1.3%
23	Virginia	172,192,000	1.2%
24	North Carolina	171,672,000	1.2%
25	Maine	154,825,000	1.1%
26	Alabama	154,321,000	1.1%
27	New Hampshire	149,985,000	1.0%
28	Arkansas	148,879,000	1.0%
29	Nevada	138,813,000	1.0%
30	Rhode Island	125,911,000	0.9%
31	Tennessee	124,923,000	0.9%
32	Kansas	122,991,000	0.8%
33	West Virginia	112,027,000	0.8%
34	Missouri	111,322,000	0.8%
35	Iowa	98,936,000	0.7%
36	Louisiana	96,762,000	0.7%
37	Montana	89,299,000	0.6%
38	Delaware	88,526,000	0.6%
39	Hawaii	88,261,000	0.6%
40	Nebraska	67,026,000	0.5%
41	Alaska	64,106,000	0.4%
42	Utah	60,300,000	0.4%
43	Mississippi	58,098,000	0.4%
44	Idaho	53,525,000	0.4%
45	Vermont	48,931,000	0.3%
46	New Mexico	48,405,000	0.3%
47	South Carolina	32,056,000	0.2%
48	South Dakota	28,185,000	0.2%
49	Wyoming	25,999,000	0.2%
50	North Dakota	23,490,000	0.2%
	District of Columbia*	NA	NA

Source: U.S. Bureau of the Census, Governments Division
"2006 State Government Tax Collections" (http://www.census.gov/govs/www/statetax06.html)
*Not applicable.

Per Capita State Government Tobacco Sales Tax Revenue in 2006

National Per Capita = $48.47

ALPHA ORDER

RANK	STATE	PER CAPITA
36	Alabama	$33.62
7	Alaska	94.63
28	Arizona	48.33
23	Arkansas	53.00
38	California	30.03
29	Colorado	48.09
14	Connecticut	73.35
5	Delaware	103.81
40	Florida	25.30
39	Georgia	26.07
16	Hawaii	69.03
34	Idaho	36.56
26	Illinois	50.12
21	Indiana	56.41
37	Iowa	33.28
31	Kansas	44.63
30	Kentucky	45.96
44	Louisiana	22.80
2	Maine	117.75
27	Maryland	50.04
17	Massachusetts	67.66
3	Michigan	116.00
10	Minnesota	86.55
47	Mississippi	20.04
49	Missouri	19.07
8	Montana	94.32
32	Nebraska	38.00
22	Nevada	55.69
4	New Hampshire	114.33
9	New Jersey	92.48
41	New Mexico	24.92
25	New York	50.37
48	North Carolina	19.36
33	North Dakota	36.85
6	Ohio	94.80
18	Oklahoma	62.30
15	Oregon	73.13
11	Pennsylvania	83.33
1	Rhode Island	118.60
50	South Carolina	7.40
35	South Dakota	35.75
46	Tennessee	20.56
43	Texas	23.32
42	Utah	23.38
12	Vermont	78.82
45	Virginia	22.54
13	Washington	74.50
19	West Virginia	61.94
20	Wisconsin	57.05
24	Wyoming	50.70

RANK ORDER

RANK	STATE	PER CAPITA
1	Rhode Island	$118.60
2	Maine	117.75
3	Michigan	116.00
4	New Hampshire	114.33
5	Delaware	103.81
6	Ohio	94.80
7	Alaska	94.63
8	Montana	94.32
9	New Jersey	92.48
10	Minnesota	86.55
11	Pennsylvania	83.33
12	Vermont	78.82
13	Washington	74.50
14	Connecticut	73.35
15	Oregon	73.13
16	Hawaii	69.03
17	Massachusetts	67.66
18	Oklahoma	62.30
19	West Virginia	61.94
20	Wisconsin	57.05
21	Indiana	56.41
22	Nevada	55.69
23	Arkansas	53.00
24	Wyoming	50.70
25	New York	50.37
26	Illinois	50.12
27	Maryland	50.04
28	Arizona	48.33
29	Colorado	48.09
30	Kentucky	45.96
31	Kansas	44.63
32	Nebraska	38.00
33	North Dakota	36.85
34	Idaho	36.56
35	South Dakota	35.75
36	Alabama	33.62
37	Iowa	33.28
38	California	30.03
39	Georgia	26.07
40	Florida	25.30
41	New Mexico	24.92
42	Utah	23.38
43	Texas	23.32
44	Louisiana	22.80
45	Virginia	22.54
46	Tennessee	20.56
47	Mississippi	20.04
48	North Carolina	19.36
49	Missouri	19.07
50	South Carolina	7.40
	District of Columbia*	NA

Source: CQ Press using data from U.S. Bureau of the Census, Governments Division
"2006 State Government Tax Collections" (http://www.census.gov/govs/www/statetax06.html)
*Not applicable.

State Tax on a Pack of Cigarettes in 2007

National Median = 80.0 Cents per Pack*

ALPHA ORDER

RANK	STATE	CENTS PER PACK
39	Alabama	42.5
7	Alaska**	180.0
4	Arizona	200.0
32	Arkansas	59.0
23	California	87.0
24	Colorado	84.0
11	Connecticut	151.0
35	Delaware	55.0
44	Florida	33.9
40	Georgia	37.0
10	Hawaii**	160.0
33	Idaho	57.0
21	Illinois	98.0
34	Indiana	55.5
41	Iowa	36.0
27	Kansas	79.0
45	Kentucky	30.0
41	Louisiana	36.0
4	Maine	200.0
20	Maryland	100.0
11	Massachusetts	151.0
4	Michigan	200.0
17	Minnesota	123.0
48	Mississippi	18.0
49	Missouri	17.0
9	Montana	170.0
30	Nebraska	64.0
25	Nevada	80.0
25	New Hampshire	80.0
1	New Jersey	257.5
22	New Mexico	91.0
13	New York	150.0
43	North Carolina	35.0
38	North Dakota	44.0
16	Ohio	125.0
19	Oklahoma	103.0
18	Oregon	118.0
15	Pennsylvania	135.0
2	Rhode Island	246.0
50	South Carolina	7.0
37	South Dakota	53.0
47	Tennessee	20.0
14	Texas	141.0
29	Utah	69.5
8	Vermont	179.0
45	Virginia	30.0
3	Washington	202.5
35	West Virginia	55.0
28	Wisconsin	77.0
31	Wyoming	60.0

RANK ORDER

RANK	STATE	CENTS PER PACK
1	New Jersey	257.5
2	Rhode Island	246.0
3	Washington	202.5
4	Arizona	200.0
4	Maine	200.0
4	Michigan	200.0
7	Alaska**	180.0
8	Vermont	179.0
9	Montana	170.0
10	Hawaii**	160.0
11	Connecticut	151.0
11	Massachusetts	151.0
13	New York	150.0
14	Texas	141.0
15	Pennsylvania	135.0
16	Ohio	125.0
17	Minnesota	123.0
18	Oregon	118.0
19	Oklahoma	103.0
20	Maryland	100.0
21	Illinois	98.0
22	New Mexico	91.0
23	California	87.0
24	Colorado	84.0
25	Nevada	80.0
25	New Hampshire	80.0
27	Kansas	79.0
28	Wisconsin	77.0
29	Utah	69.5
30	Nebraska	64.0
31	Wyoming	60.0
32	Arkansas	59.0
33	Idaho	57.0
34	Indiana	55.5
35	Delaware	55.0
35	West Virginia	55.0
37	South Dakota	53.0
38	North Dakota	44.0
39	Alabama	42.5
40	Georgia	37.0
41	Iowa	36.0
41	Louisiana	36.0
43	North Carolina	35.0
44	Florida	33.9
45	Kentucky	30.0
45	Virginia	30.0
47	Tennessee	20.0
48	Mississippi	18.0
49	Missouri	17.0
50	South Carolina	7.0

District of Columbia	100.0

Source: Federation of Tax Administrators
   "State Cigarette Excise Tax Rates" (http://www.taxadmin.org/fta/rate/cigarett.html)
*As of January 1, 2007. Many states also allow additional local option taxes on cigarettes.
**The rate per pack was scheduled to raise to $2.00 per pack on July 1, 2007 in Alaska and on September 30, 2007 in Hawaii.

State Government Alcoholic Beverage Sales Tax Revenue in 2006

National Total = $4,925,400,000

RANK	STATE	LIQUOR TAX	% of USA
13	Alabama	$120,662,000	2.4%
32	Alaska	35,225,000	0.7%
22	Arizona	61,147,000	1.2%
26	Arkansas	45,541,000	0.9%
3	California	318,276,000	6.5%
33	Colorado	33,217,000	0.7%
28	Connecticut	41,068,000	0.8%
41	Delaware	14,238,000	0.3%
2	Florida	642,926,000	13.1%
9	Georgia	156,124,000	3.2%
25	Hawaii	45,955,000	0.9%
48	Idaho	7,089,000	0.1%
10	Illinois	152,300,000	3.1%
30	Indiana	37,375,000	0.8%
40	Iowa	14,269,000	0.3%
17	Kansas	95,867,000	1.9%
16	Kentucky	97,582,000	2.0%
23	Louisiana	53,132,000	1.1%
42	Maine	14,090,000	0.3%
36	Maryland	27,943,000	0.6%
21	Massachusetts	69,526,000	1.4%
12	Michigan	133,284,000	2.7%
20	Minnesota	70,938,000	1.4%
27	Mississippi	42,200,000	0.9%
35	Missouri	29,543,000	0.6%
38	Montana	23,574,000	0.5%
37	Nebraska	24,819,000	0.5%
29	Nevada	38,262,000	0.8%
45	New Hampshire	12,624,000	0.3%
15	New Jersey	101,965,000	2.1%
31	New Mexico	37,100,000	0.8%
7	New York	191,681,000	3.9%
6	North Carolina	232,768,000	4.7%
49	North Dakota	6,341,000	0.1%
18	Ohio	91,855,000	1.9%
19	Oklahoma	74,304,000	1.5%
43	Oregon	13,643,000	0.3%
4	Pennsylvania	249,194,000	5.1%
46	Rhode Island	11,254,000	0.2%
11	South Carolina	143,034,000	2.9%
44	South Dakota	12,654,000	0.3%
14	Tennessee	105,470,000	2.1%
1	Texas	680,748,000	13.8%
34	Utah	33,049,000	0.7%
39	Vermont	18,614,000	0.4%
8	Virginia	160,703,000	3.3%
5	Washington	240,744,000	4.9%
47	West Virginia	9,053,000	0.2%
24	Wisconsin	50,782,000	1.0%
50	Wyoming	1,648,000	0.0%

RANK	STATE	LIQUOR TAX	% of USA
1	Texas	$680,748,000	13.8%
2	Florida	642,926,000	13.1%
3	California	318,276,000	6.5%
4	Pennsylvania	249,194,000	5.1%
5	Washington	240,744,000	4.9%
6	North Carolina	232,768,000	4.7%
7	New York	191,681,000	3.9%
8	Virginia	160,703,000	3.3%
9	Georgia	156,124,000	3.2%
10	Illinois	152,300,000	3.1%
11	South Carolina	143,034,000	2.9%
12	Michigan	133,284,000	2.7%
13	Alabama	120,662,000	2.4%
14	Tennessee	105,470,000	2.1%
15	New Jersey	101,965,000	2.1%
16	Kentucky	97,582,000	2.0%
17	Kansas	95,867,000	1.9%
18	Ohio	91,855,000	1.9%
19	Oklahoma	74,304,000	1.5%
20	Minnesota	70,938,000	1.4%
21	Massachusetts	69,526,000	1.4%
22	Arizona	61,147,000	1.2%
23	Louisiana	53,132,000	1.1%
24	Wisconsin	50,782,000	1.0%
25	Hawaii	45,955,000	0.9%
26	Arkansas	45,541,000	0.9%
27	Mississippi	42,200,000	0.9%
28	Connecticut	41,068,000	0.8%
29	Nevada	38,262,000	0.8%
30	Indiana	37,375,000	0.8%
31	New Mexico	37,100,000	0.8%
32	Alaska	35,225,000	0.7%
33	Colorado	33,217,000	0.7%
34	Utah	33,049,000	0.7%
35	Missouri	29,543,000	0.6%
36	Maryland	27,943,000	0.6%
37	Nebraska	24,819,000	0.5%
38	Montana	23,574,000	0.5%
39	Vermont	18,614,000	0.4%
40	Iowa	14,269,000	0.3%
41	Delaware	14,238,000	0.3%
42	Maine	14,090,000	0.3%
43	Oregon	13,643,000	0.3%
44	South Dakota	12,654,000	0.3%
45	New Hampshire	12,624,000	0.3%
46	Rhode Island	11,254,000	0.2%
47	West Virginia	9,053,000	0.2%
48	Idaho	7,089,000	0.1%
49	North Dakota	6,341,000	0.1%
50	Wyoming	1,648,000	0.0%
	District of Columbia*	NA	NA

Source: U.S. Bureau of the Census, Governments Division
   "2006 State Government Tax Collections" (http://www.census.gov/govs/www/statetax06.html)
*Not applicable.

Per Capita State Government Alcoholic Beverage Sales Tax Revenue in 2006

National Per Capita = $16.49

ALPHA ORDER

RANK	STATE	PER CAPITA
9	Alabama	$26.29
1	Alaska	52.00
37	Arizona	9.92
20	Arkansas	16.21
40	California	8.78
42	Colorado	6.97
31	Connecticut	11.75
19	Delaware	16.70
4	Florida	35.60
18	Georgia	16.71
3	Hawaii	35.94
47	Idaho	4.84
29	Illinois	11.92
43	Indiana	5.93
48	Iowa	4.80
5	Kansas	34.79
12	Kentucky	23.21
28	Louisiana	12.52
33	Maine	10.72
46	Maryland	4.99
32	Massachusetts	10.81
26	Michigan	13.19
25	Minnesota	13.76
23	Mississippi	14.56
44	Missouri	5.06
11	Montana	24.90
24	Nebraska	14.07
22	Nevada	15.35
38	New Hampshire	9.62
30	New Jersey	11.77
16	New Mexico	19.10
36	New York	9.94
10	North Carolina	26.24
35	North Dakota	9.95
41	Ohio	8.01
14	Oklahoma	20.77
49	Oregon	3.70
15	Pennsylvania	20.09
34	Rhode Island	10.60
6	South Carolina	33.03
21	South Dakota	16.05
17	Tennessee	17.36
8	Texas	29.08
27	Utah	12.81
7	Vermont	29.98
13	Virginia	21.03
2	Washington	37.76
45	West Virginia	5.01
39	Wisconsin	9.11
50	Wyoming	3.21

RANK ORDER

RANK	STATE	PER CAPITA
1	Alaska	$52.00
2	Washington	37.76
3	Hawaii	35.94
4	Florida	35.60
5	Kansas	34.79
6	South Carolina	33.03
7	Vermont	29.98
8	Texas	29.08
9	Alabama	26.29
10	North Carolina	26.24
11	Montana	24.90
12	Kentucky	23.21
13	Virginia	21.03
14	Oklahoma	20.77
15	Pennsylvania	20.09
16	New Mexico	19.10
17	Tennessee	17.36
18	Georgia	16.71
19	Delaware	16.70
20	Arkansas	16.21
21	South Dakota	16.05
22	Nevada	15.35
23	Mississippi	14.56
24	Nebraska	14.07
25	Minnesota	13.76
26	Michigan	13.19
27	Utah	12.81
28	Louisiana	12.52
29	Illinois	11.92
30	New Jersey	11.77
31	Connecticut	11.75
32	Massachusetts	10.81
33	Maine	10.72
34	Rhode Island	10.60
35	North Dakota	9.95
36	New York	9.94
37	Arizona	9.92
38	New Hampshire	9.62
39	Wisconsin	9.11
40	California	8.78
41	Ohio	8.01
42	Colorado	6.97
43	Indiana	5.93
44	Missouri	5.06
45	West Virginia	5.01
46	Maryland	4.99
47	Idaho	4.84
48	Iowa	4.80
49	Oregon	3.70
50	Wyoming	3.21

District of Columbia*   NA

Source: CQ Press using data from U.S. Bureau of the Census, Governments Division
   "2006 State Government Tax Collections" (http://www.census.gov/govs/www/statetax06.html)
*Not applicable.

State Government Total Expenditures in 2005

National Total = $1,470,456,615,000*

ALPHA ORDER

RANK	STATE	EXPENDITURES	% of USA
24	Alabama	$21,046,841,000	1.4%
39	Alaska	8,055,975,000	0.5%
20	Arizona	23,957,058,000	1.6%
32	Arkansas	13,634,214,000	0.9%
1	California	209,771,313,000	14.3%
28	Colorado	18,769,570,000	1.3%
25	Connecticut	20,203,170,000	1.4%
44	Delaware	5,904,256,000	0.4%
4	Florida	70,417,744,000	4.8%
12	Georgia	33,806,582,000	2.3%
38	Hawaii	8,405,444,000	0.6%
43	Idaho	6,137,489,000	0.4%
7	Illinois	55,666,989,000	3.8%
18	Indiana	26,451,543,000	1.8%
31	Iowa	14,142,676,000	1.0%
34	Kansas	11,765,208,000	0.8%
26	Kentucky	20,091,176,000	1.4%
23	Louisiana	21,402,115,000	1.5%
40	Maine	7,484,638,000	0.5%
17	Maryland	26,803,282,000	1.8%
11	Massachusetts	38,025,089,000	2.6%
8	Michigan	51,408,421,000	3.5%
15	Minnesota	30,169,448,000	2.1%
30	Mississippi	14,704,763,000	1.0%
21	Missouri	23,147,448,000	1.6%
46	Montana	4,800,120,000	0.3%
41	Nebraska	7,273,406,000	0.5%
37	Nevada	9,158,273,000	0.6%
45	New Hampshire	5,783,853,000	0.4%
9	New Jersey	49,230,773,000	3.3%
33	New Mexico	12,599,040,000	0.9%
2	New York	136,786,401,000	9.3%
10	North Carolina	39,482,250,000	2.7%
49	North Dakota	3,490,904,000	0.2%
6	Ohio	60,554,060,000	4.1%
29	Oklahoma	15,710,022,000	1.1%
27	Oregon	19,216,554,000	1.3%
5	Pennsylvania	62,833,258,000	4.3%
42	Rhode Island	6,753,641,000	0.5%
22	South Carolina	22,708,996,000	1.5%
50	South Dakota	3,261,813,000	0.2%
19	Tennessee	23,989,642,000	1.6%
3	Texas	81,368,646,000	5.5%
35	Utah	11,148,591,000	0.8%
47	Vermont	4,435,774,000	0.3%
14	Virginia	32,784,615,000	2.2%
13	Washington	33,059,244,000	2.2%
36	West Virginia	9,826,128,000	0.7%
16	Wisconsin	28,828,334,000	2.0%
48	Wyoming	3,999,825,000	0.3%

RANK ORDER

RANK	STATE	EXPENDITURES	% of USA
1	California	$209,771,313,000	14.3%
2	New York	136,786,401,000	9.3%
3	Texas	81,368,646,000	5.5%
4	Florida	70,417,744,000	4.8%
5	Pennsylvania	62,833,258,000	4.3%
6	Ohio	60,554,060,000	4.1%
7	Illinois	55,666,989,000	3.8%
8	Michigan	51,408,421,000	3.5%
9	New Jersey	49,230,773,000	3.3%
10	North Carolina	39,482,250,000	2.7%
11	Massachusetts	38,025,089,000	2.6%
12	Georgia	33,806,582,000	2.3%
13	Washington	33,059,244,000	2.2%
14	Virginia	32,784,615,000	2.2%
15	Minnesota	30,169,448,000	2.1%
16	Wisconsin	28,828,334,000	2.0%
17	Maryland	26,803,282,000	1.8%
18	Indiana	26,451,543,000	1.8%
19	Tennessee	23,989,642,000	1.6%
20	Arizona	23,957,058,000	1.6%
21	Missouri	23,147,448,000	1.6%
22	South Carolina	22,708,996,000	1.5%
23	Louisiana	21,402,115,000	1.5%
24	Alabama	21,046,841,000	1.4%
25	Connecticut	20,203,170,000	1.4%
26	Kentucky	20,091,176,000	1.4%
27	Oregon	19,216,554,000	1.3%
28	Colorado	18,769,570,000	1.3%
29	Oklahoma	15,710,022,000	1.1%
30	Mississippi	14,704,763,000	1.0%
31	Iowa	14,142,676,000	1.0%
32	Arkansas	13,634,214,000	0.9%
33	New Mexico	12,599,040,000	0.9%
34	Kansas	11,765,208,000	0.8%
35	Utah	11,148,591,000	0.8%
36	West Virginia	9,826,128,000	0.7%
37	Nevada	9,158,273,000	0.6%
38	Hawaii	8,405,444,000	0.6%
39	Alaska	8,055,975,000	0.5%
40	Maine	7,484,638,000	0.5%
41	Nebraska	7,273,406,000	0.5%
42	Rhode Island	6,753,641,000	0.5%
43	Idaho	6,137,489,000	0.4%
44	Delaware	5,904,256,000	0.4%
45	New Hampshire	5,783,853,000	0.4%
46	Montana	4,800,120,000	0.3%
47	Vermont	4,435,774,000	0.3%
48	Wyoming	3,999,825,000	0.3%
49	North Dakota	3,490,904,000	0.2%
50	South Dakota	3,261,813,000	0.2%
	District of Columbia**	NA	NA

Source: U.S. Bureau of the Census, Governments Division
"State and Local Government Finances: 2004-2005" (http://www.census.gov/govs/www/estimate05.html)
*Total expenditures includes all money paid other than for retirement of debt and extension of loans. Includes payments from all sources of funds including current revenues and proceeds from borrowing and prior year fund balances. Includes intergovernmental transfers and expenditures for government owned utilities and other commercial or auxiliary enterprise, and insurance trust expenditures. **Not applicable.

Per Capita State Government Total Expenditures in 2005

National Per Capita = $4,979*

ALPHA ORDER

RANK	STATE	PER CAPITA
31	Alabama	$4,636
1	Alaska	12,034
43	Arizona	4,025
26	Arkansas	4,918
11	California	5,829
44	Colorado	4,016
12	Connecticut	5,795
5	Delaware	7,024
47	Florida	3,970
49	Georgia	3,712
6	Hawaii	6,631
38	Idaho	4,304
36	Illinois	4,376
40	Indiana	4,227
29	Iowa	4,785
39	Kansas	4,291
27	Kentucky	4,817
30	Louisiana	4,761
13	Maine	5,704
28	Maryland	4,809
9	Massachusetts	5,914
23	Michigan	5,086
10	Minnesota	5,900
25	Mississippi	5,070
46	Missouri	3,999
22	Montana	5,130
42	Nebraska	4,147
48	Nevada	3,802
35	New Hampshire	4,438
14	New Jersey	5,687
7	New Mexico	6,575
4	New York	7,101
32	North Carolina	4,549
15	North Dakota	5,489
19	Ohio	5,284
34	Oklahoma	4,443
18	Oregon	5,294
24	Pennsylvania	5,081
8	Rhode Island	6,331
17	South Carolina	5,337
41	South Dakota	4,182
45	Tennessee	4,005
50	Texas	3,562
33	Utah	4,451
3	Vermont	7,158
37	Virginia	4,338
20	Washington	5,272
16	West Virginia	5,442
21	Wisconsin	5,203
2	Wyoming	7,896

RANK ORDER

RANK	STATE	PER CAPITA
1	Alaska	$12,034
2	Wyoming	7,896
3	Vermont	7,158
4	New York	7,101
5	Delaware	7,024
6	Hawaii	6,631
7	New Mexico	6,575
8	Rhode Island	6,331
9	Massachusetts	5,914
10	Minnesota	5,900
11	California	5,829
12	Connecticut	5,795
13	Maine	5,704
14	New Jersey	5,687
15	North Dakota	5,489
16	West Virginia	5,442
17	South Carolina	5,337
18	Oregon	5,294
19	Ohio	5,284
20	Washington	5,272
21	Wisconsin	5,203
22	Montana	5,130
23	Michigan	5,086
24	Pennsylvania	5,081
25	Mississippi	5,070
26	Arkansas	4,918
27	Kentucky	4,817
28	Maryland	4,809
29	Iowa	4,785
30	Louisiana	4,761
31	Alabama	4,636
32	North Carolina	4,549
33	Utah	4,451
34	Oklahoma	4,443
35	New Hampshire	4,438
36	Illinois	4,376
37	Virginia	4,338
38	Idaho	4,304
39	Kansas	4,291
40	Indiana	4,227
41	South Dakota	4,182
42	Nebraska	4,147
43	Arizona	4,025
44	Colorado	4,016
45	Tennessee	4,005
46	Missouri	3,999
47	Florida	3,970
48	Nevada	3,802
49	Georgia	3,712
50	Texas	3,562

District of Columbia**   NA

Source: CQ Press using data from U.S. Bureau of the Census, Governments Division
    "State and Local Government Finances: 2004-2005" (http://www.census.gov/govs/www/estimate05.html)
*Total expenditures includes all money paid other than for retirement of debt and extension of loans. Includes payments from all sources of funds including current revenues and proceeds from borrowing and prior year fund balances. Includes intergovernmental transfers and expenditures for government owned utilities and other commercial or auxiliary enterprise, and insurance trust expenditures. **Not applicable.

State Government Direct General Expenditures in 2005

National Total = $872,147,900,000*

ALPHA ORDER

RANK ORDER

RANK	STATE	EXPENDITURES	% of USA	RANK	STATE	EXPENDITURES	% of USA
22	Alabama	$14,616,340,000	1.7%	1	California	$95,719,606,000	11.0%
38	Alaska	5,969,923,000	0.7%	2	New York	68,138,096,000	7.8%
26	Arizona	13,553,470,000	1.6%	3	Texas	54,397,859,000	6.2%
32	Arkansas	8,796,218,000	1.0%	4	Florida	45,016,565,000	5.2%
1	California	95,719,606,000	11.0%	5	Pennsylvania	40,511,267,000	4.6%
28	Colorado	10,495,620,000	1.2%	6	Illinois	34,086,679,000	3.9%
24	Connecticut	13,962,165,000	1.6%	7	Ohio	33,122,899,000	3.8%
43	Delaware	4,468,947,000	0.5%	8	Massachusetts	27,525,324,000	3.2%
4	Florida	45,016,565,000	5.2%	9	New Jersey	27,432,793,000	3.1%
13	Georgia	20,938,542,000	2.4%	10	Michigan	26,985,462,000	3.1%
35	Hawaii	7,472,675,000	0.9%	11	North Carolina	24,968,188,000	2.9%
44	Idaho	3,961,236,000	0.5%	12	Washington	20,987,297,000	2.4%
6	Illinois	34,086,679,000	3.9%	13	Georgia	20,938,542,000	2.4%
18	Indiana	16,568,803,000	1.9%	14	Virginia	20,299,813,000	2.3%
31	Iowa	9,092,591,000	1.0%	15	Maryland	17,825,082,000	2.0%
36	Kansas	7,427,004,000	0.9%	16	Tennessee	16,798,942,000	1.9%
25	Kentucky	13,760,016,000	1.6%	17	Minnesota	16,764,179,000	1.9%
23	Louisiana	14,221,004,000	1.6%	18	Indiana	16,568,803,000	1.9%
39	Maine	5,789,830,000	0.7%	19	Wisconsin	15,967,421,000	1.8%
15	Maryland	17,825,082,000	2.0%	20	Missouri	15,190,931,000	1.7%
8	Massachusetts	27,525,324,000	3.2%	21	South Carolina	14,875,455,000	1.7%
10	Michigan	26,985,462,000	3.1%	22	Alabama	14,616,340,000	1.7%
17	Minnesota	16,764,179,000	1.9%	23	Louisiana	14,221,004,000	1.6%
30	Mississippi	9,165,866,000	1.1%	24	Connecticut	13,962,165,000	1.6%
20	Missouri	15,190,931,000	1.7%	25	Kentucky	13,760,016,000	1.6%
46	Montana	3,224,574,000	0.4%	26	Arizona	13,553,470,000	1.6%
40	Nebraska	5,162,551,000	0.6%	27	Oregon	10,737,735,000	1.2%
42	Nevada	4,803,305,000	0.6%	28	Colorado	10,495,620,000	1.2%
45	New Hampshire	3,799,914,000	0.4%	29	Oklahoma	9,928,908,000	1.1%
9	New Jersey	27,432,793,000	3.1%	30	Mississippi	9,165,866,000	1.1%
33	New Mexico	7,934,368,000	0.9%	31	Iowa	9,092,591,000	1.0%
2	New York	68,138,096,000	7.8%	32	Arkansas	8,796,218,000	1.0%
11	North Carolina	24,968,188,000	2.9%	33	New Mexico	7,934,368,000	0.9%
48	North Dakota	2,455,763,000	0.3%	34	Utah	7,932,800,000	0.9%
7	Ohio	33,122,899,000	3.8%	35	Hawaii	7,472,675,000	0.9%
29	Oklahoma	9,928,908,000	1.1%	36	Kansas	7,427,004,000	0.9%
27	Oregon	10,737,735,000	1.2%	37	West Virginia	6,931,956,000	0.8%
5	Pennsylvania	40,511,267,000	4.6%	38	Alaska	5,969,923,000	0.7%
41	Rhode Island	4,813,857,000	0.6%	39	Maine	5,789,830,000	0.7%
21	South Carolina	14,875,455,000	1.7%	40	Nebraska	5,162,551,000	0.6%
49	South Dakota	2,371,200,000	0.3%	41	Rhode Island	4,813,857,000	0.6%
16	Tennessee	16,798,942,000	1.9%	42	Nevada	4,803,305,000	0.6%
3	Texas	54,397,859,000	6.2%	43	Delaware	4,468,947,000	0.5%
34	Utah	7,932,800,000	0.9%	44	Idaho	3,961,236,000	0.5%
47	Vermont	2,921,026,000	0.3%	45	New Hampshire	3,799,914,000	0.4%
14	Virginia	20,299,813,000	2.3%	46	Montana	3,224,574,000	0.4%
12	Washington	20,987,297,000	2.4%	47	Vermont	2,921,026,000	0.3%
37	West Virginia	6,931,956,000	0.8%	48	North Dakota	2,455,763,000	0.3%
19	Wisconsin	15,967,421,000	1.8%	49	South Dakota	2,371,200,000	0.3%
50	Wyoming	2,255,835,000	0.3%	50	Wyoming	2,255,835,000	0.3%
					District of Columbia**	NA	NA

Source: U.S. Bureau of the Census, Governments Division
"State and Local Government Finances: 2004-2005" (http://www.census.gov/govs/www/estimate05.html)
*Direct general expenditures include expenditures for current operations, assistance and subsidies, interest on debt, and capital outlay. Excludes intergovernmental transfers, expenditures for government owned utilities and other commercial or auxiliary enterprise, and insurance trust expenditures.
**Not applicable.

Per Capita State Government Direct General Expenditures in 2005

National Per Capita = $2,953*

ALPHA ORDER

RANK	STATE	PER CAPITA
20	Alabama	$3,220
1	Alaska	8,918
48	Arizona	2,277
22	Arkansas	3,173
42	California	2,660
49	Colorado	2,246
10	Connecticut	4,005
3	Delaware	5,317
45	Florida	2,538
47	Georgia	2,299
2	Hawaii	5,895
37	Idaho	2,778
40	Illinois	2,680
43	Indiana	2,648
27	Iowa	3,076
38	Kansas	2,709
17	Kentucky	3,299
25	Louisiana	3,163
7	Maine	4,412
21	Maryland	3,198
8	Massachusetts	4,281
41	Michigan	2,670
18	Minnesota	3,278
26	Mississippi	3,160
44	Missouri	2,625
15	Montana	3,446
30	Nebraska	2,943
50	Nevada	1,994
31	New Hampshire	2,916
23	New Jersey	3,169
9	New Mexico	4,140
13	New York	3,537
34	North Carolina	2,877
11	North Dakota	3,862
32	Ohio	2,890
35	Oklahoma	2,808
29	Oregon	2,958
19	Pennsylvania	3,276
5	Rhode Island	4,513
14	South Carolina	3,496
28	South Dakota	3,040
36	Tennessee	2,805
46	Texas	2,381
24	Utah	3,167
4	Vermont	4,713
39	Virginia	2,686
16	Washington	3,347
12	West Virginia	3,839
33	Wisconsin	2,882
6	Wyoming	4,453

RANK ORDER

RANK	STATE	PER CAPITA
1	Alaska	$8,918
2	Hawaii	5,895
3	Delaware	5,317
4	Vermont	4,713
5	Rhode Island	4,513
6	Wyoming	4,453
7	Maine	4,412
8	Massachusetts	4,281
9	New Mexico	4,140
10	Connecticut	4,005
11	North Dakota	3,862
12	West Virginia	3,839
13	New York	3,537
14	South Carolina	3,496
15	Montana	3,446
16	Washington	3,347
17	Kentucky	3,299
18	Minnesota	3,278
19	Pennsylvania	3,276
20	Alabama	3,220
21	Maryland	3,198
22	Arkansas	3,173
23	New Jersey	3,169
24	Utah	3,167
25	Louisiana	3,163
26	Mississippi	3,160
27	Iowa	3,076
28	South Dakota	3,040
29	Oregon	2,958
30	Nebraska	2,943
31	New Hampshire	2,916
32	Ohio	2,890
33	Wisconsin	2,882
34	North Carolina	2,877
35	Oklahoma	2,808
36	Tennessee	2,805
37	Idaho	2,778
38	Kansas	2,709
39	Virginia	2,686
40	Illinois	2,680
41	Michigan	2,670
42	California	2,660
43	Indiana	2,648
44	Missouri	2,625
45	Florida	2,538
46	Texas	2,381
47	Georgia	2,299
48	Arizona	2,277
49	Colorado	2,246
50	Nevada	1,994

District of Columbia**   NA

Source: CQ Press using data from U.S. Bureau of the Census, Governments Division
"State and Local Government Finances: 2004-2005" (http://www.census.gov/govs/www/estimate05.html)
*Direct general expenditures include expenditures for current operations, assistance and subsidies, interest on debt, and capital outlay. Excludes intergovernmental transfers, expenditures for government owned utilities and other commercial or auxiliary enterprise, and insurance trust expenditures.
**Not applicable.

State Government Debt Outstanding in 2005

National Total = $797,561,459,000*

ALPHA ORDER

RANK	STATE	DEBT	% of USA
30	Alabama	$6,261,529,000	0.8%
33	Alaska	5,766,931,000	0.7%
25	Arizona	8,037,412,000	1.0%
41	Arkansas	4,298,350,000	0.5%
1	California	107,372,729,000	13.5%
20	Colorado	12,409,574,000	1.6%
10	Connecticut	23,046,930,000	2.9%
39	Delaware	4,351,256,000	0.5%
8	Florida	25,879,751,000	3.2%
24	Georgia	8,188,637,000	1.0%
32	Hawaii	5,844,308,000	0.7%
47	Idaho	2,385,704,000	0.3%
4	Illinois	48,257,297,000	6.1%
19	Indiana	13,349,947,000	1.7%
37	Iowa	4,930,582,000	0.6%
35	Kansas	5,116,742,000	0.6%
23	Kentucky	8,564,204,000	1.1%
21	Louisiana	11,493,832,000	1.4%
38	Maine	4,626,581,000	0.6%
17	Maryland	13,722,618,000	1.7%
3	Massachusetts	55,993,986,000	7.0%
7	Michigan	26,167,479,000	3.3%
27	Minnesota	7,265,044,000	0.9%
40	Mississippi	4,328,368,000	0.5%
15	Missouri	16,183,549,000	2.0%
43	Montana	3,681,679,000	0.5%
48	Nebraska	1,743,156,000	0.2%
42	Nevada	3,910,573,000	0.5%
28	New Hampshire	6,864,120,000	0.9%
5	New Jersey	42,313,155,000	5.3%
31	New Mexico	5,872,748,000	0.7%
2	New York	101,992,376,000	12.8%
16	North Carolina	15,773,058,000	2.0%
49	North Dakota	1,683,444,000	0.2%
9	Ohio	23,124,057,000	2.9%
26	Oklahoma	7,468,710,000	0.9%
22	Oregon	10,464,215,000	1.3%
6	Pennsylvania	27,690,775,000	3.5%
29	Rhode Island	6,829,330,000	0.9%
18	South Carolina	13,369,988,000	1.7%
46	South Dakota	2,572,928,000	0.3%
44	Tennessee	3,574,196,000	0.4%
12	Texas	18,153,032,000	2.3%
34	Utah	5,267,269,000	0.7%
45	Vermont	2,799,851,000	0.4%
14	Virginia	16,901,057,000	2.1%
13	Washington	17,023,263,000	2.1%
36	West Virginia	5,014,053,000	0.6%
11	Wisconsin	18,763,197,000	2.4%
50	Wyoming	867,889,000	0.1%

RANK ORDER

RANK	STATE	DEBT	% of USA
1	California	$107,372,729,000	13.5%
2	New York	101,992,376,000	12.8%
3	Massachusetts	55,993,986,000	7.0%
4	Illinois	48,257,297,000	6.1%
5	New Jersey	42,313,155,000	5.3%
6	Pennsylvania	27,690,775,000	3.5%
7	Michigan	26,167,479,000	3.3%
8	Florida	25,879,751,000	3.2%
9	Ohio	23,124,057,000	2.9%
10	Connecticut	23,046,930,000	2.9%
11	Wisconsin	18,763,197,000	2.4%
12	Texas	18,153,032,000	2.3%
13	Washington	17,023,263,000	2.1%
14	Virginia	16,901,057,000	2.1%
15	Missouri	16,183,549,000	2.0%
16	North Carolina	15,773,058,000	2.0%
17	Maryland	13,722,618,000	1.7%
18	South Carolina	13,369,988,000	1.7%
19	Indiana	13,349,947,000	1.7%
20	Colorado	12,409,574,000	1.6%
21	Louisiana	11,493,832,000	1.4%
22	Oregon	10,464,215,000	1.3%
23	Kentucky	8,564,204,000	1.1%
24	Georgia	8,188,637,000	1.0%
25	Arizona	8,037,412,000	1.0%
26	Oklahoma	7,468,710,000	0.9%
27	Minnesota	7,265,044,000	0.9%
28	New Hampshire	6,864,120,000	0.9%
29	Rhode Island	6,829,330,000	0.9%
30	Alabama	6,261,529,000	0.8%
31	New Mexico	5,872,748,000	0.7%
32	Hawaii	5,844,308,000	0.7%
33	Alaska	5,766,931,000	0.7%
34	Utah	5,267,269,000	0.7%
35	Kansas	5,116,742,000	0.6%
36	West Virginia	5,014,053,000	0.6%
37	Iowa	4,930,582,000	0.6%
38	Maine	4,626,581,000	0.6%
39	Delaware	4,351,256,000	0.5%
40	Mississippi	4,328,368,000	0.5%
41	Arkansas	4,298,350,000	0.5%
42	Nevada	3,910,573,000	0.5%
43	Montana	3,681,679,000	0.5%
44	Tennessee	3,574,196,000	0.4%
45	Vermont	2,799,851,000	0.4%
46	South Dakota	2,572,928,000	0.3%
47	Idaho	2,385,704,000	0.3%
48	Nebraska	1,743,156,000	0.2%
49	North Dakota	1,683,444,000	0.2%
50	Wyoming	867,889,000	0.1%
	District of Columbia**	NA	NA

Source: U.S. Bureau of the Census, Governments Division
"State and Local Government Finances: 2004-2005" (http://www.census.gov/govs/www/estimate05.html)
*Includes short-term, long-term, full faith and credit, nonguaranteed, and public debt for private purposes.
**Not applicable.

Per Capita State Government Debt Outstanding in 2005

National Per Capita = $2,701*

ALPHA ORDER			RANK ORDER		
RANK	STATE	PER CAPITA	RANK	STATE	PER CAPITA
45	Alabama	$1,379	1	Massachusetts	$8,709
2	Alaska	8,615	2	Alaska	8,615
46	Arizona	1,350	3	Connecticut	6,610
41	Arkansas	1,551	4	Rhode Island	6,402
18	California	2,983	5	New York	5,295
23	Colorado	2,655	6	New Hampshire	5,267
3	Connecticut	6,610	7	Delaware	5,177
7	Delaware	5,177	8	New Jersey	4,887
43	Florida	1,459	9	Hawaii	4,611
48	Georgia	899	10	Vermont	4,518
9	Hawaii	4,611	11	Montana	3,934
38	Idaho	1,673	12	Illinois	3,794
12	Illinois	3,794	13	Maine	3,526
30	Indiana	2,134	14	Wisconsin	3,387
39	Iowa	1,668	15	South Dakota	3,298
35	Kansas	1,866	16	South Carolina	3,142
33	Kentucky	2,053	17	New Mexico	3,065
26	Louisiana	2,557	18	California	2,983
13	Maine	3,526	19	Oregon	2,883
27	Maryland	2,462	20	Missouri	2,796
1	Massachusetts	8,709	21	West Virginia	2,777
25	Michigan	2,589	22	Washington	2,715
44	Minnesota	1,421	23	Colorado	2,655
42	Mississippi	1,492	24	North Dakota	2,647
20	Missouri	2,796	25	Michigan	2,589
11	Montana	3,934	26	Louisiana	2,557
47	Nebraska	994	27	Maryland	2,462
40	Nevada	1,623	28	Pennsylvania	2,239
6	New Hampshire	5,267	29	Virginia	2,236
8	New Jersey	4,887	30	Indiana	2,134
17	New Mexico	3,065	31	Oklahoma	2,112
5	New York	5,295	32	Utah	2,103
36	North Carolina	1,817	33	Kentucky	2,053
24	North Dakota	2,647	34	Ohio	2,018
34	Ohio	2,018	35	Kansas	1,866
31	Oklahoma	2,112	36	North Carolina	1,817
19	Oregon	2,883	37	Wyoming	1,713
28	Pennsylvania	2,239	38	Idaho	1,673
4	Rhode Island	6,402	39	Iowa	1,668
16	South Carolina	3,142	40	Nevada	1,623
15	South Dakota	3,298	41	Arkansas	1,551
50	Tennessee	597	42	Mississippi	1,492
49	Texas	795	43	Florida	1,459
32	Utah	2,103	44	Minnesota	1,421
10	Vermont	4,518	45	Alabama	1,379
29	Virginia	2,236	46	Arizona	1,350
22	Washington	2,715	47	Nebraska	994
21	West Virginia	2,777	48	Georgia	899
14	Wisconsin	3,387	49	Texas	795
37	Wyoming	1,713	50	Tennessee	597
				District of Columbia**	NA

Source: CQ Press using data from U.S. Bureau of the Census, Governments Division
   "State and Local Government Finances: 2004-2005" (http://www.census.gov/govs/www/estimate05.html)
*Includes short-term, long-term, full faith and credit, nonguaranteed, and public debt for private purposes.
**Not applicable.

State Government Full-Time Equivalent Employees in 2006

National Total = 4,250,554 FTE Employees*

<u>ALPHA ORDER</u>

RANK	STATE	EMPLOYEES	% of USA
18	Alabama	85,223	2.0%
41	Alaska	25,151	0.6%
27	Arizona	66,858	1.6%
29	Arkansas	58,147	1.4%
1	California	393,609	9.3%
25	Colorado	67,451	1.6%
28	Connecticut	61,971	1.5%
40	Delaware	25,614	0.6%
4	Florida	191,215	4.5%
11	Georgia	124,361	2.9%
32	Hawaii	54,958	1.3%
42	Idaho	22,259	0.5%
10	Illinois	131,859	3.1%
17	Indiana	89,799	2.1%
33	Iowa	53,258	1.3%
36	Kansas	44,393	1.0%
21	Kentucky	79,266	1.9%
19	Louisiana	83,358	2.0%
43	Maine	21,680	0.5%
15	Maryland	90,262	2.1%
14	Massachusetts	90,989	2.1%
9	Michigan	134,918	3.2%
22	Minnesota	76,795	1.8%
31	Mississippi	55,036	1.3%
16	Missouri	90,228	2.1%
46	Montana	18,933	0.4%
38	Nebraska	32,904	0.8%
39	Nevada	25,859	0.6%
45	New Hampshire	19,076	0.4%
6	New Jersey	156,768	3.7%
34	New Mexico	50,783	1.2%
3	New York	249,208	5.9%
7	North Carolina	139,117	3.3%
47	North Dakota	18,127	0.4%
8	Ohio	136,840	3.2%
26	Oklahoma	67,424	1.6%
30	Oregon	57,485	1.4%
5	Pennsylvania	161,136	3.8%
44	Rhode Island	20,594	0.5%
23	South Carolina	76,468	1.8%
49	South Dakota	13,905	0.3%
20	Tennessee	83,117	2.0%
2	Texas	281,722	6.6%
35	Utah	50,277	1.2%
48	Vermont	14,615	0.3%
12	Virginia	122,634	2.9%
13	Washington	116,943	2.8%
37	West Virginia	37,004	0.9%
24	Wisconsin	68,143	1.6%
50	Wyoming	12,814	0.3%

<u>RANK ORDER</u>

RANK	STATE	EMPLOYEES	% of USA
1	California	393,609	9.3%
2	Texas	281,722	6.6%
3	New York	249,208	5.9%
4	Florida	191,215	4.5%
5	Pennsylvania	161,136	3.8%
6	New Jersey	156,768	3.7%
7	North Carolina	139,117	3.3%
8	Ohio	136,840	3.2%
9	Michigan	134,918	3.2%
10	Illinois	131,859	3.1%
11	Georgia	124,361	2.9%
12	Virginia	122,634	2.9%
13	Washington	116,943	2.8%
14	Massachusetts	90,989	2.1%
15	Maryland	90,262	2.1%
16	Missouri	90,228	2.1%
17	Indiana	89,799	2.1%
18	Alabama	85,223	2.0%
19	Louisiana	83,358	2.0%
20	Tennessee	83,117	2.0%
21	Kentucky	79,266	1.9%
22	Minnesota	76,795	1.8%
23	South Carolina	76,468	1.8%
24	Wisconsin	68,143	1.6%
25	Colorado	67,451	1.6%
26	Oklahoma	67,424	1.6%
27	Arizona	66,858	1.6%
28	Connecticut	61,971	1.5%
29	Arkansas	58,147	1.4%
30	Oregon	57,485	1.4%
31	Mississippi	55,036	1.3%
32	Hawaii	54,958	1.3%
33	Iowa	53,258	1.3%
34	New Mexico	50,783	1.2%
35	Utah	50,277	1.2%
36	Kansas	44,393	1.0%
37	West Virginia	37,004	0.9%
38	Nebraska	32,904	0.8%
39	Nevada	25,859	0.6%
40	Delaware	25,614	0.6%
41	Alaska	25,151	0.6%
42	Idaho	22,259	0.5%
43	Maine	21,680	0.5%
44	Rhode Island	20,594	0.5%
45	New Hampshire	19,076	0.4%
46	Montana	18,933	0.4%
47	North Dakota	18,127	0.4%
48	Vermont	14,615	0.3%
49	South Dakota	13,905	0.3%
50	Wyoming	12,814	0.3%
	District of Columbia**	NA	NA

Source: U.S. Bureau of the Census, Governments Division
    "2006 State Government Employment and Payroll" (http://www.census.gov/govs/www/apesst06.html)
*As of March 2006.
**Not applicable.

Rate of State Government Full-Time Equivalent Employees in 2006

National Rate = 143 State Government Employees per 10,000 Population*

ALPHA ORDER

RANK	STATE	RATE
18	Alabama	186
2	Alaska	371
47	Arizona	108
8	Arkansas	207
46	California	109
35	Colorado	142
22	Connecticut	177
3	Delaware	300
48	Florida	106
40	Georgia	133
1	Hawaii	430
32	Idaho	152
50	Illinois	103
35	Indiana	142
21	Iowa	179
26	Kansas	161
15	Kentucky	189
11	Louisiana	196
25	Maine	165
26	Maryland	161
37	Massachusetts	141
39	Michigan	134
33	Minnesota	149
14	Mississippi	190
31	Missouri	155
10	Montana	200
17	Nebraska	187
49	Nevada	104
34	New Hampshire	145
20	New Jersey	181
5	New Mexico	261
42	New York	129
29	North Carolina	157
4	North Dakota	284
45	Ohio	119
16	Oklahoma	188
30	Oregon	156
41	Pennsylvania	130
13	Rhode Island	194
22	South Carolina	177
24	South Dakota	176
38	Tennessee	137
44	Texas	120
12	Utah	195
7	Vermont	235
26	Virginia	161
19	Washington	183
9	West Virginia	205
43	Wisconsin	122
6	Wyoming	250

RANK ORDER

RANK	STATE	RATE
1	Hawaii	430
2	Alaska	371
3	Delaware	300
4	North Dakota	284
5	New Mexico	261
6	Wyoming	250
7	Vermont	235
8	Arkansas	207
9	West Virginia	205
10	Montana	200
11	Louisiana	196
12	Utah	195
13	Rhode Island	194
14	Mississippi	190
15	Kentucky	189
16	Oklahoma	188
17	Nebraska	187
18	Alabama	186
19	Washington	183
20	New Jersey	181
21	Iowa	179
22	Connecticut	177
22	South Carolina	177
24	South Dakota	176
25	Maine	165
26	Kansas	161
26	Maryland	161
26	Virginia	161
29	North Carolina	157
30	Oregon	156
31	Missouri	155
32	Idaho	152
33	Minnesota	149
34	New Hampshire	145
35	Colorado	142
35	Indiana	142
37	Massachusetts	141
38	Tennessee	137
39	Michigan	134
40	Georgia	133
41	Pennsylvania	130
42	New York	129
43	Wisconsin	122
44	Texas	120
45	Ohio	119
46	California	109
47	Arizona	108
48	Florida	106
49	Nevada	104
50	Illinois	103

District of Columbia**   NA

Source: CQ Press using data from U.S. Bureau of the Census, Governments Division
"2006 State Government Employment and Payroll" (http://www.census.gov/govs/www/apesst06.html)
*Full-time equivalent as of March 2006.
**Not applicable.

Average Annual Earnings of Full-Time State Government Employees in 2006

National Average = $49,173*

ALPHA ORDER				RANK ORDER		
RANK	STATE	EARNINGS		RANK	STATE	EARNINGS
26	Alabama	$44,177		1	California	$65,967
13	Alaska	52,771		2	Connecticut	60,756
25	Arizona	45,454		3	New Jersey	60,579
48	Arkansas	37,650		4	New York	58,322
1	California	65,967		5	Minnesota	57,143
8	Colorado	56,321		6	Iowa	56,926
2	Connecticut	60,756		7	Rhode Island	56,394
19	Delaware	47,352		8	Colorado	56,321
35	Florida	42,233		9	Massachusetts	55,036
38	Georgia	41,898		10	Wisconsin	53,577
22	Hawaii	46,143		11	Michigan	53,426
33	Idaho	42,945		12	Illinois	53,259
12	Illinois	53,259		13	Alaska	52,771
29	Indiana	43,585		14	Maryland	51,530
6	Iowa	56,926		15	Washington	50,473
32	Kansas	42,964		16	Nevada	50,425
34	Kentucky	42,350		17	Vermont	48,642
36	Louisiana	42,188		18	Ohio	48,631
27	Maine	44,107		19	Delaware	47,352
14	Maryland	51,530		20	Pennsylvania	46,861
9	Massachusetts	55,036		21	New Hampshire	46,782
11	Michigan	53,426		22	Hawaii	46,143
5	Minnesota	57,143		23	Virginia	46,031
47	Mississippi	38,369		24	Oregon	45,981
49	Missouri	37,643		25	Arizona	45,454
37	Montana	41,957		26	Alabama	44,177
42	Nebraska	40,141		27	Maine	44,107
16	Nevada	50,425		28	Texas	43,687
21	New Hampshire	46,782		29	Indiana	43,585
3	New Jersey	60,579		30	Utah	43,575
46	New Mexico	39,595		31	North Carolina	43,365
4	New York	58,322		32	Kansas	42,964
31	North Carolina	43,365		33	Idaho	42,945
40	North Dakota	40,419		34	Kentucky	42,350
18	Ohio	48,631		35	Florida	42,233
41	Oklahoma	40,256		36	Louisiana	42,188
24	Oregon	45,981		37	Montana	41,957
20	Pennsylvania	46,861		38	Georgia	41,898
7	Rhode Island	56,394		39	Wyoming	41,777
45	South Carolina	39,748		40	North Dakota	40,419
43	South Dakota	40,109		41	Oklahoma	40,256
44	Tennessee	40,041		42	Nebraska	40,141
28	Texas	43,687		43	South Dakota	40,109
30	Utah	43,575		44	Tennessee	40,041
17	Vermont	48,642		45	South Carolina	39,748
23	Virginia	46,031		46	New Mexico	39,595
15	Washington	50,473		47	Mississippi	38,369
50	West Virginia	37,099		48	Arkansas	37,650
10	Wisconsin	53,577		49	Missouri	37,643
39	Wyoming	41,777		50	West Virginia	37,099
				District of Columbia**		NA

Source: CQ Press using data from U.S. Bureau of the Census, Governments Division
"2006 State Government Employment and Payroll" (http://www.census.gov/govs/www/apesst06.html)
*March 2006 full-time payroll (multiplied by 12) divided by full-time employees.
**Not applicable.

Local Government Total Revenue in 2005

National Total = $1,307,002,281,000*

ALPHA ORDER

RANK	STATE	REVENUE	% of USA
23	Alabama	$16,384,891,000	1.3%
44	Alaska	3,138,314,000	0.2%
17	Arizona	23,810,340,000	1.8%
36	Arkansas	7,647,567,000	0.6%
1	California	213,405,216,000	16.3%
21	Colorado	21,279,245,000	1.6%
27	Connecticut	13,827,133,000	1.1%
46	Delaware	2,567,559,000	0.2%
4	Florida	76,375,964,000	5.8%
10	Georgia	33,531,351,000	2.6%
48	Hawaii	2,107,119,000	0.2%
39	Idaho	4,372,519,000	0.3%
5	Illinois	56,026,794,000	4.3%
15	Indiana	24,362,027,000	1.9%
29	Iowa	11,179,351,000	0.9%
30	Kansas	10,657,056,000	0.8%
31	Kentucky	10,617,446,000	0.8%
24	Louisiana	15,723,957,000	1.2%
41	Maine	4,065,686,000	0.3%
20	Maryland	22,042,499,000	1.7%
14	Massachusetts	28,731,432,000	2.2%
8	Michigan	43,839,330,000	3.4%
19	Minnesota	23,138,478,000	1.8%
33	Mississippi	9,312,483,000	0.7%
22	Missouri	19,808,884,000	1.5%
45	Montana	2,675,184,000	0.2%
34	Nebraska	8,907,501,000	0.7%
28	Nevada	11,672,253,000	0.9%
40	New Hampshire	4,284,300,000	0.3%
9	New Jersey	38,303,150,000	2.9%
37	New Mexico	6,638,415,000	0.5%
2	New York	139,053,802,000	10.6%
11	North Carolina	31,787,168,000	2.4%
49	North Dakota	2,057,021,000	0.2%
7	Ohio	47,236,180,000	3.6%
32	Oklahoma	10,262,794,000	0.8%
26	Oregon	14,481,455,000	1.1%
6	Pennsylvania	50,881,365,000	3.9%
42	Rhode Island	3,586,759,000	0.3%
25	South Carolina	14,719,037,000	1.1%
47	South Dakota	2,339,035,000	0.2%
16	Tennessee	24,210,624,000	1.9%
3	Texas	86,839,801,000	6.6%
35	Utah	8,460,539,000	0.6%
50	Vermont	2,032,373,000	0.2%
13	Virginia	29,000,925,000	2.2%
12	Washington	29,306,953,000	2.2%
38	West Virginia	4,464,762,000	0.3%
18	Wisconsin	23,287,862,000	1.8%
43	Wyoming	3,233,638,000	0.2%

RANK ORDER

RANK	STATE	REVENUE	% of USA
1	California	$213,405,216,000	16.3%
2	New York	139,053,802,000	10.6%
3	Texas	86,839,801,000	6.6%
4	Florida	76,375,964,000	5.8%
5	Illinois	56,026,794,000	4.3%
6	Pennsylvania	50,881,365,000	3.9%
7	Ohio	47,236,180,000	3.6%
8	Michigan	43,839,330,000	3.4%
9	New Jersey	38,303,150,000	2.9%
10	Georgia	33,531,351,000	2.6%
11	North Carolina	31,787,168,000	2.4%
12	Washington	29,306,953,000	2.2%
13	Virginia	29,000,925,000	2.2%
14	Massachusetts	28,731,432,000	2.2%
15	Indiana	24,362,027,000	1.9%
16	Tennessee	24,210,624,000	1.9%
17	Arizona	23,810,340,000	1.8%
18	Wisconsin	23,287,862,000	1.8%
19	Minnesota	23,138,478,000	1.8%
20	Maryland	22,042,499,000	1.7%
21	Colorado	21,279,245,000	1.6%
22	Missouri	19,808,884,000	1.5%
23	Alabama	16,384,891,000	1.3%
24	Louisiana	15,723,957,000	1.2%
25	South Carolina	14,719,037,000	1.1%
26	Oregon	14,481,455,000	1.1%
27	Connecticut	13,827,133,000	1.1%
28	Nevada	11,672,253,000	0.9%
29	Iowa	11,179,351,000	0.9%
30	Kansas	10,657,056,000	0.8%
31	Kentucky	10,617,446,000	0.8%
32	Oklahoma	10,262,794,000	0.8%
33	Mississippi	9,312,483,000	0.7%
34	Nebraska	8,907,501,000	0.7%
35	Utah	8,460,539,000	0.6%
36	Arkansas	7,647,567,000	0.6%
37	New Mexico	6,638,415,000	0.5%
38	West Virginia	4,464,762,000	0.3%
39	Idaho	4,372,519,000	0.3%
40	New Hampshire	4,284,300,000	0.3%
41	Maine	4,065,686,000	0.3%
42	Rhode Island	3,586,759,000	0.3%
43	Wyoming	3,233,638,000	0.2%
44	Alaska	3,138,314,000	0.2%
45	Montana	2,675,184,000	0.2%
46	Delaware	2,567,559,000	0.2%
47	South Dakota	2,339,035,000	0.2%
48	Hawaii	2,107,119,000	0.2%
49	North Dakota	2,057,021,000	0.2%
50	Vermont	2,032,373,000	0.2%
	District of Columbia	9,326,744,000	0.7%

Source: U.S. Bureau of the Census, Governments Division
"State and Local Government Finances: 2004-2005" (http://www.census.gov/govs/www/estimate05.html)
*Total revenue includes all money received from external sources. This includes taxes, intergovernmental transfers and insurance trust revenue, and revenue from government owned utilities and other commercial or auxiliary enterprise.

Per Capita Local Government Total Revenue in 2005

National Per Capita = $4,417*

ALPHA ORDER

RANK	STATE	PER CAPITA
30	Alabama	$3,609
6	Alaska	4,688
19	Arizona	4,000
47	Arkansas	2,759
3	California	5,930
8	Colorado	4,553
21	Connecticut	3,966
43	Delaware	3,055
14	Florida	4,306
28	Georgia	3,682
50	Hawaii	1,662
42	Idaho	3,067
12	Illinois	4,405
23	Indiana	3,893
27	Iowa	3,782
24	Kansas	3,887
48	Kentucky	2,546
31	Louisiana	3,498
41	Maine	3,098
22	Maryland	3,955
10	Massachusetts	4,469
13	Michigan	4,337
9	Minnesota	4,525
40	Mississippi	3,211
34	Missouri	3,422
46	Montana	2,859
4	Nebraska	5,078
5	Nevada	4,845
37	New Hampshire	3,288
11	New Jersey	4,424
32	New Mexico	3,464
1	New York	7,219
29	North Carolina	3,663
39	North Dakota	3,235
16	Ohio	4,122
45	Oklahoma	2,902
20	Oregon	3,989
17	Pennsylvania	4,114
36	Rhode Island	3,362
33	South Carolina	3,459
44	South Dakota	2,999
18	Tennessee	4,042
26	Texas	3,801
35	Utah	3,377
38	Vermont	3,279
25	Virginia	3,837
7	Washington	4,674
49	West Virginia	2,473
15	Wisconsin	4,203
2	Wyoming	6,384

RANK ORDER

RANK	STATE	PER CAPITA
1	New York	$7,219
2	Wyoming	6,384
3	California	5,930
4	Nebraska	5,078
5	Nevada	4,845
6	Alaska	4,688
7	Washington	4,674
8	Colorado	4,553
9	Minnesota	4,525
10	Massachusetts	4,469
11	New Jersey	4,424
12	Illinois	4,405
13	Michigan	4,337
14	Florida	4,306
15	Wisconsin	4,203
16	Ohio	4,122
17	Pennsylvania	4,114
18	Tennessee	4,042
19	Arizona	4,000
20	Oregon	3,989
21	Connecticut	3,966
22	Maryland	3,955
23	Indiana	3,893
24	Kansas	3,887
25	Virginia	3,837
26	Texas	3,801
27	Iowa	3,782
28	Georgia	3,682
29	North Carolina	3,663
30	Alabama	3,609
31	Louisiana	3,498
32	New Mexico	3,464
33	South Carolina	3,459
34	Missouri	3,422
35	Utah	3,377
36	Rhode Island	3,362
37	New Hampshire	3,288
38	Vermont	3,279
39	North Dakota	3,235
40	Mississippi	3,211
41	Maine	3,098
42	Idaho	3,067
43	Delaware	3,055
44	South Dakota	2,999
45	Oklahoma	2,902
46	Montana	2,859
47	Arkansas	2,759
48	Kentucky	2,546
49	West Virginia	2,473
50	Hawaii	1,662

District of Columbia   16,024

Source: CQ Press using data from U.S. Bureau of the Census, Governments Division
"State and Local Government Finances: 2004-2005" (http://www.census.gov/govs/www/estimate05.html)
*Total revenue includes all money received from external sources. This includes taxes, intergovernmental transfers and insurance trust revenue, and revenue from government owned utilities and other commercial or auxiliary enterprise.

Local Government Revenue from the Federal Government in 2005

National Total = $52,128,887,000

ALPHA ORDER

RANK	STATE	REVENUE	% of USA
24	Alabama	$589,213,000	1.1%
37	Alaska	240,388,000	0.5%
11	Arizona	1,136,657,000	2.2%
36	Arkansas	253,400,000	0.5%
1	California	7,432,651,000	14.3%
22	Colorado	632,559,000	1.2%
26	Connecticut	448,636,000	0.9%
49	Delaware	61,826,000	0.1%
6	Florida	2,935,290,000	5.6%
16	Georgia	871,963,000	1.7%
41	Hawaii	180,225,000	0.3%
45	Idaho	136,949,000	0.3%
3	Illinois	3,041,836,000	5.8%
28	Indiana	429,300,000	0.8%
27	Iowa	431,368,000	0.8%
38	Kansas	240,146,000	0.5%
34	Kentucky	293,489,000	0.6%
20	Louisiana	803,007,000	1.5%
47	Maine	127,687,000	0.2%
12	Maryland	1,036,875,000	2.0%
9	Massachusetts	1,306,559,000	2.5%
8	Michigan	1,797,471,000	3.4%
17	Minnesota	871,093,000	1.7%
30	Mississippi	372,863,000	0.7%
18	Missouri	817,530,000	1.6%
39	Montana	202,605,000	0.4%
40	Nebraska	197,021,000	0.4%
25	Nevada	496,765,000	1.0%
46	New Hampshire	134,116,000	0.3%
15	New Jersey	933,281,000	1.8%
29	New Mexico	378,137,000	0.7%
2	New York	5,517,484,000	10.6%
14	North Carolina	947,853,000	1.8%
43	North Dakota	140,705,000	0.3%
7	Ohio	1,805,523,000	3.5%
31	Oklahoma	364,333,000	0.7%
19	Oregon	812,819,000	1.6%
5	Pennsylvania	2,966,150,000	5.7%
44	Rhode Island	140,511,000	0.3%
32	South Carolina	334,543,000	0.6%
42	South Dakota	151,739,000	0.3%
23	Tennessee	612,808,000	1.2%
4	Texas	3,026,624,000	5.8%
33	Utah	332,939,000	0.6%
50	Vermont	53,179,000	0.1%
13	Virginia	973,352,000	1.9%
10	Washington	1,296,937,000	2.5%
35	West Virginia	264,052,000	0.5%
21	Wisconsin	652,857,000	1.3%
48	Wyoming	88,999,000	0.2%

RANK ORDER

RANK	STATE	REVENUE	% of USA
1	California	$7,432,651,000	14.3%
2	New York	5,517,484,000	10.6%
3	Illinois	3,041,836,000	5.8%
4	Texas	3,026,624,000	5.8%
5	Pennsylvania	2,966,150,000	5.7%
6	Florida	2,935,290,000	5.6%
7	Ohio	1,805,523,000	3.5%
8	Michigan	1,797,471,000	3.4%
9	Massachusetts	1,306,559,000	2.5%
10	Washington	1,296,937,000	2.5%
11	Arizona	1,136,657,000	2.2%
12	Maryland	1,036,875,000	2.0%
13	Virginia	973,352,000	1.9%
14	North Carolina	947,853,000	1.8%
15	New Jersey	933,281,000	1.8%
16	Georgia	871,963,000	1.7%
17	Minnesota	871,093,000	1.7%
18	Missouri	817,530,000	1.6%
19	Oregon	812,819,000	1.6%
20	Louisiana	803,007,000	1.5%
21	Wisconsin	652,857,000	1.3%
22	Colorado	632,559,000	1.2%
23	Tennessee	612,808,000	1.2%
24	Alabama	589,213,000	1.1%
25	Nevada	496,765,000	1.0%
26	Connecticut	448,636,000	0.9%
27	Iowa	431,368,000	0.8%
28	Indiana	429,300,000	0.8%
29	New Mexico	378,137,000	0.7%
30	Mississippi	372,863,000	0.7%
31	Oklahoma	364,333,000	0.7%
32	South Carolina	334,543,000	0.6%
33	Utah	332,939,000	0.6%
34	Kentucky	293,489,000	0.6%
35	West Virginia	264,052,000	0.5%
36	Arkansas	253,400,000	0.5%
37	Alaska	240,388,000	0.5%
38	Kansas	240,146,000	0.5%
39	Montana	202,605,000	0.4%
40	Nebraska	197,021,000	0.4%
41	Hawaii	180,225,000	0.3%
42	South Dakota	151,739,000	0.3%
43	North Dakota	140,705,000	0.3%
44	Rhode Island	140,511,000	0.3%
45	Idaho	136,949,000	0.3%
46	New Hampshire	134,116,000	0.3%
47	Maine	127,687,000	0.2%
48	Wyoming	88,999,000	0.2%
49	Delaware	61,826,000	0.1%
50	Vermont	53,179,000	0.1%
	District of Columbia	2,814,574,000	5.4%

Source: U.S. Bureau of the Census, Governments Division
"State and Local Government Finances: 2004-2005" (http://www.census.gov/govs/www/estimate05.html)

Per Capita Local Government Revenue from the Federal Government in 2005

National Per Capita = $176

ALPHA ORDER

ALPHA ORDER

RANK	STATE	PER CAPITA
30	Alabama	$130
1	Alaska	359
14	Arizona	191
44	Arkansas	91
8	California	207
26	Colorado	135
31	Connecticut	129
48	Delaware	74
20	Florida	165
42	Georgia	96
24	Hawaii	142
42	Idaho	96
4	Illinois	239
50	Indiana	69
22	Iowa	146
45	Kansas	88
49	Kentucky	70
16	Louisiana	179
41	Maine	97
15	Maryland	186
11	Massachusetts	203
17	Michigan	178
19	Minnesota	170
31	Mississippi	129
25	Missouri	141
7	Montana	217
35	Nebraska	112
10	Nevada	206
38	New Hampshire	103
37	New Jersey	108
12	New Mexico	197
2	New York	286
36	North Carolina	109
6	North Dakota	221
21	Ohio	158
38	Oklahoma	103
5	Oregon	224
3	Pennsylvania	240
28	Rhode Island	132
47	South Carolina	79
13	South Dakota	195
40	Tennessee	102
28	Texas	132
27	Utah	133
46	Vermont	86
31	Virginia	129
8	Washington	207
22	West Virginia	146
34	Wisconsin	118
18	Wyoming	176

RANK ORDER

RANK	STATE	PER CAPITA
1	Alaska	$359
2	New York	286
3	Pennsylvania	240
4	Illinois	239
5	Oregon	224
6	North Dakota	221
7	Montana	217
8	California	207
8	Washington	207
10	Nevada	206
11	Massachusetts	203
12	New Mexico	197
13	South Dakota	195
14	Arizona	191
15	Maryland	186
16	Louisiana	179
17	Michigan	178
18	Wyoming	176
19	Minnesota	170
20	Florida	165
21	Ohio	158
22	Iowa	146
22	West Virginia	146
24	Hawaii	142
25	Missouri	141
26	Colorado	135
27	Utah	133
28	Rhode Island	132
28	Texas	132
30	Alabama	130
31	Connecticut	129
31	Mississippi	129
31	Virginia	129
34	Wisconsin	118
35	Nebraska	112
36	North Carolina	109
37	New Jersey	108
38	New Hampshire	103
38	Oklahoma	103
40	Tennessee	102
41	Maine	97
42	Georgia	96
42	Idaho	96
44	Arkansas	91
45	Kansas	88
46	Vermont	86
47	South Carolina	79
48	Delaware	74
49	Kentucky	70
50	Indiana	69

District of Columbia — 4,836

Source: CQ Press using data from U.S. Bureau of the Census, Governments Division
"State and Local Government Finances: 2004-2005" (http://www.census.gov/govs/www/estimate05.html)

Local Government Own Source Revenue in 2005

National Total = $708,901,221,000*

<table>
<tr><td colspan="4">ALPHA ORDER</td><td colspan="4">RANK ORDER</td></tr>
<tr><td>RANK</td><td>STATE</td><td>REVENUE</td><td>% of USA</td><td>RANK</td><td>STATE</td><td>REVENUE</td><td>% of USA</td></tr>
<tr><td>26</td><td>Alabama</td><td>$8,471,251,000</td><td>1.2%</td><td>1</td><td>California</td><td>$96,123,618,000</td><td>13.6%</td></tr>
<tr><td>44</td><td>Alaska</td><td>1,708,171,000</td><td>0.2%</td><td>2</td><td>New York</td><td>81,646,031,000</td><td>11.5%</td></tr>
<tr><td>20</td><td>Arizona</td><td>11,612,236,000</td><td>1.6%</td><td>3</td><td>Texas</td><td>53,931,746,000</td><td>7.6%</td></tr>
<tr><td>36</td><td>Arkansas</td><td>2,957,780,000</td><td>0.4%</td><td>4</td><td>Florida</td><td>47,164,205,000</td><td>6.7%</td></tr>
<tr><td>1</td><td>California</td><td>96,123,618,000</td><td>13.6%</td><td>5</td><td>Illinois</td><td>31,548,561,000</td><td>4.5%</td></tr>
<tr><td>17</td><td>Colorado</td><td>13,358,547,000</td><td>1.9%</td><td>6</td><td>Pennsylvania</td><td>27,338,637,000</td><td>3.9%</td></tr>
<tr><td>25</td><td>Connecticut</td><td>8,560,185,000</td><td>1.2%</td><td>7</td><td>Ohio</td><td>26,689,800,000</td><td>3.8%</td></tr>
<tr><td>48</td><td>Delaware</td><td>1,146,331,000</td><td>0.2%</td><td>8</td><td>New Jersey</td><td>25,199,509,000</td><td>3.6%</td></tr>
<tr><td>4</td><td>Florida</td><td>47,164,205,000</td><td>6.7%</td><td>9</td><td>Michigan</td><td>19,822,936,000</td><td>2.8%</td></tr>
<tr><td>10</td><td>Georgia</td><td>19,414,399,000</td><td>2.7%</td><td>10</td><td>Georgia</td><td>19,414,399,000</td><td>2.7%</td></tr>
<tr><td>45</td><td>Hawaii</td><td>1,511,548,000</td><td>0.2%</td><td>11</td><td>Virginia</td><td>16,595,719,000</td><td>2.3%</td></tr>
<tr><td>40</td><td>Idaho</td><td>2,492,913,000</td><td>0.4%</td><td>12</td><td>North Carolina</td><td>16,366,938,000</td><td>2.3%</td></tr>
<tr><td>5</td><td>Illinois</td><td>31,548,561,000</td><td>4.5%</td><td>13</td><td>Indiana</td><td>14,401,432,000</td><td>2.0%</td></tr>
<tr><td>13</td><td>Indiana</td><td>14,401,432,000</td><td>2.0%</td><td>14</td><td>Washington</td><td>14,353,858,000</td><td>2.0%</td></tr>
<tr><td>28</td><td>Iowa</td><td>6,573,232,000</td><td>0.9%</td><td>15</td><td>Massachusetts</td><td>13,842,877,000</td><td>2.0%</td></tr>
<tr><td>30</td><td>Kansas</td><td>6,195,899,000</td><td>0.9%</td><td>16</td><td>Maryland</td><td>13,765,132,000</td><td>1.9%</td></tr>
<tr><td>32</td><td>Kentucky</td><td>5,398,750,000</td><td>0.8%</td><td>17</td><td>Colorado</td><td>13,358,547,000</td><td>1.9%</td></tr>
<tr><td>24</td><td>Louisiana</td><td>8,949,763,000</td><td>1.3%</td><td>18</td><td>Missouri</td><td>11,846,914,000</td><td>1.7%</td></tr>
<tr><td>38</td><td>Maine</td><td>2,718,384,000</td><td>0.4%</td><td>19</td><td>Wisconsin</td><td>11,702,531,000</td><td>1.7%</td></tr>
<tr><td>16</td><td>Maryland</td><td>13,765,132,000</td><td>1.9%</td><td>20</td><td>Arizona</td><td>11,612,236,000</td><td>1.6%</td></tr>
<tr><td>15</td><td>Massachusetts</td><td>13,842,877,000</td><td>2.0%</td><td>21</td><td>Tennessee</td><td>11,150,289,000</td><td>1.6%</td></tr>
<tr><td>9</td><td>Michigan</td><td>19,822,936,000</td><td>2.8%</td><td>22</td><td>Minnesota</td><td>10,869,338,000</td><td>1.5%</td></tr>
<tr><td>22</td><td>Minnesota</td><td>10,869,338,000</td><td>1.5%</td><td>23</td><td>South Carolina</td><td>8,958,481,000</td><td>1.3%</td></tr>
<tr><td>33</td><td>Mississippi</td><td>4,745,000,000</td><td>0.7%</td><td>24</td><td>Louisiana</td><td>8,949,763,000</td><td>1.3%</td></tr>
<tr><td>18</td><td>Missouri</td><td>11,846,914,000</td><td>1.7%</td><td>25</td><td>Connecticut</td><td>8,560,185,000</td><td>1.2%</td></tr>
<tr><td>46</td><td>Montana</td><td>1,477,876,000</td><td>0.2%</td><td>26</td><td>Alabama</td><td>8,471,251,000</td><td>1.2%</td></tr>
<tr><td>35</td><td>Nebraska</td><td>4,309,844,000</td><td>0.6%</td><td>27</td><td>Oregon</td><td>7,775,818,000</td><td>1.1%</td></tr>
<tr><td>29</td><td>Nevada</td><td>6,261,183,000</td><td>0.9%</td><td>28</td><td>Iowa</td><td>6,573,232,000</td><td>0.9%</td></tr>
<tr><td>37</td><td>New Hampshire</td><td>2,786,349,000</td><td>0.4%</td><td>29</td><td>Nevada</td><td>6,261,183,000</td><td>0.9%</td></tr>
<tr><td>8</td><td>New Jersey</td><td>25,199,509,000</td><td>3.6%</td><td>30</td><td>Kansas</td><td>6,195,899,000</td><td>0.9%</td></tr>
<tr><td>39</td><td>New Mexico</td><td>2,601,555,000</td><td>0.4%</td><td>31</td><td>Oklahoma</td><td>5,542,743,000</td><td>0.8%</td></tr>
<tr><td>2</td><td>New York</td><td>81,646,031,000</td><td>11.5%</td><td>32</td><td>Kentucky</td><td>5,398,750,000</td><td>0.8%</td></tr>
<tr><td>12</td><td>North Carolina</td><td>16,366,938,000</td><td>2.3%</td><td>33</td><td>Mississippi</td><td>4,745,000,000</td><td>0.7%</td></tr>
<tr><td>49</td><td>North Dakota</td><td>1,137,290,000</td><td>0.2%</td><td>34</td><td>Utah</td><td>4,341,111,000</td><td>0.6%</td></tr>
<tr><td>7</td><td>Ohio</td><td>26,689,800,000</td><td>3.8%</td><td>35</td><td>Nebraska</td><td>4,309,844,000</td><td>0.6%</td></tr>
<tr><td>31</td><td>Oklahoma</td><td>5,542,743,000</td><td>0.8%</td><td>36</td><td>Arkansas</td><td>2,957,780,000</td><td>0.4%</td></tr>
<tr><td>27</td><td>Oregon</td><td>7,775,818,000</td><td>1.1%</td><td>37</td><td>New Hampshire</td><td>2,786,349,000</td><td>0.4%</td></tr>
<tr><td>6</td><td>Pennsylvania</td><td>27,338,637,000</td><td>3.9%</td><td>38</td><td>Maine</td><td>2,718,384,000</td><td>0.4%</td></tr>
<tr><td>41</td><td>Rhode Island</td><td>2,222,878,000</td><td>0.3%</td><td>39</td><td>New Mexico</td><td>2,601,555,000</td><td>0.4%</td></tr>
<tr><td>23</td><td>South Carolina</td><td>8,958,481,000</td><td>1.3%</td><td>40</td><td>Idaho</td><td>2,492,913,000</td><td>0.4%</td></tr>
<tr><td>47</td><td>South Dakota</td><td>1,394,169,000</td><td>0.2%</td><td>41</td><td>Rhode Island</td><td>2,222,878,000</td><td>0.3%</td></tr>
<tr><td>21</td><td>Tennessee</td><td>11,150,289,000</td><td>1.6%</td><td>42</td><td>West Virginia</td><td>2,177,384,000</td><td>0.3%</td></tr>
<tr><td>3</td><td>Texas</td><td>53,931,746,000</td><td>7.6%</td><td>43</td><td>Wyoming</td><td>1,899,679,000</td><td>0.3%</td></tr>
<tr><td>34</td><td>Utah</td><td>4,341,111,000</td><td>0.6%</td><td>44</td><td>Alaska</td><td>1,708,171,000</td><td>0.2%</td></tr>
<tr><td>50</td><td>Vermont</td><td>550,004,000</td><td>0.1%</td><td>45</td><td>Hawaii</td><td>1,511,548,000</td><td>0.2%</td></tr>
<tr><td>11</td><td>Virginia</td><td>16,595,719,000</td><td>2.3%</td><td>46</td><td>Montana</td><td>1,477,876,000</td><td>0.2%</td></tr>
<tr><td>14</td><td>Washington</td><td>14,353,858,000</td><td>2.0%</td><td>47</td><td>South Dakota</td><td>1,394,169,000</td><td>0.2%</td></tr>
<tr><td>42</td><td>West Virginia</td><td>2,177,384,000</td><td>0.3%</td><td>48</td><td>Delaware</td><td>1,146,331,000</td><td>0.2%</td></tr>
<tr><td>19</td><td>Wisconsin</td><td>11,702,531,000</td><td>1.7%</td><td>49</td><td>North Dakota</td><td>1,137,290,000</td><td>0.2%</td></tr>
<tr><td>43</td><td>Wyoming</td><td>1,899,679,000</td><td>0.3%</td><td>50</td><td>Vermont</td><td>550,004,000</td><td>0.1%</td></tr>
<tr><td></td><td></td><td></td><td></td><td></td><td>District of Columbia</td><td>5,290,397,000</td><td>0.7%</td></tr>
</table>

Source: U.S. Bureau of the Census, Governments Division
"State and Local Government Finances: 2004-2005" (http://www.census.gov/govs/www/estimate05.html)
*Own source revenue includes taxes, current charges, and miscellaneous general revenue. Excluded are intergovernmental transfers, insurance trust revenue, and revenue from government owned utilities and other commercial or auxiliary enterprise.

Per Capita Local Government Own Source Revenue in 2005

National Per Capita = $2,396*

ALPHA ORDER

RANK	STATE	PER CAPITA
35	Alabama	$1,866
8	Alaska	2,552
33	Arizona	1,951
49	Arkansas	1,067
5	California	2,671
4	Colorado	2,858
12	Connecticut	2,455
44	Delaware	1,364
6	Florida	2,659
24	Georgia	2,132
48	Hawaii	1,192
39	Idaho	1,748
9	Illinois	2,480
15	Indiana	2,302
18	Iowa	2,224
17	Kansas	2,260
46	Kentucky	1,294
31	Louisiana	1,991
29	Maine	2,072
10	Maryland	2,470
21	Massachusetts	2,153
32	Michigan	1,961
25	Minnesota	2,125
41	Mississippi	1,636
30	Missouri	2,047
42	Montana	1,579
11	Nebraska	2,457
7	Nevada	2,599
23	New Hampshire	2,138
3	New Jersey	2,911
45	New Mexico	1,358
1	New York	4,239
34	North Carolina	1,886
37	North Dakota	1,788
14	Ohio	2,329
43	Oklahoma	1,568
22	Oregon	2,142
19	Pennsylvania	2,211
28	Rhode Island	2,084
27	South Carolina	2,105
38	South Dakota	1,787
36	Tennessee	1,862
13	Texas	2,361
40	Utah	1,733
50	Vermont	887
20	Virginia	2,196
16	Washington	2,289
47	West Virginia	1,206
26	Wisconsin	2,112
2	Wyoming	3,750

RANK ORDER

RANK	STATE	PER CAPITA
1	New York	$4,239
2	Wyoming	3,750
3	New Jersey	2,911
4	Colorado	2,858
5	California	2,671
6	Florida	2,659
7	Nevada	2,599
8	Alaska	2,552
9	Illinois	2,480
10	Maryland	2,470
11	Nebraska	2,457
12	Connecticut	2,455
13	Texas	2,361
14	Ohio	2,329
15	Indiana	2,302
16	Washington	2,289
17	Kansas	2,260
18	Iowa	2,224
19	Pennsylvania	2,211
20	Virginia	2,196
21	Massachusetts	2,153
22	Oregon	2,142
23	New Hampshire	2,138
24	Georgia	2,132
25	Minnesota	2,125
26	Wisconsin	2,112
27	South Carolina	2,105
28	Rhode Island	2,084
29	Maine	2,072
30	Missouri	2,047
31	Louisiana	1,991
32	Michigan	1,961
33	Arizona	1,951
34	North Carolina	1,886
35	Alabama	1,866
36	Tennessee	1,862
37	North Dakota	1,788
38	South Dakota	1,787
39	Idaho	1,748
40	Utah	1,733
41	Mississippi	1,636
42	Montana	1,579
43	Oklahoma	1,568
44	Delaware	1,364
45	New Mexico	1,358
46	Kentucky	1,294
47	West Virginia	1,206
48	Hawaii	1,192
49	Arkansas	1,067
50	Vermont	887

District of Columbia 9,089

Source: CQ Press using data from U.S. Bureau of the Census, Governments Division
  "State and Local Government Finances: 2004-2005" (http://www.census.gov/govs/www/estimate05.html)
*Own source revenue includes taxes, current charges, and miscellaneous general revenue. Excluded are intergovernmental transfers, insurance trust revenue, and revenue from government owned utilities and other commercial or auxiliary enterprise.

Local Government Tax Revenue in 2005

National Total = $448,273,481,000

ALPHA ORDER

ALPHA ORDER | RANK ORDER

RANK	STATE	TAX REVENUE	% of USA
28	Alabama	$3,886,727,000	0.9%
44	Alaska	1,088,723,000	0.2%
20	Arizona	7,322,689,000	1.6%
40	Arkansas	1,501,477,000	0.3%
2	California	48,182,202,000	10.7%
18	Colorado	8,032,365,000	1.8%
21	Connecticut	7,312,084,000	1.6%
49	Delaware	687,170,000	0.2%
4	Florida	25,968,913,000	5.8%
9	Georgia	11,810,454,000	2.6%
43	Hawaii	1,089,391,000	0.2%
42	Idaho	1,248,087,000	0.3%
5	Illinois	22,726,806,000	5.1%
15	Indiana	8,483,101,000	1.9%
27	Iowa	3,954,232,000	0.9%
29	Kansas	3,786,796,000	0.8%
32	Kentucky	3,170,930,000	0.7%
23	Louisiana	5,663,321,000	1.3%
36	Maine	2,148,547,000	0.5%
13	Maryland	10,401,774,000	2.3%
12	Massachusetts	10,742,281,000	2.4%
10	Michigan	11,769,971,000	2.6%
24	Minnesota	5,075,508,000	1.1%
37	Mississippi	2,058,529,000	0.5%
19	Missouri	7,830,450,000	1.7%
47	Montana	847,157,000	0.2%
33	Nebraska	2,789,687,000	0.6%
30	Nevada	3,373,401,000	0.8%
35	New Hampshire	2,297,631,000	0.5%
6	New Jersey	19,623,355,000	4.4%
39	New Mexico	1,597,851,000	0.4%
1	New York	60,917,223,000	13.6%
14	North Carolina	8,667,490,000	1.9%
48	North Dakota	718,095,000	0.2%
8	Ohio	17,708,194,000	4.0%
31	Oklahoma	3,214,072,000	0.7%
25	Oregon	4,584,326,000	1.0%
7	Pennsylvania	18,756,289,000	4.2%
38	Rhode Island	1,870,877,000	0.4%
26	South Carolina	4,482,252,000	1.0%
45	South Dakota	993,785,000	0.2%
22	Tennessee	5,985,844,000	1.3%
3	Texas	36,348,920,000	8.1%
34	Utah	2,617,583,000	0.6%
50	Vermont	331,859,000	0.1%
11	Virginia	11,740,339,000	2.6%
17	Washington	8,134,408,000	1.8%
41	West Virginia	1,249,590,000	0.3%
16	Wisconsin	8,251,276,000	1.8%
46	Wyoming	932,207,000	0.2%

RANK ORDER

RANK	STATE	TAX REVENUE	% of USA
1	New York	$60,917,223,000	13.6%
2	California	48,182,202,000	10.7%
3	Texas	36,348,920,000	8.1%
4	Florida	25,968,913,000	5.8%
5	Illinois	22,726,806,000	5.1%
6	New Jersey	19,623,355,000	4.4%
7	Pennsylvania	18,756,289,000	4.2%
8	Ohio	17,708,194,000	4.0%
9	Georgia	11,810,454,000	2.6%
10	Michigan	11,769,971,000	2.6%
11	Virginia	11,740,339,000	2.6%
12	Massachusetts	10,742,281,000	2.4%
13	Maryland	10,401,774,000	2.3%
14	North Carolina	8,667,490,000	1.9%
15	Indiana	8,483,101,000	1.9%
16	Wisconsin	8,251,276,000	1.8%
17	Washington	8,134,408,000	1.8%
18	Colorado	8,032,365,000	1.8%
19	Missouri	7,830,450,000	1.7%
20	Arizona	7,322,689,000	1.6%
21	Connecticut	7,312,084,000	1.6%
22	Tennessee	5,985,844,000	1.3%
23	Louisiana	5,663,321,000	1.3%
24	Minnesota	5,075,508,000	1.1%
25	Oregon	4,584,326,000	1.0%
26	South Carolina	4,482,252,000	1.0%
27	Iowa	3,954,232,000	0.9%
28	Alabama	3,886,727,000	0.9%
29	Kansas	3,786,796,000	0.8%
30	Nevada	3,373,401,000	0.8%
31	Oklahoma	3,214,072,000	0.7%
32	Kentucky	3,170,930,000	0.7%
33	Nebraska	2,789,687,000	0.6%
34	Utah	2,617,583,000	0.6%
35	New Hampshire	2,297,631,000	0.5%
36	Maine	2,148,547,000	0.5%
37	Mississippi	2,058,529,000	0.5%
38	Rhode Island	1,870,877,000	0.4%
39	New Mexico	1,597,851,000	0.4%
40	Arkansas	1,501,477,000	0.3%
41	West Virginia	1,249,590,000	0.3%
42	Idaho	1,248,087,000	0.3%
43	Hawaii	1,089,391,000	0.2%
44	Alaska	1,088,723,000	0.2%
45	South Dakota	993,785,000	0.2%
46	Wyoming	932,207,000	0.2%
47	Montana	847,157,000	0.2%
48	North Dakota	718,095,000	0.2%
49	Delaware	687,170,000	0.2%
50	Vermont	331,859,000	0.1%
	District of Columbia	4,297,242,000	1.0%

Source: U.S. Bureau of the Census, Governments Division
"State and Local Government Finances: 2004-2005" (http://www.census.gov/govs/www/estimate05.html)

Per Capita Local Government Tax Revenue in 2005

National Per Capita = $1,515

ALPHA ORDER

ALPHA ORDER

RANK	STATE	PER CAPITA
43	Alabama	$856
12	Alaska	1,626
31	Arizona	1,230
49	Arkansas	542
24	California	1,339
9	Colorado	1,719
3	Connecticut	2,097
45	Delaware	818
19	Florida	1,464
26	Georgia	1,297
42	Hawaii	859
41	Idaho	875
6	Illinois	1,787
22	Indiana	1,356
25	Iowa	1,338
21	Kansas	1,381
46	Kentucky	760
30	Louisiana	1,260
11	Maine	1,637
4	Maryland	1,866
10	Massachusetts	1,671
32	Michigan	1,164
38	Minnesota	993
47	Mississippi	710
23	Missouri	1,353
40	Montana	905
14	Nebraska	1,590
20	Nevada	1,400
7	New Hampshire	1,763
2	New Jersey	2,267
44	New Mexico	834
1	New York	3,162
36	North Carolina	999
33	North Dakota	1,129
16	Ohio	1,545
39	Oklahoma	909
29	Oregon	1,263
17	Pennsylvania	1,517
8	Rhode Island	1,754
34	South Carolina	1,053
28	South Dakota	1,274
36	Tennessee	999
13	Texas	1,591
35	Utah	1,045
50	Vermont	535
15	Virginia	1,553
26	Washington	1,297
48	West Virginia	692
18	Wisconsin	1,489
5	Wyoming	1,840

RANK ORDER

RANK	STATE	PER CAPITA
1	New York	$3,162
2	New Jersey	2,267
3	Connecticut	2,097
4	Maryland	1,866
5	Wyoming	1,840
6	Illinois	1,787
7	New Hampshire	1,763
8	Rhode Island	1,754
9	Colorado	1,719
10	Massachusetts	1,671
11	Maine	1,637
12	Alaska	1,626
13	Texas	1,591
14	Nebraska	1,590
15	Virginia	1,553
16	Ohio	1,545
17	Pennsylvania	1,517
18	Wisconsin	1,489
19	Florida	1,464
20	Nevada	1,400
21	Kansas	1,381
22	Indiana	1,356
23	Missouri	1,353
24	California	1,339
25	Iowa	1,338
26	Georgia	1,297
26	Washington	1,297
28	South Dakota	1,274
29	Oregon	1,263
30	Louisiana	1,260
31	Arizona	1,230
32	Michigan	1,164
33	North Dakota	1,129
34	South Carolina	1,053
35	Utah	1,045
36	North Carolina	999
36	Tennessee	999
38	Minnesota	993
39	Oklahoma	909
40	Montana	905
41	Idaho	875
42	Hawaii	859
43	Alabama	856
44	New Mexico	834
45	Delaware	818
46	Kentucky	760
47	Mississippi	710
48	West Virginia	692
49	Arkansas	542
50	Vermont	535
	District of Columbia	7,383

Source: CQ Press using data from U.S. Bureau of the Census, Governments Division
"State and Local Government Finances: 2004-2005" (http://www.census.gov/govs/www/estimate05.html)

Local Government Total Expenditures in 2005

National Total = $1,313,749,897,000*

ALPHA ORDER

ALPHA ORDER

RANK	STATE	EXPENDITURES	% of USA
23	Alabama	$16,681,407,000	1.3%
43	Alaska	3,116,050,000	0.2%
16	Arizona	23,677,895,000	1.8%
36	Arkansas	7,490,510,000	0.6%
1	California	211,374,618,000	16.1%
20	Colorado	21,521,354,000	1.6%
27	Connecticut	13,243,211,000	1.0%
45	Delaware	2,616,621,000	0.2%
4	Florida	77,536,569,000	5.9%
10	Georgia	34,715,027,000	2.6%
48	Hawaii	2,275,690,000	0.2%
39	Idaho	4,293,830,000	0.3%
5	Illinois	56,580,687,000	4.3%
17	Indiana	23,653,334,000	1.8%
29	Iowa	11,260,572,000	0.9%
31	Kansas	10,423,806,000	0.8%
30	Kentucky	10,790,869,000	0.8%
24	Louisiana	15,767,960,000	1.2%
41	Maine	3,817,593,000	0.3%
21	Maryland	20,521,383,000	1.6%
14	Massachusetts	27,985,376,000	2.1%
8	Michigan	43,900,244,000	3.3%
18	Minnesota	23,595,774,000	1.8%
33	Mississippi	9,343,278,000	0.7%
22	Missouri	19,521,456,000	1.5%
46	Montana	2,612,108,000	0.2%
34	Nebraska	8,746,784,000	0.7%
28	Nevada	11,521,343,000	0.9%
40	New Hampshire	4,190,359,000	0.3%
9	New Jersey	39,835,246,000	3.0%
37	New Mexico	6,611,740,000	0.5%
2	New York	142,356,603,000	10.8%
11	North Carolina	32,622,820,000	2.5%
49	North Dakota	2,015,616,000	0.2%
7	Ohio	48,041,861,000	3.7%
32	Oklahoma	10,002,317,000	0.8%
25	Oregon	15,100,196,000	1.1%
6	Pennsylvania	50,751,766,000	3.9%
42	Rhode Island	3,507,914,000	0.3%
26	South Carolina	14,580,758,000	1.1%
47	South Dakota	2,306,544,000	0.2%
15	Tennessee	24,664,582,000	1.9%
3	Texas	89,237,530,000	6.8%
35	Utah	8,318,433,000	0.6%
50	Vermont	2,009,783,000	0.2%
13	Virginia	28,552,375,000	2.2%
12	Washington	30,403,665,000	2.3%
38	West Virginia	4,451,125,000	0.3%
19	Wisconsin	23,546,006,000	1.8%
44	Wyoming	2,957,713,000	0.2%

RANK ORDER

RANK	STATE	EXPENDITURES	% of USA
1	California	$211,374,618,000	16.1%
2	New York	142,356,603,000	10.8%
3	Texas	89,237,530,000	6.8%
4	Florida	77,536,569,000	5.9%
5	Illinois	56,580,687,000	4.3%
6	Pennsylvania	50,751,766,000	3.9%
7	Ohio	48,041,861,000	3.7%
8	Michigan	43,900,244,000	3.3%
9	New Jersey	39,835,246,000	3.0%
10	Georgia	34,715,027,000	2.6%
11	North Carolina	32,622,820,000	2.5%
12	Washington	30,403,665,000	2.3%
13	Virginia	28,552,375,000	2.2%
14	Massachusetts	27,985,376,000	2.1%
15	Tennessee	24,664,582,000	1.9%
16	Arizona	23,677,895,000	1.8%
17	Indiana	23,653,334,000	1.8%
18	Minnesota	23,595,774,000	1.8%
19	Wisconsin	23,546,006,000	1.8%
20	Colorado	21,521,354,000	1.6%
21	Maryland	20,521,383,000	1.6%
22	Missouri	19,521,456,000	1.5%
23	Alabama	16,681,407,000	1.3%
24	Louisiana	15,767,960,000	1.2%
25	Oregon	15,100,196,000	1.1%
26	South Carolina	14,580,758,000	1.1%
27	Connecticut	13,243,211,000	1.0%
28	Nevada	11,521,343,000	0.9%
29	Iowa	11,260,572,000	0.9%
30	Kentucky	10,790,869,000	0.8%
31	Kansas	10,423,806,000	0.8%
32	Oklahoma	10,002,317,000	0.8%
33	Mississippi	9,343,278,000	0.7%
34	Nebraska	8,746,784,000	0.7%
35	Utah	8,318,433,000	0.6%
36	Arkansas	7,490,510,000	0.6%
37	New Mexico	6,611,740,000	0.5%
38	West Virginia	4,451,125,000	0.3%
39	Idaho	4,293,830,000	0.3%
40	New Hampshire	4,190,359,000	0.3%
41	Maine	3,817,593,000	0.3%
42	Rhode Island	3,507,914,000	0.3%
43	Alaska	3,116,050,000	0.2%
44	Wyoming	2,957,713,000	0.2%
45	Delaware	2,616,621,000	0.2%
46	Montana	2,612,108,000	0.2%
47	South Dakota	2,306,544,000	0.2%
48	Hawaii	2,275,690,000	0.2%
49	North Dakota	2,015,616,000	0.2%
50	Vermont	2,009,783,000	0.2%
	District of Columbia	9,099,596,000	0.7%

Source: U.S. Bureau of the Census, Governments Division
   "State and Local Government Finances: 2004-2005" (http://www.census.gov/govs/www/estimate05.html)
*Total expenditures includes all money paid other than for retirement of debt and extension of loans. Includes payments from all sources of funds including current revenues and proceeds from borrowing and prior year fund balances. Includes intergovernmental transfers and expenditures for government owned utilities and other commercial or auxiliary enterprise and insurance trust expenditures.

Per Capita Local Government Total Expenditures in 2005

National Per Capita = $4,440*

ALPHA ORDER				RANK ORDER		
RANK	STATE	PER CAPITA		RANK	STATE	PER CAPITA
30	Alabama	$3,675		1	New York	$7,390
7	Alaska	4,655		2	California	5,873
20	Arizona	3,978		3	Wyoming	5,839
47	Arkansas	2,702		4	Nebraska	4,987
2	California	5,873		5	Washington	4,848
9	Colorado	4,605		6	Nevada	4,783
25	Connecticut	3,798		7	Alaska	4,655
41	Delaware	3,113		8	Minnesota	4,614
12	Florida	4,372		9	Colorado	4,605
22	Georgia	3,812		10	New Jersey	4,601
50	Hawaii	1,795		11	Illinois	4,448
42	Idaho	3,011		12	Florida	4,372
11	Illinois	4,448		13	Massachusetts	4,353
26	Indiana	3,780		14	Michigan	4,343
23	Iowa	3,810		15	Wisconsin	4,250
24	Kansas	3,802		16	Ohio	4,192
48	Kentucky	2,587		17	Oregon	4,160
31	Louisiana	3,507		18	Tennessee	4,118
44	Maine	2,909		19	Pennsylvania	4,104
29	Maryland	3,682		20	Arizona	3,978
13	Massachusetts	4,353		21	Texas	3,906
14	Michigan	4,343		22	Georgia	3,812
8	Minnesota	4,614		23	Iowa	3,810
38	Mississippi	3,221		24	Kansas	3,802
34	Missouri	3,373		25	Connecticut	3,798
46	Montana	2,791		26	Indiana	3,780
4	Nebraska	4,987		27	Virginia	3,778
6	Nevada	4,783		28	North Carolina	3,759
39	New Hampshire	3,216		29	Maryland	3,682
10	New Jersey	4,601		30	Alabama	3,675
32	New Mexico	3,450		31	Louisiana	3,507
1	New York	7,390		32	New Mexico	3,450
28	North Carolina	3,759		33	South Carolina	3,427
40	North Dakota	3,170		34	Missouri	3,373
16	Ohio	4,192		35	Utah	3,321
45	Oklahoma	2,829		36	Rhode Island	3,289
17	Oregon	4,160		37	Vermont	3,243
19	Pennsylvania	4,104		38	Mississippi	3,221
36	Rhode Island	3,289		39	New Hampshire	3,216
33	South Carolina	3,427		40	North Dakota	3,170
43	South Dakota	2,957		41	Delaware	3,113
18	Tennessee	4,118		42	Idaho	3,011
21	Texas	3,906		43	South Dakota	2,957
35	Utah	3,321		44	Maine	2,909
37	Vermont	3,243		45	Oklahoma	2,829
27	Virginia	3,778		46	Montana	2,791
5	Washington	4,848		47	Arkansas	2,702
49	West Virginia	2,465		48	Kentucky	2,587
15	Wisconsin	4,250		49	West Virginia	2,465
3	Wyoming	5,839		50	Hawaii	1,795
					District of Columbia	15,634

Source: CQ Press using data from U.S. Bureau of the Census, Governments Division
   "State and Local Government Finances: 2004-2005" (http://www.census.gov/govs/www/estimate05.html)
*Total expenditures includes all money paid other than for retirement of debt and extension of loans. Includes payments from all sources of funds including current revenues and proceeds from borrowing and prior year fund balances. Includes intergovernmental transfers and expenditures for government owned utilities and other commercial or auxiliary enterprise and insurance trust expenditures.

Local Government Direct General Expenditures in 2005

National Total = $1,137,496,048,000*

ALPHA ORDER

RANK	STATE	EXPENDITURES	% of USA
23	Alabama	$14,413,113,000	1.3%
43	Alaska	2,825,527,000	0.2%
18	Arizona	19,375,284,000	1.7%
34	Arkansas	6,708,146,000	0.6%
1	California	179,995,469,000	15.8%
20	Colorado	18,495,767,000	1.6%
27	Connecticut	12,249,653,000	1.1%
46	Delaware	2,353,432,000	0.2%
4	Florida	67,620,655,000	5.9%
10	Georgia	29,762,306,000	2.6%
49	Hawaii	1,856,435,000	0.2%
39	Idaho	4,100,977,000	0.4%
5	Illinois	48,171,678,000	4.2%
16	Indiana	21,628,215,000	1.9%
28	Iowa	10,363,809,000	0.9%
31	Kansas	9,369,013,000	0.8%
30	Kentucky	9,682,429,000	0.9%
24	Louisiana	14,306,882,000	1.3%
41	Maine	3,722,221,000	0.3%
19	Maryland	18,829,466,000	1.7%
14	Massachusetts	22,209,970,000	2.0%
8	Michigan	40,122,385,000	3.5%
17	Minnesota	21,244,592,000	1.9%
33	Mississippi	8,680,640,000	0.8%
21	Missouri	17,423,072,000	1.5%
45	Montana	2,521,974,000	0.2%
37	Nebraska	5,801,593,000	0.5%
29	Nevada	10,130,063,000	0.9%
40	New Hampshire	4,033,970,000	0.4%
9	New Jersey	38,558,838,000	3.4%
36	New Mexico	6,158,380,000	0.5%
2	New York	115,983,353,000	10.2%
11	North Carolina	27,628,189,000	2.4%
48	North Dakota	1,893,682,000	0.2%
7	Ohio	44,807,540,000	3.9%
32	Oklahoma	9,152,247,000	0.8%
26	Oregon	12,988,567,000	1.1%
6	Pennsylvania	45,791,559,000	4.0%
42	Rhode Island	3,229,427,000	0.3%
25	South Carolina	13,126,089,000	1.2%
47	South Dakota	2,074,766,000	0.2%
22	Tennessee	17,093,810,000	1.5%
3	Texas	76,938,323,000	6.8%
35	Utah	6,588,799,000	0.6%
50	Vermont	1,807,592,000	0.2%
12	Virginia	26,304,137,000	2.3%
13	Washington	23,372,805,000	2.1%
38	West Virginia	4,177,113,000	0.4%
15	Wisconsin	21,756,311,000	1.9%
44	Wyoming	2,821,480,000	0.2%

RANK ORDER

RANK	STATE	EXPENDITURES	% of USA
1	California	$179,995,469,000	15.8%
2	New York	115,983,353,000	10.2%
3	Texas	76,938,323,000	6.8%
4	Florida	67,620,655,000	5.9%
5	Illinois	48,171,678,000	4.2%
6	Pennsylvania	45,791,559,000	4.0%
7	Ohio	44,807,540,000	3.9%
8	Michigan	40,122,385,000	3.5%
9	New Jersey	38,558,838,000	3.4%
10	Georgia	29,762,306,000	2.6%
11	North Carolina	27,628,189,000	2.4%
12	Virginia	26,304,137,000	2.3%
13	Washington	23,372,805,000	2.1%
14	Massachusetts	22,209,970,000	2.0%
15	Wisconsin	21,756,311,000	1.9%
16	Indiana	21,628,215,000	1.9%
17	Minnesota	21,244,592,000	1.9%
18	Arizona	19,375,284,000	1.7%
19	Maryland	18,829,466,000	1.7%
20	Colorado	18,495,767,000	1.6%
21	Missouri	17,423,072,000	1.5%
22	Tennessee	17,093,810,000	1.5%
23	Alabama	14,413,113,000	1.3%
24	Louisiana	14,306,882,000	1.3%
25	South Carolina	13,126,089,000	1.2%
26	Oregon	12,988,567,000	1.1%
27	Connecticut	12,249,653,000	1.1%
28	Iowa	10,363,809,000	0.9%
29	Nevada	10,130,063,000	0.9%
30	Kentucky	9,682,429,000	0.9%
31	Kansas	9,369,013,000	0.8%
32	Oklahoma	9,152,247,000	0.8%
33	Mississippi	8,680,640,000	0.8%
34	Arkansas	6,708,146,000	0.6%
35	Utah	6,588,799,000	0.6%
36	New Mexico	6,158,380,000	0.5%
37	Nebraska	5,801,593,000	0.5%
38	West Virginia	4,177,113,000	0.4%
39	Idaho	4,100,977,000	0.4%
40	New Hampshire	4,033,970,000	0.4%
41	Maine	3,722,221,000	0.3%
42	Rhode Island	3,229,427,000	0.3%
43	Alaska	2,825,527,000	0.2%
44	Wyoming	2,821,480,000	0.2%
45	Montana	2,521,974,000	0.2%
46	Delaware	2,353,432,000	0.2%
47	South Dakota	2,074,766,000	0.2%
48	North Dakota	1,893,682,000	0.2%
49	Hawaii	1,856,435,000	0.2%
50	Vermont	1,807,592,000	0.2%
	District of Columbia	7,244,305,000	0.6%

Source: U.S. Bureau of the Census, Governments Division
"State and Local Government Finances: 2004-2005" (http://www.census.gov/govs/www/estimate05.html)
*Direct general expenditures include expenditures for current operations, assistance and subsidies, interest on debt, and capital outlay. Excludes intergovernmental transfers, expenditures for government owned utilities and other commercial or auxiliary enterprise, and insurance trust expenditures.

Per Capita Local Government Direct General Expenditures in 2005

National Per Capita = $3,844*

ALPHA ORDER

RANK	STATE	PER CAPITA
31	Alabama	$3,175
5	Alaska	4,221
27	Arizona	3,255
47	Arkansas	2,420
3	California	5,001
9	Colorado	3,957
17	Connecticut	3,513
42	Delaware	2,800
12	Florida	3,813
26	Georgia	3,268
50	Hawaii	1,465
39	Idaho	2,876
13	Illinois	3,787
20	Indiana	3,457
18	Iowa	3,507
22	Kansas	3,417
48	Kentucky	2,321
30	Louisiana	3,182
41	Maine	2,837
23	Maryland	3,379
21	Massachusetts	3,455
8	Michigan	3,969
7	Minnesota	4,154
36	Mississippi	2,993
35	Missouri	3,010
43	Montana	2,695
25	Nebraska	3,308
6	Nevada	4,205
32	New Hampshire	3,096
4	New Jersey	4,454
28	New Mexico	3,214
1	New York	6,021
29	North Carolina	3,183
37	North Dakota	2,978
11	Ohio	3,910
46	Oklahoma	2,588
16	Oregon	3,578
15	Pennsylvania	3,703
34	Rhode Island	3,027
33	South Carolina	3,085
44	South Dakota	2,660
40	Tennessee	2,854
24	Texas	3,368
45	Utah	2,630
38	Vermont	2,917
19	Virginia	3,480
14	Washington	3,727
49	West Virginia	2,313
10	Wisconsin	3,927
2	Wyoming	5,570

RANK ORDER

RANK	STATE	PER CAPITA
1	New York	$6,021
2	Wyoming	5,570
3	California	5,001
4	New Jersey	4,454
5	Alaska	4,221
6	Nevada	4,205
7	Minnesota	4,154
8	Michigan	3,969
9	Colorado	3,957
10	Wisconsin	3,927
11	Ohio	3,910
12	Florida	3,813
13	Illinois	3,787
14	Washington	3,727
15	Pennsylvania	3,703
16	Oregon	3,578
17	Connecticut	3,513
18	Iowa	3,507
19	Virginia	3,480
20	Indiana	3,457
21	Massachusetts	3,455
22	Kansas	3,417
23	Maryland	3,379
24	Texas	3,368
25	Nebraska	3,308
26	Georgia	3,268
27	Arizona	3,255
28	New Mexico	3,214
29	North Carolina	3,183
30	Louisiana	3,182
31	Alabama	3,175
32	New Hampshire	3,096
33	South Carolina	3,085
34	Rhode Island	3,027
35	Missouri	3,010
36	Mississippi	2,993
37	North Dakota	2,978
38	Vermont	2,917
39	Idaho	2,876
40	Tennessee	2,854
41	Maine	2,837
42	Delaware	2,800
43	Montana	2,695
44	South Dakota	2,660
45	Utah	2,630
46	Oklahoma	2,588
47	Arkansas	2,420
48	Kentucky	2,321
49	West Virginia	2,313
50	Hawaii	1,465
	District of Columbia	12,446

Source: CQ Press using data from U.S. Bureau of the Census, Governments Division
"State and Local Government Finances: 2004-2005" (http://www.census.gov/govs/www/estimate05.html)
*Direct general expenditures include expenditures for current operations, assistance and subsidies, interest on debt, and capital outlay. Excludes intergovernmental transfers, expenditures for government owned utilities and other commercial or auxiliary enterprise, and insurance trust expenditures.

Local Government Debt Outstanding in 2005

National Total = $1,269,193,627,000*

ALPHA ORDER

RANK	STATE	DEBT	% of USA
23	Alabama	$16,270,201,000	1.3%
40	Alaska	2,991,565,000	0.2%
16	Arizona	24,792,418,000	2.0%
33	Arkansas	6,904,261,000	0.5%
1	California	176,326,278,000	13.9%
14	Colorado	26,698,352,000	2.1%
31	Connecticut	8,003,012,000	0.6%
43	Delaware	1,875,777,000	0.1%
4	Florida	84,833,485,000	6.7%
11	Georgia	29,728,723,000	2.3%
38	Hawaii	3,447,832,000	0.3%
46	Idaho	1,592,932,000	0.1%
6	Illinois	55,428,508,000	4.4%
21	Indiana	17,175,572,000	1.4%
35	Iowa	6,718,434,000	0.5%
29	Kansas	12,435,805,000	1.0%
19	Kentucky	21,632,975,000	1.7%
28	Louisiana	13,260,444,000	1.0%
42	Maine	2,335,333,000	0.2%
27	Maryland	14,234,102,000	1.1%
18	Massachusetts	21,995,998,000	1.7%
7	Michigan	42,650,050,000	3.4%
12	Minnesota	28,997,121,000	2.3%
36	Mississippi	5,860,921,000	0.5%
25	Missouri	15,149,888,000	1.2%
47	Montana	1,415,531,000	0.1%
34	Nebraska	6,812,674,000	0.5%
26	Nevada	14,583,613,000	1.1%
41	New Hampshire	2,427,979,000	0.2%
10	New Jersey	30,580,977,000	2.4%
37	New Mexico	4,570,576,000	0.4%
3	New York	131,115,115,000	10.3%
15	North Carolina	25,133,405,000	2.0%
45	North Dakota	1,630,644,000	0.1%
8	Ohio	37,524,508,000	3.0%
32	Oklahoma	6,944,280,000	0.5%
24	Oregon	15,392,737,000	1.2%
5	Pennsylvania	72,900,511,000	5.7%
44	Rhode Island	1,869,399,000	0.1%
22	South Carolina	16,547,141,000	1.3%
48	South Dakota	1,266,834,000	0.1%
17	Tennessee	21,998,793,000	1.7%
2	Texas	132,452,572,000	10.4%
30	Utah	9,563,560,000	0.8%
50	Vermont	840,419,000	0.1%
13	Virginia	27,634,226,000	2.2%
9	Washington	36,025,804,000	2.8%
39	West Virginia	3,419,222,000	0.3%
20	Wisconsin	18,162,180,000	1.4%
49	Wyoming	1,031,431,000	0.1%

RANK ORDER

RANK	STATE	DEBT	% of USA
1	California	$176,326,278,000	13.9%
2	Texas	132,452,572,000	10.4%
3	New York	131,115,115,000	10.3%
4	Florida	84,833,485,000	6.7%
5	Pennsylvania	72,900,511,000	5.7%
6	Illinois	55,428,508,000	4.4%
7	Michigan	42,650,050,000	3.4%
8	Ohio	37,524,508,000	3.0%
9	Washington	36,025,804,000	2.8%
10	New Jersey	30,580,977,000	2.4%
11	Georgia	29,728,723,000	2.3%
12	Minnesota	28,997,121,000	2.3%
13	Virginia	27,634,226,000	2.2%
14	Colorado	26,698,352,000	2.1%
15	North Carolina	25,133,405,000	2.0%
16	Arizona	24,792,418,000	2.0%
17	Tennessee	21,998,793,000	1.7%
18	Massachusetts	21,995,998,000	1.7%
19	Kentucky	21,632,975,000	1.7%
20	Wisconsin	18,162,180,000	1.4%
21	Indiana	17,175,572,000	1.4%
22	South Carolina	16,547,141,000	1.3%
23	Alabama	16,270,201,000	1.3%
24	Oregon	15,392,737,000	1.2%
25	Missouri	15,149,888,000	1.2%
26	Nevada	14,583,613,000	1.1%
27	Maryland	14,234,102,000	1.1%
28	Louisiana	13,260,444,000	1.0%
29	Kansas	12,435,805,000	1.0%
30	Utah	9,563,560,000	0.8%
31	Connecticut	8,003,012,000	0.6%
32	Oklahoma	6,944,280,000	0.5%
33	Arkansas	6,904,261,000	0.5%
34	Nebraska	6,812,674,000	0.5%
35	Iowa	6,718,434,000	0.5%
36	Mississippi	5,860,921,000	0.5%
37	New Mexico	4,570,576,000	0.4%
38	Hawaii	3,447,832,000	0.3%
39	West Virginia	3,419,222,000	0.3%
40	Alaska	2,991,565,000	0.2%
41	New Hampshire	2,427,979,000	0.2%
42	Maine	2,335,333,000	0.2%
43	Delaware	1,875,777,000	0.1%
44	Rhode Island	1,869,399,000	0.1%
45	North Dakota	1,630,644,000	0.1%
46	Idaho	1,592,932,000	0.1%
47	Montana	1,415,531,000	0.1%
48	South Dakota	1,266,834,000	0.1%
49	Wyoming	1,031,431,000	0.1%
50	Vermont	840,419,000	0.1%
	District of Columbia	6,009,509,000	0.5%

Source: U.S. Bureau of the Census, Governments Division
"State and Local Government Finances: 2004-2005" (http://www.census.gov/govs/www/estimate05.html)
*Includes short-term, long-term, full faith and credit, nonguaranteed, and public debt for private purposes.

Per Capita Local Government Debt Outstanding in 2005

National Per Capita = $4,289*

ALPHA ORDER

RANK	STATE	PER CAPITA
22	Alabama	$3,584
12	Alaska	4,469
16	Arizona	4,165
35	Arkansas	2,491
9	California	4,899
6	Colorado	5,712
37	Connecticut	2,295
39	Delaware	2,232
10	Florida	4,783
27	Georgia	3,264
31	Hawaii	2,720
50	Idaho	1,117
13	Illinois	4,358
30	Indiana	2,745
38	Iowa	2,273
11	Kansas	4,536
8	Kentucky	5,187
28	Louisiana	2,950
45	Maine	1,780
34	Maryland	2,554
24	Massachusetts	3,421
15	Michigan	4,219
7	Minnesota	5,670
41	Mississippi	2,021
32	Missouri	2,618
48	Montana	1,513
18	Nebraska	3,884
2	Nevada	6,054
44	New Hampshire	1,863
23	New Jersey	3,532
36	New Mexico	2,385
1	New York	6,807
29	North Carolina	2,896
33	North Dakota	2,564
26	Ohio	3,274
42	Oklahoma	1,964
14	Oregon	4,240
3	Pennsylvania	5,895
46	Rhode Island	1,752
17	South Carolina	3,889
47	South Dakota	1,624
20	Tennessee	3,673
4	Texas	5,798
19	Utah	3,818
49	Vermont	1,356
21	Virginia	3,656
5	Washington	5,745
43	West Virginia	1,894
25	Wisconsin	3,278
40	Wyoming	2,036

RANK ORDER

RANK	STATE	PER CAPITA
1	New York	$6,807
2	Nevada	6,054
3	Pennsylvania	5,895
4	Texas	5,798
5	Washington	5,745
6	Colorado	5,712
7	Minnesota	5,670
8	Kentucky	5,187
9	California	4,899
10	Florida	4,783
11	Kansas	4,536
12	Alaska	4,469
13	Illinois	4,358
14	Oregon	4,240
15	Michigan	4,219
16	Arizona	4,165
17	South Carolina	3,889
18	Nebraska	3,884
19	Utah	3,818
20	Tennessee	3,673
21	Virginia	3,656
22	Alabama	3,584
23	New Jersey	3,532
24	Massachusetts	3,421
25	Wisconsin	3,278
26	Ohio	3,274
27	Georgia	3,264
28	Louisiana	2,950
29	North Carolina	2,896
30	Indiana	2,745
31	Hawaii	2,720
32	Missouri	2,618
33	North Dakota	2,564
34	Maryland	2,554
35	Arkansas	2,491
36	New Mexico	2,385
37	Connecticut	2,295
38	Iowa	2,273
39	Delaware	2,232
40	Wyoming	2,036
41	Mississippi	2,021
42	Oklahoma	1,964
43	West Virginia	1,894
44	New Hampshire	1,863
45	Maine	1,780
46	Rhode Island	1,752
47	South Dakota	1,624
48	Montana	1,513
49	Vermont	1,356
50	Idaho	1,117

District of Columbia — 10,325

Source: CQ Press using data from U.S. Bureau of the Census, Governments Division
"State and Local Government Finances: 2004-2005" (http://www.census.gov/govs/www/estimate05.html)
*Includes short-term, long-term, full faith and credit, nonguaranteed, and public debt for private purposes.

Local Government Full-Time Equivalent Employees in 2006

National Total = 11,885,145 FTE Employees*

ALPHA ORDER

RANK	STATE	EMPLOYEES	% of USA
23	Alabama	187,312	1.6%
44	Alaska	27,480	0.2%
18	Arizona	218,226	1.8%
31	Arkansas	103,776	0.9%
1	California	1,425,123	12.0%
22	Colorado	187,551	1.6%
29	Connecticut	126,251	1.1%
46	Delaware	23,874	0.2%
4	Florida	676,044	5.7%
8	Georgia	381,283	3.2%
48	Hawaii	14,636	0.1%
37	Idaho	57,154	0.5%
5	Illinois	503,131	4.2%
13	Indiana	243,050	2.0%
28	Iowa	132,663	1.1%
27	Kansas	140,550	1.2%
25	Kentucky	164,532	1.4%
NA	Louisiana**	NA	NA
38	Maine	55,925	0.5%
20	Maryland	200,878	1.7%
14	Massachusetts	241,083	2.0%
11	Michigan	351,779	3.0%
21	Minnesota	195,599	1.6%
NA	Mississippi**	NA	NA
16	Missouri	229,855	1.9%
40	Montana	35,255	0.3%
32	Nebraska	84,592	0.7%
34	Nevada	77,445	0.7%
39	New Hampshire	50,701	0.4%
10	New Jersey	354,987	3.0%
35	New Mexico	77,146	0.6%
3	New York	941,079	7.9%
9	North Carolina	372,146	3.1%
47	North Dakota	23,046	0.2%
6	Ohio	479,899	4.0%
26	Oklahoma	146,919	1.2%
30	Oregon	124,226	1.0%
7	Pennsylvania	407,214	3.4%
43	Rhode Island	30,638	0.3%
24	South Carolina	172,498	1.5%
42	South Dakota	31,281	0.3%
15	Tennessee	240,556	2.0%
2	Texas	1,033,284	8.7%
33	Utah	78,508	0.7%
45	Vermont	25,527	0.2%
12	Virginia	307,987	2.6%
19	Washington	216,253	1.8%
36	West Virginia	60,387	0.5%
17	Wisconsin	219,930	1.9%
41	Wyoming	32,988	0.3%

RANK ORDER

RANK	STATE	EMPLOYEES	% of USA
1	California	1,425,123	12.0%
2	Texas	1,033,284	8.7%
3	New York	941,079	7.9%
4	Florida	676,044	5.7%
5	Illinois	503,131	4.2%
6	Ohio	479,899	4.0%
7	Pennsylvania	407,214	3.4%
8	Georgia	381,283	3.2%
9	North Carolina	372,146	3.1%
10	New Jersey	354,987	3.0%
11	Michigan	351,779	3.0%
12	Virginia	307,987	2.6%
13	Indiana	243,050	2.0%
14	Massachusetts	241,083	2.0%
15	Tennessee	240,556	2.0%
16	Missouri	229,855	1.9%
17	Wisconsin	219,930	1.9%
18	Arizona	218,226	1.8%
19	Washington	216,253	1.8%
20	Maryland	200,878	1.7%
21	Minnesota	195,599	1.6%
22	Colorado	187,551	1.6%
23	Alabama	187,312	1.6%
24	South Carolina	172,498	1.5%
25	Kentucky	164,532	1.4%
26	Oklahoma	146,919	1.2%
27	Kansas	140,550	1.2%
28	Iowa	132,663	1.1%
29	Connecticut	126,251	1.1%
30	Oregon	124,226	1.0%
31	Arkansas	103,776	0.9%
32	Nebraska	84,592	0.7%
33	Utah	78,508	0.7%
34	Nevada	77,445	0.7%
35	New Mexico	77,146	0.6%
36	West Virginia	60,387	0.5%
37	Idaho	57,154	0.5%
38	Maine	55,925	0.5%
39	New Hampshire	50,701	0.4%
40	Montana	35,255	0.3%
41	Wyoming	32,988	0.3%
42	South Dakota	31,281	0.3%
43	Rhode Island	30,638	0.3%
44	Alaska	27,480	0.2%
45	Vermont	25,527	0.2%
46	Delaware	23,874	0.2%
47	North Dakota	23,046	0.2%
48	Hawaii	14,636	0.1%
NA	Louisiana**	NA	NA
NA	Mississippi**	NA	NA
	District of Columbia	46,611	0.4%

Source: U.S. Bureau of the Census, Governments Division
"Local Government Employment and Payroll - March 2006" (http://www.census.gov/govs/www/apesloc06.html)
*As of March 2006.
**Not available.

Rate of Local Government Full-Time Equivalent Employees in 2006

National Rate = 398 Local Government Employees per 10,000 Population*

ALPHA ORDER

RANK	STATE	RATE
13	Alabama	408
15	Alaska	406
38	Arizona	354
34	Arkansas	369
24	California	393
24	Colorado	393
36	Connecticut	361
47	Delaware	280
32	Florida	374
13	Georgia	408
48	Hawaii	114
27	Idaho	390
22	Illinois	394
28	Indiana	386
5	Iowa	446
2	Kansas	510
26	Kentucky	391
NA	Louisiana**	NA
7	Maine	425
37	Maryland	359
31	Massachusetts	375
39	Michigan	348
30	Minnesota	379
NA	Mississippi**	NA
22	Missouri	394
33	Montana	372
4	Nebraska	480
44	Nevada	311
28	New Hampshire	386
12	New Jersey	410
18	New Mexico	397
3	New York	488
8	North Carolina	420
35	North Dakota	362
9	Ohio	419
10	Oklahoma	411
41	Oregon	337
43	Pennsylvania	328
46	Rhode Island	289
17	South Carolina	398
18	South Dakota	397
20	Tennessee	396
6	Texas	441
45	Utah	304
10	Vermont	411
16	Virginia	403
40	Washington	339
42	West Virginia	334
21	Wisconsin	395
1	Wyoming	643

RANK ORDER

RANK	STATE	RATE
1	Wyoming	643
2	Kansas	510
3	New York	488
4	Nebraska	480
5	Iowa	446
6	Texas	441
7	Maine	425
8	North Carolina	420
9	Ohio	419
10	Oklahoma	411
10	Vermont	411
12	New Jersey	410
13	Alabama	408
13	Georgia	408
15	Alaska	406
16	Virginia	403
17	South Carolina	398
18	New Mexico	397
18	South Dakota	397
20	Tennessee	396
21	Wisconsin	395
22	Illinois	394
22	Missouri	394
24	California	393
24	Colorado	393
26	Kentucky	391
27	Idaho	390
28	Indiana	386
28	New Hampshire	386
30	Minnesota	379
31	Massachusetts	375
32	Florida	374
33	Montana	372
34	Arkansas	369
35	North Dakota	362
36	Connecticut	361
37	Maryland	359
38	Arizona	354
39	Michigan	348
40	Washington	339
41	Oregon	337
42	West Virginia	334
43	Pennsylvania	328
44	Nevada	311
45	Utah	304
46	Rhode Island	289
47	Delaware	280
48	Hawaii	114
NA	Louisiana**	NA
NA	Mississippi**	NA
	District of Columbia	796

Source: CQ Press using data from U.S. Bureau of the Census, Governments Division
   "Local Government Employment and Payroll - March 2006" (http://www.census.gov/govs/www/apesloc06.html)
*Full-time equivalent as of March 2006.
**Not available.

Average Annual Earnings of Full-Time Local Government Employees in 2006

National Average = $45,687*

ALPHA ORDER				RANK ORDER		
RANK	STATE	EARNINGS		RANK	STATE	EARNINGS
43	Alabama	$34,831		1	California	$60,777
10	Alaska	50,311		2	New Jersey	56,437
19	Arizona	46,021		3	New York	55,692
47	Arkansas	32,691		4	Washington	55,430
1	California	60,777		5	Connecticut	54,504
20	Colorado	45,678		6	Nevada	54,046
5	Connecticut	54,504		7	Rhode Island	53,992
12	Delaware	49,765		8	Maryland	52,794
22	Florida	43,291		9	Hawaii	51,036
30	Georgia	38,599		10	Alaska	50,311
9	Hawaii	51,036		11	Massachusetts	50,048
41	Idaho	35,156		12	Delaware	49,765
14	Illinois	47,887		13	Michigan	48,140
27	Indiana	39,908		14	Illinois	47,887
32	Iowa	37,606		15	Minnesota	47,832
39	Kansas	36,013		16	Pennsylvania	47,093
46	Kentucky	33,470		17	Oregon	47,003
NA	Louisiana**	NA		18	Wisconsin	46,089
35	Maine	36,850		19	Arizona	46,021
8	Maryland	52,794		20	Colorado	45,678
11	Massachusetts	50,048		21	Ohio	43,595
13	Michigan	48,140		22	Florida	43,291
15	Minnesota	47,832		23	Virginia	42,442
NA	Mississippi**	NA		24	North Dakota	41,398
38	Missouri	36,719		25	Nebraska	40,602
42	Montana	34,949		26	Utah	39,913
25	Nebraska	40,602		27	Indiana	39,908
6	Nevada	54,046		28	New Hampshire	39,809
28	New Hampshire	39,809		29	Wyoming	39,347
2	New Jersey	56,437		30	Georgia	38,599
40	New Mexico	35,260		31	North Carolina	37,813
3	New York	55,692		32	Iowa	37,606
31	North Carolina	37,813		33	Texas	37,513
24	North Dakota	41,398		34	Tennessee	37,254
21	Ohio	43,595		35	Maine	36,850
48	Oklahoma	32,644		36	Vermont	36,848
17	Oregon	47,003		37	South Carolina	36,758
16	Pennsylvania	47,093		38	Missouri	36,719
7	Rhode Island	53,992		39	Kansas	36,013
37	South Carolina	36,758		40	New Mexico	35,260
44	South Dakota	34,757		41	Idaho	35,156
34	Tennessee	37,254		42	Montana	34,949
33	Texas	37,513		43	Alabama	34,831
26	Utah	39,913		44	South Dakota	34,757
36	Vermont	36,848		45	West Virginia	33,501
23	Virginia	42,442		46	Kentucky	33,470
4	Washington	55,430		47	Arkansas	32,691
45	West Virginia	33,501		48	Oklahoma	32,644
18	Wisconsin	46,089		NA	Louisiana**	NA
29	Wyoming	39,347		NA	Mississippi**	NA
					District of Columbia	59,901

Source: CQ Press using data from U.S. Bureau of the Census, Governments Division
"Local Government Employment and Payroll - March 2006" (http://www.census.gov/govs/www/apesloc06.html)
*March 2006 full-time payroll (multiplied by 12) divided by full-time employees.
**Not available.

XI. Health

Average Medical Malpractice Payment in 2005

National Average = $294,153*

ALPHA ORDER

RANK	STATE	AVERAGE PAYMENT
29	Alabama	$256,056
3	Alaska	533,524
22	Arizona	304,851
19	Arkansas	311,623
39	California	210,060
25	Colorado	277,620
1	Connecticut	735,569
6	Delaware	456,677
34	Florida**	240,256
16	Georgia	337,322
2	Hawaii	577,834
43	Idaho	190,122
4	Illinois	510,668
26	Indiana**	271,139
40	Iowa	199,179
47	Kansas**	156,552
37	Kentucky	234,316
44	Louisiana**	181,897
35	Maine	239,414
10	Maryland	371,299
5	Massachusetts	476,428
49	Michigan	134,837
7	Minnesota	449,819
41	Mississippi	199,155
23	Missouri	303,064
28	Montana	259,141
50	Nebraska**	98,998
32	Nevada	245,924
13	New Hampshire	358,227
9	New Jersey	374,247
36	New Mexico**	239,150
8	New York	390,802
20	North Carolina	308,528
31	North Dakota	254,147
21	Ohio	305,501
33	Oklahoma	243,224
18	Oregon	314,973
15	Pennsylvania**	346,832
12	Rhode Island	362,268
45	South Carolina**	167,587
27	South Dakota	268,200
30	Tennessee	254,960
42	Texas	191,060
48	Utah	153,393
46	Vermont	161,478
14	Virginia	353,882
17	Washington	331,034
38	West Virginia	231,753
11	Wisconsin**	370,236
24	Wyoming	290,464

RANK ORDER

RANK	STATE	AVERAGE PAYMENT
1	Connecticut	$735,569
2	Hawaii	577,834
3	Alaska	533,524
4	Illinois	510,668
5	Massachusetts	476,428
6	Delaware	456,677
7	Minnesota	449,819
8	New York	390,802
9	New Jersey	374,247
10	Maryland	371,299
11	Wisconsin**	370,236
12	Rhode Island	362,268
13	New Hampshire	358,227
14	Virginia	353,882
15	Pennsylvania**	346,832
16	Georgia	337,322
17	Washington	331,034
18	Oregon	314,973
19	Arkansas	311,623
20	North Carolina	308,528
21	Ohio	305,501
22	Arizona	304,851
23	Missouri	303,064
24	Wyoming	290,464
25	Colorado	277,620
26	Indiana**	271,139
27	South Dakota	268,200
28	Montana	259,141
29	Alabama	256,056
30	Tennessee	254,960
31	North Dakota	254,147
32	Nevada	245,924
33	Oklahoma	243,224
34	Florida**	240,256
35	Maine	239,414
36	New Mexico**	239,150
37	Kentucky	234,316
38	West Virginia	231,753
39	California	210,060
40	Iowa	199,179
41	Mississippi	199,155
42	Texas	191,060
43	Idaho	190,122
44	Louisiana**	181,897
45	South Carolina**	167,587
46	Vermont	161,478
47	Kansas**	156,552
48	Utah	153,393
49	Michigan	134,837
50	Nebraska**	98,998
	District of Columbia	367,541

Source: U.S. Department of Health and Human Services, Bureau of Health Professions
"National Practitioner Data Bank, 2005 Annual Report" (http://www.npdb-hipdb.com/annualrpt.html)
*National figure includes U.S. territories and U.S. Armed Forces locations overseas.
**The figures for these states have not been adjusted for payments by state compensation funds and other similar funds.
Average payments for these states understate the actual average amounts received by claimants.

Average Annual Single Coverage Health Insurance Premium per Enrolled Employee in 2005
National Average = $3,991*

ALPHA ORDER

RANK	STATE	PREMIUM
48	Alabama	$3,419
1	Alaska	5,088
8	Arizona	4,294
46	Arkansas	3,590
33	California	3,823
30	Colorado	3,891
5	Connecticut	4,390
2	Delaware	4,623
23	Florida	4,003
31	Georgia	3,861
50	Hawaii	3,339
19	Idaho	4,078
21	Illinois	4,049
22	Indiana	4,042
44	Iowa	3,686
40	Kansas	3,755
33	Kentucky	3,823
27	Louisiana	3,931
9	Maine	4,290
32	Maryland	3,834
12	Massachusetts	4,235
10	Michigan	4,287
26	Minnesota	3,932
49	Mississippi	3,402
42	Missouri	3,741
29	Montana	3,898
39	Nebraska	3,777
41	Nevada	3,752
15	New Hampshire	4,175
7	New Jersey	4,332
36	New Mexico	3,813
11	New York	4,239
37	North Carolina	3,802
47	North Dakota	3,438
28	Ohio	3,928
18	Oklahoma	4,088
20	Oregon	4,051
14	Pennsylvania	4,195
3	Rhode Island	4,417
25	South Carolina	3,943
38	South Dakota	3,796
35	Tennessee	3,822
17	Texas	4,108
45	Utah	3,633
4	Vermont	4,392
43	Virginia	3,734
24	Washington	3,975
16	West Virginia	4,128
13	Wisconsin	4,223
6	Wyoming	4,388

RANK ORDER

RANK	STATE	PREMIUM
1	Alaska	$5,088
2	Delaware	4,623
3	Rhode Island	4,417
4	Vermont	4,392
5	Connecticut	4,390
6	Wyoming	4,388
7	New Jersey	4,332
8	Arizona	4,294
9	Maine	4,290
10	Michigan	4,287
11	New York	4,239
12	Massachusetts	4,235
13	Wisconsin	4,223
14	Pennsylvania	4,195
15	New Hampshire	4,175
16	West Virginia	4,128
17	Texas	4,108
18	Oklahoma	4,088
19	Idaho	4,078
20	Oregon	4,051
21	Illinois	4,049
22	Indiana	4,042
23	Florida	4,003
24	Washington	3,975
25	South Carolina	3,943
26	Minnesota	3,932
27	Louisiana	3,931
28	Ohio	3,928
29	Montana	3,898
30	Colorado	3,891
31	Georgia	3,861
32	Maryland	3,834
33	California	3,823
33	Kentucky	3,823
35	Tennessee	3,822
36	New Mexico	3,813
37	North Carolina	3,802
38	South Dakota	3,796
39	Nebraska	3,777
40	Kansas	3,755
41	Nevada	3,752
42	Missouri	3,741
43	Virginia	3,734
44	Iowa	3,686
45	Utah	3,633
46	Arkansas	3,590
47	North Dakota	3,438
48	Alabama	3,419
49	Mississippi	3,402
50	Hawaii	3,339

District of Columbia	4,220

Source: U.S. Department of Health and Human Services, Agency for Healthcare Research and Quality
"Private-Sector Data by Firm Size and State" (Table II Series, Medical Expenditures Panel Survey)
(http://www.meps.ahrq.gov/mepsweb/survey_comp/Insurance.jsp)
*Enrolled employees at private-sector establishments that offer health insurance coverage.

Average Annual Family Coverage Health Insurance Premium per Enrolled Employee in 2005
National Average = $10,728*

ALPHA ORDER

RANK	STATE	PREMIUM
46	Alabama	$9,420
4	Alaska	11,542
37	Arizona	10,268
49	Arkansas	9,190
29	California	10,551
21	Colorado	10,850
3	Connecticut	11,717
17	Delaware	10,964
20	Florida	10,852
38	Georgia	10,262
47	Hawaii	9,392
32	Idaho	10,398
28	Illinois	10,574
23	Indiana	10,678
48	Iowa	9,359
44	Kansas	9,734
26	Kentucky	10,617
27	Louisiana	10,602
10	Maine	11,289
30	Maryland	10,528
7	Massachusetts	11,435
14	Michigan	11,005
22	Minnesota	10,846
41	Mississippi	9,987
42	Missouri	9,948
39	Montana	10,058
43	Nebraska	9,805
40	Nevada	10,011
2	New Hampshire	11,835
9	New Jersey	11,403
25	New Mexico	10,637
11	New York	11,280
45	North Carolina	9,657
50	North Dakota	8,334
24	Ohio	10,662
15	Oklahoma	10,985
19	Oregon	10,898
12	Pennsylvania	11,108
1	Rhode Island	11,924
31	South Carolina	10,436
34	South Dakota	10,312
33	Tennessee	10,361
5	Texas	11,533
36	Utah	10,282
8	Vermont	11,420
35	Virginia	10,292
13	Washington	11,018
18	West Virginia	10,900
16	Wisconsin	10,983
6	Wyoming	11,467

RANK ORDER

RANK	STATE	PREMIUM
1	Rhode Island	$11,924
2	New Hampshire	11,835
3	Connecticut	11,717
4	Alaska	11,542
5	Texas	11,533
6	Wyoming	11,467
7	Massachusetts	11,435
8	Vermont	11,420
9	New Jersey	11,403
10	Maine	11,289
11	New York	11,280
12	Pennsylvania	11,108
13	Washington	11,018
14	Michigan	11,005
15	Oklahoma	10,985
16	Wisconsin	10,983
17	Delaware	10,964
18	West Virginia	10,900
19	Oregon	10,898
20	Florida	10,852
21	Colorado	10,850
22	Minnesota	10,846
23	Indiana	10,678
24	Ohio	10,662
25	New Mexico	10,637
26	Kentucky	10,617
27	Louisiana	10,602
28	Illinois	10,574
29	California	10,551
30	Maryland	10,528
31	South Carolina	10,436
32	Idaho	10,398
33	Tennessee	10,361
34	South Dakota	10,312
35	Virginia	10,292
36	Utah	10,282
37	Arizona	10,268
38	Georgia	10,262
39	Montana	10,058
40	Nevada	10,011
41	Mississippi	9,987
42	Missouri	9,948
43	Nebraska	9,805
44	Kansas	9,734
45	North Carolina	9,657
46	Alabama	9,420
47	Hawaii	9,392
48	Iowa	9,359
49	Arkansas	9,190
50	North Dakota	8,334
	District of Columbia	11,623

Source: U.S. Department of Health and Human Services, Agency for Healthcare Research and Quality
"Private-Sector Data by Firm Size and State" (Table II Series, Medical Expenditures Panel Survey)
(http://www.meps.ahrq.gov/mepsweb/survey_comp/Insurance.jsp)
*Enrolled employees at private-sector establishments that offer health insurance coverage.

Percent of Private-Sector Establishments That Offer Health Insurance: 2005

National Percent = 56.3%

ALPHA ORDER

RANK	STATE	PERCENT
11	Alabama	59.8
47	Alaska	42.4
23	Arizona	55.0
48	Arkansas	40.8
11	California	59.8
26	Colorado	54.1
4	Connecticut	63.8
15	Delaware	57.6
33	Florida	51.2
32	Georgia	52.3
1	Hawaii	89.6
46	Idaho	43.8
28	Illinois	53.3
21	Indiana	55.9
42	Iowa	47.9
35	Kansas	50.8
16	Kentucky	57.1
31	Louisiana	52.6
22	Maine	55.6
3	Maryland	64.1
5	Massachusetts	63.3
10	Michigan	59.9
25	Minnesota	54.3
43	Mississippi	45.3
36	Missouri	50.6
49	Montana	39.2
44	Nebraska	45.2
30	Nevada	52.8
7	New Hampshire	62.0
2	New Jersey	69.3
33	New Mexico	51.2
9	New York	60.1
18	North Carolina	56.7
38	North Dakota	49.1
6	Ohio	62.8
40	Oklahoma	48.3
18	Oregon	56.7
8	Pennsylvania	61.5
13	Rhode Island	59.5
29	South Carolina	53.2
41	South Dakota	48.1
24	Tennessee	54.7
37	Texas	50.1
45	Utah	44.1
17	Vermont	56.8
18	Virginia	56.7
27	Washington	53.8
39	West Virginia	48.8
14	Wisconsin	59.3
50	Wyoming	38.6

RANK ORDER

RANK	STATE	PERCENT
1	Hawaii	89.6
2	New Jersey	69.3
3	Maryland	64.1
4	Connecticut	63.8
5	Massachusetts	63.3
6	Ohio	62.8
7	New Hampshire	62.0
8	Pennsylvania	61.5
9	New York	60.1
10	Michigan	59.9
11	Alabama	59.8
11	California	59.8
13	Rhode Island	59.5
14	Wisconsin	59.3
15	Delaware	57.6
16	Kentucky	57.1
17	Vermont	56.8
18	North Carolina	56.7
18	Oregon	56.7
18	Virginia	56.7
21	Indiana	55.9
22	Maine	55.6
23	Arizona	55.0
24	Tennessee	54.7
25	Minnesota	54.3
26	Colorado	54.1
27	Washington	53.8
28	Illinois	53.3
29	South Carolina	53.2
30	Nevada	52.8
31	Louisiana	52.6
32	Georgia	52.3
33	Florida	51.2
33	New Mexico	51.2
35	Kansas	50.8
36	Missouri	50.6
37	Texas	50.1
38	North Dakota	49.1
39	West Virginia	48.8
40	Oklahoma	48.3
41	South Dakota	48.1
42	Iowa	47.9
43	Mississippi	45.3
44	Nebraska	45.2
45	Utah	44.1
46	Idaho	43.8
47	Alaska	42.4
48	Arkansas	40.8
49	Montana	39.2
50	Wyoming	38.6

District of Columbia	74.3

Source: U.S. Department of Health and Human Services, Agency for Healthcare Research and Quality
"Private-Sector Data by Firm Size and State" (Table II Series, Medical Expenditures Panel Survey)
(http://www.meps.ahrq.gov/mepsweb/survey_comp/Insurance.jsp)

Persons Not Covered by Health Insurance in 2006

National Total = 46,995,000 Uninsured

ALPHA ORDER

RANK	STATE	UNINSURED	% of USA
21	Alabama	689,000	1.5%
44	Alaska	109,000	0.2%
9	Arizona	1,311,000	2.8%
28	Arkansas	521,000	1.1%
1	California	6,791,000	14.5%
15	Colorado	826,000	1.8%
35	Connecticut	325,000	0.7%
45	Delaware	105,000	0.2%
3	Florida	3,828,000	8.1%
6	Georgia	1,659,000	3.5%
43	Hawaii	110,000	0.2%
38	Idaho	227,000	0.5%
5	Illinois	1,776,000	3.8%
19	Indiana	748,000	1.6%
36	Iowa	307,000	0.7%
34	Kansas	335,000	0.7%
26	Kentucky	639,000	1.4%
14	Louisiana	921,000	2.0%
42	Maine	122,000	0.3%
17	Maryland	776,000	1.7%
25	Massachusetts	657,000	1.4%
12	Michigan	1,043,000	2.2%
31	Minnesota	475,000	1.0%
27	Mississippi	600,000	1.3%
18	Missouri	772,000	1.6%
40	Montana	160,000	0.3%
39	Nebraska	217,000	0.5%
29	Nevada	496,000	1.1%
41	New Hampshire	150,000	0.3%
8	New Jersey	1,341,000	2.9%
32	New Mexico	445,000	0.9%
4	New York	2,662,000	5.7%
7	North Carolina	1,585,000	3.4%
48	North Dakota	75,000	0.2%
11	Ohio	1,138,000	2.4%
24	Oklahoma	661,000	1.4%
23	Oregon	665,000	1.4%
10	Pennsylvania	1,237,000	2.6%
46	Rhode Island	91,000	0.2%
22	South Carolina	672,000	1.4%
46	South Dakota	91,000	0.2%
16	Tennessee	809,000	1.7%
2	Texas	5,704,000	12.1%
33	Utah	442,000	0.9%
50	Vermont	63,000	0.1%
13	Virginia	1,006,000	2.1%
20	Washington	746,000	1.6%
37	West Virginia	245,000	0.5%
30	Wisconsin	481,000	1.0%
48	Wyoming	75,000	0.2%

RANK ORDER

RANK	STATE	UNINSURED	% of USA
1	California	6,791,000	14.5%
2	Texas	5,704,000	12.1%
3	Florida	3,828,000	8.1%
4	New York	2,662,000	5.7%
5	Illinois	1,776,000	3.8%
6	Georgia	1,659,000	3.5%
7	North Carolina	1,585,000	3.4%
8	New Jersey	1,341,000	2.9%
9	Arizona	1,311,000	2.8%
10	Pennsylvania	1,237,000	2.6%
11	Ohio	1,138,000	2.4%
12	Michigan	1,043,000	2.2%
13	Virginia	1,006,000	2.1%
14	Louisiana	921,000	2.0%
15	Colorado	826,000	1.8%
16	Tennessee	809,000	1.7%
17	Maryland	776,000	1.7%
18	Missouri	772,000	1.6%
19	Indiana	748,000	1.6%
20	Washington	746,000	1.6%
21	Alabama	689,000	1.5%
22	South Carolina	672,000	1.4%
23	Oregon	665,000	1.4%
24	Oklahoma	661,000	1.4%
25	Massachusetts	657,000	1.4%
26	Kentucky	639,000	1.4%
27	Mississippi	600,000	1.3%
28	Arkansas	521,000	1.1%
29	Nevada	496,000	1.1%
30	Wisconsin	481,000	1.0%
31	Minnesota	475,000	1.0%
32	New Mexico	445,000	0.9%
33	Utah	442,000	0.9%
34	Kansas	335,000	0.7%
35	Connecticut	325,000	0.7%
36	Iowa	307,000	0.7%
37	West Virginia	245,000	0.5%
38	Idaho	227,000	0.5%
39	Nebraska	217,000	0.5%
40	Montana	160,000	0.3%
41	New Hampshire	150,000	0.3%
42	Maine	122,000	0.3%
43	Hawaii	110,000	0.2%
44	Alaska	109,000	0.2%
45	Delaware	105,000	0.2%
46	Rhode Island	91,000	0.2%
46	South Dakota	91,000	0.2%
48	North Dakota	75,000	0.2%
48	Wyoming	75,000	0.2%
50	Vermont	63,000	0.1%
	District of Columbia	66,000	0.1%

Source: U.S. Bureau of the Census
"Health Insurance Coverage Status by State for All People: 2006" (http://www.census.gov/hhes/www/hlthins/hlthin06.html)

Percent of Population Not Covered by Health Insurance in 2006

National Percent = 15.3% of Population*

ALPHA ORDER

RANK	STATE	PERCENT
22	Alabama	14.1
13	Alaska	16.7
4	Arizona	19.0
11	Arkansas	17.5
6	California	18.5
14	Colorado	16.6
41	Connecticut	10.4
31	Delaware	12.5
3	Florida	20.3
10	Georgia	17.6
49	Hawaii	8.6
20	Idaho	14.9
25	Illinois	13.6
30	Indiana	13.1
48	Iowa	9.3
35	Kansas	11.1
24	Kentucky	13.8
6	Louisiana	18.5
46	Maine	9.5
26	Maryland	13.5
43	Massachusetts	10.3
40	Michigan	10.6
50	Minnesota	8.5
9	Mississippi	18.1
33	Missouri	12.3
12	Montana	17.0
35	Nebraska	11.1
8	Nevada	18.3
41	New Hampshire	10.4
21	New Jersey	14.6
2	New Mexico	21.0
28	New York	13.2
16	North Carolina	16.0
35	North Dakota	11.1
39	Ohio	10.7
5	Oklahoma	18.7
14	Oregon	16.6
44	Pennsylvania	10.2
44	Rhode Island	10.2
16	South Carolina	16.0
34	South Dakota	11.6
27	Tennessee	13.4
1	Texas	24.1
18	Utah	15.7
38	Vermont	10.8
28	Virginia	13.2
31	Washington	12.5
19	West Virginia	15.5
47	Wisconsin	9.4
23	Wyoming	14.0

RANK ORDER

RANK	STATE	PERCENT
1	Texas	24.1
2	New Mexico	21.0
3	Florida	20.3
4	Arizona	19.0
5	Oklahoma	18.7
6	California	18.5
6	Louisiana	18.5
8	Nevada	18.3
9	Mississippi	18.1
10	Georgia	17.6
11	Arkansas	17.5
12	Montana	17.0
13	Alaska	16.7
14	Colorado	16.6
14	Oregon	16.6
16	North Carolina	16.0
16	South Carolina	16.0
18	Utah	15.7
19	West Virginia	15.5
20	Idaho	14.9
21	New Jersey	14.6
22	Alabama	14.1
23	Wyoming	14.0
24	Kentucky	13.8
25	Illinois	13.6
26	Maryland	13.5
27	Tennessee	13.4
28	New York	13.2
28	Virginia	13.2
30	Indiana	13.1
31	Delaware	12.5
31	Washington	12.5
33	Missouri	12.3
34	South Dakota	11.6
35	Kansas	11.1
35	Nebraska	11.1
35	North Dakota	11.1
38	Vermont	10.8
39	Ohio	10.7
40	Michigan	10.6
41	Connecticut	10.4
41	New Hampshire	10.4
43	Massachusetts	10.3
44	Pennsylvania	10.2
44	Rhode Island	10.2
46	Maine	9.5
47	Wisconsin	9.4
48	Iowa	9.3
49	Hawaii	8.6
50	Minnesota	8.5
	District of Columbia	12.4

Source: U.S. Bureau of the Census
"Health Insurance Coverage Status by State for All People: 2006" (http://www.census.gov/hhes/www/hlthins/hlthin06.html)
*Three-year average for 2004 through 2006.

Percent of Population Lacking Access to Primary Care in 2007

National Percent = 11.1% of Population*

ALPHA ORDER

RANK	STATE	PERCENT
5	Alabama	22.0
25	Alaska	10.6
18	Arizona	13.1
28	Arkansas	9.8
32	California	8.9
30	Colorado	9.4
34	Connecticut	8.5
17	Delaware	13.2
12	Florida	14.9
14	Georgia	14.4
48	Hawaii	3.6
10	Idaho	16.9
11	Illinois	15.7
35	Indiana	8.1
36	Iowa	7.7
26	Kansas	10.3
22	Kentucky	11.3
1	Louisiana	35.8
41	Maine	5.9
47	Maryland	4.8
39	Massachusetts	6.3
23	Michigan	11.0
43	Minnesota	5.5
2	Mississippi	31.7
9	Missouri	19.6
8	Montana	20.2
46	Nebraska	5.1
15	Nevada	14.3
45	New Hampshire	5.3
50	New Jersey	2.2
3	New Mexico	30.0
24	New York	10.9
43	North Carolina	5.5
6	North Dakota	20.9
37	Ohio	6.7
13	Oklahoma	14.7
38	Oregon	6.4
42	Pennsylvania	5.8
39	Rhode Island	6.3
15	South Carolina	14.3
4	South Dakota	24.5
19	Tennessee	12.1
19	Texas	12.1
21	Utah	11.4
49	Vermont	2.7
33	Virginia	8.6
31	Washington	9.1
27	West Virginia	10.1
29	Wisconsin	9.6
7	Wyoming	20.5

RANK ORDER

RANK	STATE	PERCENT
1	Louisiana	35.8
2	Mississippi	31.7
3	New Mexico	30.0
4	South Dakota	24.5
5	Alabama	22.0
6	North Dakota	20.9
7	Wyoming	20.5
8	Montana	20.2
9	Missouri	19.6
10	Idaho	16.9
11	Illinois	15.7
12	Florida	14.9
13	Oklahoma	14.7
14	Georgia	14.4
15	Nevada	14.3
15	South Carolina	14.3
17	Delaware	13.2
18	Arizona	13.1
19	Tennessee	12.1
19	Texas	12.1
21	Utah	11.4
22	Kentucky	11.3
23	Michigan	11.0
24	New York	10.9
25	Alaska	10.6
26	Kansas	10.3
27	West Virginia	10.1
28	Arkansas	9.8
29	Wisconsin	9.6
30	Colorado	9.4
31	Washington	9.1
32	California	8.9
33	Virginia	8.6
34	Connecticut	8.5
35	Indiana	8.1
36	Iowa	7.7
37	Ohio	6.7
38	Oregon	6.4
39	Massachusetts	6.3
39	Rhode Island	6.3
41	Maine	5.9
42	Pennsylvania	5.8
43	Minnesota	5.5
43	North Carolina	5.5
45	New Hampshire	5.3
46	Nebraska	5.1
47	Maryland	4.8
48	Hawaii	3.6
49	Vermont	2.7
50	New Jersey	2.2

District of Columbia 25.7

Source: CQ Press using data from U.S. Dept. of Health and Human Services, Div. of Shortage Designation
   "Selected Statistics on Health Professional Shortage Areas" (as of June 30, 2007)
*Percent of population considered under-served by primary medical practitioners (Family and General Practice doctors, Internists, Ob/Gyns, and Pediatricians). An under-served population does not have primary medical care within reasonable economic and geographic bounds.

Physicians in 2006

National Total = 908,065 Physicians*

ALPHA ORDER					RANK ORDER			
RANK	STATE	PHYSICIANS	% of USA		RANK	STATE	PHYSICIANS	% of USA
27	Alabama	10,994	1.2%		1	California	110,406	12.2%
49	Alaska	1,697	0.2%		2	New York	83,826	9.2%
21	Arizona	15,127	1.7%		3	Texas	54,971	6.1%
31	Arkansas	6,464	0.7%		4	Florida	53,566	5.9%
1	California	110,406	12.2%		5	Pennsylvania	42,204	4.6%
23	Colorado	14,175	1.6%		6	Illinois	39,240	4.3%
22	Connecticut	14,488	1.6%		7	Ohio	34,091	3.8%
46	Delaware	2,414	0.3%		8	Massachusetts	32,575	3.6%
4	Florida	53,566	5.9%		9	New Jersey	30,183	3.3%
14	Georgia	22,805	2.5%		10	Michigan	27,877	3.1%
39	Hawaii	4,599	0.5%		11	Maryland	25,969	2.9%
43	Idaho	2,934	0.3%		12	North Carolina	25,385	2.8%
6	Illinois	39,240	4.3%		13	Virginia	23,545	2.6%
20	Indiana	15,229	1.7%		14	Georgia	22,805	2.5%
32	Iowa	6,428	0.7%		15	Washington	19,864	2.2%
30	Kansas	7,079	0.8%		16	Tennessee	17,791	2.0%
28	Kentucky	10,828	1.2%		17	Minnesota	16,756	1.8%
24	Louisiana	12,643	1.4%		18	Wisconsin	16,154	1.8%
41	Maine	4,197	0.5%		19	Missouri	15,586	1.7%
11	Maryland	25,969	2.9%		20	Indiana	15,229	1.7%
8	Massachusetts	32,575	3.6%		21	Arizona	15,127	1.7%
10	Michigan	27,877	3.1%		22	Connecticut	14,488	1.6%
17	Minnesota	16,756	1.8%		23	Colorado	14,175	1.6%
34	Mississippi	5,890	0.6%		24	Louisiana	12,643	1.4%
19	Missouri	15,586	1.7%		25	Oregon	11,741	1.3%
45	Montana	2,548	0.3%		26	South Carolina	11,241	1.2%
37	Nebraska	4,852	0.5%		27	Alabama	10,994	1.2%
36	Nevada	5,384	0.6%		28	Kentucky	10,828	1.2%
42	New Hampshire	4,079	0.4%		29	Oklahoma	7,111	0.8%
9	New Jersey	30,183	3.3%		30	Kansas	7,079	0.8%
35	New Mexico	5,424	0.6%		31	Arkansas	6,464	0.7%
2	New York	83,826	9.2%		32	Iowa	6,428	0.7%
12	North Carolina	25,385	2.8%		33	Utah	6,093	0.7%
48	North Dakota	1,745	0.2%		34	Mississippi	5,890	0.6%
7	Ohio	34,091	3.8%		35	New Mexico	5,424	0.6%
29	Oklahoma	7,111	0.8%		36	Nevada	5,384	0.6%
25	Oregon	11,741	1.3%		37	Nebraska	4,852	0.5%
5	Pennsylvania	42,204	4.6%		38	West Virginia	4,710	0.5%
40	Rhode Island	4,368	0.5%		39	Hawaii	4,599	0.5%
26	South Carolina	11,241	1.2%		40	Rhode Island	4,368	0.5%
47	South Dakota	1,975	0.2%		41	Maine	4,197	0.5%
16	Tennessee	17,791	2.0%		42	New Hampshire	4,079	0.4%
3	Texas	54,971	6.1%		43	Idaho	2,934	0.3%
33	Utah	6,093	0.7%		44	Vermont	2,659	0.3%
44	Vermont	2,659	0.3%		45	Montana	2,548	0.3%
13	Virginia	23,545	2.6%		46	Delaware	2,414	0.3%
15	Washington	19,864	2.2%		47	South Dakota	1,975	0.2%
38	West Virginia	4,710	0.5%		48	North Dakota	1,745	0.2%
18	Wisconsin	16,154	1.8%		49	Alaska	1,697	0.2%
50	Wyoming	1,132	0.1%		50	Wyoming	1,132	0.1%
						District of Columbia	5,023	0.6%

Source: American Medical Association (Chicago, Illinois)
    "Physician Characteristics and Distribution in the U.S." (2008 Edition)
*As of December 31, 2006. Total does not include 13,839 physicians in the U.S. territories and possessions, at APO's and FPO's or whose addresses are unknown.

Rate of Physicians in 2006

National Rate = 304 Physicians per 100,000 Population*

ALPHA ORDER

RANK	STATE	RATE
41	Alabama	240
36	Alaska	250
38	Arizona	245
44	Arkansas	230
17	California	305
19	Colorado	297
5	Connecticut	414
25	Delaware	283
19	Florida	297
39	Georgia	244
7	Hawaii	360
49	Idaho	200
16	Illinois	307
40	Indiana	242
46	Iowa	216
35	Kansas	257
34	Kentucky	258
18	Louisiana	298
11	Maine	319
2	Maryland	464
1	Massachusetts	506
27	Michigan	276
10	Minnesota	325
48	Mississippi	203
31	Missouri	267
30	Montana	269
28	Nebraska	275
46	Nevada	216
14	New Hampshire	311
8	New Jersey	348
26	New Mexico	279
3	New York	435
24	North Carolina	286
29	North Dakota	274
19	Ohio	297
50	Oklahoma	199
12	Oregon	318
9	Pennsylvania	340
6	Rhode Island	411
32	South Carolina	260
36	South Dakota	250
22	Tennessee	293
43	Texas	235
42	Utah	236
4	Vermont	428
15	Virginia	308
13	Washington	312
32	West Virginia	260
23	Wisconsin	290
45	Wyoming	221

RANK ORDER

RANK	STATE	RATE
1	Massachusetts	506
2	Maryland	464
3	New York	435
4	Vermont	428
5	Connecticut	414
6	Rhode Island	411
7	Hawaii	360
8	New Jersey	348
9	Pennsylvania	340
10	Minnesota	325
11	Maine	319
12	Oregon	318
13	Washington	312
14	New Hampshire	311
15	Virginia	308
16	Illinois	307
17	California	305
18	Louisiana	298
19	Colorado	297
19	Florida	297
19	Ohio	297
22	Tennessee	293
23	Wisconsin	290
24	North Carolina	286
25	Delaware	283
26	New Mexico	279
27	Michigan	276
28	Nebraska	275
29	North Dakota	274
30	Montana	269
31	Missouri	267
32	South Carolina	260
32	West Virginia	260
34	Kentucky	258
35	Kansas	257
36	Alaska	250
36	South Dakota	250
38	Arizona	245
39	Georgia	244
40	Indiana	242
41	Alabama	240
42	Utah	236
43	Texas	235
44	Arkansas	230
45	Wyoming	221
46	Iowa	216
46	Nevada	216
48	Mississippi	203
49	Idaho	200
50	Oklahoma	199

District of Columbia 858

Source: CQ Press using data from American Medical Association (Chicago, Illinois)
"Physician Characteristics and Distribution in the U.S." (2008 Edition)
*As of December 31, 2006. National rate does not include physicians in the U.S. territories and possessions, at APO's and FPO's or whose addresses are unknown.

Rate of Registered Nurses in 2006

National Rate = 809 Nurses per 100,000 Population*

ALPHA ORDER

RANK	STATE	RATE
19	Alabama	872
33	Alaska	776
50	Arizona	517
38	Arkansas	748
45	California	646
40	Colorado	724
8	Connecticut	993
16	Delaware	918
30	Florida	810
44	Georgia	651
37	Hawaii	752
47	Idaho	622
31	Illinois	807
28	Indiana	839
4	Iowa	1,044
23	Kansas	856
17	Kentucky	907
18	Louisiana	894
5	Maine	1,041
26	Maryland	849
2	Massachusetts	1,187
27	Michigan	840
10	Minnesota	962
22	Mississippi	866
12	Missouri	950
34	Montana	770
11	Nebraska	955
49	Nevada	564
13	New Hampshire	948
15	New Jersey	927
48	New Mexico	601
23	New York	856
28	North Carolina	839
3	North Dakota	1,082
9	Ohio	976
42	Oklahoma	691
35	Oregon	761
6	Pennsylvania	1,017
7	Rhode Island	994
39	South Carolina	735
1	South Dakota	1,195
21	Tennessee	869
43	Texas	669
46	Utah	640
14	Vermont	946
40	Virginia	724
36	Washington	756
25	West Virginia	850
20	Wisconsin	870
32	Wyoming	782

RANK ORDER

RANK	STATE	RATE
1	South Dakota	1,195
2	Massachusetts	1,187
3	North Dakota	1,082
4	Iowa	1,044
5	Maine	1,041
6	Pennsylvania	1,017
7	Rhode Island	994
8	Connecticut	993
9	Ohio	976
10	Minnesota	962
11	Nebraska	955
12	Missouri	950
13	New Hampshire	948
14	Vermont	946
15	New Jersey	927
16	Delaware	918
17	Kentucky	907
18	Louisiana	894
19	Alabama	872
20	Wisconsin	870
21	Tennessee	869
22	Mississippi	866
23	Kansas	856
23	New York	856
25	West Virginia	850
26	Maryland	849
27	Michigan	840
28	Indiana	839
28	North Carolina	839
30	Florida	810
31	Illinois	807
32	Wyoming	782
33	Alaska	776
34	Montana	770
35	Oregon	761
36	Washington	756
37	Hawaii	752
38	Arkansas	748
39	South Carolina	735
40	Colorado	724
40	Virginia	724
42	Oklahoma	691
43	Texas	669
44	Georgia	651
45	California	646
46	Utah	640
47	Idaho	622
48	New Mexico	601
49	Nevada	564
50	Arizona	517
	District of Columbia	1,354

Source: CQ Press using data from U.S. Department of Labor, Bureau of Labor Statistics
   "Occupational Employment and Wages, 2006" (http://www.bls.gov/oes/)
*Does not include self-employed.

Rate of Dentists in 2005

National Rate = 60 Dentists per 100,000 Population*

RANK	STATE	RATE
46	Alabama	44
8	Alaska	73
32	Arizona	50
49	Arkansas	41
6	California	74
11	Colorado	65
5	Connecticut	76
39	Delaware	47
27	Florida	52
46	Georgia	44
2	Hawaii	82
21	Idaho	57
13	Illinois	64
37	Indiana	48
25	Iowa	53
30	Kansas	51
24	Kentucky	55
40	Louisiana	46
32	Maine	50
6	Maryland	74
1	Massachusetts	83
16	Michigan	61
18	Minnesota	60
50	Mississippi	39
37	Missouri	48
21	Montana	57
14	Nebraska	63
42	Nevada	45
16	New Hampshire	61
3	New Jersey	80
46	New Mexico	44
4	New York	78
42	North Carolina	45
34	North Dakota	49
25	Ohio	53
34	Oklahoma	49
10	Oregon	68
14	Pennsylvania	63
27	Rhode Island	52
42	South Carolina	45
34	South Dakota	49
30	Tennessee	51
42	Texas	45
11	Utah	65
19	Vermont	59
20	Virginia	58
9	Washington	70
40	West Virginia	46
21	Wisconsin	57
27	Wyoming	52

RANK	STATE	RATE
1	Massachusetts	83
2	Hawaii	82
3	New Jersey	80
4	New York	78
5	Connecticut	76
6	California	74
6	Maryland	74
8	Alaska	73
9	Washington	70
10	Oregon	68
11	Colorado	65
11	Utah	65
13	Illinois	64
14	Nebraska	63
14	Pennsylvania	63
16	Michigan	61
16	New Hampshire	61
18	Minnesota	60
19	Vermont	59
20	Virginia	58
21	Idaho	57
21	Montana	57
21	Wisconsin	57
24	Kentucky	55
25	Iowa	53
25	Ohio	53
27	Florida	52
27	Rhode Island	52
27	Wyoming	52
30	Kansas	51
30	Tennessee	51
32	Arizona	50
32	Maine	50
34	North Dakota	49
34	Oklahoma	49
34	South Dakota	49
37	Indiana	48
37	Missouri	48
39	Delaware	47
40	Louisiana	46
40	West Virginia	46
42	Nevada	45
42	North Carolina	45
42	South Carolina	45
42	Texas	45
46	Alabama	44
46	Georgia	44
46	New Mexico	44
49	Arkansas	41
50	Mississippi	39

District of Columbia — 108

Source: CQ Press using data from American Dental Association
"Distribution of Dentists, by Region and State, 2005"
*Professionally active dentists. National rate includes dentists for whom state is not known. National rate does not include dentists in territories nor dentists in the Armed Forces stationed overseas.

Community Hospitals in 2006

National Total = 4,927 Hospitals*

ALPHA ORDER

RANK	STATE	HOSPITALS	% of USA
20	Alabama	109	2.2%
47	Alaska	22	0.4%
30	Arizona	66	1.3%
26	Arkansas	84	1.7%
2	California	357	7.2%
29	Colorado	73	1.5%
42	Connecticut	35	0.7%
50	Delaware	6	0.1%
3	Florida	203	4.1%
8	Georgia	147	3.0%
45	Hawaii	24	0.5%
39	Idaho	38	0.8%
5	Illinois	190	3.9%
17	Indiana	114	2.3%
16	Iowa	117	2.4%
13	Kansas	129	2.6%
21	Kentucky	104	2.1%
10	Louisiana	132	2.7%
40	Maine	37	0.8%
36	Maryland	50	1.0%
27	Massachusetts	80	1.6%
9	Michigan	142	2.9%
11	Minnesota	131	2.7%
22	Mississippi	94	1.9%
15	Missouri	119	2.4%
34	Montana	52	1.1%
25	Nebraska	85	1.7%
43	Nevada	33	0.7%
44	New Hampshire	28	0.6%
28	New Jersey	79	1.6%
41	New Mexico	36	0.7%
3	New York	203	4.1%
17	North Carolina	114	2.3%
38	North Dakota	41	0.8%
7	Ohio	171	3.5%
19	Oklahoma	112	2.3%
32	Oregon	58	1.2%
6	Pennsylvania	188	3.8%
49	Rhode Island	11	0.2%
30	South Carolina	66	1.3%
34	South Dakota	52	1.1%
12	Tennessee	130	2.6%
1	Texas	417	8.5%
37	Utah	43	0.9%
48	Vermont	14	0.3%
23	Virginia	88	1.8%
23	Washington	88	1.8%
33	West Virginia	56	1.1%
14	Wisconsin	124	2.5%
45	Wyoming	24	0.5%

RANK ORDER

RANK	STATE	HOSPITALS	% of USA
1	Texas	417	8.5%
2	California	357	7.2%
3	Florida	203	4.1%
3	New York	203	4.1%
5	Illinois	190	3.9%
6	Pennsylvania	188	3.8%
7	Ohio	171	3.5%
8	Georgia	147	3.0%
9	Michigan	142	2.9%
10	Louisiana	132	2.7%
11	Minnesota	131	2.7%
12	Tennessee	130	2.6%
13	Kansas	129	2.6%
14	Wisconsin	124	2.5%
15	Missouri	119	2.4%
16	Iowa	117	2.4%
17	Indiana	114	2.3%
17	North Carolina	114	2.3%
19	Oklahoma	112	2.3%
20	Alabama	109	2.2%
21	Kentucky	104	2.1%
22	Mississippi	94	1.9%
23	Virginia	88	1.8%
23	Washington	88	1.8%
25	Nebraska	85	1.7%
26	Arkansas	84	1.7%
27	Massachusetts	80	1.6%
28	New Jersey	79	1.6%
29	Colorado	73	1.5%
30	Arizona	66	1.3%
30	South Carolina	66	1.3%
32	Oregon	58	1.2%
33	West Virginia	56	1.1%
34	Montana	52	1.1%
34	South Dakota	52	1.1%
36	Maryland	50	1.0%
37	Utah	43	0.9%
38	North Dakota	41	0.8%
39	Idaho	38	0.8%
40	Maine	37	0.8%
41	New Mexico	36	0.7%
42	Connecticut	35	0.7%
43	Nevada	33	0.7%
44	New Hampshire	28	0.6%
45	Hawaii	24	0.5%
45	Wyoming	24	0.5%
47	Alaska	22	0.4%
48	Vermont	14	0.3%
49	Rhode Island	11	0.2%
50	Delaware	6	0.1%
	District of Columbia	11	0.2%

Source: American Hospital Association (Chicago, IL)
   "Hospital Statistics" (2008 edition)

*Community hospitals are all nonfederal, short-term, general, and special hospitals whose facilities and services are available to the public.

Rate of Community Hospitals in 2005

National Rate = 1.6 Community Hospitals per 100,000 Population*

ALPHA ORDER

RANK	STATE	RATE
18	Alabama	2.4
8	Alaska	3.2
42	Arizona	1.1
13	Arkansas	3.0
45	California	1.0
31	Colorado	1.5
45	Connecticut	1.0
50	Delaware	0.7
42	Florida	1.1
29	Georgia	1.6
24	Hawaii	1.9
15	Idaho	2.6
31	Illinois	1.5
26	Indiana	1.8
7	Iowa	3.9
5	Kansas	4.7
16	Kentucky	2.5
10	Louisiana	3.1
14	Maine	2.8
48	Maryland	0.9
40	Massachusetts	1.2
36	Michigan	1.4
16	Minnesota	2.5
8	Mississippi	3.2
23	Missouri	2.0
3	Montana	5.5
4	Nebraska	4.8
38	Nevada	1.3
21	New Hampshire	2.1
48	New Jersey	0.9
24	New Mexico	1.9
42	New York	1.1
38	North Carolina	1.3
2	North Dakota	6.4
31	Ohio	1.5
10	Oklahoma	3.1
29	Oregon	1.6
31	Pennsylvania	1.5
45	Rhode Island	1.0
31	South Carolina	1.5
1	South Dakota	6.6
21	Tennessee	2.1
26	Texas	1.8
28	Utah	1.7
19	Vermont	2.3
40	Virginia	1.2
36	Washington	1.4
10	West Virginia	3.1
20	Wisconsin	2.2
5	Wyoming	4.7

RANK ORDER

RANK	STATE	RATE
1	South Dakota	6.6
2	North Dakota	6.4
3	Montana	5.5
4	Nebraska	4.8
5	Kansas	4.7
5	Wyoming	4.7
7	Iowa	3.9
8	Alaska	3.2
8	Mississippi	3.2
10	Louisiana	3.1
10	Oklahoma	3.1
10	West Virginia	3.1
13	Arkansas	3.0
14	Maine	2.8
15	Idaho	2.6
16	Kentucky	2.5
16	Minnesota	2.5
18	Alabama	2.4
19	Vermont	2.3
20	Wisconsin	2.2
21	New Hampshire	2.1
21	Tennessee	2.1
23	Missouri	2.0
24	Hawaii	1.9
24	New Mexico	1.9
26	Indiana	1.8
26	Texas	1.8
28	Utah	1.7
29	Georgia	1.6
29	Oregon	1.6
31	Colorado	1.5
31	Illinois	1.5
31	Ohio	1.5
31	Pennsylvania	1.5
31	South Carolina	1.5
36	Michigan	1.4
36	Washington	1.4
38	Nevada	1.3
38	North Carolina	1.3
40	Massachusetts	1.2
40	Virginia	1.2
42	Arizona	1.1
42	Florida	1.1
42	New York	1.1
45	California	1.0
45	Connecticut	1.0
45	Rhode Island	1.0
48	Maryland	0.9
48	New Jersey	0.9
50	Delaware	0.7

| | District of Columbia | 1.9 |

Source: CQ Press using data from American Hospital Association (Chicago, IL)
    "Hospital Statistics" (2008 edition)
*Community hospitals are all nonfederal, short-term, general, and special hospitals whose facilities and services are available to the public.

Births in 2006

National Total = 4,265,996 Live Births*

<table>
<tr><td colspan="4">ALPHA ORDER</td><td colspan="4">RANK ORDER</td></tr>
<tr><th>RANK</th><th>STATE</th><th>BIRTHS</th><th>% of USA</th><th>RANK</th><th>STATE</th><th>BIRTHS</th><th>% of USA</th></tr>
<tr><td>24</td><td>Alabama</td><td>63,235</td><td>1.5%</td><td>1</td><td>California</td><td>562,431</td><td>13.2%</td></tr>
<tr><td>47</td><td>Alaska</td><td>10,991</td><td>0.3%</td><td>2</td><td>Texas</td><td>399,612</td><td>9.4%</td></tr>
<tr><td>13</td><td>Arizona</td><td>102,475</td><td>2.4%</td><td>3</td><td>New York</td><td>250,091</td><td>5.9%</td></tr>
<tr><td>32</td><td>Arkansas</td><td>40,973</td><td>1.0%</td><td>4</td><td>Florida</td><td>236,882</td><td>5.6%</td></tr>
<tr><td>1</td><td>California</td><td>562,431</td><td>13.2%</td><td>5</td><td>Illinois</td><td>180,583</td><td>4.2%</td></tr>
<tr><td>22</td><td>Colorado</td><td>70,750</td><td>1.7%</td><td>6</td><td>Ohio</td><td>150,590</td><td>3.5%</td></tr>
<tr><td>31</td><td>Connecticut</td><td>41,807</td><td>1.0%</td><td>7</td><td>Pennsylvania</td><td>149,082</td><td>3.5%</td></tr>
<tr><td>45</td><td>Delaware</td><td>11,988</td><td>0.3%</td><td>8</td><td>Georgia</td><td>148,619</td><td>3.5%</td></tr>
<tr><td>4</td><td>Florida</td><td>236,882</td><td>5.6%</td><td>9</td><td>North Carolina</td><td>127,841</td><td>3.0%</td></tr>
<tr><td>8</td><td>Georgia</td><td>148,619</td><td>3.5%</td><td>10</td><td>Michigan</td><td>127,476</td><td>3.0%</td></tr>
<tr><td>40</td><td>Hawaii</td><td>18,982</td><td>0.4%</td><td>11</td><td>New Jersey</td><td>115,006</td><td>2.7%</td></tr>
<tr><td>38</td><td>Idaho</td><td>24,184</td><td>0.6%</td><td>12</td><td>Virginia</td><td>107,817</td><td>2.5%</td></tr>
<tr><td>5</td><td>Illinois</td><td>180,583</td><td>4.2%</td><td>13</td><td>Arizona</td><td>102,475</td><td>2.4%</td></tr>
<tr><td>14</td><td>Indiana</td><td>88,674</td><td>2.1%</td><td>14</td><td>Indiana</td><td>88,674</td><td>2.1%</td></tr>
<tr><td>34</td><td>Iowa</td><td>40,610</td><td>1.0%</td><td>15</td><td>Washington</td><td>86,848</td><td>2.0%</td></tr>
<tr><td>33</td><td>Kansas</td><td>40,964</td><td>1.0%</td><td>16</td><td>Tennessee</td><td>84,345</td><td>2.0%</td></tr>
<tr><td>26</td><td>Kentucky</td><td>58,291</td><td>1.4%</td><td>17</td><td>Missouri</td><td>81,388</td><td>1.9%</td></tr>
<tr><td>23</td><td>Louisiana</td><td>63,399</td><td>1.5%</td><td>18</td><td>Massachusetts</td><td>77,769</td><td>1.8%</td></tr>
<tr><td>42</td><td>Maine</td><td>14,151</td><td>0.3%</td><td>19</td><td>Maryland</td><td>77,478</td><td>1.8%</td></tr>
<tr><td>19</td><td>Maryland</td><td>77,478</td><td>1.8%</td><td>20</td><td>Minnesota</td><td>73,559</td><td>1.7%</td></tr>
<tr><td>18</td><td>Massachusetts</td><td>77,769</td><td>1.8%</td><td>21</td><td>Wisconsin</td><td>72,335</td><td>1.7%</td></tr>
<tr><td>10</td><td>Michigan</td><td>127,476</td><td>3.0%</td><td>22</td><td>Colorado</td><td>70,750</td><td>1.7%</td></tr>
<tr><td>20</td><td>Minnesota</td><td>73,559</td><td>1.7%</td><td>23</td><td>Louisiana</td><td>63,399</td><td>1.5%</td></tr>
<tr><td>30</td><td>Mississippi</td><td>46,069</td><td>1.1%</td><td>24</td><td>Alabama</td><td>63,235</td><td>1.5%</td></tr>
<tr><td>17</td><td>Missouri</td><td>81,388</td><td>1.9%</td><td>25</td><td>South Carolina</td><td>62,271</td><td>1.5%</td></tr>
<tr><td>43</td><td>Montana</td><td>12,506</td><td>0.3%</td><td>26</td><td>Kentucky</td><td>58,291</td><td>1.4%</td></tr>
<tr><td>37</td><td>Nebraska</td><td>26,733</td><td>0.6%</td><td>27</td><td>Oklahoma</td><td>54,018</td><td>1.3%</td></tr>
<tr><td>35</td><td>Nevada</td><td>40,085</td><td>0.9%</td><td>28</td><td>Utah</td><td>53,499</td><td>1.3%</td></tr>
<tr><td>41</td><td>New Hampshire</td><td>14,380</td><td>0.3%</td><td>29</td><td>Oregon</td><td>48,717</td><td>1.1%</td></tr>
<tr><td>11</td><td>New Jersey</td><td>115,006</td><td>2.7%</td><td>30</td><td>Mississippi</td><td>46,069</td><td>1.1%</td></tr>
<tr><td>36</td><td>New Mexico</td><td>29,937</td><td>0.7%</td><td>31</td><td>Connecticut</td><td>41,807</td><td>1.0%</td></tr>
<tr><td>3</td><td>New York</td><td>250,091</td><td>5.9%</td><td>32</td><td>Arkansas</td><td>40,973</td><td>1.0%</td></tr>
<tr><td>9</td><td>North Carolina</td><td>127,841</td><td>3.0%</td><td>33</td><td>Kansas</td><td>40,964</td><td>1.0%</td></tr>
<tr><td>48</td><td>North Dakota</td><td>8,622</td><td>0.2%</td><td>34</td><td>Iowa</td><td>40,610</td><td>1.0%</td></tr>
<tr><td>6</td><td>Ohio</td><td>150,590</td><td>3.5%</td><td>35</td><td>Nevada</td><td>40,085</td><td>0.9%</td></tr>
<tr><td>27</td><td>Oklahoma</td><td>54,018</td><td>1.3%</td><td>36</td><td>New Mexico</td><td>29,937</td><td>0.7%</td></tr>
<tr><td>29</td><td>Oregon</td><td>48,717</td><td>1.1%</td><td>37</td><td>Nebraska</td><td>26,733</td><td>0.6%</td></tr>
<tr><td>7</td><td>Pennsylvania</td><td>149,082</td><td>3.5%</td><td>38</td><td>Idaho</td><td>24,184</td><td>0.6%</td></tr>
<tr><td>44</td><td>Rhode Island</td><td>12,379</td><td>0.3%</td><td>39</td><td>West Virginia</td><td>20,928</td><td>0.5%</td></tr>
<tr><td>25</td><td>South Carolina</td><td>62,271</td><td>1.5%</td><td>40</td><td>Hawaii</td><td>18,982</td><td>0.4%</td></tr>
<tr><td>46</td><td>South Dakota</td><td>11,917</td><td>0.3%</td><td>41</td><td>New Hampshire</td><td>14,380</td><td>0.3%</td></tr>
<tr><td>16</td><td>Tennessee</td><td>84,345</td><td>2.0%</td><td>42</td><td>Maine</td><td>14,151</td><td>0.3%</td></tr>
<tr><td>2</td><td>Texas</td><td>399,612</td><td>9.4%</td><td>43</td><td>Montana</td><td>12,506</td><td>0.3%</td></tr>
<tr><td>28</td><td>Utah</td><td>53,499</td><td>1.3%</td><td>44</td><td>Rhode Island</td><td>12,379</td><td>0.3%</td></tr>
<tr><td>50</td><td>Vermont</td><td>6,509</td><td>0.2%</td><td>45</td><td>Delaware</td><td>11,988</td><td>0.3%</td></tr>
<tr><td>12</td><td>Virginia</td><td>107,817</td><td>2.5%</td><td>46</td><td>South Dakota</td><td>11,917</td><td>0.3%</td></tr>
<tr><td>15</td><td>Washington</td><td>86,848</td><td>2.0%</td><td>47</td><td>Alaska</td><td>10,991</td><td>0.3%</td></tr>
<tr><td>39</td><td>West Virginia</td><td>20,928</td><td>0.5%</td><td>48</td><td>North Dakota</td><td>8,622</td><td>0.2%</td></tr>
<tr><td>21</td><td>Wisconsin</td><td>72,335</td><td>1.7%</td><td>49</td><td>Wyoming</td><td>7,670</td><td>0.2%</td></tr>
<tr><td>49</td><td>Wyoming</td><td>7,670</td><td>0.2%</td><td>50</td><td>Vermont</td><td>6,509</td><td>0.2%</td></tr>
<tr><td></td><td></td><td></td><td></td><td></td><td>District of Columbia</td><td>8,529</td><td>0.2%</td></tr>
</table>

Source: U.S. Department of Health and Human Services, National Center for Health Statistics
     "National Vital Statistics Reports" (Vol. 56, No. 7, December 5, 2007, http://www.cdc.gov/nchs/births.htm)
*Preliminary data by state of residence.

Birth Rate in 2006

National Rate = 14.2 Live Births per 1,000 Population*

ALPHA ORDER

RANK	STATE	RATE
31	Alabama	13.7
5	Alaska	16.4
3	Arizona	16.6
19	Arkansas	14.6
9	California	15.4
14	Colorado	14.9
45	Connecticut	11.9
25	Delaware	14.0
38	Florida	13.1
7	Georgia	15.9
16	Hawaii	14.8
4	Idaho	16.5
23	Illinois	14.1
25	Indiana	14.0
32	Iowa	13.6
16	Kansas	14.8
28	Kentucky	13.9
16	Louisiana	14.8
49	Maine	10.7
30	Maryland	13.8
43	Massachusetts	12.1
42	Michigan	12.6
22	Minnesota	14.2
8	Mississippi	15.8
28	Missouri	13.9
35	Montana	13.2
12	Nebraska	15.1
6	Nevada	16.1
48	New Hampshire	10.9
35	New Jersey	13.2
10	New Mexico	15.3
40	New York	13.0
20	North Carolina	14.4
32	North Dakota	13.6
38	Ohio	13.1
12	Oklahoma	15.1
35	Oregon	13.2
44	Pennsylvania	12.0
46	Rhode Island	11.6
20	South Carolina	14.4
11	South Dakota	15.2
25	Tennessee	14.0
2	Texas	17.0
1	Utah	21.0
50	Vermont	10.4
23	Virginia	14.1
32	Washington	13.6
47	West Virginia	11.5
40	Wisconsin	13.0
14	Wyoming	14.9

RANK ORDER

RANK	STATE	RATE
1	Utah	21.0
2	Texas	17.0
3	Arizona	16.6
4	Idaho	16.5
5	Alaska	16.4
6	Nevada	16.1
7	Georgia	15.9
8	Mississippi	15.8
9	California	15.4
10	New Mexico	15.3
11	South Dakota	15.2
12	Nebraska	15.1
12	Oklahoma	15.1
14	Colorado	14.9
14	Wyoming	14.9
16	Hawaii	14.8
16	Kansas	14.8
16	Louisiana	14.8
19	Arkansas	14.6
20	North Carolina	14.4
20	South Carolina	14.4
22	Minnesota	14.2
23	Illinois	14.1
23	Virginia	14.1
25	Delaware	14.0
25	Indiana	14.0
25	Tennessee	14.0
28	Kentucky	13.9
28	Missouri	13.9
30	Maryland	13.8
31	Alabama	13.7
32	Iowa	13.6
32	North Dakota	13.6
32	Washington	13.6
35	Montana	13.2
35	New Jersey	13.2
35	Oregon	13.2
38	Florida	13.1
38	Ohio	13.1
40	New York	13.0
40	Wisconsin	13.0
42	Michigan	12.6
43	Massachusetts	12.1
44	Pennsylvania	12.0
45	Connecticut	11.9
46	Rhode Island	11.6
47	West Virginia	11.5
48	New Hampshire	10.9
49	Maine	10.7
50	Vermont	10.4

District of Columbia	14.7

Source: U.S. Department of Health and Human Services, National Center for Health Statistics
"National Vital Statistics Reports" (Vol. 56, No. 7, December 5, 2007, http://www.cdc.gov/nchs/births.htm)
*Preliminary data by state of residence.

Births of Low Birthweight as a Percent of All Births in 2006

National Percent = 8.3% of Live Births*

ALPHA ORDER			RANK ORDER		
RANK	STATE	PERCENT	RANK	STATE	PERCENT
3	Alabama	10.5	1	Mississippi	12.4
50	Alaska	6.0	2	Louisiana	11.3
35	Arizona	7.1	3	Alabama	10.5
10	Arkansas	9.2	4	South Carolina	10.1
44	California	6.8	5	West Virginia	9.7
13	Colorado	8.9	6	Georgia	9.6
28	Connecticut	8.1	6	Tennessee	9.6
9	Delaware	9.3	8	Maryland	9.4
17	Florida	8.7	9	Delaware	9.3
6	Georgia	9.6	10	Arkansas	9.2
28	Hawaii	8.1	11	Kentucky	9.1
38	Idaho	6.9	11	North Carolina	9.1
18	Illinois	8.6	13	Colorado	8.9
27	Indiana	8.2	13	New Mexico	8.9
38	Iowa	6.9	13	Wyoming	8.9
34	Kansas	7.2	16	Ohio	8.8
11	Kentucky	9.1	17	Florida	8.7
2	Louisiana	11.3	18	Illinois	8.6
44	Maine	6.8	18	New Jersey	8.6
8	Maryland	9.4	20	Pennsylvania	8.4
32	Massachusetts	7.9	20	Texas	8.4
22	Michigan	8.3	22	Michigan	8.3
47	Minnesota	6.5	22	Nevada	8.3
1	Mississippi	12.4	22	New York	8.3
28	Missouri	8.1	22	Oklahoma	8.3
33	Montana	7.3	22	Virginia	8.3
35	Nebraska	7.1	27	Indiana	8.2
22	Nevada	8.3	28	Connecticut	8.1
38	New Hampshire	6.9	28	Hawaii	8.1
18	New Jersey	8.6	28	Missouri	8.1
13	New Mexico	8.9	31	Rhode Island	8.0
22	New York	8.3	32	Massachusetts	7.9
11	North Carolina	9.1	33	Montana	7.3
46	North Dakota	6.7	34	Kansas	7.2
16	Ohio	8.8	35	Arizona	7.1
22	Oklahoma	8.3	35	Nebraska	7.1
49	Oregon	6.1	37	South Dakota	7.0
20	Pennsylvania	8.4	38	Idaho	6.9
31	Rhode Island	8.0	38	Iowa	6.9
4	South Carolina	10.1	38	New Hampshire	6.9
37	South Dakota	7.0	38	Utah	6.9
6	Tennessee	9.6	38	Vermont	6.9
20	Texas	8.4	38	Wisconsin	6.9
38	Utah	6.9	44	California	6.8
38	Vermont	6.9	44	Maine	6.8
22	Virginia	8.3	46	North Dakota	6.7
47	Washington	6.5	47	Minnesota	6.5
5	West Virginia	9.7	47	Washington	6.5
38	Wisconsin	6.9	49	Oregon	6.1
13	Wyoming	8.9	50	Alaska	6.0
				District of Columbia	11.5

Source: U.S. Department of Health and Human Services, National Center for Health Statistics
    "Births: Preliminary data for 2006" (unpublished data)
*Preliminary data by state of residence. Births of less than 2,500 grams (5 pounds 8 ounces).

Teenage Birth Rate in 2006

National Rate = 43.3 Live Births per 1,000 Women 15 to 19 Years Old*

ALPHA ORDER

RANK	STATE	RATE
9	Alabama	55.9
27	Alaska	39.9
4	Arizona	64.0
5	Arkansas	63.0
23	California	41.4
20	Colorado	44.0
47	Connecticut	23.9
17	Delaware	46.1
19	Florida	45.3
7	Georgia	57.2
27	Hawaii	39.9
26	Idaho	40.3
24	Illinois	40.9
21	Indiana	43.9
34	Iowa	34.6
22	Kansas	42.7
12	Kentucky	54.9
13	Louisiana	52.7
45	Maine	25.1
35	Maryland	34.5
48	Massachusetts	23.2
36	Michigan	34.4
43	Minnesota	28.1
1	Mississippi	71.3
18	Missouri	45.8
30	Montana	38.3
37	Nebraska	34.1
9	Nevada	55.9
50	New Hampshire	18.5
46	New Jersey	24.6
3	New Mexico	64.7
44	New York	27.6
14	North Carolina	52.1
42	North Dakota	28.6
25	Ohio	40.5
6	Oklahoma	59.6
33	Oregon	35.8
39	Pennsylvania	32.6
40	Rhode Island	32.0
8	South Carolina	56.9
29	South Dakota	39.3
11	Tennessee	55.8
2	Texas	64.9
31	Utah	37.0
49	Vermont	21.1
32	Virginia	36.4
38	Washington	33.2
16	West Virginia	46.3
41	Wisconsin	30.7
15	Wyoming	46.6

RANK ORDER

RANK	STATE	RATE
1	Mississippi	71.3
2	Texas	64.9
3	New Mexico	64.7
4	Arizona	64.0
5	Arkansas	63.0
6	Oklahoma	59.6
7	Georgia	57.2
8	South Carolina	56.9
9	Alabama	55.9
9	Nevada	55.9
11	Tennessee	55.8
12	Kentucky	54.9
13	Louisiana	52.7
14	North Carolina	52.1
15	Wyoming	46.6
16	West Virginia	46.3
17	Delaware	46.1
18	Missouri	45.8
19	Florida	45.3
20	Colorado	44.0
21	Indiana	43.9
22	Kansas	42.7
23	California	41.4
24	Illinois	40.9
25	Ohio	40.5
26	Idaho	40.3
27	Alaska	39.9
27	Hawaii	39.9
29	South Dakota	39.3
30	Montana	38.3
31	Utah	37.0
32	Virginia	36.4
33	Oregon	35.8
34	Iowa	34.6
35	Maryland	34.5
36	Michigan	34.4
37	Nebraska	34.1
38	Washington	33.2
39	Pennsylvania	32.6
40	Rhode Island	32.0
41	Wisconsin	30.7
42	North Dakota	28.6
43	Minnesota	28.1
44	New York	27.6
45	Maine	25.1
46	New Jersey	24.6
47	Connecticut	23.9
48	Massachusetts	23.2
49	Vermont	21.1
50	New Hampshire	18.5

District of Columbia   76.1

Source: CQ Press using data from U.S. Department of Health and Human Services, National Center for Health Statistics
    "Births: Preliminary data for 2006" (unpublished data)
*Preliminary data by state of residence.

Births to Unmarried Women as a Percent of All Births in 2006

National Percent = 38.5% of Live Births*

ALPHA ORDER

RANK	STATE	PERCENT
29	Alabama	36.6
28	Alaska	36.8
7	Arizona	44.0
9	Arkansas	41.8
25	California	37.6
48	Colorado	27.6
37	Connecticut	34.0
4	Delaware	45.6
6	Florida	44.5
8	Georgia	42.4
30	Hawaii	36.0
49	Idaho	24.3
21	Illinois	38.7
10	Indiana	41.4
38	Iowa	33.8
33	Kansas	35.2
32	Kentucky	35.4
3	Louisiana	49.1
26	Maine	37.1
18	Maryland	39.7
43	Massachusetts	32.2
22	Michigan	38.3
45	Minnesota	31.7
1	Mississippi	52.8
20	Missouri	39.3
30	Montana	36.0
42	Nebraska	32.3
12	Nevada	41.2
47	New Hampshire	29.4
40	New Jersey	33.0
2	New Mexico	51.2
17	New York	40.0
16	North Carolina	40.1
45	North Dakota	31.7
14	Ohio	40.5
13	Oklahoma	40.9
35	Oregon	34.3
22	Pennsylvania	38.3
14	Rhode Island	40.5
5	South Carolina	45.5
26	South Dakota	37.1
10	Tennessee	41.4
19	Texas	39.4
50	Utah	18.8
34	Vermont	34.5
38	Virginia	33.8
44	Washington	31.8
24	West Virginia	37.9
36	Wisconsin	34.1
40	Wyoming	33.0

RANK ORDER

RANK	STATE	PERCENT
1	Mississippi	52.8
2	New Mexico	51.2
3	Louisiana	49.1
4	Delaware	45.6
5	South Carolina	45.5
6	Florida	44.5
7	Arizona	44.0
8	Georgia	42.4
9	Arkansas	41.8
10	Indiana	41.4
10	Tennessee	41.4
12	Nevada	41.2
13	Oklahoma	40.9
14	Ohio	40.5
14	Rhode Island	40.5
16	North Carolina	40.1
17	New York	40.0
18	Maryland	39.7
19	Texas	39.4
20	Missouri	39.3
21	Illinois	38.7
22	Michigan	38.3
22	Pennsylvania	38.3
24	West Virginia	37.9
25	California	37.6
26	Maine	37.1
26	South Dakota	37.1
28	Alaska	36.8
29	Alabama	36.6
30	Hawaii	36.0
30	Montana	36.0
32	Kentucky	35.4
33	Kansas	35.2
34	Vermont	34.5
35	Oregon	34.3
36	Wisconsin	34.1
37	Connecticut	34.0
38	Iowa	33.8
38	Virginia	33.8
40	New Jersey	33.0
40	Wyoming	33.0
42	Nebraska	32.3
43	Massachusetts	32.2
44	Washington	31.8
45	Minnesota	31.7
45	North Dakota	31.7
47	New Hampshire	29.4
48	Colorado	27.6
49	Idaho	24.3
50	Utah	18.8
	District of Columbia	57.6

Source: U.S. Department of Health and Human Services, National Center for Health Statistics
   "Births: Preliminary data for 2006" (unpublished data)
*Preliminary data by state of residence. By race of mother.

Percent of Mothers Receiving Late or No Prenatal Care in 2005

National Percent = 3.5% of Mothers*

ALPHA ORDER				RANK ORDER		
RANK	STATE	PERCENT		RANK	STATE	PERCENT
14	Alabama	4.1		1	Nevada	8.2
5	Alaska	4.9		2	New Mexico	7.7
3	Arizona	6.2		3	Arizona	6.2
9	Arkansas	4.7		4	Oklahoma	5.5
26	California	2.7		5	Alaska	4.9
10	Colorado	4.5		5	Delaware	4.9
37	Connecticut	1.9		5	New York*	4.9
5	Delaware	4.9		8	New Jersey	4.8
NA	Florida**	NA		9	Arkansas	4.7
16	Georgia	3.8		10	Colorado	4.5
18	Hawaii	3.6		11	Maryland	4.3
NA	Idaho**	NA		11	Utah	4.3
31	Illinois	2.6		13	Indiana	4.2
13	Indiana	4.2		14	Alabama	4.1
34	Iowa	2.2		14	Oregon	4.1
NA	Kansas**	NA		16	Georgia	3.8
NA	Kentucky**	NA		16	Virginia	3.8
26	Louisiana	2.7		18	Hawaii	3.6
38	Maine	1.7		18	South Dakota	3.6
11	Maryland	4.3		20	Wyoming	3.3
34	Massachusetts	2.2		21	Michigan	3.0
21	Michigan	3.0		21	Mississippi	3.0
32	Minnesota	2.3		23	North Carolina	2.9
21	Mississippi	3.0		23	Ohio	2.9
32	Missouri	2.3		23	Wisconsin	2.9
26	Montana	2.7		26	California	2.7
NA	Nebraska**	NA		26	Louisiana	2.7
1	Nevada	8.2		26	Montana	2.7
NA	New Hampshire**	NA		26	North Dakota	2.7
8	New Jersey	4.8		26	West Virginia	2.7
2	New Mexico	7.7		31	Illinois	2.6
5	New York*	4.9		32	Minnesota	2.3
23	North Carolina	2.9		32	Missouri	2.3
26	North Dakota	2.7		34	Iowa	2.2
23	Ohio	2.9		34	Massachusetts	2.2
4	Oklahoma	5.5		34	Rhode Island	2.2
14	Oregon	4.1		37	Connecticut	1.9
NA	Pennsylvania**	NA		38	Maine	1.7
34	Rhode Island	2.2		NA	Florida**	NA
NA	South Carolina**	NA		NA	Idaho**	NA
18	South Dakota	3.6		NA	Kansas**	NA
NA	Tennessee**	NA		NA	Kentucky**	NA
NA	Texas**	NA		NA	Nebraska**	NA
11	Utah	4.3		NA	New Hampshire**	NA
NA	Vermont**	NA		NA	Pennsylvania**	NA
16	Virginia	3.8		NA	South Carolina**	NA
NA	Washington**	NA		NA	Tennessee**	NA
26	West Virginia	2.7		NA	Texas**	NA
23	Wisconsin	2.9		NA	Vermont**	NA
20	Wyoming	3.3		NA	Washington**	NA
					District of Columbia	5.1

Source: U.S. Department of Health and Human Services, National Center for Health Statistics
    "National Vital Statistics Reports" (Vol. 56, No. 6, December 5, 2007, http://www.cdc.gov/nchs/births.htm)
*Final data by state of residence. "Late" means care begun in third trimester. New York's figure is for New York City only.
**Not available. These states have implemented the 2003 Revision of the U.S. Certificate of Live Birth and their prenatal care data are not comparable with those based on the 1989 revision.

Reported Legal Abortions in 2004

Reporting States' Total = 839,226 Abortions*

ALPHA ORDER

RANK	STATE	ABORTIONS	% of USA
20	Alabama	11,370	1.4%
42	Alaska	1,937	0.2%
16	Arizona	12,690	1.5%
33	Arkansas	4,644	0.6%
NA	California**	NA	NA
19	Colorado	11,415	1.4%
17	Connecticut	12,189	1.5%
34	Delaware	4,588	0.5%
2	Florida	91,710	10.9%
9	Georgia	32,513	3.9%
39	Hawaii	3,467	0.4%
45	Idaho	963	0.1%
4	Illinois	43,537	5.2%
23	Indiana	10,514	1.3%
31	Iowa	6,022	0.7%
21	Kansas	11,357	1.4%
37	Kentucky	3,557	0.4%
22	Louisiana	11,224	1.3%
40	Maine	2,593	0.3%
24	Maryland	10,096	1.2%
13	Massachusetts	24,366	2.9%
10	Michigan	26,269	3.1%
15	Minnesota	13,791	1.6%
38	Mississippi	3,500	0.4%
27	Missouri	8,072	1.0%
41	Montana	2,256	0.3%
36	Nebraska	3,584	0.4%
26	Nevada	9,856	1.2%
NA	New Hampshire**	NA	NA
8	New Jersey	32,642	3.9%
30	New Mexico	6,070	0.7%
1	New York	126,002	15.0%
7	North Carolina	33,954	4.0%
44	North Dakota	1,357	0.2%
6	Ohio	34,242	4.1%
28	Oklahoma	6,712	0.8%
18	Oregon	11,443	1.4%
5	Pennsylvania	36,030	4.3%
32	Rhode Island	5,587	0.7%
29	South Carolina	6,565	0.8%
46	South Dakota	814	0.1%
14	Tennessee	16,400	2.0%
3	Texas	74,801	8.9%
35	Utah	3,665	0.4%
43	Vermont	1,725	0.2%
11	Virginia	26,117	3.1%
12	Washington	24,664	2.9%
NA	West Virginia**	NA	NA
25	Wisconsin	9,943	1.2%
47	Wyoming	12	0.0%

RANK ORDER

RANK	STATE	ABORTIONS	% of USA
1	New York	126,002	15.0%
2	Florida	91,710	10.9%
3	Texas	74,801	8.9%
4	Illinois	43,537	5.2%
5	Pennsylvania	36,030	4.3%
6	Ohio	34,242	4.1%
7	North Carolina	33,954	4.0%
8	New Jersey	32,642	3.9%
9	Georgia	32,513	3.9%
10	Michigan	26,269	3.1%
11	Virginia	26,117	3.1%
12	Washington	24,664	2.9%
13	Massachusetts	24,366	2.9%
14	Tennessee	16,400	2.0%
15	Minnesota	13,791	1.6%
16	Arizona	12,690	1.5%
17	Connecticut	12,189	1.5%
18	Oregon	11,443	1.4%
19	Colorado	11,415	1.4%
20	Alabama	11,370	1.4%
21	Kansas	11,357	1.4%
22	Louisiana	11,224	1.3%
23	Indiana	10,514	1.3%
24	Maryland	10,096	1.2%
25	Wisconsin	9,943	1.2%
26	Nevada	9,856	1.2%
27	Missouri	8,072	1.0%
28	Oklahoma	6,712	0.8%
29	South Carolina	6,565	0.8%
30	New Mexico	6,070	0.7%
31	Iowa	6,022	0.7%
32	Rhode Island	5,587	0.7%
33	Arkansas	4,644	0.6%
34	Delaware	4,588	0.5%
35	Utah	3,665	0.4%
36	Nebraska	3,584	0.4%
37	Kentucky	3,557	0.4%
38	Mississippi	3,500	0.4%
39	Hawaii	3,467	0.4%
40	Maine	2,593	0.3%
41	Montana	2,256	0.3%
42	Alaska	1,937	0.2%
43	Vermont	1,725	0.2%
44	North Dakota	1,357	0.2%
45	Idaho	963	0.1%
46	South Dakota	814	0.1%
47	Wyoming	12	0.0%
NA	California**	NA	NA
NA	New Hampshire**	NA	NA
NA	West Virginia**	NA	NA
	District of Columbia	2,401	0.3%

Source: U.S. Department of Health and Human Services, Centers for Disease Control and Prevention
   "Abortion Surveillance-United States, 2004" (Morbidity and Mortality Weekly Report, Vol. 56, No. SS-9, 11/23/07)
*By state of occurrence. Total is for reporting states only.
**Not reported.

Reported Legal Abortions per 1,000 Live Births in 2004

Reporting States' Ratio = 238 Abortions per 1,000 Live Births*

ALPHA ORDER

RANK	STATE	RATIO
25	Alabama	191
27	Alaska	187
35	Arizona	135
39	Arkansas	120
NA	California**	NA
30	Colorado	167
7	Connecticut	290
4	Delaware	404
3	Florida	421
17	Georgia	234
26	Hawaii	190
46	Idaho	43
16	Illinois	241
38	Indiana	121
32	Iowa	157
8	Kansas	286
45	Kentucky	64
29	Louisiana	172
28	Maine	186
35	Maryland	135
5	Massachusetts	311
21	Michigan	202
24	Minnesota	195
42	Mississippi	82
41	Missouri	104
22	Montana	196
34	Nebraska	136
11	Nevada	280
NA	New Hampshire**	NA
9	New Jersey	283
19	New Mexico	214
1	New York	504
9	North Carolina	283
31	North Dakota	166
18	Ohio	230
37	Oklahoma	131
13	Oregon	251
15	Pennsylvania	249
2	Rhode Island	442
40	South Carolina	116
43	South Dakota	72
20	Tennessee	206
22	Texas	196
43	Utah	72
12	Vermont	261
13	Virginia	251
6	Washington	302
NA	West Virginia**	NA
33	Wisconsin	142
NA	Wyoming**	NA

RANK ORDER

RANK	STATE	RATIO
1	New York	504
2	Rhode Island	442
3	Florida	421
4	Delaware	404
5	Massachusetts	311
6	Washington	302
7	Connecticut	290
8	Kansas	286
9	New Jersey	283
9	North Carolina	283
11	Nevada	280
12	Vermont	261
13	Oregon	251
13	Virginia	251
15	Pennsylvania	249
16	Illinois	241
17	Georgia	234
18	Ohio	230
19	New Mexico	214
20	Tennessee	206
21	Michigan	202
22	Montana	196
22	Texas	196
24	Minnesota	195
25	Alabama	191
26	Hawaii	190
27	Alaska	187
28	Maine	186
29	Louisiana	172
30	Colorado	167
31	North Dakota	166
32	Iowa	157
33	Wisconsin	142
34	Nebraska	136
35	Arizona	135
35	Maryland	135
37	Oklahoma	131
38	Indiana	121
39	Arkansas	120
40	South Carolina	116
41	Missouri	104
42	Mississippi	82
43	South Dakota	72
43	Utah	72
45	Kentucky	64
46	Idaho	43
NA	California**	NA
NA	New Hampshire**	NA
NA	West Virginia**	NA
NA	Wyoming**	NA

District of Columbia 303

Source: U.S. Department of Health and Human Services, Centers for Disease Control and Prevention
"Abortion Surveillance-United States, 2004" (Morbidity and Mortality Weekly Report, Vol. 56, No. SS-9, 11/23/07)
*By state of occurrence. National figure is for reporting states only.
**Not reported.

Infant Deaths in 2005

National Total = 28,440 Infant Deaths*

ALPHA ORDER

RANK	STATE	DEATHS	% of USA
18	Alabama	568	2.0%
47	Alaska	62	0.2%
14	Arizona	662	2.3%
29	Arkansas	309	1.1%
1	California	2,930	10.3%
23	Colorado	444	1.6%
32	Connecticut	243	0.9%
41	Delaware	105	0.4%
3	Florida	1,629	5.7%
7	Georgia	1,159	4.1%
40	Hawaii	116	0.4%
39	Idaho	141	0.5%
5	Illinois	1,328	4.7%
13	Indiana	698	2.5%
35	Iowa	210	0.7%
30	Kansas	294	1.0%
27	Kentucky	375	1.3%
15	Louisiana	613	2.2%
42	Maine	97	0.3%
19	Maryland	547	1.9%
26	Massachusetts	396	1.4%
10	Michigan	1,012	3.6%
28	Minnesota	362	1.3%
21	Mississippi	481	1.7%
17	Missouri	590	2.1%
45	Montana	81	0.3%
38	Nebraska	147	0.5%
34	Nevada	215	0.8%
46	New Hampshire	76	0.3%
16	New Jersey	595	2.1%
36	New Mexico	177	0.6%
4	New York	1,431	5.0%
8	North Carolina	1,083	3.8%
48	North Dakota	50	0.2%
6	Ohio	1,225	4.3%
25	Oklahoma	417	1.5%
31	Oregon	269	0.9%
9	Pennsylvania	1,061	3.7%
44	Rhode Island	82	0.3%
20	South Carolina	543	1.9%
43	South Dakota	83	0.3%
12	Tennessee	724	2.5%
2	Texas	2,537	8.9%
33	Utah	230	0.8%
50	Vermont	42	0.1%
11	Virginia	781	2.7%
24	Washington	421	1.5%
37	West Virginia	169	0.6%
22	Wisconsin	469	1.6%
49	Wyoming	49	0.2%

RANK ORDER

RANK	STATE	DEATHS	% of USA
1	California	2,930	10.3%
2	Texas	2,537	8.9%
3	Florida	1,629	5.7%
4	New York	1,431	5.0%
5	Illinois	1,328	4.7%
6	Ohio	1,225	4.3%
7	Georgia	1,159	4.1%
8	North Carolina	1,083	3.8%
9	Pennsylvania	1,061	3.7%
10	Michigan	1,012	3.6%
11	Virginia	781	2.7%
12	Tennessee	724	2.5%
13	Indiana	698	2.5%
14	Arizona	662	2.3%
15	Louisiana	613	2.2%
16	New Jersey	595	2.1%
17	Missouri	590	2.1%
18	Alabama	568	2.0%
19	Maryland	547	1.9%
20	South Carolina	543	1.9%
21	Mississippi	481	1.7%
22	Wisconsin	469	1.6%
23	Colorado	444	1.6%
24	Washington	421	1.5%
25	Oklahoma	417	1.5%
26	Massachusetts	396	1.4%
27	Kentucky	375	1.3%
28	Minnesota	362	1.3%
29	Arkansas	309	1.1%
30	Kansas	294	1.0%
31	Oregon	269	0.9%
32	Connecticut	243	0.9%
33	Utah	230	0.8%
34	Nevada	215	0.8%
35	Iowa	210	0.7%
36	New Mexico	177	0.6%
37	West Virginia	169	0.6%
38	Nebraska	147	0.5%
39	Idaho	141	0.5%
40	Hawaii	116	0.4%
41	Delaware	105	0.4%
42	Maine	97	0.3%
43	South Dakota	83	0.3%
44	Rhode Island	82	0.3%
45	Montana	81	0.3%
46	New Hampshire	76	0.3%
47	Alaska	62	0.2%
48	North Dakota	50	0.2%
49	Wyoming	49	0.2%
50	Vermont	42	0.1%
	District of Columbia	112	0.4%

Source: U.S. Department of Health and Human Services, National Center for Health Statistics
   "National Vital Statistics Reports" (Vol. 56, No. 10, January 2008, http://www.cdc.gov/nchs/deaths.htm)
*Final data. Deaths under 1 year old by state of residence.

Infant Mortality Rate in 2005

National Rate = 6.9 Infant Deaths per 1,000 Live Births*

ALPHA ORDER

RANK	STATE	RATE
3	Alabama	9.4
37	Alaska	5.9
24	Arizona	6.9
13	Arkansas	7.9
43	California	5.3
33	Colorado	6.4
39	Connecticut	5.8
5	Delaware	9.0
21	Florida	7.2
9	Georgia	8.2
31	Hawaii	6.5
34	Idaho	6.1
17	Illinois	7.4
12	Indiana	8.0
43	Iowa	5.3
17	Kansas	7.4
28	Kentucky	6.6
2	Louisiana	10.1
24	Maine	6.9
19	Maryland	7.3
46	Massachusetts	5.2
13	Michigan	7.9
48	Minnesota	5.1
1	Mississippi	11.4
15	Missouri	7.5
23	Montana	7.0
42	Nebraska	5.6
39	Nevada	5.8
43	New Hampshire	5.3
46	New Jersey	5.2
34	New Mexico	6.1
39	New York	5.8
7	North Carolina	8.8
36	North Dakota	6.0
8	Ohio	8.3
10	Oklahoma	8.1
37	Oregon	5.9
19	Pennsylvania	7.3
31	Rhode Island	6.5
3	South Carolina	9.4
21	South Dakota	7.2
6	Tennessee	8.9
28	Texas	6.6
50	Utah	4.5
27	Vermont	6.7
15	Virginia	7.5
48	Washington	5.1
10	West Virginia	8.1
28	Wisconsin	6.6
26	Wyoming	6.8

RANK ORDER

RANK	STATE	RATE
1	Mississippi	11.4
2	Louisiana	10.1
3	Alabama	9.4
3	South Carolina	9.4
5	Delaware	9.0
6	Tennessee	8.9
7	North Carolina	8.8
8	Ohio	8.3
9	Georgia	8.2
10	Oklahoma	8.1
10	West Virginia	8.1
12	Indiana	8.0
13	Arkansas	7.9
13	Michigan	7.9
15	Missouri	7.5
15	Virginia	7.5
17	Illinois	7.4
17	Kansas	7.4
19	Maryland	7.3
19	Pennsylvania	7.3
21	Florida	7.2
21	South Dakota	7.2
23	Montana	7.0
24	Arizona	6.9
24	Maine	6.9
26	Wyoming	6.8
27	Vermont	6.7
28	Kentucky	6.6
28	Texas	6.6
28	Wisconsin	6.6
31	Hawaii	6.5
31	Rhode Island	6.5
33	Colorado	6.4
34	Idaho	6.1
34	New Mexico	6.1
36	North Dakota	6.0
37	Alaska	5.9
37	Oregon	5.9
39	Connecticut	5.8
39	Nevada	5.8
39	New York	5.8
42	Nebraska	5.6
43	California	5.3
43	Iowa	5.3
43	New Hampshire	5.3
46	Massachusetts	5.2
46	New Jersey	5.2
48	Minnesota	5.1
48	Washington	5.1
50	Utah	4.5

| | District of Columbia | 14.1 |

Source: U.S. Department of Health and Human Services, National Center for Health Statistics
    "National Vital Statistics Reports" (Vol. 56, No. 10, January 2008, http://www.cdc.gov/nchs/deaths.htm)
*Final data. Deaths under 1 year old by state of residence.

Deaths in 2005

National Total = 2,447,903 Deaths*

ALPHA ORDER

ALPHA ORDER

RANK	STATE	DEATHS	% of USA
17	Alabama	47,088	1.9%
50	Alaska	3,170	0.1%
20	Arizona	45,837	1.9%
31	Arkansas	28,055	1.1%
1	California	237,079	9.7%
28	Colorado	29,628	1.2%
29	Connecticut	29,466	1.2%
45	Delaware	7,472	0.3%
2	Florida	170,787	7.0%
11	Georgia	66,735	2.7%
43	Hawaii	9,137	0.4%
40	Idaho	10,554	0.4%
7	Illinois	103,977	4.2%
14	Indiana	55,676	2.3%
32	Iowa	27,812	1.1%
33	Kansas	24,684	1.0%
23	Kentucky	40,223	1.6%
21	Louisiana	44,333	1.8%
39	Maine	12,871	0.5%
22	Maryland	43,893	1.8%
16	Massachusetts	53,872	2.2%
8	Michigan	86,868	3.5%
25	Minnesota	37,537	1.5%
30	Mississippi	29,198	1.2%
15	Missouri	54,658	2.2%
44	Montana	8,529	0.3%
37	Nebraska	14,964	0.6%
35	Nevada	19,037	0.8%
41	New Hampshire	10,194	0.4%
10	New Jersey	71,970	2.9%
36	New Mexico	14,984	0.6%
4	New York	152,427	6.2%
9	North Carolina	74,639	3.0%
47	North Dakota	5,744	0.2%
6	Ohio	109,030	4.5%
26	Oklahoma	36,181	1.5%
27	Oregon	31,099	1.3%
5	Pennsylvania	129,536	5.3%
42	Rhode Island	10,007	0.4%
24	South Carolina	38,483	1.6%
46	South Dakota	7,087	0.3%
13	Tennessee	57,270	2.3%
3	Texas	156,474	6.4%
38	Utah	13,434	0.5%
48	Vermont	5,066	0.2%
12	Virginia	57,857	2.4%
19	Washington	46,212	1.9%
34	West Virginia	20,780	0.8%
18	Wisconsin	46,709	1.9%
49	Wyoming	4,100	0.2%

RANK ORDER

RANK	STATE	DEATHS	% of USA
1	California	237,079	9.7%
2	Florida	170,787	7.0%
3	Texas	156,474	6.4%
4	New York	152,427	6.2%
5	Pennsylvania	129,536	5.3%
6	Ohio	109,030	4.5%
7	Illinois	103,977	4.2%
8	Michigan	86,868	3.5%
9	North Carolina	74,639	3.0%
10	New Jersey	71,970	2.9%
11	Georgia	66,735	2.7%
12	Virginia	57,857	2.4%
13	Tennessee	57,270	2.3%
14	Indiana	55,676	2.3%
15	Missouri	54,658	2.2%
16	Massachusetts	53,872	2.2%
17	Alabama	47,088	1.9%
18	Wisconsin	46,709	1.9%
19	Washington	46,212	1.9%
20	Arizona	45,837	1.9%
21	Louisiana	44,333	1.8%
22	Maryland	43,893	1.8%
23	Kentucky	40,223	1.6%
24	South Carolina	38,483	1.6%
25	Minnesota	37,537	1.5%
26	Oklahoma	36,181	1.5%
27	Oregon	31,099	1.3%
28	Colorado	29,628	1.2%
29	Connecticut	29,466	1.2%
30	Mississippi	29,198	1.2%
31	Arkansas	28,055	1.1%
32	Iowa	27,812	1.1%
33	Kansas	24,684	1.0%
34	West Virginia	20,780	0.8%
35	Nevada	19,037	0.8%
36	New Mexico	14,984	0.6%
37	Nebraska	14,964	0.6%
38	Utah	13,434	0.5%
39	Maine	12,871	0.5%
40	Idaho	10,554	0.4%
41	New Hampshire	10,194	0.4%
42	Rhode Island	10,007	0.4%
43	Hawaii	9,137	0.4%
44	Montana	8,529	0.3%
45	Delaware	7,472	0.3%
46	South Dakota	7,087	0.3%
47	North Dakota	5,744	0.2%
48	Vermont	5,066	0.2%
49	Wyoming	4,100	0.2%
50	Alaska	3,170	0.1%
	District of Columbia	5,483	0.2%

Source: U.S. Department of Health and Human Services, National Center for Health Statistics
"Deaths: Preliminary Data for 2005" (http://www.cdc.gov/nchs/deaths.htm)
*Preliminary data by state of residence.

Age-Adjusted Death Rate in 2005

National Rate = 798.8 Deaths per 100,000 Population*

RANK	STATE	RATE
3	Alabama	997.9
33	Alaska	750.8
29	Arizona	771.8
8	Arkansas	930.2
46	California	713.1
38	Colorado	742.8
48	Connecticut	696.0
16	Delaware	830.5
35	Florida	749.4
9	Georgia	905.8
50	Hawaii	609.1
30	Idaho	766.4
25	Illinois	798.2
14	Indiana	858.7
39	Iowa	742.0
21	Kansas	806.8
7	Kentucky	958.4
2	Louisiana	1,020.6
19	Maine	813.2
26	Maryland	796.4
44	Massachusetts	721.9
20	Michigan	812.3
49	Minnesota	683.9
1	Mississippi	1,026.9
13	Missouri	869.4
24	Montana	798.4
34	Nebraska	749.5
11	Nevada	892.3
41	New Hampshire	732.3
37	New Jersey	745.9
27	New Mexico	795.0
45	New York	718.0
12	North Carolina	876.0
47	North Dakota	699.1
15	Ohio	856.8
4	Oklahoma	980.8
28	Oregon	773.7
18	Pennsylvania	814.8
36	Rhode Island	747.3
10	South Carolina	899.1
31	South Dakota	757.0
6	Tennessee	959.9
17	Texas	828.8
42	Utah	731.3
43	Vermont	728.4
22	Virginia	801.5
40	Washington	738.2
5	West Virginia	960.4
32	Wisconsin	752.2
23	Wyoming	801.4

RANK	STATE	RATE
1	Mississippi	1,026.9
2	Louisiana	1,020.6
3	Alabama	997.9
4	Oklahoma	980.8
5	West Virginia	960.4
6	Tennessee	959.9
7	Kentucky	958.4
8	Arkansas	930.2
9	Georgia	905.8
10	South Carolina	899.1
11	Nevada	892.3
12	North Carolina	876.0
13	Missouri	869.4
14	Indiana	858.7
15	Ohio	856.8
16	Delaware	830.5
17	Texas	828.8
18	Pennsylvania	814.8
19	Maine	813.2
20	Michigan	812.3
21	Kansas	806.8
22	Virginia	801.5
23	Wyoming	801.4
24	Montana	798.4
25	Illinois	798.2
26	Maryland	796.4
27	New Mexico	795.0
28	Oregon	773.7
29	Arizona	771.8
30	Idaho	766.4
31	South Dakota	757.0
32	Wisconsin	752.2
33	Alaska	750.8
34	Nebraska	749.5
35	Florida	749.4
36	Rhode Island	747.3
37	New Jersey	745.9
38	Colorado	742.8
39	Iowa	742.0
40	Washington	738.2
41	New Hampshire	732.3
42	Utah	731.3
43	Vermont	728.4
44	Massachusetts	721.9
45	New York	718.0
46	California	713.1
47	North Dakota	699.1
48	Connecticut	696.0
49	Minnesota	683.9
50	Hawaii	609.1

	District of Columbia	971.4

Source: U.S. Department of Health and Human Services, National Center for Health Statistics
"Deaths: Preliminary Data for 2005" (http://www.cdc.gov/nchs/deaths.htm)
*Preliminary data by state of residence. Age-adjusted rates eliminate the distorting effects of the aging of the population. Rates based on the year 2000 standard population.

Estimated Deaths by Cancer in 2007

National Estimated Total = 559,650 Deaths

ALPHA ORDER

RANK	STATE	DEATHS	% of USA
21	Alabama	9,740	1.7%
50	Alaska	810	0.1%
20	Arizona	10,120	1.8%
31	Arkansas	6,240	1.1%
1	California	54,890	9.8%
29	Colorado	6,660	1.2%
28	Connecticut	6,990	1.2%
45	Delaware	1,810	0.3%
2	Florida	40,430	7.2%
11	Georgia	14,950	2.7%
43	Hawaii	2,260	0.4%
41	Idaho	2,370	0.4%
7	Illinois	23,870	4.3%
15	Indiana	12,730	2.3%
30	Iowa	6,510	1.2%
33	Kansas	5,290	0.9%
23	Kentucky	9,390	1.7%
22	Louisiana	9,550	1.7%
38	Maine	3,190	0.6%
19	Maryland	10,210	1.8%
13	Massachusetts	13,240	2.4%
8	Michigan	19,180	3.4%
24	Minnesota	9,380	1.7%
32	Mississippi	5,990	1.1%
16	Missouri	12,610	2.3%
44	Montana	1,920	0.3%
36	Nebraska	3,320	0.6%
34	Nevada	4,660	0.8%
40	New Hampshire	2,630	0.5%
9	New Jersey	17,140	3.1%
37	New Mexico	3,270	0.6%
3	New York	35,270	6.3%
10	North Carolina	16,880	3.0%
47	North Dakota	1,220	0.2%
6	Ohio	24,600	4.4%
26	Oklahoma	7,380	1.3%
27	Oregon	7,370	1.3%
5	Pennsylvania	29,140	5.2%
41	Rhode Island	2,370	0.4%
25	South Carolina	8,940	1.6%
46	South Dakota	1,600	0.3%
14	Tennessee	12,920	2.3%
4	Texas	34,170	6.1%
39	Utah	2,690	0.5%
48	Vermont	1,160	0.2%
12	Virginia	13,740	2.5%
17	Washington	11,370	2.0%
35	West Virginia	4,610	0.8%
18	Wisconsin	10,870	1.9%
49	Wyoming	980	0.2%

RANK ORDER

RANK	STATE	DEATHS	% of USA
1	California	54,890	9.8%
2	Florida	40,430	7.2%
3	New York	35,270	6.3%
4	Texas	34,170	6.1%
5	Pennsylvania	29,140	5.2%
6	Ohio	24,600	4.4%
7	Illinois	23,870	4.3%
8	Michigan	19,180	3.4%
9	New Jersey	17,140	3.1%
10	North Carolina	16,880	3.0%
11	Georgia	14,950	2.7%
12	Virginia	13,740	2.5%
13	Massachusetts	13,240	2.4%
14	Tennessee	12,920	2.3%
15	Indiana	12,730	2.3%
16	Missouri	12,610	2.3%
17	Washington	11,370	2.0%
18	Wisconsin	10,870	1.9%
19	Maryland	10,210	1.8%
20	Arizona	10,120	1.8%
21	Alabama	9,740	1.7%
22	Louisiana	9,550	1.7%
23	Kentucky	9,390	1.7%
24	Minnesota	9,380	1.7%
25	South Carolina	8,940	1.6%
26	Oklahoma	7,380	1.3%
27	Oregon	7,370	1.3%
28	Connecticut	6,990	1.2%
29	Colorado	6,660	1.2%
30	Iowa	6,510	1.2%
31	Arkansas	6,240	1.1%
32	Mississippi	5,990	1.1%
33	Kansas	5,290	0.9%
34	Nevada	4,660	0.8%
35	West Virginia	4,610	0.8%
36	Nebraska	3,320	0.6%
37	New Mexico	3,270	0.6%
38	Maine	3,190	0.6%
39	Utah	2,690	0.5%
40	New Hampshire	2,630	0.5%
41	Idaho	2,370	0.4%
41	Rhode Island	2,370	0.4%
43	Hawaii	2,260	0.4%
44	Montana	1,920	0.3%
45	Delaware	1,810	0.3%
46	South Dakota	1,600	0.3%
47	North Dakota	1,220	0.2%
48	Vermont	1,160	0.2%
49	Wyoming	980	0.2%
50	Alaska	810	0.1%
	District of Columbia	1,020	0.2%

Source: American Cancer Society
"Cancer Facts & Figures 2007" (Copyright 2007, American Cancer Society)

Estimated Death Rate by Cancer in 2007

National Estimated Rate = 186.9 Deaths per 100,000 Population*

ALPHA ORDER

RANK	STATE	RATE
14	Alabama	211.8
49	Alaska	120.9
43	Arizona	164.1
7	Arkansas	222.0
46	California	150.6
48	Colorado	140.1
23	Connecticut	199.4
13	Delaware	212.1
4	Florida	223.5
45	Georgia	159.7
41	Hawaii	175.8
44	Idaho	161.6
34	Illinois	186.0
21	Indiana	201.6
9	Iowa	218.3
28	Kansas	191.4
5	Kentucky	223.2
6	Louisiana	222.7
2	Maine	241.4
37	Maryland	181.8
18	Massachusetts	205.7
31	Michigan	190.0
38	Minnesota	181.5
17	Mississippi	205.8
10	Missouri	215.8
20	Montana	203.3
32	Nebraska	187.7
33	Nevada	186.7
22	New Hampshire	200.0
25	New Jersey	196.5
42	New Mexico	167.3
36	New York	182.7
29	North Carolina	190.6
27	North Dakota	191.9
11	Ohio	214.3
16	Oklahoma	206.2
24	Oregon	199.1
3	Pennsylvania	234.2
7	Rhode Island	222.0
15	South Carolina	206.9
19	South Dakota	204.6
12	Tennessee	213.9
47	Texas	145.4
50	Utah	105.5
35	Vermont	185.9
39	Virginia	179.8
40	Washington	177.8
1	West Virginia	253.5
26	Wisconsin	195.6
30	Wyoming	190.3

RANK ORDER

RANK	STATE	RATE
1	West Virginia	253.5
2	Maine	241.4
3	Pennsylvania	234.2
4	Florida	223.5
5	Kentucky	223.2
6	Louisiana	222.7
7	Arkansas	222.0
7	Rhode Island	222.0
9	Iowa	218.3
10	Missouri	215.8
11	Ohio	214.3
12	Tennessee	213.9
13	Delaware	212.1
14	Alabama	211.8
15	South Carolina	206.9
16	Oklahoma	206.2
17	Mississippi	205.8
18	Massachusetts	205.7
19	South Dakota	204.6
20	Montana	203.3
21	Indiana	201.6
22	New Hampshire	200.0
23	Connecticut	199.4
24	Oregon	199.1
25	New Jersey	196.5
26	Wisconsin	195.6
27	North Dakota	191.9
28	Kansas	191.4
29	North Carolina	190.6
30	Wyoming	190.3
31	Michigan	190.0
32	Nebraska	187.7
33	Nevada	186.7
34	Illinois	186.0
35	Vermont	185.9
36	New York	182.7
37	Maryland	181.8
38	Minnesota	181.5
39	Virginia	179.8
40	Washington	177.8
41	Hawaii	175.8
42	New Mexico	167.3
43	Arizona	164.1
44	Idaho	161.6
45	Georgia	159.7
46	California	150.6
47	Texas	145.4
48	Colorado	140.1
49	Alaska	120.9
50	Utah	105.5
	District of Columbia	175.4

Source: CQ Press using data from American Cancer Society
"Cancer Facts & Figures 2007" (Copyright 2007, American Cancer Society)
*Rates calculated using 2006 Census resident population estimates. Not age-adjusted.

Estimated New Cancer Cases in 2007

National Estimated Total = 1,444,920 New Cases*

ALPHA ORDER

RANK	STATE	CASES	% of USA
25	Alabama	20,590	1.4%
49	Alaska	2,500	0.2%
20	Arizona	26,270	1.8%
31	Arkansas	14,130	1.0%
1	California	151,250	10.5%
27	Colorado	19,190	1.3%
26	Connecticut	19,780	1.4%
45	Delaware	4,530	0.3%
2	Florida	106,560	7.4%
11	Georgia	35,440	2.5%
43	Hawaii	6,020	0.4%
42	Idaho	6,140	0.4%
6	Illinois	62,010	4.3%
15	Indiana	30,040	2.1%
30	Iowa	16,540	1.1%
32	Kansas	12,760	0.9%
22	Kentucky	22,850	1.6%
23	Louisiana	22,540	1.6%
37	Maine	8,340	0.6%
19	Maryland	26,390	1.8%
13	Massachusetts	34,920	2.4%
8	Michigan	54,410	3.8%
21	Minnesota	25,420	1.8%
33	Mississippi	12,470	0.9%
16	Missouri	29,930	2.1%
44	Montana	4,920	0.3%
36	Nebraska	8,720	0.6%
34	Nevada	11,030	0.8%
40	New Hampshire	7,140	0.5%
9	New Jersey	49,370	3.4%
38	New Mexico	8,030	0.6%
3	New York	100,960	7.0%
10	North Carolina	38,210	2.6%
48	North Dakota	3,340	0.2%
7	Ohio	59,220	4.1%
29	Oklahoma	17,170	1.2%
28	Oregon	18,630	1.3%
5	Pennsylvania	75,130	5.2%
41	Rhode Island	6,360	0.4%
24	South Carolina	21,370	1.5%
46	South Dakota	3,990	0.3%
17	Tennessee	28,440	2.0%
4	Texas	91,020	6.3%
39	Utah	7,660	0.5%
47	Vermont	3,500	0.2%
12	Virginia	35,090	2.4%
14	Washington	31,080	2.2%
35	West Virginia	10,490	0.7%
18	Wisconsin	28,130	1.9%
50	Wyoming	2,340	0.2%

RANK ORDER

RANK	STATE	CASES	% of USA
1	California	151,250	10.5%
2	Florida	106,560	7.4%
3	New York	100,960	7.0%
4	Texas	91,020	6.3%
5	Pennsylvania	75,130	5.2%
6	Illinois	62,010	4.3%
7	Ohio	59,220	4.1%
8	Michigan	54,410	3.8%
9	New Jersey	49,370	3.4%
10	North Carolina	38,210	2.6%
11	Georgia	35,440	2.5%
12	Virginia	35,090	2.4%
13	Massachusetts	34,920	2.4%
14	Washington	31,080	2.2%
15	Indiana	30,040	2.1%
16	Missouri	29,930	2.1%
17	Tennessee	28,440	2.0%
18	Wisconsin	28,130	1.9%
19	Maryland	26,390	1.8%
20	Arizona	26,270	1.8%
21	Minnesota	25,420	1.8%
22	Kentucky	22,850	1.6%
23	Louisiana	22,540	1.6%
24	South Carolina	21,370	1.5%
25	Alabama	20,590	1.4%
26	Connecticut	19,780	1.4%
27	Colorado	19,190	1.3%
28	Oregon	18,630	1.3%
29	Oklahoma	17,170	1.2%
30	Iowa	16,540	1.1%
31	Arkansas	14,130	1.0%
32	Kansas	12,760	0.9%
33	Mississippi	12,470	0.9%
34	Nevada	11,030	0.8%
35	West Virginia	10,490	0.7%
36	Nebraska	8,720	0.6%
37	Maine	8,340	0.6%
38	New Mexico	8,030	0.6%
39	Utah	7,660	0.5%
40	New Hampshire	7,140	0.5%
41	Rhode Island	6,360	0.4%
42	Idaho	6,140	0.4%
43	Hawaii	6,020	0.4%
44	Montana	4,920	0.3%
45	Delaware	4,530	0.3%
46	South Dakota	3,990	0.3%
47	Vermont	3,500	0.2%
48	North Dakota	3,340	0.2%
49	Alaska	2,500	0.2%
50	Wyoming	2,340	0.2%
	District of Columbia	2,540	0.2%

Source: American Cancer Society
"Cancer Facts & Figures 2007" (Copyright 2007, American Cancer Society)
*These estimates are offered as a rough guide and should not be regarded as definitive. They are calculated according to the distribution of estimated 2007 cancer deaths by state. Totals do not include basal and squamous cell skin cancers or in situ carcinomas except urinary bladder.

Estimated Rate of New Cancer Cases in 2007

National Estimated Rate = 482.6 New Cases per 100,000 Population*

ALPHA ORDER

RANK	STATE	RATE
38	Alabama	447.7
49	Alaska	373.1
42	Arizona	426.0
24	Arkansas	502.7
44	California	414.9
46	Colorado	403.7
7	Connecticut	564.4
14	Delaware	530.8
4	Florida	589.1
48	Georgia	378.5
34	Hawaii	468.3
43	Idaho	418.7
29	Illinois	483.2
31	Indiana	475.8
9	Iowa	554.6
35	Kansas	461.6
10	Kentucky	543.3
15	Louisiana	525.7
1	Maine	631.1
33	Maryland	469.9
12	Massachusetts	542.5
13	Michigan	538.9
27	Minnesota	492.0
41	Mississippi	428.4
20	Missouri	512.3
18	Montana	520.8
26	Nebraska	493.1
39	Nevada	442.0
11	New Hampshire	543.0
6	New Jersey	565.9
45	New Mexico	410.8
17	New York	522.9
40	North Carolina	431.4
16	North Dakota	525.3
19	Ohio	515.9
30	Oklahoma	479.7
23	Oregon	503.4
2	Pennsylvania	603.9
3	Rhode Island	595.7
25	South Carolina	494.5
21	South Dakota	510.3
32	Tennessee	471.0
47	Texas	387.2
50	Utah	300.4
8	Vermont	561.0
36	Virginia	459.1
28	Washington	485.9
5	West Virginia	576.9
22	Wisconsin	506.3
37	Wyoming	454.4

RANK ORDER

RANK	STATE	RATE
1	Maine	631.1
2	Pennsylvania	603.9
3	Rhode Island	595.7
4	Florida	589.1
5	West Virginia	576.9
6	New Jersey	565.9
7	Connecticut	564.4
8	Vermont	561.0
9	Iowa	554.6
10	Kentucky	543.3
11	New Hampshire	543.0
12	Massachusetts	542.5
13	Michigan	538.9
14	Delaware	530.8
15	Louisiana	525.7
16	North Dakota	525.3
17	New York	522.9
18	Montana	520.8
19	Ohio	515.9
20	Missouri	512.3
21	South Dakota	510.3
22	Wisconsin	506.3
23	Oregon	503.4
24	Arkansas	502.7
25	South Carolina	494.5
26	Nebraska	493.1
27	Minnesota	492.0
28	Washington	485.9
29	Illinois	483.2
30	Oklahoma	479.7
31	Indiana	475.8
32	Tennessee	471.0
33	Maryland	469.9
34	Hawaii	468.3
35	Kansas	461.6
36	Virginia	459.1
37	Wyoming	454.4
38	Alabama	447.7
39	Nevada	442.0
40	North Carolina	431.4
41	Mississippi	428.4
42	Arizona	426.0
43	Idaho	418.7
44	California	414.9
45	New Mexico	410.8
46	Colorado	403.7
47	Texas	387.2
48	Georgia	378.5
49	Alaska	373.1
50	Utah	300.4

District of Columbia 436.8

Source: CQ Press using data from American Cancer Society
    "Cancer Facts & Figures 2007" (Copyright 2007, American Cancer Society)
*These estimates are offered as a rough guide and should not be regarded as definitive. They are calculated according to the distribution of estimated 2007 cancer deaths by state. Totals do not include basal and squamous cell skin cancers or in situ carcinomas except urinary bladder. Rates calculated using 2006 Census resident population estimates.

Deaths by Accidents in 2004

National Total = 112,012 Deaths*

ALPHA ORDER

RANK	STATE	DEATHS	% of USA
15	Alabama	2,403	2.1%
45	Alaska	326	0.3%
12	Arizona	2,770	2.5%
29	Arkansas	1,406	1.3%
1	California	10,633	9.5%
25	Colorado	1,810	1.6%
31	Connecticut	1,261	1.1%
47	Delaware	294	0.3%
3	Florida	8,229	7.3%
9	Georgia	3,667	3.3%
44	Hawaii	390	0.3%
39	Idaho	593	0.5%
7	Illinois	4,133	3.7%
16	Indiana	2,395	2.1%
35	Iowa	1,108	1.0%
33	Kansas	1,144	1.0%
21	Kentucky	2,260	2.0%
20	Louisiana	2,300	2.1%
41	Maine	480	0.4%
28	Maryland	1,412	1.3%
30	Massachusetts	1,366	1.2%
10	Michigan	3,312	3.0%
24	Minnesota	1,867	1.7%
26	Mississippi	1,703	1.5%
13	Missouri	2,728	2.4%
40	Montana	535	0.5%
37	Nebraska	743	0.7%
36	Nevada	1,021	0.9%
42	New Hampshire	445	0.4%
18	New Jersey	2,324	2.1%
32	New Mexico	1,223	1.1%
5	New York	4,530	4.0%
8	North Carolina	4,019	3.6%
48	North Dakota	274	0.2%
6	Ohio	4,234	3.8%
23	Oklahoma	1,947	1.7%
27	Oregon	1,444	1.3%
4	Pennsylvania	5,200	4.6%
46	Rhode Island	298	0.3%
22	South Carolina	2,094	1.9%
43	South Dakota	416	0.4%
11	Tennessee	3,156	2.8%
2	Texas	8,323	7.4%
38	Utah	697	0.6%
49	Vermont	253	0.2%
14	Virginia	2,630	2.3%
17	Washington	2,341	2.1%
34	West Virginia	1,110	1.0%
19	Wisconsin	2,303	2.1%
50	Wyoming	243	0.2%

RANK ORDER

RANK	STATE	DEATHS	% of USA
1	California	10,633	9.5%
2	Texas	8,323	7.4%
3	Florida	8,229	7.3%
4	Pennsylvania	5,200	4.6%
5	New York	4,530	4.0%
6	Ohio	4,234	3.8%
7	Illinois	4,133	3.7%
8	North Carolina	4,019	3.6%
9	Georgia	3,667	3.3%
10	Michigan	3,312	3.0%
11	Tennessee	3,156	2.8%
12	Arizona	2,770	2.5%
13	Missouri	2,728	2.4%
14	Virginia	2,630	2.3%
15	Alabama	2,403	2.1%
16	Indiana	2,395	2.1%
17	Washington	2,341	2.1%
18	New Jersey	2,324	2.1%
19	Wisconsin	2,303	2.1%
20	Louisiana	2,300	2.1%
21	Kentucky	2,260	2.0%
22	South Carolina	2,094	1.9%
23	Oklahoma	1,947	1.7%
24	Minnesota	1,867	1.7%
25	Colorado	1,810	1.6%
26	Mississippi	1,703	1.5%
27	Oregon	1,444	1.3%
28	Maryland	1,412	1.3%
29	Arkansas	1,406	1.3%
30	Massachusetts	1,366	1.2%
31	Connecticut	1,261	1.1%
32	New Mexico	1,223	1.1%
33	Kansas	1,144	1.0%
34	West Virginia	1,110	1.0%
35	Iowa	1,108	1.0%
36	Nevada	1,021	0.9%
37	Nebraska	743	0.7%
38	Utah	697	0.6%
39	Idaho	593	0.5%
40	Montana	535	0.5%
41	Maine	480	0.4%
42	New Hampshire	445	0.4%
43	South Dakota	416	0.4%
44	Hawaii	390	0.3%
45	Alaska	326	0.3%
46	Rhode Island	298	0.3%
47	Delaware	294	0.3%
48	North Dakota	274	0.2%
49	Vermont	253	0.2%
50	Wyoming	243	0.2%
	District of Columbia	219	0.2%

Source: U.S. Department of Health and Human Services, National Center for Health Statistics
   "National Vital Statistics Reports" (Vol. 55, No. 19, August 21, 2007, http://www.cdc.gov/nchs/deaths.htm)
*Final data by state of residence. Includes motor vehicle deaths, poisoning, falls, drowning, and other accidents.

Age-Adjusted Death Rate by Accidents in 2004

National Rate = 37.7 Deaths per 100,000 Population*

ALPHA ORDER

RANK	STATE	RATE
9	Alabama	52.8
4	Alaska	56.1
14	Arizona	48.6
12	Arkansas	50.4
44	California	30.4
22	Colorado	42.1
39	Connecticut	33.4
37	Delaware	34.9
20	Florida	44.7
19	Georgia	44.8
45	Hawaii	29.2
21	Idaho	43.1
42	Illinois	32.3
30	Indiana	38.0
41	Iowa	33.0
23	Kansas	40.3
6	Kentucky	54.6
10	Louisiana	51.6
35	Maine	35.2
46	Maryland	25.8
50	Massachusetts	19.6
43	Michigan	32.2
36	Minnesota	35.1
2	Mississippi	59.5
17	Missouri	46.1
6	Montana	54.6
25	Nebraska	39.4
18	Nevada	45.4
38	New Hampshire	33.6
46	New Jersey	25.8
1	New Mexico	65.6
49	New York	22.6
15	North Carolina	47.7
31	North Dakota	37.9
34	Ohio	35.6
5	Oklahoma	54.9
29	Oregon	38.3
28	Pennsylvania	38.6
48	Rhode Island	24.2
13	South Carolina	49.9
11	South Dakota	50.5
8	Tennessee	53.4
24	Texas	39.7
40	Utah	33.3
27	Vermont	38.7
33	Virginia	36.0
32	Washington	37.3
3	West Virginia	58.7
26	Wisconsin	39.1
16	Wyoming	47.0

RANK ORDER

RANK	STATE	RATE
1	New Mexico	65.6
2	Mississippi	59.5
3	West Virginia	58.7
4	Alaska	56.1
5	Oklahoma	54.9
6	Kentucky	54.6
6	Montana	54.6
8	Tennessee	53.4
9	Alabama	52.8
10	Louisiana	51.6
11	South Dakota	50.5
12	Arkansas	50.4
13	South Carolina	49.9
14	Arizona	48.6
15	North Carolina	47.7
16	Wyoming	47.0
17	Missouri	46.1
18	Nevada	45.4
19	Georgia	44.8
20	Florida	44.7
21	Idaho	43.1
22	Colorado	42.1
23	Kansas	40.3
24	Texas	39.7
25	Nebraska	39.4
26	Wisconsin	39.1
27	Vermont	38.7
28	Pennsylvania	38.6
29	Oregon	38.3
30	Indiana	38.0
31	North Dakota	37.9
32	Washington	37.3
33	Virginia	36.0
34	Ohio	35.6
35	Maine	35.2
36	Minnesota	35.1
37	Delaware	34.9
38	New Hampshire	33.6
39	Connecticut	33.4
40	Utah	33.3
41	Iowa	33.0
42	Illinois	32.3
43	Michigan	32.2
44	California	30.4
45	Hawaii	29.2
46	Maryland	25.8
46	New Jersey	25.8
48	Rhode Island	24.2
49	New York	22.6
50	Massachusetts	19.6
	District of Columbia	39.4

Source: U.S. Department of Health and Human Services, National Center for Health Statistics
   "National Vital Statistics Reports" (Vol. 55, No. 19, August 21, 2007, http://www.cdc.gov/nchs/deaths.htm)
*Final data by state of residence. Includes motor vehicle deaths, poisoning, falls, drowning, and other accidents. Age-adjusted rates based on the year 2000 standard population.

Deaths by Cerebrovascular Diseases in 2004

National Total = 150,074 Deaths*

RANK	STATE	DEATHS	% of USA
19	Alabama	2,986	2.0%
50	Alaska	172	0.1%
24	Arizona	2,446	1.6%
29	Arkansas	1,948	1.3%
1	California	16,882	11.2%
31	Colorado	1,638	1.1%
32	Connecticut	1,635	1.1%
47	Delaware	350	0.2%
3	Florida	9,715	6.5%
10	Georgia	4,063	2.7%
40	Hawaii	714	0.5%
41	Idaho	712	0.5%
7	Illinois	6,489	4.3%
15	Indiana	3,454	2.3%
28	Iowa	1,960	1.3%
33	Kansas	1,611	1.1%
25	Kentucky	2,339	1.6%
23	Louisiana	2,489	1.7%
37	Maine	801	0.5%
20	Maryland	2,718	1.8%
16	Massachusetts	3,254	2.2%
8	Michigan	5,290	3.5%
22	Minnesota	2,542	1.7%
30	Mississippi	1,651	1.1%
14	Missouri	3,503	2.3%
44	Montana	484	0.3%
36	Nebraska	978	0.7%
35	Nevada	1,030	0.7%
42	New Hampshire	586	0.4%
12	New Jersey	3,781	2.5%
39	New Mexico	721	0.5%
5	New York	6,927	4.6%
9	North Carolina	4,955	3.3%
45	North Dakota	475	0.3%
6	Ohio	6,501	4.3%
27	Oklahoma	2,183	1.5%
26	Oregon	2,328	1.6%
4	Pennsylvania	7,792	5.2%
43	Rhode Island	522	0.3%
21	South Carolina	2,643	1.8%
46	South Dakota	469	0.3%
13	Tennessee	3,680	2.5%
2	Texas	9,853	6.6%
38	Utah	790	0.5%
48	Vermont	302	0.2%
11	Virginia	3,788	2.5%
17	Washington	3,243	2.2%
34	West Virginia	1,178	0.8%
18	Wisconsin	3,071	2.0%
49	Wyoming	214	0.1%

RANK	STATE	DEATHS	% of USA
1	California	16,882	11.2%
2	Texas	9,853	6.6%
3	Florida	9,715	6.5%
4	Pennsylvania	7,792	5.2%
5	New York	6,927	4.6%
6	Ohio	6,501	4.3%
7	Illinois	6,489	4.3%
8	Michigan	5,290	3.5%
9	North Carolina	4,955	3.3%
10	Georgia	4,063	2.7%
11	Virginia	3,788	2.5%
12	New Jersey	3,781	2.5%
13	Tennessee	3,680	2.5%
14	Missouri	3,503	2.3%
15	Indiana	3,454	2.3%
16	Massachusetts	3,254	2.2%
17	Washington	3,243	2.2%
18	Wisconsin	3,071	2.0%
19	Alabama	2,986	2.0%
20	Maryland	2,718	1.8%
21	South Carolina	2,643	1.8%
22	Minnesota	2,542	1.7%
23	Louisiana	2,489	1.7%
24	Arizona	2,446	1.6%
25	Kentucky	2,339	1.6%
26	Oregon	2,328	1.6%
27	Oklahoma	2,183	1.5%
28	Iowa	1,960	1.3%
29	Arkansas	1,948	1.3%
30	Mississippi	1,651	1.1%
31	Colorado	1,638	1.1%
32	Connecticut	1,635	1.1%
33	Kansas	1,611	1.1%
34	West Virginia	1,178	0.8%
35	Nevada	1,030	0.7%
36	Nebraska	978	0.7%
37	Maine	801	0.5%
38	Utah	790	0.5%
39	New Mexico	721	0.5%
40	Hawaii	714	0.5%
41	Idaho	712	0.5%
42	New Hampshire	586	0.4%
43	Rhode Island	522	0.3%
44	Montana	484	0.3%
45	North Dakota	475	0.3%
46	South Dakota	469	0.3%
47	Delaware	350	0.2%
48	Vermont	302	0.2%
49	Wyoming	214	0.1%
50	Alaska	172	0.1%
	District of Columbia	218	0.1%

Source: U.S. Department of Health and Human Services, National Center for Health Statistics
   "National Vital Statistics Reports" (Vol. 55, No. 19, August 21, 2007, http://www.cdc.gov/nchs/deaths.htm)
*Final data by state of residence. Cerebrovascular diseases include stroke and other disorders of the blood vessels of the brain.

Age-Adjusted Death Rate by Cerebrovascular Diseases in 2004

National Rate = 50.0 Deaths per 100,000 Population*

ALPHA ORDER

RANK	STATE	RATE
2	Alabama	65.0
22	Alaska	52.1
42	Arizona	43.3
2	Arkansas	65.0
21	California	52.7
38	Colorado	44.6
49	Connecticut	37.6
45	Delaware	40.6
44	Florida	42.0
7	Georgia	60.5
34	Hawaii	47.1
17	Idaho	53.8
27	Illinois	50.0
18	Indiana	53.7
29	Iowa	49.5
23	Kansas	51.8
11	Kentucky	58.0
9	Louisiana	59.4
25	Maine	51.0
24	Maryland	51.5
43	Massachusetts	42.5
28	Michigan	49.9
36	Minnesota	46.2
8	Mississippi	60.1
13	Missouri	56.0
37	Montana	45.7
32	Nebraska	48.0
20	Nevada	53.4
39	New Hampshire	44.2
47	New Jersey	39.2
46	New Mexico	40.5
50	New York	32.9
5	North Carolina	61.1
15	North Dakota	54.6
26	Ohio	50.9
6	Oklahoma	60.6
10	Oregon	58.2
34	Pennsylvania	47.1
48	Rhode Island	38.1
1	South Carolina	65.2
31	South Dakota	48.1
4	Tennessee	64.7
12	Texas	56.9
33	Utah	47.7
41	Vermont	43.5
14	Virginia	55.5
19	Washington	53.5
16	West Virginia	54.1
30	Wisconsin	48.8
40	Wyoming	43.9

RANK ORDER

RANK	STATE	RATE
1	South Carolina	65.2
2	Alabama	65.0
2	Arkansas	65.0
4	Tennessee	64.7
5	North Carolina	61.1
6	Oklahoma	60.6
7	Georgia	60.5
8	Mississippi	60.1
9	Louisiana	59.4
10	Oregon	58.2
11	Kentucky	58.0
12	Texas	56.9
13	Missouri	56.0
14	Virginia	55.5
15	North Dakota	54.6
16	West Virginia	54.1
17	Idaho	53.8
18	Indiana	53.7
19	Washington	53.5
20	Nevada	53.4
21	California	52.7
22	Alaska	52.1
23	Kansas	51.8
24	Maryland	51.5
25	Maine	51.0
26	Ohio	50.9
27	Illinois	50.0
28	Michigan	49.9
29	Iowa	49.5
30	Wisconsin	48.8
31	South Dakota	48.1
32	Nebraska	48.0
33	Utah	47.7
34	Hawaii	47.1
34	Pennsylvania	47.1
36	Minnesota	46.2
37	Montana	45.7
38	Colorado	44.6
39	New Hampshire	44.2
40	Wyoming	43.9
41	Vermont	43.5
42	Arizona	43.3
43	Massachusetts	42.5
44	Florida	42.0
45	Delaware	40.6
46	New Mexico	40.5
47	New Jersey	39.2
48	Rhode Island	38.1
49	Connecticut	37.6
50	New York	32.9
	District of Columbia	38.9

Source: U.S. Department of Health and Human Services, National Center for Health Statistics
"National Vital Statistics Reports" (Vol. 55, No. 19, August 21, 2007, http://www.cdc.gov/nchs/deaths.htm)
*Final data by state of residence. Cerebrovascular diseases include stroke and other disorders of the blood vessels of the brain.
Age-adjusted rates based on the year 2000 standard population.

Deaths by Diseases of the Heart in 2004

National Total = 652,486 Deaths*

ALPHA ORDER

RANK	STATE	DEATHS	% of USA
17	Alabama	12,774	2.0%
50	Alaska	589	0.1%
22	Arizona	10,539	1.6%
29	Arkansas	7,534	1.2%
1	California	64,999	10.0%
32	Colorado	6,079	0.9%
28	Connecticut	7,868	1.2%
44	Delaware	2,015	0.3%
3	Florida	47,160	7.2%
11	Georgia	16,557	2.5%
42	Hawaii	2,457	0.4%
43	Idaho	2,450	0.4%
7	Illinois	28,284	4.3%
14	Indiana	14,636	2.2%
30	Iowa	7,299	1.1%
33	Kansas	6,048	0.9%
23	Kentucky	10,465	1.6%
20	Louisiana	10,852	1.7%
39	Maine	2,948	0.5%
19	Maryland	11,346	1.7%
16	Massachusetts	13,824	2.1%
8	Michigan	24,825	3.8%
27	Minnesota	7,891	1.2%
26	Mississippi	8,282	1.3%
12	Missouri	15,500	2.4%
45	Montana	1,838	0.3%
36	Nebraska	3,738	0.6%
35	Nevada	4,693	0.7%
41	New Hampshire	2,639	0.4%
9	New Jersey	20,560	3.2%
37	New Mexico	3,264	0.5%
2	New York	52,480	8.0%
10	North Carolina	17,607	2.7%
47	North Dakota	1,470	0.2%
6	Ohio	29,078	4.5%
24	Oklahoma	10,335	1.6%
31	Oregon	6,725	1.0%
5	Pennsylvania	36,434	5.6%
38	Rhode Island	2,969	0.5%
25	South Carolina	9,182	1.4%
46	South Dakota	1,783	0.3%
13	Tennessee	15,038	2.3%
4	Texas	40,196	6.2%
40	Utah	2,942	0.5%
48	Vermont	1,289	0.2%
15	Virginia	14,284	2.2%
21	Washington	10,644	1.6%
34	West Virginia	5,674	0.9%
18	Wisconsin	11,909	1.8%
49	Wyoming	950	0.1%

RANK ORDER

RANK	STATE	DEATHS	% of USA
1	California	64,999	10.0%
2	New York	52,480	8.0%
3	Florida	47,160	7.2%
4	Texas	40,196	6.2%
5	Pennsylvania	36,434	5.6%
6	Ohio	29,078	4.5%
7	Illinois	28,284	4.3%
8	Michigan	24,825	3.8%
9	New Jersey	20,560	3.2%
10	North Carolina	17,607	2.7%
11	Georgia	16,557	2.5%
12	Missouri	15,500	2.4%
13	Tennessee	15,038	2.3%
14	Indiana	14,636	2.2%
15	Virginia	14,284	2.2%
16	Massachusetts	13,824	2.1%
17	Alabama	12,774	2.0%
18	Wisconsin	11,909	1.8%
19	Maryland	11,346	1.7%
20	Louisiana	10,852	1.7%
21	Washington	10,644	1.6%
22	Arizona	10,539	1.6%
23	Kentucky	10,465	1.6%
24	Oklahoma	10,335	1.6%
25	South Carolina	9,182	1.4%
26	Mississippi	8,282	1.3%
27	Minnesota	7,891	1.2%
28	Connecticut	7,868	1.2%
29	Arkansas	7,534	1.2%
30	Iowa	7,299	1.1%
31	Oregon	6,725	1.0%
32	Colorado	6,079	0.9%
33	Kansas	6,048	0.9%
34	West Virginia	5,674	0.9%
35	Nevada	4,693	0.7%
36	Nebraska	3,738	0.6%
37	New Mexico	3,264	0.5%
38	Rhode Island	2,969	0.5%
39	Maine	2,948	0.5%
40	Utah	2,942	0.5%
41	New Hampshire	2,639	0.4%
42	Hawaii	2,457	0.4%
43	Idaho	2,450	0.4%
44	Delaware	2,015	0.3%
45	Montana	1,838	0.3%
46	South Dakota	1,783	0.3%
47	North Dakota	1,470	0.2%
48	Vermont	1,289	0.2%
49	Wyoming	950	0.1%
50	Alaska	589	0.1%
	District of Columbia	1,544	0.2%

Source: U.S. Department of Health and Human Services, National Center for Health Statistics
"National Vital Statistics Reports" (Vol. 55, No. 19, August 21, 2007, http://www.cdc.gov/nchs/deaths.htm)
*Final data by state of residence.

Age-Adjusted Death Rate by Diseases of the Heart in 2004

National Rate = 217.0 Deaths per 100,000 Population*

ALPHA ORDER

RANK	STATE	RATE
3	Alabama	276.3
49	Alaska	158.3
36	Arizona	185.7
8	Arkansas	250.9
27	California	202.1
48	Colorado	162.7
40	Connecticut	182.5
14	Delaware	232.3
26	Florida	204.9
11	Georgia	239.7
47	Hawaii	167.3
38	Idaho	184.3
20	Illinois	219.1
16	Indiana	228.0
30	Iowa	191.9
29	Kansas	197.3
7	Kentucky	254.9
6	Louisiana	256.6
33	Maine	188.3
24	Maryland	212.4
39	Massachusetts	183.3
13	Michigan	234.3
50	Minnesota	144.3
1	Mississippi	300.1
9	Missouri	248.4
45	Montana	173.6
37	Nebraska	185.3
12	Nevada	236.6
28	New Hampshire	197.6
23	New Jersey	213.0
41	New Mexico	180.4
10	New York	247.9
22	North Carolina	214.4
42	North Dakota	175.8
15	Ohio	229.0
2	Oklahoma	284.3
46	Oregon	169.3
18	Pennsylvania	223.7
21	Rhode Island	216.0
19	South Carolina	222.0
34	South Dakota	187.1
5	Tennessee	259.1
17	Texas	227.0
43	Utah	175.0
35	Vermont	186.6
25	Virginia	206.5
44	Washington	174.7
4	West Virginia	260.9
31	Wisconsin	191.8
32	Wyoming	191.0

RANK ORDER

RANK	STATE	RATE
1	Mississippi	300.1
2	Oklahoma	284.3
3	Alabama	276.3
4	West Virginia	260.9
5	Tennessee	259.1
6	Louisiana	256.6
7	Kentucky	254.9
8	Arkansas	250.9
9	Missouri	248.4
10	New York	247.9
11	Georgia	239.7
12	Nevada	236.6
13	Michigan	234.3
14	Delaware	232.3
15	Ohio	229.0
16	Indiana	228.0
17	Texas	227.0
18	Pennsylvania	223.7
19	South Carolina	222.0
20	Illinois	219.1
21	Rhode Island	216.0
22	North Carolina	214.4
23	New Jersey	213.0
24	Maryland	212.4
25	Virginia	206.5
26	Florida	204.9
27	California	202.1
28	New Hampshire	197.6
29	Kansas	197.3
30	Iowa	191.9
31	Wisconsin	191.8
32	Wyoming	191.0
33	Maine	188.3
34	South Dakota	187.1
35	Vermont	186.6
36	Arizona	185.7
37	Nebraska	185.3
38	Idaho	184.3
39	Massachusetts	183.3
40	Connecticut	182.5
41	New Mexico	180.4
42	North Dakota	175.8
43	Utah	175.0
44	Washington	174.7
45	Montana	173.6
46	Oregon	169.3
47	Hawaii	167.3
48	Colorado	162.7
49	Alaska	158.3
50	Minnesota	144.3
	District of Columbia	274.9

Source: U.S. Department of Health and Human Services, National Center for Health Statistics
"National Vital Statistics Reports" (Vol. 55, No. 19, August 21, 2007, http://www.cdc.gov/nchs/deaths.htm)
*Final data by state of residence. Age-adjusted rates based on the year 2000 standard population.

Deaths by Suicide in 2004

National Total = 32,439 Suicides*

ALPHA ORDER

RANK	STATE	SUICIDES	% of USA
22	Alabama	541	1.7%
42	Alaska	155	0.5%
11	Arizona	880	2.7%
32	Arkansas	361	1.1%
1	California	3,368	10.4%
14	Colorado	797	2.5%
36	Connecticut	294	0.9%
46	Delaware	93	0.3%
2	Florida	2,389	7.4%
10	Georgia	973	3.0%
44	Hawaii	116	0.4%
38	Idaho	236	0.7%
8	Illinois	1,028	3.2%
17	Indiana	704	2.2%
35	Iowa	343	1.1%
31	Kansas	370	1.1%
20	Kentucky	560	1.7%
23	Louisiana	537	1.7%
40	Maine	171	0.5%
26	Maryland	500	1.5%
29	Massachusetts	425	1.3%
7	Michigan	1,098	3.4%
24	Minnesota	524	1.6%
34	Mississippi	350	1.1%
16	Missouri	715	2.2%
39	Montana	175	0.5%
41	Nebraska	166	0.5%
28	Nevada	440	1.4%
43	New Hampshire	133	0.4%
19	New Jersey	597	1.8%
33	New Mexico	356	1.1%
6	New York	1,187	3.7%
9	North Carolina	1,027	3.2%
50	North Dakota	73	0.2%
5	Ohio	1,319	4.1%
25	Oklahoma	506	1.6%
21	Oregon	555	1.7%
4	Pennsylvania	1,410	4.3%
49	Rhode Island	85	0.3%
27	South Carolina	482	1.5%
45	South Dakota	112	0.3%
15	Tennessee	792	2.4%
3	Texas	2,300	7.1%
30	Utah	377	1.2%
46	Vermont	93	0.3%
13	Virginia	828	2.6%
12	Washington	830	2.6%
37	West Virginia	285	0.9%
18	Wisconsin	662	2.0%
48	Wyoming	88	0.3%

RANK ORDER

RANK	STATE	SUICIDES	% of USA
1	California	3,368	10.4%
2	Florida	2,389	7.4%
3	Texas	2,300	7.1%
4	Pennsylvania	1,410	4.3%
5	Ohio	1,319	4.1%
6	New York	1,187	3.7%
7	Michigan	1,098	3.4%
8	Illinois	1,028	3.2%
9	North Carolina	1,027	3.2%
10	Georgia	973	3.0%
11	Arizona	880	2.7%
12	Washington	830	2.6%
13	Virginia	828	2.6%
14	Colorado	797	2.5%
15	Tennessee	792	2.4%
16	Missouri	715	2.2%
17	Indiana	704	2.2%
18	Wisconsin	662	2.0%
19	New Jersey	597	1.8%
20	Kentucky	560	1.7%
21	Oregon	555	1.7%
22	Alabama	541	1.7%
23	Louisiana	537	1.7%
24	Minnesota	524	1.6%
25	Oklahoma	506	1.6%
26	Maryland	500	1.5%
27	South Carolina	482	1.5%
28	Nevada	440	1.4%
29	Massachusetts	425	1.3%
30	Utah	377	1.2%
31	Kansas	370	1.1%
32	Arkansas	361	1.1%
33	New Mexico	356	1.1%
34	Mississippi	350	1.1%
35	Iowa	343	1.1%
36	Connecticut	294	0.9%
37	West Virginia	285	0.9%
38	Idaho	236	0.7%
39	Montana	175	0.5%
40	Maine	171	0.5%
41	Nebraska	166	0.5%
42	Alaska	155	0.5%
43	New Hampshire	133	0.4%
44	Hawaii	116	0.4%
45	South Dakota	112	0.3%
46	Delaware	93	0.3%
46	Vermont	93	0.3%
48	Wyoming	88	0.3%
49	Rhode Island	85	0.3%
50	North Dakota	73	0.2%
	District of Columbia	33	0.1%

Source: U.S. Department of Health and Human Services, National Center for Health Statistics
    "National Vital Statistics Reports" (Vol. 55, No. 19, August 21, 2007, http://www.cdc.gov/nchs/deaths.htm)
*Final data by state of residence.

Age-Adjusted Death Rate by Suicide in 2004

National Rate = 10.9 Deaths per 100,000 Population*

ALPHA ORDER

RANK	STATE	RATE
27	Alabama	11.7
1	Alaska	23.4
9	Arizona	15.7
20	Arkansas	12.9
41	California	9.6
7	Colorado	17.3
45	Connecticut	8.1
36	Delaware	10.9
18	Florida	13.1
28	Georgia	11.3
43	Hawaii	9.0
5	Idaho	17.4
45	Illinois	8.1
28	Indiana	11.3
28	Iowa	11.3
15	Kansas	13.5
16	Kentucky	13.2
24	Louisiana	12.0
22	Maine	12.2
44	Maryland	8.9
49	Massachusetts	6.4
37	Michigan	10.8
39	Minnesota	10.1
23	Mississippi	12.1
21	Missouri	12.3
4	Montana	18.6
42	Nebraska	9.5
2	Nevada	19.2
40	New Hampshire	9.8
48	New Jersey	6.8
3	New Mexico	18.7
50	New York	6.0
24	North Carolina	12.0
33	North Dakota	11.2
28	Ohio	11.3
13	Oklahoma	14.3
11	Oregon	15.0
34	Pennsylvania	11.1
47	Rhode Island	7.5
28	South Carolina	11.3
12	South Dakota	14.7
18	Tennessee	13.1
38	Texas	10.7
7	Utah	17.3
13	Vermont	14.3
35	Virginia	11.0
16	Washington	13.2
10	West Virginia	15.3
26	Wisconsin	11.8
5	Wyoming	17.4

RANK ORDER

RANK	STATE	RATE
1	Alaska	23.4
2	Nevada	19.2
3	New Mexico	18.7
4	Montana	18.6
5	Idaho	17.4
5	Wyoming	17.4
7	Colorado	17.3
7	Utah	17.3
9	Arizona	15.7
10	West Virginia	15.3
11	Oregon	15.0
12	South Dakota	14.7
13	Oklahoma	14.3
13	Vermont	14.3
15	Kansas	13.5
16	Kentucky	13.2
16	Washington	13.2
18	Florida	13.1
18	Tennessee	13.1
20	Arkansas	12.9
21	Missouri	12.3
22	Maine	12.2
23	Mississippi	12.1
24	Louisiana	12.0
24	North Carolina	12.0
26	Wisconsin	11.8
27	Alabama	11.7
28	Georgia	11.3
28	Indiana	11.3
28	Iowa	11.3
28	Ohio	11.3
28	South Carolina	11.3
33	North Dakota	11.2
34	Pennsylvania	11.1
35	Virginia	11.0
36	Delaware	10.9
37	Michigan	10.8
38	Texas	10.7
39	Minnesota	10.1
40	New Hampshire	9.8
41	California	9.6
42	Nebraska	9.5
43	Hawaii	9.0
44	Maryland	8.9
45	Connecticut	8.1
45	Illinois	8.1
47	Rhode Island	7.5
48	New Jersey	6.8
49	Massachusetts	6.4
50	New York	6.0
	District of Columbia	5.7

Source: U.S. Department of Health and Human Services, National Center for Health Statistics
    "National Vital Statistics Reports" (Vol. 55, No. 19, August 21, 2007, http://www.cdc.gov/nchs/deaths.htm)
*Final data by state of residence. Age-adjusted rates based on the year 2000 standard population.

Deaths by AIDS in 2004

National Total = 13,063 Deaths*

ALPHA ORDER

RANK	STATE	DEATHS	% of USA
17	Alabama	207	1.6%
44	Alaska	8	0.1%
21	Arizona	158	1.2%
27	Arkansas	77	0.6%
3	California	1,379	10.6%
25	Colorado	88	0.7%
18	Connecticut	189	1.4%
31	Delaware	58	0.4%
2	Florida	1,719	13.2%
5	Georgia	700	5.4%
39	Hawaii	23	0.2%
48	Idaho	3	0.0%
9	Illinois	414	3.2%
24	Indiana	112	0.9%
37	Iowa	27	0.2%
38	Kansas	26	0.2%
29	Kentucky	66	0.5%
11	Louisiana	393	3.0%
42	Maine	13	0.1%
7	Maryland	557	4.3%
16	Massachusetts	213	1.6%
15	Michigan	215	1.6%
32	Minnesota	51	0.4%
20	Mississippi	164	1.3%
22	Missouri	145	1.1%
50	Montana	0	0.0%
43	Nebraska	11	0.1%
26	Nevada	79	0.6%
41	New Hampshire	16	0.1%
6	New Jersey	671	5.1%
40	New Mexico	22	0.2%
1	New York	1,722	13.2%
10	North Carolina	407	3.1%
48	North Dakota	3	0.0%
19	Ohio	172	1.3%
28	Oklahoma	73	0.6%
30	Oregon	63	0.5%
8	Pennsylvania	469	3.6%
36	Rhode Island	28	0.2%
13	South Carolina	268	2.1%
44	South Dakota	8	0.1%
12	Tennessee	289	2.2%
4	Texas	1,052	8.1%
34	Utah	31	0.2%
46	Vermont	4	0.0%
14	Virginia	229	1.8%
23	Washington	122	0.9%
34	West Virginia	31	0.2%
33	Wisconsin	48	0.4%
46	Wyoming	4	0.0%

RANK ORDER

RANK	STATE	DEATHS	% of USA
1	New York	1,722	13.2%
2	Florida	1,719	13.2%
3	California	1,379	10.6%
4	Texas	1,052	8.1%
5	Georgia	700	5.4%
6	New Jersey	671	5.1%
7	Maryland	557	4.3%
8	Pennsylvania	469	3.6%
9	Illinois	414	3.2%
10	North Carolina	407	3.1%
11	Louisiana	393	3.0%
12	Tennessee	289	2.2%
13	South Carolina	268	2.1%
14	Virginia	229	1.8%
15	Michigan	215	1.6%
16	Massachusetts	213	1.6%
17	Alabama	207	1.6%
18	Connecticut	189	1.4%
19	Ohio	172	1.3%
20	Mississippi	164	1.3%
21	Arizona	158	1.2%
22	Missouri	145	1.1%
23	Washington	122	0.9%
24	Indiana	112	0.9%
25	Colorado	88	0.7%
26	Nevada	79	0.6%
27	Arkansas	77	0.6%
28	Oklahoma	73	0.6%
29	Kentucky	66	0.5%
30	Oregon	63	0.5%
31	Delaware	58	0.4%
32	Minnesota	51	0.4%
33	Wisconsin	48	0.4%
34	Utah	31	0.2%
34	West Virginia	31	0.2%
36	Rhode Island	28	0.2%
37	Iowa	27	0.2%
38	Kansas	26	0.2%
39	Hawaii	23	0.2%
40	New Mexico	22	0.2%
41	New Hampshire	16	0.1%
42	Maine	13	0.1%
43	Nebraska	11	0.1%
44	Alaska	8	0.1%
44	South Dakota	8	0.1%
46	Vermont	4	0.0%
46	Wyoming	4	0.0%
48	Idaho	3	0.0%
48	North Dakota	3	0.0%
50	Montana	0	0.0%
	District of Columbia	236	1.8%

Source: U.S. Department of Health and Human Services, National Center for Health Statistics
"National Vital Statistics Reports" (Vol. 55, No. 19, August 21, 2007, http://www.cdc.gov/nchs/deaths.htm)
*AIDS is Acquired Immunodeficiency Syndrome. It is a specific group of diseases or conditions which are indicative of severe immunosuppression related to infection with the Human Immunodeficiency Virus (HIV).

Age-Adjusted Death Rate by AIDS in 2004

National Rate = 4.5 Deaths per 100,000 Population*

RANK	STATE	RATE
13	Alabama	4.7
NA	Alaska**	NA
22	Arizona	2.9
20	Arkansas	3.0
15	California	3.9
27	Colorado	1.9
10	Connecticut	5.1
7	Delaware	6.8
1	Florida	10.0
5	Georgia	7.9
29	Hawaii	1.8
NA	Idaho**	NA
18	Illinois	3.3
29	Indiana	1.8
39	Iowa	0.9
37	Kansas	1.0
33	Kentucky	1.6
3	Louisiana	9.0
NA	Maine**	NA
2	Maryland	9.6
19	Massachusetts	3.2
25	Michigan	2.1
37	Minnesota	1.0
9	Mississippi	5.9
23	Missouri	2.6
NA	Montana**	NA
NA	Nebraska**	NA
17	Nevada	3.4
NA	New Hampshire**	NA
6	New Jersey	7.4
36	New Mexico	1.2
4	New York	8.7
13	North Carolina	4.7
NA	North Dakota**	NA
35	Ohio	1.5
25	Oklahoma	2.1
29	Oregon	1.8
16	Pennsylvania	3.7
23	Rhode Island	2.6
8	South Carolina	6.4
NA	South Dakota**	NA
12	Tennessee	4.8
11	Texas	4.9
33	Utah	1.6
NA	Vermont**	NA
20	Virginia	3.0
27	Washington	1.9
32	West Virginia	1.7
39	Wisconsin	0.9
NA	Wyoming**	NA

RANK	STATE	RATE
1	Florida	10.0
2	Maryland	9.6
3	Louisiana	9.0
4	New York	8.7
5	Georgia	7.9
6	New Jersey	7.4
7	Delaware	6.8
8	South Carolina	6.4
9	Mississippi	5.9
10	Connecticut	5.1
11	Texas	4.9
12	Tennessee	4.8
13	Alabama	4.7
13	North Carolina	4.7
15	California	3.9
16	Pennsylvania	3.7
17	Nevada	3.4
18	Illinois	3.3
19	Massachusetts	3.2
20	Arkansas	3.0
20	Virginia	3.0
22	Arizona	2.9
23	Missouri	2.6
23	Rhode Island	2.6
25	Michigan	2.1
25	Oklahoma	2.1
27	Colorado	1.9
27	Washington	1.9
29	Hawaii	1.8
29	Indiana	1.8
29	Oregon	1.8
32	West Virginia	1.7
33	Kentucky	1.6
33	Utah	1.6
35	Ohio	1.5
36	New Mexico	1.2
37	Kansas	1.0
37	Minnesota	1.0
39	Iowa	0.9
39	Wisconsin	0.9
NA	Alaska**	NA
NA	Idaho**	NA
NA	Maine**	NA
NA	Montana**	NA
NA	Nebraska**	NA
NA	New Hampshire**	NA
NA	North Dakota**	NA
NA	South Dakota**	NA
NA	Vermont**	NA
NA	Wyoming**	NA
	District of Columbia	42.0

Source: U.S. Department of Health and Human Services, National Center for Health Statistics
"National Vital Statistics Reports" (Vol. 55, No. 19, August 21, 2007, http://www.cdc.gov/nchs/deaths.htm)
*AIDS is Acquired Immunodeficiency Syndrome. It is a specific group of diseases or conditions which are indicative of severe immunosuppression related to infection with the Human Immunodeficiency Virus (HIV). Age-adjusted rates based on the year 2000 standard population.
**Insufficient data to determine a reliable rate.

Adult Per Capita Alcohol Consumption in 2005

National Per Capita = 2.6 Gallons Consumed per Adult 21 Years and Older*

ALPHA ORDER

RANK	STATE	PER CAPITA
40	Alabama	2.2
5	Alaska	3.1
12	Arizona	2.8
46	Arkansas	2.0
24	California	2.6
5	Colorado	3.1
30	Connecticut	2.5
3	Delaware	3.7
8	Florida	3.0
37	Georgia	2.3
12	Hawaii	2.8
12	Idaho	2.8
24	Illinois	2.6
37	Indiana	2.3
35	Iowa	2.4
40	Kansas	2.2
46	Kentucky	2.0
12	Louisiana	2.8
22	Maine	2.7
35	Maryland	2.4
12	Massachusetts	2.8
30	Michigan	2.5
12	Minnesota	2.8
30	Mississippi	2.5
24	Missouri	2.6
8	Montana	3.0
24	Nebraska	2.6
2	Nevada	4.0
1	New Hampshire	4.7
24	New Jersey	2.6
12	New Mexico	2.8
40	New York	2.2
40	North Carolina	2.2
5	North Dakota	3.1
40	Ohio	2.2
49	Oklahoma	1.7
12	Oregon	2.8
30	Pennsylvania	2.5
12	Rhode Island	2.8
12	South Carolina	2.8
10	South Dakota	2.9
40	Tennessee	2.2
30	Texas	2.5
50	Utah	1.5
10	Vermont	2.9
37	Virginia	2.3
24	Washington	2.6
48	West Virginia	1.9
4	Wisconsin	3.3
22	Wyoming	2.7

RANK ORDER

RANK	STATE	PER CAPITA
1	New Hampshire	4.7
2	Nevada	4.0
3	Delaware	3.7
4	Wisconsin	3.3
5	Alaska	3.1
5	Colorado	3.1
5	North Dakota	3.1
8	Florida	3.0
8	Montana	3.0
10	South Dakota	2.9
10	Vermont	2.9
12	Arizona	2.8
12	Hawaii	2.8
12	Idaho	2.8
12	Louisiana	2.8
12	Massachusetts	2.8
12	Minnesota	2.8
12	New Mexico	2.8
12	Oregon	2.8
12	Rhode Island	2.8
12	South Carolina	2.8
22	Maine	2.7
22	Wyoming	2.7
24	California	2.6
24	Illinois	2.6
24	Missouri	2.6
24	Nebraska	2.6
24	New Jersey	2.6
24	Washington	2.6
30	Connecticut	2.5
30	Michigan	2.5
30	Mississippi	2.5
30	Pennsylvania	2.5
30	Texas	2.5
35	Iowa	2.4
35	Maryland	2.4
37	Georgia	2.3
37	Indiana	2.3
37	Virginia	2.3
40	Alabama	2.2
40	Kansas	2.2
40	New York	2.2
40	North Carolina	2.2
40	Ohio	2.2
40	Tennessee	2.2
46	Arkansas	2.0
46	Kentucky	2.0
48	West Virginia	1.9
49	Oklahoma	1.7
50	Utah	1.5

District of Columbia 4.3

Source: CQ Press using data from U.S. Dept of Health and Human Services, National Institute on Alcohol Abuse and Alcoholism
"Volume Beverage and Ethanol Consumption for States" (http://www.niaaa.nih.gov/Resources/)

*This is apparent consumption of actual alcohol, not entire volume of an alcoholic beverage (e.g. wine is roughly 11% absolute alcohol content). Apparent consumption is based on several sources which together approximate sales but do not actually measure consumption. Accordingly, figures for some states may be skewed by purchases by nonresidents.

Percent of Adults Who Smoke: 2006

National Median = 20.1% of Adults*

<table>
<tr><td colspan="3">ALPHA ORDER</td><td colspan="3">RANK ORDER</td></tr>
<tr><td>RANK</td><td>STATE</td><td>PERCENT</td><td>RANK</td><td>STATE</td><td>PERCENT</td></tr>
<tr><td>9</td><td>Alabama</td><td>23.2</td><td>1</td><td>Kentucky</td><td>28.5</td></tr>
<tr><td>6</td><td>Alaska</td><td>24.0</td><td>2</td><td>West Virginia</td><td>25.7</td></tr>
<tr><td>37</td><td>Arizona</td><td>18.2</td><td>3</td><td>Mississippi</td><td>25.1</td></tr>
<tr><td>7</td><td>Arkansas</td><td>23.7</td><td>3</td><td>Oklahoma</td><td>25.1</td></tr>
<tr><td>49</td><td>California</td><td>14.9</td><td>5</td><td>Indiana</td><td>24.1</td></tr>
<tr><td>41</td><td>Colorado</td><td>17.9</td><td>6</td><td>Alaska</td><td>24.0</td></tr>
<tr><td>47</td><td>Connecticut</td><td>17.0</td><td>7</td><td>Arkansas</td><td>23.7</td></tr>
<tr><td>17</td><td>Delaware</td><td>21.7</td><td>8</td><td>Louisiana</td><td>23.4</td></tr>
<tr><td>21</td><td>Florida</td><td>21.0</td><td>9</td><td>Alabama</td><td>23.2</td></tr>
<tr><td>28</td><td>Georgia</td><td>19.9</td><td>9</td><td>Missouri</td><td>23.2</td></tr>
<tr><td>45</td><td>Hawaii</td><td>17.5</td><td>11</td><td>Tennessee</td><td>22.6</td></tr>
<tr><td>48</td><td>Idaho</td><td>16.8</td><td>12</td><td>Michigan</td><td>22.4</td></tr>
<tr><td>24</td><td>Illinois</td><td>20.5</td><td>12</td><td>Ohio</td><td>22.4</td></tr>
<tr><td>5</td><td>Indiana</td><td>24.1</td><td>14</td><td>South Carolina</td><td>22.3</td></tr>
<tr><td>20</td><td>Iowa</td><td>21.4</td><td>15</td><td>Nevada</td><td>22.2</td></tr>
<tr><td>27</td><td>Kansas</td><td>20.0</td><td>16</td><td>North Carolina</td><td>22.1</td></tr>
<tr><td>1</td><td>Kentucky</td><td>28.5</td><td>17</td><td>Delaware</td><td>21.7</td></tr>
<tr><td>8</td><td>Louisiana</td><td>23.4</td><td>18</td><td>Wyoming</td><td>21.6</td></tr>
<tr><td>22</td><td>Maine</td><td>20.9</td><td>19</td><td>Pennsylvania</td><td>21.5</td></tr>
<tr><td>44</td><td>Maryland</td><td>17.7</td><td>20</td><td>Iowa</td><td>21.4</td></tr>
<tr><td>43</td><td>Massachusetts</td><td>17.8</td><td>21</td><td>Florida</td><td>21.0</td></tr>
<tr><td>12</td><td>Michigan</td><td>22.4</td><td>22</td><td>Maine</td><td>20.9</td></tr>
<tr><td>36</td><td>Minnesota</td><td>18.3</td><td>23</td><td>Wisconsin</td><td>20.8</td></tr>
<tr><td>3</td><td>Mississippi</td><td>25.1</td><td>24</td><td>Illinois</td><td>20.5</td></tr>
<tr><td>9</td><td>Missouri</td><td>23.2</td><td>25</td><td>South Dakota</td><td>20.3</td></tr>
<tr><td>32</td><td>Montana</td><td>18.9</td><td>26</td><td>New Mexico</td><td>20.1</td></tr>
<tr><td>33</td><td>Nebraska</td><td>18.7</td><td>27</td><td>Kansas</td><td>20.0</td></tr>
<tr><td>15</td><td>Nevada</td><td>22.2</td><td>28</td><td>Georgia</td><td>19.9</td></tr>
<tr><td>33</td><td>New Hampshire</td><td>18.7</td><td>29</td><td>North Dakota</td><td>19.5</td></tr>
<tr><td>39</td><td>New Jersey</td><td>18.0</td><td>30</td><td>Virginia</td><td>19.3</td></tr>
<tr><td>26</td><td>New Mexico</td><td>20.1</td><td>31</td><td>Rhode Island</td><td>19.2</td></tr>
<tr><td>37</td><td>New York</td><td>18.2</td><td>32</td><td>Montana</td><td>18.9</td></tr>
<tr><td>16</td><td>North Carolina</td><td>22.1</td><td>33</td><td>Nebraska</td><td>18.7</td></tr>
<tr><td>29</td><td>North Dakota</td><td>19.5</td><td>33</td><td>New Hampshire</td><td>18.7</td></tr>
<tr><td>12</td><td>Ohio</td><td>22.4</td><td>35</td><td>Oregon</td><td>18.5</td></tr>
<tr><td>3</td><td>Oklahoma</td><td>25.1</td><td>36</td><td>Minnesota</td><td>18.3</td></tr>
<tr><td>35</td><td>Oregon</td><td>18.5</td><td>37</td><td>Arizona</td><td>18.2</td></tr>
<tr><td>19</td><td>Pennsylvania</td><td>21.5</td><td>37</td><td>New York</td><td>18.2</td></tr>
<tr><td>31</td><td>Rhode Island</td><td>19.2</td><td>39</td><td>New Jersey</td><td>18.0</td></tr>
<tr><td>14</td><td>South Carolina</td><td>22.3</td><td>39</td><td>Vermont</td><td>18.0</td></tr>
<tr><td>25</td><td>South Dakota</td><td>20.3</td><td>41</td><td>Colorado</td><td>17.9</td></tr>
<tr><td>11</td><td>Tennessee</td><td>22.6</td><td>41</td><td>Texas</td><td>17.9</td></tr>
<tr><td>41</td><td>Texas</td><td>17.9</td><td>43</td><td>Massachusetts</td><td>17.8</td></tr>
<tr><td>50</td><td>Utah</td><td>9.8</td><td>44</td><td>Maryland</td><td>17.7</td></tr>
<tr><td>39</td><td>Vermont</td><td>18.0</td><td>45</td><td>Hawaii</td><td>17.5</td></tr>
<tr><td>30</td><td>Virginia</td><td>19.3</td><td>46</td><td>Washington</td><td>17.1</td></tr>
<tr><td>46</td><td>Washington</td><td>17.1</td><td>47</td><td>Connecticut</td><td>17.0</td></tr>
<tr><td>2</td><td>West Virginia</td><td>25.7</td><td>48</td><td>Idaho</td><td>16.8</td></tr>
<tr><td>23</td><td>Wisconsin</td><td>20.8</td><td>49</td><td>California</td><td>14.9</td></tr>
<tr><td>18</td><td>Wyoming</td><td>21.6</td><td>50</td><td>Utah</td><td>9.8</td></tr>
<tr><td></td><td></td><td></td><td></td><td>District of Columbia</td><td>17.9</td></tr>
</table>

Source: U.S. Department of Health and Human Services, Centers for Disease Control and Prevention
    "2006 Behavioral Risk Factor Surveillance Summary Prevalence Data" (http://apps.nccd.cdc.gov/brfss/)
*Persons 18 and older who have smoked more than 100 cigarettes during their lifetime and who currently smoke every day or some days.

Percent of Adults Overweight or Obese: 2006

National Median = 61.8% of Adults*

ALPHA ORDER

RANK	STATE	PERCENT
6	Alabama	64.9
10	Alaska	64.2
40	Arizona	59.6
14	Arkansas	63.8
43	California	58.8
49	Colorado	54.9
43	Connecticut	58.8
14	Delaware	63.8
41	Florida	59.5
26	Georgia	61.8
46	Hawaii	56.1
37	Idaho	59.7
28	Illinois	61.7
22	Indiana	62.8
18	Iowa	63.0
24	Kansas	62.3
3	Kentucky	66.4
18	Louisiana	63.0
37	Maine	59.7
32	Maryland	60.7
48	Massachusetts	55.5
7	Michigan	64.8
23	Minnesota	62.7
2	Mississippi	66.7
20	Missouri	62.9
42	Montana	59.3
12	Nebraska	63.9
16	Nevada	63.6
32	New Hampshire	60.7
36	New Jersey	59.9
37	New Mexico	59.7
45	New York	58.4
20	North Carolina	62.9
9	North Dakota	64.5
12	Ohio	63.9
8	Oklahoma	64.7
32	Oregon	60.7
29	Pennsylvania	61.3
31	Rhode Island	61.0
4	South Carolina	65.4
10	South Dakota	64.2
5	Tennessee	65.3
24	Texas	62.3
49	Utah	54.9
47	Vermont	56.0
26	Virginia	61.8
32	Washington	60.7
1	West Virginia	67.0
17	Wisconsin	63.4
29	Wyoming	61.3

RANK ORDER

RANK	STATE	PERCENT
1	West Virginia	67.0
2	Mississippi	66.7
3	Kentucky	66.4
4	South Carolina	65.4
5	Tennessee	65.3
6	Alabama	64.9
7	Michigan	64.8
8	Oklahoma	64.7
9	North Dakota	64.5
10	Alaska	64.2
10	South Dakota	64.2
12	Nebraska	63.9
12	Ohio	63.9
14	Arkansas	63.8
14	Delaware	63.8
16	Nevada	63.6
17	Wisconsin	63.4
18	Iowa	63.0
18	Louisiana	63.0
20	Missouri	62.9
20	North Carolina	62.9
22	Indiana	62.8
23	Minnesota	62.7
24	Kansas	62.3
24	Texas	62.3
26	Georgia	61.8
26	Virginia	61.8
28	Illinois	61.7
29	Pennsylvania	61.3
29	Wyoming	61.3
31	Rhode Island	61.0
32	Maryland	60.7
32	New Hampshire	60.7
32	Oregon	60.7
32	Washington	60.7
36	New Jersey	59.9
37	Idaho	59.7
37	Maine	59.7
37	New Mexico	59.7
40	Arizona	59.6
41	Florida	59.5
42	Montana	59.3
43	California	58.8
43	Connecticut	58.8
45	New York	58.4
46	Hawaii	56.1
47	Vermont	56.0
48	Massachusetts	55.5
49	Colorado	54.9
49	Utah	54.9

District of Columbia 54.6

Source: CQ Press using data from U.S. Department of Health and Human Services, Centers for Disease Control and Prevention
"2006 Behavioral Risk Factor Surveillance Summary Prevalence Data" (http://apps.nccd.cdc.gov/brfss/)
*Persons 18 and older. Overweight is defined as a Body Mass Index (BMI) of 25.0 to 29.9 regardless of sex. Obese is a BMI of 30.0 or greater. BMI is a ratio of height to weight. As an example, a person 5' 8" and weighing 165 pounds has a BMI of 25. The same height at 197 pounds has a BMI of 30. See http://www.cdc.gov/nccdphp/dnpa/bmi/bmi-adult.htm.

Percent of Children Aged 19 to 35 Months Fully Immunized in 2006

National Percent = 77.0%*

ALPHA ORDER

RANK	STATE	PERCENT
13	Alabama	79.1
47	Alaska	67.3
42	Arizona	70.6
39	Arkansas	72.9
18	California	78.6
28	Colorado	75.9
2	Connecticut	82.0
9	Delaware	80.3
10	Florida	80.2
4	Georgia	81.4
16	Hawaii	78.8
45	Idaho	68.8
36	Illinois	74.1
28	Indiana	75.9
14	Iowa	79.0
43	Kansas	70.1
14	Kentucky	79.0
44	Louisiana	69.6
30	Maine	75.7
19	Maryland	78.3
1	Massachusetts	83.6
21	Michigan	77.9
22	Minnesota	77.6
37	Mississippi	73.3
6	Missouri	80.7
48	Montana	65.6
33	Nebraska	74.9
50	Nevada	59.5
26	New Hampshire	76.3
27	New Jersey	76.1
40	New Mexico	71.6
17	New York	78.7
3	North Carolina	81.5
11	North Dakota	80.1
32	Ohio	75.0
22	Oklahoma	77.6
38	Oregon	73.2
5	Pennsylvania	80.8
7	Rhode Island	80.6
12	South Carolina	79.6
35	South Dakota	74.4
25	Tennessee	76.8
34	Texas	74.7
20	Utah	78.0
31	Vermont	75.2
24	Virginia	77.4
41	Washington	71.4
46	West Virginia	68.4
8	Wisconsin	80.5
49	Wyoming	63.5

RANK ORDER

RANK	STATE	PERCENT
1	Massachusetts	83.6
2	Connecticut	82.0
3	North Carolina	81.5
4	Georgia	81.4
5	Pennsylvania	80.8
6	Missouri	80.7
7	Rhode Island	80.6
8	Wisconsin	80.5
9	Delaware	80.3
10	Florida	80.2
11	North Dakota	80.1
12	South Carolina	79.6
13	Alabama	79.1
14	Iowa	79.0
14	Kentucky	79.0
16	Hawaii	78.8
17	New York	78.7
18	California	78.6
19	Maryland	78.3
20	Utah	78.0
21	Michigan	77.9
22	Minnesota	77.6
22	Oklahoma	77.6
24	Virginia	77.4
25	Tennessee	76.8
26	New Hampshire	76.3
27	New Jersey	76.1
28	Colorado	75.9
28	Indiana	75.9
30	Maine	75.7
31	Vermont	75.2
32	Ohio	75.0
33	Nebraska	74.9
34	Texas	74.7
35	South Dakota	74.4
36	Illinois	74.1
37	Mississippi	73.3
38	Oregon	73.2
39	Arkansas	72.9
40	New Mexico	71.6
41	Washington	71.4
42	Arizona	70.6
43	Kansas	70.1
44	Louisiana	69.6
45	Idaho	68.8
46	West Virginia	68.4
47	Alaska	67.3
48	Montana	65.6
49	Wyoming	63.5
50	Nevada	59.5

District of Columbia   78.4

Source: U.S. Department of Health and Human Services, Centers for Disease Control and Prevention
    "State Vaccination Coverage Levels" (Morbidity and Mortality Weekly Report, Vol. 56, No. 34, August 31, 2007)
*Fully immunized (4:3:1:3:3:1 series) children received four doses of DTP/DT/DTaP (Diphtheria, Tetanus, Pertussis (Whooping Cough), Acellular Pertussis), three doses of OPV (Oral Poliovirus Vaccine), one dose of MCV (Measles-Containing Vaccine), three doses of Hib (Haemophilus influenzae type b), three doses of Hepatitis B vaccine and one dose of Varicella (chickenpox) vaccine. This differs from previous "fully" immunized tables.

XII. Households and Housing

Households in 2006

National Total = 111,617,402 Households*

<table>
<tr><td colspan="4">ALPHA ORDER</td><td colspan="4">RANK ORDER</td></tr>
<tr><th>RANK</th><th>STATE</th><th>HOUSEHOLDS</th><th>% of USA</th><th>RANK</th><th>STATE</th><th>HOUSEHOLDS</th><th>% of USA</th></tr>
<tr><td>23</td><td>Alabama</td><td>1,796,058</td><td>1.6%</td><td>1</td><td>California</td><td>12,151,227</td><td>10.9%</td></tr>
<tr><td>49</td><td>Alaska</td><td>229,878</td><td>0.2%</td><td>2</td><td>Texas</td><td>8,109,388</td><td>7.3%</td></tr>
<tr><td>19</td><td>Arizona</td><td>2,224,992</td><td>2.0%</td><td>3</td><td>Florida</td><td>7,106,042</td><td>6.4%</td></tr>
<tr><td>31</td><td>Arkansas</td><td>1,103,428</td><td>1.0%</td><td>4</td><td>New York</td><td>7,088,376</td><td>6.4%</td></tr>
<tr><td>1</td><td>California</td><td>12,151,227</td><td>10.9%</td><td>5</td><td>Pennsylvania</td><td>4,845,603</td><td>4.3%</td></tr>
<tr><td>22</td><td>Colorado</td><td>1,846,988</td><td>1.7%</td><td>6</td><td>Illinois</td><td>4,724,252</td><td>4.2%</td></tr>
<tr><td>29</td><td>Connecticut</td><td>1,325,443</td><td>1.2%</td><td>7</td><td>Ohio</td><td>4,499,506</td><td>4.0%</td></tr>
<tr><td>45</td><td>Delaware</td><td>320,110</td><td>0.3%</td><td>8</td><td>Michigan</td><td>3,869,117</td><td>3.5%</td></tr>
<tr><td>3</td><td>Florida</td><td>7,106,042</td><td>6.4%</td><td>9</td><td>North Carolina</td><td>3,454,068</td><td>3.1%</td></tr>
<tr><td>10</td><td>Georgia</td><td>3,376,763</td><td>3.0%</td><td>10</td><td>Georgia</td><td>3,376,763</td><td>3.0%</td></tr>
<tr><td>42</td><td>Hawaii</td><td>432,632</td><td>0.4%</td><td>11</td><td>New Jersey</td><td>3,135,490</td><td>2.8%</td></tr>
<tr><td>39</td><td>Idaho</td><td>548,555</td><td>0.5%</td><td>12</td><td>Virginia</td><td>2,905,071</td><td>2.6%</td></tr>
<tr><td>6</td><td>Illinois</td><td>4,724,252</td><td>4.2%</td><td>13</td><td>Washington</td><td>2,471,912</td><td>2.2%</td></tr>
<tr><td>15</td><td>Indiana</td><td>2,435,274</td><td>2.2%</td><td>14</td><td>Massachusetts</td><td>2,446,485</td><td>2.2%</td></tr>
<tr><td>30</td><td>Iowa</td><td>1,208,765</td><td>1.1%</td><td>15</td><td>Indiana</td><td>2,435,274</td><td>2.2%</td></tr>
<tr><td>32</td><td>Kansas</td><td>1,088,288</td><td>1.0%</td><td>16</td><td>Tennessee</td><td>2,375,123</td><td>2.1%</td></tr>
<tr><td>25</td><td>Kentucky</td><td>1,651,911</td><td>1.5%</td><td>17</td><td>Missouri</td><td>2,305,027</td><td>2.1%</td></tr>
<tr><td>26</td><td>Louisiana</td><td>1,564,978</td><td>1.4%</td><td>18</td><td>Wisconsin</td><td>2,230,060</td><td>2.0%</td></tr>
<tr><td>40</td><td>Maine</td><td>548,247</td><td>0.5%</td><td>19</td><td>Arizona</td><td>2,224,992</td><td>2.0%</td></tr>
<tr><td>20</td><td>Maryland</td><td>2,089,031</td><td>1.9%</td><td>20</td><td>Maryland</td><td>2,089,031</td><td>1.9%</td></tr>
<tr><td>14</td><td>Massachusetts</td><td>2,446,485</td><td>2.2%</td><td>21</td><td>Minnesota</td><td>2,042,297</td><td>1.8%</td></tr>
<tr><td>8</td><td>Michigan</td><td>3,869,117</td><td>3.5%</td><td>22</td><td>Colorado</td><td>1,846,988</td><td>1.7%</td></tr>
<tr><td>21</td><td>Minnesota</td><td>2,042,297</td><td>1.8%</td><td>23</td><td>Alabama</td><td>1,796,058</td><td>1.6%</td></tr>
<tr><td>33</td><td>Mississippi</td><td>1,075,521</td><td>1.0%</td><td>24</td><td>South Carolina</td><td>1,656,978</td><td>1.5%</td></tr>
<tr><td>17</td><td>Missouri</td><td>2,305,027</td><td>2.1%</td><td>25</td><td>Kentucky</td><td>1,651,911</td><td>1.5%</td></tr>
<tr><td>44</td><td>Montana</td><td>372,190</td><td>0.3%</td><td>26</td><td>Louisiana</td><td>1,564,978</td><td>1.4%</td></tr>
<tr><td>38</td><td>Nebraska</td><td>700,888</td><td>0.6%</td><td>27</td><td>Oregon</td><td>1,449,662</td><td>1.3%</td></tr>
<tr><td>34</td><td>Nevada</td><td>936,828</td><td>0.8%</td><td>28</td><td>Oklahoma</td><td>1,385,300</td><td>1.2%</td></tr>
<tr><td>41</td><td>New Hampshire</td><td>504,503</td><td>0.5%</td><td>29</td><td>Connecticut</td><td>1,325,443</td><td>1.2%</td></tr>
<tr><td>11</td><td>New Jersey</td><td>3,135,490</td><td>2.8%</td><td>30</td><td>Iowa</td><td>1,208,765</td><td>1.1%</td></tr>
<tr><td>37</td><td>New Mexico</td><td>726,033</td><td>0.7%</td><td>31</td><td>Arkansas</td><td>1,103,428</td><td>1.0%</td></tr>
<tr><td>4</td><td>New York</td><td>7,088,376</td><td>6.4%</td><td>32</td><td>Kansas</td><td>1,088,288</td><td>1.0%</td></tr>
<tr><td>9</td><td>North Carolina</td><td>3,454,068</td><td>3.1%</td><td>33</td><td>Mississippi</td><td>1,075,521</td><td>1.0%</td></tr>
<tr><td>47</td><td>North Dakota</td><td>272,352</td><td>0.2%</td><td>34</td><td>Nevada</td><td>936,828</td><td>0.8%</td></tr>
<tr><td>7</td><td>Ohio</td><td>4,499,506</td><td>4.0%</td><td>35</td><td>Utah</td><td>814,028</td><td>0.7%</td></tr>
<tr><td>28</td><td>Oklahoma</td><td>1,385,300</td><td>1.2%</td><td>36</td><td>West Virginia</td><td>743,064</td><td>0.7%</td></tr>
<tr><td>27</td><td>Oregon</td><td>1,449,662</td><td>1.3%</td><td>37</td><td>New Mexico</td><td>726,033</td><td>0.7%</td></tr>
<tr><td>5</td><td>Pennsylvania</td><td>4,845,603</td><td>4.3%</td><td>38</td><td>Nebraska</td><td>700,888</td><td>0.6%</td></tr>
<tr><td>43</td><td>Rhode Island</td><td>405,627</td><td>0.4%</td><td>39</td><td>Idaho</td><td>548,555</td><td>0.5%</td></tr>
<tr><td>24</td><td>South Carolina</td><td>1,656,978</td><td>1.5%</td><td>40</td><td>Maine</td><td>548,247</td><td>0.5%</td></tr>
<tr><td>46</td><td>South Dakota</td><td>312,477</td><td>0.3%</td><td>41</td><td>New Hampshire</td><td>504,503</td><td>0.5%</td></tr>
<tr><td>16</td><td>Tennessee</td><td>2,375,123</td><td>2.1%</td><td>42</td><td>Hawaii</td><td>432,632</td><td>0.4%</td></tr>
<tr><td>2</td><td>Texas</td><td>8,109,388</td><td>7.3%</td><td>43</td><td>Rhode Island</td><td>405,627</td><td>0.4%</td></tr>
<tr><td>35</td><td>Utah</td><td>814,028</td><td>0.7%</td><td>44</td><td>Montana</td><td>372,190</td><td>0.3%</td></tr>
<tr><td>48</td><td>Vermont</td><td>253,808</td><td>0.2%</td><td>45</td><td>Delaware</td><td>320,110</td><td>0.3%</td></tr>
<tr><td>12</td><td>Virginia</td><td>2,905,071</td><td>2.6%</td><td>46</td><td>South Dakota</td><td>312,477</td><td>0.3%</td></tr>
<tr><td>13</td><td>Washington</td><td>2,471,912</td><td>2.2%</td><td>47</td><td>North Dakota</td><td>272,352</td><td>0.2%</td></tr>
<tr><td>36</td><td>West Virginia</td><td>743,064</td><td>0.7%</td><td>48</td><td>Vermont</td><td>253,808</td><td>0.2%</td></tr>
<tr><td>18</td><td>Wisconsin</td><td>2,230,060</td><td>2.0%</td><td>49</td><td>Alaska</td><td>229,878</td><td>0.2%</td></tr>
<tr><td>50</td><td>Wyoming</td><td>207,302</td><td>0.2%</td><td>50</td><td>Wyoming</td><td>207,302</td><td>0.2%</td></tr>
<tr><td></td><td></td><td></td><td></td><td></td><td>District of Columbia</td><td>250,456</td><td>0.2%</td></tr>
</table>

Source: U.S. Bureau of the Census
 "2006 American Community Survey" (http://www.census.gov/acs/www/index.html)
*A household includes all persons who occupy a housing unit. A household consists of a single family, one person living alone,
two or more families living together, or any other group of related or unrelated persons who share living arrangements.

Persons per Household in 2006

National Rate = 2.61 Persons per Household*

ALPHA ORDER				RANK ORDER		
RANK	STATE	PERSONS		RANK	STATE	PERSONS
28	Alabama	2.50		1	Utah	3.08
5	Alaska	2.81		2	California	2.93
6	Arizona	2.72		3	Hawaii	2.88
33	Arkansas	2.48		4	Texas	2.83
2	California	2.93		5	Alaska	2.81
25	Colorado	2.52		6	Arizona	2.72
18	Connecticut	2.56		6	New Jersey	2.72
17	Delaware	2.59		8	Georgia	2.69
31	Florida	2.49		9	Louisiana	2.66
8	Georgia	2.69		10	Illinois	2.65
3	Hawaii	2.88		11	New Mexico	2.64
16	Idaho	2.61		11	New York	2.64
10	Illinois	2.65		13	Nevada	2.63
25	Indiana	2.52		14	Maryland	2.62
47	Iowa	2.38		14	Mississippi	2.62
39	Kansas	2.46		16	Idaho	2.61
33	Kentucky	2.48		17	Delaware	2.59
9	Louisiana	2.66		18	Connecticut	2.56
49	Maine	2.34		19	Virginia	2.55
14	Maryland	2.62		20	Massachusetts	2.54
20	Massachusetts	2.54		20	Michigan	2.54
20	Michigan	2.54		22	New Hampshire	2.53
39	Minnesota	2.46		22	Rhode Island	2.53
14	Mississippi	2.62		22	Washington	2.53
39	Missouri	2.46		25	Colorado	2.52
37	Montana	2.47		25	Indiana	2.52
42	Nebraska	2.45		25	South Carolina	2.52
13	Nevada	2.63		28	Alabama	2.50
22	New Hampshire	2.53		28	Oklahoma	2.50
6	New Jersey	2.72		28	Oregon	2.50
11	New Mexico	2.64		31	Florida	2.49
11	New York	2.64		31	North Carolina	2.49
31	North Carolina	2.49		33	Arkansas	2.48
50	North Dakota	2.23		33	Kentucky	2.48
33	Ohio	2.48		33	Ohio	2.48
28	Oklahoma	2.50		33	Tennessee	2.48
28	Oregon	2.50		37	Montana	2.47
37	Pennsylvania	2.47		37	Pennsylvania	2.47
22	Rhode Island	2.53		39	Kansas	2.46
25	South Carolina	2.52		39	Minnesota	2.46
45	South Dakota	2.41		39	Missouri	2.46
33	Tennessee	2.48		42	Nebraska	2.45
4	Texas	2.83		43	Wisconsin	2.42
1	Utah	3.08		43	Wyoming	2.42
47	Vermont	2.38		45	South Dakota	2.41
19	Virginia	2.55		46	West Virginia	2.39
22	Washington	2.53		47	Iowa	2.38
46	West Virginia	2.39		47	Vermont	2.38
43	Wisconsin	2.42		49	Maine	2.34
43	Wyoming	2.42		50	North Dakota	2.23
					District of Columbia	2.18

Source: U.S. Bureau of the Census
   "2006 American Community Survey" (http://www.census.gov/acs/www/index.html)
*A household includes all persons who occupy a housing unit. A household consists of a single family, one person living alone, two or more families living together, or any other group of related or unrelated persons who share living arrangements.

Percent of Households with One Person in 2006

National Percent = 27.3% of Households

ALPHA ORDER

RANK	STATE	PERCENT
27	Alabama	27.7
45	Alaska	24.9
37	Arizona	26.8
37	Arkansas	26.8
47	California	24.6
14	Colorado	28.2
36	Connecticut	27.1
33	Delaware	27.2
19	Florida	28.0
42	Georgia	26.4
48	Hawaii	24.5
49	Idaho	23.9
17	Illinois	28.1
33	Indiana	27.2
22	Iowa	27.9
22	Kansas	27.9
14	Kentucky	28.2
41	Louisiana	26.5
33	Maine	27.2
39	Maryland	26.7
5	Massachusetts	28.9
19	Michigan	28.0
17	Minnesota	28.1
30	Mississippi	27.4
7	Missouri	28.8
5	Montana	28.9
10	Nebraska	28.3
40	Nevada	26.6
43	New Hampshire	25.6
43	New Jersey	25.6
9	New Mexico	28.4
2	New York	29.4
24	North Carolina	27.8
1	North Dakota	30.6
4	Ohio	29.1
10	Oklahoma	28.3
19	Oregon	28.0
3	Pennsylvania	29.3
8	Rhode Island	28.7
31	South Carolina	27.3
10	South Dakota	28.3
24	Tennessee	27.8
45	Texas	24.9
50	Utah	19.1
29	Vermont	27.5
24	Virginia	27.8
10	Washington	28.3
28	West Virginia	27.6
14	Wisconsin	28.2
31	Wyoming	27.3

RANK ORDER

RANK	STATE	PERCENT
1	North Dakota	30.6
2	New York	29.4
3	Pennsylvania	29.3
4	Ohio	29.1
5	Massachusetts	28.9
5	Montana	28.9
7	Missouri	28.8
8	Rhode Island	28.7
9	New Mexico	28.4
10	Nebraska	28.3
10	Oklahoma	28.3
10	South Dakota	28.3
10	Washington	28.3
14	Colorado	28.2
14	Kentucky	28.2
14	Wisconsin	28.2
17	Illinois	28.1
17	Minnesota	28.1
19	Florida	28.0
19	Michigan	28.0
19	Oregon	28.0
22	Iowa	27.9
22	Kansas	27.9
24	North Carolina	27.8
24	Tennessee	27.8
24	Virginia	27.8
27	Alabama	27.7
28	West Virginia	27.6
29	Vermont	27.5
30	Mississippi	27.4
31	South Carolina	27.3
31	Wyoming	27.3
33	Delaware	27.2
33	Indiana	27.2
33	Maine	27.2
36	Connecticut	27.1
37	Arizona	26.8
37	Arkansas	26.8
39	Maryland	26.7
40	Nevada	26.6
41	Louisiana	26.5
42	Georgia	26.4
43	New Hampshire	25.6
43	New Jersey	25.6
45	Alaska	24.9
45	Texas	24.9
47	California	24.6
48	Hawaii	24.5
49	Idaho	23.9
50	Utah	19.1

District of Columbia — 47.2

Source: CQ Press using data from U.S. Bureau of the Census
   "2006 American Community Survey" (http://www.census.gov/acs/www/index.html)
*A household includes all persons who occupy a housing unit. A household consists of a single family, one person living alone,
two or more families living together, or any other group of related or unrelated persons who share living arrangements.

Percent of Households Headed by Married Couples in 2006

National Percent = 49.7% of Households

ALPHA ORDER

ALPHA ORDER

RANK	STATE	PERCENT
36	Alabama	49.5
19	Alaska	51.0
32	Arizona	49.7
16	Arkansas	51.4
31	California	49.8
21	Colorado	50.6
16	Connecticut	51.4
38	Delaware	49.1
41	Florida	48.6
42	Georgia	48.5
13	Hawaii	51.5
2	Idaho	57.2
30	Illinois	49.9
18	Indiana	51.3
5	Iowa	53.1
9	Kansas	52.5
25	Kentucky	50.4
45	Louisiana	47.8
22	Maine	50.5
40	Maryland	48.7
44	Massachusetts	48.1
26	Michigan	50.1
11	Minnesota	52.1
49	Mississippi	46.3
26	Missouri	50.1
7	Montana	53.0
8	Nebraska	52.9
47	Nevada	47.4
5	New Hampshire	53.1
12	New Jersey	52.0
46	New Mexico	47.6
50	New York	45.1
37	North Carolina	49.4
20	North Dakota	50.8
39	Ohio	48.9
22	Oklahoma	50.5
33	Oregon	49.6
33	Pennsylvania	49.6
48	Rhode Island	47.0
43	South Carolina	48.2
3	South Dakota	53.2
33	Tennessee	49.6
13	Texas	51.5
1	Utah	61.9
26	Vermont	50.1
22	Virginia	50.5
29	Washington	50.0
9	West Virginia	52.5
13	Wisconsin	51.5
3	Wyoming	53.2

RANK ORDER

RANK	STATE	PERCENT
1	Utah	61.9
2	Idaho	57.2
3	South Dakota	53.2
3	Wyoming	53.2
5	Iowa	53.1
5	New Hampshire	53.1
7	Montana	53.0
8	Nebraska	52.9
9	Kansas	52.5
9	West Virginia	52.5
11	Minnesota	52.1
12	New Jersey	52.0
13	Hawaii	51.5
13	Texas	51.5
13	Wisconsin	51.5
16	Arkansas	51.4
16	Connecticut	51.4
18	Indiana	51.3
19	Alaska	51.0
20	North Dakota	50.8
21	Colorado	50.6
22	Maine	50.5
22	Oklahoma	50.5
22	Virginia	50.5
25	Kentucky	50.4
26	Michigan	50.1
26	Missouri	50.1
26	Vermont	50.1
29	Washington	50.0
30	Illinois	49.9
31	California	49.8
32	Arizona	49.7
33	Oregon	49.6
33	Pennsylvania	49.6
33	Tennessee	49.6
36	Alabama	49.5
37	North Carolina	49.4
38	Delaware	49.1
39	Ohio	48.9
40	Maryland	48.7
41	Florida	48.6
42	Georgia	48.5
43	South Carolina	48.2
44	Massachusetts	48.1
45	Louisiana	47.8
46	New Mexico	47.6
47	Nevada	47.4
48	Rhode Island	47.0
49	Mississippi	46.3
50	New York	45.1
	District of Columbia	22.3

Source: U.S. Bureau of the Census
    "2006 American Community Survey" (http://www.census.gov/acs/www/index.html)
*A household includes all persons who occupy a housing unit. A household consists of a single family, one person living alone, two or more families living together, or any other group of related or unrelated persons who share living arrangements.

Percent of Households Headed by Single Mothers in 2006

National Percent = 7.4% of Households*

ALPHA ORDER				RANK ORDER		
RANK	STATE	PERCENT		RANK	STATE	PERCENT
7	Alabama	8.3		1	Mississippi	10.8
5	Alaska	8.5		2	Louisiana	9.3
24	Arizona	7.2		3	Georgia	9.0
15	Arkansas	7.6		3	South Carolina	9.0
23	California	7.3		5	Alaska	8.5
37	Colorado	6.4		5	Texas	8.5
24	Connecticut	7.2		7	Alabama	8.3
21	Delaware	7.4		7	Rhode Island	8.3
28	Florida	7.0		9	New Mexico	8.1
3	Georgia	9.0		10	Maryland	8.0
48	Hawaii	5.4		10	New York	8.0
45	Idaho	5.7		10	North Carolina	8.0
21	Illinois	7.4		10	Tennessee	8.0
17	Indiana	7.5		14	Ohio	7.8
39	Iowa	6.2		15	Arkansas	7.6
32	Kansas	6.7		15	Oklahoma	7.6
17	Kentucky	7.5		17	Indiana	7.5
2	Louisiana	9.3		17	Kentucky	7.5
32	Maine	6.7		17	Michigan	7.5
10	Maryland	8.0		17	Missouri	7.5
30	Massachusetts	6.8		21	Delaware	7.4
17	Michigan	7.5		21	Illinois	7.4
40	Minnesota	6.1		23	California	7.3
1	Mississippi	10.8		24	Arizona	7.2
17	Missouri	7.5		24	Connecticut	7.2
50	Montana	5.1		24	Nevada	7.2
40	Nebraska	6.1		27	Virginia	7.1
24	Nevada	7.2		28	Florida	7.0
42	New Hampshire	5.9		28	New Jersey	7.0
28	New Jersey	7.0		30	Massachusetts	6.8
9	New Mexico	8.1		30	Vermont	6.8
10	New York	8.0		32	Kansas	6.7
10	North Carolina	8.0		32	Maine	6.7
49	North Dakota	5.2		34	Pennsylvania	6.6
14	Ohio	7.8		34	Washington	6.6
15	Oklahoma	7.6		34	Wisconsin	6.6
37	Oregon	6.4		37	Colorado	6.4
34	Pennsylvania	6.6		37	Oregon	6.4
7	Rhode Island	8.3		39	Iowa	6.2
3	South Carolina	9.0		40	Minnesota	6.1
47	South Dakota	5.6		40	Nebraska	6.1
10	Tennessee	8.0		42	New Hampshire	5.9
5	Texas	8.5		42	West Virginia	5.9
45	Utah	5.7		44	Wyoming	5.8
30	Vermont	6.8		45	Idaho	5.7
27	Virginia	7.1		45	Utah	5.7
34	Washington	6.6		47	South Dakota	5.6
42	West Virginia	5.9		48	Hawaii	5.4
34	Wisconsin	6.6		49	North Dakota	5.2
44	Wyoming	5.8		50	Montana	5.1
				District of Columbia		8.4

Source: CQ Press using data from U.S. Bureau of the Census
   "2006 American Community Survey" (http://www.census.gov/acs/www/index.html)
*No spouse present in household with children under 18 years old. A household includes all persons who occupy a housing unit.
A household consists of a single family, one person living alone, two or more families living together, or any other group of
related or unrelated persons who share living arrangements.

Percent of Households Headed by Single Fathers in 2006

National Percent = 2.2% of Households*

ALPHA ORDER

RANK	STATE	PERCENT
45	Alabama	1.9
2	Alaska	3.2
6	Arizona	2.6
22	Arkansas	2.2
4	California	2.8
14	Colorado	2.3
45	Connecticut	1.9
14	Delaware	2.3
36	Florida	2.0
22	Georgia	2.2
36	Hawaii	2.0
14	Idaho	2.3
36	Illinois	2.0
6	Indiana	2.6
28	Iowa	2.1
14	Kansas	2.3
28	Kentucky	2.1
28	Louisiana	2.1
6	Maine	2.6
14	Maryland	2.3
49	Massachusetts	1.7
22	Michigan	2.2
14	Minnesota	2.3
14	Mississippi	2.3
28	Missouri	2.1
36	Montana	2.0
36	Nebraska	2.0
1	Nevada	3.5
12	New Hampshire	2.4
36	New Jersey	2.0
3	New Mexico	3.0
36	New York	2.0
28	North Carolina	2.1
49	North Dakota	1.7
22	Ohio	2.2
9	Oklahoma	2.5
9	Oregon	2.5
28	Pennsylvania	2.1
45	Rhode Island	1.9
36	South Carolina	2.0
45	South Dakota	1.9
22	Tennessee	2.2
12	Texas	2.4
28	Utah	2.1
28	Vermont	2.1
36	Virginia	2.0
9	Washington	2.5
22	West Virginia	2.2
14	Wisconsin	2.3
5	Wyoming	2.7

RANK ORDER

RANK	STATE	PERCENT
1	Nevada	3.5
2	Alaska	3.2
3	New Mexico	3.0
4	California	2.8
5	Wyoming	2.7
6	Arizona	2.6
6	Indiana	2.6
6	Maine	2.6
9	Oklahoma	2.5
9	Oregon	2.5
9	Washington	2.5
12	New Hampshire	2.4
12	Texas	2.4
14	Colorado	2.3
14	Delaware	2.3
14	Idaho	2.3
14	Kansas	2.3
14	Maryland	2.3
14	Minnesota	2.3
14	Mississippi	2.3
14	Wisconsin	2.3
22	Arkansas	2.2
22	Georgia	2.2
22	Michigan	2.2
22	Ohio	2.2
22	Tennessee	2.2
22	West Virginia	2.2
28	Iowa	2.1
28	Kentucky	2.1
28	Louisiana	2.1
28	Missouri	2.1
28	North Carolina	2.1
28	Pennsylvania	2.1
28	Utah	2.1
28	Vermont	2.1
36	Florida	2.0
36	Hawaii	2.0
36	Illinois	2.0
36	Montana	2.0
36	Nebraska	2.0
36	New Jersey	2.0
36	New York	2.0
36	South Carolina	2.0
36	Virginia	2.0
45	Alabama	1.9
45	Connecticut	1.9
45	Rhode Island	1.9
45	South Dakota	1.9
49	Massachusetts	1.7
49	North Dakota	1.7

| | District of Columbia | 1.1 |

Source: CQ Press using data from U.S. Bureau of the Census
"2006 American Community Survey" (http://www.census.gov/acs/www/index.html)
*No spouse present in household with children under 18 years old. A household includes all persons who occupy a housing unit.
A household consists of a single family, one person living alone, two or more families living together, or any other group of
related or unrelated persons who share living arrangements.

Housing Units in 2006

National Total = 126,316,181 Housing Units*

ALPHA ORDER

RANK	STATE	HOUSING UNITS	% of USA
22	Alabama	2,110,154	1.7%
49	Alaska	276,571	0.2%
18	Arizona	2,605,283	2.1%
31	Arkansas	1,273,615	1.0%
1	California	13,174,378	10.4%
23	Colorado	2,094,898	1.7%
29	Connecticut	1,432,241	1.1%
45	Delaware	382,828	0.3%
3	Florida	8,533,419	6.8%
10	Georgia	3,873,183	3.1%
42	Hawaii	500,036	0.4%
40	Idaho	615,624	0.5%
6	Illinois	5,199,589	4.1%
13	Indiana	2,756,331	2.2%
30	Iowa	1,320,331	1.0%
33	Kansas	1,207,987	1.0%
25	Kentucky	1,888,164	1.5%
26	Louisiana	1,830,073	1.4%
39	Maine	691,132	0.5%
20	Maryland	2,300,567	1.8%
14	Massachusetts	2,708,986	2.1%
8	Michigan	4,513,726	3.6%
21	Minnesota	2,283,453	1.8%
32	Mississippi	1,241,489	1.0%
17	Missouri	2,623,094	2.1%
44	Montana	432,023	0.3%
38	Nebraska	774,843	0.6%
34	Nevada	1,065,197	0.8%
41	New Hampshire	589,812	0.5%
11	New Jersey	3,472,643	2.7%
37	New Mexico	850,095	0.7%
4	New York	7,907,420	6.3%
9	North Carolina	4,028,959	3.2%
48	North Dakota	307,802	0.2%
7	Ohio	5,044,709	4.0%
27	Oklahoma	1,607,349	1.3%
28	Oregon	1,586,498	1.3%
5	Pennsylvania	5,453,228	4.3%
43	Rhode Island	449,582	0.4%
24	South Carolina	1,975,638	1.6%
46	South Dakota	352,813	0.3%
16	Tennessee	2,681,150	2.1%
2	Texas	9,224,361	7.3%
35	Utah	901,283	0.7%
47	Vermont	309,557	0.2%
12	Virginia	3,230,803	2.6%
15	Washington	2,699,333	2.1%
36	West Virginia	877,784	0.7%
19	Wisconsin	2,534,075	2.0%
50	Wyoming	239,178	0.2%

RANK ORDER

RANK	STATE	HOUSING UNITS	% of USA
1	California	13,174,378	10.4%
2	Texas	9,224,361	7.3%
3	Florida	8,533,419	6.8%
4	New York	7,907,420	6.3%
5	Pennsylvania	5,453,228	4.3%
6	Illinois	5,199,589	4.1%
7	Ohio	5,044,709	4.0%
8	Michigan	4,513,726	3.6%
9	North Carolina	4,028,959	3.2%
10	Georgia	3,873,183	3.1%
11	New Jersey	3,472,643	2.7%
12	Virginia	3,230,803	2.6%
13	Indiana	2,756,331	2.2%
14	Massachusetts	2,708,986	2.1%
15	Washington	2,699,333	2.1%
16	Tennessee	2,681,150	2.1%
17	Missouri	2,623,094	2.1%
18	Arizona	2,605,283	2.1%
19	Wisconsin	2,534,075	2.0%
20	Maryland	2,300,567	1.8%
21	Minnesota	2,283,453	1.8%
22	Alabama	2,110,154	1.7%
23	Colorado	2,094,898	1.7%
24	South Carolina	1,975,638	1.6%
25	Kentucky	1,888,164	1.5%
26	Louisiana	1,830,073	1.4%
27	Oklahoma	1,607,349	1.3%
28	Oregon	1,586,498	1.3%
29	Connecticut	1,432,241	1.1%
30	Iowa	1,320,331	1.0%
31	Arkansas	1,273,615	1.0%
32	Mississippi	1,241,489	1.0%
33	Kansas	1,207,987	1.0%
34	Nevada	1,065,197	0.8%
35	Utah	901,283	0.7%
36	West Virginia	877,784	0.7%
37	New Mexico	850,095	0.7%
38	Nebraska	774,843	0.6%
39	Maine	691,132	0.5%
40	Idaho	615,624	0.5%
41	New Hampshire	589,812	0.5%
42	Hawaii	500,036	0.4%
43	Rhode Island	449,582	0.4%
44	Montana	432,023	0.3%
45	Delaware	382,828	0.3%
46	South Dakota	352,813	0.3%
47	Vermont	309,557	0.2%
48	North Dakota	307,802	0.2%
49	Alaska	276,571	0.2%
50	Wyoming	239,178	0.2%
	District of Columbia	282,894	0.2%

Source: U.S. Bureau of the Census
   "Housing Unit Estimates" (http://www.census.gov/popest/housing/HU-EST2006.html)
*A housing unit is a house, an apartment, a mobile home, a group of rooms, or a single room that is occupied (or if vacant, is intended for occupancy) as separate living quarters. Separate living quarters are those in which the occupants live and eat separately from any other persons in the building and which have direct access from the outside of the building or through a common hall.

Housing Units per Square Mile in 2006

National Average = 35.7 Housing Units*

ALPHA ORDER

RANK	STATE	HOUSING UNITS
25	Alabama	41.6
50	Alaska	0.5
36	Arizona	22.9
33	Arkansas	24.5
12	California	84.5
38	Colorado	20.2
4	Connecticut	295.6
6	Delaware	195.9
8	Florida	158.2
18	Georgia	66.9
16	Hawaii	77.9
44	Idaho	7.4
11	Illinois	93.5
17	Indiana	76.8
34	Iowa	23.6
40	Kansas	14.8
22	Kentucky	47.5
24	Louisiana	42.0
37	Maine	22.4
5	Maryland	235.4
3	Massachusetts	345.5
15	Michigan	79.5
31	Minnesota	28.7
32	Mississippi	26.5
27	Missouri	38.1
48	Montana	3.0
42	Nebraska	10.1
43	Nevada	9.7
19	New Hampshire	65.8
1	New Jersey	468.2
45	New Mexico	7.0
7	New York	167.5
13	North Carolina	82.7
47	North Dakota	4.5
9	Ohio	123.2
35	Oklahoma	23.4
39	Oregon	16.5
10	Pennsylvania	121.7
2	Rhode Island	430.2
20	South Carolina	65.6
46	South Dakota	4.6
21	Tennessee	65.0
29	Texas	35.2
41	Utah	11.0
30	Vermont	33.5
14	Virginia	81.6
26	Washington	40.6
28	West Virginia	36.5
23	Wisconsin	46.7
49	Wyoming	2.5

RANK ORDER

RANK	STATE	HOUSING UNITS
1	New Jersey	468.2
2	Rhode Island	430.2
3	Massachusetts	345.5
4	Connecticut	295.6
5	Maryland	235.4
6	Delaware	195.9
7	New York	167.5
8	Florida	158.2
9	Ohio	123.2
10	Pennsylvania	121.7
11	Illinois	93.5
12	California	84.5
13	North Carolina	82.7
14	Virginia	81.6
15	Michigan	79.5
16	Hawaii	77.9
17	Indiana	76.8
18	Georgia	66.9
19	New Hampshire	65.8
20	South Carolina	65.6
21	Tennessee	65.0
22	Kentucky	47.5
23	Wisconsin	46.7
24	Louisiana	42.0
25	Alabama	41.6
26	Washington	40.6
27	Missouri	38.1
28	West Virginia	36.5
29	Texas	35.2
30	Vermont	33.5
31	Minnesota	28.7
32	Mississippi	26.5
33	Arkansas	24.5
34	Iowa	23.6
35	Oklahoma	23.4
36	Arizona	22.9
37	Maine	22.4
38	Colorado	20.2
39	Oregon	16.5
40	Kansas	14.8
41	Utah	11.0
42	Nebraska	10.1
43	Nevada	9.7
44	Idaho	7.4
45	New Mexico	7.0
46	South Dakota	4.6
47	North Dakota	4.5
48	Montana	3.0
49	Wyoming	2.5
50	Alaska	0.5

District of Columbia 4,637.6

Source: CQ Press using data from U.S. Bureau of the Census
 "Housing Unit Estimates" (http://www.census.gov/popest/housing/HU-EST2006.html)
*Based on land area. A housing unit is a house, an apartment, a mobile home, a group of rooms, or a single room that is occupied (or if vacant, is intended for occupancy) as separate living quarters. Separate living quarters are those in which the occupants live and eat separately from any other persons in the building and which have direct access from the outside of the building or through a common hall.

Percent of Housing Units That are Owner-Occupied: 2006

National Percent = 67.3% of Housing Units*

ALPHA ORDER

RANK	STATE	PERCENT CHANGE
11	Alabama	71.8
45	Alaska	64.5
33	Arizona	68.5
35	Arkansas	68.3
49	California	58.4
31	Colorado	68.7
27	Connecticut	69.5
4	Delaware	74.4
18	Florida	70.3
38	Georgia	67.7
48	Hawaii	59.5
13	Idaho	71.3
21	Illinois	69.9
7	Indiana	72.1
5	Iowa	73.3
21	Kansas	69.9
14	Kentucky	70.7
33	Louisiana	68.5
6	Maine	72.8
29	Maryland	69.4
43	Massachusetts	64.9
2	Michigan	75.2
1	Minnesota	76.3
14	Mississippi	70.7
14	Missouri	70.7
21	Montana	69.9
37	Nebraska	67.9
47	Nevada	62.0
7	New Hampshire	72.1
39	New Jersey	67.3
26	New Mexico	69.7
50	New York	55.6
36	North Carolina	68.1
40	North Dakota	66.7
20	Ohio	70.0
32	Oklahoma	68.6
44	Oregon	64.8
12	Pennsylvania	71.7
46	Rhode Island	63.0
18	South Carolina	70.3
30	South Dakota	69.2
21	Tennessee	69.9
42	Texas	65.2
9	Utah	72.0
10	Vermont	71.9
21	Virginia	69.9
41	Washington	65.5
3	West Virginia	74.7
17	Wisconsin	70.5
27	Wyoming	69.5

RANK ORDER

RANK	STATE	PERCENT CHANGE
1	Minnesota	76.3
2	Michigan	75.2
3	West Virginia	74.7
4	Delaware	74.4
5	Iowa	73.3
6	Maine	72.8
7	Indiana	72.1
7	New Hampshire	72.1
9	Utah	72.0
10	Vermont	71.9
11	Alabama	71.8
12	Pennsylvania	71.7
13	Idaho	71.3
14	Kentucky	70.7
14	Mississippi	70.7
14	Missouri	70.7
17	Wisconsin	70.5
18	Florida	70.3
18	South Carolina	70.3
20	Ohio	70.0
21	Illinois	69.9
21	Kansas	69.9
21	Montana	69.9
21	Tennessee	69.9
21	Virginia	69.9
26	New Mexico	69.7
27	Connecticut	69.5
27	Wyoming	69.5
29	Maryland	69.4
30	South Dakota	69.2
31	Colorado	68.7
32	Oklahoma	68.6
33	Arizona	68.5
33	Louisiana	68.5
35	Arkansas	68.3
36	North Carolina	68.1
37	Nebraska	67.9
38	Georgia	67.7
39	New Jersey	67.3
40	North Dakota	66.7
41	Washington	65.5
42	Texas	65.2
43	Massachusetts	64.9
44	Oregon	64.8
45	Alaska	64.5
46	Rhode Island	63.0
47	Nevada	62.0
48	Hawaii	59.5
49	California	58.4
50	New York	55.6
	District of Columbia	45.8

Source: U.S. Bureau of the Census
  "2006 American Community Survey" (http://www.census.gov/acs/www/index.html)
*For occupied housing units.

New Housing Units Authorized in 2007

National Total = 1,380,470 Units*

ALPHA ORDER

RANK	STATE	UNITS	% of USA
19	Alabama	23,911	1.7%
50	Alaska	1,712	0.1%
7	Arizona	49,072	3.6%
35	Arkansas	10,318	0.7%
2	California	104,788	7.6%
15	Colorado	30,420	2.2%
38	Connecticut	7,576	0.5%
42	Delaware	5,192	0.4%
3	Florida	104,292	7.6%
5	Georgia	70,322	5.1%
39	Hawaii	6,946	0.5%
32	Idaho	12,706	0.9%
9	Illinois	42,666	3.1%
18	Indiana	24,130	1.7%
33	Iowa	10,580	0.8%
34	Kansas	10,499	0.8%
31	Kentucky	14,008	1.0%
20	Louisiana	22,537	1.6%
40	Maine	5,690	0.4%
24	Maryland	19,940	1.4%
29	Massachusetts	14,874	1.1%
26	Michigan	18,690	1.4%
27	Minnesota	17,529	1.3%
28	Mississippi	16,314	1.2%
25	Missouri	19,469	1.4%
43	Montana	4,609	0.3%
37	Nebraska	7,905	0.6%
16	Nevada	27,168	2.0%
44	New Hampshire	4,528	0.3%
17	New Jersey	25,828	1.9%
36	New Mexico	9,239	0.7%
6	New York	55,736	4.0%
4	North Carolina	82,907	6.0%
46	North Dakota	3,073	0.2%
14	Ohio	32,828	2.4%
30	Oklahoma	14,555	1.1%
21	Oregon	21,773	1.6%
13	Pennsylvania	33,776	2.4%
49	Rhode Island	1,949	0.1%
10	South Carolina	39,080	2.8%
41	South Dakota	5,227	0.4%
12	Tennessee	36,248	2.6%
1	Texas	174,391	12.6%
23	Utah	21,194	1.5%
48	Vermont	1,988	0.1%
11	Virginia	36,621	2.7%
8	Washington	44,944	3.3%
45	West Virginia	4,322	0.3%
22	Wisconsin	21,322	1.5%
47	Wyoming	3,050	0.2%

RANK ORDER

RANK	STATE	UNITS	% of USA
1	Texas	174,391	12.6%
2	California	104,788	7.6%
3	Florida	104,292	7.6%
4	North Carolina	82,907	6.0%
5	Georgia	70,322	5.1%
6	New York	55,736	4.0%
7	Arizona	49,072	3.6%
8	Washington	44,944	3.3%
9	Illinois	42,666	3.1%
10	South Carolina	39,080	2.8%
11	Virginia	36,621	2.7%
12	Tennessee	36,248	2.6%
13	Pennsylvania	33,776	2.4%
14	Ohio	32,828	2.4%
15	Colorado	30,420	2.2%
16	Nevada	27,168	2.0%
17	New Jersey	25,828	1.9%
18	Indiana	24,130	1.7%
19	Alabama	23,911	1.7%
20	Louisiana	22,537	1.6%
21	Oregon	21,773	1.6%
22	Wisconsin	21,322	1.5%
23	Utah	21,194	1.5%
24	Maryland	19,940	1.4%
25	Missouri	19,469	1.4%
26	Michigan	18,690	1.4%
27	Minnesota	17,529	1.3%
28	Mississippi	16,314	1.2%
29	Massachusetts	14,874	1.1%
30	Oklahoma	14,555	1.1%
31	Kentucky	14,008	1.0%
32	Idaho	12,706	0.9%
33	Iowa	10,580	0.8%
34	Kansas	10,499	0.8%
35	Arkansas	10,318	0.7%
36	New Mexico	9,239	0.7%
37	Nebraska	7,905	0.6%
38	Connecticut	7,576	0.5%
39	Hawaii	6,946	0.5%
40	Maine	5,690	0.4%
41	South Dakota	5,227	0.4%
42	Delaware	5,192	0.4%
43	Montana	4,609	0.3%
44	New Hampshire	4,528	0.3%
45	West Virginia	4,322	0.3%
46	North Dakota	3,073	0.2%
47	Wyoming	3,050	0.2%
48	Vermont	1,988	0.1%
49	Rhode Island	1,949	0.1%
50	Alaska	1,712	0.1%
	District of Columbia	2,028	0.1%

Source: U.S. Bureau of the Census
   "New Privately Owned Housing Units Authorized" (http://www.census.gov/const/www/C40/table2.html)
*Preliminary and unadjusted year to date as of December 2007. Includes single and multifamily privately owned units. Based on approximately 19,000 places in the U.S. having building permit systems.

Value of New Housing Units Authorized in 2007

National Total = $222,122,482,000*

ALPHA ORDER

RANK	STATE	VALUE	% of USA
24	Alabama	$3,142,494,000	1.4%
49	Alaska	326,909,000	0.1%
6	Arizona	8,001,353,000	3.6%
38	Arkansas	1,362,156,000	0.6%
2	California	20,050,235,000	9.0%
10	Colorado	6,322,163,000	2.8%
36	Connecticut	1,639,862,000	0.7%
46	Delaware	628,827,000	0.3%
3	Florida	18,337,316,000	8.3%
5	Georgia	10,067,488,000	4.5%
33	Hawaii	1,718,023,000	0.8%
29	Idaho	2,123,995,000	1.0%
9	Illinois	6,962,593,000	3.1%
19	Indiana	3,895,057,000	1.8%
35	Iowa	1,659,197,000	0.7%
37	Kansas	1,603,515,000	0.7%
31	Kentucky	1,847,223,000	0.8%
25	Louisiana	3,066,426,000	1.4%
40	Maine	874,897,000	0.4%
21	Maryland	3,701,487,000	1.7%
28	Massachusetts	2,760,761,000	1.2%
26	Michigan	3,048,407,000	1.4%
23	Minnesota	3,247,883,000	1.5%
32	Mississippi	1,772,953,000	0.8%
27	Missouri	2,906,900,000	1.3%
42	Montana	696,993,000	0.3%
39	Nebraska	1,051,479,000	0.5%
16	Nevada	4,308,336,000	1.9%
41	New Hampshire	866,604,000	0.4%
20	New Jersey	3,853,977,000	1.7%
34	New Mexico	1,697,281,000	0.8%
8	New York	7,171,001,000	3.2%
4	North Carolina	13,809,590,000	6.2%
47	North Dakota	414,569,000	0.2%
14	Ohio	5,368,237,000	2.4%
30	Oklahoma	2,092,639,000	0.9%
18	Oregon	4,086,668,000	1.8%
13	Pennsylvania	5,456,458,000	2.5%
50	Rhode Island	323,571,000	0.1%
12	South Carolina	5,979,087,000	2.7%
43	South Dakota	680,264,000	0.3%
15	Tennessee	5,087,212,000	2.3%
1	Texas	24,490,444,000	11.0%
17	Utah	4,162,225,000	1.9%
48	Vermont	329,276,000	0.1%
11	Virginia	6,212,207,000	2.8%
7	Washington	7,799,315,000	3.5%
44	West Virginia	676,699,000	0.3%
22	Wisconsin	3,563,740,000	1.6%
45	Wyoming	641,380,000	0.3%

RANK ORDER

RANK	STATE	VALUE	% of USA
1	Texas	$24,490,444,000	11.0%
2	California	20,050,235,000	9.0%
3	Florida	18,337,316,000	8.3%
4	North Carolina	13,809,590,000	6.2%
5	Georgia	10,067,488,000	4.5%
6	Arizona	8,001,353,000	3.6%
7	Washington	7,799,315,000	3.5%
8	New York	7,171,001,000	3.2%
9	Illinois	6,962,593,000	3.1%
10	Colorado	6,322,163,000	2.8%
11	Virginia	6,212,207,000	2.8%
12	South Carolina	5,979,087,000	2.7%
13	Pennsylvania	5,456,458,000	2.5%
14	Ohio	5,368,237,000	2.4%
15	Tennessee	5,087,212,000	2.3%
16	Nevada	4,308,336,000	1.9%
17	Utah	4,162,225,000	1.9%
18	Oregon	4,086,668,000	1.8%
19	Indiana	3,895,057,000	1.8%
20	New Jersey	3,853,977,000	1.7%
21	Maryland	3,701,487,000	1.7%
22	Wisconsin	3,563,740,000	1.6%
23	Minnesota	3,247,883,000	1.5%
24	Alabama	3,142,494,000	1.4%
25	Louisiana	3,066,426,000	1.4%
26	Michigan	3,048,407,000	1.4%
27	Missouri	2,906,900,000	1.3%
28	Massachusetts	2,760,761,000	1.2%
29	Idaho	2,123,995,000	1.0%
30	Oklahoma	2,092,639,000	0.9%
31	Kentucky	1,847,223,000	0.8%
32	Mississippi	1,772,953,000	0.8%
33	Hawaii	1,718,023,000	0.8%
34	New Mexico	1,697,281,000	0.8%
35	Iowa	1,659,197,000	0.7%
36	Connecticut	1,639,862,000	0.7%
37	Kansas	1,603,515,000	0.7%
38	Arkansas	1,362,156,000	0.6%
39	Nebraska	1,051,479,000	0.5%
40	Maine	874,897,000	0.4%
41	New Hampshire	866,604,000	0.4%
42	Montana	696,993,000	0.3%
43	South Dakota	680,264,000	0.3%
44	West Virginia	676,699,000	0.3%
45	Wyoming	641,380,000	0.3%
46	Delaware	628,827,000	0.3%
47	North Dakota	414,569,000	0.2%
48	Vermont	329,276,000	0.1%
49	Alaska	326,909,000	0.1%
50	Rhode Island	323,571,000	0.1%
	District of Columbia	235,119,000	0.1%

Source: U.S. Bureau of the Census
   "New Privately Owned Housing Units Authorized" (http://www.census.gov/const/www/C40/table2.html)
*Preliminary and unadjusted year to date as of December 2007. Includes single and multifamily privately owned units. Based on approximately 19,000 places in the U.S. having building permit systems.

Average Value of New Housing Units in 2007

National Average = $160,904 per Unit*

ALPHA ORDER

RANK	STATE	VALUE
46	Alabama	$131,425
8	Alaska	190,952
25	Arizona	163,053
44	Arkansas	132,017
7	California	191,341
4	Colorado	207,829
2	Connecticut	216,455
49	Delaware	121,115
14	Florida	175,827
38	Georgia	143,163
1	Hawaii	247,340
17	Idaho	167,165
23	Illinois	163,188
27	Indiana	161,420
29	Iowa	156,824
33	Kansas	152,730
45	Kentucky	131,869
41	Louisiana	136,062
31	Maine	153,760
10	Maryland	185,631
11	Massachusetts	185,610
24	Michigan	163,104
12	Minnesota	185,286
50	Mississippi	108,677
35	Missouri	149,309
34	Montana	151,224
43	Nebraska	133,014
28	Nevada	158,581
6	New Hampshire	191,388
36	New Jersey	149,217
13	New Mexico	183,708
48	New York	128,660
19	North Carolina	166,567
42	North Dakota	134,907
22	Ohio	163,526
37	Oklahoma	143,775
9	Oregon	187,694
26	Pennsylvania	161,548
20	Rhode Island	166,019
32	South Carolina	152,996
47	South Dakota	130,144
40	Tennessee	140,345
39	Texas	140,434
5	Utah	196,387
21	Vermont	165,632
16	Virginia	169,635
15	Washington	173,534
30	West Virginia	156,571
18	Wisconsin	167,139
3	Wyoming	210,289

RANK ORDER

RANK	STATE	VALUE
1	Hawaii	$247,340
2	Connecticut	216,455
3	Wyoming	210,289
4	Colorado	207,829
5	Utah	196,387
6	New Hampshire	191,388
7	California	191,341
8	Alaska	190,952
9	Oregon	187,694
10	Maryland	185,631
11	Massachusetts	185,610
12	Minnesota	185,286
13	New Mexico	183,708
14	Florida	175,827
15	Washington	173,534
16	Virginia	169,635
17	Idaho	167,165
18	Wisconsin	167,139
19	North Carolina	166,567
20	Rhode Island	166,019
21	Vermont	165,632
22	Ohio	163,526
23	Illinois	163,188
24	Michigan	163,104
25	Arizona	163,053
26	Pennsylvania	161,548
27	Indiana	161,420
28	Nevada	158,581
29	Iowa	156,824
30	West Virginia	156,571
31	Maine	153,760
32	South Carolina	152,996
33	Kansas	152,730
34	Montana	151,224
35	Missouri	149,309
36	New Jersey	149,217
37	Oklahoma	143,775
38	Georgia	143,163
39	Texas	140,434
40	Tennessee	140,345
41	Louisiana	136,062
42	North Dakota	134,907
43	Nebraska	133,014
44	Arkansas	132,017
45	Kentucky	131,869
46	Alabama	131,425
47	South Dakota	130,144
48	New York	128,660
49	Delaware	121,115
50	Mississippi	108,677
	District of Columbia	115,936

Source: CQ Press using data from U.S. Bureau of the Census
"New Privately Owned Housing Units Authorized" (http://www.census.gov/const/www/C40/table2.html)
*Preliminary and unadjusted year to date as of December 2007. Includes single and multifamily privately owned units. Based on approximately 19,000 places in the U.S. having building permit systems.

Median Value of Owner-Occupied Housing in 2006

National Median = $185,200*

ALPHA ORDER

RANK	STATE	MEDIAN
45	Alabama	$107,000
18	Alaska	213,200
14	Arizona	236,500
48	Arkansas	93,900
1	California	535,700
15	Colorado	232,900
8	Connecticut	298,900
17	Delaware	227,100
16	Florida	230,600
26	Georgia	156,800
2	Hawaii	529,700
24	Idaho	163,900
20	Illinois	200,200
37	Indiana	120,700
42	Iowa	112,600
40	Kansas	114,400
44	Kentucky	111,000
39	Louisiana	114,700
23	Maine	170,500
5	Maryland	334,700
3	Massachusetts	370,400
28	Michigan	153,300
19	Minnesota	208,200
50	Mississippi	88,600
34	Missouri	131,900
27	Montana	155,500
38	Nebraska	119,200
6	Nevada	315,200
11	New Hampshire	253,200
4	New Jersey	366,600
31	New Mexico	141,200
7	New York	303,400
32	North Carolina	137,200
46	North Dakota	99,700
33	Ohio	135,200
47	Oklahoma	94,500
13	Oregon	236,600
30	Pennsylvania	145,200
9	Rhode Island	295,700
36	South Carolina	122,400
42	South Dakota	112,600
35	Tennessee	123,100
41	Texas	114,000
22	Utah	188,500
21	Vermont	193,000
12	Virginia	244,200
10	Washington	267,600
49	West Virginia	89,700
25	Wisconsin	163,500
29	Wyoming	148,900

RANK ORDER

RANK	STATE	MEDIAN
1	California	$535,700
2	Hawaii	529,700
3	Massachusetts	370,400
4	New Jersey	366,600
5	Maryland	334,700
6	Nevada	315,200
7	New York	303,400
8	Connecticut	298,900
9	Rhode Island	295,700
10	Washington	267,600
11	New Hampshire	253,200
12	Virginia	244,200
13	Oregon	236,600
14	Arizona	236,500
15	Colorado	232,900
16	Florida	230,600
17	Delaware	227,100
18	Alaska	213,200
19	Minnesota	208,200
20	Illinois	200,200
21	Vermont	193,000
22	Utah	188,500
23	Maine	170,500
24	Idaho	163,900
25	Wisconsin	163,500
26	Georgia	156,800
27	Montana	155,500
28	Michigan	153,300
29	Wyoming	148,900
30	Pennsylvania	145,200
31	New Mexico	141,200
32	North Carolina	137,200
33	Ohio	135,200
34	Missouri	131,900
35	Tennessee	123,100
36	South Carolina	122,400
37	Indiana	120,700
38	Nebraska	119,200
39	Louisiana	114,700
40	Kansas	114,400
41	Texas	114,000
42	Iowa	112,600
42	South Dakota	112,600
44	Kentucky	111,000
45	Alabama	107,000
46	North Dakota	99,700
47	Oklahoma	94,500
48	Arkansas	93,900
49	West Virginia	89,700
50	Mississippi	88,600
	District of Columbia	437,700

Source: U.S. Bureau of the Census
"2006 American Community Survey" (http://www.census.gov/acs/www/index.html)
*Housing units with a mortgage.

Percent Change in House Prices: 2003 to 2007

National Percent Change = 46.9% Increase*

ALPHA ORDER

RANK	STATE	PERCENT CHANGE
29	Alabama	33.1
20	Alaska	51.3
3	Arizona	85.3
32	Arkansas	32.2
6	California	80.4
47	Colorado	18.3
23	Connecticut	46.3
12	Delaware	62.1
2	Florida	85.9
42	Georgia	25.6
1	Hawaii	99.9
11	Idaho	64.1
27	Illinois	37.1
48	Indiana	15.1
45	Iowa	22.4
44	Kansas	22.7
43	Kentucky	23.5
24	Louisiana	41.1
22	Maine	47.0
4	Maryland	85.1
38	Massachusetts	30.2
50	Michigan	6.6
37	Minnesota	30.7
32	Mississippi	32.2
39	Missouri	28.4
13	Montana	61.9
46	Nebraska	18.8
5	Nevada	84.3
26	New Hampshire	37.6
14	New Jersey	61.6
16	New Mexico	56.8
19	New York	53.4
32	North Carolina	32.2
25	North Dakota	40.6
49	Ohio	12.1
40	Oklahoma	27.7
8	Oregon	68.6
21	Pennsylvania	50.5
17	Rhode Island	56.1
29	South Carolina	33.1
31	South Dakota	32.7
35	Tennessee	32.0
41	Texas	26.0
18	Utah	54.4
15	Vermont	59.2
7	Virginia	70.2
9	Washington	67.3
28	West Virginia	34.3
36	Wisconsin	31.3
10	Wyoming	66.2

RANK ORDER

RANK	STATE	PERCENT CHANGE
1	Hawaii	99.9
2	Florida	85.9
3	Arizona	85.3
4	Maryland	85.1
5	Nevada	84.3
6	California	80.4
7	Virginia	70.2
8	Oregon	68.6
9	Washington	67.3
10	Wyoming	66.2
11	Idaho	64.1
12	Delaware	62.1
13	Montana	61.9
14	New Jersey	61.6
15	Vermont	59.2
16	New Mexico	56.8
17	Rhode Island	56.1
18	Utah	54.4
19	New York	53.4
20	Alaska	51.3
21	Pennsylvania	50.5
22	Maine	47.0
23	Connecticut	46.3
24	Louisiana	41.1
25	North Dakota	40.6
26	New Hampshire	37.6
27	Illinois	37.1
28	West Virginia	34.3
29	Alabama	33.1
29	South Carolina	33.1
31	South Dakota	32.7
32	Arkansas	32.2
32	Mississippi	32.2
32	North Carolina	32.2
35	Tennessee	32.0
36	Wisconsin	31.3
37	Minnesota	30.7
38	Massachusetts	30.2
39	Missouri	28.4
40	Oklahoma	27.7
41	Texas	26.0
42	Georgia	25.6
43	Kentucky	23.5
44	Kansas	22.7
45	Iowa	22.4
46	Nebraska	18.8
47	Colorado	18.3
48	Indiana	15.1
49	Ohio	12.1
50	Michigan	6.6

	District of Columbia	96.2

Source: Office of Federal Housing Enterprise Oversight
"House Price Index" (http://www.ofheo.gov/HPI.aspx)
*Single-family house prices. As of September 30, 2007.

Median Monthly Mortgage Payment in 2006

National Median = $1,402*

ALPHA ORDER

RANK	STATE	MORTGAGE
46	Alabama	$988
11	Alaska	1,611
20	Arizona	1,359
49	Arkansas	908
1	California	2,142
15	Colorado	1,534
5	Connecticut	1,870
19	Delaware	1,371
17	Florida	1,425
26	Georgia	1,289
3	Hawaii	1,959
34	Idaho	1,099
13	Illinois	1,566
36	Indiana	1,089
40	Iowa	1,063
32	Kansas	1,141
45	Kentucky	989
44	Louisiana	1,017
29	Maine	1,177
7	Maryland	1,736
4	Massachusetts	1,925
24	Michigan	1,302
16	Minnesota	1,436
48	Mississippi	940
35	Missouri	1,097
33	Montana	1,108
30	Nebraska	1,163
10	Nevada	1,617
9	New Hampshire	1,702
2	New Jersey	2,130
37	New Mexico	1,076
6	New York	1,789
31	North Carolina	1,144
43	North Dakota	1,043
28	Ohio	1,216
47	Oklahoma	971
18	Oregon	1,412
27	Pennsylvania	1,271
8	Rhode Island	1,707
42	South Carolina	1,055
37	South Dakota	1,076
39	Tennessee	1,072
23	Texas	1,309
25	Utah	1,294
21	Vermont	1,342
14	Virginia	1,540
12	Washington	1,573
50	West Virginia	853
22	Wisconsin	1,338
41	Wyoming	1,059

RANK ORDER

RANK	STATE	MORTGAGE
1	California	$2,142
2	New Jersey	2,130
3	Hawaii	1,959
4	Massachusetts	1,925
5	Connecticut	1,870
6	New York	1,789
7	Maryland	1,736
8	Rhode Island	1,707
9	New Hampshire	1,702
10	Nevada	1,617
11	Alaska	1,611
12	Washington	1,573
13	Illinois	1,566
14	Virginia	1,540
15	Colorado	1,534
16	Minnesota	1,436
17	Florida	1,425
18	Oregon	1,412
19	Delaware	1,371
20	Arizona	1,359
21	Vermont	1,342
22	Wisconsin	1,338
23	Texas	1,309
24	Michigan	1,302
25	Utah	1,294
26	Georgia	1,289
27	Pennsylvania	1,271
28	Ohio	1,216
29	Maine	1,177
30	Nebraska	1,163
31	North Carolina	1,144
32	Kansas	1,141
33	Montana	1,108
34	Idaho	1,099
35	Missouri	1,097
36	Indiana	1,089
37	New Mexico	1,076
37	South Dakota	1,076
39	Tennessee	1,072
40	Iowa	1,063
41	Wyoming	1,059
42	South Carolina	1,055
43	North Dakota	1,043
44	Louisiana	1,017
45	Kentucky	989
46	Alabama	988
47	Oklahoma	971
48	Mississippi	940
49	Arkansas	908
50	West Virginia	853
	District of Columbia	1,949

Source: U.S. Bureau of the Census
   "2006 American Community Survey" (http://www.census.gov/acs/www/index.html)
*For owner-occupied housing.

Percent of Home Owners Spending 30% or More of Household Income on Housing Costs: 2006
National Percent = 36.9% of Home Owners*

ALPHA ORDER

RANK	STATE	PERCENT
37	Alabama	28.8
20	Alaska	34.2
15	Arizona	37.4
42	Arkansas	26.9
1	California	51.8
14	Colorado	38.5
10	Connecticut	39.6
34	Delaware	31.3
4	Florida	44.9
24	Georgia	33.6
2	Hawaii	45.7
22	Idaho	33.9
13	Illinois	38.7
46	Indiana	26.7
48	Iowa	25.1
47	Kansas	25.8
40	Kentucky	27.7
38	Louisiana	28.7
25	Maine	33.4
18	Maryland	35.0
7	Massachusetts	41.8
17	Michigan	35.2
22	Minnesota	33.9
28	Mississippi	33.1
38	Missouri	28.7
19	Montana	34.7
41	Nebraska	27.5
3	Nevada	45.4
12	New Hampshire	39.0
5	New Jersey	44.7
36	New Mexico	31.0
8	New York	40.9
34	North Carolina	31.3
50	North Dakota	23.0
31	Ohio	31.8
44	Oklahoma	26.8
11	Oregon	39.1
30	Pennsylvania	32.6
6	Rhode Island	43.5
31	South Carolina	31.8
44	South Dakota	26.8
33	Tennessee	31.5
27	Texas	33.3
28	Utah	33.1
16	Vermont	36.5
20	Virginia	34.2
9	Washington	39.8
49	West Virginia	24.5
25	Wisconsin	33.4
42	Wyoming	26.9

RANK ORDER

RANK	STATE	PERCENT
1	California	51.8
2	Hawaii	45.7
3	Nevada	45.4
4	Florida	44.9
5	New Jersey	44.7
6	Rhode Island	43.5
7	Massachusetts	41.8
8	New York	40.9
9	Washington	39.8
10	Connecticut	39.6
11	Oregon	39.1
12	New Hampshire	39.0
13	Illinois	38.7
14	Colorado	38.5
15	Arizona	37.4
16	Vermont	36.5
17	Michigan	35.2
18	Maryland	35.0
19	Montana	34.7
20	Alaska	34.2
20	Virginia	34.2
22	Idaho	33.9
22	Minnesota	33.9
24	Georgia	33.6
25	Maine	33.4
25	Wisconsin	33.4
27	Texas	33.3
28	Mississippi	33.1
28	Utah	33.1
30	Pennsylvania	32.6
31	Ohio	31.8
31	South Carolina	31.8
33	Tennessee	31.5
34	Delaware	31.3
34	North Carolina	31.3
36	New Mexico	31.0
37	Alabama	28.8
38	Louisiana	28.7
38	Missouri	28.7
40	Kentucky	27.7
41	Nebraska	27.5
42	Arkansas	26.9
42	Wyoming	26.9
44	Oklahoma	26.8
44	South Dakota	26.8
46	Indiana	26.7
47	Kansas	25.8
48	Iowa	25.1
49	West Virginia	24.5
50	North Dakota	23.0
	District of Columbia	37.8

Source: U.S. Bureau of the Census
"2006 American Community Survey" (http://www.census.gov/acs/www/index.html)
*For owner-occupied housing units with a mortgage.

Existing Home Sales in 2007

National Total = 5,423,000 Homes*

ALPHA ORDER

RANK	STATE	HOMES	% of USA
15	Alabama	117,200	2.2%
39	Alaska	26,500	0.5%
23	Arizona	91,200	1.7%
29	Arkansas	71,200	1.3%
2	California	313,600	5.8%
19	Colorado	107,600	2.0%
32	Connecticut	62,400	1.2%
46	Delaware	14,800	0.3%
4	Florida	252,800	4.7%
8	Georgia	204,000	3.8%
38	Hawaii	28,000	0.5%
42	Idaho	24,800	0.5%
7	Illinois	232,400	4.3%
13	Indiana	130,800	2.4%
31	Iowa	66,000	1.2%
30	Kansas	67,200	1.2%
25	Kentucky	87,200	1.6%
27	Louisiana	76,400	1.4%
40	Maine	25,600	0.5%
26	Maryland	78,000	1.4%
15	Massachusetts	117,200	2.2%
10	Michigan	170,800	3.1%
24	Minnesota	90,000	1.7%
33	Mississippi	58,800	1.1%
17	Missouri	116,400	2.1%
43	Montana	22,400	0.4%
37	Nebraska	37,200	0.7%
35	Nevada	40,400	0.7%
NA	New Hampshire**	NA	NA
14	New Jersey	130,100	2.4%
34	New Mexico	42,400	0.8%
3	New York	291,200	5.4%
9	North Carolina	202,800	3.7%
47	North Dakota	14,400	0.3%
5	Ohio	238,400	4.4%
22	Oklahoma	97,600	1.8%
28	Oregon	74,000	1.4%
6	Pennsylvania	237,300	4.4%
45	Rhode Island	17,200	0.3%
21	South Carolina	101,600	1.9%
44	South Dakota	18,000	0.3%
11	Tennessee	153,600	2.8%
1	Texas	549,600	10.1%
36	Utah	39,600	0.7%
48	Vermont	13,300	0.2%
18	Virginia	108,400	2.0%
12	Washington	133,600	2.5%
40	West Virginia	25,600	0.5%
20	Wisconsin	103,200	1.9%
49	Wyoming	12,400	0.2%

RANK ORDER

RANK	STATE	HOMES	% of USA
1	Texas	549,600	10.1%
2	California	313,600	5.8%
3	New York	291,200	5.4%
4	Florida	252,800	4.7%
5	Ohio	238,400	4.4%
6	Pennsylvania	237,300	4.4%
7	Illinois	232,400	4.3%
8	Georgia	204,000	3.8%
9	North Carolina	202,800	3.7%
10	Michigan	170,800	3.1%
11	Tennessee	153,600	2.8%
12	Washington	133,600	2.5%
13	Indiana	130,800	2.4%
14	New Jersey	130,100	2.4%
15	Alabama	117,200	2.2%
15	Massachusetts	117,200	2.2%
17	Missouri	116,400	2.1%
18	Virginia	108,400	2.0%
19	Colorado	107,600	2.0%
20	Wisconsin	103,200	1.9%
21	South Carolina	101,600	1.9%
22	Oklahoma	97,600	1.8%
23	Arizona	91,200	1.7%
24	Minnesota	90,000	1.7%
25	Kentucky	87,200	1.6%
26	Maryland	78,000	1.4%
27	Louisiana	76,400	1.4%
28	Oregon	74,000	1.4%
29	Arkansas	71,200	1.3%
30	Kansas	67,200	1.2%
31	Iowa	66,000	1.2%
32	Connecticut	62,400	1.2%
33	Mississippi	58,800	1.1%
34	New Mexico	42,400	0.8%
35	Nevada	40,400	0.7%
36	Utah	39,600	0.7%
37	Nebraska	37,200	0.7%
38	Hawaii	28,000	0.5%
39	Alaska	26,500	0.5%
40	Maine	25,600	0.5%
40	West Virginia	25,600	0.5%
42	Idaho	24,800	0.5%
43	Montana	22,400	0.4%
44	South Dakota	18,000	0.3%
45	Rhode Island	17,200	0.3%
46	Delaware	14,800	0.3%
47	North Dakota	14,400	0.3%
48	Vermont	13,300	0.2%
49	Wyoming	12,400	0.2%
NA	New Hampshire**	NA	NA
	District of Columbia	9,200	0.2%

Source: National Association of Realtors®, Economics and Research Division
   "Existing Home Sales" (http://www.realtor.org/Research.nsf/Pages/MetroPrice)
*Seasonally adjusted preliminary data as of September 2007. Includes existing houses, apartment condos, and co-ops. Excludes new construction.
**Not available.

Percent Change in Existing Home Sales: 2006 to 2007

National Percent Change = 13.7% Decrease*

RANK	STATE (ALPHA ORDER)	PERCENT CHANGE		RANK	STATE (RANK ORDER)	PERCENT CHANGE
12	Alabama	(5.2)		1	North Dakota	2.9
36	Alaska	(17.2)		2	Vermont	0.8
46	Arizona	(30.9)		3	Hawaii	(1.4)
28	Arkansas	(12.3)		4	South Dakota	(2.2)
44	California	(27.8)		5	New York	(2.8)
18	Colorado	(9.4)		6	Nebraska	(3.1)
20	Connecticut	(9.8)		7	Pennsylvania	(3.2)
33	Delaware	(14.0)		8	Massachusetts	(3.3)
47	Florida	(32.0)		8	Mississippi	(3.3)
37	Georgia	(17.5)		10	Michigan	(4.0)
3	Hawaii	(1.4)		11	Texas	(5.0)
NA	Idaho**	NA		12	Alabama	(5.2)
38	Illinois	(17.6)		13	Kentucky	(7.2)
18	Indiana	(9.4)		13	Oklahoma	(7.2)
17	Iowa	(9.3)		15	Kansas	(8.7)
15	Kansas	(8.7)		16	Wyoming	(8.8)
13	Kentucky	(7.2)		17	Iowa	(9.3)
35	Louisiana	(17.0)		18	Colorado	(9.4)
32	Maine	(13.5)		18	Indiana	(9.4)
45	Maryland	(28.6)		20	Connecticut	(9.8)
8	Massachusetts	(3.3)		20	Wisconsin	(9.8)
10	Michigan	(4.0)		22	Washington	(10.2)
41	Minnesota	(20.2)		23	South Carolina	(10.6)
8	Mississippi	(3.3)		24	Missouri	(11.0)
24	Missouri	(11.0)		25	Tennessee	(11.3)
34	Montana	(16.4)		26	Ohio	(11.6)
6	Nebraska	(3.1)		27	Oregon	(11.9)
48	Nevada	(35.3)		28	Arkansas	(12.3)
NA	New Hampshire**	NA		29	North Carolina	(13.0)
31	New Jersey	(13.4)		30	Rhode Island	(13.1)
43	New Mexico	(23.7)		31	New Jersey	(13.4)
5	New York	(2.8)		32	Maine	(13.5)
29	North Carolina	(13.0)		33	Delaware	(14.0)
1	North Dakota	2.9		34	Montana	(16.4)
26	Ohio	(11.6)		35	Louisiana	(17.0)
13	Oklahoma	(7.2)		36	Alaska	(17.2)
27	Oregon	(11.9)		37	Georgia	(17.5)
7	Pennsylvania	(3.2)		38	Illinois	(17.6)
30	Rhode Island	(13.1)		39	West Virginia	(19.0)
23	South Carolina	(10.6)		40	Virginia	(19.1)
4	South Dakota	(2.2)		41	Minnesota	(20.2)
25	Tennessee	(11.3)		42	Utah	(21.4)
11	Texas	(5.0)		43	New Mexico	(23.7)
42	Utah	(21.4)		44	California	(27.8)
2	Vermont	0.8		45	Maryland	(28.6)
40	Virginia	(19.1)		46	Arizona	(30.9)
22	Washington	(10.2)		47	Florida	(32.0)
39	West Virginia	(19.0)		48	Nevada	(35.3)
20	Wisconsin	(9.8)		NA	Idaho**	NA
16	Wyoming	(8.8)		NA	New Hampshire**	NA
					District of Columbia	(11.5)

Source: National Association of Realtors®, Economics and Research Division
    "Existing Home Sales" (http://www.realtor.org/Research.nsf/Pages/MetroPrice)
*Seasonally adjusted preliminary data as of September 2007. Includes existing houses, apartment condos, and co-ops. Excludes new construction.
**Not available.

Homeownership Rate in 2006

National Rate = 68.8%*

ALPHA ORDER

RANK	STATE	PERCENT
8	Alabama	74.2
42	Alaska	67.2
23	Arizona	71.6
29	Arkansas	70.8
48	California	60.2
34	Colorado	70.1
27	Connecticut	71.1
3	Delaware	76.8
18	Florida	72.4
38	Georgia	68.5
49	Hawaii	59.9
7	Idaho	75.1
31	Illinois	70.4
8	Indiana	74.2
12	Iowa	74.0
35	Kansas	70.0
22	Kentucky	71.7
25	Louisiana	71.3
6	Maine	75.3
17	Maryland	72.6
46	Massachusetts	65.2
2	Michigan	77.4
5	Minnesota	75.6
4	Mississippi	76.2
21	Missouri	71.9
36	Montana	69.5
41	Nebraska	67.6
45	Nevada	65.7
8	New Hampshire	74.2
37	New Jersey	69.0
20	New Mexico	72.0
50	New York	55.7
32	North Carolina	70.2
39	North Dakota	68.3
19	Ohio	72.1
23	Oklahoma	71.6
40	Oregon	68.1
16	Pennsylvania	73.2
47	Rhode Island	64.6
8	South Carolina	74.2
30	South Dakota	70.6
25	Tennessee	71.3
44	Texas	66.0
15	Utah	73.5
12	Vermont	74.0
27	Virginia	71.1
43	Washington	66.7
1	West Virginia	78.4
32	Wisconsin	70.2
14	Wyoming	73.7

RANK ORDER

RANK	STATE	PERCENT
1	West Virginia	78.4
2	Michigan	77.4
3	Delaware	76.8
4	Mississippi	76.2
5	Minnesota	75.6
6	Maine	75.3
7	Idaho	75.1
8	Alabama	74.2
8	Indiana	74.2
8	New Hampshire	74.2
8	South Carolina	74.2
12	Iowa	74.0
12	Vermont	74.0
14	Wyoming	73.7
15	Utah	73.5
16	Pennsylvania	73.2
17	Maryland	72.6
18	Florida	72.4
19	Ohio	72.1
20	New Mexico	72.0
21	Missouri	71.9
22	Kentucky	71.7
23	Arizona	71.6
23	Oklahoma	71.6
25	Louisiana	71.3
25	Tennessee	71.3
27	Connecticut	71.1
27	Virginia	71.1
29	Arkansas	70.8
30	South Dakota	70.6
31	Illinois	70.4
32	North Carolina	70.2
32	Wisconsin	70.2
34	Colorado	70.1
35	Kansas	70.0
36	Montana	69.5
37	New Jersey	69.0
38	Georgia	68.5
39	North Dakota	68.3
40	Oregon	68.1
41	Nebraska	67.6
42	Alaska	67.2
43	Washington	66.7
44	Texas	66.0
45	Nevada	65.7
46	Massachusetts	65.2
47	Rhode Island	64.6
48	California	60.2
49	Hawaii	59.9
50	New York	55.7
	District of Columbia	45.9

Source: U.S. Bureau of the Census
"Housing Vacancies and Homeownership, Annual Statistics: 2006"
(http://www.census.gov/hhes/www/housing/hvs/annual06/ann06t13.html)
*Percent of households occupied by the owner.

Foreclosure Filings in 2007

National Total = 2,203,295 Foreclosures Filings*

ALPHA ORDER					RANK ORDER			
RANK	STATE	FILINGS	% of USA		RANK	STATE	FILINGS	% of USA
30	Alabama	7,903	0.4%		1	California	481,392	21.8%
40	Alaska	1,650	0.1%		2	Florida	279,325	12.7%
9	Arizona	69,970	3.2%		3	Ohio	153,196	7.0%
24	Arkansas	14,310	0.6%		4	Texas	149,703	6.8%
1	California	481,392	21.8%		5	Michigan	136,205	6.2%
8	Colorado	71,149	3.2%		6	Georgia	99,578	4.5%
22	Connecticut	23,470	1.1%		7	Illinois	90,782	4.1%
41	Delaware	1,430	0.1%		8	Colorado	71,149	3.2%
2	Florida	279,325	12.7%		9	Arizona	69,970	3.2%
6	Georgia	99,578	4.5%		10	Nevada	66,316	3.0%
43	Hawaii	1,270	0.1%		11	New York	57,350	2.6%
33	Idaho	6,032	0.3%		12	New Jersey	53,652	2.4%
7	Illinois	90,782	4.1%		13	Indiana	52,930	2.4%
13	Indiana	52,930	2.4%		14	Tennessee	45,834	2.1%
31	Iowa	7,404	0.3%		15	Massachusetts	41,487	1.9%
35	Kansas	4,978	0.2%		16	North Carolina	37,426	1.7%
29	Kentucky	8,793	0.4%		17	Pennsylvania	34,089	1.5%
32	Louisiana	7,331	0.3%		18	Missouri	32,022	1.5%
NA	Maine**	NA	NA		19	Maryland	25,109	1.1%
19	Maryland	25,109	1.1%		20	Virginia	24,199	1.1%
15	Massachusetts	41,487	1.9%		21	Washington	23,705	1.1%
5	Michigan	136,205	6.2%		22	Connecticut	23,470	1.1%
25	Minnesota	13,615	0.6%		23	Wisconsin	17,503	0.8%
39	Mississippi	1,997	0.1%		24	Arkansas	14,310	0.6%
18	Missouri	32,022	1.5%		25	Minnesota	13,615	0.6%
42	Montana	1,378	0.1%		26	Oklahoma	13,594	0.6%
36	Nebraska	3,971	0.2%		27	Oregon	10,746	0.5%
10	Nevada	66,316	3.0%		28	Utah	9,668	0.4%
NA	New Hampshire**	NA	NA		29	Kentucky	8,793	0.4%
12	New Jersey	53,652	2.4%		30	Alabama	7,903	0.4%
37	New Mexico	3,893	0.2%		31	Iowa	7,404	0.3%
11	New York	57,350	2.6%		32	Louisiana	7,331	0.3%
16	North Carolina	37,426	1.7%		33	Idaho	6,032	0.3%
46	North Dakota	308	0.0%		34	South Carolina	5,038	0.2%
3	Ohio	153,196	7.0%		35	Kansas	4,978	0.2%
26	Oklahoma	13,594	0.6%		36	Nebraska	3,971	0.2%
27	Oregon	10,746	0.5%		37	New Mexico	3,893	0.2%
17	Pennsylvania	34,089	1.5%		38	Rhode Island	3,241	0.1%
38	Rhode Island	3,241	0.1%		39	Mississippi	1,997	0.1%
34	South Carolina	5,038	0.2%		40	Alaska	1,650	0.1%
NA	South Dakota**	NA	NA		41	Delaware	1,430	0.1%
14	Tennessee	45,834	2.1%		42	Montana	1,378	0.1%
4	Texas	149,703	6.8%		43	Hawaii	1,270	0.1%
28	Utah	9,668	0.4%		44	West Virginia	1,135	0.1%
47	Vermont	61	0.0%		45	Wyoming	497	0.0%
20	Virginia	24,199	1.1%		46	North Dakota	308	0.0%
21	Washington	23,705	1.1%		47	Vermont	61	0.0%
44	West Virginia	1,135	0.1%		NA	Maine**	NA	NA
23	Wisconsin	17,503	0.8%		NA	New Hampshire**	NA	NA
45	Wyoming	497	0.0%		NA	South Dakota**	NA	NA
						District of Columbia	800	0.0%

Source: RealtyTrac

"U.S. Foreclosure Activity Increases 75 Percent in 2007" (Press Release, 01/29/08, www.realtytrac.com)

*Foreclosure filings include foreclosure-related documents filed in all phases of foreclosure.

**Not available.

Foreclosure Filings Rate in 2007

National Rate = 1.0% of Households*

ALPHA ORDER				RANK ORDER		
RANK	STATE	PERCENT		RANK	STATE	PERCENT
33	Alabama	0.3		1	Nevada	3.4
22	Alaska	0.5		2	Florida	2.0
8	Arizona	1.5		3	California	1.9
22	Arkansas	0.5		3	Colorado	1.9
3	California	1.9		3	Michigan	1.9
3	Colorado	1.9		6	Ohio	1.8
16	Connecticut	0.8		7	Georgia	1.6
33	Delaware	0.3		8	Arizona	1.5
2	Florida	2.0		9	Illinois	1.3
7	Georgia	1.6		10	Indiana	1.0
39	Hawaii	0.2		10	Tennessee	1.0
20	Idaho	0.6		12	Missouri	0.9
9	Illinois	1.3		12	New Jersey	0.9
10	Indiana	1.0		12	Texas	0.9
33	Iowa	0.3		12	Utah	0.9
39	Kansas	0.2		16	Connecticut	0.8
33	Kentucky	0.3		16	Maryland	0.8
39	Louisiana	0.2		18	Massachusetts	0.7
48	Maine	0.0		18	North Carolina	0.7
16	Maryland	0.8		20	Idaho	0.6
18	Massachusetts	0.7		20	Washington	0.6
3	Michigan	1.9		22	Alaska	0.5
22	Minnesota	0.5		22	Arkansas	0.5
45	Mississippi	0.1		22	Minnesota	0.5
12	Missouri	0.9		22	Nebraska	0.5
33	Montana	0.3		22	New York	0.5
22	Nebraska	0.5		22	Oklahoma	0.5
1	Nevada	3.4		22	Oregon	0.5
39	New Hampshire	0.2		22	Virginia	0.5
12	New Jersey	0.9		22	Wisconsin	0.5
31	New Mexico	0.4		31	New Mexico	0.4
22	New York	0.5		31	Rhode Island	0.4
18	North Carolina	0.7		33	Alabama	0.3
45	North Dakota	0.1		33	Delaware	0.3
6	Ohio	1.8		33	Iowa	0.3
22	Oklahoma	0.5		33	Kentucky	0.3
22	Oregon	0.5		33	Montana	0.3
33	Pennsylvania	0.3		33	Pennsylvania	0.3
31	Rhode Island	0.4		39	Hawaii	0.2
39	South Carolina	0.2		39	Kansas	0.2
48	South Dakota	0.0		39	Louisiana	0.2
10	Tennessee	1.0		39	New Hampshire	0.2
12	Texas	0.9		39	South Carolina	0.2
12	Utah	0.9		39	Wyoming	0.2
48	Vermont	0.0		45	Mississippi	0.1
22	Virginia	0.5		45	North Dakota	0.1
20	Washington	0.6		45	West Virginia	0.1
45	West Virginia	0.1		48	Maine	0.0
22	Wisconsin	0.5		48	South Dakota	0.0
39	Wyoming	0.2		48	Vermont	0.0
				District of Columbia		0.3

Source: RealtyTrac
"U.S. Foreclosure Activity Increases 75 Percent in 2007" (Press Release, 01/29/08, www.realtytrac.com)
*Foreclosure filings include foreclosure-related documents filed in all phases of foreclosure. Household numbers are based on the U.S. Census 2005 estimate of total housing units.

Percent Change in Foreclosure Filings: 2006 to 2007

National Percent Change = 75.0% Increase*

ALPHA ORDER

RANK	STATE	PERCENT CHANGE
11	Alabama	81.8
16	Alaska	54.6
6	Arizona	150.9
25	Arkansas	26.4
3	California	238.0
22	Colorado	30.0
NA	Connecticut**	NA
NA	Delaware**	NA
7	Florida	124.0
19	Georgia	31.1
9	Hawaii	88.7
NA	Idaho**	NA
26	Illinois	25.3
32	Indiana	11.3
NA	Iowa**	NA
30	Kansas	20.9
28	Kentucky	23.5
NA	Louisiana**	NA
NA	Maine**	NA
2	Maryland	455.3
5	Massachusetts	161.1
14	Michigan	68.3
NA	Minnesota**	NA
8	Mississippi	91.7
12	Missouri	80.9
23	Montana	29.3
20	Nebraska	30.9
4	Nevada	215.1
NA	New Hampshire**	NA
18	New Jersey	34.1
38	New Mexico	(26.0)
33	New York	10.2
15	North Carolina	66.5
13	North Dakota	74.0
10	Ohio	87.9
36	Oklahoma	(12.8)
31	Oregon	12.3
35	Pennsylvania	(11.1)
NA	Rhode Island**	NA
39	South Carolina	(27.6)
NA	South Dakota**	NA
27	Tennessee	24.6
34	Texas	(4.6)
37	Utah	(25.9)
17	Vermont	35.6
1	Virginia	456.3
24	Washington	28.0
21	West Virginia	30.3
NA	Wisconsin**	NA
29	Wyoming	21.5

RANK ORDER

RANK	STATE	PERCENT CHANGE
1	Virginia	456.3
2	Maryland	455.3
3	California	238.0
4	Nevada	215.1
5	Massachusetts	161.1
6	Arizona	150.9
7	Florida	124.0
8	Mississippi	91.7
9	Hawaii	88.7
10	Ohio	87.9
11	Alabama	81.8
12	Missouri	80.9
13	North Dakota	74.0
14	Michigan	68.3
15	North Carolina	66.5
16	Alaska	54.6
17	Vermont	35.6
18	New Jersey	34.1
19	Georgia	31.1
20	Nebraska	30.9
21	West Virginia	30.3
22	Colorado	30.0
23	Montana	29.3
24	Washington	28.0
25	Arkansas	26.4
26	Illinois	25.3
27	Tennessee	24.6
28	Kentucky	23.5
29	Wyoming	21.5
30	Kansas	20.9
31	Oregon	12.3
32	Indiana	11.3
33	New York	10.2
34	Texas	(4.6)
35	Pennsylvania	(11.1)
36	Oklahoma	(12.8)
37	Utah	(25.9)
38	New Mexico	(26.0)
39	South Carolina	(27.6)
NA	Connecticut**	NA
NA	Delaware**	NA
NA	Idaho**	NA
NA	Iowa**	NA
NA	Louisiana**	NA
NA	Maine**	NA
NA	Minnesota**	NA
NA	New Hampshire**	NA
NA	Rhode Island**	NA
NA	South Dakota**	NA
NA	Wisconsin**	NA
	District of Columbia**	NA

Source: RealtyTrac

"U.S. Foreclosure Activity Increases 75 Percent in 2007" (Press Release, 01/29/08, www.realtytrac.com)

*Foreclosure filings include foreclosure-related documents filed in all phases of foreclosure.

**Not available or no comparable data.

Median Monthly Rental Payment in 2006

National Median = $763*

ALPHA ORDER				RANK ORDER		
RANK	STATE	RENT		RANK	STATE	RENT
44	Alabama	$573		1	Hawaii	$1,116
8	Alaska	883		2	California	1,029
17	Arizona	762		3	New Jersey	974
46	Arkansas	566		4	Maryland	953
2	California	1,029		5	Massachusetts	933
15	Colorado	780		6	Nevada	917
7	Connecticut	886		7	Connecticut	886
14	Delaware	830		8	Alaska	883
10	Florida	872		9	New York	875
19	Georgia	738		10	Florida	872
1	Hawaii	1,116		11	New Hampshire	861
33	Idaho	623		12	Virginia	846
18	Illinois	761		13	Rhode Island	840
30	Indiana	638		14	Delaware	830
41	Iowa	584		15	Colorado	780
37	Kansas	609		16	Washington	779
47	Kentucky	548		17	Arizona	762
34	Louisiana	618		18	Illinois	761
31	Maine	636		19	Georgia	738
4	Maryland	953		20	Vermont	716
5	Massachusetts	933		21	Oregon	714
25	Michigan	675		22	Texas	711
23	Minnesota	701		23	Minnesota	701
41	Mississippi	584		24	Utah	697
38	Missouri	607		25	Michigan	675
45	Montana	571		26	Pennsylvania	664
40	Nebraska	593		27	Wisconsin	658
6	Nevada	917		28	North Carolina	656
11	New Hampshire	861		29	South Carolina	640
3	New Jersey	974		30	Indiana	638
35	New Mexico	617		31	Maine	636
9	New York	875		32	Ohio	627
28	North Carolina	656		33	Idaho	623
50	North Dakota	497		34	Louisiana	618
32	Ohio	627		35	New Mexico	617
43	Oklahoma	580		36	Tennessee	613
21	Oregon	714		37	Kansas	609
26	Pennsylvania	664		38	Missouri	607
13	Rhode Island	840		39	Wyoming	601
29	South Carolina	640		40	Nebraska	593
48	South Dakota	522		41	Iowa	584
36	Tennessee	613		41	Mississippi	584
22	Texas	711		43	Oklahoma	580
24	Utah	697		44	Alabama	573
20	Vermont	716		45	Montana	571
12	Virginia	846		46	Arkansas	566
16	Washington	779		47	Kentucky	548
49	West Virginia	499		48	South Dakota	522
27	Wisconsin	658		49	West Virginia	499
39	Wyoming	601		50	North Dakota	497
					District of Columbia	914

Source: U.S. Bureau of the Census
 "2006 American Community Survey" (http://www.census.gov/acs/www/index.html)
*For renter-occupied housing.

Percent of Renters Spending 30% or More of
Household Income on Rent and Utilities: 2006
National Percent = 46.0% of Renters

ALPHA ORDER

ALPHA ORDER

RANK ORDER

RANK	STATE	PERCENT	RANK	STATE	PERCENT
38	Alabama	41.0	1	Florida	52.0
47	Alaska	37.8	2	California	51.9
17	Arizona	45.2	3	Massachusetts	48.6
30	Arkansas	42.3	4	Nevada	48.1
2	California	51.9	4	New York	48.1
9	Colorado	47.1	6	Michigan	47.8
7	Connecticut	47.6	7	Connecticut	47.6
13	Delaware	46.0	8	New Jersey	47.3
1	Florida	52.0	9	Colorado	47.1
16	Georgia	45.6	9	Vermont	47.1
15	Hawaii	45.7	11	Oregon	47.0
46	Idaho	38.7	12	New Hampshire	46.4
13	Illinois	46.0	13	Delaware	46.0
22	Indiana	44.5	13	Illinois	46.0
40	Iowa	40.3	15	Hawaii	45.7
39	Kansas	40.8	16	Georgia	45.6
42	Kentucky	40.0	17	Arizona	45.2
29	Louisiana	42.5	18	Ohio	44.9
33	Maine	42.2	18	Rhode Island	44.9
24	Maryland	43.7	18	Washington	44.9
3	Massachusetts	48.6	21	Minnesota	44.6
6	Michigan	47.8	22	Indiana	44.5
21	Minnesota	44.6	23	Texas	44.4
27	Mississippi	42.7	24	Maryland	43.7
30	Missouri	42.3	25	Wisconsin	43.3
42	Montana	40.0	26	Pennsylvania	43.0
45	Nebraska	39.0	27	Mississippi	42.7
4	Nevada	48.1	27	North Carolina	42.7
12	New Hampshire	46.4	29	Louisiana	42.5
8	New Jersey	47.3	30	Arkansas	42.3
36	New Mexico	41.9	30	Missouri	42.3
4	New York	48.1	30	Tennessee	42.3
27	North Carolina	42.7	33	Maine	42.2
48	North Dakota	36.0	34	Utah	42.1
18	Ohio	44.9	34	Virginia	42.1
37	Oklahoma	41.4	36	New Mexico	41.9
11	Oregon	47.0	37	Oklahoma	41.4
26	Pennsylvania	43.0	38	Alabama	41.0
18	Rhode Island	44.9	39	Kansas	40.8
40	South Carolina	40.3	40	Iowa	40.3
49	South Dakota	34.0	40	South Carolina	40.3
30	Tennessee	42.3	42	Kentucky	40.0
23	Texas	44.4	42	Montana	40.0
34	Utah	42.1	44	West Virginia	39.3
9	Vermont	47.1	45	Nebraska	39.0
34	Virginia	42.1	46	Idaho	38.7
18	Washington	44.9	47	Alaska	37.8
44	West Virginia	39.3	48	North Dakota	36.0
25	Wisconsin	43.3	49	South Dakota	34.0
50	Wyoming	30.0	50	Wyoming	30.0
				District of Columbia	45.3

Source: U.S. Bureau of the Census
    "2006 American Community Survey" (http://www.census.gov/acs/www/index.html)

State and Local Government Expenditures
for Housing and Community Development in 2005
National Total = $39,994,594,000*

ALPHA ORDER

RANK	STATE	EXPENDITURES	% of USA
25	Alabama	$438,805,000	1.1%
33	Alaska	230,287,000	0.6%
26	Arizona	397,802,000	1.0%
39	Arkansas	170,969,000	0.4%
1	California	8,092,499,000	20.2%
19	Colorado	625,180,000	1.6%
18	Connecticut	635,018,000	1.6%
45	Delaware	118,890,000	0.3%
8	Florida	1,492,383,000	3.7%
13	Georgia	868,939,000	2.2%
40	Hawaii	166,368,000	0.4%
49	Idaho	45,050,000	0.1%
3	Illinois	1,929,632,000	4.8%
16	Indiana	764,719,000	1.9%
42	Iowa	157,678,000	0.4%
31	Kansas	232,968,000	0.6%
27	Kentucky	357,382,000	0.9%
22	Louisiana	515,312,000	1.3%
36	Maine	213,563,000	0.5%
11	Maryland	968,965,000	2.4%
7	Massachusetts	1,494,073,000	3.7%
12	Michigan	888,776,000	2.2%
17	Minnesota	752,848,000	1.9%
34	Mississippi	221,421,000	0.6%
20	Missouri	569,554,000	1.4%
46	Montana	104,802,000	0.3%
41	Nebraska	161,722,000	0.4%
30	Nevada	248,789,000	0.6%
35	New Hampshire	215,805,000	0.5%
10	New Jersey	1,068,972,000	2.7%
32	New Mexico	231,912,000	0.6%
2	New York	4,372,497,000	10.9%
15	North Carolina	777,576,000	1.9%
48	North Dakota	57,331,000	0.1%
5	Ohio	1,738,516,000	4.3%
38	Oklahoma	205,694,000	0.5%
23	Oregon	474,256,000	1.2%
4	Pennsylvania	1,891,980,000	4.7%
37	Rhode Island	210,416,000	0.5%
28	South Carolina	354,018,000	0.9%
47	South Dakota	84,294,000	0.2%
21	Tennessee	559,380,000	1.4%
6	Texas	1,635,618,000	4.1%
29	Utah	253,934,000	0.6%
44	Vermont	123,243,000	0.3%
14	Virginia	858,036,000	2.1%
9	Washington	1,108,546,000	2.8%
43	West Virginia	140,011,000	0.4%
24	Wisconsin	440,748,000	1.1%
50	Wyoming	15,703,000	0.0%

RANK ORDER

RANK	STATE	EXPENDITURES	% of USA
1	California	$8,092,499,000	20.2%
2	New York	4,372,497,000	10.9%
3	Illinois	1,929,632,000	4.8%
4	Pennsylvania	1,891,980,000	4.7%
5	Ohio	1,738,516,000	4.3%
6	Texas	1,635,618,000	4.1%
7	Massachusetts	1,494,073,000	3.7%
8	Florida	1,492,383,000	3.7%
9	Washington	1,108,546,000	2.8%
10	New Jersey	1,068,972,000	2.7%
11	Maryland	968,965,000	2.4%
12	Michigan	888,776,000	2.2%
13	Georgia	868,939,000	2.2%
14	Virginia	858,036,000	2.1%
15	North Carolina	777,576,000	1.9%
16	Indiana	764,719,000	1.9%
17	Minnesota	752,848,000	1.9%
18	Connecticut	635,018,000	1.6%
19	Colorado	625,180,000	1.6%
20	Missouri	569,554,000	1.4%
21	Tennessee	559,380,000	1.4%
22	Louisiana	515,312,000	1.3%
23	Oregon	474,256,000	1.2%
24	Wisconsin	440,748,000	1.1%
25	Alabama	438,805,000	1.1%
26	Arizona	397,802,000	1.0%
27	Kentucky	357,382,000	0.9%
28	South Carolina	354,018,000	0.9%
29	Utah	253,934,000	0.6%
30	Nevada	248,789,000	0.6%
31	Kansas	232,968,000	0.6%
32	New Mexico	231,912,000	0.6%
33	Alaska	230,287,000	0.6%
34	Mississippi	221,421,000	0.6%
35	New Hampshire	215,805,000	0.5%
36	Maine	213,563,000	0.5%
37	Rhode Island	210,416,000	0.5%
38	Oklahoma	205,694,000	0.5%
39	Arkansas	170,969,000	0.4%
40	Hawaii	166,368,000	0.4%
41	Nebraska	161,722,000	0.4%
42	Iowa	157,678,000	0.4%
43	West Virginia	140,011,000	0.4%
44	Vermont	123,243,000	0.3%
45	Delaware	118,890,000	0.3%
46	Montana	104,802,000	0.3%
47	South Dakota	84,294,000	0.2%
48	North Dakota	57,331,000	0.1%
49	Idaho	45,050,000	0.1%
50	Wyoming	15,703,000	0.0%
	District of Columbia	311,714,000	0.8%

Source: U.S. Bureau of the Census, Governments Division
"State and Local Government Finances: 2004-2005" (http://www.census.gov/govs/www/estimate05.html)
*Direct general expenditures.

Per Capita State and Local Government Expenditures
for Housing and Community Development in 2005
National Per Capita = $135*

ALPHA ORDER

RANK	STATE	PER CAPITA
30	Alabama	$97
1	Alaska	344
45	Arizona	67
46	Arkansas	62
4	California	225
17	Colorado	134
7	Connecticut	182
16	Delaware	141
39	Florida	84
31	Georgia	95
18	Hawaii	131
49	Idaho	32
13	Illinois	152
21	Indiana	122
48	Iowa	53
38	Kansas	85
37	Kentucky	86
23	Louisiana	115
11	Maine	163
9	Maryland	174
2	Massachusetts	232
36	Michigan	88
15	Minnesota	147
43	Mississippi	76
29	Missouri	98
25	Montana	112
33	Nebraska	92
27	Nevada	103
10	New Hampshire	166
20	New Jersey	123
22	New Mexico	121
3	New York	227
34	North Carolina	90
34	North Dakota	90
13	Ohio	152
47	Oklahoma	58
18	Oregon	131
12	Pennsylvania	153
6	Rhode Island	197
40	South Carolina	83
26	South Dakota	108
32	Tennessee	93
44	Texas	72
28	Utah	101
5	Vermont	199
24	Virginia	114
8	Washington	177
42	West Virginia	78
41	Wisconsin	80
50	Wyoming	31

RANK ORDER

RANK	STATE	PER CAPITA
1	Alaska	$344
2	Massachusetts	232
3	New York	227
4	California	225
5	Vermont	199
6	Rhode Island	197
7	Connecticut	182
8	Washington	177
9	Maryland	174
10	New Hampshire	166
11	Maine	163
12	Pennsylvania	153
13	Illinois	152
13	Ohio	152
15	Minnesota	147
16	Delaware	141
17	Colorado	134
18	Hawaii	131
18	Oregon	131
20	New Jersey	123
21	Indiana	122
22	New Mexico	121
23	Louisiana	115
24	Virginia	114
25	Montana	112
26	South Dakota	108
27	Nevada	103
28	Utah	101
29	Missouri	98
30	Alabama	97
31	Georgia	95
32	Tennessee	93
33	Nebraska	92
34	North Carolina	90
34	North Dakota	90
36	Michigan	88
37	Kentucky	86
38	Kansas	85
39	Florida	84
40	South Carolina	83
41	Wisconsin	80
42	West Virginia	78
43	Mississippi	76
44	Texas	72
45	Arizona	67
46	Arkansas	62
47	Oklahoma	58
48	Iowa	53
49	Idaho	32
50	Wyoming	31

	District of Columbia	536

Source: CQ Press using data from U.S. Bureau of the Census, Governments Division
"State and Local Government Finances: 2004-2005" (http://www.census.gov/govs/www/estimate05.html)
*Direct general expenditures.

XIII. Population

Population in 2007

National Total = 301,621,157*

ALPHA ORDER

RANK	STATE	POPULATION	% of USA
23	Alabama	4,627,851	1.5%
47	Alaska	683,478	0.2%
16	Arizona	6,338,755	2.1%
32	Arkansas	2,834,797	0.9%
1	California	36,553,215	12.1%
22	Colorado	4,861,515	1.6%
29	Connecticut	3,502,309	1.2%
45	Delaware	864,764	0.3%
4	Florida	18,251,243	6.1%
9	Georgia	9,544,750	3.2%
42	Hawaii	1,283,388	0.4%
39	Idaho	1,499,402	0.5%
5	Illinois	12,852,548	4.3%
15	Indiana	6,345,289	2.1%
30	Iowa	2,988,046	1.0%
33	Kansas	2,775,997	0.9%
26	Kentucky	4,241,474	1.4%
25	Louisiana	4,293,204	1.4%
40	Maine	1,317,207	0.4%
19	Maryland	5,618,344	1.9%
14	Massachusetts	6,449,755	2.1%
8	Michigan	10,071,822	3.3%
21	Minnesota	5,197,621	1.7%
31	Mississippi	2,918,785	1.0%
18	Missouri	5,878,415	1.9%
44	Montana	957,861	0.3%
38	Nebraska	1,774,571	0.6%
35	Nevada	2,565,382	0.9%
41	New Hampshire	1,315,828	0.4%
11	New Jersey	8,685,920	2.9%
36	New Mexico	1,969,915	0.7%
3	New York	19,297,729	6.4%
10	North Carolina	9,061,032	3.0%
48	North Dakota	639,715	0.2%
7	Ohio	11,466,917	3.8%
28	Oklahoma	3,617,316	1.2%
27	Oregon	3,747,455	1.2%
6	Pennsylvania	12,432,792	4.1%
43	Rhode Island	1,057,832	0.4%
24	South Carolina	4,407,709	1.5%
46	South Dakota	796,214	0.3%
17	Tennessee	6,156,719	2.0%
2	Texas	23,904,380	7.9%
34	Utah	2,645,330	0.9%
49	Vermont	621,254	0.2%
12	Virginia	7,712,091	2.6%
13	Washington	6,468,424	2.1%
37	West Virginia	1,812,035	0.6%
20	Wisconsin	5,601,640	1.9%
50	Wyoming	522,830	0.2%

RANK ORDER

RANK	STATE	POPULATION	% of USA
1	California	36,553,215	12.1%
2	Texas	23,904,380	7.9%
3	New York	19,297,729	6.4%
4	Florida	18,251,243	6.1%
5	Illinois	12,852,548	4.3%
6	Pennsylvania	12,432,792	4.1%
7	Ohio	11,466,917	3.8%
8	Michigan	10,071,822	3.3%
9	Georgia	9,544,750	3.2%
10	North Carolina	9,061,032	3.0%
11	New Jersey	8,685,920	2.9%
12	Virginia	7,712,091	2.6%
13	Washington	6,468,424	2.1%
14	Massachusetts	6,449,755	2.1%
15	Indiana	6,345,289	2.1%
16	Arizona	6,338,755	2.1%
17	Tennessee	6,156,719	2.0%
18	Missouri	5,878,415	1.9%
19	Maryland	5,618,344	1.9%
20	Wisconsin	5,601,640	1.9%
21	Minnesota	5,197,621	1.7%
22	Colorado	4,861,515	1.6%
23	Alabama	4,627,851	1.5%
24	South Carolina	4,407,709	1.5%
25	Louisiana	4,293,204	1.4%
26	Kentucky	4,241,474	1.4%
27	Oregon	3,747,455	1.2%
28	Oklahoma	3,617,316	1.2%
29	Connecticut	3,502,309	1.2%
30	Iowa	2,988,046	1.0%
31	Mississippi	2,918,785	1.0%
32	Arkansas	2,834,797	0.9%
33	Kansas	2,775,997	0.9%
34	Utah	2,645,330	0.9%
35	Nevada	2,565,382	0.9%
36	New Mexico	1,969,915	0.7%
37	West Virginia	1,812,035	0.6%
38	Nebraska	1,774,571	0.6%
39	Idaho	1,499,402	0.5%
40	Maine	1,317,207	0.4%
41	New Hampshire	1,315,828	0.4%
42	Hawaii	1,283,388	0.4%
43	Rhode Island	1,057,832	0.4%
44	Montana	957,861	0.3%
45	Delaware	864,764	0.3%
46	South Dakota	796,214	0.3%
47	Alaska	683,478	0.2%
48	North Dakota	639,715	0.2%
49	Vermont	621,254	0.2%
50	Wyoming	522,830	0.2%
	District of Columbia	588,292	0.2%

Source: U.S. Bureau of the Census
   "Population Estimates" (December 21, 2007, http://www.census.gov/popest/estimates.php)
*Resident population.

Population in 2006

National Total = 298,754,819*

RANK	STATE	POPULATION	% of USA
23	Alabama	4,590,240	1.5%
47	Alaska	677,450	0.2%
16	Arizona	6,165,689	2.1%
32	Arkansas	2,809,111	0.9%
1	California	36,249,872	12.1%
22	Colorado	4,766,248	1.6%
29	Connecticut	3,495,753	1.2%
45	Delaware	852,747	0.3%
4	Florida	18,057,508	6.0%
9	Georgia	9,342,080	3.1%
42	Hawaii	1,278,635	0.4%
39	Idaho	1,463,878	0.5%
5	Illinois	12,777,042	4.3%
15	Indiana	6,302,646	2.1%
30	Iowa	2,972,566	1.0%
33	Kansas	2,755,817	0.9%
26	Kentucky	4,204,444	1.4%
25	Louisiana	4,243,288	1.4%
40	Maine	1,314,910	0.4%
19	Maryland	5,602,017	1.9%
13	Massachusetts	6,434,389	2.2%
8	Michigan	10,102,322	3.4%
21	Minnesota	5,154,586	1.7%
31	Mississippi	2,899,112	1.0%
18	Missouri	5,837,639	2.0%
44	Montana	946,795	0.3%
38	Nebraska	1,763,765	0.6%
35	Nevada	2,492,427	0.8%
41	New Hampshire	1,311,821	0.4%
11	New Jersey	8,666,075	2.9%
36	New Mexico	1,942,302	0.7%
3	New York	19,281,988	6.5%
10	North Carolina	8,869,442	3.0%
48	North Dakota	637,460	0.2%
7	Ohio	11,463,513	3.8%
28	Oklahoma	3,577,536	1.2%
27	Oregon	3,691,084	1.2%
6	Pennsylvania	12,402,817	4.2%
43	Rhode Island	1,061,641	0.4%
24	South Carolina	4,330,108	1.4%
46	South Dakota	788,467	0.3%
17	Tennessee	6,074,913	2.0%
2	Texas	23,407,629	7.8%
34	Utah	2,579,535	0.9%
49	Vermont	620,778	0.2%
12	Virginia	7,640,249	2.6%
14	Washington	6,374,910	2.1%
37	West Virginia	1,808,699	0.6%
20	Wisconsin	5,572,660	1.9%
50	Wyoming	512,757	0.2%

RANK	STATE	POPULATION	% of USA
1	California	36,249,872	12.1%
2	Texas	23,407,629	7.8%
3	New York	19,281,988	6.5%
4	Florida	18,057,508	6.0%
5	Illinois	12,777,042	4.3%
6	Pennsylvania	12,402,817	4.2%
7	Ohio	11,463,513	3.8%
8	Michigan	10,102,322	3.4%
9	Georgia	9,342,080	3.1%
10	North Carolina	8,869,442	3.0%
11	New Jersey	8,666,075	2.9%
12	Virginia	7,640,249	2.6%
13	Massachusetts	6,434,389	2.2%
14	Washington	6,374,910	2.1%
15	Indiana	6,302,646	2.1%
16	Arizona	6,165,689	2.1%
17	Tennessee	6,074,913	2.0%
18	Missouri	5,837,639	2.0%
19	Maryland	5,602,017	1.9%
20	Wisconsin	5,572,660	1.9%
21	Minnesota	5,154,586	1.7%
22	Colorado	4,766,248	1.6%
23	Alabama	4,590,240	1.5%
24	South Carolina	4,330,108	1.4%
25	Louisiana	4,243,288	1.4%
26	Kentucky	4,204,444	1.4%
27	Oregon	3,691,084	1.2%
28	Oklahoma	3,577,536	1.2%
29	Connecticut	3,495,753	1.2%
30	Iowa	2,972,566	1.0%
31	Mississippi	2,899,112	1.0%
32	Arkansas	2,809,111	0.9%
33	Kansas	2,755,817	0.9%
34	Utah	2,579,535	0.9%
35	Nevada	2,492,427	0.8%
36	New Mexico	1,942,302	0.7%
37	West Virginia	1,808,699	0.6%
38	Nebraska	1,763,765	0.6%
39	Idaho	1,463,878	0.5%
40	Maine	1,314,910	0.4%
41	New Hampshire	1,311,821	0.4%
42	Hawaii	1,278,635	0.4%
43	Rhode Island	1,061,641	0.4%
44	Montana	946,795	0.3%
45	Delaware	852,747	0.3%
46	South Dakota	788,467	0.3%
47	Alaska	677,450	0.2%
48	North Dakota	637,460	0.2%
49	Vermont	620,778	0.2%
50	Wyoming	512,757	0.2%
	District of Columbia	585,459	0.2%

Source: U.S. Bureau of the Census
"Population Estimates" (December 21, 2007, http://www.census.gov/popest/estimates.php)
*Resident population. Revised estimates.

Numerical Population Change: 2006 to 2007

National Total = 2,866,338 Increase*

ALPHA ORDER

RANK	STATE	GAIN/LOSS	% of USA
21	Alabama	37,611	1.3%
41	Alaska	6,028	0.2%
6	Arizona	173,066	6.0%
27	Arkansas	25,686	0.9%
2	California	303,343	10.6%
7	Colorado	95,267	3.3%
40	Connecticut	6,556	0.2%
35	Delaware	12,017	0.4%
4	Florida	193,735	6.8%
3	Georgia	202,670	7.1%
42	Hawaii	4,753	0.2%
23	Idaho	35,524	1.2%
11	Illinois	75,506	2.6%
18	Indiana	42,643	1.5%
33	Iowa	15,480	0.5%
28	Kansas	20,180	0.7%
22	Kentucky	37,030	1.3%
16	Louisiana	49,916	1.7%
46	Maine	2,297	0.1%
31	Maryland	16,327	0.6%
34	Massachusetts	15,366	0.5%
50	Michigan	(30,500)	
17	Minnesota	43,035	1.5%
30	Mississippi	19,673	0.7%
19	Missouri	40,776	1.4%
36	Montana	11,066	0.4%
37	Nebraska	10,806	0.4%
12	Nevada	72,955	2.5%
43	New Hampshire	4,007	0.1%
29	New Jersey	19,845	0.7%
26	New Mexico	27,613	1.0%
32	New York	15,741	0.5%
5	North Carolina	191,590	6.7%
47	North Dakota	2,255	0.1%
44	Ohio	3,404	0.1%
20	Oklahoma	39,780	1.4%
15	Oregon	56,371	2.0%
24	Pennsylvania	29,975	1.0%
49	Rhode Island	(3,809)	
10	South Carolina	77,601	2.7%
39	South Dakota	7,747	0.3%
9	Tennessee	81,806	2.9%
1	Texas	496,751	17.3%
14	Utah	65,795	2.3%
48	Vermont	476	0.0%
13	Virginia	71,842	2.5%
8	Washington	93,514	3.3%
45	West Virginia	3,336	0.1%
25	Wisconsin	28,980	1.0%
38	Wyoming	10,073	0.4%

RANK ORDER

RANK	STATE	GAIN/LOSS	% of USA
1	Texas	496,751	17.3%
2	California	303,343	10.6%
3	Georgia	202,670	7.1%
4	Florida	193,735	6.8%
5	North Carolina	191,590	6.7%
6	Arizona	173,066	6.0%
7	Colorado	95,267	3.3%
8	Washington	93,514	3.3%
9	Tennessee	81,806	2.9%
10	South Carolina	77,601	2.7%
11	Illinois	75,506	2.6%
12	Nevada	72,955	2.5%
13	Virginia	71,842	2.5%
14	Utah	65,795	2.3%
15	Oregon	56,371	2.0%
16	Louisiana	49,916	1.7%
17	Minnesota	43,035	1.5%
18	Indiana	42,643	1.5%
19	Missouri	40,776	1.4%
20	Oklahoma	39,780	1.4%
21	Alabama	37,611	1.3%
22	Kentucky	37,030	1.3%
23	Idaho	35,524	1.2%
24	Pennsylvania	29,975	1.0%
25	Wisconsin	28,980	1.0%
26	New Mexico	27,613	1.0%
27	Arkansas	25,686	0.9%
28	Kansas	20,180	0.7%
29	New Jersey	19,845	0.7%
30	Mississippi	19,673	0.7%
31	Maryland	16,327	0.6%
32	New York	15,741	0.5%
33	Iowa	15,480	0.5%
34	Massachusetts	15,366	0.5%
35	Delaware	12,017	0.4%
36	Montana	11,066	0.4%
37	Nebraska	10,806	0.4%
38	Wyoming	10,073	0.4%
39	South Dakota	7,747	0.3%
40	Connecticut	6,556	0.2%
41	Alaska	6,028	0.2%
42	Hawaii	4,753	0.2%
43	New Hampshire	4,007	0.1%
44	Ohio	3,404	0.1%
45	West Virginia	3,336	0.1%
46	Maine	2,297	0.1%
47	North Dakota	2,255	0.1%
48	Vermont	476	0.0%
49	Rhode Island	(3,809)	
50	Michigan	(30,500)	
	District of Columbia	2,833	0.1%

Source: U.S. Bureau of the Census
  "Population Estimates" (December 21, 2007, http://www.census.gov/popest/estimates.php)
*Resident population from July 1, 2006 to July 1, 2007.

Percent Change in Population: 2006 to 2007

National Percent Change = 1.0% Increase*

ALPHA ORDER

RANK	STATE	PERCENT CHANGE
25	Alabama	0.8
21	Alaska	0.9
2	Arizona	2.8
21	Arkansas	0.9
25	California	0.8
8	Colorado	2.0
40	Connecticut	0.2
13	Delaware	1.4
18	Florida	1.1
5	Georgia	2.2
36	Hawaii	0.4
4	Idaho	2.4
32	Illinois	0.6
28	Indiana	0.7
34	Iowa	0.5
28	Kansas	0.7
21	Kentucky	0.9
16	Louisiana	1.2
40	Maine	0.2
38	Maryland	0.3
40	Massachusetts	0.2
49	Michigan	(0.3)
25	Minnesota	0.8
28	Mississippi	0.7
28	Missouri	0.7
16	Montana	1.2
32	Nebraska	0.6
1	Nevada	2.9
38	New Hampshire	0.3
40	New Jersey	0.2
13	New Mexico	1.4
46	New York	0.1
5	North Carolina	2.2
36	North Dakota	0.4
48	Ohio	0.0
18	Oklahoma	1.1
11	Oregon	1.5
40	Pennsylvania	0.2
50	Rhode Island	(0.4)
10	South Carolina	1.8
20	South Dakota	1.0
15	Tennessee	1.3
7	Texas	2.1
3	Utah	2.6
46	Vermont	0.1
21	Virginia	0.9
11	Washington	1.5
40	West Virginia	0.2
34	Wisconsin	0.5
8	Wyoming	2.0

RANK ORDER

RANK	STATE	PERCENT CHANGE
1	Nevada	2.9
2	Arizona	2.8
3	Utah	2.6
4	Idaho	2.4
5	Georgia	2.2
5	North Carolina	2.2
7	Texas	2.1
8	Colorado	2.0
8	Wyoming	2.0
10	South Carolina	1.8
11	Oregon	1.5
11	Washington	1.5
13	Delaware	1.4
13	New Mexico	1.4
15	Tennessee	1.3
16	Louisiana	1.2
16	Montana	1.2
18	Florida	1.1
18	Oklahoma	1.1
20	South Dakota	1.0
21	Alaska	0.9
21	Arkansas	0.9
21	Kentucky	0.9
21	Virginia	0.9
25	Alabama	0.8
25	California	0.8
25	Minnesota	0.8
28	Indiana	0.7
28	Kansas	0.7
28	Mississippi	0.7
28	Missouri	0.7
32	Illinois	0.6
32	Nebraska	0.6
34	Iowa	0.5
34	Wisconsin	0.5
36	Hawaii	0.4
36	North Dakota	0.4
38	Maryland	0.3
38	New Hampshire	0.3
40	Connecticut	0.2
40	Maine	0.2
40	Massachusetts	0.2
40	New Jersey	0.2
40	Pennsylvania	0.2
40	West Virginia	0.2
46	New York	0.1
46	Vermont	0.1
48	Ohio	0.0
49	Michigan	(0.3)
50	Rhode Island	(0.4)
	District of Columbia	0.5

Source: U.S. Bureau of the Census
   "Population Estimates" (December 21, 2007, http://www.census.gov/popest/estimates.php)
*Resident population from July 1, 2006 to July 1, 2007.

Population in 2000 Census

National Total = 281,421,906*

ALPHA ORDER

RANK	STATE	POPULATION	% of USA
23	Alabama	4,447,100	1.6%
48	Alaska	626,932	0.2%
20	Arizona	5,130,632	1.8%
33	Arkansas	2,673,400	0.9%
1	California	33,871,648	12.0%
24	Colorado	4,301,261	1.5%
29	Connecticut	3,405,565	1.2%
45	Delaware	783,600	0.3%
4	Florida	15,982,378	5.7%
10	Georgia	8,186,453	2.9%
42	Hawaii	1,211,537	0.4%
39	Idaho	1,293,953	0.5%
5	Illinois	12,419,293	4.4%
14	Indiana	6,080,485	2.2%
30	Iowa	2,926,324	1.0%
32	Kansas	2,688,418	1.0%
25	Kentucky	4,041,769	1.4%
22	Louisiana	4,468,976	1.6%
40	Maine	1,274,923	0.5%
19	Maryland	5,296,486	1.9%
13	Massachusetts	6,349,097	2.3%
8	Michigan	9,938,444	3.5%
21	Minnesota	4,919,479	1.7%
31	Mississippi	2,844,658	1.0%
17	Missouri	5,595,211	2.0%
44	Montana	902,195	0.3%
38	Nebraska	1,711,263	0.6%
35	Nevada	1,998,257	0.7%
41	New Hampshire	1,235,786	0.4%
9	New Jersey	8,414,350	3.0%
36	New Mexico	1,819,046	0.6%
3	New York	18,976,457	6.7%
11	North Carolina	8,049,313	2.9%
47	North Dakota	642,200	0.2%
7	Ohio	11,353,140	4.0%
27	Oklahoma	3,450,654	1.2%
28	Oregon	3,421,399	1.2%
6	Pennsylvania	12,281,054	4.4%
43	Rhode Island	1,048,319	0.4%
26	South Carolina	4,012,012	1.4%
46	South Dakota	754,844	0.3%
16	Tennessee	5,689,283	2.0%
2	Texas	20,851,820	7.4%
34	Utah	2,233,169	0.8%
49	Vermont	608,827	0.2%
12	Virginia	7,078,515	2.5%
15	Washington	5,894,121	2.1%
37	West Virginia	1,808,344	0.6%
18	Wisconsin	5,363,675	1.9%
50	Wyoming	493,782	0.2%

RANK ORDER

RANK	STATE	POPULATION	% of USA
1	California	33,871,648	12.0%
2	Texas	20,851,820	7.4%
3	New York	18,976,457	6.7%
4	Florida	15,982,378	5.7%
5	Illinois	12,419,293	4.4%
6	Pennsylvania	12,281,054	4.4%
7	Ohio	11,353,140	4.0%
8	Michigan	9,938,444	3.5%
9	New Jersey	8,414,350	3.0%
10	Georgia	8,186,453	2.9%
11	North Carolina	8,049,313	2.9%
12	Virginia	7,078,515	2.5%
13	Massachusetts	6,349,097	2.3%
14	Indiana	6,080,485	2.2%
15	Washington	5,894,121	2.1%
16	Tennessee	5,689,283	2.0%
17	Missouri	5,595,211	2.0%
18	Wisconsin	5,363,675	1.9%
19	Maryland	5,296,486	1.9%
20	Arizona	5,130,632	1.8%
21	Minnesota	4,919,479	1.7%
22	Louisiana	4,468,976	1.6%
23	Alabama	4,447,100	1.6%
24	Colorado	4,301,261	1.5%
25	Kentucky	4,041,769	1.4%
26	South Carolina	4,012,012	1.4%
27	Oklahoma	3,450,654	1.2%
28	Oregon	3,421,399	1.2%
29	Connecticut	3,405,565	1.2%
30	Iowa	2,926,324	1.0%
31	Mississippi	2,844,658	1.0%
32	Kansas	2,688,418	1.0%
33	Arkansas	2,673,400	0.9%
34	Utah	2,233,169	0.8%
35	Nevada	1,998,257	0.7%
36	New Mexico	1,819,046	0.6%
37	West Virginia	1,808,344	0.6%
38	Nebraska	1,711,263	0.6%
39	Idaho	1,293,953	0.5%
40	Maine	1,274,923	0.5%
41	New Hampshire	1,235,786	0.4%
42	Hawaii	1,211,537	0.4%
43	Rhode Island	1,048,319	0.4%
44	Montana	902,195	0.3%
45	Delaware	783,600	0.3%
46	South Dakota	754,844	0.3%
47	North Dakota	642,200	0.2%
48	Alaska	626,932	0.2%
49	Vermont	608,827	0.2%
50	Wyoming	493,782	0.2%
	District of Columbia	572,059	0.2%

Source: U.S. Bureau of the Census
   "First Census 2000 Results" (December 28, 2000, http://www.census.gov/main/www/cen2000.html)
*Resident population as of April 2000 Census.

Population per Square Mile in 2007

National Rate = 85.3 Persons per Square Mile*

ALPHA ORDER

RANK	STATE	RATE
27	Alabama	91.2
50	Alaska	1.2
33	Arizona	55.8
34	Arkansas	54.4
11	California	234.4
37	Colorado	46.9
4	Connecticut	722.9
6	Delaware	442.6
8	Florida	338.4
18	Georgia	164.8
13	Hawaii	199.8
44	Idaho	18.1
12	Illinois	231.2
17	Indiana	176.9
35	Iowa	53.5
40	Kansas	33.9
22	Kentucky	106.8
24	Louisiana	98.6
38	Maine	42.7
5	Maryland	574.8
3	Massachusetts	822.7
16	Michigan	177.3
31	Minnesota	65.3
32	Mississippi	62.2
28	Missouri	85.3
48	Montana	6.6
43	Nebraska	23.1
42	Nevada	23.4
20	New Hampshire	146.7
1	New Jersey	1,171.1
45	New Mexico	16.2
7	New York	408.7
15	North Carolina	186.0
47	North Dakota	9.3
9	Ohio	280.0
36	Oklahoma	52.7
39	Oregon	39.0
10	Pennsylvania	277.4
2	Rhode Island	1,012.3
21	South Carolina	146.4
46	South Dakota	10.5
19	Tennessee	149.4
26	Texas	91.3
41	Utah	32.2
30	Vermont	67.2
14	Virginia	194.8
25	Washington	97.2
29	West Virginia	75.3
23	Wisconsin	103.1
49	Wyoming	5.4

RANK ORDER

RANK	STATE	RATE
1	New Jersey	1,171.1
2	Rhode Island	1,012.3
3	Massachusetts	822.7
4	Connecticut	722.9
5	Maryland	574.8
6	Delaware	442.6
7	New York	408.7
8	Florida	338.4
9	Ohio	280.0
10	Pennsylvania	277.4
11	California	234.4
12	Illinois	231.2
13	Hawaii	199.8
14	Virginia	194.8
15	North Carolina	186.0
16	Michigan	177.3
17	Indiana	176.9
18	Georgia	164.8
19	Tennessee	149.4
20	New Hampshire	146.7
21	South Carolina	146.4
22	Kentucky	106.8
23	Wisconsin	103.1
24	Louisiana	98.6
25	Washington	97.2
26	Texas	91.3
27	Alabama	91.2
28	Missouri	85.3
29	West Virginia	75.3
30	Vermont	67.2
31	Minnesota	65.3
32	Mississippi	62.2
33	Arizona	55.8
34	Arkansas	54.4
35	Iowa	53.5
36	Oklahoma	52.7
37	Colorado	46.9
38	Maine	42.7
39	Oregon	39.0
40	Kansas	33.9
41	Utah	32.2
42	Nevada	23.4
43	Nebraska	23.1
44	Idaho	18.1
45	New Mexico	16.2
46	South Dakota	10.5
47	North Dakota	9.3
48	Montana	6.6
49	Wyoming	5.4
50	Alaska	1.2
	District of Columbia	9,644.1

Source: CQ Press using data from U.S. Bureau of the Census
"Population Estimates" (December 21, 2007, http://www.census.gov/popest/estimates.php)
*Resident population. Based on land area of states.

Male Population in 2006

National Total = 147,512,152 Males

RANK	STATE	MALES	% of USA
23	Alabama	2,229,469	1.5%
47	Alaska	346,411	0.2%
16	Arizona	3,085,755	2.1%
32	Arkansas	1,377,711	0.9%
1	California	18,224,444	12.4%
22	Colorado	2,393,004	1.6%
29	Connecticut	1,706,188	1.2%
45	Delaware	414,244	0.3%
4	Florida	8,884,135	6.0%
9	Georgia	4,611,078	3.1%
42	Hawaii	643,328	0.4%
39	Idaho	738,366	0.5%
5	Illinois	6,317,460	4.3%
15	Indiana	3,110,503	2.1%
30	Iowa	1,472,810	1.0%
33	Kansas	1,371,446	0.9%
26	Kentucky	2,061,310	1.4%
25	Louisiana	2,085,761	1.4%
41	Maine	646,427	0.4%
20	Maryland	2,716,854	1.8%
14	Massachusetts	3,117,205	2.1%
8	Michigan	4,969,692	3.4%
21	Minnesota	2,568,869	1.7%
31	Mississippi	1,409,348	1.0%
18	Missouri	2,854,715	1.9%
44	Montana	472,660	0.3%
38	Nebraska	876,754	0.6%
35	Nevada	1,268,894	0.9%
40	New Hampshire	648,568	0.4%
11	New Jersey	4,262,291	2.9%
36	New Mexico	964,808	0.7%
3	New York	9,355,020	6.3%
10	North Carolina	4,341,298	2.9%
48	North Dakota	319,427	0.2%
7	Ohio	5,597,677	3.8%
28	Oklahoma	1,764,514	1.2%
27	Oregon	1,839,688	1.2%
6	Pennsylvania	6,047,537	4.1%
43	Rhode Island	516,213	0.3%
24	South Carolina	2,103,713	1.4%
46	South Dakota	390,578	0.3%
17	Tennessee	2,950,890	2.0%
2	Texas	11,714,068	7.9%
34	Utah	1,282,401	0.9%
49	Vermont	307,023	0.2%
12	Virginia	3,756,771	2.5%
13	Washington	3,189,630	2.2%
37	West Virginia	890,588	0.6%
19	Wisconsin	2,760,942	1.9%
50	Wyoming	261,002	0.2%

RANK	STATE	MALES	% of USA
1	California	18,224,444	12.4%
2	Texas	11,714,068	7.9%
3	New York	9,355,020	6.3%
4	Florida	8,884,135	6.0%
5	Illinois	6,317,460	4.3%
6	Pennsylvania	6,047,537	4.1%
7	Ohio	5,597,677	3.8%
8	Michigan	4,969,692	3.4%
9	Georgia	4,611,078	3.1%
10	North Carolina	4,341,298	2.9%
11	New Jersey	4,262,291	2.9%
12	Virginia	3,756,771	2.5%
13	Washington	3,189,630	2.2%
14	Massachusetts	3,117,205	2.1%
15	Indiana	3,110,503	2.1%
16	Arizona	3,085,755	2.1%
17	Tennessee	2,950,890	2.0%
18	Missouri	2,854,715	1.9%
19	Wisconsin	2,760,942	1.9%
20	Maryland	2,716,854	1.8%
21	Minnesota	2,568,869	1.7%
22	Colorado	2,393,004	1.6%
23	Alabama	2,229,469	1.5%
24	South Carolina	2,103,713	1.4%
25	Louisiana	2,085,761	1.4%
26	Kentucky	2,061,310	1.4%
27	Oregon	1,839,688	1.2%
28	Oklahoma	1,764,514	1.2%
29	Connecticut	1,706,188	1.2%
30	Iowa	1,472,810	1.0%
31	Mississippi	1,409,348	1.0%
32	Arkansas	1,377,711	0.9%
33	Kansas	1,371,446	0.9%
34	Utah	1,282,401	0.9%
35	Nevada	1,268,894	0.9%
36	New Mexico	964,808	0.7%
37	West Virginia	890,588	0.6%
38	Nebraska	876,754	0.6%
39	Idaho	738,366	0.5%
40	New Hampshire	648,568	0.4%
41	Maine	646,427	0.4%
42	Hawaii	643,328	0.4%
43	Rhode Island	516,213	0.3%
44	Montana	472,660	0.3%
45	Delaware	414,244	0.3%
46	South Dakota	390,578	0.3%
47	Alaska	346,411	0.2%
48	North Dakota	319,427	0.2%
49	Vermont	307,023	0.2%
50	Wyoming	261,002	0.2%
	District of Columbia	272,664	0.2%

Source: CQ Press using data from U.S. Bureau of the Census
"SC-EST2006-AGESEX_RES - State Characteristic Estimates" (http://www.census.gov/popest/datasets.html)

Female Population in 2006

National Total = 151,886,332 Females

ALPHA ORDER					RANK ORDER			
RANK	STATE	FEMALES	% of USA		RANK	STATE	FEMALES	% of USA
22	Alabama	2,369,561	1.6%		1	California	18,233,105	12.0%
47	Alaska	323,642	0.2%		2	Texas	11,793,715	7.8%
17	Arizona	3,080,563	2.0%		3	New York	9,951,163	6.6%
32	Arkansas	1,433,161	0.9%		4	Florida	9,205,753	6.1%
1	California	18,233,105	12.0%		5	Illinois	6,514,510	4.3%
23	Colorado	2,360,373	1.6%		6	Pennsylvania	6,393,084	4.2%
29	Connecticut	1,798,621	1.2%		7	Ohio	5,880,329	3.9%
45	Delaware	439,232	0.3%		8	Michigan	5,125,951	3.4%
4	Florida	9,205,753	6.1%		9	Georgia	4,752,863	3.1%
9	Georgia	4,752,863	3.1%		10	North Carolina	4,515,207	3.0%
42	Hawaii	642,170	0.4%		11	New Jersey	4,462,269	2.9%
39	Idaho	728,099	0.5%		12	Virginia	3,886,113	2.6%
5	Illinois	6,514,510	4.3%		13	Massachusetts	3,319,988	2.2%
15	Indiana	3,203,017	2.1%		14	Washington	3,206,168	2.1%
30	Iowa	1,509,275	1.0%		15	Indiana	3,203,017	2.1%
33	Kansas	1,392,629	0.9%		16	Tennessee	3,087,913	2.0%
26	Kentucky	2,144,764	1.4%		17	Arizona	3,080,563	2.0%
25	Louisiana	2,202,007	1.4%		18	Missouri	2,987,998	2.0%
40	Maine	675,147	0.4%		19	Maryland	2,898,873	1.9%
19	Maryland	2,898,873	1.9%		20	Wisconsin	2,795,564	1.8%
13	Massachusetts	3,319,988	2.2%		21	Minnesota	2,598,232	1.7%
8	Michigan	5,125,951	3.4%		22	Alabama	2,369,561	1.6%
21	Minnesota	2,598,232	1.7%		23	Colorado	2,360,373	1.6%
31	Mississippi	1,501,192	1.0%		24	South Carolina	2,217,536	1.5%
18	Missouri	2,987,998	2.0%		25	Louisiana	2,202,007	1.4%
44	Montana	471,972	0.3%		26	Kentucky	2,144,764	1.4%
38	Nebraska	891,577	0.6%		27	Oregon	1,861,070	1.2%
35	Nevada	1,226,635	0.8%		28	Oklahoma	1,814,698	1.2%
41	New Hampshire	666,327	0.4%		29	Connecticut	1,798,621	1.2%
11	New Jersey	4,462,269	2.9%		30	Iowa	1,509,275	1.0%
36	New Mexico	989,791	0.7%		31	Mississippi	1,501,192	1.0%
3	New York	9,951,163	6.6%		32	Arkansas	1,433,161	0.9%
10	North Carolina	4,515,207	3.0%		33	Kansas	1,392,629	0.9%
49	North Dakota	316,440	0.2%		34	Utah	1,267,662	0.8%
7	Ohio	5,880,329	3.9%		35	Nevada	1,226,635	0.8%
28	Oklahoma	1,814,698	1.2%		36	New Mexico	989,791	0.7%
27	Oregon	1,861,070	1.2%		37	West Virginia	927,882	0.6%
6	Pennsylvania	6,393,084	4.2%		38	Nebraska	891,577	0.6%
43	Rhode Island	551,397	0.4%		39	Idaho	728,099	0.5%
24	South Carolina	2,217,536	1.5%		40	Maine	675,147	0.4%
46	South Dakota	391,341	0.3%		41	New Hampshire	666,327	0.4%
16	Tennessee	3,087,913	2.0%		42	Hawaii	642,170	0.4%
2	Texas	11,793,715	7.8%		43	Rhode Island	551,397	0.4%
34	Utah	1,267,662	0.8%		44	Montana	471,972	0.3%
48	Vermont	316,885	0.2%		45	Delaware	439,232	0.3%
12	Virginia	3,886,113	2.6%		46	South Dakota	391,341	0.3%
14	Washington	3,206,168	2.1%		47	Alaska	323,642	0.2%
37	West Virginia	927,882	0.6%		48	Vermont	316,885	0.2%
20	Wisconsin	2,795,564	1.8%		49	North Dakota	316,440	0.2%
50	Wyoming	254,002	0.2%		50	Wyoming	254,002	0.2%
					District of Columbia		308,866	0.2%

Source: CQ Press using data from U.S. Bureau of the Census
"SC-EST2006-AGESEX_RES - State Characteristic Estimates" (http://www.census.gov/popest/datasets.html)

Male to Female Ratio in 2006

National Ratio = 97.1 Males per 100 Females

ALPHA ORDER				RANK ORDER		
RANK	STATE	RATIO		RANK	STATE	RATIO
45	Alabama	94.1		1	Alaska	107.0
1	Alaska	107.0		2	Nevada	103.4
8	Arizona	100.2		3	Wyoming	102.8
31	Arkansas	96.1		4	Colorado	101.4
11	California	100.0		4	Idaho	101.4
4	Colorado	101.4		6	Utah	101.2
40	Connecticut	94.9		7	North Dakota	100.9
44	Delaware	94.3		8	Arizona	100.2
30	Florida	96.5		8	Hawaii	100.2
25	Georgia	97.0		10	Montana	100.1
8	Hawaii	100.2		11	California	100.0
4	Idaho	101.4		12	South Dakota	99.8
25	Illinois	97.0		13	Washington	99.5
24	Indiana	97.1		14	Texas	99.3
20	Iowa	97.6		15	Minnesota	98.9
18	Kansas	98.5		15	Oregon	98.9
31	Kentucky	96.1		17	Wisconsin	98.8
42	Louisiana	94.7		18	Kansas	98.5
35	Maine	95.7		19	Nebraska	98.3
49	Maryland	93.7		20	Iowa	97.6
47	Massachusetts	93.9		21	New Mexico	97.5
25	Michigan	97.0		22	New Hampshire	97.3
15	Minnesota	98.9		23	Oklahoma	97.2
47	Mississippi	93.9		24	Indiana	97.1
37	Missouri	95.5		25	Georgia	97.0
10	Montana	100.1		25	Illinois	97.0
19	Nebraska	98.3		25	Michigan	97.0
2	Nevada	103.4		28	Vermont	96.9
22	New Hampshire	97.3		29	Virginia	96.7
37	New Jersey	95.5		30	Florida	96.5
21	New Mexico	97.5		31	Arkansas	96.1
46	New York	94.0		31	Kentucky	96.1
31	North Carolina	96.1		31	North Carolina	96.1
7	North Dakota	100.9		34	West Virginia	96.0
39	Ohio	95.2		35	Maine	95.7
23	Oklahoma	97.2		36	Tennessee	95.6
15	Oregon	98.9		37	Missouri	95.5
43	Pennsylvania	94.6		37	New Jersey	95.5
50	Rhode Island	93.6		39	Ohio	95.2
40	South Carolina	94.9		40	Connecticut	94.9
12	South Dakota	99.8		40	South Carolina	94.9
36	Tennessee	95.6		42	Louisiana	94.7
14	Texas	99.3		43	Pennsylvania	94.6
6	Utah	101.2		44	Delaware	94.3
28	Vermont	96.9		45	Alabama	94.1
29	Virginia	96.7		46	New York	94.0
13	Washington	99.5		47	Massachusetts	93.9
34	West Virginia	96.0		47	Mississippi	93.9
17	Wisconsin	98.8		49	Maryland	93.7
3	Wyoming	102.8		50	Rhode Island	93.6
					District of Columbia	88.3

Source: CQ Press using data from U.S. Bureau of the Census
"SC-EST2006-AGESEX_RES - State Characteristic Estimates" (http://www.census.gov/popest/datasets.html)

White Population in 2006

National Total = 239,746,254 White Persons*

ALPHA ORDER

RANK	STATE	WHITES	% of USA
25	Alabama	3,276,561	1.4%
49	Alaska	473,645	0.2%
16	Arizona	5,380,815	2.2%
33	Arkansas	2,279,839	1.0%
1	California	28,043,733	11.7%
21	Colorado	4,282,804	1.8%
26	Connecticut	2,966,187	1.2%
45	Delaware	636,116	0.3%
3	Florida	14,503,894	6.0%
11	Georgia	6,158,769	2.6%
50	Hawaii	367,230	0.2%
39	Idaho	1,396,543	0.6%
6	Illinois	10,169,966	4.2%
13	Indiana	5,575,402	2.3%
28	Iowa	2,820,425	1.2%
31	Kansas	2,462,232	1.0%
22	Kentucky	3,793,438	1.6%
30	Louisiana	2,802,347	1.2%
40	Maine	1,278,398	0.5%
23	Maryland	3,573,922	1.5%
14	Massachusetts	5,568,643	2.3%
8	Michigan	8,198,927	3.4%
20	Minnesota	4,615,613	1.9%
35	Mississippi	1,771,596	0.7%
18	Missouri	4,974,983	2.1%
43	Montana	858,140	0.4%
38	Nebraska	1,622,682	0.7%
34	Nevada	2,038,372	0.9%
41	New Hampshire	1,259,738	0.5%
9	New Jersey	6,665,390	2.8%
37	New Mexico	1,653,876	0.7%
4	New York	14,220,047	5.9%
10	North Carolina	6,558,154	2.7%
47	North Dakota	584,116	0.2%
7	Ohio	9,747,752	4.1%
29	Oklahoma	2,803,755	1.2%
24	Oregon	3,348,473	1.4%
5	Pennsylvania	10,660,136	4.4%
42	Rhode Island	947,030	0.4%
27	South Carolina	2,958,982	1.2%
44	South Dakota	691,100	0.3%
19	Tennessee	4,855,937	2.0%
2	Texas	19,452,577	8.1%
32	Utah	2,383,544	1.0%
46	Vermont	603,345	0.3%
12	Virginia	5,605,240	2.3%
15	Washington	5,420,961	2.3%
36	West Virginia	1,725,687	0.7%
17	Wisconsin	4,999,679	2.1%
48	Wyoming	486,480	0.2%

RANK ORDER

RANK	STATE	WHITES	% of USA
1	California	28,043,733	11.7%
2	Texas	19,452,577	8.1%
3	Florida	14,503,894	6.0%
4	New York	14,220,047	5.9%
5	Pennsylvania	10,660,136	4.4%
6	Illinois	10,169,966	4.2%
7	Ohio	9,747,752	4.1%
8	Michigan	8,198,927	3.4%
9	New Jersey	6,665,390	2.8%
10	North Carolina	6,558,154	2.7%
11	Georgia	6,158,769	2.6%
12	Virginia	5,605,240	2.3%
13	Indiana	5,575,402	2.3%
14	Massachusetts	5,568,643	2.3%
15	Washington	5,420,961	2.3%
16	Arizona	5,380,815	2.2%
17	Wisconsin	4,999,679	2.1%
18	Missouri	4,974,983	2.1%
19	Tennessee	4,855,937	2.0%
20	Minnesota	4,615,613	1.9%
21	Colorado	4,282,804	1.8%
22	Kentucky	3,793,438	1.6%
23	Maryland	3,573,922	1.5%
24	Oregon	3,348,473	1.4%
25	Alabama	3,276,561	1.4%
26	Connecticut	2,966,187	1.2%
27	South Carolina	2,958,982	1.2%
28	Iowa	2,820,425	1.2%
29	Oklahoma	2,803,755	1.2%
30	Louisiana	2,802,347	1.2%
31	Kansas	2,462,232	1.0%
32	Utah	2,383,544	1.0%
33	Arkansas	2,279,839	1.0%
34	Nevada	2,038,372	0.9%
35	Mississippi	1,771,596	0.7%
36	West Virginia	1,725,687	0.7%
37	New Mexico	1,653,876	0.7%
38	Nebraska	1,622,682	0.7%
39	Idaho	1,396,543	0.6%
40	Maine	1,278,398	0.5%
41	New Hampshire	1,259,738	0.5%
42	Rhode Island	947,030	0.4%
43	Montana	858,140	0.4%
44	South Dakota	691,100	0.3%
45	Delaware	636,116	0.3%
46	Vermont	603,345	0.3%
47	North Dakota	584,116	0.2%
48	Wyoming	486,480	0.2%
49	Alaska	473,645	0.2%
50	Hawaii	367,230	0.2%
	District of Columbia	223,033	0.1%

Source: U.S. Bureau of the Census
    "State Population Estimates - Characteristics" (http://www.census.gov/popest/states/asrh/)
*"White" is defined by Census as a person having origins in any of the original peoples of Europe, North Africa, or the Middle East. There are 198,744,494 non-Hispanic whites. Census states "Race is a self-identification data item in which respondents choose the race or races with which they most closely identify."

Percent of Population White in 2006

National Percent = 80.1% White*

ALPHA ORDER

RANK	STATE	PERCENT
43	Alabama	71.2
44	Alaska	70.7
21	Arizona	87.3
32	Arkansas	81.1
37	California	76.9
14	Colorado	90.1
27	Connecticut	84.6
39	Delaware	74.5
34	Florida	80.2
46	Georgia	65.8
50	Hawaii	28.6
4	Idaho	95.2
35	Illinois	79.3
20	Indiana	88.3
6	Iowa	94.6
17	Kansas	89.1
13	Kentucky	90.2
47	Louisiana	65.4
1	Maine	96.7
48	Maryland	63.6
22	Massachusetts	86.5
31	Michigan	81.2
16	Minnesota	89.3
49	Mississippi	60.9
24	Missouri	85.1
11	Montana	90.8
10	Nebraska	91.8
30	Nevada	81.7
3	New Hampshire	95.8
38	New Jersey	76.4
27	New Mexico	84.6
41	New York	73.7
40	North Carolina	74.0
9	North Dakota	91.9
25	Ohio	84.9
36	Oklahoma	78.3
12	Oregon	90.5
23	Pennsylvania	85.7
18	Rhode Island	88.7
45	South Carolina	68.5
19	South Dakota	88.4
33	Tennessee	80.4
29	Texas	82.7
8	Utah	93.5
1	Vermont	96.7
42	Virginia	73.3
26	Washington	84.8
5	West Virginia	94.9
15	Wisconsin	90.0
7	Wyoming	94.5

RANK ORDER

RANK	STATE	PERCENT
1	Maine	96.7
1	Vermont	96.7
3	New Hampshire	95.8
4	Idaho	95.2
5	West Virginia	94.9
6	Iowa	94.6
7	Wyoming	94.5
8	Utah	93.5
9	North Dakota	91.9
10	Nebraska	91.8
11	Montana	90.8
12	Oregon	90.5
13	Kentucky	90.2
14	Colorado	90.1
15	Wisconsin	90.0
16	Minnesota	89.3
17	Kansas	89.1
18	Rhode Island	88.7
19	South Dakota	88.4
20	Indiana	88.3
21	Arizona	87.3
22	Massachusetts	86.5
23	Pennsylvania	85.7
24	Missouri	85.1
25	Ohio	84.9
26	Washington	84.8
27	Connecticut	84.6
27	New Mexico	84.6
29	Texas	82.7
30	Nevada	81.7
31	Michigan	81.2
32	Arkansas	81.1
33	Tennessee	80.4
34	Florida	80.2
35	Illinois	79.3
36	Oklahoma	78.3
37	California	76.9
38	New Jersey	76.4
39	Delaware	74.5
40	North Carolina	74.0
41	New York	73.7
42	Virginia	73.3
43	Alabama	71.2
44	Alaska	70.7
45	South Carolina	68.5
46	Georgia	65.8
47	Louisiana	65.4
48	Maryland	63.6
49	Mississippi	60.9
50	Hawaii	28.6
	District of Columbia	38.4

Source: CQ Press using data from U.S. Bureau of the Census
 "State Population Estimates - Characteristics" (http://www.census.gov/popest/states/asrh/)
*"White" is defined by Census as a person having origins in any of the original peoples of Europe, North Africa, or the Middle East. Non-Hispanic whites comprise 66.4% of the total population. Census states "Race is a self-identification data item in which respondents choose the race or races with which they most closely identify."

Black Population in 2006

National Total = 38,342,549 Black Persons*

ALPHA ORDER

RANK	STATE	BLACKS	% of USA
16	Alabama	1,211,583	3.2%
42	Alaska	25,108	0.1%
27	Arizona	231,677	0.6%
22	Arkansas	442,155	1.2%
5	California	2,445,228	6.4%
31	Colorado	195,978	0.5%
23	Connecticut	358,210	0.9%
32	Delaware	178,201	0.5%
2	Florida	2,864,423	7.5%
4	Georgia	2,799,625	7.3%
40	Hawaii	31,761	0.1%
45	Idaho	9,534	0.0%
6	Illinois	1,928,153	5.0%
20	Indiana	563,037	1.5%
35	Iowa	73,086	0.2%
33	Kansas	164,507	0.4%
25	Kentucky	316,945	0.8%
12	Louisiana	1,357,661	3.5%
44	Maine	10,918	0.0%
8	Maryland	1,656,615	4.3%
21	Massachusetts	446,721	1.2%
10	Michigan	1,444,451	3.8%
28	Minnesota	231,053	0.6%
17	Mississippi	1,080,796	2.8%
19	Missouri	673,075	1.8%
50	Montana	4,094	0.0%
34	Nebraska	77,636	0.2%
30	Nevada	196,075	0.5%
43	New Hampshire	13,905	0.0%
14	New Jersey	1,264,681	3.3%
39	New Mexico	49,161	0.1%
1	New York	3,352,874	8.7%
7	North Carolina	1,921,307	5.0%
47	North Dakota	5,262	0.0%
11	Ohio	1,377,161	3.6%
26	Oklahoma	278,849	0.7%
36	Oregon	68,610	0.2%
13	Pennsylvania	1,336,278	3.5%
37	Rhode Island	67,328	0.2%
15	South Carolina	1,253,131	3.3%
46	South Dakota	7,389	0.0%
18	Tennessee	1,019,528	2.7%
3	Texas	2,804,949	7.3%
41	Utah	25,838	0.1%
49	Vermont	4,329	0.0%
9	Virginia	1,519,812	4.0%
29	Washington	227,926	0.6%
38	West Virginia	60,196	0.2%
24	Wisconsin	332,296	0.9%
48	Wyoming	4,867	0.0%

RANK ORDER

RANK	STATE	BLACKS	% of USA
1	New York	3,352,874	8.7%
2	Florida	2,864,423	7.5%
3	Texas	2,804,949	7.3%
4	Georgia	2,799,625	7.3%
5	California	2,445,228	6.4%
6	Illinois	1,928,153	5.0%
7	North Carolina	1,921,307	5.0%
8	Maryland	1,656,615	4.3%
9	Virginia	1,519,812	4.0%
10	Michigan	1,444,451	3.8%
11	Ohio	1,377,161	3.6%
12	Louisiana	1,357,661	3.5%
13	Pennsylvania	1,336,278	3.5%
14	New Jersey	1,264,681	3.3%
15	South Carolina	1,253,131	3.3%
16	Alabama	1,211,583	3.2%
17	Mississippi	1,080,796	2.8%
18	Tennessee	1,019,528	2.7%
19	Missouri	673,075	1.8%
20	Indiana	563,037	1.5%
21	Massachusetts	446,721	1.2%
22	Arkansas	442,155	1.2%
23	Connecticut	358,210	0.9%
24	Wisconsin	332,296	0.9%
25	Kentucky	316,945	0.8%
26	Oklahoma	278,849	0.7%
27	Arizona	231,677	0.6%
28	Minnesota	231,053	0.6%
29	Washington	227,926	0.6%
30	Nevada	196,075	0.5%
31	Colorado	195,978	0.5%
32	Delaware	178,201	0.5%
33	Kansas	164,507	0.4%
34	Nebraska	77,636	0.2%
35	Iowa	73,086	0.2%
36	Oregon	68,610	0.2%
37	Rhode Island	67,328	0.2%
38	West Virginia	60,196	0.2%
39	New Mexico	49,161	0.1%
40	Hawaii	31,761	0.1%
41	Utah	25,838	0.1%
42	Alaska	25,108	0.1%
43	New Hampshire	13,905	0.0%
44	Maine	10,918	0.0%
45	Idaho	9,534	0.0%
46	South Dakota	7,389	0.0%
47	North Dakota	5,262	0.0%
48	Wyoming	4,867	0.0%
49	Vermont	4,329	0.0%
50	Montana	4,094	0.0%
	District of Columbia	328,566	0.9%

Source: U.S. Bureau of the Census
"State Population Estimates - Characteristics" (http://www.census.gov/popest/states/asrh/)
*"Black" is defined by Census as a person having origins in any of the Black racial groups of Africa. Census states "Race is a self-identification data item in which respondents choose the race or races with which they most closely identify."

Percent of Population Black in 2006

National Percent = 12.8% Black*

RANK	STATE	PERCENT
6	Alabama	26.3
35	Alaska	3.7
34	Arizona	3.8
13	Arkansas	15.7
27	California	6.7
33	Colorado	4.1
21	Connecticut	10.2
8	Delaware	20.9
12	Florida	15.8
3	Georgia	29.9
38	Hawaii	2.5
48	Idaho	0.7
14	Illinois	15.0
22	Indiana	8.9
38	Iowa	2.5
29	Kansas	6.0
25	Kentucky	7.5
2	Louisiana	31.7
46	Maine	0.8
4	Maryland	29.5
26	Massachusetts	6.9
16	Michigan	14.3
31	Minnesota	4.5
1	Mississippi	37.1
19	Missouri	11.5
50	Montana	0.4
32	Nebraska	4.4
23	Nevada	7.9
42	New Hampshire	1.1
15	New Jersey	14.5
38	New Mexico	2.5
10	New York	17.4
7	North Carolina	21.7
46	North Dakota	0.8
17	Ohio	12.0
24	Oklahoma	7.8
41	Oregon	1.9
20	Pennsylvania	10.7
28	Rhode Island	6.3
5	South Carolina	29.0
44	South Dakota	0.9
11	Tennessee	16.9
18	Texas	11.9
43	Utah	1.0
48	Vermont	0.7
9	Virginia	19.9
36	Washington	3.6
37	West Virginia	3.3
29	Wisconsin	6.0
44	Wyoming	0.9

RANK	STATE	PERCENT
1	Mississippi	37.1
2	Louisiana	31.7
3	Georgia	29.9
4	Maryland	29.5
5	South Carolina	29.0
6	Alabama	26.3
7	North Carolina	21.7
8	Delaware	20.9
9	Virginia	19.9
10	New York	17.4
11	Tennessee	16.9
12	Florida	15.8
13	Arkansas	15.7
14	Illinois	15.0
15	New Jersey	14.5
16	Michigan	14.3
17	Ohio	12.0
18	Texas	11.9
19	Missouri	11.5
20	Pennsylvania	10.7
21	Connecticut	10.2
22	Indiana	8.9
23	Nevada	7.9
24	Oklahoma	7.8
25	Kentucky	7.5
26	Massachusetts	6.9
27	California	6.7
28	Rhode Island	6.3
29	Kansas	6.0
29	Wisconsin	6.0
31	Minnesota	4.5
32	Nebraska	4.4
33	Colorado	4.1
34	Arizona	3.8
35	Alaska	3.7
36	Washington	3.6
37	West Virginia	3.3
38	Hawaii	2.5
38	Iowa	2.5
38	New Mexico	2.5
41	Oregon	1.9
42	New Hampshire	1.1
43	Utah	1.0
44	South Dakota	0.9
44	Wyoming	0.9
46	Maine	0.8
46	North Dakota	0.8
48	Idaho	0.7
48	Vermont	0.7
50	Montana	0.4

District of Columbia — 56.5

Source: CQ Press using data from U.S. Bureau of the Census
  "State Population Estimates - Characteristics" (http://www.census.gov/popest/states/asrh/)
*"Black" is defined by Census as a person having origins in any of the Black racial groups of Africa. Census states "Race is a self-identification data item in which respondents choose the race or races with which they most closely identify."

Hispanic Population in 2006

National Total = 44,321,038 Hispanics*

RANK	STATE	HISPANICS	% of USA
37	Alabama	113,890	0.3%
42	Alaska	37,548	0.1%
6	Arizona	1,803,378	4.1%
31	Arkansas	141,053	0.3%
1	California	13,074,156	29.5%
8	Colorado	934,413	2.1%
18	Connecticut	391,935	0.9%
40	Delaware	53,835	0.1%
3	Florida	3,646,499	8.2%
10	Georgia	703,246	1.6%
38	Hawaii	99,663	0.2%
32	Idaho	138,870	0.3%
5	Illinois	1,886,933	4.3%
21	Indiana	300,857	0.7%
36	Iowa	114,700	0.3%
26	Kansas	237,426	0.5%
39	Kentucky	85,938	0.2%
34	Louisiana	124,481	0.3%
48	Maine	13,529	0.0%
20	Maryland	337,341	0.8%
15	Massachusetts	511,014	1.2%
17	Michigan	393,281	0.9%
27	Minnesota	196,135	0.4%
41	Mississippi	53,381	0.1%
29	Missouri	164,194	0.4%
45	Montana	23,818	0.1%
33	Nebraska	130,304	0.3%
11	Nevada	610,052	1.4%
44	New Hampshire	29,872	0.1%
7	New Jersey	1,364,696	3.1%
9	New Mexico	860,688	1.9%
4	New York	3,139,456	7.1%
12	North Carolina	593,896	1.3%
49	North Dakota	10,637	0.0%
23	Ohio	267,750	0.6%
25	Oklahoma	247,450	0.6%
19	Oregon	379,038	0.9%
14	Pennsylvania	526,976	1.2%
35	Rhode Island	117,701	0.3%
30	South Carolina	151,289	0.3%
46	South Dakota	16,773	0.0%
28	Tennessee	194,706	0.4%
2	Texas	8,385,139	18.9%
22	Utah	286,113	0.6%
50	Vermont	7,135	0.0%
16	Virginia	479,530	1.1%
13	Washington	581,357	1.3%
47	West Virginia	16,767	0.0%
24	Wisconsin	258,696	0.6%
43	Wyoming	35,729	0.1%

RANK	STATE	HISPANICS	% of USA
1	California	13,074,156	29.5%
2	Texas	8,385,139	18.9%
3	Florida	3,646,499	8.2%
4	New York	3,139,456	7.1%
5	Illinois	1,886,933	4.3%
6	Arizona	1,803,378	4.1%
7	New Jersey	1,364,696	3.1%
8	Colorado	934,413	2.1%
9	New Mexico	860,688	1.9%
10	Georgia	703,246	1.6%
11	Nevada	610,052	1.4%
12	North Carolina	593,896	1.3%
13	Washington	581,357	1.3%
14	Pennsylvania	526,976	1.2%
15	Massachusetts	511,014	1.2%
16	Virginia	479,530	1.1%
17	Michigan	393,281	0.9%
18	Connecticut	391,935	0.9%
19	Oregon	379,038	0.9%
20	Maryland	337,341	0.8%
21	Indiana	300,857	0.7%
22	Utah	286,113	0.6%
23	Ohio	267,750	0.6%
24	Wisconsin	258,696	0.6%
25	Oklahoma	247,450	0.6%
26	Kansas	237,426	0.5%
27	Minnesota	196,135	0.4%
28	Tennessee	194,706	0.4%
29	Missouri	164,194	0.4%
30	South Carolina	151,289	0.3%
31	Arkansas	141,053	0.3%
32	Idaho	138,870	0.3%
33	Nebraska	130,304	0.3%
34	Louisiana	124,481	0.3%
35	Rhode Island	117,701	0.3%
36	Iowa	114,700	0.3%
37	Alabama	113,890	0.3%
38	Hawaii	99,663	0.2%
39	Kentucky	85,938	0.2%
40	Delaware	53,835	0.1%
41	Mississippi	53,381	0.1%
42	Alaska	37,548	0.1%
43	Wyoming	35,729	0.1%
44	New Hampshire	29,872	0.1%
45	Montana	23,818	0.1%
46	South Dakota	16,773	0.0%
47	West Virginia	16,767	0.0%
48	Maine	13,529	0.0%
49	North Dakota	10,637	0.0%
50	Vermont	7,135	0.0%
	District of Columbia	47,774	0.1%

Source: U.S. Bureau of the Census
   "State Population Estimates - Characteristics" (http://www.census.gov/popest/states/asrh/)
*Persons of Hispanic origin may be of any race. Census states "Race is a self-identification data item in which respondents choose the race or races with which they most closely identify."

Percent of Population Hispanic in 2006

National Percent = 14.8% Hispanic*

ALPHA ORDER

RANK	STATE	PERCENT
40	Alabama	2.5
28	Alaska	5.6
4	Arizona	29.2
29	Arkansas	5.0
2	California	35.9
7	Colorado	19.7
11	Connecticut	11.2
25	Delaware	6.3
6	Florida	20.2
20	Georgia	7.5
19	Hawaii	7.8
15	Idaho	9.5
10	Illinois	14.7
30	Indiana	4.8
34	Iowa	3.8
17	Kansas	8.6
45	Kentucky	2.0
38	Louisiana	2.9
49	Maine	1.0
27	Maryland	6.0
18	Massachusetts	7.9
33	Michigan	3.9
34	Minnesota	3.8
46	Mississippi	1.8
39	Missouri	2.8
40	Montana	2.5
21	Nebraska	7.4
5	Nevada	24.4
42	New Hampshire	2.3
9	New Jersey	15.6
1	New Mexico	44.0
8	New York	16.3
24	North Carolina	6.7
47	North Dakota	1.7
42	Ohio	2.3
22	Oklahoma	6.9
14	Oregon	10.2
32	Pennsylvania	4.2
13	Rhode Island	11.0
36	South Carolina	3.5
44	South Dakota	2.1
37	Tennessee	3.2
3	Texas	35.7
11	Utah	11.2
48	Vermont	1.1
25	Virginia	6.3
16	Washington	9.1
50	West Virginia	0.9
31	Wisconsin	4.7
22	Wyoming	6.9

RANK ORDER

RANK	STATE	PERCENT
1	New Mexico	44.0
2	California	35.9
3	Texas	35.7
4	Arizona	29.2
5	Nevada	24.4
6	Florida	20.2
7	Colorado	19.7
8	New York	16.3
9	New Jersey	15.6
10	Illinois	14.7
11	Connecticut	11.2
11	Utah	11.2
13	Rhode Island	11.0
14	Oregon	10.2
15	Idaho	9.5
16	Washington	9.1
17	Kansas	8.6
18	Massachusetts	7.9
19	Hawaii	7.8
20	Georgia	7.5
21	Nebraska	7.4
22	Oklahoma	6.9
22	Wyoming	6.9
24	North Carolina	6.7
25	Delaware	6.3
25	Virginia	6.3
27	Maryland	6.0
28	Alaska	5.6
29	Arkansas	5.0
30	Indiana	4.8
31	Wisconsin	4.7
32	Pennsylvania	4.2
33	Michigan	3.9
34	Iowa	3.8
34	Minnesota	3.8
36	South Carolina	3.5
37	Tennessee	3.2
38	Louisiana	2.9
39	Missouri	2.8
40	Alabama	2.5
40	Montana	2.5
42	New Hampshire	2.3
42	Ohio	2.3
44	South Dakota	2.1
45	Kentucky	2.0
46	Mississippi	1.8
47	North Dakota	1.7
48	Vermont	1.1
49	Maine	1.0
50	West Virginia	0.9

District of Columbia   8.2

Source: CQ Press using data from U.S. Bureau of the Census
"State Population Estimates - Characteristics" (http://www.census.gov/popest/states/asrh/)
*Persons of Hispanic origin may be of any race. Census states "Race is a self-identification data item in which respondents choose the race or races with which they most closely identify."

Asian Population in 2006

National Total = 13,159,343 Asians*

ALPHA ORDER					RANK ORDER			

ALPHA ORDER

ALPHA ORDER

RANK	STATE	ASIANS	% of USA
33	Alabama	41,881	0.3%
35	Alaska	31,113	0.2%
19	Arizona	146,725	1.1%
36	Arkansas	29,312	0.2%
1	California	4,510,534	34.3%
21	Colorado	125,724	1.0%
22	Connecticut	117,986	0.9%
41	Delaware	23,680	0.2%
8	Florida	397,143	3.0%
13	Georgia	261,401	2.0%
6	Hawaii	514,395	3.9%
43	Idaho	15,918	0.1%
5	Illinois	541,218	4.1%
24	Indiana	83,583	0.6%
32	Iowa	46,553	0.4%
27	Kansas	60,870	0.5%
34	Kentucky	41,752	0.3%
28	Louisiana	60,455	0.5%
45	Maine	11,490	0.1%
12	Maryland	277,697	2.1%
10	Massachusetts	313,942	2.4%
14	Michigan	237,389	1.8%
15	Minnesota	181,065	1.4%
42	Mississippi	22,399	0.2%
25	Missouri	83,216	0.6%
48	Montana	5,699	0.0%
37	Nebraska	29,253	0.2%
18	Nevada	149,621	1.1%
40	New Hampshire	24,389	0.2%
4	New Jersey	647,986	4.9%
39	New Mexico	26,140	0.2%
2	New York	1,326,089	10.1%
17	North Carolina	164,111	1.2%
49	North Dakota	4,743	0.0%
16	Ohio	177,215	1.3%
29	Oklahoma	60,201	0.5%
20	Oregon	133,740	1.0%
11	Pennsylvania	292,507	2.2%
38	Rhode Island	29,177	0.2%
31	South Carolina	49,681	0.4%
47	South Dakota	5,808	0.0%
26	Tennessee	79,665	0.6%
3	Texas	788,356	6.0%
30	Utah	50,230	0.4%
46	Vermont	6,847	0.1%
9	Virginia	363,094	2.8%
7	Washington	422,039	3.2%
44	West Virginia	11,778	0.1%
23	Wisconsin	111,057	0.8%
50	Wyoming	3,605	0.0%

RANK ORDER

RANK	STATE	ASIANS	% of USA
1	California	4,510,534	34.3%
2	New York	1,326,089	10.1%
3	Texas	788,356	6.0%
4	New Jersey	647,986	4.9%
5	Illinois	541,218	4.1%
6	Hawaii	514,395	3.9%
7	Washington	422,039	3.2%
8	Florida	397,143	3.0%
9	Virginia	363,094	2.8%
10	Massachusetts	313,942	2.4%
11	Pennsylvania	292,507	2.2%
12	Maryland	277,697	2.1%
13	Georgia	261,401	2.0%
14	Michigan	237,389	1.8%
15	Minnesota	181,065	1.4%
16	Ohio	177,215	1.3%
17	North Carolina	164,111	1.2%
18	Nevada	149,621	1.1%
19	Arizona	146,725	1.1%
20	Oregon	133,740	1.0%
21	Colorado	125,724	1.0%
22	Connecticut	117,986	0.9%
23	Wisconsin	111,057	0.8%
24	Indiana	83,583	0.6%
25	Missouri	83,216	0.6%
26	Tennessee	79,665	0.6%
27	Kansas	60,870	0.5%
28	Louisiana	60,455	0.5%
29	Oklahoma	60,201	0.5%
30	Utah	50,230	0.4%
31	South Carolina	49,681	0.4%
32	Iowa	46,553	0.4%
33	Alabama	41,881	0.3%
34	Kentucky	41,752	0.3%
35	Alaska	31,113	0.2%
36	Arkansas	29,312	0.2%
37	Nebraska	29,253	0.2%
38	Rhode Island	29,177	0.2%
39	New Mexico	26,140	0.2%
40	New Hampshire	24,389	0.2%
41	Delaware	23,680	0.2%
42	Mississippi	22,399	0.2%
43	Idaho	15,918	0.1%
44	West Virginia	11,778	0.1%
45	Maine	11,490	0.1%
46	Vermont	6,847	0.1%
47	South Dakota	5,808	0.0%
48	Montana	5,699	0.0%
49	North Dakota	4,743	0.0%
50	Wyoming	3,605	0.0%
	District of Columbia	18,871	0.1%

Source: U.S. Bureau of the Census
"State Population Estimates - Characteristics" (http://www.census.gov/popest/states/asrh/)
*Census states "Race is a self-identification data item in which respondents choose the race or races with which they most closely identify."

Percent of Population Asian in 2006

National Percent = 4.4% Asian*

ALPHA ORDER

RANK	STATE	PERCENT
43	Alabama	0.9
10	Alaska	4.6
20	Arizona	2.4
41	Arkansas	1.0
2	California	12.4
19	Colorado	2.6
14	Connecticut	3.4
16	Delaware	2.8
23	Florida	2.2
16	Georgia	2.8
1	Hawaii	40.0
38	Idaho	1.1
11	Illinois	4.2
35	Indiana	1.3
31	Iowa	1.6
23	Kansas	2.2
41	Kentucky	1.0
33	Louisiana	1.4
43	Maine	0.9
7	Maryland	4.9
7	Massachusetts	4.9
20	Michigan	2.4
13	Minnesota	3.5
45	Mississippi	0.8
33	Missouri	1.4
49	Montana	0.6
29	Nebraska	1.7
6	Nevada	6.0
27	New Hampshire	1.9
3	New Jersey	7.4
35	New Mexico	1.3
4	New York	6.9
27	North Carolina	1.9
46	North Dakota	0.7
32	Ohio	1.5
29	Oklahoma	1.7
12	Oregon	3.6
20	Pennsylvania	2.4
18	Rhode Island	2.7
38	South Carolina	1.1
46	South Dakota	0.7
35	Tennessee	1.3
14	Texas	3.4
25	Utah	2.0
38	Vermont	1.1
9	Virginia	4.8
5	Washington	6.6
49	West Virginia	0.6
25	Wisconsin	2.0
46	Wyoming	0.7

RANK ORDER

RANK	STATE	PERCENT
1	Hawaii	40.0
2	California	12.4
3	New Jersey	7.4
4	New York	6.9
5	Washington	6.6
6	Nevada	6.0
7	Maryland	4.9
7	Massachusetts	4.9
9	Virginia	4.8
10	Alaska	4.6
11	Illinois	4.2
12	Oregon	3.6
13	Minnesota	3.5
14	Connecticut	3.4
14	Texas	3.4
16	Delaware	2.8
16	Georgia	2.8
18	Rhode Island	2.7
19	Colorado	2.6
20	Arizona	2.4
20	Michigan	2.4
20	Pennsylvania	2.4
23	Florida	2.2
23	Kansas	2.2
25	Utah	2.0
25	Wisconsin	2.0
27	New Hampshire	1.9
27	North Carolina	1.9
29	Nebraska	1.7
29	Oklahoma	1.7
31	Iowa	1.6
32	Ohio	1.5
33	Louisiana	1.4
33	Missouri	1.4
35	Indiana	1.3
35	New Mexico	1.3
35	Tennessee	1.3
38	Idaho	1.1
38	South Carolina	1.1
38	Vermont	1.1
41	Arkansas	1.0
41	Kentucky	1.0
43	Alabama	0.9
43	Maine	0.9
45	Mississippi	0.8
46	North Dakota	0.7
46	South Dakota	0.7
46	Wyoming	0.7
49	Montana	0.6
49	West Virginia	0.6

District of Columbia	3.2

Source: CQ Press using data from U.S. Bureau of the Census
  "State Population Estimates - Characteristics" (http://www.census.gov/popest/states/asrh/)
*Census states "Race is a self-identification data item in which respondents choose the race or races with which they most closely identify."

American Indian Population in 2006

National Total = 2,902,851 American Indians*

ALPHA ORDER

RANK	STATE	INDIANS	% of USA
30	Alabama	23,799	0.8%
9	Alaska	103,497	3.6%
2	Arizona	294,118	10.1%
31	Arkansas	21,635	0.7%
1	California	421,346	14.5%
15	Colorado	54,626	1.9%
41	Connecticut	12,497	0.4%
49	Delaware	3,454	0.1%
10	Florida	80,369	2.8%
22	Georgia	30,893	1.1%
46	Hawaii	6,378	0.2%
32	Idaho	20,897	0.7%
18	Illinois	41,231	1.4%
35	Indiana	18,603	0.6%
42	Iowa	11,145	0.4%
26	Kansas	27,374	0.9%
43	Kentucky	9,988	0.3%
27	Louisiana	27,042	0.9%
44	Maine	7,582	0.3%
36	Maryland	18,584	0.6%
33	Massachusetts	19,044	0.7%
12	Michigan	60,820	2.1%
14	Minnesota	60,491	2.1%
39	Mississippi	13,816	0.5%
23	Missouri	28,332	1.0%
13	Montana	60,725	2.1%
37	Nebraska	17,103	0.6%
19	Nevada	34,813	1.2%
48	New Hampshire	3,458	0.1%
24	New Jersey	27,970	1.0%
4	New Mexico	190,826	6.6%
7	New York	104,936	3.6%
6	North Carolina	111,148	3.8%
20	North Dakota	34,190	1.2%
25	Ohio	27,546	0.9%
3	Oklahoma	287,728	9.9%
17	Oregon	51,209	1.8%
29	Pennsylvania	24,077	0.8%
45	Rhode Island	6,574	0.2%
38	South Carolina	16,849	0.6%
11	South Dakota	66,665	2.3%
34	Tennessee	18,733	0.6%
5	Texas	163,455	5.6%
21	Utah	33,663	1.2%
50	Vermont	2,386	0.1%
28	Virginia	26,020	0.9%
8	Washington	104,405	3.6%
47	West Virginia	4,045	0.1%
16	Wisconsin	51,937	1.8%
40	Wyoming	12,668	0.4%

RANK ORDER

RANK	STATE	INDIANS	% of USA
1	California	421,346	14.5%
2	Arizona	294,118	10.1%
3	Oklahoma	287,728	9.9%
4	New Mexico	190,826	6.6%
5	Texas	163,455	5.6%
6	North Carolina	111,148	3.8%
7	New York	104,936	3.6%
8	Washington	104,405	3.6%
9	Alaska	103,497	3.6%
10	Florida	80,369	2.8%
11	South Dakota	66,665	2.3%
12	Michigan	60,820	2.1%
13	Montana	60,725	2.1%
14	Minnesota	60,491	2.1%
15	Colorado	54,626	1.9%
16	Wisconsin	51,937	1.8%
17	Oregon	51,209	1.8%
18	Illinois	41,231	1.4%
19	Nevada	34,813	1.2%
20	North Dakota	34,190	1.2%
21	Utah	33,663	1.2%
22	Georgia	30,893	1.1%
23	Missouri	28,332	1.0%
24	New Jersey	27,970	1.0%
25	Ohio	27,546	0.9%
26	Kansas	27,374	0.9%
27	Louisiana	27,042	0.9%
28	Virginia	26,020	0.9%
29	Pennsylvania	24,077	0.8%
30	Alabama	23,799	0.8%
31	Arkansas	21,635	0.7%
32	Idaho	20,897	0.7%
33	Massachusetts	19,044	0.7%
34	Tennessee	18,733	0.6%
35	Indiana	18,603	0.6%
36	Maryland	18,584	0.6%
37	Nebraska	17,103	0.6%
38	South Carolina	16,849	0.6%
39	Mississippi	13,816	0.5%
40	Wyoming	12,668	0.4%
41	Connecticut	12,497	0.4%
42	Iowa	11,145	0.4%
43	Kentucky	9,988	0.3%
44	Maine	7,582	0.3%
45	Rhode Island	6,574	0.2%
46	Hawaii	6,378	0.2%
47	West Virginia	4,045	0.1%
48	New Hampshire	3,458	0.1%
49	Delaware	3,454	0.1%
50	Vermont	2,386	0.1%
	District of Columbia	2,161	0.1%

Source: U.S. Bureau of the Census
   "State Population Estimates - Characteristics" (http://www.census.gov/popest/states/asrh/)
*Includes Alaska Native populations. Census states "Race is a self-identification data item in which respondents choose the race or races with which they most closely identify."

Percent of Population American Indian in 2006

National Percent = 1.0% American Indian*

ALPHA ORDER

RANK	STATE	PERCENT
27	Alabama	0.5
1	Alaska	15.4
7	Arizona	4.8
21	Arkansas	0.8
15	California	1.2
17	Colorado	1.1
32	Connecticut	0.4
32	Delaware	0.4
32	Florida	0.4
38	Georgia	0.3
27	Hawaii	0.5
10	Idaho	1.4
38	Illinois	0.3
38	Indiana	0.3
32	Iowa	0.4
18	Kansas	1.0
47	Kentucky	0.2
23	Louisiana	0.6
23	Maine	0.6
38	Maryland	0.3
38	Massachusetts	0.3
23	Michigan	0.6
15	Minnesota	1.2
27	Mississippi	0.5
27	Missouri	0.5
5	Montana	6.4
18	Nebraska	1.0
10	Nevada	1.4
38	New Hampshire	0.3
38	New Jersey	0.3
2	New Mexico	9.8
27	New York	0.5
13	North Carolina	1.3
6	North Dakota	5.4
47	Ohio	0.2
4	Oklahoma	8.0
10	Oregon	1.4
47	Pennsylvania	0.2
23	Rhode Island	0.6
32	South Carolina	0.4
3	South Dakota	8.5
38	Tennessee	0.3
22	Texas	0.7
13	Utah	1.3
32	Vermont	0.4
38	Virginia	0.3
9	Washington	1.6
47	West Virginia	0.2
20	Wisconsin	0.9
8	Wyoming	2.5

RANK ORDER

RANK	STATE	PERCENT
1	Alaska	15.4
2	New Mexico	9.8
3	South Dakota	8.5
4	Oklahoma	8.0
5	Montana	6.4
6	North Dakota	5.4
7	Arizona	4.8
8	Wyoming	2.5
9	Washington	1.6
10	Idaho	1.4
10	Nevada	1.4
10	Oregon	1.4
13	North Carolina	1.3
13	Utah	1.3
15	California	1.2
15	Minnesota	1.2
17	Colorado	1.1
18	Kansas	1.0
18	Nebraska	1.0
20	Wisconsin	0.9
21	Arkansas	0.8
22	Texas	0.7
23	Louisiana	0.6
23	Maine	0.6
23	Michigan	0.6
23	Rhode Island	0.6
27	Alabama	0.5
27	Hawaii	0.5
27	Mississippi	0.5
27	Missouri	0.5
27	New York	0.5
32	Connecticut	0.4
32	Delaware	0.4
32	Florida	0.4
32	Iowa	0.4
32	South Carolina	0.4
32	Vermont	0.4
38	Georgia	0.3
38	Illinois	0.3
38	Indiana	0.3
38	Maryland	0.3
38	Massachusetts	0.3
38	New Hampshire	0.3
38	New Jersey	0.3
38	Tennessee	0.3
38	Virginia	0.3
47	Kentucky	0.2
47	Ohio	0.2
47	Pennsylvania	0.2
47	West Virginia	0.2
	District of Columbia	0.4

Source: CQ Press using data from U.S. Bureau of the Census
"State Population Estimates - Characteristics" (http://www.census.gov/popest/states/asrh/)
*Includes Alaska Native populations. Census states "Race is a self-identification data item in which respondents choose the race or races with which they most closely identify."

Mixed Race Population in 2006

National Total = 4,718,669 Mixed Race*

<u>ALPHA ORDER</u>

RANK	STATE	MIXED RACE	% of USA
29	Alabama	43,457	0.9%
35	Alaska	32,552	0.7%
15	Arizona	100,851	2.1%
34	Arkansas	35,282	0.7%
1	California	883,515	18.7%
18	Colorado	87,490	1.9%
27	Connecticut	47,332	1.0%
46	Delaware	11,527	0.2%
5	Florida	228,658	4.8%
14	Georgia	105,857	2.2%
4	Hawaii	248,767	5.3%
38	Idaho	21,732	0.5%
10	Illinois	142,954	3.0%
23	Indiana	70,045	1.5%
37	Iowa	29,476	0.6%
28	Kansas	47,229	1.0%
30	Kentucky	42,186	0.9%
32	Louisiana	38,653	0.8%
45	Maine	12,753	0.3%
19	Maryland	85,394	1.8%
20	Massachusetts	83,717	1.8%
7	Michigan	150,299	3.2%
22	Minnesota	76,113	1.6%
39	Mississippi	20,998	0.4%
21	Missouri	78,734	1.7%
43	Montana	15,447	0.3%
40	Nebraska	20,432	0.4%
24	Nevada	64,207	1.4%
44	New Hampshire	12,891	0.3%
13	New Jersey	111,655	2.4%
36	New Mexico	31,941	0.7%
2	New York	283,074	6.0%
16	North Carolina	96,030	2.0%
48	North Dakota	7,259	0.2%
9	Ohio	144,545	3.1%
8	Oklahoma	145,250	3.1%
17	Oregon	88,449	1.9%
12	Pennsylvania	122,177	2.6%
42	Rhode Island	16,214	0.3%
31	South Carolina	40,319	0.9%
47	South Dakota	10,576	0.2%
25	Tennessee	61,862	1.3%
3	Texas	271,543	5.8%
33	Utah	37,511	0.8%
50	Vermont	6,829	0.1%
11	Virginia	123,094	2.6%
6	Washington	190,764	4.0%
41	West Virginia	16,233	0.3%
26	Wisconsin	59,409	1.3%
49	Wyoming	6,999	0.1%

<u>RANK ORDER</u>

RANK	STATE	MIXED RACE	% of USA
1	California	883,515	18.7%
2	New York	283,074	6.0%
3	Texas	271,543	5.8%
4	Hawaii	248,767	5.3%
5	Florida	228,658	4.8%
6	Washington	190,764	4.0%
7	Michigan	150,299	3.2%
8	Oklahoma	145,250	3.1%
9	Ohio	144,545	3.1%
10	Illinois	142,954	3.0%
11	Virginia	123,094	2.6%
12	Pennsylvania	122,177	2.6%
13	New Jersey	111,655	2.4%
14	Georgia	105,857	2.2%
15	Arizona	100,851	2.1%
16	North Carolina	96,030	2.0%
17	Oregon	88,449	1.9%
18	Colorado	87,490	1.9%
19	Maryland	85,394	1.8%
20	Massachusetts	83,717	1.8%
21	Missouri	78,734	1.7%
22	Minnesota	76,113	1.6%
23	Indiana	70,045	1.5%
24	Nevada	64,207	1.4%
25	Tennessee	61,862	1.3%
26	Wisconsin	59,409	1.3%
27	Connecticut	47,332	1.0%
28	Kansas	47,229	1.0%
29	Alabama	43,457	0.9%
30	Kentucky	42,186	0.9%
31	South Carolina	40,319	0.9%
32	Louisiana	38,653	0.8%
33	Utah	37,511	0.8%
34	Arkansas	35,282	0.7%
35	Alaska	32,552	0.7%
36	New Mexico	31,941	0.7%
37	Iowa	29,476	0.6%
38	Idaho	21,732	0.5%
39	Mississippi	20,998	0.4%
40	Nebraska	20,432	0.4%
41	West Virginia	16,233	0.3%
42	Rhode Island	16,214	0.3%
43	Montana	15,447	0.3%
44	New Hampshire	12,891	0.3%
45	Maine	12,753	0.3%
46	Delaware	11,527	0.2%
47	South Dakota	10,576	0.2%
48	North Dakota	7,259	0.2%
49	Wyoming	6,999	0.1%
50	Vermont	6,829	0.1%
	District of Columbia	8,388	0.2%

Source: U.S. Bureau of the Census
  "State Population Estimates - Characteristics" (http://www.census.gov/popest/states/asrh/)
*Census states "Race is a self-identification data item in which respondents choose the race or races with which they most closely identify." The 2000 Census was the first to allow respondents to identify themselves as one or more races.

Percent of Population of Mixed Race in 2006

National Percent = 1.6% Mixed Race*

ALPHA ORDER

RANK	STATE	PERCENT
46	Alabama	0.9
2	Alaska	4.9
10	Arizona	1.6
25	Arkansas	1.3
6	California	2.4
8	Colorado	1.8
21	Connecticut	1.4
21	Delaware	1.4
25	Florida	1.3
33	Georgia	1.1
1	Hawaii	19.4
14	Idaho	1.5
33	Illinois	1.1
33	Indiana	1.1
40	Iowa	1.0
9	Kansas	1.7
40	Kentucky	1.0
46	Louisiana	0.9
40	Maine	1.0
14	Maryland	1.5
25	Massachusetts	1.3
14	Michigan	1.5
14	Minnesota	1.5
50	Mississippi	0.7
25	Missouri	1.3
10	Montana	1.6
31	Nebraska	1.2
5	Nevada	2.6
40	New Hampshire	1.0
25	New Jersey	1.3
10	New Mexico	1.6
14	New York	1.5
33	North Carolina	1.1
33	North Dakota	1.1
25	Ohio	1.3
3	Oklahoma	4.1
6	Oregon	2.4
40	Pennsylvania	1.0
14	Rhode Island	1.5
46	South Carolina	0.9
21	South Dakota	1.4
40	Tennessee	1.0
31	Texas	1.2
14	Utah	1.5
33	Vermont	1.1
10	Virginia	1.6
4	Washington	3.0
46	West Virginia	0.9
33	Wisconsin	1.1
21	Wyoming	1.4

RANK ORDER

RANK	STATE	PERCENT
1	Hawaii	19.4
2	Alaska	4.9
3	Oklahoma	4.1
4	Washington	3.0
5	Nevada	2.6
6	California	2.4
6	Oregon	2.4
8	Colorado	1.8
9	Kansas	1.7
10	Arizona	1.6
10	Montana	1.6
10	New Mexico	1.6
10	Virginia	1.6
14	Idaho	1.5
14	Maryland	1.5
14	Michigan	1.5
14	Minnesota	1.5
14	New York	1.5
14	Rhode Island	1.5
14	Utah	1.5
21	Connecticut	1.4
21	Delaware	1.4
21	South Dakota	1.4
21	Wyoming	1.4
25	Arkansas	1.3
25	Florida	1.3
25	Massachusetts	1.3
25	Missouri	1.3
25	New Jersey	1.3
25	Ohio	1.3
31	Nebraska	1.2
31	Texas	1.2
33	Georgia	1.1
33	Illinois	1.1
33	Indiana	1.1
33	North Carolina	1.1
33	North Dakota	1.1
33	Vermont	1.1
33	Wisconsin	1.1
40	Iowa	1.0
40	Kentucky	1.0
40	Maine	1.0
40	New Hampshire	1.0
40	Pennsylvania	1.0
40	Tennessee	1.0
46	Alabama	0.9
46	Louisiana	0.9
46	South Carolina	0.9
46	West Virginia	0.9
50	Mississippi	0.7

District of Columbia 1.4

Source: CQ Press using data from U.S. Bureau of the Census
"State Population Estimates - Characteristics" (http://www.census.gov/popest/states/asrh/)
*Census states "Race is a self-identification data item in which respondents choose the race or races with which they most closely identify." The 2000 Census was the first to allow respondents to identify themselves as one or more races.

Projected State Population in 2030

National Total = 363,584,435

RANK	STATE	POPULATION	% of USA
24	Alabama	4,874,243	1.3%
46	Alaska	867,674	0.2%
10	Arizona	10,712,397	2.9%
32	Arkansas	3,240,208	0.9%
1	California	46,444,861	12.8%
22	Colorado	5,792,357	1.6%
30	Connecticut	3,688,630	1.0%
45	Delaware	1,012,658	0.3%
3	Florida	28,685,769	7.9%
8	Georgia	12,017,838	3.3%
41	Hawaii	1,466,046	0.4%
37	Idaho	1,969,624	0.5%
5	Illinois	13,432,892	3.7%
18	Indiana	6,810,108	1.9%
34	Iowa	2,955,172	0.8%
35	Kansas	2,940,084	0.8%
27	Kentucky	4,554,998	1.3%
26	Louisiana	4,802,633	1.3%
42	Maine	1,411,097	0.4%
16	Maryland	7,022,251	1.9%
17	Massachusetts	7,012,009	1.9%
11	Michigan	10,694,172	2.9%
20	Minnesota	6,306,130	1.7%
33	Mississippi	3,092,410	0.9%
19	Missouri	6,430,173	1.8%
44	Montana	1,044,898	0.3%
38	Nebraska	1,820,247	0.5%
28	Nevada	4,282,102	1.2%
40	New Hampshire	1,646,471	0.5%
13	New Jersey	9,802,440	2.7%
36	New Mexico	2,099,708	0.6%
4	New York	19,477,429	5.4%
7	North Carolina	12,227,739	3.4%
49	North Dakota	606,566	0.2%
9	Ohio	11,550,528	3.2%
29	Oklahoma	3,913,251	1.1%
25	Oregon	4,833,918	1.3%
6	Pennsylvania	12,768,184	3.5%
43	Rhode Island	1,152,941	0.3%
23	South Carolina	5,148,569	1.4%
47	South Dakota	800,462	0.2%
15	Tennessee	7,380,634	2.0%
2	Texas	33,317,744	9.2%
31	Utah	3,485,367	1.0%
48	Vermont	711,867	0.2%
12	Virginia	9,825,019	2.7%
14	Washington	8,624,801	2.4%
39	West Virginia	1,719,959	0.5%
21	Wisconsin	6,150,764	1.7%
50	Wyoming	522,979	0.1%

RANK	STATE	POPULATION	% of USA
1	California	46,444,861	12.8%
2	Texas	33,317,744	9.2%
3	Florida	28,685,769	7.9%
4	New York	19,477,429	5.4%
5	Illinois	13,432,892	3.7%
6	Pennsylvania	12,768,184	3.5%
7	North Carolina	12,227,739	3.4%
8	Georgia	12,017,838	3.3%
9	Ohio	11,550,528	3.2%
10	Arizona	10,712,397	2.9%
11	Michigan	10,694,172	2.9%
12	Virginia	9,825,019	2.7%
13	New Jersey	9,802,440	2.7%
14	Washington	8,624,801	2.4%
15	Tennessee	7,380,634	2.0%
16	Maryland	7,022,251	1.9%
17	Massachusetts	7,012,009	1.9%
18	Indiana	6,810,108	1.9%
19	Missouri	6,430,173	1.8%
20	Minnesota	6,306,130	1.7%
21	Wisconsin	6,150,764	1.7%
22	Colorado	5,792,357	1.6%
23	South Carolina	5,148,569	1.4%
24	Alabama	4,874,243	1.3%
25	Oregon	4,833,918	1.3%
26	Louisiana	4,802,633	1.3%
27	Kentucky	4,554,998	1.3%
28	Nevada	4,282,102	1.2%
29	Oklahoma	3,913,251	1.1%
30	Connecticut	3,688,630	1.0%
31	Utah	3,485,367	1.0%
32	Arkansas	3,240,208	0.9%
33	Mississippi	3,092,410	0.9%
34	Iowa	2,955,172	0.8%
35	Kansas	2,940,084	0.8%
36	New Mexico	2,099,708	0.6%
37	Idaho	1,969,624	0.5%
38	Nebraska	1,820,247	0.5%
39	West Virginia	1,719,959	0.5%
40	New Hampshire	1,646,471	0.5%
41	Hawaii	1,466,046	0.4%
42	Maine	1,411,097	0.4%
43	Rhode Island	1,152,941	0.3%
44	Montana	1,044,898	0.3%
45	Delaware	1,012,658	0.3%
46	Alaska	867,674	0.2%
47	South Dakota	800,462	0.2%
48	Vermont	711,867	0.2%
49	North Dakota	606,566	0.2%
50	Wyoming	522,979	0.1%
	District of Columbia	433,414	0.1%

Source: U.S. Bureau of the Census
"State Interim Population Projections: 2004-2030 "
(http://www.census.gov/population/www/projections/projectionsagesex.html)

Projected Percent Change in Population: 2000 to 2030

National Projected Percent Change = 29.2% Increase*

ALPHA ORDER

RANK	STATE	PERCENT CHANGE
35	Alabama	9.6
12	Alaska	38.4
2	Arizona	108.8
21	Arkansas	21.2
13	California	37.1
14	Colorado	34.7
38	Connecticut	8.3
18	Delaware	29.2
3	Florida	79.5
8	Georgia	46.8
22	Hawaii	21.0
6	Idaho	52.2
39	Illinois	8.2
31	Indiana	12.0
48	Iowa	1.0
36	Kansas	9.4
30	Kentucky	12.7
41	Louisiana	7.5
32	Maine	10.7
16	Maryland	32.6
33	Massachusetts	10.4
40	Michigan	7.6
20	Minnesota	28.2
37	Mississippi	8.7
27	Missouri	14.9
25	Montana	15.8
42	Nebraska	6.4
1	Nevada	114.3
15	New Hampshire	33.2
24	New Jersey	16.5
26	New Mexico	15.4
46	New York	2.6
7	North Carolina	51.9
50	North Dakota	(5.5)
47	Ohio	1.7
29	Oklahoma	13.4
10	Oregon	41.3
45	Pennsylvania	4.0
34	Rhode Island	10.0
19	South Carolina	28.3
43	South Dakota	6.0
17	Tennessee	29.7
4	Texas	59.8
5	Utah	56.1
23	Vermont	16.9
11	Virginia	38.8
9	Washington	46.3
49	West Virginia	(4.9)
28	Wisconsin	14.7
44	Wyoming	5.9

RANK ORDER

RANK	STATE	PERCENT CHANGE
1	Nevada	114.3
2	Arizona	108.8
3	Florida	79.5
4	Texas	59.8
5	Utah	56.1
6	Idaho	52.2
7	North Carolina	51.9
8	Georgia	46.8
9	Washington	46.3
10	Oregon	41.3
11	Virginia	38.8
12	Alaska	38.4
13	California	37.1
14	Colorado	34.7
15	New Hampshire	33.2
16	Maryland	32.6
17	Tennessee	29.7
18	Delaware	29.2
19	South Carolina	28.3
20	Minnesota	28.2
21	Arkansas	21.2
22	Hawaii	21.0
23	Vermont	16.9
24	New Jersey	16.5
25	Montana	15.8
26	New Mexico	15.4
27	Missouri	14.9
28	Wisconsin	14.7
29	Oklahoma	13.4
30	Kentucky	12.7
31	Indiana	12.0
32	Maine	10.7
33	Massachusetts	10.4
34	Rhode Island	10.0
35	Alabama	9.6
36	Kansas	9.4
37	Mississippi	8.7
38	Connecticut	8.3
39	Illinois	8.2
40	Michigan	7.6
41	Louisiana	7.5
42	Nebraska	6.4
43	South Dakota	6.0
44	Wyoming	5.9
45	Pennsylvania	4.0
46	New York	2.6
47	Ohio	1.7
48	Iowa	1.0
49	West Virginia	(4.9)
50	North Dakota	(5.5)

District of Columbia   (24.2)

Source: U.S. Bureau of the Census
"State Interim Population Projections: 2004-2030 "
(http://www.census.gov/population/www/projections/projectionsagesex.html)

Projected Percent of State Population Under Age 18 in 2030

National Percent = 23.6%

ALPHA ORDER

RANK	STATE	PERCENT
27	Alabama	22.8
2	Alaska	28.7
14	Arizona	24.3
17	Arkansas	24.2
21	California	23.8
5	Colorado	25.3
32	Connecticut	22.3
41	Delaware	21.6
45	Florida	20.1
4	Georgia	26.2
33	Hawaii	22.2
11	Idaho	24.7
14	Illinois	24.3
9	Indiana	25.0
31	Iowa	22.4
18	Kansas	24.1
30	Kentucky	22.6
19	Louisiana	23.9
50	Maine	18.1
12	Maryland	24.5
38	Massachusetts	22.0
27	Michigan	22.8
19	Minnesota	23.9
25	Mississippi	23.0
23	Missouri	23.3
45	Montana	20.1
7	Nebraska	25.1
7	Nevada	25.1
41	New Hampshire	21.6
33	New Jersey	22.2
40	New Mexico	21.7
33	New York	22.2
6	North Carolina	25.2
44	North Dakota	21.2
26	Ohio	22.9
9	Oklahoma	25.0
24	Oregon	23.1
43	Pennsylvania	21.5
39	Rhode Island	21.9
33	South Carolina	22.2
12	South Dakota	24.5
14	Tennessee	24.3
3	Texas	27.0
1	Utah	30.4
47	Vermont	19.5
22	Virginia	23.6
27	Washington	22.8
49	West Virginia	18.9
33	Wisconsin	22.2
48	Wyoming	19.1

RANK ORDER

RANK	STATE	PERCENT
1	Utah	30.4
2	Alaska	28.7
3	Texas	27.0
4	Georgia	26.2
5	Colorado	25.3
6	North Carolina	25.2
7	Nebraska	25.1
7	Nevada	25.1
9	Indiana	25.0
9	Oklahoma	25.0
11	Idaho	24.7
12	Maryland	24.5
12	South Dakota	24.5
14	Arizona	24.3
14	Illinois	24.3
14	Tennessee	24.3
17	Arkansas	24.2
18	Kansas	24.1
19	Louisiana	23.9
19	Minnesota	23.9
21	California	23.8
22	Virginia	23.6
23	Missouri	23.3
24	Oregon	23.1
25	Mississippi	23.0
26	Ohio	22.9
27	Alabama	22.8
27	Michigan	22.8
27	Washington	22.8
30	Kentucky	22.6
31	Iowa	22.4
32	Connecticut	22.3
33	Hawaii	22.2
33	New Jersey	22.2
33	New York	22.2
33	South Carolina	22.2
33	Wisconsin	22.2
38	Massachusetts	22.0
39	Rhode Island	21.9
40	New Mexico	21.7
41	Delaware	21.6
41	New Hampshire	21.6
43	Pennsylvania	21.5
44	North Dakota	21.2
45	Florida	20.1
45	Montana	20.1
47	Vermont	19.5
48	Wyoming	19.1
49	West Virginia	18.9
50	Maine	18.1
	District of Columbia	23.2

Source: U.S. Bureau of the Census
"State Interim Population Projections: 2004-2030 "
(http://www.census.gov/population/www/projections/projectionsagesex.html)

Projected Percent of State Population Age 65 and Older in 2030

National Percent = 19.7%

ALPHA ORDER

RANK	STATE	PERCENT
19	Alabama	21.3
49	Alaska	14.7
14	Arizona	22.1
25	Arkansas	20.3
43	California	17.8
46	Colorado	16.5
16	Connecticut	21.5
9	Delaware	23.5
1	Florida	27.1
47	Georgia	15.9
13	Hawaii	22.3
38	Idaho	18.3
42	Illinois	18.0
40	Indiana	18.1
12	Iowa	22.4
26	Kansas	20.2
30	Kentucky	19.8
31	Louisiana	19.7
2	Maine	26.5
45	Maryland	17.6
21	Massachusetts	20.9
32	Michigan	19.5
35	Minnesota	18.9
23	Mississippi	20.5
26	Missouri	20.2
5	Montana	25.8
22	Nebraska	20.6
37	Nevada	18.6
17	New Hampshire	21.4
29	New Jersey	20.0
4	New Mexico	26.4
28	New York	20.1
43	North Carolina	17.8
6	North Dakota	25.1
24	Ohio	20.4
33	Oklahoma	19.4
39	Oregon	18.2
11	Pennsylvania	22.6
17	Rhode Island	21.4
15	South Carolina	22.0
10	South Dakota	23.1
34	Tennessee	19.2
48	Texas	15.6
50	Utah	13.2
8	Vermont	24.4
36	Virginia	18.8
40	Washington	18.1
7	West Virginia	24.8
19	Wisconsin	21.3
2	Wyoming	26.5

RANK ORDER

RANK	STATE	PERCENT
1	Florida	27.1
2	Maine	26.5
2	Wyoming	26.5
4	New Mexico	26.4
5	Montana	25.8
6	North Dakota	25.1
7	West Virginia	24.8
8	Vermont	24.4
9	Delaware	23.5
10	South Dakota	23.1
11	Pennsylvania	22.6
12	Iowa	22.4
13	Hawaii	22.3
14	Arizona	22.1
15	South Carolina	22.0
16	Connecticut	21.5
17	New Hampshire	21.4
17	Rhode Island	21.4
19	Alabama	21.3
19	Wisconsin	21.3
21	Massachusetts	20.9
22	Nebraska	20.6
23	Mississippi	20.5
24	Ohio	20.4
25	Arkansas	20.3
26	Kansas	20.2
26	Missouri	20.2
28	New York	20.1
29	New Jersey	20.0
30	Kentucky	19.8
31	Louisiana	19.7
32	Michigan	19.5
33	Oklahoma	19.4
34	Tennessee	19.2
35	Minnesota	18.9
36	Virginia	18.8
37	Nevada	18.6
38	Idaho	18.3
39	Oregon	18.2
40	Indiana	18.1
40	Washington	18.1
42	Illinois	18.0
43	California	17.8
43	North Carolina	17.8
45	Maryland	17.6
46	Colorado	16.5
47	Georgia	15.9
48	Texas	15.6
49	Alaska	14.7
50	Utah	13.2

District of Columbia	13.4

Source: U.S. Bureau of the Census
"State Interim Population Projections: 2004-2030 "
(http://www.census.gov/population/www/projections/projectionsagesex.html)

Median Age in 2006

National Median = 36.4 Years Old

ALPHA ORDER				RANK ORDER		
RANK	STATE	MEDIAN AGE		RANK	STATE	MEDIAN AGE
23	Alabama	37.1		1	Maine	41.1
48	Alaska	33.4		2	Vermont	40.4
44	Arizona	34.6		3	West Virginia	40.2
30	Arkansas	36.8		4	Florida	39.6
46	California	34.4		5	Pennsylvania	39.5
41	Colorado	35.4		6	New Hampshire	39.4
8	Connecticut	39.0		7	Montana	39.2
15	Delaware	37.5		8	Connecticut	39.0
4	Florida	39.6		9	Massachusetts	38.2
44	Georgia	34.6		9	New Jersey	38.2
17	Hawaii	37.3		9	Rhode Island	38.2
47	Idaho	34.2		12	Iowa	37.8
38	Illinois	35.7		13	Wisconsin	37.7
34	Indiana	36.3		14	Ohio	37.6
12	Iowa	37.8		15	Delaware	37.5
35	Kansas	36.0		15	Oregon	37.5
19	Kentucky	37.2		17	Hawaii	37.3
38	Louisiana	35.7		17	New York	37.3
1	Maine	41.1		19	Kentucky	37.2
19	Maryland	37.2		19	Maryland	37.2
9	Massachusetts	38.2		19	Michigan	37.2
19	Michigan	37.2		19	North Dakota	37.2
30	Minnesota	36.8		23	Alabama	37.1
42	Mississippi	35.3		23	Missouri	37.1
23	Missouri	37.1		23	South Carolina	37.1
7	Montana	39.2		23	Tennessee	37.1
35	Nebraska	36.0		23	Wyoming	37.1
40	Nevada	35.5		28	South Dakota	36.9
6	New Hampshire	39.4		28	Virginia	36.9
9	New Jersey	38.2		30	Arkansas	36.8
42	New Mexico	35.3		30	Minnesota	36.8
17	New York	37.3		32	Washington	36.7
33	North Carolina	36.6		33	North Carolina	36.6
19	North Dakota	37.2		34	Indiana	36.3
14	Ohio	37.6		35	Kansas	36.0
35	Oklahoma	36.0		35	Nebraska	36.0
15	Oregon	37.5		35	Oklahoma	36.0
5	Pennsylvania	39.5		38	Illinois	35.7
9	Rhode Island	38.2		38	Louisiana	35.7
23	South Carolina	37.1		40	Nevada	35.5
28	South Dakota	36.9		41	Colorado	35.4
23	Tennessee	37.1		42	Mississippi	35.3
49	Texas	33.1		42	New Mexico	35.3
50	Utah	28.3		44	Arizona	34.6
2	Vermont	40.4		44	Georgia	34.6
28	Virginia	36.9		46	California	34.4
32	Washington	36.7		47	Idaho	34.2
3	West Virginia	40.2		48	Alaska	33.4
13	Wisconsin	37.7		49	Texas	33.1
23	Wyoming	37.1		50	Utah	28.3
					District of Columbia	35.0

Source: U.S. Bureau of the Census
"2006 American Community Survey" (http://www.census.gov/acs/www/index.html)

Population Under 5 Years Old in 2006

National Total = 20,417,636

ALPHA ORDER

RANK	STATE	POPULATION	% of USA
24	Alabama	299,377	1.5%
47	Alaska	49,771	0.2%
13	Arizona	480,491	2.4%
33	Arkansas	192,891	0.9%
1	California	2,678,019	13.1%
22	Colorado	341,069	1.7%
31	Connecticut	202,831	1.0%
45	Delaware	56,692	0.3%
4	Florida	1,122,849	5.5%
8	Georgia	702,134	3.4%
40	Hawaii	87,321	0.4%
38	Idaho	112,963	0.6%
5	Illinois	887,605	4.3%
14	Indiana	431,089	2.1%
34	Iowa	192,055	0.9%
32	Kansas	194,100	1.0%
26	Kentucky	275,751	1.4%
23	Louisiana	301,375	1.5%
42	Maine	70,245	0.3%
19	Maryland	368,199	1.8%
17	Massachusetts	387,863	1.9%
9	Michigan	638,195	3.1%
21	Minnesota	345,250	1.7%
30	Mississippi	209,457	1.0%
18	Missouri	386,752	1.9%
44	Montana	57,916	0.3%
37	Nebraska	127,665	0.6%
35	Nevada	183,588	0.9%
41	New Hampshire	73,575	0.4%
11	New Jersey	558,994	2.7%
36	New Mexico	141,969	0.7%
3	New York	1,220,468	6.0%
10	North Carolina	611,110	3.0%
48	North Dakota	39,556	0.2%
6	Ohio	734,735	3.6%
27	Oklahoma	254,718	1.2%
29	Oregon	230,660	1.1%
7	Pennsylvania	724,687	3.5%
43	Rhode Island	61,961	0.3%
25	South Carolina	283,481	1.4%
46	South Dakota	54,828	0.3%
16	Tennessee	398,252	2.0%
2	Texas	1,925,197	9.4%
28	Utah	247,801	1.2%
50	Vermont	32,779	0.2%
12	Virginia	508,965	2.5%
15	Washington	408,158	2.0%
39	West Virginia	104,964	0.5%
20	Wisconsin	348,764	1.7%
49	Wyoming	33,553	0.2%

RANK ORDER

RANK	STATE	POPULATION	% of USA
1	California	2,678,019	13.1%
2	Texas	1,925,197	9.4%
3	New York	1,220,468	6.0%
4	Florida	1,122,849	5.5%
5	Illinois	887,605	4.3%
6	Ohio	734,735	3.6%
7	Pennsylvania	724,687	3.5%
8	Georgia	702,134	3.4%
9	Michigan	638,195	3.1%
10	North Carolina	611,110	3.0%
11	New Jersey	558,994	2.7%
12	Virginia	508,965	2.5%
13	Arizona	480,491	2.4%
14	Indiana	431,089	2.1%
15	Washington	408,158	2.0%
16	Tennessee	398,252	2.0%
17	Massachusetts	387,863	1.9%
18	Missouri	386,752	1.9%
19	Maryland	368,199	1.8%
20	Wisconsin	348,764	1.7%
21	Minnesota	345,250	1.7%
22	Colorado	341,069	1.7%
23	Louisiana	301,375	1.5%
24	Alabama	299,377	1.5%
25	South Carolina	283,481	1.4%
26	Kentucky	275,751	1.4%
27	Oklahoma	254,718	1.2%
28	Utah	247,801	1.2%
29	Oregon	230,660	1.1%
30	Mississippi	209,457	1.0%
31	Connecticut	202,831	1.0%
32	Kansas	194,100	1.0%
33	Arkansas	192,891	0.9%
34	Iowa	192,055	0.9%
35	Nevada	183,588	0.9%
36	New Mexico	141,969	0.7%
37	Nebraska	127,665	0.6%
38	Idaho	112,963	0.6%
39	West Virginia	104,964	0.5%
40	Hawaii	87,321	0.4%
41	New Hampshire	73,575	0.4%
42	Maine	70,245	0.3%
43	Rhode Island	61,961	0.3%
44	Montana	57,916	0.3%
45	Delaware	56,692	0.3%
46	South Dakota	54,828	0.3%
47	Alaska	49,771	0.2%
48	North Dakota	39,556	0.2%
49	Wyoming	33,553	0.2%
50	Vermont	32,779	0.2%
	District of Columbia	34,948	0.2%

Source: U.S. Bureau of the Census
"State Population Estimates - Characteristics" (http://www.census.gov/popest/states/asrh/)

Percent of Population Under 5 Years Old in 2006

National Percent = 6.8% of Population

ALPHA ORDER

RANK	STATE	PERCENT
30	Alabama	6.5
6	Alaska	7.4
3	Arizona	7.8
17	Arkansas	6.9
8	California	7.3
10	Colorado	7.2
44	Connecticut	5.8
24	Delaware	6.6
39	Florida	6.2
5	Georgia	7.5
20	Hawaii	6.8
4	Idaho	7.7
17	Illinois	6.9
20	Indiana	6.8
32	Iowa	6.4
14	Kansas	7.0
24	Kentucky	6.6
14	Louisiana	7.0
49	Maine	5.3
24	Maryland	6.6
43	Massachusetts	6.0
36	Michigan	6.3
22	Minnesota	6.7
10	Mississippi	7.2
24	Missouri	6.6
42	Montana	6.1
10	Nebraska	7.2
6	Nevada	7.4
48	New Hampshire	5.6
32	New Jersey	6.4
8	New Mexico	7.3
36	New York	6.3
17	North Carolina	6.9
39	North Dakota	6.2
32	Ohio	6.4
13	Oklahoma	7.1
39	Oregon	6.2
44	Pennsylvania	5.8
44	Rhode Island	5.8
24	South Carolina	6.6
14	South Dakota	7.0
24	Tennessee	6.6
2	Texas	8.2
1	Utah	9.7
49	Vermont	5.3
22	Virginia	6.7
32	Washington	6.4
44	West Virginia	5.8
36	Wisconsin	6.3
30	Wyoming	6.5

RANK ORDER

RANK	STATE	PERCENT
1	Utah	9.7
2	Texas	8.2
3	Arizona	7.8
4	Idaho	7.7
5	Georgia	7.5
6	Alaska	7.4
6	Nevada	7.4
8	California	7.3
8	New Mexico	7.3
10	Colorado	7.2
10	Mississippi	7.2
10	Nebraska	7.2
13	Oklahoma	7.1
14	Kansas	7.0
14	Louisiana	7.0
14	South Dakota	7.0
17	Arkansas	6.9
17	Illinois	6.9
17	North Carolina	6.9
20	Hawaii	6.8
20	Indiana	6.8
22	Minnesota	6.7
22	Virginia	6.7
24	Delaware	6.6
24	Kentucky	6.6
24	Maryland	6.6
24	Missouri	6.6
24	South Carolina	6.6
24	Tennessee	6.6
30	Alabama	6.5
30	Wyoming	6.5
32	Iowa	6.4
32	New Jersey	6.4
32	Ohio	6.4
32	Washington	6.4
36	Michigan	6.3
36	New York	6.3
36	Wisconsin	6.3
39	Florida	6.2
39	North Dakota	6.2
39	Oregon	6.2
42	Montana	6.1
43	Massachusetts	6.0
44	Connecticut	5.8
44	Pennsylvania	5.8
44	Rhode Island	5.8
44	West Virginia	5.8
48	New Hampshire	5.6
49	Maine	5.3
49	Vermont	5.3
	District of Columbia	6.0

Source: CQ Press using data from U.S. Bureau of the Census
"State Population Estimates - Characteristics" (http://www.census.gov/popest/states/asrh/)

Population 5 to 17 Years Old in 2006

National Total = 53,317,926

ALPHA ORDER				RANK ORDER			
RANK	**STATE**	**POPULATION**	**% of USA**	**RANK**	**STATE**	**POPULATION**	**% of USA**
23	Alabama	814,924	1.5%	1	California	6,854,595	12.9%
47	Alaska	131,663	0.2%	2	Texas	4,568,768	8.6%
13	Arizona	1,147,707	2.2%	3	New York	3,293,874	6.2%
34	Arkansas	498,295	0.9%	4	Florida	2,898,706	5.4%
1	California	6,854,595	12.9%	5	Illinois	2,327,639	4.4%
22	Colorado	828,232	1.6%	6	Pennsylvania	2,080,186	3.9%
29	Connecticut	615,455	1.2%	7	Ohio	2,035,300	3.8%
45	Delaware	146,674	0.3%	8	Michigan	1,840,161	3.5%
4	Florida	2,898,706	5.4%	9	Georgia	1,752,886	3.3%
9	Georgia	1,752,886	3.3%	10	North Carolina	1,544,277	2.9%
41	Hawaii	210,760	0.4%	11	New Jersey	1,530,344	2.9%
39	Idaho	281,317	0.5%	12	Virginia	1,297,882	2.4%
5	Illinois	2,327,639	4.4%	13	Arizona	1,147,707	2.2%
14	Indiana	1,146,540	2.2%	14	Indiana	1,146,540	2.2%
32	Iowa	518,139	1.0%	15	Washington	1,118,109	2.1%
33	Kansas	501,737	0.9%	16	Massachusetts	1,061,021	2.0%
26	Kentucky	723,780	1.4%	17	Tennessee	1,044,341	2.0%
24	Louisiana	788,626	1.5%	18	Missouri	1,029,840	1.9%
42	Maine	210,749	0.4%	19	Maryland	992,332	1.9%
19	Maryland	992,332	1.9%	20	Wisconsin	963,766	1.8%
16	Massachusetts	1,061,021	2.0%	21	Minnesota	912,014	1.7%
8	Michigan	1,840,161	3.5%	22	Colorado	828,232	1.6%
21	Minnesota	912,014	1.7%	23	Alabama	814,924	1.5%
30	Mississippi	549,948	1.0%	24	Louisiana	788,626	1.5%
18	Missouri	1,029,840	1.9%	25	South Carolina	756,172	1.4%
44	Montana	159,932	0.3%	26	Kentucky	723,780	1.4%
37	Nebraska	317,368	0.6%	27	Oklahoma	639,316	1.2%
35	Nevada	450,932	0.8%	28	Oregon	625,599	1.2%
40	New Hampshire	224,050	0.4%	29	Connecticut	615,455	1.2%
11	New Jersey	1,530,344	2.9%	30	Mississippi	549,948	1.0%
36	New Mexico	366,961	0.7%	31	Utah	543,397	1.0%
3	New York	3,293,874	6.2%	32	Iowa	518,139	1.0%
10	North Carolina	1,544,277	2.9%	33	Kansas	501,737	0.9%
48	North Dakota	105,378	0.2%	34	Arkansas	498,295	0.9%
7	Ohio	2,035,300	3.8%	35	Nevada	450,932	0.8%
27	Oklahoma	639,316	1.2%	36	New Mexico	366,961	0.7%
28	Oregon	625,599	1.2%	37	Nebraska	317,368	0.6%
6	Pennsylvania	2,080,186	3.9%	38	West Virginia	284,107	0.5%
43	Rhode Island	175,490	0.3%	39	Idaho	281,317	0.5%
25	South Carolina	756,172	1.4%	40	New Hampshire	224,050	0.4%
46	South Dakota	139,853	0.3%	41	Hawaii	210,760	0.4%
17	Tennessee	1,044,341	2.0%	42	Maine	210,749	0.4%
2	Texas	4,568,768	8.6%	43	Rhode Island	175,490	0.3%
31	Utah	543,397	1.0%	44	Montana	159,932	0.3%
49	Vermont	100,610	0.2%	45	Delaware	146,674	0.3%
12	Virginia	1,297,882	2.4%	46	South Dakota	139,853	0.3%
15	Washington	1,118,109	2.1%	47	Alaska	131,663	0.2%
38	West Virginia	284,107	0.5%	48	North Dakota	105,378	0.2%
20	Wisconsin	963,766	1.8%	49	Vermont	100,610	0.2%
50	Wyoming	88,241	0.2%	50	Wyoming	88,241	0.2%
					District of Columbia	79,933	0.1%

Source: U.S. Bureau of the Census
"State Population Estimates - Characteristics" (http://www.census.gov/popest/states/asrh/)

Percent of Population 5 to 17 Years Old in 2006

National Percent = 17.8% of Population

ALPHA ORDER

RANK	STATE	PERCENT
19	Alabama	17.7
2	Alaska	19.6
9	Arizona	18.6
19	Arkansas	17.7
6	California	18.8
29	Colorado	17.4
24	Connecticut	17.6
34	Delaware	17.2
48	Florida	16.0
8	Georgia	18.7
45	Hawaii	16.4
4	Idaho	19.2
14	Illinois	18.1
11	Indiana	18.2
29	Iowa	17.4
11	Kansas	18.2
34	Kentucky	17.2
10	Louisiana	18.4
49	Maine	15.9
19	Maryland	17.7
44	Massachusetts	16.5
11	Michigan	18.2
19	Minnesota	17.7
5	Mississippi	18.9
24	Missouri	17.6
40	Montana	16.9
16	Nebraska	17.9
14	Nevada	18.1
38	New Hampshire	17.0
26	New Jersey	17.5
6	New Mexico	18.8
36	New York	17.1
29	North Carolina	17.4
43	North Dakota	16.6
19	Ohio	17.7
16	Oklahoma	17.9
40	Oregon	16.9
42	Pennsylvania	16.7
45	Rhode Island	16.4
26	South Carolina	17.5
16	South Dakota	17.9
32	Tennessee	17.3
3	Texas	19.4
1	Utah	21.3
47	Vermont	16.1
38	Virginia	17.0
26	Washington	17.5
50	West Virginia	15.6
32	Wisconsin	17.3
36	Wyoming	17.1

RANK ORDER

RANK	STATE	PERCENT
1	Utah	21.3
2	Alaska	19.6
3	Texas	19.4
4	Idaho	19.2
5	Mississippi	18.9
6	California	18.8
6	New Mexico	18.8
8	Georgia	18.7
9	Arizona	18.6
10	Louisiana	18.4
11	Indiana	18.2
11	Kansas	18.2
11	Michigan	18.2
14	Illinois	18.1
14	Nevada	18.1
16	Nebraska	17.9
16	Oklahoma	17.9
16	South Dakota	17.9
19	Alabama	17.7
19	Arkansas	17.7
19	Maryland	17.7
19	Minnesota	17.7
19	Ohio	17.7
24	Connecticut	17.6
24	Missouri	17.6
26	New Jersey	17.5
26	South Carolina	17.5
26	Washington	17.5
29	Colorado	17.4
29	Iowa	17.4
29	North Carolina	17.4
32	Tennessee	17.3
32	Wisconsin	17.3
34	Delaware	17.2
34	Kentucky	17.2
36	New York	17.1
36	Wyoming	17.1
38	New Hampshire	17.0
38	Virginia	17.0
40	Montana	16.9
40	Oregon	16.9
42	Pennsylvania	16.7
43	North Dakota	16.6
44	Massachusetts	16.5
45	Hawaii	16.4
45	Rhode Island	16.4
47	Vermont	16.1
48	Florida	16.0
49	Maine	15.9
50	West Virginia	15.6

District of Columbia 13.7

Source: CQ Press using data from U.S. Bureau of the Census
"State Population Estimates - Characteristics" (http://www.census.gov/popest/states/asrh/)

Population 18 Years Old and Older in 2006

National Total = 225,662,922

ALPHA ORDER

RANK	STATE	POPULATION	% of USA
23	Alabama	3,484,729	1.5%
49	Alaska	488,619	0.2%
17	Arizona	4,538,120	2.0%
32	Arkansas	2,119,686	0.9%
1	California	26,924,935	11.9%
22	Colorado	3,584,076	1.6%
28	Connecticut	2,686,523	1.2%
45	Delaware	650,110	0.3%
4	Florida	14,068,333	6.2%
9	Georgia	6,908,921	3.1%
42	Hawaii	987,417	0.4%
39	Idaho	1,072,185	0.5%
6	Illinois	9,616,726	4.3%
15	Indiana	4,735,891	2.1%
30	Iowa	2,271,891	1.0%
33	Kansas	2,068,238	0.9%
25	Kentucky	3,206,543	1.4%
26	Louisiana	3,197,767	1.4%
40	Maine	1,040,580	0.5%
19	Maryland	4,255,196	1.9%
13	Massachusetts	4,988,309	2.2%
8	Michigan	7,617,287	3.4%
21	Minnesota	3,909,837	1.7%
31	Mississippi	2,151,135	1.0%
18	Missouri	4,426,121	2.0%
44	Montana	726,784	0.3%
38	Nebraska	1,323,298	0.6%
34	Nevada	1,861,009	0.8%
41	New Hampshire	1,017,270	0.5%
11	New Jersey	6,635,222	2.9%
36	New Mexico	1,445,669	0.6%
3	New York	14,791,841	6.6%
10	North Carolina	6,701,118	3.0%
47	North Dakota	490,933	0.2%
7	Ohio	8,707,971	3.9%
29	Oklahoma	2,685,178	1.2%
27	Oregon	2,844,499	1.3%
5	Pennsylvania	9,635,748	4.3%
43	Rhode Island	830,159	0.4%
24	South Carolina	3,281,596	1.5%
46	South Dakota	587,238	0.3%
16	Tennessee	4,596,210	2.0%
2	Texas	17,013,818	7.5%
35	Utah	1,758,865	0.8%
48	Vermont	490,519	0.2%
12	Virginia	5,836,037	2.6%
14	Washington	4,869,531	2.2%
37	West Virginia	1,429,399	0.6%
20	Wisconsin	4,243,976	1.9%
50	Wyoming	393,210	0.2%

RANK ORDER

RANK	STATE	POPULATION	% of USA
1	California	26,924,935	11.9%
2	Texas	17,013,818	7.5%
3	New York	14,791,841	6.6%
4	Florida	14,068,333	6.2%
5	Pennsylvania	9,635,748	4.3%
6	Illinois	9,616,726	4.3%
7	Ohio	8,707,971	3.9%
8	Michigan	7,617,287	3.4%
9	Georgia	6,908,921	3.1%
10	North Carolina	6,701,118	3.0%
11	New Jersey	6,635,222	2.9%
12	Virginia	5,836,037	2.6%
13	Massachusetts	4,988,309	2.2%
14	Washington	4,869,531	2.2%
15	Indiana	4,735,891	2.1%
16	Tennessee	4,596,210	2.0%
17	Arizona	4,538,120	2.0%
18	Missouri	4,426,121	2.0%
19	Maryland	4,255,196	1.9%
20	Wisconsin	4,243,976	1.9%
21	Minnesota	3,909,837	1.7%
22	Colorado	3,584,076	1.6%
23	Alabama	3,484,729	1.5%
24	South Carolina	3,281,596	1.5%
25	Kentucky	3,206,543	1.4%
26	Louisiana	3,197,767	1.4%
27	Oregon	2,844,499	1.3%
28	Connecticut	2,686,523	1.2%
29	Oklahoma	2,685,178	1.2%
30	Iowa	2,271,891	1.0%
31	Mississippi	2,151,135	1.0%
32	Arkansas	2,119,686	0.9%
33	Kansas	2,068,238	0.9%
34	Nevada	1,861,009	0.8%
35	Utah	1,758,865	0.8%
36	New Mexico	1,445,669	0.6%
37	West Virginia	1,429,399	0.6%
38	Nebraska	1,323,298	0.6%
39	Idaho	1,072,185	0.5%
40	Maine	1,040,580	0.5%
41	New Hampshire	1,017,270	0.5%
42	Hawaii	987,417	0.4%
43	Rhode Island	830,159	0.4%
44	Montana	726,784	0.3%
45	Delaware	650,110	0.3%
46	South Dakota	587,238	0.3%
47	North Dakota	490,933	0.2%
48	Vermont	490,519	0.2%
49	Alaska	488,619	0.2%
50	Wyoming	393,210	0.2%
	District of Columbia	466,649	0.2%

Source: U.S. Bureau of the Census
  "State Population Estimates - Characteristics" (http://www.census.gov/popest/states/asrh/)

Percent of Population 18 Years Old and Older in 2006

National Percent = 75.4% of Population

ALPHA ORDER

RANK	STATE	PERCENT
26	Alabama	75.8
48	Alaska	72.9
46	Arizona	73.6
32	Arkansas	75.4
43	California	73.9
32	Colorado	75.4
13	Connecticut	76.7
18	Delaware	76.2
4	Florida	77.8
45	Georgia	73.8
12	Hawaii	76.8
47	Idaho	73.1
37	Illinois	74.9
35	Indiana	75.0
18	Iowa	76.2
38	Kansas	74.8
18	Kentucky	76.2
40	Louisiana	74.6
1	Maine	78.7
26	Maryland	75.8
6	Massachusetts	77.5
31	Michigan	75.5
29	Minnesota	75.7
43	Mississippi	73.9
26	Missouri	75.8
10	Montana	76.9
38	Nebraska	74.8
40	Nevada	74.6
8	New Hampshire	77.4
21	New Jersey	76.1
42	New Mexico	74.0
14	New York	76.6
29	North Carolina	75.7
9	North Dakota	77.2
24	Ohio	75.9
35	Oklahoma	75.0
10	Oregon	76.9
6	Pennsylvania	77.5
4	Rhode Island	77.8
24	South Carolina	75.9
34	South Dakota	75.1
21	Tennessee	76.1
49	Texas	72.4
50	Utah	69.0
2	Vermont	78.6
15	Virginia	76.4
21	Washington	76.1
2	West Virginia	78.6
15	Wisconsin	76.4
15	Wyoming	76.4

RANK ORDER

RANK	STATE	PERCENT
1	Maine	78.7
2	Vermont	78.6
2	West Virginia	78.6
4	Florida	77.8
4	Rhode Island	77.8
6	Massachusetts	77.5
6	Pennsylvania	77.5
8	New Hampshire	77.4
9	North Dakota	77.2
10	Montana	76.9
10	Oregon	76.9
12	Hawaii	76.8
13	Connecticut	76.7
14	New York	76.6
15	Virginia	76.4
15	Wisconsin	76.4
15	Wyoming	76.4
18	Delaware	76.2
18	Iowa	76.2
18	Kentucky	76.2
21	New Jersey	76.1
21	Tennessee	76.1
21	Washington	76.1
24	Ohio	75.9
24	South Carolina	75.9
26	Alabama	75.8
26	Maryland	75.8
26	Missouri	75.8
29	Minnesota	75.7
29	North Carolina	75.7
31	Michigan	75.5
32	Arkansas	75.4
32	Colorado	75.4
34	South Dakota	75.1
35	Indiana	75.0
35	Oklahoma	75.0
37	Illinois	74.9
38	Kansas	74.8
38	Nebraska	74.8
40	Louisiana	74.6
40	Nevada	74.6
42	New Mexico	74.0
43	California	73.9
43	Mississippi	73.9
45	Georgia	73.8
46	Arizona	73.6
47	Idaho	73.1
48	Alaska	72.9
49	Texas	72.4
50	Utah	69.0

District of Columbia	80.2

Source: CQ Press using data from U.S. Bureau of the Census
"State Population Estimates - Characteristics" (http://www.census.gov/popest/states/asrh/)

Population 18 to 24 Years Old in 2006

National Total = 29,454,784

Source: U.S. Bureau of the Census
"State Population Estimates - Characteristics" (http://www.census.gov/popest/states/asrh/)

Percent of Population 18 to 24 Years Old in 2006

National Percent = 9.8% of Population

ALPHA ORDER

RANK	STATE	PERCENT
28	Alabama	9.7
4	Alaska	10.7
36	Arizona	9.5
36	Arkansas	9.5
12	California	10.4
28	Colorado	9.7
42	Connecticut	9.1
28	Delaware	9.7
47	Florida	8.8
23	Georgia	9.8
28	Hawaii	9.7
16	Idaho	10.2
20	Illinois	10.0
23	Indiana	9.8
9	Iowa	10.5
6	Kansas	10.6
42	Kentucky	9.1
6	Louisiana	10.6
47	Maine	8.8
36	Maryland	9.5
23	Massachusetts	9.8
28	Michigan	9.7
17	Minnesota	10.1
12	Mississippi	10.4
28	Missouri	9.7
17	Montana	10.1
4	Nebraska	10.7
50	Nevada	8.5
42	New Hampshire	9.1
47	New Jersey	8.8
9	New Mexico	10.5
20	New York	10.0
40	North Carolina	9.4
1	North Dakota	12.9
34	Ohio	9.6
15	Oklahoma	10.3
41	Oregon	9.2
34	Pennsylvania	9.6
3	Rhode Island	10.9
23	South Carolina	9.8
6	South Dakota	10.6
42	Tennessee	9.1
12	Texas	10.4
2	Utah	12.5
20	Vermont	10.0
23	Virginia	9.8
36	Washington	9.5
46	West Virginia	9.0
17	Wisconsin	10.1
9	Wyoming	10.5

RANK ORDER

RANK	STATE	PERCENT
1	North Dakota	12.9
2	Utah	12.5
3	Rhode Island	10.9
4	Alaska	10.7
4	Nebraska	10.7
6	Kansas	10.6
6	Louisiana	10.6
6	South Dakota	10.6
9	Iowa	10.5
9	New Mexico	10.5
9	Wyoming	10.5
12	California	10.4
12	Mississippi	10.4
12	Texas	10.4
15	Oklahoma	10.3
16	Idaho	10.2
17	Minnesota	10.1
17	Montana	10.1
17	Wisconsin	10.1
20	Illinois	10.0
20	New York	10.0
20	Vermont	10.0
23	Georgia	9.8
23	Indiana	9.8
23	Massachusetts	9.8
23	South Carolina	9.8
23	Virginia	9.8
28	Alabama	9.7
28	Colorado	9.7
28	Delaware	9.7
28	Hawaii	9.7
28	Michigan	9.7
28	Missouri	9.7
34	Ohio	9.6
34	Pennsylvania	9.6
36	Arizona	9.5
36	Arkansas	9.5
36	Maryland	9.5
36	Washington	9.5
40	North Carolina	9.4
41	Oregon	9.2
42	Connecticut	9.1
42	Kentucky	9.1
42	New Hampshire	9.1
42	Tennessee	9.1
46	West Virginia	9.0
47	Florida	8.8
47	Maine	8.8
47	New Jersey	8.8
50	Nevada	8.5

| | District of Columbia | 12.3 |

Source: CQ Press using data from U.S. Bureau of the Census
"State Population Estimates - Characteristics" (http://www.census.gov/popest/states/asrh/)

Population 25 to 44 Years Old in 2006

National Total = 84,082,929

ALPHA ORDER

RANK	STATE	POPULATION	% of USA
23	Alabama	1,239,397	1.5%
46	Alaska	195,833	0.2%
15	Arizona	1,752,098	2.1%
32	Arkansas	758,800	0.9%
1	California	10,767,783	12.8%
21	Colorado	1,439,861	1.7%
28	Connecticut	953,997	1.1%
44	Delaware	234,313	0.3%
4	Florida	4,868,204	5.8%
8	Georgia	2,831,306	3.4%
41	Hawaii	357,386	0.4%
39	Idaho	398,349	0.5%
5	Illinois	3,659,718	4.4%
16	Indiana	1,743,780	2.1%
31	Iowa	760,212	0.9%
34	Kansas	730,431	0.9%
24	Kentucky	1,192,239	1.4%
26	Louisiana	1,141,815	1.4%
42	Maine	346,919	0.4%
18	Maryland	1,603,325	1.9%
14	Massachusetts	1,822,110	2.2%
9	Michigan	2,735,111	3.3%
22	Minnesota	1,435,721	1.7%
30	Mississippi	771,521	0.9%
19	Missouri	1,586,140	1.9%
45	Montana	232,961	0.3%
38	Nebraska	462,507	0.6%
33	Nevada	755,681	0.9%
40	New Hampshire	362,548	0.4%
11	New Jersey	2,472,454	2.9%
36	New Mexico	515,837	0.6%
3	New York	5,423,867	6.5%
10	North Carolina	2,548,840	3.0%
49	North Dakota	154,174	0.2%
7	Ohio	3,081,056	3.7%
29	Oklahoma	952,911	1.1%
27	Oregon	1,032,934	1.2%
6	Pennsylvania	3,224,626	3.8%
43	Rhode Island	290,587	0.3%
25	South Carolina	1,180,743	1.4%
47	South Dakota	195,426	0.2%
17	Tennessee	1,715,517	2.0%
2	Texas	6,894,417	8.2%
35	Utah	719,745	0.9%
48	Vermont	161,919	0.2%
12	Virginia	2,226,126	2.6%
13	Washington	1,843,166	2.2%
37	West Virginia	477,853	0.6%
20	Wisconsin	1,508,475	1.8%
50	Wyoming	133,401	0.2%

RANK ORDER

RANK	STATE	POPULATION	% of USA
1	California	10,767,783	12.8%
2	Texas	6,894,417	8.2%
3	New York	5,423,867	6.5%
4	Florida	4,868,204	5.8%
5	Illinois	3,659,718	4.4%
6	Pennsylvania	3,224,626	3.8%
7	Ohio	3,081,056	3.7%
8	Georgia	2,831,306	3.4%
9	Michigan	2,735,111	3.3%
10	North Carolina	2,548,840	3.0%
11	New Jersey	2,472,454	2.9%
12	Virginia	2,226,126	2.6%
13	Washington	1,843,166	2.2%
14	Massachusetts	1,822,110	2.2%
15	Arizona	1,752,098	2.1%
16	Indiana	1,743,780	2.1%
17	Tennessee	1,715,517	2.0%
18	Maryland	1,603,325	1.9%
19	Missouri	1,586,140	1.9%
20	Wisconsin	1,508,475	1.8%
21	Colorado	1,439,861	1.7%
22	Minnesota	1,435,721	1.7%
23	Alabama	1,239,397	1.5%
24	Kentucky	1,192,239	1.4%
25	South Carolina	1,180,743	1.4%
26	Louisiana	1,141,815	1.4%
27	Oregon	1,032,934	1.2%
28	Connecticut	953,997	1.1%
29	Oklahoma	952,911	1.1%
30	Mississippi	771,521	0.9%
31	Iowa	760,212	0.9%
32	Arkansas	758,800	0.9%
33	Nevada	755,681	0.9%
34	Kansas	730,431	0.9%
35	Utah	719,745	0.9%
36	New Mexico	515,837	0.6%
37	West Virginia	477,853	0.6%
38	Nebraska	462,507	0.6%
39	Idaho	398,349	0.5%
40	New Hampshire	362,548	0.4%
41	Hawaii	357,386	0.4%
42	Maine	346,919	0.4%
43	Rhode Island	290,587	0.3%
44	Delaware	234,313	0.3%
45	Montana	232,961	0.3%
46	Alaska	195,833	0.2%
47	South Dakota	195,426	0.2%
48	Vermont	161,919	0.2%
49	North Dakota	154,174	0.2%
50	Wyoming	133,401	0.2%
	District of Columbia	188,789	0.2%

Source: CQ Press using data from U.S. Bureau of the Census
"SC-EST2006-AGESEX_RES - State Characteristic Estimates" (http://www.census.gov/popest/datasets.html)

Percent of Population 25 to 44 Years Old in 2006

National Percent = 28.1% of Population

ALPHA ORDER				RANK ORDER		
RANK	STATE	PERCENT		RANK	STATE	PERCENT
33	Alabama	26.9		1	Colorado	30.3
6	Alaska	29.2		1	Nevada	30.3
12	Arizona	28.4		3	Georgia	30.2
32	Arkansas	27.0		4	California	29.5
4	California	29.5		5	Texas	29.3
1	Colorado	30.3		6	Alaska	29.2
26	Connecticut	27.2		7	Virginia	29.1
24	Delaware	27.5		8	North Carolina	28.8
33	Florida	26.9		8	Washington	28.8
3	Georgia	30.2		10	Maryland	28.6
20	Hawaii	27.8		11	Illinois	28.5
26	Idaho	27.2		12	Arizona	28.4
11	Illinois	28.5		12	Tennessee	28.4
22	Indiana	27.6		14	Kentucky	28.3
47	Iowa	25.5		14	Massachusetts	28.3
39	Kansas	26.4		14	New Jersey	28.3
14	Kentucky	28.3		17	Utah	28.2
36	Louisiana	26.6		18	New York	28.1
41	Maine	26.3		19	Oregon	27.9
10	Maryland	28.6		20	Hawaii	27.8
14	Massachusetts	28.3		20	Minnesota	27.8
29	Michigan	27.1		22	Indiana	27.6
20	Minnesota	27.8		22	New Hampshire	27.6
38	Mississippi	26.5		24	Delaware	27.5
29	Missouri	27.1		25	South Carolina	27.3
49	Montana	24.7		26	Connecticut	27.2
43	Nebraska	26.2		26	Idaho	27.2
1	Nevada	30.3		26	Rhode Island	27.2
22	New Hampshire	27.6		29	Michigan	27.1
14	New Jersey	28.3		29	Missouri	27.1
39	New Mexico	26.4		29	Wisconsin	27.1
18	New York	28.1		32	Arkansas	27.0
8	North Carolina	28.8		33	Alabama	26.9
50	North Dakota	24.2		33	Florida	26.9
35	Ohio	26.8		35	Ohio	26.8
36	Oklahoma	26.6		36	Louisiana	26.6
19	Oregon	27.9		36	Oklahoma	26.6
45	Pennsylvania	25.9		38	Mississippi	26.5
26	Rhode Island	27.2		39	Kansas	26.4
25	South Carolina	27.3		39	New Mexico	26.4
48	South Dakota	25.0		41	Maine	26.3
12	Tennessee	28.4		41	West Virginia	26.3
5	Texas	29.3		43	Nebraska	26.2
17	Utah	28.2		44	Vermont	26.0
44	Vermont	26.0		45	Pennsylvania	25.9
7	Virginia	29.1		45	Wyoming	25.9
8	Washington	28.8		47	Iowa	25.5
41	West Virginia	26.3		48	South Dakota	25.0
29	Wisconsin	27.1		49	Montana	24.7
45	Wyoming	25.9		50	North Dakota	24.2
					District of Columbia	32.5

Source: CQ Press using data from U.S. Bureau of the Census
"SC-EST2006-AGESEX_RES - State Characteristic Estimates" (http://www.census.gov/popest/datasets.html)

Population 45 to 64 Years Old in 2006

National Total = 74,864,857

ALPHA ORDER

RANK	STATE	POPULATION	% of USA
23	Alabama	1,182,168	1.6%
48	Alaska	175,435	0.2%
20	Arizona	1,407,556	1.9%
32	Arkansas	703,685	0.9%
1	California	8,441,510	11.3%
22	Colorado	1,207,574	1.6%
28	Connecticut	942,319	1.3%
45	Delaware	218,018	0.3%
4	Florida	4,567,909	6.1%
10	Georgia	2,250,173	3.0%
42	Hawaii	325,559	0.4%
41	Idaho	355,576	0.5%
6	Illinois	3,140,765	4.2%
15	Indiana	1,592,056	2.1%
30	Iowa	764,140	1.0%
33	Kansas	687,278	0.9%
25	Kentucky	1,092,852	1.5%
26	Louisiana	1,077,344	1.4%
39	Maine	385,279	0.5%
18	Maryland	1,468,280	2.0%
14	Massachusetts	1,676,959	2.2%
8	Michigan	2,638,489	3.5%
21	Minnesota	1,326,978	1.8%
31	Mississippi	713,757	1.0%
17	Missouri	1,492,451	2.0%
44	Montana	268,176	0.4%
38	Nebraska	437,323	0.6%
34	Nevada	615,096	0.8%
40	New Hampshire	372,043	0.5%
9	New Jersey	2,271,077	3.0%
37	New Mexico	482,330	0.6%
3	New York	4,906,189	6.6%
11	North Carolina	2,240,580	3.0%
49	North Dakota	162,115	0.2%
7	Ohio	2,998,192	4.0%
29	Oklahoma	889,603	1.2%
27	Oregon	993,430	1.3%
5	Pennsylvania	3,326,901	4.4%
43	Rhode Island	275,533	0.4%
24	South Carolina	1,124,361	1.5%
46	South Dakota	197,495	0.3%
16	Tennessee	1,562,696	2.1%
2	Texas	5,336,206	7.1%
36	Utah	494,529	0.7%
47	Vermont	183,419	0.2%
12	Virginia	1,975,035	2.6%
13	Washington	1,680,777	2.2%
35	West Virginia	509,356	0.7%
19	Wisconsin	1,450,541	1.9%
50	Wyoming	142,797	0.2%

RANK ORDER

RANK	STATE	POPULATION	% of USA
1	California	8,441,510	11.3%
2	Texas	5,336,206	7.1%
3	New York	4,906,189	6.6%
4	Florida	4,567,909	6.1%
5	Pennsylvania	3,326,901	4.4%
6	Illinois	3,140,765	4.2%
7	Ohio	2,998,192	4.0%
8	Michigan	2,638,489	3.5%
9	New Jersey	2,271,077	3.0%
10	Georgia	2,250,173	3.0%
11	North Carolina	2,240,580	3.0%
12	Virginia	1,975,035	2.6%
13	Washington	1,680,777	2.2%
14	Massachusetts	1,676,959	2.2%
15	Indiana	1,592,056	2.1%
16	Tennessee	1,562,696	2.1%
17	Missouri	1,492,451	2.0%
18	Maryland	1,468,280	2.0%
19	Wisconsin	1,450,541	1.9%
20	Arizona	1,407,556	1.9%
21	Minnesota	1,326,978	1.8%
22	Colorado	1,207,574	1.6%
23	Alabama	1,182,168	1.6%
24	South Carolina	1,124,361	1.5%
25	Kentucky	1,092,852	1.5%
26	Louisiana	1,077,344	1.4%
27	Oregon	993,430	1.3%
28	Connecticut	942,319	1.3%
29	Oklahoma	889,603	1.2%
30	Iowa	764,140	1.0%
31	Mississippi	713,757	1.0%
32	Arkansas	703,685	0.9%
33	Kansas	687,278	0.9%
34	Nevada	615,096	0.8%
35	West Virginia	509,356	0.7%
36	Utah	494,529	0.7%
37	New Mexico	482,330	0.6%
38	Nebraska	437,323	0.6%
39	Maine	385,279	0.5%
40	New Hampshire	372,043	0.5%
41	Idaho	355,576	0.5%
42	Hawaii	325,559	0.4%
43	Rhode Island	275,533	0.4%
44	Montana	268,176	0.4%
45	Delaware	218,018	0.3%
46	South Dakota	197,495	0.3%
47	Vermont	183,419	0.2%
48	Alaska	175,435	0.2%
49	North Dakota	162,115	0.2%
50	Wyoming	142,797	0.2%
	District of Columbia	134,947	0.2%

Source: U.S. Bureau of the Census
"State Population Estimates - Characteristics" (http://www.census.gov/popest/states/asrh/)

Percent of Population 45 to 64 Years Old in 2006

National Percent = 25.0% of Population

RANK	STATE	PERCENT
23	Alabama	25.7
11	Alaska	26.2
48	Arizona	22.8
37	Arkansas	25.0
47	California	23.2
29	Colorado	25.4
7	Connecticut	26.9
26	Delaware	25.5
31	Florida	25.3
46	Georgia	24.0
31	Hawaii	25.3
45	Idaho	24.2
43	Illinois	24.5
35	Indiana	25.2
25	Iowa	25.6
38	Kansas	24.9
17	Kentucky	26.0
36	Louisiana	25.1
2	Maine	29.2
12	Maryland	26.1
12	Massachusetts	26.1
12	Michigan	26.1
23	Minnesota	25.7
43	Mississippi	24.5
26	Missouri	25.5
3	Montana	28.4
40	Nebraska	24.7
42	Nevada	24.6
4	New Hampshire	28.3
17	New Jersey	26.0
40	New Mexico	24.7
29	New York	25.4
31	North Carolina	25.3
26	North Dakota	25.5
12	Ohio	26.1
38	Oklahoma	24.9
8	Oregon	26.8
9	Pennsylvania	26.7
21	Rhode Island	25.8
17	South Carolina	26.0
31	South Dakota	25.3
20	Tennessee	25.9
49	Texas	22.7
50	Utah	19.4
1	Vermont	29.4
21	Virginia	25.8
10	Washington	26.3
5	West Virginia	28.0
12	Wisconsin	26.1
6	Wyoming	27.7

RANK	STATE	PERCENT
1	Vermont	29.4
2	Maine	29.2
3	Montana	28.4
4	New Hampshire	28.3
5	West Virginia	28.0
6	Wyoming	27.7
7	Connecticut	26.9
8	Oregon	26.8
9	Pennsylvania	26.7
10	Washington	26.3
11	Alaska	26.2
12	Maryland	26.1
12	Massachusetts	26.1
12	Michigan	26.1
12	Ohio	26.1
12	Wisconsin	26.1
17	Kentucky	26.0
17	New Jersey	26.0
17	South Carolina	26.0
20	Tennessee	25.9
21	Rhode Island	25.8
21	Virginia	25.8
23	Alabama	25.7
23	Minnesota	25.7
25	Iowa	25.6
26	Delaware	25.5
26	Missouri	25.5
26	North Dakota	25.5
29	Colorado	25.4
29	New York	25.4
31	Florida	25.3
31	Hawaii	25.3
31	North Carolina	25.3
31	South Dakota	25.3
35	Indiana	25.2
36	Louisiana	25.1
37	Arkansas	25.0
38	Kansas	24.9
38	Oklahoma	24.9
40	Nebraska	24.7
40	New Mexico	24.7
42	Nevada	24.6
43	Illinois	24.5
43	Mississippi	24.5
45	Idaho	24.2
46	Georgia	24.0
47	California	23.2
48	Arizona	22.8
49	Texas	22.7
50	Utah	19.4
	District of Columbia	23.2

Source: CQ Press using data from U.S. Bureau of the Census
"State Population Estimates - Characteristics" (http://www.census.gov/popest/states/asrh/)

Population 65 Years Old and Older in 2006

National Total = 37,260,352

ALPHA ORDER

RANK	STATE	POPULATION	% of USA
22	Alabama	615,597	1.7%
50	Alaska	45,630	0.1%
14	Arizona	790,286	2.1%
31	Arkansas	390,421	1.0%
1	California	3,931,514	10.6%
27	Colorado	477,186	1.3%
29	Connecticut	470,443	1.3%
45	Delaware	114,574	0.3%
2	Florida	3,037,704	8.2%
11	Georgia	912,874	2.4%
40	Hawaii	179,370	0.5%
41	Idaho	169,173	0.5%
6	Illinois	1,534,476	4.1%
15	Indiana	784,219	2.1%
30	Iowa	435,657	1.2%
33	Kansas	357,709	1.0%
24	Kentucky	537,294	1.4%
25	Louisiana	523,346	1.4%
39	Maine	192,639	0.5%
20	Maryland	650,568	1.7%
13	Massachusetts	855,962	2.3%
8	Michigan	1,260,864	3.4%
21	Minnesota	627,394	1.7%
32	Mississippi	362,172	1.0%
16	Missouri	778,891	2.1%
44	Montana	130,592	0.4%
37	Nebraska	234,655	0.6%
35	Nevada	276,943	0.7%
42	New Hampshire	162,629	0.4%
9	New Jersey	1,127,742	3.0%
36	New Mexico	242,600	0.7%
3	New York	2,522,686	6.8%
10	North Carolina	1,076,951	2.9%
47	North Dakota	92,874	0.2%
7	Ohio	1,531,994	4.1%
28	Oklahoma	473,545	1.3%
26	Oregon	478,180	1.3%
5	Pennsylvania	1,885,323	5.1%
43	Rhode Island	147,966	0.4%
23	South Carolina	553,396	1.5%
46	South Dakota	111,183	0.3%
17	Tennessee	769,222	2.1%
4	Texas	2,334,459	6.3%
38	Utah	225,539	0.6%
48	Vermont	82,966	0.2%
12	Virginia	887,768	2.4%
18	Washington	738,369	2.0%
34	West Virginia	278,692	0.7%
19	Wisconsin	724,034	1.9%
49	Wyoming	62,750	0.2%

RANK ORDER

RANK	STATE	POPULATION	% of USA
1	California	3,931,514	10.6%
2	Florida	3,037,704	8.2%
3	New York	2,522,686	6.8%
4	Texas	2,334,459	6.3%
5	Pennsylvania	1,885,323	5.1%
6	Illinois	1,534,476	4.1%
7	Ohio	1,531,994	4.1%
8	Michigan	1,260,864	3.4%
9	New Jersey	1,127,742	3.0%
10	North Carolina	1,076,951	2.9%
11	Georgia	912,874	2.4%
12	Virginia	887,768	2.4%
13	Massachusetts	855,962	2.3%
14	Arizona	790,286	2.1%
15	Indiana	784,219	2.1%
16	Missouri	778,891	2.1%
17	Tennessee	769,222	2.1%
18	Washington	738,369	2.0%
19	Wisconsin	724,034	1.9%
20	Maryland	650,568	1.7%
21	Minnesota	627,394	1.7%
22	Alabama	615,597	1.7%
23	South Carolina	553,396	1.5%
24	Kentucky	537,294	1.4%
25	Louisiana	523,346	1.4%
26	Oregon	478,180	1.3%
27	Colorado	477,186	1.3%
28	Oklahoma	473,545	1.3%
29	Connecticut	470,443	1.3%
30	Iowa	435,657	1.2%
31	Arkansas	390,421	1.0%
32	Mississippi	362,172	1.0%
33	Kansas	357,709	1.0%
34	West Virginia	278,692	0.7%
35	Nevada	276,943	0.7%
36	New Mexico	242,600	0.7%
37	Nebraska	234,655	0.6%
38	Utah	225,539	0.6%
39	Maine	192,639	0.5%
40	Hawaii	179,370	0.5%
41	Idaho	169,173	0.5%
42	New Hampshire	162,629	0.4%
43	Rhode Island	147,966	0.4%
44	Montana	130,592	0.4%
45	Delaware	114,574	0.3%
46	South Dakota	111,183	0.3%
47	North Dakota	92,874	0.2%
48	Vermont	82,966	0.2%
49	Wyoming	62,750	0.2%
50	Alaska	45,630	0.1%
	District of Columbia	71,331	0.2%

Source: U.S. Bureau of the Census
"State Population Estimates - Characteristics" (http://www.census.gov/popest/states/asrh/)

Percent of Population 65 Years Old and Older in 2006

National Percent = 12.4% of Population

ALPHA ORDER				RANK ORDER		
RANK	STATE	PERCENT		RANK	STATE	PERCENT
12	Alabama	13.4		1	Florida	16.8
50	Alaska	6.8		2	West Virginia	15.3
26	Arizona	12.8		3	Pennsylvania	15.2
9	Arkansas	13.9		4	Iowa	14.6
45	California	10.8		4	Maine	14.6
46	Colorado	10.0		4	North Dakota	14.6
12	Connecticut	13.4		7	South Dakota	14.2
12	Delaware	13.4		8	Hawaii	14.0
1	Florida	16.8		9	Arkansas	13.9
48	Georgia	9.7		9	Rhode Island	13.9
8	Hawaii	14.0		11	Montana	13.8
42	Idaho	11.5		12	Alabama	13.4
39	Illinois	12.0		12	Connecticut	13.4
31	Indiana	12.4		12	Delaware	13.4
4	Iowa	14.6		15	Massachusetts	13.3
23	Kansas	12.9		15	Missouri	13.3
26	Kentucky	12.8		15	Nebraska	13.3
35	Louisiana	12.2		15	Ohio	13.3
4	Maine	14.6		15	Vermont	13.3
40	Maryland	11.6		20	Oklahoma	13.2
15	Massachusetts	13.3		21	New York	13.1
30	Michigan	12.5		22	Wisconsin	13.0
38	Minnesota	12.1		23	Kansas	12.9
31	Mississippi	12.4		23	New Jersey	12.9
15	Missouri	13.3		23	Oregon	12.9
11	Montana	13.8		26	Arizona	12.8
15	Nebraska	13.3		26	Kentucky	12.8
44	Nevada	11.1		26	South Carolina	12.8
31	New Hampshire	12.4		29	Tennessee	12.7
23	New Jersey	12.9		30	Michigan	12.5
31	New Mexico	12.4		31	Indiana	12.4
21	New York	13.1		31	Mississippi	12.4
35	North Carolina	12.2		31	New Hampshire	12.4
4	North Dakota	14.6		31	New Mexico	12.4
15	Ohio	13.3		35	Louisiana	12.2
20	Oklahoma	13.2		35	North Carolina	12.2
23	Oregon	12.9		35	Wyoming	12.2
3	Pennsylvania	15.2		38	Minnesota	12.1
9	Rhode Island	13.9		39	Illinois	12.0
26	South Carolina	12.8		40	Maryland	11.6
7	South Dakota	14.2		40	Virginia	11.6
29	Tennessee	12.7		42	Idaho	11.5
47	Texas	9.9		42	Washington	11.5
49	Utah	8.8		44	Nevada	11.1
15	Vermont	13.3		45	California	10.8
40	Virginia	11.6		46	Colorado	10.0
42	Washington	11.5		47	Texas	9.9
2	West Virginia	15.3		48	Georgia	9.7
22	Wisconsin	13.0		49	Utah	8.8
35	Wyoming	12.2		50	Alaska	6.8
				District of Columbia		12.3

Source: CQ Press using data from U.S. Bureau of the Census
"State Population Estimates - Characteristics" (http://www.census.gov/popest/states/asrh/)

Population 85 Years Old and Older in 2006

National Total = 5,296,817

ALPHA ORDER

RANK	STATE	POPULATION	% of USA
22	Alabama	79,530	1.5%
50	Alaska	4,148	0.1%
18	Arizona	105,104	2.0%
32	Arkansas	54,889	1.0%
1	California	555,473	10.5%
30	Colorado	61,232	1.2%
23	Connecticut	76,395	1.4%
47	Delaware	14,553	0.3%
2	Florida	462,545	8.7%
13	Georgia	113,362	2.1%
40	Hawaii	26,888	0.5%
42	Idaho	23,384	0.4%
6	Illinois	227,074	4.3%
15	Indiana	111,190	2.1%
24	Iowa	75,180	1.4%
31	Kansas	59,518	1.1%
26	Kentucky	69,463	1.3%
28	Louisiana	67,599	1.3%
39	Maine	27,012	0.5%
21	Maryland	85,783	1.6%
10	Massachusetts	137,022	2.6%
8	Michigan	174,758	3.3%
19	Minnesota	101,634	1.9%
33	Mississippi	49,582	0.9%
12	Missouri	113,789	2.1%
45	Montana	19,000	0.4%
34	Nebraska	39,128	0.7%
38	Nevada	27,841	0.5%
43	New Hampshire	23,118	0.4%
9	New Jersey	166,529	3.1%
36	New Mexico	31,309	0.6%
3	New York	371,667	7.0%
11	North Carolina	136,229	2.6%
46	North Dakota	16,797	0.3%
7	Ohio	216,992	4.1%
29	Oklahoma	65,571	1.2%
25	Oregon	70,969	1.3%
5	Pennsylvania	294,824	5.6%
41	Rhode Island	25,123	0.5%
27	South Carolina	68,701	1.3%
44	South Dakota	19,075	0.4%
20	Tennessee	97,712	1.8%
4	Texas	302,646	5.7%
37	Utah	29,235	0.6%
48	Vermont	11,714	0.2%
14	Virginia	112,129	2.1%
17	Washington	107,032	2.0%
35	West Virginia	36,073	0.7%
16	Wisconsin	111,159	2.1%
49	Wyoming	8,367	0.2%

RANK ORDER

RANK	STATE	POPULATION	% of USA
1	California	555,473	10.5%
2	Florida	462,545	8.7%
3	New York	371,667	7.0%
4	Texas	302,646	5.7%
5	Pennsylvania	294,824	5.6%
6	Illinois	227,074	4.3%
7	Ohio	216,992	4.1%
8	Michigan	174,758	3.3%
9	New Jersey	166,529	3.1%
10	Massachusetts	137,022	2.6%
11	North Carolina	136,229	2.6%
12	Missouri	113,789	2.1%
13	Georgia	113,362	2.1%
14	Virginia	112,129	2.1%
15	Indiana	111,190	2.1%
16	Wisconsin	111,159	2.1%
17	Washington	107,032	2.0%
18	Arizona	105,104	2.0%
19	Minnesota	101,634	1.9%
20	Tennessee	97,712	1.8%
21	Maryland	85,783	1.6%
22	Alabama	79,530	1.5%
23	Connecticut	76,395	1.4%
24	Iowa	75,180	1.4%
25	Oregon	70,969	1.3%
26	Kentucky	69,463	1.3%
27	South Carolina	68,701	1.3%
28	Louisiana	67,599	1.3%
29	Oklahoma	65,571	1.2%
30	Colorado	61,232	1.2%
31	Kansas	59,518	1.1%
32	Arkansas	54,889	1.0%
33	Mississippi	49,582	0.9%
34	Nebraska	39,128	0.7%
35	West Virginia	36,073	0.7%
36	New Mexico	31,309	0.6%
37	Utah	29,235	0.6%
38	Nevada	27,841	0.5%
39	Maine	27,012	0.5%
40	Hawaii	26,888	0.5%
41	Rhode Island	25,123	0.5%
42	Idaho	23,384	0.4%
43	New Hampshire	23,118	0.4%
44	South Dakota	19,075	0.4%
45	Montana	19,000	0.4%
46	North Dakota	16,797	0.3%
47	Delaware	14,553	0.3%
48	Vermont	11,714	0.2%
49	Wyoming	8,367	0.2%
50	Alaska	4,148	0.1%
	District of Columbia	10,770	0.2%

Source: U.S. Bureau of the Census
"State Population Estimates - Characteristics" (http://www.census.gov/popest/states/asrh/)

Percent of Population 85 Years Old and Older in 2006

National Percent = 1.8% of Population

<table>
<tr><td colspan="3">ALPHA ORDER</td><td colspan="3">RANK ORDER</td></tr>
<tr><td>RANK</td><td>STATE</td><td>PERCENT</td><td>RANK</td><td>STATE</td><td>PERCENT</td></tr>
<tr><td>28</td><td>Alabama</td><td>1.7</td><td>1</td><td>Florida</td><td>2.6</td></tr>
<tr><td>50</td><td>Alaska</td><td>0.6</td><td>1</td><td>North Dakota</td><td>2.6</td></tr>
<tr><td>28</td><td>Arizona</td><td>1.7</td><td>3</td><td>Iowa</td><td>2.5</td></tr>
<tr><td>12</td><td>Arkansas</td><td>2.0</td><td>4</td><td>Pennsylvania</td><td>2.4</td></tr>
<tr><td>41</td><td>California</td><td>1.5</td><td>4</td><td>Rhode Island</td><td>2.4</td></tr>
<tr><td>45</td><td>Colorado</td><td>1.3</td><td>4</td><td>South Dakota</td><td>2.4</td></tr>
<tr><td>7</td><td>Connecticut</td><td>2.2</td><td>7</td><td>Connecticut</td><td>2.2</td></tr>
<tr><td>28</td><td>Delaware</td><td>1.7</td><td>7</td><td>Kansas</td><td>2.2</td></tr>
<tr><td>1</td><td>Florida</td><td>2.6</td><td>7</td><td>Nebraska</td><td>2.2</td></tr>
<tr><td>47</td><td>Georgia</td><td>1.2</td><td>10</td><td>Hawaii</td><td>2.1</td></tr>
<tr><td>10</td><td>Hawaii</td><td>2.1</td><td>10</td><td>Massachusetts</td><td>2.1</td></tr>
<tr><td>35</td><td>Idaho</td><td>1.6</td><td>12</td><td>Arkansas</td><td>2.0</td></tr>
<tr><td>24</td><td>Illinois</td><td>1.8</td><td>12</td><td>Maine</td><td>2.0</td></tr>
<tr><td>24</td><td>Indiana</td><td>1.8</td><td>12</td><td>Minnesota</td><td>2.0</td></tr>
<tr><td>3</td><td>Iowa</td><td>2.5</td><td>12</td><td>Montana</td><td>2.0</td></tr>
<tr><td>7</td><td>Kansas</td><td>2.2</td><td>12</td><td>West Virginia</td><td>2.0</td></tr>
<tr><td>28</td><td>Kentucky</td><td>1.7</td><td>12</td><td>Wisconsin</td><td>2.0</td></tr>
<tr><td>35</td><td>Louisiana</td><td>1.6</td><td>18</td><td>Missouri</td><td>1.9</td></tr>
<tr><td>12</td><td>Maine</td><td>2.0</td><td>18</td><td>New Jersey</td><td>1.9</td></tr>
<tr><td>41</td><td>Maryland</td><td>1.5</td><td>18</td><td>New York</td><td>1.9</td></tr>
<tr><td>10</td><td>Massachusetts</td><td>2.1</td><td>18</td><td>Ohio</td><td>1.9</td></tr>
<tr><td>28</td><td>Michigan</td><td>1.7</td><td>18</td><td>Oregon</td><td>1.9</td></tr>
<tr><td>12</td><td>Minnesota</td><td>2.0</td><td>18</td><td>Vermont</td><td>1.9</td></tr>
<tr><td>28</td><td>Mississippi</td><td>1.7</td><td>24</td><td>Illinois</td><td>1.8</td></tr>
<tr><td>18</td><td>Missouri</td><td>1.9</td><td>24</td><td>Indiana</td><td>1.8</td></tr>
<tr><td>12</td><td>Montana</td><td>2.0</td><td>24</td><td>New Hampshire</td><td>1.8</td></tr>
<tr><td>7</td><td>Nebraska</td><td>2.2</td><td>24</td><td>Oklahoma</td><td>1.8</td></tr>
<tr><td>48</td><td>Nevada</td><td>1.1</td><td>28</td><td>Alabama</td><td>1.7</td></tr>
<tr><td>24</td><td>New Hampshire</td><td>1.8</td><td>28</td><td>Arizona</td><td>1.7</td></tr>
<tr><td>18</td><td>New Jersey</td><td>1.9</td><td>28</td><td>Delaware</td><td>1.7</td></tr>
<tr><td>35</td><td>New Mexico</td><td>1.6</td><td>28</td><td>Kentucky</td><td>1.7</td></tr>
<tr><td>18</td><td>New York</td><td>1.9</td><td>28</td><td>Michigan</td><td>1.7</td></tr>
<tr><td>41</td><td>North Carolina</td><td>1.5</td><td>28</td><td>Mississippi</td><td>1.7</td></tr>
<tr><td>1</td><td>North Dakota</td><td>2.6</td><td>28</td><td>Washington</td><td>1.7</td></tr>
<tr><td>18</td><td>Ohio</td><td>1.9</td><td>35</td><td>Idaho</td><td>1.6</td></tr>
<tr><td>24</td><td>Oklahoma</td><td>1.8</td><td>35</td><td>Louisiana</td><td>1.6</td></tr>
<tr><td>18</td><td>Oregon</td><td>1.9</td><td>35</td><td>New Mexico</td><td>1.6</td></tr>
<tr><td>4</td><td>Pennsylvania</td><td>2.4</td><td>35</td><td>South Carolina</td><td>1.6</td></tr>
<tr><td>4</td><td>Rhode Island</td><td>2.4</td><td>35</td><td>Tennessee</td><td>1.6</td></tr>
<tr><td>35</td><td>South Carolina</td><td>1.6</td><td>35</td><td>Wyoming</td><td>1.6</td></tr>
<tr><td>4</td><td>South Dakota</td><td>2.4</td><td>41</td><td>California</td><td>1.5</td></tr>
<tr><td>35</td><td>Tennessee</td><td>1.6</td><td>41</td><td>Maryland</td><td>1.5</td></tr>
<tr><td>45</td><td>Texas</td><td>1.3</td><td>41</td><td>North Carolina</td><td>1.5</td></tr>
<tr><td>48</td><td>Utah</td><td>1.1</td><td>41</td><td>Virginia</td><td>1.5</td></tr>
<tr><td>18</td><td>Vermont</td><td>1.9</td><td>45</td><td>Colorado</td><td>1.3</td></tr>
<tr><td>41</td><td>Virginia</td><td>1.5</td><td>45</td><td>Texas</td><td>1.3</td></tr>
<tr><td>28</td><td>Washington</td><td>1.7</td><td>47</td><td>Georgia</td><td>1.2</td></tr>
<tr><td>12</td><td>West Virginia</td><td>2.0</td><td>48</td><td>Nevada</td><td>1.1</td></tr>
<tr><td>12</td><td>Wisconsin</td><td>2.0</td><td>48</td><td>Utah</td><td>1.1</td></tr>
<tr><td>35</td><td>Wyoming</td><td>1.6</td><td>50</td><td>Alaska</td><td>0.6</td></tr>
<tr><td></td><td></td><td></td><td></td><td>District of Columbia</td><td>1.9</td></tr>
</table>

Source: CQ Press using data from U.S. Bureau of the Census
"State Population Estimates - Characteristics" (http://www.census.gov/popest/states/asrh/)

Percent of Native Population Born in Their State of Residence: 2006

National Percent = 67.4%

ALPHA ORDER

RANK	STATE	PERCENT
13	Alabama	73.0
48	Alaska	41.8
47	Arizona	42.0
31	Arkansas	63.7
17	California	71.9
44	Colorado	46.9
30	Connecticut	64.0
41	Delaware	51.1
49	Florida	41.5
34	Georgia	61.1
25	Hawaii	65.9
43	Idaho	47.8
6	Illinois	77.6
18	Indiana	71.6
8	Iowa	75.1
33	Kansas	63.1
12	Kentucky	73.8
2	Louisiana	82.2
23	Maine	67.1
39	Maryland	54.4
9	Massachusetts	74.6
3	Michigan	80.4
10	Minnesota	74.0
10	Mississippi	74.0
21	Missouri	68.6
38	Montana	54.5
19	Nebraska	69.4
50	Nevada	28.5
45	New Hampshire	44.2
26	New Jersey	65.6
35	New Mexico	56.6
1	New York	82.3
29	North Carolina	64.1
15	North Dakota	72.6
5	Ohio	77.9
28	Oklahoma	64.9
42	Oregon	49.9
4	Pennsylvania	79.6
22	Rhode Island	67.7
32	South Carolina	63.4
24	South Dakota	66.6
27	Tennessee	65.2
16	Texas	72.4
20	Utah	68.7
37	Vermont	54.8
36	Virginia	56.5
40	Washington	53.9
13	West Virginia	73.0
7	Wisconsin	75.5
46	Wyoming	43.8

RANK ORDER

RANK	STATE	PERCENT
1	New York	82.3
2	Louisiana	82.2
3	Michigan	80.4
4	Pennsylvania	79.6
5	Ohio	77.9
6	Illinois	77.6
7	Wisconsin	75.5
8	Iowa	75.1
9	Massachusetts	74.6
10	Minnesota	74.0
10	Mississippi	74.0
12	Kentucky	73.8
13	Alabama	73.0
13	West Virginia	73.0
15	North Dakota	72.6
16	Texas	72.4
17	California	71.9
18	Indiana	71.6
19	Nebraska	69.4
20	Utah	68.7
21	Missouri	68.6
22	Rhode Island	67.7
23	Maine	67.1
24	South Dakota	66.6
25	Hawaii	65.9
26	New Jersey	65.6
27	Tennessee	65.2
28	Oklahoma	64.9
29	North Carolina	64.1
30	Connecticut	64.0
31	Arkansas	63.7
32	South Carolina	63.4
33	Kansas	63.1
34	Georgia	61.1
35	New Mexico	56.6
36	Virginia	56.5
37	Vermont	54.8
38	Montana	54.5
39	Maryland	54.4
40	Washington	53.9
41	Delaware	51.1
42	Oregon	49.9
43	Idaho	47.8
44	Colorado	46.9
45	New Hampshire	44.2
46	Wyoming	43.8
47	Arizona	42.0
48	Alaska	41.8
49	Florida	41.5
50	Nevada	28.5

District of Columbia — 45.9

Source: U.S. Bureau of the Census
"2006 American Community Survey" (http://www.census.gov/acs/www/index.html)

Domestic Migration of Population: 2006 to 2007

National Net Migration = 0 People*

ALPHA ORDER

RANK	STATE	NET MIGRATION
15	Alabama	18,427
34	Alaska	(2,805)
4	Arizona	90,402
19	Arkansas	8,323
50	California	(263,035)
9	Colorado	33,438
42	Connecticut	(19,377)
23	Delaware	5,224
8	Florida	35,301
3	Georgia	94,004
40	Hawaii	(9,673)
14	Idaho	19,569
46	Illinois	(60,265)
28	Indiana	(505)
35	Iowa	(2,947)
33	Kansas	(2,550)
16	Kentucky	17,357
11	Louisiana	28,854
29	Maine	(717)
44	Maryland	(36,270)
43	Massachusetts	(35,121)
48	Michigan	(94,420)
37	Minnesota	(6,025)
26	Mississippi	2,473
22	Missouri	6,205
21	Montana	6,463
36	Nebraska	(4,869)
7	Nevada	41,338
32	New Hampshire	(2,389)
47	New Jersey	(69,160)
18	New Mexico	8,530
49	New York	(189,765)
2	North Carolina	111,963
30	North Dakota	(1,136)
45	Ohio	(51,842)
17	Oklahoma	13,578
12	Oregon	26,811
39	Pennsylvania	(7,377)
41	Rhode Island	(10,031)
5	South Carolina	53,993
27	South Dakota	1,910
6	Tennessee	48,665
1	Texas	141,280
13	Utah	24,657
31	Vermont	(1,788)
24	Virginia	2,959
10	Washington	31,009
25	West Virginia	2,553
38	Wisconsin	(6,732)
20	Wyoming	6,654

RANK ORDER

RANK	STATE	NET MIGRATION
1	Texas	141,280
2	North Carolina	111,963
3	Georgia	94,004
4	Arizona	90,402
5	South Carolina	53,993
6	Tennessee	48,665
7	Nevada	41,338
8	Florida	35,301
9	Colorado	33,438
10	Washington	31,009
11	Louisiana	28,854
12	Oregon	26,811
13	Utah	24,657
14	Idaho	19,569
15	Alabama	18,427
16	Kentucky	17,357
17	Oklahoma	13,578
18	New Mexico	8,530
19	Arkansas	8,323
20	Wyoming	6,654
21	Montana	6,463
22	Missouri	6,205
23	Delaware	5,224
24	Virginia	2,959
25	West Virginia	2,553
26	Mississippi	2,473
27	South Dakota	1,910
28	Indiana	(505)
29	Maine	(717)
30	North Dakota	(1,136)
31	Vermont	(1,788)
32	New Hampshire	(2,389)
33	Kansas	(2,550)
34	Alaska	(2,805)
35	Iowa	(2,947)
36	Nebraska	(4,869)
37	Minnesota	(6,025)
38	Wisconsin	(6,732)
39	Pennsylvania	(7,377)
40	Hawaii	(9,673)
41	Rhode Island	(10,031)
42	Connecticut	(19,377)
43	Massachusetts	(35,121)
44	Maryland	(36,270)
45	Ohio	(51,842)
46	Illinois	(60,265)
47	New Jersey	(69,160)
48	Michigan	(94,420)
49	New York	(189,765)
50	California	(263,035)
	District of Columbia	(3,141)

Source: U.S. Bureau of the Census
   "Components of Population Change" (http://www.census.gov/popest/datasets.html)
*From July 1, 2006 to July 1, 2007. Includes armed forces residing in each state. Net Domestic Migration is the difference between domestic inmigration to an area and domestic outmigration from it during the period. Domestic inmigration and outmigration consist of moves where both the origins and destinations are within the United States (excluding Puerto Rico).

Net International Migration: 2006 to 2007

National Net = 1,037,657 Immigrants*

RANK	STATE	IMMIGRANTS	% of USA
33	Alabama	4,077	0.4%
45	Alaska	602	0.1%
8	Arizona	27,708	2.7%
36	Arkansas	3,526	0.3%
1	California	233,810	22.5%
14	Colorado	18,381	1.8%
17	Connecticut	12,867	1.2%
40	Delaware	1,823	0.2%
4	Florida	88,111	8.5%
7	Georgia	31,330	3.0%
32	Hawaii	4,112	0.4%
39	Idaho	2,268	0.2%
5	Illinois	54,402	5.2%
22	Indiana	9,038	0.9%
30	Iowa	4,689	0.5%
27	Kansas	6,017	0.6%
34	Kentucky	4,062	0.4%
38	Louisiana	2,999	0.3%
43	Maine	699	0.1%
15	Maryland	17,704	1.7%
9	Massachusetts	27,014	2.6%
13	Michigan	20,153	1.9%
20	Minnesota	11,522	1.1%
42	Mississippi	1,433	0.1%
26	Missouri	6,760	0.7%
49	Montana	284	0.0%
35	Nebraska	3,583	0.3%
21	Nevada	10,979	1.1%
41	New Hampshire	1,813	0.2%
6	New Jersey	48,944	4.7%
31	New Mexico	4,386	0.4%
2	New York	111,607	10.8%
10	North Carolina	24,465	2.4%
48	North Dakota	440	0.0%
18	Ohio	12,332	1.2%
28	Oklahoma	5,475	0.5%
19	Oregon	11,848	1.1%
16	Pennsylvania	16,829	1.6%
37	Rhode Island	3,162	0.3%
29	South Carolina	5,339	0.5%
46	South Dakota	601	0.1%
24	Tennessee	7,919	0.8%
3	Texas	109,086	10.5%
23	Utah	8,202	0.8%
44	Vermont	649	0.1%
11	Virginia	21,455	2.1%
12	Washington	21,422	2.1%
47	West Virginia	571	0.1%
25	Wisconsin	7,523	0.7%
50	Wyoming	278	0.0%

RANK	STATE	IMMIGRANTS	% of USA
1	California	233,810	22.5%
2	New York	111,607	10.8%
3	Texas	109,086	10.5%
4	Florida	88,111	8.5%
5	Illinois	54,402	5.2%
6	New Jersey	48,944	4.7%
7	Georgia	31,330	3.0%
8	Arizona	27,708	2.7%
9	Massachusetts	27,014	2.6%
10	North Carolina	24,465	2.4%
11	Virginia	21,455	2.1%
12	Washington	21,422	2.1%
13	Michigan	20,153	1.9%
14	Colorado	18,381	1.8%
15	Maryland	17,704	1.7%
16	Pennsylvania	16,829	1.6%
17	Connecticut	12,867	1.2%
18	Ohio	12,332	1.2%
19	Oregon	11,848	1.1%
20	Minnesota	11,522	1.1%
21	Nevada	10,979	1.1%
22	Indiana	9,038	0.9%
23	Utah	8,202	0.8%
24	Tennessee	7,919	0.8%
25	Wisconsin	7,523	0.7%
26	Missouri	6,760	0.7%
27	Kansas	6,017	0.6%
28	Oklahoma	5,475	0.5%
29	South Carolina	5,339	0.5%
30	Iowa	4,689	0.5%
31	New Mexico	4,386	0.4%
32	Hawaii	4,112	0.4%
33	Alabama	4,077	0.4%
34	Kentucky	4,062	0.4%
35	Nebraska	3,583	0.3%
36	Arkansas	3,526	0.3%
37	Rhode Island	3,162	0.3%
38	Louisiana	2,999	0.3%
39	Idaho	2,268	0.2%
40	Delaware	1,823	0.2%
41	New Hampshire	1,813	0.2%
42	Mississippi	1,433	0.1%
43	Maine	699	0.1%
44	Vermont	649	0.1%
45	Alaska	602	0.1%
46	South Dakota	601	0.1%
47	West Virginia	571	0.1%
48	North Dakota	440	0.0%
49	Montana	284	0.0%
50	Wyoming	278	0.0%
	District of Columbia	3,358	0.3%

Source: U.S. Bureau of the Census
    "Components of Population Change" (http://www.census.gov/popest/datasets.html)
*From July 1, 2006 to July 1, 2007. Net International Migration is the difference between migration to an area from outside the United States (immigration) and migration from the area to outside the United States (emigration) during the period. Includes legal immigration and estimates of undocumented immigration.

Percent of Population Foreign Born: 2006

National Percent = 12.5% of Population*

ALPHA ORDER

RANK	STATE	PERCENT
43	Alabama	2.8
22	Alaska	7.0
8	Arizona	15.1
37	Arkansas	3.8
1	California	27.2
15	Colorado	10.3
11	Connecticut	12.9
21	Delaware	8.1
5	Florida	18.9
19	Georgia	9.2
6	Hawaii	16.3
27	Idaho	5.6
10	Illinois	13.8
33	Indiana	4.2
37	Iowa	3.8
25	Kansas	6.3
44	Kentucky	2.7
42	Louisiana	2.9
41	Maine	3.2
14	Maryland	12.2
9	Massachusetts	14.1
26	Michigan	5.9
24	Minnesota	6.6
49	Mississippi	1.8
40	Missouri	3.3
48	Montana	1.9
27	Nebraska	5.6
4	Nevada	19.1
29	New Hampshire	5.4
3	New Jersey	20.1
16	New Mexico	10.1
2	New York	21.6
23	North Carolina	6.9
47	North Dakota	2.1
39	Ohio	3.6
31	Oklahoma	4.9
18	Oregon	9.7
30	Pennsylvania	5.1
12	Rhode Island	12.6
34	South Carolina	4.1
46	South Dakota	2.2
35	Tennessee	3.9
7	Texas	15.9
20	Utah	8.3
35	Vermont	3.9
16	Virginia	10.1
13	Washington	12.4
50	West Virginia	1.2
32	Wisconsin	4.4
44	Wyoming	2.7

RANK ORDER

RANK	STATE	PERCENT
1	California	27.2
2	New York	21.6
3	New Jersey	20.1
4	Nevada	19.1
5	Florida	18.9
6	Hawaii	16.3
7	Texas	15.9
8	Arizona	15.1
9	Massachusetts	14.1
10	Illinois	13.8
11	Connecticut	12.9
12	Rhode Island	12.6
13	Washington	12.4
14	Maryland	12.2
15	Colorado	10.3
16	New Mexico	10.1
16	Virginia	10.1
18	Oregon	9.7
19	Georgia	9.2
20	Utah	8.3
21	Delaware	8.1
22	Alaska	7.0
23	North Carolina	6.9
24	Minnesota	6.6
25	Kansas	6.3
26	Michigan	5.9
27	Idaho	5.6
27	Nebraska	5.6
29	New Hampshire	5.4
30	Pennsylvania	5.1
31	Oklahoma	4.9
32	Wisconsin	4.4
33	Indiana	4.2
34	South Carolina	4.1
35	Tennessee	3.9
35	Vermont	3.9
37	Arkansas	3.8
37	Iowa	3.8
39	Ohio	3.6
40	Missouri	3.3
41	Maine	3.2
42	Louisiana	2.9
43	Alabama	2.8
44	Kentucky	2.7
44	Wyoming	2.7
46	South Dakota	2.2
47	North Dakota	2.1
48	Montana	1.9
49	Mississippi	1.8
50	West Virginia	1.2

District of Columbia   12.7

Source: U.S. Bureau of the Census
   "2006 American Community Survey" (http://www.census.gov/acs/www/index.html)
*"Foreign born" are persons not born in the United States, Puerto Rico, a U.S. Island Area, or abroad of American parent or parents.

Percent of Population Speaking a Language Other Than English at Home in 2006
National Percent = 19.7%*

ALPHA ORDER

RANK	STATE	PERCENT
47	Alabama	4.2
16	Alaska	15.4
5	Arizona	28.0
40	Arkansas	6.1
1	California	42.5
14	Colorado	17.2
13	Connecticut	20.1
21	Delaware	12.1
8	Florida	25.7
22	Georgia	11.9
9	Hawaii	23.5
24	Idaho	10.1
10	Illinois	21.8
35	Indiana	7.6
38	Iowa	6.4
23	Kansas	10.3
48	Kentucky	4.1
30	Louisiana	8.4
34	Maine	7.7
17	Maryland	14.9
12	Massachusetts	20.2
29	Michigan	9.0
25	Minnesota	9.6
49	Mississippi	3.1
42	Missouri	5.6
46	Montana	4.7
28	Nebraska	9.1
7	Nevada	26.9
32	New Hampshire	8.2
6	New Jersey	27.6
2	New Mexico	36.5
4	New York	28.8
25	North Carolina	9.6
45	North Dakota	5.2
39	Ohio	6.2
31	Oklahoma	8.3
19	Oregon	14.2
27	Pennsylvania	9.2
11	Rhode Island	20.4
41	South Carolina	6.0
37	South Dakota	6.5
43	Tennessee	5.5
3	Texas	33.8
18	Utah	14.3
44	Vermont	5.3
20	Virginia	13.1
15	Washington	16.6
50	West Virginia	2.3
33	Wisconsin	8.1
36	Wyoming	6.6

RANK ORDER

RANK	STATE	PERCENT
1	California	42.5
2	New Mexico	36.5
3	Texas	33.8
4	New York	28.8
5	Arizona	28.0
6	New Jersey	27.6
7	Nevada	26.9
8	Florida	25.7
9	Hawaii	23.5
10	Illinois	21.8
11	Rhode Island	20.4
12	Massachusetts	20.2
13	Connecticut	20.1
14	Colorado	17.2
15	Washington	16.6
16	Alaska	15.4
17	Maryland	14.9
18	Utah	14.3
19	Oregon	14.2
20	Virginia	13.1
21	Delaware	12.1
22	Georgia	11.9
23	Kansas	10.3
24	Idaho	10.1
25	Minnesota	9.6
25	North Carolina	9.6
27	Pennsylvania	9.2
28	Nebraska	9.1
29	Michigan	9.0
30	Louisiana	8.4
31	Oklahoma	8.3
32	New Hampshire	8.2
33	Wisconsin	8.1
34	Maine	7.7
35	Indiana	7.6
36	Wyoming	6.6
37	South Dakota	6.5
38	Iowa	6.4
39	Ohio	6.2
40	Arkansas	6.1
41	South Carolina	6.0
42	Missouri	5.6
43	Tennessee	5.5
44	Vermont	5.3
45	North Dakota	5.2
46	Montana	4.7
47	Alabama	4.2
48	Kentucky	4.1
49	Mississippi	3.1
50	West Virginia	2.3
	District of Columbia	15.3

Source: U.S. Bureau of the Census
   "2006 American Community Survey" (http://www.census.gov/acs/www/index.html)
*Population five years old and older.

Percent of Population Speaking Spanish at Home in 2006

National Percent = 12.2%*

ALPHA ORDER

RANK	STATE	PERCENT
38	Alabama	2.5
32	Alaska	3.6
4	Arizona	21.9
26	Arkansas	4.4
3	California	28.4
10	Colorado	12.3
12	Connecticut	9.4
20	Delaware	6.5
6	Florida	18.7
17	Georgia	7.0
45	Hawaii	1.5
15	Idaho	7.7
9	Illinois	12.7
27	Indiana	4.3
33	Iowa	3.5
19	Kansas	6.6
42	Kentucky	2.0
37	Louisiana	2.7
49	Maine	1.0
24	Maryland	5.7
18	Massachusetts	6.8
35	Michigan	3.1
33	Minnesota	3.5
44	Mississippi	1.7
39	Missouri	2.4
45	Montana	1.5
22	Nebraska	6.0
5	Nevada	19.3
40	New Hampshire	2.1
8	New Jersey	13.9
2	New Mexico	28.8
7	New York	14.2
20	North Carolina	6.5
45	North Dakota	1.5
40	Ohio	2.1
25	Oklahoma	5.2
14	Oregon	8.5
30	Pennsylvania	3.7
11	Rhode Island	10.0
30	South Carolina	3.7
42	South Dakota	2.0
36	Tennessee	3.0
1	Texas	29.1
12	Utah	9.4
49	Vermont	1.0
23	Virginia	5.8
16	Washington	7.2
48	West Virginia	1.1
28	Wisconsin	4.2
29	Wyoming	4.1

RANK ORDER

RANK	STATE	PERCENT
1	Texas	29.1
2	New Mexico	28.8
3	California	28.4
4	Arizona	21.9
5	Nevada	19.3
6	Florida	18.7
7	New York	14.2
8	New Jersey	13.9
9	Illinois	12.7
10	Colorado	12.3
11	Rhode Island	10.0
12	Connecticut	9.4
12	Utah	9.4
14	Oregon	8.5
15	Idaho	7.7
16	Washington	7.2
17	Georgia	7.0
18	Massachusetts	6.8
19	Kansas	6.6
20	Delaware	6.5
20	North Carolina	6.5
22	Nebraska	6.0
23	Virginia	5.8
24	Maryland	5.7
25	Oklahoma	5.2
26	Arkansas	4.4
27	Indiana	4.3
28	Wisconsin	4.2
29	Wyoming	4.1
30	Pennsylvania	3.7
30	South Carolina	3.7
32	Alaska	3.6
33	Iowa	3.5
33	Minnesota	3.5
35	Michigan	3.1
36	Tennessee	3.0
37	Louisiana	2.7
38	Alabama	2.5
39	Missouri	2.4
40	New Hampshire	2.1
40	Ohio	2.1
42	Kentucky	2.0
42	South Dakota	2.0
44	Mississippi	1.7
45	Hawaii	1.5
45	Montana	1.5
45	North Dakota	1.5
48	West Virginia	1.1
49	Maine	1.0
49	Vermont	1.0

District of Columbia	8.2

Source: U.S. Bureau of the Census
"2006 American Community Survey" (http://www.census.gov/acs/www/index.html)
*Population five years old and older.

Marriages in 2006

National Total = 2,161,812 Marriages*

RANK	STATE	MARRIAGES	% of USA
18	Alabama	39,627	1.8%
46	Alaska	5,309	0.2%
19	Arizona	38,983	1.8%
24	Arkansas	34,261	1.6%
1	California	215,985	10.0%
23	Colorado	36,121	1.7%
34	Connecticut	17,382	0.8%
47	Delaware	5,153	0.2%
3	Florida	155,505	7.2%
9	Georgia	66,456	3.1%
28	Hawaii	28,662	1.3%
36	Idaho	14,811	0.7%
6	Illinois	77,981	3.6%
14	Indiana	50,854	2.4%
32	Iowa	20,024	0.9%
33	Kansas	18,862	0.9%
21	Kentucky	36,905	1.7%
NA	Louisiana**	NA	NA
40	Maine	9,740	0.5%
22	Maryland	36,495	1.7%
20	Massachusetts	38,494	1.8%
12	Michigan	59,162	2.7%
27	Minnesota	30,916	1.4%
35	Mississippi	16,861	0.8%
17	Missouri	40,746	1.9%
43	Montana	6,757	0.3%
39	Nebraska	12,037	0.6%
4	Nevada	131,826	6.1%
41	New Hampshire	9,328	0.4%
15	New Jersey	42,398	2.0%
37	New Mexico	13,423	0.6%
5	New York	127,401	5.9%
13	North Carolina	55,343	2.6%
49	North Dakota	4,331	0.2%
7	Ohio	73,100	3.4%
30	Oklahoma	26,266	1.2%
29	Oregon	26,888	1.2%
8	Pennsylvania	68,584	3.2%
42	Rhode Island	6,916	0.3%
25	South Carolina	32,846	1.5%
44	South Dakota	6,272	0.3%
10	Tennessee	64,028	3.0%
2	Texas	174,989	8.1%
31	Utah	23,678	1.1%
45	Vermont	5,385	0.2%
11	Virginia	60,760	2.8%
16	Washington	40,967	1.9%
38	West Virginia	13,129	0.6%
26	Wisconsin	32,562	1.5%
48	Wyoming	5,027	0.2%

RANK	STATE	MARRIAGES	% of USA
1	California	215,985	10.0%
2	Texas	174,989	8.1%
3	Florida	155,505	7.2%
4	Nevada	131,826	6.1%
5	New York	127,401	5.9%
6	Illinois	77,981	3.6%
7	Ohio	73,100	3.4%
8	Pennsylvania	68,584	3.2%
9	Georgia	66,456	3.1%
10	Tennessee	64,028	3.0%
11	Virginia	60,760	2.8%
12	Michigan	59,162	2.7%
13	North Carolina	55,343	2.6%
14	Indiana	50,854	2.4%
15	New Jersey	42,398	2.0%
16	Washington	40,967	1.9%
17	Missouri	40,746	1.9%
18	Alabama	39,627	1.8%
19	Arizona	38,983	1.8%
20	Massachusetts	38,494	1.8%
21	Kentucky	36,905	1.7%
22	Maryland	36,495	1.7%
23	Colorado	36,121	1.7%
24	Arkansas	34,261	1.6%
25	South Carolina	32,846	1.5%
26	Wisconsin	32,562	1.5%
27	Minnesota	30,916	1.4%
28	Hawaii	28,662	1.3%
29	Oregon	26,888	1.2%
30	Oklahoma	26,266	1.2%
31	Utah	23,678	1.1%
32	Iowa	20,024	0.9%
33	Kansas	18,862	0.9%
34	Connecticut	17,382	0.8%
35	Mississippi	16,861	0.8%
36	Idaho	14,811	0.7%
37	New Mexico	13,423	0.6%
38	West Virginia	13,129	0.6%
39	Nebraska	12,037	0.6%
40	Maine	9,740	0.5%
41	New Hampshire	9,328	0.4%
42	Rhode Island	6,916	0.3%
43	Montana	6,757	0.3%
44	South Dakota	6,272	0.3%
45	Vermont	5,385	0.2%
46	Alaska	5,309	0.2%
47	Delaware	5,153	0.2%
48	Wyoming	5,027	0.2%
49	North Dakota	4,331	0.2%
NA	Louisiana**	NA	NA
	District of Columbia	2,276	0.1%

Source: U.S. Department of Health and Human Services, National Center for Health Statistics
　　"National Vital Statistics Reports" (Vol. 55, No. 20, August 28, 2007)
*Provisional data by state of occurrence.
**Not available.

Marriage Rate in 2006

National Rate = 7.3 Marriages per 1,000 Population*

ALPHA ORDER

RANK	STATE	RATE
10	Alabama	8.6
15	Alaska	7.8
37	Arizona	6.3
3	Arkansas	12.2
40	California	6.0
16	Colorado	7.6
48	Connecticut	5.0
40	Delaware	6.0
10	Florida	8.6
23	Georgia	7.1
2	Hawaii	22.4
5	Idaho	10.1
39	Illinois	6.1
12	Indiana	8.1
31	Iowa	6.7
28	Kansas	6.8
8	Kentucky	8.8
NA	Louisiana**	NA
19	Maine	7.4
33	Maryland	6.5
40	Massachusetts	6.0
44	Michigan	5.9
40	Minnesota	6.0
45	Mississippi	5.8
26	Missouri	7.0
23	Montana	7.1
28	Nebraska	6.8
1	Nevada	52.9
23	New Hampshire	7.1
49	New Jersey	4.9
27	New Mexico	6.9
32	New York	6.6
38	North Carolina	6.2
28	North Dakota	6.8
35	Ohio	6.4
20	Oklahoma	7.3
20	Oregon	7.3
47	Pennsylvania	5.5
33	Rhode Island	6.5
16	South Carolina	7.6
13	South Dakota	8.0
4	Tennessee	10.5
18	Texas	7.5
7	Utah	9.2
9	Vermont	8.7
13	Virginia	8.0
35	Washington	6.4
20	West Virginia	7.3
45	Wisconsin	5.8
6	Wyoming	9.8

RANK ORDER

RANK	STATE	RATE
1	Nevada	52.9
2	Hawaii	22.4
3	Arkansas	12.2
4	Tennessee	10.5
5	Idaho	10.1
6	Wyoming	9.8
7	Utah	9.2
8	Kentucky	8.8
9	Vermont	8.7
10	Alabama	8.6
10	Florida	8.6
12	Indiana	8.1
13	South Dakota	8.0
13	Virginia	8.0
15	Alaska	7.8
16	Colorado	7.6
16	South Carolina	7.6
18	Texas	7.5
19	Maine	7.4
20	Oklahoma	7.3
20	Oregon	7.3
20	West Virginia	7.3
23	Georgia	7.1
23	Montana	7.1
23	New Hampshire	7.1
26	Missouri	7.0
27	New Mexico	6.9
28	Kansas	6.8
28	Nebraska	6.8
28	North Dakota	6.8
31	Iowa	6.7
32	New York	6.6
33	Maryland	6.5
33	Rhode Island	6.5
35	Ohio	6.4
35	Washington	6.4
37	Arizona	6.3
38	North Carolina	6.2
39	Illinois	6.1
40	California	6.0
40	Delaware	6.0
40	Massachusetts	6.0
40	Minnesota	6.0
44	Michigan	5.9
45	Mississippi	5.8
45	Wisconsin	5.8
47	Pennsylvania	5.5
48	Connecticut	5.0
49	New Jersey	4.9
NA	Louisiana**	NA

District of Columbia 3.9

Source: CQ Press using data from U.S. Department of Health and Human Services, National Center for Health Statistics
"National Vital Statistics Reports" (Vol. 55, No. 20, August 28, 2007)

*Provisional data by state of occurrence.

**Not available.

Estimated Median Age of Men at First Marriage: 2006

National Median = 27.5 Years*

ALPHA ORDER

RANK	STATE	AGE
32	Alabama	26.8
23	Alaska	27.4
21	Arizona	27.5
48	Arkansas	25.3
8	California	28.4
37	Colorado	26.6
6	Connecticut	28.8
19	Delaware	27.6
11	Florida	28.0
29	Georgia	27.0
6	Hawaii	28.8
49	Idaho	25.0
11	Illinois	28.0
32	Indiana	26.8
29	Iowa	27.0
44	Kansas	26.2
41	Kentucky	26.4
40	Louisiana	26.5
13	Maine	27.9
10	Maryland	28.3
1	Massachusetts	29.6
21	Michigan	27.5
28	Minnesota	27.1
19	Mississippi	27.6
42	Missouri	26.3
36	Montana	26.7
42	Nebraska	26.3
27	Nevada	27.2
5	New Hampshire	28.9
2	New Jersey	29.5
23	New Mexico	27.4
4	New York	29.4
29	North Carolina	27.0
37	North Dakota	26.6
23	Ohio	27.4
46	Oklahoma	25.9
15	Oregon	27.8
8	Pennsylvania	28.4
2	Rhode Island	29.5
16	South Carolina	27.7
46	South Dakota	25.9
37	Tennessee	26.6
32	Texas	26.8
50	Utah	24.9
16	Vermont	27.7
26	Virginia	27.3
13	Washington	27.9
45	West Virginia	26.1
16	Wisconsin	27.7
32	Wyoming	26.8

RANK ORDER

RANK	STATE	AGE
1	Massachusetts	29.6
2	New Jersey	29.5
2	Rhode Island	29.5
4	New York	29.4
5	New Hampshire	28.9
6	Connecticut	28.8
6	Hawaii	28.8
8	California	28.4
8	Pennsylvania	28.4
10	Maryland	28.3
11	Florida	28.0
11	Illinois	28.0
13	Maine	27.9
13	Washington	27.9
15	Oregon	27.8
16	South Carolina	27.7
16	Vermont	27.7
16	Wisconsin	27.7
19	Delaware	27.6
19	Mississippi	27.6
21	Arizona	27.5
21	Michigan	27.5
23	Alaska	27.4
23	New Mexico	27.4
23	Ohio	27.4
26	Virginia	27.3
27	Nevada	27.2
28	Minnesota	27.1
29	Georgia	27.0
29	Iowa	27.0
29	North Carolina	27.0
32	Alabama	26.8
32	Indiana	26.8
32	Texas	26.8
32	Wyoming	26.8
36	Montana	26.7
37	Colorado	26.6
37	North Dakota	26.6
37	Tennessee	26.6
40	Louisiana	26.5
41	Kentucky	26.4
42	Missouri	26.3
42	Nebraska	26.3
44	Kansas	26.2
45	West Virginia	26.1
46	Oklahoma	25.9
46	South Dakota	25.9
48	Arkansas	25.3
49	Idaho	25.0
50	Utah	24.9

| | District of Columbia | 30.3 |

Source: U.S. Bureau of the Census
   "2006 American Community Survey" (http://www.census.gov/acs/www/index.html)
*The median age at first marriage is calculated indirectly by estimating the proportion of young people who will marry during their lifetime, calculating one-half of this proportion, and determining the age (at the time of the survey) of people at this half-way mark. It does not represent the actual median age of the population who married during the calendar year.

Estimated Median Age of Women at First Marriage: 2006

National Median = 25.9 Years*

<table>
<tr><td colspan="3">ALPHA ORDER</td><td colspan="3">RANK ORDER</td></tr>
<tr><td>RANK</td><td>STATE</td><td>AGE</td><td>RANK</td><td>STATE</td><td>AGE</td></tr>
<tr><td>38</td><td>Alabama</td><td>25.0</td><td>1</td><td>Massachusetts</td><td>27.7</td></tr>
<tr><td>20</td><td>Alaska</td><td>25.9</td><td>1</td><td>New York</td><td>27.7</td></tr>
<tr><td>28</td><td>Arizona</td><td>25.6</td><td>3</td><td>Hawaii</td><td>27.6</td></tr>
<tr><td>47</td><td>Arkansas</td><td>23.9</td><td>3</td><td>New Jersey</td><td>27.6</td></tr>
<tr><td>16</td><td>California</td><td>26.2</td><td>5</td><td>Delaware</td><td>27.2</td></tr>
<tr><td>31</td><td>Colorado</td><td>25.4</td><td>6</td><td>New Hampshire</td><td>27.1</td></tr>
<tr><td>7</td><td>Connecticut</td><td>27.0</td><td>7</td><td>Connecticut</td><td>27.0</td></tr>
<tr><td>5</td><td>Delaware</td><td>27.2</td><td>8</td><td>Vermont</td><td>26.9</td></tr>
<tr><td>23</td><td>Florida</td><td>25.8</td><td>9</td><td>Maryland</td><td>26.8</td></tr>
<tr><td>30</td><td>Georgia</td><td>25.5</td><td>9</td><td>Rhode Island</td><td>26.8</td></tr>
<tr><td>3</td><td>Hawaii</td><td>27.6</td><td>11</td><td>Maine</td><td>26.7</td></tr>
<tr><td>50</td><td>Idaho</td><td>22.5</td><td>11</td><td>Pennsylvania</td><td>26.7</td></tr>
<tr><td>14</td><td>Illinois</td><td>26.4</td><td>13</td><td>Michigan</td><td>26.5</td></tr>
<tr><td>31</td><td>Indiana</td><td>25.4</td><td>14</td><td>Illinois</td><td>26.4</td></tr>
<tr><td>35</td><td>Iowa</td><td>25.2</td><td>15</td><td>South Carolina</td><td>26.3</td></tr>
<tr><td>45</td><td>Kansas</td><td>24.7</td><td>16</td><td>California</td><td>26.2</td></tr>
<tr><td>44</td><td>Kentucky</td><td>24.8</td><td>17</td><td>Ohio</td><td>26.0</td></tr>
<tr><td>23</td><td>Louisiana</td><td>25.8</td><td>17</td><td>Virginia</td><td>26.0</td></tr>
<tr><td>11</td><td>Maine</td><td>26.7</td><td>17</td><td>Wisconsin</td><td>26.0</td></tr>
<tr><td>9</td><td>Maryland</td><td>26.8</td><td>20</td><td>Alaska</td><td>25.9</td></tr>
<tr><td>1</td><td>Massachusetts</td><td>27.7</td><td>20</td><td>Oregon</td><td>25.9</td></tr>
<tr><td>13</td><td>Michigan</td><td>26.5</td><td>20</td><td>Washington</td><td>25.9</td></tr>
<tr><td>23</td><td>Minnesota</td><td>25.8</td><td>23</td><td>Florida</td><td>25.8</td></tr>
<tr><td>31</td><td>Mississippi</td><td>25.4</td><td>23</td><td>Louisiana</td><td>25.8</td></tr>
<tr><td>35</td><td>Missouri</td><td>25.2</td><td>23</td><td>Minnesota</td><td>25.8</td></tr>
<tr><td>23</td><td>Montana</td><td>25.8</td><td>23</td><td>Montana</td><td>25.8</td></tr>
<tr><td>42</td><td>Nebraska</td><td>24.9</td><td>27</td><td>New Mexico</td><td>25.7</td></tr>
<tr><td>37</td><td>Nevada</td><td>25.1</td><td>28</td><td>Arizona</td><td>25.6</td></tr>
<tr><td>6</td><td>New Hampshire</td><td>27.1</td><td>28</td><td>North Dakota</td><td>25.6</td></tr>
<tr><td>3</td><td>New Jersey</td><td>27.6</td><td>30</td><td>Georgia</td><td>25.5</td></tr>
<tr><td>27</td><td>New Mexico</td><td>25.7</td><td>31</td><td>Colorado</td><td>25.4</td></tr>
<tr><td>1</td><td>New York</td><td>27.7</td><td>31</td><td>Indiana</td><td>25.4</td></tr>
<tr><td>31</td><td>North Carolina</td><td>25.4</td><td>31</td><td>Mississippi</td><td>25.4</td></tr>
<tr><td>28</td><td>North Dakota</td><td>25.6</td><td>31</td><td>North Carolina</td><td>25.4</td></tr>
<tr><td>17</td><td>Ohio</td><td>26.0</td><td>35</td><td>Iowa</td><td>25.2</td></tr>
<tr><td>46</td><td>Oklahoma</td><td>24.3</td><td>35</td><td>Missouri</td><td>25.2</td></tr>
<tr><td>20</td><td>Oregon</td><td>25.9</td><td>37</td><td>Nevada</td><td>25.1</td></tr>
<tr><td>11</td><td>Pennsylvania</td><td>26.7</td><td>38</td><td>Alabama</td><td>25.0</td></tr>
<tr><td>9</td><td>Rhode Island</td><td>26.8</td><td>38</td><td>South Dakota</td><td>25.0</td></tr>
<tr><td>15</td><td>South Carolina</td><td>26.3</td><td>38</td><td>Tennessee</td><td>25.0</td></tr>
<tr><td>38</td><td>South Dakota</td><td>25.0</td><td>38</td><td>West Virginia</td><td>25.0</td></tr>
<tr><td>38</td><td>Tennessee</td><td>25.0</td><td>42</td><td>Nebraska</td><td>24.9</td></tr>
<tr><td>42</td><td>Texas</td><td>24.9</td><td>42</td><td>Texas</td><td>24.9</td></tr>
<tr><td>49</td><td>Utah</td><td>22.7</td><td>44</td><td>Kentucky</td><td>24.8</td></tr>
<tr><td>8</td><td>Vermont</td><td>26.9</td><td>45</td><td>Kansas</td><td>24.7</td></tr>
<tr><td>17</td><td>Virginia</td><td>26.0</td><td>46</td><td>Oklahoma</td><td>24.3</td></tr>
<tr><td>20</td><td>Washington</td><td>25.9</td><td>47</td><td>Arkansas</td><td>23.9</td></tr>
<tr><td>38</td><td>West Virginia</td><td>25.0</td><td>48</td><td>Wyoming</td><td>23.8</td></tr>
<tr><td>17</td><td>Wisconsin</td><td>26.0</td><td>49</td><td>Utah</td><td>22.7</td></tr>
<tr><td>48</td><td>Wyoming</td><td>23.8</td><td>50</td><td>Idaho</td><td>22.5</td></tr>
<tr><td></td><td></td><td></td><td></td><td>District of Columbia</td><td>29.5</td></tr>
</table>

Source: U.S. Bureau of the Census
   "2006 American Community Survey" (http://www.census.gov/acs/www/index.html)
*The median age at first marriage is calculated indirectly by estimating the proportion of young people who will marry during their lifetime, calculating one-half of this proportion, and determining the age (at the time of the survey) of people at this half-way mark. It does not represent the actual median age of the population who married during the calendar year.

Ratio of Unmarried Men to Unmarried Women: 2006

National Ratio = 113.0 Unmarried Men for Every 100 Unmarried Women*

ALPHA ORDER

RANK ORDER

RANK	STATE	RATIO
43	Alabama	107.6
1	Alaska	124.7
5	Arizona	120.8
34	Arkansas	111.7
9	California	117.8
6	Colorado	120.6
38	Connecticut	109.6
48	Delaware	105.6
22	Florida	114.9
36	Georgia	110.3
4	Hawaii	122.1
8	Idaho	119.6
30	Illinois	112.3
27	Indiana	112.9
16	Iowa	116.3
13	Kansas	116.6
32	Kentucky	111.8
46	Louisiana	106.3
44	Maine	106.7
50	Maryland	103.7
42	Massachusetts	107.9
31	Michigan	112.0
19	Minnesota	115.6
45	Mississippi	106.4
37	Missouri	109.7
9	Montana	117.8
20	Nebraska	115.2
3	Nevada	122.5
24	New Hampshire	114.5
35	New Jersey	111.6
32	New Mexico	111.8
46	New York	106.3
25	North Carolina	113.8
17	North Dakota	116.2
40	Ohio	109.4
18	Oklahoma	115.7
21	Oregon	115.0
39	Pennsylvania	109.5
49	Rhode Island	105.5
41	South Carolina	109.0
2	South Dakota	123.1
27	Tennessee	112.9
13	Texas	116.6
12	Utah	117.7
26	Vermont	113.7
29	Virginia	112.4
15	Washington	116.4
23	West Virginia	114.8
9	Wisconsin	117.8
7	Wyoming	119.9

RANK	STATE	RATIO
1	Alaska	124.7
2	South Dakota	123.1
3	Nevada	122.5
4	Hawaii	122.1
5	Arizona	120.8
6	Colorado	120.6
7	Wyoming	119.9
8	Idaho	119.6
9	California	117.8
9	Montana	117.8
9	Wisconsin	117.8
12	Utah	117.7
13	Kansas	116.6
13	Texas	116.6
15	Washington	116.4
16	Iowa	116.3
17	North Dakota	116.2
18	Oklahoma	115.7
19	Minnesota	115.6
20	Nebraska	115.2
21	Oregon	115.0
22	Florida	114.9
23	West Virginia	114.8
24	New Hampshire	114.5
25	North Carolina	113.8
26	Vermont	113.7
27	Indiana	112.9
27	Tennessee	112.9
29	Virginia	112.4
30	Illinois	112.3
31	Michigan	112.0
32	Kentucky	111.8
32	New Mexico	111.8
34	Arkansas	111.7
35	New Jersey	111.6
36	Georgia	110.3
37	Missouri	109.7
38	Connecticut	109.6
39	Pennsylvania	109.5
40	Ohio	109.4
41	South Carolina	109.0
42	Massachusetts	107.9
43	Alabama	107.6
44	Maine	106.7
45	Mississippi	106.4
46	Louisiana	106.3
46	New York	106.3
48	Delaware	105.6
49	Rhode Island	105.5
50	Maryland	103.7
	District of Columbia	92.1

Source: U.S. Bureau of the Census
"2006 American Community Survey" (http://www.census.gov/acs/www/index.html)
*Population 15 to 44 years old.

Divorces in 2006

Reporting States' Total = 853,972 Divorces*

ALPHA ORDER

RANK	STATE	DIVORCES	% of USA
15	Alabama	22,054	2.6%
40	Alaska	2,968	0.3%
12	Arizona	24,274	2.8%
21	Arkansas	16,150	1.9%
NA	California**	NA	NA
17	Colorado	21,138	2.5%
28	Connecticut	9,773	1.1%
37	Delaware	3,849	0.5%
1	Florida	87,789	10.3%
NA	Georgia**	NA	NA
NA	Hawaii**	NA	NA
33	Idaho	7,500	0.9%
7	Illinois	32,158	3.8%
NA	Indiana**	NA	NA
32	Iowa	8,024	0.9%
29	Kansas	9,158	1.1%
16	Kentucky	21,489	2.5%
NA	Louisiana**	NA	NA
36	Maine	4,752	0.6%
19	Maryland	17,012	2.0%
23	Massachusetts	14,607	1.7%
6	Michigan	35,596	4.2%
NA	Minnesota**	NA	NA
25	Mississippi	13,658	1.6%
14	Missouri	22,935	2.7%
38	Montana	3,372	0.4%
34	Nebraska	6,173	0.7%
20	Nevada	16,737	2.0%
35	New Hampshire	5,258	0.6%
11	New Jersey	25,794	3.0%
31	New Mexico	8,383	1.0%
3	New York	55,627	6.5%
5	North Carolina	36,378	4.3%
44	North Dakota	1,673	0.2%
4	Ohio	41,035	4.8%
18	Oklahoma	19,023	2.2%
24	Oregon	14,214	1.7%
9	Pennsylvania	27,357	3.2%
39	Rhode Island	3,115	0.4%
26	South Carolina	12,821	1.5%
42	South Dakota	2,502	0.3%
10	Tennessee	25,886	3.0%
2	Texas	78,072	9.1%
27	Utah	9,890	1.2%
43	Vermont	2,167	0.3%
8	Virginia	31,087	3.6%
13	Washington	24,014	2.8%
30	West Virginia	8,541	1.0%
22	Wisconsin	15,966	1.9%
41	Wyoming	2,749	0.3%

RANK ORDER

RANK	STATE	DIVORCES	% of USA
1	Florida	87,789	10.3%
2	Texas	78,072	9.1%
3	New York	55,627	6.5%
4	Ohio	41,035	4.8%
5	North Carolina	36,378	4.3%
6	Michigan	35,596	4.2%
7	Illinois	32,158	3.8%
8	Virginia	31,087	3.6%
9	Pennsylvania	27,357	3.2%
10	Tennessee	25,886	3.0%
11	New Jersey	25,794	3.0%
12	Arizona	24,274	2.8%
13	Washington	24,014	2.8%
14	Missouri	22,935	2.7%
15	Alabama	22,054	2.6%
16	Kentucky	21,489	2.5%
17	Colorado	21,138	2.5%
18	Oklahoma	19,023	2.2%
19	Maryland	17,012	2.0%
20	Nevada	16,737	2.0%
21	Arkansas	16,150	1.9%
22	Wisconsin	15,966	1.9%
23	Massachusetts	14,607	1.7%
24	Oregon	14,214	1.7%
25	Mississippi	13,658	1.6%
26	South Carolina	12,821	1.5%
27	Utah	9,890	1.2%
28	Connecticut	9,773	1.1%
29	Kansas	9,158	1.1%
30	West Virginia	8,541	1.0%
31	New Mexico	8,383	1.0%
32	Iowa	8,024	0.9%
33	Idaho	7,500	0.9%
34	Nebraska	6,173	0.7%
35	New Hampshire	5,258	0.6%
36	Maine	4,752	0.6%
37	Delaware	3,849	0.5%
38	Montana	3,372	0.4%
39	Rhode Island	3,115	0.4%
40	Alaska	2,968	0.3%
41	Wyoming	2,749	0.3%
42	South Dakota	2,502	0.3%
43	Vermont	2,167	0.3%
44	North Dakota	1,673	0.2%
NA	California**	NA	NA
NA	Georgia**	NA	NA
NA	Hawaii**	NA	NA
NA	Indiana**	NA	NA
NA	Louisiana**	NA	NA
NA	Minnesota**	NA	NA
	District of Columbia	1,254	0.1%

Source: U.S. Department of Health and Human Services, National Center for Health Statistics
   "National Vital Statistics Reports" (Vol. 55, No. 20, August 28, 2007)
*Provisional data by state of occurrence. National total is only for reporting states.
**Not available.

Divorce Rate in 2006

Reporting States' Rate = 2.9 Divorces per 1,000 Population*

ALPHA ORDER

RANK	STATE	RATE
8	Alabama	4.8
12	Alaska	4.4
19	Arizona	3.9
2	Arkansas	5.7
NA	California**	NA
12	Colorado	4.4
39	Connecticut	2.8
11	Delaware	4.5
7	Florida	4.9
NA	Georgia**	NA
NA	Hawaii**	NA
5	Idaho	5.1
42	Illinois	2.5
NA	Indiana**	NA
40	Iowa	2.7
30	Kansas	3.3
5	Kentucky	5.1
NA	Louisiana**	NA
24	Maine	3.6
33	Maryland	3.0
43	Massachusetts	2.3
27	Michigan	3.5
NA	Minnesota**	NA
9	Mississippi	4.7
19	Missouri	3.9
24	Montana	3.6
27	Nebraska	3.5
1	Nevada	6.7
18	New Hampshire	4.0
33	New Jersey	3.0
14	New Mexico	4.3
36	New York	2.9
16	North Carolina	4.1
41	North Dakota	2.6
24	Ohio	3.6
4	Oklahoma	5.3
19	Oregon	3.9
44	Pennsylvania	2.2
36	Rhode Island	2.9
33	South Carolina	3.0
32	South Dakota	3.2
14	Tennessee	4.3
30	Texas	3.3
22	Utah	3.8
27	Vermont	3.5
16	Virginia	4.1
22	Washington	3.8
9	West Virginia	4.7
36	Wisconsin	2.9
3	Wyoming	5.4

RANK ORDER

RANK	STATE	RATE
1	Nevada	6.7
2	Arkansas	5.7
3	Wyoming	5.4
4	Oklahoma	5.3
5	Idaho	5.1
5	Kentucky	5.1
7	Florida	4.9
8	Alabama	4.8
9	Mississippi	4.7
9	West Virginia	4.7
11	Delaware	4.5
12	Alaska	4.4
12	Colorado	4.4
14	New Mexico	4.3
14	Tennessee	4.3
16	North Carolina	4.1
16	Virginia	4.1
18	New Hampshire	4.0
19	Arizona	3.9
19	Missouri	3.9
19	Oregon	3.9
22	Utah	3.8
22	Washington	3.8
24	Maine	3.6
24	Montana	3.6
24	Ohio	3.6
27	Michigan	3.5
27	Nebraska	3.5
27	Vermont	3.5
30	Kansas	3.3
30	Texas	3.3
32	South Dakota	3.2
33	Maryland	3.0
33	New Jersey	3.0
33	South Carolina	3.0
36	New York	2.9
36	Rhode Island	2.9
36	Wisconsin	2.9
39	Connecticut	2.8
40	Iowa	2.7
41	North Dakota	2.6
42	Illinois	2.5
43	Massachusetts	2.3
44	Pennsylvania	2.2
NA	California**	NA
NA	Georgia**	NA
NA	Hawaii**	NA
NA	Indiana**	NA
NA	Louisiana**	NA
NA	Minnesota**	NA

District of Columbia 2.1

Source: CQ Press using data from U.S. Department of Health and Human Services, National Center for Health Statistics
"National Vital Statistics Reports" (Vol. 55, No. 20, August 28, 2007)

*Provisional data by state of occurrence. National rate is only for reporting states.
**Not available.

Average Family Size in 2006

National Average = 3.20 Persons per Family

RANK	STATE	PERSONS
30	Alabama	3.06
5	Alaska	3.36
6	Arizona	3.33
42	Arkansas	2.99
2	California	3.54
22	Colorado	3.11
18	Connecticut	3.13
17	Delaware	3.15
32	Florida	3.05
10	Georgia	3.27
3	Hawaii	3.45
22	Idaho	3.11
8	Illinois	3.29
30	Indiana	3.06
46	Iowa	2.92
40	Kansas	3.02
35	Kentucky	3.04
12	Louisiana	3.25
49	Maine	2.82
14	Maryland	3.19
16	Massachusetts	3.17
18	Michigan	3.13
38	Minnesota	3.03
14	Mississippi	3.19
35	Missouri	3.04
32	Montana	3.05
40	Nebraska	3.02
13	Nevada	3.20
32	New Hampshire	3.05
8	New Jersey	3.29
11	New Mexico	3.26
7	New York	3.31
35	North Carolina	3.04
49	North Dakota	2.82
25	Ohio	3.08
26	Oklahoma	3.07
26	Oregon	3.07
26	Pennsylvania	3.07
18	Rhode Island	3.13
26	South Carolina	3.07
44	South Dakota	2.97
38	Tennessee	3.03
4	Texas	3.41
1	Utah	3.56
47	Vermont	2.90
21	Virginia	3.12
22	Washington	3.11
48	West Virginia	2.89
43	Wisconsin	2.98
45	Wyoming	2.94

RANK	STATE	PERSONS
1	Utah	3.56
2	California	3.54
3	Hawaii	3.45
4	Texas	3.41
5	Alaska	3.36
6	Arizona	3.33
7	New York	3.31
8	Illinois	3.29
8	New Jersey	3.29
10	Georgia	3.27
11	New Mexico	3.26
12	Louisiana	3.25
13	Nevada	3.20
14	Maryland	3.19
14	Mississippi	3.19
16	Massachusetts	3.17
17	Delaware	3.15
18	Connecticut	3.13
18	Michigan	3.13
18	Rhode Island	3.13
21	Virginia	3.12
22	Colorado	3.11
22	Idaho	3.11
22	Washington	3.11
25	Ohio	3.08
26	Oklahoma	3.07
26	Oregon	3.07
26	Pennsylvania	3.07
26	South Carolina	3.07
30	Alabama	3.06
30	Indiana	3.06
32	Florida	3.05
32	Montana	3.05
32	New Hampshire	3.05
35	Kentucky	3.04
35	Missouri	3.04
35	North Carolina	3.04
38	Minnesota	3.03
38	Tennessee	3.03
40	Kansas	3.02
40	Nebraska	3.02
42	Arkansas	2.99
43	Wisconsin	2.98
44	South Dakota	2.97
45	Wyoming	2.94
46	Iowa	2.92
47	Vermont	2.90
48	West Virginia	2.89
49	Maine	2.82
49	North Dakota	2.82
	District of Columbia	3.24

Source: U.S. Bureau of the Census
"2006 American Community Survey" (http://www.census.gov/acs/www/index.html)

Seats in the U.S. House of Representatives in 2008

National Total = 435 Seats*

ALPHA ORDER

RANK	STATE	SEATS	% of USA
22	Alabama	7	1.6%
44	Alaska	1	0.2%
18	Arizona	8	1.8%
31	Arkansas	4	0.9%
1	California	53	12.2%
22	Colorado	7	1.6%
27	Connecticut	5	1.1%
44	Delaware	1	0.2%
4	Florida	25	5.7%
9	Georgia	13	3.0%
39	Hawaii	2	0.5%
39	Idaho	2	0.5%
5	Illinois	19	4.4%
14	Indiana	9	2.1%
27	Iowa	5	1.1%
31	Kansas	4	0.9%
25	Kentucky	6	1.4%
22	Louisiana	7	1.6%
39	Maine	2	0.5%
18	Maryland	8	1.8%
13	Massachusetts	10	2.3%
8	Michigan	15	3.4%
18	Minnesota	8	1.8%
31	Mississippi	4	0.9%
14	Missouri	9	2.1%
44	Montana	1	0.2%
34	Nebraska	3	0.7%
34	Nevada	3	0.7%
39	New Hampshire	2	0.5%
9	New Jersey	13	3.0%
34	New Mexico	3	0.7%
3	New York	29	6.7%
9	North Carolina	13	3.0%
44	North Dakota	1	0.2%
7	Ohio	18	4.1%
27	Oklahoma	5	1.1%
27	Oregon	5	1.1%
5	Pennsylvania	19	4.4%
39	Rhode Island	2	0.5%
25	South Carolina	6	1.4%
44	South Dakota	1	0.2%
14	Tennessee	9	2.1%
2	Texas	32	7.4%
34	Utah	3	0.7%
44	Vermont	1	0.2%
12	Virginia	11	2.5%
14	Washington	9	2.1%
34	West Virginia	3	0.7%
18	Wisconsin	8	1.8%
44	Wyoming	1	0.2%

RANK ORDER

RANK	STATE	SEATS	% of USA
1	California	53	12.2%
2	Texas	32	7.4%
3	New York	29	6.7%
4	Florida	25	5.7%
5	Illinois	19	4.4%
5	Pennsylvania	19	4.4%
7	Ohio	18	4.1%
8	Michigan	15	3.4%
9	Georgia	13	3.0%
9	New Jersey	13	3.0%
9	North Carolina	13	3.0%
12	Virginia	11	2.5%
13	Massachusetts	10	2.3%
14	Indiana	9	2.1%
14	Missouri	9	2.1%
14	Tennessee	9	2.1%
14	Washington	9	2.1%
18	Arizona	8	1.8%
18	Maryland	8	1.8%
18	Minnesota	8	1.8%
18	Wisconsin	8	1.8%
22	Alabama	7	1.6%
22	Colorado	7	1.6%
22	Louisiana	7	1.6%
25	Kentucky	6	1.4%
25	South Carolina	6	1.4%
27	Connecticut	5	1.1%
27	Iowa	5	1.1%
27	Oklahoma	5	1.1%
27	Oregon	5	1.1%
31	Arkansas	4	0.9%
31	Kansas	4	0.9%
31	Mississippi	4	0.9%
34	Nebraska	3	0.7%
34	Nevada	3	0.7%
34	New Mexico	3	0.7%
34	Utah	3	0.7%
34	West Virginia	3	0.7%
39	Hawaii	2	0.5%
39	Idaho	2	0.5%
39	Maine	2	0.5%
39	New Hampshire	2	0.5%
39	Rhode Island	2	0.5%
44	Alaska	1	0.2%
44	Delaware	1	0.2%
44	Montana	1	0.2%
44	North Dakota	1	0.2%
44	South Dakota	1	0.2%
44	Vermont	1	0.2%
44	Wyoming	1	0.2%
	District of Columbia**	0	0.0%

Source: U.S. Bureau of the Census
"Congressional Apportionment" (http://www.census.gov/population/www/censusdata/apportionment.html)
*This table shows the number of seats after reapportionment of the 2000 Census. This apportionment became effective with the Congress elected in November 2002 and that took office in January 2003.
**The District of Columbia has one non-voting delegate. Each state has two members in the U.S. Senate.

Estimated Population per U.S. House Seat in 2008

National Rate = 692,030 Persons per House Member*

<u>ALPHA ORDER</u>

RANK	STATE	RATE
33	Alabama	661,122
28	Alaska	683,478
6	Arizona	792,344
16	Arkansas	708,699
26	California	689,683
24	Colorado	694,502
21	Connecticut	700,462
3	Delaware	864,764
12	Florida	730,050
11	Georgia	734,212
41	Hawaii	641,694
7	Idaho	749,701
29	Illinois	676,450
18	Indiana	705,032
47	Iowa	597,609
25	Kansas	693,999
17	Kentucky	706,912
45	Louisiana	613,315
34	Maine	658,604
19	Maryland	702,293
40	Massachusetts	644,976
30	Michigan	671,455
39	Minnesota	649,703
13	Mississippi	729,696
38	Missouri	653,157
1	Montana	957,861
48	Nebraska	591,524
4	Nevada	855,127
35	New Hampshire	657,914
31	New Jersey	668,148
36	New Mexico	656,638
32	New York	665,439
23	North Carolina	697,002
42	North Dakota	639,715
43	Ohio	637,051
14	Oklahoma	723,463
8	Oregon	749,491
37	Pennsylvania	654,357
49	Rhode Island	528,916
10	South Carolina	734,618
5	South Dakota	796,214
27	Tennessee	684,080
9	Texas	747,012
2	Utah	881,777
44	Vermont	621,254
20	Virginia	701,099
15	Washington	718,714
46	West Virginia	604,012
22	Wisconsin	700,205
50	Wyoming	522,830

<u>RANK ORDER</u>

RANK	STATE	RATE
1	Montana	957,861
2	Utah	881,777
3	Delaware	864,764
4	Nevada	855,127
5	South Dakota	796,214
6	Arizona	792,344
7	Idaho	749,701
8	Oregon	749,491
9	Texas	747,012
10	South Carolina	734,618
11	Georgia	734,212
12	Florida	730,050
13	Mississippi	729,696
14	Oklahoma	723,463
15	Washington	718,714
16	Arkansas	708,699
17	Kentucky	706,912
18	Indiana	705,032
19	Maryland	702,293
20	Virginia	701,099
21	Connecticut	700,462
22	Wisconsin	700,205
23	North Carolina	697,002
24	Colorado	694,502
25	Kansas	693,999
26	California	689,683
27	Tennessee	684,080
28	Alaska	683,478
29	Illinois	676,450
30	Michigan	671,455
31	New Jersey	668,148
32	New York	665,439
33	Alabama	661,122
34	Maine	658,604
35	New Hampshire	657,914
36	New Mexico	656,638
37	Pennsylvania	654,357
38	Missouri	653,157
39	Minnesota	649,703
40	Massachusetts	644,976
41	Hawaii	641,694
42	North Dakota	639,715
43	Ohio	637,051
44	Vermont	621,254
45	Louisiana	613,315
46	West Virginia	604,012
47	Iowa	597,609
48	Nebraska	591,524
49	Rhode Island	528,916
50	Wyoming	522,830
	District of Columbia**	NA

Source: CQ Press using data from U.S. Bureau of the Census

"Congressional Apportionment" (http://www.census.gov/population/www/censusdata/apportionment.html)

*National rate does not include population of the District of Columbia. D.C. has one non-voting delegate. Each state has two members in the U.S. Senate. This table is based only on U.S. Representatives and not U.S. Senate members. This table reflects reapportionment resulting from the 2000 census.

**Not applicable.

State Legislators in 2008

National Total = 7,382 Legislators*

ALPHA ORDER

RANK	STATE	LEGISLATORS	% of USA
27	Alabama	140	1.9%
49	Alaska	60	0.8%
43	Arizona	90	1.2%
30	Arkansas	135	1.8%
35	California	120	1.6%
42	Colorado	100	1.4%
9	Connecticut	187	2.5%
48	Delaware	62	0.8%
18	Florida	160	2.2%
3	Georgia	236	3.2%
46	Hawaii	76	1.0%
39	Idaho	105	1.4%
13	Illinois	177	2.4%
19	Indiana	150	2.0%
19	Iowa	150	2.0%
17	Kansas	165	2.2%
29	Kentucky	138	1.9%
25	Louisiana	144	2.0%
10	Maine	186	2.5%
8	Maryland	188	2.5%
6	Massachusetts	200	2.7%
23	Michigan	148	2.0%
5	Minnesota	201	2.7%
14	Mississippi	174	2.4%
7	Missouri	197	2.7%
19	Montana	150	2.0%
50	Nebraska	49	0.7%
47	Nevada	63	0.9%
1	New Hampshire	424	5.7%
35	New Jersey	120	1.6%
38	New Mexico	112	1.5%
4	New York	212	2.9%
15	North Carolina	170	2.3%
26	North Dakota	141	1.9%
32	Ohio	132	1.8%
22	Oklahoma	149	2.0%
43	Oregon	90	1.2%
2	Pennsylvania	253	3.4%
37	Rhode Island	113	1.5%
15	South Carolina	170	2.3%
39	South Dakota	105	1.4%
32	Tennessee	132	1.8%
11	Texas	181	2.5%
41	Utah	104	1.4%
12	Vermont	180	2.4%
27	Virginia	140	1.9%
24	Washington	147	2.0%
31	West Virginia	134	1.8%
32	Wisconsin	132	1.8%
43	Wyoming	90	1.2%

RANK ORDER

RANK	STATE	LEGISLATORS	% of USA
1	New Hampshire	424	5.7%
2	Pennsylvania	253	3.4%
3	Georgia	236	3.2%
4	New York	212	2.9%
5	Minnesota	201	2.7%
6	Massachusetts	200	2.7%
7	Missouri	197	2.7%
8	Maryland	188	2.5%
9	Connecticut	187	2.5%
10	Maine	186	2.5%
11	Texas	181	2.5%
12	Vermont	180	2.4%
13	Illinois	177	2.4%
14	Mississippi	174	2.4%
15	North Carolina	170	2.3%
15	South Carolina	170	2.3%
17	Kansas	165	2.2%
18	Florida	160	2.2%
19	Indiana	150	2.0%
19	Iowa	150	2.0%
19	Montana	150	2.0%
22	Oklahoma	149	2.0%
23	Michigan	148	2.0%
24	Washington	147	2.0%
25	Louisiana	144	2.0%
26	North Dakota	141	1.9%
27	Alabama	140	1.9%
27	Virginia	140	1.9%
29	Kentucky	138	1.9%
30	Arkansas	135	1.8%
31	West Virginia	134	1.8%
32	Ohio	132	1.8%
32	Tennessee	132	1.8%
32	Wisconsin	132	1.8%
35	California	120	1.6%
35	New Jersey	120	1.6%
37	Rhode Island	113	1.5%
38	New Mexico	112	1.5%
39	Idaho	105	1.4%
39	South Dakota	105	1.4%
41	Utah	104	1.4%
42	Colorado	100	1.4%
43	Arizona	90	1.2%
43	Oregon	90	1.2%
43	Wyoming	90	1.2%
46	Hawaii	76	1.0%
47	Nevada	63	0.9%
48	Delaware	62	0.8%
49	Alaska	60	0.8%
50	Nebraska	49	0.7%
	District of Columbia**	NA	NA

Source: National Conference of State Legislatures (Denver, CO)
"2006 Post-Election Partisan Composition of State Legislatures"
(http://www.ncsl.org/programs/legismgt/statevote/partycomptable2007.htm)

*There are 1,971 state senators (including Nebraska's 49 unicameral seats) and 5,411 state house members.
**Not applicable.

Population per State Legislator in 2008

National Rate = 40,779 Population per Legislator*

ALPHA ORDER

RANK	STATE	RATE
22	Alabama	33,056
42	Alaska	11,391
8	Arizona	70,431
32	Arkansas	20,998
1	California	304,610
13	Colorado	48,615
34	Connecticut	18,729
40	Delaware	13,948
3	Florida	114,070
20	Georgia	40,444
36	Hawaii	16,887
39	Idaho	14,280
6	Illinois	72,613
17	Indiana	42,302
33	Iowa	19,920
37	Kansas	16,824
24	Kentucky	30,735
27	Louisiana	29,814
45	Maine	7,082
25	Maryland	29,885
23	Massachusetts	32,249
9	Michigan	68,053
29	Minnesota	25,859
38	Mississippi	16,775
26	Missouri	29,840
46	Montana	6,386
21	Nebraska	36,216
19	Nevada	40,720
50	New Hampshire	3,103
7	New Jersey	72,383
35	New Mexico	17,589
4	New York	91,027
11	North Carolina	53,300
48	North Dakota	4,537
5	Ohio	86,871
31	Oklahoma	24,277
18	Oregon	41,638
12	Pennsylvania	49,141
43	Rhode Island	9,361
28	South Carolina	25,928
44	South Dakota	7,583
14	Tennessee	46,642
2	Texas	132,068
30	Utah	25,436
49	Vermont	3,451
10	Virginia	55,086
15	Washington	44,003
41	West Virginia	13,523
16	Wisconsin	42,437
47	Wyoming	5,809

RANK ORDER

RANK	STATE	RATE
1	California	304,610
2	Texas	132,068
3	Florida	114,070
4	New York	91,027
5	Ohio	86,871
6	Illinois	72,613
7	New Jersey	72,383
8	Arizona	70,431
9	Michigan	68,053
10	Virginia	55,086
11	North Carolina	53,300
12	Pennsylvania	49,141
13	Colorado	48,615
14	Tennessee	46,642
15	Washington	44,003
16	Wisconsin	42,437
17	Indiana	42,302
18	Oregon	41,638
19	Nevada	40,720
20	Georgia	40,444
21	Nebraska	36,216
22	Alabama	33,056
23	Massachusetts	32,249
24	Kentucky	30,735
25	Maryland	29,885
26	Missouri	29,840
27	Louisiana	29,814
28	South Carolina	25,928
29	Minnesota	25,859
30	Utah	25,436
31	Oklahoma	24,277
32	Arkansas	20,998
33	Iowa	19,920
34	Connecticut	18,729
35	New Mexico	17,589
36	Hawaii	16,887
37	Kansas	16,824
38	Mississippi	16,775
39	Idaho	14,280
40	Delaware	13,948
41	West Virginia	13,523
42	Alaska	11,391
43	Rhode Island	9,361
44	South Dakota	7,583
45	Maine	7,082
46	Montana	6,386
47	Wyoming	5,809
48	North Dakota	4,537
49	Vermont	3,451
50	New Hampshire	3,103
	District of Columbia**	NA

Source: CQ Press using data from National Conference of State Legislatures (Denver, CO)
   "2006 Post-Election Partisan Composition of State Legislatures"
   (http://www.ncsl.org/programs/legismgt/statevote/partycomptable2007.htm)
*There are 1,971 state senators (including Nebraska's 49 unicameral seats) and 5,411 state house members. National rate does not include population for the District of Columbia.
**Not applicable.

Registered Voters in 2004

National Total = 142,070,000

RANK	STATE	REGISTERED	% of USA
22	Alabama	2,418,000	1.7%
49	Alaska	334,000	0.2%
21	Arizona	2,485,000	1.7%
33	Arkansas	1,328,000	0.9%
1	California	14,193,000	10.0%
24	Colorado	2,307,000	1.6%
29	Connecticut	1,695,000	1.2%
46	Delaware	415,000	0.3%
4	Florida	8,219,000	5.8%
11	Georgia	3,948,000	2.8%
44	Hawaii	497,000	0.3%
41	Idaho	663,000	0.5%
6	Illinois	6,437,000	4.5%
18	Indiana	3,031,000	2.1%
30	Iowa	1,674,000	1.2%
32	Kansas	1,338,000	0.9%
26	Kentucky	2,231,000	1.6%
23	Louisiana	2,413,000	1.7%
39	Maine	824,000	0.6%
20	Maryland	2,676,000	1.9%
12	Massachusetts	3,483,000	2.5%
8	Michigan	5,364,000	3.8%
17	Minnesota	3,080,000	2.2%
31	Mississippi	1,510,000	1.1%
14	Missouri	3,336,000	2.3%
43	Montana	519,000	0.4%
38	Nebraska	918,000	0.6%
35	Nevada	965,000	0.7%
40	New Hampshire	716,000	0.5%
10	New Jersey	4,085,000	2.9%
36	New Mexico	936,000	0.7%
3	New York	8,624,000	6.1%
9	North Carolina	4,292,000	3.0%
47	North Dakota	412,000	0.3%
7	Ohio	6,003,000	4.2%
28	Oklahoma	1,781,000	1.3%
27	Oregon	2,049,000	1.4%
5	Pennsylvania	6,481,000	4.6%
42	Rhode Island	522,000	0.4%
25	South Carolina	2,238,000	1.6%
45	South Dakota	425,000	0.3%
19	Tennessee	2,739,000	1.9%
2	Texas	9,681,000	6.8%
34	Utah	1,141,000	0.8%
48	Vermont	354,000	0.2%
13	Virginia	3,441,000	2.4%
16	Washington	3,133,000	2.2%
37	West Virginia	935,000	0.7%
15	Wisconsin	3,225,000	2.3%
50	Wyoming	265,000	0.2%

RANK	STATE	REGISTERED	% of USA
1	California	14,193,000	10.0%
2	Texas	9,681,000	6.8%
3	New York	8,624,000	6.1%
4	Florida	8,219,000	5.8%
5	Pennsylvania	6,481,000	4.6%
6	Illinois	6,437,000	4.5%
7	Ohio	6,003,000	4.2%
8	Michigan	5,364,000	3.8%
9	North Carolina	4,292,000	3.0%
10	New Jersey	4,085,000	2.9%
11	Georgia	3,948,000	2.8%
12	Massachusetts	3,483,000	2.5%
13	Virginia	3,441,000	2.4%
14	Missouri	3,336,000	2.3%
15	Wisconsin	3,225,000	2.3%
16	Washington	3,133,000	2.2%
17	Minnesota	3,080,000	2.2%
18	Indiana	3,031,000	2.1%
19	Tennessee	2,739,000	1.9%
20	Maryland	2,676,000	1.9%
21	Arizona	2,485,000	1.7%
22	Alabama	2,418,000	1.7%
23	Louisiana	2,413,000	1.7%
24	Colorado	2,307,000	1.6%
25	South Carolina	2,238,000	1.6%
26	Kentucky	2,231,000	1.6%
27	Oregon	2,049,000	1.4%
28	Oklahoma	1,781,000	1.3%
29	Connecticut	1,695,000	1.2%
30	Iowa	1,674,000	1.2%
31	Mississippi	1,510,000	1.1%
32	Kansas	1,338,000	0.9%
33	Arkansas	1,328,000	0.9%
34	Utah	1,141,000	0.8%
35	Nevada	965,000	0.7%
36	New Mexico	936,000	0.7%
37	West Virginia	935,000	0.7%
38	Nebraska	918,000	0.6%
39	Maine	824,000	0.6%
40	New Hampshire	716,000	0.5%
41	Idaho	663,000	0.5%
42	Rhode Island	522,000	0.4%
43	Montana	519,000	0.4%
44	Hawaii	497,000	0.3%
45	South Dakota	425,000	0.3%
46	Delaware	415,000	0.3%
47	North Dakota	412,000	0.3%
48	Vermont	354,000	0.2%
49	Alaska	334,000	0.2%
50	Wyoming	265,000	0.2%
	District of Columbia	293,000	0.2%

Source: U.S. Bureau of the Census
   "Voting and Registration" (Table 4c, http://www.census.gov/population/www/socdemo/voting.html)

Percent of Eligible Voters Reported Registered in 2004

National Percent = 72.1%*

ALPHA ORDER				RANK ORDER		
RANK	STATE	PERCENT		RANK	STATE	PERCENT
21	Alabama	74.2		1	North Dakota	89.3
9	Alaska	77.0		2	Minnesota	84.5
37	Arizona	70.8		3	Wisconsin	82.1
43	Arkansas	68.4		4	Maine	81.8
42	California	68.6		5	Missouri	81.2
21	Colorado	74.2		6	Oregon	78.8
38	Connecticut	70.3		7	Iowa	78.4
33	Delaware	71.6		8	Massachusetts	77.5
32	Florida	71.7		9	Alaska	77.0
46	Georgia	67.3		10	South Dakota	76.8
50	Hawaii	58.4		11	Utah	75.7
39	Idaho	69.9		12	New Hampshire	75.6
20	Illinois	74.5		12	Vermont	75.6
44	Indiana	68.3		14	Montana	75.5
7	Iowa	78.4		14	Nebraska	75.5
28	Kansas	72.3		16	Kentucky	75.1
16	Kentucky	75.1		17	Louisiana	75.0
17	Louisiana	75.0		18	Michigan	74.7
4	Maine	81.8		19	South Carolina	74.6
26	Maryland	72.7		20	Illinois	74.5
8	Massachusetts	77.5		21	Alabama	74.2
18	Michigan	74.7		21	Colorado	74.2
2	Minnesota	84.5		21	Washington	74.2
24	Mississippi	73.7		24	Mississippi	73.7
5	Missouri	81.2		25	New Jersey	73.1
14	Montana	75.5		26	Maryland	72.7
14	Nebraska	75.5		27	North Carolina	72.5
48	Nevada	65.3		28	Kansas	72.3
12	New Hampshire	75.6		28	Ohio	72.3
25	New Jersey	73.1		30	New Mexico	72.0
30	New Mexico	72.0		31	Oklahoma	71.9
45	New York	67.5		32	Florida	71.7
27	North Carolina	72.5		33	Delaware	71.6
1	North Dakota	89.3		33	Pennsylvania	71.6
28	Ohio	72.3		33	Wyoming	71.6
31	Oklahoma	71.9		36	Rhode Island	71.3
6	Oregon	78.8		37	Arizona	70.8
33	Pennsylvania	71.6		38	Connecticut	70.3
36	Rhode Island	71.3		39	Idaho	69.9
19	South Carolina	74.6		40	Texas	69.5
10	South Dakota	76.8		41	Virginia	69.2
49	Tennessee	64.4		42	California	68.6
40	Texas	69.5		43	Arkansas	68.4
11	Utah	75.7		44	Indiana	68.3
12	Vermont	75.6		45	New York	67.5
41	Virginia	69.2		46	Georgia	67.3
21	Washington	74.2		47	West Virginia	67.1
47	West Virginia	67.1		48	Nevada	65.3
3	Wisconsin	82.1		49	Tennessee	64.4
33	Wyoming	71.6		50	Hawaii	58.4
					District of Columbia	75.2

Source: U.S. Bureau of the Census
"Voting and Registration" (Table 4c, http://www.census.gov/population/www/socdemo/voting.html)
*As a percent of citizen population 18 and older.

Persons Voting in 2004

National Total = 125,736,000

ALPHA ORDER

RANK	STATE	VOTERS	% of USA
24	Alabama	2,060,000	1.6%
49	Alaska	293,000	0.2%
21	Arizona	2,239,000	1.8%
33	Arkansas	1,140,000	0.9%
1	California	12,807,000	10.2%
22	Colorado	2,097,000	1.7%
29	Connecticut	1,524,000	1.2%
45	Delaware	385,000	0.3%
4	Florida	7,372,000	5.9%
11	Georgia	3,332,000	2.6%
44	Hawaii	433,000	0.3%
41	Idaho	585,000	0.5%
6	Illinois	5,672,000	4.5%
18	Indiana	2,598,000	2.1%
30	Iowa	1,522,000	1.2%
32	Kansas	1,188,000	0.9%
25	Kentucky	1,930,000	1.5%
23	Louisiana	2,067,000	1.6%
39	Maine	736,000	0.6%
19	Maryland	2,413,000	1.9%
13	Massachusetts	3,085,000	2.5%
8	Michigan	4,818,000	3.8%
15	Minnesota	2,887,000	2.3%
31	Mississippi	1,263,000	1.0%
17	Missouri	2,815,000	2.2%
42	Montana	482,000	0.4%
38	Nebraska	793,000	0.6%
35	Nevada	871,000	0.7%
40	New Hampshire	677,000	0.5%
9	New Jersey	3,693,000	2.9%
36	New Mexico	837,000	0.7%
3	New York	7,698,000	6.1%
10	North Carolina	3,639,000	2.9%
47	North Dakota	330,000	0.3%
7	Ohio	5,485,000	4.4%
28	Oklahoma	1,541,000	1.2%
26	Oregon	1,924,000	1.5%
5	Pennsylvania	5,845,000	4.6%
43	Rhode Island	467,000	0.4%
27	South Carolina	1,899,000	1.5%
46	South Dakota	378,000	0.3%
20	Tennessee	2,319,000	1.8%
2	Texas	7,950,000	6.3%
34	Utah	1,022,000	0.8%
48	Vermont	316,000	0.3%
12	Virginia	3,134,000	2.5%
16	Washington	2,851,000	2.3%
37	West Virginia	798,000	0.6%
14	Wisconsin	3,010,000	2.4%
50	Wyoming	247,000	0.2%

RANK ORDER

RANK	STATE	VOTERS	% of USA
1	California	12,807,000	10.2%
2	Texas	7,950,000	6.3%
3	New York	7,698,000	6.1%
4	Florida	7,372,000	5.9%
5	Pennsylvania	5,845,000	4.6%
6	Illinois	5,672,000	4.5%
7	Ohio	5,485,000	4.4%
8	Michigan	4,818,000	3.8%
9	New Jersey	3,693,000	2.9%
10	North Carolina	3,639,000	2.9%
11	Georgia	3,332,000	2.6%
12	Virginia	3,134,000	2.5%
13	Massachusetts	3,085,000	2.5%
14	Wisconsin	3,010,000	2.4%
15	Minnesota	2,887,000	2.3%
16	Washington	2,851,000	2.3%
17	Missouri	2,815,000	2.2%
18	Indiana	2,598,000	2.1%
19	Maryland	2,413,000	1.9%
20	Tennessee	2,319,000	1.8%
21	Arizona	2,239,000	1.8%
22	Colorado	2,097,000	1.7%
23	Louisiana	2,067,000	1.6%
24	Alabama	2,060,000	1.6%
25	Kentucky	1,930,000	1.5%
26	Oregon	1,924,000	1.5%
27	South Carolina	1,899,000	1.5%
28	Oklahoma	1,541,000	1.2%
29	Connecticut	1,524,000	1.2%
30	Iowa	1,522,000	1.2%
31	Mississippi	1,263,000	1.0%
32	Kansas	1,188,000	0.9%
33	Arkansas	1,140,000	0.9%
34	Utah	1,022,000	0.8%
35	Nevada	871,000	0.7%
36	New Mexico	837,000	0.7%
37	West Virginia	798,000	0.6%
38	Nebraska	793,000	0.6%
39	Maine	736,000	0.6%
40	New Hampshire	677,000	0.5%
41	Idaho	585,000	0.5%
42	Montana	482,000	0.4%
43	Rhode Island	467,000	0.4%
44	Hawaii	433,000	0.3%
45	Delaware	385,000	0.3%
46	South Dakota	378,000	0.3%
47	North Dakota	330,000	0.3%
48	Vermont	316,000	0.3%
49	Alaska	293,000	0.2%
50	Wyoming	247,000	0.2%
	District of Columbia	270,000	0.2%

Source: U.S. Bureau of the Census
"Voting and Registration" (Table 4c, http://www.census.gov/population/www/socdemo/voting.html)

Percent of Eligible Population Reported Voting in 2004

National Percent = 63.8%

ALPHA ORDER

RANK	STATE	PERCENT
33	Alabama	63.2
13	Alaska	67.6
31	Arizona	63.8
44	Arkansas	58.7
38	California	61.9
15	Colorado	67.5
33	Connecticut	63.2
19	Delaware	66.4
28	Florida	64.3
48	Georgia	56.8
50	Hawaii	50.8
40	Idaho	61.6
22	Illinois	65.6
45	Indiana	58.6
7	Iowa	71.3
29	Kansas	64.2
25	Kentucky	65.0
29	Louisiana	64.2
4	Maine	73.1
22	Maryland	65.6
9	Massachusetts	68.6
17	Michigan	67.1
1	Minnesota	79.2
39	Mississippi	61.7
10	Missouri	68.5
8	Montana	70.2
24	Nebraska	65.3
43	Nevada	58.9
5	New Hampshire	71.5
21	New Jersey	66.0
27	New Mexico	64.4
42	New York	60.2
41	North Carolina	61.4
5	North Dakota	71.5
20	Ohio	66.1
37	Oklahoma	62.3
3	Oregon	74.0
26	Pennsylvania	64.5
32	Rhode Island	63.7
33	South Carolina	63.2
11	South Dakota	68.3
49	Tennessee	54.6
47	Texas	57.1
12	Utah	67.8
16	Vermont	67.3
36	Virginia	63.1
13	Washington	67.6
46	West Virginia	57.2
2	Wisconsin	76.6
18	Wyoming	66.9

RANK ORDER

RANK	STATE	PERCENT
1	Minnesota	79.2
2	Wisconsin	76.6
3	Oregon	74.0
4	Maine	73.1
5	New Hampshire	71.5
5	North Dakota	71.5
7	Iowa	71.3
8	Montana	70.2
9	Massachusetts	68.6
10	Missouri	68.5
11	South Dakota	68.3
12	Utah	67.8
13	Alaska	67.6
13	Washington	67.6
15	Colorado	67.5
16	Vermont	67.3
17	Michigan	67.1
18	Wyoming	66.9
19	Delaware	66.4
20	Ohio	66.1
21	New Jersey	66.0
22	Illinois	65.6
22	Maryland	65.6
24	Nebraska	65.3
25	Kentucky	65.0
26	Pennsylvania	64.5
27	New Mexico	64.4
28	Florida	64.3
29	Kansas	64.2
29	Louisiana	64.2
31	Arizona	63.8
32	Rhode Island	63.7
33	Alabama	63.2
33	Connecticut	63.2
33	South Carolina	63.2
36	Virginia	63.1
37	Oklahoma	62.3
38	California	61.9
39	Mississippi	61.7
40	Idaho	61.6
41	North Carolina	61.4
42	New York	60.2
43	Nevada	58.9
44	Arkansas	58.7
45	Indiana	58.6
46	West Virginia	57.2
47	Texas	57.1
48	Georgia	56.8
49	Tennessee	54.6
50	Hawaii	50.8
	District of Columbia	69.2

Source: U.S. Bureau of the Census
"Voting and Registration" (Table 4c, http://www.census.gov/population/www/socdemo/voting.html)
*As a percent of citizen population 18 and older.

XIV. Social Welfare

Poverty Rate in 2006

National Rate = 12.5% of Population in Poverty*

RANK	STATE	PERCENT		RANK	STATE	PERCENT
	ALPHA ORDER				RANK ORDER	
6	Alabama	16.0		1	Mississippi	19.8
41	Alaska	9.3		2	Louisiana	17.4
10	Arizona	14.7		3	New Mexico	17.1
7	Arkansas	15.6		4	Kentucky	16.5
17	California	12.9		5	Texas	16.4
34	Colorado	10.4		6	Alabama	16.0
44	Connecticut	9.1		7	Arkansas	15.6
43	Delaware	9.2		8	Tennessee	15.2
27	Florida	11.4		9	West Virginia	15.0
16	Georgia	13.3		10	Arizona	14.7
46	Hawaii	8.8		11	New York	14.5
38	Idaho	9.8		12	Oklahoma	13.9
25	Illinois	11.5		13	Montana	13.8
24	Indiana	11.6		13	North Carolina	13.8
31	Iowa	10.8		15	South Carolina	13.7
19	Kansas	12.2		16	Georgia	13.3
4	Kentucky	16.5		17	California	12.9
2	Louisiana	17.4		17	Michigan	12.9
25	Maine	11.5		19	Kansas	12.2
41	Maryland	9.3		20	Ohio	12.0
33	Massachusetts	10.5		20	South Dakota	12.0
17	Michigan	12.9		22	Oregon	11.9
48	Minnesota	7.7		23	Missouri	11.7
1	Mississippi	19.8		24	Indiana	11.6
23	Missouri	11.7		25	Illinois	11.5
13	Montana	13.8		25	Maine	11.5
39	Nebraska	9.7		27	Florida	11.4
34	Nevada	10.4		28	Pennsylvania	11.3
50	New Hampshire	5.5		28	Rhode Island	11.3
47	New Jersey	7.9		30	Wisconsin	10.9
3	New Mexico	17.1		31	Iowa	10.8
11	New York	14.5		31	North Dakota	10.8
13	North Carolina	13.8		33	Massachusetts	10.5
31	North Dakota	10.8		34	Colorado	10.4
20	Ohio	12.0		34	Nevada	10.4
12	Oklahoma	13.9		36	Wyoming	10.2
22	Oregon	11.9		37	Washington	9.9
28	Pennsylvania	11.3		38	Idaho	9.8
28	Rhode Island	11.3		39	Nebraska	9.7
15	South Carolina	13.7		40	Utah	9.5
20	South Dakota	12.0		41	Alaska	9.3
8	Tennessee	15.2		41	Maryland	9.3
5	Texas	16.4		43	Delaware	9.2
40	Utah	9.5		44	Connecticut	9.1
48	Vermont	7.7		44	Virginia	9.1
44	Virginia	9.1		46	Hawaii	8.8
37	Washington	9.9		47	New Jersey	7.9
9	West Virginia	15.0		48	Minnesota	7.7
30	Wisconsin	10.9		48	Vermont	7.7
36	Wyoming	10.2		50	New Hampshire	5.5
					District of Columbia	18.8

Source: U.S. Bureau of the Census
   "Income, Poverty and Health Insurance Coverage in the United States: 2006"
   (http://www.census.gov/hhes/www/poverty/poverty06.html)
*Three-year average: 2004-2006. The poverty threshold for a family of four (two children) in 2006 was $20,614.

Percent of Senior Citizens Living in Poverty in 2006

National Percent = 9.9%*

<u>ALPHA ORDER</u>				<u>RANK ORDER</u>		
RANK	STATE	PERCENT		RANK	STATE	PERCENT
6	Alabama	12.6		1	Mississippi	15.7
50	Alaska	4.2		2	Louisiana	13.9
41	Arizona	8.0		3	Kentucky	13.5
9	Arkansas	12.3		4	Tennessee	13.4
35	California	8.4		5	New Mexico	13.0
36	Colorado	8.3		6	Alabama	12.6
48	Connecticut	6.1		6	Georgia	12.6
46	Delaware	6.9		8	South Dakota	12.5
18	Florida	10.1		9	Arkansas	12.3
6	Georgia	12.6		9	Texas	12.3
24	Hawaii	9.1		11	New York	12.1
31	Idaho	8.7		12	South Carolina	12.0
25	Illinois	9.0		13	North Carolina	11.2
44	Indiana	7.8		14	North Dakota	11.0
41	Iowa	8.0		15	West Virginia	10.5
26	Kansas	8.9		16	Maine	10.3
3	Kentucky	13.5		16	Missouri	10.3
2	Louisiana	13.9		18	Florida	10.1
16	Maine	10.3		18	Oklahoma	10.1
38	Maryland	8.2		20	Nebraska	9.5
22	Massachusetts	9.3		21	Vermont	9.4
31	Michigan	8.7		22	Massachusetts	9.3
40	Minnesota	8.1		23	Virginia	9.2
1	Mississippi	15.7		24	Hawaii	9.1
16	Missouri	10.3		25	Illinois	9.0
26	Montana	8.9		26	Kansas	8.9
20	Nebraska	9.5		26	Montana	8.9
45	Nevada	7.2		26	Pennsylvania	8.9
43	New Hampshire	7.9		26	Rhode Island	8.9
38	New Jersey	8.2		30	Washington	8.8
5	New Mexico	13.0		31	Idaho	8.7
11	New York	12.1		31	Michigan	8.7
13	North Carolina	11.2		33	Ohio	8.5
14	North Dakota	11.0		33	Oregon	8.5
33	Ohio	8.5		35	California	8.4
18	Oklahoma	10.1		36	Colorado	8.3
33	Oregon	8.5		36	Wisconsin	8.3
26	Pennsylvania	8.9		38	Maryland	8.2
26	Rhode Island	8.9		38	New Jersey	8.2
12	South Carolina	12.0		40	Minnesota	8.1
8	South Dakota	12.5		41	Arizona	8.0
4	Tennessee	13.4		41	Iowa	8.0
9	Texas	12.3		43	New Hampshire	7.9
47	Utah	6.7		44	Indiana	7.8
21	Vermont	9.4		45	Nevada	7.2
23	Virginia	9.2		46	Delaware	6.9
30	Washington	8.8		47	Utah	6.7
15	West Virginia	10.5		48	Connecticut	6.1
36	Wisconsin	8.3		48	Wyoming	6.1
48	Wyoming	6.1		50	Alaska	4.2
				District of Columbia		15.2

Source: U.S. Bureau of the Census
   "2006 American Community Survey" (http://www.census.gov/acs/www/index.html)
*People 65 years and older living with incomes below the poverty level.

Percent of Children Living in Poverty in 2006

National Percent = 17.9%*

<table>
<tr><td colspan="3">ALPHA ORDER</td><td colspan="3">RANK ORDER</td></tr>
<tr><th>RANK</th><th>STATE</th><th>PERCENT</th><th>RANK</th><th>STATE</th><th>PERCENT</th></tr>
<tr><td>8</td><td>Alabama</td><td>22.7</td><td>1</td><td>Mississippi</td><td>29.2</td></tr>
<tr><td>33</td><td>Alaska</td><td>14.7</td><td>2</td><td>Louisiana</td><td>27.5</td></tr>
<tr><td>15</td><td>Arizona</td><td>19.1</td><td>3</td><td>New Mexico</td><td>25.3</td></tr>
<tr><td>5</td><td>Arkansas</td><td>23.8</td><td>4</td><td>West Virginia</td><td>24.6</td></tr>
<tr><td>19</td><td>California</td><td>17.7</td><td>5</td><td>Arkansas</td><td>23.8</td></tr>
<tr><td>28</td><td>Colorado</td><td>15.3</td><td>5</td><td>Oklahoma</td><td>23.8</td></tr>
<tr><td>47</td><td>Connecticut</td><td>10.7</td><td>7</td><td>Texas</td><td>23.5</td></tr>
<tr><td>28</td><td>Delaware</td><td>15.3</td><td>8</td><td>Alabama</td><td>22.7</td></tr>
<tr><td>21</td><td>Florida</td><td>17.0</td><td>9</td><td>Kentucky</td><td>22.3</td></tr>
<tr><td>13</td><td>Georgia</td><td>19.7</td><td>9</td><td>Tennessee</td><td>22.3</td></tr>
<tr><td>47</td><td>Hawaii</td><td>10.7</td><td>11</td><td>South Carolina</td><td>21.7</td></tr>
<tr><td>34</td><td>Idaho</td><td>14.5</td><td>12</td><td>North Carolina</td><td>19.8</td></tr>
<tr><td>22</td><td>Illinois</td><td>16.8</td><td>13</td><td>Georgia</td><td>19.7</td></tr>
<tr><td>20</td><td>Indiana</td><td>17.4</td><td>13</td><td>New York</td><td>19.7</td></tr>
<tr><td>38</td><td>Iowa</td><td>13.2</td><td>15</td><td>Arizona</td><td>19.1</td></tr>
<tr><td>30</td><td>Kansas</td><td>15.1</td><td>16</td><td>Ohio</td><td>18.3</td></tr>
<tr><td>9</td><td>Kentucky</td><td>22.3</td><td>17</td><td>Missouri</td><td>18.2</td></tr>
<tr><td>2</td><td>Louisiana</td><td>27.5</td><td>18</td><td>Michigan</td><td>17.8</td></tr>
<tr><td>23</td><td>Maine</td><td>16.7</td><td>19</td><td>California</td><td>17.7</td></tr>
<tr><td>49</td><td>Maryland</td><td>9.3</td><td>20</td><td>Indiana</td><td>17.4</td></tr>
<tr><td>41</td><td>Massachusetts</td><td>12.0</td><td>21</td><td>Florida</td><td>17.0</td></tr>
<tr><td>18</td><td>Michigan</td><td>17.8</td><td>22</td><td>Illinois</td><td>16.8</td></tr>
<tr><td>42</td><td>Minnesota</td><td>11.8</td><td>23</td><td>Maine</td><td>16.7</td></tr>
<tr><td>1</td><td>Mississippi</td><td>29.2</td><td>24</td><td>Montana</td><td>16.6</td></tr>
<tr><td>17</td><td>Missouri</td><td>18.2</td><td>25</td><td>Pennsylvania</td><td>16.5</td></tr>
<tr><td>24</td><td>Montana</td><td>16.6</td><td>26</td><td>Oregon</td><td>16.2</td></tr>
<tr><td>36</td><td>Nebraska</td><td>13.8</td><td>27</td><td>South Dakota</td><td>16.1</td></tr>
<tr><td>37</td><td>Nevada</td><td>13.4</td><td>28</td><td>Colorado</td><td>15.3</td></tr>
<tr><td>50</td><td>New Hampshire</td><td>9.0</td><td>28</td><td>Delaware</td><td>15.3</td></tr>
<tr><td>45</td><td>New Jersey</td><td>11.5</td><td>30</td><td>Kansas</td><td>15.1</td></tr>
<tr><td>3</td><td>New Mexico</td><td>25.3</td><td>31</td><td>Rhode Island</td><td>14.9</td></tr>
<tr><td>13</td><td>New York</td><td>19.7</td><td>32</td><td>Washington</td><td>14.8</td></tr>
<tr><td>12</td><td>North Carolina</td><td>19.8</td><td>33</td><td>Alaska</td><td>14.7</td></tr>
<tr><td>39</td><td>North Dakota</td><td>12.4</td><td>34</td><td>Idaho</td><td>14.5</td></tr>
<tr><td>16</td><td>Ohio</td><td>18.3</td><td>35</td><td>Wisconsin</td><td>14.3</td></tr>
<tr><td>5</td><td>Oklahoma</td><td>23.8</td><td>36</td><td>Nebraska</td><td>13.8</td></tr>
<tr><td>26</td><td>Oregon</td><td>16.2</td><td>37</td><td>Nevada</td><td>13.4</td></tr>
<tr><td>25</td><td>Pennsylvania</td><td>16.5</td><td>38</td><td>Iowa</td><td>13.2</td></tr>
<tr><td>31</td><td>Rhode Island</td><td>14.9</td><td>39</td><td>North Dakota</td><td>12.4</td></tr>
<tr><td>11</td><td>South Carolina</td><td>21.7</td><td>39</td><td>Vermont</td><td>12.4</td></tr>
<tr><td>27</td><td>South Dakota</td><td>16.1</td><td>41</td><td>Massachusetts</td><td>12.0</td></tr>
<tr><td>9</td><td>Tennessee</td><td>22.3</td><td>42</td><td>Minnesota</td><td>11.8</td></tr>
<tr><td>7</td><td>Texas</td><td>23.5</td><td>43</td><td>Virginia</td><td>11.7</td></tr>
<tr><td>44</td><td>Utah</td><td>11.6</td><td>44</td><td>Utah</td><td>11.6</td></tr>
<tr><td>39</td><td>Vermont</td><td>12.4</td><td>45</td><td>New Jersey</td><td>11.5</td></tr>
<tr><td>43</td><td>Virginia</td><td>11.7</td><td>46</td><td>Wyoming</td><td>11.4</td></tr>
<tr><td>32</td><td>Washington</td><td>14.8</td><td>47</td><td>Connecticut</td><td>10.7</td></tr>
<tr><td>4</td><td>West Virginia</td><td>24.6</td><td>47</td><td>Hawaii</td><td>10.7</td></tr>
<tr><td>35</td><td>Wisconsin</td><td>14.3</td><td>49</td><td>Maryland</td><td>9.3</td></tr>
<tr><td>46</td><td>Wyoming</td><td>11.4</td><td>50</td><td>New Hampshire</td><td>9.0</td></tr>
<tr><td></td><td></td><td></td><td></td><td>District of Columbia</td><td>32.1</td></tr>
</table>

Source: U.S. Bureau of the Census
    "2006 American Community Survey" (http://www.census.gov/acs/www/index.html)
*Children 17 and under living in families with incomes below the poverty level.

Percent of Families Living in Poverty in 2006

National Percent = 9.8%*

<table>
<tr><td colspan="3"><u>ALPHA ORDER</u></td><td colspan="3"><u>RANK ORDER</u></td></tr>
<tr><th>RANK</th><th>STATE</th><th>PERCENT</th><th>RANK</th><th>STATE</th><th>PERCENT</th></tr>
<tr><td>9</td><td>Alabama</td><td>12.6</td><td>1</td><td>Mississippi</td><td>16.8</td></tr>
<tr><td>30</td><td>Alaska</td><td>8.2</td><td>2</td><td>Louisiana</td><td>14.4</td></tr>
<tr><td>15</td><td>Arizona</td><td>10.1</td><td>3</td><td>New Mexico</td><td>13.8</td></tr>
<tr><td>5</td><td>Arkansas</td><td>13.1</td><td>4</td><td>Texas</td><td>13.3</td></tr>
<tr><td>18</td><td>California</td><td>9.7</td><td>5</td><td>Arkansas</td><td>13.1</td></tr>
<tr><td>28</td><td>Colorado</td><td>8.4</td><td>5</td><td>Kentucky</td><td>13.1</td></tr>
<tr><td>48</td><td>Connecticut</td><td>5.9</td><td>7</td><td>Oklahoma</td><td>12.8</td></tr>
<tr><td>36</td><td>Delaware</td><td>7.6</td><td>8</td><td>West Virginia</td><td>12.7</td></tr>
<tr><td>23</td><td>Florida</td><td>9.0</td><td>9</td><td>Alabama</td><td>12.6</td></tr>
<tr><td>12</td><td>Georgia</td><td>11.1</td><td>10</td><td>Tennessee</td><td>12.4</td></tr>
<tr><td>40</td><td>Hawaii</td><td>7.1</td><td>11</td><td>South Carolina</td><td>11.9</td></tr>
<tr><td>20</td><td>Idaho</td><td>9.3</td><td>12</td><td>Georgia</td><td>11.1</td></tr>
<tr><td>22</td><td>Illinois</td><td>9.1</td><td>13</td><td>New York</td><td>10.9</td></tr>
<tr><td>23</td><td>Indiana</td><td>9.0</td><td>14</td><td>North Carolina</td><td>10.7</td></tr>
<tr><td>38</td><td>Iowa</td><td>7.3</td><td>15</td><td>Arizona</td><td>10.1</td></tr>
<tr><td>26</td><td>Kansas</td><td>8.6</td><td>16</td><td>Missouri</td><td>10.0</td></tr>
<tr><td>5</td><td>Kentucky</td><td>13.1</td><td>17</td><td>Ohio</td><td>9.8</td></tr>
<tr><td>2</td><td>Louisiana</td><td>14.4</td><td>18</td><td>California</td><td>9.7</td></tr>
<tr><td>25</td><td>Maine</td><td>8.7</td><td>19</td><td>Michigan</td><td>9.6</td></tr>
<tr><td>49</td><td>Maryland</td><td>5.3</td><td>20</td><td>Idaho</td><td>9.3</td></tr>
<tr><td>41</td><td>Massachusetts</td><td>7.0</td><td>21</td><td>Oregon</td><td>9.2</td></tr>
<tr><td>19</td><td>Michigan</td><td>9.6</td><td>22</td><td>Illinois</td><td>9.1</td></tr>
<tr><td>45</td><td>Minnesota</td><td>6.5</td><td>23</td><td>Florida</td><td>9.0</td></tr>
<tr><td>1</td><td>Mississippi</td><td>16.8</td><td>23</td><td>Indiana</td><td>9.0</td></tr>
<tr><td>16</td><td>Missouri</td><td>10.0</td><td>25</td><td>Maine</td><td>8.7</td></tr>
<tr><td>26</td><td>Montana</td><td>8.6</td><td>26</td><td>Kansas</td><td>8.6</td></tr>
<tr><td>33</td><td>Nebraska</td><td>7.8</td><td>26</td><td>Montana</td><td>8.6</td></tr>
<tr><td>36</td><td>Nevada</td><td>7.6</td><td>28</td><td>Colorado</td><td>8.4</td></tr>
<tr><td>50</td><td>New Hampshire</td><td>4.9</td><td>28</td><td>South Dakota</td><td>8.4</td></tr>
<tr><td>46</td><td>New Jersey</td><td>6.4</td><td>30</td><td>Alaska</td><td>8.2</td></tr>
<tr><td>3</td><td>New Mexico</td><td>13.8</td><td>30</td><td>Pennsylvania</td><td>8.2</td></tr>
<tr><td>13</td><td>New York</td><td>10.9</td><td>32</td><td>Washington</td><td>8.0</td></tr>
<tr><td>14</td><td>North Carolina</td><td>10.7</td><td>33</td><td>Nebraska</td><td>7.8</td></tr>
<tr><td>41</td><td>North Dakota</td><td>7.0</td><td>33</td><td>Rhode Island</td><td>7.8</td></tr>
<tr><td>17</td><td>Ohio</td><td>9.8</td><td>33</td><td>Utah</td><td>7.8</td></tr>
<tr><td>7</td><td>Oklahoma</td><td>12.8</td><td>36</td><td>Delaware</td><td>7.6</td></tr>
<tr><td>21</td><td>Oregon</td><td>9.2</td><td>36</td><td>Nevada</td><td>7.6</td></tr>
<tr><td>30</td><td>Pennsylvania</td><td>8.2</td><td>38</td><td>Iowa</td><td>7.3</td></tr>
<tr><td>33</td><td>Rhode Island</td><td>7.8</td><td>38</td><td>Wisconsin</td><td>7.3</td></tr>
<tr><td>11</td><td>South Carolina</td><td>11.9</td><td>40</td><td>Hawaii</td><td>7.1</td></tr>
<tr><td>28</td><td>South Dakota</td><td>8.4</td><td>41</td><td>Massachusetts</td><td>7.0</td></tr>
<tr><td>10</td><td>Tennessee</td><td>12.4</td><td>41</td><td>North Dakota</td><td>7.0</td></tr>
<tr><td>4</td><td>Texas</td><td>13.3</td><td>43</td><td>Virginia</td><td>6.8</td></tr>
<tr><td>33</td><td>Utah</td><td>7.8</td><td>44</td><td>Vermont</td><td>6.7</td></tr>
<tr><td>44</td><td>Vermont</td><td>6.7</td><td>45</td><td>Minnesota</td><td>6.5</td></tr>
<tr><td>43</td><td>Virginia</td><td>6.8</td><td>46</td><td>New Jersey</td><td>6.4</td></tr>
<tr><td>32</td><td>Washington</td><td>8.0</td><td>47</td><td>Wyoming</td><td>6.3</td></tr>
<tr><td>8</td><td>West Virginia</td><td>12.7</td><td>48</td><td>Connecticut</td><td>5.9</td></tr>
<tr><td>38</td><td>Wisconsin</td><td>7.3</td><td>49</td><td>Maryland</td><td>5.3</td></tr>
<tr><td>47</td><td>Wyoming</td><td>6.3</td><td>50</td><td>New Hampshire</td><td>4.9</td></tr>
<tr><td></td><td></td><td></td><td></td><td>District of Columbia</td><td>16.3</td></tr>
</table>

Source: CQ Press using data from U.S. Bureau of the Census
"2006 American Community Survey" (http://www.census.gov/acs/www/index.html)
*Families living with incomes below the poverty level.

Percent of Female-Headed Families with Children Living in Poverty in 2006

National Percent = 36.9%*

<table>
<tr><td colspan="3">ALPHA ORDER</td><td colspan="3">RANK ORDER</td></tr>
<tr><td>RANK</td><td>STATE</td><td>PERCENT</td><td>RANK</td><td>STATE</td><td>PERCENT</td></tr>
<tr><td>6</td><td>Alabama</td><td>46.3</td><td>1</td><td>West Virginia</td><td>50.6</td></tr>
<tr><td>42</td><td>Alaska</td><td>30.4</td><td>2</td><td>Mississippi</td><td>50.3</td></tr>
<tr><td>35</td><td>Arizona</td><td>33.8</td><td>3</td><td>Louisiana</td><td>50.2</td></tr>
<tr><td>4</td><td>Arkansas</td><td>47.7</td><td>4</td><td>Arkansas</td><td>47.7</td></tr>
<tr><td>41</td><td>California</td><td>31.7</td><td>5</td><td>New Mexico</td><td>46.5</td></tr>
<tr><td>30</td><td>Colorado</td><td>35.2</td><td>6</td><td>Alabama</td><td>46.3</td></tr>
<tr><td>45</td><td>Connecticut</td><td>28.4</td><td>7</td><td>Kentucky</td><td>45.2</td></tr>
<tr><td>34</td><td>Delaware</td><td>34.1</td><td>8</td><td>Oklahoma</td><td>44.5</td></tr>
<tr><td>37</td><td>Florida</td><td>33.0</td><td>8</td><td>Tennessee</td><td>44.5</td></tr>
<tr><td>21</td><td>Georgia</td><td>37.7</td><td>10</td><td>Texas</td><td>42.0</td></tr>
<tr><td>44</td><td>Hawaii</td><td>29.0</td><td>11</td><td>South Carolina</td><td>41.5</td></tr>
<tr><td>32</td><td>Idaho</td><td>34.7</td><td>12</td><td>Ohio</td><td>39.9</td></tr>
<tr><td>23</td><td>Illinois</td><td>37.0</td><td>13</td><td>North Carolina</td><td>39.7</td></tr>
<tr><td>17</td><td>Indiana</td><td>38.2</td><td>14</td><td>Michigan</td><td>39.0</td></tr>
<tr><td>28</td><td>Iowa</td><td>36.5</td><td>15</td><td>Kansas</td><td>38.8</td></tr>
<tr><td>15</td><td>Kansas</td><td>38.8</td><td>15</td><td>Maine</td><td>38.8</td></tr>
<tr><td>7</td><td>Kentucky</td><td>45.2</td><td>17</td><td>Indiana</td><td>38.2</td></tr>
<tr><td>3</td><td>Louisiana</td><td>50.2</td><td>17</td><td>Missouri</td><td>38.2</td></tr>
<tr><td>15</td><td>Maine</td><td>38.8</td><td>19</td><td>Oregon</td><td>38.1</td></tr>
<tr><td>50</td><td>Maryland</td><td>21.8</td><td>20</td><td>Nebraska</td><td>38.0</td></tr>
<tr><td>37</td><td>Massachusetts</td><td>33.0</td><td>21</td><td>Georgia</td><td>37.7</td></tr>
<tr><td>14</td><td>Michigan</td><td>39.0</td><td>22</td><td>Montana</td><td>37.1</td></tr>
<tr><td>43</td><td>Minnesota</td><td>30.3</td><td>23</td><td>Illinois</td><td>37.0</td></tr>
<tr><td>2</td><td>Mississippi</td><td>50.3</td><td>23</td><td>New York</td><td>37.0</td></tr>
<tr><td>17</td><td>Missouri</td><td>38.2</td><td>25</td><td>Pennsylvania</td><td>36.9</td></tr>
<tr><td>22</td><td>Montana</td><td>37.1</td><td>26</td><td>Wisconsin</td><td>36.8</td></tr>
<tr><td>20</td><td>Nebraska</td><td>38.0</td><td>27</td><td>North Dakota</td><td>36.7</td></tr>
<tr><td>47</td><td>Nevada</td><td>28.2</td><td>28</td><td>Iowa</td><td>36.5</td></tr>
<tr><td>49</td><td>New Hampshire</td><td>24.9</td><td>29</td><td>Wyoming</td><td>36.1</td></tr>
<tr><td>48</td><td>New Jersey</td><td>27.3</td><td>30</td><td>Colorado</td><td>35.2</td></tr>
<tr><td>5</td><td>New Mexico</td><td>46.5</td><td>31</td><td>Utah</td><td>34.8</td></tr>
<tr><td>23</td><td>New York</td><td>37.0</td><td>32</td><td>Idaho</td><td>34.7</td></tr>
<tr><td>13</td><td>North Carolina</td><td>39.7</td><td>33</td><td>South Dakota</td><td>34.3</td></tr>
<tr><td>27</td><td>North Dakota</td><td>36.7</td><td>34</td><td>Delaware</td><td>34.1</td></tr>
<tr><td>12</td><td>Ohio</td><td>39.9</td><td>35</td><td>Arizona</td><td>33.8</td></tr>
<tr><td>8</td><td>Oklahoma</td><td>44.5</td><td>36</td><td>Washington</td><td>33.3</td></tr>
<tr><td>19</td><td>Oregon</td><td>38.1</td><td>37</td><td>Florida</td><td>33.0</td></tr>
<tr><td>25</td><td>Pennsylvania</td><td>36.9</td><td>37</td><td>Massachusetts</td><td>33.0</td></tr>
<tr><td>40</td><td>Rhode Island</td><td>31.8</td><td>39</td><td>Vermont</td><td>32.5</td></tr>
<tr><td>11</td><td>South Carolina</td><td>41.5</td><td>40</td><td>Rhode Island</td><td>31.8</td></tr>
<tr><td>33</td><td>South Dakota</td><td>34.3</td><td>41</td><td>California</td><td>31.7</td></tr>
<tr><td>8</td><td>Tennessee</td><td>44.5</td><td>42</td><td>Alaska</td><td>30.4</td></tr>
<tr><td>10</td><td>Texas</td><td>42.0</td><td>43</td><td>Minnesota</td><td>30.3</td></tr>
<tr><td>31</td><td>Utah</td><td>34.8</td><td>44</td><td>Hawaii</td><td>29.0</td></tr>
<tr><td>39</td><td>Vermont</td><td>32.5</td><td>45</td><td>Connecticut</td><td>28.4</td></tr>
<tr><td>45</td><td>Virginia</td><td>28.4</td><td>45</td><td>Virginia</td><td>28.4</td></tr>
<tr><td>36</td><td>Washington</td><td>33.3</td><td>47</td><td>Nevada</td><td>28.2</td></tr>
<tr><td>1</td><td>West Virginia</td><td>50.6</td><td>48</td><td>New Jersey</td><td>27.3</td></tr>
<tr><td>26</td><td>Wisconsin</td><td>36.8</td><td>49</td><td>New Hampshire</td><td>24.9</td></tr>
<tr><td>29</td><td>Wyoming</td><td>36.1</td><td>50</td><td>Maryland</td><td>21.8</td></tr>
<tr><td></td><td></td><td></td><td></td><td>District of Columbia</td><td>40.2</td></tr>
</table>

Source: CQ Press using data from U.S. Bureau of the Census
"2006 American Community Survey" (http://www.census.gov/acs/www/index.html)
*Households headed by females with own children under 18 years living with them with incomes below the poverty level as a percent of all such female-headed households.

State and Local Government Expenditures for Public Welfare Programs in 2005

National Total = $362,007,160,000*

ALPHA ORDER

RANK	STATE	EXPENDITURES	% of USA
24	Alabama	$5,023,054,000	1.4%
44	Alaska	1,379,291,000	0.4%
21	Arizona	5,911,588,000	1.6%
31	Arkansas	3,304,340,000	0.9%
1	California	44,225,552,000	12.2%
32	Colorado	3,232,470,000	0.9%
26	Connecticut	4,360,233,000	1.2%
45	Delaware	1,122,499,000	0.3%
5	Florida	17,235,436,000	4.8%
13	Georgia	8,823,389,000	2.4%
42	Hawaii	1,439,657,000	0.4%
43	Idaho	1,405,225,000	0.4%
7	Illinois	13,148,278,000	3.6%
19	Indiana	6,284,135,000	1.7%
30	Iowa	3,480,923,000	1.0%
34	Kansas	2,762,589,000	0.8%
22	Kentucky	5,419,363,000	1.5%
25	Louisiana	4,479,959,000	1.2%
36	Maine	2,333,561,000	0.6%
20	Maryland	5,958,690,000	1.6%
8	Massachusetts	10,788,057,000	3.0%
9	Michigan	10,690,757,000	3.0%
10	Minnesota	9,715,876,000	2.7%
27	Mississippi	4,047,342,000	1.1%
18	Missouri	6,348,378,000	1.8%
47	Montana	804,487,000	0.2%
39	Nebraska	2,021,555,000	0.6%
40	Nevada	1,627,597,000	0.4%
41	New Hampshire	1,623,726,000	0.4%
12	New Jersey	9,124,735,000	2.5%
33	New Mexico	3,156,357,000	0.9%
2	New York	42,637,700,000	11.8%
11	North Carolina	9,645,781,000	2.7%
49	North Dakota	714,382,000	0.2%
6	Ohio	15,303,390,000	4.2%
29	Oklahoma	3,764,841,000	1.0%
28	Oregon	3,806,197,000	1.1%
3	Pennsylvania	20,420,553,000	5.6%
38	Rhode Island	2,045,215,000	0.6%
23	South Carolina	5,202,766,000	1.4%
48	South Dakota	744,940,000	0.2%
14	Tennessee	8,656,756,000	2.4%
4	Texas	19,387,475,000	5.4%
37	Utah	2,225,791,000	0.6%
46	Vermont	1,100,504,000	0.3%
17	Virginia	6,731,566,000	1.9%
16	Washington	6,757,968,000	1.9%
35	West Virginia	2,340,248,000	0.6%
15	Wisconsin	7,002,387,000	1.9%
50	Wyoming	550,249,000	0.2%

RANK ORDER

RANK	STATE	EXPENDITURES	% of USA
1	California	$44,225,552,000	12.2%
2	New York	42,637,700,000	11.8%
3	Pennsylvania	20,420,553,000	5.6%
4	Texas	19,387,475,000	5.4%
5	Florida	17,235,436,000	4.8%
6	Ohio	15,303,390,000	4.2%
7	Illinois	13,148,278,000	3.6%
8	Massachusetts	10,788,057,000	3.0%
9	Michigan	10,690,757,000	3.0%
10	Minnesota	9,715,876,000	2.7%
11	North Carolina	9,645,781,000	2.7%
12	New Jersey	9,124,735,000	2.5%
13	Georgia	8,823,389,000	2.4%
14	Tennessee	8,656,756,000	2.4%
15	Wisconsin	7,002,387,000	1.9%
16	Washington	6,757,968,000	1.9%
17	Virginia	6,731,566,000	1.9%
18	Missouri	6,348,378,000	1.8%
19	Indiana	6,284,135,000	1.7%
20	Maryland	5,958,690,000	1.6%
21	Arizona	5,911,588,000	1.6%
22	Kentucky	5,419,363,000	1.5%
23	South Carolina	5,202,766,000	1.4%
24	Alabama	5,023,054,000	1.4%
25	Louisiana	4,479,959,000	1.2%
26	Connecticut	4,360,233,000	1.2%
27	Mississippi	4,047,342,000	1.1%
28	Oregon	3,806,197,000	1.1%
29	Oklahoma	3,764,841,000	1.0%
30	Iowa	3,480,923,000	1.0%
31	Arkansas	3,304,340,000	0.9%
32	Colorado	3,232,470,000	0.9%
33	New Mexico	3,156,357,000	0.9%
34	Kansas	2,762,589,000	0.8%
35	West Virginia	2,340,248,000	0.6%
36	Maine	2,333,561,000	0.6%
37	Utah	2,225,791,000	0.6%
38	Rhode Island	2,045,215,000	0.6%
39	Nebraska	2,021,555,000	0.6%
40	Nevada	1,627,597,000	0.4%
41	New Hampshire	1,623,726,000	0.4%
42	Hawaii	1,439,657,000	0.4%
43	Idaho	1,405,225,000	0.4%
44	Alaska	1,379,291,000	0.4%
45	Delaware	1,122,499,000	0.3%
46	Vermont	1,100,504,000	0.3%
47	Montana	804,487,000	0.2%
48	South Dakota	744,940,000	0.2%
49	North Dakota	714,382,000	0.2%
50	Wyoming	550,249,000	0.2%
	District of Columbia	1,689,352,000	0.5%

Source: U.S. Bureau of the Census, Governments Division
"State and Local Government Finances: 2004-2005" (http://www.census.gov/govs/www/estimate05.html)
*Direct general expenditures. Includes funds for cash assistance programs, medical and other vendor payments, welfare institutions, and other public welfare programs.

Per Capita State and Local Government Expenditures
for Public Welfare Programs in 2005
National Per Capita = $1,223*

ALPHA ORDER

RANK	STATE	PER CAPITA
27	Alabama	$1,106
2	Alaska	2,060
40	Arizona	993
21	Arkansas	1,192
19	California	1,229
49	Colorado	692
17	Connecticut	1,251
12	Delaware	1,335
42	Florida	972
43	Georgia	969
24	Hawaii	1,136
41	Idaho	986
36	Illinois	1,034
38	Indiana	1,004
22	Iowa	1,178
37	Kansas	1,008
14	Kentucky	1,299
39	Louisiana	997
5	Maine	1,778
31	Maryland	1,069
7	Massachusetts	1,678
33	Michigan	1,058
4	Minnesota	1,900
11	Mississippi	1,395
28	Missouri	1,097
47	Montana	860
23	Nebraska	1,153
50	Nevada	676
18	New Hampshire	1,246
34	New Jersey	1,054
9	New Mexico	1,647
1	New York	2,214
26	North Carolina	1,111
25	North Dakota	1,123
12	Ohio	1,335
32	Oklahoma	1,065
35	Oregon	1,049
8	Pennsylvania	1,651
3	Rhode Island	1,917
20	South Carolina	1,223
44	South Dakota	955
10	Tennessee	1,445
48	Texas	849
46	Utah	889
6	Vermont	1,776
45	Virginia	891
30	Washington	1,078
15	West Virginia	1,296
16	Wisconsin	1,264
29	Wyoming	1,086

RANK ORDER

RANK	STATE	PER CAPITA
1	New York	$2,214
2	Alaska	2,060
3	Rhode Island	1,917
4	Minnesota	1,900
5	Maine	1,778
6	Vermont	1,776
7	Massachusetts	1,678
8	Pennsylvania	1,651
9	New Mexico	1,647
10	Tennessee	1,445
11	Mississippi	1,395
12	Delaware	1,335
12	Ohio	1,335
14	Kentucky	1,299
15	West Virginia	1,296
16	Wisconsin	1,264
17	Connecticut	1,251
18	New Hampshire	1,246
19	California	1,229
20	South Carolina	1,223
21	Arkansas	1,192
22	Iowa	1,178
23	Nebraska	1,153
24	Hawaii	1,136
25	North Dakota	1,123
26	North Carolina	1,111
27	Alabama	1,106
28	Missouri	1,097
29	Wyoming	1,086
30	Washington	1,078
31	Maryland	1,069
32	Oklahoma	1,065
33	Michigan	1,058
34	New Jersey	1,054
35	Oregon	1,049
36	Illinois	1,034
37	Kansas	1,008
38	Indiana	1,004
39	Louisiana	997
40	Arizona	993
41	Idaho	986
42	Florida	972
43	Georgia	969
44	South Dakota	955
45	Virginia	891
46	Utah	889
47	Montana	860
48	Texas	849
49	Colorado	692
50	Nevada	676

District of Columbia   2,902

Source: CQ Press using data from U.S. Bureau of the Census, Governments Division
"State and Local Government Finances: 2004-2005" (http://www.census.gov/govs/www/estimate05.html)
*Direct general expenditures. Includes funds for cash assistance programs, medical and other vendor payments, welfare institutions, and other public welfare programs.

State and Local Government Spending for Public Welfare Programs as a Percent of All State and Local Government Expenditures in 2005
National Percent = 18.0%*

<table>
<tr><td colspan="3">ALPHA ORDER</td><td colspan="3">RANK ORDER</td></tr>
<tr><td>RANK</td><td>STATE</td><td>PERCENT</td><td>RANK</td><td>STATE</td><td>PERCENT</td></tr>
<tr><td>26</td><td>Alabama</td><td>17.3</td><td>1</td><td>Minnesota</td><td>25.6</td></tr>
<tr><td>38</td><td>Alaska</td><td>15.7</td><td>2</td><td>Tennessee</td><td>25.5</td></tr>
<tr><td>22</td><td>Arizona</td><td>18.0</td><td>3</td><td>Rhode Island</td><td>25.4</td></tr>
<tr><td>12</td><td>Arkansas</td><td>21.3</td><td>4</td><td>Maine</td><td>24.5</td></tr>
<tr><td>34</td><td>California</td><td>16.0</td><td>5</td><td>Pennsylvania</td><td>23.7</td></tr>
<tr><td>48</td><td>Colorado</td><td>11.1</td><td>6</td><td>Vermont</td><td>23.3</td></tr>
<tr><td>28</td><td>Connecticut</td><td>16.6</td><td>7</td><td>New York</td><td>23.2</td></tr>
<tr><td>29</td><td>Delaware</td><td>16.5</td><td>8</td><td>Kentucky</td><td>23.1</td></tr>
<tr><td>41</td><td>Florida</td><td>15.3</td><td>9</td><td>Mississippi</td><td>22.7</td></tr>
<tr><td>24</td><td>Georgia</td><td>17.4</td><td>10</td><td>New Mexico</td><td>22.4</td></tr>
<tr><td>40</td><td>Hawaii</td><td>15.4</td><td>11</td><td>Massachusetts</td><td>21.7</td></tr>
<tr><td>24</td><td>Idaho</td><td>17.4</td><td>12</td><td>Arkansas</td><td>21.3</td></tr>
<tr><td>34</td><td>Illinois</td><td>16.0</td><td>13</td><td>West Virginia</td><td>21.1</td></tr>
<tr><td>29</td><td>Indiana</td><td>16.5</td><td>14</td><td>New Hampshire</td><td>20.7</td></tr>
<tr><td>23</td><td>Iowa</td><td>17.9</td><td>15</td><td>Oklahoma</td><td>19.7</td></tr>
<tr><td>31</td><td>Kansas</td><td>16.4</td><td>16</td><td>Ohio</td><td>19.6</td></tr>
<tr><td>8</td><td>Kentucky</td><td>23.1</td><td>17</td><td>Missouri</td><td>19.5</td></tr>
<tr><td>38</td><td>Louisiana</td><td>15.7</td><td>18</td><td>South Carolina</td><td>18.6</td></tr>
<tr><td>4</td><td>Maine</td><td>24.5</td><td>18</td><td>Wisconsin</td><td>18.6</td></tr>
<tr><td>33</td><td>Maryland</td><td>16.3</td><td>20</td><td>Nebraska</td><td>18.4</td></tr>
<tr><td>11</td><td>Massachusetts</td><td>21.7</td><td>21</td><td>North Carolina</td><td>18.3</td></tr>
<tr><td>37</td><td>Michigan</td><td>15.9</td><td>22</td><td>Arizona</td><td>18.0</td></tr>
<tr><td>1</td><td>Minnesota</td><td>25.6</td><td>23</td><td>Iowa</td><td>17.9</td></tr>
<tr><td>9</td><td>Mississippi</td><td>22.7</td><td>24</td><td>Georgia</td><td>17.4</td></tr>
<tr><td>17</td><td>Missouri</td><td>19.5</td><td>24</td><td>Idaho</td><td>17.4</td></tr>
<tr><td>46</td><td>Montana</td><td>14.0</td><td>26</td><td>Alabama</td><td>17.3</td></tr>
<tr><td>20</td><td>Nebraska</td><td>18.4</td><td>27</td><td>South Dakota</td><td>16.8</td></tr>
<tr><td>49</td><td>Nevada</td><td>10.9</td><td>28</td><td>Connecticut</td><td>16.6</td></tr>
<tr><td>14</td><td>New Hampshire</td><td>20.7</td><td>29</td><td>Delaware</td><td>16.5</td></tr>
<tr><td>47</td><td>New Jersey</td><td>13.8</td><td>29</td><td>Indiana</td><td>16.5</td></tr>
<tr><td>10</td><td>New Mexico</td><td>22.4</td><td>31</td><td>Kansas</td><td>16.4</td></tr>
<tr><td>7</td><td>New York</td><td>23.2</td><td>31</td><td>North Dakota</td><td>16.4</td></tr>
<tr><td>21</td><td>North Carolina</td><td>18.3</td><td>33</td><td>Maryland</td><td>16.3</td></tr>
<tr><td>31</td><td>North Dakota</td><td>16.4</td><td>34</td><td>California</td><td>16.0</td></tr>
<tr><td>16</td><td>Ohio</td><td>19.6</td><td>34</td><td>Illinois</td><td>16.0</td></tr>
<tr><td>15</td><td>Oklahoma</td><td>19.7</td><td>34</td><td>Oregon</td><td>16.0</td></tr>
<tr><td>34</td><td>Oregon</td><td>16.0</td><td>37</td><td>Michigan</td><td>15.9</td></tr>
<tr><td>5</td><td>Pennsylvania</td><td>23.7</td><td>38</td><td>Alaska</td><td>15.7</td></tr>
<tr><td>3</td><td>Rhode Island</td><td>25.4</td><td>38</td><td>Louisiana</td><td>15.7</td></tr>
<tr><td>18</td><td>South Carolina</td><td>18.6</td><td>40</td><td>Hawaii</td><td>15.4</td></tr>
<tr><td>27</td><td>South Dakota</td><td>16.8</td><td>41</td><td>Florida</td><td>15.3</td></tr>
<tr><td>2</td><td>Tennessee</td><td>25.5</td><td>41</td><td>Utah</td><td>15.3</td></tr>
<tr><td>44</td><td>Texas</td><td>14.8</td><td>43</td><td>Washington</td><td>15.2</td></tr>
<tr><td>41</td><td>Utah</td><td>15.3</td><td>44</td><td>Texas</td><td>14.8</td></tr>
<tr><td>6</td><td>Vermont</td><td>23.3</td><td>45</td><td>Virginia</td><td>14.4</td></tr>
<tr><td>45</td><td>Virginia</td><td>14.4</td><td>46</td><td>Montana</td><td>14.0</td></tr>
<tr><td>43</td><td>Washington</td><td>15.2</td><td>47</td><td>New Jersey</td><td>13.8</td></tr>
<tr><td>13</td><td>West Virginia</td><td>21.1</td><td>48</td><td>Colorado</td><td>11.1</td></tr>
<tr><td>18</td><td>Wisconsin</td><td>18.6</td><td>49</td><td>Nevada</td><td>10.9</td></tr>
<tr><td>50</td><td>Wyoming</td><td>10.8</td><td>50</td><td>Wyoming</td><td>10.8</td></tr>
<tr><td></td><td></td><td></td><td></td><td>District of Columbia</td><td>23.3</td></tr>
</table>

Source: CQ Press using data from U.S. Bureau of the Census, Governments Division
"State and Local Government Finances: 2004-2005" (http://www.census.gov/govs/www/estimate05.html)
*As a percent of direct general expenditures. Includes funds for cash assistance programs, medical and other vendor payments, welfare institutions, and other public welfare programs.

Social Security (OASDI) Payments in 2005

National Total = $520,561,000,000*

ALPHA ORDER

RANK	STATE	PAYMENTS	% of USA
20	Alabama	$9,259,000,000	1.8%
50	Alaska	659,000,000	0.1%
19	Arizona	10,030,000,000	1.9%
31	Arkansas	5,564,000,000	1.1%
1	California	48,106,000,000	9.2%
29	Colorado	6,227,000,000	1.2%
26	Connecticut	6,917,000,000	1.3%
45	Delaware	1,725,000,000	0.3%
2	Florida	36,891,000,000	7.1%
11	Georgia	12,846,000,000	2.5%
42	Hawaii	2,162,000,000	0.4%
41	Idaho	2,379,000,000	0.5%
7	Illinois	21,364,000,000	4.1%
13	Indiana	11,872,000,000	2.3%
30	Iowa	5,946,000,000	1.1%
33	Kansas	4,974,000,000	1.0%
23	Kentucky	8,129,000,000	1.6%
25	Louisiana	7,378,000,000	1.4%
39	Maine	2,686,000,000	0.5%
22	Maryland	8,512,000,000	1.6%
14	Massachusetts	11,691,000,000	2.2%
8	Michigan	20,106,000,000	3.9%
21	Minnesota	8,525,000,000	1.6%
32	Mississippi	5,395,000,000	1.0%
16	Missouri	11,281,000,000	2.2%
44	Montana	1,748,000,000	0.3%
36	Nebraska	3,120,000,000	0.6%
35	Nevada	3,830,000,000	0.7%
40	New Hampshire	2,485,000,000	0.5%
9	New Jersey	16,474,000,000	3.2%
37	New Mexico	3,079,000,000	0.6%
3	New York	34,797,000,000	6.7%
10	North Carolina	15,856,000,000	3.0%
48	North Dakota	1,174,000,000	0.2%
6	Ohio	21,546,000,000	4.1%
28	Oklahoma	6,606,000,000	1.3%
27	Oregon	6,837,000,000	1.3%
5	Pennsylvania	27,072,000,000	5.2%
43	Rhode Island	2,089,000,000	0.4%
24	South Carolina	8,100,000,000	1.6%
46	South Dakota	1,415,000,000	0.3%
15	Tennessee	11,406,000,000	2.2%
4	Texas	30,684,000,000	5.9%
38	Utah	2,913,000,000	0.6%
47	Vermont	1,184,000,000	0.2%
12	Virginia	12,115,000,000	2.3%
18	Washington	10,474,000,000	2.0%
34	West Virginia	4,417,000,000	0.8%
17	Wisconsin	10,551,000,000	2.0%
49	Wyoming	908,000,000	0.2%

RANK ORDER

RANK	STATE	PAYMENTS	% of USA
1	California	$48,106,000,000	9.2%
2	Florida	36,891,000,000	7.1%
3	New York	34,797,000,000	6.7%
4	Texas	30,684,000,000	5.9%
5	Pennsylvania	27,072,000,000	5.2%
6	Ohio	21,546,000,000	4.1%
7	Illinois	21,364,000,000	4.1%
8	Michigan	20,106,000,000	3.9%
9	New Jersey	16,474,000,000	3.2%
10	North Carolina	15,856,000,000	3.0%
11	Georgia	12,846,000,000	2.5%
12	Virginia	12,115,000,000	2.3%
13	Indiana	11,872,000,000	2.3%
14	Massachusetts	11,691,000,000	2.2%
15	Tennessee	11,406,000,000	2.2%
16	Missouri	11,281,000,000	2.2%
17	Wisconsin	10,551,000,000	2.0%
18	Washington	10,474,000,000	2.0%
19	Arizona	10,030,000,000	1.9%
20	Alabama	9,259,000,000	1.8%
21	Minnesota	8,525,000,000	1.6%
22	Maryland	8,512,000,000	1.6%
23	Kentucky	8,129,000,000	1.6%
24	South Carolina	8,100,000,000	1.6%
25	Louisiana	7,378,000,000	1.4%
26	Connecticut	6,917,000,000	1.3%
27	Oregon	6,837,000,000	1.3%
28	Oklahoma	6,606,000,000	1.3%
29	Colorado	6,227,000,000	1.2%
30	Iowa	5,946,000,000	1.1%
31	Arkansas	5,564,000,000	1.1%
32	Mississippi	5,395,000,000	1.0%
33	Kansas	4,974,000,000	1.0%
34	West Virginia	4,417,000,000	0.8%
35	Nevada	3,830,000,000	0.7%
36	Nebraska	3,120,000,000	0.6%
37	New Mexico	3,079,000,000	0.6%
38	Utah	2,913,000,000	0.6%
39	Maine	2,686,000,000	0.5%
40	New Hampshire	2,485,000,000	0.5%
41	Idaho	2,379,000,000	0.5%
42	Hawaii	2,162,000,000	0.4%
43	Rhode Island	2,089,000,000	0.4%
44	Montana	1,748,000,000	0.3%
45	Delaware	1,725,000,000	0.3%
46	South Dakota	1,415,000,000	0.3%
47	Vermont	1,184,000,000	0.2%
48	North Dakota	1,174,000,000	0.2%
49	Wyoming	908,000,000	0.2%
50	Alaska	659,000,000	0.1%
	District of Columbia	674,000,000	0.1%

Source: Social Security Administration
"Social Security Bulletin, Annual Statistical Supplement 2006"
(http://www.ssa.gov/policy/docs/statcomps/supplement/2006/5j.html)
*"OASDI" is Old Age, Survivors and Disability Insurance. National total includes $8,383,000,000 in payments to recipients in
U.S. territories and foreign countries.

Per Capita Social Security (OASDI) Payments in 2005

National Per Capita = $1,727*

ALPHA ORDER

RANK	STATE	PER CAPITA
6	Alabama	$2,036
50	Alaska	994
35	Arizona	1,685
7	Arkansas	2,005
48	California	1,331
47	Colorado	1,335
10	Connecticut	1,976
4	Delaware	2,049
3	Florida	2,076
45	Georgia	1,407
34	Hawaii	1,698
38	Idaho	1,664
36	Illinois	1,674
19	Indiana	1,895
7	Iowa	2,005
30	Kansas	1,810
11	Kentucky	1,948
40	Louisiana	1,637
5	Maine	2,038
44	Maryland	1,523
29	Massachusetts	1,817
9	Michigan	1,991
39	Minnesota	1,663
25	Mississippi	1,855
12	Missouri	1,946
23	Montana	1,870
33	Nebraska	1,775
43	Nevada	1,588
17	New Hampshire	1,902
20	New Jersey	1,893
42	New Mexico	1,599
31	New York	1,801
27	North Carolina	1,828
26	North Dakota	1,850
22	Ohio	1,878
24	Oklahoma	1,864
21	Oregon	1,879
2	Pennsylvania	2,182
12	Rhode Island	1,946
16	South Carolina	1,907
28	South Dakota	1,826
14	Tennessee	1,915
46	Texas	1,338
49	Utah	1,170
17	Vermont	1,902
41	Virginia	1,602
37	Washington	1,665
1	West Virginia	2,435
15	Wisconsin	1,909
32	Wyoming	1,785

RANK ORDER

RANK	STATE	PER CAPITA
1	West Virginia	$2,435
2	Pennsylvania	2,182
3	Florida	2,076
4	Delaware	2,049
5	Maine	2,038
6	Alabama	2,036
7	Arkansas	2,005
7	Iowa	2,005
9	Michigan	1,991
10	Connecticut	1,976
11	Kentucky	1,948
12	Missouri	1,946
12	Rhode Island	1,946
14	Tennessee	1,915
15	Wisconsin	1,909
16	South Carolina	1,907
17	New Hampshire	1,902
17	Vermont	1,902
19	Indiana	1,895
20	New Jersey	1,893
21	Oregon	1,879
22	Ohio	1,878
23	Montana	1,870
24	Oklahoma	1,864
25	Mississippi	1,855
26	North Dakota	1,850
27	North Carolina	1,828
28	South Dakota	1,826
29	Massachusetts	1,817
30	Kansas	1,810
31	New York	1,801
32	Wyoming	1,785
33	Nebraska	1,775
34	Hawaii	1,698
35	Arizona	1,685
36	Illinois	1,674
37	Washington	1,665
38	Idaho	1,664
39	Minnesota	1,663
40	Louisiana	1,637
41	Virginia	1,602
42	New Mexico	1,599
43	Nevada	1,588
44	Maryland	1,523
45	Georgia	1,407
46	Texas	1,338
47	Colorado	1,335
48	California	1,331
49	Utah	1,170
50	Alaska	994
	District of Columbia	1,158

Source: CQ Press using data from Social Security Administration
"Social Security Bulletin, Annual Statistical Supplement 2006"
(http://www.ssa.gov/policy/docs/statcomps/supplement/2006/5j.html)
*"OASDI" is Old Age, Survivors and Disability Insurance. National per capita does not include payments or population in U.S. territories and foreign countries.

Social Security (OASDI) Monthly Payments in 2005

National Total = $44,359,836,000*

ALPHA ORDER

RANK	STATE	PAYMENTS	% of USA
20	Alabama	$777,647,000	1.8%
50	Alaska	55,990,000	0.1%
19	Arizona	863,964,000	1.9%
31	Arkansas	469,576,000	1.1%
1	California	4,109,753,000	9.3%
29	Colorado	534,372,000	1.2%
26	Connecticut	596,201,000	1.3%
45	Delaware	148,333,000	0.3%
2	Florida	3,175,662,000	7.2%
11	Georgia	1,092,624,000	2.5%
42	Hawaii	187,948,000	0.4%
41	Idaho	204,866,000	0.5%
7	Illinois	1,818,840,000	4.1%
13	Indiana	1,013,004,000	2.3%
30	Iowa	507,038,000	1.1%
33	Kansas	424,873,000	1.0%
24	Kentucky	678,321,000	1.5%
25	Louisiana	597,689,000	1.3%
39	Maine	227,989,000	0.5%
22	Maryland	726,632,000	1.6%
14	Massachusetts	998,122,000	2.3%
8	Michigan	1,711,034,000	3.9%
21	Minnesota	732,320,000	1.7%
32	Mississippi	449,824,000	1.0%
16	Missouri	959,484,000	2.2%
44	Montana	149,841,000	0.3%
36	Nebraska	266,702,000	0.6%
35	Nevada	329,889,000	0.7%
40	New Hampshire	213,879,000	0.5%
9	New Jersey	1,415,475,000	3.2%
37	New Mexico	262,240,000	0.6%
3	New York	2,977,656,000	6.7%
10	North Carolina	1,357,989,000	3.1%
48	North Dakota	99,339,000	0.2%
6	Ohio	1,820,160,000	4.1%
28	Oklahoma	560,122,000	1.3%
27	Oregon	588,217,000	1.3%
5	Pennsylvania	2,304,192,000	5.2%
43	Rhode Island	178,943,000	0.4%
23	South Carolina	691,809,000	1.6%
46	South Dakota	120,721,000	0.3%
15	Tennessee	967,708,000	2.2%
4	Texas	2,602,270,000	5.9%
38	Utah	251,754,000	0.6%
47	Vermont	101,594,000	0.2%
12	Virginia	1,033,327,000	2.3%
18	Washington	902,750,000	2.0%
34	West Virginia	365,344,000	0.8%
17	Wisconsin	906,644,000	2.0%
49	Wyoming	78,015,000	0.2%

RANK ORDER

RANK	STATE	PAYMENTS	% of USA
1	California	$4,109,753,000	9.3%
2	Florida	3,175,662,000	7.2%
3	New York	2,977,656,000	6.7%
4	Texas	2,602,270,000	5.9%
5	Pennsylvania	2,304,192,000	5.2%
6	Ohio	1,820,160,000	4.1%
7	Illinois	1,818,840,000	4.1%
8	Michigan	1,711,034,000	3.9%
9	New Jersey	1,415,475,000	3.2%
10	North Carolina	1,357,989,000	3.1%
11	Georgia	1,092,624,000	2.5%
12	Virginia	1,033,327,000	2.3%
13	Indiana	1,013,004,000	2.3%
14	Massachusetts	998,122,000	2.3%
15	Tennessee	967,708,000	2.2%
16	Missouri	959,484,000	2.2%
17	Wisconsin	906,644,000	2.0%
18	Washington	902,750,000	2.0%
19	Arizona	863,964,000	1.9%
20	Alabama	777,647,000	1.8%
21	Minnesota	732,320,000	1.7%
22	Maryland	726,632,000	1.6%
23	South Carolina	691,809,000	1.6%
24	Kentucky	678,321,000	1.5%
25	Louisiana	597,689,000	1.3%
26	Connecticut	596,201,000	1.3%
27	Oregon	588,217,000	1.3%
28	Oklahoma	560,122,000	1.3%
29	Colorado	534,372,000	1.2%
30	Iowa	507,038,000	1.1%
31	Arkansas	469,576,000	1.1%
32	Mississippi	449,824,000	1.0%
33	Kansas	424,873,000	1.0%
34	West Virginia	365,344,000	0.8%
35	Nevada	329,889,000	0.7%
36	Nebraska	266,702,000	0.6%
37	New Mexico	262,240,000	0.6%
38	Utah	251,754,000	0.6%
39	Maine	227,989,000	0.5%
40	New Hampshire	213,879,000	0.5%
41	Idaho	204,866,000	0.5%
42	Hawaii	187,948,000	0.4%
43	Rhode Island	178,943,000	0.4%
44	Montana	149,841,000	0.3%
45	Delaware	148,333,000	0.3%
46	South Dakota	120,721,000	0.3%
47	Vermont	101,594,000	0.2%
48	North Dakota	99,339,000	0.2%
49	Wyoming	78,015,000	0.2%
50	Alaska	55,990,000	0.1%
	District of Columbia	57,217,000	0.1%

Source: Social Security Administration
   "Social Security Bulletin, Annual Statistical Supplement 2006"
      (http://www.ssa.gov/policy/docs/statcomps/supplement/2006/5j.html)
*For December 2005. "OASDI" is Old Age, Survivors and Disability Insurance. National total includes $693,933,000 in payments to recipients in U.S. territories and foreign countries.

Social Security (OASDI) Beneficiaries in 2005

National Total = 48,445,900*

RANK	STATE	BENEFICIARIES	% of USA
20	Alabama	903,830	1.9%
50	Alaska	65,040	0.1%
19	Arizona	918,830	1.9%
30	Arkansas	558,200	1.2%
1	California	4,460,390	9.2%
28	Colorado	587,740	1.2%
29	Connecticut	585,320	1.2%
45	Delaware	152,340	0.3%
2	Florida	3,423,660	7.1%
11	Georgia	1,231,430	2.5%
42	Hawaii	202,890	0.4%
40	Idaho	227,580	0.5%
7	Illinois	1,898,060	3.9%
16	Indiana	1,055,020	2.2%
32	Iowa	548,480	1.1%
33	Kansas	450,980	0.9%
21	Kentucky	798,940	1.6%
25	Louisiana	716,000	1.5%
39	Maine	269,310	0.6%
24	Maryland	772,340	1.6%
14	Massachusetts	1,071,720	2.2%
8	Michigan	1,742,680	3.6%
22	Minnesota	786,430	1.6%
31	Mississippi	551,860	1.1%
15	Missouri	1,064,020	2.2%
44	Montana	168,970	0.3%
37	Nebraska	293,510	0.6%
35	Nevada	348,040	0.7%
41	New Hampshire	225,550	0.5%
10	New Jersey	1,379,170	2.8%
36	New Mexico	311,120	0.6%
3	New York	3,063,640	6.3%
9	North Carolina	1,510,710	3.1%
47	North Dakota	115,260	0.2%
6	Ohio	1,965,370	4.1%
26	Oklahoma	635,170	1.3%
27	Oregon	624,670	1.3%
5	Pennsylvania	2,424,590	5.0%
43	Rhode Island	191,930	0.4%
23	South Carolina	773,700	1.6%
46	South Dakota	142,070	0.3%
13	Tennessee	1,097,610	2.3%
4	Texas	2,955,290	6.1%
38	Utah	272,080	0.6%
48	Vermont	112,190	0.2%
12	Virginia	1,138,720	2.4%
18	Washington	937,180	1.9%
34	West Virginia	412,910	0.9%
17	Wisconsin	951,670	2.0%
49	Wyoming	84,240	0.2%

RANK	STATE	BENEFICIARIES	% of USA
1	California	4,460,390	9.2%
2	Florida	3,423,660	7.1%
3	New York	3,063,640	6.3%
4	Texas	2,955,290	6.1%
5	Pennsylvania	2,424,590	5.0%
6	Ohio	1,965,370	4.1%
7	Illinois	1,898,060	3.9%
8	Michigan	1,742,680	3.6%
9	North Carolina	1,510,710	3.1%
10	New Jersey	1,379,170	2.8%
11	Georgia	1,231,430	2.5%
12	Virginia	1,138,720	2.4%
13	Tennessee	1,097,610	2.3%
14	Massachusetts	1,071,720	2.2%
15	Missouri	1,064,020	2.2%
16	Indiana	1,055,020	2.2%
17	Wisconsin	951,670	2.0%
18	Washington	937,180	1.9%
19	Arizona	918,830	1.9%
20	Alabama	903,830	1.9%
21	Kentucky	798,940	1.6%
22	Minnesota	786,430	1.6%
23	South Carolina	773,700	1.6%
24	Maryland	772,340	1.6%
25	Louisiana	716,000	1.5%
26	Oklahoma	635,170	1.3%
27	Oregon	624,670	1.3%
28	Colorado	587,740	1.2%
29	Connecticut	585,320	1.2%
30	Arkansas	558,200	1.2%
31	Mississippi	551,860	1.1%
32	Iowa	548,480	1.1%
33	Kansas	450,980	0.9%
34	West Virginia	412,910	0.9%
35	Nevada	348,040	0.7%
36	New Mexico	311,120	0.6%
37	Nebraska	293,510	0.6%
38	Utah	272,080	0.6%
39	Maine	269,310	0.6%
40	Idaho	227,580	0.5%
41	New Hampshire	225,550	0.5%
42	Hawaii	202,890	0.4%
43	Rhode Island	191,930	0.4%
44	Montana	168,970	0.3%
45	Delaware	152,340	0.3%
46	South Dakota	142,070	0.3%
47	North Dakota	115,260	0.2%
48	Vermont	112,190	0.2%
49	Wyoming	84,240	0.2%
50	Alaska	65,040	0.1%
	District of Columbia	71,190	0.1%

Source: Social Security Administration
"Social Security Bulletin, Annual Statistical Supplement 2006"
(http://www.ssa.gov/policy/docs/statcomps/supplement/2006/5j.html)
*For December 2005. "OASDI" is Old Age, Survivors and Disability Insurance. National total includes 1,196,260 beneficiaries in U.S. territories and foreign countries.

Average Monthly Social Security (OASDI) Payment in 2005

National Average = $924 Each Month per Beneficiary*

ALPHA ORDER

RANK	STATE	AVERAGE BENEFIT
43	Alabama	$860
42	Alaska	861
16	Arizona	940
48	Arkansas	841
26	California	921
27	Colorado	909
2	Connecticut	1,019
4	Delaware	974
20	Florida	928
35	Georgia	887
21	Hawaii	926
32	Idaho	900
8	Illinois	958
7	Indiana	960
25	Iowa	924
13	Kansas	942
45	Kentucky	849
49	Louisiana	835
46	Maine	847
15	Maryland	941
18	Massachusetts	931
3	Michigan	982
18	Minnesota	931
50	Mississippi	815
31	Missouri	902
35	Montana	887
27	Nebraska	909
11	Nevada	948
11	New Hampshire	948
1	New Jersey	1,026
47	New Mexico	843
5	New York	972
33	North Carolina	899
41	North Dakota	862
21	Ohio	926
38	Oklahoma	882
13	Oregon	942
10	Pennsylvania	950
17	Rhode Island	932
34	South Carolina	894
44	South Dakota	850
38	Tennessee	882
40	Texas	881
24	Utah	925
30	Vermont	906
29	Virginia	907
6	Washington	963
37	West Virginia	885
9	Wisconsin	953
21	Wyoming	926

RANK ORDER

RANK	STATE	AVERAGE BENEFIT
1	New Jersey	$1,026
2	Connecticut	1,019
3	Michigan	982
4	Delaware	974
5	New York	972
6	Washington	963
7	Indiana	960
8	Illinois	958
9	Wisconsin	953
10	Pennsylvania	950
11	Nevada	948
11	New Hampshire	948
13	Kansas	942
13	Oregon	942
15	Maryland	941
16	Arizona	940
17	Rhode Island	932
18	Massachusetts	931
18	Minnesota	931
20	Florida	928
21	Hawaii	926
21	Ohio	926
21	Wyoming	926
24	Utah	925
25	Iowa	924
26	California	921
27	Colorado	909
27	Nebraska	909
29	Virginia	907
30	Vermont	906
31	Missouri	902
32	Idaho	900
33	North Carolina	899
34	South Carolina	894
35	Georgia	887
35	Montana	887
37	West Virginia	885
38	Oklahoma	882
38	Tennessee	882
40	Texas	881
41	North Dakota	862
42	Alaska	861
43	Alabama	860
44	South Dakota	850
45	Kentucky	849
46	Maine	847
47	New Mexico	843
48	Arkansas	841
49	Louisiana	835
50	Mississippi	815

District of Columbia   804

Source: CQ Press using data from Social Security Administration
"Social Security Bulletin, Annual Statistical Supplement 2006"
(http://www.ssa.gov/policy/docs/statcomps/supplement/2006/5j.html)
*As of December 2005. "OASDI" is Old Age, Survivors and Disability Insurance. National average does not include beneficiaries or payments in U.S. territories or foreign countries.

Social Security Supplemental Security Income Beneficiaries in 2005

National Total = 7,113,879 Beneficiaries*

ALPHA ORDER

RANK	STATE	BENEFICIARIES	% of USA
13	Alabama	163,709	2.3%
48	Alaska	11,027	0.2%
23	Arizona	97,703	1.4%
26	Arkansas	91,043	1.3%
1	California	1,212,069	17.0%
31	Colorado	55,441	0.8%
33	Connecticut	52,147	0.7%
44	Delaware	13,664	0.2%
4	Florida	422,466	5.9%
9	Georgia	202,747	2.9%
39	Hawaii	22,689	0.3%
42	Idaho	22,200	0.3%
6	Illinois	258,553	3.6%
22	Indiana	98,555	1.4%
34	Iowa	43,388	0.6%
35	Kansas	39,154	0.6%
11	Kentucky	180,225	2.5%
15	Louisiana	155,803	2.2%
37	Maine	31,978	0.4%
24	Maryland	94,418	1.3%
12	Massachusetts	171,488	2.4%
8	Michigan	222,073	3.1%
29	Minnesota	72,915	1.0%
18	Mississippi	124,561	1.8%
19	Missouri	117,613	1.7%
43	Montana	14,784	0.2%
41	Nebraska	22,334	0.3%
36	Nevada	32,977	0.5%
45	New Hampshire	13,636	0.2%
16	New Jersey	152,352	2.1%
32	New Mexico	53,773	0.8%
2	New York	635,079	8.9%
10	North Carolina	199,270	2.8%
49	North Dakota	7,917	0.1%
7	Ohio	250,283	3.5%
27	Oklahoma	79,564	1.1%
30	Oregon	60,557	0.9%
5	Pennsylvania	317,462	4.5%
38	Rhode Island	30,194	0.4%
21	South Carolina	105,341	1.5%
47	South Dakota	12,573	0.2%
14	Tennessee	161,099	2.3%
3	Texas	501,762	7.1%
40	Utah	22,587	0.3%
46	Vermont	13,138	0.2%
17	Virginia	137,340	1.9%
20	Washington	115,563	1.6%
28	West Virginia	76,728	1.1%
25	Wisconsin	92,225	1.3%
50	Wyoming	5,797	0.1%

RANK ORDER

RANK	STATE	BENEFICIARIES	% of USA
1	California	1,212,069	17.0%
2	New York	635,079	8.9%
3	Texas	501,762	7.1%
4	Florida	422,466	5.9%
5	Pennsylvania	317,462	4.5%
6	Illinois	258,553	3.6%
7	Ohio	250,283	3.5%
8	Michigan	222,073	3.1%
9	Georgia	202,747	2.9%
10	North Carolina	199,270	2.8%
11	Kentucky	180,225	2.5%
12	Massachusetts	171,488	2.4%
13	Alabama	163,709	2.3%
14	Tennessee	161,099	2.3%
15	Louisiana	155,803	2.2%
16	New Jersey	152,352	2.1%
17	Virginia	137,340	1.9%
18	Mississippi	124,561	1.8%
19	Missouri	117,613	1.7%
20	Washington	115,563	1.6%
21	South Carolina	105,341	1.5%
22	Indiana	98,555	1.4%
23	Arizona	97,703	1.4%
24	Maryland	94,418	1.3%
25	Wisconsin	92,225	1.3%
26	Arkansas	91,043	1.3%
27	Oklahoma	79,564	1.1%
28	West Virginia	76,728	1.1%
29	Minnesota	72,915	1.0%
30	Oregon	60,557	0.9%
31	Colorado	55,441	0.8%
32	New Mexico	53,773	0.8%
33	Connecticut	52,147	0.7%
34	Iowa	43,388	0.6%
35	Kansas	39,154	0.6%
36	Nevada	32,977	0.5%
37	Maine	31,978	0.4%
38	Rhode Island	30,194	0.4%
39	Hawaii	22,689	0.3%
40	Utah	22,587	0.3%
41	Nebraska	22,334	0.3%
42	Idaho	22,200	0.3%
43	Montana	14,784	0.2%
44	Delaware	13,664	0.2%
45	New Hampshire	13,636	0.2%
46	Vermont	13,138	0.2%
47	South Dakota	12,573	0.2%
48	Alaska	11,027	0.2%
49	North Dakota	7,917	0.1%
50	Wyoming	5,797	0.1%
	District of Columbia	21,166	0.3%

Source: Social Security Administration
"Social Security Bulletin, Annual Statistical Supplement 2006" (http://www.ssa.gov/policy/docs/statcomps/supplement/2006/)
*For December 2005. National total includes 749 beneficiaries in U.S. territories or otherwise not distributed by state. The SSI program provides income support to persons age 65 and older and blind or disabled adults and children.

Average Monthly Social Security Supplemental Security Income Payment: 2005

National Average = $439.09 Each Month per Beneficiary*

ALPHA ORDER

RANK	STATE	AVERAGE BENEFIT
38	Alabama	$385.73
27	Alaska	397.16
13	Arizona	416.47
44	Arkansas	377.16
1	California	570.55
32	Colorado	391.00
14	Connecticut	414.43
22	Delaware	404.79
21	Florida	405.29
39	Georgia	383.69
4	Hawaii	444.02
31	Idaho	394.64
6	Illinois	437.63
17	Indiana	411.12
40	Iowa	382.89
28	Kansas	396.69
23	Kentucky	403.57
25	Louisiana	399.42
47	Maine	375.20
12	Maryland	420.15
3	Massachusetts	447.61
7	Michigan	435.65
16	Minnesota	411.54
41	Mississippi	381.05
26	Missouri	397.98
34	Montana	388.51
43	Nebraska	378.64
18	Nevada	408.11
36	New Hampshire	387.34
11	New Jersey	424.36
33	New Mexico	388.61
2	New York	468.67
48	North Carolina	371.97
50	North Dakota	349.64
10	Ohio	429.73
30	Oklahoma	394.76
19	Oregon	406.66
8	Pennsylvania	435.03
5	Rhode Island	440.35
42	South Carolina	380.18
49	South Dakota	364.66
37	Tennessee	387.18
45	Texas	377.04
20	Utah	406.21
29	Vermont	395.99
35	Virginia	387.94
9	Washington	433.41
15	West Virginia	412.45
24	Wisconsin	400.56
46	Wyoming	376.84

RANK ORDER

RANK	STATE	AVERAGE BENEFIT
1	California	$570.55
2	New York	468.67
3	Massachusetts	447.61
4	Hawaii	444.02
5	Rhode Island	440.35
6	Illinois	437.63
7	Michigan	435.65
8	Pennsylvania	435.03
9	Washington	433.41
10	Ohio	429.73
11	New Jersey	424.36
12	Maryland	420.15
13	Arizona	416.47
14	Connecticut	414.43
15	West Virginia	412.45
16	Minnesota	411.54
17	Indiana	411.12
18	Nevada	408.11
19	Oregon	406.66
20	Utah	406.21
21	Florida	405.29
22	Delaware	404.79
23	Kentucky	403.57
24	Wisconsin	400.56
25	Louisiana	399.42
26	Missouri	397.98
27	Alaska	397.16
28	Kansas	396.69
29	Vermont	395.99
30	Oklahoma	394.76
31	Idaho	394.64
32	Colorado	391.00
33	New Mexico	388.61
34	Montana	388.51
35	Virginia	387.94
36	New Hampshire	387.34
37	Tennessee	387.18
38	Alabama	385.73
39	Georgia	383.69
40	Iowa	382.89
41	Mississippi	381.05
42	South Carolina	380.18
43	Nebraska	378.64
44	Arkansas	377.16
45	Texas	377.04
46	Wyoming	376.84
47	Maine	375.20
48	North Carolina	371.97
49	South Dakota	364.66
50	North Dakota	349.64
	District of Columbia	443.02

Source: Social Security Administration
"Social Security Bulletin, Annual Statistical Supplement 2006" (http://www.ssa.gov/policy/docs/statcomps/supplement/2006/)
*As of December 2005. National average includes payments to beneficiaries in U.S. territories and foreign countries. The SSI program provides income support to persons age 65 and older and blind or disabled adults and children.

Medicare Enrollees in 2006

National Total = 43,338,571 Enrollees*

ALPHA ORDER

RANK	STATE	ENROLLEES	% of USA
20	Alabama	772,280	1.8%
50	Alaska	54,305	0.1%
19	Arizona	815,115	1.9%
31	Arkansas	484,836	1.1%
1	California	4,275,113	9.9%
28	Colorado	539,883	1.2%
29	Connecticut	530,034	1.2%
45	Delaware	131,832	0.3%
2	Florida	3,079,554	7.1%
11	Georgia	1,075,265	2.5%
42	Hawaii	185,449	0.4%
40	Idaho	199,505	0.5%
7	Illinois	1,712,828	4.0%
16	Indiana	922,553	2.1%
30	Iowa	494,523	1.1%
33	Kansas	406,456	0.9%
23	Kentucky	694,894	1.6%
25	Louisiana	624,151	1.4%
39	Maine	240,568	0.6%
22	Maryland	708,049	1.6%
13	Massachusetts	981,691	2.3%
8	Michigan	1,510,532	3.5%
21	Minnesota	713,242	1.6%
32	Mississippi	461,641	1.1%
15	Missouri	929,501	2.1%
44	Montana	151,738	0.4%
37	Nebraska	264,307	0.6%
35	Nevada	306,777	0.7%
41	New Hampshire	197,821	0.5%
10	New Jersey	1,241,698	2.9%
36	New Mexico	275,806	0.6%
3	New York	2,804,725	6.5%
9	North Carolina	1,317,754	3.0%
47	North Dakota	104,418	0.2%
6	Ohio	1,778,058	4.1%
26	Oklahoma	553,545	1.3%
27	Oregon	552,856	1.3%
5	Pennsylvania	2,155,832	5.0%
43	Rhode Island	173,776	0.4%
24	South Carolina	673,965	1.6%
46	South Dakota	127,044	0.3%
14	Tennessee	949,263	2.2%
4	Texas	2,625,612	6.1%
38	Utah	245,960	0.6%
48	Vermont	99,071	0.2%
12	Virginia	1,017,880	2.3%
17	Washington	846,793	2.0%
34	West Virginia	361,308	0.8%
18	Wisconsin	839,806	1.9%
49	Wyoming	72,402	0.2%

RANK ORDER

RANK	STATE	ENROLLEES	% of USA
1	California	4,275,113	9.9%
2	Florida	3,079,554	7.1%
3	New York	2,804,725	6.5%
4	Texas	2,625,612	6.1%
5	Pennsylvania	2,155,832	5.0%
6	Ohio	1,778,058	4.1%
7	Illinois	1,712,828	4.0%
8	Michigan	1,510,532	3.5%
9	North Carolina	1,317,754	3.0%
10	New Jersey	1,241,698	2.9%
11	Georgia	1,075,265	2.5%
12	Virginia	1,017,880	2.3%
13	Massachusetts	981,691	2.3%
14	Tennessee	949,263	2.2%
15	Missouri	929,501	2.1%
16	Indiana	922,553	2.1%
17	Washington	846,793	2.0%
18	Wisconsin	839,806	1.9%
19	Arizona	815,115	1.9%
20	Alabama	772,280	1.8%
21	Minnesota	713,242	1.6%
22	Maryland	708,049	1.6%
23	Kentucky	694,894	1.6%
24	South Carolina	673,965	1.6%
25	Louisiana	624,151	1.4%
26	Oklahoma	553,545	1.3%
27	Oregon	552,856	1.3%
28	Colorado	539,883	1.2%
29	Connecticut	530,034	1.2%
30	Iowa	494,523	1.1%
31	Arkansas	484,836	1.1%
32	Mississippi	461,641	1.1%
33	Kansas	406,456	0.9%
34	West Virginia	361,308	0.8%
35	Nevada	306,777	0.7%
36	New Mexico	275,806	0.6%
37	Nebraska	264,307	0.6%
38	Utah	245,960	0.6%
39	Maine	240,568	0.6%
40	Idaho	199,505	0.5%
41	New Hampshire	197,821	0.5%
42	Hawaii	185,449	0.4%
43	Rhode Island	173,776	0.4%
44	Montana	151,738	0.4%
45	Delaware	131,832	0.3%
46	South Dakota	127,044	0.3%
47	North Dakota	104,418	0.2%
48	Vermont	99,071	0.2%
49	Wyoming	72,402	0.2%
50	Alaska	54,305	0.1%
	District of Columbia	73,575	0.2%

Source: U.S. Department of Health and Human Services, Centers for Medicare and Medicaid Services
"2007 Data Compendium" (http://www.cms.hhs.gov/DataCompendium/)
*Includes aged and disabled enrollees. Total includes 609,956 enrollees in Puerto Rico and other outlying areas, foreign countries or whose address is unknown.

Percent of Population Enrolled in Medicare in 2006

National Percent = 14.3% of Population*

ALPHA ORDER

RANK	STATE	PERCENT
6	Alabama	16.9
50	Alaska	8.2
39	Arizona	13.7
3	Arkansas	17.4
46	California	11.8
47	Colorado	11.6
25	Connecticut	15.1
18	Delaware	15.6
4	Florida	17.3
45	Georgia	11.9
32	Hawaii	14.5
36	Idaho	14.0
42	Illinois	13.4
30	Indiana	14.7
7	Iowa	16.7
29	Kansas	14.8
7	Kentucky	16.7
38	Louisiana	13.8
2	Maine	18.2
44	Maryland	12.6
21	Massachusetts	15.3
28	Michigan	14.9
37	Minnesota	13.9
16	Mississippi	15.8
13	Missouri	16.0
11	Montana	16.2
27	Nebraska	15.0
43	Nevada	12.7
25	New Hampshire	15.1
34	New Jersey	14.2
33	New Mexico	14.3
31	New York	14.6
22	North Carolina	15.2
9	North Dakota	16.4
20	Ohio	15.5
18	Oklahoma	15.6
22	Oregon	15.2
4	Pennsylvania	17.3
12	Rhode Island	16.1
16	South Carolina	15.8
9	South Dakota	16.4
14	Tennessee	15.9
48	Texas	11.5
49	Utah	10.0
14	Vermont	15.9
40	Virginia	13.5
40	Washington	13.5
1	West Virginia	19.9
22	Wisconsin	15.2
34	Wyoming	14.2

RANK ORDER

RANK	STATE	PERCENT
1	West Virginia	19.9
2	Maine	18.2
3	Arkansas	17.4
4	Florida	17.3
4	Pennsylvania	17.3
6	Alabama	16.9
7	Iowa	16.7
7	Kentucky	16.7
9	North Dakota	16.4
9	South Dakota	16.4
11	Montana	16.2
12	Rhode Island	16.1
13	Missouri	16.0
14	Tennessee	15.9
14	Vermont	15.9
16	Mississippi	15.8
16	South Carolina	15.8
18	Delaware	15.6
18	Oklahoma	15.6
20	Ohio	15.5
21	Massachusetts	15.3
22	North Carolina	15.2
22	Oregon	15.2
22	Wisconsin	15.2
25	Connecticut	15.1
25	New Hampshire	15.1
27	Nebraska	15.0
28	Michigan	14.9
29	Kansas	14.8
30	Indiana	14.7
31	New York	14.6
32	Hawaii	14.5
33	New Mexico	14.3
34	New Jersey	14.2
34	Wyoming	14.2
36	Idaho	14.0
37	Minnesota	13.9
38	Louisiana	13.8
39	Arizona	13.7
40	Virginia	13.5
40	Washington	13.5
42	Illinois	13.4
43	Nevada	12.7
44	Maryland	12.6
45	Georgia	11.9
46	California	11.8
47	Colorado	11.6
48	Texas	11.5
49	Utah	10.0
50	Alaska	8.2
	District of Columbia	13.4

Source: U.S. Department of Health and Human Services, Centers for Medicare and Medicaid Services
    "2007 Data Compendium" (http://www.cms.hhs.gov/DataCompendium/)
*Includes aged and disabled enrollees. National rate includes only residents of the 50 states and the District of Columbia.

Medicare Program Payments in 2006

National Total = $279,452,000,000*

<table>
<tr><td colspan="4">ALPHA ORDER</td><td colspan="4">RANK ORDER</td></tr>
<tr><th>RANK</th><th>STATE</th><th>BENEFITS</th><th>% of USA</th><th>RANK</th><th>STATE</th><th>BENEFITS</th><th>% of USA</th></tr>
<tr><td>18</td><td>Alabama</td><td>$5,052,000,000</td><td>1.8%</td><td>1</td><td>California</td><td>$23,204,000,000</td><td>8.3%</td></tr>
<tr><td>50</td><td>Alaska</td><td>350,000,000</td><td>0.1%</td><td>2</td><td>Florida</td><td>21,997,000,000</td><td>7.9%</td></tr>
<tr><td>26</td><td>Arizona</td><td>3,772,000,000</td><td>1.3%</td><td>3</td><td>Texas</td><td>20,915,000,000</td><td>7.5%</td></tr>
<tr><td>29</td><td>Arkansas</td><td>3,137,000,000</td><td>1.1%</td><td>4</td><td>New York</td><td>19,313,000,000</td><td>6.9%</td></tr>
<tr><td>1</td><td>California</td><td>23,204,000,000</td><td>8.3%</td><td>5</td><td>Illinois</td><td>13,124,000,000</td><td>4.7%</td></tr>
<tr><td>32</td><td>Colorado</td><td>2,705,000,000</td><td>1.0%</td><td>6</td><td>Ohio</td><td>12,104,000,000</td><td>4.3%</td></tr>
<tr><td>24</td><td>Connecticut</td><td>4,235,000,000</td><td>1.5%</td><td>7</td><td>Michigan</td><td>12,073,000,000</td><td>4.3%</td></tr>
<tr><td>42</td><td>Delaware</td><td>995,000,000</td><td>0.4%</td><td>8</td><td>Pennsylvania</td><td>11,818,000,000</td><td>4.2%</td></tr>
<tr><td>2</td><td>Florida</td><td>21,997,000,000</td><td>7.9%</td><td>9</td><td>New Jersey</td><td>10,356,000,000</td><td>3.7%</td></tr>
<tr><td>11</td><td>Georgia</td><td>7,388,000,000</td><td>2.6%</td><td>10</td><td>North Carolina</td><td>8,673,000,000</td><td>3.1%</td></tr>
<tr><td>47</td><td>Hawaii</td><td>599,000,000</td><td>0.2%</td><td>11</td><td>Georgia</td><td>7,388,000,000</td><td>2.6%</td></tr>
<tr><td>41</td><td>Idaho</td><td>1,013,000,000</td><td>0.4%</td><td>12</td><td>Massachusetts</td><td>6,957,000,000</td><td>2.5%</td></tr>
<tr><td>5</td><td>Illinois</td><td>13,124,000,000</td><td>4.7%</td><td>13</td><td>Indiana</td><td>6,407,000,000</td><td>2.3%</td></tr>
<tr><td>13</td><td>Indiana</td><td>6,407,000,000</td><td>2.3%</td><td>14</td><td>Virginia</td><td>6,352,000,000</td><td>2.3%</td></tr>
<tr><td>30</td><td>Iowa</td><td>2,869,000,000</td><td>1.0%</td><td>15</td><td>Maryland</td><td>6,350,000,000</td><td>2.3%</td></tr>
<tr><td>31</td><td>Kansas</td><td>2,731,000,000</td><td>1.0%</td><td>16</td><td>Tennessee</td><td>6,261,000,000</td><td>2.2%</td></tr>
<tr><td>21</td><td>Kentucky</td><td>4,766,000,000</td><td>1.7%</td><td>17</td><td>Missouri</td><td>5,883,000,000</td><td>2.1%</td></tr>
<tr><td>19</td><td>Louisiana</td><td>4,947,000,000</td><td>1.8%</td><td>18</td><td>Alabama</td><td>5,052,000,000</td><td>1.8%</td></tr>
<tr><td>37</td><td>Maine</td><td>1,466,000,000</td><td>0.5%</td><td>19</td><td>Louisiana</td><td>4,947,000,000</td><td>1.8%</td></tr>
<tr><td>15</td><td>Maryland</td><td>6,350,000,000</td><td>2.3%</td><td>20</td><td>Wisconsin</td><td>4,788,000,000</td><td>1.7%</td></tr>
<tr><td>12</td><td>Massachusetts</td><td>6,957,000,000</td><td>2.5%</td><td>21</td><td>Kentucky</td><td>4,766,000,000</td><td>1.7%</td></tr>
<tr><td>7</td><td>Michigan</td><td>12,073,000,000</td><td>4.3%</td><td>22</td><td>South Carolina</td><td>4,718,000,000</td><td>1.7%</td></tr>
<tr><td>27</td><td>Minnesota</td><td>3,674,000,000</td><td>1.3%</td><td>23</td><td>Washington</td><td>4,507,000,000</td><td>1.6%</td></tr>
<tr><td>28</td><td>Mississippi</td><td>3,555,000,000</td><td>1.3%</td><td>24</td><td>Connecticut</td><td>4,235,000,000</td><td>1.5%</td></tr>
<tr><td>17</td><td>Missouri</td><td>5,883,000,000</td><td>2.1%</td><td>25</td><td>Oklahoma</td><td>3,854,000,000</td><td>1.4%</td></tr>
<tr><td>44</td><td>Montana·</td><td>840,000,000</td><td>0.3%</td><td>26</td><td>Arizona</td><td>3,772,000,000</td><td>1.3%</td></tr>
<tr><td>35</td><td>Nebraska</td><td>1,679,000,000</td><td>0.6%</td><td>27</td><td>Minnesota</td><td>3,674,000,000</td><td>1.3%</td></tr>
<tr><td>36</td><td>Nevada</td><td>1,631,000,000</td><td>0.6%</td><td>28</td><td>Mississippi</td><td>3,555,000,000</td><td>1.3%</td></tr>
<tr><td>39</td><td>New Hampshire</td><td>1,337,000,000</td><td>0.5%</td><td>29</td><td>Arkansas</td><td>3,137,000,000</td><td>1.1%</td></tr>
<tr><td>9</td><td>New Jersey</td><td>10,356,000,000</td><td>3.7%</td><td>30</td><td>Iowa</td><td>2,869,000,000</td><td>1.0%</td></tr>
<tr><td>38</td><td>New Mexico</td><td>1,353,000,000</td><td>0.5%</td><td>31</td><td>Kansas</td><td>2,731,000,000</td><td>1.0%</td></tr>
<tr><td>4</td><td>New York</td><td>19,313,000,000</td><td>6.9%</td><td>32</td><td>Colorado</td><td>2,705,000,000</td><td>1.0%</td></tr>
<tr><td>10</td><td>North Carolina</td><td>8,673,000,000</td><td>3.1%</td><td>33</td><td>West Virginia</td><td>2,367,000,000</td><td>0.8%</td></tr>
<tr><td>48</td><td>North Dakota</td><td>591,000,000</td><td>0.2%</td><td>34</td><td>Oregon</td><td>2,141,000,000</td><td>0.8%</td></tr>
<tr><td>6</td><td>Ohio</td><td>12,104,000,000</td><td>4.3%</td><td>35</td><td>Nebraska</td><td>1,679,000,000</td><td>0.6%</td></tr>
<tr><td>25</td><td>Oklahoma</td><td>3,854,000,000</td><td>1.4%</td><td>36</td><td>Nevada</td><td>1,631,000,000</td><td>0.6%</td></tr>
<tr><td>34</td><td>Oregon</td><td>2,141,000,000</td><td>0.8%</td><td>37</td><td>Maine</td><td>1,466,000,000</td><td>0.5%</td></tr>
<tr><td>8</td><td>Pennsylvania</td><td>11,818,000,000</td><td>4.2%</td><td>38</td><td>New Mexico</td><td>1,353,000,000</td><td>0.5%</td></tr>
<tr><td>43</td><td>Rhode Island</td><td>858,000,000</td><td>0.3%</td><td>39</td><td>New Hampshire</td><td>1,337,000,000</td><td>0.5%</td></tr>
<tr><td>22</td><td>South Carolina</td><td>4,718,000,000</td><td>1.7%</td><td>40</td><td>Utah</td><td>1,300,000,000</td><td>0.5%</td></tr>
<tr><td>45</td><td>South Dakota</td><td>720,000,000</td><td>0.3%</td><td>41</td><td>Idaho</td><td>1,013,000,000</td><td>0.4%</td></tr>
<tr><td>16</td><td>Tennessee</td><td>6,261,000,000</td><td>2.2%</td><td>42</td><td>Delaware</td><td>995,000,000</td><td>0.4%</td></tr>
<tr><td>3</td><td>Texas</td><td>20,915,000,000</td><td>7.5%</td><td>43</td><td>Rhode Island</td><td>858,000,000</td><td>0.3%</td></tr>
<tr><td>40</td><td>Utah</td><td>1,300,000,000</td><td>0.5%</td><td>44</td><td>Montana</td><td>840,000,000</td><td>0.3%</td></tr>
<tr><td>46</td><td>Vermont</td><td>655,000,000</td><td>0.2%</td><td>45</td><td>South Dakota</td><td>720,000,000</td><td>0.3%</td></tr>
<tr><td>14</td><td>Virginia</td><td>6,352,000,000</td><td>2.3%</td><td>46</td><td>Vermont</td><td>655,000,000</td><td>0.2%</td></tr>
<tr><td>23</td><td>Washington</td><td>4,507,000,000</td><td>1.6%</td><td>47</td><td>Hawaii</td><td>599,000,000</td><td>0.2%</td></tr>
<tr><td>33</td><td>West Virginia</td><td>2,367,000,000</td><td>0.8%</td><td>48</td><td>North Dakota</td><td>591,000,000</td><td>0.2%</td></tr>
<tr><td>20</td><td>Wisconsin</td><td>4,788,000,000</td><td>1.7%</td><td>49</td><td>Wyoming</td><td>444,000,000</td><td>0.2%</td></tr>
<tr><td>49</td><td>Wyoming</td><td>444,000,000</td><td>0.2%</td><td>50</td><td>Alaska</td><td>350,000,000</td><td>0.1%</td></tr>
<tr><td></td><td></td><td></td><td></td><td></td><td>District of Columbia</td><td>630,000,000</td><td>0.2%</td></tr>
</table>

Source: U.S. Department of Health and Human Services, Centers for Medicare and Medicaid Services
  "Health Care Financing Review, 2007 Statistical Supplement" (http://cms.hhs.gov/MedicareMedicaidStatSupp)
*Figures for calendar year 2006. Includes payments to aged and disabled enrollees. Total does not include payments to beneficiaries in Puerto Rico and other outlying areas.

Medicare Program Payments per Enrollee in 2006

National Rate = $7,941*

ALPHA ORDER				RANK ORDER		
RANK	STATE	PER ENROLLEE		RANK	STATE	PER ENROLLEE
21	Alabama	$7,479		1	Maryland	$9,427
37	Alaska	6,625		2	Florida	9,273
29	Arizona	7,202		3	Louisiana	9,234
31	Arkansas	6,974		4	Texas	9,076
11	California	8,088		5	New Jersey	9,069
30	Colorado	7,135		6	New York	8,794
7	Connecticut	8,554		7	Connecticut	8,554
18	Delaware	7,548		8	Michigan	8,486
2	Florida	9,273		9	Massachusetts	8,474
25	Georgia	7,363		10	Illinois	8,193
50	Hawaii	4,953		11	California	8,088
46	Idaho	6,056		12	Mississippi	8,025
10	Illinois	8,193		13	Ohio	7,997
20	Indiana	7,481		14	Pennsylvania	7,898
39	Iowa	6,505		15	Oklahoma	7,795
27	Kansas	7,252		16	Tennessee	7,744
24	Kentucky	7,367		17	South Carolina	7,562
3	Louisiana	9,234		18	Delaware	7,548
44	Maine	6,187		19	Rhode Island	7,517
1	Maryland	9,427		20	Indiana	7,481
9	Massachusetts	8,474		21	Alabama	7,479
8	Michigan	8,486		22	Nevada	7,448
32	Minnesota	6,961		23	North Carolina	7,412
12	Mississippi	8,025		24	Kentucky	7,367
26	Missouri	7,348		25	Georgia	7,363
47	Montana	5,946		26	Missouri	7,348
35	Nebraska	6,792		27	Kansas	7,252
22	Nevada	7,448		28	West Virginia	7,204
33	New Hampshire	6,949		29	Arizona	7,202
5	New Jersey	9,069		30	Colorado	7,135
43	New Mexico	6,245		31	Arkansas	6,974
6	New York	8,794		32	Minnesota	6,961
23	North Carolina	7,412		33	New Hampshire	6,949
48	North Dakota	5,898		34	Wisconsin	6,829
13	Ohio	7,997		35	Nebraska	6,792
15	Oklahoma	7,795		36	Virginia	6,709
45	Oregon	6,125		37	Alaska	6,625
14	Pennsylvania	7,898		38	Vermont	6,564
19	Rhode Island	7,517		39	Iowa	6,505
17	South Carolina	7,562		40	Washington	6,485
49	South Dakota	5,840		41	Utah	6,477
16	Tennessee	7,744		42	Wyoming	6,276
4	Texas	9,076		43	New Mexico	6,245
41	Utah	6,477		44	Maine	6,187
38	Vermont	6,564		45	Oregon	6,125
36	Virginia	6,709		46	Idaho	6,056
40	Washington	6,485		47	Montana	5,946
28	West Virginia	7,204		48	North Dakota	5,898
34	Wisconsin	6,829		49	South Dakota	5,840
42	Wyoming	6,276		50	Hawaii	4,953
					District of Columbia	9,149

Source: U.S. Department of Health and Human Services, Centers for Medicare and Medicaid Services
"Health Care Financing Review, 2007 Statistical Supplement" (http://cms.hhs.gov/MedicareMedicaidStatSupp)
*Figures for calendar year 2006. Includes payments to aged and disabled enrollees. National figure does not include enrollees in managed care plans in the denominator used to calculate average payments. National rate also does not include payments or enrollees in Puerto Rico and other outlying areas.

Medicaid Enrollment in 2006

National Total = 45,156,803 Enrollees*

ALPHA ORDER

RANK	STATE	ENROLLEES	% of USA
20	Alabama	738,971	1.6%
46	Alaska	103,671	0.2%
14	Arizona	970,967	2.2%
25	Arkansas	630,671	1.4%
1	California	6,435,557	14.3%
32	Colorado	390,520	0.9%
30	Connecticut	404,719	0.9%
43	Delaware	146,807	0.3%
4	Florida	2,206,524	4.9%
10	Georgia	1,271,472	2.8%
38	Hawaii	199,903	0.4%
42	Idaho	165,187	0.4%
5	Illinois	1,993,000	4.4%
19	Indiana	824,938	1.8%
33	Iowa	323,966	0.7%
35	Kansas	261,457	0.6%
21	Kentucky	708,837	1.6%
15	Louisiana	942,734	2.1%
36	Maine	251,060	0.6%
23	Maryland	692,437	1.5%
12	Massachusetts	1,091,128	2.4%
8	Michigan	1,475,917	3.3%
27	Minnesota	579,528	1.3%
28	Mississippi	555,881	1.2%
18	Missouri	825,378	1.8%
48	Montana	79,598	0.2%
37	Nebraska	208,836	0.5%
41	Nevada	166,471	0.4%
45	New Hampshire	110,117	0.2%
16	New Jersey	863,641	1.9%
29	New Mexico	426,118	0.9%
2	New York	4,024,784	8.9%
9	North Carolina	1,287,498	2.9%
50	North Dakota	51,447	0.1%
7	Ohio	1,729,515	3.8%
26	Oklahoma	581,308	1.3%
31	Oregon	402,371	0.9%
6	Pennsylvania	1,802,430	4.0%
40	Rhode Island	183,111	0.4%
24	South Carolina	667,581	1.5%
47	South Dakota	99,647	0.2%
11	Tennessee	1,179,335	2.6%
3	Texas	2,778,761	6.2%
39	Utah	198,243	0.4%
44	Vermont	130,608	0.3%
22	Virginia	701,193	1.6%
13	Washington	999,031	2.2%
34	West Virginia	293,056	0.6%
17	Wisconsin	844,962	1.9%
49	Wyoming	62,459	0.1%

RANK ORDER

RANK	STATE	ENROLLEES	% of USA
1	California	6,435,557	14.3%
2	New York	4,024,784	8.9%
3	Texas	2,778,761	6.2%
4	Florida	2,206,524	4.9%
5	Illinois	1,993,000	4.4%
6	Pennsylvania	1,802,430	4.0%
7	Ohio	1,729,515	3.8%
8	Michigan	1,475,917	3.3%
9	North Carolina	1,287,498	2.9%
10	Georgia	1,271,472	2.8%
11	Tennessee	1,179,335	2.6%
12	Massachusetts	1,091,128	2.4%
13	Washington	999,031	2.2%
14	Arizona	970,967	2.2%
15	Louisiana	942,734	2.1%
16	New Jersey	863,641	1.9%
17	Wisconsin	844,962	1.9%
18	Missouri	825,378	1.8%
19	Indiana	824,938	1.8%
20	Alabama	738,971	1.6%
21	Kentucky	708,837	1.6%
22	Virginia	701,193	1.6%
23	Maryland	692,437	1.5%
24	South Carolina	667,581	1.5%
25	Arkansas	630,671	1.4%
26	Oklahoma	581,308	1.3%
27	Minnesota	579,528	1.3%
28	Mississippi	555,881	1.2%
29	New Mexico	426,118	0.9%
30	Connecticut	404,719	0.9%
31	Oregon	402,371	0.9%
32	Colorado	390,520	0.9%
33	Iowa	323,966	0.7%
34	West Virginia	293,056	0.6%
35	Kansas	261,457	0.6%
36	Maine	251,060	0.6%
37	Nebraska	208,836	0.5%
38	Hawaii	199,903	0.4%
39	Utah	198,243	0.4%
40	Rhode Island	183,111	0.4%
41	Nevada	166,471	0.4%
42	Idaho	165,187	0.4%
43	Delaware	146,807	0.3%
44	Vermont	130,608	0.3%
45	New Hampshire	110,117	0.2%
46	Alaska	103,671	0.2%
47	South Dakota	99,647	0.2%
48	Montana	79,598	0.2%
49	Wyoming	62,459	0.1%
50	North Dakota	51,447	0.1%
	District of Columbia	146,014	0.3%

Source: U.S. Department of Health and Human Services, Centers for Medicare and Medicaid Services
   "Medicaid Managed Care State Enrollment" (http://www.cms.hhs.gov/MedicaidDataSourcesGenInfo/)
*Unduplicated enrollment as of December 31, 2006. National total includes 947,438 Medicaid enrollees in Puerto Rico and the Virgin Islands.

Percent of Population Enrolled in Medicaid in 2006

National Percent = 14.8% of Population*

ALPHA ORDER

RANK ORDER

RANK	STATE	PERCENT		RANK	STATE	PERCENT
16	Alabama	16.1		1	Arkansas	22.5
22	Alaska	15.3		2	Louisiana	22.2
17	Arizona	15.7		3	New Mexico	21.9
1	Arkansas	22.5		4	Vermont	21.0
9	California	17.8		5	New York	20.9
47	Colorado	8.2		6	Tennessee	19.4
37	Connecticut	11.6		7	Mississippi	19.2
10	Delaware	17.2		8	Maine	19.1
33	Florida	12.2		9	California	17.8
29	Georgia	13.6		10	Delaware	17.2
19	Hawaii	15.6		10	Rhode Island	17.2
38	Idaho	11.3		12	Massachusetts	17.0
19	Illinois	15.6		13	Kentucky	16.9
30	Indiana	13.1		14	Oklahoma	16.2
40	Iowa	10.9		14	West Virginia	16.2
43	Kansas	9.5		16	Alabama	16.1
13	Kentucky	16.9		17	Arizona	15.7
2	Louisiana	22.2		17	Washington	15.7
8	Maine	19.1		19	Hawaii	15.6
32	Maryland	12.4		19	Illinois	15.6
12	Massachusetts	17.0		21	South Carolina	15.4
25	Michigan	14.6		22	Alaska	15.3
39	Minnesota	11.2		23	Wisconsin	15.2
7	Mississippi	19.2		24	Ohio	15.1
28	Missouri	14.1		25	Michigan	14.6
45	Montana	8.4		26	North Carolina	14.5
36	Nebraska	11.8		26	Pennsylvania	14.5
50	Nevada	6.7		28	Missouri	14.1
45	New Hampshire	8.4		29	Georgia	13.6
42	New Jersey	10.0		30	Indiana	13.1
3	New Mexico	21.9		31	South Dakota	12.6
5	New York	20.9		32	Maryland	12.4
26	North Carolina	14.5		33	Florida	12.2
48	North Dakota	8.1		33	Wyoming	12.2
24	Ohio	15.1		35	Texas	11.9
14	Oklahoma	16.2		36	Nebraska	11.8
40	Oregon	10.9		37	Connecticut	11.6
26	Pennsylvania	14.5		38	Idaho	11.3
10	Rhode Island	17.2		39	Minnesota	11.2
21	South Carolina	15.4		40	Iowa	10.9
31	South Dakota	12.6		40	Oregon	10.9
6	Tennessee	19.4		42	New Jersey	10.0
35	Texas	11.9		43	Kansas	9.5
49	Utah	7.7		44	Virginia	9.2
4	Vermont	21.0		45	Montana	8.4
44	Virginia	9.2		45	New Hampshire	8.4
17	Washington	15.7		47	Colorado	8.2
14	West Virginia	16.2		48	North Dakota	8.1
23	Wisconsin	15.2		49	Utah	7.7
33	Wyoming	12.2		50	Nevada	6.7

District of Columbia   24.9

Source: CQ Press using data from U.S. Department of Health and Human Services, Centers for Medicare and Medicaid Services
"Medicaid Managed Care State Enrollment" (http://www.cms.hhs.gov/MedicaidDataSourcesGenInfo/)
*Unduplicated enrollment as of December 31, 2006. National percent does not include recipients or population in U.S. territories.

Estimated Medicaid Expenditures in 2007

National Total = $308,801,000,000*

ALPHA ORDER

RANK	STATE	EXPENDITURES	% of USA
24	Alabama	$4,497,000,000	1.5%
40	Alaska	1,218,000,000	0.4%
15	Arizona	6,508,000,000	2.1%
28	Arkansas	3,470,000,000	1.1%
1	California	35,488,000,000	11.5%
32	Colorado	2,651,000,000	0.9%
26	Connecticut	3,915,000,000	1.3%
45	Delaware	994,000,000	0.3%
5	Florida	14,574,000,000	4.7%
13	Georgia	7,219,000,000	2.3%
44	Hawaii	1,057,000,000	0.3%
42	Idaho	1,121,000,000	0.4%
7	Illinois	13,686,000,000	4.4%
22	Indiana	4,803,000,000	1.6%
33	Iowa	2,612,000,000	0.8%
35	Kansas	2,295,000,000	0.7%
25	Kentucky	4,381,000,000	1.4%
18	Louisiana	5,373,000,000	1.7%
34	Maine	2,334,000,000	0.8%
19	Maryland	5,348,000,000	1.7%
11	Massachusetts	7,583,000,000	2.5%
9	Michigan	9,233,000,000	3.0%
17	Minnesota	5,962,000,000	1.9%
27	Mississippi	3,747,000,000	1.2%
14	Missouri	6,576,000,000	2.1%
47	Montana	730,000,000	0.2%
37	Nebraska	1,646,000,000	0.5%
43	Nevada	1,079,000,000	0.3%
41	New Hampshire	1,150,000,000	0.4%
10	New Jersey	8,388,000,000	2.7%
31	New Mexico	2,767,000,000	0.9%
2	New York	32,388,000,000	10.5%
8	North Carolina	9,614,000,000	3.1%
49	North Dakota	513,000,000	0.2%
6	Ohio	14,137,000,000	4.6%
29	Oklahoma	3,321,000,000	1.1%
30	Oregon	3,144,000,000	1.0%
4	Pennsylvania	17,671,000,000	5.7%
38	Rhode Island	1,641,000,000	0.5%
21	South Carolina	4,908,000,000	1.6%
48	South Dakota	694,000,000	0.2%
12	Tennessee	7,475,000,000	2.4%
3	Texas	19,841,000,000	6.4%
39	Utah	1,560,000,000	0.5%
46	Vermont	809,000,000	0.3%
20	Virginia	5,042,000,000	1.6%
16	Washington	6,183,000,000	2.0%
36	West Virginia	2,214,000,000	0.7%
23	Wisconsin	4,787,000,000	1.6%
50	Wyoming	454,000,000	0.1%

RANK ORDER

RANK	STATE	EXPENDITURES	% of USA
1	California	$35,488,000,000	11.5%
2	New York	32,388,000,000	10.5%
3	Texas	19,841,000,000	6.4%
4	Pennsylvania	17,671,000,000	5.7%
5	Florida	14,574,000,000	4.7%
6	Ohio	14,137,000,000	4.6%
7	Illinois	13,686,000,000	4.4%
8	North Carolina	9,614,000,000	3.1%
9	Michigan	9,233,000,000	3.0%
10	New Jersey	8,388,000,000	2.7%
11	Massachusetts	7,583,000,000	2.5%
12	Tennessee	7,475,000,000	2.4%
13	Georgia	7,219,000,000	2.3%
14	Missouri	6,576,000,000	2.1%
15	Arizona	6,508,000,000	2.1%
16	Washington	6,183,000,000	2.0%
17	Minnesota	5,962,000,000	1.9%
18	Louisiana	5,373,000,000	1.7%
19	Maryland	5,348,000,000	1.7%
20	Virginia	5,042,000,000	1.6%
21	South Carolina	4,908,000,000	1.6%
22	Indiana	4,803,000,000	1.6%
23	Wisconsin	4,787,000,000	1.6%
24	Alabama	4,497,000,000	1.5%
25	Kentucky	4,381,000,000	1.4%
26	Connecticut	3,915,000,000	1.3%
27	Mississippi	3,747,000,000	1.2%
28	Arkansas	3,470,000,000	1.1%
29	Oklahoma	3,321,000,000	1.1%
30	Oregon	3,144,000,000	1.0%
31	New Mexico	2,767,000,000	0.9%
32	Colorado	2,651,000,000	0.9%
33	Iowa	2,612,000,000	0.8%
34	Maine	2,334,000,000	0.8%
35	Kansas	2,295,000,000	0.7%
36	West Virginia	2,214,000,000	0.7%
37	Nebraska	1,646,000,000	0.5%
38	Rhode Island	1,641,000,000	0.5%
39	Utah	1,560,000,000	0.5%
40	Alaska	1,218,000,000	0.4%
41	New Hampshire	1,150,000,000	0.4%
42	Idaho	1,121,000,000	0.4%
43	Nevada	1,079,000,000	0.3%
44	Hawaii	1,057,000,000	0.3%
45	Delaware	994,000,000	0.3%
46	Vermont	809,000,000	0.3%
47	Montana	730,000,000	0.2%
48	South Dakota	694,000,000	0.2%
49	North Dakota	513,000,000	0.2%
50	Wyoming	454,000,000	0.1%
	District of Columbia **	NA	NA

Source: National Association of State Budget Officers
   "2006 State Expenditure Report" (http://www.nasbo.org)
*Estimates for fiscal year 2007.
**Not available.

Percent Change in Medicaid Expenditures: 2006 to 2007

National Percent Change = 7.3% Increase*

<table>
<tr><td colspan="3">ALPHA ORDER</td><td colspan="3">RANK ORDER</td></tr>
<tr><td>RANK</td><td>STATE</td><td>PERCENT</td><td>RANK</td><td>STATE</td><td>PERCENT</td></tr>
<tr><td>27</td><td>Alabama</td><td>6.3</td><td>1</td><td>South Carolina</td><td>26.6</td></tr>
<tr><td>3</td><td>Alaska</td><td>14.3</td><td>2</td><td>Illinois</td><td>20.1</td></tr>
<tr><td>23</td><td>Arizona</td><td>6.7</td><td>3</td><td>Alaska</td><td>14.3</td></tr>
<tr><td>10</td><td>Arkansas</td><td>10.4</td><td>4</td><td>California</td><td>13.8</td></tr>
<tr><td>4</td><td>California</td><td>13.8</td><td>5</td><td>Nebraska</td><td>13.4</td></tr>
<tr><td>40</td><td>Colorado</td><td>1.6</td><td>6</td><td>Mississippi</td><td>13.1</td></tr>
<tr><td>45</td><td>Connecticut</td><td>(0.2)</td><td>7</td><td>Louisiana</td><td>13.0</td></tr>
<tr><td>19</td><td>Delaware</td><td>7.7</td><td>8</td><td>Oklahoma</td><td>11.1</td></tr>
<tr><td>29</td><td>Florida</td><td>5.3</td><td>9</td><td>Wyoming</td><td>11.0</td></tr>
<tr><td>21</td><td>Georgia</td><td>7.2</td><td>10</td><td>Arkansas</td><td>10.4</td></tr>
<tr><td>15</td><td>Hawaii</td><td>8.4</td><td>11</td><td>Michigan</td><td>10.0</td></tr>
<tr><td>37</td><td>Idaho</td><td>2.3</td><td>12</td><td>Massachusetts</td><td>9.6</td></tr>
<tr><td>2</td><td>Illinois</td><td>20.1</td><td>13</td><td>New Mexico</td><td>8.8</td></tr>
<tr><td>39</td><td>Indiana</td><td>1.9</td><td>13</td><td>North Carolina</td><td>8.8</td></tr>
<tr><td>46</td><td>Iowa</td><td>(1.7)</td><td>15</td><td>Hawaii</td><td>8.4</td></tr>
<tr><td>28</td><td>Kansas</td><td>6.0</td><td>15</td><td>South Dakota</td><td>8.4</td></tr>
<tr><td>47</td><td>Kentucky</td><td>(2.4)</td><td>17</td><td>Tennessee</td><td>8.1</td></tr>
<tr><td>7</td><td>Louisiana</td><td>13.0</td><td>18</td><td>Texas</td><td>7.9</td></tr>
<tr><td>35</td><td>Maine</td><td>2.8</td><td>19</td><td>Delaware</td><td>7.7</td></tr>
<tr><td>24</td><td>Maryland</td><td>6.5</td><td>19</td><td>Minnesota</td><td>7.7</td></tr>
<tr><td>12</td><td>Massachusetts</td><td>9.6</td><td>21</td><td>Georgia</td><td>7.2</td></tr>
<tr><td>11</td><td>Michigan</td><td>10.0</td><td>21</td><td>New York</td><td>7.2</td></tr>
<tr><td>19</td><td>Minnesota</td><td>7.7</td><td>23</td><td>Arizona</td><td>6.7</td></tr>
<tr><td>6</td><td>Mississippi</td><td>13.1</td><td>24</td><td>Maryland</td><td>6.5</td></tr>
<tr><td>40</td><td>Missouri</td><td>1.6</td><td>24</td><td>Virginia</td><td>6.5</td></tr>
<tr><td>42</td><td>Montana</td><td>0.8</td><td>24</td><td>Wisconsin</td><td>6.5</td></tr>
<tr><td>5</td><td>Nebraska</td><td>13.4</td><td>27</td><td>Alabama</td><td>6.3</td></tr>
<tr><td>49</td><td>Nevada</td><td>(7.2)</td><td>28</td><td>Kansas</td><td>6.0</td></tr>
<tr><td>33</td><td>New Hampshire</td><td>4.4</td><td>29</td><td>Florida</td><td>5.3</td></tr>
<tr><td>48</td><td>New Jersey</td><td>(6.6)</td><td>30</td><td>Ohio</td><td>5.2</td></tr>
<tr><td>13</td><td>New Mexico</td><td>8.8</td><td>31</td><td>Rhode Island</td><td>5.1</td></tr>
<tr><td>21</td><td>New York</td><td>7.2</td><td>32</td><td>West Virginia</td><td>4.7</td></tr>
<tr><td>13</td><td>North Carolina</td><td>8.8</td><td>33</td><td>New Hampshire</td><td>4.4</td></tr>
<tr><td>42</td><td>North Dakota</td><td>0.8</td><td>34</td><td>Utah</td><td>3.0</td></tr>
<tr><td>30</td><td>Ohio</td><td>5.2</td><td>35</td><td>Maine</td><td>2.8</td></tr>
<tr><td>8</td><td>Oklahoma</td><td>11.1</td><td>36</td><td>Pennsylvania</td><td>2.6</td></tr>
<tr><td>44</td><td>Oregon</td><td>0.0</td><td>37</td><td>Idaho</td><td>2.3</td></tr>
<tr><td>36</td><td>Pennsylvania</td><td>2.6</td><td>38</td><td>Washington</td><td>2.0</td></tr>
<tr><td>31</td><td>Rhode Island</td><td>5.1</td><td>39</td><td>Indiana</td><td>1.9</td></tr>
<tr><td>1</td><td>South Carolina</td><td>26.6</td><td>40</td><td>Colorado</td><td>1.6</td></tr>
<tr><td>15</td><td>South Dakota</td><td>8.4</td><td>40</td><td>Missouri</td><td>1.6</td></tr>
<tr><td>17</td><td>Tennessee</td><td>8.1</td><td>42</td><td>Montana</td><td>0.8</td></tr>
<tr><td>18</td><td>Texas</td><td>7.9</td><td>42</td><td>North Dakota</td><td>0.8</td></tr>
<tr><td>34</td><td>Utah</td><td>3.0</td><td>44</td><td>Oregon</td><td>0.0</td></tr>
<tr><td>50</td><td>Vermont</td><td>(9.1)</td><td>45</td><td>Connecticut</td><td>(0.2)</td></tr>
<tr><td>24</td><td>Virginia</td><td>6.5</td><td>46</td><td>Iowa</td><td>(1.7)</td></tr>
<tr><td>38</td><td>Washington</td><td>2.0</td><td>47</td><td>Kentucky</td><td>(2.4)</td></tr>
<tr><td>32</td><td>West Virginia</td><td>4.7</td><td>48</td><td>New Jersey</td><td>(6.6)</td></tr>
<tr><td>24</td><td>Wisconsin</td><td>6.5</td><td>49</td><td>Nevada</td><td>(7.2)</td></tr>
<tr><td>9</td><td>Wyoming</td><td>11.0</td><td>50</td><td>Vermont</td><td>(9.1)</td></tr>
<tr><td></td><td></td><td></td><td></td><td>District of Columbia **</td><td>NA</td></tr>
</table>

Source: National Association of State Budget Officers
   "2006 State Expenditure Report" (http://www.nasbo.org)
*Estimates for fiscal year 2007.
**Not available.

Percent of Population Receiving Public Aid in 2005

National Percent = 3.9% of Population*

ALPHA ORDER

ALPHA ORDER

RANK	STATE	PERCENT		RANK	STATE	PERCENT
9	Alabama	4.7		1	California	6.3
25	Alaska	3.1		2	Kentucky	6.0
22	Arizona	3.2		3	Tennessee	5.7
16	Arkansas	3.9		4	West Virginia	5.6
1	California	6.3		5	Mississippi	5.4
46	Colorado	2.0		6	New Mexico	5.2
38	Connecticut	2.6		6	Rhode Island	5.2
22	Delaware	3.2		8	New York	5.0
32	Florida	2.9		9	Alabama	4.7
27	Georgia	3.0		10	Pennsylvania	4.6
22	Hawaii	3.2		11	Maine	4.3
48	Idaho	1.8		11	Michigan	4.3
34	Illinois	2.8		13	Louisiana	4.2
20	Indiana	3.5		13	Massachusetts	4.2
32	Iowa	2.9		15	Washington	4.0
25	Kansas	3.1		16	Arkansas	3.9
2	Kentucky	6.0		16	Vermont	3.9
13	Louisiana	4.2		18	Missouri	3.7
11	Maine	4.3		18	Ohio	3.7
38	Maryland	2.6		20	Indiana	3.5
13	Massachusetts	4.2		21	South Carolina	3.3
11	Michigan	4.3		22	Arizona	3.2
36	Minnesota	2.7		22	Delaware	3.2
5	Mississippi	5.4		22	Hawaii	3.2
18	Missouri	3.7		25	Alaska	3.1
36	Montana	2.7		25	Kansas	3.1
38	Nebraska	2.6		27	Georgia	3.0
47	Nevada	1.9		27	New Jersey	3.0
45	New Hampshire	2.1		27	North Carolina	3.0
27	New Jersey	3.0		27	Oklahoma	3.0
6	New Mexico	5.2		27	Texas	3.0
8	New York	5.0		32	Florida	2.9
27	North Carolina	3.0		32	Iowa	2.9
41	North Dakota	2.4		34	Illinois	2.8
18	Ohio	3.7		34	Oregon	2.8
27	Oklahoma	3.0		36	Minnesota	2.7
34	Oregon	2.8		36	Montana	2.7
10	Pennsylvania	4.6		38	Connecticut	2.6
6	Rhode Island	5.2		38	Maryland	2.6
21	South Carolina	3.3		38	Nebraska	2.6
41	South Dakota	2.4		41	North Dakota	2.4
3	Tennessee	5.7		41	South Dakota	2.4
27	Texas	3.0		41	Wisconsin	2.4
49	Utah	1.7		44	Virginia	2.2
16	Vermont	3.9		45	New Hampshire	2.1
44	Virginia	2.2		46	Colorado	2.0
15	Washington	4.0		47	Nevada	1.9
4	West Virginia	5.6		48	Idaho	1.8
41	Wisconsin	2.4		49	Utah	1.7
50	Wyoming	1.2		50	Wyoming	1.2

District of Columbia 10.5

Source: CQ Press using data from U.S. Social Security Administration and
    U.S. Department of Health and Human Services

*As of December 2005. Includes recipients of Temporary Assistance to Needy Families (TANF) and/or Supplemental Security Income payments.

Recipients of Temporary Assistance to Needy Families (TANF) Payments: 2007

National Total = 3,901,890 Monthly Recipients*

ALPHA ORDER

RANK	STATE	RECIPIENTS	% of USA
24	Alabama	40,475	1.0%
45	Alaska	8,738	0.2%
13	Arizona	75,324	1.9%
36	Arkansas	19,165	0.5%
1	California	1,157,566	29.7%
30	Colorado	25,360	0.6%
28	Connecticut	34,002	0.9%
44	Delaware	9,564	0.2%
14	Florida	73,528	1.9%
20	Georgia	43,542	1.1%
40	Hawaii	14,376	0.4%
49	Idaho	2,357	0.1%
15	Illinois	67,870	1.7%
8	Indiana	117,110	3.0%
22	Iowa	41,177	1.1%
25	Kansas	36,053	0.9%
18	Kentucky	58,738	1.5%
31	Louisiana	23,685	0.6%
32	Maine	23,661	0.6%
23	Maryland	40,706	1.0%
11	Massachusetts	89,727	2.3%
3	Michigan	190,353	4.9%
17	Minnesota	63,573	1.6%
33	Mississippi	22,944	0.6%
10	Missouri	102,522	2.6%
46	Montana	8,148	0.2%
39	Nebraska	16,851	0.4%
38	Nevada	17,542	0.4%
43	New Hampshire	10,492	0.3%
12	New Jersey	80,849	2.1%
27	New Mexico	34,243	0.9%
2	New York	261,015	6.7%
19	North Carolina	46,489	1.2%
48	North Dakota	5,233	0.1%
4	Ohio	163,122	4.2%
37	Oklahoma	18,718	0.5%
21	Oregon	42,253	1.1%
6	Pennsylvania	149,196	3.8%
35	Rhode Island	20,193	0.5%
29	South Carolina	32,430	0.8%
47	South Dakota	5,956	0.2%
5	Tennessee	156,046	4.0%
7	Texas	130,881	3.4%
41	Utah	11,557	0.3%
42	Vermont	11,105	0.3%
16	Virginia	66,204	1.7%
9	Washington	115,543	3.0%
34	West Virginia	22,112	0.6%
26	Wisconsin	35,912	0.9%
50	Wyoming	460	0.0%

RANK ORDER

RANK	STATE	RECIPIENTS	% of USA
1	California	1,157,566	29.7%
2	New York	261,015	6.7%
3	Michigan	190,353	4.9%
4	Ohio	163,122	4.2%
5	Tennessee	156,046	4.0%
6	Pennsylvania	149,196	3.8%
7	Texas	130,881	3.4%
8	Indiana	117,110	3.0%
9	Washington	115,543	3.0%
10	Missouri	102,522	2.6%
11	Massachusetts	89,727	2.3%
12	New Jersey	80,849	2.1%
13	Arizona	75,324	1.9%
14	Florida	73,528	1.9%
15	Illinois	67,870	1.7%
16	Virginia	66,204	1.7%
17	Minnesota	63,573	1.6%
18	Kentucky	58,738	1.5%
19	North Carolina	46,489	1.2%
20	Georgia	43,542	1.1%
21	Oregon	42,253	1.1%
22	Iowa	41,177	1.1%
23	Maryland	40,706	1.0%
24	Alabama	40,475	1.0%
25	Kansas	36,053	0.9%
26	Wisconsin	35,912	0.9%
27	New Mexico	34,243	0.9%
28	Connecticut	34,002	0.9%
29	South Carolina	32,430	0.8%
30	Colorado	25,360	0.6%
31	Louisiana	23,685	0.6%
32	Maine	23,661	0.6%
33	Mississippi	22,944	0.6%
34	West Virginia	22,112	0.6%
35	Rhode Island	20,193	0.5%
36	Arkansas	19,165	0.5%
37	Oklahoma	18,718	0.5%
38	Nevada	17,542	0.4%
39	Nebraska	16,851	0.4%
40	Hawaii	14,376	0.4%
41	Utah	11,557	0.3%
42	Vermont	11,105	0.3%
43	New Hampshire	10,492	0.3%
44	Delaware	9,564	0.2%
45	Alaska	8,738	0.2%
46	Montana	8,148	0.2%
47	South Dakota	5,956	0.2%
48	North Dakota	5,233	0.1%
49	Idaho	2,357	0.1%
50	Wyoming	460	0.0%
	District of Columbia	11,915	0.3%

Source: U.S. Department of Health and Human Services, Administration for Children and Families
"TANF Caseload Data" (http://www.acf.hhs.gov/programs/ofa/caseload/caseloadindex.htm)
*As of June 2007. Welfare reform replaced the Aid to Families with Dependent Children program (AFDC) with Temporary Assistance to Needy Families (TANF) as of July 1, 1997. National total includes 45,475 recipients in U.S. territories (33,320 in Puerto Rico).

Percent Change in TANF Recipients: 2006 to 2007

National Percent Change = 5.5% Decrease*

<table>
<tr><td colspan="3">ALPHA ORDER</td><td colspan="3">RANK ORDER</td></tr>
<tr><td>RANK</td><td>STATE</td><td>PERCENT CHANGE</td><td>RANK</td><td>STATE</td><td>PERCENT CHANGE</td></tr>
<tr><td>15</td><td>Alabama</td><td>(4.7)</td><td>1</td><td>Virginia</td><td>160.4</td></tr>
<tr><td>27</td><td>Alaska</td><td>(11.5)</td><td>2</td><td>Nevada</td><td>45.3</td></tr>
<tr><td>23</td><td>Arizona</td><td>(9.1)</td><td>3</td><td>Arkansas</td><td>12.9</td></tr>
<tr><td>3</td><td>Arkansas</td><td>12.9</td><td>4</td><td>Missouri</td><td>12.7</td></tr>
<tr><td>5</td><td>California</td><td>11.1</td><td>5</td><td>California</td><td>11.1</td></tr>
<tr><td>48</td><td>Colorado</td><td>(30.1)</td><td>6</td><td>Iowa</td><td>4.1</td></tr>
<tr><td>16</td><td>Connecticut</td><td>(5.5)</td><td>7</td><td>Vermont</td><td>3.6</td></tr>
<tr><td>40</td><td>Delaware</td><td>(18.2)</td><td>8</td><td>Oregon</td><td>1.6</td></tr>
<tr><td>24</td><td>Florida</td><td>(9.3)</td><td>9</td><td>Louisiana</td><td>0.9</td></tr>
<tr><td>43</td><td>Georgia</td><td>(21.6)</td><td>10</td><td>Indiana</td><td>0.8</td></tr>
<tr><td>35</td><td>Hawaii</td><td>(14.9)</td><td>11</td><td>West Virginia</td><td>(1.0)</td></tr>
<tr><td>42</td><td>Idaho</td><td>(20.2)</td><td>12</td><td>Massachusetts</td><td>(1.5)</td></tr>
<tr><td>44</td><td>Illinois</td><td>(21.8)</td><td>13</td><td>Ohio</td><td>(2.1)</td></tr>
<tr><td>10</td><td>Indiana</td><td>0.8</td><td>14</td><td>South Dakota</td><td>(3.6)</td></tr>
<tr><td>6</td><td>Iowa</td><td>4.1</td><td>15</td><td>Alabama</td><td>(4.7)</td></tr>
<tr><td>40</td><td>Kansas</td><td>(18.2)</td><td>16</td><td>Connecticut</td><td>(5.5)</td></tr>
<tr><td>33</td><td>Kentucky</td><td>(14.2)</td><td>16</td><td>South Carolina</td><td>(5.5)</td></tr>
<tr><td>9</td><td>Louisiana</td><td>0.9</td><td>18</td><td>Minnesota</td><td>(5.6)</td></tr>
<tr><td>19</td><td>Maine</td><td>(6.5)</td><td>19</td><td>Maine</td><td>(6.5)</td></tr>
<tr><td>20</td><td>Maryland</td><td>(6.9)</td><td>20</td><td>Maryland</td><td>(6.9)</td></tr>
<tr><td>12</td><td>Massachusetts</td><td>(1.5)</td><td>21</td><td>Washington</td><td>(7.0)</td></tr>
<tr><td>32</td><td>Michigan</td><td>(13.5)</td><td>22</td><td>Wisconsin</td><td>(8.5)</td></tr>
<tr><td>18</td><td>Minnesota</td><td>(5.6)</td><td>23</td><td>Arizona</td><td>(9.1)</td></tr>
<tr><td>25</td><td>Mississippi</td><td>(11.2)</td><td>24</td><td>Florida</td><td>(9.3)</td></tr>
<tr><td>4</td><td>Missouri</td><td>12.7</td><td>25</td><td>Mississippi</td><td>(11.2)</td></tr>
<tr><td>37</td><td>Montana</td><td>(16.7)</td><td>25</td><td>Wyoming</td><td>(11.2)</td></tr>
<tr><td>47</td><td>Nebraska</td><td>(29.3)</td><td>27</td><td>Alaska</td><td>(11.5)</td></tr>
<tr><td>2</td><td>Nevada</td><td>45.3</td><td>28</td><td>Tennessee</td><td>(11.8)</td></tr>
<tr><td>45</td><td>New Hampshire</td><td>(22.5)</td><td>29</td><td>Texas</td><td>(12.1)</td></tr>
<tr><td>39</td><td>New Jersey</td><td>(17.8)</td><td>30</td><td>Oklahoma</td><td>(12.9)</td></tr>
<tr><td>36</td><td>New Mexico</td><td>(16.5)</td><td>31</td><td>New York</td><td>(13.4)</td></tr>
<tr><td>31</td><td>New York</td><td>(13.4)</td><td>32</td><td>Michigan</td><td>(13.5)</td></tr>
<tr><td>38</td><td>North Carolina</td><td>(17.6)</td><td>33</td><td>Kentucky</td><td>(14.2)</td></tr>
<tr><td>46</td><td>North Dakota</td><td>(24.5)</td><td>34</td><td>Rhode Island</td><td>(14.3)</td></tr>
<tr><td>13</td><td>Ohio</td><td>(2.1)</td><td>35</td><td>Hawaii</td><td>(14.9)</td></tr>
<tr><td>30</td><td>Oklahoma</td><td>(12.9)</td><td>36</td><td>New Mexico</td><td>(16.5)</td></tr>
<tr><td>8</td><td>Oregon</td><td>1.6</td><td>37</td><td>Montana</td><td>(16.7)</td></tr>
<tr><td>50</td><td>Pennsylvania</td><td>(37.5)</td><td>38</td><td>North Carolina</td><td>(17.6)</td></tr>
<tr><td>34</td><td>Rhode Island</td><td>(14.3)</td><td>39</td><td>New Jersey</td><td>(17.8)</td></tr>
<tr><td>16</td><td>South Carolina</td><td>(5.5)</td><td>40</td><td>Delaware</td><td>(18.2)</td></tr>
<tr><td>14</td><td>South Dakota</td><td>(3.6)</td><td>40</td><td>Kansas</td><td>(18.2)</td></tr>
<tr><td>28</td><td>Tennessee</td><td>(11.8)</td><td>42</td><td>Idaho</td><td>(20.2)</td></tr>
<tr><td>29</td><td>Texas</td><td>(12.1)</td><td>43</td><td>Georgia</td><td>(21.6)</td></tr>
<tr><td>49</td><td>Utah</td><td>(32.5)</td><td>44</td><td>Illinois</td><td>(21.8)</td></tr>
<tr><td>7</td><td>Vermont</td><td>3.6</td><td>45</td><td>New Hampshire</td><td>(22.5)</td></tr>
<tr><td>1</td><td>Virginia</td><td>160.4</td><td>46</td><td>North Dakota</td><td>(24.5)</td></tr>
<tr><td>21</td><td>Washington</td><td>(7.0)</td><td>47</td><td>Nebraska</td><td>(29.3)</td></tr>
<tr><td>11</td><td>West Virginia</td><td>(1.0)</td><td>48</td><td>Colorado</td><td>(30.1)</td></tr>
<tr><td>22</td><td>Wisconsin</td><td>(8.5)</td><td>49</td><td>Utah</td><td>(32.5)</td></tr>
<tr><td>25</td><td>Wyoming</td><td>(11.2)</td><td>50</td><td>Pennsylvania</td><td>(37.5)</td></tr>
<tr><td></td><td></td><td></td><td></td><td>District of Columbia</td><td>(69.3)</td></tr>
</table>

Source: CQ Press using data from U.S. Department of Health and Human Services, Administration for Children and Families "TANF Caseload Data" (http://www.acf.hhs.gov/programs/ofa/caseload/caseloadindex.htm)
*June 2006 to June 2007. Welfare reform replaced the Aid to Families with Dependent Children program (AFDC) with Temporary Assistance to Needy Families (TANF) as of July 1, 1997. National percent includes recipients in U.S. territories.

TANF Work Participation Rates in 2006

National Rate = 32.5%*

RANK	STATE	PERCENT
20	Alabama	41.6
13	Alaska	45.6
35	Arizona	29.6
37	Arkansas	27.9
45	California	22.2
34	Colorado	30.0
32	Connecticut	30.8
42	Delaware	25.3
21	Florida	41.0
4	Georgia	64.9
25	Hawaii	37.3
16	Idaho	44.2
9	Illinois	53.0
38	Indiana	26.7
22	Iowa	39.0
2	Kansas	77.2
14	Kentucky	44.6
23	Louisiana	38.4
39	Maine	26.6
15	Maryland	44.5
50	Massachusetts	13.6
47	Michigan	21.6
33	Minnesota	30.3
28	Mississippi	35.5
48	Missouri	18.7
1	Montana	79.2
31	Nebraska	32.0
12	Nevada	47.8
44	New Hampshire	24.1
36	New Jersey	29.2
18	New Mexico	42.3
24	New York	37.8
30	North Carolina	32.4
10	North Dakota	51.9
7	Ohio	54.9
29	Oklahoma	32.9
49	Oregon	15.2
41	Pennsylvania	26.1
43	Rhode Island	24.9
11	South Carolina	49.5
5	South Dakota	57.9
6	Tennessee	57.2
19	Texas	42.0
17	Utah	42.5
45	Vermont	22.2
8	Virginia	53.9
27	Washington	36.1
40	West Virginia	26.2
26	Wisconsin	36.2
2	Wyoming	77.2

RANK	STATE	PERCENT
1	Montana	79.2
2	Kansas	77.2
2	Wyoming	77.2
4	Georgia	64.9
5	South Dakota	57.9
6	Tennessee	57.2
7	Ohio	54.9
8	Virginia	53.9
9	Illinois	53.0
10	North Dakota	51.9
11	South Carolina	49.5
12	Nevada	47.8
13	Alaska	45.6
14	Kentucky	44.6
15	Maryland	44.5
16	Idaho	44.2
17	Utah	42.5
18	New Mexico	42.3
19	Texas	42.0
20	Alabama	41.6
21	Florida	41.0
22	Iowa	39.0
23	Louisiana	38.4
24	New York	37.8
25	Hawaii	37.3
26	Wisconsin	36.2
27	Washington	36.1
28	Mississippi	35.5
29	Oklahoma	32.9
30	North Carolina	32.4
31	Nebraska	32.0
32	Connecticut	30.8
33	Minnesota	30.3
34	Colorado	30.0
35	Arizona	29.6
36	New Jersey	29.2
37	Arkansas	27.9
38	Indiana	26.7
39	Maine	26.6
40	West Virginia	26.2
41	Pennsylvania	26.1
42	Delaware	25.3
43	Rhode Island	24.9
44	New Hampshire	24.1
45	California	22.2
45	Vermont	22.2
47	Michigan	21.6
48	Missouri	18.7
49	Oregon	15.2
50	Massachusetts	13.6
	District of Columbia	17.1

Source: U.S. Department of Health and Human Services, Administration for Children and Families
    "Table 1A: TANF Work Participation Rates" (http://www.acf.hhs.gov/programs/ofa/particip/2006/tab1a.htm)
*For fiscal year 2006. Percent of parents in TANF families who work for at least 30 hours per week, or 20 hours per week if they
have children under age six. Welfare reform replaced the Aid to Families with Dependent Children program (AFDC) with
Temporary Assistance to Needy Families (TANF) as of July 1, 1997. National average includes recipients in U.S. territories.

Average Monthly TANF Assistance per Family in 2006

National Average = $372.17*

ALPHA ORDER				RANK ORDER		
RANK	STATE	PER FAMILY		RANK	STATE	PER FAMILY
44	Alabama	$197.25		1	Alaska	$602.09
1	Alaska	602.09		2	California	536.50
33	Arizona	269.99		3	Hawaii	517.88
50	Arkansas	147.49		4	Vermont	500.77
2	California	536.50		5	Massachusetts	499.61
31	Colorado	293.92		6	New York	499.09
11	Connecticut	413.42		7	New Hampshire	463.01
37	Delaware	246.84		8	Wisconsin	428.08
38	Florida	232.99		9	Washington	427.84
42	Georgia	204.65		10	Rhode Island	417.18
3	Hawaii	517.88		11	Connecticut	413.42
29	Idaho	301.79		12	Utah	399.73
36	Illinois	247.30		13	Oregon	389.45
43	Indiana	203.05		14	Michigan	386.65
26	Iowa	320.03		15	Montana	377.06
28	Kansas	305.73		16	Maryland	373.42
35	Kentucky	248.63		17	Maine	361.33
32	Louisiana	275.47		18	South Dakota	350.48
17	Maine	361.33		19	Minnesota	348.30
16	Maryland	373.42		20	Nevada	346.50
5	Massachusetts	499.61		21	New Jersey	324.58
14	Michigan	386.65		22	Ohio	323.76
19	Minnesota	348.30		23	Virginia	323.16
49	Mississippi	163.58		24	North Dakota	322.75
39	Missouri	229.71		25	Pennsylvania	321.70
15	Montana	377.06		26	Iowa	320.03
30	Nebraska	299.61		27	New Mexico	306.45
20	Nevada	346.50		28	Kansas	305.73
7	New Hampshire	463.01		29	Idaho	301.79
21	New Jersey	324.58		30	Nebraska	299.61
27	New Mexico	306.45		31	Colorado	293.92
6	New York	499.09		32	Louisiana	275.47
41	North Carolina	213.59		33	Arizona	269.99
24	North Dakota	322.75		34	West Virginia	269.70
22	Ohio	323.76		35	Kentucky	248.63
46	Oklahoma	188.59		36	Illinois	247.30
13	Oregon	389.45		37	Delaware	246.84
25	Pennsylvania	321.70		38	Florida	232.99
10	Rhode Island	417.18		39	Missouri	229.71
47	South Carolina	172.39		40	Wyoming	218.23
18	South Dakota	350.48		41	North Carolina	213.59
48	Tennessee	167.39		42	Georgia	204.65
45	Texas	195.01		43	Indiana	203.05
12	Utah	399.73		44	Alabama	197.25
4	Vermont	500.77		45	Texas	195.01
23	Virginia	323.16		46	Oklahoma	188.59
9	Washington	427.84		47	South Carolina	172.39
34	West Virginia	269.70		48	Tennessee	167.39
8	Wisconsin	428.08		49	Mississippi	163.58
40	Wyoming	218.23		50	Arkansas	147.49
					District of Columbia	327.14

Source: U.S. Department of Health and Human Services, Administration for Children and Families
    "Average Monthly Amount of Assistance" (http://www.acf.hhs.gov/programs/ofa/character/FY2006/tab41.htm)
*For fiscal year 2006.   Welfare reform replaced the Aid to Families with Dependent Children program (AFDC) with Temporary
Assistance to Needy Families (TANF) as of July 1, 1997. National average includes families in U.S. territories.

Percent of Households with Food Insecurity: 2006

National Percent = 11.3% of Households*

RANK	STATE	PERCENT
21	Alabama	12.1
15	Alaska	12.6
10	Arizona	13.1
8	Arkansas	14.3
26	California	10.9
22	Colorado	12.0
42	Connecticut	8.6
46	Delaware	7.8
39	Florida	8.9
15	Georgia	12.6
46	Hawaii	7.8
13	Idaho	12.7
32	Illinois	9.8
27	Indiana	10.8
24	Iowa	11.4
17	Kansas	12.5
9	Kentucky	13.6
7	Louisiana	14.4
11	Maine	12.9
35	Maryland	9.5
44	Massachusetts	8.1
20	Michigan	12.2
43	Minnesota	8.2
1	Mississippi	18.1
19	Missouri	12.3
31	Montana	9.9
35	Nebraska	9.5
41	Nevada	8.8
49	New Hampshire	7.4
48	New Jersey	7.7
2	New Mexico	16.1
32	New York	9.8
11	North Carolina	12.9
50	North Dakota	6.4
13	Ohio	12.7
5	Oklahoma	14.6
23	Oregon	11.9
30	Pennsylvania	10.0
25	Rhode Island	11.3
4	South Carolina	14.7
35	South Dakota	9.5
17	Tennessee	12.5
3	Texas	15.9
6	Utah	14.5
34	Vermont	9.6
45	Virginia	7.9
29	Washington	10.3
38	West Virginia	9.3
39	Wisconsin	8.9
28	Wyoming	10.6

RANK	STATE	PERCENT
1	Mississippi	18.1
2	New Mexico	16.1
3	Texas	15.9
4	South Carolina	14.7
5	Oklahoma	14.6
6	Utah	14.5
7	Louisiana	14.4
8	Arkansas	14.3
9	Kentucky	13.6
10	Arizona	13.1
11	Maine	12.9
11	North Carolina	12.9
13	Idaho	12.7
13	Ohio	12.7
15	Alaska	12.6
15	Georgia	12.6
17	Kansas	12.5
17	Tennessee	12.5
19	Missouri	12.3
20	Michigan	12.2
21	Alabama	12.1
22	Colorado	12.0
23	Oregon	11.9
24	Iowa	11.4
25	Rhode Island	11.3
26	California	10.9
27	Indiana	10.8
28	Wyoming	10.6
29	Washington	10.3
30	Pennsylvania	10.0
31	Montana	9.9
32	Illinois	9.8
32	New York	9.8
34	Vermont	9.6
35	Maryland	9.5
35	Nebraska	9.5
35	South Dakota	9.5
38	West Virginia	9.3
39	Florida	8.9
39	Wisconsin	8.9
41	Nevada	8.8
42	Connecticut	8.6
43	Minnesota	8.2
44	Massachusetts	8.1
45	Virginia	7.9
46	Delaware	7.8
46	Hawaii	7.8
48	New Jersey	7.7
49	New Hampshire	7.4
50	North Dakota	6.4

District of Columbia	12.5

Source: U.S. Department of Agriculture, Economic Research Service
   "Household Food Security in the United States, 2006" (http://www.ers.usda.gov/Publications/ERR24/)
*Three-year average for 2004-2006. Refers to households for which access to enough food is limited by a lack of money and other resources. About one-third of food-insecure households have very low food security, meaning that at times the food intake of some household members is reduced and their normal eating patterns are disrupted.

Food Stamp Benefits in 2007

National Total = $30,373,188,625*

ALPHA ORDER

RANK	STATE	BENEFITS	% of USA
18	Alabama	$601,413,135	2.0%
44	Alaska	86,084,132	0.3%
16	Arizona	646,750,299	2.1%
26	Arkansas	412,445,881	1.4%
2	California	2,569,814,590	8.5%
29	Colorado	310,583,982	1.0%
33	Connecticut	253,062,794	0.8%
45	Delaware	74,729,045	0.2%
5	Florida	1,400,153,858	4.6%
9	Georgia	1,125,954,322	3.7%
37	Hawaii	156,542,027	0.5%
41	Idaho	95,992,768	0.3%
4	Illinois	1,565,198,255	5.2%
14	Indiana	677,097,583	2.2%
32	Iowa	265,450,404	0.9%
35	Kansas	192,850,959	0.6%
15	Kentucky	674,261,809	2.2%
12	Louisiana	746,127,346	2.5%
36	Maine	170,581,745	0.6%
28	Maryland	357,244,132	1.2%
23	Massachusetts	471,901,175	1.6%
6	Michigan	1,367,629,622	4.5%
30	Minnesota	296,304,235	1.0%
25	Mississippi	443,797,523	1.5%
13	Missouri	745,311,957	2.5%
42	Montana	89,698,694	0.3%
40	Nebraska	126,459,764	0.4%
38	Nevada	133,739,897	0.4%
47	New Hampshire	62,477,686	0.2%
21	New Jersey	483,425,455	1.6%
34	New Mexico	248,844,870	0.8%
3	New York	2,324,294,916	7.7%
11	North Carolina	972,290,890	3.2%
49	North Dakota	51,891,080	0.2%
7	Ohio	1,292,695,103	4.3%
24	Oklahoma	458,907,034	1.5%
22	Oregon	477,442,080	1.6%
8	Pennsylvania	1,258,604,269	4.1%
43	Rhode Island	89,354,659	0.3%
17	South Carolina	618,164,263	2.0%
46	South Dakota	70,614,077	0.2%
10	Tennessee	1,003,609,007	3.3%
1	Texas	2,718,158,343	8.9%
39	Utah	133,204,438	0.4%
48	Vermont	55,659,902	0.2%
20	Virginia	551,446,240	1.8%
19	Washington	600,647,715	2.0%
31	West Virginia	274,884,537	0.9%
27	Wisconsin	363,438,582	1.2%
50	Wyoming	25,284,892	0.1%

RANK ORDER

RANK	STATE	BENEFITS	% of USA
1	Texas	$2,718,158,343	8.9%
2	California	2,569,814,590	8.5%
3	New York	2,324,294,916	7.7%
4	Illinois	1,565,198,255	5.2%
5	Florida	1,400,153,858	4.6%
6	Michigan	1,367,629,622	4.5%
7	Ohio	1,292,695,103	4.3%
8	Pennsylvania	1,258,604,269	4.1%
9	Georgia	1,125,954,322	3.7%
10	Tennessee	1,003,609,007	3.3%
11	North Carolina	972,290,890	3.2%
12	Louisiana	746,127,346	2.5%
13	Missouri	745,311,957	2.5%
14	Indiana	677,097,583	2.2%
15	Kentucky	674,261,809	2.2%
16	Arizona	646,750,299	2.1%
17	South Carolina	618,164,263	2.0%
18	Alabama	601,413,135	2.0%
19	Washington	600,647,715	2.0%
20	Virginia	551,446,240	1.8%
21	New Jersey	483,425,455	1.6%
22	Oregon	477,442,080	1.6%
23	Massachusetts	471,901,175	1.6%
24	Oklahoma	458,907,034	1.5%
25	Mississippi	443,797,523	1.5%
26	Arkansas	412,445,881	1.4%
27	Wisconsin	363,438,582	1.2%
28	Maryland	357,244,132	1.2%
29	Colorado	310,583,982	1.0%
30	Minnesota	296,304,235	1.0%
31	West Virginia	274,884,537	0.9%
32	Iowa	265,450,404	0.9%
33	Connecticut	253,062,794	0.8%
34	New Mexico	248,844,870	0.8%
35	Kansas	192,850,959	0.6%
36	Maine	170,581,745	0.6%
37	Hawaii	156,542,027	0.5%
38	Nevada	133,739,897	0.4%
39	Utah	133,204,438	0.4%
40	Nebraska	126,459,764	0.4%
41	Idaho	95,992,768	0.3%
42	Montana	89,698,694	0.3%
43	Rhode Island	89,354,659	0.3%
44	Alaska	86,084,132	0.3%
45	Delaware	74,729,045	0.2%
46	South Dakota	70,614,077	0.2%
47	New Hampshire	62,477,686	0.2%
48	Vermont	55,659,902	0.2%
49	North Dakota	51,891,080	0.2%
50	Wyoming	25,284,892	0.1%
	District of Columbia	103,950,879	0.3%

Source: U.S. Department of Agriculture, Food, Nutrition and Consumer Services
   "Food Stamp Program: Benefits" (http://www.fns.usda.gov/pd/fspmain.htm)
*Preliminary data. National total includes $76,715,775 to U.S. territories. Costs are for benefits only and exclude administrative expenditures.

Monthly Food Stamp Recipients in 2007

National Total = 26,465,816 Recipients*

ALPHA ORDER

RANK ORDER

RANK	STATE	RECIPIENTS	% of USA		RANK	STATE	RECIPIENTS	% of USA
16	Alabama	545,955	2.1%		1	Texas	2,422,198	9.2%
47	Alaska	56,181	0.2%		2	California	2,048,185	7.7%
18	Arizona	544,688	2.1%		3	New York	1,801,984	6.8%
27	Arkansas	379,768	1.4%		4	Illinois	1,246,400	4.7%
2	California	2,048,185	7.7%		5	Florida	1,232,803	4.7%
31	Colorado	250,704	0.9%		6	Michigan	1,204,409	4.6%
34	Connecticut	212,562	0.8%		7	Pennsylvania	1,135,146	4.3%
44	Delaware	67,185	0.3%		8	Ohio	1,076,764	4.1%
5	Florida	1,232,803	4.7%		9	Georgia	950,038	3.6%
9	Georgia	950,038	3.6%		10	North Carolina	882,946	3.3%
40	Hawaii	89,629	0.3%		11	Tennessee	864,870	3.3%
41	Idaho	87,068	0.3%		12	Missouri	823,915	3.1%
4	Illinois	1,246,400	4.7%		13	Louisiana	650,357	2.5%
15	Indiana	587,156	2.2%		14	Kentucky	602,022	2.3%
32	Iowa	238,349	0.9%		15	Indiana	587,156	2.2%
35	Kansas	182,407	0.7%		16	Alabama	545,955	2.1%
14	Kentucky	602,022	2.3%		17	South Carolina	545,293	2.1%
13	Louisiana	650,357	2.5%		18	Arizona	544,688	2.1%
36	Maine	162,602	0.6%		19	Washington	536,333	2.0%
28	Maryland	317,825	1.2%		20	Virginia	515,032	1.9%
21	Massachusetts	456,192	1.7%		21	Massachusetts	456,192	1.7%
6	Michigan	1,204,409	4.6%		22	Oregon	438,498	1.7%
29	Minnesota	276,414	1.0%		23	Mississippi	426,116	1.6%
23	Mississippi	426,116	1.6%		24	Oklahoma	421,316	1.6%
12	Missouri	823,915	3.1%		25	New Jersey	414,503	1.6%
42	Montana	79,969	0.3%		26	Wisconsin	382,770	1.4%
39	Nebraska	120,634	0.5%		27	Arkansas	379,768	1.4%
38	Nevada	122,224	0.5%		28	Maryland	317,825	1.2%
46	New Hampshire	59,101	0.2%		29	Minnesota	276,414	1.0%
25	New Jersey	414,503	1.6%		30	West Virginia	269,343	1.0%
33	New Mexico	233,918	0.9%		31	Colorado	250,704	0.9%
3	New York	1,801,984	6.8%		32	Iowa	238,349	0.9%
10	North Carolina	882,946	3.3%		33	New Mexico	233,918	0.9%
49	North Dakota	45,122	0.2%		34	Connecticut	212,562	0.8%
8	Ohio	1,076,764	4.1%		35	Kansas	182,407	0.7%
24	Oklahoma	421,316	1.6%		36	Maine	162,602	0.6%
22	Oregon	438,498	1.7%		37	Utah	123,475	0.5%
7	Pennsylvania	1,135,146	4.3%		38	Nevada	122,224	0.5%
43	Rhode Island	76,315	0.3%		39	Nebraska	120,634	0.5%
17	South Carolina	545,293	2.1%		40	Hawaii	89,629	0.3%
45	South Dakota	60,246	0.2%		41	Idaho	87,068	0.3%
11	Tennessee	864,870	3.3%		42	Montana	79,969	0.3%
1	Texas	2,422,198	9.2%		43	Rhode Island	76,315	0.3%
37	Utah	123,475	0.5%		44	Delaware	67,185	0.3%
48	Vermont	49,865	0.2%		45	South Dakota	60,246	0.2%
20	Virginia	515,032	1.9%		46	New Hampshire	59,101	0.2%
19	Washington	536,333	2.0%		47	Alaska	56,181	0.2%
30	West Virginia	269,343	1.0%		48	Vermont	49,865	0.2%
26	Wisconsin	382,770	1.4%		49	North Dakota	45,122	0.2%
50	Wyoming	22,608	0.1%		50	Wyoming	22,608	0.1%
						District of Columbia	86,519	0.3%

Source: U.S. Department of Agriculture, Food, Nutrition and Consumer Services
    "Food Stamp Program" (http://www.fns.usda.gov/pd/fspmain.htm)
*Preliminary for fiscal year 2007. National total includes 39,895 recipients in U.S. territories.

Average Monthly Food Stamp Benefit per Recipient in 2007

National Average = $95.64 per Recipient*

<u>ALPHA ORDER</u>				<u>RANK ORDER</u>		
RANK	STATE	PER RECIPIENT		RANK	STATE	PER RECIPIENT
32	Alabama	$91.80		1	Hawaii	$145.55
2	Alaska	127.69		2	Alaska	127.69
9	Arizona	98.95		3	New York	107.49
37	Arkansas	90.50		4	Illinois	104.65
5	California	104.56		5	California	104.56
6	Colorado	103.24		6	Colorado	103.24
8	Connecticut	99.21		7	Ohio	100.04
29	Delaware	92.69		8	Connecticut	99.21
18	Florida	94.65		9	Arizona	98.95
10	Georgia	98.76		10	Georgia	98.76
1	Hawaii	145.55		11	South Dakota	97.67
31	Idaho	91.88		12	Rhode Island	97.57
4	Illinois	104.65		13	New Jersey	97.19
15	Indiana	96.10		14	Tennessee	96.70
28	Iowa	92.81		15	Indiana	96.10
42	Kansas	88.10		16	North Dakota	95.83
24	Kentucky	93.33		17	Louisiana	95.60
17	Louisiana	95.60		18	Florida	94.65
44	Maine	87.42		19	Michigan	94.63
21	Maryland	93.67		20	South Carolina	94.47
47	Massachusetts	86.20		21	Maryland	93.67
19	Michigan	94.63		22	Texas	93.52
39	Minnesota	89.33		23	Montana	93.47
46	Mississippi	86.79		24	Kentucky	93.33
50	Missouri	75.38		24	Washington	93.33
23	Montana	93.47		26	Wyoming	93.20
45	Nebraska	87.36		27	Vermont	93.02
34	Nevada	91.18		28	Iowa	92.81
42	New Hampshire	88.10		29	Delaware	92.69
13	New Jersey	97.19		30	Pennsylvania	92.40
41	New Mexico	88.65		31	Idaho	91.88
3	New York	107.49		32	Alabama	91.80
33	North Carolina	91.77		33	North Carolina	91.77
16	North Dakota	95.83		34	Nevada	91.18
7	Ohio	100.04		35	Oklahoma	90.77
35	Oklahoma	90.77		36	Oregon	90.73
36	Oregon	90.73		37	Arkansas	90.50
30	Pennsylvania	92.40		38	Utah	89.90
12	Rhode Island	97.57		39	Minnesota	89.33
20	South Carolina	94.47		40	Virginia	89.23
11	South Dakota	97.67		41	New Mexico	88.65
14	Tennessee	96.70		42	Kansas	88.10
22	Texas	93.52		42	New Hampshire	88.10
38	Utah	89.90		44	Maine	87.42
27	Vermont	93.02		45	Nebraska	87.36
40	Virginia	89.23		46	Mississippi	86.79
24	Washington	93.33		47	Massachusetts	86.20
48	West Virginia	85.05		48	West Virginia	85.05
49	Wisconsin	79.12		49	Wisconsin	79.12
26	Wyoming	93.20		50	Missouri	75.38
					District of Columbia	100.12

Source: U.S. Department of Agriculture, Food, Nutrition and Consumer Services
    "Food Stamp Program" (http://www.fns.usda.gov/pd/fspmain.htm)
*Preliminary for fiscal year 2007. National average includes recipients in U.S. territories.

Percent of Population Receiving Food Stamps in 2007

National Percent = 8.8%*

ALPHA ORDER

RANK	STATE	PERCENT
12	Alabama	11.8
26	Alaska	8.2
23	Arizona	8.6
7	Arkansas	13.4
43	California	5.6
45	Colorado	5.2
40	Connecticut	6.1
29	Delaware	7.8
35	Florida	6.8
16	Georgia	10.0
34	Hawaii	7.0
41	Idaho	5.8
17	Illinois	9.7
20	Indiana	9.3
27	Iowa	8.0
39	Kansas	6.6
4	Kentucky	14.2
1	Louisiana	15.1
9	Maine	12.3
42	Maryland	5.7
32	Massachusetts	7.1
10	Michigan	12.0
44	Minnesota	5.3
3	Mississippi	14.6
5	Missouri	14.0
24	Montana	8.3
35	Nebraska	6.8
46	Nevada	4.8
49	New Hampshire	4.5
46	New Jersey	4.8
11	New Mexico	11.9
20	New York	9.3
17	North Carolina	9.7
32	North Dakota	7.1
19	Ohio	9.4
14	Oklahoma	11.6
13	Oregon	11.7
22	Pennsylvania	9.1
31	Rhode Island	7.2
8	South Carolina	12.4
30	South Dakota	7.6
5	Tennessee	14.0
15	Texas	10.1
48	Utah	4.7
27	Vermont	8.0
38	Virginia	6.7
24	Washington	8.3
2	West Virginia	14.9
35	Wisconsin	6.8
50	Wyoming	4.3

RANK ORDER

RANK	STATE	PERCENT
1	Louisiana	15.1
2	West Virginia	14.9
3	Mississippi	14.6
4	Kentucky	14.2
5	Missouri	14.0
5	Tennessee	14.0
7	Arkansas	13.4
8	South Carolina	12.4
9	Maine	12.3
10	Michigan	12.0
11	New Mexico	11.9
12	Alabama	11.8
13	Oregon	11.7
14	Oklahoma	11.6
15	Texas	10.1
16	Georgia	10.0
17	Illinois	9.7
17	North Carolina	9.7
19	Ohio	9.4
20	Indiana	9.3
20	New York	9.3
22	Pennsylvania	9.1
23	Arizona	8.6
24	Montana	8.3
24	Washington	8.3
26	Alaska	8.2
27	Iowa	8.0
27	Vermont	8.0
29	Delaware	7.8
30	South Dakota	7.6
31	Rhode Island	7.2
32	Massachusetts	7.1
32	North Dakota	7.1
34	Hawaii	7.0
35	Florida	6.8
35	Nebraska	6.8
35	Wisconsin	6.8
38	Virginia	6.7
39	Kansas	6.6
40	Connecticut	6.1
41	Idaho	5.8
42	Maryland	5.7
43	California	5.6
44	Minnesota	5.3
45	Colorado	5.2
46	Nevada	4.8
46	New Jersey	4.8
48	Utah	4.7
49	New Hampshire	4.5
50	Wyoming	4.3
	District of Columbia	14.7

Source: CQ Press using data from U.S. Department of Agriculture, Food, Nutrition and Consumer Services
    "Food Stamp Program" (http://www.fns.usda.gov/pd/fspmain.htm)
*Preliminary data for fiscal year 2007. National rate does not include recipients in U.S. territories.

Percent of Households Receiving Food Stamps in 2007

National Percent = 10.6% of Households*

ALPHA ORDER

RANK	STATE	PERCENT
15	Alabama	12.3
29	Alaska	9.3
25	Arizona	10.0
9	Arkansas	14.3
42	California	6.8
48	Colorado	5.8
34	Connecticut	8.5
30	Delaware	9.1
33	Florida	8.8
18	Georgia	11.5
23	Hawaii	10.5
43	Idaho	6.6
16	Illinois	12.0
24	Indiana	10.4
32	Iowa	8.9
37	Kansas	7.6
5	Kentucky	16.1
1	Louisiana	17.0
7	Maine	14.9
41	Maryland	7.0
26	Massachusetts	9.8
8	Michigan	14.4
44	Minnesota	6.5
2	Mississippi	16.6
12	Missouri	13.1
28	Montana	9.4
39	Nebraska	7.4
47	Nevada	6.1
49	New Hampshire	5.7
45	New Jersey	6.3
13	New Mexico	12.7
11	New York	13.4
19	North Carolina	11.3
38	North Dakota	7.5
20	Ohio	11.0
13	Oklahoma	12.7
6	Oregon	15.6
22	Pennsylvania	10.9
31	Rhode Island	9.0
10	South Carolina	14.1
35	South Dakota	7.9
3	Tennessee	16.3
17	Texas	11.7
46	Utah	6.2
26	Vermont	9.8
35	Virginia	7.9
20	Washington	11.0
4	West Virginia	16.2
40	Wisconsin	7.3
50	Wyoming	4.6

RANK ORDER

RANK	STATE	PERCENT
1	Louisiana	17.0
2	Mississippi	16.6
3	Tennessee	16.3
4	West Virginia	16.2
5	Kentucky	16.1
6	Oregon	15.6
7	Maine	14.9
8	Michigan	14.4
9	Arkansas	14.3
10	South Carolina	14.1
11	New York	13.4
12	Missouri	13.1
13	New Mexico	12.7
13	Oklahoma	12.7
15	Alabama	12.3
16	Illinois	12.0
17	Texas	11.7
18	Georgia	11.5
19	North Carolina	11.3
20	Ohio	11.0
20	Washington	11.0
22	Pennsylvania	10.9
23	Hawaii	10.5
24	Indiana	10.4
25	Arizona	10.0
26	Massachusetts	9.8
26	Vermont	9.8
28	Montana	9.4
29	Alaska	9.3
30	Delaware	9.1
31	Rhode Island	9.0
32	Iowa	8.9
33	Florida	8.8
34	Connecticut	8.5
35	South Dakota	7.9
35	Virginia	7.9
37	Kansas	7.6
38	North Dakota	7.5
39	Nebraska	7.4
40	Wisconsin	7.3
41	Maryland	7.0
42	California	6.8
43	Idaho	6.6
44	Minnesota	6.5
45	New Jersey	6.3
46	Utah	6.2
47	Nevada	6.1
48	Colorado	5.8
49	New Hampshire	5.7
50	Wyoming	4.6

District of Columbia — 18.0

Source: CQ Press using data from U.S. Department of Agriculture, Food, Nutrition and Consumer Services
"Food Stamp Program" (http://www.fns.usda.gov/pd/fspmain.htm)
*Food stamp program households are preliminary data for fiscal year 2007. Percent calculated using 2006 estimated total households. National percent excludes households in U.S. territories.

Average Monthly Participants in Women, Infants and Children (WIC) Special Nutrition Program in 2007
National Total = 8,285,902 Participants*

ALPHA ORDER

RANK	STATE	PARTICIPANTS	% of USA
21	Alabama	126,280	1.5%
41	Alaska	25,205	0.3%
11	Arizona	186,470	2.3%
30	Arkansas	84,457	1.0%
1	California	1,378,748	16.6%
29	Colorado	91,062	1.1%
35	Connecticut	53,206	0.6%
45	Delaware	20,405	0.2%
4	Florida	420,518	5.1%
5	Georgia	283,107	3.4%
40	Hawaii	32,612	0.4%
39	Idaho	38,087	0.5%
7	Illinois	279,982	3.4%
16	Indiana	140,891	1.7%
31	Iowa	69,468	0.8%
32	Kansas	69,067	0.8%
19	Kentucky	129,644	1.6%
20	Louisiana	129,054	1.6%
42	Maine	24,686	0.3%
22	Maryland	123,868	1.5%
24	Massachusetts	118,112	1.4%
10	Michigan	232,007	2.8%
17	Minnesota	134,662	1.6%
28	Mississippi	102,669	1.2%
18	Missouri	134,642	1.6%
46	Montana	19,279	0.2%
38	Nebraska	42,087	0.5%
36	Nevada	52,343	0.6%
47	New Hampshire	17,411	0.2%
14	New Jersey	150,502	1.8%
33	New Mexico	64,417	0.8%
3	New York	482,787	5.8%
9	North Carolina	242,088	2.9%
49	North Dakota	14,545	0.2%
6	Ohio	281,607	3.4%
23	Oklahoma	119,759	1.4%
27	Oregon	103,753	1.3%
8	Pennsylvania	244,155	2.9%
43	Rhode Island	24,220	0.3%
26	South Carolina	114,737	1.4%
44	South Dakota	21,795	0.3%
13	Tennessee	160,058	1.9%
2	Texas	900,396	10.9%
34	Utah	64,218	0.8%
48	Vermont	16,308	0.2%
15	Virginia	143,271	1.7%
12	Washington	165,206	2.0%
37	West Virginia	49,588	0.6%
25	Wisconsin	116,761	1.4%
50	Wyoming	12,341	0.1%

RANK ORDER

RANK	STATE	PARTICIPANTS	% of USA
1	California	1,378,748	16.6%
2	Texas	900,396	10.9%
3	New York	482,787	5.8%
4	Florida	420,518	5.1%
5	Georgia	283,107	3.4%
6	Ohio	281,607	3.4%
7	Illinois	279,982	3.4%
8	Pennsylvania	244,155	2.9%
9	North Carolina	242,088	2.9%
10	Michigan	232,007	2.8%
11	Arizona	186,470	2.3%
12	Washington	165,206	2.0%
13	Tennessee	160,058	1.9%
14	New Jersey	150,502	1.8%
15	Virginia	143,271	1.7%
16	Indiana	140,891	1.7%
17	Minnesota	134,662	1.6%
18	Missouri	134,642	1.6%
19	Kentucky	129,644	1.6%
20	Louisiana	129,054	1.6%
21	Alabama	126,280	1.5%
22	Maryland	123,868	1.5%
23	Oklahoma	119,759	1.4%
24	Massachusetts	118,112	1.4%
25	Wisconsin	116,761	1.4%
26	South Carolina	114,737	1.4%
27	Oregon	103,753	1.3%
28	Mississippi	102,669	1.2%
29	Colorado	91,062	1.1%
30	Arkansas	84,457	1.0%
31	Iowa	69,468	0.8%
32	Kansas	69,067	0.8%
33	New Mexico	64,417	0.8%
34	Utah	64,218	0.8%
35	Connecticut	53,206	0.6%
36	Nevada	52,343	0.6%
37	West Virginia	49,588	0.6%
38	Nebraska	42,087	0.5%
39	Idaho	38,087	0.5%
40	Hawaii	32,612	0.4%
41	Alaska	25,205	0.3%
42	Maine	24,686	0.3%
43	Rhode Island	24,220	0.3%
44	South Dakota	21,795	0.3%
45	Delaware	20,405	0.2%
46	Montana	19,279	0.2%
47	New Hampshire	17,411	0.2%
48	Vermont	16,308	0.2%
49	North Dakota	14,545	0.2%
50	Wyoming	12,341	0.1%
	District of Columbia	15,190	0.2%

Source: U.S. Department of Agriculture, Food, Nutrition and Consumer Services
"WIC Program (http://www.fns.usda.gov/pd/wicmain.htm)
*Preliminary data for fiscal year 2007. National total includes 218,174 participants in outlying areas not shown separately (Puerto Rico has 199,540 participants).

Average Monthly Benefit per Participant in Women, Infant and Children (WIC) Special Nutrition Program in 2007
National Average = $39.13*

ALPHA ORDER

RANK	STATE	AVERAGE BENEFIT
2	Alabama	$49.02
4	Alaska	47.75
38	Arizona	35.43
18	Arkansas	40.04
26	California	36.82
45	Colorado	32.43
3	Connecticut	48.18
44	Delaware	32.62
11	Florida	42.85
10	Georgia	43.41
1	Hawaii	56.11
46	Idaho	32.07
12	Illinois	42.64
34	Indiana	36.09
39	Iowa	35.25
41	Kansas	34.06
15	Kentucky	42.36
8	Louisiana	43.80
24	Maine	37.98
36	Maryland	35.84
17	Massachusetts	40.74
21	Michigan	39.22
28	Minnesota	36.47
14	Mississippi	42.37
43	Missouri	33.78
25	Montana	37.68
35	Nebraska	35.94
48	Nevada	30.88
29	New Hampshire	36.39
20	New Jersey	39.61
23	New Mexico	38.85
5	New York	46.88
22	North Carolina	39.05
13	North Dakota	42.43
33	Ohio	36.14
27	Oklahoma	36.65
40	Oregon	34.89
32	Pennsylvania	36.21
9	Rhode Island	43.56
16	South Carolina	41.15
42	South Dakota	33.88
7	Tennessee	45.41
47	Texas	31.02
50	Utah	27.41
6	Vermont	46.10
30	Virginia	36.36
19	Washington	39.89
31	West Virginia	36.28
37	Wisconsin	35.69
49	Wyoming	27.59

RANK ORDER

RANK	STATE	AVERAGE BENEFIT
1	Hawaii	$56.11
2	Alabama	49.02
3	Connecticut	48.18
4	Alaska	47.75
5	New York	46.88
6	Vermont	46.10
7	Tennessee	45.41
8	Louisiana	43.80
9	Rhode Island	43.56
10	Georgia	43.41
11	Florida	42.85
12	Illinois	42.64
13	North Dakota	42.43
14	Mississippi	42.37
15	Kentucky	42.36
16	South Carolina	41.15
17	Massachusetts	40.74
18	Arkansas	40.04
19	Washington	39.89
20	New Jersey	39.61
21	Michigan	39.22
22	North Carolina	39.05
23	New Mexico	38.85
24	Maine	37.98
25	Montana	37.68
26	California	36.82
27	Oklahoma	36.65
28	Minnesota	36.47
29	New Hampshire	36.39
30	Virginia	36.36
31	West Virginia	36.28
32	Pennsylvania	36.21
33	Ohio	36.14
34	Indiana	36.09
35	Nebraska	35.94
36	Maryland	35.84
37	Wisconsin	35.69
38	Arizona	35.43
39	Iowa	35.25
40	Oregon	34.89
41	Kansas	34.06
42	South Dakota	33.88
43	Missouri	33.78
44	Delaware	32.62
45	Colorado	32.43
46	Idaho	32.07
47	Texas	31.02
48	Nevada	30.88
49	Wyoming	27.59
50	Utah	27.41
	District of Columbia	39.26

Source: U.S. Department of Agriculture, Food, Nutrition and Consumer Services
  "WIC Program (http://www.fns.usda.gov/pd/wicmain.htm)
*Preliminary data for fiscal year 2007. National average includes outlying areas and Indian reservations not shown separately.

Percent of Public Elementary and Secondary School Students Eligible for Free or Reduced-Price Meals in 2006
Reporting States' Percent = 41.6%*

ALPHA ORDER

RANK	STATE	PERCENT
7	Alabama	51.7
40	Alaska	31.4
15	Arizona	45.0
5	Arkansas	52.9
11	California	48.5
33	Colorado	33.1
48	Connecticut	26.5
26	Delaware	36.1
14	Florida	45.8
9	Georgia	49.8
20	Hawaii	40.5
23	Idaho	37.8
24	Illinois	37.2
26	Indiana	36.1
36	Iowa	32.1
22	Kansas	38.8
6	Kentucky	52.4
2	Louisiana	61.2
32	Maine	33.8
38	Maryland	31.6
46	Massachusetts	28.2
28	Michigan	35.6
43	Minnesota	30.3
1	Mississippi	69.5
21	Missouri	39.1
31	Montana	34.5
30	Nebraska	34.7
19	Nevada	41.3
50	New Hampshire	17.1
47	New Jersey	26.8
3	New Mexico	55.7
16	New York	44.4
18	North Carolina	42.6
44	North Dakota	29.6
34	Ohio	32.5
4	Oklahoma	54.5
17	Oregon	43.2
40	Pennsylvania	31.4
29	Rhode Island	35.3
8	South Carolina	51.5
37	South Dakota	32.0
13	Tennessee	47.1
12	Texas	48.2
35	Utah	32.3
49	Vermont	26.4
42	Virginia	31.1
25	Washington	36.5
10	West Virginia	49.1
45	Wisconsin	29.3
38	Wyoming	31.6

RANK ORDER

RANK	STATE	PERCENT
1	Mississippi	69.5
2	Louisiana	61.2
3	New Mexico	55.7
4	Oklahoma	54.5
5	Arkansas	52.9
6	Kentucky	52.4
7	Alabama	51.7
8	South Carolina	51.5
9	Georgia	49.8
10	West Virginia	49.1
11	California	48.5
12	Texas	48.2
13	Tennessee	47.1
14	Florida	45.8
15	Arizona	45.0
16	New York	44.4
17	Oregon	43.2
18	North Carolina	42.6
19	Nevada	41.3
20	Hawaii	40.5
21	Missouri	39.1
22	Kansas	38.8
23	Idaho	37.8
24	Illinois	37.2
25	Washington	36.5
26	Delaware	36.1
26	Indiana	36.1
28	Michigan	35.6
29	Rhode Island	35.3
30	Nebraska	34.7
31	Montana	34.5
32	Maine	33.8
33	Colorado	33.1
34	Ohio	32.5
35	Utah	32.3
36	Iowa	32.1
37	South Dakota	32.0
38	Maryland	31.6
38	Wyoming	31.6
40	Alaska	31.4
40	Pennsylvania	31.4
42	Virginia	31.1
43	Minnesota	30.3
44	North Dakota	29.6
45	Wisconsin	29.3
46	Massachusetts	28.2
47	New Jersey	26.8
48	Connecticut	26.5
49	Vermont	26.4
50	New Hampshire	17.1

District of Columbia — 53.4

Source: CQ Press using data from U.S. Department of Education, National Center for Education Statistics "Common Core of Data (CCD) Database" (http://nces.ed.gov/ccd/)
*Preliminary data for school year 2005-2006.

Child Support Collections in 2006

National Total = $23,647,978,991*

ALPHA ORDER					RANK ORDER			
RANK	STATE	COLLECTIONS	% of USA		RANK	STATE	COLLECTIONS	% of USA
27	Alabama	$246,440,868	1.0%		1	California	$2,187,632,783	9.3%
41	Alaska	86,408,926	0.4%		2	Texas	2,002,840,203	8.5%
25	Arizona	283,504,310	1.2%		3	Ohio	1,694,575,743	7.2%
33	Arkansas	166,999,427	0.7%		4	New York	1,457,168,830	6.2%
1	California	2,187,632,783	9.3%		5	Pennsylvania	1,441,881,350	6.1%
26	Colorado	251,838,691	1.1%		6	Michigan	1,399,561,029	5.9%
29	Connecticut	238,378,851	1.0%		7	Florida	1,130,847,009	4.8%
44	Delaware	69,753,316	0.3%		8	New Jersey	962,286,549	4.1%
7	Florida	1,130,847,009	4.8%		9	Washington	626,886,724	2.7%
15	Georgia	525,393,042	2.2%		10	Illinois	621,004,002	2.6%
40	Hawaii	87,502,455	0.4%		11	Wisconsin	607,234,700	2.6%
38	Idaho	121,483,643	0.5%		12	North Carolina	591,558,146	2.5%
10	Illinois	621,004,002	2.6%		13	Minnesota	584,188,523	2.5%
16	Indiana	507,821,721	2.1%		14	Virginia	539,893,786	2.3%
23	Iowa	298,238,365	1.3%		15	Georgia	525,393,042	2.2%
35	Kansas	157,720,315	0.7%		16	Indiana	507,821,721	2.1%
21	Kentucky	356,470,107	1.5%		17	Missouri	489,006,349	2.1%
24	Louisiana	292,527,410	1.2%		18	Massachusetts	482,694,886	2.0%
39	Maine	101,111,420	0.4%		19	Maryland	461,979,714	2.0%
19	Maryland	461,979,714	2.0%		20	Tennessee	442,106,732	1.9%
18	Massachusetts	482,694,886	2.0%		21	Kentucky	356,470,107	1.5%
6	Michigan	1,399,561,029	5.9%		22	Oregon	314,467,562	1.3%
13	Minnesota	584,188,523	2.5%		23	Iowa	298,238,365	1.3%
30	Mississippi	206,634,659	0.9%		24	Louisiana	292,527,410	1.2%
17	Missouri	489,006,349	2.1%		25	Arizona	283,504,310	1.2%
49	Montana	49,925,528	0.2%		26	Colorado	251,838,691	1.1%
34	Nebraska	165,087,441	0.7%		27	Alabama	246,440,868	1.0%
37	Nevada	126,945,166	0.5%		28	South Carolina	243,280,928	1.0%
42	New Hampshire	82,334,492	0.3%		29	Connecticut	238,378,851	1.0%
8	New Jersey	962,286,549	4.1%		30	Mississippi	206,634,659	0.9%
43	New Mexico	74,411,789	0.3%		31	Oklahoma	204,527,099	0.9%
4	New York	1,457,168,830	6.2%		32	West Virginia	174,791,834	0.7%
12	North Carolina	591,558,146	2.5%		33	Arkansas	166,999,427	0.7%
45	North Dakota	68,450,313	0.3%		34	Nebraska	165,087,441	0.7%
3	Ohio	1,694,575,743	7.2%		35	Kansas	157,720,315	0.7%
31	Oklahoma	204,527,099	0.9%		36	Utah	157,604,724	0.7%
22	Oregon	314,467,562	1.3%		37	Nevada	126,945,166	0.5%
5	Pennsylvania	1,441,881,350	6.1%		38	Idaho	121,483,643	0.5%
47	Rhode Island	55,199,480	0.2%		39	Maine	101,111,420	0.4%
28	South Carolina	243,280,928	1.0%		40	Hawaii	87,502,455	0.4%
46	South Dakota	61,483,282	0.3%		41	Alaska	86,408,926	0.4%
20	Tennessee	442,106,732	1.9%		42	New Hampshire	82,334,492	0.3%
2	Texas	2,002,840,203	8.5%		43	New Mexico	74,411,789	0.3%
36	Utah	157,604,724	0.7%		44	Delaware	69,753,316	0.3%
50	Vermont	46,077,875	0.2%		45	North Dakota	68,450,313	0.3%
14	Virginia	539,893,786	2.3%		46	South Dakota	61,483,282	0.3%
9	Washington	626,886,724	2.7%		47	Rhode Island	55,199,480	0.2%
32	West Virginia	174,791,834	0.7%		48	Wyoming	53,383,171	0.2%
11	Wisconsin	607,234,700	2.6%		49	Montana	49,925,528	0.2%
48	Wyoming	53,383,171	0.2%		50	Vermont	46,077,875	0.2%
						District of Columbia	48,433,723	0.2%

Source: U.S. Department of Health and Human Services, Office of Child Support Enforcement
   "Child Support Enforcement Preliminary Data Report"
      (http://www.acf.hhs.gov/programs/cse/pubs/2007/preliminary_report/table_7.html)
*Fiscal year 2006. Total does not include $285,405,266 collected in U.S. territories.

XV. Transportation

Federal Highway Funding in 2008

National Total = $35,055,002,251*

ALPHA ORDER

RANK	STATE	FUNDS	% of USA
16	Alabama	$710,720,554	2.0%
37	Alaska	306,306,135	0.9%
17	Arizona	700,661,621	2.0%
29	Arkansas	440,218,090	1.3%
1	California	3,072,609,148	8.8%
27	Colorado	468,740,372	1.3%
28	Connecticut	456,399,814	1.3%
50	Delaware	138,734,856	0.4%
3	Florida	1,834,882,760	5.2%
7	Georgia	1,264,015,559	3.6%
49	Hawaii	145,122,250	0.4%
38	Idaho	263,639,385	0.8%
8	Illinois	1,185,552,195	3.4%
13	Indiana	918,193,377	2.6%
32	Iowa	383,685,042	1.1%
34	Kansas	349,764,917	1.0%
19	Kentucky	611,525,066	1.7%
26	Louisiana	535,919,991	1.5%
46	Maine	156,764,742	0.4%
22	Maryland	574,572,443	1.6%
23	Massachusetts	571,310,223	1.6%
9	Michigan	1,067,883,675	3.0%
24	Minnesota	556,216,742	1.6%
30	Mississippi	420,591,580	1.2%
14	Missouri	819,067,814	2.3%
35	Montana	340,798,820	1.0%
39	Nebraska	260,480,797	0.7%
41	Nevada	247,562,225	0.7%
47	New Hampshire	154,277,121	0.4%
11	New Jersey	965,160,761	2.8%
36	New Mexico	319,692,805	0.9%
4	New York	1,555,255,114	4.4%
10	North Carolina	1,029,268,822	2.9%
44	North Dakota	220,852,077	0.6%
6	Ohio	1,281,578,350	3.7%
25	Oklahoma	539,736,528	1.5%
31	Oregon	396,476,085	1.1%
5	Pennsylvania	1,550,106,911	4.4%
45	Rhode Island	172,577,938	0.5%
20	South Carolina	604,243,496	1.7%
42	South Dakota	232,706,992	0.7%
15	Tennessee	776,136,114	2.2%
2	Texas	3,044,120,750	8.7%
40	Utah	258,063,203	0.7%
48	Vermont	145,770,002	0.4%
12	Virginia	960,322,612	2.7%
21	Washington	603,842,118	1.7%
33	West Virginia	377,587,272	1.1%
18	Wisconsin	694,085,538	2.0%
43	Wyoming	230,375,556	0.7%

RANK ORDER

RANK	STATE	FUNDS	% of USA
1	California	$3,072,609,148	8.8%
2	Texas	3,044,120,750	8.7%
3	Florida	1,834,882,760	5.2%
4	New York	1,555,255,114	4.4%
5	Pennsylvania	1,550,106,911	4.4%
6	Ohio	1,281,578,350	3.7%
7	Georgia	1,264,015,559	3.6%
8	Illinois	1,185,552,195	3.4%
9	Michigan	1,067,883,675	3.0%
10	North Carolina	1,029,268,822	2.9%
11	New Jersey	965,160,761	2.8%
12	Virginia	960,322,612	2.7%
13	Indiana	918,193,377	2.6%
14	Missouri	819,067,814	2.3%
15	Tennessee	776,136,114	2.2%
16	Alabama	710,720,554	2.0%
17	Arizona	700,661,621	2.0%
18	Wisconsin	694,085,538	2.0%
19	Kentucky	611,525,066	1.7%
20	South Carolina	604,243,496	1.7%
21	Washington	603,842,118	1.7%
22	Maryland	574,572,443	1.6%
23	Massachusetts	571,310,223	1.6%
24	Minnesota	556,216,742	1.6%
25	Oklahoma	539,736,528	1.5%
26	Louisiana	535,919,991	1.5%
27	Colorado	468,740,372	1.3%
28	Connecticut	456,399,814	1.3%
29	Arkansas	440,218,090	1.3%
30	Mississippi	420,591,580	1.2%
31	Oregon	396,476,085	1.1%
32	Iowa	383,685,042	1.1%
33	West Virginia	377,587,272	1.1%
34	Kansas	349,764,917	1.0%
35	Montana	340,798,820	1.0%
36	New Mexico	319,692,805	0.9%
37	Alaska	306,306,135	0.9%
38	Idaho	263,639,385	0.8%
39	Nebraska	260,480,797	0.7%
40	Utah	258,063,203	0.7%
41	Nevada	247,562,225	0.7%
42	South Dakota	232,706,992	0.7%
43	Wyoming	230,375,556	0.7%
44	North Dakota	220,852,077	0.6%
45	Rhode Island	172,577,938	0.5%
46	Maine	156,764,742	0.4%
47	New Hampshire	154,277,121	0.4%
48	Vermont	145,770,002	0.4%
49	Hawaii	145,122,250	0.4%
50	Delaware	138,734,856	0.4%
	District of Columbia	140,825,893	0.4%

Source: U.S. Department of Transportation, Federal Highway Administration
"FHWA Apportionment" (http://www.fhwa.dot.gov/legsregs/directives/notices/n4510648t8.htm)
*Fiscal Year 2008 apportionments after penalty and after programmatic distribution.

Per Capita Federal Highway Funding in 2008

National Per Capita = $116*

ALPHA ORDER

RANK	STATE	PER CAPITA
13	Alabama	$154
1	Alaska	448
36	Arizona	111
12	Arkansas	155
49	California	84
45	Colorado	96
22	Connecticut	130
11	Delaware	160
42	Florida	101
21	Georgia	132
34	Hawaii	113
8	Idaho	176
47	Illinois	92
16	Indiana	145
23	Iowa	128
25	Kansas	126
17	Kentucky	144
27	Louisiana	125
31	Maine	119
41	Maryland	102
48	Massachusetts	89
39	Michigan	106
38	Minnesota	107
17	Mississippi	144
19	Missouri	139
3	Montana	356
15	Nebraska	147
44	Nevada	97
32	New Hampshire	117
36	New Jersey	111
10	New Mexico	162
50	New York	81
33	North Carolina	114
4	North Dakota	345
35	Ohio	112
14	Oklahoma	149
39	Oregon	106
27	Pennsylvania	125
9	Rhode Island	163
20	South Carolina	137
5	South Dakota	292
25	Tennessee	126
24	Texas	127
43	Utah	98
6	Vermont	235
27	Virginia	125
46	Washington	93
7	West Virginia	208
30	Wisconsin	124
2	Wyoming	441

RANK ORDER

RANK	STATE	PER CAPITA
1	Alaska	$448
2	Wyoming	441
3	Montana	356
4	North Dakota	345
5	South Dakota	292
6	Vermont	235
7	West Virginia	208
8	Idaho	176
9	Rhode Island	163
10	New Mexico	162
11	Delaware	160
12	Arkansas	155
13	Alabama	154
14	Oklahoma	149
15	Nebraska	147
16	Indiana	145
17	Kentucky	144
17	Mississippi	144
19	Missouri	139
20	South Carolina	137
21	Georgia	132
22	Connecticut	130
23	Iowa	128
24	Texas	127
25	Kansas	126
25	Tennessee	126
27	Louisiana	125
27	Pennsylvania	125
27	Virginia	125
30	Wisconsin	124
31	Maine	119
32	New Hampshire	117
33	North Carolina	114
34	Hawaii	113
35	Ohio	112
36	Arizona	111
36	New Jersey	111
38	Minnesota	107
39	Michigan	106
39	Oregon	106
41	Maryland	102
42	Florida	101
43	Utah	98
44	Nevada	97
45	Colorado	96
46	Washington	93
47	Illinois	92
48	Massachusetts	89
49	California	84
50	New York	81

District of Columbia   239

Source: CQ Press using data from U.S. Department of Transportation, Federal Highway Administration
"FHWA Apportionment" (http://www.fhwa.dot.gov/legsregs/directives/notices/n4510648t8.htm)
*Fiscal Year 2008 apportionments after penalty and after programmatic distribution. Calculated with 2007 population estimates.

Public Road and Street Mileage in 2005

National Total = 3,995,644 Miles*

ALPHA ORDER

RANK	STATE	MILES	% of USA
18	Alabama	96,045	2.4%
47	Alaska	14,369	0.4%
34	Arizona	59,790	1.5%
17	Arkansas	98,659	2.5%
2	California	169,906	4.3%
22	Colorado	87,598	2.2%
44	Connecticut	21,194	0.5%
49	Delaware	6,094	0.2%
10	Florida	120,557	3.0%
11	Georgia	117,645	2.9%
50	Hawaii	4,321	0.1%
35	Idaho	47,129	1.2%
3	Illinois	138,833	3.5%
19	Indiana	95,575	2.4%
13	Iowa	113,972	2.9%
4	Kansas	135,462	3.4%
26	Kentucky	78,021	2.0%
33	Louisiana	60,953	1.5%
43	Maine	22,807	0.6%
41	Maryland	30,962	0.8%
39	Massachusetts	35,897	0.9%
8	Michigan	121,456	3.0%
5	Minnesota	132,048	3.3%
27	Mississippi	74,181	1.9%
6	Missouri	125,822	3.1%
29	Montana	69,338	1.7%
20	Nebraska	93,310	2.3%
40	Nevada	34,624	0.9%
45	New Hampshire	15,566	0.4%
37	New Jersey	38,552	1.0%
32	New Mexico	63,758	1.6%
14	New York	113,343	2.8%
16	North Carolina	103,128	2.6%
23	North Dakota	86,793	2.2%
7	Ohio	124,840	3.1%
15	Oklahoma	112,937	2.8%
31	Oregon	64,543	1.6%
9	Pennsylvania	120,668	3.0%
48	Rhode Island	6,491	0.2%
30	South Carolina	66,238	1.7%
24	South Dakota	83,911	2.1%
21	Tennessee	90,451	2.3%
1	Texas	304,171	7.6%
36	Utah	43,575	1.1%
46	Vermont	14,399	0.4%
28	Virginia	71,961	1.8%
25	Washington	83,381	2.1%
38	West Virginia	37,028	0.9%
12	Wisconsin	114,142	2.9%
42	Wyoming	27,700	0.7%

RANK ORDER

RANK	STATE	MILES	% of USA
1	Texas	304,171	7.6%
2	California	169,906	4.3%
3	Illinois	138,833	3.5%
4	Kansas	135,462	3.4%
5	Minnesota	132,048	3.3%
6	Missouri	125,822	3.1%
7	Ohio	124,840	3.1%
8	Michigan	121,456	3.0%
9	Pennsylvania	120,668	3.0%
10	Florida	120,557	3.0%
11	Georgia	117,645	2.9%
12	Wisconsin	114,142	2.9%
13	Iowa	113,972	2.9%
14	New York	113,343	2.8%
15	Oklahoma	112,937	2.8%
16	North Carolina	103,128	2.6%
17	Arkansas	98,659	2.5%
18	Alabama	96,045	2.4%
19	Indiana	95,575	2.4%
20	Nebraska	93,310	2.3%
21	Tennessee	90,451	2.3%
22	Colorado	87,598	2.2%
23	North Dakota	86,793	2.2%
24	South Dakota	83,911	2.1%
25	Washington	83,381	2.1%
26	Kentucky	78,021	2.0%
27	Mississippi	74,181	1.9%
28	Virginia	71,961	1.8%
29	Montana	69,338	1.7%
30	South Carolina	66,238	1.7%
31	Oregon	64,543	1.6%
32	New Mexico	63,758	1.6%
33	Louisiana	60,953	1.5%
34	Arizona	59,790	1.5%
35	Idaho	47,129	1.2%
36	Utah	43,575	1.1%
37	New Jersey	38,552	1.0%
38	West Virginia	37,028	0.9%
39	Massachusetts	35,897	0.9%
40	Nevada	34,624	0.9%
41	Maryland	30,962	0.8%
42	Wyoming	27,700	0.7%
43	Maine	22,807	0.6%
44	Connecticut	21,194	0.5%
45	New Hampshire	15,566	0.4%
46	Vermont	14,399	0.4%
47	Alaska	14,369	0.4%
48	Rhode Island	6,491	0.2%
49	Delaware	6,094	0.2%
50	Hawaii	4,321	0.1%
	District of Columbia	1,500	0.0%

Source: U.S. Department of Transportation, Federal Highway Administration
"Highway Statistics 2005" (Table HM-10) (http://www.fhwa.dot.gov/policy/ohpi/hss/index.htm)
*Does not include 15,991 miles of roads and streets in Puerto Rico.

Percent of Public Road and Street Mileage Federally-Funded in 2005

National Percent = 24.5% of Public Road and Street Mileage*

ALPHA ORDER

RANK	STATE	PERCENT
24	Alabama	25.0
5	Alaska	30.3
39	Arizona	21.8
40	Arkansas	21.4
2	California	32.0
45	Colorado	20.0
8	Connecticut	29.0
21	Delaware	25.2
40	Florida	21.4
18	Georgia	26.2
1	Hawaii	36.1
31	Idaho	23.2
21	Illinois	25.2
29	Indiana	23.3
35	Iowa	22.6
19	Kansas	25.7
50	Kentucky	17.7
36	Louisiana	22.0
13	Maine	27.7
21	Maryland	25.2
4	Massachusetts	31.0
7	Michigan	29.5
26	Minnesota	24.1
9	Mississippi	28.5
27	Missouri	24.0
42	Montana	21.1
36	Nebraska	22.0
48	Nevada	18.4
36	New Hampshire	22.0
16	New Jersey	26.8
49	New Mexico	17.9
32	New York	23.1
42	North Carolina	21.1
44	North Dakota	21.0
32	Ohio	23.1
10	Oklahoma	28.0
11	Oregon	27.9
29	Pennsylvania	23.3
15	Rhode Island	26.9
3	South Carolina	31.7
28	South Dakota	23.5
46	Tennessee	19.3
19	Texas	25.7
47	Utah	19.1
16	Vermont	26.8
6	Virginia	29.6
34	Washington	22.8
11	West Virginia	27.9
25	Wisconsin	24.9
13	Wyoming	27.7

RANK ORDER

RANK	STATE	PERCENT
1	Hawaii	36.1
2	California	32.0
3	South Carolina	31.7
4	Massachusetts	31.0
5	Alaska	30.3
6	Virginia	29.6
7	Michigan	29.5
8	Connecticut	29.0
9	Mississippi	28.5
10	Oklahoma	28.0
11	Oregon	27.9
11	West Virginia	27.9
13	Maine	27.7
13	Wyoming	27.7
15	Rhode Island	26.9
16	New Jersey	26.8
16	Vermont	26.8
18	Georgia	26.2
19	Kansas	25.7
19	Texas	25.7
21	Delaware	25.2
21	Illinois	25.2
21	Maryland	25.2
24	Alabama	25.0
25	Wisconsin	24.9
26	Minnesota	24.1
27	Missouri	24.0
28	South Dakota	23.5
29	Indiana	23.3
29	Pennsylvania	23.3
31	Idaho	23.2
32	New York	23.1
32	Ohio	23.1
34	Washington	22.8
35	Iowa	22.6
36	Louisiana	22.0
36	Nebraska	22.0
36	New Hampshire	22.0
39	Arizona	21.8
40	Arkansas	21.4
40	Florida	21.4
42	Montana	21.1
42	North Carolina	21.1
44	North Dakota	21.0
45	Colorado	20.0
46	Tennessee	19.3
47	Utah	19.1
48	Nevada	18.4
49	New Mexico	17.9
50	Kentucky	17.7

District of Columbia	30.1

Source: CQ Press using data from U.S. Department of Transportation, Federal Highway Administration
"Highway Statistics 2005" (Table HM-15) (http://www.fhwa.dot.gov/policy/ohpi/hss/index.htm)
*National percent does not include federally-funded highway miles in Puerto Rico.

Interstate Highway Mileage in 2005

National Total = 46,608 Miles*

ALPHA ORDER

RANK	STATE	MILES	% of USA
24	Alabama	909	2.0%
17	Alaska	1,081	2.3%
12	Arizona	1,169	2.5%
35	Arkansas	656	1.4%
2	California	2,460	5.3%
19	Colorado	956	2.1%
45	Connecticut	346	0.7%
50	Delaware	41	0.1%
7	Florida	1,471	3.2%
8	Georgia	1,243	2.7%
49	Hawaii	55	0.1%
36	Idaho	612	1.3%
3	Illinois	2,169	4.7%
12	Indiana	1,169	2.5%
28	Iowa	781	1.7%
26	Kansas	874	1.9%
30	Kentucky	762	1.6%
25	Louisiana	903	1.9%
44	Maine	367	0.8%
42	Maryland	481	1.0%
37	Massachusetts	573	1.2%
8	Michigan	1,243	2.7%
22	Minnesota	915	2.0%
33	Mississippi	682	1.5%
11	Missouri	1,182	2.5%
10	Montana	1,192	2.6%
41	Nebraska	482	1.0%
39	Nevada	562	1.2%
47	New Hampshire	225	0.5%
43	New Jersey	431	0.9%
18	New Mexico	1,000	2.1%
5	New York	1,674	3.6%
16	North Carolina	1,083	2.3%
38	North Dakota	571	1.2%
6	Ohio	1,574	3.4%
21	Oklahoma	933	2.0%
32	Oregon	728	1.6%
4	Pennsylvania	1,758	3.8%
48	Rhode Island	71	0.2%
27	South Carolina	843	1.8%
34	South Dakota	678	1.5%
15	Tennessee	1,104	2.4%
1	Texas	3,233	6.9%
20	Utah	940	2.0%
46	Vermont	320	0.7%
14	Virginia	1,118	2.4%
29	Washington	764	1.6%
40	West Virginia	554	1.2%
31	Wisconsin	743	1.6%
23	Wyoming	914	2.0%

RANK ORDER

RANK	STATE	MILES	% of USA
1	Texas	3,233	6.9%
2	California	2,460	5.3%
3	Illinois	2,169	4.7%
4	Pennsylvania	1,758	3.8%
5	New York	1,674	3.6%
6	Ohio	1,574	3.4%
7	Florida	1,471	3.2%
8	Georgia	1,243	2.7%
8	Michigan	1,243	2.7%
10	Montana	1,192	2.6%
11	Missouri	1,182	2.5%
12	Arizona	1,169	2.5%
12	Indiana	1,169	2.5%
14	Virginia	1,118	2.4%
15	Tennessee	1,104	2.4%
16	North Carolina	1,083	2.3%
17	Alaska	1,081	2.3%
18	New Mexico	1,000	2.1%
19	Colorado	956	2.1%
20	Utah	940	2.0%
21	Oklahoma	933	2.0%
22	Minnesota	915	2.0%
23	Wyoming	914	2.0%
24	Alabama	909	2.0%
25	Louisiana	903	1.9%
26	Kansas	874	1.9%
27	South Carolina	843	1.8%
28	Iowa	781	1.7%
29	Washington	764	1.6%
30	Kentucky	762	1.6%
31	Wisconsin	743	1.6%
32	Oregon	728	1.6%
33	Mississippi	682	1.5%
34	South Dakota	678	1.5%
35	Arkansas	656	1.4%
36	Idaho	612	1.3%
37	Massachusetts	573	1.2%
38	North Dakota	571	1.2%
39	Nevada	562	1.2%
40	West Virginia	554	1.2%
41	Nebraska	482	1.0%
42	Maryland	481	1.0%
43	New Jersey	431	0.9%
44	Maine	367	0.8%
45	Connecticut	346	0.7%
46	Vermont	320	0.7%
47	New Hampshire	225	0.5%
48	Rhode Island	71	0.2%
49	Hawaii	55	0.1%
50	Delaware	41	0.1%
	District of Columbia	13	0.0%

Source: U.S. Department of Transportation, Federal Highway Administration
"Highway Statistics 2005" (Table HM-15) (http://www.fhwa.dot.gov/policy/ohpi/hss/index.htm)
*Does not include 265 miles of highway in Puerto Rico that are part of the interstate system.

Toll Road Mileage in 2005

National Total = 4,622 Miles

ALPHA ORDER					RANK ORDER			

RANK	STATE	MILES	% of USA		RANK	STATE	MILES	% of USA
25	Alabama	1	0.0%		1	Florida	679	14.7%
27	Alaska	0	0.0%		2	Oklahoma	597	12.9%
27	Arizona	0	0.0%		3	Pennsylvania	533	11.5%
27	Arkansas	0	0.0%		4	New York	518	11.2%
13	California	96	2.1%		5	Ohio	392	8.5%
17	Colorado	58	1.3%		6	New Jersey	326	7.1%
27	Connecticut	0	0.0%		7	Illinois	239	5.2%
19	Delaware	47	1.0%		8	Kansas	237	5.1%
1	Florida	679	14.7%		9	Texas	164	3.5%
22	Georgia	6	0.1%		10	Indiana	157	3.4%
27	Hawaii	0	0.0%		11	Massachusetts	138	3.0%
27	Idaho	0	0.0%		12	Maine	106	2.3%
7	Illinois	239	5.2%		13	California	96	2.1%
10	Indiana	157	3.4%		14	West Virginia	87	1.9%
27	Iowa	0	0.0%		15	Kentucky	80	1.7%
8	Kansas	237	5.1%		16	New Hampshire	59	1.3%
15	Kentucky	80	1.7%		17	Colorado	58	1.3%
24	Louisiana	2	0.0%		17	Virginia	58	1.3%
12	Maine	106	2.3%		19	Delaware	47	1.0%
27	Maryland	0	0.0%		20	South Carolina	24	0.5%
11	Massachusetts	138	3.0%		21	Vermont	12	0.3%
27	Michigan	0	0.0%		22	Georgia	6	0.1%
27	Minnesota	0	0.0%		22	Nevada	6	0.1%
27	Mississippi	0	0.0%		24	Louisiana	2	0.0%
27	Missouri	0	0.0%		25	Alabama	1	0.0%
27	Montana	0	0.0%		25	Utah	1	0.0%
27	Nebraska	0	0.0%		27	Alaska	0	0.0%
22	Nevada	6	0.1%		27	Arizona	0	0.0%
16	New Hampshire	59	1.3%		27	Arkansas	0	0.0%
6	New Jersey	326	7.1%		27	Connecticut	0	0.0%
27	New Mexico	0	0.0%		27	Hawaii	0	0.0%
4	New York	518	11.2%		27	Idaho	0	0.0%
27	North Carolina	0	0.0%		27	Iowa	0	0.0%
27	North Dakota	0	0.0%		27	Maryland	0	0.0%
5	Ohio	392	8.5%		27	Michigan	0	0.0%
2	Oklahoma	597	12.9%		27	Minnesota	0	0.0%
27	Oregon	0	0.0%		27	Mississippi	0	0.0%
3	Pennsylvania	533	11.5%		27	Missouri	0	0.0%
27	Rhode Island	0	0.0%		27	Montana	0	0.0%
20	South Carolina	24	0.5%		27	Nebraska	0	0.0%
27	South Dakota	0	0.0%		27	New Mexico	0	0.0%
27	Tennessee	0	0.0%		27	North Carolina	0	0.0%
9	Texas	164	3.5%		27	North Dakota	0	0.0%
25	Utah	1	0.0%		27	Oregon	0	0.0%
21	Vermont	12	0.3%		27	Rhode Island	0	0.0%
17	Virginia	58	1.3%		27	South Dakota	0	0.0%
27	Washington	0	0.0%		27	Tennessee	0	0.0%
14	West Virginia	87	1.9%		27	Washington	0	0.0%
27	Wisconsin	0	0.0%		27	Wisconsin	0	0.0%
27	Wyoming	0	0.0%		27	Wyoming	0	0.0%
						District of Columbia	0	0.0%

Source: U.S. Department of Transportation, Bureau of Transportation Statistics
"State Transportation Statistics 2005" (http://www.bts.gov/publications/state_transportation_profiles/)

Rural Road and Street Mileage in 2005

National Total = 2,985,804 Rural Miles*

ALPHA ORDER					RANK ORDER			
RANK	STATE	MILES	% of USA		RANK	STATE	MILES	% of USA
18	Alabama	74,418	2.5%		1	Texas	220,722	7.4%
43	Alaska	12,114	0.4%		2	Kansas	123,695	4.1%
35	Arizona	37,068	1.2%		3	Minnesota	115,641	3.9%
9	Arkansas	87,726	2.9%		4	Missouri	106,473	3.6%
13	California	84,471	2.8%		5	Iowa	102,858	3.4%
23	Colorado	68,779	2.3%		6	Illinois	100,358	3.4%
47	Connecticut	6,154	0.2%		7	Oklahoma	97,621	3.3%
48	Delaware	3,209	0.1%		8	Wisconsin	92,210	3.1%
34	Florida	39,468	1.3%		9	Arkansas	87,726	2.9%
15	Georgia	80,658	2.7%		10	Nebraska	87,250	2.9%
49	Hawaii	2,034	0.1%		11	Michigan	86,033	2.9%
33	Idaho	42,388	1.4%		12	North Dakota	84,947	2.8%
6	Illinois	100,358	3.4%		13	California	84,471	2.8%
19	Indiana	74,345	2.5%		14	South Dakota	81,286	2.7%
5	Iowa	102,858	3.4%		15	Georgia	80,658	2.7%
2	Kansas	123,695	4.1%		16	Ohio	80,370	2.7%
25	Kentucky	65,701	2.2%		17	Pennsylvania	76,186	2.6%
32	Louisiana	45,434	1.5%		18	Alabama	74,418	2.5%
40	Maine	19,836	0.7%		19	Indiana	74,345	2.5%
41	Maryland	13,964	0.5%		20	New York	72,117	2.4%
45	Massachusetts	7,952	0.3%		21	North Carolina	71,015	2.4%
11	Michigan	86,033	2.9%		22	Tennessee	69,032	2.3%
3	Minnesota	115,641	3.9%		23	Colorado	68,779	2.3%
26	Mississippi	63,550	2.1%		24	Montana	66,585	2.2%
4	Missouri	106,473	3.6%		25	Kentucky	65,701	2.2%
24	Montana	66,585	2.2%		26	Mississippi	63,550	2.1%
10	Nebraska	87,250	2.9%		27	Washington	63,234	2.1%
38	Nevada	27,696	0.9%		28	New Mexico	55,785	1.9%
44	New Hampshire	10,845	0.4%		29	Oregon	51,748	1.7%
46	New Jersey	7,319	0.2%		30	Virginia	50,474	1.7%
28	New Mexico	55,785	1.9%		31	South Carolina	49,787	1.7%
20	New York	72,117	2.4%		32	Louisiana	45,434	1.5%
21	North Carolina	71,015	2.4%		33	Idaho	42,388	1.4%
12	North Dakota	84,947	2.8%		34	Florida	39,468	1.3%
16	Ohio	80,370	2.7%		35	Arizona	37,068	1.2%
7	Oklahoma	97,621	3.3%		36	Utah	32,996	1.1%
29	Oregon	51,748	1.7%		37	West Virginia	32,845	1.1%
17	Pennsylvania	76,186	2.6%		38	Nevada	27,696	0.9%
50	Rhode Island	1,266	0.0%		39	Wyoming	25,139	0.8%
31	South Carolina	49,787	1.7%		40	Maine	19,836	0.7%
14	South Dakota	81,286	2.7%		41	Maryland	13,964	0.5%
22	Tennessee	69,032	2.3%		42	Vermont	13,002	0.4%
1	Texas	220,722	7.4%		43	Alaska	12,114	0.4%
36	Utah	32,996	1.1%		44	New Hampshire	10,845	0.4%
42	Vermont	13,002	0.4%		45	Massachusetts	7,952	0.3%
30	Virginia	50,474	1.7%		46	New Jersey	7,319	0.2%
27	Washington	63,234	2.1%		47	Connecticut	6,154	0.2%
37	West Virginia	32,845	1.1%		48	Delaware	3,209	0.1%
8	Wisconsin	92,210	3.1%		49	Hawaii	2,034	0.1%
39	Wyoming	25,139	0.8%		50	Rhode Island	1,266	0.0%
						District of Columbia	0	0.0%

Source: U.S. Department of Transportation, Federal Highway Administration
"Highway Statistics 2005" (Table HM-10) (http://www.fhwa.dot.gov/policy/ohpi/hss/index.htm)
*Does not include 3,106 miles of rural roads and streets in Puerto Rico.

Urban Road and Street Mileage in 2005

National Total = 1,009,840 Urban Miles*

ALPHA ORDER

RANK	STATE	MILES	% of USA
15	Alabama	21,627	2.1%
48	Alaska	2,255	0.2%
13	Arizona	22,722	2.3%
32	Arkansas	10,933	1.1%
1	California	85,435	8.5%
21	Colorado	18,819	1.9%
27	Connecticut	15,040	1.5%
43	Delaware	2,885	0.3%
3	Florida	81,089	8.0%
8	Georgia	36,987	3.7%
47	Hawaii	2,287	0.2%
39	Idaho	4,741	0.5%
7	Illinois	38,475	3.8%
18	Indiana	21,230	2.1%
31	Iowa	11,114	1.1%
30	Kansas	11,767	1.2%
29	Kentucky	12,320	1.2%
25	Louisiana	15,519	1.5%
42	Maine	2,971	0.3%
22	Maryland	16,998	1.7%
12	Massachusetts	27,945	2.8%
9	Michigan	35,423	3.5%
24	Minnesota	16,407	1.6%
33	Mississippi	10,631	1.1%
20	Missouri	19,349	1.9%
44	Montana	2,753	0.3%
37	Nebraska	6,060	0.6%
36	Nevada	6,928	0.7%
40	New Hampshire	4,721	0.5%
11	New Jersey	31,233	3.1%
35	New Mexico	7,973	0.8%
6	New York	41,226	4.1%
10	North Carolina	32,113	3.2%
49	North Dakota	1,846	0.2%
5	Ohio	44,470	4.4%
26	Oklahoma	15,316	1.5%
28	Oregon	12,795	1.3%
4	Pennsylvania	44,482	4.4%
38	Rhode Island	5,225	0.5%
23	South Carolina	16,451	1.6%
45	South Dakota	2,625	0.3%
17	Tennessee	21,419	2.1%
2	Texas	83,449	8.3%
34	Utah	10,579	1.0%
50	Vermont	1,397	0.1%
16	Virginia	21,487	2.1%
19	Washington	20,147	2.0%
41	West Virginia	4,183	0.4%
14	Wisconsin	21,932	2.2%
46	Wyoming	2,561	0.3%

RANK ORDER

RANK	STATE	MILES	% of USA
1	California	85,435	8.5%
2	Texas	83,449	8.3%
3	Florida	81,089	8.0%
4	Pennsylvania	44,482	4.4%
5	Ohio	44,470	4.4%
6	New York	41,226	4.1%
7	Illinois	38,475	3.8%
8	Georgia	36,987	3.7%
9	Michigan	35,423	3.5%
10	North Carolina	32,113	3.2%
11	New Jersey	31,233	3.1%
12	Massachusetts	27,945	2.8%
13	Arizona	22,722	2.3%
14	Wisconsin	21,932	2.2%
15	Alabama	21,627	2.1%
16	Virginia	21,487	2.1%
17	Tennessee	21,419	2.1%
18	Indiana	21,230	2.1%
19	Washington	20,147	2.0%
20	Missouri	19,349	1.9%
21	Colorado	18,819	1.9%
22	Maryland	16,998	1.7%
23	South Carolina	16,451	1.6%
24	Minnesota	16,407	1.6%
25	Louisiana	15,519	1.5%
26	Oklahoma	15,316	1.5%
27	Connecticut	15,040	1.5%
28	Oregon	12,795	1.3%
29	Kentucky	12,320	1.2%
30	Kansas	11,767	1.2%
31	Iowa	11,114	1.1%
32	Arkansas	10,933	1.1%
33	Mississippi	10,631	1.1%
34	Utah	10,579	1.0%
35	New Mexico	7,973	0.8%
36	Nevada	6,928	0.7%
37	Nebraska	6,060	0.6%
38	Rhode Island	5,225	0.5%
39	Idaho	4,741	0.5%
40	New Hampshire	4,721	0.5%
41	West Virginia	4,183	0.4%
42	Maine	2,971	0.3%
43	Delaware	2,885	0.3%
44	Montana	2,753	0.3%
45	South Dakota	2,625	0.3%
46	Wyoming	2,561	0.3%
47	Hawaii	2,287	0.2%
48	Alaska	2,255	0.2%
49	North Dakota	1,846	0.2%
50	Vermont	1,397	0.1%
	District of Columbia	1,500	0.1%

Source: U.S. Department of Transportation, Federal Highway Administration
"Highway Statistics 2005" (Table HM-10) (http://www.fhwa.dot.gov/policy/ohpi/hss/index.htm)
*Does not include 12,885 miles of urban roads and streets in Puerto Rico.

Percent of Roadways in Mediocre or Poor Condition: 2005

National Percent = 17.4%*

ALPHA ORDER

RANK	STATE	PERCENT
36	Alabama	10.3
18	Alaska	21.0
41	Arizona	8.7
11	Arkansas	25.4
2	California	38.8
34	Colorado	11.6
29	Connecticut	14.3
26	Delaware	17.2
49	Florida	3.0
50	Georgia	1.0
17	Hawaii	22.2
3	Idaho	35.1
25	Illinois	17.8
23	Indiana	18.2
27	Iowa	15.9
6	Kansas	31.7
48	Kentucky	4.4
13	Louisiana	25.0
14	Maine	24.6
4	Maryland	34.7
5	Massachusetts	33.7
16	Michigan	22.6
38	Minnesota	9.2
20	Mississippi	19.6
21	Missouri	18.9
43	Montana	6.1
30	Nebraska	13.6
42	Nevada	8.0
32	New Hampshire	12.5
1	New Jersey	49.9
7	New Mexico	31.4
24	New York	17.9
31	North Carolina	12.8
37	North Dakota	9.7
39	Ohio	9.1
9	Oklahoma	29.5
45	Oregon	5.6
10	Pennsylvania	25.8
8	Rhode Island	29.9
28	South Carolina	15.0
19	South Dakota	19.7
43	Tennessee	6.1
33	Texas	12.0
46	Utah	5.1
12	Vermont	25.2
40	Virginia	8.9
35	Washington	10.8
15	West Virginia	24.0
22	Wisconsin	18.6
47	Wyoming	4.6

RANK ORDER

RANK	STATE	PERCENT
1	New Jersey	49.9
2	California	38.8
3	Idaho	35.1
4	Maryland	34.7
5	Massachusetts	33.7
6	Kansas	31.7
7	New Mexico	31.4
8	Rhode Island	29.9
9	Oklahoma	29.5
10	Pennsylvania	25.8
11	Arkansas	25.4
12	Vermont	25.2
13	Louisiana	25.0
14	Maine	24.6
15	West Virginia	24.0
16	Michigan	22.6
17	Hawaii	22.2
18	Alaska	21.0
19	South Dakota	19.7
20	Mississippi	19.6
21	Missouri	18.9
22	Wisconsin	18.6
23	Indiana	18.2
24	New York	17.9
25	Illinois	17.8
26	Delaware	17.2
27	Iowa	15.9
28	South Carolina	15.0
29	Connecticut	14.3
30	Nebraska	13.6
31	North Carolina	12.8
32	New Hampshire	12.5
33	Texas	12.0
34	Colorado	11.6
35	Washington	10.8
36	Alabama	10.3
37	North Dakota	9.7
38	Minnesota	9.2
39	Ohio	9.1
40	Virginia	8.9
41	Arizona	8.7
42	Nevada	8.0
43	Montana	6.1
43	Tennessee	6.1
45	Oregon	5.6
46	Utah	5.1
47	Wyoming	4.6
48	Kentucky	4.4
49	Florida	3.0
50	Georgia	1.0

District of Columbia — 25.2

Source: CQ Press using data from U.S. Department of Transportation, Bureau of Transportation Statistics
"State Transportation Statistics 2006" (http://www.bts.gov/publications/state_transportation_profiles/)
*Does not include 4,416 miles for which the condition is not reported. Road condition ratings are derived from the International Roughness Index (IRI) and the Present Serviceability Rating (PSR). States are required to report to the Federal Highway Administration (FHWA) IRI data for the Interstate system, other principal arterials, rural minor arterials, and the National Highway System regardless of functional system.

Bridges in 2007

National Total = 597,620 Bridges*

ALPHA ORDER

RANK	STATE	BRIDGES	% of USA
15	Alabama	15,881	2.7%
47	Alaska	1,229	0.2%
29	Arizona	7,348	1.2%
23	Arkansas	12,531	2.1%
6	California	24,184	4.0%
27	Colorado	8,366	1.4%
38	Connecticut	4,175	0.7%
49	Delaware	857	0.1%
24	Florida	11,663	2.0%
17	Georgia	14,563	2.4%
48	Hawaii	1,115	0.2%
39	Idaho	4,104	0.7%
3	Illinois	25,998	4.4%
11	Indiana	18,494	3.1%
5	Iowa	24,776	4.1%
4	Kansas	25,461	4.3%
19	Kentucky	13,637	2.3%
21	Louisiana	13,342	2.2%
44	Maine	2,387	0.4%
34	Maryland	5,127	0.9%
35	Massachusetts	5,018	0.8%
25	Michigan	10,923	1.8%
22	Minnesota	13,067	2.2%
14	Mississippi	17,007	2.8%
7	Missouri	24,071	4.0%
36	Montana	4,980	0.8%
16	Nebraska	15,475	2.6%
46	Nevada	1,705	0.3%
45	New Hampshire	2,364	0.4%
32	New Jersey	6,448	1.1%
40	New Mexico	3,850	0.6%
13	New York	17,361	2.9%
12	North Carolina	17,783	3.0%
37	North Dakota	4,458	0.7%
2	Ohio	27,998	4.7%
8	Oklahoma	23,524	3.9%
30	Oregon	7,318	1.2%
9	Pennsylvania	22,325	3.7%
50	Rhode Island	748	0.1%
26	South Carolina	9,221	1.5%
33	South Dakota	5,924	1.0%
10	Tennessee	19,838	3.3%
1	Texas	50,271	8.4%
42	Utah	2,851	0.5%
43	Vermont	2,712	0.5%
20	Virginia	13,417	2.2%
28	Washington	7,651	1.3%
31	West Virginia	7,001	1.2%
18	Wisconsin	13,798	2.3%
41	Wyoming	3,030	0.5%

RANK ORDER

RANK	STATE	BRIDGES	% of USA
1	Texas	50,271	8.4%
2	Ohio	27,998	4.7%
3	Illinois	25,998	4.4%
4	Kansas	25,461	4.3%
5	Iowa	24,776	4.1%
6	California	24,184	4.0%
7	Missouri	24,071	4.0%
8	Oklahoma	23,524	3.9%
9	Pennsylvania	22,325	3.7%
10	Tennessee	19,838	3.3%
11	Indiana	18,494	3.1%
12	North Carolina	17,783	3.0%
13	New York	17,361	2.9%
14	Mississippi	17,007	2.8%
15	Alabama	15,881	2.7%
16	Nebraska	15,475	2.6%
17	Georgia	14,563	2.4%
18	Wisconsin	13,798	2.3%
19	Kentucky	13,637	2.3%
20	Virginia	13,417	2.2%
21	Louisiana	13,342	2.2%
22	Minnesota	13,067	2.2%
23	Arkansas	12,531	2.1%
24	Florida	11,663	2.0%
25	Michigan	10,923	1.8%
26	South Carolina	9,221	1.5%
27	Colorado	8,366	1.4%
28	Washington	7,651	1.3%
29	Arizona	7,348	1.2%
30	Oregon	7,318	1.2%
31	West Virginia	7,001	1.2%
32	New Jersey	6,448	1.1%
33	South Dakota	5,924	1.0%
34	Maryland	5,127	0.9%
35	Massachusetts	5,018	0.8%
36	Montana	4,980	0.8%
37	North Dakota	4,458	0.7%
38	Connecticut	4,175	0.7%
39	Idaho	4,104	0.7%
40	New Mexico	3,850	0.6%
41	Wyoming	3,030	0.5%
42	Utah	2,851	0.5%
43	Vermont	2,712	0.5%
44	Maine	2,387	0.4%
45	New Hampshire	2,364	0.4%
46	Nevada	1,705	0.3%
47	Alaska	1,229	0.2%
48	Hawaii	1,115	0.2%
49	Delaware	857	0.1%
50	Rhode Island	748	0.1%
	District of Columbia	245	0.0%

Source: U.S. Department of Transportation, Federal Highway Administration
"Deficient Bridges by State and Highway System, 2007" (http://www.fhwa.dot.gov/bridge/deficient.htm)
*As of December 2007. Includes federal-aid and nonfederal-aid system bridges. National total does not include 2,146 bridges in Puerto Rico.

Deficient Bridges in 2007

National Total = 151,253 Deficient Bridges*

RANK	STATE	BRIDGES	% of USA
15	Alabama	4,057	2.7%
48	Alaska	334	0.2%
41	Arizona	781	0.5%
21	Arkansas	2,905	1.9%
5	California	6,977	4.6%
33	Colorado	1,404	0.9%
34	Connecticut	1,400	0.9%
50	Delaware	132	0.1%
29	Florida	1,994	1.3%
20	Georgia	2,916	1.9%
45	Hawaii	500	0.3%
40	Idaho	801	0.5%
11	Illinois	4,341	2.9%
16	Indiana	4,034	2.7%
8	Iowa	6,608	4.4%
9	Kansas	5,363	3.5%
13	Kentucky	4,290	2.8%
17	Louisiana	3,960	2.6%
39	Maine	817	0.5%
35	Maryland	1,368	0.9%
24	Massachusetts	2,572	1.7%
22	Michigan	2,888	1.9%
31	Minnesota	1,579	1.0%
12	Mississippi	4,317	2.9%
3	Missouri	7,541	5.0%
36	Montana	1,014	0.7%
18	Nebraska	3,623	2.4%
49	Nevada	203	0.1%
42	New Hampshire	741	0.5%
25	New Jersey	2,251	1.5%
43	New Mexico	698	0.5%
7	New York	6,646	4.4%
10	North Carolina	5,059	3.3%
37	North Dakota	992	0.7%
6	Ohio	6,863	4.5%
4	Oklahoma	7,407	4.9%
30	Oregon	1,669	1.1%
2	Pennsylvania	9,736	6.4%
47	Rhode Island	396	0.3%
27	South Carolina	2,068	1.4%
32	South Dakota	1,477	1.0%
14	Tennessee	4,101	2.7%
1	Texas	10,037	6.6%
46	Utah	487	0.3%
38	Vermont	967	0.6%
19	Virginia	3,442	2.3%
28	Washington	2,061	1.4%
23	West Virginia	2,573	1.7%
26	Wisconsin	2,091	1.4%
44	Wyoming	620	0.4%

RANK	STATE	BRIDGES	% of USA
1	Texas	10,037	6.6%
2	Pennsylvania	9,736	6.4%
3	Missouri	7,541	5.0%
4	Oklahoma	7,407	4.9%
5	California	6,977	4.6%
6	Ohio	6,863	4.5%
7	New York	6,646	4.4%
8	Iowa	6,608	4.4%
9	Kansas	5,363	3.5%
10	North Carolina	5,059	3.3%
11	Illinois	4,341	2.9%
12	Mississippi	4,317	2.9%
13	Kentucky	4,290	2.8%
14	Tennessee	4,101	2.7%
15	Alabama	4,057	2.7%
16	Indiana	4,034	2.7%
17	Louisiana	3,960	2.6%
18	Nebraska	3,623	2.4%
19	Virginia	3,442	2.3%
20	Georgia	2,916	1.9%
21	Arkansas	2,905	1.9%
22	Michigan	2,888	1.9%
23	West Virginia	2,573	1.7%
24	Massachusetts	2,572	1.7%
25	New Jersey	2,251	1.5%
26	Wisconsin	2,091	1.4%
27	South Carolina	2,068	1.4%
28	Washington	2,061	1.4%
29	Florida	1,994	1.3%
30	Oregon	1,669	1.1%
31	Minnesota	1,579	1.0%
32	South Dakota	1,477	1.0%
33	Colorado	1,404	0.9%
34	Connecticut	1,400	0.9%
35	Maryland	1,368	0.9%
36	Montana	1,014	0.7%
37	North Dakota	992	0.7%
38	Vermont	967	0.6%
39	Maine	817	0.5%
40	Idaho	801	0.5%
41	Arizona	781	0.5%
42	New Hampshire	741	0.5%
43	New Mexico	698	0.5%
44	Wyoming	620	0.4%
45	Hawaii	500	0.3%
46	Utah	487	0.3%
47	Rhode Island	396	0.3%
48	Alaska	334	0.2%
49	Nevada	203	0.1%
50	Delaware	132	0.1%
	District of Columbia	152	0.1%

Source: U.S. Department of Transportation, Federal Highway Administration
   "Deficient Bridges by State and Highway System, 2007" (http://www.fhwa.dot.gov/bridge/deficient.htm)
*As of December 2007. Includes federal-aid and nonfederal-aid system bridges. National total does not include 1,063 deficient bridges in Puerto Rico. Bridges classified as deficient are either functionally obsolete or structurally deficient and are not necessarily unsafe.

Deficient Bridges as a Percent of Total Bridges in 2007

National Percent = 25.3% of Bridges are Deficient*

<table>
<tr><td colspan="3">ALPHA ORDER</td><td colspan="3">RANK ORDER</td></tr>
<tr><td>RANK</td><td>STATE</td><td>PERCENT</td><td>RANK</td><td>STATE</td><td>PERCENT</td></tr>
<tr><td>24</td><td>Alabama</td><td>25.5</td><td>1</td><td>Rhode Island</td><td>52.9</td></tr>
<tr><td>18</td><td>Alaska</td><td>27.2</td><td>2</td><td>Massachusetts</td><td>51.3</td></tr>
<tr><td>50</td><td>Arizona</td><td>10.6</td><td>3</td><td>Hawaii</td><td>44.8</td></tr>
<tr><td>29</td><td>Arkansas</td><td>23.2</td><td>4</td><td>Pennsylvania</td><td>43.6</td></tr>
<tr><td>16</td><td>California</td><td>28.8</td><td>5</td><td>New York</td><td>38.3</td></tr>
<tr><td>44</td><td>Colorado</td><td>16.8</td><td>6</td><td>West Virginia</td><td>36.8</td></tr>
<tr><td>10</td><td>Connecticut</td><td>33.5</td><td>7</td><td>Vermont</td><td>35.7</td></tr>
<tr><td>46</td><td>Delaware</td><td>15.4</td><td>8</td><td>New Jersey</td><td>34.9</td></tr>
<tr><td>42</td><td>Florida</td><td>17.1</td><td>9</td><td>Maine</td><td>34.2</td></tr>
<tr><td>38</td><td>Georgia</td><td>20.0</td><td>10</td><td>Connecticut</td><td>33.5</td></tr>
<tr><td>3</td><td>Hawaii</td><td>44.8</td><td>11</td><td>Kentucky</td><td>31.5</td></tr>
<tr><td>40</td><td>Idaho</td><td>19.5</td><td>11</td><td>Oklahoma</td><td>31.5</td></tr>
<tr><td>45</td><td>Illinois</td><td>16.7</td><td>13</td><td>Missouri</td><td>31.3</td></tr>
<tr><td>33</td><td>Indiana</td><td>21.8</td><td>13</td><td>New Hampshire</td><td>31.3</td></tr>
<tr><td>20</td><td>Iowa</td><td>26.7</td><td>15</td><td>Louisiana</td><td>29.7</td></tr>
<tr><td>34</td><td>Kansas</td><td>21.1</td><td>16</td><td>California</td><td>28.8</td></tr>
<tr><td>11</td><td>Kentucky</td><td>31.5</td><td>17</td><td>North Carolina</td><td>28.4</td></tr>
<tr><td>15</td><td>Louisiana</td><td>29.7</td><td>18</td><td>Alaska</td><td>27.2</td></tr>
<tr><td>9</td><td>Maine</td><td>34.2</td><td>19</td><td>Washington</td><td>26.9</td></tr>
<tr><td>20</td><td>Maryland</td><td>26.7</td><td>20</td><td>Iowa</td><td>26.7</td></tr>
<tr><td>2</td><td>Massachusetts</td><td>51.3</td><td>20</td><td>Maryland</td><td>26.7</td></tr>
<tr><td>22</td><td>Michigan</td><td>26.4</td><td>22</td><td>Michigan</td><td>26.4</td></tr>
<tr><td>48</td><td>Minnesota</td><td>12.1</td><td>23</td><td>Virginia</td><td>25.7</td></tr>
<tr><td>25</td><td>Mississippi</td><td>25.4</td><td>24</td><td>Alabama</td><td>25.5</td></tr>
<tr><td>13</td><td>Missouri</td><td>31.3</td><td>25</td><td>Mississippi</td><td>25.4</td></tr>
<tr><td>37</td><td>Montana</td><td>20.4</td><td>26</td><td>South Dakota</td><td>24.9</td></tr>
<tr><td>28</td><td>Nebraska</td><td>23.4</td><td>27</td><td>Ohio</td><td>24.5</td></tr>
<tr><td>49</td><td>Nevada</td><td>11.9</td><td>28</td><td>Nebraska</td><td>23.4</td></tr>
<tr><td>13</td><td>New Hampshire</td><td>31.3</td><td>29</td><td>Arkansas</td><td>23.2</td></tr>
<tr><td>8</td><td>New Jersey</td><td>34.9</td><td>30</td><td>Oregon</td><td>22.8</td></tr>
<tr><td>41</td><td>New Mexico</td><td>18.1</td><td>31</td><td>South Carolina</td><td>22.4</td></tr>
<tr><td>5</td><td>New York</td><td>38.3</td><td>32</td><td>North Dakota</td><td>22.3</td></tr>
<tr><td>17</td><td>North Carolina</td><td>28.4</td><td>33</td><td>Indiana</td><td>21.8</td></tr>
<tr><td>32</td><td>North Dakota</td><td>22.3</td><td>34</td><td>Kansas</td><td>21.1</td></tr>
<tr><td>27</td><td>Ohio</td><td>24.5</td><td>35</td><td>Tennessee</td><td>20.7</td></tr>
<tr><td>11</td><td>Oklahoma</td><td>31.5</td><td>36</td><td>Wyoming</td><td>20.5</td></tr>
<tr><td>30</td><td>Oregon</td><td>22.8</td><td>37</td><td>Montana</td><td>20.4</td></tr>
<tr><td>4</td><td>Pennsylvania</td><td>43.6</td><td>38</td><td>Georgia</td><td>20.0</td></tr>
<tr><td>1</td><td>Rhode Island</td><td>52.9</td><td>38</td><td>Texas</td><td>20.0</td></tr>
<tr><td>31</td><td>South Carolina</td><td>22.4</td><td>40</td><td>Idaho</td><td>19.5</td></tr>
<tr><td>26</td><td>South Dakota</td><td>24.9</td><td>41</td><td>New Mexico</td><td>18.1</td></tr>
<tr><td>35</td><td>Tennessee</td><td>20.7</td><td>42</td><td>Florida</td><td>17.1</td></tr>
<tr><td>38</td><td>Texas</td><td>20.0</td><td>42</td><td>Utah</td><td>17.1</td></tr>
<tr><td>42</td><td>Utah</td><td>17.1</td><td>44</td><td>Colorado</td><td>16.8</td></tr>
<tr><td>7</td><td>Vermont</td><td>35.7</td><td>45</td><td>Illinois</td><td>16.7</td></tr>
<tr><td>23</td><td>Virginia</td><td>25.7</td><td>46</td><td>Delaware</td><td>15.4</td></tr>
<tr><td>19</td><td>Washington</td><td>26.9</td><td>47</td><td>Wisconsin</td><td>15.2</td></tr>
<tr><td>6</td><td>West Virginia</td><td>36.8</td><td>48</td><td>Minnesota</td><td>12.1</td></tr>
<tr><td>47</td><td>Wisconsin</td><td>15.2</td><td>49</td><td>Nevada</td><td>11.9</td></tr>
<tr><td>36</td><td>Wyoming</td><td>20.5</td><td>50</td><td>Arizona</td><td>10.6</td></tr>
<tr><td colspan="3"></td><td colspan="2">District of Columbia</td><td>62.0</td></tr>
</table>

Source: CQ Press using data from U.S. Department of Transportation, Federal Highway Administration
   "Deficient Bridges by State and Highway System, 2007" (http://www.fhwa.dot.gov/bridge/deficient.htm)
*As of December 2007. Includes federal-aid and nonfederal-aid system bridges. National percent does not include bridges in
Puerto Rico. Bridges classified as deficient are either functionally obsolete or structurally deficient and are not necessarily
unsafe.

Vehicle-Miles of Travel in 2005

National Total = 2,989,807,000,000 Miles

ALPHA ORDER

RANK	STATE	MILES	% of USA
18	Alabama	59,661,000,000	2.0%
50	Alaska	5,035,000,000	0.2%
17	Arizona	59,799,000,000	2.0%
30	Arkansas	31,972,000,000	1.1%
1	California	329,267,000,000	11.0%
24	Colorado	47,962,000,000	1.6%
31	Connecticut	31,675,000,000	1.1%
44	Delaware	9,508,000,000	0.3%
3	Florida	201,531,000,000	6.7%
5	Georgia	113,509,000,000	3.8%
43	Hawaii	10,083,000,000	0.3%
40	Idaho	14,866,000,000	0.5%
8	Illinois	107,706,000,000	3.6%
13	Indiana	71,799,000,000	2.4%
32	Iowa	31,060,000,000	1.0%
33	Kansas	29,621,000,000	1.0%
25	Kentucky	47,466,000,000	1.6%
27	Louisiana	44,979,000,000	1.5%
39	Maine	14,925,000,000	0.5%
20	Maryland	56,319,000,000	1.9%
22	Massachusetts	55,458,000,000	1.9%
9	Michigan	104,052,000,000	3.5%
19	Minnesota	56,904,000,000	1.9%
28	Mississippi	42,186,000,000	1.4%
15	Missouri	68,754,000,000	2.3%
42	Montana	11,126,000,000	0.4%
38	Nebraska	19,291,000,000	0.6%
36	Nevada	20,776,000,000	0.7%
41	New Hampshire	13,429,000,000	0.4%
12	New Jersey	73,819,000,000	2.5%
35	New Mexico	23,966,000,000	0.8%
4	New York	137,521,000,000	4.6%
10	North Carolina	101,268,000,000	3.4%
49	North Dakota	7,570,000,000	0.3%
6	Ohio	110,491,000,000	3.7%
26	Oklahoma	47,019,000,000	1.6%
29	Oregon	35,282,000,000	1.2%
7	Pennsylvania	108,042,000,000	3.6%
47	Rhode Island	8,300,000,000	0.3%
23	South Carolina	49,434,000,000	1.7%
46	South Dakota	8,397,000,000	0.3%
14	Tennessee	70,814,000,000	2.4%
2	Texas	235,170,000,000	7.9%
34	Utah	25,158,000,000	0.8%
48	Vermont	7,713,000,000	0.3%
11	Virginia	80,337,000,000	2.7%
21	Washington	55,476,000,000	1.9%
37	West Virginia	20,523,000,000	0.7%
16	Wisconsin	60,017,000,000	2.0%
45	Wyoming	9,058,000,000	0.3%

RANK ORDER

RANK	STATE	MILES	% of USA
1	California	329,267,000,000	11.0%
2	Texas	235,170,000,000	7.9%
3	Florida	201,531,000,000	6.7%
4	New York	137,521,000,000	4.6%
5	Georgia	113,509,000,000	3.8%
6	Ohio	110,491,000,000	3.7%
7	Pennsylvania	108,042,000,000	3.6%
8	Illinois	107,706,000,000	3.6%
9	Michigan	104,052,000,000	3.5%
10	North Carolina	101,268,000,000	3.4%
11	Virginia	80,337,000,000	2.7%
12	New Jersey	73,819,000,000	2.5%
13	Indiana	71,799,000,000	2.4%
14	Tennessee	70,814,000,000	2.4%
15	Missouri	68,754,000,000	2.3%
16	Wisconsin	60,017,000,000	2.0%
17	Arizona	59,799,000,000	2.0%
18	Alabama	59,661,000,000	2.0%
19	Minnesota	56,904,000,000	1.9%
20	Maryland	56,319,000,000	1.9%
21	Washington	55,476,000,000	1.9%
22	Massachusetts	55,458,000,000	1.9%
23	South Carolina	49,434,000,000	1.7%
24	Colorado	47,962,000,000	1.6%
25	Kentucky	47,466,000,000	1.6%
26	Oklahoma	47,019,000,000	1.6%
27	Louisiana	44,979,000,000	1.5%
28	Mississippi	42,186,000,000	1.4%
29	Oregon	35,282,000,000	1.2%
30	Arkansas	31,972,000,000	1.1%
31	Connecticut	31,675,000,000	1.1%
32	Iowa	31,060,000,000	1.0%
33	Kansas	29,621,000,000	1.0%
34	Utah	25,158,000,000	0.8%
35	New Mexico	23,966,000,000	0.8%
36	Nevada	20,776,000,000	0.7%
37	West Virginia	20,523,000,000	0.7%
38	Nebraska	19,291,000,000	0.6%
39	Maine	14,925,000,000	0.5%
40	Idaho	14,866,000,000	0.5%
41	New Hampshire	13,429,000,000	0.4%
42	Montana	11,126,000,000	0.4%
43	Hawaii	10,083,000,000	0.3%
44	Delaware	9,508,000,000	0.3%
45	Wyoming	9,058,000,000	0.3%
46	South Dakota	8,397,000,000	0.3%
47	Rhode Island	8,300,000,000	0.3%
48	Vermont	7,713,000,000	0.3%
49	North Dakota	7,570,000,000	0.3%
50	Alaska	5,035,000,000	0.2%
	District of Columbia	3,713,000,000	0.1%

Source: U.S. Department of Transportation, Federal Highway Administration
"Highway Statistics 2005" (Table VM-2) (http://www.fhwa.dot.gov/policy/ohpi/hss/index.htm)

Highway Fatalities in 2005

National Total = 43,443 Fatalities

ALPHA ORDER

RANK	STATE	FATALITIES	% of USA
13	Alabama	1,131	2.6%
50	Alaska	72	0.2%
12	Arizona	1,177	2.7%
24	Arkansas	648	1.5%
1	California	4,329	10.0%
27	Colorado	606	1.4%
39	Connecticut	274	0.6%
46	Delaware	134	0.3%
2	Florida	3,543	8.2%
4	Georgia	1,729	4.0%
45	Hawaii	140	0.3%
38	Idaho	275	0.6%
8	Illinois	1,361	3.1%
19	Indiana	938	2.2%
31	Iowa	450	1.0%
33	Kansas	428	1.0%
16	Kentucky	985	2.3%
17	Louisiana	955	2.2%
43	Maine	169	0.4%
26	Maryland	614	1.4%
32	Massachusetts	442	1.0%
14	Michigan	1,129	2.6%
28	Minnesota	559	1.3%
20	Mississippi	931	2.1%
11	Missouri	1,257	2.9%
40	Montana	251	0.6%
37	Nebraska	276	0.6%
34	Nevada	427	1.0%
44	New Hampshire	166	0.4%
23	New Jersey	748	1.7%
29	New Mexico	488	1.1%
7	New York	1,429	3.3%
6	North Carolina	1,534	3.5%
47	North Dakota	123	0.3%
9	Ohio	1,323	3.0%
22	Oklahoma	802	1.8%
29	Oregon	488	1.1%
5	Pennsylvania	1,616	3.7%
48	Rhode Island	87	0.2%
15	South Carolina	1,093	2.5%
41	South Dakota	186	0.4%
10	Tennessee	1,270	2.9%
3	Texas	3,504	8.1%
36	Utah	282	0.6%
49	Vermont	73	0.2%
18	Virginia	947	2.2%
25	Washington	647	1.5%
35	West Virginia	374	0.9%
21	Wisconsin	815	1.9%
42	Wyoming	170	0.4%

RANK ORDER

RANK	STATE	FATALITIES	% of USA
1	California	4,329	10.0%
2	Florida	3,543	8.2%
3	Texas	3,504	8.1%
4	Georgia	1,729	4.0%
5	Pennsylvania	1,616	3.7%
6	North Carolina	1,534	3.5%
7	New York	1,429	3.3%
8	Illinois	1,361	3.1%
9	Ohio	1,323	3.0%
10	Tennessee	1,270	2.9%
11	Missouri	1,257	2.9%
12	Arizona	1,177	2.7%
13	Alabama	1,131	2.6%
14	Michigan	1,129	2.6%
15	South Carolina	1,093	2.5%
16	Kentucky	985	2.3%
17	Louisiana	955	2.2%
18	Virginia	947	2.2%
19	Indiana	938	2.2%
20	Mississippi	931	2.1%
21	Wisconsin	815	1.9%
22	Oklahoma	802	1.8%
23	New Jersey	748	1.7%
24	Arkansas	648	1.5%
25	Washington	647	1.5%
26	Maryland	614	1.4%
27	Colorado	606	1.4%
28	Minnesota	559	1.3%
29	New Mexico	488	1.1%
29	Oregon	488	1.1%
31	Iowa	450	1.0%
32	Massachusetts	442	1.0%
33	Kansas	428	1.0%
34	Nevada	427	1.0%
35	West Virginia	374	0.9%
36	Utah	282	0.6%
37	Nebraska	276	0.6%
38	Idaho	275	0.6%
39	Connecticut	274	0.6%
40	Montana	251	0.6%
41	South Dakota	186	0.4%
42	Wyoming	170	0.4%
43	Maine	169	0.4%
44	New Hampshire	166	0.4%
45	Hawaii	140	0.3%
46	Delaware	134	0.3%
47	North Dakota	123	0.3%
48	Rhode Island	87	0.2%
49	Vermont	73	0.2%
50	Alaska	72	0.2%
	District of Columbia	48	0.1%

Source: U.S. Department of Transportation, National Highway Traffic Safety Administration
"Traffic Safety Facts-Speeding" (http://www-nrd.nhtsa.dot.gov/Pubs/810629.PDF)

Highway Fatality Rate in 2005

National Rate = 1.45 Fatalities per 100 Million Vehicle-Miles of Travel

ALPHA ORDER

RANK	STATE	RATE
11	Alabama	1.90
26	Alaska	1.43
10	Arizona	1.97
9	Arkansas	2.03
32	California	1.31
34	Colorado	1.26
49	Connecticut	0.87
28	Delaware	1.41
17	Florida	1.76
20	Georgia	1.52
29	Hawaii	1.39
13	Idaho	1.85
34	Illinois	1.26
32	Indiana	1.31
24	Iowa	1.45
25	Kansas	1.44
6	Kentucky	2.08
5	Louisiana	2.12
40	Maine	1.13
42	Maryland	1.09
50	Massachusetts	0.80
42	Michigan	1.09
47	Minnesota	0.98
3	Mississippi	2.21
14	Missouri	1.83
1	Montana	2.26
26	Nebraska	1.43
7	Nevada	2.06
36	New Hampshire	1.24
46	New Jersey	1.01
8	New Mexico	2.04
45	New York	1.04
21	North Carolina	1.51
19	North Dakota	1.62
37	Ohio	1.20
18	Oklahoma	1.71
30	Oregon	1.38
22	Pennsylvania	1.50
44	Rhode Island	1.05
3	South Carolina	2.21
2	South Dakota	2.22
16	Tennessee	1.79
23	Texas	1.49
41	Utah	1.12
48	Vermont	0.95
38	Virginia	1.18
39	Washington	1.17
15	West Virginia	1.82
31	Wisconsin	1.36
12	Wyoming	1.88

RANK ORDER

RANK	STATE	RATE
1	Montana	2.26
2	South Dakota	2.22
3	Mississippi	2.21
3	South Carolina	2.21
5	Louisiana	2.12
6	Kentucky	2.08
7	Nevada	2.06
8	New Mexico	2.04
9	Arkansas	2.03
10	Arizona	1.97
11	Alabama	1.90
12	Wyoming	1.88
13	Idaho	1.85
14	Missouri	1.83
15	West Virginia	1.82
16	Tennessee	1.79
17	Florida	1.76
18	Oklahoma	1.71
19	North Dakota	1.62
20	Georgia	1.52
21	North Carolina	1.51
22	Pennsylvania	1.50
23	Texas	1.49
24	Iowa	1.45
25	Kansas	1.44
26	Alaska	1.43
26	Nebraska	1.43
28	Delaware	1.41
29	Hawaii	1.39
30	Oregon	1.38
31	Wisconsin	1.36
32	California	1.31
32	Indiana	1.31
34	Colorado	1.26
34	Illinois	1.26
36	New Hampshire	1.24
37	Ohio	1.20
38	Virginia	1.18
39	Washington	1.17
40	Maine	1.13
41	Utah	1.12
42	Maryland	1.09
42	Michigan	1.09
44	Rhode Island	1.05
45	New York	1.04
46	New Jersey	1.01
47	Minnesota	0.98
48	Vermont	0.95
49	Connecticut	0.87
50	Massachusetts	0.80

| | District of Columbia | 1.29 |

Source: CQ Press using data from U.S. Department of Transportation, National Highway Traffic Safety Administration "Traffic Safety Facts-Speeding" (http://www-nrd.nhtsa.dot.gov/Pubs/810629.PDF)

Percent of Traffic Fatalities That Were Speeding-Related: 2005

National Percent = 30.2%*

ALPHA ORDER

RANK	STATE	PERCENT
7	Alabama	43.6
15	Alaska	37.5
10	Arizona	39.1
47	Arkansas	16.0
22	California	34.0
24	Colorado	33.7
26	Connecticut	33.6
11	Delaware	38.8
50	Florida	6.7
43	Georgia	19.7
2	Hawaii	49.3
21	Idaho	34.5
12	Illinois	38.6
34	Indiana	27.5
49	Iowa	9.8
33	Kansas	27.8
44	Kentucky	19.0
45	Louisiana	18.8
1	Maine	50.9
20	Maryland	34.9
29	Massachusetts	33.0
40	Michigan	21.5
36	Minnesota	27.2
35	Mississippi	27.3
8	Missouri	42.1
12	Montana	38.6
46	Nebraska	18.5
15	Nevada	37.5
24	New Hampshire	33.7
48	New Jersey	10.6
23	New Mexico	33.8
32	New York	31.9
17	North Carolina	36.5
38	North Dakota	22.8
41	Ohio	20.9
18	Oklahoma	36.4
29	Oregon	33.0
3	Pennsylvania	46.8
4	Rhode Island	46.0
6	South Carolina	43.9
27	South Dakota	33.3
41	Tennessee	20.9
9	Texas	40.7
37	Utah	26.6
5	Vermont	45.2
28	Virginia	33.1
14	Washington	38.2
39	West Virginia	21.9
19	Wisconsin	36.1
31	Wyoming	32.9

RANK ORDER

RANK	STATE	PERCENT
1	Maine	50.9
2	Hawaii	49.3
3	Pennsylvania	46.8
4	Rhode Island	46.0
5	Vermont	45.2
6	South Carolina	43.9
7	Alabama	43.6
8	Missouri	42.1
9	Texas	40.7
10	Arizona	39.1
11	Delaware	38.8
12	Illinois	38.6
12	Montana	38.6
14	Washington	38.2
15	Alaska	37.5
15	Nevada	37.5
17	North Carolina	36.5
18	Oklahoma	36.4
19	Wisconsin	36.1
20	Maryland	34.9
21	Idaho	34.5
22	California	34.0
23	New Mexico	33.8
24	Colorado	33.7
24	New Hampshire	33.7
26	Connecticut	33.6
27	South Dakota	33.3
28	Virginia	33.1
29	Massachusetts	33.0
29	Oregon	33.0
31	Wyoming	32.9
32	New York	31.9
33	Kansas	27.8
34	Indiana	27.5
35	Mississippi	27.3
36	Minnesota	27.2
37	Utah	26.6
38	North Dakota	22.8
39	West Virginia	21.9
40	Michigan	21.5
41	Ohio	20.9
41	Tennessee	20.9
43	Georgia	19.7
44	Kentucky	19.0
45	Louisiana	18.8
46	Nebraska	18.5
47	Arkansas	16.0
48	New Jersey	10.6
49	Iowa	9.8
50	Florida	6.7

| | District of Columbia | 35.4 |

Source: CQ Press using data from U.S. Department of Transportation, National Highway Traffic Safety Administration
    "Traffic Safety Facts-Speeding" (http://www-nrd.nhtsa.dot.gov/Pubs/810629.PDF)
*A speeding-related crash is if the driver was charged with a speeding-related offense or if an officer indicated that racing, driving too fast for conditions, or exceeding the posted speed limit was a contributing factor in the crash.

Percent of Vehicles Involved in Fatal Crashes That Were Large Trucks: 2005

National Percent = 8.3%*

ALPHA ORDER

RANK	STATE	PERCENT
30	Alabama	7.7
48	Alaska	3.9
43	Arizona	5.5
1	Arkansas	14.8
40	California	6.5
33	Colorado	7.6
45	Connecticut	4.6
46	Delaware	4.1
28	Florida	7.8
13	Georgia	9.6
49	Hawaii	2.3
15	Idaho	9.2
8	Illinois	10.1
6	Indiana	10.4
5	Iowa	10.9
2	Kansas	12.5
20	Kentucky	8.8
16	Louisiana	9.1
27	Maine	8.0
42	Maryland	6.3
47	Massachusetts	4.0
40	Michigan	6.5
28	Minnesota	7.8
37	Mississippi	6.9
16	Missouri	9.1
30	Montana	7.7
2	Nebraska	12.5
23	Nevada	8.4
44	New Hampshire	4.8
9	New Jersey	10.0
10	New Mexico	9.8
35	New York	7.3
16	North Carolina	9.1
34	North Dakota	7.5
19	Ohio	9.0
6	Oklahoma	10.4
21	Oregon	8.7
25	Pennsylvania	8.2
50	Rhode Island	0.9
23	South Carolina	8.4
38	South Dakota	6.6
25	Tennessee	8.2
14	Texas	9.5
30	Utah	7.7
10	Vermont	9.8
22	Virginia	8.5
38	Washington	6.6
10	West Virginia	9.8
35	Wisconsin	7.3
4	Wyoming	12.3

RANK ORDER

RANK	STATE	PERCENT
1	Arkansas	14.8
2	Kansas	12.5
2	Nebraska	12.5
4	Wyoming	12.3
5	Iowa	10.9
6	Indiana	10.4
6	Oklahoma	10.4
8	Illinois	10.1
9	New Jersey	10.0
10	New Mexico	9.8
10	Vermont	9.8
10	West Virginia	9.8
13	Georgia	9.6
14	Texas	9.5
15	Idaho	9.2
16	Louisiana	9.1
16	Missouri	9.1
16	North Carolina	9.1
19	Ohio	9.0
20	Kentucky	8.8
21	Oregon	8.7
22	Virginia	8.5
23	Nevada	8.4
23	South Carolina	8.4
25	Pennsylvania	8.2
25	Tennessee	8.2
27	Maine	8.0
28	Florida	7.8
28	Minnesota	7.8
30	Alabama	7.7
30	Montana	7.7
30	Utah	7.7
33	Colorado	7.6
34	North Dakota	7.5
35	New York	7.3
35	Wisconsin	7.3
37	Mississippi	6.9
38	South Dakota	6.6
38	Washington	6.6
40	California	6.5
40	Michigan	6.5
42	Maryland	6.3
43	Arizona	5.5
44	New Hampshire	4.8
45	Connecticut	4.6
46	Delaware	4.1
47	Massachusetts	4.0
48	Alaska	3.9
49	Hawaii	2.3
50	Rhode Island	0.9
	District of Columbia	5.3

Source: U.S. Department of Transportation, National Highway Traffic Safety Administration
   "Traffic Safety Facts-Large Trucks" (http://www-nrd.nhtsa.dot.gov/Pubs/largetruckstsf05.pdf)
*Large trucks are those with gross vehicle weight greater than 10,000 pounds. In 2005, 4,932 large trucks were involved in fatal crashes.

Lives Saved by Child Restraints, Seat Belts and Air Bags in 2006

National Total = 18,604 Lives

ALPHA ORDER

ALPHA ORDER

RANK	STATE	LIVES	% of USA
9	Alabama	549	3.0%
49	Alaska	37	0.2%
13	Arizona	451	2.4%
27	Arkansas	237	1.3%
1	California	2,158	11.6%
30	Colorado	210	1.1%
37	Connecticut	140	0.8%
43	Delaware	65	0.3%
3	Florida	1,132	6.1%
5	Georgia	802	4.3%
44	Hawaii	57	0.3%
38	Idaho	125	0.7%
8	Illinois	574	3.1%
16	Indiana	394	2.1%
28	Iowa	232	1.2%
32	Kansas	206	1.1%
22	Kentucky	317	1.7%
14	Louisiana	436	2.3%
42	Maine	80	0.4%
21	Maryland	338	1.8%
36	Massachusetts	148	0.8%
6	Michigan	618	3.3%
29	Minnesota	220	1.2%
20	Mississippi	345	1.9%
18	Missouri	364	2.0%
40	Montana	98	0.5%
39	Nebraska	119	0.6%
33	Nevada	193	1.0%
48	New Hampshire	38	0.2%
31	New Jersey	207	1.1%
26	New Mexico	241	1.3%
7	New York	584	3.1%
4	North Carolina	805	4.3%
47	North Dakota	46	0.2%
12	Ohio	511	2.7%
19	Oklahoma	359	1.9%
25	Oregon	284	1.5%
10	Pennsylvania	534	2.9%
50	Rhode Island	15	0.1%
17	South Carolina	385	2.1%
46	South Dakota	48	0.3%
11	Tennessee	530	2.8%
2	Texas	1,887	10.1%
34	Utah	166	0.9%
45	Vermont	50	0.3%
15	Virginia	402	2.2%
23	Washington	316	1.7%
35	West Virginia	157	0.8%
24	Wisconsin	292	1.6%
41	Wyoming	89	0.5%

RANK ORDER

RANK	STATE	LIVES	% of USA
1	California	2,158	11.6%
2	Texas	1,887	10.1%
3	Florida	1,132	6.1%
4	North Carolina	805	4.3%
5	Georgia	802	4.3%
6	Michigan	618	3.3%
7	New York	584	3.1%
8	Illinois	574	3.1%
9	Alabama	549	3.0%
10	Pennsylvania	534	2.9%
11	Tennessee	530	2.8%
12	Ohio	511	2.7%
13	Arizona	451	2.4%
14	Louisiana	436	2.3%
15	Virginia	402	2.2%
16	Indiana	394	2.1%
17	South Carolina	385	2.1%
18	Missouri	364	2.0%
19	Oklahoma	359	1.9%
20	Mississippi	345	1.9%
21	Maryland	338	1.8%
22	Kentucky	317	1.7%
23	Washington	316	1.7%
24	Wisconsin	292	1.6%
25	Oregon	284	1.5%
26	New Mexico	241	1.3%
27	Arkansas	237	1.3%
28	Iowa	232	1.2%
29	Minnesota	220	1.2%
30	Colorado	210	1.1%
31	New Jersey	207	1.1%
32	Kansas	206	1.1%
33	Nevada	193	1.0%
34	Utah	166	0.9%
35	West Virginia	157	0.8%
36	Massachusetts	148	0.8%
37	Connecticut	140	0.8%
38	Idaho	125	0.7%
39	Nebraska	119	0.6%
40	Montana	98	0.5%
41	Wyoming	89	0.5%
42	Maine	80	0.4%
43	Delaware	65	0.3%
44	Hawaii	57	0.3%
45	Vermont	50	0.3%
46	South Dakota	48	0.3%
47	North Dakota	46	0.2%
48	New Hampshire	38	0.2%
49	Alaska	37	0.2%
50	Rhode Island	15	0.1%
	District of Columbia	13	0.1%

Source: CQ Press using data from U.S. Department of Transportation, National Highway Traffic Safety Administration "Traffic Safety Crash Stats" (http://www-nrd.nhtsa.dot.gov/Pubs/810869.PDF)

Safety Belt Usage Rate in 2006

National Rate = 81.0% Use Safety Belts*

ALPHA ORDER			RANK ORDER		
RANK	STATE	PERCENT	RANK	STATE	PERCENT
20	Alabama	82.9	1	Washington	96.3
18	Alaska	83.2	2	Michigan	94.3
NA	Arizona**	NA	3	Oregon	94.1
38	Arkansas	69.3	4	California	93.4
4	California	93.4	5	Hawaii	92.5
23	Colorado	80.3	6	Texas	90.4
16	Connecticut	83.5	7	New Jersey	90.0
13	Delaware	86.1	8	Iowa	89.6
NA	Florida**	NA	8	New Mexico	89.6
NA	Georgia**	NA	10	Utah	88.6
5	Hawaii	92.5	11	North Carolina	88.5
24	Idaho	79.8	12	Illinois	87.8
12	Illinois	87.8	13	Delaware	86.1
14	Indiana	84.3	14	Indiana	84.3
8	Iowa	89.6	15	Oklahoma	83.7
35	Kansas	73.5	16	Connecticut	83.5
39	Kentucky	67.2	17	Minnesota	83.3
33	Louisiana	74.8	18	Alaska	83.2
29	Maine	77.2	19	New York	83.0
NA	Maryland**	NA	20	Alabama	82.9
40	Massachusetts	66.9	21	Vermont	82.4
2	Michigan	94.3	22	Ohio	81.7
17	Minnesota	83.3	23	Colorado	80.3
34	Mississippi	73.6	24	Idaho	79.8
32	Missouri	75.2	25	Montana	79.0
25	Montana	79.0	25	North Dakota	79.0
30	Nebraska	76.0	27	Virginia	78.7
NA	Nevada**	NA	28	Tennessee	78.6
NA	New Hampshire**	NA	29	Maine	77.2
7	New Jersey	90.0	30	Nebraska	76.0
8	New Mexico	89.6	31	Wisconsin	75.4
19	New York	83.0	32	Missouri	75.2
11	North Carolina	88.5	33	Louisiana	74.8
25	North Dakota	79.0	34	Mississippi	73.6
22	Ohio	81.7	35	Kansas	73.5
15	Oklahoma	83.7	36	South Carolina	72.5
3	Oregon	94.1	37	South Dakota	71.3
NA	Pennsylvania**	NA	38	Arkansas	69.3
NA	Rhode Island**	NA	39	Kentucky	67.2
36	South Carolina	72.5	40	Massachusetts	66.9
37	South Dakota	71.3	41	Wyoming	63.5
28	Tennessee	78.6	NA	Arizona**	NA
6	Texas	90.4	NA	Florida**	NA
10	Utah	88.6	NA	Georgia**	NA
21	Vermont	82.4	NA	Maryland**	NA
27	Virginia	78.7	NA	Nevada**	NA
1	Washington	96.3	NA	New Hampshire**	NA
NA	West Virginia**	NA	NA	Pennsylvania**	NA
31	Wisconsin	75.4	NA	Rhode Island**	NA
41	Wyoming	63.5	NA	West Virginia**	NA
				District of Columbia	85.4

Source: U.S. Department of Transportation, National Highway Traffic Safety Administration
   "Safety Belt Use in 2006" (http://www-nrd.nhtsa.dot.gov/pdf/nrd-30/NCSA/RNotes/2007/810690.pdf)
*National estimate is from the National Occupant Protection Use Survey (NOPUS) using a different methodology.
**Not available.

Percent of Passenger Car Occupant Fatalities
Where Victim Used a Seat Belt in 2005
National Percent = 41% of Passenger Car Occupant Fatalities*

ALPHA ORDER

RANK	STATE	PERCENT
27	Alabama	38
8	Alaska	50
32	Arizona	35
43	Arkansas	29
2	California	55
19	Colorado	42
24	Connecticut	39
16	Delaware	43
24	Florida	39
27	Georgia	38
19	Hawaii	42
19	Idaho	42
14	Illinois	44
23	Indiana	41
11	Iowa	46
41	Kansas	30
32	Kentucky	35
32	Louisiana	35
29	Maine	36
4	Maryland	52
45	Massachusetts	28
2	Michigan	55
16	Minnesota	43
47	Mississippi	26
40	Missouri	31
47	Montana	26
45	Nebraska	28
16	Nevada	43
43	New Hampshire	29
5	New Jersey	51
10	New Mexico	48
9	New York	49
11	North Carolina	46
50	North Dakota	23
19	Ohio	42
24	Oklahoma	39
1	Oregon	63
39	Pennsylvania	32
36	Rhode Island	34
41	South Carolina	30
49	South Dakota	24
29	Tennessee	36
5	Texas	51
14	Utah	44
13	Vermont	45
38	Virginia	33
5	Washington	51
29	West Virginia	36
32	Wisconsin	35
36	Wyoming	34

RANK ORDER

RANK	STATE	PERCENT
1	Oregon	63
2	California	55
2	Michigan	55
4	Maryland	52
5	New Jersey	51
5	Texas	51
5	Washington	51
8	Alaska	50
9	New York	49
10	New Mexico	48
11	Iowa	46
11	North Carolina	46
13	Vermont	45
14	Illinois	44
14	Utah	44
16	Delaware	43
16	Minnesota	43
16	Nevada	43
19	Colorado	42
19	Hawaii	42
19	Idaho	42
19	Ohio	42
23	Indiana	41
24	Connecticut	39
24	Florida	39
24	Oklahoma	39
27	Alabama	38
27	Georgia	38
29	Maine	36
29	Tennessee	36
29	West Virginia	36
32	Arizona	35
32	Kentucky	35
32	Louisiana	35
32	Wisconsin	35
36	Rhode Island	34
36	Wyoming	34
38	Virginia	33
39	Pennsylvania	32
40	Missouri	31
41	Kansas	30
41	South Carolina	30
43	Arkansas	29
43	New Hampshire	29
45	Massachusetts	28
45	Nebraska	28
47	Mississippi	26
47	Montana	26
49	South Dakota	24
50	North Dakota	23

District of Columbia   36

Source: U.S. Department of Transportation, National Highway Safety Administration
   "Traffic Safety Facts-Occupant Protection" (www-nrd.nhtsa.dot.gov/Pubs/occupantprotectiontsf05.PDF)
*Only those fatalities where seat belts are known to have been used are counted.

Fatalities in Alcohol-Related Crashes in 2005

National Total = 15,172 Fatalities*

ALPHA ORDER

RANK	STATE	FATALITIES	% of USA
14	Alabama	399	2.6%
49	Alaska	32	0.2%
13	Arizona	417	2.7%
26	Arkansas	219	1.4%
1	California	1,478	9.7%
24	Colorado	229	1.5%
37	Connecticut	109	0.7%
43	Delaware	59	0.4%
3	Florida	1,207	8.0%
6	Georgia	489	3.2%
41	Hawaii	65	0.4%
39	Idaho	86	0.6%
5	Illinois	535	3.5%
20	Indiana	302	2.0%
36	Iowa	112	0.7%
32	Kansas	145	1.0%
21	Kentucky	293	1.9%
16	Louisiana	357	2.4%
44	Maine	58	0.4%
27	Maryland	203	1.3%
30	Massachusetts	153	1.0%
15	Michigan	373	2.5%
28	Minnesota	187	1.2%
18	Mississippi	342	2.3%
8	Missouri	479	3.2%
35	Montana	116	0.8%
38	Nebraska	88	0.6%
33	Nevada	143	0.9%
44	New Hampshire	58	0.4%
25	New Jersey	222	1.5%
29	New Mexico	160	1.1%
10	New York	443	2.9%
9	North Carolina	475	3.1%
46	North Dakota	57	0.4%
7	Ohio	480	3.2%
23	Oklahoma	263	1.7%
30	Oregon	153	1.0%
4	Pennsylvania	595	3.9%
47	Rhode Island	38	0.3%
12	South Carolina	425	2.8%
40	South Dakota	73	0.5%
11	Tennessee	434	2.9%
2	Texas	1,408	9.3%
48	Utah	35	0.2%
50	Vermont	29	0.2%
19	Virginia	323	2.1%
22	Washington	272	1.8%
34	West Virginia	118	0.8%
17	Wisconsin	353	2.3%
42	Wyoming	63	0.4%

RANK ORDER

RANK	STATE	FATALITIES	% of USA
1	California	1,478	9.7%
2	Texas	1,408	9.3%
3	Florida	1,207	8.0%
4	Pennsylvania	595	3.9%
5	Illinois	535	3.5%
6	Georgia	489	3.2%
7	Ohio	480	3.2%
8	Missouri	479	3.2%
9	North Carolina	475	3.1%
10	New York	443	2.9%
11	Tennessee	434	2.9%
12	South Carolina	425	2.8%
13	Arizona	417	2.7%
14	Alabama	399	2.6%
15	Michigan	373	2.5%
16	Louisiana	357	2.4%
17	Wisconsin	353	2.3%
18	Mississippi	342	2.3%
19	Virginia	323	2.1%
20	Indiana	302	2.0%
21	Kentucky	293	1.9%
22	Washington	272	1.8%
23	Oklahoma	263	1.7%
24	Colorado	229	1.5%
25	New Jersey	222	1.5%
26	Arkansas	219	1.4%
27	Maryland	203	1.3%
28	Minnesota	187	1.2%
29	New Mexico	160	1.1%
30	Massachusetts	153	1.0%
30	Oregon	153	1.0%
32	Kansas	145	1.0%
33	Nevada	143	0.9%
34	West Virginia	118	0.8%
35	Montana	116	0.8%
36	Iowa	112	0.7%
37	Connecticut	109	0.7%
38	Nebraska	88	0.6%
39	Idaho	86	0.6%
40	South Dakota	73	0.5%
41	Hawaii	65	0.4%
42	Wyoming	63	0.4%
43	Delaware	59	0.4%
44	Maine	58	0.4%
44	New Hampshire	58	0.4%
46	North Dakota	57	0.4%
47	Rhode Island	38	0.3%
48	Utah	35	0.2%
49	Alaska	32	0.2%
50	Vermont	29	0.2%
	District of Columbia	22	0.1%

Source: U.S. Department of Transportation, National Highway Traffic Safety Administration
   "Traffic Safety Facts-Alcohol" (http://www-nrd.nhtsa.dot.gov/Pubs/alcoholtsf05.pdf)
*Drivers with Blood Alcohol Content (BAC) of .01 or more. "Legally Drunk" BAC differs from state to state but is often .08 or higher.

Fatalities in Alcohol-Related Crashes
as a Percent of All Highway Fatalities in 2005
National Percent = 35% of Highway Fatalities*

ALPHA ORDER

RANK	STATE	PERCENT
23	Alabama	35
4	Alaska	44
21	Arizona	36
26	Arkansas	34
26	California	34
15	Colorado	38
9	Connecticut	40
4	Delaware	44
26	Florida	34
48	Georgia	28
1	Hawaii	47
40	Idaho	32
12	Illinois	39
40	Indiana	32
49	Iowa	25
26	Kansas	34
46	Kentucky	30
17	Louisiana	37
26	Maine	34
34	Maryland	33
23	Massachusetts	35
34	Michigan	33
26	Minnesota	34
17	Mississippi	37
15	Missouri	38
1	Montana	47
34	Nebraska	33
34	Nevada	33
23	New Hampshire	35
46	New Jersey	30
34	New Mexico	33
43	New York	31
43	North Carolina	31
3	North Dakota	46
21	Ohio	36
34	Oklahoma	33
43	Oregon	31
17	Pennsylvania	37
4	Rhode Island	44
12	South Carolina	39
12	South Dakota	39
26	Tennessee	34
9	Texas	40
50	Utah	13
9	Vermont	40
26	Virginia	34
8	Washington	42
40	West Virginia	32
4	Wisconsin	44
17	Wyoming	37

RANK ORDER

RANK	STATE	PERCENT
1	Hawaii	47
1	Montana	47
3	North Dakota	46
4	Alaska	44
4	Delaware	44
4	Rhode Island	44
4	Wisconsin	44
8	Washington	42
9	Connecticut	40
9	Texas	40
9	Vermont	40
12	Illinois	39
12	South Carolina	39
12	South Dakota	39
15	Colorado	38
15	Missouri	38
17	Louisiana	37
17	Mississippi	37
17	Pennsylvania	37
17	Wyoming	37
21	Arizona	36
21	Ohio	36
23	Alabama	35
23	Massachusetts	35
23	New Hampshire	35
26	Arkansas	34
26	California	34
26	Florida	34
26	Kansas	34
26	Maine	34
26	Minnesota	34
26	Tennessee	34
26	Virginia	34
34	Maryland	33
34	Michigan	33
34	Nebraska	33
34	Nevada	33
34	New Mexico	33
34	Oklahoma	33
40	Idaho	32
40	Indiana	32
40	West Virginia	32
43	New York	31
43	North Carolina	31
43	Oregon	31
46	Kentucky	30
46	New Jersey	30
48	Georgia	28
49	Iowa	25
50	Utah	13
	District of Columbia	47

Source: U.S. Department of Transportation, National Highway Traffic Safety Administration
"Traffic Safety Facts-Alcohol" (http://www-nrd.nhtsa.dot.gov/Pubs/alcoholtsf05.pdf)
*Drivers with Blood Alcohol Content (BAC) of .01 or more. "Legally Drunk" BAC differs from state to state but is often .08 or higher.

Percent of Fatal Traffic Accidents Involving Older Drivers in 2005

National Percent = 10.5%*

ALPHA ORDER

RANK	STATE	PERCENT
39	Alabama	10.1
50	Alaska	5.9
43	Arizona	8.9
18	Arkansas	11.3
46	California	8.0
42	Colorado	9.0
30	Connecticut	10.9
16	Delaware	11.4
22	Florida	11.2
33	Georgia	10.7
49	Hawaii	6.3
8	Idaho	12.8
14	Illinois	11.5
34	Indiana	10.6
1	Iowa	14.7
11	Kansas	12.0
22	Kentucky	11.2
48	Louisiana	6.7
6	Maine	13.3
39	Maryland	10.1
13	Massachusetts	11.7
14	Michigan	11.5
36	Minnesota	10.4
38	Mississippi	10.2
29	Missouri	11.0
18	Montana	11.3
22	Nebraska	11.2
25	Nevada	11.1
2	New Hampshire	14.6
18	New Jersey	11.3
45	New Mexico	8.4
9	New York	12.3
36	North Carolina	10.4
3	North Dakota	14.4
25	Ohio	11.1
16	Oklahoma	11.4
4	Oregon	13.4
7	Pennsylvania	12.9
46	Rhode Island	8.0
30	South Carolina	10.9
25	South Dakota	11.1
25	Tennessee	11.1
44	Texas	8.7
35	Utah	10.5
32	Vermont	10.8
10	Virginia	12.1
41	Washington	9.6
12	West Virginia	11.9
18	Wisconsin	11.3
4	Wyoming	13.4

RANK ORDER

RANK	STATE	PERCENT
1	Iowa	14.7
2	New Hampshire	14.6
3	North Dakota	14.4
4	Oregon	13.4
4	Wyoming	13.4
6	Maine	13.3
7	Pennsylvania	12.9
8	Idaho	12.8
9	New York	12.3
10	Virginia	12.1
11	Kansas	12.0
12	West Virginia	11.9
13	Massachusetts	11.7
14	Illinois	11.5
14	Michigan	11.5
16	Delaware	11.4
16	Oklahoma	11.4
18	Arkansas	11.3
18	Montana	11.3
18	New Jersey	11.3
18	Wisconsin	11.3
22	Florida	11.2
22	Kentucky	11.2
22	Nebraska	11.2
25	Nevada	11.1
25	Ohio	11.1
25	South Dakota	11.1
25	Tennessee	11.1
29	Missouri	11.0
30	Connecticut	10.9
30	South Carolina	10.9
32	Vermont	10.8
33	Georgia	10.7
34	Indiana	10.6
35	Utah	10.5
36	Minnesota	10.4
36	North Carolina	10.4
38	Mississippi	10.2
39	Alabama	10.1
39	Maryland	10.1
41	Washington	9.6
42	Colorado	9.0
43	Arizona	8.9
44	Texas	8.7
45	New Mexico	8.4
46	California	8.0
46	Rhode Island	8.0
48	Louisiana	6.7
49	Hawaii	6.3
50	Alaska	5.9

District of Columbia — 8.8

Source: CQ Press using data from U.S. Department of Transportation, National Highway Traffic Safety Administration "Traffic Safety Facts-Older Population" (http://www-nrd.nhtsa.dot.gov/Pubs/OlderPopulationTSF05.pdf)
*Drivers 65 years old and older. Twelve percent of the total U.S. population is 65 or older.

Percent of Highway Fatalities Who Were Young Drivers: 2005

National Percent = 8.0% of Fatalities*

ALPHA ORDER				RANK ORDER		
RANK	STATE	PERCENT		RANK	STATE	PERCENT
8	Alabama	9.5		1	Vermont	15.1
49	Alaska	5.6		2	Iowa	10.9
43	Arizona	6.5		3	Kansas	10.3
5	Arkansas	10.0		3	Missouri	10.3
41	California	7.0		5	Arkansas	10.0
35	Colorado	7.4		6	Nebraska	9.8
19	Connecticut	8.4		6	North Dakota	9.8
20	Delaware	8.2		8	Alabama	9.5
38	Florida	7.3		8	Maine	9.5
30	Georgia	7.9		8	Massachusetts	9.5
50	Hawaii	5.0		11	Minnesota	9.3
32	Idaho	7.6		12	Mississippi	9.1
30	Illinois	7.9		12	Ohio	9.1
16	Indiana	8.7		14	Oklahoma	8.9
2	Iowa	10.9		15	North Carolina	8.8
3	Kansas	10.3		16	Indiana	8.7
22	Kentucky	8.1		16	Virginia	8.7
35	Louisiana	7.4		18	New Mexico	8.6
8	Maine	9.5		19	Connecticut	8.4
39	Maryland	7.2		20	Delaware	8.2
8	Massachusetts	9.5		20	Wyoming	8.2
28	Michigan	8.0		22	Kentucky	8.1
11	Minnesota	9.3		22	Pennsylvania	8.1
12	Mississippi	9.1		22	South Dakota	8.1
3	Missouri	10.3		22	Tennessee	8.1
47	Montana	6.0		22	Texas	8.1
6	Nebraska	9.8		22	Wisconsin	8.1
42	Nevada	6.6		28	Michigan	8.0
47	New Hampshire	6.0		28	Rhode Island	8.0
46	New Jersey	6.1		30	Georgia	7.9
18	New Mexico	8.6		30	Illinois	7.9
43	New York	6.5		32	Idaho	7.6
15	North Carolina	8.8		32	Oregon	7.6
6	North Dakota	9.8		34	West Virginia	7.5
12	Ohio	9.1		35	Colorado	7.4
14	Oklahoma	8.9		35	Louisiana	7.4
32	Oregon	7.6		35	Utah	7.4
22	Pennsylvania	8.1		38	Florida	7.3
28	Rhode Island	8.0		39	Maryland	7.2
39	South Carolina	7.2		39	South Carolina	7.2
22	South Dakota	8.1		41	California	7.0
22	Tennessee	8.1		42	Nevada	6.6
22	Texas	8.1		43	Arizona	6.5
35	Utah	7.4		43	New York	6.5
1	Vermont	15.1		43	Washington	6.5
16	Virginia	8.7		46	New Jersey	6.1
43	Washington	6.5		47	Montana	6.0
34	West Virginia	7.5		47	New Hampshire	6.0
22	Wisconsin	8.1		49	Alaska	5.6
20	Wyoming	8.2		50	Hawaii	5.0
					District of Columbia	4.2

Source: CQ Press using data from U.S. Department of Transportation, National Highway Traffic Safety Administration "Traffic Safety Facts-Young Drivers" (http://www-nrd.nhtsa.dot.gov/Pubs/YoungDriversTSF05.pdf)
*Drivers 15 to 20 years old. Based on 3,467 fatalities of young drivers. An additional 4,726 passengers and nonoccupants were killed in crashes involving young drivers. Young drivers accounted for 6.3 percent of all drivers.

Licensed Drivers in 2005

National Total = 200,665,267 Licensed Drivers

<table>
<tr><td colspan="4">ALPHA ORDER</td><td colspan="4">RANK ORDER</td></tr>
<tr><td>RANK</td><td>STATE</td><td>DRIVERS</td><td>% of USA</td><td>RANK</td><td>STATE</td><td>DRIVERS</td><td>% of USA</td></tr>
<tr><td>21</td><td>Alabama</td><td>3,637,414</td><td>1.8%</td><td>1</td><td>California</td><td>22,895,965</td><td>11.4%</td></tr>
<tr><td>48</td><td>Alaska</td><td>482,532</td><td>0.2%</td><td>2</td><td>Texas</td><td>14,659,390</td><td>7.3%</td></tr>
<tr><td>19</td><td>Arizona</td><td>3,943,180</td><td>2.0%</td><td>3</td><td>Florida</td><td>13,373,700</td><td>6.7%</td></tr>
<tr><td>31</td><td>Arkansas</td><td>2,024,466</td><td>1.0%</td><td>4</td><td>New York</td><td>11,071,911</td><td>5.5%</td></tr>
<tr><td>1</td><td>California</td><td>22,895,965</td><td>11.4%</td><td>5</td><td>Pennsylvania</td><td>8,460,530</td><td>4.2%</td></tr>
<tr><td>22</td><td>Colorado</td><td>3,341,275</td><td>1.7%</td><td>6</td><td>Illinois</td><td>7,870,872</td><td>3.9%</td></tr>
<tr><td>27</td><td>Connecticut</td><td>2,740,270</td><td>1.4%</td><td>7</td><td>Ohio</td><td>7,707,842</td><td>3.8%</td></tr>
<tr><td>47</td><td>Delaware</td><td>533,943</td><td>0.3%</td><td>8</td><td>Michigan</td><td>7,105,272</td><td>3.5%</td></tr>
<tr><td>3</td><td>Florida</td><td>13,373,700</td><td>6.7%</td><td>9</td><td>North Carolina</td><td>6,227,817</td><td>3.1%</td></tr>
<tr><td>10</td><td>Georgia</td><td>5,939,513</td><td>3.0%</td><td>10</td><td>Georgia</td><td>5,939,513</td><td>3.0%</td></tr>
<tr><td>42</td><td>Hawaii</td><td>856,163</td><td>0.4%</td><td>11</td><td>New Jersey</td><td>5,870,720</td><td>2.9%</td></tr>
<tr><td>41</td><td>Idaho</td><td>978,450</td><td>0.5%</td><td>12</td><td>Virginia</td><td>5,112,523</td><td>2.5%</td></tr>
<tr><td>6</td><td>Illinois</td><td>7,870,872</td><td>3.9%</td><td>13</td><td>Washington</td><td>4,681,927</td><td>2.3%</td></tr>
<tr><td>15</td><td>Indiana</td><td>4,521,329</td><td>2.3%</td><td>14</td><td>Massachusetts</td><td>4,612,829</td><td>2.3%</td></tr>
<tr><td>30</td><td>Iowa</td><td>2,033,157</td><td>1.0%</td><td>15</td><td>Indiana</td><td>4,521,329</td><td>2.3%</td></tr>
<tr><td>32</td><td>Kansas</td><td>1,974,238</td><td>1.0%</td><td>16</td><td>Tennessee</td><td>4,351,868</td><td>2.2%</td></tr>
<tr><td>26</td><td>Kentucky</td><td>2,860,729</td><td>1.4%</td><td>17</td><td>Missouri</td><td>4,135,394</td><td>2.1%</td></tr>
<tr><td>24</td><td>Louisiana</td><td>3,083,516</td><td>1.5%</td><td>18</td><td>Wisconsin</td><td>3,993,348</td><td>2.0%</td></tr>
<tr><td>39</td><td>Maine</td><td>1,003,972</td><td>0.5%</td><td>19</td><td>Arizona</td><td>3,943,180</td><td>2.0%</td></tr>
<tr><td>20</td><td>Maryland</td><td>3,709,594</td><td>1.8%</td><td>20</td><td>Maryland</td><td>3,709,594</td><td>1.8%</td></tr>
<tr><td>14</td><td>Massachusetts</td><td>4,612,829</td><td>2.3%</td><td>21</td><td>Alabama</td><td>3,637,414</td><td>1.8%</td></tr>
<tr><td>8</td><td>Michigan</td><td>7,105,272</td><td>3.5%</td><td>22</td><td>Colorado</td><td>3,341,275</td><td>1.7%</td></tr>
<tr><td>23</td><td>Minnesota</td><td>3,083,757</td><td>1.5%</td><td>23</td><td>Minnesota</td><td>3,083,757</td><td>1.5%</td></tr>
<tr><td>33</td><td>Mississippi</td><td>1,965,464</td><td>1.0%</td><td>24</td><td>Louisiana</td><td>3,083,516</td><td>1.5%</td></tr>
<tr><td>17</td><td>Missouri</td><td>4,135,394</td><td>2.1%</td><td>25</td><td>South Carolina</td><td>2,987,593</td><td>1.5%</td></tr>
<tr><td>44</td><td>Montana</td><td>715,512</td><td>0.4%</td><td>26</td><td>Kentucky</td><td>2,860,729</td><td>1.4%</td></tr>
<tr><td>37</td><td>Nebraska</td><td>1,320,617</td><td>0.7%</td><td>27</td><td>Connecticut</td><td>2,740,270</td><td>1.4%</td></tr>
<tr><td>35</td><td>Nevada</td><td>1,596,353</td><td>0.8%</td><td>28</td><td>Oregon</td><td>2,692,948</td><td>1.3%</td></tr>
<tr><td>40</td><td>New Hampshire</td><td>985,775</td><td>0.5%</td><td>29</td><td>Oklahoma</td><td>2,234,114</td><td>1.1%</td></tr>
<tr><td>11</td><td>New Jersey</td><td>5,870,720</td><td>2.9%</td><td>30</td><td>Iowa</td><td>2,033,157</td><td>1.0%</td></tr>
<tr><td>38</td><td>New Mexico</td><td>1,304,721</td><td>0.7%</td><td>31</td><td>Arkansas</td><td>2,024,466</td><td>1.0%</td></tr>
<tr><td>4</td><td>New York</td><td>11,071,911</td><td>5.5%</td><td>32</td><td>Kansas</td><td>1,974,238</td><td>1.0%</td></tr>
<tr><td>9</td><td>North Carolina</td><td>6,227,817</td><td>3.1%</td><td>33</td><td>Mississippi</td><td>1,965,464</td><td>1.0%</td></tr>
<tr><td>49</td><td>North Dakota</td><td>466,701</td><td>0.2%</td><td>34</td><td>Utah</td><td>1,599,514</td><td>0.8%</td></tr>
<tr><td>7</td><td>Ohio</td><td>7,707,842</td><td>3.8%</td><td>35</td><td>Nevada</td><td>1,596,353</td><td>0.8%</td></tr>
<tr><td>29</td><td>Oklahoma</td><td>2,234,114</td><td>1.1%</td><td>36</td><td>West Virginia</td><td>1,327,569</td><td>0.7%</td></tr>
<tr><td>28</td><td>Oregon</td><td>2,692,948</td><td>1.3%</td><td>37</td><td>Nebraska</td><td>1,320,617</td><td>0.7%</td></tr>
<tr><td>5</td><td>Pennsylvania</td><td>8,460,530</td><td>4.2%</td><td>38</td><td>New Mexico</td><td>1,304,721</td><td>0.7%</td></tr>
<tr><td>43</td><td>Rhode Island</td><td>746,465</td><td>0.4%</td><td>39</td><td>Maine</td><td>1,003,972</td><td>0.5%</td></tr>
<tr><td>25</td><td>South Carolina</td><td>2,987,593</td><td>1.5%</td><td>40</td><td>New Hampshire</td><td>985,775</td><td>0.5%</td></tr>
<tr><td>45</td><td>South Dakota</td><td>566,255</td><td>0.3%</td><td>41</td><td>Idaho</td><td>978,450</td><td>0.5%</td></tr>
<tr><td>16</td><td>Tennessee</td><td>4,351,868</td><td>2.2%</td><td>42</td><td>Hawaii</td><td>856,163</td><td>0.4%</td></tr>
<tr><td>2</td><td>Texas</td><td>14,659,390</td><td>7.3%</td><td>43</td><td>Rhode Island</td><td>746,465</td><td>0.4%</td></tr>
<tr><td>34</td><td>Utah</td><td>1,599,514</td><td>0.8%</td><td>44</td><td>Montana</td><td>715,512</td><td>0.4%</td></tr>
<tr><td>46</td><td>Vermont</td><td>563,162</td><td>0.3%</td><td>45</td><td>South Dakota</td><td>566,255</td><td>0.3%</td></tr>
<tr><td>12</td><td>Virginia</td><td>5,112,523</td><td>2.5%</td><td>46</td><td>Vermont</td><td>563,162</td><td>0.3%</td></tr>
<tr><td>13</td><td>Washington</td><td>4,681,927</td><td>2.3%</td><td>47</td><td>Delaware</td><td>533,943</td><td>0.3%</td></tr>
<tr><td>36</td><td>West Virginia</td><td>1,327,569</td><td>0.7%</td><td>48</td><td>Alaska</td><td>482,532</td><td>0.2%</td></tr>
<tr><td>18</td><td>Wisconsin</td><td>3,993,348</td><td>2.0%</td><td>49</td><td>North Dakota</td><td>466,701</td><td>0.2%</td></tr>
<tr><td>50</td><td>Wyoming</td><td>382,735</td><td>0.2%</td><td>50</td><td>Wyoming</td><td>382,735</td><td>0.2%</td></tr>
<tr><td></td><td></td><td></td><td></td><td></td><td>District of Columbia</td><td>330,363</td><td>0.2%</td></tr>
</table>

Source: U.S. Department of Transportation, Federal Highway Administration
"Highway Statistics 2005" (Table DL-1C) (http://www.fhwa.dot.gov/policy/ohpi/hss/index.htm)

Licensed Drivers per 1,000 Driving Age Population in 2005

National Ratio = 867 Licensed Drivers

ALPHA ORDER

RANK	STATE	RATIO
2	Alabama	1,012
4	Alaska	969
30	Arizona	871
14	Arkansas	928
45	California	833
16	Colorado	925
3	Connecticut	987
47	Delaware	797
8	Florida	942
40	Georgia	852
44	Hawaii	849
27	Idaho	891
48	Illinois	796
11	Indiana	932
38	Iowa	855
19	Kansas	918
34	Kentucky	866
29	Louisiana	879
13	Maine	928
42	Maryland	851
21	Massachusetts	903
24	Michigan	900
49	Minnesota	761
32	Mississippi	870
22	Missouri	902
6	Montana	944
5	Nebraska	959
37	Nevada	859
7	New Hampshire	943
35	New Jersey	863
31	New Mexico	871
50	New York	727
18	North Carolina	919
23	North Dakota	901
39	Ohio	853
46	Oklahoma	800
12	Oregon	932
43	Pennsylvania	849
33	Rhode Island	868
26	South Carolina	892
15	South Dakota	927
17	Tennessee	919
41	Texas	852
28	Utah	887
1	Vermont	1,107
36	Virginia	859
9	Washington	940
25	West Virginia	897
20	Wisconsin	907
10	Wyoming	934

RANK ORDER

RANK	STATE	RATIO
1	Vermont	1,107
2	Alabama	1,012
3	Connecticut	987
4	Alaska	969
5	Nebraska	959
6	Montana	944
7	New Hampshire	943
8	Florida	942
9	Washington	940
10	Wyoming	934
11	Indiana	932
12	Oregon	932
13	Maine	928
14	Arkansas	928
15	South Dakota	927
16	Colorado	925
17	Tennessee	919
18	North Carolina	919
19	Kansas	918
20	Wisconsin	907
21	Massachusetts	903
22	Missouri	902
23	North Dakota	901
24	Michigan	900
25	West Virginia	897
26	South Carolina	892
27	Idaho	891
28	Utah	887
29	Louisiana	879
30	Arizona	871
31	New Mexico	871
32	Mississippi	870
33	Rhode Island	868
34	Kentucky	866
35	New Jersey	863
36	Virginia	859
37	Nevada	859
38	Iowa	855
39	Ohio	853
40	Georgia	852
41	Texas	852
42	Maryland	851
43	Pennsylvania	849
44	Hawaii	849
45	California	833
46	Oklahoma	800
47	Delaware	797
48	Illinois	796
49	Minnesota	761
50	New York	727

	District of Columbia	737

Source: U.S. Department of Transportation, Federal Highway Administration
"Highway Statistics 2005" (Table DL-1C) (http://www.fhwa.dot.gov/policy/ohpi/hss/index.htm)

Motor Vehicle Registrations in 2005

National Total = 241,193,974 Motor Vehicles*

ALPHA ORDER

RANK	STATE	VEHICLES	% of USA
20	Alabama	4,544,518	1.9%
48	Alaska	672,766	0.3%
22	Arizona	3,971,515	1.6%
33	Arkansas	1,939,533	0.8%
1	California	32,487,477	13.5%
34	Colorado	1,807,879	0.7%
28	Connecticut	3,058,553	1.3%
46	Delaware	736,542	0.3%
3	Florida	15,691,438	6.5%
9	Georgia	8,062,838	3.3%
43	Hawaii	947,548	0.4%
37	Idaho	1,374,056	0.6%
7	Illinois	9,458,252	3.9%
16	Indiana	4,955,476	2.1%
26	Iowa	3,397,604	1.4%
30	Kansas	2,368,115	1.0%
25	Kentucky	3,427,718	1.4%
23	Louisiana	3,819,198	1.6%
41	Maine	1,074,895	0.4%
21	Maryland	4,321,813	1.8%
14	Massachusetts	5,420,206	2.2%
8	Michigan	8,247,447	3.4%
18	Minnesota	4,646,923	1.9%
32	Mississippi	1,978,111	0.8%
19	Missouri	4,589,356	1.9%
42	Montana	1,008,930	0.4%
35	Nebraska	1,702,790	0.7%
39	Nevada	1,349,313	0.6%
40	New Hampshire	1,174,380	0.5%
11	New Jersey	6,261,501	2.6%
36	New Mexico	1,548,371	0.6%
4	New York	11,862,504	4.9%
12	North Carolina	6,148,316	2.5%
47	North Dakota	695,225	0.3%
5	Ohio	10,634,083	4.4%
24	Oklahoma	3,725,279	1.5%
29	Oregon	2,897,385	1.2%
6	Pennsylvania	9,863,785	4.1%
45	Rhode Island	811,610	0.3%
27	South Carolina	3,339,456	1.4%
44	South Dakota	853,548	0.4%
15	Tennessee	4,980,010	2.1%
2	Texas	17,469,547	7.2%
31	Utah	2,209,833	0.9%
50	Vermont	507,706	0.2%
10	Virginia	6,591,497	2.7%
13	Washington	5,598,446	2.3%
38	West Virginia	1,351,746	0.6%
17	Wisconsin	4,725,425	2.0%
49	Wyoming	646,230	0.3%

RANK ORDER

RANK	STATE	VEHICLES	% of USA
1	California	32,487,477	13.5%
2	Texas	17,469,547	7.2%
3	Florida	15,691,438	6.5%
4	New York	11,862,504	4.9%
5	Ohio	10,634,083	4.4%
6	Pennsylvania	9,863,785	4.1%
7	Illinois	9,458,252	3.9%
8	Michigan	8,247,447	3.4%
9	Georgia	8,062,838	3.3%
10	Virginia	6,591,497	2.7%
11	New Jersey	6,261,501	2.6%
12	North Carolina	6,148,316	2.5%
13	Washington	5,598,446	2.3%
14	Massachusetts	5,420,206	2.2%
15	Tennessee	4,980,010	2.1%
16	Indiana	4,955,476	2.1%
17	Wisconsin	4,725,425	2.0%
18	Minnesota	4,646,923	1.9%
19	Missouri	4,589,356	1.9%
20	Alabama	4,544,518	1.9%
21	Maryland	4,321,813	1.8%
22	Arizona	3,971,515	1.6%
23	Louisiana	3,819,198	1.6%
24	Oklahoma	3,725,279	1.5%
25	Kentucky	3,427,718	1.4%
26	Iowa	3,397,604	1.4%
27	South Carolina	3,339,456	1.4%
28	Connecticut	3,058,553	1.3%
29	Oregon	2,897,385	1.2%
30	Kansas	2,368,115	1.0%
31	Utah	2,209,833	0.9%
32	Mississippi	1,978,111	0.8%
33	Arkansas	1,939,533	0.8%
34	Colorado	1,807,879	0.7%
35	Nebraska	1,702,790	0.7%
36	New Mexico	1,548,371	0.6%
37	Idaho	1,374,056	0.6%
38	West Virginia	1,351,746	0.6%
39	Nevada	1,349,313	0.6%
40	New Hampshire	1,174,380	0.5%
41	Maine	1,074,895	0.4%
42	Montana	1,008,930	0.4%
43	Hawaii	947,548	0.4%
44	South Dakota	853,548	0.4%
45	Rhode Island	811,610	0.3%
46	Delaware	736,542	0.3%
47	North Dakota	695,225	0.3%
48	Alaska	672,766	0.3%
49	Wyoming	646,230	0.3%
50	Vermont	507,706	0.2%
	District of Columbia	237,281	0.1%

Source: U.S. Department of Transportation, Federal Highway Administration
   "Highway Statistics 2005" (Table MV-1) (http://www.fhwa.dot.gov/policy/ohpi/hss/index.htm)
*Includes automobiles, trucks and buses. Does not include motorcycles.

Motor Vehicles per Driving Age Population in 2005

National Rate = 1.04 Motor Vehicles*

ALPHA ORDER		
RANK	STATE	RATE
8	Alabama	1.26
4	Alaska	1.35
46	Arizona	0.88
45	Arkansas	0.89
12	California	1.18
50	Colorado	0.50
20	Connecticut	1.10
20	Delaware	1.10
18	Florida	1.11
14	Georgia	1.16
40	Hawaii	0.94
9	Idaho	1.25
39	Illinois	0.96
30	Indiana	1.02
2	Iowa	1.43
20	Kansas	1.10
27	Kentucky	1.04
23	Louisiana	1.09
36	Maine	0.99
36	Maryland	0.99
25	Massachusetts	1.06
27	Michigan	1.04
15	Minnesota	1.15
46	Mississippi	0.88
32	Missouri	1.00
6	Montana	1.33
10	Nebraska	1.24
49	Nevada	0.73
16	New Hampshire	1.12
42	New Jersey	0.92
29	New Mexico	1.03
48	New York	0.78
43	North Carolina	0.91
5	North Dakota	1.34
12	Ohio	1.18
6	Oklahoma	1.33
32	Oregon	1.00
36	Pennsylvania	0.99
40	Rhode Island	0.94
32	South Carolina	1.00
3	South Dakota	1.40
26	Tennessee	1.05
30	Texas	1.02
11	Utah	1.23
32	Vermont	1.00
18	Virginia	1.11
16	Washington	1.12
43	West Virginia	0.91
24	Wisconsin	1.07
1	Wyoming	1.58

RANK ORDER		
RANK	STATE	RATE
1	Wyoming	1.58
2	Iowa	1.43
3	South Dakota	1.40
4	Alaska	1.35
5	North Dakota	1.34
6	Montana	1.33
6	Oklahoma	1.33
8	Alabama	1.26
9	Idaho	1.25
10	Nebraska	1.24
11	Utah	1.23
12	California	1.18
12	Ohio	1.18
14	Georgia	1.16
15	Minnesota	1.15
16	New Hampshire	1.12
16	Washington	1.12
18	Florida	1.11
18	Virginia	1.11
20	Connecticut	1.10
20	Delaware	1.10
20	Kansas	1.10
23	Louisiana	1.09
24	Wisconsin	1.07
25	Massachusetts	1.06
26	Tennessee	1.05
27	Kentucky	1.04
27	Michigan	1.04
29	New Mexico	1.03
30	Indiana	1.02
30	Texas	1.02
32	Missouri	1.00
32	Oregon	1.00
32	South Carolina	1.00
32	Vermont	1.00
36	Maine	0.99
36	Maryland	0.99
36	Pennsylvania	0.99
39	Illinois	0.96
40	Hawaii	0.94
40	Rhode Island	0.94
42	New Jersey	0.92
43	North Carolina	0.91
43	West Virginia	0.91
45	Arkansas	0.89
46	Arizona	0.88
46	Mississippi	0.88
48	New York	0.78
49	Nevada	0.73
50	Colorado	0.50

	District of Columbia	0.53

Source: CQ Press using data from U.S. Department of Transportation, Federal Highway Administration
"Highway Statistics 2005" (Table MV-1) (http://www.fhwa.dot.gov/policy/ohpi/hss/index.htm)
*Persons age 16 and older. Motor Vehicles include automobiles, trucks and buses. Motorcycles are not included.

Average Travel Time to Work in 2006

National Average = 25.0 Minutes*

RANK	STATE	MINUTES
22	Alabama	23.6
46	Alaska	17.7
14	Arizona	25.0
40	Arkansas	20.7
7	California	26.8
21	Colorado	23.9
19	Connecticut	24.1
22	Delaware	23.6
9	Florida	25.9
5	Georgia	27.3
11	Hawaii	25.5
41	Idaho	20.1
4	Illinois	27.9
30	Indiana	22.3
44	Iowa	18.2
43	Kansas	18.5
29	Kentucky	22.4
13	Louisiana	25.1
30	Maine	22.3
2	Maryland	30.6
8	Massachusetts	26.6
25	Michigan	23.4
34	Minnesota	22.0
20	Mississippi	24.0
27	Missouri	22.9
48	Montana	17.6
46	Nebraska	17.7
18	Nevada	24.2
16	New Hampshire	24.6
3	New Jersey	29.1
37	New Mexico	20.9
1	New York	30.9
25	North Carolina	23.4
50	North Dakota	15.5
33	Ohio	22.1
42	Oklahoma	20.0
35	Oregon	21.8
14	Pennsylvania	25.0
30	Rhode Island	22.3
27	South Carolina	22.9
49	South Dakota	15.9
24	Tennessee	23.5
16	Texas	24.6
38	Utah	20.8
36	Vermont	21.2
6	Virginia	26.9
12	Washington	25.2
10	West Virginia	25.6
38	Wisconsin	20.8
45	Wyoming	17.9

RANK	STATE	MINUTES
1	New York	30.9
2	Maryland	30.6
3	New Jersey	29.1
4	Illinois	27.9
5	Georgia	27.3
6	Virginia	26.9
7	California	26.8
8	Massachusetts	26.6
9	Florida	25.9
10	West Virginia	25.6
11	Hawaii	25.5
12	Washington	25.2
13	Louisiana	25.1
14	Arizona	25.0
14	Pennsylvania	25.0
16	New Hampshire	24.6
16	Texas	24.6
18	Nevada	24.2
19	Connecticut	24.1
20	Mississippi	24.0
21	Colorado	23.9
22	Alabama	23.6
22	Delaware	23.6
24	Tennessee	23.5
25	Michigan	23.4
25	North Carolina	23.4
27	Missouri	22.9
27	South Carolina	22.9
29	Kentucky	22.4
30	Indiana	22.3
30	Maine	22.3
30	Rhode Island	22.3
33	Ohio	22.1
34	Minnesota	22.0
35	Oregon	21.8
36	Vermont	21.2
37	New Mexico	20.9
38	Utah	20.8
38	Wisconsin	20.8
40	Arkansas	20.7
41	Idaho	20.1
42	Oklahoma	20.0
43	Kansas	18.5
44	Iowa	18.2
45	Wyoming	17.9
46	Alaska	17.7
46	Nebraska	17.7
48	Montana	17.6
49	South Dakota	15.9
50	North Dakota	15.5
	District of Columbia	29.2

Source: U.S. Bureau of the Census
    "2006 American Community Survey" (http://www.census.gov/acs/www/)
*Workers 16 and older not working at home.

Percent of Commuters Who Drive to Work Alone: 2006

National Percent = 76.0%*

ALPHA ORDER				RANK ORDER		
RANK	STATE	PERCENT		RANK	STATE	PERCENT
1	Alabama	83.6		1	Alabama	83.6
48	Alaska	67.7		2	Tennessee	83.3
39	Arizona	74.6		3	Ohio	83.1
16	Arkansas	80.2		4	Michigan	82.9
42	California	73.0		5	Indiana	82.4
37	Colorado	75.1		6	Mississippi	82.2
20	Connecticut	79.7		7	Kansas	81.8
13	Delaware	80.8		8	New Hampshire	81.7
21	Florida	79.3		9	Louisiana	81.6
26	Georgia	78.2		10	Kentucky	81.5
49	Hawaii	67.0		11	Rhode Island	81.1
31	Idaho	77.2		11	South Carolina	81.1
40	Illinois	74.3		13	Delaware	80.8
5	Indiana	82.4		13	Missouri	80.8
24	Iowa	78.5		15	Oklahoma	80.4
7	Kansas	81.8		16	Arkansas	80.2
10	Kentucky	81.5		17	West Virginia	80.0
9	Louisiana	81.6		18	Wisconsin	79.9
29	Maine	77.6		19	North Carolina	79.8
43	Maryland	72.8		20	Connecticut	79.7
41	Massachusetts	73.7		21	Florida	79.3
4	Michigan	82.9		21	North Dakota	79.3
28	Minnesota	78.1		23	Nebraska	79.1
6	Mississippi	82.2		24	Iowa	78.5
13	Missouri	80.8		24	Texas	78.5
45	Montana	72.7		26	Georgia	78.2
23	Nebraska	79.1		26	New Mexico	78.2
33	Nevada	76.7		28	Minnesota	78.1
8	New Hampshire	81.7		29	Maine	77.6
46	New Jersey	71.9		30	South Dakota	77.5
26	New Mexico	78.2		31	Idaho	77.2
50	New York	54.4		32	Virginia	77.0
19	North Carolina	79.8		33	Nevada	76.7
21	North Dakota	79.3		34	Pennsylvania	76.4
3	Ohio	83.1		35	Wyoming	76.0
15	Oklahoma	80.4		36	Utah	75.2
47	Oregon	71.4		37	Colorado	75.1
34	Pennsylvania	76.4		37	Vermont	75.1
11	Rhode Island	81.1		39	Arizona	74.6
11	South Carolina	81.1		40	Illinois	74.3
30	South Dakota	77.5		41	Massachusetts	73.7
2	Tennessee	83.3		42	California	73.0
24	Texas	78.5		43	Maryland	72.8
36	Utah	75.2		43	Washington	72.8
37	Vermont	75.1		45	Montana	72.7
32	Virginia	77.0		46	New Jersey	71.9
43	Washington	72.8		47	Oregon	71.4
17	West Virginia	80.0		48	Alaska	67.7
18	Wisconsin	79.9		49	Hawaii	67.0
35	Wyoming	76.0		50	New York	54.4
					District of Columbia	35.4

Source: U.S. Bureau of the Census
"2006 American Community Survey" (http://www.census.gov/acs/www/)
*Workers 16 and older who traveled to work by car, truck or van.

Percent of Commuters Who Drive to Work in Carpools: 2006

National Percent = 10.7%*

ALPHA ORDER

RANK	STATE	PERCENT
22	Alabama	11.3
5	Alaska	12.7
2	Arizona	13.9
4	Arkansas	12.9
10	California	12.4
30	Colorado	10.6
48	Connecticut	8.4
37	Delaware	9.4
27	Florida	10.9
20	Georgia	11.5
1	Hawaii	16.0
16	Idaho	11.7
38	Illinois	9.3
34	Indiana	9.9
28	Iowa	10.8
41	Kansas	9.2
22	Kentucky	11.3
18	Louisiana	11.6
26	Maine	11.0
29	Maryland	10.7
47	Massachusetts	8.5
44	Michigan	9.1
38	Minnesota	9.3
12	Mississippi	12.1
31	Missouri	10.4
14	Montana	12.0
31	Nebraska	10.4
11	Nevada	12.3
46	New Hampshire	8.6
38	New Jersey	9.3
7	New Mexico	12.5
50	New York	7.6
7	North Carolina	12.5
41	North Dakota	9.2
49	Ohio	8.3
18	Oklahoma	11.6
16	Oregon	11.7
34	Pennsylvania	9.9
45	Rhode Island	8.9
22	South Carolina	11.3
36	South Dakota	9.6
33	Tennessee	10.2
5	Texas	12.7
3	Utah	13.1
25	Vermont	11.2
21	Virginia	11.4
15	Washington	11.8
12	West Virginia	12.1
41	Wisconsin	9.2
7	Wyoming	12.5

RANK ORDER

RANK	STATE	PERCENT
1	Hawaii	16.0
2	Arizona	13.9
3	Utah	13.1
4	Arkansas	12.9
5	Alaska	12.7
5	Texas	12.7
7	New Mexico	12.5
7	North Carolina	12.5
7	Wyoming	12.5
10	California	12.4
11	Nevada	12.3
12	Mississippi	12.1
12	West Virginia	12.1
14	Montana	12.0
15	Washington	11.8
16	Idaho	11.7
16	Oregon	11.7
18	Louisiana	11.6
18	Oklahoma	11.6
20	Georgia	11.5
21	Virginia	11.4
22	Alabama	11.3
22	Kentucky	11.3
22	South Carolina	11.3
25	Vermont	11.2
26	Maine	11.0
27	Florida	10.9
28	Iowa	10.8
29	Maryland	10.7
30	Colorado	10.6
31	Missouri	10.4
31	Nebraska	10.4
33	Tennessee	10.2
34	Indiana	9.9
34	Pennsylvania	9.9
36	South Dakota	9.6
37	Delaware	9.4
38	Illinois	9.3
38	Minnesota	9.3
38	New Jersey	9.3
41	Kansas	9.2
41	North Dakota	9.2
41	Wisconsin	9.2
44	Michigan	9.1
45	Rhode Island	8.9
46	New Hampshire	8.6
47	Massachusetts	8.5
48	Connecticut	8.4
49	Ohio	8.3
50	New York	7.6
	District of Columbia	6.3

Source: U.S. Bureau of the Census
"2006 American Community Survey" (http://www.census.gov/acs/www/)
*Workers 16 and older who traveled to work by car, truck or van.

Percent of Commuters Who Travel to Work by Public Transportation: 2006

National Percent = 4.8%*

<table>
<tr><td colspan="3"><u>ALPHA ORDER</u></td><td colspan="3"><u>RANK ORDER</u></td></tr>
<tr><th>RANK</th><th>STATE</th><th>PERCENT</th><th>RANK</th><th>STATE</th><th>PERCENT</th></tr>
<tr><td>44</td><td>Alabama</td><td>0.5</td><td>1</td><td>New York</td><td>26.1</td></tr>
<tr><td>28</td><td>Alaska</td><td>1.1</td><td>2</td><td>New Jersey</td><td>10.3</td></tr>
<tr><td>20</td><td>Arizona</td><td>2.1</td><td>3</td><td>Maryland</td><td>8.8</td></tr>
<tr><td>47</td><td>Arkansas</td><td>0.4</td><td>4</td><td>Massachusetts</td><td>8.6</td></tr>
<tr><td>9</td><td>California</td><td>5.0</td><td>5</td><td>Illinois</td><td>8.4</td></tr>
<tr><td>14</td><td>Colorado</td><td>3.2</td><td>6</td><td>Hawaii</td><td>5.4</td></tr>
<tr><td>11</td><td>Connecticut</td><td>4.1</td><td>7</td><td>Pennsylvania</td><td>5.2</td></tr>
<tr><td>16</td><td>Delaware</td><td>2.8</td><td>7</td><td>Washington</td><td>5.2</td></tr>
<tr><td>21</td><td>Florida</td><td>2.0</td><td>9</td><td>California</td><td>5.0</td></tr>
<tr><td>19</td><td>Georgia</td><td>2.4</td><td>10</td><td>Oregon</td><td>4.4</td></tr>
<tr><td>6</td><td>Hawaii</td><td>5.4</td><td>11</td><td>Connecticut</td><td>4.1</td></tr>
<tr><td>37</td><td>Idaho</td><td>0.8</td><td>11</td><td>Virginia</td><td>4.1</td></tr>
<tr><td>5</td><td>Illinois</td><td>8.4</td><td>13</td><td>Nevada</td><td>3.6</td></tr>
<tr><td>30</td><td>Indiana</td><td>1.0</td><td>14</td><td>Colorado</td><td>3.2</td></tr>
<tr><td>30</td><td>Iowa</td><td>1.0</td><td>15</td><td>Minnesota</td><td>3.0</td></tr>
<tr><td>42</td><td>Kansas</td><td>0.6</td><td>16</td><td>Delaware</td><td>2.8</td></tr>
<tr><td>30</td><td>Kentucky</td><td>1.0</td><td>17</td><td>Rhode Island</td><td>2.6</td></tr>
<tr><td>28</td><td>Louisiana</td><td>1.1</td><td>17</td><td>Utah</td><td>2.6</td></tr>
<tr><td>39</td><td>Maine</td><td>0.7</td><td>19</td><td>Georgia</td><td>2.4</td></tr>
<tr><td>3</td><td>Maryland</td><td>8.8</td><td>20</td><td>Arizona</td><td>2.1</td></tr>
<tr><td>4</td><td>Massachusetts</td><td>8.6</td><td>21</td><td>Florida</td><td>2.0</td></tr>
<tr><td>27</td><td>Michigan</td><td>1.2</td><td>21</td><td>Ohio</td><td>2.0</td></tr>
<tr><td>15</td><td>Minnesota</td><td>3.0</td><td>23</td><td>Wisconsin</td><td>1.9</td></tr>
<tr><td>47</td><td>Mississippi</td><td>0.4</td><td>24</td><td>Texas</td><td>1.7</td></tr>
<tr><td>25</td><td>Missouri</td><td>1.4</td><td>25</td><td>Missouri</td><td>1.4</td></tr>
<tr><td>35</td><td>Montana</td><td>0.9</td><td>26</td><td>Wyoming</td><td>1.3</td></tr>
<tr><td>44</td><td>Nebraska</td><td>0.5</td><td>27</td><td>Michigan</td><td>1.2</td></tr>
<tr><td>13</td><td>Nevada</td><td>3.6</td><td>28</td><td>Alaska</td><td>1.1</td></tr>
<tr><td>39</td><td>New Hampshire</td><td>0.7</td><td>28</td><td>Louisiana</td><td>1.1</td></tr>
<tr><td>2</td><td>New Jersey</td><td>10.3</td><td>30</td><td>Indiana</td><td>1.0</td></tr>
<tr><td>35</td><td>New Mexico</td><td>0.9</td><td>30</td><td>Iowa</td><td>1.0</td></tr>
<tr><td>1</td><td>New York</td><td>26.1</td><td>30</td><td>Kentucky</td><td>1.0</td></tr>
<tr><td>30</td><td>North Carolina</td><td>1.0</td><td>30</td><td>North Carolina</td><td>1.0</td></tr>
<tr><td>47</td><td>North Dakota</td><td>0.4</td><td>30</td><td>West Virginia</td><td>1.0</td></tr>
<tr><td>21</td><td>Ohio</td><td>2.0</td><td>35</td><td>Montana</td><td>0.9</td></tr>
<tr><td>44</td><td>Oklahoma</td><td>0.5</td><td>35</td><td>New Mexico</td><td>0.9</td></tr>
<tr><td>10</td><td>Oregon</td><td>4.4</td><td>37</td><td>Idaho</td><td>0.8</td></tr>
<tr><td>7</td><td>Pennsylvania</td><td>5.2</td><td>37</td><td>Vermont</td><td>0.8</td></tr>
<tr><td>17</td><td>Rhode Island</td><td>2.6</td><td>39</td><td>Maine</td><td>0.7</td></tr>
<tr><td>42</td><td>South Carolina</td><td>0.6</td><td>39</td><td>New Hampshire</td><td>0.7</td></tr>
<tr><td>47</td><td>South Dakota</td><td>0.4</td><td>39</td><td>Tennessee</td><td>0.7</td></tr>
<tr><td>39</td><td>Tennessee</td><td>0.7</td><td>42</td><td>Kansas</td><td>0.6</td></tr>
<tr><td>24</td><td>Texas</td><td>1.7</td><td>42</td><td>South Carolina</td><td>0.6</td></tr>
<tr><td>17</td><td>Utah</td><td>2.6</td><td>44</td><td>Alabama</td><td>0.5</td></tr>
<tr><td>37</td><td>Vermont</td><td>0.8</td><td>44</td><td>Nebraska</td><td>0.5</td></tr>
<tr><td>11</td><td>Virginia</td><td>4.1</td><td>44</td><td>Oklahoma</td><td>0.5</td></tr>
<tr><td>7</td><td>Washington</td><td>5.2</td><td>47</td><td>Arkansas</td><td>0.4</td></tr>
<tr><td>30</td><td>West Virginia</td><td>1.0</td><td>47</td><td>Mississippi</td><td>0.4</td></tr>
<tr><td>23</td><td>Wisconsin</td><td>1.9</td><td>47</td><td>North Dakota</td><td>0.4</td></tr>
<tr><td>26</td><td>Wyoming</td><td>1.3</td><td>47</td><td>South Dakota</td><td>0.4</td></tr>
<tr><td></td><td></td><td></td><td></td><td>District of Columbia</td><td>39.0</td></tr>
</table>

Source: U.S. Bureau of the Census
   "2006 American Community Survey" (http://www.census.gov/acs/www/)
*Workers 16 and older.

Annual Miles per Vehicle in 2005

National Annual Average = 12,396 Miles*

ALPHA ORDER

RANK	STATE	MILES		RANK	STATE	MILES
19	Alabama	13,128		1	Colorado	26,529
50	Alaska	7,484		2	Mississippi	21,326
9	Arizona	15,057		3	Arkansas	16,484
3	Arkansas	16,484		4	North Carolina	16,471
46	California	10,135		5	New Mexico	15,478
1	Colorado	26,529		6	Nevada	15,397
43	Connecticut	10,356		7	Vermont	15,192
21	Delaware	12,909		8	West Virginia	15,183
22	Florida	12,843		9	Arizona	15,057
14	Georgia	14,078		10	Missouri	14,981
41	Hawaii	10,641		11	South Carolina	14,803
40	Idaho	10,819		12	Indiana	14,489
34	Illinois	11,388		13	Tennessee	14,220
12	Indiana	14,489		14	Georgia	14,078
49	Iowa	9,142		15	Wyoming	14,017
26	Kansas	12,508		16	Maine	13,885
17	Kentucky	13,848		17	Kentucky	13,848
31	Louisiana	11,777		18	Texas	13,462
16	Maine	13,885		19	Alabama	13,128
20	Maryland	13,031		20	Maryland	13,031
44	Massachusetts	10,232		21	Delaware	12,909
25	Michigan	12,616		22	Florida	12,843
27	Minnesota	12,246		23	Wisconsin	12,701
2	Mississippi	21,326		24	Oklahoma	12,622
10	Missouri	14,981		25	Michigan	12,616
37	Montana	11,028		26	Kansas	12,508
36	Nebraska	11,329		27	Minnesota	12,246
6	Nevada	15,397		28	Virginia	12,188
33	New Hampshire	11,435		29	Oregon	12,177
30	New Jersey	11,789		30	New Jersey	11,789
5	New Mexico	15,478		31	Louisiana	11,777
32	New York	11,593		32	New York	11,593
4	North Carolina	16,471		33	New Hampshire	11,435
39	North Dakota	10,889		34	Illinois	11,388
42	Ohio	10,390		35	Utah	11,385
24	Oklahoma	12,622		36	Nebraska	11,329
29	Oregon	12,177		37	Montana	11,028
38	Pennsylvania	10,953		38	Pennsylvania	10,953
45	Rhode Island	10,227		39	North Dakota	10,889
11	South Carolina	14,803		40	Idaho	10,819
48	South Dakota	9,838		41	Hawaii	10,641
13	Tennessee	14,220		42	Ohio	10,390
18	Texas	13,462		43	Connecticut	10,356
35	Utah	11,385		44	Massachusetts	10,232
7	Vermont	15,192		45	Rhode Island	10,227
28	Virginia	12,188		46	California	10,135
47	Washington	9,909		47	Washington	9,909
8	West Virginia	15,183		48	South Dakota	9,838
23	Wisconsin	12,701		49	Iowa	9,142
15	Wyoming	14,017		50	Alaska	7,484

RANK ORDER

District of Columbia   15,648

Source: CQ Press using data from U.S. Department of Transportation, Federal Highway Administration
   "Highway Statistics 2005" (Tables MV-1 and VM-2) (http://www.fhwa.dot.gov/policy/ohpi/hss/index.htm)
*Includes automobiles, trucks, buses and motorcycles.

Average Miles per Gallon in 2005

National Average = 17.2 Miles per Gallon*

ALPHA ORDER			RANK ORDER		
RANK	STATE	MILES PER GALLON	RANK	STATE	MILES PER GALLON
16	Alabama	17.8	1	Hawaii	20.3
50	Alaska	10.1	2	Florida	20.0
32	Arizona	16.5	3	New York	19.6
38	Arkansas	16.0	4	Mississippi	19.3
18	California	17.6	5	Kansas	19.2
13	Colorado	18.2	5	Vermont	19.2
26	Connecticut	16.9	7	Rhode Island	19.1
8	Delaware	19.0	8	Delaware	19.0
2	Florida	20.0	8	North Carolina	19.0
24	Georgia	17.0	8	Wisconsin	19.0
1	Hawaii	20.3	11	Oklahoma	18.5
16	Idaho	17.8	12	West Virginia	18.4
33	Illinois	16.4	13	Colorado	18.2
37	Indiana	16.1	14	Michigan	18.1
45	Iowa	14.7	14	Utah	18.1
5	Kansas	19.2	16	Alabama	17.8
40	Kentucky	15.8	16	Idaho	17.8
43	Louisiana	15.4	18	California	17.6
29	Maine	16.7	18	Maryland	17.6
18	Maryland	17.6	20	Minnesota	17.4
22	Massachusetts	17.3	20	Tennessee	17.4
14	Michigan	18.1	22	Massachusetts	17.3
20	Minnesota	17.4	23	Oregon	17.2
4	Mississippi	19.3	24	Georgia	17.0
30	Missouri	16.6	24	New Mexico	17.0
41	Montana	15.7	26	Connecticut	16.9
35	Nebraska	16.2	26	New Hampshire	16.9
48	Nevada	13.9	26	Washington	16.9
26	New Hampshire	16.9	29	Maine	16.7
47	New Jersey	14.3	30	Missouri	16.6
24	New Mexico	17.0	30	Ohio	16.6
3	New York	19.6	32	Arizona	16.5
8	North Carolina	19.0	33	Illinois	16.4
44	North Dakota	14.9	34	Pennsylvania	16.3
30	Ohio	16.6	35	Nebraska	16.2
11	Oklahoma	18.5	35	Virginia	16.2
23	Oregon	17.2	37	Indiana	16.1
34	Pennsylvania	16.3	38	Arkansas	16.0
7	Rhode Island	19.1	38	South Carolina	16.0
38	South Carolina	16.0	40	Kentucky	15.8
46	South Dakota	14.5	41	Montana	15.7
20	Tennessee	17.4	41	Texas	15.7
41	Texas	15.7	43	Louisiana	15.4
14	Utah	18.1	44	North Dakota	14.9
5	Vermont	19.2	45	Iowa	14.7
35	Virginia	16.2	46	South Dakota	14.5
26	Washington	16.9	47	New Jersey	14.3
12	West Virginia	18.4	48	Nevada	13.9
8	Wisconsin	19.0	48	Wyoming	13.9
48	Wyoming	13.9	50	Alaska	10.1
				District of Columbia	24.1

Source: CQ Press using data from U.S. Department of Transportation, Federal Highway Administration
"Highway Statistics 2005" (http://www.fhwa.dot.gov/policy/ohpi/hss/index.htm)
*Total vehicle-miles for 2005 divided by total highway motor-fuel use. Includes gasoline, gasohol, diesel, and other "special fuels."

Airports in 2006

National Total = 13,813 Airports*

ALPHA ORDER

RANK	STATE	AIRPORTS	% of USA
32	Alabama	184	1.3%
4	Alaska	520	3.8%
31	Arizona	189	1.4%
26	Arkansas	239	1.7%
3	California	533	3.9%
22	Colorado	265	1.9%
46	Connecticut	54	0.4%
48	Delaware	33	0.2%
7	Florida	487	3.5%
17	Georgia	346	2.5%
49	Hawaii	31	0.2%
28	Idaho	212	1.5%
2	Illinois	563	4.1%
6	Indiana	491	3.6%
27	Iowa	233	1.7%
14	Kansas	371	2.7%
35	Kentucky	151	1.1%
24	Louisiana	247	1.8%
39	Maine	107	0.8%
36	Maryland	146	1.1%
43	Massachusetts	75	0.5%
12	Michigan	383	2.8%
13	Minnesota	380	2.8%
30	Mississippi	194	1.4%
10	Missouri	402	2.9%
25	Montana	240	1.7%
23	Nebraska	259	1.9%
41	Nevada	98	0.7%
47	New Hampshire	51	0.4%
38	New Jersey	115	0.8%
37	New Mexico	144	1.0%
11	New York	394	2.9%
19	North Carolina	311	2.3%
21	North Dakota	291	2.1%
5	Ohio	513	3.7%
15	Oklahoma	349	2.5%
16	Oregon	347	2.5%
8	Pennsylvania	461	3.3%
50	Rhode Island	10	0.1%
33	South Carolina	163	1.2%
34	South Dakota	157	1.1%
29	Tennessee	203	1.5%
1	Texas	1,451	10.5%
40	Utah	99	0.7%
45	Vermont	62	0.4%
20	Virginia	292	2.1%
18	Washington	344	2.5%
44	West Virginia	74	0.5%
9	Wisconsin	458	3.3%
42	Wyoming	89	0.6%

RANK ORDER

RANK	STATE	AIRPORTS	% of USA
1	Texas	1,451	10.5%
2	Illinois	563	4.1%
3	California	533	3.9%
4	Alaska	520	3.8%
5	Ohio	513	3.7%
6	Indiana	491	3.6%
7	Florida	487	3.5%
8	Pennsylvania	461	3.3%
9	Wisconsin	458	3.3%
10	Missouri	402	2.9%
11	New York	394	2.9%
12	Michigan	383	2.8%
13	Minnesota	380	2.8%
14	Kansas	371	2.7%
15	Oklahoma	349	2.5%
16	Oregon	347	2.5%
17	Georgia	346	2.5%
18	Washington	344	2.5%
19	North Carolina	311	2.3%
20	Virginia	292	2.1%
21	North Dakota	291	2.1%
22	Colorado	265	1.9%
23	Nebraska	259	1.9%
24	Louisiana	247	1.8%
25	Montana	240	1.7%
26	Arkansas	239	1.7%
27	Iowa	233	1.7%
28	Idaho	212	1.5%
29	Tennessee	203	1.5%
30	Mississippi	194	1.4%
31	Arizona	189	1.4%
32	Alabama	184	1.3%
33	South Carolina	163	1.2%
34	South Dakota	157	1.1%
35	Kentucky	151	1.1%
36	Maryland	146	1.1%
37	New Mexico	144	1.0%
38	New Jersey	115	0.8%
39	Maine	107	0.8%
40	Utah	99	0.7%
41	Nevada	98	0.7%
42	Wyoming	89	0.6%
43	Massachusetts	75	0.5%
44	West Virginia	74	0.5%
45	Vermont	62	0.4%
46	Connecticut	54	0.4%
47	New Hampshire	51	0.4%
48	Delaware	33	0.2%
49	Hawaii	31	0.2%
50	Rhode Island	10	0.1%
	District of Columbia	2	0.0%

Source: U.S. Department of Transportation, Bureau of Transportation Statistics
   "State Transportation Statistics 2006" (http://www.bts.gov/publications/state_transportation_profiles/)
*This table comprises all U.S. public use and private use airports. Public use facilities are open to the public with no prior authorization or permission required. Private use facilities are not open to the general public and include medical, law enforcement, corporate, and other such facilities.

Inland Waterway Mileage in 2005

National Total = 29,627 Miles*

ALPHA ORDER

RANK	STATE	MILES	% of USA
6	Alabama	1,270	4.3%
1	Alaska	5,497	18.6%
40	Arizona	0	0.0%
3	Arkansas	1,860	6.3%
26	California	286	1.0%
40	Colorado	0	0.0%
32	Connecticut	117	0.4%
34	Delaware	99	0.3%
5	Florida	1,540	5.2%
14	Georgia	721	2.4%
40	Hawaii	0	0.0%
33	Idaho	111	0.4%
8	Illinois	1,095	3.7%
24	Indiana	353	1.2%
19	Iowa	492	1.7%
31	Kansas	120	0.4%
4	Kentucky	1,591	5.4%
2	Louisiana	2,823	9.5%
37	Maine	73	0.2%
18	Maryland	532	1.8%
35	Massachusetts	90	0.3%
40	Michigan	0	0.0%
28	Minnesota	258	0.9%
12	Mississippi	873	2.9%
10	Missouri	1,033	3.5%
40	Montana	0	0.0%
25	Nebraska	318	1.1%
40	Nevada	0	0.0%
39	New Hampshire	8	0.0%
23	New Jersey	360	1.2%
40	New Mexico	0	0.0%
22	New York	394	1.3%
7	North Carolina	1,152	3.9%
40	North Dakota	0	0.0%
21	Ohio	444	1.5%
30	Oklahoma	150	0.5%
16	Oregon	681	2.3%
27	Pennsylvania	259	0.9%
38	Rhode Island	39	0.1%
20	South Carolina	482	1.6%
36	South Dakota	75	0.3%
11	Tennessee	946	3.2%
13	Texas	834	2.8%
40	Utah	0	0.0%
40	Vermont	0	0.0%
17	Virginia	674	2.3%
9	Washington	1,057	3.6%
15	West Virginia	682	2.3%
29	Wisconsin	231	0.8%
40	Wyoming	0	0.0%

RANK ORDER

RANK	STATE	MILES	% of USA
1	Alaska	5,497	18.6%
2	Louisiana	2,823	9.5%
3	Arkansas	1,860	6.3%
4	Kentucky	1,591	5.4%
5	Florida	1,540	5.2%
6	Alabama	1,270	4.3%
7	North Carolina	1,152	3.9%
8	Illinois	1,095	3.7%
9	Washington	1,057	3.6%
10	Missouri	1,033	3.5%
11	Tennessee	946	3.2%
12	Mississippi	873	2.9%
13	Texas	834	2.8%
14	Georgia	721	2.4%
15	West Virginia	682	2.3%
16	Oregon	681	2.3%
17	Virginia	674	2.3%
18	Maryland	532	1.8%
19	Iowa	492	1.7%
20	South Carolina	482	1.6%
21	Ohio	444	1.5%
22	New York	394	1.3%
23	New Jersey	360	1.2%
24	Indiana	353	1.2%
25	Nebraska	318	1.1%
26	California	286	1.0%
27	Pennsylvania	259	0.9%
28	Minnesota	258	0.9%
29	Wisconsin	231	0.8%
30	Oklahoma	150	0.5%
31	Kansas	120	0.4%
32	Connecticut	117	0.4%
33	Idaho	111	0.4%
34	Delaware	99	0.3%
35	Massachusetts	90	0.3%
36	South Dakota	75	0.3%
37	Maine	73	0.2%
38	Rhode Island	39	0.1%
39	New Hampshire	8	0.0%
40	Arizona	0	0.0%
40	Colorado	0	0.0%
40	Hawaii	0	0.0%
40	Michigan	0	0.0%
40	Montana	0	0.0%
40	Nevada	0	0.0%
40	New Mexico	0	0.0%
40	North Dakota	0	0.0%
40	Utah	0	0.0%
40	Vermont	0	0.0%
40	Wyoming	0	0.0%
	District of Columbia	7	0.0%

Source: U.S. Department of Transportation, Bureau of Transportation Statistics
   "State Transportation Statistics 2005" (http://www.bts.gov/publications/state_transportation_profiles/)
*Waterway mileage was determined by including the length of channels 1) with a controlling draft of nine feet or greater, 2) with commercial cargo traffic reported for 1998 and 1999, but 3) were not offshore. Channels within major bays are included (e.g., Chesapeake Bay, San Francisco Bay, Puget Sound, Long Island Sound, and major sounds and straits in southeastern Alaska). Channels in the Great Lakes are not included.

Percent of Recreational Boating Accidents Involving Alcohol: 2006

National Percent = 8.1% of Accidents*

ALPHA ORDER

RANK	STATE	PERCENT
10	Alabama	14.9
15	Alaska	12.5
35	Arizona	4.8
18	Arkansas	10.9
36	California	4.6
31	Colorado	6.8
42	Connecticut	2.4
17	Delaware	11.1
37	Florida	4.4
32	Georgia	6.0
45	Hawaii	0.0
10	Idaho	14.9
5	Illinois	18.6
39	Indiana	3.9
2	Iowa	25.0
41	Kansas	2.6
8	Kentucky	15.4
24	Louisiana	8.4
45	Maine	0.0
28	Maryland	7.2
43	Massachusetts	2.2
30	Michigan	7.0
13	Minnesota	14.2
14	Mississippi	12.9
16	Missouri	12.0
4	Montana	18.8
20	Nebraska	9.1
27	Nevada	7.3
26	New Hampshire	7.6
29	New Jersey	7.1
40	New Mexico	2.9
6	New York	15.8
20	North Carolina	9.1
45	North Dakota	0.0
9	Ohio	15.3
34	Oklahoma	5.6
45	Oregon	0.0
12	Pennsylvania	14.3
45	Rhode Island	0.0
38	South Carolina	4.3
1	South Dakota	31.3
23	Tennessee	8.7
25	Texas	8.2
44	Utah	1.2
45	Vermont	0.0
33	Virginia	5.8
3	Washington	24.0
19	West Virginia	9.5
20	Wisconsin	9.1
6	Wyoming	15.8

RANK ORDER

RANK	STATE	PERCENT
1	South Dakota	31.3
2	Iowa	25.0
3	Washington	24.0
4	Montana	18.8
5	Illinois	18.6
6	New York	15.8
6	Wyoming	15.8
8	Kentucky	15.4
9	Ohio	15.3
10	Alabama	14.9
10	Idaho	14.9
12	Pennsylvania	14.3
13	Minnesota	14.2
14	Mississippi	12.9
15	Alaska	12.5
16	Missouri	12.0
17	Delaware	11.1
18	Arkansas	10.9
19	West Virginia	9.5
20	Nebraska	9.1
20	North Carolina	9.1
20	Wisconsin	9.1
23	Tennessee	8.7
24	Louisiana	8.4
25	Texas	8.2
26	New Hampshire	7.6
27	Nevada	7.3
28	Maryland	7.2
29	New Jersey	7.1
30	Michigan	7.0
31	Colorado	6.8
32	Georgia	6.0
33	Virginia	5.8
34	Oklahoma	5.6
35	Arizona	4.8
36	California	4.6
37	Florida	4.4
38	South Carolina	4.3
39	Indiana	3.9
40	New Mexico	2.9
41	Kansas	2.6
42	Connecticut	2.4
43	Massachusetts	2.2
44	Utah	1.2
45	Hawaii	0.0
45	Maine	0.0
45	North Dakota	0.0
45	Oregon	0.0
45	Rhode Island	0.0
45	Vermont	0.0
	District of Columbia	0.0

Source: CQ Press using data from United States Coast Guard
"Boating Statistics 2006" (http://www.uscgboating.org/statistics/accident_stats.htm)
*Alcohol involvement in a boating accident includes any accident in which alcoholic beverages are consumed in the boat and the investigating official has determined that the operator was impaired or affected while operating the boat.

Railroad Accidents and Incidents in 2006

National Total = 13,369*

ALPHA ORDER					RANK ORDER			
RANK	STATE	ACCIDENTS	% of USA		RANK	STATE	ACCIDENTS	% of USA
12	Alabama	315	2.4%		1	Texas	1,201	9.0%
46	Alaska	42	0.3%		2	Illinois	1,068	8.0%
26	Arizona	205	1.5%		3	New York	905	6.8%
15	Arkansas	274	2.0%		4	California	900	6.7%
4	California	900	6.7%		5	Pennsylvania	698	5.2%
22	Colorado	229	1.7%		6	New Jersey	468	3.5%
34	Connecticut	140	1.0%		7	Ohio	406	3.0%
42	Delaware	68	0.5%		8	Indiana	366	2.7%
11	Florida	343	2.6%		9	Louisiana	364	2.7%
10	Georgia	356	2.7%		10	Georgia	356	2.7%
50	Hawaii	3	0.0%		11	Florida	343	2.6%
38	Idaho	98	0.7%		12	Alabama	315	2.4%
2	Illinois	1,068	8.0%		13	Nebraska	299	2.2%
8	Indiana	366	2.7%		14	Kansas	276	2.1%
18	Iowa	246	1.8%		15	Arkansas	274	2.0%
14	Kansas	276	2.1%		16	Washington	264	2.0%
23	Kentucky	215	1.6%		17	Missouri	252	1.9%
9	Louisiana	364	2.7%		18	Iowa	246	1.8%
45	Maine	43	0.3%		18	Michigan	246	1.8%
36	Maryland	122	0.9%		20	Minnesota	242	1.8%
29	Massachusetts	194	1.5%		21	Tennessee	239	1.8%
18	Michigan	246	1.8%		22	Colorado	229	1.7%
20	Minnesota	242	1.8%		23	Kentucky	215	1.6%
31	Mississippi	169	1.3%		24	Virginia	207	1.5%
17	Missouri	252	1.9%		25	North Carolina	206	1.5%
32	Montana	150	1.1%		26	Arizona	205	1.5%
13	Nebraska	299	2.2%		27	Oklahoma	197	1.5%
42	Nevada	68	0.5%		27	Oregon	197	1.5%
49	New Hampshire	7	0.1%		29	Massachusetts	194	1.5%
6	New Jersey	468	3.5%		30	Wisconsin	190	1.4%
39	New Mexico	93	0.7%		31	Mississippi	169	1.3%
3	New York	905	6.8%		32	Montana	150	1.1%
25	North Carolina	206	1.5%		33	Wyoming	142	1.1%
41	North Dakota	80	0.6%		34	Connecticut	140	1.0%
7	Ohio	406	3.0%		35	South Carolina	130	1.0%
27	Oklahoma	197	1.5%		36	Maryland	122	0.9%
27	Oregon	197	1.5%		37	West Virginia	116	0.9%
5	Pennsylvania	698	5.2%		38	Idaho	98	0.7%
47	Rhode Island	21	0.2%		39	New Mexico	93	0.7%
35	South Carolina	130	1.0%		40	Utah	86	0.6%
44	South Dakota	52	0.4%		41	North Dakota	80	0.6%
21	Tennessee	239	1.8%		42	Delaware	68	0.5%
1	Texas	1,201	9.0%		42	Nevada	68	0.5%
40	Utah	86	0.6%		44	South Dakota	52	0.4%
48	Vermont	18	0.1%		45	Maine	43	0.3%
24	Virginia	207	1.5%		46	Alaska	42	0.3%
16	Washington	264	2.0%		47	Rhode Island	21	0.2%
37	West Virginia	116	0.9%		48	Vermont	18	0.1%
30	Wisconsin	190	1.4%		49	New Hampshire	7	0.1%
33	Wyoming	142	1.1%		50	Hawaii	3	0.0%
						District of Columbia	153	1.1%

Source: U.S. Department of Transportation, Federal Railroad Administration
"Railroad Safety Statistics, 2006 Preliminary Annual Report" (http://safetydata.fra.dot.gov/officeofsafety/)
*Accidents or incidents include all events reportable to the U.S. Department of Transportation. These include train accidents causing damage above an established threshold; highway-rail grade crossing incidents involving impact between railroad equipment and highway users at crossings; and all other reportable incidents that cause a fatality or injury to any person or an occupational illness to a railroad employee.

Railroad Mileage Operated in 2005

National Total = 140,810 Miles of Railroad*

ALPHA ORDER

RANK	STATE	MILES	% of USA
17	Alabama	3,335	2.4%
45	Alaska	506	0.4%
36	Arizona	1,815	1.3%
25	Arkansas	2,730	1.9%
3	California	5,791	4.1%
28	Colorado	2,529	1.8%
47	Connecticut	331	0.2%
48	Delaware	218	0.2%
24	Florida	2,871	2.0%
7	Georgia	4,738	3.4%
50	Hawaii	0	0.0%
37	Idaho	1,601	1.1%
2	Illinois	7,196	5.1%
9	Indiana	4,165	3.0%
11	Iowa	3,931	2.8%
6	Kansas	4,878	3.5%
26	Kentucky	2,621	1.9%
23	Louisiana	2,947	2.1%
40	Maine	1,162	0.8%
43	Maryland	774	0.5%
41	Massachusetts	1,076	0.8%
12	Michigan	3,607	2.6%
8	Minnesota	4,599	3.3%
30	Mississippi	2,459	1.7%
10	Missouri	4,096	2.9%
18	Montana	3,280	2.3%
16	Nebraska	3,394	2.4%
39	Nevada	1,200	0.9%
46	New Hampshire	421	0.3%
42	New Jersey	949	0.7%
33	New Mexico	1,993	1.4%
14	New York	3,532	2.5%
19	North Carolina	3,255	2.3%
13	North Dakota	3,590	2.5%
4	Ohio	5,354	3.8%
20	Oklahoma	3,237	2.3%
29	Oregon	2,486	1.8%
5	Pennsylvania	5,002	3.6%
49	Rhode Island	87	0.1%
31	South Carolina	2,283	1.6%
35	South Dakota	1,833	1.3%
27	Tennessee	2,595	1.8%
1	Texas	10,386	7.4%
38	Utah	1,469	1.0%
44	Vermont	568	0.4%
21	Virginia	3,204	2.3%
22	Washington	3,166	2.2%
32	West Virginia	2,264	1.6%
15	Wisconsin	3,405	2.4%
34	Wyoming	1,857	1.3%

RANK ORDER

RANK	STATE	MILES	% of USA
1	Texas	10,386	7.4%
2	Illinois	7,196	5.1%
3	California	5,791	4.1%
4	Ohio	5,354	3.8%
5	Pennsylvania	5,002	3.6%
6	Kansas	4,878	3.5%
7	Georgia	4,738	3.4%
8	Minnesota	4,599	3.3%
9	Indiana	4,165	3.0%
10	Missouri	4,096	2.9%
11	Iowa	3,931	2.8%
12	Michigan	3,607	2.6%
13	North Dakota	3,590	2.5%
14	New York	3,532	2.5%
15	Wisconsin	3,405	2.4%
16	Nebraska	3,394	2.4%
17	Alabama	3,335	2.4%
18	Montana	3,280	2.3%
19	North Carolina	3,255	2.3%
20	Oklahoma	3,237	2.3%
21	Virginia	3,204	2.3%
22	Washington	3,166	2.2%
23	Louisiana	2,947	2.1%
24	Florida	2,871	2.0%
25	Arkansas	2,730	1.9%
26	Kentucky	2,621	1.9%
27	Tennessee	2,595	1.8%
28	Colorado	2,529	1.8%
29	Oregon	2,486	1.8%
30	Mississippi	2,459	1.7%
31	South Carolina	2,283	1.6%
32	West Virginia	2,264	1.6%
33	New Mexico	1,993	1.4%
34	Wyoming	1,857	1.3%
35	South Dakota	1,833	1.3%
36	Arizona	1,815	1.3%
37	Idaho	1,601	1.1%
38	Utah	1,469	1.0%
39	Nevada	1,200	0.9%
40	Maine	1,162	0.8%
41	Massachusetts	1,076	0.8%
42	New Jersey	949	0.7%
43	Maryland	774	0.5%
44	Vermont	568	0.4%
45	Alaska	506	0.4%
46	New Hampshire	421	0.3%
47	Connecticut	331	0.2%
48	Delaware	218	0.2%
49	Rhode Island	87	0.1%
50	Hawaii	0	0.0%
	District of Columbia	24	0.0%

Source: Association of American Railroads

"Railroads and States 2005" (www.aar.org/PubCommon/Documents/AboutTheIndustry/RRState_Rankings.pdf)

*Includes Class I and non-Class I miles. Excludes trackage rights. Synonymous with route-miles, so that a mile of single track is counted the same as a mile of double track.

Sources

ACT, Inc.
500 ACT Drive, P.O. Box 168
Iowa City, IA 52243-0168
319-337-1000
www.act.org

Administration for Children and Families
U.S. Dept. of Health and Human Services
370 L'Enfant Promenade, SW
Washington, D.C. 20447
202-401-9215
www.acf.dhhs.gov

American Cancer Society, Inc.
1599 Clifton Road, NE
Atlanta, GA 30329-4251
800-227-2345
www.cancer.org

American Dental Association
211 E. Chicago Ave.
Chicago, IL 60611-2678
312-440-2500
www.ada.org

American Hospital Association
One North Franklin
Chicago, IL 60606-3421
312-422-3000
www.aha.org

American Medical Association
515 North State Street
Chicago, IL 60610
800-621-8335
www.ama-assn.org

Association of American Railroads
50 F Street, NW
Washington, D.C. 20001-1564
202-639-2100
www.aar.org

Bureau of the Census
4700 Silver Hill Road
Washington, D.C. 20233-0001
301-457-2800
www.census.gov

Bureau of Economic Analysis
U.S. Department of Commerce
1441 L Street, NW
Washington, D.C. 20230
202-606-9900
www.bea.gov

Bureau of Justice Statistics
U.S. Department of Justice
810 Seventh St., NW
Washington, D.C. 20531
202-307-0765
www.ojp.usdoj.gov/bjs/

Bureau of Labor Statistics
U.S.Department of Labor
2 Massachusetts Ave., NE.
Washington, D.C. 20212-0001
202-691-5200
www.bls.gov

Bureau of Transportation Statistics
1200 New Jersey Ave., SE
Washington, D.C. 20590
800-853-1351
www.bts.gov

Centers for Disease Control and Prevention
1600 Clifton Road
Atlanta, GA   30333
800-311-3435
www.cdc.gov

Centers for Medicare and Medicaid Services
7500 Security Boulevard
Baltimore, MD   21244-1850
877-267-2323
www.cms.hhs.gov

College Board
The College Board
45 Columbus Avenue
New York, NY   10023
212-713-8000
www.collegeboard.com

Economic Research Service
U.S. Department of Agriculture
1800 M Street, NW
Washington, D.C.   20036-5831
202-694-5050
www.ers.usda.gov

Energy Information Administration
1000 Independence Avenue, SW
Washington, D.C.   20585
202-586-8800
www.eia.doe.gov

Environmental Protection Agency
Ariel Rios Building
1200 Pennsylvania Ave, NW
Washington, D.C.   20464
202-272-0167
www.epa.gov

Federal Bureau of Investigation
935 Pennsylvania Avenue, NW
Washington, D.C.   20535
202-324-3000
www.fbi.gov

Federal Election Commission
999 E Street, NW
Washington, D.C.   20463
800-424-9530
www.fec.gov

Federal Highway Administration
1200 New Jersey Ave., SE
Washington, D.C.   20590
202-366-0660
www.fhwa.dot.gov

Federation of Tax Administrators
444 North Capitol St., NW, Ste 348
Washington, D.C.   20001
202-624-5890
www.taxadmin.org

Food and Nutrition Service
U.S. Department of Agriculture
3101 Park Center Drive
Alexandria, VA   22302
703-305-2281
www.fns.usda.gov/fns/

General Services Administration
1800 F Street, NW
Washington, D.C.   20405
202-501-1231
www.gsa.gov

Health Resources and Services Administration
Division of Practitioner Data Banks
5600 Fishers Lane
Rockville, MD   20857
800-767-6732
www.hrsa.gov

Internal Revenue Service
U.S. Department of the Treasury
1111 Constitution Avenue, NW
Washington, D.C.   20224
800-829-1040
www.irs.gov

Medical Expenditure Panel Survey
Agency for Healthcare Research and Quality
540 Gaither Road
Rockville, MD   20850
301-427-1364
www.meps.ahrq.gov

National Agricultural Statistics Service
1400 Independence Avenue, SW
Washington, D.C.   20250
800-727-9540
www.nass.usda.gov

National Assembly of State Arts Agencies
1029 Vermont Ave., NW 2nd Fl
Washington, D.C.   20005
202-347-6352
www.nasaa-arts.org

National Association of Realtors
430 N. Michigan Ave
Chicago, IL   60611
800-874-6500
www.realtor.org

National Association of State Park Directors
8829 Woodyhill Road
Raleigh, NC 27613
919-676-8365
www.naspd.org

National Center for Education Statistics
U.S. Department of Education
1990 K Street, NW
Washington, D.C. 20006
202-502-7300
http://nces.ed.gov

National Center for Health Statistics
U.S. Department of Health and Human Services
3311 Toledo Road
Hyattsville, MD 20782
800-232-4636
www.cdc.gov/nchs/

National Conference of State Legislatures
770 E. First Place
Denver, CO 80230
303-346-7700
www.ncsl.org

National Education Association
1201 16th Street, NW
Washington, D.C. 20036-3290
202-833-4000
www.nea.org

National Highway Traffic Safety Administration
1200 New Jersey Ave., SE
Washington, D.C. 20590
888-327-4236
www.nhtsa.dot.gov

National Institute on Alcohol Abuse And Alcoholism
5635 Fishers Lane, MSC 9304
Bethesda, MD 20892-9304
301-443-3860
www.niaaa.nih.gov/

National Oceanic and Atmospheric Administration
U.S. Department of Commerce
1401 Constitution Ave., NW. Rm 6217
Washington, D.C. 20230
202-482-6090
www.noaa.gov

National Weather Service
Storm Prediction Center
120 David Boren Blvd
Norman, OK 73072
405-579-0771
www.spc.noaa.gov

Social Security Administration
Windsor Park Building
6401 Security Boulevard
Baltimore, MD 21235
800-772-1213 (information)
www.ssa.gov

Tax Foundation
2001 L Street, NW, Ste 1050
Washington, D.C. 20036
202-464-6200
www.taxfoundation.org

U.S. Department of Defense
Directorate for Public Inquiry and Analysis
Room 2E565 The Pentagon
1400 Defense Pentagon
Washington, D.C. 20301-1400
703-428-0711
www.defenselink.mil

U.S. Department of Veterans Affairs
810 Vermont Avenue, NW
Washington, D.C. 20420
202-273-5700
www.va.gov

U.S. Geological Survey
12201 Sunrise Valley Drive
Reston, VA 20192
1-888-275-8747
www.usgs.gov

Index